To Shireen

Credits

Executive Editor
Carol Long

Senior Development Editor
Tom Dinse

Production Editor
Tim Tate

Editorial Manager
Mary Beth Wakefield

Production Manager
Tim Tate

Vice President and Executive Group Publisher
Richard Swadley

Vice President and Executive Publisher
Joseph B. Wikert

Project Coordinator, Cover
Lynsey Stanford

Proofreader
Nancy Bell

Indexer
Jack Lewis

Cover Image
© Digital Vision/Getty Images

Cover Design
Michael E. Trent

Contents at a Glance

Contents

Preface to the Second Edition

The first edition of *Security Engineering* was published in May 2001. Since then the world has changed.

System security was one of Microsoft's lowest priorities then; it's now one of the highest. The volume of malware continues to increase along with the nuisance that it causes. Although a lot of effort has gone into defence — we have seen Windows NT replaced by XP and then Vista, and occasional service packs replaced by monthly security patches — the effort put into attacks has increased far more. People who write viruses no longer do so for fun, but for profit; the last few years have seen the emergence of a criminal economy that supports diverse specialists. Spammers, virus writers, phishermen, money launderers and spies trade busily with each other.

Cryptography has also moved on. The Advanced Encryption Standard is being embedded into more and more products, and we have some interesting developments on the public-key side of things too. But just as our algorithm problems get solved, so we face a host of implementation issues. Side channels, poorly designed APIs and protocol failures continue to break systems. Applied cryptography is harder than ever to do well.

Pervasive computing also opens up new challenges. As computers and communications become embedded invisibly everywhere, so problems that used to only afflict 'proper computers' crop up in all sorts of other devices too. What does it mean for a thermometer to be secure, or an air-conditioner?

The great diversity of intelligent devices brings with it a great diversity of interests and actors. Security is not just about keeping the bad guys out, but increasingly concerned with tussles for power and control. DRM pits the content and platform industries against consumers, and against each other; accessory control is used to tie printers to their vendors' cartridges, but leads to antitrust lawsuits and government intervention. Security also interacts with safety in applications from cars through utilities to electronic healthcare. The security engineer needs to understand not just crypto and operating systems, but economics and human factors as well.

And the ubiquity of digital devices means that 'computer security' is no longer just a problem for a few systems specialists. Almost all white-collar crime (and much crime of the serious violent sort) now involves computers or mobile phones, so a detective needs to understand computer forensics just as she needs to know how to drive. More and more lawyers, accountants, managers and other people with no formal engineering training are going to have to understand system security in order to do their jobs well.

The rapid growth of online services, from Google and Facebook to massively multiplayer games, has also changed the world. Bugs in online applications can be fixed rapidly once they're noticed, but the applications get ever more complex and their side-effects harder to predict. We may have a reasonably good idea what it means for an operating system or even a banking service to be secure, but we can't make any such claims for online lifestyles that evolve all the time. We're entering a novel world of evolving socio-technical systems, and that raises profound questions about how the evolution is driven and who is in control.

The largest changes, however, may be those driven by the tragic events of September 2001 and by our reaction to them. These have altered perceptions and priorities in many ways, and changed the shape of the security industry. Terrorism is not just about risk, but about the perception of risk, and about the manipulation of perception. This adds psychology and politics to the mix. Security engineers also have a duty to contribute to the political debate. Where inappropriate reactions to terrorist crimes have led to major waste of resources and unforced policy errors, we have to keep on educating people to ask a few simple questions: what are we seeking to prevent, and will the proposed mechanisms actually work?

Ross Anderson
Cambridge, January 2008

Foreword

In a paper he wrote with Roger Needham, Ross Anderson coined the phrase "programming Satan's computer" to describe the problems faced by computer-security engineers. It's the sort of evocative image I've come to expect from Ross, and a phrase I've used ever since.

Programming a computer is straightforward: keep hammering away at the problem until the computer does what it's supposed to do. Large application programs and operating systems are a lot more complicated, but the methodology is basically the same. Writing a reliable computer program is much harder, because the program needs to work even in the face of random errors and mistakes: Murphy's computer, if you will. Significant research has gone into reliable software design, and there are many mission-critical software applications that are designed to withstand Murphy's Law.

Writing a *secure* computer program is another matter entirely. Security involves making sure things work, not in the presence of random faults, but in the face of an intelligent and malicious adversary trying to ensure that things fail in the worst possible way at the worst possible time ... again and again. It truly is programming Satan's computer.

Security engineering is different from any other kind of programming. It's a point I made over and over again: in my own book, *Secrets and Lies*, in my monthly newsletter *Crypto-Gram*, and in my other writings. And it's a point Ross makes in every chapter of this book. This is why, if you're doing any security engineering ... if you're even *thinking* of doing any security engineering, you need to read this book. It's the first, and only, end-to-end modern security design and engineering book ever written.

And it comes just in time. You can divide the history of the Internet into three waves. The first wave centered around mainframes and terminals.

Computers were expensive and rare. The second wave, from about 1992 until now, centered around personal computers, browsers, and large application programs. And the third, starting now, will see the connection of all sorts of devices that are currently in proprietary networks, standalone, and non-computerized. By 2003, there will be more mobile phones connected to the Internet than computers. Within a few years we'll see many of the world's refrigerators, heart monitors, bus and train ticket dispensers, burglar alarms, and electricity meters talking IP. Personal computers will be a minority player on the Internet.

Security engineering, especially in this third wave, requires you to think differently. You need to figure out not how something works, but how something can be made to not work. You have to imagine an intelligent and malicious adversary inside your system (remember Satan's computer), constantly trying new ways to subvert it. You have to consider all the ways your system can fail, most of them having nothing to do with the design itself. You have to look at everything backwards, upside down, and sideways. You have to think like an alien.

As the late great science fiction editor John W. Campbell, said: "An alien thinks as well as a human, but not like a human." Computer security is a lot like that. Ross is one of those rare people who can think like an alien, and then explain that thinking to humans. Have fun reading.

Bruce Schneier
January 2001

Preface

For generations, people have defined and protected their property and their privacy using locks, fences, signatures, seals, account books, and meters. These have been supported by a host of social constructs ranging from international treaties through national laws to manners and customs.

This is changing, and quickly. Most records are now electronic, from bank accounts to registers of real property; and transactions are increasingly electronic, as shopping moves to the Internet. Just as important, but less obvious, are the many everyday systems that have been quietly automated. Burglar alarms no longer wake up the neighborhood, but send silent messages to the police; students no longer fill their dormitory washers and dryers with coins, but credit them using a smartcard they recharge at the college bookstore; locks are no longer simple mechanical affairs, but are operated by electronic remote controls or swipe cards; and instead of renting videocassettes, millions of people get their movies from satellite or cable channels. Even the humble banknote is no longer just ink on paper, but may contain digital watermarks that enable many forgeries to be detected by machine.

How good is all this new security technology? Unfortunately, the honest answer is 'nowhere near as good as it should be'. New systems are often rapidly broken, and the same elementary mistakes are repeated in one application after another. It often takes four or five attempts to get a security design right, and that is far too many.

The media regularly report security breaches on the Internet; banks fight their customers over 'phantom withdrawals' from cash machines; VISA reports huge increases in the number of disputed Internet credit card transactions; satellite TV companies hound pirates who copy their smartcards; and law enforcement agencies try to stake out territory in cyberspace with laws controlling the use of encryption. Worse still, features interact. A mobile phone that calls the last number again if one of the keys is pressed by accident may be just a minor nuisance — until someone invents a machine that dispenses a can of soft drink every time its phone number is called. When all of a sudden you find 50 cans of Coke on your phone bill, who is responsible, the phone company, the handset manufacturer, or the vending machine operator? Once almost every electronic device that affects your life is connected to the Internet — which Microsoft expects to happen by 2010 — what does 'Internet security' mean to you, and how do you cope with it?

As well as the systems that fail, many systems just don't work well enough. Medical record systems don't let doctors share personal health information as they would like, but still don't protect it against inquisitive private eyes. Zillion-dollar military systems prevent anyone without a 'top secret' clearance from getting at intelligence data, but are often designed so that almost everyone needs this clearance to do any work. Passenger ticket systems are designed to prevent customers cheating, but when trustbusters break up the railroad, they cannot stop the new rail companies cheating each other. Many of these failures could have been foreseen if designers had just a little bit more knowledge of what had been tried, and had failed, elsewhere.

Security engineering is the new discipline that is starting to emerge out of all this chaos.

Although most of the underlying technologies (cryptology, software reliability, tamper resistance, security printing, auditing, etc.) are relatively well understood, the knowledge and experience of how to apply them effectively is much scarcer. And since the move from mechanical to digital mechanisms is happening everywhere at once, there just has not been time for the lessons learned to percolate through the engineering community. Time and again, we see the same old square wheels being reinvented.

The industries that have managed the transition most capably are often those that have been able to borrow an appropriate technology from another discipline. Examples include the reuse of technology designed for military identify-friend-or-foe equipment in bank cash machines and even prepayment gas meters. So even if a security designer has serious expertise in some particular speciality — whether as a mathematician working with ciphers or a chemist developing banknote inks — it is still prudent to have an overview of the whole subject. The essence of good security engineering is understanding the potential threats to a system, then applying an appropriate mix of protective measures — both technological and organizational — to control them. Knowing what has worked, and more importantly what has failed, in other applications is a great help in developing judgment. It can also save a lot of money.

The purpose of this book is to give a solid introduction to security engineering, as we understand it at the beginning of the twenty-first century. My goal is that it works at four different levels:

1. *As a textbook that you can read from one end to the other over a few days as an introduction to the subject.* The book is to be used mainly by the working IT professional who needs to learn about the subject, but it can also be used in a one-semester course in a university.

2. *As a reference book to which you can come for an overview of the workings of some particular type of system.* These systems include cash machines, taxi meters, radar jammers, anonymous medical record databases, and so on.

3. *As an introduction to the underlying technologies, such as crypto, access control, inference control, tamper resistance, and seals.* Space prevents me from going into great depth; but I provide a basic road map for each subject, plus a reading list for the curious (and a list of open research problems for the prospective graduate student).

4. *As an original scientific contribution in which I have tried to draw out the common principles that underlie security engineering, and the lessons that people building one kind of system should have learned from others.* In the many years I have been working in security, I keep coming across these. For example, a simple attack on stream ciphers wasn't known to the people who designed a common antiaircraft fire control radar so it was easy to jam; while a trick well known to the radar community wasn't understood by banknote printers and people who design copyright marking schemes, which led to a quite general attack on most digital watermarks.

I have tried to keep this book resolutely mid-Atlantic; a security engineering book has to be, as many of the fundamental technologies are American, while many of the interesting applications are European. (This isn't surprising given the better funding of U.S. universities and research labs, and the greater diversity of nations and markets in Europe.) What's more, many of the successful European innovations — from the smart-card to the GSM mobile phone to the pay-per-view TV service — have crossed the Atlantic and now thrive in the Americas. Both the science, and the case studies, are necessary.

This book grew out of the security engineering courses I teach at Cambridge University, but I have rewritten my notes to make them self-contained and added at least as much material again. It should be useful to the established professional security manager or consultant as a first-line reference; to the computer science professor doing research in cryptology; to the working police detective trying to figure out the latest computer scam; and to policy wonks struggling with the conflicts involved in regulating cryptography and anonymity. Above all, it is aimed at Dilbert. My main audience is the working programmer or engineer who is trying to design real systems that will keep on working despite the best efforts of customers, managers, and everybody else.

This book is divided into three parts.

- The first looks at basic concepts, starting with the central concept of a security protocol, and going on to human-computer interface issues, access controls, cryptology, and distributed system issues. It does not assume any particular technical background other than basic computer literacy. It is based on an Introduction to Security course that I teach to second-year undergraduates.

- The second part looks in much more detail at a number of important applications, such as military communications, medical record systems, cash machines, mobile phones, and pay-TV. These are used to introduce more of the advanced technologies and concepts. It also considers information security from the viewpoint of a number of different interest groups, such as companies, consumers, criminals, police, and spies. This material is drawn from my senior course on security, from research work, and from experience consulting.

- The third part looks at the organizational and policy issues: how computer security interacts with law, with evidence, and with corporate politics; how we can gain confidence that a system will perform as intended; and how the whole business of security engineering can best be managed.

I believe that building systems that continue to perform robustly in the face of malice is one of the most important, interesting, and difficult tasks facing engineers in the twenty-first century.

Ross Anderson
Cambridge, January 2001

About the Author

Why should I have been the person to write this book? Well, I seem to have accumulated the right mix of experience and qualifications over the last 25 years. I graduated in mathematics and natural science from Cambridge (England) in the 1970s, and got a qualification in computer engineering; my first proper job was in avionics; and I became interested in cryptology and computer security in the mid-1980s. After working in the banking industry for several years, I started doing consultancy for companies that designed equipment for banks, and then working on other applications of this technology, such as prepayment electricity meters.

I moved to academia in 1992, but continued to consult to industry on security technology. During the 1990s, the number of applications that employed cryptology rose rapidly: burglar alarms, car door locks, road toll tags, and satellite TV encryption systems all made their appearance. As the first legal disputes about these systems came along, I was lucky enough to be an expert witness in some of the important cases. The research team I lead had the good fortune to be in the right place at the right time when several crucial technologies, such as tamper resistance and digital watermarking, became hot topics.

By about 1996, it started to become clear to me that the existing textbooks were too specialized. The security textbooks focused on the access control mechanisms in operating systems, while the cryptology books gave very detailed expositions of the design of cryptographic algorithms and protocols. These topics are interesting, and important. However they are only part of the story. Most system designers are not overly concerned with crypto or operating system internals, but with how to use these tools effectively. They are quite right in this, as the inappropriate use of mechanisms is one of the main causes of security failure. I was encouraged by the success of a number of articles I wrote on security engineering (starting with 'Why Cryptosystems Fail' in 1993); and the need to teach an undergraduate class in security led to the development of a set of lecture notes that made up about half of this book. Finally, in 1999, I got round to rewriting them for a general technical audience.

I have learned a lot in the process; writing down what you think you know is a good way of finding out what you don't. I have also had a lot of fun. I hope you have as much fun reading it!

Acknowledgments

A great many people have helped in various ways with this book. I probably owe the greatest thanks to those who read the manuscript (or a large part of it) looking for errors and obscurities. They were Anne Anderson, Ian Brown, Nick Bohm, Richard Bondi, Caspar Bowden, Richard Clayton, Steve Early, Rich Graveman, Markus Kuhn, Dan Lough, David MacKay, John McHugh, Bob Morris, Roger Needham, Jerry Saltzer, Marv Schaefer, Karen Spärck Jones and Frank Stajano. Much credit also goes to my editor, Carol Long, who (among many other things) went through the first six chapters and coached me on the style appropriate for a professional (as opposed to academic) book. At the proofreading stage, I got quite invaluable help from Carola Bohm, Mike Bond, Richard Clayton, George Danezis, and Bruce Godfrey.

A large number of subject experts also helped me with particular chapters or sections. Richard Bondi helped me refine the definitions in Chapter 1; Jianxin Yan, Alan Blackwell and Alasdair Grant helped me investigate the applied psychology aspects of passwords; John Gordon and Sergei Skorobogatov were my main sources on remote key entry devices; Whit Diffie and Mike Brown on IFF; Steve Early on Unix security (although some of my material is based on lectures given by Ian Jackson); Mike Roe, Ian Kelly, Paul Leyland, and Fabien Petitcolas on the security of Windows NT4 and Win2K; Virgil Gligor on the history of memory overwriting attacks, and on mandatory integrity policies; and Jean Bacon on distributed systems. Gary Graunke told me the history of protection in Intel processors; Orr Dunkelman found many bugs in a draft of the crypto chapter and John Brazier pointed me to the Humpty Dumpty quote.

Moving to the second part of the book, the chapter on multilevel security was much improved by input from Jeremy Epstein, Virgil Gligor, Jong-Hyeon Lee, Ira Moskowitz, Paul Karger, Rick Smith, Frank Stajano, and Simon Wiseman, while Frank also helped with the following two chapters. The material on medical systems was originally developed with a number of people at the British Medical Association, most notably Fleur Fisher, Simon Jenkins, and Grant Kelly. Denise Schmandt-Besserat taught the world about bullae, which provided the background for the chapter on banking systems; that chapter was also strengthened by input from Fay Hider and Willie List. The chapter on alarms contains much that I was taught by Roger Needham, Peter Dean, John Martin, Frank Clish, and Gary Geldart. Nuclear command and control systems are much the brainchild of Gus Simmons; he and Bob Morris taught me much of what's in that chapter.

Sijbrand Spannenburg reviewed the chapter on security printing; and Roger Johnston has taught us all an enormous amount about seals. John Daugman helped polish the chapter on biometrics, as well as inventing iris scanning which I describe there. My tutors on tamper resistance were Oliver Kömmerling and Markus Kuhn; Markus also worked with me on emission security. I had substantial input on electronic warfare from Mike Brown and Owen Lewis. The chapter on phone fraud owes a lot to Duncan Campbell, Richard Cox, Rich Graveman, Udi Manber, Andrew Odlyzko and Roy Paterson. Ian Jackson contributed some ideas on network security. Fabien Petitcolas 'wrote the book' on copyright marking, and helped polish my chapter on it. Johann Bezuidenhoudt made perceptive comments on both phone fraud and electronic commerce, while Peter Landrock gave valuable input on bookkeeping and electronic commerce systems. Alistair Kelman was a fount of knowledge on the legal aspects of copyright; and Hal Varian kept me straight on matters of economics, and particularly the chapters on e-commerce and assurance.

As for the third part of the book, the chapter on e-policy was heavily influenced by colleagues at the Foundation for Information Policy Research, notably Caspar Bowden, Nick Bohm, Fleur Fisher, Brian Gladman, Ian Brown, Richard Clayton — and by the many others involved in the fight, including Whit Diffie, John Gilmore, Susan Landau, Brian Omotani and Mark Rotenberg. The chapter on management benefited from input from Robert Brady, Jack Lang, and Willie List. Finally, my thinking on assurance has been influenced by many people, including Robin Ball, Robert Brady, Willie List, and Robert Morris.

There were also many people over the years who taught me my trade. The foremost of them is Roger Needham, who was my thesis advisor; but I also learned a lot from hundreds of engineers, programmers, auditors, lawyers, and policemen with whom I worked on various consultancy jobs over the last 15 years. Of course, I take the rap for all the remaining errors and omissions.

Finally, I owe a huge debt to my family, especially to my wife Shireen for putting up with over a year in which I neglected household duties and was generally preoccupied. Daughter Bavani and dogs Jimmy, Bess, Belle, Hobbes, Bigfoot, Cat, and Dogmatix also had to compete for a diminished quantum of attention, and I thank them for their forbearance.

Further Acknowledgments for the Second Edition

Many of the folks who helped me with the first edition have also helped update the same material this time. In addition, I've had useful input, feedback or debugging assistance from Edmond Alyanakian, Johann Bezuidenhoudt, Richard Clayton, Jolyon Clulow, Dan Cvrcek, Roger Dingledine, Saar Drimer, Mike Ellims, Dan Geer, Gary Geldart, Wendy Grossman, Dan Hagon, Feng Hao, Roger Johnston, Markus Kuhn, Susan Landau, Stephen Lewis, Nick Mathewson, Tyler Moore, Steven Murdoch, Shishir Nagaraja, Roger Nebel, Andy Ozment, Mike Roe, Frank Stajano, Mark Staples, Don Taylor, Marc Tobias, Robert Watson and Jeff Yan. The members of our security group in Cambridge, and the Advisory Council of the Foundation for Information Policy Research, have been an invaluable sounding-board for many ideas. And I am also grateful to the many readers of the first edition who pointed out typos and other improvements: Piotr Carlson, Peter Chambers, Nick Drage, Austin Donnelly, Ben Dougall, Shawn Fitzgerald, Paul Gillingwater, Pieter Hartel, David Håsäther, Konstantin Hyppönen, Oliver Jorns, Markus Kuhn, Garry McKay, Joe Osborne, Avi Rubin, Sam Simpson, M Taylor, Peter Taylor, Paul Thomas, Nick Volenec, Randall Walker, Keith Willis, Stuart Wray and Stefek Zaba.

A number of typos have been corrected in the second printing (2010). Thanks to Adam Atkinson, Alastair Beresford, Antonomasia, David Boddie, Kristof Boeynaems, Martin Brain, James Davenport, Dan Eble, Shailendra Fuloria, Dan Hasather, Neil Jenkins, Hyoung Joong Kim, Patrick Koeberl, Simon Kramer, Stephan Neuhaus, Mark Oeltjenbruns, Alexandros Papadopoulos, Chris Pepper, Oscar Pereira, Raphael Phan, Matthew Slyman, Daniel Wagner-Hall, Randall Walker, and Stuart Wray for pointing them out!

Legal Notice

I cannot emphasize too strongly that the tricks taught in this book are intended only to enable you to build better systems. They are not in any way given as a means of helping you to break into systems, subvert copyright protection mechanisms, or do anything else unethical or illegal.

Where possible I have tried to give case histories at a level of detail that illustrates the underlying principles without giving a 'hacker's cookbook'.

Should This Book Be Published at All?

There are people who believe that the knowledge contained in this book should not be published. This is an old debate; in previous centuries, people objected to the publication of books on locksmithing, on the grounds that they were likely to help the bad guys more than the good guys.

I think that these fears are answered in the first book in English that discussed cryptology. This was a treatise on optical and acoustic telegraphy written by Bishop John Wilkins in 1641 [805]. He traced scientific censorship back to the Egyptian priests who forbade the use of alphabetic writing on the grounds that it would spread literacy among the common people and thus foster dissent. As he said:

> It will not follow that everything must be suppresst which may be abused...
> If all those useful inventions that are liable to abuse should therefore be
> concealed there is not any Art or Science which may be lawfully profest.

The question was raised again in the nineteenth century, when some well-meaning people wanted to ban books on locksmithing. A contemporary writer on the subject replied [750]:

Many well-meaning persons suppose that the discussion respecting the means for baffling the supposed safety of locks offers a premium for dishonesty, by showing others how to be dishonest. This is a fallacy. Rogues are very keen in their profession, and already know much more than we can teach them respecting their several kinds of roguery. Rogues knew a good deal about lockpicking long before locksmiths discussed it among themselves ... if there be harm, it will be much more than counterbalanced by good.

These views have been borne out by long experience since. As for me, I worked for two separate banks for three and a half years on cash machine security, but I learned significant new tricks from a document written by a convicted card fraudster that circulated in the U.K. prison system. Many government agencies are now coming round to this point of view. It is encouraging to see, for example, that the U.S. National Security Agency has published the specifications of the encryption algorithm (Skipjack) and the key management protocol (KEA) used to protect secret U.S. government traffic. Their judgment is clearly that the potential harm done by letting the Iraqis use a decent encryption algorithm is less than the good that will be done by having commercial off-the-shelf software compatible with Federal encryption standards.

In short, while some bad guys will benefit from a book such as this, they mostly know the tricks already, and the good guys will benefit much more.

PART

I

In this section of the book, I cover the basics of security engineering technology. The first chapter sets out to define the subject matter by giving an overview of the secure distributed systems found in four environments: a bank, an air force base, a hospital, and the home. The second chapter then plunges into the thick of things by tackling usability. The interface between the user and the machine is where the most intractable problems lurk. Phishing is the most rapidly growing online crime; pretexting is the main way in which privacy is compromised; and psychology is likely to be one of the most fruitful areas of security research in coming years. We need to know more about how people can be deceived, so we can design systems that make deception harder. There is also the problem that risk perceptions and realities have drifted ever further apart, specially since 9/11.

The following chapters dig progressively deeper into the technical meat. The third chapter is on security protocols, which specify how the players in a system — whether people, computers, or other electronic devices — communicate with each other. The fourth is on access control: even once a client (be it a phone, a PC, or whatever) has authenticated itself satisfactorily to a server, we still need mechanisms to control which data it can read or write on the server and which transactions it can execute. These mechanisms operate at different levels — operating system, database, application — but share some interesting characteristics and failure modes.

The fifth chapter is on the 'duct tape' that underlies most of the protocols and holds distributed systems together: cryptography. This is the art (and science) of codes and ciphers; it is much more than a clever means for keeping messages secret from an eavesdropper. Nowadays its job is 'taking trust from where it exists to where it's needed' [853].

The next chapter is on distributed systems. Researchers in this field are interested in topics such as concurrency control, fault tolerance, and naming. These take on subtle new meanings when systems must be made resilient against malice as well as against accidental failure. Using old data — replaying old transactions or reusing the credentials of a user who has left some time ago — is a serious problem, as is the multitude of names by which people are known to different systems (email addresses, credit card numbers, subscriber numbers, etc.). Many systems fail because their designers don't appreciate these issues.

The final chapter in this part is on economics. Security economics has grown hugely since this book first appeared in 2001; we have come to realise that many security failures are often due to perverse incentives rather than to the lack of suitable technical protection mechanisms. (Indeed, the former often explain the latter.) Security mechanisms are increasingly used not to keep 'bad' people out of 'good' systems, but to enable one principal to exert power over another: examples are authentication mechanisms that compel you to buy ink cartridges from your printer maker; and digital rights management mechanisms that restrict the owner of a computer. (This was marketed as a technology to protect the rights of the music industry, but in practice has turned out to often maximise the income of the vendor of the rights-management system). Ethical decisions are no longer a matter of 'black hat' versus 'white hat', but can turn on whether the intended effect is anticompetitive. So the modern security engineer needs to understand basic economic theory along with the theories underlying ciphers, protocols and access controls.

Most of the material in these chapters is standard textbook fare, and the chapters are intended to be pedagogic rather than encyclopaedic, so I have not put in as many citations as in the rest of the book. I hope, however, that even experts will find some of the case studies of value.

What Is Security Engineering?

Out of the crooked timber of humanity, no straight thing was ever made.
— **Immanuel Kant**

The world is never going to be perfect, either on- or offline; so let's not set impossibly high standards for online.
— **Esther Dyson**

1.1   Introduction

Security engineering is about building systems to remain dependable in the face of malice, error, or mischance. As a discipline, it focuses on the tools, processes, and methods needed to design, implement, and test complete systems, and to adapt existing systems as their environment evolves.

Security engineering requires cross-disciplinary expertise, ranging from cryptography and computer security through hardware tamper-resistance and formal methods to a knowledge of economics, applied psychology, organizations and the law. System engineering skills, from business process analysis through software engineering to evaluation and testing, are also important; but they are not sufficient, as they deal only with error and mischance rather than malice.

Many security systems have critical assurance requirements. Their failure may endanger human life and the environment (as with nuclear safety and control systems), do serious damage to major economic infrastructure (cash machines and other bank systems), endanger personal privacy (medical record systems), undermine the viability of whole business sectors (pay-TV), and facilitate crime (burglar and car alarms). Even the perception that a system is more vulnerable than it really is (paying with a credit card over the Internet) can significantly hold up economic development.

The conventional view is that while software engineering is about ensuring that certain things happen ('John can read this file'), security is about ensuring that they don't ('The Chinese government can't read this file'). Reality is much more complex. Security requirements differ greatly from one system to another. One typically needs some combination of user authentication, transaction integrity and accountability, fault-tolerance, message secrecy, and covertness. But many systems fail because their designers protect the wrong things, or protect the right things but in the wrong way.

Getting protection right thus depends on several different types of process. You have to figure out what needs protecting, and how to do it. You also need to ensure that the people who will guard the system and maintain it are properly motivated. In the next section, I'll set out a framework for thinking about this. Then, in order to illustrate the range of different things that security systems have to do, I will take a quick look at four application areas: a bank, an air force base, a hospital, and the home. Once we have given some concrete examples of the stuff that security engineers have to understand and build, we will be in a position to attempt some definitions.

1.2   A Framework

Good security engineering requires four things to come together. There's policy: what you're supposed to achieve. There's mechanism: the ciphers, access controls, hardware tamper-resistance and other machinery that you assemble in order to implement the policy. There's assurance: the amount of reliance you can place on each particular mechanism. Finally, there's incentive: the motive that the people guarding and maintaining the system have to do their job properly, and also the motive that the attackers have to try to defeat your policy. All of these interact (see Fig. 1.1).

As an example, let's think of the 9/11 terrorist attacks. The hijackers' success in getting knives through airport security was not a mechanism failure but a policy one; at that time, knives with blades up to three inches were permitted, and the screeners did their task of keeping guns and explosives off as far as we know. Policy has changed since then: first to prohibit all knives, then most weapons (baseball bats are now forbidden but whiskey bottles are OK); it's flip-flopped on many details (butane lighters forbidden then allowed again). Mechanism is weak, because of things like composite knives and explosives that don't contain nitrogen. Assurance is always poor; many tons of harmless passengers' possessions are consigned to the trash each month, while well

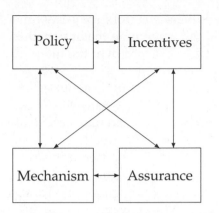

Figure 1.1: Security Engineering Analysis Framework

below half of all the weapons taken through screening (whether accidentally or for test purposes) are picked up.

Serious analysts point out major problems with priorities. For example, the TSA has spent $14.7 billion on aggressive passenger screening, which is fairly ineffective, while $100 m spent on reinforcing cockpit doors would remove most of the risk [1024]. The President of the Airline Pilots Security Alliance notes that most ground staff aren't screened, and almost no care is taken to guard aircraft parked on the ground overnight. As most airliners don't have locks, there's not much to stop a bad guy wheeling steps up to a plane and placing a bomb on board; if he had piloting skills and a bit of chutzpah, he could file a flight plan and make off with it [820]. Yet screening staff and guarding planes are just not a priority.

Why are such poor policy choices made? Quite simply, the incentives on the decision makers favour visible controls over effective ones. The result is what Bruce Schneier calls 'security theatre' — measures designed to produce a feeling of security rather than the reality. Most players also have an incentive to exaggerate the threat from terrorism: politicians to scare up the vote, journalists to sell more papers, companies to sell more equipment, government officials to build their empires, and security academics to get grants. The upshot of all this is that most of the damage done by terrorists to democratic countries comes from the overreaction. Fortunately, electorates figure this out over time. In Britain, where the IRA bombed us intermittently for a generation, the public reaction to the 7/7 bombings was mostly a shrug.

Security engineers have to understand all this; we need to be able to put risks and threats in context, make realistic assessments of what might go wrong, and give our clients good advice. That depends on a wide understanding of what has gone wrong over time with various systems; what sort of attacks have worked, what their consequences were, and how they were stopped (if it was worthwhile to do so). This book is full of case histories. I'll talk about terrorism specifically in Part III. For now, in order to set the scene, I'll give a few brief examples here of interesting security systems and what they are designed to prevent.

1.3   Example 1 — A Bank

Banks operate a surprisingly large range of security-critical computer systems.

1. The core of a bank's operations is usually a branch bookkeeping system. This keeps customer account master files plus a number of journals that record the day's transactions. The main threat to this system is the bank's own staff; about one percent of bankers are fired each year, mostly for petty dishonesty (the average theft is only a few thousand dollars). The main defense comes from bookkeeping procedures that have evolved over centuries. For example, each debit against one account must be matched by an equal and opposite credit against another; so money can only be moved within a bank, never created or destroyed. In addition, large transfers of money might need two or three people to authorize them. There are also alarm systems that look for unusual volumes or patterns of transactions, and staff are required to take regular vacations during which they have no access to the bank's premises or systems.

2. One public face of the bank is its automatic teller machines. Authenticating transactions based on a customer's card and personal identification number — in such a way as to defend against both outside and inside attack — is harder than it looks! There have been many epidemics of 'phantom withdrawals' in various countries when local villains (or bank staff) have found and exploited loopholes in the system. Automatic teller machines are also interesting as they were the first large scale commercial use of cryptography, and they helped establish a number of crypto standards.

3. Another public face is the bank's website. Many customers now do more of their routine business, such as bill payments and transfers between savings and checking accounts, online rather than at a branch. Bank websites have come under heavy attack recently from *phishing* — from bogus websites into which customers are invited to enter their passwords. The 'standard' internet security mechanisms designed in the 1990s, such as SSL/TLS, turned out to be ineffective once capable motivated opponents started attacking the customers rather than the bank. Phishing is a fascinating security engineering problem mixing elements from authentication, usability, psychology, operations and economics. I'll discuss it in detail in the next chapter.

4. Behind the scenes are a number of high-value messaging systems. These are used to move large sums of money (whether between local banks or between banks internationally); to trade in securities; to issue letters of credit and guarantees; and so on. An attack on such a system is the dream of the sophisticated white-collar criminal. The defense is a mixture of bookkeeping procedures, access controls, and cryptography.

5. The bank's branches will often appear to be large, solid and prosperous, giving customers the psychological message that their money is safe. This is theatre rather than reality: the stone facade gives no real protection. If you walk in with a gun, the tellers will give you all the cash you can see; and if you break in at night, you can cut into the safe or strongroom in a couple of minutes with an abrasive wheel. The effective controls these days center on the alarm systems — which are in constant communication with a security company's control center. Cryptography is used to prevent a robber or burglar manipulating the communications and making the alarm appear to say 'all's well' when it isn't.

I'll look at these applications in later chapters. Banking computer security is important: until quite recently, banks were the main non-military market for many computer security products, so they had a disproportionate influence on security standards. Secondly, even where their technology isn't blessed by an international standard, it is often widely used in other sectors anyway.

1.4   Example 2 — A Military Base

Military systems have also been an important technology driver. They have motivated much of the academic research that governments have funded into computer security in the last 20 years. As with banking, there is not one single application but many.

1. Some of the most sophisticated installations are the electronic warfare systems whose goals include trying to jam enemy radars while preventing the enemy from jamming yours. This area of information warfare is particularly instructive because for decades, well-funded research labs have been developing sophisticated countermeasures, counter-countermeasures and so on — with a depth, subtlety and range of deception strategies that are still not found elsewhere. As I write, in 2007, a lot of work is being done on adapting jammers to disable improvised explosive devices that make life hazardous for allied troops in Iraq. Electronic warfare has given many valuable insights: issues such as spoofing and service-denial attacks were live there long before bankers and bookmakers started having problems with bad guys targeting their websites.

2. Military communication systems have some interesting requirements. It is often not sufficient to just encipher messages: the enemy, on seeing traffic encrypted with somebody else's keys, may simply locate the transmitter and attack it. *Low-probability-of-intercept* (LPI) radio links are one answer; they use a number of tricks that are now being adopted in applications such as copyright marking. Covert communications are also important in some privacy applications, such as in defeating the Internet censorship imposed by repressive regimes.

3. Military organizations have some of the biggest systems for logistics and inventory management, which differ from commercial systems in having a number of special assurance requirements. For example, one may have a separate stores management system at each different security level: a general system for things like jet fuel and boot polish, plus a second secret system for stores and equipment whose location might give away tactical intentions. (This is very like the businessman who keeps separate sets of books for his partners and for the tax man, and can cause similar problems for the poor auditor.) There may also be intelligence systems and command systems with even higher protection requirements. The general rule is that sensitive information may not flow down to less restrictive classifications. So you can copy a file from a *Secret* stores system to a *Top Secret* command system, but not vice versa. The same rule applies to intelligence systems which collect data using wiretaps: information must flow up to the intelligence analyst from the target of investigation, but the target must not know which of his communications have been intercepted. Managing multiple systems with information flow restrictions is a hard problem and has inspired a lot of research. Since 9/11, for example, the drive to link up intelligence systems has led people to invent search engines that can index material at multiple levels and show users only the answers they are cleared to know.

4. The particular problems of protecting nuclear weapons have given rise over the last two generations to a lot of interesting security technology, ranging from electronic authentication systems that prevent weapons being used without the permission of the national command authority, through seals and alarm systems, to methods of identifying people with a high degree of certainty using biometrics such as iris patterns.

The civilian security engineer can learn a lot from all this. For example, many early systems for inserting copyright marks into digital audio and video, which used ideas from spread-spectrum radio, were vulnerable to desynchronisation attacks that are also a problem for some spread-spectrum systems. Another example comes from munitions management. There, a typical system enforces rules such as 'Don't put explosives and detonators in the same truck'. Such techniques can be recycled in food logistics — where hygiene rules forbid raw and cooked meats being handled together.

1.5   Example 3 — A Hospital

From soldiers and food hygiene we move on to healthcare. Hospitals have a number of interesting protection requirements — mostly to do with patient safety and privacy.

1. Patient record systems should not let all the staff see every patient's record, or privacy violations can be expected. They need to implement rules such as 'nurses can see the records of any patient who has been cared for in their department at any time during the previous 90 days'. This can be hard to do with traditional computer security mechanisms as roles can change (nurses move from one department to another) and there are cross-system dependencies (if the patient records system ends up relying on the personnel system for access control decisions, then the personnel system may just have become critical for safety, for privacy or for both).

2. Patient records are often anonymized for use in research, but this is hard to do well. Simply encrypting patient names is usually not enough as an enquiry such as 'show me all records of 59 year old males who were treated for a broken collarbone on September 15th 1966' would usually be enough to find the record of a politician who was known to have sustained such an injury at college. But if records cannot be anonymized properly, then much stricter rules have to be followed when handling the data, and this increases the cost of medical research.

3. Web-based technologies present interesting new assurance problems in healthcare. For example, as reference books — such as directories of drugs — move online, doctors need assurance that life-critical data, such as the figures for dosage per body weight, are exactly as published by the relevant authority, and have not been mangled in some way. Another example is that as doctors start to access patients' records from home or from laptops or even PDAs during house calls, suitable electronic authentication and encryption tools are starting to be required.

4. New technology can introduce risks that are just not understood. Hospital administrators understand the need for backup procedures to deal with outages of power, telephone service and so on; but medical practice is rapidly coming to depend on the net in ways that are often not documented. For example, hospitals in Britain are starting to use online radiology systems: X-rays no longer travel from the X-ray machine to the

operating theatre in an envelope, but via a server in a distant town. So a network failure can stop doctors operating just as much as a power failure. All of a sudden, the Internet turns into a safety-critical system, and denial-of-service attacks might kill people.

We will look at medical system security too in more detail later. This is a much younger field than banking IT or military systems, but as healthcare accounts for a larger proportion of GNP than either of them in all developed countries, and as hospitals are adopting IT at an increasing rate, it looks set to become important. In the USA in particular, the HIPAA legislation — which sets minimum standards for privacy — has made the sector a major client of the information security industry.

1.6   Example 4 — The Home

You might not think that the typical family operates any secure systems. But consider the following.

1. Many families use some of the systems we've already described. You may use a web-based electronic banking system to pay bills, and in a few years you may have encrypted online access to your medical records. Your burglar alarm may send an encrypted 'all's well' signal to the security company every few minutes, rather than waking up the neighborhood when something happens.

2. Your car probably has an electronic immobilizer that sends an encrypted challenge to a radio transponder in the key fob; the transponder has to respond correctly before the car will start. This makes theft harder and cuts your insurance premiums. But it also increases the number of car thefts from homes, where the house is burgled to get the car keys. The really hard edge is a surge in car-jackings: criminals who want a getaway car may just take one at gunpoint.

3. Early mobile phones were easy for villains to 'clone': users could suddenly find their bills inflated by hundreds or even thousands of dollars. The current GSM digital mobile phones authenticate themselves to the network by a cryptographic challenge-response protocol similar to the ones used in car door locks and immobilizers.

4. Satellite TV set-top boxes decipher movies so long as you keep paying your subscription. DVD players use copy control mechanisms based on cryptography and copyright marking to make it harder to copy disks (or to play them outside a certain geographic area). Authentication protocols can now also be used to set up secure communications on home networks (including WiFi, Bluetooth and HomePlug).

5. In many countries, households who can't get credit can get prepayment meters for electricity and gas, which they top up using a smartcard or other electronic key which they refill at a local store. Many universities use similar technologies to get students to pay for photocopier use, washing machines and even soft drinks.

6. Above all, the home provides a haven of physical security and seclusion. Technological progress will impact this in many ways. Advances in locksmithing mean that most common house locks can be defeated easily; does this matter? Research suggests that burglars aren't worried by locks as much as by occupants, so perhaps it doesn't matter much — but then maybe alarms will become more important for keeping intruders at bay when no-one's at home. Electronic intrusion might over time become a bigger issue, as more and more devices start to communicate with central services. The security of your home may come to depend on remote systems over which you have little control.

So you probably already use many systems that are designed to enforce some protection policy or other using largely electronic mechanisms. Over the next few decades, the number of such systems is going to increase rapidly. On past experience, many of them will be badly designed. The necessary skills are just not spread widely enough.

The aim of this book is to enable you to design such systems better. To do this, an engineer or programmer needs to learn about what systems there are, how they work, and — at least as important — how they have failed in the past. Civil engineers learn far more from the one bridge that falls down than from the hundred that stay up; exactly the same holds in security engineering.

1.7 Definitions

Many of the terms used in security engineering are straightforward, but some are misleading or even controversial. There are more detailed definitions of technical terms in the relevant chapters, which you can find using the index. In this section, I'll try to point out where the main problems lie.

The first thing we need to clarify is what we mean by *system*. In practice, this can denote:

1. a product or component, such as a cryptographic protocol, a smartcard or the hardware of a PC;

2. a collection of the above plus an operating system, communications and other things that go to make up an organization's infrastructure;

3. the above plus one or more applications (media player, browser, word processor, accounts / payroll package, and so on);

4. any or all of the above plus IT staff;

5. any or all of the above plus internal users and management;

6. any or all of the above plus customers and other external users.

Confusion between the above definitions is a fertile source of errors and vulnerabilities. Broadly speaking, the vendor and evaluator communities focus on the first (and occasionally) the second of them, while a business will focus on the sixth (and occasionally the fifth). We will come across many examples of systems that were advertised or even certified as secure because the hardware was, but that broke badly when a particular application was run, or when the equipment was used in a way the designers didn't anticipate. Ignoring the human components, and thus neglecting usability issues, is one of the largest causes of security failure. So we will generally use definition 6; when we take a more restrictive view, it should be clear from the context.

The next set of problems comes from lack of clarity about who the players are and what they are trying to prove. In the literature on security and cryptology, it's a convention that principals in security protocols are identified by names chosen with (usually) successive initial letters — much like hurricanes — and so we see lots of statements such as 'Alice authenticates herself to Bob'. This makes things much more readable, but often at the expense of precision. Do we mean that Alice proves to Bob that her name actually is Alice, or that she proves she's got a particular credential? Do we mean that the authentication is done by Alice the human being, or by a smartcard or software tool acting as Alice's agent? In that case, are we sure it's Alice, and not perhaps Cherie to whom Alice lent her card, or David who stole her card, or Eve who hacked her PC?

By a *subject* I will mean a physical person (human, ET, . . .), in any role including that of an operator, principal or victim. By a *person*, I will mean either a physical person or a legal person such as a company or government[1].

A *principal* is an entity that participates in a security system. This entity can be a subject, a person, a role, or a piece of equipment such as a PC, smartcard, or card reader terminal. A principal can also be a communications channel (which might be a port number, or a crypto key, depending on the circumstance). A principal can also be a compound of other principals; examples are a group (Alice or Bob), a conjunction (Alice and Bob acting together), a compound role (Alice acting as Bob's manager) and a delegation (Bob acting for Alice in her absence). Beware that groups and roles are not the same. By a *group* I will mean a set of principals, while a *role* is a set of functions assumed by different persons in succession (such as 'the officer of the watch on the USS Nimitz' or 'the president for the time being of the Icelandic Medical Association'). A principal may be considered at more than one level of abstraction: e.g. 'Bob

---

[1]That some persons are not people may seem slightly confusing but it's well established. Blame the lawyers.

acting for Alice in her absence' might mean 'Bob's smartcard representing Bob who is acting for Alice in her absence' or even 'Bob operating Alice's smartcard in her absence'. When we have to consider more detail, I'll be more specific.

The meaning of the word *identity* is controversial. When we have to be careful, I will use it to mean a correspondence between the names of two principals signifying that they refer to the same person or equipment. For example, it may be important to know that the Bob in 'Alice acting as Bob's manager' is the same as the Bob in 'Bob acting as Charlie's manager' and in 'Bob as branch manager signing a bank draft jointly with David'. Often, identity is abused to mean simply 'name', an abuse entrenched by such phrases as 'user identity' and 'citizen's identity card'. Where there is no possibility of being ambiguous, I'll sometimes lapse into this vernacular usage in order to avoid pomposity.

The definitions of *trust* and *trustworthy* are often confused. The following example illustrates the difference: if an NSA employee is observed in a toilet stall at Baltimore Washington International airport selling key material to a Chinese diplomat, then (assuming his operation was not authorized) we can describe him as 'trusted but not trustworthy'. Hereafter, we'll use the NSA definition that a *trusted* system or component is one whose failure can break the security policy, while a *trustworthy* system or component is one that won't fail.

Beware, though, that there are many alternative definitions of trust. A UK military view stresses auditability and fail-secure properties: a trusted systems element is one 'whose integrity cannot be assured by external observation of its behaviour whilst in operation'. Other definitions often have to do with whether a particular system is approved by authority: a trusted system might be 'a system which won't get me fired if it gets hacked on my watch' or even 'a system which we can insure'. I won't use either of these definitions. When we mean a system which isn't failure-evident, or an approved system, or an insured system, I'll say so.

The definition of *confidentiality* versus *privacy* versus *secrecy* opens another can of worms. These terms clearly overlap, but equally clearly are not exactly the same. If my neighbor cuts down some ivy at our common fence with the result that his kids can look into my garden and tease my dogs, it's not my confidentiality that has been invaded. And the duty to keep quiet about the affairs of a former employer is a duty of confidence, not of privacy.

The way I'll use these words is as follows.

- *Secrecy* is a technical term which refers to the effect of the mechanisms used to limit the number of principals who can access information, such as cryptography or computer access controls.

- *Confidentiality* involves an obligation to protect some other person's or organization's secrets if you know them.

- *Privacy* is the ability and/or right to protect your personal information and extends to the ability and/or right to prevent invasions of your personal space (the exact definition of which varies quite sharply from one country to another). Privacy can extend to families but not to legal persons such as corporations.

For example, hospital patients have a right to privacy, and in order to uphold this right the doctors, nurses and other staff have a duty of confidence towards their patients. The hospital has no right of privacy in respect of its business dealings but those employees who are privy to them may have a duty of confidence. In short, privacy is secrecy for the benefit of the individual while confidentiality is secrecy for the benefit of the organization.

There is a further complexity in that it's often not sufficient to protect data, such as the contents of messages; we also have to protect metadata, such as logs of who spoke to whom. For example, many countries have laws making the treatment of sexually transmitted diseases secret, and yet if a private eye could find out that you were exchanging encrypted messages with an STD clinic, he might well draw the conclusion that you were being treated there. (A famous model in Britain recently won a privacy lawsuit against a tabloid newspaper which printed a photograph of her leaving a meeting of Narcotics Anonymous.) So *anonymity* can be just as important a factor in privacy (or confidentiality) as secrecy. To make things even more complex, some writers refer to what we've called secrecy as *message content confidentiality* and to what we've called anonymity as *message source (or destination) confidentiality*. In general, anonymity is hard. It's difficult to be anonymous on your own; you usually need a crowd to hide in. Also, our legal codes are not designed to support anonymity: it's much easier for the police to get itemized billing information from the phone company, which tells them who called whom, than it is to get an actual wiretap. (And it's often very useful.)

The meanings of *authenticity* and *integrity* can also vary subtly. In the academic literature on security protocols, authenticity means integrity plus freshness: you have established that you are speaking to a genuine principal, not a replay of previous messages. We have a similar idea in banking protocols. In a country whose banking laws state that checks are no longer valid after six months, a seven month old uncashed check has integrity (assuming it's not been altered) but is no longer valid. The military usage tends to be that authenticity applies to the identity of principals and orders they give, while integrity applies to stored data. Thus we can talk about the integrity of a database of electronic warfare threats (it's not been corrupted, whether by the other side or by Murphy) but the authenticity of a general's orders (which has an overlap with the academic usage). However, there are some strange usages. For example, one can talk about an *authentic copy* of a deceptive order given by the other side's electronic warfare people; here the authenticity refers to the act of copying and storage. Similarly, a police crime scene officer will talk about preserving the integrity of a forged check, by placing it in an evidence bag.

The last matter I'll clarify here is the terminology which describes what we're trying to achieve. A *vulnerability* is a property of a system or its environment which, in conjunction with an internal or external *threat*, can lead to a *security failure*, which is a breach of the system's security policy. By *security policy* I will mean a succinct statement of a system's protection strategy (for example, 'each credit must be matched by an equal and opposite debit, and all transactions over $1,000 must be authorized by two managers'). A *security target* is a more detailed specification which sets out the means by which a security policy will be implemented in a particular product — encryption and digital signature mechanisms, access controls, audit logs and so on — and which will be used as the yardstick to evaluate whether the designers and implementers have done a proper job. Between these two levels you may find a *protection profile* which is like a security target except written in a sufficiently device-independent way to allow comparative evaluations among different products and different versions of the same product. I'll elaborate on security policies, security targets and protection profiles in later chapters. In general, the word *protection* will mean a property such as confidentiality or integrity, defined in a sufficiently abstract way for us to reason about it in the context of general systems rather than specific implementations.

1.8   Summary

There is a lot of terminological confusion in security engineering, much of which is due to the element of conflict. 'Security' is a terribly overloaded word, which often means quite incompatible things to different people.

To a corporation, it might mean the ability to monitor all employees' email and web browsing; to the employees, it might mean being able to use email and the web without being monitored. As time goes on, and security mechanisms are used more and more by the people who control a system's design to gain some commercial advantage over the other people who use it, we can expect conflicts, confusion and the deceptive use of language to increase.

One is reminded of a passage from Lewis Carroll:

> *"When I use a word," Humpty Dumpty said, in a rather scornful tone, "it means just what I choose it to mean — neither more nor less." "The question is," said Alice, "whether you can make words mean so many different things." "The question is," said Humpty Dumpty, "which is to be master — that's all."*

The security engineer should develop sensitivity to the different nuances of meaning that common words acquire in different applications, and to be able to formalize what the security policy and target actually are. That may sometimes be inconvenient for clients who wish to get away with something, but, in general, robust security design requires that the protection goals are made explicit.

CHAPTER 2

Usability and Psychology

Humans are incapable of securely storing high-quality cryptographic keys, and they have unacceptable speed and accuracy when performing cryptographic operations. (They are also large, expensive to maintain, difficult to manage, and they pollute the environment. It is astonishing that these devices continue to be manufactured and deployed. But they are sufficiently pervasive that we must design our protocols around their limitations.)

— Kaufmann, Perlman and Speciner [698]

Only amateurs attack machines; professionals target people.

— Bruce Schneier

2.1 Introduction

Many real attacks exploit psychology at least as much as technology. The fastest-growing online crime is *phishing*, in which victims are lured by an email to log on to a website that appears genuine but that's actually designed to steal their passwords. Online frauds like phishing are often easier to do, and harder to stop, than similar real-world frauds because most online protection mechanisms are not anything like as intuitively usable or as difficult to forge convincingly as their real-world equivalents; it is much easier for crooks to build a bogus bank website that passes casual inspection than it is for them to create a bogus bank in a shopping mall.

We've evolved social and psychological tools over millions of years to help us deal with deception in face-to-face contexts, but these are little use to us when we're presented with an email that asks us to do something. It seems to be harder to create useful asymmetry in usability, by which I mean that good use is easier than bad use. We have some examples of asymmetry in physical objects: a potato peeler is easier to use for peeling potatoes than a knife is, but a lot harder to use for murder. However, much of the asymmetry on which we rely in our daily business doesn't just depend on formal exchanges — which can be automated easily — but on some combination of physical objects, judgment of people, and the supporting social protocols. (I'll discuss this further in the Introduction to Chapter 3.) So, as our relationships with employers, banks and government become more formalised via online communication, and we lose both physical and human context, the forgery of these communications becomes more of a risk.

Deception, of various kinds, is now the greatest threat to online security. It can be used to get passwords, or to compromise confidential information or manipulate financial transactions directly. The most common way for private investigators to steal personal information is *pretexting* — phoning someone who has the information under a false pretext, usually by pretending to be someone authorised to be told it. Such attacks are sometimes known collectively as *social engineering.* There are many other flavours. The quote from Bruce Schneier at the head of this chapter appeared in a report of a stock scam, where a bogus press release said that a company's CEO had resigned and its earnings would be restated. Several wire services passed this on, and the stock dropped 61% until the hoax was exposed [1128]. Hoaxes and frauds have always happened, but the Internet makes some of them easier, and lets others be repackaged in ways that may bypass our existing controls (be they personal intuitions, company procedures or even laws). We will be playing catch-up for some time.

Another driver for the surge in attacks based on social engineering is that people are getting better at technology. As designers learn how to forestall the easier techie attacks, psychological manipulation of system users or operators becomes ever more attractive. So the security engineer simply must understand basic psychology and 'security usability', and one of the biggest opportunities facing the research community is to learn more about what works and why.

2.2   Attacks Based on Psychology

Hacking systems through the people who operate them may be growing rapidly but is not new. Military and intelligence organisations have always targeted each other's staff; most of the intelligence successes of the old Soviet Union were of this kind [77]. Private investigation agencies have not been far behind. The classic attack of this type is pretexting.

2.2.1 Pretexting

Colleagues of mine did an experiment in England in 1996 to determine the threat posed by pretexting to medical privacy. We trained the staff at a health authority (a government-owned health insurer that purchased medical services for a district of maybe 250,000 people) to identify and report false-pretext calls. A typical private eye would pretend to be a doctor involved in the emergency care of a patient, and he could be detected because the phone number he gave wasn't that of the hospital at which he claimed to work. (The story is told in detail later in the chapter on Multilateral Security.) We detected about 30 false-pretext calls a week. Unfortunately, we were unable to persuade the UK government to make this training mandatory for health authority staff. Thirty attacks per week times 52 weeks in a year times 200 health authorities in England is a lot of privacy compromise! Many countries have laws against pretexting, including both the UK and the USA, yet there are people in both countries who earn their living from it [411]. A typical case is reported in [449], where a private eye collecting debts for General Motors was fined for conning civil servants into giving out 250 people's home addresses over the phone.

The year 2002 saw the publication of perhaps the most disturbing security book ever, Kevin Mitnick's *'Art of Deception'*. Mitnick, who got extensive press coverage when he was arrested and convicted after breaking into phone systems, related after his release from prison how almost all of his exploits had involved social engineering. His typical hack was to pretend to a phone company employee that he was a colleague, and solicit 'help' such as a password. Ways of getting past a company's switchboard and winning its people's trust have been taught for years in sales-training courses; Mitnick became an expert at using them to defeat company security procedures, and his book recounts a fascinating range of tricks [896].

Pretexting became world headline news in September 2006 when it emerged that Hewlett-Packard chairwoman Patricia Dunn had hired private investigators who had used pretexting to obtain the phone records of other board members of whom she was suspicious, and of journalists she considered hostile. She was forced to resign. The following month, the California Attorney General filed felony charges and arrest warrants against her and three private eyes. The charges were online crime, wire fraud, taking computer data and using personal identifying information without authorization. In March 2007, charges against her were dropped; a factor was that she was suffering from cancer. Her codefendants pleaded no contest to lesser counts of fraudulent wire communications, a misdemeanor, and got community service [93].

But fixing the problem is hard. Despite continuing publicity about pretexting, there was an audit of the IRS in 2007 by the Treasury Inspector General for Tax Administration, whose staff called 102 IRS employees at all levels, asked for their user ids, and told them to change their passwords to a known value.

62 did so. Now nearly 100,000 IRS employees have access to tax return data, so if you're a US taxpayer there might be 60,000 people who might be fooled into letting an intruder breach your financial privacy. What's worse, this happened despite similar audit tests in 2001 and 2004 [1131]. Now a number of government departments, including Homeland Security, are planning to launch phishing attacks on their own staff in order to gauge the effectiveness of security education. In the UK, the privacy authorities announced a crackdown and prosecuted a private detective agency that did blagging for top law firms [779].

Resisting attempts by outsiders to inveigle your staff into revealing secrets is known in military circles as *operational security*. Protecting really valuable secrets, such as unpublished financial data, not-yet-patented industrial research or military plans, depends on limiting the number of people with access, and also having strict doctrines about with whom they may be discussed and how. It's not enough for rules to exist; you have to train all the staff who have access to the confidential material, and explain to them the reasons behind the rules. In our medical privacy example, we educated staff about pretexting and trained them not to discuss medical records on the phone unless they had initiated the call, and made it to a number they had got from the phone book rather than from a caller. And once the staff have encountered, detected and defeated a few pretexting attempts, they talk about it and the message gets across loud and clear. Often the hardest people to educate are the most senior; a consultancy sent the finance directors of 500 publicly-quoted companies a USB memory stick as part of an anonymous invitation saying 'For Your Chance to Attend the Party of a Lifetime', and 46% of them put it into their computers [701].

Intelligence-agency rules are very much tougher. Most of the operational security effort goes into training staff in what not to do, instilling a culture of discretion that shades well over into anonymity. And since foreign intelligence agencies make many fewer approaches to spooks than private eyes make to medical-record clerks, a spymaster can't rely on a robust detection culture to spring up of its own accord. He has to have his own red team constantly testing his staff to ensure that they take the paranoia business seriously.

Some operational security measures are common sense, such as not tossing out sensitive stuff in the trash. Less obvious is the need to train the people you trust, even if they're old friends. A leak of embarrassing emails that appeared to come from the office of the UK Prime Minister and was initially blamed on 'hackers' turned out to have been fished out of the trash at his personal pollster's home by a private detective called 'Benji the Binman' who achieved instant celebrity status [828]. Governments have mostly adopted a set of procedures whereby sensitive information is 'classified' and can only be passed to people with an appropriate 'clearance', that is, background checks and training. While this can become monstrously bureaucratic and wasteful, it does still give a useful baseline for thinking about operational security, and has led to the development of some protection technologies which I'll discuss later in the chapter on Multilevel Security. The disciplines used by banks to prevent a rogue from talking a manager into sending him money are similar in spirit but differ in detail; I discuss them in the chapter on Banking and Bookkeeping.

Pretexting is mostly used for attacks on companies, but it's starting to be used more against individuals. Here's the scam du jour in the USA, as I write this in 2007: the bad guy phones you pretending to be a court official, tells you you've been selected for jury duty, and demands your SSN and date of birth. If you tell him, he applies for a credit card in your name. If you tell him to get lost, he threatens you with arrest and imprisonment. Not everyone has the self-confidence and legal knowledge to resist this kind of sting.

2.2.2 Phishing

Phishing is in many ways a harder problem for a company to deal with than pretexting, since (as with the last scam I mentioned) the targets are not your staff but your customers. It is difficult enough to train the average customer — and you can't design simply for the average. If your security systems are unusable by people who don't speak English well, or who are dyslexic, or who have learning difficulties, you are asking for serious legal trouble, at least if you do business in civilised countries.

Phishing attacks against banks started in 2003, with half-a-dozen attempts reported [299]. The early attacks imitated bank websites, but were both crude and greedy; the attackers asked for all sorts of information such as ATM PINs, and were also written in poor English. Most customers smelt a rat. The attackers now use better psychology; they often reuse genuine bank emails, with just the URLs changed, or send an email saying something like 'Thank you for adding a new email address to your PayPal account' to provoke the customer to log on to complain that they hadn't. Of course, customers who use the provided link rather than typing in www.paypal.com or using an existing bookmark are likely to get their accounts emptied.

Losses are growing extremely rapidly (maybe $200 m in the USA in 2006, £35 m / $70 m in the UK) although they are hard to tie down exactly as some banks try to hold the customer liable and/or manipulate the accounting rules to avoid reporting frauds. The phishing business has plenty room for growth. Most UK losses in 2006 were sustained by one bank, while in the USA there are perhaps half-a-dozen principal victims. We are only just starting to see large-scale attacks on firms like eBay and Amazon, but I'm sure we will see many more; when compromising a password lets you change the target's email and street addresses to your own, and then use their credit card to order a wide-screen TV, the temptation is clear.

If you are a bank or an online retail business, then a number of factors influence whether you get targeted. Some have to do with whether you're thought to be a wimp; banks that pursue fraudsters viciously and relentlessly in the courts, well past the point of economic rationality, seem able to deter attacks. The phishermen also prefer banks whose poor internal controls allow large amounts of money to be moved abroad quickly, which lack effective intrusion alarms, which take several days to check whether suspicious payments were authorised, and which don't try too hard to retrieve those that weren't. (I will discuss internal controls later — see the chapter on Banking and Bookkeeping.)

In the rest of this chapter, I'll first visit some relevant basic psychology and then apply it to the study of passwords — how you get users to choose good passwords and enter them accurately, and what you can do to stop users disclosing them to third parties. Finally there will be a brief section on CAPTCHAs, the tests websites use to check that a user is a human rather than a robot; these provide another angle on the differences between human minds and software.

2.3   Insights from Psychology Research

I expect the interaction between security and psychology to be a big research area over the next five years, just as security economics has been over the last five. This is not just because of the growing number of attacks that target users instead of (or as well as) technology. For example, terrorism is largely about manipulating perceptions of risk; and even outside the national-security context, many protection mechanisms are sold using scaremongering. (I'll return to the broader policy issues in Part III.)

Psychology is a huge subject, ranging from neuroscience through to clinical topics, and spilling over into cognate disciplines from philosophy through artificial intelligence to sociology. Although it has been studied for much longer than computer science, our understanding of the mind is much less complete: the brain is so much more complex. We still do not understand one central problem — the nature of consciousness. We know that 'the mind is what the brain does', yet the mechanisms that underlie our sense of self and of personal history remain quite obscure.

Nonetheless a huge amount is known about the functioning of the mind and the brain, and I expect we'll get many valuable insights once we get psychologists working together with security researchers on real problems. In what follows I can only offer a helicopter tour of some ideas that appear relevant to our trade.

2.3.1 What the Brain Does Worse Than the Computer

Cognitive psychology deals with how we think, remember, make decisions and even daydream. There are many well-known results; for example, it is easier to memorise things that are repeated frequently, and it is easier to store things in context. However, many of these insights are poorly understood by systems developers. For example, most people have heard of George Miller's result that human short-term memory can cope with about seven (plus or minus two) simultaneous choices [891] and, as a result, many designers limit menu choices to about five. But this is not the right conclusion to draw. People search for information first by recalling where to look, and then by scanning; once you have found the relevant menu, scanning ten items is only twice as hard as scanning five. The real limit on menu size is with spoken menus, where the average user has difficulty dealing with more than three or four choices [1039].

Our knowledge in this field has been significantly enhanced by the empirical know-how gained not just from lab experiments, but from the iterative improvement of fielded systems. As a result, the centre of gravity has been shifting from applied psychology to the human-computer interaction (HCI) research community. HCI researchers not only model and measure human performance, including perception, motor control, memory and problem-solving; they have also developed an understanding of how people's mental models of systems work, and of the techniques (such as task analysis and cognitive walkthrough) that we can use to explore how people learn to use systems and understand them.

Security researchers need to find ways of turning these ploughshares into swords (the bad guys are already working on it). There are some obvious low-hanging fruit; for example, the safety research community has done a lot of work on characterising the errors people make when operating equipment [1060]. It's said that 'to err is human' and error research confirms this: the predictable varieties of human error are rooted in the very nature of cognition. The schemata, or mental models, that enable us to recognise people, sounds and concepts so much better than computers do, also make us vulnerable when the wrong model gets activated.

Human errors made while operating equipment fall into broadly three categories, depending on where they occur in the 'stack': slips and lapses at the level of skill, mistakes at the level of rules, and mistakes at the cognitive level.

- Actions performed often become a matter of skill, but this comes with a downside: inattention can cause a practised action to be performed instead of an intended one. We are all familiar with such *capture errors*; an example is when you intend to go to the supermarket on the way home from work but take the road home by mistake — as that's what you do most days. In computer systems, people are trained to click 'OK' to pop-up boxes as that's often the only way to get the work done; some attacks have used the fact that enough people will do this even when they know they shouldn't. (Thus Apple, unlike Microsoft, makes you enter your password when installing software — as this is something you do less often, you might just pause for thought.) Errors also commonly follow interruptions and perceptual confusion. One example is the *post-completion error*: once they've accomplished their immediate goal, people are easily distracted from tidying-up actions. More people leave cards behind in ATMs that give them the money first and the card back second.

▪ Actions that people take by following rules are open to errors when they follow the wrong rule. Various circumstances — such as information overload — can cause people to follow the strongest rule they know, or the most general rule, rather than the best one. Examples of phishermen getting people to follow the wrong rule include using `https` (because 'it's secure') and starting URLs with the impersonated bank's name, as `www.citibank.secureauthentication.com` — looking for the name being for many people a stronger rule than parsing its position.

▪ The third category of mistakes are those made by people for cognitive reasons — they simply don't understand the problem. For example, Microsoft's latest (IE7) anti-phishing toolbar is easily defeated by a picture-in-picture attack, which I'll describe later.

What makes security harder than safety is that we have a sentient attacker who will try to provoke exploitable errors.

What can the defender do? Well, we expect the attacker to use errors whose effect is predictable, such as capture errors. We also expect him to look for, or subtly create, exploitable dissonances between users' mental models of a system and its actual logic. Given a better understanding of this, we might try to engineer countermeasures — perhaps a form of cognitive walkthrough aimed at identifying attack points, just as a code walkthough can be used to search for software vulnerabilities.

2.3.2 Perceptual Bias and Behavioural Economics

Perhaps the most promising field of psychology for security folks to mine in the short term is that which studies the heuristics that people use, and the biases that influence them, when making decisions. This discipline, known as *behavioural economics* or *decision science*, sits at the boundary of psychology and economics. It examines the ways in which people's decision processes depart from the rational behaviour modeled by economists; Daniel Kahneman won the Nobel Prize in economics in 2002 for launching this field (along with the late Amos Tversky). One of his insights was that the heuristics we use in everyday judgement and decision making lie somewhere between rational thought and the unmediated input from the senses [679].

Kahneman and Tversky did extensive experimental work on how people made decisions faced with uncertainty. They developed *prospect theory* which models risk aversion, among other things: in many circumstances, people dislike losing $100 they already have more than they value winning $100. That's why marketers talk in terms of 'discount' and 'saving' — by *framing* an action as a gain rather than as a loss makes people more likely to take it. We're also bad at calculating probabilities, and use all sorts of heuristics to help us make decisions: we base inferences on familiar or easily-imagined analogies (the *availability heuristic* whereby easily-remembered data have more weight in mental processing), and by comparison with recent experiences (the *anchoring effect* whereby we base a judgement on an initial guess or comparison and then adjust it if need be). We also worry too much about unlikely events.

The channels through which we experience things also matter (we're more likely to be sceptical about things we've heard than about things we've seen). Another factor is that we evolved in small social groups, and the behaviour appropriate here isn't the same as in markets; indeed, many frauds work by appealing to our atavistic instincts to trust people more in certain situations or over certain types of decision. Other traditional vices now studied by behavioural economists range from our tendency to procrastinate to our imperfect self-control.

This tradition is not just relevant to working out how likely people are to click on links in phishing emails, but to the much deeper problem of the public perception of risk. Many people perceive terrorism to be a much worse threat than food poisoning or road traffic accidents: this is irrational, but hardly surprising to a behavioural economist, as we overestimate the small risk of dying in a terrorist attack not just because it's small but because of the visual effect of the 9/11 TV coverage and the ease of remembering the event. (There are further factors, which I'll discuss in Chapter 24 when we discuss terrorism.)

The misperception of risk underlies many other public-policy problems. The psychologist Daniel Gilbert, in an article provocatively entitled 'If only gay sex caused global warming', discusses why we are much more afraid of terrorism than of climate change. First, we evolved to be much more wary of hostile intent than of nature; 100,000 years ago, a man with a club (or a hungry lion) was a much worse threat than a thunderstorm. Second, global warming doesn't violate anyone's moral sensibilities; third, it's a long-term threat rather than a clear and present danger; and fourth, we're sensitive to rapid changes in the environment rather than slow ones [526].

Bruce Schneier lists more biases: we are less afraid when we're in control, such as when driving a car, as opposed to being a passenger in a car or airplane; we are more afraid of risks to which we've been sensitised, for example by gruesome news coverage; and we are more afraid of uncertainty, that is, when the magnitude of the risk is unknown (even when it's small). And a lot is known on the specific mistakes we're likely to make when working out probabilities and doing mental accounting [1129, 1133].

Most of us are not just more afraid of losing something we have, than of not making a gain of equivalent value, as prospect theory models. We're also risk-averse in that most people opt for a bird in the hand rather than two in the bush. This is thought to be an aspect of *satisficing* — as situations are often too hard to assess accurately, we have a tendency to plump for the alternative that's 'good enough' rather than face the cognitive strain of trying to work out the odds perfectly, especially when faced with a small transaction. Another aspect of this is that many people just plump for the standard configuration of a system, as they assume it will be good enough. This is one reason why secure defaults matter[1].

There is a vast amount of material here that can be exploited by the fraudster and the terrorist, as well as by politicians and other marketers. And as behavioural psychology gets better understood, the practice of marketing gets sharper too, and the fraudsters are never far behind. And the costs to business come not just from crime directly, but even more from the fear of crime. For example, many people don't use electronic banking because of a fear of fraud that is exaggerated (at least in the USA with its tough consumer-protection laws): so banks pay a fortune for the time of branch and call-center staff. So it's not enough for the security engineer to stop bad things happening; you also have to reassure people. The appearance of protection can matter just as much as the reality.

2.3.3 Different Aspects of Mental Processing

Many psychologists see the mind as composed of interacting rational and emotional components — 'heart' and 'head', or 'affective' and 'cognitive' systems. Studies of developmental biology have shown that, from an early age, we have different mental processing systems for social phenomena (such as recognising parents and siblings) and physical phenomena. Paul Bloom has written a provocative book arguing that the tension between them explains why many people are natural dualists — that is, they believe that mind and body are basically different [194]. Children try to explain what they see using their understanding of physics, but when this falls short, they explain phenomena in terms of deliberate action. This tendency to look for affective

---

[1]In fact, behavioral economics has fostered a streak of libertarian paternalism in the policy world that aims at setting good defaults in many spheres. An example is the attempt to reduce poverty in old age by making pension plans opt-out rather than opt-in.

explanations in the absence of material ones has survival value to the young, as it disposes them to get advice from parents or other adults about novel natural phenomena. According to Bloom, it has a significant side-effect: it predisposes humans to believe that body and soul are different, and thus lays the ground for religious belief. This argument may not overwhelm the faithful (who can retort that Bloom simply stumbled across a mechanism created by the Intelligent Designer to cause us to have faith in Him). But it may have relevance for the security engineer.

First, it goes some way to explaining the *fundamental attribution error* — people often err by trying to explain things by intentionality rather than by situation. Second, attempts to curb phishing by teaching users about the gory design details of the Internet — for example, by telling them to parse URLs in emails that seem to come from a bank — will be of limited value if users get bewildered. If the emotional is programmed to take over whenever the rational runs out, then engaging in a war of technical measures and counter-measures with the phishermen is fundamentally unsound. Safe defaults would be better — such as 'Our bank will never, ever send you email. Any email that purports to come from us is fraudulent.'

It has spilled over recently into behavioural economics via the *affect heuristic*, explored by Paul Slovic and colleagues [1189]. The idea is that by asking an emotional question (such as 'How many dates did you have last month?') you can get people to answer subsequent questions using their hearts more than their minds, which can make people insensitive to probability. This work starts to give us a handle on issues from people's risky behaviour with porn websites to the use of celebrities in marketing (and indeed in malware). Cognitive overload also increases reliance on affect: so a bank that builds a busy website may be able to sell more life insurance, but it's also likely to make its customers more vulnerable to phishing. In the other direction, events that evoke a feeling of dread — from cancer to terrorism — scare people more than the naked probabilities justify.

Our tendency to explain things by intent rather than by situation is reinforced by a tendency to frame decisions in social contexts; for example, we're more likely to trust people against whom we can take vengeance. (I'll discuss evolutionary game theory, which underlies this, in the chapter on Economics.)

2.3.4 Differences Between People

Most information systems are designed by men, and yet over half their users may be women. Recently people have realised that software can create barriers to females, and this has led to research work on 'gender HCI' — on how software should be designed so that women as well as men can use it effectively. For example, it's known that women navigate differently from men in the real world, using peripheral vision more, and it duly turns out that larger displays reduce gender bias. Other work has focused on female programmers, especially end-user programmers working with tools like spreadsheets. It turns out that women tinker less than males, but more effectively [139]. They appear to be more thoughtful, but lower self-esteem and higher risk-aversion leads them to use fewer features. Given that many of the world's spreadsheet users are women, this work has significant implications for product design.

No-one seems to have done any work on gender and security usability, yet reviews of work on gender psychology (such as [1012]) suggest many points of leverage. One formulation, by Simon Baron-Cohen, classifies human brains into type S (systematizers) and type E (empathizers) [120]. Type S people are better at geometry and some kinds of symbolic reasoning, while type Es are better at language and multiprocessing. Most men are type S, while most women are type E, a relationship that Baron-Cohen believes is due to fetal testosterone levels. Of course, innate abilities can be modulated by many developmental and social factors. Yet, even at a casual reading, this material makes me suspect that many security mechanisms are far from gender-neutral. Is it unlawful sex discrimination for a bank to expect its customers to detect phishing attacks by parsing URLs?

2.3.5 Social Psychology

This discipline attempts to explain how the thoughts, feelings, and behaviour of individuals are influenced by the actual, imagined, or implied presence of others. It has many aspects, from the identity that people derive from belonging to groups, through the self-esteem we get by comparing ourselves with others. It may be particularly useful in understanding persuasion; after all, deception is the twin brother of marketing. The growth of social-networking systems will lead to peer pressure being used as a tool for deception, just as it is currently used as a tool for marketing fashions.

Social psychology has been entangled with the security world longer than many other parts of psychology through its relevance to propaganda, interrogation and aggression. Three particularly famous experiments in the 20th century illuminated this. In 1951, Solomon Asch showed that people could be induced to deny the evidence of their own eyes in order to conform to a group. Subjects judged the lengths of lines after hearing wrong opinions from other group members, who were actually the experimenter's associates. Most subjects gave in and conformed, with only 29% resisting the bogus majority [90].

Stanley Milgram was inspired by the 1961 trial of Adolf Eichmann to investigate how many experimental subjects were prepared to administer severe electric shocks to an actor playing the role of a 'learner' at the behest of an experimenter playing the role of the 'teacher' — even when the 'learner' appeared to be in severe pain and begged the subject to stop. This experiment was designed to measure what proportion of people will obey an authority rather than their conscience. Most will — consistently over 60% of people will do downright immoral things if they are told to [888].

The third of these was the Stanford Prisoner Experiment which showed that normal people can behave wickedly even in the absence of orders. In 1971, experimenter Philip Zimbardo set up a 'prison' at Stanford where 24 students were assigned at random to the roles of 12 warders and 12 inmates. The aim of the experiment was to discover whether prison abuses occurred because warders (and possibly prisoners) were self-selecting. However, the students playing the role of warders rapidly became sadistic authoritarians, and the experiment was halted after six days on ethical grounds [1377].

Abuse of authority, whether real or ostensible, is a major issue for people designing operational security measures. During the period 1995–2005, a hoaxer calling himself 'Officer Scott' ordered the managers of over 68 US stores and restaurants in 32 US states (including at least 17 McDonalds' stores) to detain some young employee on suspicion of theft and strip-search her or him. Various other degradations were ordered, including beatings and sexual assaults [1351]. A former prison guard was tried for impersonating a police officer but acquitted. At least 13 people who obeyed the caller and did searches were charged with crimes, and seven were convicted. MacDonald's got sued for not training its store managers properly, even years after the pattern of hoax calls was established; and in October 2007, a jury ordered McDonalds to pay $6.1 million dollars to Louise Ogborn, one of the victims, who had been strip-searched when an 18-year-old employee. It was an unusually nasty case, as the victim was then left by the store manager in the custody of her boyfriend, who forced her to perform oral sex on him. The boyfriend got five years, and the manager pleaded guilty to unlawfully detaining Ogborn. When it came to the matter of damages, McDonalds argued that Ogborn was responsible for whatever damages she suffered for not realizing it was a hoax, and that the store manager had failed to apply common sense. A Kentucky jury didn't buy this and ordered McDonalds to pay up. The store manager also sued, saying she too was the victim of McDonalds' negligence to warn her of the hoax, and got $1.1 million [740]. So as of 2007, US employers seem to have a legal duty to train their staff to resist pretexting.

But what about a firm's customers? There is a lot of scope for phishermen to simply order bank customers to reveal their security data. Bank staff routinely tell their customers to do this, even when making unsolicited calls. I've personally received an unsolicited call from my bank saying 'Hello, this is Lloyds TSB, can you tell me your mother's maiden name?' and caused the caller much annoyance by telling her to get lost. Most people don't, though. ATM card thieves already called their victims in the 1980s and, impersonating bank or police officers, have ordered them to reveal PINs 'so that your card can be deactivated'. The current scam — as of December 2007 — is that callers who pretend to be from Visa say they are conducting a fraud investigation. After some rigmarole they say that some transactions to your card were fraudulent, so they'll be issuing a credit. But they need to satisfy themselves that you are still in possession of your card: so can you please read out the three security digits on the signature strip? A prudent system designer will expect a lot more of this, and will expect the courts to side with the customers eventually. If you train your customers to do something that causes them to come to harm, you can expect no other outcome.

Another interesting offshoot of social psychology is cognitive dissonance theory. People are uncomfortable when they hold conflicting views; they seek out information that confirms their existing views of the world and of themselves, and try to reject information that conflicts with their views or might undermine their self-esteem. One practical consequence is that people are remarkably able to persist in wrong courses of action in the face of mounting evidence that things have gone wrong [1241]. Admitting to yourself or to others that you were duped can be painful; hustlers know this and exploit it. A security professional should 'feel the hustle' — that is, be alert for a situation in which recently established social cues and expectations place you under pressure to 'just do' something about which you'd normally have reservations, so that you can step back and ask yourself whether you're being had. But training people to perceive this is hard enough, and getting the average person to break the social flow and say 'stop!' is really hard.

2.3.6   What the Brain Does Better Than the Computer

Psychology isn't all doom and gloom for our trade, though. There are tasks that the human brain performs much better than a computer. We are extremely good at recognising other humans visually, an ability shared by many primates. We are good at image recognition generally; a task such as 'pick out all scenes in this movie where a girl rides a horse next to water' is trivial for a human child yet a hard research problem in image processing. We're also better than machines at understanding speech, particularly in noisy environments, and at identifying speakers.

These abilities mean that it's possible to devise tests that are easy for humans to pass but hard for machines — the so-called 'CAPTCHA' tests that you often come across when trying to set up an online account or posting to a bulletin board. I will describe CAPTCHAs in more detail later in this chapter. They are a useful first step towards introducing some asymmetry into the interactions between people and machines, so as to make the bad guy's job harder than the legitimate user's.

2.4   Passwords

In this section, I will focus on the management of passwords as a simple, important and instructive context in which usability, applied psychology and security meet. Passwords are one of the biggest practical problems facing security engineers today. In fact, as the usability researcher Angela Sasse puts it, it's hard to think of a worse authentication mechanism than passwords, given what we know about human memory: people can't remember infrequently-used, frequently-changed, or many similar items; we can't forget on demand; recall is harder than recognition; and non-meaningful words are more difficult. The use of passwords imposes real costs on business: the UK phone company BT has a hundred people in its password-reset centre.

There are system and policy issues too: as people become principals in more and more electronic systems, the same passwords get used over and over again. Not only may attacks be carried out by outsiders guessing passwords, but by insiders in other systems. People are now asked to choose passwords for a large number of websites that they visit rarely. Does this impose an unreasonable burden?

Passwords are not, of course, the only way of authenticating users to systems. There are basically three options. The person may retain physical control of the device — as with a remote car door key. The second is that she presents something she knows, such as a password. The third is to use something like a fingerprint or iris pattern, which I'll discuss in the chapter on Biometrics. (These options are commonly summed up as 'something you have, something you know, or something you are' — or, as Simson Garfinkel engagingly puts it, 'something you had once, something you've forgotten, or something you once were'.) But for reasons of cost, most systems take the second option; and even where we use a physical token such as a one-time password generator, it is common to use another password as well (whether to lock it, or as an additional logon check) in case it gets stolen. Biometrics are also commonly used in conjunction with passwords, as you can't change your fingerprint once the Mafia gets to know it. So, like it or not, passwords are the (often shaky) foundation on which much of information security is built.

Some passwords have to be 'harder' than others, the principal reason being that sometimes we can limit the number of guesses an opponent can make and sometimes we cannot. With an ATM PIN, the bank can freeze the account after three wrong guesses, so a four-digit number will do. But there are many applications where it isn't feasible to put a hard limit on the number of guesses, such as where you encrypt a document with a password; someone who gets hold of the ciphertext can try passwords till the cows come home. In such applications, we have to try to get people to use longer passwords that are really hard to guess.

In addition to things that are 'obviously' passwords, such as your computer password and your bank card PIN, many other things (and combinations of things) are used for the same purpose. The most notorious are social security numbers, and your mother's maiden name, which many organisations use to recognize you. The ease with which such data can be guessed, or found out from more or less public sources, has given rise to a huge industry of so-called *'identity theft'* [458]. Criminals obtain credit cards, mobile phones and other assets in your name, loot them, and leave you to sort out the mess. In the USA, about half a million people are the 'victims' of this kind of fraud each year[2].

So passwords matter, and managing them is a serious real world problem that mixes issues of psychology with technical issues. There are basically three broad concerns, in ascending order of importance and difficulty:

1. Will the user enter the password correctly with a high enough probability?

2. Will the user remember the password, or will they have to either write it down or choose one that's easy for the attacker to guess?

3. Will the user break the system security by disclosing the password to a third party, whether accidentally, on purpose, or as a result of deception?

2.4.1 Difficulties with Reliable Password Entry

Our first human-factors issue is that if a password is too long or complex, users might have difficulty entering it correctly. If the operation they are trying to perform is urgent, this might have safety implications. If customers have difficulty entering software product activation codes, this can generate expensive calls to your support desk.

One application in which this is important is encrypted access codes. By quoting a reservation number, we get access to a hotel room, a rental car or an airline ticket. Activation codes for software and other products are often alphanumeric representations of encrypted data, which can be a 64-bit or 128-bit string with symmetric ciphers and hundreds of bits when public-key cryptography is used. As the numbers get longer, what happens to the error rate?

---

[2]I write 'identity theft' in quotes as it's a propaganda term for the old-fashioned offence of impersonation. In the old days, if someone went to a bank, pretended to be me, borrowed money from them and vanished, then that was the bank's problem, not mine. In the USA and the UK, banks have recently taken to claiming that it's my identity that's been stolen rather than their money, and that this somehow makes me liable. So I also parenthesise 'victims' — the banks are the real victims, except insofar as they commit secondary fraud against the customer. There's an excellent discussion of this by Adam Shostack and Paul Syverson in [1166].

An interesting study was done in South Africa in the context of prepaid electricity meters used to sell electricity in areas where the customers have no credit rating and often not even an address. With the most common make of meter, the customer hands some money to a sales agent, and in return gets one or more 20-digit numbers printed out on a receipt. He takes this receipt home and enters the numbers at a keypad in his meter. These numbers are encrypted commands, whether to dispense electricity, to change the tariff or whatever; the meter decrypts them and acts on them.

When this meter was introduced, its designers worried that since a third of the population was illiterate, and since people might get lost halfway through entering the number, the system might be unusable. But it turned out that illiteracy was not a problem: even people who could not read had no difficulty with numbers ('everybody can use a phone', as one of the engineers said). Entry errors were a greater problem, but were solved by printing the twenty digits in two rows, with three and two groups of four digits respectively [59].

A quite different application is the firing codes for U.S. nuclear weapons. These consist of only 12 decimal digits. If they are ever used, the operators may be under extreme stress, and possibly using improvised or obsolete communications channels. Experiments suggested that 12 digits was the maximum that could be conveyed reliably in such circumstances.

2.4.2 Difficulties with Remembering the Password

Our second psychological issue with passwords is that people often find them hard to remember [245, 1379]. Twelve to twenty digits may be fine when they are simply copied from a telegram or a meter ticket, but when customers are expected to memorize passwords, they either choose values which are easy for attackers to guess, or write them down, or both. In fact, the password problem has been neatly summed up as: "Choose a password you can't remember, and don't write it down."

The problems are not limited to computer access. For example, one chain of hotels in France introduced completely unattended service. You would turn up at the hotel, swipe your credit card in the reception machine, and get a receipt with a numerical access code which would unlock your room door. To keep costs down, the rooms did not have en-suite bathrooms, so guests had to use communal facilities. The usual failure mode was that a guest, having gone to the bathroom, would forget his access code. Unless he had taken the receipt with him, he'd end up having to sleep on the bathroom floor until the staff arrived the following morning.

Problems related to password memorability can be discussed under four main headings: naive password choice, user abilities and training, design errors, and operational failures.

2.4.3   Naive Password Choice

Since at least the mid-1980s, people have studied what sort of passwords are chosen by users who are left to their own devices. The results are depressing. People will use spouses' names, single letters, or even just hit carriage return giving an empty string as their password. So some systems started to require minimum password lengths, or even check user entered passwords against a dictionary of bad choices. However, password quality enforcement is harder than you might think. Fred Grampp and Robert Morris's classic paper on Unix security [550] reports that after software became available which forced passwords to be at least six characters long and have at least one nonletter, they made a file of the 20 most common female names, each followed by a single digit. Of these 200 passwords, at least one was in use on each of several dozen machines they examined.

A well-known study was conducted by Daniel Klein who gathered 25,000 Unix passwords in the form of encrypted password files and ran cracking software to guess them [720]. He found that 21–25% of passwords could be guessed depending on the amount of effort put in. Dictionary words accounted for 7.4%, common names for 4%, combinations of user and account name 2.7%, and so on down a list of less probable choices such as words from science fiction (0.4%) and sports terms (0.2%). Some of these were straighforward dictionary searches; others used patterns. For example, the algorithm for constructing combinations of user and account names would take an account *'klone'* belonging to the user 'Daniel V. Klein' and try passwords such as klone, klone1, klone 123, dvk, dvkdvk, leinad, neilk, DvkkvD, and so on.

Many firms require users to change passwords regularly, but this tends to backfire. According to one report, when users were compelled to change their passwords and prevented from using the previous few choices, they changed passwords rapidly to exhaust the history list and get back to their favorite password. A response, of forbidding password changes until after 15 days, meant that users couldn't change compromised passwords without help from an administrator [1008]. A large healthcare organisation in England is only now moving away from a monthly change policy; the predictable result was a large number of password resets at month end (to cope with which, sysadmins reset passwords to a well-known value). In my own experience, insisting on alphanumeric passwords and also forcing a password change once a month led people to choose passwords such as 'julia03' for March, 'julia04' for April, and so on.

So when our university's auditors write in their annual report each year that we should have a policy of monthly enforced password change, my response is to ask the chair of our Audit Committee when we'll get a new lot of auditors.

Even among the general population, there is some evidence that many peo ple now choose slightly better passwords; passwords retrieved from phishing sites typically contain numbers as well as letters, while the average password length has gone up from six to eight characters and the most common password is not 'password' but 'password1' [1130]. One possible explanation is that many people try to use the same password everywhere, and the deployment of password checking programs on some websites trains them to use longer passwords with numbers as well as letters [302].

2.4.4 User Abilities and Training

Sometimes you really can train users. In a corporate or military environment you can try to teach them to choose good passwords, or issue them with random passwords, and insist that passwords are treated the same way as the data they protect. So bank master passwords go in the vault overnight, while military 'Top Secret' passwords must be sealed in an envelope, in a safe, in a room that's locked when not occupied, in a building patrolled by guards. You can run background checks on everyone with access to any terminals where the passwords can be used. You can encrypt passwords along with data in transit between secure sites. You can send guards round at night to check that no-one's left a note of a password lying around. You can operate a clean desk policy so that a password can't be overlooked in a pile of papers on a desk. You can send your guards round the building every night to clean all desks every night.

Even if you're running an e-commerce website, you are not completely helpless: you can give your users negative feedback if they choose bad passwords. For example, you might require that passwords be at least eight characters long and contain at least one nonletter. But you will not want to drive your customers away. And even in the Army, you do not want to order your soldiers to do things they can't; then reality and regulations will drift apart, you won't really know what's going on, and discipline will be undermined. So what can you realistically expect from users when it comes to choosing and remembering passwords?

Colleagues and I studied the benefits that can be obtained by training users [1365]. While writing the first edition of this book, I could not find any account of experiments on this that would hold water by the standards of applied psychology (i.e., randomized controlled trials with big enough groups for the results to be statistically significant). The closest I found was a study of the recall rates, forgetting rates, and guessing rates of various types of password [245]; this didn't tell us the actual (as opposed to likely) effects of giving users various kinds of advice. We therefore selected three groups of about a hundred volunteers from our first year science students.

- The red (control) group was given the usual advice (password at least six characters long, including one nonletter).

- The green group was told to think of a passphrase and select letters from it to build a password. So 'It's 12 noon and I am hungry' would give `'I'S12&IAH'`.

- The yellow group was told to select eight characters (alpha or numeric) at random from a table we gave them, write them down, and destroy this note after a week or two once they'd memorized the password.

What we expected to find was that the red group's passwords would be easier to guess than the green group's which would in turn be easier than the yellow group's; and that the yellow group would have the most difficulty remembering their passwords (or would be forced to reset them more often), followed by green and then red. But that's not what we found.

About 30% of the control group chose passwords that could be guessed using cracking software (which I discuss later), versus about 10 percent for the other two groups. So passphrases and random passwords seemed to be about equally effective. When we looked at password reset rates, there was no significant difference between the three groups. When we asked the students whether they'd found their passwords hard to remember (or had written them down), the yellow group had significantly more problems than the other two; but there was no significant difference between red and green.

The conclusions we drew were as follows.

- For users who follow instructions, passwords based on mnemonic phrases offer the best of both worlds. They are as easy to remember as naively selected passwords, and as hard to guess as random passwords.

- The problem then becomes one of *user compliance*. A significant number of users (perhaps a third of them) just don't do what they're told.

So, while a policy of centrally-assigned, randomly selected passwords may work for the military, its value comes from the fact that the passwords are centrally assigned (thus compelling user compliance) rather than from the fact that they're random (as mnemonic phrases would do just as well).

But centrally-assigned passwords are often inappropriate. When you are offering a service to the public, your customers expect you to present broadly the same interfaces as your competitors. So you must let users choose their own website passwords, subject to some lightweight algorithm to reject passwords that are too short or otherwise 'clearly bad'. In the case of bank cards, users expect a bank-issued initial PIN plus the ability to change the PIN afterwards to one of their choosing (though again you may block a 'clearly bad' PIN such as 0000 or 1234). There can also be policy reasons not to issue passwords: for example, in Europe you can't issue passwords for devices that generate electronic signatures, as this could enable the system administrator to get at the signing key and forge messages, which would destroy the evidential value of the signature. By law, users must choose their own passwords.

So the best compromise will often be a password checking program that rejects 'clearly bad' user choices, plus a training program to get your compliant users to choose mnemonic passwords. Password checking can be done using a program like *crack* to filter user choices; other programs understand language statistics and reject passwords that are too likely to be chosen by others at random [353, 163]; another option is to mix the two ideas using a suitable coding scheme [1207].

2.4.4.1 *Design Errors*

Attempts to make passwords memorable are a frequent source of severe design errors — especially with the many systems built rapidly by unskilled people in the dotcom rush by businesses to get online.

An important example of how not to do it is to ask for 'your mother's maiden name'. A surprising number of banks, government departments and other organisations authenticate their customers in this way. But there are two rather obvious problems. First, your mother's maiden name is easy for a thief to find out, whether by asking around or using online genealogical databases. Second, asking for a maiden name makes assumptions which don't hold for all cultures, so you can end up accused of discrimination: Icelanders have no surnames, and women from many other countries don't change their names on marriage. Third, there is often no provision for changing 'your mother's maiden name', so if it ever becomes known to a thief your customer would have to close bank accounts (and presumably reopen them elsewhere). And even if changes are possible, and a cautious customer decides that from now on her mother's maiden name is going to be Yngstrom (or even 'yGt5r4ad') rather than Smith, there are further problems. She might be worried about breaking her credit card agreement, and perhaps invalidating her insurance cover, by giving false data. So smart customers will avoid your business; famous ones, whose mothers' maiden names are in Who's Who, should certainly shun you. Finally, people are asked to give their mother's maiden name to a lot of organisations, any one of which might have a crooked employee. (You could always try to tell 'Yngstrom' to your bank, 'Jones' to the phone company, 'Geraghty' to the travel agent, and so on; but data are shared extensively between companies, so you could easily end up confusing their systems — not to mention yourself).

Some organisations use contextual security information. My bank asks its business customers the value of the last check from their account that was cleared. In theory, this could be helpful: even if someone compromises my password — such as by overhearing me doing a transaction on the telephone — the security of the system usually recovers more or less automatically. The details bear some attention though. When this system was first introduced, I wondered about the risk that a supplier, to whom I'd just written a check, had a chance of impersonating me, and concluded that asking for the last three checks' values would be safer. But the problem I actually had was unexpected. Having given the checkbook to our accountant for the annual audit, I couldn't authenticate myself to get a balance over the phone. There is also a further liability shift: banks with such systems may expect customers to either keep all statements securely, or shred them. If someone who steals my physical post can also steal my money, I'd rather bank elsewhere.

Many e-commerce sites ask for a password explicitly rather than (or as well as) 'security questions' like a maiden name. But the sheer number of applications demanding a password nowadays exceeds the powers of human memory. Even though web browsers cache passwords, many customers will write passwords down (despite being told not to), or use the same password for many different purposes; relying on your browser cache makes life difficult when you're travelling and have to use an Internet café. The upshot is that the password you use to authenticate the customer of the electronic banking system you've just designed, may be known to a Mafia-operated porn site as well.

Twenty years ago, when I was working in the banking industry, we security folks opposed letting customers choose their own PINs for just this sort of reason. But the marketing folks were in favour, and they won the argument. Most banks allow the customer to choose their own PIN. It is believed that about a third of customers use a birthdate, in which case the odds against the thief are no longer over 3000 to 1 (getting four digits right in three guesses) but a bit over a hundred to one (and much shorter if he knows the victim). Even if this risk is thought acceptable, the PIN might still be set to the same value as the PIN used with a mobile phone that's shared with family members.

The risk you face as a consumer is not just a direct loss through 'identity theft' or fraud. Badly-designed password mechanisms that lead to password reuse can cause you to lose a genuine legal claim. For example, if a thief forges your cash machine card and loots your bank account, the bank will ask whether you have ever shared your PIN with any other person or company. If you admit to using the same PIN for your mobile phone, then the bank can say you were grossly negligent by allowing someone to see you using the phone, or maybe somebody at the phone company did it — so it's up to you to find them and sue them. Eventually, courts may find such contract terms unreasonable — especially as banks give different and conflicting advice. For example, the UK bankers' association has advised customers to change all their PINs to the same value, then more recently that this is acceptable but discouraged; their most recent leaflet also suggests using a keyboard pattern such as 'C' (3179) or 'U' (1793) [84].

Many attempts to find alternative solutions have hit the rocks. One bank sent its customers a letter warning them against writing down their PIN, and instead supplied a distinctive piece of cardboard on which they were supposed to conceal their PIN in the following way. Suppose your PIN is 2256. Choose a four-letter word, say 'blue'. Write these four letters down in the second, second, fifth and sixth columns of the card respectively, as shown in Figure 2.1. Then fill up the empty boxes with random letters.

1	2	3	4	5	6	7	8	9	0
	b								
	l								
				u					
					e				

Figure 2.1: A bad mnemonic system for bank PINs

This is clearly a bad idea. Even if the random letters aren't written in a slightly different way, a quick check shows that a four by ten matrix of random letters may yield about two dozen words (unless there's an 's' on the bottom row, when you can get 40–50). So the odds that the thief can guess the PIN, given three attempts, have just shortened from 1 in 3000-odd to 1 in 8.

2.4.4.2 *Operational Issues*

It's not just the customer end where things go wrong. One important case in Britain in the late 1980's was R v Gold and Schifreen. The defendants saw a phone number for the development system for Prestel (an early public email service run by British Telecom) in a note stuck on a terminal at an exhibition. They dialed in later, and found that the welcome screen had an all-powerful maintenance password displayed on it. They tried this on the live system too, and it worked! They proceeded to hack into the Duke of Edinburgh's electronic mail account, and sent mail 'from' him to someone they didn't like, announcing the award of a knighthood. This heinous crime so shocked the establishment that when prosecutors failed to convict the defendants under the laws then in force, parliament passed Britain's first specific computer crime law.

A similar and very general error is failing to reset the default passwords supplied with certain system services. For example, one top-selling dial access system in the 1980's had a default software support user name of 999999 and a password of 9999. It also had a default supervisor name of 777777 with a password of 7777. Most sites didn't change these passwords, and many of them were hacked once the practice became widely known. Failure to change default passwords as supplied by the equipment vendor has affected a wide range of systems. To this day there are web applications running on databases that use well-known default master passwords — and websites listing the defaults for everything in sight.

2.4.5 Social-Engineering Attacks

The biggest practical threat to passwords nowadays is that the user will break system security by disclosing the password to a third party, whether accidentally or as a result of deception. This is the core of the 'phishing' problem.

Although the first phishing attacks happened in 2003, the word 'phishing' itself is older, having appeared in 1996 in the context of the theft of AOL passwords. Even by 1995, attempts to harvest these to send spam had become sufficiently common for AOL to have a 'report password solicitation' button on its web page; and the first reference to 'password fishing' is in 1990, in the context of people altering terminal firmware to collect Unix logon passwords [301][3].

Phishing brings together several threads of attack technology. The first is pretexting, which has long been a practical way of getting passwords and PINs. An old thieves' trick, having stolen a bank card, is to ring up the victim and say 'This is the security department of your bank. We see that your card has been used fraudulently to buy gold coins. I wonder if you can tell me the PIN, so I can get into the computer and cancel it?'

There are many variants. A harassed system administrator is called once or twice on trivial matters by someone who claims to be a very senior manager's personal assistant; once he has accepted her as an employee, she calls and demands a new password for her boss. (See Mitnick's book [896] for dozens more examples.) It even works by email. In a systematic experimental study, 336 computer science students at the University of Sydney were sent an email message asking them to supply their password on the pretext that it was required to 'validate' the password database after a suspected breakin. 138 of them returned a valid password. Some were suspicious: 30 returned a plausible looking but invalid password, while over 200 changed their passwords without official prompting. But very few of them reported the email to authority [556].

Within a tightly-run company, such risks can just about be controlled. We've a policy at our lab that initial passwords are always handed by the sysadmin to the user on paper. Sun Microsystems had a policy that the root password for each machine is a 16-character random alphanumeric string, kept in an envelope with the machine, and which may never be divulged over the phone or sent over the network. If a rule like this is rigidly enforced throughout an organization, it will make any pretext attack on a root password conspicuous. The people who can get at it must be only those who can physically access the machine anyway. (The problem is of course that you have to teach staff not

---

[3]The first recorded spam is much earlier: in 1865, a London dentist annoyed polite society by sending out telegrams advertising his practice [415]. Manners and other social mechanisms have long lagged behind technological progress!

just a rule, but the reasoning behind the rule. Otherwise you end up with the password stuck to the terminal, as in the Prestel case.)

Another approach, used at the NSA, is to have different colored internal and external telephones which are not connected to each other, and a policy that when the external phone in a room is off-hook, classified material can't even be discussed in the room — let alone on the phone. A somewhat less extreme approach (used at our laboratory) is to have different ring tones for internal and external phones. This works so long as you have alert system administrators.

Outside of controlled environments, things are harder. A huge problem is that many banks and other businesses train their customers to act in unsafe ways. It's not prudent to click on links in emails, so if you want to contact your bank you should type in the URL or use a bookmark — yet bank marketing departments continue to send out emails containing clickable links. Many email clients — including Apple's, Microsoft's, and Google's — make plaintext URLs clickable, and indeed their users may never see a URL that isn't. This makes it harder for banks to do the right thing.

A prudent customer ought to be cautious if a web service directs him somewhere else — yet bank systems can use all sorts of strange URLs for their services. It's not prudent to give out security information over the phone to unidentified callers — yet we all get phoned by bank staff who aggressively demand security information without having any well-thought-out means of identifying themselves. Yet I've had this experience now from two of the banks with which I've done business — once from the fraud department that had got suspicious about a transaction my wife had made. If even the fraud department doesn't understand that banks ought to be able to identify themselves, and that customers should not be trained to give out security information on the phone, what hope is there?

You might expect that a dotcom such as eBay would know better, yet its banking subsidiary PayPal sent its UK customers an email in late 2006 directing them to a competition at `www.paypalchristmas.co.uk`, a domain belonging to a small marketing company I'd never heard of; and despite the fact that they're the most heavily phished site on the web, and boast of the technical prowess of their anti-fraud team when speaking at conferences, the marketing folks seem to have retained the upper hand over the security folks. In November 2007 they sent an email to a colleague of mine which had a sidebar warning him to always type in the URL when logging in to his account — and a text body that asked him to click on a link! (My colleague closed his account in disgust.)

Citibank reassures its customers that it will never send emails to customers to verify personal information, and asks them to disregard and report emails that ask for such information, including PIN and account details. So what happened? You guessed it — it sent its Australian customers an email in October 2006 asking customers 'as part of a security upgrade' to log on to the bank's website and authenticate themselves using a card number and an ATM PIN [739]. Meanwhile a marketing spam from the Bank of America directed UK customers to `mynewcard.com`. Not only is spam illegal in Britain, and the domain name inconsistent, and clickable links a bad idea; but BoA got the certificate wrong (it was for `mynewcard.bankofamerica.com`). The 'mynewcard' problem had been pointed out in 2003 and not fixed. Such bad practices are rife among major banks, who thereby train their customers to practice unsafe computing — by disregarding domain names, ignoring certificate warnings, and merrily clicking links [399]. As a result, even security experts have difficulty telling bank spam from phish [301].

But perhaps the worst example of all came from Halifax Share Dealing Services, part of a large well-known bank in the UK, which sent out a spam with a URL not registered to the bank. The Halifax's web page at the time sensibly advised its customers not to reply to emails, click on links or disclose details — and the spam itself had a similar warning at the end. The mother of a student of ours received this spam and contacted the bank's security department, which told her it was a phish. The student then contacted the ISP to report abuse, and found that the URL and the service were genuine — although provided to the Halifax by a third party [842]. When even a bank's security department can't tell spam from phish, how are their customers supposed to?

2.4.6 Trusted Path

The second thread in the background of phishing is *trusted path*, which refers to some means of being sure that you're logging into a genuine machine through a channel that isn't open to eavesdropping. Here the deception is more technical than psychological; rather than inveigling a bank customer into revealing her PIN to you by claiming to be a policeman, you steal her PIN directly by putting a false ATM in a shopping mall.

Such attacks go back to the dawn of time-shared computing. A public terminal would be left running an attack program that looks just like the usual logon screen — asking for a user name and password. When an unsuspecting user does this, it will save the password somewhere in the system, reply 'sorry, wrong password' and then vanish, invoking the genuine password program. The user will assume that he made a typing error first time and think no more of it. This is why Windows has a *secure attention sequence*, namely `ctrl-alt-del`, which is guaranteed to take you to a genuine password prompt.

If the whole terminal is bogus, then of course all bets are off. We once caught a student installing modified keyboards in our public terminal room to capture passwords. When the attacker is prepared to take this much trouble, then all the `ctrl-alt-del` sequence achieves is to make his software design task simpler.

Crooked cash machines and point-of-sale terminals are now a big deal. In one early case in Connecticut in 1993 the bad guys even bought genuine cash machines (on credit), installed them in a shopping mall, and proceeded to collect PINs and card details from unsuspecting bank customers who tried to use them [33]. Within a year, crooks in London had copied the idea, and scaled it up to a whole bogus bank branch [635]. Since about 2003, there has been a spate of *skimmers* — devices fitted over the front of genuine cash machines which copy the card data as it's inserted and use a pinhole camera to record the customer PIN. Since about 2005, we have also seen skimmers that clip on to the wires linking point-of-sale terminals in stores to their PIN pads, and which contain mobile phones to send captured card and PIN data to the crooks by SMS. (I'll discuss such devices in much more detail later in the chapter on Banking and Bookkeeping.)

2.4.7 Phishing Countermeasures

What makes phishing hard to deal with is the combination of psychology and technology. On the one hand, users have been trained to act insecurely by their bankers and service providers, and there are many ways in which people can be conned into clicking on a web link. Indeed much of the marketing industry is devoted to getting people to click on links. In April 2007 there was the first reported case of attackers buying Google AdWords in an attempt to install keyloggers on PCs. This cost them maybe a couple of dollars per click but enabled them to target the PCs of users thinking of setting up a new business [1248].

On the other hand, so long as online service providers want to save money by using the open systems platform provided by web servers and browsers, the technology does not provide any really effective way for users to identify the website into which they are about to enter a password.

Anyway, a large number of phishing countermeasures have been tried or proposed.

2.4.7.1 Password Manglers

A number of people have designed browser plug-ins that take the user-entered password and transparently turn it into a strong, domain-specific password. A typical mechanism is to hash it using a secret key and the domain name of the web site into which it's being entered [1085]. Even if the user always uses the same password (even if he uses 'password' as his password), each web site he visits will be provided with a different and hard-to-guess password that is unique to him. Thus if he mistakenly enters his Citibank password into a phishing site, the phisherman gets a different password and cannot use it to impersonate him.

This works fine in theory but can be tricky to implement in practice. Banks and shops that use multiple domain names are one headache; another comes from the different rules that websites use for password syntax (some insist on alphanumeric, others alpha; some are case sensitive and others not; and so on). There is also a cost to the user in terms of convenience: roaming becomes difficult. If only your home machine knows the secret key, then how do you log on to eBay from a cyber-café when you're on holiday?

2.4.7.2   Client Certs or Specialist Apps

One of the earliest electronic banking systems I used was one from Bank of America in the 1980s. This came as a bootable floppy disk; you put it in your PC, hit ctrl-alt-del, and your PC was suddenly transformed into a bank terminal. As the disk contained its own copy of the operating system, this terminal was fairly secure. There are still some online banking systems (particularly at the corporate end of the market) using such bespoke software. Of course, if a bank were to give enough customers a special banking application for them to be a worthwhile target, the phishermen will just tell them to 'please apply the attached upgrade'.

A lower-cost equivalent is the *client certificate*. The SSL protocol supports certificates for the client as well as the server. I'll discuss the technical details later, but for now a certificate is supposed to identify its holder to the other principals in a transaction and to enable the traffic between them to be securely encrypted. Server certificates identify web sites to your browser, causing the lock icon to appear when the name on the certificate corresponds to the name in the toolbar. Client certificates can be used to make the authentication mutual, and some UK stockbrokers started using them in about 2006. As of 2007, the mechanism is still not bulletproof, as certification systems are a pain to manage, and Javascript can be used to fool common browsers into performing cryptographic operations they shouldn't [1163]. Even once that's fixed, the risk is that malware could steal them, or that the phisherman will just tell the customer 'Your certificates have expired, so please send them back to us for secure destruction'.

2.4.7.3   Using the Browser's Password Database

Choosing random passwords and letting your browser cache remember them can be a pragmatic way of operating. It gets much of the benefit of a password mangler, as the browser will only enter the password into a web page with the right URL (IE) or the same hostname and field name (Firefox). It suffers from some of the same drawbacks (dealing with amazon.com versus amazon.co.uk, and with roaming). As passwords are stored unencrypted, they are at some small risk of compromise from malware. Whether you use this strategy may depend on whether you reckon the greater risk comes from phishing or from keyloggers. (Firefox lets you encrypt the password database but this is not the default so many users won't invoke it.) I personally use this approach with many low-to-medium-grade web passwords.

Many banks try to disable this feature by setting `autocomplete="off"` in their web pages. This stops Firefox and Internet Explorer storing the password. Banks seem to think this improves security, but I doubt it. There may be a small benefit in that a virus can't steal the password from the browser database, but the phishing defence provided by the browser is disabled — which probably exposes the customer to much greater risk [913].

2.4.7.4 Soft Keyboards

This was a favorite of banks in Latin America for a while. Rather than using the keyboard, they would flash up a keyboard on the screen on which the customer had to type out their password using mouse clicks. The bankers thought the bad guys would not be able to capture this, as the keyboard could appear differently to different customers and in different sessions.

However the phishing suppliers managed to write software to defeat it. At present, they simply capture the screen for 40 pixels around each mouse click and send these images back to the phisherman for him to inspect and decipher. As computers get faster, more complex image processing becomes possible.

2.4.7.5 Customer Education

Banks have put some effort into trying to train their customers to look for certain features in websites. This has partly been due diligence — seeing to it that customers who don't understand or can't follow instructions can be held liable — and partly a bona fide attempt at risk reduction. However, the general pattern is that as soon as customers are trained to follow some particular rule, the phisherman exploit this, as the reasons for the rule are not adequately explained.

At the beginning, the advice was 'Check the English', so the bad guys either got someone who could write English, or simply started using the banks' own emails but with the URLs changed. Then it was 'Look for the lock symbol', so the phishing sites started to use SSL (or just forging it by putting graphics of lock symbols on their web pages). Some banks started putting the last four digits of the customer account number into emails; the phishermen responded by putting in the first four (which are constant for a given bank and card product). Next the advice was that it was OK to click on images, but not on

URLs; the phishermen promptly put in links that appeared to be images but actually pointed at executables. The advice then was to check where a link would really go by hovering your mouse over it; the bad guys then either inserted a non-printing character into the URL to stop Internet Explorer from displaying the rest, or used an unmanageably long URL (as many banks also did).

As I remarked earlier, this sort of arms race is most likely to benefit the attackers. The countermeasures become so complex and counterintuitive that they confuse more and more users — exactly what the phishermen need. The safety and usability communities have known for years that 'blame and train' is not the way to deal with unusable systems–the only remedy is to make the systems properly usable in the first place [972].

2.4.7.6 *Microsoft Passport*

Microsoft Passport was on the face of it a neat idea — a system for using Microsoft's logon facilities to authenticate the users of any merchant website. Anyone with an account on a Microsoft service, such as Hotmail, could log on automatically to a participating website using a proprietary protocol adapted from Kerberos to send tickets back and forth in cookies.

One downside was that putting all your eggs in one basket gives people an incentive to try to kick the basket over. There were many juicy security flaws. At one time, if you logged in to Passport using your own ID and password, and then as soon as you'd entered that you backtracked and changed the ID to somebody else's, then when the system had checked your password against the file entry for the first ID, it would authenticate you as the owner of the second. This is a classic example of a *race condition* or time-of-check-to-time-of-use (TOCTTOU) vulnerability, and a spectacular one it was too: anyone in the world could masquerade as anyone else to any system that relied on Passport for authentication. Other flaws included cookie-stealing attacks, password reset attacks and logout failures. On a number of occasions, Microsoft had to change the logic of Passport rapidly when such flaws came to light. (At least, being centralised, it could be fixed quickly.)

Another downside came from the business model. Participating sites had to use Microsoft web servers rather than free products such as Apache, and it was feared that Microsoft's access to a mass of data about who was doing what business with which website would enable it to extend its dominant position in browser software into a dominant position in the market for consumer profiling data. Extending a monopoly from one market to another is against European law. There was an industry outcry that led to the establishment of the Liberty Alliance, a consortium of Microsoft's competitors, which developed open protocols for the same purpose. (These are now used in some application areas, such as the car industry, but have not caught on for general consumer use.)

2.4.7.7   *Phishing Alert Toolbars*

Some companies have produced browser toolbars that use a number of heuristics to parse URLs and look for wicked ones. Microsoft offers such a toolbar in Internet Explorer version 7. The idea is that if the user visits a known phishing site, the browser toolbar turns red; if she visits a suspect site, it turns yellow; a normal site leaves it white; while a site with an 'extended validation' certificate — a new, expensive type of certificate that's only sold to websites after their credentials have been checked slightly more diligently than used to be the case — then it will turn green.

The initial offering has already been broken, according to a paper jointly authored by researchers from Stanford and from Microsoft itself [650]. Attackers can present users with a 'picture-in-picture' website which simply displays a picture of a browser with a nice green toolbar in the frame of the normal browser. (No doubt the banks will say 'maximise the browser before entering your password' but this won't work for the reasons discussed above.) The new scheme can also be attacked using similar URLs: for example, `www.bankofthewest.com` can be impersonated as `www.bankofthevvest.com`. Even if the interface problem can be fixed, there are problems with using heuristics to spot dodgy sites. The testing cannot be static; if it were, the phishermen would just tinker with their URLs until they passed the current tests. Thus the toolbar has to call a server at least some of the time, and check in real time whether a URL is good or bad. The privacy aspects bear thinking about, and it's not entirely clear that the competition-policy issues with Passport have been solved either.

2.4.7.8   *Two-Factor Authentication*

Various firms sell security tokens that produce a one-time password. This can be in response to a challenge sent by the machine to which you want to log on, or more simply a function of time; you can get a keyfob device that displays a new eight-digit password every few seconds. I'll describe the technology in more detail in the next chapter. These devices were invented in the early 1980s and are widely used to log on to corporate systems. They are often referred to as *two-factor authentication*, as the system typically asks for a memorised password as well; thus your logon consists of 'something you have' and also 'something you know'. Password calculators are now used by some exclusive London private banks, such as the Queen's bankers, Coutts, to authenticate their online customers, and we're now seeing them at a handful of big money-centre banks too.

There is some pressure[4] for banks to move to two-factor authentication and issue all their customers with password calculators. But small banks are chronically short of development resources, and even big banks' security staff resist the move on grounds of cost; everyone also knows that the phishermen will simply switch to real-time man-in-the-middle attacks. I'll discuss these in detail in the next chapter, but the basic idea is that the phisherman pretends to the customer to be the bank and pretends to the bank to be the customer at the same time, simply taking over the session once it's established. As of early 2007, only one or two such phishing attacks have been detected, but the attack technology could be upgraded easily enough.

The favoured two-factor technology in Europe is the chip authentication program (CAP) device which I'll also describe in the next chapter. This can be used either to calculate a logon password, or (once man-in-the-middle attacks become widespread) to compute a message authentication code on the actual transaction contents. This means that to pay money to someone you'll probably have to type in their account number and the amount twice — once into the bank's website and once into your CAP calculator. This will clearly be a nuisance: tedious, fiddly and error-prone.

2.4.7.9 Trusted Computing

The 'Trusted Computing' initiative, which has led to TPM security chips in PC motherboards, may make it possible to tie down a transaction to a particular PC motherboard. The TPM chip can support functions equivalent to those of the CAP device. Having hardware bank transaction support integrated into the PC will be less fiddly than retyping data at the CAP as well as the PC; on the other hand, roaming will be a problem, as it is with password manglers or with relying on the browser cache.

Vista was supposed to ship with a mechanism (remote attestation) that would have made it easy for bank software developers to identify customer PCs with high confidence and to stop the bad guys from easily tinkering with the PC software. However, as I'll describe later in the chapter on access control, Microsoft appears to have been unable to make this work yet, so bank programmers will have to roll their own. As Vista has just been released into consumer markets in 2007, it may be 2011 before most customers could have this option available, and it remains to be seen how the banks would cope with Apple or Linux users. It might be fair to say that this technology has not so far lived up to the initial hype.

---

[4]In the USA, from the Federal Financial Institutions Examination Council — which, as of September 2007, 98% of banks were still resisting [1003].

2.4.7.10 Fortified Password Protocols

In 1992, Steve Bellovin and Michael Merritt looked at the problem of how a guessable password could be used in an authentication protocol between two machines [158]. They came up with a series of protocols for encrypted key exchange, whereby a key exchange is combined with a shared password in such a way that a man-in-the-middle could not guess the password. Various other researchers came up with other protocols to do the same job.

Some people believe that these protocols could make a significant dent in the phishing industry in a few years' time, once the patents run out and the technology gets incorporated as a standard feature into browsers.

2.4.7.11 Two-Channel Authentication

Perhaps the most hopeful technical innovation is two-channel authentication. This involves sending an access code to the user via a separate channel, such as their mobile phone. The Bank of America has recently introduced a version of this called SafePass in which a user who tried to log on is sent a six-digit code to their mobile phone; they use this as an additional password [868]. The problem with this is the same as with the two-factor authentication already tried in Europe: the bad guys will just use a real-time man-in-the-middle attack.

However, two-channel comes into its own when you authenticate transaction data as well. If your customer tries to do a suspicious transaction, you can send him the details and ask for confirmation: 'If you really wanted to send $7500 to Russia, please enter 4716 now in your browser.' Implemented like this, it has the potential to give the level of authentication aimed at by the CAP designers but with a much more usable interface. Banks have held back from using two-channel in this way because of worries that usability problems might drive up their call-centre costs; however the first banks to implement it report that it hasn't pushed up support call volumes, and a number of sites have been implementing it through 2007, with South African banks being in the forefront. We have already seen the first serious fraud — some Johannesburg crooks social-engineered the phone company to send them a new SIM for the phone number of the CFO of Ubuntu, a charity that looks after orphaned and vulnerable children, and emptied its bank account [1017]. The bank and the phone company are arguing about liability, although the phone company says it's fixing its procedures.

Even once the phone-company end of things gets sorted, there are still limits. Two-channel authentication relies for its security on the independence of the channels: although the phishermen may be able to infect both PCs and mobile phones with viruses, so long as both processes are statistically independent, only a very small number of people will have both platforms compromised at the same time. However, if everyone starts using an iPhone, or doing VoIP telephony over wireless access points, then the assumption of independence breaks down.

Nonetheless, if I were working for a bank and looking for a front-end authentication solution today, two-channel would be the first thing I would look at. I'd be cautious about high-value clients, because of possible attacks on the phone company, but for normal electronic banking it seems to give the most bang for the buck.

2.4.8   The Future of Phishing

It's always dangerous to predict the future, but it's maybe worth the risk of wondering where phishing might go over the next seven years. What might I be writing about in the next edition of this book?

I'd expect to see the phishing trade grow substantially, with attacks on many non-banks. In November 2007, there was a phishing attack on Salesforce.com in which the phisherman got a password from a staff member, following which customers started receiving bogus invoices [614]. If it gets hard to phish the banks, the next obvious step is to phish their suppliers (such as Salesforce). In a world of increasing specialisation and outsourcing, how can you track dependencies and identify vulnerabilities?

Second, research has shown that the bad guys can greatly improve their yields if they match the context of their phish to the targets [658]; so phish will get smarter and harder to tell from real emails, just as spam has. Authority can be impersonated: 80% of West Point cadets bit a phish sent from a bogus colonel, and a phisherman who uses a social network can do almost as well: while emails from a random university address got 16% of students to visit an off-campus website and enter their university password to access it, this shot up to 72% if the email appeared to come from one of the target's friends — with the friendship data collected by spidering open-access social-networking websites [653]. Future phishermen won't ask you for your mother's maiden name: they'll forge emails from your mother.

On the technical side, more man-in-the-middle attacks seem likely, as do more compromises of endpoints such as PCs and mobile phones. If a banking application running on Vista can only do business on the genuine motherboard, then the attacker will look for ways to run his software on that motherboard. If 'trusted computing' features in later releases of Vista can stop malware actually pressing keys and overwriting the screen while a banking application is running, this might bring real benefits (but I'm not holding my breath).

Starting from the top end of the market, I would not be surprised to see exclusive private banks issuing their customers with dedicated payment devices — 'Keep your account $50,000 in credit and get a Free Gold Blackberry!' Such a device could do wireless payments securely and perhaps even double as a credit card. (I expect it would fail when the marketing department also decided it should handle ordinary email, and the crooks figured out ways of pretexting the rich accountholders into doing things they didn't really mean to.)

At the middle of the market, I'd expect to see phishing become less distinguishable from more conventional confidence tricks. I mentioned earlier that the marketing industry nowadays was largely about getting people to click on links. Now Google has built a twelve-figure business out of this, so if you're a crook, why not just advertise there for victims? It's already started. And indeed, research by Ben Edelman has found that while 2.73% of companies ranked top in a web search were bad, 4.44% of companies who had bought ads from the search engine were bad [416]. (Edelman's conclusion — 'Don't click on ads' — could be bad news in the medium term for the search industry.)

On the regulatory side of things, I expect more attempts to interfere in the identity market, as governments such as America's and Britain's look for ways to issue citizens with identity cards, and as international bodies try to muscle in. The International Telecommunications Union tried this in 2006 [131]; it won't be the last. We will see more pressures to use two-factor authentication, and to use biometrics. Those parts of the security-industrial complex have been well fed since 9/11 and will lobby hard for corporate welfare.

However, I don't believe it will be effective to rely entirely on front-end controls, whether passwords or fancy widgets. Tricksters will still be able to con people (especially the old and the less educated), and systems will continue to get more and more complex, limited only by the security, usability and other failures inflicted by feature interaction. I believe that the back-end controls will be at least as important. The very first home banking system — introduced by the Bank of Scotland in 1984 — allowed payments only to accounts that you had previously 'nominated' in writing. The idea was that you'd write to the bank to nominate your landlord, your gas company, your phone company and so on, and then you could pay your bills by email. You set a monthly limit on how much could be paid to each of them. These early systems suffered almost no fraud; there was no easy way for a bad man to extract cash. But the recipient controls were dismantled during the dotcom boom and then phishing took off.

Some banks are now starting to reintroduce controls — for example, by imposing a delay and requiring extra authentication the first time a customer makes a payment to someone they haven't paid before. Were I designing an online banking system now, I would invest most of the security budget in the back end. The phishermen target banks that are slow at recovering stolen funds [55]. If your asset-recovery team is really on the ball, checks up quickly on attempts to send money to known cash-extraction channels, claws it back vigorously, and is ruthless about using the law against miscreants, then the phishermen will go after your competitors instead. (I'll discuss what makes controls effective later, in the chapter on Banking and Bookkeeping, especially section 10.3.2.)

2.5   System Issues

Although the fastest-growing public concern surrounding passwords is phishing, and the biggest research topic is psychology, there are a number of other circumstances in which attackers try to steal or guess passwords, or compromise systems in other ways. There are also technical issues to do with password entry and storage that I'll also cover briefly here for the sake of completeness.

I already noted that the biggest system issue was whether it is possible to restrict the number of password guesses. Security engineers sometimes refer to password systems as 'online' if guessing is limited (as with ATM PINs) and 'offline' if it is not (this originally meant systems where a user could fetch the password file and take it away to try to guess the passwords of other users, including more privileged users). The terms are no longer really accurate. Some offline systems restrict password guesses, such as the smartcards used in more and more countries for ATMs and retail transactions; these check the PIN in the smartcard chip and rely on its tamper-resistance to limit guessing. Many online systems cannot restrict guesses; for example, if you log on using Kerberos, an opponent who taps the line can observe your key encrypted with your password flowing from the server to your client, and then data encrypted with that key flowing on the line; so she can take her time to try out all possible passwords.

Password guessability is not the only system-level design question, though; there are others (and they interact). In this section I'll describe a number of issues concerning threat models and technical protection, which you might care to consider next time you design a password system.

Just as we can only talk about the soundness of a security protocol in the context of a specific threat model, so we can only judge whether a given password scheme is sound by considering the type of attacks we are trying to defend against. Broadly speaking, these are:

Targeted attack on one account: an intruder tries to guess a particular user's password. He might try to guess the PIN for Bill Gates's bank account, or a rival's logon password at the office, in order to do mischief directly. When this involves sending emails, it is known as *spear phishing*.

Attempt to penetrate any account on a system: the intruder tries to get a logon as any user of the system. This is the classic case of the phisherman trying to get a password for any user of a target bank's online service.

Attempt to penetrate any account on any system: the intruder merely wants an account at any system in a given domain but doesn't care which one. Examples are bad guys trying to guess passwords on an online service so they can send spam from the compromised account, or use its web space to host a phishing site for a few hours. The modus operandi is often to try one or two common passwords (such as 'password1') on large numbers of randomly-selected accounts. Other possible attackers might be teens looking for somewhere to hide pornography, or a private eye tasked to get access to a company's intranet who is looking for a beachhead in the form of a logon to some random machine in their domain.

Service denial attack: the attacker may wish to prevent the legitimate user from using the system. This might be targeted on a particular account or system-wide.

This taxonomy helps us ask relevant questions when evaluating a password system.

2.5.1   Can You Deny Service?

Banks often have a rule that a terminal and user account are frozen after three bad password attempts; after that, an administrator has to reactivate them. This could be rather dangerous in a military system, as an enemy who got access to the network could use a flood of false logon attempts to mount a service denial attack; if he had a list of all the user names on a machine he might well take it out of service completely. Many commercial websites nowadays don't limit guessing because of the possibility of such an attack.

When deciding whether this might be a problem, you have to consider not just the case in which someone attacks one of your customers, but also the case in which someone attacks your whole system. Can a flood of false logon attempts bring down your service? Could it be used to blackmail you? Or can you turn off account blocking quickly in the event that such an attack materialises? And if you do turn it off, what sort of attacks might follow?

2.5.2   Protecting Oneself or Others?

Next, to what extent does the system need to protect users from each other? In some systems — such as mobile phone systems and cash machine systems — no-one should be able to use the service at someone else's expense. It is assumed that the attackers are already legitimate users of the system. So systems are (or at least should be) carefully designed so that knowledge of one user's password will not allow another identifiable user's account to be compromised.

Where a user who chooses a password that is easy to guess harms only himself, a wide variation in password strength can more easily be tolerated. (Bear in mind that the passwords people choose are very often easy for their spouses or partners to guess [245]: so some thought needs to be given to issues such as what happens when a cheated partner seeks vengeance.)

But many systems do not provide strong separation between users. Operating systems such as Unix and Windows may have been designed to protect one user against accidental interference by another, but they are not hardened to protect against capable malicious actions by other users. They have many well-publicized vulnerabilities, with more being published constantly on the web. A competent opponent who can get a single account on a shared computer system that is not professionally managed can usually become the system administrator fairly quickly, and from there he can do whatever he likes.

2.5.3   Attacks on Password Entry

Password entry is often poorly protected.

2.5.3.1   *Interface Design*

Sometimes the problem is thoughtless interface design. Some common makes of cash machine had a vertical keyboard at head height, making it simple for a pickpocket to watch a customer enter her PIN before lifting her purse from her shopping bag. The keyboards were at a reasonable height for the men who designed them, but women — and men in many countries — are a few inches shorter and were highly exposed. One of these machines 'protected client privacy' by forcing the customer to gaze at the screen through a narrow slot. Your balance was private, but your PIN was not! Many pay-telephones have a similar problem, and *shoulder surfing* of calling card details (as it's known in the industry) has been endemic at some locations such as major US train stations and airports.

I usually cover my dialling hand with my body or my other hand when entering a card number or PIN in a public place — but you shouldn't design systems on the assumption that all your customers will do this. Many people are uncomfortable shielding a PIN from others as it's a visible signal of distrust; the discomfort can be particularly acute if someone's in a supermarket queue and a friend is standing nearby. In the UK, for example, the banks say that 20% of users never shield their PIN when entering it, as if to blame any customer whose PIN is compromised by an overhead CCTV camera [84]; yet in court cases where I've acted as an expert witness, only a few percent of customers shield their PIN well enough to protect it from an overhead camera. (And just wait till the bad guys start using infrared imaging.)

2.5.3.2 Eavesdropping

Taking care with password entry may stop the bad guys looking over your shoulder as you use your calling card at an airport telephone. But it won't stop other eavesdropping attacks. The latest modus operandi is for bad people to offer free WiFi access in public places, and harvest the passwords that users enter into websites. It is trivial to grab passwords entered into the many websites that don't use encryption, and with a bit more work you can get passwords entered into most of them that do, by using a middleperson attack.

Such attacks have been around for ages. In the old days, a hotel manager might abuse his switchboard facilities to log the keystrokes you enter at the phone in your room. That way, he might get a credit card number you used — and if this wasn't the card number you used to pay your hotel bill, he could plunder your account with much less risk. And in the corporate world, many networked computer systems still send passwords in clear over local area networks; anyone who can program a machine on the network, or attach his own sniffer equipment, can harvest them. (I'll describe in the next chapter how Windows uses the Kerberos authentication protocol to stop this, and `ssh` is also widely used — but there are still many unprotected systems.)

2.5.3.3 Technical Defeats of Password Retry Counters

Many kids find out that a bicycle combination lock can usually be broken in a few minutes by solving each ring in order of looseness. The same idea worked against a number of computer systems. The PDP-10 TENEX operating system checked passwords one character at a time, and stopped as soon as one of them was wrong. This opened up a *timing attack*: the attacker would repeatedly place a guessed password in memory at a suitable location, have it verified as part of a file access request, and wait to see how long it took to be rejected [774]. An error in the first character would be reported almost at once, an error in the second character would take a little longer to report, and in the third character a little longer still, and so on. So you could guess the characters once after another, and instead of a password of N characters drawn from an alphabet of A characters taking $A^N/2$ guesses on average, it took $AN/2$. (Bear in mind that in thirty years' time, all that might remain of the system you're building today is the memory of its more newsworthy security failures.)

These same mistakes are being made all over again in the world of embedded systems. With one remote car locking device, as soon as a wrong byte was transmitted from the key fob, the red telltale light on the receiver came on. With some smartcards, it has been possible to determine the customer PIN by trying each possible input value and looking at the card's power consumption, then issuing a reset if the input was wrong. The reason was that a wrong PIN caused a PIN retry counter to be decremented, and writing to the EEPROM memory which held this counter caused a current surge of several milliamps — which could be detected in time to reset the card before the write was complete [753]. These implementation details matter.

2.5.4   Attacks on Password Storage

Passwords have often been vulnerable where they are stored. There was a horrendous bug in one operating system update in the 1980s: a user who entered a wrong password, and was told "sorry, wrong password" merely had to hit carriage return to get into the system anyway. This was spotted quickly, and a patch was shipped, but almost a hundred U.S. government systems in Germany were using unlicensed copies of the software and didn't get the patch, with the result that hackers were able to get in and steal information, which they are rumored to have sold to the KGB.

Another horrible programming error struck a U.K. bank, which issued all its customers the same PIN by mistake. It happened because the standard equipment in use at the time for PIN generation required the bank programmer to first create and store an encrypted PIN, and then use another command to print out a clear version on a PIN mailer. A bug meant that all customers got the same encrypted PIN. As the procedures for handling PINs were carefully controlled, no one in the bank got access to anyone's PIN other than his or her own, so the mistake wasn't spotted until after thousands of customer cards had been shipped.

Auditing provides another hazard. In systems that log failed password attempts, the log usually contains a large number of passwords, as users get the 'username, password' sequence out of phase. If the logs are not well protected then attacks become easy. Someone who sees an audit record of a failed login with a non-existent user name of `e5gv,8yp` can be fairly sure that this string is a password for one of the valid user names on the system.

2.5.4.1   One-Way Encryption

Password storage has also been a problem for some systems. Keeping a plaintext file of passwords can be dangerous. In MIT's 'Compatible Time Sharing System', `ctss` (a predecessor of Multics), it once happened that one person was editing the message of the day, while another was editing the password file. Because of a software bug, the two editor temporary files got swapped, with the result that everyone who logged on was greeted with a copy of the password file!

As a result of such incidents, passwords are often protected by encrypting them using a one-way algorithm, an innovation due to Roger Needham and Mike Guy. The password, when entered, is passed through a one-way function and the user is logged on only if it matches a previously stored value. However, it's often implemented wrong. The right way to do it is to generate a random salt, hash the password with the salt, and store both the salt and the hash in the file. The popular blog software Wordpress, as of October 2007, simply stores a hash of the password — so if the attacker can download the password file for a Wordpress blog, he can look for weak passwords by comparing the file against a precomputed file of hashes of words in the dictionary. What's even worse is that Wordpress then uses a hash of this hash as the cookie that it sets on your browser once you've logged on. As a result, someone who can look at the password file can also get in by computing cookies from password hashes, so he can attack even an adminstrator account with a strong password. In this case, the one-way algorithm went the wrong way. They should have chosen a random cookie, and stored a hash of that too.

2.5.4.2 *Password Cracking*

However, some systems that do use an encrypted password file make it widely readable (Unix used to be the prime example — the password file was by default readable by all users). So a user who can fetch this file can then try to break passwords offline using a dictionary; he encrypts the values in his dictionary and compares them with those in the file (an activity called a *dictionary attack*, or more colloquially, *password cracking*). The upshot was that he could impersonate other users, perhaps including a privileged user. Windows NT was slightly better, but the password file could still be accessed by users who knew what they were doing.

Most modern operating systems have fixed this problem, but the attack is still implemented in commercially available password recovery tools. If you've encrypted an Office document with a password you've forgotten, there are programs that will try 350,000 passwords a second [1132]. Such tools can just as easily be used by a bad man who has got a copy of your data, and in older systems of your password file. So password cracking is still worth some attention. Well-designed password protection routines slow down the guessing by using a complicated function to derive the crypto key from the password and from a locally-stored salt that changes with each file; the latest WinZip, for example, allows less than 1000 guesses a second. You can also complicate a guessing attack by using an odd form of password; most password guessers try common words first, then passwords consisting of a root followed by an appendage, such as 'Kevin06'. Users who avoid such patterns can slow down the attacker.

2.5.5 Absolute Limits

Regardless of how well passwords are managed, there can be absolute limits imposed by the design of the platform. For example, Unix systems used to limit the length of the password to eight characters (you could often enter more than this, but the ninth and subsequent characters were ignored). The effort required to try all possible passwords — the *total exhaust time*, in cryptanalytic jargon — is 96^8 or about 2^{52}, and the average effort for a search is half of this. A well-financed government agency (or a well-organised hacker group) can now break any encrypted password in a standard Unix password file.

This motivates more technical defenses against password cracking, including 'shadow passwords', that is, encrypted passwords hidden in a private file (most modern Unices), using an obscure mechanism to do the encryption (Novell), or using a secret key with the encryption (MVS). The strength of these mechanisms may vary.

For the above reasons, military system administrators often prefer to issue random passwords. This also lets the probability of password guessing attacks be estimated and managed. For example, if L is the maximum password lifetime, R is login attempt rate, S is the size of the password space, then the probability that a password can be guessed in its lifetime is $P = LR/S$, according to the US Department of Defense password management guideline [377].

There are various problems with this doctrine, of which the worst may be that the attacker's goal is often not to guess some particular user's password but to get access to any account. If a large defense network has a million possible passwords and a million users, and the alarm goes off after three bad password attempts on any account, then the attack is to try one password for every single account. Thus the quantity of real interest is the probability that the password space can be exhausted in the lifetime of the system at the maximum feasible password guess rate.

To take a concrete example, UK government systems tend to issue passwords randomly selected with a fixed template of consonants, vowels and numbers designed to make them easier to remember, such as CVCNCVCN (eg `fuR5xEb8`). If passwords are not case sensitive, the guess probability is only $21^4.5^2.10^2$, or about 2^{29}. So if an attacker could guess 100 passwords a second — perhaps distributed across 10,000 accounts on hundreds of machines on a network, so as not to raise the alarm — then he'd need about 5 million seconds, or two months, to get in. With a million-machine botnet, he could obviously try to speed this up. So if you're responsible for such a system, you might find it prudent to do rate control: prevent more than one password guess every few seconds per user account, or (if you can) by source IP address. You might also keep a count of all the failed logon attempts and analyse them: is there a constant series of guesses that could indicate an attempted intrusion? (And what would you do if you noticed one?) With a commercial website, 100 passwords per second may translate to one compromised user account per second. That may not be a big deal for a web service with 100 million accounts — but it may still be worth trying to identify the source of any industrial-scale password-guessing attacks. If they're from a small number of IP addresses, you can block them, but this won't work so well if the attacker has a botnet. But if an automated-guessing attack does emerge, then another way of dealing with it is the CAPTCHA, which I'll describe next.

2.6   CAPTCHAs

Recently people have tried to design protection mechanisms that use the brain's strengths rather than its weaknesses. One early attempt was *Passfaces*: this is an authentication system that presents users with nine faces, only one of which is of a person they know; they have to pick the right face several times in a row to log on [356]. The rationale is that people are very good at recognising other people's faces, but very bad at describing them: so you could build a system where it was all but impossible for people to give away their passwords, whether by accident or on purpose. Other proposals of this general type have people selecting a series of points on an image — again, easy to remember but hard to disclose. Both types of system make shoulder surfing harder, as well as deliberate disclosure offline.

The most successful innovation in this field, however, is the CAPTCHA — which stands for 'Completely Automated Public Turing Test to Tell Computers and Humans Apart.' You will probably have seen these: they are the little visual puzzles that you often have to solve to post to a blog, or register for a free email account. The idea is that a program generates some random text, and produces a distorted version of it that the user must decipher. Humans are good at reading distorted text, while programs are less good. CAPTCHAs first came into use in a big way in 2003 to stop spammers using scripts to open thousands of accounts on free email services, and their judicious use can make it a lot harder for attackers to try a few simple passwords with each of a large number of existing accounts.

The CAPTCHA was devised by Luis von Ahn and colleagues [1304]. It is inspired by the test famously posed by Alan Turing as to whether a computer was intelligent, where you put a computer in one room and a human in another, and invite a human to try to tell them apart. The innovation is that the test is designed so that a computer can tell the difference between human and machine, using a known 'hard problem' in AI such as the recognition of distorted text against a noisy background. The idea is that breaking the CAPTCHA is equivalent to solving the AI problem.

As with all new security technologies, the CAPTCHA is undergoing a period of rapid coevolution of attack and defence. Many of the image recognition problems posed by early systems turned out not to be too hard at all. There are also possible protocol-level attacks; von Ahn mentioned in 2001 that in theory a spammer could use a porn site to solve them, by getting people to solve them as the price of access to free porn [1303]. This has since become a folk legend, and finally, in October 2007, it actually started to happen: spammers created a game in which you undress a woman by solving one CAPTCHA after another [134]. Also in that month, we saw the first commercial CAPTCHA-breaking tools arrive on the market [571].

Finally, the technology can be integrated with authentication and authorisation controls in potentially useful new ways. An interesting example comes from the banks in Germany, who are introducing an anti-phishing measure whereby if you authorise a payment online the bank sends you the payee, the amount and your date of birth, integrated into a CAPTCHA that also contains a challenge, such as 'if you want to authorize this payment please enter the thirteenth password from your list'. This lets them use a static list of one-time passwords to authenticate actual amounts and beneficiaries, by ensuring that a real-time man-in-the-middle attack would require a human in the loop. It may be a better technology than the CAP calculator; it will certainly be less fiddly than entering transaction details twice. Time will tell if it works.

2.7   Summary

Usability is one of the most important and yet hardest design problems in many secure systems. It was long neglected as having less techie glamour then operating systems or cryptographic algorithms; yet most real attacks nowadays target the user. Phishing is the most rapidly growing threat to online banking systems, and is starting to be a problem for other sites too. Other forms of deception are also likely to increase; as technical protection improves, the bad guys will target the users.

Much of the early work on security usability focused on passwords. Critical questions to ask when designing a password system include not just whether people might re-use passwords, but also whether they need to be protected from each other, whether they can be trained and disciplined, and whether accounts can be frozen after a fixed number of bad guesses. You also have to consider whether attackers will target a particular account, or be happy with breaking any account on a machine or a network; and technical protection issues such as whether passwords can be snooped by malicious software, false terminals or network eavesdropping.

However, there is no 'magic bullet' in sight. As minor improvements in protection are devised and fielded, so the phishermen adapt their tactics. At present, the practical advice is that you should not be a soft touch — harden your system enough for the phishermen to hit your competitors instead. This involves not just security usability issues but also your internal controls, which we will discuss in later chapters. You should assume that some user accounts will be compromised, and work out how to spot this and limit the damage when it does happen.

Research Problems

There is a lot of work being done on phishing, but (as we discussed here) none of it is no far a really convincing solution to the problem. We could do with some fresh thinking. Are there any neat ways to combine things like passwords, CAPTCHAs, images and games so as to provide sufficiently dependable two-way authentication between humans and computers? In general, are there any ways of making middleperson attacks sufficiently harder that it doesn't matter if the Mafia owns your ISP?

We also need more fundamental thinking about the relationship between psychology and security. Between the first edition of this book in 2001 and the second in 2007, the whole field of security economics sprang into life; now there are two regular conferences and numerous other relevant events. So far, security usability is in a fairly embryonic state. Will it also grow big and prosperous? If so, which parts of existing psychology research will be the interesting areas to mine?

Further Reading

When I wrote the first edition of this book, there was only a small handful of notable papers on passwords, including classic papers by Morris and Thompson [906], Grampp and Morris [550], and Klein [720], and some DoD guidelines [377]. Since then there has arisen a large research literature on phishing, with a compendium of papers published as [659]. Perhaps the greatest gains will come when security engineers start paying attention to standard HCI texts such as [1039], and researchers start reading widely in the psychology literature.

A text I've found helpful is James Reason's '*Human Error*', which essentially tells us what the safety-critical systems community has learned from many years studying the cognate problems in their field [1060]. Recently, we've seen the first book on security usability — a collection of the early research papers [333]. There is also an annual workshop, the Symposium On Usable Privacy and Security (SOUPS) [1240].

I'm loth to provide much of a guide to the psychology literature, as I don't know it as well as I ought to, and we've only just started on the project of building 'security psychology' as a discipline. It will take some years for us to find which psychological theories and experimental results provide us with useful insights. But here are some pointers. Tom Gilovich, Dale Griffin and Danny Kahneman put together a volume of papers summarising the state of play in the heuristics and biases tradition in 2002 [529]; while a more gentle introduction might be a book chapter by Richard Samuels, Steven Stich and Luc Faucher discussing the tensions between that tradition and the evolutionary psychologists [1106]. It may also be of interest that a number of psychologists and primatologists (such as Nicholas Humphrey, Richard Byrne and Andy Whiten) have argued that we evolved intelligence because people who were better at deception, or at detecting deception in others, had more surviving offspring — the so-called 'Machiavellian Brain' hypothesis [250]. This might lead us to wonder whether security engineering is the culmination of millions of years of evolution! (Other psychologists, such as Simon Baron-Cohen, would deflate any such hubris by arguing that nurturing the young was at least as important.) Further fascinating analogies with evolutionary biology have been collected by Raphael Sagarin and Terence Taylor in their book *'Natural Security'*.

Finally, if you're interested in the dark side, *'The Manipulation of Human Behavior'* by Albert Biderman and Herb Zimmer reports experiments on interrogation carried out after the Korean War with US Government funding [162]. It's also known as the Torturer's Bible, and describes the relative effectiveness of sensory deprivation, drugs, hypnosis, social pressure and so on when interrogating and brainwashing prisoners.

CHAPTER 3

Protocols

It is impossible to foresee the consequences of being clever.
— **Christopher Strachey**

Every thing secret degenerates, even the administration of justice; nothing is safe that does not show how it can bear discussion and publicity.
— **Lord Acton**

3.1   Introduction

If security engineering has a deep unifying theme, it is the study of security protocols. We've come across a few protocols informally already — I've mentioned challenge-response authentication and Kerberos. In this chapter, I'll dig down into the details. Rather than starting off with a formal definition of a security protocol, I will give a rough indication and then refine it using a number of examples. As this is an engineering book, I will also give many examples of how protocols fail.

A typical security system consists of a number of principals such as people, companies, computers and magnetic card readers, which communicate using a variety of channels including phones, email, radio, infrared, and by carrying data on physical devices such as bank cards and transport tickets. The security protocols are the rules that govern these communications. They are typically designed so that the system will survive malicious acts such as people telling lies on the phone, hostile governments jamming radio, or forgers altering the data on train tickets. Protection against all possible attacks is often too expensive, so protocols are typically designed under certain assumptions about the threats. For example, the logon protocol that consists of a user entering a password into a machine assumes that she can enter it into the right machine. In the old days of hard-wired terminals in the workplace, this was reasonable; now that people log on to websites over the Internet, it is much less so. Evaluating a protocol thus involves answering two questions: first, is the threat model realistic? Second, does the protocol deal with it?

Protocols may be extremely simple, such as swiping a badge through a reader in order to enter a building. They often involve interaction, and do not necessarily involve technical measures like cryptography. For example, when we order a bottle of fine wine in a restaurant, the standard wine-waiter protocol provides some privacy (the other diners at our table don't learn the price), some integrity (we can be sure we got the right bottle and that it wasn't switched for, or refilled with, cheap plonk) and non-repudiation (it's hard for the diner to complain afterwards that the wine was off). Blaze gives other examples from applications as diverse as ticket inspection, aviation security and voting in [185].

At the technical end of things, protocols can be much more complex. The world's bank card payment system has dozens of protocols specifying how customers interact with cash machines and retail terminals, how a cash machine or terminal talks to the bank that operates it, how the bank communicates with the network operator, how money gets settled between banks, how encryption keys are set up between the various cards and machines, and what sort of alarm messages may be transmitted (such as instructions to capture a card). All these protocols have to work together in a large and complex system.

Often a seemingly innocuous design feature opens up a serious flaw. For example, a number of banks encrypted the customer's PIN using a key known only to their central computers and cash machines, and wrote it to the card magnetic strip. The idea was to let the cash machine verify PINs locally, which saved on communications and even allowed a limited service to be provided when the cash machine was offline. After this system had been used for many years without incident, a programmer (who was playing around with a card reader used in a building access control system) discovered that he could alter the magnetic strip of his own bank card by substituting his wife's bank account number for his own. He could then take money out of her account using the modified card and his own PIN. He realised that this enabled him to loot any other customer's account too, and went on to steal hundreds of thousands over a period of years. The affected banks had to spend millions on changing their systems. And some security upgrades can take years; at the time of writing, much of Europe has moved from magnetic-strip cards to smartcards, while America has not. Old and new systems have to work side by side so that European cardholders can buy from American stores and vice versa. This also opens up opportunities for the crooks; clones of European cards are often used in magnetic-strip cash machines in other countries, as the two systems' protection mechanisms don't quite mesh.

So we need to look systematically at security protocols and how they fail. As they are widely deployed and often very badly designed, I will give a number of examples from different applications.

3.2 Password Eavesdropping Risks

Passwords and PINs are still the foundation on which much of computer security rests, as they are the main mechanism used to authenticate humans to machines. I discussed their usability and 'human interface' problems of passwords in the last chapter. Now let us consider some more technical attacks, of the kind that we have to consider when designing more general protocols that operate between one machine and another. A good case study comes from simple embedded systems, such as the remote control used to open your garage or to unlock the doors of cars manufactured up to the mid-1990's. These primitive remote controls just broadcast their serial number, which also acts as the password.

An attack that became common was to use a 'grabber', a device that would record a code broadcast locally and replay it later. These devices, seemingly from Taiwan, arrived on the market in about 1995; they enabled thieves lurking in parking lots to record the signal used to lock a car door and then replay it to unlock the car once the owner had left[1].

One countermeasure was to use separate codes for lock and unlock. But this is still not ideal. First, the thief can lurk outside your house and record the unlock code before you drive away in the morning; he can then come back at night and help himself. Second, sixteen-bit passwords are too short. It occasionally happened that people found they could unlock the wrong car by mistake (or even set the alarm on a car whose owner didn't know he had one [217]). And by the mid-1990's, devices appeared which could try all possible codes one after the other. A code will be found on average after about 2^{15} tries, which at ten per second takes under an hour. A thief operating in a parking lot with a hundred vehicles within range would be rewarded in less than a minute with a car helpfully flashing its lights.

So another countermeasure was to double the length of the password from 16 to 32 bits. The manufacturers proudly advertised 'over 4 billion codes'. But this only showed they hadn't really understood the problem. There was still

---

[1]With garage doors it's even worse. A common chip is the Princeton PT2262, which uses 12 tri-state pins to encode 3^{12} or 531,441 address codes. However implementers often don't read the data sheet carefully enough to understand tri-state inputs and treat them as binary instead, getting 2^{12}. Many of them only use eight inputs, as the other four are on the other side of the chip. And as the chip has no retry-lockout logic, an attacker can cycle through the combinations quickly and open your garage door after 2^7 attempts on average.

only one code (or two codes) for each car, and although guessing was now impractical, grabbers still worked fine.

Using a serial number as a password has a further vulnerability: there may be many people with access to it. In the case of a car, this might mean all the dealer staff, and perhaps the state motor vehicle registration agency. Some burglar alarms have also used serial numbers as master passwords, and here it's even worse: the serial number may appear on the order, the delivery note, the invoice and all the other standard commercial paperwork.

Simple passwords are sometimes the appropriate technology, even when they double as serial numbers. For example, my monthly season ticket for the swimming pool simply has a barcode. I'm sure I could make a passable forgery with our photocopier and laminating machine, but as the turnstile is attended and the attendants get to know the 'regulars', there is no need for anything more expensive. My card keys for getting into the laboratory where I work are slightly harder to forge: the one for student areas uses an infrared barcode, while the card for staff areas has an RFID chip that states its serial number when interrogated over short-range radio. Again, these are probably quite adequate — our more expensive equipment is in rooms with fairly good mechanical door locks. But for things that lots of people want to steal, like cars, a better technology is needed. This brings us to cryptographic authentication protocols.

3.3   Who Goes There? — Simple Authentication

A simple example of an authentication device is an infrared token used in some multistorey parking garages to enable subscribers to raise the barrier. This first transmits its serial number and then sends an authentication block consisting of the same serial number, followed by a random number, all encrypted using a key which is unique to the device. We will postpone discussion of how to encrypt data and what properties the cipher should have; we will simply use the notation $\{X\}_K$ for the message X encrypted under the key K.

Then the protocol between the access token in the car and the parking garage can be written as:

$$T \rightarrow G : T, \{T, N\}_{KT}$$

This is the standard protocol engineering notation, and can be a bit confusing at first, so we'll take it slowly.

The in-car token sends its name T followed by the encrypted value of T concatenated with N, where N stands for 'number used once', or *nonce*. Everything within the braces is encrypted, and the encryption binds T and N together as well as obscuring their values. The purpose of the nonce is to assure the recipient that the message is *fresh*, that is, it is not a replay of an old message that an attacker observed. Verification is simple: the parking garage server reads T, gets the corresponding key KT, deciphers the rest of the message, checks that the nonce N has not been seen before, and finally that the plaintext contains T (which stops a thief in a car park from attacking all the cars in parallel with successive guessed ciphertexts).

One reason many people get confused is that to the left of the colon, T identifies one of the principals (the token which represents the subscriber) whereas to the right it means the name (that is, the serial number) of the token. Another is that once we start discussing attacks on protocols, we can suddenly start finding that the token T's message intended for the parking garage G was actually intercepted by the freeloader F and played back at some later time. So the notation is unfortunate, but it's too well entrenched now to change easily. Professionals often think of the $T \rightarrow G$ to the left of the colon is simply a hint as to what the protocol designer had in mind.

The term *nonce* can mean anything that guarantees the freshness of a message. A nonce can, according to the context, be a random number, a serial number, a random challenge received from a third party, or even a timestamp. There are subtle differences between these approaches, such as in the level of resistance they offer to various kinds of replay attack, and they increase system complexity in different ways. But in very low-cost systems, the first two predominate as it tends to be cheaper to have a communication channel in one direction only, and cheap devices usually don't have clocks.

Key management in such devices can be very simple. In a typical garage token product, each token's key is simply its serial number encrypted under a global master key KM known to the central server:

$$KT = \{T\}_{KM}$$

This is known as *key diversification*. It's a common way of implementing access tokens, and is very widely used in smartcard-based systems as well. But there is still plenty of room for error. One old failure mode that seems to have returned is for the serial numbers not to be long enough, so that someone occasionally finds that their remote control works for another car in the car park as well. Having 128-bit keys doesn't help if the key is derived by encrypting a 16-bit serial number.

Weak ciphers also turn up. One token technology used by a number of car makers in their door locks and immobilisers employs a block cipher known as Keeloq, which was designed in the late 1980s to use the minimum number of gates; it consists of a large number of iterations of a simple round function. However in recent years an attack has been found on ciphers of this type, and it works against Keeloq; it takes about an hour's access to your key to collect enough data for the attack, and then about a day on a PC to process it and recover the embedded cryptographic key [172]. You might not think this a practical attack, as someone who gets access to your key can just drive off with your car. However, in some implementations, there is also a terrible protocol vulnerability, in that the key diversification is not done using the block cipher itself, but using exclusive-or: $KT = T \oplus KM$. So once you have broken a single vehicle key for that type of car, you can immediately work out the key for any other car of that type. The researchers who found this attack suggested 'Soon, cryptographers will drive expensive cars.'

Indeed protocol vulnerabilities usually give rise to more, and simpler, attacks than cryptographic weaknesses do. At least two manufacturers have made the mistake of only checking that the nonce is different from last time, so that given two valid codes A and B, the series $ABABAB...$ was interpreted as a series of independently valid codes. A thief could open a car by replaying the last-but-one code. A further example comes from the world of prepayment utility meters. Over a million households in the UK, plus many millions in developing countries, have an electricity or gas meter that accepts encrypted tokens; the householder buys a token, takes it home and inserts it into the meter, which then dispenses the purchased quantity of energy. One electricity meter widely used in South Africa checked only that the nonce in the decrypted command was different from last time. So the customer could charge the meter up to the limit by buying two low-value power tickets and then repeatedly feeding them in one after the other [59].

So the question of whether to use a random number or a counter is not as easy as it might seem [316]. If you use random numbers, the lock has to remember a reasonable number of past codes. You might want to remember enough of them to defeat the *valet attack*. Here, someone who has temporary access to the token — such as a valet parking attendant — can record a number of access codes and replay them later to steal your car. Providing enough nonvolatile memory to remember hundreds or even thousands of old codes might push you to a more expensive microcontroller, and add a few cents to the cost of your lock.

If you opt for counters, the problem is synchronization. The key may be used for more than one lock; it may also be activated repeatedly by jostling against something in your pocket (I once took an experimental token home where it was gnawed by my dogs). So there has to be a way to recover after the counter has been incremented hundreds or possibly even thousands of times. This can be turned to advantage by allowing the lock to 'learn', or synchronise on, a key under certain conditions; but the details are not always designed thoughtfully. One common product uses a sixteen bit counter, and allows access when the deciphered counter value is the last valid code incremented by no more than sixteen. To cope with cases where the token has been used more than sixteen times elsewhere (or gnawed by a family pet), the lock will open on a second press provided that the counter value has been incremented between 17 and 32,767 times since a valid code was entered (the counter rolls over so that 0 is the successor of 65,535). This is fine in many applications, but a thief who can get six well-chosen access codes — say for values 0, 1, 20,000, 20,001, 40,000 and 40,001 — can break the system completely. So you would have to think hard about whether your threat model includes a valet able to get access codes corresponding to chosen counter values, either by patience or by hardware hacking.

A recent example of design failure comes from TinyOS, an operating system used in sensor networks based on the IEEE 802.15.4 ad-hoc networking standard. The TinySec library commonly used for security protocols contains not one, but three counters. The first is lost as the radio chip driver overwrites it, the second isn't remembered by the receiver, and although the third is functional, it's used for reliability rather than security. So if someone monkeys with the traffic, the outcome is 'error' rather than 'alarm', and the network will resynchronise itself on a bad counter [340].

So designing even a simple token authentication mechanism is not at all straightforward. There are many attacks that do not involve 'breaking' the encryption. Such attacks are likely to become more common as cryptographic authentication mechanisms proliferate, many of them designed by programmers who thought the problem was easy and never bothered to read a book like this one. And there are capable agencies trying to find ways to defeat these remote key entry systems; in Thailand, for example, Muslim insurgents use them to detonate bombs, and the army has responded by deploying jammers [1000].

Another important example of authentication, and one that's politically contentious for different reasons, is 'accessory control'. Many printer companies embed authentication mechanisms in printers to ensure that genuine toner cartridges are used. If a competitor's product is loaded instead, the printer may quietly downgrade from 1200 dpi to 300 dpi, or simply refuse to work at all. Mobile phone vendors make a lot of money from replacement batteries, and now use authentication protocols to spot competitors' products so they can be blocked or even drained more quickly. All sorts of other industries are getting in on the act; there's talk in the motor trade of cars that authenticate their major spare parts. I'll discuss this in more detail in Chapter 22 along with copyright and rights management generally. Suffice it to say here that security mechanisms are used more and more to support business models, by accessory control, rights management, product tying and bundling. It is wrong to assume blindly that security protocols exist to keep 'bad' guys 'out'. They are increasingly used to constrain the lawful owner of the equipment in which they are built; their purpose may be of questionable legality or contrary to public policy.

3.3.1   Challenge and Response

Most cars nowadays have remote-controlled door unlocking, though most also have a fallback metal key to ensure that you can still get into your car even if the RF environment is noisy. Many also use a more sophisticated two-pass protocol, called challenge-response, to actually authorise engine start. As the car key is inserted into the steering lock, the engine controller sends a challenge consisting of a random n-bit number to the key using short-range radio. The car key computes a response by encrypting the challenge. So, writing E for the engine controller, T for the transponder in the car key, K for the cryptographic key shared between the transponder and the engine controller, and N for the random challenge, the protocol may look something like:

$$E \rightarrow T : \quad N$$
$$T \rightarrow E : \quad \{T, N\}_K$$

This is still not bulletproof.

In one system, the random numbers generated by the engine management unit turned out to be predictable, so it was possible for a thief to interrogate the key in the car owner's pocket, as he passed, with the anticipated next challenge. In fact, many products that incorporate encryption have been broken at some time or another because their random number generators weren't random enough [533, 395]. The fix varies from one application to another. It's possible to build hardware random number generators using radioactive decay, but this isn't common because of health and safety concerns. There are various sources of usable randomness in large systems such as PCs, such as the small variations in the rotation speed of the hard disk caused by air turbulence [358]. PC software products often mix together the randomness from a number of environmental sources such as network traffic and keystroke timing and from internal system sources [567]; and the way these sources are combined is often critical [703]. But in a typical embedded system such as a car lock, the random challenge is generated by encrypting a counter using a special key which is kept inside the device and not used for any other purpose.

Locks are not the only application of challenge-response protocols. In HTTP Digest Authentication, a web server challenges a client or proxy, with whom it shares a password, by sending it a nonce. The response consists of the hash of the nonce, the password, and the requested URI [493]. This provides a mechanism that's not vulnerable to password snooping. It's used, for example, to authenticate clients and servers in SIP, the protocol for Voice-Over-IP (VOIP) telephony. It is much better than sending a password in the clear, but suffers from various weaknesses — the most serious being middleperson attacks, which I'll discuss shortly.

A much more visible use of challenge-response is in *two-factor authentication*. Many organizations issue their staff with password generators to let them log on to corporate computer systems [1354]. These may look like calculators (and some even function as calculators) but their main function is as follows. When you want to log in to a machine on the network, you call up a logon screen and are presented with a random challenge of maybe seven digits. You key this into your password generator, together with a PIN of maybe four digits. The device encrypts these eleven digits using a secret key shared with the corporate security server, and displays the first seven digits of the result. You enter these seven digits as your password. This protocol is illustrated in Figure 3.1. If you had a password generator with the right secret key, and you entered the PIN right, and you typed in the result correctly, then the corporate computer system lets you in. But if you do not have a genuine password generator for which you know the PIN, your chance of logging on is small.

Formally, with S for the server, P for the password generator, PIN for the user's Personal Identification Number that bootstraps the password generator, U for the user and N for the random nonce:

$$
\begin{aligned}
S \rightarrow U: & \quad N \\
U \rightarrow P: & \quad N, PIN \\
P \rightarrow U: & \quad \{N, PIN\}_K \\
U \rightarrow S: & \quad \{N, PIN\}_K
\end{aligned}
$$

Figure 3.1: Password generator use

These devices appeared from the early 1980s and caught on first with phone companies, then in the 1990s with banks for use by staff. There are simplified versions that don't have a keyboard, but just generate a new access code every minute or so by encrypting a counter: the RSA SecurID is the best known. One sector after another has been adopting authentication tokens of one kind or another to replace or supplement passwords; the US Defense Department announced in 2007 that the introduction of an authentication system based on the DoD Common Access Card had cut network intrusions by 46% in the previous year [225].

The technology is now starting to spread to the customer side of things. By 2001, password generators were used by some exclusive private banks, such as Coutts, to authenticate their online customers. These banks never suffered any phishing fraud. By 2006, some banks in the Netherlands and Scandinavia had rolled out the technology to all their millions of customers; then the frauds started. The phishermen typically use real-time man-in-the-middle attacks (which I'll describe in the next section) to take over a session once the user has authenticated herself to the bank. As of late 2007, some banks in the UK and elsewhere in Europe have been introducing the Chip Authentication Program (CAP), which is implemented by giving bank customers a calculator that uses their bank card to do crypto[2]. This calculator, when loaded with a bank card, will ask for the customer's PIN and, if it's entered correctly, will compute a response code based on either a counter (as a one-off authentication code for a card transaction, or a one-step logon to a banking website) or a challenge (for a two-step logon). There is also a third mode of operation: if session takeover becomes a problem, the CAP calculator can also be used to authenticate transaction data. In this case, it's planned to have the customer enter the amount and the last eight digits of the payee account number into her CAP calculator.

But the result might not be as good in banking as it has been in the armed forces. First, when your wallet is stolen the thief might be able to read your PIN digits from the calculator — they will be the dirty and worn keys. If you just use one bank card, then the thief's chance of guessing your PIN in 3 tries has just come down from about 1 in 3000 to about 1 in 10. Second, when you use your card in a Mafia-owned shop (or in a shop whose terminals have been quietly reprogrammed without the owner's knowledge), the bad guys have everything they need to loot your account. Not only that — they can compute a series of CAP codes to give them access in the future, and use your account for wicked purposes such as money laundering. Third, someone who takes your bank card from you at knifepoint can now verify that you've told them

---

[2]Bank cards in many European countries have an EMV smartcard chip on them, and new UK bank cards have software to compute authentication codes as well as to operate ATMs and shop terminals.

the right PIN. A further problem is that the mechanisms can be used in a range of protocols; if you have to give a one-off authentication code over the phone to buy a book with your bank card, and the bookseller can then use that code to log on to your bank, it's clearly a bad thing. A deeper problem is that once lots of banks use one-time passwords, the phishermen will just rewrite their scripts to do real-time man-in-the-middle attacks. These have already been used against the early adopter banks in the Netherlands and Scandinavia. To see how they work, we will now look at a military example.

3.3.2 The MIG-in-the-Middle Attack

The ever-increasing speeds of warplanes in the 1930s and 1940s, together with the invention of the jet engine, radar and rocketry, made it ever more difficult for air defence forces to tell their own craft apart from the enemy's. This led to a serious risk of 'fratricide' — people shooting down their colleagues by mistake — and drove the development of systems to 'identify-friend-or-foe' (IFF). These were first fielded in World War II, and in their early form enabled an airplane illuminated by radar to broadcast an identifying number to signal friendly intent. In 1952, this system was adopted to identify civil aircraft to air traffic controllers and, worried about the loss of security once it became widely used, the U.S. Air Force started a research programme to incorporate cryptographic protection in the system. Nowadays, the typical air defense system sends random challenges with its radar signals, and friendly aircraft have equipment and keys that enable them to identify themselves with correct responses. The chapter on electronic warfare has more details on modern systems.

It's tricky to design a good IFF system. One of the problems is illustrated by the following story, which I heard from an officer in the South African Air Force (SAAF). After it was published in the first edition of this book, the story was disputed — as I'll discuss below. Be that as it may, similar games have been played with other electronic warfare systems since World War 2. The 'Mig-in-the-middle' story has in any event become part of the folklore, and it nicely illustrates how attacks can be carried out in real time on challenge-response authentication protocols.

In the late 1980's, South African troops were fighting a war in northern Namibia and southern Angola. The goals were to keep Namibia under white rule, and impose a client government (UNITA) on Angola. Because the South African Defence Force consisted largely of conscripts from a small white population, it was important to limit casualties, so most South African soldiers remained in Namibia on policing duties while the fighting to the north was done by UNITA troops. The role of the SAAF was twofold: to provide tactical support to UNITA by bombing targets in Angola, and to ensure that the Angolans and their Cuban allies did not return the compliment in Namibia.

Suddenly, the Cubans broke through the South African air defenses and carried out a bombing raid on a South African camp in northern Namibia, killing a number of white conscripts. This proof that their air supremacy had been lost helped the Pretoria government decide to hand over Namibia to the insurgents — itself a huge step on the road to majority rule in South Africa several years later. The raid may also have been the last successful military operation ever carried out by Soviet bloc forces.

Some years afterwards, a SAAF officer told me how the Cubans had pulled it off. Several MIGs had loitered in southern Angola, just north of the South African air defense belt, until a flight of SAAF Impala bombers raided a target in Angola. Then the MIGs turned sharply and flew openly through the SAAF's air defenses, which sent IFF challenges. The MIGs relayed them to the Angolan air defense batteries, which transmitted them at a SAAF bomber; the responses were relayed back in real time to the MIGs, who retransmitted them and were allowed through — as in Figure 3.2. According to my informant, this had a significant effect on the general staff in Pretoria. Being not only outfought by black opponents, but actually outsmarted, was not consistent with the world view they had held up till then.

After this tale was published in the first edition of my book, I was contacted by a former officer in SA Communications Security Agency who disputed the story's details. He said that their IFF equipment did not use cryptography yet at the time of the Angolan war, and was always switched off over enemy territory. Thus, he said, any electronic trickery must have been of a more primitive kind. However, others tell me that 'Mig-in-the-middle' tricks were significant in Korea, Vietnam and various Middle Eastern conflicts.

In any case, the tale illustrates the basic idea behind an attack known to the cryptographic community as the *man-in-the-middle* or (more recently) the *middleperson* attack. It applies in a straightforward way to the challenge-response authentication performed by password calculators: the phishing site invites the mark to log on and simultaneously opens a logon session with his bank. The bank sends a challenge; the phisherman relays this to the mark, who uses his device to respond to it; the phisherman relays it to the bank, and is now authenticated to the bank as the mark. This is why, as I discussed above, European banks are introducing not just a simple response to a single challenge, but an authentication code based on input fields such as the amount, the payee account number and a transaction sequence number.

However, once the protocol-level vulnerabilities are fixed by including all the transaction data, the big problem will be usability. If it takes two minutes and the entry of dozens of digits to make a payment, then a lot of customers will get digits wrong, give up, and then either call the call center or send paper checks — undermining the cost savings of online banking. Also, the bad guys will be able to exploit the fallback mechanisms, perhaps by spoofing customers

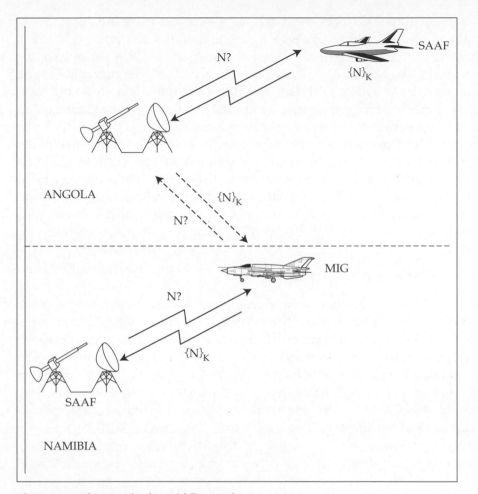

Figure 3.2: The MIG-in-the middle attack

into calling voice phishing phone numbers that run a middleperson attack between the customer and the call center.

We will come across the man-in-the-middle attack again and again in applications ranging from pay-TV to Internet security protocols. It even applies in online gaming. As the mathematician John Conway once remarked, it's easy to get at least a draw against a grandmaster at postal chess: just play two grandmasters at once, one as white and the other as black, and relay the moves between them!

In many cases, middleperson attacks are possible but not economic. In the case of car keys, it should certainly be possible to steal a car by having an accomplice follow the driver and electronically relay the radio challenge to you as you work the lock. (One of our students has actually demonstrated this for our RFID door locks.) But, for the average car thief, it would be a lot simpler to just pick the target's pocket or mug him.

In early 2007, it became clear that there is a practical middleperson attack on the protocols used by the EMV smartcards issued to bank customers in Europe. A bad man could build a wicked terminal that masqueraded, for example, as a parking meter; when you entered your card and PIN to pay a £2.50 parking fee, the transaction could be relayed to a crook loitering near a self-service terminal in a hardware store, who would use a card emulator to order goods. When you get your statement, you might find you've been debited £2,500 for a wide-screen TV [915]. The basic problem here is the lack of a trustworthy user interface on the card; the cardholder doesn't really know which terminal his card is doing business with. I'll discuss such attacks further in the chapter on Banking and Bookkeeping.

3.3.3   Reflection Attacks

Further interesting problems arise with mutual authentication, that is, when two principals have to identify each other. Suppose, for example, that a simple challenge-response IFF system designed to prevent anti-aircraft gunners attacking friendly aircraft had to be deployed in a fighter-bomber too. Now suppose that the air force simply installed one of their air gunners' challenge units in each aircraft and connected it to the fire-control radar. But now an enemy bomber might reflect a challenge back at our fighter, get a correct response, and then reflect that back as its own response:

$$F \rightarrow B : N$$

$$B \rightarrow F : N$$

$$F \rightarrow B : \{N\}_K$$

$$B \rightarrow F : \{N\}_K$$

So we will want to integrate the challenge system with the response generator. It is still not enough just for the two units to be connected and share a list of outstanding challenges, as an enemy attacked by two of our aircraft might reflect a challenge from one of them to be answered by the other. It might also not be acceptable to switch manually from 'attack' to 'defense' during combat.

There are a number of ways of stopping this 'reflection attack': in many cases, it is sufficient to include the names of the two parties in the authentication exchange. In the above example, we might require a friendly bomber to reply to the challenge:

$$F \rightarrow B : N$$

with a response such as:

$$B \rightarrow F : \{B, N\}_K$$

Thus a reflected response $\{F, N\}$ (or even $\{F', N\}$ from the fighter pilot's wingman) could be detected.

This is a much simplified account of IFF, but it serves to illustrate the subtelty of the trust assumptions that underlie an authentication protocol. If you send out a challenge N and receive, within 20 milliseconds, a response $\{N\}_K$, then — since light can travel a bit under 3,730 miles in 20 ms — you know that there is someone with the key K within 2000 miles. But that's all you know. If you can be sure that the response was not computed using your own equipment, you now know that there is someone *else* with the key K within two thousand miles. If you make the further assumption that all copies of the key K are securely held in equipment which may be trusted to operate properly, and you see $\{B, N\}_K$, you might be justified in deducing that the aircraft with callsign B is within 2000 miles. A clear understanding of trust assumptions and their consequences is at the heart of security protocol design.

By now you might think that the protocol design aspects of IFF have been exhaustively discussed. But we've omitted one of the most important problems — and one which the designers of early IFF systems did not anticipate. As radar returns are weak, the signal from the IFF transmitter on board an aircraft will often be audible at a much greater range than the return. The Allies learned this the hard way; in January 1944, decrypts of Enigma messages revealed that the Germans were plotting British and American bombers at twice the normal radar range by interrogating their IFF. So many modern systems authenticate the challenge as well as the response. The NATO mode XII, for example, has a 32 bit encrypted challenge, and a different valid challenge is generated for every interrogation signal, of which there are typically 250 per second. Theoretically there is no need to switch off over enemy territory, but in practice an enemy who can record valid challenges can replay them as part of an attack. Relays are also possible, as with the Mig in the middle.

Many other IFF design problems are less protocol-related, such as the difficulties posed by neutrals, error rates in dense operational environments, how to deal with equipment failure, how to manage keys, and how to cope with multinational coalitions such as that put together for Operation Desert Storm. I'll return to IFF in Chapter 19. For now, the spurious-challenge problem serves to reinforce an important point: that the correctness of a security protocol depends on the assumptions made about the requirements. A protocol that can protect against one kind of attack (being shot down by your own side) but which increases the exposure to an even more likely attack (being shot down by the other side) does more harm than good. In fact, the spurious-challenge problem became so serious in World War II that some experts advocated abandoning IFF altogether, rather than taking the risk that one bomber pilot in a formation of hundreds would ignore orders and leave his IFF switched on while over enemy territory.

3.4   Manipulating the Message

We've now seen a number of middleperson attacks that reflect or spoof the information used to authenticate a participant's identity — from ATM cards that could be reprogrammed to 'identify' the wrong customer, to attacks on IFF. However, there are more complex attacks where the attacker does not just obtain false identification, but manipulates the message content in some way.

An example is when dishonest cabbies insert pulse generators in the cable that connects their taximeter to a sensor in their taxi's gearbox. The sensor sends pulses as the prop shaft turns, which lets the meter work out how far the taxi has gone. A pirate device, which inserts extra pulses, makes the taxi appear to have gone further. We'll discuss such attacks at much greater length in the chapter on 'Monitoring Systems', in section 12.3.

Another example is a key log attack which defeated many pay-TV systems in Europe in the 1990s and still appears to work in China. The attack is also known as *delayed data transfer*, or DDT. First-generation pay-TV equipment has a decoder, which deciphers the video signal, and a customer smartcard which generates the deciphering keys. These keys are recomputed every few hundred milliseconds by using a one-way encryption function applied to various 'entitlement control messages' that appear in the signal. Such systems can be very elaborate (and we'll discuss some more complex attacks on them later) but there is a very simple attack which works against a lot of them. If the messages that pass between the smartcard and the decoder are the same for all decoders (which is usually the case) then a subscriber can log all the keys sent by his card to his decoder and post it online somewhere. People without a subscription, but who have video-recorded the enciphered program, can then download the key log and use it to decipher the tape.

Changing pay-TV protocols to prevent DDT attacks can be difficult. The base of installed equipment is huge, and many of the obvious countermeasures have an adverse effect on legitimate customers (such as by preventing them videotaping movies). Pay-TV companies generally ignore this attack, since connecting a PC up to a satellite TV decoder through a special hardware adaptor is something only hobbyists do; it is too inconvenient to be a real threat to their revenue stream. In the rare cases where it becomes a nuisance, the strategy is usually to identify the troublesome subscribers and send entitlement control messages that deactivate their cards.

Message-manipulation attacks aren't limited to 'consumer' grade systems. The Intelsat satellites used for international telephone and data traffic have robust mechanisms to prevent a command being accepted twice — otherwise an attacker could repeatedly order the same maneuver to be carried out until the satellite ran out of fuel [1027].

3.5 Changing the Environment

A very common cause of protocol failure is that the environment changes, so that assumptions which were originally true no longer hold and the security protocols cannot cope with the new threats.

One nice example comes from the ticketing systems used by the urban transport authority in London. In the early 1980's, passengers devised a number of scams to cut the cost of commuting. For example, a passenger who commuted a long distance from a suburban station to downtown might buy two cheaper, short distance season tickets — one between his suburban station and a nearby one, and the other between his destination and another downtown station. These would let him get through the barriers, and on the rare occasions he was challenged by an inspector in between, he would claim that he'd boarded at a rural station which had a broken ticket machine.

A large investment later, the system had all the features necessary to stop such scams: all barriers were automatic, tickets could retain state, and the laws had been changed so that people caught without tickets got fined on the spot.

But suddenly the whole environment changed, as the national transport system was privatized to create dozens of rail and bus companies. Some of the new operating companies started cheating each other, and there was nothing the system could do about it! For example, when a one-day travel pass was sold, the revenue was distributed between the various bus, train and subway operators using a formula that depended on where it was sold. Suddenly, the train companies had a motive to book all their ticket sales through the outlet that let them keep the largest percentage. As well as bad outsiders (passengers), we now had bad insiders (rail companies), and the design just hadn't allowed for them. Chaos and litigation ensued.

The transport system's problem was not new; it had been observed in the Italian ski resort of Val di Fassa in the mid-1970's. There, one could buy a monthly pass for all the ski lifts in the valley. An attendant at one of the lifts was observed with a deck of cards, one of which he swiped through the reader between each of the guests. It turned out that the revenue was divided up between the various lift operators according to the number of people who had passed their turnstiles. So each operator sought to inflate its own figures as much as it could [1217].

Another nice example comes from the world of cash machine fraud. In 1993 and 1994, Holland suffered an epidemic of 'phantom withdrawals'; there was much controversy in the press, with the banks claiming that their systems were secure while many people wrote in to the papers claiming to have been cheated. Eventually the banks were shamed into actively investigating the claims, and noticed that many of the victims had used their bank cards at a certain filling station near Utrecht. This was staked out and one of the staff was arrested. It turned out that he had tapped the line from the card reader to the PC that controlled it; his tap recorded the magnetic stripe details from their cards while he used his eyeballs to capture their PINs [33].

Why had the system been designed so badly? Well, when the standards for managing magnetic stripe cards and PINs were developed in the early 1980's by organizations such as IBM and VISA, the engineers had made two assumptions. The first was that the contents of the magnetic strip — the card number, version number and expiration date — were not secret, while the PIN was [880]. (The analogy used was that the magnetic strip was your name and the PIN your password. I will have more to say on the difficulties of naming below.) The second assumption was that bank card equipment would only be operated in trustworthy environments, such as in a physically robust automatic teller machine, or by a bank clerk at a teller station. So it was 'clearly' only necessary to encrypt the PIN, on its way from the PIN pad to the server; the magnetic strip data could be sent in clear from the card reader.

Both of these assumptions had changed by 1993. An epidemic of card forgery, mostly in the Far East in the late 1980's, drove banks to introduce authentication codes on the magnetic strips. Also, the commercial success of the bank card industry led banks in many countries to extend the use of debit cards from ATMs to terminals in all manner of shops. The combination of these two environmental changes undermined the original system design: instead of putting a card whose magnetic strip contained no security data into a trusted machine, people were putting a card with security data in clear on the strip into an untrusted machine. These changes had come about so gradually, and over such a long period, that the industry didn't see the problem coming.

3.6   Chosen Protocol Attacks

Some firms are trying to sell the idea of a 'multifunction smartcard' — an authentication device that could be used in a wide range of transactions to save you having to carry around dozens of different cards and keys. Governments keen to push ID cards in the wake of 9/11 have tried to get them used for many other transactions; some want a single card to be used for ID, banking and even transport ticketing. Singapore went so far as to experiment with a bank card that doubled as military ID. This introduced some interesting new risks: if a Navy captain tries to withdraw some cash from an ATM after a good dinner and forgets his PIN, will he be unable to take his ship to sea until Monday morning when they open the bank and give him his card back?

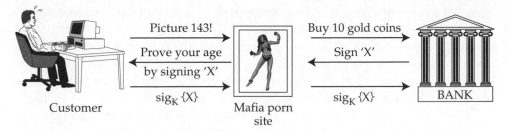

Figure 3.3: The Mafia-in-the-middle attack

Suppose that the banks in Europe were to introduce the CAP protocol to get their customers to authenticate themselves to electronic banking websites, but rather than forcing their customers to fiddle about with a calculator device they just issued all customers with smartcard readers that could be attached to their PC. This would certainly improve convenience and usability. You might think it would improve security too; the EMV protocol enables the card to calculate a message authentication code (MAC) on transaction data such as the amount, merchant number, date and transaction serial number. Message manipulation attacks against electronic banking payments would be prevented.

Or would they? The idea behind the 'Chosen Protocol Attack' is that given a target protocol, you design a new protocol that will attack it if the users can be inveigled into reusing the same token or crypto key. So how might the Mafia design a protocol to attack CAP?

Here's one approach. It used to be common for people visiting a porn website to be asked for 'proof of age,' which usually involves giving a credit card number, whether to the site itself or to an age checking service. If credit and debit cards become usable in PCs, it would be natural for the porn site to ask the customer to authenticate a random challenge as proof of age. A porn site can then mount a 'Mafia-in-the-middle' attack as shown in Figure 3.3. They wait until an unsuspecting customer visits their site, then order something resellable (such as gold coins) from a dealer, playing the role of the coin dealer's customer. When the coin dealer sends them the transaction data for authentication, they relay it through their porn site to the waiting customer. The poor man OKs it, the Mafia gets the gold coins, and when thousands of people suddenly complain about the huge charges to their cards at the end of the month, the porn site has vanished — along with the gold [702].

This is a more extreme variant on the Utrecht scam, and in the 1990s a vulnerability of this kind found its way into international standards: the standards for digital signature and authentication could be run back-to-back in this way. It has since been shown that many protocols, though secure in themselves, can be broken if their users can be inveigled into reusing the same keys in other applications [702]. This is why, for CAP to be secure, it may well have to be implemented in a stand-alone device into which the customer enters all the transaction parameters directly. Even so, some way has to be found to make it hard for the phishermen to trick the customer into computing an authentication code on data that they supply to the victim. The use of the customer's bank card in the CAP calculator may at least help to bring home that a banking transaction is being done.

In general, using crypto keys (or other authentication mechanisms) in more than one application is dangerous, while letting other people bootstrap their own application security off yours can be downright foolish. If a bank lets its smartcards also be used to load credit into prepayment electricity meters, it would have to worry very hard about whether bad software could be used in electricity vending stations (or even electricity meters) to steal money. Even if those risks could be controlled somehow, liability issues can arise from unplanned or emergent dependencies. A bank that changed its card specification might break the metering system — leaving its customers literally in the dark and risking a lawsuit from the power company. If the bank heeds these risks and tests system changes properly with all the dependant systems, then changes will be much more expensive. Crooks who hack the bank could black out the neighbourhood. The bank might still want to take this risk, though, reckoning that power company customers would be locked in more tightly to the bank, enabling it to charge them more. Security dependencies can have all sorts of strange effects, and we will return to this subject again and again later.

3.7   Managing Encryption Keys

The examples of security protocols that we have discussed so far are mostly about authenticating a principal's name, or application data such as the impulses driving a taximeter. There is one further class of authentication protocols that is very important — the protocols used to manage cryptographic keys. Until recently, such protocols were largely used in the background to support other operations; much of the technology was developed to manage the keys used by cash machines and banks to communicate with each other. But now, systems such as pay-TV use key management to control access to the system directly.

Authentication protocols are now also used in distributed computer systems for general key management purposes, and are therefore becoming ever more important. Kerberos was the first such system to come into widespread use, and a variant of it is used in Windows. I'll now lay the foundations for an understanding of Kerberos.

3.7.1 Basic Key Management

The basic idea behind key distribution protocols is that where two principals want to communicate, they may use a trusted third party to effect an introduction.

When discussing authentication protocols, it is conventional to give the principals human names in order to avoid getting lost in too much algebraic notation. So we will call the two communicating principals 'Alice' and 'Bob', and the trusted third party 'Sam'. But please don't assume that we are talking about human principals. Alice and Bob are likely to be programs while Sam is a server; for example, Alice might be a program in a taximeter, Bob the program in a gearbox sensor and Sam the computer at the taxi inspection station.

Anyway, a simple authentication protocol could run as follows.

1. Alice first calls Sam and asks for a key for communicating with Bob.

2. Sam responds by sending Alice a pair of certificates. Each contains a copy of a key, the first encrypted so only Alice can read it, and the second encrypted so only Bob can read it.

3. Alice then calls Bob and presents the second certificate as her introduction. Each of them decrypts the appropriate certificate under the key they share with Sam and thereby gets access to the new key. Alice can now use the key to send encrypted messages to Bob, and to receive messages from him in return.

Replay attacks are a known problem with authentication protocols, so in order that both Bob and Alice can check that the certificates are fresh, Sam may include a timestamp in each of them. If certificates never expire, there might be serious problems dealing with users whose privileges have been revoked.

Using our protocol notation, we could describe this as

$$A \rightarrow S: \quad A, B$$
$$S \rightarrow A: \quad \{A, B, K_{AB}, T\}_{K_{AS}}, \{A, B, K_{AB}, T\}_{K_{BS}}$$
$$A \rightarrow B: \quad \{A, B, K_{AB}, T\}_{K_{BS}}, \{M\}_{K_{AB}}$$

Expanding the notation, Alice calls Sam and says she'd like to talk to Bob. Sam makes up a session key message consisting of Alice's name, Bob's name, a key for them to use, and a timestamp. He encrypts all this under the key he shares with Alice, and he encrypts another copy of it under the key he shares with Bob. He gives both ciphertexts to Alice. Alice retrieves the key from the ciphertext that was encrypted to her, and passes on to Bob the ciphertext encrypted for him. She now sends him whatever message she wanted to send, encrypted using this key.

3.7.2   The Needham-Schroeder Protocol

Many things can go wrong, and here is a famous historical example. Many existing key distribution protocols are derived from the Needham-Schroeder protocol, which appeared in 1978 [960]. It is somewhat similar to the above, but uses nonces rather than timestamps. It runs as follows:

Message 1	$A \rightarrow S$:	A, B, N_A
Message 2	$S \rightarrow A$:	$\{N_A, B, K_{AB}, \{K_{AB}, A\}_{K_{BS}}\}_{K_{AS}}$
Message 3	$A \rightarrow B$:	$\{K_{AB}, A\}_{K_{BS}}$
Message 4	$B \rightarrow A$:	$\{N_B\}_{K_{AB}}$
Message 5	$A \rightarrow B$:	$\{N_B - 1\}_{K_{AB}}$

Here Alice takes the initiative, and tells Sam: 'I'm Alice, I want to talk to Bob, and my random nonce is N_A.' Sam provides her with a session key, encrypted using the key she shares with him. This ciphertext also contains her nonce so she can confirm it's not a replay. He also gives her a certificate to convey this key to Bob. She passes it to Bob, who then does a challenge-response to check that she is present and alert.

There is a subtle problem with this protocol — Bob has to assume that the key K_{AB} he receives from Sam (via Alice) is fresh. This is not necessarily so: Alice could have waited a year between steps 2 and 3. In many applications this may not be important; it might even help Alice to cache keys against possible server failures. But if an opponent — say Charlie — ever got hold of Alice's key, he could use it to set up session keys with many other principals.

Suppose, for example, that Alice had also asked for and received a key to communicate with Dave, and after Charlie stole her key he sent messages to Sam pretending to be Alice and got keys for Freddie and Ginger. He might also have observed message 2 in her protocol exchanges with Dave. So now Charlie could impersonate Alice to Dave, Freddie and Ginger. So when Alice finds out that her key has been stolen, perhaps by comparing message logs with Dave, she'd have to get Sam to contact everyone for whom she'd ever been issued a key, and tell them that her old key was no longer valid. She could not do this herself as she doesn't know anything about Freddie and Ginger. In other words, revocation is a problem: Sam may have to keep complete logs of everything he's ever done, and these logs would grow in size forever unless the principals' names expired at some fixed time in the future.

Almost 30 years later, this example still generates controversy in the security protocols community. The simplistic view is that Needham and Schroeder just got it wrong; the view argued by Susan Pancho and Dieter Gollmann (for which I have much sympathy) is that this is one more example of a protocol failure brought on by shifting assumptions [538, 1002]. 1978 was a kinder, gentler world; computer security then concerned itself with keeping 'bad guys' out, while nowadays we expect the 'enemy' to be the users of the system. The Needham-Schroeder paper explicitly assumes that all principals behave themselves, and that all attacks come from outsiders [960]. With these assumptions, the protocol remains sound.

3.7.3 Kerberos

An important practical derivative of the Needham-Schroeder protocol may be found in Kerberos, a distributed access control system that originated at MIT and is now one of the standard authentication tools in Windows [1224]. Instead of a single trusted third party, Kerberos has two kinds: an authentication server to which users log on, and a ticket granting server which gives them tickets allowing access to various resources such as files. This enables more scalable access management. In a university, for example, one might manage students through their halls of residence but manage file servers by departments; in a company, the personnel people might register users to the payroll system while departmental administrators manage resources such as servers and printers.

First, Alice logs on to the authentication server using a password. The client software in her PC fetches a ticket from this server that is encrypted under her password and that contains a session key K_{AS}. Assuming she gets the password right, she now controls K_{AS} and to get access to a resource B controlled by the ticket granting server S, the following protocol takes place. Its outcome is a key K_{AB} with timestamp T_S and lifetime L, which will be used to authenticate Alice's subsequent traffic with that resource:

$$
\begin{aligned}
A \to S: \quad & A, B \\
S \to A: \quad & \{T_S, L, K_{AB}, B, \{T_S, L, K_{AB}, A\}_{K_{BS}}\}_{K_{AS}} \\
A \to B: \quad & \{T_S, L, K_{AB}, A\}_{K_{BS}}, \{A, T_A\}_{K_{AB}} \\
B \to A: \quad & \{T_A + 1\}_{K_{AB}}
\end{aligned}
$$

Translating this into English: Alice asks the ticket granting server for access to B. If this is permissible, the ticket $\{T_S, L, K_{AB}, A\}_{K_{BS}}$ is created containing a suitable key K_{AB} and given to Alice to use. She also gets a copy of the key in a form readable by her, namely encrypted under K_{AS}. She now verifies the ticket by sending a timestamp T_A to the resource, which confirms it's alive by sending back the timestamp incremented by one (this shows it was able to decrypt the ticket correctly and extract the key K_{AB}).

The vulnerability of Needham-Schroeder has been fixed by introducing timestamps rather than random nonces. But, as in most of life, we get little in security for free. There is now a new vulnerability, namely that the clocks on our various clients and servers might get out of synch; they might even be desynchronized deliberately as part of a more complex attack.

3.7.4   Practical Key Management

So we can use a protocol like Kerberos to set up and manage working keys between users given that each user shares one or more long-term keys with a server that acts as a key distribution centre. I'll describe a number of other similar protocols later; for example, in the chapter on 'Banking and Bookkeeping' I'll discuss how a bank can set up a long-term key with each of its ATMs and with each of the interbank networks with which it's associated. The bank then uses protocols not too unlike Kerberos to establish a 'key of the day' with each ATM and with each network switch; so when you turn up at the ATM belonging to a foreign bank and ask for money from your own bank via the Cirrus network, the ATM will encrypt the transaction using the working key it shares with the bank that owns it, and the bank will then pass on the transaction to Cirrus encrypted with the key of the day for that network.

So far so good. But a moment's thought will reveal that the bank has to maintain several keys for each of the several hundred ATMs that it owns — a long-term master key, plus perhaps an encryption key and an authentication key; several keys for each of the several dozen bank networks of which it's a member; passwords and other security information for each of several million electronic banking customers, and perhaps keys for them as well if they're given client software that uses cryptography. Oh, and there may be encrypted passwords for each of several thousand employees, which might also take the form of Kerberos keys encrypted under user passwords. That's a lot of key material. How is it to be managed?

Key management is a complex and difficult business and is often got wrong because it's left as an afterthought. A good engineer will sit down and think about how many keys are needed, how they're to be generated, how long they need to remain in service and how they'll eventually be destroyed. There is a much longer list of concerns — many of them articulated in the Federal Information Processing Standard for key management [948]. In addition, things go wrong as applications evolve; it's important to provide extra keys to support next year's functionality, so that you don't compromise your existing ones by reusing them in protocols that turn out to be incompatible. It's also important to support recovery from security failure. Yet there are no standard ways of doing either.

As for practical strategies, there are a number — none of them straightforward. Public-key crypto, which I'll discuss in Chapter 5, can slightly simplify the key management task. Long-term keys can be split into a private part and a public part; you don't have to keep the public part secret (as its name implies) but you do have to guarantee its integrity. In banking the usual answer is to use dedicated cryptographic processors called security modules, which I'll describe in detail in the chapter on 'Tamper Resistance'. These do all the cryptography and contain internal keys with which application keys are protected.

Thus you get your security module to generate master keys for each of your ATMs; you store their encrypted values in your ATM master file. Whenever a transaction comes in from that ATM, you retrieve the encrypted key from the file and pass it to the security module along with the encrypted data. The module then does what's necessary: it decrypts the PIN and verifies it, perhaps against an encrypted value kept locally. Unfortunately, the protocols used to set all this up are also liable to failure. Many attacks have been found that exploit the application programming interface, or API, of the security module, where these protocols are exposed. I will describe these attacks in detail in the chapter on API Security. For now, it's enough to note that getting security protocols right is hard. You should not design them at home, any more than you design your own explosives.

3.8 Getting Formal

Subtle difficulties of the kind we have seen with the above protocols, and the many ways in which protection properties depend on quite subtle starting assumptions that protocol designers may get wrong (or that may be misunderstood later), have led researchers to apply formal methods to key distribution protocols. The goal of this exercise was originally to decide whether a protocol was right or wrong: it should either be proved correct, or an attack should be exhibited. More recently this has expanded to clarifying the assumptions that underlie a given protocol.

There are a number of different approaches to verifying the correctness of protocols. The best known is the *logic of belief*, or *BAN logic*, named after its inventors Burrows, Abadi and Needham [249]. It reasons about what a principal might reasonably believe having seen of certain messages, timestamps and so on. A second is the *random oracle model*, which I touch on in the chapter on cryptology and which is favored by people working on the theory of cryptography; this appears less expressive than logics of belief, but can tie protocol properties to the properties of the underlying encryption algorithms. Finally, a number of researchers have applied mainstream formal methods such as CSP and verification tools such as Isabelle.

Some history exists of flaws being found in protocols that had been proved correct using formal methods; the following subsection offers a typical example.

3.8.1 A Typical Smartcard Banking Protocol

The COPAC system is an electronic purse used by VISA in countries with poor telecommunications [48]. It was the first live financial system whose underlying protocol suite was designed and verified using such formal techniques, and in particular a variant of the BAN logic. A similar protocol is now used in the 'Geldkarte,' an electronic purse issued by banks in Germany, and adopted also by French banks as 'Moneo'. There's also a system in Belgium called 'Proton'. The European applications focus on low-value transactions with devices such as parking meters and vending machines for which it may not be economical to provide a network connection.

Transactions take place from a customer smartcard to a merchant smartcard (which in the case of a vending machine is kept in the machine and changed when it's replenished). The customer gives the merchant an electronic check with two authentication codes on it; one that can be checked by the network, and one that can be checked by the customer's bank. A simplified version of the protocol is as follows.

$$C \rightarrow R: \quad \{C, N_C\}_K$$
$$R \rightarrow C: \quad \{R, N_R, C, N_C\}_K$$
$$C \rightarrow R: \quad \{C, N_C, R, N_R, X\}_K$$

In English: the customer and the retailer share a key K. Using this key, the customer encrypts a message containing its account number C and a customer transaction serial number N_C. The retailer confirms its own account number R and his own transaction serial number N_R, as well as the information it's just received from the customer. The customer now sends the electronic check X, along with all the data exchanged so far in the protocol. One can think of the electronic check as being stapled to a payment advice with the customer's and retailer's account numbers and their respective reference numbers. (The reason for repeating all previous data in each message is to prevent message manipulation attacks using cut-and-paste.)

3.8.2 The BAN Logic

The BAN logic provides a formal method for reasoning about the beliefs of principals in cryptographic protocols. Its underlying idea is that we will believe that a message is authentic if it is encrypted with a relevant key and it is also fresh (that is, generated during the current run of the protocol). Further assumptions include that principals will only assert statements they believe in, and that some principals are authorities for certain kinds of statement. This is formalized using a notation which includes:

$A \mid\equiv X$ *A believes X*, or, more accurately, that A is entitled to believe X;

$A \mid\sim X$ *A once said X* (without implying that this utterance was recent or not);

$A \mid\rightarrow X$ *A has jurisdiction over X*, in other words A is the authority on X and is to be trusted on it;

$A \lhd X$ A *sees* X, that is, someone sent a message to A containing X in such a way that he can read and repeat it;

$\sharp X$ X *is fresh*, that is, contains a current timestamp or some information showing that it was uttered by the relevant principal during the current run of the protocol;

$\{X\}_K$ X *encrypted under the key* K, as in the rest of this chapter;

$A \leftrightarrow^K B$ A *and* B *share the key* K, in other words it is an appropriate key for them to use to communicate.

There are further symbols dealing, for example, with public key operations and with passwords, that need not concern us here.

These symbols are manipulated using a set of postulates which include:

the message meaning rule states that if A sees a message encrypted under K, and K is a good key for communicating with B, then he will believe that the message was once said by B. (We assume that each principal can recognize and ignore his or her own messages.) Formally, $\dfrac{A \mid\equiv A \leftrightarrow^K B, A \lhd \{X\}_K}{A \mid\equiv B \mid\sim X}$

the nonce-verification rule states that if a principal once said a message, and the message is fresh, then that principal still believes it. Formally, $\dfrac{A \mid\equiv \sharp X, A \mid\equiv B \mid\sim X}{A \mid\equiv B \mid\equiv X}$

the jurisdiction rule states that if a principal believes something, and is an authority on the matter, then he or she should be believed. Formally, we write that $\dfrac{A \mid\equiv B \mid\Rightarrow X, A \mid\equiv B \mid\equiv X}{A \mid\equiv X}$

In this notation, the statements on the top are the conditions, and the one on the bottom is the result. There are a number of further rules to cover the more mechanical aspects of manipulation; for example, if A sees a statement then he sees its components provided he knows the necessary keys, and if part of a formula is known to be fresh, then the whole formula must be.

3.8.3 Verifying the Payment Protocol

Assuming that the key K is only available to principals who can be trusted to execute the protocol faithfully, formal verification is now straightforward. The trick is to start from the desired result and work backwards. In this case, we wish to prove that the retailer should trust the check, i.e., $R \mid\equiv X$ (the syntax of checks and cryptographic keys is similar for our purposes here; a check is good if and only if it is genuine and the date on it is sufficiently recent).

Now $R \mid\equiv X$ will follow under the jurisdiction rule from $R \mid\equiv C \mid\Rightarrow X$ (R believes C has jurisdiction over X) and $R \mid\equiv C \mid\equiv X$ (R believes C believes X).

The former condition follows from the hardware constraint, that no-one except C could have uttered a text of the form $\{C, \ldots\}_K$.

The latter, that $R \mid\equiv C \mid\equiv X$, must be deduced using the nonce verification rule from $\sharp X$ (X is fresh) and $R \mid\equiv C \mid\sim X$ (R believes C uttered X).

$\sharp X$ follows from its occurrence in $\{C, N_C, R, N_R, X\}_K$ which contains the sequence number N_R, while $R \mid\equiv C \mid\sim X$ follows from the hardware constraint.

The above summary of the proof is, of necessity, telegraphic. If you want to understand logics of authentication in detail, you should consult the original papers [48] and see the recommendations for further reading at the end of this chapter.

3.8.4   Limitations of Formal Verification

Formal methods can be an excellent way of finding bugs in security protocol designs as they force the designer to make everything explicit and thus confront difficult design choices that might otherwise be fudged. However, they have their limitations, too.

One problem is in the external assumptions we make. For example, we assumed that the key wasn't available to anyone who might use it in an unauthorized manner. In practice, this is not always true. Although our purse protocol is executed in tamper-resistant smartcards, their software can have bugs, and in any case the tamper-resistance they offer is never complete. (I'll discuss this in the chapter on Tamper Resistance.) So the system has various fallback mechanisms to detect and react to card forgery, such as shadow accounts which track the amount of money that should be on each card and which are updated as transactions are cleared. It also has lists of hot cards that are distributed to terminals; these are needed anyway for stolen cards, and can be used for forged cards too.

Second, there are often problems with the idealisation of the protocol. An interesting flaw was found in an early version of this system. The key K actually consisted of two keys — the encryption was done first with a 'transaction key' which was diversified (that is, each card had its own variant) and then again with a 'bank key', which was not diversified. The former was done by the network operator, and the latter by the bank which issued the card. The reasons for this included dual control, and to ensure that even if an attacker managed to drill the keys out of a single card, he would only be able to forge that card, not make forgeries which would pass as other cards (and thus defeat the hot card mechanism). But since the bank key was not diversified, it must be assumed to be known to any attacker who has broken a card. This means that he can undo the outer wrapping of encryption, and in some circumstances message replay was possible. (The bank key was diversified in a later version before any villains discovered and exploited the flaw.)

In this case there was no failure of the formal method, as no attempt was ever made to verify the diversification mechanism. But it does illustrate a common problem in security engineering — that vulnerabilities arise at the boundary between two protection technologies. In this case, there were three technologies: the hardware tamper resistance, the authentication protocol and the shadow account / hot card list mechanisms. Different protection technologies are often the domain of different experts who don't completely understand the assumptions made by the others. (In fact, that's one reason security engineers need a book such as this one: to help subject specialists understand each others' tools and communicate with each other more effectively.)

For these reasons, people have explored alternative ways of assuring the design of authentication protocols, including the idea of *protocol robustness*. Just as structured programming techniques aim to ensure that software is designed methodically and nothing of importance is left out, so robust protocol design is largely about explicitness. Robustness principles include that the interpretation of a protocol should depend only on its content, not its context; so everything of importance (such as principals' names) should be stated explicitly in the messages. There are other issues concerning the freshness provided by serial numbers, timestamps and random challenges, and on the way encryption is used. If the protocol uses public key cryptography or digital signature mechanisms, there are further more technical robustness issues.

3.9   Summary

Passwords are just one (simple) example of a more general concept, the security protocol. Protocols specify the series of steps that principals use to establish trust relationships in a system, such as authenticating a claim to identity, demonstrating ownership of a credential, or granting a claim on a resource. Cryptographic authentication protocols, whether one-pass (e.g., using random nonces) or two-pass (challenge-response) are used for a wide range of such purposes, from basic entity authentication to provide infrastructure for distributed systems that allows trust to be taken from where it exists to where it is needed. Security protocols are fielded in all sorts of systems from remote car door locks through military IFF systems to authentication in distributed computer systems.

It is difficult to design effective security protocols. They suffer from a number of potential problems, including middleperson attacks, modification attacks, reflection attacks, and replay attacks. These threats can interact with implementation vulnerabilities such as poor random number generators. Using mathematical techniques to verify the correctness of protocols can help, but it won't catch all the bugs. Some of the most pernicious failures are caused by creeping changes in the environment for which a protocol was designed, so that the protection it gives is no longer adequate.

Research Problems

At several times during the past 20 years, some people have thought that protocols had been 'done' and that we should turn to new research topics. They have been repeatedly proved wrong by the emergence of new protocol applications with a new crop of errors and attacks to be explored. Formal methods blossomed in the early 1990s, then key management protocols; during the mid-1990's the flood of proposals for electronic commerce mechanisms kept us busy; and in the later 1990's a whole series of mechanisms proposed for protecting copyright on the Internet provided us with targets. Since 2000, one strand of protocol research has acquired an economic flavour as security mechanisms are used more and more to support business models; the designer's 'enemy' is often a commercial competitor, or even the customer. Another has applied protocol analysis tools to look at the security of application programming interfaces (APIs), a topic to which I'll return later.

Will people continue to develop faulty protocols which other people attack, or will we manage to develop a methodology for designing them right first time? What are the exact uses and limitations of formal methods, and other mathematical approaches such as the random oracle model?

At the system level, how do we manage the tension between the principle that robust protocols are generally those in which everything is completely specified and checked (principals' names, roles, security policy statement, protocol version, time, date, sequence number, security context, maker of grandmother's kitchen sink) and the system engineering principle that a good specification should not overconstrain the implementer?

Further Reading

Research papers on security protocols are scattered fairly widely throughout the literature. The main introductory papers to read are probably the original Needham-Schroeder paper [960]; the Burrows-Abadi-Needham authentication logic [249]; papers by Abadi and Needham, and Anderson and Needham, on protocol robustness [2, 73]; and there is a survey paper by Anderson and Needham [74]. In [707] there is an analysis of a defective security protocol, carried out using three different formal methods. Beyond that, the proceedings of the security protocols workshops [290, 291] provide leads to current research, and there are many papers scattered around a wide range of conferences.

Access Control

Going all the way back to early time-sharing systems we systems people regarded the users, and any code they wrote, as the mortal enemies of us and each other. We were like the police force in a violent slum.

— Roger Needham

Microsoft could have incorporated effective security measures as standard, but good sense prevailed. Security systems have a nasty habit of backfiring and there is no doubt they would cause enormous problems.

— Rick Maybury

4.1 Introduction

Access control is the traditional center of gravity of computer security. It is where security engineering meets computer science. Its function is to control which principals (persons, processes, machines, . . .) have access to which resources in the system — which files they can read, which programs they can execute, how they share data with other principals, and so on.

Access control works at a number of levels (Figure 4.1).

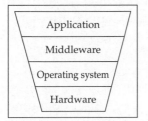

Figure 4.1: Access controls at different levels in a system

1. The access control mechanisms the user sees at the application level may express a very rich and complex security policy. A modern online business could assign staff to one of dozens of different roles, each of which could initiate some subset of several hundred possible transactions in the system. Some of these (such as refunds) might require dual control or approval from a supervisor. And that's nothing compared with the complexity of the access controls on a modern social networking site, which will have a thicket of rules and options about who can see, copy, and search what data from whom.

2. The applications may be written on top of middleware, such as a database management system or bookkeeping package, which enforces a number of protection properties. For example, bookkeeping software may ensure that a transaction which debits one ledger for a certain amount must credit another ledger for the same amount, while database software typically has access controls specifying which dictionaries a given user can select, and which procedures they can run.

3. The middleware will use facilities provided by the underlying operating system. As this constructs resources such as files and communications ports from lower level components, it acquires the responsibility for providing ways to control access to them.

4. Finally, the operating system access controls will usually rely on hardware features provided by the processor or by associated memory management hardware. These control which memory addresses a given process can access.

As we work up from the hardware through the operating system and middleware to the application layer, the controls become progressively more complex and less reliable. Most actual computer frauds involve staff accidentally discovering features of the application code that they can exploit in an opportunistic way, or just abusing features of the application that they were trusted not to. However, loopholes in access-control mechanisms — such as in database software used in a large number of web servers — can expose many systems simultaneously and compel large numbers of companies to patch or rewrite their products. So in this chapter, we will focus on the fundamentals: access control at the hardware, operating system and database levels. You have to understand the basic principles to design serviceable application-level controls too (I give many examples in Part II of how to combine access controls with the needs of specific applications).

As with the other building blocks discussed so far, access control makes sense only in the context of a protection goal, typically expressed as a security policy. PCs carry an unfortunate legacy, in that the old single-user operating systems such as DOS and Win95/98 let any process modify any data; as a result many applications won't run unless they are run with administrator privileges and thus given access to the whole machine. Insisting that your software run as administrator is also more convenient for the programmer. But people do have implicit protection goals; you don't expect a shrink-wrap program to trash your hard disk. So an explicit security policy is a good idea.

Now one of the biggest challenges in computer security is preventing one program from interfering with another. You don't want a virus to be able to steal the passwords from your browser, or to patch a banking application so as to steal your money. In addition, many everyday reliability problems stem from applications interacting with each other or with the system configuration. However, it's difficult to separate applications when the customer wants to share data. It would make phishing much harder if people were simply unable to paste URLs from emails into a browser, but that would make everyday life much harder too. The single-user history of personal computing has got people used to all sorts of ways of working that are not really consistent with separating applications and their data in useful ways. Indeed, one senior manager at Microsoft took the view in 2000 that there was really nothing for operating-system access controls to do, as client PCs were single-user and server PCs were single-application.

The pendulum is now swinging back. Hosting centres make increasing use of virtualization; having machines exclusively for your own use costs several times what you pay for the same resource on shared machines. The Trusted Computing initiative, and Microsoft Vista, place more emphasis on separating applications from each other; even if you don't care about security, preventing your programs from overwriting each others' configuration files should make your PC much more reliable. More secure operating systems have led to ever more technical attacks on software other than the operating system; you don't want your brokerage account hacked via a computer game you downloaded that later turns out to be insecure. And employers would like ways of ensuring that employees' laptops don't pick up malware at home, so it makes sense to have one partition (or virtual machine) for work and another for play. Undoing the damage done by many years of information-sharing promiscuity will be hard, but in the medium term we might reasonably hope for a framework that enables interactions between applications to be restricted to controllable interfaces.

Many access control systems build on the mechanisms provided by the operating system. I will start off by discussing operating-system protection mechanisms that support the isolation of multiple processes. These came first historically — being invented along with the first time-sharing systems in the

1960s — and they remain the foundation on which many higher-layer mechanisms are built. I will then go on to discuss database systems, which provide broadly similar access control mechanisms that may or may not be tied to the operating-systems mechanisms. Finally I'll discuss three advanced protection techniques — *sandboxing, virtualization* and *'Trusted Computing'*. Sandboxing is an application-level control, run for example in a browser to restrict what mobile code can do; virtualization runs underneath the operating system, creating two or more independent virtual machines between which information flows can be controlled or prevented; and Trusted Computing is a project to create two virtual machines side-by-side, one being the 'old, insecure' version of an operating system and the second being a more restricted environment in which security-critical operations such as cryptography can be carried out.

The latest Microsoft system, Vista, is trying to move away from running all code with administrator privilege, and these three modern techniques are each, independently, trying to achieve the same thing — to get us back where we'd be if all applications had to run with user privileges rather than as the administrator. That is more or less where computing was in the 1970s, when people ran their code as unprivileged processes on time-shared minicomputers and mainframes. Only time will tell whether we can recapture the lost Eden of order and control alluded to in the quote from Roger Needham at the start of this chapter, and to escape the messy reality of today to which Rick Maybury's quote refers; but certainly the attempt is worth making.

4.2   Operating System Access Controls

The access controls provided with an operating system typically authenticate principals using a mechanism such as passwords or Kerberos, then mediate their access to files, communications ports and other system resources.

Their effect can often be modelled by a matrix of access permissions, with columns for files and rows for users. We'll write r for permission to read, w for permission to write, x for permission to execute a program, and - for no access at all, as shown in Figure 4.2.

	Operating System	Accounts Program	Accounting Data	Audit Trail
Sam	rwx	rwx	rw	r
Alice	x	x	rw	–
Bob	rx	r	r	r

Figure 4.2: Naive access control matrix

In this simplified example, Sam is the system administrator and has universal access (except to the audit trail, which even he should only be able to read). Alice, the manager, needs to execute the operating system and application, but only through the approved interfaces — she mustn't have the ability to tamper with them. She also needs to read and write the data. Bob, the auditor, can read everything.

This is often enough, but in the specific case of a bookkeeping system it's not quite what we need. We want to ensure that transactions are well-formed — that each debit is matched by a credit somewhere else — so we would not want Alice to have uninhibited write access to the account file. We would also rather that Sam didn't have this access. So we would prefer that write access to the accounting data file be possible only via the accounting program. The access permissions might now look like in Figure 4.3:

User	Operating System	Accounts Program	Accounting Data	Audit Trail
Sam	rwx	rwx	r	r
Alice	rx	x	–	–
Accounts program	rx	r	rw	w
Bob	rx	r	r	r

Figure 4.3: Access control matrix for bookkeeping

Another way of expressing a policy of this type would be with *access triples* of *(user, program, file)*. In the general case, our concern isn't with a program so much as a *protection domain* which is a set of processes or threads which share access to the same resources (though at any given time they might have different files open or different scheduling priorities).

Access control matrices (whether in two or three dimensions) can be used to implement protection mechanisms as well as just model them. But they do not scale well. For instance, a bank with 50,000 staff and 300 applications would have an access control matrix of 15,000,000 entries. This is inconveniently large. It might not only impose a performance problem but also be vulnerable to administrators' mistakes. We will usually need a more compact way of storing and managing this information. The two main ways of doing this are to compress the users and to compress the rights. As for the first of these, the simplest is to use groups or roles to manage the privileges of large sets of users simultaneously, while in the second we may store the access control matrix either by columns (access control lists) or rows (capabilities, sometimes known as 'tickets') [1102, 1344]. (There are more complex approaches involving policy engines, but let's learn to walk before we try to run.)

4.2.1   Groups and Roles

When we look at large organisations, we usually find that most staff fit into one or other of a small number of categories. A bank might have 40 or 50: teller, chief teller, branch accountant, branch manager, and so on. Only a few dozen people (security manager, chief foreign exchange dealer, ...) will need to have their access rights defined individually.

So we want a small number of pre-defined groups, or functional roles, to which staff can be assigned. Some people use the words *group* and *role* interchangeably, and with many systems they are; but the more careful definition is that a group is a list of principals, while a role is a fixed set of access permissions that one or more principals may assume for a period of time using some defined procedure. The classic example of a role is the officer of the watch on a ship. There is exactly one watchkeeper at any one time, and there is a formal procedure whereby one officer relieves another when the watch changes. In fact, in most government and business applications, it's the role that matters rather than the individual.

Groups and roles can be combined. *The officers of the watch of all ships currently at sea* is a group of roles. In banking, the manager of the Cambridge branch might have his or her privileges expressed by membership of the group *manager* and assumption of the role *acting manager of Cambridge branch*. The group *manager* might express a rank in the organisation (and perhaps even a salary band) while the role *acting manager* might include an assistant accountant standing in while the manager, deputy manager, and branch accountant are all off sick.

Whether we need to be careful about this distinction is a matter for the application. In a warship, we want even an ordinary seaman to be allowed to stand watch if everyone more senior has been killed. In a bank, we might have a policy that 'transfers over \$10m must be approved by two staff, one with rank at least manager and one with rank at least assistant accountant'. If the branch manager is sick, then the assistant accountant acting as manager might have to get the regional head office to provide the second signature on a large transfer.

Operating-system level support is available for groups and roles, but its appearance has been fairly recent and its uptake is still slow. Developers used to implement this kind of functionality in application code, or as custom middleware (in the 1980s I worked on two bank projects where group support was hand-coded as extensions to the mainframe operating system). Windows 2000 introduced extensive support for groups, while academic researchers have done quite a lot of work since the mid-90s on *role-based access control* (RBAC), which I'll discuss further in Part II, and which is starting to be rolled out in some large applications.

4.2.2   Access Control Lists

Another way of simplifying the management of access rights is to store the access control matrix a column at a time, along with the resource to which the column refers. This is called an *access control list* or ACL (pronounced 'ackle'). In the first of our above examples, the ACL for file 3 (the account file) might look as shown here in Figure 4.4.

ACLs have a number of advantages and disadvantages as a means of managing security state. These can be divided into general properties of ACLs, and specific properties of particular implementations.

ACLs are a natural choice in environments where users manage their own file security, and became widespread in the Unix systems common in universities and science labs from the 1970s. They are the basic access control mechanism in Unix-based systems such as GNU/Linux and Apple's OS/X; the access controls in Windows are also based on ACLs, but have become more complex over time. Where access control policy is set centrally, ACLs are suited to environments where protection is data-oriented; they are less suited where the user population is large and constantly changing, or where users want to be able to delegate their authority to run a particular program to another user for some set period of time. ACLs are simple to implement, but are not efficient as a means of doing security checking at runtime, as the typical operating system knows which user is running a particular program, rather than what files it has been authorized to access since it was invoked. The operating system must either check the ACL at each file access, or keep track of the active access rights in some other way.

Finally, distributing the access rules into ACLs means that it can be tedious to find all the files to which a user has access. Revoking the access of an employee who has just been fired will usually have to be done by cancelling their password or other authentication mechanism. It may also be tedious to run system-wide checks; for example, verifying that no files have been left world-writable could involve checking ACLs on millions of user files.

Let's look at two important examples of ACLs — their implementation in Unix and Windows.

User	Accounting Data
Sam	rw
Alice	rw
Bob	r

Figure 4.4: Access control list (ACL)

4.2.3 Unix Operating System Security

In Unix (including its popular variant Linux), files are not allowed to have arbitrary access control lists, but simply rwx attributes for the resource owner, the group, and the world. These attributes allow the file to be read, written and executed. The access control list as normally displayed has a flag to show whether the file is a directory, then flags r, w and x for world, group and owner respectively; it then has the owner's name and the group name. A directory with all flags set would have the ACL:

```
drwxrwxrwx Alice Accounts
```

In our first example in Figure 4.3, the ACL of file 3 would be:

```
-rw-r----- Alice Accounts
```

This records that the file is not a directory; the file owner can read and write it; group members can read it but not write it; non-group members have no access at all; the file owner is Alice; and the group is *Accounts*.

In Unix, the program that gets control when the machine is booted (the operating system kernel) runs as the supervisor, and has unrestricted access to the whole machine. All other programs run as users and have their access mediated by the supervisor. Access decisions are made on the basis of the userid associated with the program. However if this is zero (root), then the access control decision is 'yes'. So root can do what it likes — access any file, become any user, or whatever. What's more, there are certain things that only root can do, such as starting certain communication processes. The root userid is typically made available to the system administrator.

This means that (with most flavours of Unix) the system administrator can do anything, so we have difficulty implementing an audit trail as a file that he cannot modify. This not only means that, in our example, Sam could tinker with the accounts, and have difficulty defending himself if he were falsely accused of tinkering, but that a hacker who managed to become the system administrator could remove all evidence of his intrusion.

The Berkeley distributions, including FreeBSD and OS/X, go some way towards fixing the problem. Files can be set to be append-only, immutable or undeletable for user, system or both. When set by a user at a sufficient security level during the boot process, they cannot be overridden or removed later, even by root. Various military variants go to even greater trouble to allow separation of duty. However the simplest and most common way to protect logs against root compromise is to keep them separate. In the old days that meant sending the system log to a printer in a locked room; nowadays, given the volumes of data, it means sending it to another machine, administered by somebody else.

Second, ACLs only contain the names of users, not of programs; so there is no straightforward way to implement access triples of (user, program, file).

Instead, Unix provides an indirect method: the *set-user-id* (`suid`) file attribute. The owner of a program can mark it as `suid`, which enables it to run with the privilege of its owner rather than the privilege of the user who has invoked it. So in order to achieve the functionality needed by our second example above, we could create a user '`account-package`' to own file 2 (the accounts package), make the file `suid` and place it in a directory to which Alice has access. This special user can then be given the access control attributes the accounts program needs.

One way of looking at this is that an access control problem that is naturally modelled in three dimensions — by triples (user, program, data) — is being implemented using two-dimensional mechanisms. These mechanisms are much less intuitive than triples and people make many mistakes implementing them. Programmers are often lazy or facing tight deadlines; so they just make the application `suid root`, so it can do anything. This practice leads to some rather shocking security holes. The responsibility for making access control decisions is moved from the operating system environment to the program, and most programmers are insufficiently experienced and careful to check everything they should. (It's hard to know what to check, as the person invoking a `suid root` program controls its environment and can often manipulate this to cause protection failures.)

Third, ACLs are not very good at expressing mutable state. Suppose we want a transaction to be authorised by a manager and an accountant before it's acted on; we can either do this at the application level (say, by having queues of transactions awaiting a second signature) or by doing something fancy with `suid`. In general, managing stateful access rules is difficult; this can even complicate the revocation of users who have just been fired, as it can be hard to track down the files they might have open.

Fourth, the Unix ACL only names one user. Older versions allow a process to hold only one group id at a time and force it to use a privileged program to access other groups; newer Unix systems put a process in all groups that the user is in. This is still much less expressive than one might like. In theory, the ACL and `suid` mechanisms can often be used to achieve the desired effect. In practice, programmers often can't be bothered to figure out how to do this, and design their code to require much more privilege than it really ought to have.

4.2.4   Apple's OS/X

Apple's OS/X operating system is based on the FreeBSD version of Unix running on top of the Mach kernel. The BSD layer provides memory protection; applications cannot access system memory (or each others') unless running with advanced permissions. This means, for example, that you can kill a wedged application using the 'Force Quit' command; you usually do not have

to reboot the system. On top of this Unix core are a number of graphics components, including OpenGL, Quartz, Quicktime and Carbon, while at the surface
the Aqua user interface provides an elegant and coherent view to the user.

At the file system level, OS/X is almost a standard Unix. The default
installation has the root account disabled, but users who may administer the
system are in a group 'wheel' that allows them to su to root. The most visible
implication is that if you are such a user, you can install programs (you are
asked for the root password when you do so). This may be a slightly better
approach than Windows (up till XP) or Linux, which in practice let only
administrators install software but do not insist on an authentication step
when they do so; the many Windows users who run as administrator for
convenience do dreadful things by mistake (and malware they download does
dreadful things deliberately). Although Microsoft is struggling to catch up
with Vista, as I'll discuss below, Apple's advantage may be increased further
by OS/X version 10.5 (Leopard), which is based on TrustedBSD, a variant of
BSD developed for government systems that incorporates mandatory access
control. (I'll discuss this in Chapter 8.)

4.2.5   Windows – Basic Architecture

The most widespread PC operating system is Windows, whose protection
has been largely based on access control lists since Windows NT. The current
version of Windows (Vista) is fairly complex, so it's helpful to trace its
antecedents. The protection in Windows NT (Windows v4) was very much
like Unix, and was inspired by it, and has since followed the Microsoft
philosophy of 'embrace and extend'.

First, rather than just *read*, *write* and *execute* there are separate attributes for
take ownership, *change permissions* and *delete*, which means that more flexible
delegation can be supported. These attributes apply to groups as well as users,
and group permissions allow you to achieve much the same effect as suid
programs in Unix. Attributes are not simply on or off, as in Unix, but have
multiple values: you can set *AccessDenied*, *AccessAllowed* or *SystemAudit*. These
are parsed in that order. If an AccessDenied is encountered in an ACL for the
relevant user or group, then no access is permitted regardless of any conflicting
AccessAllowed flags. A benefit of the richer syntax is that you can arrange
matters so that everyday configuration tasks, such as installing printers, don't
require full administrator privileges. (This is rarely done, though.)

Second, users and resources can be partitioned into domains with distinct
administrators, and trust can be inherited between domains in one direction
or both. In a typical large company, you might put all the users into a
personnel domain administered by Human Resources, while resources such
as servers and printers could be in resource domains under departmental
control; individual workstations may even be administered by their users.

Things would be arranged so that the departmental resource domains trust the user domain, but not vice versa — so a corrupt or careless departmental administrator can't do much damage outside his own domain. The individual workstations would in turn trust the department (but not vice versa) so that users can perform tasks that require local privilege (installing many software packages requires this). Administrators are still all-powerful (so you can't create truly tamper-resistant audit trails without using write-once storage devices or writing to machines controlled by others) but the damage they can do can be limited by suitable organisation. The data structure used to manage all this, and hide the ACL details from the user interface, is called the *Registry*.

Problems with designing a Windows security architecture in very large organisations include naming issues (which I'll explore in Chapter 6), the way domains scale as the number of principals increases (badly), and the restriction that a user in another domain can't be an administrator (which can cause complex interactions between local and global groups).

One peculiarity of Windows is that *everyone* is a principal, not a default or an absence of control, so 'remove everyone' means just stop a file being generally accessible. A resource can be locked quickly by setting everyone to have no access. This brings us naturally to the subject of capabilities.

4.2.6 Capabilities

The next way to manage the access control matrix is to store it by rows. These are called *capabilities*, and in our example in Figure 4.2 above, Bob's capabilities would be as in Figure 4.5 here:

User	Operating System	Accounts Program	Accounting Data	Audit Trail
Bob	rx	r	r	r

Figure 4.5: A capability

The strengths and weaknesses of capabilities are more or less the opposite of ACLs. Runtime security checking is more efficient, and we can delegate a right without much difficulty: Bob could create a certificate saying 'Here is my capability and I hereby delegate to David the right to read file 4 from 9am to 1pm, signed Bob'. On the other hand, changing a file's status can suddenly become more tricky as it can be difficult to find out which users have access. This can be tiresome when we have to investigate an incident or prepare evidence of a crime.

There were a number of experimental implementations in the 1970s, which were rather like file passwords; users would get hard-to-guess bitstrings for the various read, write and other capabilities to which they were entitled. It was found that such an arrangement could give very comprehensive protection [1344]. It was not untypical to find that almost all of an operating system could run in user mode rather than as supervisor, so operating system bugs were not security critical. (In fact, many operating system bugs caused security violations, which made debugging the operating system much easier.)

The IBM AS/400 series systems employed capability-based protection, and enjoyed some commercial success. Now capabilities have made a limited comeback in the form of *public key certificates*. I'll discuss the mechanisms of public key cryptography in Chapter 5, and give more concrete details of certificate-based systems, such as SSL/TLS, in Part II. For now, think of a public key certificate as a credential, signed by some authority, which declares that the holder of a certain cryptographic key is a certain person, or a member of some group, or the holder of some privilege.

As an example of where certificate-based capabilities can be useful, consider a hospital. If we implemented a rule like 'a nurse shall have access to all the patients who are on her ward, or who have been there in the last 90 days' naively, each access control decision in the patient record system will require several references to administrative systems, to find out which nurses and which patients were on which ward, when. So a failure of the administrative systems can now affect patient safety much more directly than before, and this is clearly a bad thing. Matters can be much simplified by giving nurses certificates which entitle them to access the files associated with their current ward. Such a system has been used for several years at our university hospital.

Public key certificates are often considered to be 'crypto' rather than 'access control', with the result that their implications for access control policies and architectures are not thought through. The lessons that could have been learned from the capability systems of the 1970s are generally having to be rediscovered (the hard way). In general, the boundary between crypto and access control is a fault line where things can easily go wrong. The experts often come from different backgrounds, and the products from different suppliers.

4.2.7 Windows – Added Features

A number of systems, from mainframe access control products to research systems, have combined ACLs and capabilities in an attempt to get the best of both worlds. But the most important application of capabilities is in Windows.

Windows 2000 added capabilities in two ways which can override or complement the ACLs of Windows NT. First, users or groups can be either whitelisted or blacklisted by means of profiles. (Some limited blacklisting was also possible in NT4.) Security policy is set by groups rather than for the system as a whole. Groups are intended to be the primary method for centralized configuration management and control (group policy overrides individual profiles). Group policy can be associated with sites, domains or organizational units, so it can start to tackle some of the real complexity problems with naming. Policies can be created using standard tools or custom coded. Groups are defined in the *Active Directory*, an object-oriented database that organises users, groups, machines, and organisational units within a domain in a hierarchical namespace, indexing them so they can be searched for on any attribute. There are also finer grained access control lists on individual resources.

As already mentioned, Windows adopted Kerberos from Windows 2000 as its main means of authenticating users across networks[1]. This is encapsulated behind the *Security Support Provider Interface* (SSPI) which enables administrators to plug in other authentication services.

This brings us to the second way in which capabilities insinuate their way into Windows: in many applications, people use the public key protocol TLS, which is widely used on the web, and which is based on public key certificates. The management of these certificates can provide another, capability-oriented, layer of access control outside the purview of the Active Directory.

The latest version of Windows, Vista, introduces a further set of protection mechanisms. Probably the most important is a package of measures aimed at getting away from the previous default situation of all software running as root. First, the kernel is closed off to developers; second, the graphics subsystem is removed from the kernel, as are most drivers; and third, User Account Control (UAC) replaces the default administrator privilege with user defaults instead. This involved extensive changes; in XP, many routine tasks required administrative privilege and this meant that enterprises usually made all their users administrators, which made it difficult to contain the effects of malware. Also, developers wrote their software on the assumption that it would have access to all system resources.

In Vista, when an administrator logs on, she is given two access tokens: a standard one and an admin one. The standard token is used to start the desktop, `explorer.exe`, which acts as the parent process for later user processes. This means, for example, that even administrators browse the web as normal users, and malware they download can't overwrite system files unless given later authorisation. When a task is started that requires admin privilege, then a user who has it gets an *elevation prompt* asking her to authorise it by entering an admin password. (This brings Windows into line with Apple's OS/X although the details under the hood differ somewhat.)

---

[1]It was in fact a proprietary variant, with changes to the ticket format which prevent Windows clients from working with existing Unix Kerberos infrastructures. The documentation for the changes was released on condition that it was not used to make compatible implementations. Microsoft's goal was to get everyone to install Win2K Kerberos servers. This caused an outcry in the open systems community [121]. Since then, the European Union prosecuted an antitrust case against Microsoft that resulted in interface specifications being made available in late 2006.

Of course, admin users are often tricked into installing malicious software, and so Vista provides further controls in the form of file integrity levels. I'll discuss these along with other mandatory access controls in Chapter 8 but the basic idea is that low-integrity processes (such as code you download from the Internet) should not be able to modify high-integrity data (such as system files). It remains to be seen how effective these measures will be; home users will probably want to bypass them to get stuff to work, while Microsoft is providing ever-more sophisticated tools to enable IT managers to lock down corporate networks — to the point, for example, of preventing most users from installing anything from removable media. UAC and mandatory integrity controls can certainly play a role in this ecology, but we'll have to wait and see how things develop.

The final problem with which the Vista developers grappled is the fact that large numbers of existing applications expect to run as root, so that they can fool about with registry settings (for a hall of shame, see [579]). According to the Microsoft folks, this is a major reason for Windows' lack of robustness: applications monkey with system resources in incompatible ways. So there is an Application Information Service that launches applications which require elevated privileges to run. Vista uses virtualization technology for legacy applications: if they modify the registry, for example, they don't modify the 'real' registry but simply the version of it that they can see. This is seen as a 'short-term fix' [885]. I expect it will be around for a long time, and I'm curious to see whether the added complexity will be worth the reduced malware risk.

Despite virtualisation, the bugbear with Vista is compatibility. As this book went to press in early January 2008, sales of Vista were still sluggish, with personal users complaining that games and other applications just didn't work, while business users were waiting for service pack 1 and postponing large-scale roll-out to late 2008 or even early 2009. It has clearly been expensive for Microsoft to move away from running everything as root, but it's clearly a necessary move and they deserve full credit for biting the bullet.

To sum up, Windows provides a richer and more flexible set of access control tools than any system previously sold in mass markets. It does still have design limitations. Implementing roles whose requirements differ from those of groups could be tricky in some applications; SSL certificates are the obvious way to do this but require an external management infrastructure. Second, Windows is still (in its consumer incarnations) a single-user operating system in the sense that only one person can operate a PC at a time. Thus if I want to run an unprivileged, sacrificial user on my PC for accessing untrustworthy web sites that might contain malicious code, I have to log off and log on again, or use other techniques which are so inconvenient that few users will bother. (On my Mac, I can run two users simultaneously and switch between them quickly.) So Vista should be seen as the latest step on a journey, rather than a destination. The initial version also has some undesirable implementation quirks. For example, it uses some odd heuristics to try to maintain backwards compatibility with programs that assume they'll run as administrator: if I compile a C++ program called `Fred Installer.exe` then Vista will ask for elevated privilege to run it, and tell it that it's running on Windows XP, while if I call the program simply `Fred.exe` it will run as user and be told that it's running on Vista [797]. Determining a program's privileges on the basis of its filename is just bizarre.

And finally, there are serious usability issues. For example, most users still run administrator accounts all the time, and will be tempted to disable UAC; if they don't, they'll become habituated to clicking away the UAC dialog box that forever asks them if they really meant to do what they just tried to. For these reasons, UAC may be much less effective in practice than it might be in theory [555]. We will no doubt see in due course.

It's interesting to think about what future access controls could support, for example, an electronic banking application that would be protected from malware running on the same machine. Microsoft did come up with some ideas in the context of its 'Trusted Computing' project, which I'll describe below in section 4.2.11, but they didn't make it into Vista.

4.2.8   Middleware

Doing access control at the level of files and programs was all very well in the early days of computing, when these were the resources that mattered. Since about the 1980s, growing scale and complexity has meant led to access control being done at other levels instead of (sometimes as well as) at the operating system level. For example, a bank's branch bookkeeping system will typically run on top of a database product, and the database looks to the operating system as one large file. This means that the access control has to be done in the database; all the operating system supplies it may be an authenticated ID for each user who logs on.

4.2.8.1   Database Access Controls

Until the dotcom boom, database security was largely a back-room concern. But it is now common for enterprises to have critical databases, that handle inventory, dispatch and e-commerce, fronted by web servers that pass transactions to the databases directly. These databases now contain much of the data of greatest relevance to our lives — such as bank accounts, vehicle registrations and employment records — and front-end failures sometimes expose the database itself to random online users.

Database products, such as Oracle, DB2 and MySQL, have their own access control mechanisms. As the database looks to the operating system as a single large file, the most the operating system can do is to identify users and to separate the database from other applications running on the same machine. The database access controls are in general modelled on operating-system mechanisms, with privileges typically available for both users and objects (so the mechanisms are a mixture of access control lists and capabilities). However, the typical database access control architecture is more complex even than Windows: Oracle 10g has 173 system privileges of which at least six can be used to take over the system completely [804]. There are more privileges because a modern database product is very complex and some of the things one wants to control involve much higher levels of abstraction than files or processes. The flip side is that unless developers know what they're doing, they are likely to leave a back door open.

Some products let developers bypass operating-system controls. For example, Oracle has both operating system accounts (whose users must be authenticated externally by the platform) and database accounts (whose users are authenticated directly by the Oracle software). It is often more convenient to use database accounts as it saves the developer from synchronising his work with the details of what other departments are doing. In many installations, the database is accessible directly from the outside; this raises all sorts of issues from default passwords to flaws in network protocols. Even where the database is shielded from the outside by a web service front-end, this often contains loopholes that let SQL code be inserted into the database.

Database security failures can also cause problems directly. The Slammer worm in January 2003 propagated itself using a stack-overflow in Microsoft SQL Server 2000 and created large amounts of traffic and compromised machines sent large numbers of attack packets to random IP addresses.

Just as Windows is trickier to configure securely, because it's more complex, so the typical database system is trickier still, and it takes specialist knowledge that's beyond the scope of this book. Database security is now a discipline in its own right; if you have to lock down a database system — or even just review one as part of a broader assignment — I'd strongly recommend that you read a specialist text, such as David Litchfield's [804].

4.2.8.2 General Middleware Issues

There are a number of aspects common to middleware security and application-level controls. The first is granularity: as the operating system works with files, these are usually the smallest objects with which its access control mechanisms can deal. The second is state. An access rule such as 'a nurse can see the records of any patient on her ward' or 'a transaction over $100,000 must be authorised by a manager and an accountant' both involve managing state: in the first case the duty roster, and in the second the list of transactions that have so far been authorised by only one principal. The third is level: we may end up with separate access control systems at the machine, network and application levels, and as these typically come from different vendors it may be difficult to keep them consistent.

Ease of administration is often a critical bottleneck. In companies I've advised, the administration of the operating system and the database system have been done by different departments, which do not talk to each other; and often user pressure drives IT departments to put in crude hacks which make the various access control systems seem to work as one, but which open up serious holes. An example is 'single sign-on'. Despite the best efforts of computer managers, most large companies accumulate systems of many different architectures, so users get more and more logons to different systems and the cost of administering them escalates. Many organisations want to give each employee a single logon to all the machines on the network. Commercial solutions may involve a single security server through which all logons must pass, and the use of a smartcard to do multiple authentication protocols for different systems. Such solutions are hard to engineer properly, and the security of the best system can very easily be reduced to that of the worst.

4.2.8.3 ORBs and Policy Languages

These problems led researchers to look for ways in which access control for a number of applications might be handled by standard middleware. Research in the 1990s focussed on *object request brokers* (ORBs). An ORB is a software component that mediates communications between objects (an object consists of code and data bundled together, an abstraction used in object-oriented languages such as C++). An ORB typically provides a means of controlling calls that are made across protection domains. The *Common Object Request Broker Architecture* (CORBA) is an attempt at an industry standard for object-oriented systems; a book on CORBA security is [182]. This technology is starting to be adopted in some industries, such as telecomms.

Research since 2000 has included work on languages to express security policy, with projects such as XACML (Sun), XrML (ISO) and SecPAL (Microsoft). They followed early work on 'Policymaker' by Matt Blaze and others [188], and vary in their expressiveness. XrML deals with subjects and objects but not relationships, so cannot easily express a concept such as 'Alice is Bob's manager'. XACML does relationships but does not support universally quantified variables, so it cannot easily express 'a child's guardian may sign its report card' (which we might want to program as 'if x is a child and y is x's guardian and z is x's report card, then y may sign z). The initial interest in these languages appears to come from the military and the rights-management industry, both of which have relatively simple state in their access control policies. Indeed, DRM engineers have already developed a number of specialised rights-management languages that are built into products such as Windows Media Player and can express concepts such as 'User X can play this file as audio until the end of September and can burn it to a CD only once.' The push for interoperable DRM may create a demand for more general mechanisms that can embrace and extend the products already in the field.

If a suitably expressive policy language emerges, and is adopted as a standard scripting language on top of the access-control interfaces that major applications provide to their administrators, it might provide some value by enabling people to link up access controls when new services are constructed on top of multiple existing services. There are perhaps two caveats. First, people who implement access control when customizing a package are not likely to do so as a full-time job, and so it may be better to let them use a language with which they are familiar, in which they will be less likely to make mistakes. Second, security composition is a hard problem; it's easy to come up with examples of systems that are secure in isolation but that break horribly when joined up together. We'll see many examples in Part II.

Finally, the higher in a system we build the protection mechanisms, the more complex they'll be, the more other software they'll rely on, and the closer they'll be to the error-prone mark 1 human being — so the less dependable they are likely to prove. Platform vendors such as Microsoft have more security PhDs, and more experience in security design, than almost any application vendor; and a customer who customises an application package usually has less experience still. Code written by users is most likely to have glaring flaws. For example, the fatal accidents that happened in healthcare as a result of the Y2K bug were not platform failures, but errors in spreadsheets developed by individual doctors, to do things like processing lab test results and calculating radiology dosages. Letting random users write security-critical code carries the same risks as letting them write safety-critical code.

4.2.9   Sandboxing and Proof-Carrying Code

The late 1990s saw the emergence of yet another way of implementing access control: the software *sandbox*. This was introduced by Sun with its Java programming language. The model is that a user wants to run some code that she has downloaded from the web as an applet, but is concerned that the applet might do something nasty, such as taking a list of all her files and mailing it off to a software marketing company.

The designers of Java tackled this problem by providing a 'sandbox' for such code — a restricted environment in which it has no access to the local hard disk (or at most only temporary access to a restricted directory), and is only allowed to communicate with the host it came from. These security objectives are met by having the code executed by an interpreter — the Java Virtual Machine (JVM) — which has only limited access rights [539]. Java is also used on smartcards but (in current implementations at least) the JVM is in effect a compiler external to the card, which raises the issue of how the code it outputs can be got to the card in a trustworthy manner. Another application is in the new Blu-ray format for high-definition DVDs; players have virtual machines that execute rights-management code bundled with the disk. (I describe the mechanisms in detail in section 22.2.6.2.)

An alternative is proof-carrying code. Here, code to be executed must carry with it a proof that it doesn't do anything that contravenes the local security policy. This way, rather than using an interpreter with the resulting speed penalty, one merely has to trust a short program that checks the proofs supplied by downloaded programs before allowing them to be executed. The overhead of a JVM is not necessary [956].

Both of these are less general alternatives to an architecture supporting proper supervisor-level confinement.

4.2.10   Virtualization

This refers to systems that enable a single machine to emulate a number of machines independently. It was invented in the 1960s by IBM [336]; back when CPUs were very expensive, a single machine could be partitioned using VM/370 into multiple virtual machines, so that a company that bought two mainframes could use one for its production environment and the other as a series of logically separate machines for development, testing, and minor applications.

The move to PCs saw the emergence of virtual machine software for this platform, with offerings from various vendors, notably VMware and (in open-source form) the Xen project. Virtualization is very attractive to the hosting industry, as clients can be sold a share of a machine in a hosting centre for much less than a whole machine. In the few years that robust products have been available, their use has become extremely widespread.

At the client end, virtualization allows people to run a host operating system on top of a guest (for example, Windows on top of Linux or OS/X) and this offers not just flexibility but the prospect of better containment. For example, an employee might have two copies of Windows running on his laptop — a locked-down version with her office environment, and another for use at home. The separation can be high-grade from the technical viewpoint; the usual problem is operational. People may feel the need to share data between the two virtual machines and resort to ad-hoc mechanisms, from USB sticks to webmail accounts, that undermine the separation. Military system designers are nonetheless very interested in virtualization; I discuss their uses of it in section 8.5.3.

4.2.11   Trusted Computing

The 'Trusted Computing' initiative was launched by Microsoft, Intel, IBM, HP and Compaq to provide a more secure PC. Their stated aim was to provide software and hardware add-ons to the PC architecture that would enable people to be sure that a given program was running on a machine with a given specification; that is, that software had not been patched (whether by the user or by other software) and was running on a identifiable type and configuration of PC rather than on an emulator. The initial motivation was to support digital rights management. The problem there was this: if Disney was going to download a copy of a high-definition movie to Windows Media Player on your PC, how could they be sure it wasn't a hacked version, or running on a copy of Windows that was itself running on top of Xen? In either case, the movie might be ripped and end up on file-sharing systems.

The hardware proposal was to add a chip, the Trusted Platform Module or TPM, which could monitor the PC at boot time and report its state to the operating system; cryptographic keys would be made available depending on this state. Thus if a platform were modified — for example, by changing the boot ROM or the hard disk controller — different keys would be derived and previously encrypted material would not be available. A PC would also be able to use its TPM to certify to other PCs that it was in an 'approved' configuration, a process called *remote attestation*. Of course, individual PCs might be hacked in less detectable ways, such as by installing dual-ported memory or interfering with the bus from the TPM to the CPU — but the idea was to exclude low-cost break-once-run-anywhere attacks. Then again, the operating system will break from time to time, and the media player; so the idea was to make the content protection depend on as little as possible, and have revocation mechanisms that would compel people to upgrade away from broken software.

Thus a vendor of digital content might only serve premium products to a machine in an approved configuration. Furthermore, data-based access control policies could be enforced. An example of these is found in the 'Information Rights Management' mechanisms introduced with Office 2003; here, a file can be marked with access controls in a rights expression language which can state, for example, that it may only be read by certain named users and only for a certain period of time. Word-processing documents (as well as movies) could be marked 'view three times only'; a drug dealer could arrange for the spreadsheet with November's cocaine shipments to be unreadable after December, and so on.

There are objections to data-based access controls based on competition policy, to which I'll return in Part III. For now, my concern is the mechanisms. The problem facing Microsoft was to maintain backwards compatibility with the bad old world where thousands of buggy and insecure applications run as administrator, while creating the possibility of new access domains to which the old buggy code has no access. One proposed architecture, Palladium, was unveiled in 2002; this envisaged running the old, insecure, software in parallel with new, more secure components.

In addition to the normal operating system, Windows would have a 'Nexus', a security kernel small enough to be verified, that would talk directly to the TPM hardware and monitor what went on in the rest of the machine; and each application would have a Nexus Control Program (NCP) that would run on top of the Nexus in the secure virtual machine and manage critical things like cryptographic keys. NCPs would have direct access to hardware. In this way, a DRM program such as a media player could keep its crypto keys in its NCP and use them to output content to the screen and speakers directly — so that the plaintext content could not be stolen by spyware.

At the time of writing, the curtained memory features are not used in Vista; presentations at Microsoft research workshops indicated that getting fine-grained access control and virtualization to work at the middle layers of such a complex operating system has turned out to be a massive task. Meanwhile the TPM is available for secure storage of root keys for utilities such as hard disk encryption; this is available as 'BitLocker' in the more expensive versions of Vista. It remains to be seen whether the more comprehensive vision of Trusted Computing can be made to work; there's a growing feeling in the industry that it was too hard and, as it's also politically toxic, it's likely to be quietly abandoned. Anyway, TPMs bring us to the more general problem of the hardware protection mechanisms on which access controls are based.

4.3   Hardware Protection

Most access control systems set out not just to control what users can do, but to limit what programs can do as well. In most systems, users can either write programs, or download and install them. So programs may be buggy or even malicious.

Preventing one process from interfering with another is the *protection problem*. The *confinement problem* is usually defined as that of preventing programs communicating outward other than through authorized channels. There are several flavours of each. The goal may be to prevent active interference, such as memory overwriting, or to stop one process reading another's memory directly. This is what commercial operating systems set out to do. Military systems may also try to protect *metadata* — data about other data, or subjects, or processes — so that, for example, a user can't find out what other users are logged on to the system or what processes they're running. In some applications, such as processing census data, confinement means allowing a program to read data but not release anything about it other than the results of certain constrained queries.

Unless one uses sandboxing techniques (which are too restrictive for general programming environments), solving the confinement problem on a single processor means, at the very least, having a mechanism that will stop one program from overwriting another's code or data. There may be areas of memory that are shared in order to allow interprocess communication; but programs must be protected from accidental or deliberate modification, and they must have access to memory that is similarly protected.

This usually means that hardware access control must be integrated with the processor's memory management functions. A typical mechanism is *segment addressing*. Memory is addressed by two registers, a segment register which points to a segment of memory, and another address register which points to a location within that segment. The segment registers are controlled by the operating system, and often by a special component of it called the *reference monitor* which links the access control mechanisms with the hardware.

The actual implementation has become more complex as the processors themselves have. Early IBM mainframes had a two state CPU: the machine was either in authorized state or it was not. In the latter case, the program was restricted to a memory segment allocated by the operating system. In the former, it could alter the segment registers at will. An authorized program was one that was loaded from an authorized library.

Any desired access control policy can be implemented on top of this, given suitable authorized libraries, but this is not always efficient; and system security depends on keeping bad code (whether malicious or buggy) out of the authorized libraries. So later processors offered more complex hardware mechanisms. Multics, an operating system developed at MIT in the 1960's and which inspired the development of Unix, introduced *rings of protection* which express differing levels of privilege: ring 0 programs had complete access to disk, supervisor states ran in ring 2, and user code at various less privileged levels [1139]. Its features have to some extent been adopted in more recent processors, such as the Intel main processor line from the 80286 onwards.

There are a number of general problems with interfacing hardware and software security mechanisms. For example, it often happens that a less privileged process such as application code needs to invoke a more privileged process such as a device driver. The mechanisms for doing this need to be designed with some care, or security bugs can be expected. The IBM mainframe operating system MVS, for example, had a bug in which a program which executed a normal and an authorized task concurrently could make the former authorized too [774]. Also, performance may depend quite drastically on whether routines at different privilege levels are called by reference or by value [1139].

4.3.1   Intel Processors, and 'Trusted Computing'

Early Intel processors, such as the 8088/8086 used in early PCs, had no distinction between system and user mode, and thus no protection at all — any running program controlled the whole machine. The 80286 added protected segment addressing and rings, so for the first time it could run proper operating systems. The 80386 had built in virtual memory, and large enough memory segments (4 Gb) that they could be ignored and the machine treated as a 32-bit flat address machine. The 486 and Pentium series chips added more performance (caches, out of order execution and MMX).

The rings of protection are supported by a number of mechanisms. The current privilege level can only be changed by a process in ring 0 (the kernel). Procedures cannot access objects in lower level rings directly but there are *gates* which allow execution of code at a different privilege level and which manage the supporting infrastructure, such as multiple stack segments for different privilege levels and exception handling. For more details, see [646].

The Pentium 3 finally added a new security feature — a processor serial number. This caused a storm of protest because privacy advocates feared it could be used for all sorts of 'big brother' purposes, which may have been irrational as computers have all sorts of unique numbers in them that software can use to tell which machine it's running on (examples range from MAC addresses to the serial numbers of hard disk controllers). At the time the serial number was launched, Intel had planned to introduce cryptographic support into the Pentium by 2000 in order to support DRM. Their thinking was that as they earned 90% of their profits from PC microprocessors, where they had 90% of the market, they could only grow their business by expanding the market for PCs; and since the business market was saturated, that meant sales to homes where, it was thought, DRM would be a requirement.

Anyway, the outcry against the Pentium serial number led Intel to set up an industry alliance, now called the Trusted Computing Group, to introduce cryptography into the PC platform by means of a separate processor, the Trusted Platform Module (TPM), which is a smartcard chip mounted on the PC motherboard. The TPM works together with *curtained memory* features introduced in the Pentium to enable operating system vendors to create memory spaces isolated from each other, and even against a process in one memory space running with administrator privileges. The mechanisms proposed by Microsoft are described above, and have not been made available in commercial releases of Windows at the time of writing.

One Intel hardware feature that has been implemented and used is the x86 virtualization support, known as Intel VT (or its development name, Vanderpool). AMD has an equivalent offering. Processor architectures such as S/370 and M68000 are easy to virtualize, and the theoretical requirements for this have been known for many years [1033]. The native Intel instruction set, however, had instructions that were hard to virtualize, requiring messy workarounds, such as patches to hosted operating systems. Processors with these extensions can use products such as Xen to run unmodified copies of guest operating systems. (It does appear, though, that if the Trusted Computing mechanisms are ever implemented, it will be complex to make them work alongside virtualization.)

4.3.2 ARM Processors

The ARM is the 32-bit processor core most commonly licensed to third party vendors of embedded systems; hundreds of millions are used in mobile phones and other consumer electronic devices. The original ARM (which stood for *Acorn Risc Machine*) was the first commercial RISC design. ARM chips are also used in many security products, from the Capstone chips used by the US government to protect secret data, to the crypto accelerator boards from firms like nCipher that do cryptography for large web sites. A fast multiply-and-accumulate instruction and low power consumption made the ARM very attractive for embedded applications doing crypto and/or signal processing. The standard reference is [508].

The ARM is licensed as a processor core, which chip designers can include in their products, plus a number of optional add-ons. The basic core contains separate banks of registers for user and system processes, plus a software interrupt mechanism that puts the processor in supervisor mode and transfers control to a process at a fixed address. The core contains no memory management, so ARM-based designs can have their hardware protection extensively customized. A system control coprocessor is available to help with this. It can support domains of processes that have similar access rights (and thus share the same translation tables) but that retain some protection from each other. This gives fast context switching. Standard product ARM CPU chips, from the model 600 onwards, have this memory support built in.

There is a version, the Amulet, which uses self-timed logic. Eliminating the clock saved power and reduces RF interference, but made it necessary to introduce hardware protection features, such as register locking, into the main processor itself so that contention between different hardware processes could be managed. This is an interesting example of protection techniques typical of an operating system being recycled in main-line processor design.

4.3.3 Security Processors

Specialist security processors range from the chips in smartcards, through the TPM chips now fixed to most PC motherboards (which are basically smartcard chips with parallel interfaces) and crypto accelerator boards, to specialist crypto devices.

Many of the lower-cost smartcards still have 8-bit processors. Some of them have memory management routines that let certain addresses be read only when passwords are entered into a register in the preceding few instructions. The goal was that the various principals with a stake in the card — perhaps a card manufacturer, an OEM, a network and a bank — can all have their secrets on the card and yet be protected from each other. This may be a matter of software; but some cards have small, hardwired access control matrices to enforce this protection.

Many of the encryption devices used in banking to handle ATM PINs have a further layer of application-level access control in the form of an 'authorized state' which must be set (by two console passwords, or a physical key) when PINs are to be printed. This is reminiscent of the old IBM mainframes, but is used for manual rather than programmatic control: it enables a shift supervisor to ensure that he is present when this job is run. Similar devices are used by the military to distribute keys. I'll discuss cryptoprocessors in more detail in Chapter 16.

4.4   What Goes Wrong

Popular operating systems such as Unix / Linux and Windows are very large and complex, so they have many bugs. They are used in a huge range of systems, so their features are tested daily by millions of users under very diverse circumstances. Consequently, many bugs are found and reported. Thanks to the net, knowledge spreads widely and rapidly. Thus at any one time, there may be dozens of security flaws that are known, and for which attack scripts are circulating on the net. A vulnerability has a typical lifecycle whereby it is discovered; reported to CERT or to the vendor; a patch is shipped; the patch is reverse-engineered, and an exploit is produced for the vulnerability; and people who did not apply the patch in time find that their machines have been recruited to a botnet when their ISP cuts them off for sending spam. There is a variant in which the vulnerability is exploited at once rather than reported — often called a *zero-day* exploit as attacks happen from day zero of the vulnerability's known existence. The economics, and the ecology, of the vulnerability lifecycle are the subject of intensive study by security economists; I'll discuss their findings in Part III.

The traditional goal of an attacker was to get a normal account on the system and then become the system administrator, so he could take over the system completely. The first step might have involved guessing, or social-engineering, a password, and then using one of the many known operating-system bugs that allow the transition from user to root. A taxonomy of such technical flaws was compiled in 1993 by Carl Landwehr [774]. These involved failures in the technical implementation, of which I will give examples in the next two sections, and also in the higher level design; for example, the user interface might induce people to mismanage access rights or do other stupid things which cause the access control to be bypassed. I will give some examples in section 4.4.3 below.

The user/root distinction has become less important in the last few years for two reasons. First, Windows PCs have predominated, running applications that insist on being run as administrator, so any application that can be compromised gives administrator access. Second, attackers have come to focus on compromising large numbers of PCs, which they can organise into a botnet in order to send spam or phish and thus make money. Even if your mail client were not running as administrator, it would still be useful to a spammer who could control it. However, botnet herders tend to install *rootkits* which, as their name suggests, run as root; and the user/root distinction does still matter in business environments, where you do not want a compromised web server or database application to expose your other applications as well. Perhaps if large numbers of ordinary users start running Vista with User Account Control enabled, it will make the botnet herders' lives a bit harder. We may at least hope.

In any case, the basic types of technical attack have not changed hugely since the early 1990s and I'll now consider them briefly.

4.4.1 Smashing the Stack

About half of the technical attacks on operating systems that are reported in *Computer Emergency Response Team* (CERT) bulletins and security mailing lists involve memory overwriting attacks, colloquially known as 'smashing the stack'. The proportion was even higher in the late 1990s and early 2000s but is now dropping slowly.

The basic idea behind the stack-smashing attack is that programmers are often careless about checking the size of arguments, so an attacker who passes a long argument to a program may find that some of it gets treated as code rather than data. A classic example was a vulnerability in the Unix `finger` command. A widespread implementation of this would accept an argument of any length, although only 256 bytes had been allocated for this argument by the program. When an attacker used the command with a longer argument, the trailing bytes of the argument ended up being executed by the system.

The usual technique is to arrange for the trailing bytes of the argument to have a *landing pad* — a long space of *no-operation* (NOP) commands, or other register commands that don't change the control flow, and whose task is to catch the processor if it executes any of them. The landing pad delivers the processor to the attack code which will do something like creating a root account with no password, or starting a shell with administrative privilege directly (see Figure 4.6).

Many of the vulnerabilities reported routinely by CERT and bugtraq are variants on this theme. I wrote in the first edition of this book, in 2001, 'There is really no excuse for the problem to continue, as it's been well known for a generation'. Yet it remains a problem.

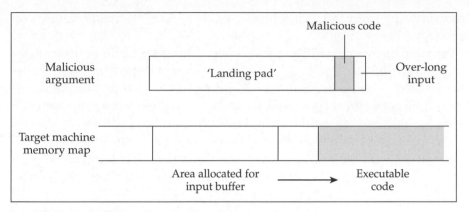

Figure 4.6: Stack smashing attack

Most of the early 1960's time sharing systems suffered from it, and fixed it [549]. Penetration analysis efforts at the System Development Corporation in the early '70s showed that the problem of 'unexpected parameters' was still one of the most frequently used attack strategies [799]. Intel's 80286 processor introduced explicit parameter checking instructions — verify read, verify write, and verify length — in 1982, but they were avoided by most software designers to prevent architecture dependencies. In 1988, large numbers of Unix computers were brought down simultaneously by the 'Internet worm', which used the `finger` vulnerability described above, and thus brought memory overwriting attacks to the notice of the mass media [1206]. A 1998 survey paper described memory overwriting attacks as the 'attack of the decade' [329].

Yet programmers still don't check the size of arguments, and holes keep on being found. The attack isn't even limited to networked computer systems: at least one smartcard could be defeated by passing it a message longer than its programmer had anticipated.

4.4.2 Other Technical Attacks

In 2002, Microsoft announced a security initiative that involved every programmer being trained in how to write secure code. (The book they produced for this, *'Writing Secure Code'* by Michael Howard and David LeBlanc, is good; I recommend it to my students [627].) Other tech companies have launched similar training programmes. Despite the training and the tools, memory overwriting attacks are still appearing, to the great frustration of software company managers. However, they are perhaps half of all new vulnerabilities now rather than the 90% they were in 2001.

The other new vulnerabilities are mostly variations on the same general theme, in that they occur when data in grammar A is interpreted as being in grammar B. A stack overflow is when data are accepted as input (e.g. a URL) and end up being executed as machine code. They are essentially failures of type safety.

A **format string vulnerability** arises when a machine accepts input data as a formatting instruction (e.g. %n in the C command printf()). These commonly arise when a programmer tries to print user-supplied data and carelessly allows the print command to interpret any formatting instructions in the string; this may allow the string's author to write to the stack. There are many other variants on the theme; buffer overflows can be induced by improper string termination, passing an inadequately sized buffer to a path manipulation function, and many other subtle errors. See Gary McGraw's book '*Software Security*' [858] for a taxonomy.

SQL insertion attacks commonly arise when a careless web developer passes user input to a back-end database without checking to see whether it contains SQL code. The game is often given away by error messages, from which a capable and motivated user may infer enough to mount an attack. (Indeed, a survey of business websites in 2006 showed that over 10% were potentially vulnerable [1234].) There are similar command-injection problems afflicting other languages used by web developers, such as PHP and perl. The remedy in general is to treat all user input as suspicious and validate it.

Checking data sizes is all very well when you get the buffer size calculation correct, but when you make a mistake — for example, if you fail to consider all the edge cases — you can end up with another type of attack called an **integer manipulation attack**. Here, an overflow, underflow, wrap-around or truncation can result in the 'security' code writing an inappropriate number of bytes to the stack.

Once such type-safety attacks are dealt with, **race conditions** are probably next. These occur when a transaction is carried out in two or more stages, and it is possible for someone to alter it after the stage which involves verifying access rights. I mentioned in Chapter 2 how a race condition can allow users to log in as other users if the userid can be overwritten while the password validation is in progress. Another classic example arose in the Unix command to create a directory, 'mkdir', which used to work in two steps: the storage was allocated, and then ownership was transferred to the user. Since these steps were separate, a user could initiate a 'mkdir' in background, and if this completed only the first step before being suspended, a second process could be used to replace the newly created directory with a link to the password file. Then the original process would resume, and change ownership of the password file to the user. The /tmp directory, used for temporary files, can often be abused in this way; the trick is to wait until an application run by a privileged user writes a file here, then change it to a symbolic link to another file somewhere else — which will be removed when the privileged user's application tries to delete the temporary file.

A wide variety of other bugs have enabled users to assume root status and take over the system. For example, the PDP-10 TENEX operating system had the bug that the program address could overflow into the next bit of the process state word which was the privilege-mode bit; this meant that a program overflow could put a program in supervisor state. In another example, some Unix implementations had the feature that if a user tried to execute the command su when the maximum number of files were open, then su was unable to open the password file and responded by giving the user root status. In more modern systems, the most intractable user-to-root problems tend to be feature interactions. For example, we've struggled with backup and recovery systems. It's convenient if you can let users recover their own files, rather than having to call a sysadmin — but how do you protect information assets from a time traveller, especially if the recovery system allows him to compose parts of pathnames to get access to directories that were always closed to him? And what if the recovery functionality is buried in an application to which he needs access in order to do his job, and can be manipulated to give root access?

There have also been many bugs that allowed service denial attacks. For example, Multics had a global limit on the number of files that could be open at once, but no local limits. So a user could exhaust this limit and lock the system so that not even the administrator could log on [774]. And until the late 1990's, most implementations of the Internet protocols allocated a fixed amount of buffer space to process the SYN packets with which TCP/IP connections are initiated. The result was *SYN flooding attacks*: by sending a large number of SYN packets, an attacker could exhaust the available buffer space and prevent the machine accepting any new connections. This is now fixed using *syncookies*, which I'll discuss in Part II.

The most recently discovered family of attacks of this kind are on *system call wrappers*. These are software products that modify software behaviour by intercepting the system calls it makes and performing some filtering or manipulation. Some wrapper products do virtualization; others provide security extensions to operating systems. However Robert Watson has discovered that such products may have synchronization bugs and race conditions that allow an attacker to become root [1325]. (I'll describe these in more detail in section 18.3.) The proliferation of concurrency mechanisms everywhere, with multiprocessor machines suddenly becoming the norm after many years in which they were a research curiosity, may lead to race conditions being the next big family of attacks.

4.4.3 User Interface Failures

One of the earliest attacks to be devised was the *Trojan Horse*, a program that the administrator is invited to run and which will do some harm if he does so. People would write games which checked occasionally whether the player was the system administrator, and if so would create another administrator account with a known password.

Another trick is to write a program that has the same name as a commonly used system utility, such as the `ls` command which lists all the files in a Unix directory, and design it to abuse the administrator privilege (if any) before invoking the genuine utility. The next step is to complain to the administrator that something is wrong with this directory. When the administrator enters the directory and types `ls` to see what's there, the damage is done. The fix is simple: an administrator's 'PATH' variable (the list of directories which will be searched for a suitably named program when a command is invoked) should not contain '.' (the symbol for the current directory). Recent Unix versions are shipped with this as a default; but it's still an unnecessary trap for the unwary.

Perhaps the most serious example of user interface failure, in terms of the number of systems at risk, is in Windows. I refer to the fact that, until Vista came along, a user needed to be the system administrator to install anything[2]. In theory this might have helped a bank preventing its branch staff from running games on their PCs at lunchtime and picking up viruses. But most environments are much less controlled, and many people need to be able to install software to get their work done. So millions of people have administrator privileges who shouldn't need them, and are vulnerable to attacks in which malicious code simply pops up a box telling them to do something. Thank goodness Vista is moving away from this, but UAC provides no protection where applications such as web servers must run as root, are visible to the outside world, and contain software bugs that enable them to be taken over.

Another example, which might be argued is an interface failure, comes from the use of active content of various kinds. These can be a menace because users have no intuitively clear way of controlling them. Javascript and ActiveX in web pages, macros in Office documents and executables in email attachments have all been used to launch serious attacks. Even Java, for all its supposed security, has suffered a number of attacks that exploited careless implementations [360]. However, many people (and many companies) are unwilling to forego the bells and whistles which active content can provide, and we saw in Chapter 2 how the marketing folks usually beat the security folks (even in applications like banking).

4.4.4 Why So Many Things Go Wrong

We've already mentioned the basic problem faced by operating system security designers: their products are huge and therefore buggy, and are tested by large

---

[2]In theory a member of the Power Users Group in XP could but that made little difference.

numbers of users in parallel, some of whom will publicize their discoveries rather than reporting them to the vendor. Even if all bugs were reported responsibly, this wouldn't make much difference; almost all of the widely exploited vulnerabilities over the last few years had already been patched. (Indeed, Microsoft's 'Patch Tuesday' each month is followed by 'Exploit Wednesday' as the malware writers reverse the new vulnerabilities and attack them before everyone's patched them.)

There are other structural problems too. One of the more serious causes of failure is *kernel bloat*. Under Unix, all device drivers, filesystems etc. must be in the kernel. Until Vista, the Windows kernel used to contain drivers for a large number of smartcards, card readers and the like, many of which were written by the equipment vendors. So large quantities of code were trusted, in that they are put inside the security perimeter. Some other systems, such as MVS, introduced mechanisms that decrease the level of trust needed by many utilities. However the means to do this in the most common operating systems are few and relatively nonstandard.

Even more seriously, most application developers make their programs run as root. The reasons for this are economic rather than technical, and are easy enough to understand. A company trying to build market share for a platform, such as an operating system, must appeal to its complementers — its application developers — as well as to its users. It is easier for developers if programs can run as root, so early Windows products allowed just that. Once the vendor has a dominant position, the business logic is to increase the security, and also to customise it so as to lock in both application developers and users more tightly. This is now happening with Windows Vista as the access control mechanisms become ever more complex, and different from Linux and OS/X. A similar pattern, or too little security in the early stages of a platform lifecycle and too much (of the wrong kind) later, has been observed in other platforms from mainframes to mobile phones.

Making many applications and utilities run as root has repeatedly introduced horrible vulnerabilities where more limited privilege could have been used with only a modicum of thought and a minor redesign. There are many systems such as `lpr/lpd` — the Unix lineprinter subsystem — which does not need to run as root but does anyway on most systems. This has also been a source of security failures in the past (e.g., getting the printer to spool to the password file).

Some applications need a certain amount of privilege. For example, mail delivery agents must be able to deal with user mailboxes. But while a prudent designer would restrict this privilege to a small part of the application, most agents are written so that the whole program needs to run as root. The classic example is `sendmail`, which has a long history of serious security holes; but many other MTAs also have problems. The general effect is that a bug which ought to compromise only one person's mail may end up giving root privilege to an outside attacker.

So we're going to have some interesting times as developers come to grips with UAC. The precedents are not all encouraging. Some programmers historically avoided the difficulty of getting non-root software installed and working securely by simply leaving important shared data structures and resources accessible to all users. Many old systems stored mail in a file per user in a world-writeable directory, which makes mail forgery easy. The Unix file utmp — the list of users logged in — was frequently used for security checking of various kinds, but is also frequently world-writeable! This should have been built as a service rather than a file — but fixing problems like these once the initial design decisions have been made can be hard. I expect to see all the old problems of 1970s multiuser systems come back again, as the complexity of using the Vista mechanisms properly just defeats many programmers who aren't security specialists and are just desparate to get something sort of working so they can end the assignment, collect their bonus and move on.

4.4.5 Remedies

Some classes of vulnerability can be fixed using automatic tools. Stack overwriting attacks, for example, are largely due to the lack of proper bounds checking in C (the language most operating systems are written in). There are various tools (including free tools) available for checking C programs for potential problems, and there is even a compiler patch called StackGuard which puts a *canary* next to the return address on the stack. This can be a random 32-bit value chosen when the program is started, and checked when a function is torn down. If the stack has been overwritten meanwhile, then with high probability the canary will change [329]. The availability of these tools, and training initiatives such as Microsoft's, have slowly reduced the number of stack overflow errors. However, attack tools also improve, and attackers are now finding bugs such as format string vulnerabilities and integer overflows to which no-one paid much attention in the 1990s.

In general, much more effort needs to be put into design, coding and testing. Architecture matters; having clean interfaces that evolve in a controlled way, under the eagle eye of someone experienced who has a long-term stake in the security of the product, can make a huge difference. (I'll discuss this at greater length in Part III.) Programs should only have as much privilege as they need: the *principle of least privilege* [1102]. Software should also be designed so that the default configuration, and in general, the easiest way of doing something, should be safe. Sound architecture is critical in achieving safe defaults and using least privilege. However, many systems are shipped with dangerous defaults and messy code that potentially exposes all sorts of interfaces to attacks like SQL injection that just shouldn't happen.

4.4.6 Environmental Creep

I have pointed out repeatedly that many security failures result from environmental change undermining a security model. Mechanisms that were adequate in a restricted environment often fail in a more general one.

Access control mechanisms are no exception. Unix, for example, was originally designed as a 'single user Multics' (hence the name). It then became an operating system to be used by a number of skilled and trustworthy people in a laboratory who were sharing a single machine. In this environment the function of the security mechanisms is mostly to contain mistakes; to prevent one user's typing errors or program crashes from deleting or overwriting another user's files. The original security mechanisms were quite adequate for this purpose.

But Unix security became a classic 'success disaster'. Unix was repeatedly extended without proper consideration being given to how the protection mechanisms also needed to be extended. The Berkeley versions assumed an extension from a single machine to a network of machines that were all on one LAN and all under one management. Mechanisms such as `rhosts` were based on a tuple *(username,hostname)* rather than just a username, and saw the beginning of the transfer of trust.

The Internet mechanisms (telnet, ftp, DNS, SMTP), which grew out of Arpanet in the 1970's, were written for mainframes on what was originally a secure WAN. Mainframes were autonomous, the network was outside the security protocols, and there was no transfer of authorization. Thus remote authentication, which the Berkeley model was starting to make prudent, was simply not supported. The Sun contributions (NFS, NIS, RPC etc.) were based on a workstation model of the universe, with a multiple LAN environment with distributed management but still usually in a single organisation. (A proper tutorial on topics such as DNS and NFS is beyond the scope of this book, but there is some more detailed background material in the section on Vulnerabilities in Network Protocols in Chapter 21.)

Mixing all these different models of computation together has resulted in chaos. Some of their initial assumptions still apply partially, but none of them apply globally any more. The Internet now has hundreds of millions of PCs, millions of LANs, thousands of interconnected WANs, and managements which are not just independent but may be in conflict (including nation states and substate groups that are at war with each other). Many PCs have no management at all, and there's a growing number of network-connected Windows and Linux boxes in the form of fax machines, routers and other embedded products that don't ever get patched.

Users, instead of being trustworthy but occasionally incompetent, are now largely incompetent — but some are both competent and hostile. Code used to be simply buggy — but now there is a significant amount of malicious code out there. Attacks on communications networks used to be the purview of national intelligence agencies — now they can be done by *script kiddies*, relatively unskilled people who have downloaded attack tools from the net and launched them without any real idea of how they work.

So Unix and Internet security gives us yet another example of a system that started out reasonably well designed but which was undermined by a changing environment.

Windows Vista and its predecessors in the NT product series have more extensive protection mechanisms than Unix, but have been around for much less time. The same goes for database products such as Oracle. Realistically, all we can say is that the jury is still out.

4.5   Summary

Access control mechanisms operate at a number of levels in a system, from applications down through middleware to the operating system and the hardware. Higher level mechanisms can be more expressive, but also tend to be more vulnerable to attack for a variety of reasons ranging from intrinsic complexity to implementer skill levels. Most attacks involve the opportunistic exploitation of bugs, and software products that are very large, very widely used, or both (as with operating systems and databases) are particularly likely to have security bugs found and publicized. Systems at all levels are also vulnerable to environmental changes which undermine the assumptions used in their design.

The main function of access control is to limit the damage that can be done by particular groups, users, and programs whether through error or malice. The most important fielded examples are Unix and Windows, which are similar in many respects, though Windows is more expressive. Database products are often more expressive still (and thus even harder to implement securely.) Access control is also an important part of the design of special purpose hardware such as smartcards and other encryption devices. New techniques are being developed to push back on the number of implementation errors, such as stack overflow attacks; but new attacks are being found continually, and the overall dependability of large software systems improves only slowly.

The general concepts of access control from read, write and execute permissions to groups and roles will crop up again and again. In some distributed systems, they may not be immediately obvious as the underlying mechanisms can be quite different. An example comes from public key infrastructures, which are a reimplementation of an old access control concept, the capability. However, the basic mechanisms (and their problems) are pervasive.

Research Problems

Most of the issues in access control were identified by the 1960's or early 1970's and were worked out on experimental systems such as Multics [1139] and the CAP [1344]. Much of the research in access control systems since has involved reworking the basic themes in new contexts, such as object oriented systems and mobile code.

Recent threads of research include how to combine access control with the admission control mechanisms used to provide quality of service guaranteed in multimedia operating systems, and how to implement and manage access control efficiently in large complex systems, using roles and policy languages. However the largest single topic of research during 2003–6 has been 'Trusted Computing', and how various trust mechanisms could be layered on top of the mechanisms proposed by the Trusted Computing Group. The failure of Windows Vista, as released in January 2007, to support remote attestation has somewhat taken the wind out of the sails of this effort.

I suspect that a useful research topic for the next few years will be how to engineer access control mechanisms that are not just robust but also usable — by both programmers and end users. Separation is easy enough in principle; one can have different machines, or different virtual machines, for different tasks. But how happy would people be with an electronic banking application that was so well walled off from the rest of the digital world that they could not export figures from their bank statement into a spreadsheet? I'll discuss this problem at greater length when we come to mandatory access controls in Chapter 8.

Further Reading

The best textbook to go to for a more detailed introduction to access control issues is Dieter Gollmann's *'Computer Security'* [537]. A technical report from Carl Landwehr gives a useful reference to many of the flaws found in operating systems over the last 30 years or so [774]. One of the earliest reports on the subject (and indeed on computer security in general) is by Willis Ware [1319]. One of the most influential early papers is by Jerry Saltzer and Mike Schroeder [1102], while Butler Lampson's influential paper on the confinement problem is at [768].

The classic description of Unix security is in the paper by Fred Grampp and Robert Morris [550]. The most comprehensive textbook on this subject is Simson Garfinkel and Eugene Spafford's *Practical Unix and Internet Security* [517], while the classic on the Internet side of things is Bill Cheswick and Steve

Bellovin's *Firewalls and Internet Security* [157], with many examples of network attacks on Unix systems.

The protection mechanisms of Windows are described briefly in Gollmann. For more detail, see the Microsoft online documentation; no doubt a number of textbooks on Vista will appear soon. There is a history of microprocessor architectures at [128], and a reference book for Java security written by its architect Li Gong [539].

The field of software security is fast moving; the attacks that are catching the headlines change significantly (at least in their details) from one year to the next. The best recent book I've read is Gary McGraw's [858]. But to keep up, you should not just read textbooks, but follow the latest notices from CERT and mailing lists such as bugtraq and books about the dark side such as Markus Jakobsson and Zulfikar Ramzan's [660].

Cryptography

ZHQM ZMGM ZMFM
— G Julius Caesar

KXJEY UREBE ZWEHE WRYTU HEYFS KREHE GOYFI WTTTU OLKSY CAJPO BOTEI
ZONTX BYBWT GONEY CUZWR GDSON SXBOU YWRHE BAAHY USEDQ
— John F Kennedy

5.1   Introduction

Cryptography is where security engineering meets mathematics. It provides us with the tools that underlie most modern security protocols. It is probably the key enabling technology for protecting distributed systems, yet it is surprisingly hard to do right. As we've already seen in Chapter 3, 'Protocols', cryptography has often been used to protect the wrong things, or used to protect them in the wrong way. We'll see plenty more examples when we start looking in detail at real applications.

Unfortunately, the computer security and cryptology communities have drifted apart over the last 25 years. Security people don't always understand the available crypto tools, and crypto people don't always understand the real-world problems. There are a number of reasons for this, such as different professional backgrounds (computer science versus mathematics) and different research funding (governments have tried to promote computer security research while suppressing cryptography). It reminds me of a story told by a medical friend. While she was young, she worked for a few years in a country where, for economic reasons, they'd shortened their medical degrees and concentrated on producing specialists as quickly as possible. One day, a patient who'd had both kidneys removed and was awaiting a transplant needed her dialysis shunt redone. The surgeon sent the patient back from the theater on the grounds that there was no urinalysis on file. It just didn't occur to him that a patient with no kidneys couldn't produce any urine.

Just as a doctor needs to understand physiology as well as surgery, so a security engineer needs to be familiar with cryptology as well as computer security (and much else). This chapter is aimed at people without any training in cryptology; cryptologists will find little in it that they don't already know. As I only have a few dozen pages, and a proper exposition of modern cryptography would run into thousands, I won't go into much of the mathematics (there are lots of books that do that; see the end of the chapter for further reading). I'll just explain the basic intuitions and constructions that seem to cause the most confusion. If you have to use cryptography in anything resembling a novel way, then I strongly recommend that you read a lot more about it — and talk to some real experts. The security engineer Paul Kocher remarked, at a keynote speech at Crypto 2007, that you could expect to break any crypto product designed by 'any company that doesn't employ someone in this room'. There is a fair bit of truth in that.

Computer security people often ask for non-mathematical definitions of cryptographic terms. The basic terminology is that *cryptography* refers to the science and art of designing ciphers; *cryptanalysis* to the science and art of breaking them; while *cryptology*, often shortened to just crypto, is the study of both. The input to an encryption process is commonly called the *plaintext*, and the output the *ciphertext*. Thereafter, things get somewhat more complicated. There are a number of *cryptographic primitives* — basic building blocks, such as *block ciphers*, *stream ciphers*, and *hash functions*. Block ciphers may either have one key for both encryption and decryption, in which case they're called *shared-key* (also *secret-key* or *symmetric*), or have separate keys for encryption and decryption, in which case they're called *public-key* or *asymmetric*. A *digital signature scheme* is a special type of asymmetric crypto primitive.

In the rest of this chapter, I will first give some simple historical examples to illustrate the basic concepts. I'll then try to fine-tune definitions by introducing the *random oracle model*, which many cryptologists use. Finally, I'll show how some of the more important cryptographic algorithms actually work, and how they can be used to protect data.

5.2 Historical Background

Suetonius tells us that Julius Caesar enciphered his dispatches by writing 'D' for 'A', 'E' for 'D' and so on [1202]. When Augustus Caesar ascended the throne, he changed the imperial cipher system so that 'C' was now written for

'A', 'D' for 'B' etcetera. In modern terminology, we would say that he changed the key from 'D' to 'C'. Remarkably, a similar code was used by Bernardo Provenzano, allegedly the *capo di tutti capi* of the Sicilian mafia, who wrote '4' for 'a', '5' for 'b' and so on. This led directly to his capture by the Italian police in 2006 after they intercepted and deciphered some of his messages [1034].

The Arabs generalised this idea to the *monoalphabetic substitution*, in which a keyword is used to permute the cipher alphabet. We will write the plaintext in lower case letters, and the ciphertext in upper case, as shown in Figure 5.1:

```
abcdefghijklmnopqrstuvwxyz
SECURITYABDFGHJKLMNOPQVWXZ
```

Figure 5.1: Monoalphabetic substitution cipher

OYAN RWSGKFR AN AH RHTFANY MSOYRM OYSH SMSEAC NCMAKO; but breaking ciphers of this kind is a straightforward pencil and paper puzzle, which you may have done in primary school. The trick is that some letters, and combinations of letters, are much more common than others; in English the most common letters are e,t,a,i,o,n,s,h,r,d,l,u in that order. Artificial intelligence researchers have shown some interest in writing programs to solve monoalphabetic substitutions. Using letter and digram (letter pair) frequencies alone, they typically succeed with about 600 letters of ciphertext, while smarter strategies such as guessing probable words can cut this to about 150 letters. A human cryptanalyst will usually require much less.

There are basically two ways to make a stronger cipher — the *stream cipher* and the *block cipher*. In the former, you make the encryption rule depend on a plaintext symbol's position in the stream of plaintext symbols, while in the latter you encrypt several plaintext symbols at once in a block. Let's look at early examples.

5.2.1 An Early Stream Cipher — The Vigenère

This early stream cipher is commonly ascribed to the Frenchman Blaise de Vigenère, a diplomat who served King Charles IX. It works by adding a key repeatedly into the plaintext using the convention that 'A' = 0, 'B' = 1, ... , 'Z' = 25, and addition is carried out modulo 26 — that is, if the result is greater than 25, we subtract as many multiples of 26 as are needed to bring is into the range [0, ... , 25], that is, [A, ... , Z]. Mathematicians write this as

$$C = P + K \bmod 26$$

So, for example, when we add P (15) to U (20) we get 35, which we reduce to 9 by subtracting 26.9 corresponds to J, so the encryption of P under the key U (and of U under the key P) is J. In this notation, Julius Caesar's system used a fixed key $K = D^1$, while Augustus Caesar's used $K = C$ and Vigenère used a repeating key, also known as a *running key*. Various means were developed to do this addition quickly, including printed tables and, for field use, cipher wheels. Whatever the implementation technology, the encryption using a repeated keyword for the key would look as shown in Figure 5.2:

Plain	`tobeornottobethatisthequestion`
Key	`runrunrunrunrunrunrunrunrunrun`
Cipher	`KIOVIEEIGKIOVNURNVJNUVKHVMGZIA`

Figure 5.2: Vigenère (polyalphabetic substitution cipher)

A number of people appear to have worked out how to solve polyalphabetic ciphers, from the womaniser Giacomo Casanova to the computing pioneer Charles Babbage. However the first published solution was in 1863 by Friedrich Kasiski, a Prussian infantry officer [695]. He noticed that given a long enough piece of ciphertext, repeated patterns will appear at multiples of the keyword length.

In Figure 5.2, for example, we see 'KIOV' repeated after nine letters, and 'NU' after six. Since three divides both six and nine, we might guess a keyword of three letters. It follows that ciphertext letters one, four, seven and so on all enciphered under the same keyletter; so we can use frequency analysis techniques to guess the most likely values of this letter, and then repeat the process for the second and third letters of the key.

5.2.2 The One-Time Pad

One way to make a stream cipher of this type proof against attacks is for the key sequence to be as long as the plaintext, and to never repeat. This was proposed by Gilbert Vernam during World War 1 [676]; its effect is that given any ciphertext, and any plaintext of the same length, there is a key which decrypts the ciphertext to the plaintext. Regardless of the amount of computation that opponents can do, they are none the wiser, as all possible plaintexts are just as likely. This system is known as the *one-time pad*. Leo Marks' engaging book on cryptography in the Special Operations Executive in World War 2 [836] relates how one-time key material was printed on silk, which agents could conceal inside their clothing; whenever a key had been used it was torn off and burnt.

An example should explain all this. Suppose you had intercepted a message from a wartime German agent which you knew started with 'Heil Hitler', and the first ten letters of ciphertext were `DGTYI BWPJA`. This means that

---

[1]modulo 23, as the alphabet Caesar used wrote U as V, J as I, and had no W.

the first ten letters of the one-time pad were `wclnb tdefj`, as shown in Figure 5.3:

Plain   `heilhitler`
Key   `wclnbtdefj`
Cipher   `DGTYIBWPJA`

Figure 5.3: A spy's message

But once he's burnt the piece of silk with his key material, the spy can claim that he's actually a member of the anti-Nazi underground resistance, and the message actually said 'Hang Hitler'. This is quite possible, as the key material could just as easily have been `wggsb tdefj`, as shown in Figure 5.4:

Cipher   `DGTYIBWPJA`
Key   `wggsbtdefj`
Plain   `hanghitler`

Figure 5.4: What the spy claimed he said

Now we rarely get anything for nothing in cryptology, and the price of the perfect secrecy of the one-time pad is that it fails completely to protect message integrity. Suppose for example that you wanted to get this spy into trouble, you could change the ciphertext to `DCYTI BWPJA` (Figure 5.5):

Cipher   `DCYTIBWPJA`
Key   `wclnbtdefj`
Plain   `hanghitler`

Figure 5.5: Manipulating the message to entrap the spy

During the Second World War, Claude Shannon proved that a cipher has perfect secrecy if and only if there are as many possible keys as possible plaintexts, and every key is equally likely; so the one-time pad is the only kind of system which offers perfect secrecy [1157, 1158].

The one-time pad is still used for some diplomatic and intelligence traffic, but it consumes as much key material as there is traffic and this is too expensive for most applications. It's more common for stream ciphers to use a suitable pseudorandom number generator to expand a short key into a long keystream. The data is then encrypted by exclusive-or'ing the keystream, one bit at a time, with the data. It's not enough for the keystream to appear "random" in the sense of passing the standard statistical randomness tests: it must also have the property that an opponent who gets his hands on even quite a lot of keystream bits should not be able to predict any more of them. I'll formalise this more tightly in the next section.

Stream ciphers are commonly used nowadays in hardware applications where the number of gates has to be minimised to save power. We'll look at some actual designs in later chapters, including the A5 algorithm used to encipher GSM mobile phone traffic (in the chapter on 'Telecom System Security'), and the shift register systems used in pay-per-view TV and DVD CSS (in the chapter on 'Copyright and Privacy Protection'). However, block ciphers are more suited for many applications where encryption is done in software, so let's look at them next.

5.2.3   An Early Block Cipher — Playfair

One of the best-known early block ciphers is the Playfair system. It was invented in 1854 by Sir Charles Wheatstone, a telegraph pioneer who also invented the concertina and the Wheatstone bridge. The reason it's not called the Wheatstone cipher is that he demonstrated it to Baron Playfair, a politician; Playfair in turn demonstrated it to Prince Albert and to Viscount Palmerston (later Prime Minister), on a napkin after dinner.

This cipher uses a 5 by 5 grid, in which we place the alphabet, permuted by the key word, and omitting the letter 'J' (see Figure 5.6):

P	A	L	M	E
R	S	T	O	N
B	C	D	F	G
H	I	K	Q	U
V	W	X	Y	Z

Figure 5.6: The Playfair enciphering tableau

The plaintext is first conditioned by replacing 'J' with 'I' wherever it occurs, then dividing it into letter pairs, preventing double letters occurring in a pair by separating them with an 'x', and finally adding a 'z' if necessary to complete the last letter pair. The example Playfair wrote on his napkin was 'Lord Granville's letter' which becomes 'lo rd gr an vi lx le sl et te rz'.

It is then enciphered two letters at a time using the following rules:

- if the two letters are in the same row or column, they are replaced by the succeeding letters. For example, 'am' enciphers to 'LE'

- otherwise the two letters stand at two of the corners of a rectangle in the table, and we replace them with the letters at the other two corners of this rectangle. For example, 'lo' enciphers to 'MT'.

We can now encipher our specimen text as follows:

Plain	lo rd gr an vi lx le sl et te rz
Cipher	MT TB BN ES WH TL MP TA LN NL NV

Figure 5.7: Example of Playfair enciphering

Variants of this cipher were used by the British army as a field cipher in World War 1, and by the Americans and Germans in World War 2. It's a substantial improvement on Vigenère as the statistics which an analyst can collect are of *digraphs* (letter pairs) rather than single letters, so the distribution is much flatter and more ciphertext is needed for an attack.

Again, it's not enough for the output of a block cipher to just look intuitively 'random'. Playfair ciphertexts look random; but they have the property that if you change a single letter of a plaintext pair, then often only a single letter of the ciphertext will change. Thus using the key in Figure 5.7, rd enciphers to TB while rf enciphers to OB and rg enciphers to NB. One consequence is that given enough ciphertext, or a few probable words, the table (or an equivalent one) can be reconstructed [512]. So we will want the effects of small changes in a block cipher's input to diffuse completely through its output: changing one input bit should, on average, cause half of the output bits to change. We'll tighten these ideas up in the next section.

The security of a block cipher can be greatly improved by choosing a longer block length than two characters. For example, the *Data Encryption Standard* (DES), which is widely used in banking, has a block length of 64 bits, which equates to eight ascii characters and the Advanced Encryption Standard (AES), which is replacing it in many applications, has a block length of twice this. I discuss the internal details of DES and AES below; for the time being, I'll just remark that an eight byte or sixteen byte block size is not enough of itself. For example, if a bank account number always appears at the same place in a transaction, then it's likely to produce the same ciphertext every time a transaction involving it is encrypted with the same key.

This might allow an opponent to cut and paste parts of two different cipher-texts in order to produce a seemingly genuine but unauthorized transaction. Suppose a bad man worked for a bank's phone company, and could intercept their traffic. If he monitored an enciphered transaction that he knew said ''Pay IBM $10,000,000'' he might wire $1,000 to his brother causing the bank computer to insert another transaction saying ''Pay John Smith $1,000'', intercept this instruction, and make up a false instruction from the two ciphertexts that decrypted as ''Pay John Smith $10,000,000''. So unless the cipher block is as large as the message, the ciphertext will contain more than one block and we will usually need some way of binding the blocks together.

5.2.4   One-Way Functions

The third classical type of cipher is the *one-way function*. This evolved to protect the integrity and authenticity of messages, which as we've seen is not protected at all by many simple ciphers where it is often easy to manipulate the ciphertext in such a way as to cause a predictable change in the plaintext.

After the invention of the telegraph in the mid-19th century, banks rapidly became its main users and developed systems for transferring money electronically. Of course, it isn't the money itself which is 'wired' but a payment instruction, such as:

> *'To Lombard Bank, London. Please pay from our account with you no. 1234567890 the sum of £1000 to John Smith of 456 Chesterton Road, who has an account with HSBC Bank Cambridge no. 301234 4567890123, and notify him that this was for "wedding present from Doreen Smith". From First Cowboy Bank of Santa Barbara, CA, USA. Charges to be paid by us.'*

Since telegraph messages were relayed from one office to another by human operators, it was possible for an operator to manipulate a payment message.

In the nineteenth century, banks, telegraph companies and shipping companies developed *code books* that could not only protect transactions but also shorten them — which was very important given the costs of international telegrams at the time. A code book was essentially a block cipher which mapped words or phrases to fixed-length groups of letters or numbers. So 'Please pay from our account with you no.' might become 'AFVCT'. A competing technology from the 1920s was *rotor machines*, mechanical cipher devices which produce a very long sequence of pseudorandom numbers and combine them with plaintext to get ciphertext; these were independently invented by a number of people, many of whom dreamed of making a fortune selling them to the banking industry. Banks weren't in general interested, but rotor machines became the main high-level ciphers used by the combatants in World War 2.

The banks realised that neither mechanical stream ciphers nor code books protect message authenticity. If, for example, the codeword for '1000' is 'mauve' and for '1,000,000' is 'magenta', then the crooked telegraph clerk who can compare the coded traffic with known transactions should be able to figure this out and substitute one for the other.

The critical innovation, for the banks' purposes, was to use a code book but to make the coding one-way by adding the code groups together into a number called a *test key*. (Modern cryptographers would describe it as a *hash value* or *message authentication code*, terms I'll define more carefully later.)

Here is a simple example. Suppose the bank has a code book with a table of numbers corresponding to payment amounts as in Figure 5.8:

	0	1	2	3	4	5	6	7	8	9
x 1000	14	22	40	87	69	93	71	35	06	58
x 10,000	73	38	15	46	91	82	00	29	64	57
x 100,000	95	70	09	54	82	63	21	47	36	18
x 1,000,000	53	77	66	29	40	12	31	05	87	94

Figure 5.8: A simple test key system

Now in order to authenticate a transaction for £376,514 we add together 53 (no millions), 54 (300,000), 29 (70,000) and 71 (6,000). (It's common to ignore the less significant digits of the amount.) This gives us a test key of 207.

Most real systems were more complex than this; they usually had tables for currency codes, dates and even recipient account numbers. In the better systems, the code groups were four digits long rather than two, and in order to make it harder for an attacker to reconstruct the tables, the test keys were compressed: a key of '7549' might become '23' by adding the first and second digits, and the third and fourth digits, and ignoring the carry.

This made such test key systems into *one-way functions* in that although given knowledge of the key it was possible to compute a test from a message, it was not possible to reverse the process and recover a message from a test — the test just did not contain enough information. Indeed, one-way functions had been around since at least the seventeenth century. The scientist Robert Hooke published in 1678 the sorted anagram 'ceiiinosssttuu' and revealed two years later that it was derived from 'Ut tensio sic uis' — 'the force varies as the tension', or what we now call Hooke's law for a spring. (The goal was to establish priority for the idea while giving him time to continue developing it.)

Test keys are not strong by the standards of modern cryptography. Given somewhere between a few dozen and a few hundred tested messages, depending on the design details, a patient analyst could reconstruct enough of the tables to forge a transaction. With a few carefully chosen messages inserted into the banking system by an accomplice, it's even easier still. But the banks got away with it: test keys worked fine from the late nineteenth century through the 1980's. In several years working as a bank security consultant, and listening to elderly bank auditors' tales over lunch, I only ever heard of two cases of fraud that exploited it: one external attempt involving cryptanalysis, which failed because the attacker didn't understand bank procedures, and one successful but small fraud involving a crooked staff member. I'll discuss the systems which replaced test keys, and the whole issue of how to tie cryptographic authentication mechanisms to procedural protection such as dual control, in the chapter on 'Banking and Bookkeeping'. For the meantime, test keys are the classic example of a one-way function used for authentication.

Later examples included functions for applications discussed in the previous chapters, such as storing passwords in a one-way encrypted password file, and computing a response from a challenge in an authentication protocol.

5.2.5   Asymmetric Primitives

Finally, some modern cryptosystems are asymmetric, in that different keys are used for encryption and decryption. So, for example, many people publish on their web page a *public key* with which people can encrypt messages to send to them; the owner of the web page can then decrypt them using the corresponding *private key*.

There are some pre-computer examples of this too; perhaps the best is the postal service. You can send me a private message just as simply by addressing it to me and dropping it into a post box. Once that's done, I'm the only person who'll be able to read it. There are of course many things that can go wrong. You might get the wrong address for me (whether by error or as a result of deception); the police might get a warrant to open my mail; the letter might be stolen by a dishonest postman; a fraudster might redirect my mail without my knowledge; or a thief might steal the letter from my mailbox. There are similar things that can go wrong with public key cryptography. False public keys can be inserted into the system, computers can be hacked, people can be coerced and so on. We'll look at these problems in more detail in later chapters.

Another asymmetric application of cryptography is the *digital signature*. The idea here is that I can sign a message using a private *signature key* and then anybody can check this using my public *signature verification key*. Again, there are pre-computer analogues in the form of manuscript signatures and seals; and again, there is a remarkably similar litany of things that can go wrong, both with the old way of doing things and with the new.

5.3   The Random Oracle Model

Before delving into the detailed design of modern ciphers, I want to take a few pages to refine the definitions of the various types of cipher. (Readers who are phobic about theoretical computer science should skip this section at a first pass; I've included it because a basic grasp of the terminology of random oracles is needed to decipher many recent research papers on cryptography.)

The random oracle model seeks to formalize the idea that a cipher is 'good' if, when viewed in a suitable way, it is indistinguishable from a random function of a certain type. I will call a cryptographic primitive *pseudorandom* if it passes all the statistical and other tests which a random function of the appropriate type would pass, in whatever model of computation we are using. Of course, the cryptographic primitive will actually be an algorithm, implemented as an array of gates in hardware or a program in software; but the outputs should 'look random' in that they're indistinguishable from a suitable random oracle given the type and the number of tests that our computation model permits.

In this way, we can hope to separate the problem of designing ciphers from the problem of using them correctly. Mathematicians who design ciphers can provide evidence that their cipher is pseudorandom. Quite separately, a computer scientist who has designed a cryptographic protocol can try to prove that it is secure on the assumption that the crypto primitives used to implement it are pseudorandom. The process isn't infallible, as we saw with proofs of protocol correctness. Theorems can have bugs, just like programs; the problem could be idealized wrongly; and the mathematicians might be using a different model of computation from the computer scientists. In fact, there is a live debate among crypto researchers about whether formal models and proofs are valuable [724]. But crypto theory can help us sharpen our understanding of how ciphers behave and how they can safely be used.

We can visualize a random oracle as an elf sitting in a black box with a source of physical randomness and some means of storage (see Figure 5.9) — represented in our picture by the dice and the scroll. The elf will accept inputs of a certain type, then look in the scroll to see whether this query has ever been answered before. If so, it will give the answer it finds there; if not, it will generate an answer at random by throwing the dice. We'll further assume that there is some kind of bandwidth limitation — that the elf will only answer so many queries every second. This ideal will turn out to be useful as a way of refining our notions of a stream cipher, a hash function, a block cipher, a public key encryption algorithm and a digital signature scheme.

Figure 5.9: The random oracle

Finally, we can get a useful simplification of our conceptual model by noting that encryption can be used to protect data across time as well as across distance. A good example is when we encrypt data before storing it with a third-party backup service, and may decrypt it later if we have to recover from a disk crash. In this case, we only need a single encryption/decryption device, rather than having one at each end of a communications link. For simplicity, let us assume it is this sort of application we are modelling here. The user takes a diskette to the cipher machine, types in a key, issues an instruction, and the data get transformed in the appropriate way. A year later, she comes back to get the data decrypted and verified.

We shall now look at this model in more detail for various different cryptographic primitives.

5.3.1   Random Functions — Hash Functions

The first type of random oracle is the random function. A random function accepts an input string of any length and outputs a random string of fixed length, say n bits long. So the elf just has a simple list of inputs and outputs, which grows steadily as it works. (We'll ignore any effects of the size of the scroll and assume that all queries are answered in constant time.)

Random functions are our model for *one-way functions*, also known as *cryptographic hash functions*, which have many practical uses. They were first used in computer systems for one-way encryption of passwords in the 1960s and, as I mentioned in the chapter on security protocols, are used today in a number of authentication systems. They are used to compute checksums on files in forensic applications: presented with a computer seized from a suspect, you can compute hash values of the files to identify which files are already known (such as system files) and which are novel (such as user data). Hash values are also used as a means of checking the integrity of files, as they will change if a file is corrupted. In messaging applications, hashes are often known as *message digests*; given a message M we can pass it through a pseudorandom function to get a digest, say $h(M)$, which can stand in for the message in various applications. One example is digital signature: signature algorithms tend to be slow if the message is long, so it's usually convenient to sign a message digest rather than the message itself.

Another application is timestamping. If we want evidence that we possessed a given electronic document by a certain date, we might submit it to an online time-stamping service. However, if the document is still secret — for example an invention which we plan to patent, and for which we merely want to establish a priority date — then we might not send the timestamping service the whole document, but just the message digest.

5.3.1.1 *Properties*

The first main property of a random function is one-wayness. Given knowledge of an input x we can easily compute the hash value $h(x)$, but it is very difficult given the hash value $h(x)$ to find a corresponding *preimage* x if one is not already known. (The elf will only pick outputs for given inputs, not the other way round.) As the output is random, the best an attacker who wants to invert a random function can do is to keep on feeding in more inputs until he gets lucky. A pseudorandom function will have the same properties, or they could be used to distinguish it from a random function, contrary to our definition. It follows that a pseudorandom function will also be a *one-way function*, provided there are enough possible outputs that the opponent can't find a desired target output by chance. This means choosing the output to be an n-bit number where the opponent can't do anything near 2^n computations.

A second property of pseudorandom functions is that the output will not give any information at all about even part of the input. Thus a one-way encryption of the value x can be accomplished by concatenating it with a secret key k and computing $h(x, k)$. If the hash function isn't random enough, though, using it for one-way encryption in this manner is asking for trouble. A topical example comes from the authentication in GSM mobile phones, where a 16 byte challenge from the base station is concatenated with a 16 byte secret key known to the phone into a 32 byte number, and passed through a hash function to give an 11 byte output [226]. The idea is that the phone company also knows k and can check this computation, while someone who eavesdrops on the radio link can only get a number of values of the random challenge x and corresponding output from $h(x, k)$. So the eavesdropper must not be able to get any information about k, or compute $h(y, k)$ for a new input y. But the one-way function used by many phone companies isn't one-way enough, with the result that an eavesdropper who can pretend to be a base station and send a phone about 150,000 suitable challenges and get the responses can compute the key. I'll discuss this failure in more detail in section 20.3.2.

A third property of pseudorandom functions with sufficiently long outputs is that it is hard to find *collisions*, that is, different messages $M_1 \neq M_2$ with $h(M_1) = h(M_2)$. Unless the opponent can find a shortcut attack (which would mean the function wasn't really pseudorandom) then the best way of finding a collision is to collect a large set of messages M_i and their corresponding hashes $h(M_i)$, sort the hashes, and look for a match. If the hash function output is an n-bit number, so that there are 2^n possible hash values, then the number of hashes the enemy will need to compute before he can expect to find a match will be about the square root of this, namely $2^{n/2}$ hashes. This fact is of huge importance in security engineering, so let's look at it more closely.

5.3.1.2   The Birthday Theorem

The birthday theorem gets its name from the following problem. A maths teacher asks a typical class of 30 pupils what they think is the probability that two of them have the same birthday. Most pupils will intuitively think it's unlikely, and the maths teacher then asks the pupils to state their birthdays one after another. As the result seems unlikely to most people, it's also known as the 'birthday paradox'. The odds of a match exceed 50% once 23 pupils have been called.

The birthday theorem was first invented in the 1930's to count fish, which led to its also being known as *capture-recapture statistics* [1123]. Suppose there are N fish in a lake and you catch m of them, ring them and throw them back, then when you first catch a fish you've ringed already, m should be 'about' the square root of N. The intuitive reason why this holds is that once you have $\sqrt{N}$ samples, each could potentially match any of the others, so the number of possible matches is about $\sqrt{N} \times \sqrt{N}$ or N, which is what you need[2].

This theorem has many applications for the security engineer. For example, if we have a biometric system which can authenticate a person's claim to identity with a probability of only one in a million that two randomly selected subjects will be falsely identified as the same person, this doesn't mean that we can use it as a reliable means of identification in a university with a user population of twenty thousand staff and students. This is because there will be almost two hundred million possible pairs. In fact, you expect to find the first *collision* — the first pair of people who can be mistaken for each other by the system — once you have somewhat over a thousand people enrolled.

There are some applications where collision-search attacks aren't a problem, such as in challenge-response protocols where an attacker would have to be able to find the answer to the challenge just issued, and where you can prevent challenges repeating. (For example, the challenge might be generated by encrypting a counter.) So in identify-friend-or-foe (IFF) systems, for example, common equipment has a response length of 48 to 80 bits.

However, there are other applications in which collisions are unacceptable. In a digital signature application, if it were possible to find collisions with $h(M_1) = h(M_2)$ but $M_1 \neq M_2$, then a Mafia owned bookstore's web site might get you to sign a message M_1 saying something like 'I hereby order a copy of Rubber Fetish volume 7 for \$32.95' and then present the signature together with an M_2 saying something like 'I hereby mortgage my house for \$75,000 and please make the funds payable to Mafia Holdings Inc., Bermuda'.

For this reason, hash functions used with digital signature schemes generally have n large enough to make them collision-free, that is, that $2^{n/2}$ computations

---

[2]More precisely, the probability that m fish chosen randomly from N fish are different is $\beta = N(N-1)\ldots(N-m+1)/N^m$ which is asymptotically solved by $N \simeq m^2/2log(1/\beta)$ [708].

are impractical for an opponent. The two most common are MD5, which has a 128-bit output and will thus require at most 2^{64} computations to break, and SHA1 with a 160-bit output and a work factor for the cryptanalyst of at most 2^{80}. However, collision search gives at best an upper bound on the strength of a hash function, and both these particular functions have turned out to be disappointing, with cryptanalytic attacks that I'll describe later in section 5.6.2. Collisions are easy to find for MD4 and MD5, while for SHA-1 it takes about 2^{60} computations to find a collision — something that a botnet of half a million machines should be able to do in a few days.

In any case, a pseudorandom function is also often referred to as being *collision free* or *collision intractable*. This doesn't mean that collisions don't exist — they must, as the set of possible inputs is larger than the set of possible outputs — just that you will never find any of them. The (usually unstated) assumptions are that the output must be long enough, and that the cryptographic design of the hash function must be sound.

5.3.2   Random Generators — Stream Ciphers

The second basic cryptographic primitive is the *random generator*, also known as a *keystream generator* or *stream cipher*. This is also a random function, but unlike in the hash function case it has a short input and a long output. (If we had a good pseudorandom function whose input and output were a billion bits long, and we never wanted to handle any objects larger than this, we could turn it into a hash function by throwing away all but a few hundred bits of the output, and turn it into a stream cipher by padding all but a few hundred bits of the input with a constant.) At the conceptual level, however, it's common to think of a stream cipher as a random oracle whose input length is fixed while the output is a very long stream of bits, known as the keystream.

It can be used quite simply to protect the confidentiality of backup data: we go to the keystream generator, enter a key, get a long file of random bits, and exclusive-or it with our plaintext data to get ciphertext, which we then send to our backup contractor. We can think of the elf generating a random tape of the required length each time he is presented with a new key as input, giving it to us and keeping a copy of it on his scroll for reference in case he's given the same input again. If we need to recover the data, we go back to the generator, enter the same key, get the same long file of random data, and exclusive-or it with our ciphertext to get our plaintext data back again. Other people with access to the keystream generator won't be able to generate the same keystream unless they know the key.

I mentioned the one-time pad, and Shannon's result that a cipher has perfect secrecy if and only if there are as many possible keys as possible plaintexts, and every key is equally likely. Such security is called *unconditional* (or *statistical*) security as it doesn't depend either on the computing power available to the opponent, or on there being no future advances in mathematics which provide a shortcut attack on the cipher.

One-time pad systems are a very close fit for our theoretical model, except in that they are typically used to secure communications across space rather than time: there are two communicating parties who have shared a copy of the randomly-generated keystream in advance. Vernam's original telegraph cipher machine used punched paper tape; a modern diplomatic system might use DVDs, shipped in a tamper-evident container in a diplomatic bag. Various techniques have been used to do the random generation. Marks describes how SOE agents' silken keys were manufactured in Oxford by little old ladies shuffling counters.

One important problem with keystream generators is that we want to prevent the same keystream being used more than once, whether to encrypt more than one backup tape or to encrypt more than one message sent on a communications channel. During World War 2, the amount of Russian diplomatic traffic exceeded the quantity of one-time tape they had distributed in advance to their embassies, so it was reused. This was a serious blunder. If $M_1 + K = C_1$ and $M_2 + K = C_2$, then the opponent can combine the two ciphertexts to get a combination of two messages: $C_1 - C_2 = M_1 - M_2$, and if the messages M_i have enough redundancy then they can be recovered. Text messages do in fact contain enough redundancy for much to be recovered, and in the case of the Russian traffic this led to the Venona project in which the US and UK decrypted large amounts of wartime Russian traffic afterwards and broke up a number of Russian spy rings. The saying is: 'Avoid the two-time tape!'

Exactly the same consideration holds for any stream cipher, and the normal engineering practice when using an algorithmic keystream generator is to have a *seed* as well as a key. Each time the cipher is used, we want it to generate a different keystream, so the key supplied to the cipher should be different. So if the long-term key which two users share is K, they may concatenate it with a seed which is a message number N (or some other nonce) and then pass it through a hash function to form a working key $h(K, N)$. This working key is the one actually fed to the cipher machine. The nonce may be a separate pre-agreed key, or it may be generated at random and sent along with the ciphertext. However, the details of key management can be quite tricky, and the designer has to watch out for attacks in which a principal is tricked into synchronising on the wrong key. In effect, a protocol has to be designed to ensure that both parties can synchronise on the right working key even in the presence of an adversary.

5.3.3   Random Permutations — Block Ciphers

The third type of primitive, and the most important in modern commercial cryptography, is the block cipher, which we model as a *random permutation*.

Here, the function is invertible, and the input plaintext and the output ciphertext are of a fixed size. With Playfair, both input and output are two characters; with DES, they're both bit strings of 64 bits. Whatever the number of symbols and the underlying alphabet, encryption acts on a block of fixed length. (So if you want to encrypt a shorter input, you have to pad it as with the final 'z' in our Playfair example.)

We can visualize block encryption as follows. As before, we have an elf in a box with dice and a scroll. This has on the left a column of plaintexts and on the right a column of ciphertexts. When we ask the elf to encrypt a message, it checks in the left hand column to see if it has a record of it. If not, it uses the dice to generate a random ciphertext of the appropriate size (and which doesn't appear yet in the right hand column of the scroll), and then writes down the plaintext/ciphertext pair in the scroll. If it does find a record, it gives us the corresponding ciphertext from the right hand column.

When asked to decrypt, the elf does the same, but with the function of the columns reversed: he takes the input ciphertext, checks it (this time on the right hand scroll) and if he finds it he gives the message with which it was previously associated. If not, he generates a message at random (which does not already appear in the left column) and notes it down.

A *block cipher* is a keyed family of pseudorandom permutations. For each key, we have a single permutation which is independent of all the others. We can think of each key as corresponding to a different scroll. The intuitive idea is that a cipher machine should output the ciphertext given the plaintext and the key, and output the plaintext given the ciphertext and the key, but given only the plaintext and the ciphertext it should output nothing.

We will write a block cipher using the notation established for encryption in the chapter on protocols:

$$C = \{M\}_K$$

The random permutation model also allows us to define different types of attack on block ciphers. In a *known plaintext attack*, the opponent is just given a number of randomly chosen inputs and outputs from the oracle corresponding to a target key. In a *chosen plaintext attack*, the opponent is allowed to put a certain number of plaintext queries and get the corresponding ciphertexts. In a *chosen ciphertext attack* he gets to make a number of ciphertext queries. In a *chosen plaintext/ciphertext attack* he is allowed to make queries of either type. Finally, in a *related key attack* he can make queries that will be answered using keys related to the target key K, such as $K + 1$ and $K + 2$.

In each case, the objective of the attacker may be either to deduce the answer to a query he hasn't already made (a *forgery attack*), or to recover the key (unsurprisingly known as a *key recovery attack*).

This precision about attacks is important. When someone discovers a vulnerability in a cryptographic primitive, it may or may not be relevant to your application. Often it won't be, but will have been hyped by the media — so you will need to be able to explain clearly to your boss and your customers why it's not a problem. So you have to look carefully to find out exactly what kind of attack has been found, and what the parameters are. For example, the first major attack announced on the Data Encryption Standard algorithm requires 2^{47} chosen plaintexts to recover the key, while the next major attack improved this to 2^{43} known plaintexts. While these attacks were of great scientific importance, their practical engineering effect was zero, as no practical systems make that much known (let alone chosen) text available to an attacker. Such attacks are often referred to as *certificational*. They can have a commercial effect, though: the attacks on DES undermined confidence in it and started moving people to other ciphers. In some other cases, an attack that started off as certificational has been developed by later ideas into an exploit.

Which sort of attacks you should be worried about depends on your application. With a broadcast entertainment system, for example, a bad man can buy a decoder, observe a lot of material and compare it with the enciphered broadcast signal; so a known-plaintext attack is the main threat. But there are surprisingly many applications where chosen-plaintext attacks are possible. Obvious ones include IFF, where the enemy can send challenges of his choice to any aircraft in range of one of his radars; and ATMs, where if you allow customers to change their PINs, an attacker can change his PIN through a range of possible values and observe the enciphered equivalents by wiretapping the line from the ATM to the bank. A more traditional example is diplomatic messaging systems, where it's been known for a host government to give an ambassador a message to transmit to his capital that's been specially designed to help the local cryptanalysts fill out the missing gaps in the ambassador's code book [676]. In general, if the opponent can insert any kind of message into your system, it's chosen-plaintext attacks you should worry about.

The other attacks are more specialized. *Chosen plaintext/ciphertext* attacks may be a worry where the threat is a *lunchtime attacker*: someone who gets temporary access to some cryptographic equipment while its authorized user is out. *Related-key attacks* are a concern where the block cipher is used as a building block in the construction of a hash function (which we'll discuss below).

5.3.4   Public Key Encryption and Trapdoor One-Way Permutations

A *public-key encryption* algorithm is a special kind of block cipher in which the elf will perform the encryption corresponding to a particular key for anyone who requests it, but will do the decryption operation only for the key's owner. To continue with our analogy, the user might give a secret name to the scroll that only she and the elf know, use the elf's public one-way function to compute a hash of this secret name, publish the hash, and instruct the elf to perform the encryption operation for anybody who quotes this hash.

This means that a principal, say Alice, can publish a key and if Bob wants to, he can now encrypt a message and send it to her, even if they have never met. All that is necessary is that they have access to the oracle. There are some more details that have to be taken care of, such as how Alice's name can be bound to the key, and indeed whether it means anything to Bob; I'll deal with these later.

A common way of implementing public key encryption is the *trapdoor one-way permutation*. This is a computation which anyone can perform, but which can be reversed only by someone who knows a *trapdoor* such as a secret key. This model is like the 'one-way function' model of a cryptographic hash function. Let us state it formally nonetheless: a public key encryption primitive consists of a function which given a random input R will return two keys, KR (the public encryption key) and KR^{-1} (the private decryption key) with the properties that

1. Given KR, it is infeasible to compute KR^{-1} (so it's not possible to compute R either);

2. There is an encryption function $\{\dots\}$ which, applied to a message M using the encryption key KR, will produce a ciphertext $C = \{M\}_{KR}$; and

3. There is a decryption function which, applied to a ciphertext C using the decryption key KR^{-1}, will produce the original message $M = \{C\}_{KR^{-1}}$.

For practical purposes, we will want the oracle to be replicated at both ends of the communications channel, and this means either using tamper-resistant hardware or (more commonly) implementing its functions using mathematics rather than metal. There are several more demanding models than this, for example to analyze security in the case where the opponent can get ciphertexts of his choice decrypted, with the exception of the target ciphertext. But this will do for now.

5.3.5 Digital Signatures

The final cryptographic primitive which we'll define here is the *digital signature*. The basic idea is that a signature on a message can be created by only one person, but checked by anyone. It can thus perform the sort of function in the electronic world that ordinary signatures do in the world of paper. Applications include signing software updates, so that a PC can tell that an update to Windows was really produced by Microsoft rather than by a villain.

Signature schemes can be *deterministic* or *randomized*: in the first, computing a signature on a message will always give the same result and in the second, it will give a different result. (The latter is more like handwritten signatures;

no two are ever alike but the bank has a means of deciding whether a given specimen is genuine or forged). Also, signature schemes may or may not support *message recovery*. If they do, then given the signature, anyone can recover the message on which it was generated; if they don't, then the verifier needs to know or guess the message before he can perform the verification. (There are further, more specialised, signature schemes such as blind signatures and threshold signatures but I'll postpone discussion of them for now.)

Formally, a signature scheme, like public key encryption scheme, has a keypair generation function which given a random input R will return two keys, σR (the private signing key) and VR (the public signature verification key) with the properties that

1. Given the public signature verification key VR, it is infeasible to compute the private signing key σR;

2. There is a digital signature function which given a message M and a private signature key σR, will produce a signature $Sig_{\sigma R}(M)$; and

3. There is a signature verification function which, given the signature $Sig_{\sigma R}(M)$ and the public signature verification key VR will output TRUE if the signature was computed correctly with σR and otherwise output FALSE.

We can model a simple digital signature algorithm as a random function that reduces any input message to a one-way hash value of fixed length, followed by a special kind of block cipher in which the elf will perform the operation in one direction, known as *signature*, for only one principal, while in the other direction, it will perform verification for anybody.

Signature verification can take two forms. In the basic scheme, the elf (or the signature verification algorithm) only outputs TRUE or FALSE depending on whether the signature is good. But in a scheme with *message recovery*, anyone can input a signature and get back the message corresponding to it. In our elf model, this means that if the elf has seen the signature before, it will give the message corresponding to it on the scroll, otherwise it will give a random value (and record the input and the random output as a signature and message pair). This is sometimes desirable: when sending short messages over a low bandwidth channel, it can save space if only the signature has to be sent rather than the signature plus the message. An example is in the machine-printed postage stamps, or *indicia*, being brought into use in many countries: the stamp may consist of a 2-d barcode with a digital signature made by the postal meter and which contains information such as the value, the date and the sender's and recipient's post codes. We give some more detail about this at the end of section 14.3.2.

However, in the general case we do not need message recovery, as the message to be signed may be of arbitrary length and so we will first pass it through a hash function and then sign the hash value. As hash functions are one-way, the resulting compound signature scheme does not have message recovery — although if the underlying signature scheme does, then the hash of the message can be recovered from the signature.

5.4 Symmetric Crypto Primitives

Now that we have defined the basic crypto primitives, we will look under the hood to see how they can be implemented in practice. While most explanations are geared towards graduate mathematics students, the presentation I'll give here is based on one I've developed over several years with computer science students. So I hope it will let the non-mathematician grasp the essentials. In fact, even at the research level, most of cryptography is as much computer science as mathematics. Modern attacks on ciphers are put together from guessing bits, searching for patterns, sorting possible results, and so on rather than from anything particularly highbrow.

We'll focus in this section on block ciphers, and then see in the next section how you can make hash functions and stream ciphers from them, and vice versa. (In later chapters, we'll also look at some special-purpose ciphers.)

5.4.1 SP-Networks

Claude Shannon suggested in the 1940's that strong ciphers could be built by combining substitution with transposition repeatedly. For example, one might add some key material to a block of input text, and then shuffle subsets of the input, and continue in this way a number of times. He described the properties of a cipher as being *confusion* and *diffusion* — adding unknown key values will confuse an attacker about the value of a plaintext symbol, while diffusion means spreading the plaintext information through the ciphertext. Block ciphers need diffusion as well as confusion.

The earliest block ciphers were simple networks which combined substitution and permutation circuits, and so were called SP-networks [681]. Figure 5.10 shows an SP-network with sixteen inputs, which we can imagine as the bits of a sixteen-bit number, and two layers of four-bit invertible substitution boxes (or *S-boxes*), each of which can be visualized as a lookup table containing some permutation of the numbers 0 to 15.

The point of this arrangement is that if we were to implement an arbitrary 16 bit to 16 bit function in digital logic, we would need 2^{20} bits of memory — one lookup table of 2^{16} bits for each single output bit. That's hundreds of thousands of gates, while a four bit to four bit function takes only 4×2^4 or 64 bits of memory. One might hope that with suitable choices of parameters, the function produced by iterating this simple structure would be indistinguishable from a random 16 bit to 16 bit function to an opponent who didn't know the value of the key. The key might consist of some choice of a number of four-bit S-boxes, or it might be added at each round to provide confusion and the resulting text fed through the S-boxes to provide diffusion.

Three things need to be done to make such a design secure:

1. the cipher needs to be "wide" enough
2. it needs to have enough rounds, and
3. the S-boxes need to be suitably chosen.

5.4.1.1 Block Size

First, a block cipher which operated on sixteen bit blocks would have rather limited applicability, as an opponent could just build a dictionary of plaintext and ciphertext blocks as he observed them. The birthday theorem tells us that even if the input plaintexts were random, he'd expect to find a match as soon as he had seen a little over 2^8 blocks. So a practical block cipher will usually deal with plaintexts and ciphertexts of 64 bits, 128 bits or even more. So if we are using four-bit to four-bit S-boxes, we may have 16 of them (for a 64 bit block size) or 32 of them (for a 128 bit block size).

5.4.1.2 Number of Rounds

Second, we have to have enough rounds. The two rounds in Figure 5.10 are completely inadequate, as an opponent can deduce the values of the S-boxes by tweaking input bits in suitable patterns. For example, he could hold the rightmost 12 bits constant and try tweaking the leftmost four bits, to deduce the values in the top left S-box. (The attack is slightly more complicated than this, as sometimes a tweak in an input bit to an S-box won't produce a change in any output bit, so we have to change one of its other inputs and tweak again. But implementing it is still a simple student exercise.)

The number of rounds we require depends on the speed with which data diffuse through the cipher. In the above simple example, diffusion is very slow because each output bit from one round of S-boxes is connected to only one input bit in the next round. Instead of having a simple permutation of the wires, it is more efficient to have a linear transformation in which each input bit in one round is the exclusive-or of several output bits in the previous round. Of course, if the block cipher is to be used for decryption as well as encryption, this linear transformation will have to be invertible. We'll see some concrete examples below in the sections on Serpent and AES.

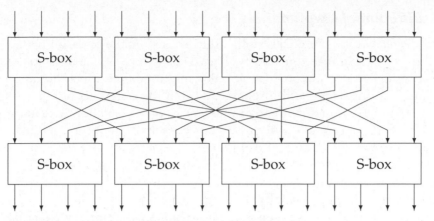

Figure 5.10: A simple 16-bit SP-network block cipher

5.4.1.3 Choice of S-Boxes

The design of the S-boxes also affects the number of rounds required for security, and studying bad choices gives us our entry into the deeper theory of block ciphers. Suppose that the S-box were the permutation that maps the inputs $(0,1,2,\ldots,15)$ to the outputs $(5,7,0,2,4,3,1,6,8,10,15,12,9,11,14,13)$. Then the most significant bit of the input would come through unchanged as the most significant bit of the output. If the same S-box were used in both rounds in the above cipher, then the most significant bit of the input would pass through to become the most significant bit of the output. This would usually be a bad thing; we certainly couldn't claim that our cipher was pseudorandom.

5.4.1.4 Linear Cryptanalysis

Attacks on real block ciphers are usually harder to spot than in this artificial example, but they use the same ideas. It might turn out that the S-box had the property that bit one of the input was equal to bit two plus bit four of the output; more commonly, there will be linear approximations to an S-box which hold with a certain probability. *Linear cryptanalysis* [602, 843] proceeds by collecting a number of relations such as 'bit 2 plus bit 5 of the input to the first S-box is equal to bit 1 plus bit 8 of the output, with probability 13/16' and then searching for ways to glue them together into an algebraic relation between input bits, output bits and key bits that holds with a probability different from one half. If we can find a linear relationship that holds over the whole cipher with probability $p = 0.5 + 1/M$, then according to probability theory we can expect to start recovering keybits once we have about M^2 known texts. If the value of M^2 for the best linear relationship is greater than the total possible number of known texts (namely 2^n where the inputs and outputs are n bits wide), then we consider the cipher to be secure against linear cryptanalysis.

5.4.1.5 Differential Cryptanalysis

Differential Cryptanalysis [170, 602] is similar but is based on the probability that a given change in the input to an S-box will give rise to a certain change in the output. A typical observation on an 8-bit S-box might be that 'if we flip input bits 2, 3, and 7 at once, then with probability 11/16 the only output bits that will flip are 0 and 1'. In fact, with any nonlinear Boolean function, tweaking some combination of input bits will cause some combination of output bits to change with a probability different from one half. The analysis procedure is to look at all possible input difference patterns and look for those values δ_i, δ_o such that an input change of δ_i will produce an output change of δ_o with particularly high (or low) probability.

As in linear cryptanalysis, we then search for ways to join things up so that an input difference which we can feed into the cipher will produce a known output difference with a useful probability over a number of rounds. Given enough chosen inputs, we will see the expected output and be able to make deductions about the key. As in linear cryptanalysis, it's common to consider the cipher to be secure if the number of texts required for an attack is greater than the total possible number of different texts for that key. (We have to be careful though of pathological cases, such as if you had a cipher with a 32-bit block and a 128-bit key with a differential attack whose success probability given a single pair was 2^{-40}. Given a lot of text under a number of keys, we'd eventually solve for the current key.)

There are a quite few variants on these two themes. For example, instead of looking for high probability differences, we can look for differences that can't happen (or that happen only rarely). This has the charming name of *impossible cryptanalysis*, but it is quite definitely possible against many systems [169]. There are also various specialised attacks on particular ciphers.

Block cipher design involves a number of trade-offs. For example, we can reduce the per-round information leakage, and thus the required number of rounds, by designing the rounds carefully. However, a complex design might be slow in software, or need a lot of gates in hardware, so using simple rounds but more of them might have been better. Simple rounds may also be easier to analyze. A prudent designer will also use more rounds than are strictly necessary to block the attacks known today, in order to give some margin of safety against improved mathematics in the future. We may be able to show that a cipher resists all the attacks we know of, but this says little about whether it will resist the attacks we don't know of yet. (A general security proof for a block cipher would appear to imply a proof about an attacker's computational powers, which might entail a result such as $P \neq NP$ that would revolutionize computer science.)

The point that the security engineer should remember is that block cipher cryptanalysis is a complex subject about which we have a fairly extensive theory. Use an off-the-shelf design that has been thoroughly scrutinized by experts, rather than rolling your own; and if there's a compelling reason to use a proprietary cipher (for example, if you want to use a patented design to stop other people copying a product) then get it reviewed by experts. Cipher design is not an amateur sport any more.

5.4.1.6 Serpent

As a concrete example, the encryption algorithm 'Serpent' is an SP-network with input and output block sizes of 128 bits. These are processed through 32 rounds, in each of which we first add 128 bits of key material, then pass the text through 32 S-boxes of 4 bits width, and then perform a linear transformation that takes each output of one round to the inputs of a number of S-boxes in the next round. Rather than each input bit in one round coming from a single output bit in the last, it is the exclusive-or of between two and seven of them. This means that a change in an input bit propagates rapidly through the cipher — a so-called *avalanche* effect which makes both linear and differential attacks harder. After the final round, a further 128 bits of key material are added to give the ciphertext. The 33 times 128 bits of key material required are computed from a user supplied key of up to 256 bits.

This is a real cipher using the structure of Figure 5.10, but modified to be 'wide' enough and to have enough rounds. The S-boxes are chosen to make linear and differential analysis hard; they have fairly tight bounds on the maximum linear correlation between input and output bits, and on the maximum effect of toggling patterns of input bits. Each of the 32 S-boxes in a given round is the same; this means that bit-slicing techniques can be used to give a very efficient software implementation on 32-bit processors.

Its simple structure makes Serpent easy to analyze, and it can be shown that it withstands all the currently known attacks. A full specification of Serpent is given in [60] and can be downloaded, together with implementations in a number of languages, from [61].

5.4.2 The Advanced Encryption Standard (AES)

This discussion has prepared us to describe the Advanced Encryption Standard, an algorithm also known as Rijndael after its inventors Vincent Rijmen and Joan Daemen [342]. This algorithm acts on 128-bit blocks and can use a key of 128, 192 or 256 bits in length. It is an SP-network; in order to specify it, we need to fix the S-boxes, the linear transformation between the rounds, and the way in which the key is added into the computation.

AES uses a single S-box which acts on a byte input to give a byte output. For implementation purposes it can be regarded simply as a lookup table of 256 bytes; it is actually defined by the equation $S(x) = M(1/x) + b$ over the field $GF(2^8)$ where M is a suitably chosen matrix and b is a constant. This construction gives tight differential and linear bounds.

The linear transformation is based on arranging the 16 bytes of the value being enciphered in a square and then doing bytewise shuffling and mixing operations. (AES is descended from an earlier cipher called Square, which introduced this technique.)

The first step in the linear transformation is the *shuffle* in which the top row of four bytes is left unchanged, while the second row is shifted one place to the left, the third row by two places and the fourth row by three places. The second step is a column mixing step in which the four bytes in a column are mixed using a matrix multiplication. This is illustrated in Figure 5.11 which shows, as an example, how a change in the value of the third byte in the first column is propagated. The effect of this combination is that a change in the input to the cipher can potentially affect all of the output after just two rounds.

The key material is added byte by byte after the linear transformation. This means that 16 bytes of key material are needed per round; they are derived from the user supplied key material by means of a recurrence relation.

The algorithm uses 10 rounds with 128-bit keys, 12 rounds with 192-bit keys and 14 rounds with 256-bit keys. These give a reasonable margin of safety; the best shortcut attacks known at the time of writing (2007) can tackle 7 rounds for 128-bit keys, and 9 rounds for 192- and 256-bit keys [16]. The general belief in the block cipher community is that even if advances in the state of the art do permit attacks on AES with the full number of rounds, they will be purely certificational attacks in that they will require infeasibly large numbers of texts. (AES's margin of safety against attacks that require only feasible numbers of texts is about 100%.) Although there is no proof of security — whether in the sense of pseudorandomness, or in the weaker sense of an absence of shortcut attacks of known types — there is now a high level of confidence that AES is secure for all practical purposes. The NSA has since 2005 approved AES with 128-bit keys for protecting information up to SECRET and with 256-bit keys for TOP SECRET.

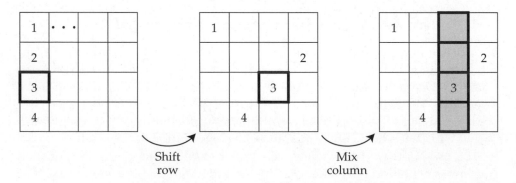

Figure 5.11: The AES linear transformation, illustrated by its effect on byte 3 of the input

Even although I was an author of Serpent which was an unsuccessful finalist in the AES competition (the winner Rijndael got 86 votes, Serpent 59 votes, Twofish 31 votes, RC6 23 votes and MARS 13 votes at the last AES conference), and although Serpent was designed to have an even larger security margin than Rijndael, I recommend to my clients that they use AES where a general-purpose block cipher is required. I recommend the 256-bit-key version, and not because I think that the 10 rounds of the 128-bit-key variant will be broken anytime soon. Longer keys are better because some key bits often leak in real products, as I'll discuss at some length in the chapters on tamper-resistance and emission security. It does not make sense to implement Serpent as well, 'just in case AES is broken': the risk of a fatal error in the algorithm negotiation protocol is orders of magnitude greater than the risk that anyone will come up with a production attack on AES. (We'll see a number of examples later where using multiple algorithms, or using an algorithm like DES multiple times, caused something to break horribly.)

The definitive specification of AES is Federal Information Processing Standard 197, and its inventors have written a book describing its design in detail [342]. Other information, from book errata to links to implementations, can be found on the AES Lounge web page [16].

One word of warning: the most likely practical attacks on a real implementation of AES include timing analysis and power analysis, both of which I discuss in Part II in the chapter on emission security. In timing analysis, the risk is that an opponent observes cache misses and uses them to work out the key. The latest versions of this attack can extract a key given the precise measurements of the time taken to do a few hundred cryptographic operations. In power analysis, an opponent uses measurements of the current drawn by the device doing the crypto — think of a bank smartcard that a customer places in a terminal in a Mafia-owned shop. The two overlap; cache misses cause a device like a smartcard to draw more power — and can also be observed on remote machines by an opponent who can measure the time taken to encrypt. The implementation details matter.

5.4.3 Feistel Ciphers

Many block ciphers use a more complex structure, which was invented by Feistel and his team while they were developing the Mark XII IFF in the late 1950's and early 1960's. Feistel then moved to IBM and founded a research group which produced the Data Encryption Standard, (DES) algorithm, which is still the mainstay of financial transaction processing security.

A Feistel cipher has the ladder structure shown in Figure 5.12. The input is split up into two blocks, the left half and the right half. A *round function f_1* of the left half is computed and combined with the right half using exclusive-or (binary addition without carry), though in some Feistel ciphers addition with carry is also used. (We use the notation ⊕ for exclusive-or.) Then, a function f_2 of the right half is computed and combined with the left half, and so on. Finally (if the number of rounds is even) the left half and right half are swapped.

LEFT HALF   RIGHT HALF

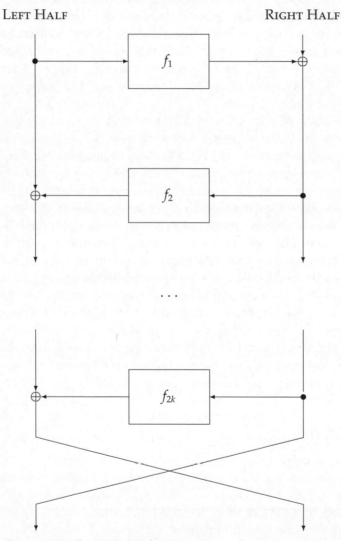

Figure 5.12: The Feistel cipher structure

A notation which you may see for the Feistel cipher is $\psi(f, g, h, \ldots)$ where $f, g, h, \ldots$ are the successive round functions. Under this notation, the above cipher is $\psi(f_1, f_2, \ldots f_{2k-1}, f_{2k})$. The basic result that enables us to decrypt a Feistel cipher — and indeed the whole point of his design — is that:

$$\psi^{-1}(f_1, f_2, \ldots, f_{2k-1}, f_{2k}) = \psi(f_{2k}, f_{2k-1}, \ldots, f_2, f_1)$$

In other words, to decrypt, we just use the round functions in the reverse order. Thus the round functions f_i do not have to be invertible, and the Feistel structure lets us turn any one-way function into a block cipher. This means that we are less constrained in trying to choose a round function with good diffusion and confusion properties, and which also satisfies any other design constraints such as code size, table size, software speed, hardware gate count, and so on.

5.4.3.1   *The Luby-Rackoff Result*

The key theoretical result on Feistel ciphers was proved by Mike Luby and Charlie Rackoff in 1988. They showed that if f_i were random functions, then $\psi(f_1, f_2, f_3)$ was indistinguishable from a random permutation under chosen plaintext attack, and this result was soon extended to show that $\psi(f_1, f_2, f_3, f_4)$ was indistinguishable under chosen plaintext/ciphertext attack — in other words, it was a pseudorandom permutation.

There are a number of technicalities we omit. In engineering terms, the effect is that given a really good round function, four rounds of Feistel are enough. So if we have a hash function in which we have confidence, it is straightforward to construct a block cipher from it: use four rounds of keyed hash in a Feistel network.

5.4.3.2   *DES*

The DES algorithm is widely used in banking, government and embedded applications. For example, it is the standard in automatic teller machine networks. It is a Feistel cipher, with a 64-bit block and 56-bit key. Its round function operates on 32-bit half blocks and consists of three operations:

- first, the block is expanded from 32 bits to 48;
- next, 48 bits of round key are mixed in using exclusive-or;
- the result is passed through a row of eight S-boxes, each of which takes a six-bit input and provides a four-bit output;
- finally, the bits of the output are permuted according to a fixed pattern.

The effect of the expansion, key mixing and S-boxes is shown in Figure 5.13:

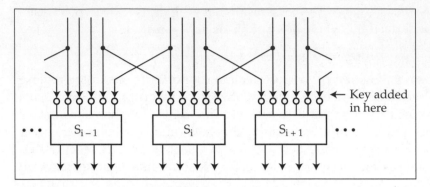

Figure 5.13: The DES round function

The round keys are derived from the user-supplied key by using each user key bit in twelve different rounds according to a slightly irregular pattern. A full specification of DES is given in [936]; code can be found in [1125] or downloaded from many places on the web.

DES was introduced in 1974 and caused some controversy. The most telling criticism was that the key is too short. Someone who wants to find a 56 bit key using brute force, that is by trying all possible keys, will have a *total exhaust time* of 2^{56} encryptions and an *average solution time* of half that, namely 2^{55} encryptions. Whit Diffie and Martin Hellman argued in 1977 that a DES keysearch machine could be built with a million chips, each testing a million keys a second; as a million is about 2^{20}, this would take on average 2^{15} seconds, or a bit over 9 hours, to find the key. They argued that such a machine could be built for $20 million dollars in 1977 [386]. IBM, whose scientists invented DES, retorted that they would charge the US government $200 million to build such a machine. (Perhaps both were right.)

During the 1980's, there were persistent rumors of DES keysearch machines being built by various intelligence agencies, but the first successful public keysearch attack took place in 1997. In a distributed effort organised over the net, 14,000 PCs took more than four months to find the key to a challenge. In 1998, the Electronic Frontier Foundation (EFF) built a DES keysearch machine called Deep Crack for under $250,000 which broke a DES challenge in 3 days. It contained 1,536 chips run at 40MHz, each chip containing 24 search units which each took 16 cycles to do a test decrypt. The search rate was thus 2.5 million test decryptions per second per search unit, or 60 million keys per second per chip. The design of the cracker is public and can be found at [423]. By 2006, Sandeep Kumar and colleagues at the universities of Bochum and Kiel built a machine using 120 FPGAs and costing $10,000, which could break DES in 7 days on average [755]. A modern botnet with half a million machines would take a few hours. So the key length of DES is now definitely inadequate, and banks have for some years been upgrading their payment systems.

Another criticism of DES was that, since IBM kept its design principles secret at the request of the US government, perhaps there was a 'trapdoor' which would give them easy access. However, the design principles were published in 1992 after differential cryptanalysis was invented and published [326]. Their story was that IBM had discovered these techniques in 1972, and the US National Security Agency (NSA) even earlier. IBM kept the design details secret at the NSA's request. We'll discuss the political aspects of all this in 24.3.9.1.

We now have a fairly thorough analysis of DES. The best known *shortcut attack*, that is, a cryptanalytic attack involving less computation than keysearch, is a linear attack using 2^{42} known texts. DES would be secure with more than 20 rounds, but for practical purposes its security is limited by its keylength. I don't know of any real applications where an attacker might get hold of even 2^{40} known texts. So the known shortcut attacks are not an issue. However, its growing vulnerability to keysearch makes DES unusable in its original form. If Moore's law continues, than by 2020 it might be possible to find a DES key on a single PC in a few months, so even low-grade systems such as taxi meters will be vulnerable to brute force-cryptanalysis. As with AES, there are also attacks based on timing analysis and power analysis, but because of DES's structure, the latter are more serious.

The usual way of dealing with the DES keysearch problem is to use the algorithm multiple times with different keys. Banking networks have largely moved to *triple-DES*, a standard since 1999 [936]. Triple-DES does an encryption, then a decryption, and then a further encryption, all done with independent keys. Formally:

$$3DES(k_0, k_1, k_2; M) = DES(k_2; DES^{-1}(k_1; DES(k_0; M)))$$

The reason for this design is that by setting the three keys equal, one gets the same result as a single DES encryption, thus giving a backwards compatibility mode with legacy equipment. (Some banking systems use *two-key triple-DES* which sets $k_2 = k_0$; this gives an intermediate step between single and triple DES). New systems now use AES as of choice, but banking systems are deeply committed to using block ciphers with an eight-byte block size, because of the message formats used in the many protocols by which ATMs, point-of-sale terminals and bank networks talk to each other, and because of the use of block ciphers to generate and protect customer PINs (which I discuss in Chapter 10). Triple DES is a perfectly serviceable block cipher for such purposes for the foreseeable future.

Another way of preventing keysearch (and making power analysis harder) is *whitening*. In addition to the 56-bit key, say k_0, we choose two 64-bit whitening keys k_1 and k_2, xor'ing the first with the plaintext before encryption and the second with the output of the encryption to get the ciphertext afterwards. This composite cipher is known as DESX, and is used in the Win2K encrypting file system. Formally,

$$DESX(k_0, k_1, k_2; M) = DES(k_0; M \oplus k_1) \oplus k_2$$

It can be shown that, on reasonable assumptions, DESX has the properties you'd expect; it inherits the differential strength of DES but its resistance to keysearch is increased by the amount of the whitening [717]. Whitened block ciphers are used in some applications.

5.5   Modes of Operation

In practice, how you use an encryption algorithm is often more important than which one you pick. An important factor is the *'mode of operation'*, which specifies how a block cipher with a fixed block size (8 bytes for DES, 16 for AES) can be extended to process messages of arbitrary length.

There are several standard modes of operation for using a block cipher on multiple blocks [944]. Understanding them, and choosing the right one for the job, is an important factor in using a block cipher securely.

5.5.1   Electronic Code Book

In electronic code book (ECB) we just encrypt each succeeding block of plaintext with our block cipher to get ciphertext, as with the Playfair cipher I gave above as an example. This is adequate for many simple operations such as challenge-response and some key management tasks; it's also used to encrypt PINs in cash machine systems. However, if we use it to encrypt redundant data the patterns will show through, letting an opponent deduce information about the plaintext. For example, if a word processing format has lots of strings of nulls, then the ciphertext will have a lot of blocks whose value is the encryption of null characters under the current key.

In one popular corporate email system from the late 1980's, the encryption used was DES ECB with the key derived from an eight character password. If you looked at a ciphertext generated by this system, you saw that a certain block was far more common than the others — the one corresponding to a plaintext of nulls. This gave one of the simplest attacks on a fielded DES encryption system: just encrypt a null block with each password in a dictionary and sort the answers. You can now break at sight any ciphertext whose password was one of those in your dictionary.

In addition, using ECB mode to encrypt messages of more than one block length which have an authenticity requirement — such as bank payment messages — would be foolish, as messages could be subject to a *cut and splice* attack along the block boundaries. For example, if a bank message said 'Please pay account number X the sum Y, and their reference number is Z' then an attacker might initiate a payment designed so that some of the digits of X could be replaced with some of the digits of Z.

5.5.2 Cipher Block Chaining

Most commercial applications which encrypt more than one block use cipher block chaining, or CBC, mode. In it, we exclusive-or the previous block of ciphertext to the current block of plaintext before encryption (see Figure 5.14).

This mode is effective at disguising any patterns in the plaintext: the encryption of each block depends on all the previous blocks. The input IV is an *initialization vector*, a random number that performs the same function as a seed in a stream cipher and ensures that stereotyped plaintext message headers won't leak information by encrypting to identical ciphertext blocks.

However, an opponent who knows some of the plaintext may be able to cut and splice a message (or parts of several messages encrypted under the same key), so the integrity protection is not total. In fact, if an error is inserted into the ciphertext, it will affect only two blocks of plaintext on decryption, so if there isn't any integrity protection on the plaintext, an enemy can insert two-block garbles of random data at locations of his choice.

5.5.3 Output Feedback

Output feedback (OFB) mode consists of repeatedly encrypting an initial value and using this as a keystream in a stream cipher of the kind discussed above.

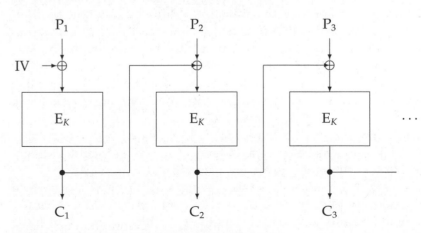

Figure 5.14: Cipher Block Chaining (CBC) mode

Writing IV for the initialization vector or seed, the i-th block of keystream will be given by

$$K_i = \{\ldots \{\{IV\}_K\}_K \ldots \textit{total of i times}\}$$

This is one standard way of turning a block cipher into a stream cipher. The key K is expanded into a long stream of blocks K_i of *keystream*. Keystream is typically combined with the blocks of a message M_i using exclusive-or to give ciphertext $C_i = M_i \oplus K_i$; this arrangement is sometimes called an *additive stream cipher* as exclusive-or is just addition module 2 (and some old hand systems used addition modulo 26).

All additive stream ciphers have an important vulnerability: they fail to protect message integrity. I mentioned this in the context of the one-time pad in section 5.2.2 above, but it's important to realise that this doesn't just affect 'perfectly secure' systems but 'real life' stream ciphers too. Suppose, for example, that a stream cipher were used to encipher fund transfer messages. These messages are very highly structured; you might know, for example, that bytes 37–42 contained the amount of money being transferred. You could then carry out the following attack. You cause the data traffic from a local bank to go via your computer, for example by a wiretap. You go into the bank and send a modest sum (say $500) to an accomplice. The ciphertext $C_i = M_i \oplus K_i$, duly arrives in your machine. You know M_i for bytes 37–42, so you know K_i and can easily construct a modified message which instructs the receiving bank to pay not $500 but $500,000! This is an example of an *attack in depth*; it is the price not just of the perfect secrecy we get from the one-time pad, but of much more humble stream ciphers too.

5.5.4   Counter Encryption

One possible drawback of feedback modes of block cipher encryption is latency: feedback modes are hard to parallelize. With CBC, a whole block of the cipher must be computed between each block input and each block output; with OFB, we can precompute keystream but storing it requires memory. This can be inconvenient in very high speed applications, such as protecting traffic on gigabit backbone links. There, as silicon is cheap, we would rather pipeline our encryption chip, so that it encrypts a new block (or generates a new block of keystream) in as few clock ticks as possible.

The simplest solution is often is to generate a keystream by just encrypting a counter: $K_i = \{IV + i\}_K$. As before, this is then added to the plaintext to get ciphertext (so it's also vulnerable to attacks in depth).

Another problem this mode solves when using a 64-bit block cipher such as triple-DES on a very high speed link is cycle length. An n-bit block cipher in OFB mode will typically have a cycle length of $2^{n/2}$ blocks, after which the birthday theorem will see to it that the keystream starts to repeat. (Once we've a little over 2^{32} 64-bit values, the odds are that two of them will match.) In

CBC mode, too, the birthday theorem ensures that after about $2^{n/2}$ blocks, we will start to see repeats. Counter mode encryption, however, has a guaranteed cycle length of 2^n rather than $2^{n/2}$.

5.5.5   Cipher Feedback

Cipher feedback, or CFB, mode is another kind of stream cipher. It was designed to be self-synchronizing, in that even if we get a burst error and drop a few bits, the system will recover synchronization after one block length. This is achieved by using our block cipher to encrypt the last n bits of ciphertext, and then adding one of the output bits to the next plaintext bit.

With decryption, the reverse operation is performed, with ciphertext feeding in from the right in Figure 5.15. Thus even if we get a burst error and drop a few bits, as soon as we've received enough ciphertext bits to fill up the shift register, the system will resynchronize.

Cipher feedback is not much used any more. It was designed for use in military HF radio links which are vulnerable to fading, in the days when digital electronics were relatively expensive. Now that silicon is cheap, people use dedicated link layer protocols for synchronization and error correction rather than trying to combine them with the cryptography.

5.5.6   Message Authentication Code

The next official mode of operation of a block cipher is not used to encipher data, but to protect its integrity and authenticity. This is the *message authentication code*, or MAC. To compute a MAC on a message using a block cipher, we encrypt it using CBC mode and throw away all the output ciphertext blocks except the last one; this last block is the MAC. (The intermediate results are kept secret in order to prevent splicing attacks.)

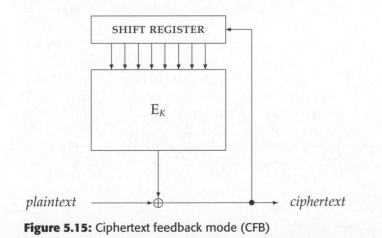

Figure 5.15: Ciphertext feedback mode (CFB)

This construction makes the MAC depend on all the plaintext blocks as well as on the key. It is secure provided the message length is fixed; Mihir Bellare, Joe Kilian and Philip Rogaway proved that any attack on a MAC under these circumstances would give an attack on the underlying block cipher [147].

If the message length is variable, you have to ensure that a MAC computed on one string can't be used as the IV for computing a MAC on a different string, so that an opponent can't cheat by getting a MAC on the composition of the two strings. In order to fix this problem, NIST has standardised CMAC, in which a variant of the key is xor-ed in before the last encryption [945]. (CMAC is based on a proposal by Tetsu Iwata and Kaoru Kurosawa [649].)

There are other possible constructions of MACs: a common one is to use a hash function with a key, which we'll look at in more detail in section 5.6.2.

5.5.7   Composite Modes of Operation

In applications needing both integrity and privacy, the standard procedure used to be to first calculate a MAC on the message using one key, and then CBC encrypt it using a different key. (If the same key is used for both encryption and authentication, then the security of the latter is no longer guaranteed; cut-and-splice attacks are still possible.)

Recently two further modes of operation have been tackled by NIST that combine encryption and authentication. The first is CCM, which combines counter-mode encryption with CBC-MAC authentication. The danger to watch for here is that the counter values used in encryption must not coincide with the initialisation vector used in the MAC; the standard requires that the formatting function prevent this [946].

The second combined mode is Galois Counter Mode (GCM), which has just been approved at the time of writing (2007). This interesting and innovative mode is designed to be parallelisable so that it can give high throughput on fast data links with low cost and low latency. As the implementation is moderately complex, and the algorithm was approved as this book was in its final edit, I don't include the details here, but refer you instead to the official specification [947]. The telegraphic summary is that the encryption is performed in a variant of counter mode; the resulting ciphertexts are also multiplied together with key material and message length information in a Galois field of 2^{128} elements to get an authenticator tag. The output is thus a ciphertext of the same length as the plaintext, plus a tag of typically 128 bits. The tag computation uses a *universal hash function* which comes from the theory of unconditionally-secure authentication codes; I'll describe this in Chapter 13, 'Nuclear Command and Control'.

Both CCM, and old-fashioned CBC plus CBC MAC, need a completely new MAC to be computed on the whole message if any bit of it is changed. However, the GCM mode of operation has an interesting incremental property: a new authenticator and ciphertext can be calculated with an amount of effort proportional to the number of bits that were changed. GCM is an invention of David McGrew and John Viega of Cisco; their goal was to create an authenticated encryption mode that is highly parallelisable for use in high-performance network hardware and that only uses one block cipher operation per block of plaintext, unlike CCM or the old-fashioned CBC plus CBC-MAC [862]. Now that GCM has been adopted as a standard, we might expect it to become the most common mode of operation for the encryption of bulk content.

5.6 Hash Functions

In section 5.4.3.1 I showed how the Luby-Rackoff theorem enables us to construct a block cipher from a hash function. It's also possible to construct a hash function from a block cipher. (In fact, we can also construct hash functions and block ciphers from stream ciphers — so, subject to some caveats I'll discuss in the next section, given any one of these three primitives we can construct the other two.)

The trick is to feed the message blocks one at a time to the key input of our block cipher, and use it to update a hash value (which starts off at say $H_0 = 0$). In order to make this operation non-invertible, we add feedforward: the $(i-1)$st hash value is exclusive or'ed with the output of round i. This is our final mode of operation of a block cipher (Figure 5.16).

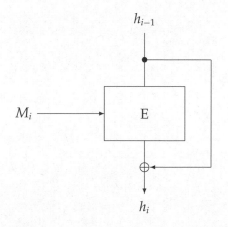

Figure 5.16: Feedforward mode (hash function)

5.6.1   Extra Requirements on the Underlying Cipher

The birthday effect makes another appearance here, in that if a hash function h is built using an n bit block cipher, it is possible to find two messages $M_1 \neq M_2$ with $h(M_1) = h(M_2)$ with about $2^{n/2}$ effort (hash slightly more than that many messages M_i and look for a match). So a 64 bit block cipher is not adequate, as the cost of forging a message would be of the order of 2^{32} messages, which is quite practical. A 128-bit cipher such as AES may be just about adequate, and in fact the AACS content protection mechanism used in the next generation of DVDs uses 'AES-H', the hash function derived from AES in this way.

The birthday limit is not the only way in which the hash function mode of operation is more demanding on the underlying block cipher than a mode such as CBC designed for confidentiality. A good illustration comes from a cipher called Treyfer which was designed to encrypt data using as little memory as possible in the 8051 microcontrollers commonly found in consumer electronics and domestic appliances [1371]. (It takes only 30 bytes of ROM.)

Treyfer 'scavenges' its S-box by using 256 bytes from the ROM, which may be code, or even — to make commercial cloning riskier — contain a copyright message. At each round, it acts on eight bytes of text with eight bytes of key by adding a byte of text to a byte of key, passing it through the S-box, adding it to the next byte and then rotating the result by one bit (see Figure 5.17). This rotation deals with some of the problems that might arise if the S-box has uneven randomness across its bitplanes (for example, if it contains ascii text

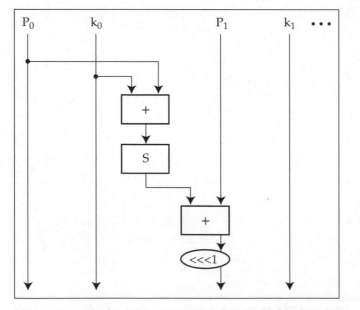

Figure 5.17: The basic component of the Treyfer block cipher

such as a copyright message). Finally, the algorithm makes up for its simple round structure and probably less than ideal S-box by having a large number of rounds (32).

Treyfer can in theory be used for confidentiality (although its effective keylength is only 44 bits). However, the algorithm does have a weakness that prevents its use in hash functions. It suffers from a *fixed-point attack*. Given any input, there is a fair chance we can find a key which will leave the input unchanged. We just have to look to see, for each byte of input, whether the S-box assumes the output which, when added to the byte on the right, has the effect of rotating it one bit to the right. If such outputs exist for each of the input bytes, then it's easy to choose key values which will leave the data unchanged after one round, and thus after 32. The probability that we can do this depends on the S-box[3]. This means that we can easily find collisions if Treyfer is used as a hash function. In effect, hash functions have to be based on block ciphers which withstand *chosen-key attacks*.

5.6.2   Common Hash Functions and Applications

Algorithms similar to Treyfer have been used in hash functions in key management protocols in some pay-TV systems, but typically they have a modification to prevent fixed-point attacks, such as a procedure to add in the round number at each round, or to mix up the bits of the key in some way (a *key scheduling* algorithm).

The most commonly used hash functions are all cryptographically suspect. They are based on variants of a block cipher with a 512 bit key and a block size of either 128 or 160 bits:

- MD4 has three rounds and a 128 bit hash value, and a collision was found for it in 1998 [394];

- MD5 has four rounds and a 128 bit hash value, and a collision was found for it in 2004 [1315, 1317];

- the US Secure Hash Standard has five rounds and a 160 bit hash value, and it was shown in 2005 that a collision can be found with a computational effort of 2^{69} steps rather than the 2^{80} that one would hope given its block size [1316].

The block ciphers underlying these hash functions are similar: their round function is a complicated mixture of the register operations available on 32 bit processors [1125].

---

[3]Curiously, an S-box which is a permutation is always vulnerable, while a randomly selected one isn't quite so bad. In many cipher designs, S-boxes which are permutations are essential or at least desirable. Treyfer is an exception.

MD5 was broken by Xiaoyun Wang and her colleagues in 2004 [1315, 1317]; collisions can now be found easily, even between strings containing meaningful text and adhering to message formats such as those used for digital certificates. Wang seriously dented SHA the following year, providing an algorithm that will find collisions in only 2^{69} steps [1316]; and at the Crypto 2007 conference, the view was that finding a collision should cost about 2^{60}. Volunteers were being recruited for the task. So it appears that soon a collision will be found and SHA-1 will be declared 'broken'.

At the time of writing, the US National Institute of Standards and Technology (NIST) recommends that people use extended block-size versions of SHA, such as SHA-256 or SHA-512. The draft FIPS 180-3 allows, though discourages, the original SHA; it specifies SHA-256 and SHA-512, and also supports 224-bit and 384-bit hashes derived from SHA-256 and SHA-512 respectively by changing the initial values and truncating the output. The NSA specifies the use of SHA-256 or SHA-382 along with AES in its Suite B of cryptographic algorithms for defense use. NIST is also organising a competition to find a replacement hash function family [949].

Whether a collision-search algorithm that requires months of work on hundreds of machines (or a few days on a large botnet) will put any given application at risk can be a complex question. If bank systems would actually take a message composed by a customer saying 'Pay X the sum Y', hash it and sign it, then a weak hash function could indeed be exploited: a bad man could find two messages 'Pay X the sum Y' and 'Pay X the sum Z' that hashed to the same value, get one signed, and swap it for the other. But bank systems don't work like that. They typically use MACs rather than digital signatures on actual transactions, relying on signatures only in public-key certificates that bootstrap key-management protocols; and as the public-key certificates are generated by trusted CAs using fairly constrained algorithms, there isn't an opportunity to insert one text of a colliding pair. Instead you'd have to find a collision with an externally-given target value, which is a much harder cryptanalytic task.

Hash functions have many uses. One of them is to compute MACs. A naive method would be to simply hash the message with a key: $MAC_k(M) = h(k, M)$. However the accepted way of doing this, called HMAC, uses an extra step in which the result of this computation is hashed again. The two hashing operations are done using variants of the key, derived by exclusive-or'ing them with two different constants. Thus $HMAC_k(M) = h(k \oplus A, h(k \oplus B, M))$. A is constructed by repeating the byte `0x36` as often as necessary, and B similarly from the byte `0x5C`. Given a hash function that may be on the weak side, this is believed to make exploitable collisions harder to find [741]. HMAC is now FIPS 198, being replaced by FIPS 198-1.

Another use of hash functions is to make commitments that are to be revealed later. For example, I might wish to timestamp a digital document in order to establish intellectual priority, but not reveal the contents yet. In that case, I can submit a hash of the document to a commercial timestamping service [572]. Later, when I reveal the document, the fact that its hash was timestamped at a given time establishes that I had written it by then. Again, an algorithm that generates colliding pairs doesn't break this, as you have to have the pair to hand when you do the timestamp. The moral, I suppose, is that engineers should be clear about whether a given application needs a hash function that's strongly collision-resistant.

But even though there may be few applications where the ability to find collisions could enable a bad guy to steal real money today, the existence of a potential vulnerability can still undermine a system's value. In 2005, a motorist accused of speeding in Sydney, Australia, was acquitted after the New South Wales Roads and Traffic Authority failed to find an expert to testify that MD5 was secure. The judge was ''not satisfied beyond reasonable doubt that the photograph [had] not been altered since it was taken'' and acquitted the motorist; this ruling was upheld on appeal the following year [964]. So even if a vulnerability doesn't present an engineering threat, it can still present a very real *certificational* threat.

Finally, before we go on to discuss asymmetric cryptography, there are two particular uses of hash functions which need mention: key updating and autokeying.

Key updating means that two or more principals who share a key pass it through a one-way hash function at agreed times: $K_i = h(K_{i-1})$. The point is that if an attacker compromises one of their systems and steals the key, he only gets the current key and is unable to decrypt back traffic. The chain of compromise is broken by the hash function's one-wayness. This property is also known as *backward security*.

Autokeying means that two or more principals who share a key hash it at agreed times with the messages they have exchanged since the last key change: $K_{+1}i = h(K_i, M_{i1}, M_{i2}, \ldots)$. The point is that if an attacker compromises one of their systems and steals the key, then as soon as they exchange a message which he doesn't observe or guess, security will be recovered in that he can no longer decrypt their traffic. Again, the chain of compromise is broken. This property is known as *forward security*. It is used, for example, in EFT payment terminals in Australia [143, 145]. The use of asymmetric crypto allows a slightly stronger form of forward security, namely that as soon as a compromised terminal exchanges a message with an uncompromised one which the opponent doesn't control, then security can be recovered even if the message is in plain sight. I'll describe how this trick works next.

5.7   Asymmetric Crypto Primitives

The commonly used building blocks in *asymmetric cryptography*, that is public key encryption and digital signature, are based on number theory. I'll give only a brief overview here, and look in more detail at some of the mechanisms used in Part II where I discuss applications. (If you find the description assumes too much mathematics, I'd suggest you skip the following two sections and read up the material from a cryptography textbook.)

The technique is to make the security of the cipher depend on the difficulty of solving a certain mathematical problem. The two problems which are used in almost all fielded systems are factorization (used in most commercial systems) and discrete logarithm (used in many government systems).

5.7.1   Cryptography Based on Factoring

The *prime numbers* are the positive whole numbers with no proper divisors; that is, the only numbers that divide a prime number are 1 and the number itself. By definition, 1 is not prime; so the primes are {2, 3, 5, 7, 11, ...}. The *fundamental theorem of arithmetic* states that each natural number greater than 1 factors into prime numbers in a way that is unique up to the order of the factors. It is easy to find prime numbers and multiply them together to give a composite number, but much harder to resolve a composite number into its factors. The largest composite product of two large random primes to have been factorized to date was RSA-200, a 663-bit number (200 decimal digits), factored in 2005. This factorization was done on a number of PCs and took the equivalent of 75 years' work on a single 2.2GHz machine. It is possible for factoring to be done surreptitiously, perhaps using a botnet; in 2001, when the state of the art was factoring 512-bit numbers, such a challenge was set in Simon Singh's 'Code Book' and solved by five Swedish students using several hundred computers to which they had access [24]. By 2007, 512-bit factorization had entered into mainstream commerce. From 2003, Intuit had protected its Quicken files with strong encryption, but left a back door based on a 512-bit RSA key so that they could offer a key recovery service. Elcomsoft appears to have factored this key and now offers a competing recovery product.

It is believed that factoring an RSA modulus of 1024 bits would require a special-purpose machine costing in the range of \$10–50m and that would take a year for each factorization [781]; but I've heard of no-one seriously planning to build such a machine. Many physicists hope that a quantum computer could be built that would make it easy to factor even large numbers. So, given that Moore's law is slowing down and that quantum computers haven't arrived yet, we can summarise the state of the art as follows. 1024-bit products of two random primes are hard to factor and cryptographic systems that rely on them are at no immediate risk from low-to-medium budget attackers; NIST expects them to be secure until 2010, while an extrapolation of the history of factoring records suggests the first factorization will be published in 2018. So risk-averse organisations that want keys to remain secure for many years are already using 2048-bit numbers.

The algorithm commonly used to do public-key encryption and digital signatures based on factoring is RSA, named after its inventors Ron Rivest, Adi Shamir and Len Adleman. It uses *Fermat's (little) theorem*, which states that for all primes p not dividing a, $a^{p-1} \equiv 1$ (mod p) (proof: take the set $\{1, 2, \ldots, p-1\}$ and multiply each of them modulo p by a, then cancel out $(p-1)!$ each side). Euler's function $\phi(n)$ is the number of positive integers less than n with which it has no divisor in common; so if n is the product of two primes pq then $\phi(n) = (p-1)(q-1)$ (the proof is similar).

The encryption key is a modulus N which is hard to factor (take $N = pq$ for two large randomly chosen primes p and q, say of 1024 bits each) plus a public exponent e that has no common factors with either $p-1$ or $q-1$. The private key is the factors p and q, which are kept secret. Where M is the message and C is the ciphertext, encryption is defined by

$$C \equiv M^e \quad (\text{mod } N)$$

Decryption is the reverse operation:

$$M \equiv \sqrt[e]{C} \quad (\text{mod } N)$$

Whoever knows the private key — the factors p and q of N — can easily calculate $\sqrt[e]{C}$ (mod N). As $\phi(N) = (p-1)(q-1)$ and e has no common factors with $\phi(N)$, the key's owner can find a number d such that $de \equiv 1$ (mod $\phi(N)$) — she finds the value of d separately modulo $p-1$ and $q-1$, and combines the answers. $\sqrt[e]{C}$ (mod N) is now computed as C^d (mod N), and decryption works because of Fermat's theorem:

$$C^d \equiv \{M^e\}^d \equiv M^{ed} \equiv M^{1+k\phi(N)} \equiv M.M^{k\phi(N)} \equiv M.1 \equiv M \quad (\text{mod } N)$$

Similarly, the owner of a private key can operate on a message with this to produce a signature

$$Sig_d(M) \equiv M^d \quad (\text{mod } N)$$

and this signature can be verified by raising it to the power e mod N (thus, using e and N as the public signature verification key) and checking that the message M is recovered:

$$M \equiv (Sig_d(M))^e \quad (\text{mod } N)$$

Neither RSA encryption nor signature is generally safe to use on its own. The reason is that, as encryption is an algebraic process, it preserves certain algebraic properties. For example, if we have a relation such as $M_1 M_2 = M_3$

that holds among plaintexts, then the same relationship will hold among ciphertexts $C_1 C_2 = C_3$ and signatures $Sig_1 Sig_2 = Sig_3$. This property is known as a *multiplicative homomorphism*; a homomorphism is a function that preserves some mathematical structure. The homomorphic nature of raw RSA means that it doesn't meet the random oracle model definitions of public key encryption or signature.

Another problem with public-key encryption is that if the plaintexts are drawn from a small set, such as 'attack' or 'retreat', and the encryption process is known to the opponent, then he can precompute possible ciphertexts and recognise them when they appear. Specific algorithms also have specific vulnerabilities: with RSA, it's dangerous to use a small exponent e to encrypt the same message to multiple recipients, as this can lead to an algebraic attack. To stop the guessing attack, the low-exponent attack and attacks based on homomorphism, it's sensible to add in some randomness, and some redundancy, into a plaintext block before encrypting it. However, there are good ways and bad ways of doing this.

In fact, crypto theoreticians have wrestled for decades to analyze all the things that can go wrong with asymmetric cryptography, and to find ways to tidy it up. Shafi Goldwasser and Silvio Micali came up with formal models of *probabilistic encryption* in which we add randomness to the encryption process, and *semantic security*, which means that an attacker cannot get any information at all about a plaintext M that was encrypted to a ciphertext C, even if he is allowed to request the decryption of any other ciphertext C' not equal to C [536]. There are a number of constructions that give provable semantic security, but they tend to be too ungainly for practical use.

The common real-world solution is *optimal asymmetric encryption padding* (OAEP), where we concatenate the message M with a random nonce N, and use a hash function h to combine them:

$$C_1 = M \oplus h(N)$$

$$C_2 = N \oplus h(C_1)$$

In effect, this is a two-round Feistel cipher that uses h as its round function. The result, the combination C_1, C_2, is then encrypted with RSA and sent. The recipient then computes N as $C_2 \oplus h(C_1)$ and recovers M as $C_1 \oplus h(N)$ [148]. (This construction came with a security proof, in which a mistake was subsequently found [1167, 234], sparking a vigorous debate on the value of mathematical proofs in security engineering [724].) RSA Data Security, which for years licensed the RSA algorithm, developed a number of public-key cryptography standards; PKCS #1 describes OAEP [672].

With signatures, things are slightly simpler. In general, it's often enough to just hash the message before applying the private key: $Sig_u - [h(M)]^d$ (mod N); PKCS #7 describes simple mechanisms for signing a message digest [680]. However, in some applications one might wish to include further data in the signature block, such as a timestamp, or some randomness in order to make side-channel attacks harder.

Many of the things that have gone wrong with real implementations have to do with error handling. Some errors can affect cryptographic mechanisms directly. The most spectacular example was when Daniel Bleichenbacher found a way to break the RSA implementation in SSL v 3.0 by sending suitably chosen ciphertexts to the victim and observing any resulting error messages. If he can learn from the target whether a given c, when decrypted as c^d (mod n), corresponds to a PKCS #1 message, then he can use this to decrypt or sign messages [189]. Other attacks have depended on measuring the precise time taken to decrypt; I'll discuss these in the chapter on emission security. Yet others have involved stack overflows, whether by sending the attack code in as keys, or as padding in poorly-implemented standards. Don't assume that the only attacks on your crypto code will be doing cryptanalysis.

5.7.2   Cryptography Based on Discrete Logarithms

While RSA is used in most web browsers in the SSL protocol, and in the SSH protocol commonly used for remote login to computer systems, there are other products, and many government systems, which base public key operations on discrete logarithms. These come in a number of flavors, some using 'normal' arithmetic while others use mathematical structures called *elliptic curves*. I'll explain the normal case. The elliptic variants use essentially the same idea but the implementation is more complex.

A *primitive root* modulo p is a number whose powers generate all the nonzero numbers mod p; for example, when working modulo 7 we find that $5^2 = 25$ which reduces to 4 (modulo 7), then we can compute 5^3 as $5^2 \times 5$ or 4×5 which is 20, which reduces to 6 (modulo 7), and so on, as in Figure 5.18:

$$
\begin{array}{llll}
5^1 & & = 5 & (\text{mod } 7) \\
5^2 = & 25 & \equiv 4 & (\text{mod } 7) \\
5^3 \equiv & 4 \times 5 & \equiv 6 & (\text{mod } 7) \\
5^4 \equiv & 6 \times 5 & \equiv 2 & (\text{mod } 7) \\
5^5 \equiv & 2 \times 5 & \equiv 3 & (\text{mod } 7) \\
5^6 \equiv & 3 \times 5 & \equiv 1 & (\text{mod } 7)
\end{array}
$$

Figure 5.18: Example of discrete logarithm calculations

Thus 5 is a primitive root modulo 7. This means that given any y, we can always solve the equation $y = 5^x$ (mod 7); x is then called the discrete logarithm of y modulo 7. Small examples like this can be solved by inspection, but for a large random prime number p, we do not know how to do this computation.

So the mapping $f : x \to g^x$ (mod p) is a one-way function, with the additional properties that $f(x + y) = f(x)f(y)$ and $f(nx) = f(x)^n$. In other words, it is a *one-way homomorphism*. As such, it can be used to construct digital signature and public key encryption algorithms.

5.7.2.1 Public Key Encryption – Diffie Hellman and ElGamal

To understand how discrete logarithms can be used to build a public-key encryption algorithm, bear in mind that we want a cryptosystem which does not need the users to start off with a shared secret key. Consider the following 'classical' scenario.

Imagine that Anthony wants to send a secret to Brutus, and the only communications channel available is an untrustworthy courier (say, a slave belonging to Caesar). Anthony can take the message, put it in a box, padlock it, and get the courier to take it to Brutus. Brutus could then put his own padlock on it too, and have it taken back to Anthony. He in turn would remove his padlock, and have it taken back to Brutus, who would now at last open it.

Exactly the same can be done using a suitable encryption function that commutes, that is, has the property that $\{\{M\}_{KA}\}_{KB} = \{\{M\}_{KB}\}_{KA}$. Alice can take the message M and encrypt it with her key KA to get $\{M\}_{KA}$ which she sends to Bob. Bob encrypts it again with his key KB getting $\{\{M\}_{KA}\}_{KB}$. But the commutativity property means that this is just $\{\{M\}_{KB}\}_{KA}$, so Alice can decrypt it using her key KA getting $\{M\}_{KB}$. She sends this to Bob and he can decrypt it with KB, finally recovering the message M. The keys KA and KB might be long-term keys if this mechanism were to be used as a conventional public-key encryption system, or they might be transient keys if the goal were to establish a key with forward secrecy.

How can a suitable commutative encryption be implemented? The one-time pad does commute, but is not suitable here. Suppose Alice chooses a random key xA and sends Bob $M \oplus xA$ while Bob returns $M \oplus xB$ and Alice finally sends him $M \oplus xA \oplus xB$, then an attacker can simply exclusive-or these three messages together; as $X \oplus X = 0$ for all X, the two values of xA and xB both cancel our leaving as an answer the plaintext M.

The discrete logarithm problem comes to the rescue. If the discrete log problem based on a primitive root modulo p is hard, then we can use discrete exponentiation as our encryption function. For example, Alice encodes her message as the primitive root g, chooses a random number xA, calculates g^{xA} modulo p and sends it, together with p, to Bob. Bob likewise chooses a random number xB and forms g^{xAxB} modulo p, which he passes back to Alice. Alice can now remove her exponentiation: using Fermat's theorem, she calculates $g^{xB} = (g^{xAxB})^{(p-xA)}$ (mod p) and sends it to Bob. Bob can now remove his exponentiation, too, and so finally gets hold of g. The security of this scheme depends on the difficulty of the discrete logarithm problem. In practice, it is tricky to encode a message to be a primitive root; but there is a much simpler means of achieving the same effect. The first public key encryption scheme to be published, by Whitfield Diffie and Martin Hellman in 1976, has a fixed primitive root g and uses g^{xAxB} modulo p as the key to a shared-key encryption system. The values xA and xB can be the private keys of the two parties.

Let's see how this might provide a public-key encryption system. The prime p and generator g are common to all users. Alice chooses a secret random number xA, calculates $yA = g^{xA}$ and publishes it opposite her name in the company phone book. Bob does the same, choosing a random number x_B and publishing $yB = g^{x_B}$. In order to communicate with Bob, Alice fetches yB from the phone book, forms yB^{xA} which is just g^{xAxB}, and uses this to encrypt the message to Bob. On receiving it, Bob looks up Alice's public key y_A and forms yA^{xB} which is also equal to g^{xAxB}, so he can decrypt her message.

Slightly more work is needed to provide a full solution. Some care is needed when choosing the parameters p and g; and there are several other details which depend on whether we want properties such as forward security. Variants on the Diffie-Hellman theme include the US government *key exchange algorithm* (KEA) [939], used in network security products such as the Fortezza card, and the so-called Royal Holloway protocol, which is used by the UK government [76].

Of course, one of the big problems with public-key systems is how to be sure that you've got a genuine copy of the phone book, and that the entry you're interested in isn't out of date. I'll discuss that in section 5.7.5.

5.7.2.2 Key Establishment

Mechanisms for providing forward security in such protocols are of independent interest, As before, let the prime p and generator g be common to all users. Alice chooses a random number R_A, calculates g^{R_A} and sends it to Bob; Bob does the same, choosing a random number R_B and sending g^{R_B} to Alice; they then both form $g^{R_A R_B}$, which they use as a session key (Figure 5.19).

$$A \to B: \qquad g^{R_A} \pmod{p}$$
$$B \to A: \qquad g^{R_B} \pmod{p}$$
$$A \to B: \qquad \{M\}_{g^{R_A R_B}}$$

Figure 5.19: The Diffie-Hellman key exchange protocol

Alice and Bob can now use the session key $g^{R_A R_B}$ to encrypt a conversation. They have managed to create a shared secret 'out of nothing'. Even if an opponent had obtained full access to both their machines before this protocol was started, and thus knew all their stored private keys, then provided some basic conditions were met (e.g., that their random number generators were not predictable) the opponent could still not eavesdrop on their traffic. This is the strong version of the forward security property to which I referred in section 5.6.2. The opponent can't work forward from knowledge of previous keys which he might have obtained. Provided that Alice and Bob both destroy the shared secret after use, they will also have backward security: an opponent who gets access to their equipment subsequently cannot work backward to break their old traffic.

But this protocol has a small problem: although Alice and Bob end up with a session key, neither of them has any idea who they share it with.

Suppose that in our padlock protocol Caesar had just ordered his slave to bring the box to him instead, and placed his own padlock on it next to Anthony's. The slave takes the box back to Anthony, who removes his padlock, and brings the box back to Caesar who opens it. Caesar can even run two instances of the protocol, pretending to Anthony that he's Brutus and to Brutus that he's Anthony. One fix is for Anthony and Brutus to apply their seals to their locks.

With the vanilla Diffie-Hellman protocol, the same idea leads to a middleperson attack. Charlie intercepts Alice's message to Bob and replies to it; at the same time, he initiates a key exchange with Bob, pretending to be Alice. He ends up with a key $g^{R_A R_C}$ which he shares with Alice, and another key $g^{R_B R_C}$ which he shares with Bob. So long as he continues to sit in the middle of the network and translate the messages between them, they may have a hard time detecting that their communications are compromised. The usual solution is to authenticate transient keys, and there are various possibilities.

In one secure telephone product, the two principals would read out an eight digit hash of the key they had generated and check that they had the same value before starting to discuss classified matters. A more general solution is for Alice and Bob to sign the messages that they send to each other.

A few other details have to be got right, such as a suitable choice of the values p and g. There's some non-trivial mathematics behind this, which is best left to specialists. There are also many things that can go wrong in implementations — examples being software that will generate or accept very weak keys and thus give only the appearance of protection; programs that leak the key by the amount of time they take to decrypt; and software vulnerabilities leading to stack overflows and other nasties. Nonspecialists implementing public-key cryptography should consult up-to-date standards documents and/or use properly accredited toolkits.

5.7.2.3 *Digital Signature*

Suppose that the base p and the generator g are public values chosen in some suitable way, and that each user who wishes to sign messages has a private signing key X and a public signature verification key $Y = g^X$. An ElGamal signature scheme works as follows. Choose a message key k at random, and form $r = g^k \pmod{p}$. Now form the signature s using a linear equation in k, r, the message M and the private key X. There are a number of equations that will do; the particular one that happens to be used in ElGamal signatures is

$$rX + sk = M$$

So s is computed as $s = (M - rX)/k$; this is done modulo $\phi(p)$. When both sides are passed through our one-way homomorphism $f(x) = g^x \bmod p$ we get:

$$g^{rX}g^{sk} \equiv g^M$$

or

$$Y^r r^s \equiv g^M$$

An ElGamal signature on the message M consists of the values r and s, and the recipient can verify it using the above equation.

A few more details need to be fixed up to get a functional digital signature scheme. As before, bad choices of p and g can weaken the algorithm. We will also want to hash the message M using a hash function so that we can sign messages of arbitrary length, and so that an opponent can't use the algorithm's algebraic structure to forge signatures on messages that were never signed. Having attended to these details and applied one or two optimisations, we get the *Digital Signature Algorithm* (DSA) which is a US standard and widely used in government applications.

DSA (also known as DSS, for Digital Signature Standard) assumes a prime p of typically 1024 bits, a prime q of 160 bits dividing $(p - 1)$, an element g of order q in the integers modulo p, a secret signing key x and a public verification key $y = g^x$. The signature on a message M, $Sig_x(M)$, is (r, s) where

$$r \equiv (g^k \pmod{p}) \pmod{q}$$

$$s \equiv (h(M) - xr)/k \pmod{q}$$

The hash function used here is SHA1.

DSA is the classic example of a randomized digital signature scheme without message recovery. The standard has changed somewhat with faster computers, as variants of the algorithm used to factor large numbers can also be used to compute discrete logarithms modulo bases of similar size[4]. Initially the prime p could be in the range 512–1024 bits, but this was changed to 1023–1024 bits in 2001 [941]; the proposed third-generation standard will allow primes p in the range 1024–3072 bits and q in the range 160–256 bits [942]. Further tweaks to the standard are also foreseeable after a new hash function standard is adopted.

---

[4]Discrete log efforts lag slightly behind, with a record set in 2006 of 440 bits.

5.7.3 Special Purpose Primitives

Researchers have discovered a large number of public-key and signature primitives with special properties. Two that have so far appeared in real products are threshold cryptography and blind signatures.

Threshold crypto is a mechanism whereby a signing key, or a decryption key, can be split up among n principals so that any k out of n can sign a message (or decrypt). For $k = n$ the construction is easy. With RSA, for example, you can split up the private key d as $d = d_1 + d_2 + \ldots + d_n$. For $k < n$ it's slightly more complex (but not much — you use the Lagrange interpolation formula) [382]. Threshold signatures are used in systems where a number of servers process transactions independently and vote independently on the outcome; they could also be used to implement business rules such as 'a check may be signed by any two of the seven directors'.

Blind signatures are a way of making a signature on a message without knowing what the message is. For example, if we are using RSA, I can take a random number R, form $R^e M$ (mod n), and give it to the signer who computes $(R^e M)^d = R.M^d$ (mod n). When he gives this back to me, I can divide out R to get the signature M^d. Now you might ask why on earth someone would want to sign a document without knowing its contents, but there are indeed applications.

The first was in *digital cash*; a bank might want to be able to issue anonymous payment tokens to customers, and this has been done by getting it to sign 'digital coins' without knowing their serial numbers. In such a system, the bank might agree to honour for \$10 any string M with a unique serial number and a specified form of redundancy, bearing a signature that verified as correct using the public key (e, n). The blind signature protocol shows how a customer can get a bank to sign a coin without the banker knowing its serial number. The effect is that the digital cash can be anonymous for the spender. (There are a few technical details that need to be sorted out, such as how you detect people who spend the same coin twice; but these are fixable.) Blind signatures and digital cash were invented by Chaum [285], along with much other supporting digital privacy technology which I'll discuss later [284]. They were used briefly in pilot projects for road tolls in the Netherlands and for electronic purses in Brussels, but failed to take off on a broader scale because of patent issues and because neither banks nor governments really want payments to be anonymous: the anti-money-laundering regulations nowadays restrict anonymous payment services to rather small amounts. Anonymous digital credentials are now talked about, for example, in the context of 'identity management': the TPM chip on your PC motherboard might prove something about you (such as your age) without actually revealing your name.

Researchers continue to suggest new applications for specialist public key mechanisms. A popular candidate is in online elections, which require a particular mixture of anonymity and accountability. Voters want to be sure that their votes have been counted, but it's also desirable that they should not be able to prove which way they voted to anybody else; if they can, then vote-buying and intimidation become easier.

5.7.4 Elliptic Curve Cryptography

Finally, discrete logarithms and their analogues exist in many other mathematical structures; thus for example *elliptic curve cryptography* uses discrete logarithms on an elliptic curve — a curve given by an equation like $y^2 = x^3 + ax + b$. These curves have the property that you can define an addition operation on them and use it for cryptography; the algebra gets a bit complex and a general book like this isn't the place to set it out. However, elliptic curve cryptosystems are interesting for two reasons.

First, they give versions of the familiar primitives such as Diffie-Hellmann key exchange and the Digital Signature Algorithm that use less computation, and also have slightly shorter variables; both can be welcome in constrained environments such as smartcards and embedded processors. Elliptic curve cryptography is used, for example, in the rights-management mechanisms of Windows Media Player, and has been adopted as a standard by the NSA for use in defense systems.

Second, some elliptic curves have a *bilinear pairing* which Dan Boneh and Matt Franklin used to construct cryptosystems where your public key is your name [207]. Recall that in RSA and Diffie-Hellmann, the user chose his private key and then computed a corresponding public key. In a so-called *identity-based cryptosystem*, you choose your identity then go to a central authority that issues you with a private key corresponding to that identity. There is a global public key, with which anyone can encrypt a message to your identity; you can decrypt this using your private key. Earlier, Adi Shamir had discovered *identity-based signature schemes* that allow you to sign messages using a private key so that anyone can verify the signature against your name [1147]. In both cases, your private key is computed by the central authority using a system-wide private key known only to itself. Identity-based primitives could have interesting implications for specialist systems, but in the context of ordinary public-key and signature systems they achieve much the same result as the certification of public keys, which I'll discuss next.

5.7.5 Certification

Now that we can do public-key encryption and digital signature, we need some mechanism to bind users to keys. The approach proposed by Diffie and Hellman when they invented digital signatures was to have a directory of the public keys of a system's authorized users, like a phone book. A more common solution, due to Loren Kohnfelder, is for a *certification authority* (CA) to sign the users' public encryption and/or signature verification keys giving certificates that contain the user's name, attributed such as authorizations, and public keys. The CA might be run by the local system administrator; or it might be a third party service such as Verisign whose business is to sign public keys after doing some due diligence about whether they belong to the principals named in them.

A certificate might be described symbolically as

$$C_A = Sig_{K_S}(T_S, L, A, K_A, V_A) \tag{5.1}$$

where (using the same notation as with Kerberos) T_S is the certificate's starting date and time, L is the length of time for which it is valid, A is the user's name, K_A is her public encryption key, and V_A is her public signature verification key. In this way, only the administrator's public signature verification key needs to be communicated to all principals in a trustworthy manner.

Certification is hard, for a whole lot of reasons. I'll discuss different aspects later — naming in Chapter 6, 'Distributed Systems', public-key infrastructures in Chapter 21, 'Network Attack and Defense', and the policy aspects in Part III. Here I'll merely point out that the protocol design aspects are much harder than they look.

One of the first proposed public-key protocols was due to Dorothy Denning and Giovanni Sacco, who in 1982 proposed that two users, say Alice and Bob, set up a shared key K_{AB} as follows. When Alice first wants to communicate with Bob, she goes to the certification authority and gets current copies of public key certificates for herself and Bob. She then makes up a key packet containing a timestamp T_A, a session key K_{AB} and a signature, which she computes on these items using her private signing key. She then encrypts this whole bundle under Bob's public key and ships it off to him. Symbolically,

$$A \rightarrow B : C_A, C_B, \{T_A, K_{AB}, Sig_{K_A}(T_A, K_{AB})\}_{K_B} \tag{5.2}$$

In 1994, Martín Abadi and Roger Needham pointed out that this protocol is fatally flawed [2]. Bob, on receiving this message, can masquerade as Alice for as long as Alice's timestamp T_A remains valid! To see how, suppose that Bob wants to masquerade as Alice to Charlie. He goes to Sam and gets a fresh certificate C_C for Charlie, and then strips off the outer encryption $\{\ldots\}_{K_B}$ from message 3 in the above protocol. He now re-encrypts the signed key packet $T_A, K_{AB}, Sig_{K_A}(T_A, K_{AB})$ with Charlie's public key — which he gets from C_C — and makes up a bogus message 3:

$$B \rightarrow C : C_A, C_C, \{T_A, K_{AB}, Sig_{K_A}(T_A, K_{AB})\}_{K_C} \tag{5.3}$$

It is quite alarming that such a simple protocol — essentially, a one line program   should have such a serious flaw remain undetected for so long. With a normal program of only a few lines of code, you might expect to find a bug in it by looking at it for a minute or two. In fact, public key protocols are if anything harder to design than protocols that use shared-key encryption, as they are prone to subtle and pernicious middleperson attacks. This further motivates the use of formal methods to prove that protocols are correct.

Often, the participants' names aren't the most important things the authentication mechanism has to establish. In the STU-III secure telephone used by the US government and defense contractors, there is a protocol for establishing transient keys with forward and backward security; to exclude middleperson attacks, users have a *crypto ignition key*, a portable electronic device that they plug into the phone to identify not just their names, but their security clearance level. In general, textbooks tend to talk about identification as the main goal of authentication and key management protocols; but in real life, it's usually authorization that matters. This is more complex, as it starts to introduce assumptions about the application into the protocol design. (In fact, the NSA security manual emphasises the importance of always knowing whether there is an uncleared person in the room. The STU-III design is a natural way of extending this to electronic communications.)

One serious weakness of relying on public-key certificates is the difficulty of getting users to understand all their implications and manage them properly, especially where they are not an exact reimplementation of a familiar manual control system [357]. There are many other things that can go wrong with certification at the level of systems engineering, which I'll start to look at in the next chapter.

5.7.6 The Strength of Asymmetric Cryptographic Primitives

In order to provide the same level of protection as a symmetric block cipher, asymmetric cryptographic primitives generally require at least twice the block length. Elliptic curve systems appear to achieve this bound; a 128-bit elliptic scheme could be about as hard to break as a 64-bit block cipher with a 64-bit key; and the only public-key encryption schemes used in the NSA's Suite B of military algorithms are 256- and 384-bit elliptic curve systems. The commoner schemes, based on factoring and discrete log, are less robust because there are shortcut attack algorithms such as the number field sieve that exploit the fact that some integers are *smooth*, that is, they have a large number of small factors. When I wrote the first edition of this book in 2000, the number field sieve had been used to attack keys up to 512 bits, a task comparable in difficulty to keysearch on 56-bit DES keys; by the time I rewrote this chapter for the second edition in 2007, 64-bit symmetric keys had been brute-forced, and the 663-bit challenge number RSA-200 had been factored. The advance in factoring has historically been due about equally to better hardware and better algorithms. I wrote in 2000 that 'The current consensus is that private keys for RSA and for standard discrete log systems should be at least 1024 bits long, while 2048 bits gives some useful safety margin'; now in 2007, 1024-bit RSA is widely believed to give about the same protection as 80-bit symmetric keys, and designers are starting to move to 2048 bits for keys intended to last many years. As I mentioned above, an extrapolation of recent factoring results suggests that it might be a decade before we see a 1024-bit challenge factored — although with Moore's law starting to slow down, it might take much longer. No-one really knows. (However I expect to see 768-bit RSA factored within a few years.)

There has been much research into *quantum computers* — devices that perform a large number of computations simultaneously using superposed quantum states. Peter Shor has shown that if a sufficiently large quantum computer can be built, then both factoring and discrete logarithm computations will become easy [1165]. So far only very small quantum computers can be built; factoring 15 is about the state of the art in 2007. Many people are sceptical about whether the technology can be scaled up to threaten real systems. But if it does, then asymmetric cryptography may have to change radically. So it is fortunate that many of the things we currently do with asymmetric mechanisms can also be done with symmetric ones; most authentication protocols in use could be redesigned to use variants on Kerberos.

5.8   Summary

Many ciphers fail because they're used improperly, so we need a clear model of what a cipher does. The random oracle model provides a useful intuition: we assume that each new value returned by the encryption engine is random in the sense of being statistically independent of all the different outputs seen before.

Block ciphers for symmetric key applications can be constructed by the careful combination of substitutions and permutations; for asymmetric applications such as public key encryption and digital signature one uses number theory. In both cases, there is quite a large body of mathematics. Other kinds of ciphers — stream ciphers and hash functions — can be constructed from block ciphers by using them in suitable modes of operation. These have different error propagation, pattern concealment and integrity protection properties.

The basic properties that the security engineer needs to understand are not too difficult to grasp, though there are many subtle things that can go wrong. In particular, it is surprisingly hard to build systems that are robust even when components fail (or are encouraged to) and where the cryptographic mechanisms are well integrated with other measures such as access control and physical security. I'll return to this repeatedly in later chapters.

Research Problems

There are many active threads in cryptography research. Many of them are where crypto meets a particular branch of mathematics (number theory, algebraic geometry, complexity theory, combinatorics, graph theory, and information theory). The empirical end of the business is concerned with designing primitives for encryption, signature and composite operations, and which perform reasonably well on available platforms. The two meet in the study of subjects ranging from cryptanalysis, through the search for primitives that combine provable security properties with decent performance, to attacks on public key protocols. Research is more driven by the existing body of knowledge than by applications, though there are exceptions: copyright protection concerns and 'Trusted Computing' have been a stimulus in recent years, as was the US government's competition in the late 1990s to find an Advanced Encryption Standard.

The best way to get a flavor of what's going on is to read the last few years' proceedings of research conferences such as Crypto, Eurocrypt, Asiacrypt, CHES and Fast Software Encryption — all published by Springer in their *Lecture Notes on Computer Science* series.

Further Reading

The classic papers by Whit Diffie and Martin Hellman [385] and by Ron Rivest, Adi Shamir and Len Adleman [1078] are the closest to required reading in this subject. The most popular introduction is Bruce Schneier's *Applied Cryptography* [1125] which covers a lot of ground at a level a non-mathematician can understand, but is slightly dated. Alfred Menezes, Paul van Oorshot and Scott Vanstone's *Handbook of Applied Cryptography* [872] is the closest to a standard reference book on the mathematical detail. For an appreciation of the recent history of cryptanalysis, try Mark Stamp and Richard Low's 'Applied Cryptanalysis' [1214]: this has recent attacks on fielded ciphers such as PKZIP, RC4, CMEA and MD5.

There are many more specialised references. The bible on differential cryptanalysis is a book by its inventors Eli Biham and Adi Shamir [170], while a good short tutorial on linear and differential cryptanalysis was written by Howard Heys [602]. A textbook by Doug Stinson has another detailed explanation of linear cryptanalysis [1226]; and the modern theory of block ciphers can be traced through the papers in the *Fast Software Encryption* conference series. The original book on modes of operation is by Carl Meyer and Steve Matyas [880]. Neal Koblitz has a good basic introduction to the mathematics behind public key cryptography [723]; and the number field sieve is described in [780].

There's a shortage of good books on the random oracle model and on theoretical cryptology in general: all the published texts I've seen are very technical and heavy going. Probably the most regarded source is a book by Oded Goldreich [535] but this is pitched at the postgraduate maths student. A less thorough but more readable introduction to randomness and algorithms is in [564]. Current research at the theoretical end of cryptology is found at the FOCS, STOC, Crypto, Eurocrypt and Asiacrypt conferences.

Four of the simple block cipher modes of operation (ECB, CBC, OFB and CFB) date back to FIPS-81; their specification was reissued, with CTR mode added, in 2001 as NIST Special Publication 800-38A [944]. The compound modes of operation are described in subsequent papers in that series.

The history of cryptology is fascinating, and so many old problems keep on recurring in modern guises that the security engineer should be familiar with it. The standard work is Kahn [676]; there are also compilations of historical articles from *Cryptologia* [363, 361, 362] as well as several books on the history of cryptology in World War 2 [296, 677, 836, 1336]. The NSA Museum at Fort George Meade, Md., is also worth a visit, as is the one at Bletchley Park in England.

Finally, no chapter that introduces public key encryption would be complete without a mention that, under the name of 'non-secret encryption,' it was first discovered by James Ellis in about 1969. However, as Ellis worked for GCHQ (Britain's Government Communications Headquarters, the equivalent of the NSA) his work remained classified. The RSA algorithm was then invented by Clifford Cocks, and also kept secret. This story is told in [427]. One effect of the secrecy was that their work was not used: although it was motivated by the expense of Army key distribution, Britain's Ministry of Defence did not start building electronic key distribution systems for its main networks until 1992. It should also be noted that the classified community did not pre-invent digital signatures; they remain the achievement of Whit Diffie and Martin Hellman.

CHAPTER 6

Distributed Systems

You know you have a distributed system when the crash of a computer you've never heard of stops you from getting any work done.

— Leslie Lamport

6.1   Introduction

We've seen in the last few chapters how people can authenticate themselves to systems (and systems can authenticate themselves to each other) using security protocols; how access controls can be used to manage which principals can perform what operations in a system; and some of the mechanics of how crypto can be used to underpin access control in distributed systems. But there's much more to building a secure distributed system than just implementing access controls, protocols and crypto. When systems become large, the scale-up problems are not linear; there is often a qualitative change in complexity, and some things that are trivial to deal with in a network of only a few machines and principals (such as naming) suddenly become a big deal.

Over the last 40 years, computer science researchers have built many distributed systems and studied issues such as concurrency, failure recovery and naming. The theory is supplemented by a growing body of experience from industry, commerce and government. These issues are central to the design of effective secure systems but are often handled rather badly. I've already described attacks on security protocols that can be seen as concurrency failures. If we replicate data to make a system fault-tolerant then we may increase the risk of a compromise of confidentiality. Finally, naming is a particularly thorny problem. Many governments and organisations are trying to build larger, flatter namespaces — using identity cards to number citizens and using RFID to number objects — and yet naming problems undermined attempts during the 1990s to build useful public key infrastructures.

6.2   Concurrency

Processes are said to be *concurrent* if they run at the same time, and concurrency gives rise to a number of well-studied problems. Processes may use old data; they can make inconsistent updates; the order of updates may or may not matter; the system might deadlock; the data in different systems might never converge to consistent values; and when it's important to make things happen in the right order, or even to know the exact time, this can be harder than you might think.

Systems are now rapidly becoming more concurrent. First, the scale of online business has grown rapidly; Google may have started off with four machines but now its server farms have hundreds of thousands. Second, devices are becoming more complex; a luxury car can now contain over forty different processors. Third, the components are also getting more complex: the microprocessor in your PC may now have two, or even four, CPU cores, and will soon have more, while the graphics card, disk controller and other accessories all have their own processors too. On top of this, virtualization technologies such as VMware and Xen may turn a handful of real CPUs into hundreds or even thousands of virtual CPUs.

Programming concurrent systems is hard; and, unfortunately, most of the textbook examples come from the relatively rarefied world of operating system internals and thread management. But concurrency control is also a security issue. Like access control, it exists in order to prevent users interfering with each other, whether accidentally or on purpose. Also, concurrency problems can occur at many levels in a system, from the hardware right up to the business environment. In what follows, I provide a number of concrete examples of the effects of concurrency on security. These are by no means exhaustive.

6.2.1   Using Old Data Versus Paying to Propagate State

I've already described two kinds of concurrency problem. First, there are replay attacks on protocols, where an attacker manages to pass off out-of-date credentials. Secondly, there are race conditions. I mentioned the 'mkdir' vulnerability from Unix, in which a privileged instruction that is executed in two phases could be attacked halfway through the process by renaming an object on which it acts. These problems have been around for a long time. In one of the first multiuser operating systems, IBM's OS/360, an attempt to open a file caused it to be read and its permissions checked; if the user was authorized to access it, it was read again. The user could arrange things so that the file was altered in between [774].

These are examples of a *time-of-check-to-time-of-use* (TOCTTOU) attack. There are systematic ways of finding such attacks in file systems [176], but as more of our infrastructure becomes concurrent, attacks crop up at other levels such as system calls in virtualised environments, which may require different approaches. (I'll discuss this specific case in detail in Chapter 18.) They also appear at the level of business logic. Preventing them isn't always economical, as propagating changes in security state can be expensive.

For example, the banking industry manages lists of all *hot* credit cards (whether stolen or abused) but there are millions of them worldwide, so it isn't possible to keep a complete hot card list in every merchant terminal, and it would be too expensive to verify all transactions with the bank that issued the card. Instead, there are multiple levels of stand-in processing. Terminals are allowed to process transactions up to a certain limit (the *floor limit*) offline; larger transactions need online verification with a local bank, which will know about all the local hot cards plus foreign cards that are being actively abused; above another limit there might be a reference to an organization such as VISA with a larger international list; while the largest transactions might need a reference to the card issuer. In effect, the only transactions that are checked immediately before use are those that are local or large.

Credit card systems are interesting as the largest systems that manage the global propagation of security state — which they do by assuming that most events are local, of low value, or both. They taught us that revoking compromised credentials quickly and on a global scale was expensive. In the 1990s, when people started to build infrastructures of public key certificates to support everything from web shopping to corporate networks, there was a fear that biggest cost would be revoking the credentials of principals who changed address, changed job, had their private key hacked, or got fired. This turned out not to be the case in general[1]. Another aspect of the costs of revocation can be seen in large web services, where it would be expensive to check a user's credentials against a database every time she visits any one of the service's thousands of machines. A common solution is to use cookies — giving the user an encrypted credential that her browser automatically presents on each visit. That way only the key has to be shared between the server farm's many machines. However, if revoking users quickly is important to the application, some other method needs to be found to do this.

---

[1]Frauds against web-based banking and shopping services don't generally involve compromised certificates. However, one application where revocation is a problem is the Deparatment of Defense, which has issued 16 million certificates to military personnel since 1999 and now has a list of 10 million revoked certificates that must be downloaded to all security servers every day [878].

6.2.2   Locking to Prevent Inconsistent Updates

When a number of people are working concurrently on a document, they may use a version control system to ensure that only one person has write access at any one time to any given part of it. This illustrates the importance of *locking* as a way to manage contention for resources such as filesystems and to reduce the likelihood of conflicting updates. Another mechanism is *callback*; a server may keep a list of all those clients which rely on it for security state, and notify them when the state changes.

Locking and callback also matter in secure distributed systems. Credit cards again provide an example. If I own a hotel, and a customer presents a credit card on checkin, I ask the card company for a *pre-authorization* which records the fact that I will want to make a debit in the near future; I might register a claim on 'up to $500' of her available credit. If the card is cancelled the following day, her bank can call me and ask me to contact the police, or to get her to pay cash. (My bank might or might not have guaranteed me the money; it all depends on what sort of contract I've managed to negotiate with it.) This is an example of the *publish-register-notify* model of how to do robust authorization in distributed systems (of which there's a more general description in [105]).

Callback mechanisms don't provide a universal solution, though. The credential issuer might not want to run a callback service, and the customer might object on privacy grounds to the issuer being told all her comings and goings. Consider passports as an example. In many countries, government ID is required for many transactions, but governments won't provide any guarantee, and most citizens would object if the government kept a record of every time an ID document was presented. Indeed, one of the frequent objections to the British government's proposal for biometric ID cards is that checking citizens' fingerprints against a database whenever they show their ID would create an audit trail of all the places where the card was used.

In general, there is a distinction between those credentials whose use gives rise to some obligation on the issuer, such as credit cards, and the others, such as passports. Among the differences is the importance of the order in which updates are made.

6.2.3   The Order of Updates

If two transactions arrive at the government's bank account — say a credit of $500,000 and a debit of $400,000 — then the order in which they are applied may not matter much. But if they're arriving at my bank account, the order will have a huge effect on the outcome! In fact, the problem of deciding the order in which transactions are applied has no clean solution. It's closely related to the problem of how to parallelize a computation, and much of the art of building efficient distributed systems lies in arranging matters so that processes are either simple sequential or completely parallel.

The usual algorithm in retail checking account systems is to batch the transactions overnight and apply all the credits for each account before applying all the debits. Inputs from devices such as ATMs and check sorters are first batched up into journals before the overnight reconciliation. The inevitable side-effect of this is that payments which bounce then have to be reversed out — and in the case of ATM and other transactions where the cash has already been dispensed, you can end up with customers borrowing money without authorization. In practice, chains of failed payments terminate, though in theory this isn't necessarily so. Some interbank payment mechanisms are moving to *real time gross settlement* in which transactions are booked in order of arrival. The downside here is that the outcome can depend on network vagaries. Some people thought this would limit the *systemic risk* that a non-terminating payment chain might bring down the world's banking system, but there is no real agreement on which practice is better. Credit cards operate a mixture of the two strategies, with credit limits run in real time or near real time (each authorization reduces the available credit limit) while settlement is run just as in a checking account. The downside here is that by putting through a large pre-authorization, a merchant can tie up your card.

The checking-account approach has recently been the subject of research in the parallel systems community. The idea is that disconnected applications propose tentative update transactions that are later applied to a master copy. Various techniques can be used to avoid instability; mechanisms for tentative update, such as with bank journals, are particularly important [553]. Application-level sanity checks are important; banks know roughly how much they expect to pay each other each day to settle net payments, and large cash flows get verified.

In other systems, the order in which transactions arrive is much less important. Passports are a good example. Passport issuers only worry about their creation and expiration dates, not the order in which visas are stamped on them. (There are exceptions, such as the Arab countries that won't let you in if you have an Israeli stamp on your passport, but most pure identification systems are stateless.)

6.2.4   Deadlock

Deadlock is another problem. Things may foul up because two systems are each waiting for the other to move first. A famous exposition of deadlock is the *dining philosophers' problem* in which a number of philosophers are seated round a table. There is a chopstick between each philosopher, who can only eat when he can pick up the two chopsticks on either side. Deadlock can follow if they all try to eat at once and each picks up (say) the chopstick on his right.

This problem, and the algorithms that can be used to avoid it, are presented in a classic paper by Dijkstra [388].

This can get horribly complex when you have multiple hierarchies of locks, and they're distributed across systems some of which fail (especially where failures can mean that the locks aren't reliable). There's a lot written on the problem in the distributed systems literature [104]. But it is not just a technical matter; there are many Catch-22 situations in business processes. So long as the process is manual, some fudge may be found to get round the catch, but when it is implemented in software, this option may no longer be available.

Sometimes it isn't possible to remove the fudge. In a well known business problem — the *battle of the forms* — one company issues an order with its own terms attached, another company accepts it subject to its own terms, and trading proceeds without any agreement about whose conditions govern the contract. The matter may only be resolved if something goes wrong and the two companies end up in court; even then, one company's terms might specify an American court while the other's specify a court in England. This kind of problem looks set to get worse as trading becomes more electronic.

6.2.5   Non-Convergent State

When designing protocols that update the state of a distributed system, the 'motherhood and apple pie' is ACID — that transactions should be *atomic, consistent, isolated and durable*. A transaction is atomic if you 'do it all or not at all' — which makes it easier to recover the system after a failure. It is consistent if some invariant is preserved, such as that the books must still balance. This is common in banking systems, and is achieved by insisting that each credit to one account is matched by an equal and opposite debit to another (I'll discuss this more in Chapter 10, 'Banking and Bookkeeping'). Transactions are isolated if they look the same to each other, that is, are serializable; and they are durable if once done they can't be undone.

These properties can be too much, or not enough, or both. On the one hand, each of them can fail or be attacked in numerous obscure ways; on the other, it's often sufficient to design the system to be *convergent*. This means that, if the transaction volume were to tail off, then eventually there would be consistent state throughout [912]. Convergence is usually achieved using semantic tricks such as timestamps and version numbers; this can often be enough where transactions get appended to files rather than overwritten.

However, in real life, you also need ways to survive things that go wrong and are not completely recoverable. The life of a security or audit manager can be a constant battle against entropy: apparent deficits (and surpluses) are always turning up, and sometimes simply can't be explained. For example, different national systems have different ideas of which fields in bank transaction records are mandatory or optional, so payment gateways often have to guess data in order to make things work. Sometimes they guess wrong; and sometimes people see and exploit vulnerabilities which aren't understood until much later (if ever). In the end, things get fudged by adding a correction factor, called something like 'branch differences', and setting a target for keeping it below a certain annual threshold.

Durability is a subject of debate in transaction processing. The advent of phishing and keylogging attacks has meant that some small proportion of bank accounts will at any time be under the control of criminals; money gets moved both from and through them. When an account compromise is detected, the bank moves to freeze it and to reverse any payments that have recently been made from it. The phishermen naturally try to move funds through institutions, or jurisdictions, that don't do transaction reversal, or do it at best slowly and grudgingly [55]. This sets up a tension between the recoverability and thus the resilience of the payment system on the one hand, and transaction durability and finality on the other. The solution may lie at the application level, namely charging customers a premium for irrevocable payments and letting the market allocate the associated risks to the bank best able to price it.

The battle of the forms mentioned in the above section gives an example of a distributed non-electronic system that doesn't converge.

In military systems, there is the further problem of dealing with users who request some data for which they don't have a clearance. For example, someone at a dockyard might ask the destination of a warship that's actually on a secret mission carrying arms to Iran. If she isn't allowed to know this, the system may conceal the ship's real destination by making up a *cover story*. Search may have to be handled differently from specific enquiries; the joining-up of intelligence databases since 9/11 has forced system builders to start sending clearances along with search queries, otherwise sorting the results became unmanageable. This all raises difficult engineering problems, with potentially severe conflicts between atomicity, consistency, isolation and durability (not to mention performance), which will be discussed at more length in Chapter 8, 'Multilevel Security'.

6.2.6 Secure Time

The final kind of concurrency problem with special interest to the security engineer is the provision of accurate time. As authentication protocols such as Kerberos can be attacked by inducing an error in the clock, it's not enough to simply trust a time source on the network. A few years ago, the worry was a *Cinderella attack*: if a security critical program such as a firewall has a license with a timelock in it, an attacker might wind your clock forward 'and cause your software to turn into a pumpkin'. Things have become more acute since the arrival of operating systems such as Vista with hardware security support, and of media players with built-in DRM; the concern now is that someone might do a large-scale service-denial attack by convincing millions of machines that their owners had tampered with the clock, causing their files to become inaccessible.

Anyway, there are several possible approaches to the provision of secure time.

- You could furnish every computer with a radio clock, but that can be expensive, and radio clocks — even GPS — can be jammed if the opponent is serious.

- There are clock synchronization protocols described in the research literature in which a number of clocks vote in a way that should make clock failures and network delays apparent. Even though these are designed to withstand random (rather than malicious) failure, they can no doubt be hardened by having the messages digitally signed.

- You can abandon absolute time and instead use *Lamport time* in which all you care about is whether event A happened before event B, rather than what date it is [766]. Using challenge-response rather than timestamps in security protocols is an example of this; another is given by timestamping services that continually hash all documents presented to them into a running total that's published, and can thus provide proof that a certain document existed by a certain date [572].

However, in most applications, you are likely to end up using the *network time protocol* (NTP). This has a moderate amount of protection, with clock voting and authentication of time servers. It is dependable enough for many purposes.

6.3 Fault Tolerance and Failure Recovery

Failure recovery is often the most important aspect of security engineering, yet it is one of the most neglected. For many years, most of the research papers on computer security have dealt with confidentiality, and most of the rest with authenticity and integrity; availability has been neglected. Yet the actual expenditures of a typical bank are the other way round. Perhaps a third of all IT costs go on availability and recovery mechanisms, such as hot standby processing sites and multiply redundant networks; a few percent more get invested in integrity mechanisms such as internal audit; and an almost insignificant amount goes on confidentiality mechanisms such as encryption boxes. As you read through this book, you'll see that many other applications, from burglar alarms through electronic warfare to protecting a company from Internet-based service denial attacks, are fundamentally about availability. Fault tolerance and failure recovery are a huge part of the security engineer's job.

Classical fault tolerance is usually based on mechanisms such as logs and locking, and is greatly complicated when it must withstand malicious attacks on these mechanisms. Fault tolerance interacts with security in a number of ways: the failure model, the nature of resilience, the location of redundancy used to provide it, and defense against service denial attacks. I'll use the following definitions: a *fault* may cause an *error*, which is an incorrect state; this may lead to a *failure* which is a deviation from the system's specified behavior. The resilience which we build into a system to tolerate faults and recover from failures will have a number of components, such as fault detection, error recovery and if necessary failure recovery. The meaning of *mean-time-before-failure* (MTBF) and *mean-time-to-repair* (MTTR) should be obvious.

6.3.1   Failure Models

In order to decide what sort of resilience we need, we must know what sort of attacks are expected. Much of this will come from an analysis of threats specific to our system's operating environment, but there are some general issues that bear mentioning.

6.3.1.1   Byzantine Failure

First, the failures with which we are concerned may be normal or *Byzantine*. The Byzantine fault model is inspired by the idea that there are n generals defending Byzantium, t of whom have been bribed by the Turks to cause as much confusion as possible in the command structure. The generals can pass oral messages by courier, and the couriers are trustworthy, so each general can exchange confidential and authentic communications with each other general (we could imagine them encrypting and computing a MAC on each message). What is the maximum number t of traitors which can be tolerated?

The key observation is that if we have only three generals, say Anthony, Basil and Charalampos, and Anthony is the traitor, then he can tell Basil 'let's attack' and Charalampos 'let's retreat'. Basil can now say to Charalampos 'Anthony says let's attack', but this doesn't let Charalampos conclude that Anthony's the traitor. It could just as easily have been Basil; Anthony could have said 'let's retreat' to both of them, but Basil lied when he said 'Anthony says let's attack'.

This beautiful insight is due to Leslie Lamport, Robert Shostak and Marshall Pease, who proved that the problem has a solution if and only if $n \geq 3t + 1$ [767]. Of course, if the generals are able to sign their messages, then no general dare say different things to two different colleagues. This illustrates the power of digital signatures in particular and of end-to-end security mechanisms in general. Relying on third parties to introduce principals to each other or to process transactions between them can give great savings, but if the third parties ever become untrustworthy then it can impose significant costs.

Another lesson is that if a component that fails (or can be induced to fail by an opponent) gives the wrong answer rather than just no answer, then it's much harder to build a resilient system using it. This has recently become a problem in avionics, leading to an emergency Airworthiness Directive in April 2005 that mandated a software upgrade for the Boeing 777, after one of these planes suffered a 'flight control outage' [762].

6.3.1.2   Interaction with Fault Tolerance

We can constrain the failure rate in a number of ways. The two most obvious are by using *redundancy* and *fail-stop processors*. The latter process error-correction information along with data, and stop when an inconsistency is detected; for example, bank transaction processing will typically stop if an out-of-balance condition is detected after a processing task. The two may be combined; IBM's System/88 minicomputer had two disks, two buses and even two CPUs, each of which would stop if it detected errors; the fail-stop CPUs were built by having two CPUs on the same card and comparing their outputs. If they disagreed the output went open-circuit, thus avoiding the Byzantine failure problem.

In general distributed systems, either redundancy or fail-stop processing can make a system more *resilient*, but their side effects are rather different. While both mechanisms may help protect the integrity of data, a fail-stop processor may be more vulnerable to service denial attacks, whereas redundancy can make confidentiality harder to achieve. If I have multiple sites with backup data, then confidentiality could be broken if any of them gets compromised; and if I have some data that I have a duty to destroy, perhaps in response to a court order, then purging it from multiple backup tapes can be a headache.

It is only a slight simplification to say that while replication provides integrity and availability, tamper resistance provides confidentiality too. I'll return to this theme later. Indeed, the prevalence of replication in commercial systems, and of tamper-resistance in military systems, echoes their differing protection priorities.

However, there are traps for the unwary. In one case in which I was called on as an expert, my client was arrested while using a credit card in a store, accused of having a forged card, and beaten up by the police. He was adamant that the card was genuine. Much later, we got the card examined by VISA who confirmed that it was indeed genuine. What happened, as well as we can reconstruct it, was this. Credit cards have two types of redundancy on the magnetic strip — a simple checksum obtained by combining together all the bytes on the track using exclusive-or, and a cryptographic checksum which we'll describe in detail later in section 10.5.2. The former is there to detect errors, and the latter to detect forgery. It appears that in this particular case, the merchant's card reader was out of alignment in such a way as to cause an even number of bit errors which cancelled each other out by chance in the simple checksum, while causing the crypto checksum to fail. The result was a false alarm, and a major disruption in my client's life.

Redundancy is hard enough to deal with in mechanical systems. For example, training pilots to handle multi-engine aircraft involves drilling them on engine failure procedures, first in the simulator and then in real aircraft with an instructor. Novice pilots are in fact more likely to be killed by an engine failure in a multi-engine plane than in a single; landing in the nearest field is less hazardous for them than coping with suddenly asymmetric thrust. The same goes for instrument failures; it doesn't help to have three artificial horizons in the cockpit if, under stress, you rely on the one that's broken. Aircraft are much simpler than many modern information systems — yet there are still regular air crashes when pilots fail to manage the redundancy that's supposed to keep them safe. All too often, system designers put in multiple protection mechanisms and hope that things will be 'all right on the night'. This might be compared to strapping a 40-hour rookie pilot into a Learjet and telling him to go play. It really isn't good enough. Please bear the aircraft analogy in mind if you have to design systems combining redundancy and security!

The proper way to do things is to consider all the possible use cases and abuse cases of a system, think through all the failure modes that can happen by chance (or be maliciously induced), and work out how all the combinations of alarms will be dealt with — and how, and by whom. Then write up your safety and security case and have it evaluated by someone who knows what they're doing. I'll have more to say on this later in the chapter on 'System Evaluation and Assurance'.

Even so, large-scale system failures very often show up dependencies that the planners didn't think of. For example, Britain suffered a fuel tanker drivers' strike in 2001, and some hospitals had to close because of staff shortages. The government allocated petrol rations to doctors and nurses, but not to schoolteachers. So schools closed, and nurses had to stay home to look after their kids, and this closed hospitals too. We are becoming increasingly dependent on each other, and this makes contingency planning harder.

6.3.2   What Is Resilience For?

When introducing redundancy or other resilience mechanisms into a system, we need to be very clear about what they're for. An important consideration is whether the resilience is contained within a single organization.

In the first case, replication can be an internal feature of the server to make it more trustworthy. AT&T built a system called *Rampart* in which a number of geographically distinct servers can perform a computation separately and combine their results using threshold decryption and signature [1065]; the idea is to use it for tasks like key management [1066]. IBM developed a variant on this idea called *Proactive Security*, where keys are regularly flushed through the system, regardless of whether an attack has been reported [597]. The idea is to recover even from attackers who break into a server and then simply bide their time until enough other servers have also been compromised. The trick of building a secure 'virtual server' on top of a number of cheap off-the-shelf machines has turned out to be attractive to people designing certification authority services because it's possible to have very robust evidence of attacks on, or mistakes made by, one of the component servers [337]. It also appeals to a number of navies, as critical resources can be spread around a ship in multiple PCs and survive most kinds of damage that don't sink it [489].

But often things are much more complicated. A server may have to protect itself against malicious clients. A prudent bank, for example, will assume that some of its customers would cheat it given the chance. Sometimes the problem is the other way round, in that we have to rely on a number of services, none of which is completely trustworthy. Since 9/11, for example, international money-laundering controls have been tightened so that people opening bank accounts are supposed to provide two different items that give evidence of their name and address — such as a gas bill and a pay slip. (This causes serious problems in Africa, where the poor also need banking services as part of their path out of poverty, but may live in huts that don't even have addresses, let alone utilities [55].)

The direction of mistrust has an effect on protocol design. A server faced with multiple untrustworthy clients, and a client relying on multiple servers that may be incompetent, unavailable or malicious, will both wish to control the flow of messages in a protocol in order to contain the effects of service denial. So a client facing several unreliable servers may wish to use an authentication protocol such as the Needham-Schroeder protocol I discussed in section 3.7.2; then the fact that the client can use old server tickets is no longer a bug but a feature. This idea can be applied to protocol design in general [1043]. It provides us with another insight into why protocols may fail if the principal responsible for the design, and the principal who carries the cost of fraud, are different; and why designing systems for the real world in which everyone (clients and servers) are unreliable and mutually suspicious, is hard.

At a still higher level, the emphasis might be on *security renewability*. Pay-TV is a good example: secret keys and other subscriber management tools are typically kept in a cheap smartcard rather than in an expensive set-top box, so that even if all the secret keys are compromised, the operator can recover by mailing new cards out to his subscribers. I'll discuss in more detail in Chapter 22, 'Copyright and Privacy Protection'

6.3.3   At What Level Is the Redundancy?

Systems may be made resilient against errors, attacks and equipment failures at a number of levels. As with access control systems, these become progressively more complex and less reliable as we go up to higher layers in the system.

Some computers have been built with redundancy at the hardware level, such as the IBM System/88 I mentioned earlier. From the late 1980's, these machines were widely used in transaction processing tasks (eventually ordinary hardware became reliable enough that banks would not pay the premium in capital cost and development effort to use non-standard hardware). Some more modern systems achieve the same goal with standard hardware either at the component level, using *redundant arrays of inexpensive disks* ('RAID' disks) or at the system level by massively parallel server farms. But none of these techniques provides a defense against faulty or malicious software, or against an intruder who exploits such software.

At the next level up, there is *process group redundancy*. Here, we may run multiple copies of a system on multiple servers in different locations, and compare their outputs. This can stop the kind of attack in which the opponent gets physical access to a machine and subverts it, whether by mechanical destruction or by inserting unauthorized software, and destroys or alters data. It can't defend against attacks by authorized users or damage by bad authorized software, which could simply order the deletion of a critical file.

The next level is *backup*. Here, we typically take a copy of the system (also known as a *checkpoint*) at regular intervals. The backup copies are usually kept on media that can't be overwritten such as write-protected tapes or DVDs. We may also keep *journals* of all the transactions applied between checkpoints. In general, systems are kept recoverable by a transaction processing strategy of logging the incoming data, trying to do the transaction, logging it again, and then checking to see whether it worked. Whatever the detail, backup and recovery mechanisms not only enable us to recover from physical asset destruction; they also ensure that if we do get an attack at the logical level — such as a time bomb in our software which deletes our customer database on a specific date — we have some hope of recovering. They are not infallible though. The closest that any bank I know of came to a catastrophic computer failure that would have closed its business was when its mainframe software got progressively more tangled as time progressed, and it just wasn't feasible to roll back processing several weeks and try again.

Backup is not the same as *fallback*. A fallback system is typically a less capable system to which processing reverts when the main system is unavailable. An example is the use of manual imprinting machines to capture credit card transactions from the card embossing when electronic terminals fail.

Fallback systems are an example of redundancy in the application layer — the highest layer we can put it. We might require that a transaction above a certain limit be authorized by two members of staff, that an audit trail be kept of all transactions, and a number of other things. We'll discuss such arrangements at greater length in the chapter on banking and bookkeeping.

It is important to realise that these are different mechanisms, which do different things. Redundant disks won't protect against a malicious programmer who deletes all your account files, and backups won't stop him if rather than just deleting files he writes code that slowly inserts more and more errors. Neither will give much protection against attacks on data confidentiality. On the other hand, the best encryption in the world won't help you if your data processing center burns down. Real world recovery plans and mechanisms can get fiendishly complex and involve a mixture of all of the above.

The remarks that I made earlier about the difficulty of redundancy, and the absolute need to plan and train for it properly, apply in spades to system backup. When I was working in banking we reckoned that we could probably get our backup system working within an hour or so of our main processing centre being destroyed, but the tests we did were limited by the fact that we didn't want to risk processing during business hours. The most impressive preparations I've ever seen were at a UK supermarket, which as a matter of policy pulls the plug on its main processing centre once a year without warning the operators. This is the only way they can be sure that the backup arrangements actually work, and that the secondary processing centre really cuts in within a minute or so. Bank tellers can keep serving customers for a few hours with the systems down; but retailers with dead checkout lanes can't do that.

6.3.4 Service-Denial Attacks

One of the reasons we want security services to be fault-tolerant is to make service-denial attacks less attractive, more difficult, or both. These attacks are often used as part of a larger attack plan. For example, one might swamp a host to take it temporarily offline, and then get another machine on the same LAN (which had already been subverted) to assume its identity for a while. Another possible attack is to take down a security server to force other servers to use cached copies of credentials.

A powerful defense against service denial is to prevent the opponent mounting a selective attack. If principals are anonymous — or at least there is no name service which will tell the opponent where to attack — then he may be ineffective. I'll discuss this further in the context of burglar alarms and electronic warfare.

Where this isn't possible, and the opponent knows where to attack, then there are some types of service-denial attacks which can be stopped by redundancy and resilience mechanisms, and others which can't. For example, the TCP/IP protocol has few effective mechanisms for hosts to protect themselves against various network flooding attacks. An opponent can send a large number of connection requests and prevent anyone else establishing a connection. Defense against this kind of attack tends to involve moving your site to a beefier hosting service with specialist packet-washing hardware — or tracing and arresting the perpetrator.

Distributed denial-of-service (DDoS) attacks had been known to the research community as a possibility for some years. They came to public notice when they were used to bring down Panix, a New York ISP, for several days in 1996. During the late 1990s they were occasionally used by script kiddies to take over chat servers. In 2000, colleagues and I suggested dealing with the problem by server replication [1366], and in 2001 I mentioned them in passing in the first edition of this book. Over the following three years, small-time extortionists started using DDoS attacks for blackmail. The modus operandi was to assemble a *botnet*, a network of compromised PCs used as attack robots, which would flood a target webserver with packet traffic until its owner paid them to desist. Typical targets were online bookmakers, and amounts of $10,000–$50,000 were typically demanded to leave them alone. The typical bookie paid up the first time this happened, but when the attacks persisted the first solution was replication: operators moved their websites to hosting services such as Akamai whose servers are so numerous (and so close to customers) that they can shrug off anything that the average botnet could throw at them. In the end, the blackmail problem was solved when the bookmakers met and agreed not to pay any more blackmail money, and the Russian police were prodded into arresting the gang responsible.

Finally, where a more vulnerable fallback system exists, a common technique is to force its use by a service denial attack. The classic example is the use of smartcards for bank payments in countries in Europe. Smartcards are generally harder to forge than magnetic strip cards, but perhaps 1% of them fail every year, thanks to static electricity and worn contacts. Also, foreign tourists still use magnetic strip cards. So card payment systems have a fallback mode that uses the magnetic strip. A typical attack nowadays is to use a false terminal, or a bug inserted into the cable between a genuine terminal and a branch server, to capture card details, and then write these details to the magnetic stripe of a card whose chip has been destroyed (connecting 20V across the contacts does the job nicely). In the same way, burglar alarms that rely on network connections for the primary response and fall back to alarm bells may be very vulnerable if the network can be interrupted by an attacker: now that online alarms are the norm, few people pay attention any more to alarm bells.

6.4 Naming

Naming is a minor if troublesome aspect of ordinary distributed systems, but it becomes surprisingly hard in security engineering. The topical example in the 1990s was the problem of what names to put on public key certificates. A certificate that says simply 'the person named Ross Anderson is allowed to administer machine X' is little use. Before the arrival of Internet search engines, I was the only Ross Anderson I knew of; now I know of dozens of us. I am also known by different names to dozens of different systems. Names exist in contexts, and naming the principals in secure systems is becoming ever more important and difficult.

Engineers observed then that using more names than you need to causes unnecessary complexity. For example, A certificate that simply says 'the bearer of this certificate is allowed to administer machine X' is a straightforward bearer token, which we know how to deal with; but once my name is involved, then presumably I have to present some kind of ID to prove who I am, and the system acquires a further dependency. Worse, if my ID is compromised the consequences could be extremely far-reaching.

Since 9/11 the terms of this debate have shifted somewhat, as many governments have rushed to issue their citizens with ID cards. In order to justify the expense and hassle, pressure is often put on commercial system operators to place some reliance on government-issue ID where this was previously not thought necessary. In the UK, for example, you can no longer board a domestic flight using just the credit card with which you bought the ticket, and you have to produce a passport or driving license to cash a check or order a bank transfer for more than £1000. Such measures cause inconvenience and introduce new failure modes into all sorts of systems.

No doubt this identity fixation will abate in time, as governments find other things to scare their citizens with. However there is a second reason that the world is moving towards larger, flatter name spaces: the move from barcodes (which code a particular product) to RFID tags (which contain a 128-bit unique identifier that code a particular item.) This has ramifications well beyond naming — into issues such as the interaction between product security, supply-chain security and competition policy.

For now, it's useful to go through what a generation of computer science researchers have learned about naming in distributed systems.

6.4.1 The Distributed Systems View of Naming

During the last quarter of the twentieth century, the distributed systems research community ran up against many naming problems. The basic algorithm used to bind names to addresses is known as *rendezvous*: the principal exporting a name advertises it somewhere, and the principal seeking to import and use it searches for it. Obvious examples include phone books, and directories in file systems.

However, the distributed systems community soon realised that naming can get fiendishly complex, and the lessons learned are set out in a classic article by Needham [958]. I'll summarize the main points, and look at which of them apply to secure systems.

1. *The function of names is to facilitate sharing.* This continues to hold: my bank account number exists in order to provide a convenient way of sharing the information that I deposited money last week with the teller from whom I am trying to withdraw money this week. In general, names are needed when the data to be shared is changeable. If I only ever wished to withdraw exactly the same sum as I'd deposited, a bearer deposit certificate would be fine. Conversely, names need not be shared — or linked — where data will not be; there is no need to link my bank account number to my telephone number unless I am going to pay my phone bill from the account.

2. *The naming information may not all be in one place, and so resolving names brings all the general problems of a distributed system.* This holds with a vengeance. A link between a bank account and a phone number assumes both of them will remain stable. So each system relies on the other, and an attack on one can affect the other. In the days when electronic banking was dial-up rather than web based, a bank which identified its customers using calling line ID was vulnerable to attacks on telephone systems (such as tapping into the distribution frame in an apartment block, hacking a phone company computer, or bribing a phone company employee). Nowadays some banks are using two-channel authorization to combat phishing — if you order a payment online you get a text message on your mobile phone saying 'if you want to pay $X to account Y, please enter the following four digit code into your browser'. This is a bit tougher, as mobile phone traffic is encrypted — but one weak link to watch for is the binding between the customer and his phone number. If you let just anyone notify you of a customer phone number change, you'll be in trouble.

3. *It is bad to assume that only so many names will be needed.* The shortage of IP addresses, which motivated the development of IP version 6 (IPv6), is well enough discussed. What is less well known is that the most expensive upgrade which the credit card industry ever had to make was not Y2K remediation, but the move from thirteen digit credit card numbers to sixteen. Issuers originally assumed that 13 digits would be enough, but the system ended up with tens of thousands of banks (many with dozens of products) so a six digit *bank identification number*

(BIN number) was needed. Some card issuers have millions of customers, so a nine digit account number is the norm. And there's also a *check digit* (a one-digit linear combination of the other digits which is appended to detect errors).

4. *Global names buy you less than you think.* For example, the 128-bit address in IPv6 can in theory enable every object in the universe to have a unique name. However, for us to do business, a local name at my end must be resolved into this unique name and back into a local name at your end. Invoking a unique name in the middle may not buy us anything; it may even get in the way if the unique naming service takes time, costs money, or occasionally fails (as it surely will). In fact, the name service itself will usually have to be a distributed system, of the same scale (and security level) as the system we're trying to protect. So we can expect no silver bullets from this quarter. One reason the banking industry was wary of initiatives such as SET that would have given each customer a public key certificate on a key with which they could sign payment instructions was that banks already have perfectly good names for their customers (account numbers). Adding an extra name has the potential to add extra costs and failure modes.

5. *Names imply commitments, so keep the scheme flexible enough to cope with organizational changes.* This sound principle was ignored in the design of a UK government's key management system for secure email [76]. There, principals' private keys are generated by encrypting their names under departmental master keys. So the frequent reorganizations meant that the security infrastructure would have to be rebuilt each time — and that money would have had to be spent solving many secondary problems such as how people would access old material.

6. *Names may double as access tickets, or capabilities.* We have already seen a number of examples of this in Chapters 2 and 3. In general, it's a bad idea to assume that today's name won't be tomorrow's password or capability — remember the Utrecht fraud we discussed in section 3.5. (This is one of the arguments for making all names public keys — 'keys speak in cyberspace' in Carl Ellison's phrase — but we've already noted the difficulties of linking keys with names.)

I've given a number of examples of how things go wrong when a name starts being used as a password. But sometimes the roles of name and password are ambiguous. In order to get entry to a car park I used to use at the university, I had to speak my surname and parking badge number into a microphone at the barrier. So if I say, 'Anderson, 123', which of these is the password? In fact it was 'Anderson', as anyone can walk through the car park and note down valid badge

numbers from the parking permits on the car windscreens. Another
example, from medical informatics, is a large database of medical
records kept by the UK government for research, where the name of the
patient has been replaced by their postcode and date of birth. Yet access
to many medical services requires the patient to give just these two
items to the receptionist to prove who they are. I will have more to say
on this later.

7. *Things are made much simpler if an incorrect name is obvious.* In standard
   distributed systems, this enables us to take a liberal attitude to cacheing.
   In payment systems, credit card numbers may be accepted while a terminal is offline so long as the credit card number appears valid (i.e., the
   last digit is a proper check digit of the first fifteen) and it is not on the
   hot card list. Certificates provide a higher-quality implementation of
   the same basic concept.

   It's important where the name is checked. The credit card check digit
   algorithm is deployed at the point of sale, so it is public. A further
   check — the *card verification value* on the magnetic strip — is computed
   with secret keys but can be checked at the issuing bank, the acquiring bank or even at a network switch (if one trusts these third parties
   with the keys). This is more expensive, and still vulnerable to network
   outages.

8. *Consistency is hard, and is often fudged. If directories are replicated, then
   you may find yourself unable to read, or to write, depending on whether too
   many or too few directories are available.* Naming consistency causes problems for e-commerce in a number of ways, of which perhaps the most
   notorious is the bar code system. Although this is simple enough in
   theory — with a unique numerical code for each product — in practice it can be a nightmare, as different manufacturers, distributors and
   retailers attach quite different descriptions to the bar codes in their
   databases. Thus a search for products by 'Kellogg's' will throw up
   quite different results depending on whether or not an apostrophe is
   inserted, and this can cause great confusion in the supply chain. Proposals to fix this problem can be surprisingly complicated [618]. There
   are also the issues of convergence discussed above; data might not be
   consistent across a system, even in theory. There are also the problems of timeliness, such as whether a product has been recalled.

   Now, many firms propose moving to RFID chips that contain a globally unique number: an item code rather than a product code. This may
   move name resolution upstream; rather than the shop's
   computer recognising that the customer has presented a packet of
   vitamin C at the checkout, it may go to the manufacturer to find this

out. Manufacturers push for this on safety grounds; they can then be sure that the product hasn't passed its sell-by date and has not been recalled. But this also increases their power over the supply chain; they can detect and stop gray-market trading that would otherwise undermine their ability to charge different prices in different towns.

9. *Don't get too smart. Phone numbers are much more robust than computer addresses.* Amen to that — but it's too often ignored by secure system designers. Bank account numbers are much easier to deal with than the public-key certificates which were once believed both necessary and sufficient to secure credit card payments online. I'll discuss specific problems of public key infrastructures in section 21.4.5.7.

10. *Some names are bound early, others not; and in general it is a bad thing to bind early if you can avoid it.* A prudent programmer will normally avoid coding absolute addresses or filenames as that would make it hard to upgrade or replace a machine. He will prefer to leave this to a configuration file or an external service such as DNS. (This is another reason not to put addresses in names.) It is true that secure systems often want stable and accountable names as any third-party service used for last minute resolution could be a point of attack. However, designers should read the story of Netgear, who got their home routers to find out the time using the Network Time Protocol from a server at the University of Wisconsin-Madison. Their product was successful; the university was swamped with hundreds of thousands of packets a second. Netgear ended up paying them $375,000 to maintain the time service for three years. Shortly afterwards, D-Link repeated the same mistake [304].

So Needham's ten principles for distributed naming apply fairly directly to distributed secure systems.

6.4.2 What Else Goes Wrong

Needham's principles, although very useful, are not sufficient. They were designed for a world in which naming systems could be designed and imposed at the system owner's convenience. When we move from distributed systems in the abstract to the reality of modern web-based (and interlinked) service industries, there is still more to say.

6.4.2.1 Naming and Identity

The most obvious difference is that the principals in security protocols may be known by many different kinds of name — a bank account number, a company registration number, a personal name plus a date of birth or a postal address, a telephone number, a passport number, a health service patient number, or a userid on a computer system.

As I mentioned in the introductory chapter, a common mistake is to confuse naming with identity. *Identity* is when two different names (or instances of the same name) correspond to the same principal (this is known in the distributed systems literature as an *indirect name* or *symbolic link*). The classic example comes from the registration of title to real estate. It is very common that someone who wishes to sell a house uses a different name than they did at the time it was purchased: they might have changed their name on marriage, or after a criminal conviction. Changes in name usage are also common. For example, the DE Bell of the Bell-LaPadula system[2] wrote his name 'D. Elliot Bell' in 1973 on that paper; but he was always known as David, which is how he now writes his name too. A land-registration system must cope with a lot of identity issues like this.

The classic example of identity failure leading to compromise is check fraud. Suppose I steal a high-value check made out to Mr Elliott Bell. I then open an account in that name and cash it; banking law in both the USA and the UK absolves the bank of liability so long as it pays the check into an account of the same name. The modern procedure of asking people who open bank accounts for two proofs of address, such as utility bills, probably makes the bad guys' job easier; there are hundreds of utility companies, many of which provide electronic copies of bills that are easy to alter. The pre-9/11 system, of taking up personal references, may well have been better.

Moving to verifying government-issue photo-ID on account opening adds to the mix statements such as 'The Elliott Bell who owns bank account number 12345678 is the Elliott James Bell with passport number 98765432 and date of birth 3/4/56'. This may be seen as a symbolic link between two separate systems — the bank's and the passport office's. Note that the latter part of this 'identity' encapsulates a further statement, which might be something like 'The US passport office's file number 98765432 corresponds to the entry in birth register for 3/4/56 of one Elliott James Bell'. In general, names may involve several steps of recursion, and this gives attackers a choice of targets. For example, a lot of passport fraud is *pre-issue fraud*: the bad guys apply for passports in the names of genuine citizens who haven't applied for a passport already and for whom copies of birth certificates are easy enough to obtain. Postmortem applications are also common. Linden Labs, the operators of Second Life, introduced in late 2007 a scheme whereby you prove you're over 18 by providing the driver's license number or social security number of someone who is. Now a web search quickly pulls up such data for many people, such as the rapper Tupac Amaru Shakur; and yes, Linden Labs did accept Mr Shakur's license number — even through the license is expired, and

[2]I'll discuss this in Chapter 8, 'Multilevel Secure Systems'.

he's dead. Indeed, someone else managed to verify their age using Mohammed Atta's driver's license [389].

6.4.2.2   *Cultural Assumptions*

The assumptions that underlie names often change from one country to another. In the English-speaking world, people may generally use as many names as they please; a name is simply what you are known by. But some countries forbid the use of aliases, and others require them to be registered. This can lead to some interesting scams: in at least one case, a British citizen evaded pursuit by foreign tax authorities by changing his name. On a less exalted plane, women who pursue academic careers and change their name on marriage may wish to retain their former name for professional use, which means that the name on their scientific papers is different from their name on the payroll. This caused a row at my university which introduced a unified ID card system, keyed to payroll names, without support for aliases.

In general, many of the really intractable problems arise when an attempt is made to unify two local naming systems which turn out to have incompatible assumptions. As electronics invades everyday life more and more, and systems become linked up, conflicts can propagate and have unexpected remote effects. For example, one of the lady professors in the dispute over our university card was also a trustee of the British Library, which issues its own admission tickets on the basis of the name on the holder's home university library card.

Even human naming conventions are not uniform. Russians are known by a forename, a patronymic and a surname; Icelanders have no surname but are known instead by a given name followed by a patronymic if they are male and a matronymic if they are female. This causes problems when they travel. When US immigration comes across 'Maria Trosttadóttir' and learns that 'Trosttadóttir' isn't a surname or even a patronymic, their standard practice was to compel her to adopt as a surname a patronymic (say, 'Carlsson' if her father was called Carl). This causes unnecessary offence.

The biggest cultural divide is often thought to be that between the English speaking countries (where identity cards were long considered to be unacceptable on privacy grounds[3]) and the countries conquered by Napoleon or by the Soviets, where identity cards are the norm.

There are further subtleties. I know Germans who have refused to believe that a country could function at all without a proper system of population registration and ID cards, yet admit they are asked for their ID card only rarely (for example, to open a bank account or get married). Their card number can't be used as a name, because it is a document number and changes every time a new card is issued. A Swiss hotelier may be happy to register a German guest on

---

[3]unless they're called drivers' licences or health service cards!

sight of an ID card rather than a credit card, but if he discovers some damage after a German guest has checked out, he may be out of luck. And the British passport office will issue a citizen with more than one passport at the same time, if he says he needs them to make business trips to (say) Cuba and the USA; so our Swiss hotelier, finding that a British guest has just left without paying, can't rely on the passport number to have him stopped at the airport.

There are many other hidden assumptions about the relationship between governments and people's names, and they vary from one country to another in ways which can cause unexpected security failures.

6.4.2.3   Semantic Content of Names

Another hazard arises on changing from one type of name to another without adequate background research. A bank got sued after they moved from storing customer data by account number to storing it by name and address. They wanted to target junk mail more accurately, so they wrote a program to link up all the accounts operated by each of their customers. The effect for one poor customer was that the bank statement for the account he maintained for his mistress got sent to his wife, who divorced him.

Sometimes naming is simple, but sometimes it merely appears to be. For example, when I got a monthly ticket for the local swimming baths, the cashier simply took the top card off a pile, swiped it through a reader to tell the system it was now live, and gave it to me. I had been assigned a random name — the serial number on the card. Many US road toll systems work in much the same way. Sometimes a random, anonymous name can add commercial value. In Hong Kong, toll tokens for the Aberdeen tunnel could be bought for cash, or at a discount in the form of a refillable card. In the run-up to the transfer of power from Britain to Beijing, many people preferred to pay extra for the less traceable version as they were worried about surveillance by the new government.

Semantics of names can change. I once got a hardware store loyalty card with a random account number (and no credit checks). I was offered the chance to change this into a bank card after the store was taken over by the supermarket and the supermarket started a bank. (This appears to have ignored money laundering regulations that all new bank customers must be subjected to due diligence.)

Assigning bank account numbers to customers might have seemed unproblematic — but as the above examples show, systems may start to construct assumptions about relationships between names that are misleading and dangerous.

6.4.2.4   Uniqueness of Names

Human names evolved when we lived in small communities. We started off with just forenames, but by the late Middle Ages the growth of travel led governments to bully people into adopting surnames. That process took a century or so, and was linked with the introduction of paper into Europe as a lower-cost and more tamper-resistant replacement for parchment; paper enabled the badges, seals and other bearer tokens, which people had previously used for road tolls and the like, to be replaced with letters that mentioned their names.

The mass movement of people, business and administration to the Internet in the decade after 1995 has been too fast to allow any such social adaptation. There are now many more people (and systems) online than we are used to dealing with. As I remarked at the beginning of this section, I used to be the only Ross Anderson I knew of, but thanks to search engines, I now know dozens of us. Some of us work in fields I've also worked in, such as software engineering and electric power distribution; the fact that I'm `www.ross-anderson.com` and `ross.anderson@iee.org` is down to luck — I got there first. (Even so, `rjanderson@iee.org` is somebody else.) So even the combination of a relatively rare name and a specialized profession is still ambiguous. Another way of putting this is that 'traditional usernames, although old-school-geeky, don't scale well to the modern Internet' [21].

Sometimes system designers are tempted to solve the uniqueness problem by just giving everything and everyone a number. This is very common in transaction processing, but it can lead to interesting failures if you don't put the uniqueness in the right place. A UK bank wanted to send £20m overseas, but the operator typed in £10m by mistake. To correct the error, a second payment of £10m was ordered. However, the sending bank's system took the transaction sequence number from the paperwork used to authorise it. Two payments were sent to SWIFT with the same date, payee, amount and sequence number — so the second was discarded as a duplicate [218].

6.4.2.5 Stability of Names and Addresses

Many names include some kind of address, yet addresses change. About a quarter of Cambridge phone book addresses change every year; with email, the turnover is probably higher. A project to develop a directory of people who use encrypted email, together with their keys, found that the main cause of changed entries was changes of email address [67]. (Some people had assumed it would be the loss or theft of keys; the contribution from this source was precisely zero.)

A serious problem could arise with IPv6. The security community assumes that v6 IP addresses will be stable, so that public key certificates can bind principals of various kinds to them. All sorts of mechanisms have been proposed to map real world names, addresses and even document content indelibly and eternally on to 128 bit strings (see, for example, [573]). The data communications community, on the other hand, assumes that IPv6 addresses will change regularly. The more significant bits will change to accommodate more efficient routing algorithms, while the less significant bits will be used to manage local networks. These assumptions can't both be right.

Distributed systems pioneers considered it a bad thing to put addresses in names [912]. But in general, there can be multiple layers of abstraction with some of the address information at each layer forming part of the name at the layer above. Also, whether a namespace is better flat depends on the application. Often people end up with different names at the departmental and organizational level (such as `rja14@cam.ac.uk` and `ross.anderson@cl.cam.ac.uk` in my own case). So a clean demarcation between names and addresses is not always possible.

Authorizations have many (but not all) of the properties of addresses. Kent's Law tells designers that if a credential contains a list of what it may be used for, then the more things are on this list the shorter its period of usefulness. A similar problem besets systems where names are composite. For example, some online businesses recognize me by the combination of email address and credit card number. This is clearly bad practice. Quite apart from the fact that I have several email addresses, I have several credit cards. The one I use will depend on which of them is currently offering the best service or the biggest bribes.

There are many good reasons to use pseudonyms. It's certainly sensible for children and young people to use online names that aren't easily linkable to their real names. This is often advocated as a child-protection measure, although the number of children abducted and murdered by strangers in developed countries remains happily low and stable at about 1 per 10,000,000 population per year. A more serious reason is that when you go for your first job on leaving college aged 22, or for a CEO's job at 45, you don't want Google to turn up all your teenage rants. Many people also change email addresses from time to time to escape spam; I give a different email address to every website where I shop. Of course, there are police and other agencies that would prefer people not to use pseudonyms, and this takes us into the whole question of traceability online, which I'll discuss in Part II.

6.4.2.6 *Adding Social Context to Naming*

The rapid growth recently of social network sites such as Facebook points to a more human and scaleable way of managing naming. Facebook does not give me a visible username: I use my own name, and build my context by having links to a few dozen friends. (Although each profile does have a unique number, this does not appear in the page itself, just in URLs.) This fixes the uniqueness problem — Facebook can have as many Ross Andersons as care to turn up — and the stability problem (though at the cost of locking me into Facebook if I try to use it for everything).

Distributed systems folks had argued for some time that no naming system can be simultaneously globally unique, decentralized, and human-meaningful. It can only have two of those attributes (Zooko's triangle) [21]. In the past, engineers tanded to look for naming systems that were unique and meaningful, like URLs, or unique and decentralised, as with public-key certificates[4]. The innovation from sites like Facebook is to show on a really large scale that naming doesn't have to be unique at all. We can use social context to build systems that are both decentralised and meaningful — which is just what our brains evolved to cope with.

6.4.2.7 *Restrictions on the Use of Names*

The interaction between naming and society brings us to a further problem: some names may be used only in restricted circumstances. This may be laid down by law, as with the US *Social Security Number* (SSN) and its equivalents in many European countries. Sometimes it is a matter of marketing. I would rather not give out my residential address (or my home phone number) when shopping online, and I avoid businesses that demand them.

Restricted naming systems interact in unexpected ways. For example, it's fairly common for hospitals to use a patient number as an index to medical record databases, as this may allow researchers to use pseudonymous records for some limited purposes without much further processing. This causes problems when a merger of health maintenance organizations, or a new policy directive in a national health service, forces the hospital to introduce uniform names. In the UK, for example, the merger of two records databases — one of which used patient names while the other was pseudonymous — has raised the prospect of legal challenges to processing on privacy grounds.

Finally, when we come to law and policy, the definition of a name turns out to be unexpectedly tricky. Regulations that allow police to collect communications data — that is, a record of who called whom and when — are often very much more lax than the regulations governing phone tapping; in many countries, police can get this data just by asking the phone company. There was an acrimonious public debate in the UK about whether this enables them to harvest the URLs which people use to fetch web pages. URLs often have embedded in them data such as the parameters passed to search engines. Clearly there are policemen who would like a list of everyone who hit a URL such as http://www.google.com/search?q=cannabis+cultivation+UK; just as clearly, many people would consider such large-scale trawling to be an unacceptable invasion of privacy. The police argued that if they were limited to

---

[4]Carl Ellison, Butler Lampson and Ron Rivest went so far as to propose the SPKI/SDSI certificate system in which naming would be relative, rather than fixed with respect to central authority. The PGP web of trust worked informally in the same way.

monitoring IP addresses, they could have difficulties tracing criminals who use transient IP addresses. In the end, Parliament resolved the debate when it passed the Regulation of Investigatory Powers Act in 2000: the police just get the identity of the machine under the laxer regime for communications data.

6.4.3 Types of Name

The complexity of naming appears at all levels — organisational, technical and political. I noted in the introduction that names can refer not just to persons (and machines acting on their behalf), but also to organizations, roles ('the officer of the watch'), groups, and compound constructions: *principal in role* — Alice as manager; *delegation* — Alice for Bob; *conjunction* — Alice and Bob. Conjunction often expresses implicit access rules: 'Alice acting as branch manager plus Bob as a member of the group of branch accountants'.

That's only the beginning. Names also apply to services (such as NFS, or a public key infrastructure) and channels (which might mean wires, ports, or crypto keys). The same name might refer to different roles: 'Alice as a computer game player' ought to have less privilege than 'Alice the system administrator'. The usual abstraction used in the security literature is to treat them as different principals. This all means that there's no easy mapping between names and principals.

Finally, there are functional tensions which come from the underlying business processes rather than from system design. Businesses mainly want to get paid, while governments want to identify people uniquely. In effect, business wants a credit card number while government wants a passport number. Building systems which try to be both — as many governments are trying to encourage — is a tar-pit. There are many semantic differences. You can show your passport to a million people, if you wish, but you had better not try that with a credit card. Banks want to open accounts for anyone who turns up with some money; governments want them to verify people's identity carefully in order to discourage money laundering. The list is a long one.

6.5 Summary

Many secure distributed systems have incurred huge costs, or developed serious vulnerabilities, because their designers ignored the basic lessons of how to build (and how not to build) distributed systems. Most of these lessons are still valid, and there are more to add.

A large number of security breaches are concurrency failures of one kind or another; systems use old data, make updates inconsistently or in the wrong order, or assume that data are consistent when they aren't and can't be. Knowing the right time is harder than it seems.

Fault tolerance and failure recovery are critical. Providing the ability to recover from security failures, and random physical disasters, is the main purpose of the protection budget for many organisations. At a more technical level, there are significant interactions between protection and resilience mechanisms. Byzantine failure — where defective processes conspire, rather than failing randomly — is an issue, and interacts with our choice of cryptographic tools. There are many different flavors of redundancy, and we have to use the right combination. We need to protect not just against failures and attempted manipulation, but also against deliberate attempts to deny service which may often be part of larger attack plans.

Many problems also arise from trying to make a name do too much, or making assumptions about it which don't hold outside of one particular system, or culture, or jurisdiction. For example, it should be possible to revoke a user's access to a system by cancelling their user name without getting sued on account of other functions being revoked. The simplest solution is often to assign each principal a unique identifier used for no other purpose, such as a bank account number or a system logon name. But many problems arise when merging two systems that use naming schemes that are incompatible for some reason. Sometimes this merging can even happen by accident — an example being when two systems use a common combination such as 'name plus date of birth' to track individuals, but in different ways.

Research Problems

In the research community, secure distributed systems tend to have been discussed as a side issue by experts on communications protocols and operating systems, rather than as a discipline in its own right. So it is a relatively open field, and one still holds much promise.

There are many technical issues which I've touched on in this chapter, such as how we design secure time protocols and the complexities of naming. But perhaps the most important research problem is to work out how to design systems that are resilient in the face of malice, that degrade gracefully, and whose security can be recovered simply once the attack is past. This may mean revisiting the definition of convergent applications. Under what conditions can one recover neatly from corrupt security state?

What lessons do we need to learn from the onset of phishing and keylogging attacks on electronic banking, which mean that at any given time a small (but nonzero) proportion of customer accounts will be under criminal control? Do we have to rework recovery (which in its classic form explores how to rebuild databases from backup tapes) into resilience, and if so how do we handle the tensions with the classic notions of atomicity, consistency, isolation and durability as the keys to convergence in distributed systems? What interactions can there be between resilience mechanisms and the various protection technologies? In what respects should the protection and resilience mechanisms be aligned, and in what respects should they be separated? What other pieces are missing from the jigsaw?

Further Reading

There are many books on distributed systems; I've found Mullender [912] to be helpful and thought-provoking for graduate students, while the textbook we recommend to our undergraduates by Bacon [104] is also worth reading. Geraint Price has a survey of the literature on the interaction between fault tolerance and security [1043]. The research literature on concurrency, such as the SIGMOD conferences, has occasional gems. There is also a 2003 report from the U.S. National Research Council, *'Who Goes There? Authentication Through the Lens of Privacy'* which discusses the tradeoffs between authentication and privacy, and how they tend to scale poorly [710].

Economics

The great fortunes of the information age lie in the hands of companies that have established proprietary architectures that are used by a large installed base of locked-in customers.

— Carl Shapiro and Hal Varian

There are two things I am sure of after all these years: there is a growing societal need for high assurance software, and market forces are never going to provide it.

— Earl Boebert

If you try to buck the markets, then the markets will buck you.

— Margaret Thatcher

7.1   Introduction

The economics of information security has recently become a thriving and fast-moving discipline. We started to realise round about 2000 that many security system failures weren't due to technical errors so much as to wrong incentives: the classic case is where the people who guard a system are not the people who suffer when it fails. Indeed, security mechanisms are often designed quite deliberately to shift liability, which often leads to trouble.

Economics has always been important to engineering, at the raw level of cost accounting; a good engineer was one who could build a bridge safely with a thousand tons of concrete when everyone else used two thousand tons. But the perverse incentives that arise in complex systems with multiple owners make economic questions both more important and more subtle for the security engineer. Truly global-scale systems like the Internet arise from the actions of millions of independent principals with divergent interests; we hope that reasonable global outcomes will result from selfish local actions. In general, people won't do something unless they have an incentive to. Markets are often the best guide we have to what sort of mechanisms work, or fail. Markets also fail; the computer industry has been dogged by monopolies since its earliest days. The reasons for this are now understood, and their interaction with security is starting to be. When someone asks 'Why is Microsoft software insecure?' we can now give a principled answer rather than simply cursing Redmond as a form of bad weather.

The new field of security economics provides valuable insights not just into 'security' topics such as privacy, bugs, spam, and phishing, but into more general areas such as system dependability. For example, what's the optimal balance of effort by programmers and testers? (For the answer, see section 7.5.1 below.) It also enables us to analyse the policy problems that security technology increasingly throws up — on issues like digital rights management. Where protection mechanisms are used by the system designer to control the owner of a machine, rather than to protect her against outside enemies, questions of competition policy and consumer rights follow, which economics provides the language to discuss. There are also questions of the balance between public and private action. Network insecurity is somewhat like air pollution or congestion, in that people who connect insecure machines to the Internet do not bear the full consequences of their actions. So how much of the protection effort can (or should) be left to individuals, and how much should be borne by vendors, regulators or the police?

7.2   Classical Economics

Modern economics is an enormous field covering many different aspects of human behaviour. The parts of it that (so far) have found application in security are largely drawn from microeconomics and game theory. I'll discuss game theory in the next section; here, I'll give a helicopter tour of the most relevant ideas from microeconomics. The object of the exercise is not to provide a tutorial on economics, or even on information economics — for that, I recommend you read Carl Shapiro and Hal Varian's book 'Information Rules' [1159] — but to familiarise you with the essential terminology and ideas, so we can move on to discuss security economics.

The modern subject started in the 18th century when the industrial revolution and growing trade changed the world, and people wanted to understand why. In 1776, Adam Smith's classic *'The Wealth of Nations'* [1192] provided a first draft: he explained how rational self-interest in a free market economy leads to economic wellbeing. Specialisation leads to productivity gains at all levels from a small factory to international trade, and the self-interested striving of many individuals and firms drives progress, as people must produce something others value to survive in a competitive market. In his famous phrase, 'It is not from the benevolence of the butcher, the brewer, or the baker, that we can expect our dinner, but from their regard to their own interest'.

These ideas were refined by nineteenth-century economists; David Ricardo clarified and strengthened Smith's arguments in favour of free trade, Stanley Jevons, Léon Walras and Carl Menger built detailed models of supply and demand, and by the end of the century Alfred Marshall had combined models of supply and demand in markets for goods, labour and capital into an overarching 'classical' model in which, at equilibrium, all the excess profits would be competed away and the economy would be functioning efficiently. By 1948, Kenneth Arrow and Gérard Debreu had put this on a rigorous mathematical foundation by proving that markets give efficient outcomes, subject to certain conditions. Much of the interest in economics — especially to the computer industry, and to security folks in particular — comes from the circumstances in which these conditions aren't met, giving rise to monopolies and other problems.

7.2.1 Monopoly

A rapid way into the subject is to consider a simple textbook case of monopoly. Suppose we have a market for apartments in a university town, and the students have different incomes. We might have one rich student able to pay $4000 a month, maybe 300 people willing to pay $2000 a month, and (to give us round numbers) 1000 prepared to pay $1000 a month. That gives us the *demand curve* shown in Figure 7.1 below.

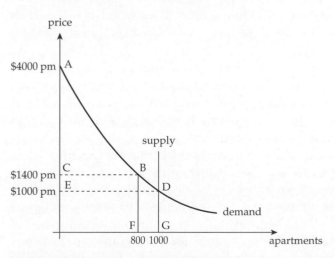

Figure 7.1: The market for apartments

So if there are 1000 apartments being let by many competing landlords, the market-clearing price will be at the intersection of the demand curve with the vertical supply curve, namely $1000. But suppose the market is rigged — say the landlords have set up a cartel, or the university makes its students rent through a tied agency. For simplicity let's assume a single monopolist landlord. He examines the demand curve, and notices that if he rents out only 800 apartments, he can get $1400 per month for each of them. Now 800 times $1400 is $1,120,000 per month, which is more than the million dollars a month he'll make from the market price at $1000. (Economists would say that his 'revenue box' is CBFO rather than EDGO.) So he sets an artificially high price, and 200 apartments remain empty.

This is clearly inefficient, and the Italian economist Vilfredo Pareto invented a neat way to formalise this. A *Pareto improvement* is any change that would make some people better off without making anyone else worse off, and an allocation is *Pareto efficient* if there isn't any Pareto improvement available. Here, the allocation is not efficient, as the monopolist could rent out one empty apartment to anyone at a lower price, making both him and them better off. Now Pareto efficiency is a rather weak criterion; both perfect communism (everyone gets the same income) and perfect dictatorship (the President gets all the income) are Pareto-efficient. In neither case can you make anyone better off without making someone worse off! Yet the simple monopoly described here is not efficient even in this very weak sense.

So what can the monopolist do? There is one possibility — if he can charge everyone a different price, then he can set each student's rent at exactly what they are prepared to pay. We call such a landlord a *discriminating monopolist*; he charges the rich student exactly $4000, and so on down to the 1000th student whom he charges exactly $1000. The same students get apartments as before, yet almost all of them are worse off. The rich student loses $3000, money that he was prepared to pay but previously didn't have to; economists refer to this money he saved as *surplus*. In effect, the discriminating monopolist manages to extract all the consumer surplus.

Merchants have tried to price-discriminate since antiquity. The carpet seller in Damascus who offers to 'make a very special price, just for you' is playing this game, as is Microsoft in offering seven different versions of Vista at different price points, and an airline in selling first, business and cattle class seats. The extent to which firms can do this depends on a number of factors, principally their market power and the amount of information they have. Market power is a measure of how close a merchant is to being a monopolist; under monopoly the merchant is a *price setter* while under perfect competition he simply has to accept whatever price the market establishes (he is a *price taker*). Technology tends to increase market power while reducing the cost of information about customers at the same time, and this combination is one of the main factors eroding privacy in the modern world.

7.2.2 Public Goods

A second type of market failure occurs when everyone gets the same quantity of some good, whether they want it or not. Classic examples are air quality, national defense and scientific research. Economists call these *public goods*, and the formal definition is that they are goods which are non-rivalrous (my using them doesn't mean there's less available for you) and non-excludable (there's no practical way to exclude people from consuming them). Uncoordinated markets are generally unable to provide public goods in socially optimal quantities.

Public goods may be supplied by governments directly, as in the case of national defense, or by using indirect mechanisms to coordinate markets. The classic example is laws on patents and copyrights to encourage people to produce inventions, literary works and musical compositions by giving them a temporary monopoly — by making the goods in question excludable for a limited period of time. Very often, public goods are provided by some mix of public and private action; scientific research is done in universities that get some public subsidy, earn some income from student fees, and get some research contracts from industry (where industry may get patents on the useful inventions while the underlying scientific research gets published for all to use). The mix can be controversial; the debate on global warming sets people who want direct government action in the form of a 'carbon tax' (which would be simple and easy to enforce) against others who want a 'cap and trade' system whereby firms and countries can trade licenses to emit carbon (which in a perfect world would cause emission reductions by the firms who could do so most cheaply, but which might well be more open to abuse and evasion).

The importance of this for us is that many aspects of security are public goods. I do not have an anti-aircraft gun on the roof of my house; air-defense threats come from a small number of actors, and are most efficiently dealt with by government action. So what about Internet security? Certainly there are strong externalities involved, and people who connect insecure machines to the Internet end up dumping costs on others, just like people who burn polluting coal fires. So what should we do about it? One might imagine a government tax on vulnerabilities, with rewards paid to researchers who discover them and larger fines imposed on the firms whose software contained them. Again, one of the early papers on security economics suggested a vulnerability cap-and-trade system; vendors who could not be bothered to make their software secure could buy permits from other vendors who were making the effort to tighten up their products [256]. (Both arrangements would be resisted by the free software community!) But is air pollution the right analogy — or air defense?

Threats such as viruses and spam used to come from a large number of small actors, but since about 2004 we've seen a lot of consolidation as malware writers and users have become commercial. By 2007, the number of serious spammers had dropped to the point that ISPs see significant fluctuations in overall spam volumes as the big spammers run particular campaigns — there is no law of large numbers operating any more [305]. This suggests a different and perhaps more centralised strategy. If our air-defense threat in 1987 was mainly the Russian airforce, and our cyber-defense threat in 2007 is mainly from a small number of Russian gangs, and they are imposing large costs on US and European Internet users and companies, then state action may be needed now as it was then. Instead of telling us to buy anti-virus software, our governments could be putting pressure on the Russians to round up and jail their cyber-gangsters. I'll discuss this in greater detail in Part III; for now, it should be clear that concepts such as 'monopoly' and 'public goods' are important to the security engineer — and indeed to everyone who works in IT. Just think of the two operating systems that dominate the world's desktops and server farms: Windows is a monopoly, while the common Unix systems (Linux and OpenBSD) are public goods maintained by volunteers. Why should this be so? Why are markets for information goods and services so odd?

7.3   Information Economics

One of the insights from the nineteenth-century economists Jevons and Menger is that the price of a good, at equilibrium, is the marginal cost of production. When coal cost nine shillings a ton in 1870, that didn't mean that every mine dug coal at this price, merely that the marginal producers — those who were only just managing to stay in business — could sell at that price. If the price went down, these mines would close; if it went up, other, even more marginal mines, would open. That's how supply responded to changes in demand.

7.3.1   The Price of Information

So in a competitive equilibrium, the price of information should be its marginal cost of production. But that is almost zero! This explains why there is so much information available for free in the Internet; zero is its fair price. If two or more suppliers compete to offer an operating system, or a map, or an encyclopaedia, that they can duplicate for no cost, then the incentive will be for them to keep on cutting their prices without limit. This is what happened with encyclopaedias; the Britannica used to cost $1,600 for 32 volumes; then Microsoft brought out Encarta for $49.95, forcing Britannica to produce a cheap CD edition; and now we have Wikipedia for free [1159]. One firm after another has had to move to a business model in which the goods are given away free, and the money comes from advertising or in some parallel market.

Linux companies give away an operating system, and make their money from support; many Linux developers give their time free to the project while at college, as their contribution strengthens their CV and helps them get a good job when they graduate.

Many other industries with high fixed costs and low marginal costs moved to an advertising or service model; think terrestrial TV. Others have moved in this direction: most newspapers made most of their money from advertising, and so have had little difficulty moving to free online editions plus paid paper editions, all putting the lucrative ads in front of eyeballs. Yet other industries, such as airlines and hotels, tended instead to become monopolists who try to dominate particular routes or areas and to charge different prices to different customers.

So what other characteristics of the information goods and services industries are particularly important?

1. There are often *network externalities*, whereby the value of a network grows more than linearly in the number of users. For example, the more people used fax machines in the 1980s, the more useful they became, until round about 1985 fax machines suddenly took off; every business needed one. Much the same happened with email in about 1995. Network effects also apply to services more generally: anyone wanting to auction some goods will usually go to the largest auction house, as it will attract more bidders. They also apply to software: firms develop software for Windows so they will have access to more users than they would if they developed for Linux or Mac, and users for their part prefer Windows because there's more software for it. (This is called a *two-sided market*.)

2. There is often technical lock-in stemming from interoperability. Once a software firm is committed to using Windows as a platform for its product, it can be expensive to change; for users, too, changing platforms can be expensive. They have to buy new software, convert files (if they can), and retrain themselves.

These features separately can lead to industries with dominant firms; together, they are even more likely to. If users simply want to be compatible with other users (and software vendors) then they will logically buy from the vendor they expect to win the biggest market share.

7.3.2 The Value of Lock-In

There is an interesting result, due to Shapiro and Varian: that the value of a software company is the total lock-in (due to both technical and network effects) of all its customers [1159]. To see how this might work, consider a firm with 100 staff each using Office, for which it has paid $500 per copy. It could save this $50,000 by moving to OpenOffice, so if the costs of installing this product, retraining its staff, converting files and so on — in other words the total switching costs — were less than $50,000, it would switch. But if the costs of switching were more than $50,000, then Microsoft would put up its prices.

Technical lock-in existed before, but the move to the digital economy has made it much more significant. If you own a Volvo car, you are locked in to Volvo spares and accessories; but when you're fed up with it you can always trade it in for a Mercedes. But if you own an Apple Mac, you'll have Mac software, a Mac printer, and quite possibly thousands of music tracks that you've ripped to iTunes. You'd also have to learn to use different commands and interfaces. Moving to Windows would be much more painful than just shelling out $700 for a new laptop. You'd have to retrain yourself; you'd have to throw away Office for Mac and buy Office for Windows. And if you'd bought a lot of music tracks from the iTunes music store, it could be more painful still (you'd probably decide to keep your iPod with your new Windows machine rather than moving to a Windows music player, even though the iPod works better with the Mac). This shows why lock-in can be so durable; although each piece of equipment — be it a Mac laptop, an iPod, or a printer — wears out, the lock-in persists in the complementary relationship between them. And this doesn't just apply to PC platforms, but to ISPs; commercial software systems such as databases; equipment such as telephone exchanges; and various online services.

This is why so much effort gets expended in standards wars and antitrust suits. It's also why so many security mechanisms now aim at controlling compatibility. In such cases, the likely hackers are not malicious outsiders, but the owners of the equipment, or new firms trying to challenge the incumbent by making compatible products. The issues are made more complex by the fact that innovation is often incremental, and products succeed when new firms find killer applications for them [607]. The PC, for example, was designed by IBM as a machine to run spreadsheets; if they had locked it down to this application alone, then a massive opportunity would have been lost. Indeed, the fact that the IBM PC was more open than the Apple Mac was a factor in its becoming the dominant desktop platform.

So the law in many countries gives companies a right to reverse-engineer their competitors' products for compatibility [1110]. More and more, security mechanisms are being used to try to circumvent that law: incumbents try to lock down their platforms using cryptography and tamper-resistance so that even if competitors have the legal right to try to reverse engineer them, they are not always going to succeed in practice. Many businesses are seeing brutal power struggles for control of the supply chain; for example, mobile phone makers' attempts to introduce sophisticated DRM into their handsets were frustrated by network operators determined to prevent the handset makers from establishing business relationships directly with their customers. These struggles set the scene in which more and more security products succeed or fail.

7.3.3 Asymmetric Information

Another of the ways in which markets can fail, beyond monopoly and public goods, is when some principals know more than others. The study of *asymmetric information* was kicked off by a famous paper in 1970 on the 'market for lemons' [19], for which George Akerlof won a Nobel prize. It presents the following simple yet profound insight: suppose that there are 100 used cars for sale in a town: 50 well-maintained cars worth $2000 each, and 50 'lemons' worth $1000. The sellers know which is which, but the buyers don't. What is the market price of a used car? You might think $1500; but at that price no good cars will be offered for sale. So the market price will be close to $1000. This is one reason poor security products predominate. When users can't tell good from bad, they might as well buy a cheap antivirus product for $10 as a better one for $20, and we may expect a race to the bottom on price.

A further distinction can be drawn between hidden information and hidden action. For example, Volvo has a reputation for building safe cars that survive accidents well, yet it is well known that Volvo drivers have more accidents. Is this because people who know they're bad drivers buy Volvos so they're less likely to get killed, or because people in Volvos drive faster? The first is the hidden-information case, also known as *adverse selection*, and the second is the hidden-action case, also known as *moral hazard*. Both effects are important in security, and both may combine in specific cases. (In the case of drivers, there seems to be a growing consensus that people adjust their driving behaviour to keep their risk exposure to the level with which they are comfortable. This also explains why mandatory seat-belt laws tend not to save lives overall, merely to move fatalities from vehicle occupants to pedestrians and cyclists [10].)

Asymmetric information explains many market failures in the real world, from low prices in used-car markets to the difficulty that older people have in getting insurance on reasonable terms (people who know they're sick will tend to buy more of it, making it uneconomic for the healthy). It tends to lead to surveillance or rationing.

7.4 Game Theory

There are really just two ways to get something you want if you can't find or make it yourself. You either make something useful and trade it; or you take what you need, by force, by the ballot box or whatever. Choices between cooperation and conflict are made every day at all sorts of levels, by both humans and animals.

The main tool we can use to study and analyse them is game theory, which I will define as 'the study of problems of cooperation and conflict among independent decision makers'. We're interested in games of strategy rather than games of chance, and we're less interested in games of perfect information (such as chess) than in games of imperfect information, which can be much more interesting. We try to get to the core of games by abstracting away much of the detail. For example, consider the school playground game of 'matching pennies': Alice and Bob toss coins and reveal them simultaneously, upon which Alice gets Bob's penny if they're different and Bob gets Alice's penny if they're the same. I'll write this as shown in Figure 7.2:

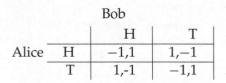

		Bob	
		H	T
Alice	H	−1,1	1,−1
	T	1,-1	−1,1

Figure 7.2: Matching pennies

Each entry in the table shows first Alice's outcome and then Bob's outcome. Thus if the coins fall (H,H) Alice loses a penny and Bob gains a penny. This is an example of a *zero-sum game*: Alice's gain is Bob's loss.

Often we can solve a game quickly by writing out a *payoff matrix* like this. Here's an example (Figure 7.3):

		Bob	
		Left	Right
Alice	Top	1,2	0,1
	Bottom	2,1	1,0

Figure 7.3: Dominant strategy equilibrium

In this game, no matter what Bob plays, Alice is better off playing 'Bottom'; and no matter what Alice plays, Bob is better off playing 'Left'. Each player has a *dominant strategy* — an optimal choice regardless of what the other does. So Alice's strategy should be a constant 'Bottom' and Bob's a constant 'Left'. (A *strategy* in game theory is just an algorithm that takes a game state and outputs a move.) We call this a *dominant strategy equilibrium*.

Another example is shown in Figure 7.4:

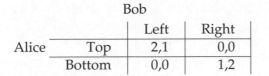

Figure 7.4: Nash equilibrium

Here each player's optimal strategy depends on what the other player does, or (perhaps more accurately) what they think the other player will do. We say that two strategies are in Nash equilibrium when Alice's choice is optimal given Bob's, and vice versa. Here there are two symmetric Nash equilibria, at top left and bottom right. You can think of them as being like local optima while a dominant strategy equilibrium is a global optimum.

7.4.1   The Prisoners' Dilemma

We're now ready to look at a famous problem posed in 1950 by John Nash, and for which he won the Nobel. It applies to many situations from international trade negotiations to free-riding in peer-to-peer file-sharing systems to cooperation between hunting animals, and Nash first studied it in the context of US and USSR defense spending; his employer, the Rand corporation, was paid to think about possible strategies in nuclear war. However, Nash presented it using the following simple example.

Two prisoners are arrested on suspicion of planning a bank robbery. The police interview them separately and tell each of them the following: "If neither of you confesses you'll each get a year for carrying a concealed firearm without a permit. If one of you confesses, he'll go free and the other will get 6 years for conspiracy to rob. If both of you confess, you will each get three years."

What should the prisoners do? Let's write the game out formally, as shown in Figure 7.5:

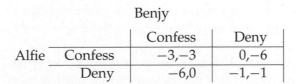

Figure 7.5: The prisoners' dilemma

When Alfie looks at this table, he will reason as follows: 'If Benjy's going to confess then I should too as then I get 3 years rather than 6; and if he's going to deny then I should still confess as that way I walk rather than doing a year'. Benjy will reason similarly. The two of them will each confess, and get three years each. This is not just a Nash equilibrium; it's a dominant strategy equilibrium. Each prisoner should logically confess regardless of what the other does.

But hang on, you say, if they had agreed to keep quiet then they'll get a year each, which is a better outcome for them! In fact the strategy (deny,deny) is Pareto efficient, while the dominant strategy equilibrium is not. (That's one reason it's useful to have concepts like 'Pareto efficient' and 'dominant strategy equilibrium' rather than just arguing over 'best'.)

So what's the solution? Well, so long as the game is going to be played once only, and this is the only game in town, there isn't a solution. Both prisoners will logically confess and get three years. We can only change this state of affairs if somehow we can change the game itself. There are many possibilities: there can be laws of various kinds from international treaties on trade to the gangster's *omertá*. In practice, a prisoner's dilemma game is changed by altering the rules or the context so as to turn it into another game where the equilibrium is more efficient.

7.4.2 Evolutionary Games

An important class of problems can be solved where the game is played repeatedly — if Alfie and Benjy are career criminals who expect to be dealing with each other again and again. Then of course there can be an incentive for them to cooperate. There are at least two ways of modelling this.

In the 1970s, Bob Axelrod started thinking about how people might play many rounds of prisoners' dilemma. He set up a series of competitions to which people could submit programs, and these programs played each other repeatedly in tournaments. He found that one of the best strategies overall was *tit-for-tat*, which is simply that you cooperate in round one, and at each subsequent round you do to your opponent what he or she did in the previous round [99]. It began to be realised that strategy evolution could explain a lot. For example, in the presence of noise, players tend to get locked into (defect, defect) whenever one player's cooperative behaviour is misread by the other as defection. So in this case it helps to 'forgive' the other player from time to time.

Simultaneously, a parallel approach was opened up by John Maynard Smith and George Price [848]. They considered what would happen if you had a mixed population of aggressive and docile individuals, 'hawks' and 'doves', with the behaviour that doves cooperate; hawks take food from doves; and hawks fight, with a risk of death. Suppose the value of the food at each interaction is V and the risk of death in a hawk fight per encounter is C. Then the payoff matrix looks like Figure 7.6:

	Hawk	Dove
Hawk	$\frac{V-C}{2}, \frac{V-C}{2}$	$V, 0$
Dove	$0, V$	$\frac{V}{2}, \frac{V}{2}$

Figure 7.6: The hawk-dove game

Here, if $V > C$, the whole population will become hawk, as that's the dominant strategy, but if $C > V$ (fighting is too expensive) then there is an equilibrium where the probability p that a bird is a hawk sets the hawk payoff and the dove payoff equal, that is

$$p\frac{V-C}{2} + (1-p)V = (1-p)\frac{V}{2}$$

which is solved by $p = V/C$. In other words, you can have aggressive and docile individuals coexisting in a population, and the proportion of aggressive individuals will at equilibrium be a function of the costs of aggression; the more dangerous it is, the fewer such individuals there will be. Of course, the costs can change over time, and diversity is a good thing in evolutionary terms as a society with a minority of combative individuals may be at an advantage when war breaks out. Again, it takes generations for a society to move to equilibrium. Perhaps our current incidence of aggression is too high because it reflects conditions in the Dark Ages, or even on the African highveld 500,000 years ago[1].

This neat insight, along with Bob Axelrod's simulation methodology for tackling problems that don't have a neat algebraic solution, got many people from moral philosophers to students of animal behaviour interested in evolutionary game theory. They give deep insights into how cooperation evolved. It turns out that many primates have an inbuilt sense of fairness and punish individuals who are seen to be cheating — the instinct for vengeance is part of the mechanism to enforce sociality. Fairness can operate in a number of different ways at different levels. For example, the philosopher Brian Skyrms found that doves can get a better result against hawks if they can recognise each other and interact preferentially, giving a model for how social movements such as freemasons and maybe even some religions establish themselves [1188].

---

[1] A number of leading anthropologists believe that, until recent times, tribal warfare was endemic among human societies [777].

Of course, the basic idea behind tit-for-tat goes back a long way. The Old Testament has 'An eye for an eye' and the New Testament 'Do unto others as you'd have them do unto you'; the latter formulation is, of course, more fault-tolerant, and versions of it can be found in Aristotle, in Confucius and elsewhere. More recently, Thomas Hobbes used primitive prisoners'-dilemma-style arguments in the seventeenth century to justify the existence of a state without the Divine Right of Kings.

The applications of evolutionary game theory keep on growing. Since 9/11, for example, there has been interest in whether hawk-dove games explain the ability of fundamentalists to take over discourse in religions at a time of stress. From the economists' viewpoint, evolutionary games explain why cartel-like behaviour can appear in industries even where there are no secret deals being done in smoke-filled rooms. For example, if there are three airlines operating a profitable route, and one lowers its prices to compete for volume, the others may well respond by cutting prices even more sharply to punish it and make the route unprofitable, in the hope that the discounts will be discontinued and everyone can go back to gouging the customer. And there are some interesting applications in security, too, which I'll come to later.

7.5   The Economics of Security and Dependability

Economists used to be well aware of the interaction between economics and security; rich nations could afford big armies. But nowadays a web search on 'economics' and 'security' turns up relatively few articles. The main reason is that, after 1945, economists drifted apart from people working on strategic studies; nuclear weapons were thought to decouple national survival from economic power [839]. A secondary factor may have been that the USA confronted the USSR over security, but Japan and the EU over trade. It has been left to the information security world to re-establish the connection.

One of the observations that rekindled interest in security economics came from banking. In the USA, banks are generally liable for the costs of card fraud; when a customer disputes a transaction, the bank must either show she is trying to cheat it, or refund her money. In the UK, banks generally got away with claiming that their systems were 'secure', and telling customers who complained that they must be mistaken or lying. 'Lucky bankers,' you might think; yet UK banks spent more on security and suffered more fraud. This was probably a moral-hazard effect: UK bank staff knew that customer complaints would not be taken seriously, so they became lazy and careless, leading to an epidemic of fraud [33, 34].

Another was that people were not spending as much money on anti-virus software as the vendors might have hoped. Now a typical virus payload then was a service-denial attack on Microsoft; and while a rational consumer might spend $20 to stop a virus trashing her hard disk, she will be less likely to do so just to protect a wealthy corporation [1290]. There are many other examples, such as hospital systems bought by medical directors and administrators that look after their interests but don't protect patient privacy. The picture that started to emerge was of system security failing because the people guarding a system were not the people who suffered the costs of failure, or of particular types of failure. Sometimes, as we'll see, security mechanisms are used to dump risks on others, and if you are one of these others you'd be better off with an insecure system. Put differently, security is often not a scalar, but a power relationship; the principals who control what it means in a given system often use it to advance their own interests.

This was the initial insight. But once we started studying security economics seriously, we found that there's a lot more to it than that.

7.5.1 Weakest Link, or Sum of Efforts?

The late Jack Hirshleifer, the founder of conflict theory, told the story of Anarchia, an island whose flood defences were constructed by individual families who each maintained a section of the flood wall. The island's flood defence thus depended on the weakest link, that is, the laziest family. He compared this with a city whose defences against missile attack depend on the single best defensive shot [609]. Another example of best-shot is medieval warfare, where there was on occasion a single combat between the two armies' champions. Hal Varian extended this model to three cases of interest to the dependability of information systems — where performance depends on the minimum effort, the best effort, or the sum-of-efforts [1292]. This last case, the sum-of-efforts, is the modern model for warfare: we pay our taxes and the government hires soldiers. It's a lot more efficient than best-shot (where most people will free-ride behind the heroes), and that in turn is miles better than weakest-link (where everyone will free-ride behind the laziest).

Program correctness can depend on minimum effort (the most careless programmer introducing a vulnerability) while software vulnerability testing may depend on the sum of everyone's efforts. Security may also depend on the best effort — the actions taken by an individual champion such as a security architect. As more agents are added, systems become more reliable in the total-effort case but less reliable in the weakest-link case. What are the implications? Well, software companies should hire more software testers and fewer (but more competent) programmers.

7.5.2 Managing the Patching Cycle

There has been much debate about 'open source security', and more generally whether actively seeking and disclosing vulnerabilities is socially desirable.

It's a debate that has flared up again and again; as we saw in the preface, the Victorians agonised over whether it was socially responsible to publish books about lockpicking, and eventually concluded that it was [1257]. People have worried more recently about the online availability of (for example) the US Army Improvised Munitions Handbook [1271]; is the risk of helping terrorists sufficient to justify online censorship?

Security economics provides both a theoretical and a quantitative framework for discussing some issues of this kind. I showed in 2002 that, under standard assumptions of reliability growth, open systems and proprietary systems are just as secure as each other; opening up a system helps the attackers and defenders equally [54]. Thus the open-security question will often be an empirical one, turning on the extent to which a given real system follows the standard model.

In 2004, Eric Rescorla argued that for software with many latent vulnerabilities, removing one bug makes little difference to the likelihood of an attacker finding another one later. Since exploits are often based on vulnerabilities inferred from patches, he argued against disclosure and frequent patching unless the same vulnerabilities are likely to be rediscovered [1071]. Ashish Arora and others responded with data showing that public disclosure made vendors respond with fixes more quickly; attacks increased to begin with, but reported vulnerabilities declined over time [88]. In 2006, Andy Ozment and Stuart Schechter found that the rate at which unique vulnerabilities were disclosed for the core OpenBSD operating system has decreased over a six-year period [998]. These results support the current system of responsible disclosure whereby people who discover vulnerabilities report them to CERT, which reports them on to vendors, and publicises them once patches are shipped.

This is by no means all that there is to say about the economics of dependability. There are tensions between vendors and their customers over the frequency and timing of patch release; issues with complementers; difficulties with metrics; companies such as iDefense and TippingPoint that buy and sell information on vulnerabilities; and even concerns that intelligence agencies with privileged access to bug reports use them for zero-day exploits against other countries' systems. I'll come back to all this in Part III.

7.5.3 Why Is Windows So Insecure?

The micromanagement of the patching cycle begs a deeper question: why are there so many bugs in the first place? In particular, why is Windows so insecure, despite Microsoft's dominant market position? It's possible to write much better software, and there are fields such as defense and healthcare where a serious effort is made to produce dependable systems. Why do we not see a comparable effort made with commodity platforms, especially since Microsoft has no real competitors?

To be honest, Microsoft's software security is improving. Windows 95 was dreadful, Windows 98 slightly better, and the improvement's continued through NT, XP and Vista. But the attackers are getting better too, and the protection in Vista isn't all for the user's benefit. As Peter Gutmann points out, enormous effort has gone into protecting premium video content, and almost no effort into protecting users' credit card numbers [570]. The same pattern has also been seen in other platform products, from the old IBM mainframe operating systems through telephone exchange switches to the Symbian operating system for mobile phones. Products are insecure at first, and although they improve over time, many of the new security features are for the vendor's benefit as much as the user's.

By now, you should not find this surprising. The combination of high fixed and low marginal costs, network effects and technical lock-in makes platform markets particularly likely to be dominated by single vendors, who stand to gain vast fortunes if they can win the race to dominate the market. In such a race, the notorious Microsoft philosophy of the 1990s — 'ship it Tuesday and get it right by version 3' — is perfectly rational behaviour. In such a race, the platform vendor must appeal at least as much to complementers — to the software companies who decide whether to write applications for its platform or for someone else's. Security gets in the way of applications, and it tends to be a lemons market anyway. So the rational vendor will enable (indeed encourage) all applications to run as root, until his position is secure. Then he will add more security — but there will still be a strong incentive to engineer it in such a way as to maximise customer lock-in, or to appeal to complementers in new markets such as digital media.

From the viewpoint of the consumer, markets with lock-in are often 'bargains then rip-offs'. You buy a nice new printer for $39.95, then find to your disgust after just a few months that you need two new printer cartridges for $19.95 each. You wonder whether you'd not be better off just buying a new printer. From the viewpoint of the application developer, markets with standards races based on lock-in look a bit like this. At first it's really easy to write code for them; later on, once you're committed, there are many more hoops to jump through. From the viewpoint of the poor consumer, they could be described as 'poor security, then security for someone else'.

Sometimes it can be worse than that. When racing to establish a dominant position, vendors are likely to engineer their products so that the cost of managing such security as there is falls on the user, rather than on the application developers. A classic example is SSL/TLS encryption. This was adopted in the mid-1990s as Microsoft and Netscape battled for dominance of the browser market. As I discussed in Chapter 2, SSL leaves it up to the user to assess the certificate offered by a web site and decide whether to trust it; and this has turned out to facilitate all kinds of phishing and other attacks. Yet dumping the compliance costs on the user made perfect sense at the time, and competing protocols such as SET, that would have required heavier investment by banks and merchants, were allowed to wither on the vine [357]. The world has ended up not just with a quite insecure system of Internet payments, but with widespread liability dumping that makes progress towards a better system difficult. Too much of the infrastructure has weakest-link rather than sum-of-efforts security.

7.5.4   Economics of Privacy

The big conundrum with privacy is that people say that they value privacy, yet act otherwise. If you stop people in the street and ask them their views, about a third say they are privacy fundamentalists and will never hand over their personal information to marketers or anyone else; about a third say they don't care; and about a third are in the middle, saying they'd take a pragmatic view of the risks and benefits of any disclosure. However, the behavior that people exhibit via their shopping behavior — both online and offline — is quite different; the great majority of people pay little heed to privacy, and will give away the most sensitive information for little benefit. Privacy-enhancing technologies have been offered for sale by various firms, yet most have failed in the marketplace. Why should this be?

Privacy is one aspect of information security that interested economists before 2000. In 1978, Richard Posner defined privacy in terms of secrecy [1035], and the following year extended this to seclusion [1036]. In 1980, Jack Hirshleifer published a seminal paper in which he argued that rather than being about withdrawing from society, privacy was a means of organising society, arising from evolved territorial behavior; internalised respect for property is what allows autonomy to persist in society. These privacy debates in the 1970s led in Europe to generic data-protection laws, while the USA limited itself to a few sector-specific laws such as HIPAA. Economists' appetite for work on privacy was further whetted recently by the Internet, the dotcom boom, and the exploding trade in personal information about online shoppers.

An early modern view of privacy can be found in a 1996 paper by Hal Varian who analysed privacy in terms of information markets [1289]. Consumers want to not be annoyed by irrelevant marketing calls while marketers do not want to waste effort. Yet both are frustrated, because of search costs, externalities and other factors. Varian suggested giving consumers rights in information about themselves, and letting them lease it to marketers with the proviso that it not be resold without permission.

The recent proliferation of complex, information-intensive business models demanded a broader approach. Andrew Odlyzko argued in 2003 that privacy erosion is a consequence of the desire to charge different prices for similar services [981]. Technology is simultaneously increasing both the incentives and the opportunities for price discrimination. Companies can mine online purchases and interactions for data revealing individuals' willingness to pay. From airline yield-management systems to complex and ever-changing software and telecommunications prices, differential pricing is economically efficient — but increasingly resented. Peter Swire argued that we should measure the costs of privacy intrusion more broadly [1237]. If a telesales operator calls 100 prospects, sells three of them insurance, and annoys 80, then the conventional analysis considers only the benefit to the three and to the insurer. However, persistent annoyance causes millions of people to go ex-directory, to not answer the phone during dinner, or to screen calls through an answering machine. The long-run societal harm can be considerable. Several empirical studies have backed this up by examining people's privacy valuations.

My own view on this is that it simply takes time for the public to assimilate the privacy risks. For thirty years or so, IT policy folks have been agonising about the death of privacy, but this remained a geek interest until recently. The significance is now starting to percolate down to sophisticated people like stock-market investors: Alessandro Acquisti and others have found that the stock price of companies reporting a security or privacy breach is likely to fall [8, 265]. It's only when tabloid newspapers and talk-radio shows give lots of coverage to stories of ordinary people who've suffered real harm as a result of 'identity theft' and phishing that the average voter will start to sit up and take notice. There are some early signs that this is starting to happen (for example in the growing number of requests that privacy experts like me get to appear on radio and TV shows). But another behavioural economist, George Loewnstein, points out that people are more sensitive to large changes in their circumstances rather than to small ones: they will get concerned if things suddenly get worse, but not if they get worse gradually. They also become habituated surprisingly easily to bad circumstances that they don't believe they can change.

It may be of particular interest that, in late 2007, the British government suffered spectacular embarrassment when it lost the electronic tax records on all the nation's children and their families — including bank account details — leading to a personal apology in Parliament from the Prime Minister and massive media coverage of subsequent privacy breaches. I'll discuss this in more detail in section 9.4; the privacy economist's interest will be in whether this changes public attitudes in any measurable way over time, and whether attitudes stay changed.

7.5.5 Economics of DRM

Rights-management technologies have also come in for economic scrutiny. Hal Varian pointed out in 2002 that DRM and similar mechanisms were also about tying, bundling and price discrimination; and that their unfettered use could damage competition [1291]. I wrote an FAQ on 'Trusted Computing' in 2003, followed by a research paper, in which I pointed out the potential for competitive abuse of rights management mechanisms; for example, by transferring control of user data from the owner of the machine on which it is stored to the creator of the file in which it is stored, the potential for lock-in is hugely increased [53]. Think of the example above, in which a law firm of 100 fee earners each has a PC on which they install Office for $500. The $50,000 they pay Microsoft is roughly equal to the total costs of switching to (say) OpenOffice, including training, converting files and so on. However, if control of the files moves to its thousands of customers, and the firm now has to contact each customer and request a digital certificate in order to migrate the file, then clearly the switching costs have increased — so you can expect the cost of Office to increase too, over time.

There are some interesting angles on the debate about rights management in music too. In 2004, Felix Oberholzer and Koleman Strumpf published a now-famous paper, in which they examined how music downloads and record sales were correlated [978]. They showed that downloads do not do significant harm to the music industry. Even in the most pessimistic interpretation, five thousand downloads are needed to displace a single album sale, while high-selling albums actually benefit from file sharing. This research was hotly disputed by music-industry spokesmen at the time, but has since been confirmed by Canadian government research that found a positive correlation between downloading and CD sales among peer-to-peer system users, and no correlation among the population as a whole [28].

In January 2005, Hal Varian made a controversial prediction [1293]: that stronger DRM would help system vendors more than the music industry, because the computer industry is more concentrated (with only three serious suppliers of DRM platforms — Microsoft, Sony, and the dominant firm, Apple). The content industry scoffed, but by the end of that year music publishers were protesting that Apple was getting too large a share of the cash from online music sales. As power in the supply chain moved from the music majors to the platform vendors, so power in the music industry appears to be shifting from the majors to the independents, just as airline deregulation favoured aircraft makers and low-cost airlines. This is a striking demonstration of the predictive power of economic analysis. By fighting a non-existent threat, the record industry helped the computer industry forge a weapon that may be its undoing.

7.6 Summary

Many systems fail because the incentives are wrong, rather than because of some technical design mistake. As a result, the security engineer needs to understand basic economics as well as the basics of crypto, protocols, access controls and psychology. Security economics is a rapidly growing research area that explains many of the things that we used to consider just 'bad weather', such as the insecurity of Windows. It constantly throws up fascinating new insights into all sorts of questions from how to optimise the patching cycle through whether people really care about privacy to what legislators might do about DRM.

Research Problems

So far, two areas of economics have been explored for their relevance to security, namely microeconomics and game theory. Behavioural economics (the boundary between economics and psychology) has also started to yield insights. But economics is a vast subject. What other ideas might it give us?

Further Reading

The best initial introduction to information economics is Shapiro and Varian's *'Information Rules'* which remains remarkably fresh and accurate for a book written ten years ago [1159]. I generally recommend that students read this first. For those who want to go on to do research in the subject, I then suggest Hal Varian's textbook *'Intermediate Microeconomics'* which covers the material from an academic viewpoint, with fewer case histories and more mathematics [1284].

The current research in security economics is published mostly at the Workshop on the Economics of Information Security (WEIS), which has been held annually since 2002; details of WEIS, and other relevant events, can be found at [58]. There is a current (2007) survey of the field, that I wrote with Tyler Moore, at [72]. There are two books of collected research papers [257, 548], and a popular account by Bruce Schneier [1129]; I also maintain an Economics and Security Resource Page at `http://www.cl.cam.ac.uk/ rja14/econsec.html`. Two other relevant papers, which are in press as this book goes to print, are a report I'm writing with Rainer Böhme, Richard Clayton and Tyler Moore on security economics in the European internal market [62], and an OECD report by Michel van Eeten and colleagues that reports extensive interviews with information security stakeholders about the incentives they face in practice [420].

A number of economists study related areas. I mentioned Jack Hirshleifer's conflict theory; a number of his papers are available in a book [610]. Another really important strand is the economics of crime, which was kick-started by Gary Becker [138], and has recently been popularised by Steve Levitt and

Stephen Dubner's 'Freakonomics' [787]. Much of this analyses volume crime by deprived young males, an issue to which I'll return in Chapter 11; but some scholars have also studied organised crime [392, 473]. As computer crime is increasingly driven by the profit motive rather than by ego and bragging rights, we can expect economic analyses to be ever more useful.

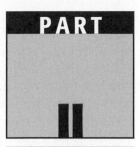

PART

II

In this second part of the book, I describe a large number of applications of secure systems, many of which introduce particular protection concepts or technologies.

There are three broad themes. Chapters 8–10 look at conventional computer security issues, and by discussing what one is trying to do and how it's done in different environments — the military, banks and healthcare — we introduce security policy models which set out the protection concepts that real systems try to implement. We introduce our first detailed case studies. An example is the worldwide network of automatic teller machines, which illustrates many of the problems of transferring familiar protection properties from a bank branch to a global distributed environment using cryptography.

Chapters 10–18 look at the hardware and system engineering aspects of information security. This includes biometrics, the design of various tokens such as smartcards, and the whole panoply of hardware security mechanisms from physical locks through chip-level tamper-resistance and emission security to security printing and seals. New applications that illustrate the technologies are described, ranging from electronic warfare and nuclear weapon control through burglar alarms, truck speed limiters and prepayment gas meters. We end up with a chapter on the security of application programming interfaces, where hardware and software security meet.

The third theme is attacks on networks, and on highly-networked systems. We start off with electronic and information warfare in Chapter 19, as these activities give some of the more extreme examples and show how far techniques of denial, deception and exploitation can be taken by a resourceful opponent under severe operational pressure. It also gives a view of surveillance and intrusion from the intelligence agencies' point of view, and introduces concepts such as anonymity and traffic analysis. We then study the lessons of history by examining frauds on phone systems, and on applications that rely on them, in Chapter 20. This sets the scene for a discussion in Chapter 21 of attacks on computer networks and defensive technologies ranging from firewalls to protocols such as SSH, TLS, IPSEC and Bluetooth. Chapter 22 deals with copyright and DRM, and related topics such as information hiding. Finally, in Chapter 23 I present four vignettes of the 'bleeding edge' of security research in 2007: computer games; web applications (such as auctions, search and social networking); privacy technology (from email anonymity and web proxies to forensics countermeasures); and elections.

One reason for this ordering is to give the chapters a logical progression. Thus, for example, I discuss frauds against magnetic stripe bank cards before going on to describe the smartcards which may replace them and the pay-TV systems which actually use smartcards today.

Sometimes a neat linear ordering isn't possible as a particular technology has evolved through a number of iterations over several applications. In such cases I try to distill what I know into a case history. To keep the book manageable for readers who use it primarily as a reference rather than as a textbook, I have put the more technical material towards the end of each chapter or section: if you get lost at a first reading then do just skip to the next section and carry on.

CHAPTER 8

Multilevel Security

Most high assurance work has been done in the area of kinetic devices and infernal machines that are controlled by stupid robots. As information processing technology becomes more important to society, these concerns spread to areas previously thought inherently harmless, like operating systems.

— Earl Boebert

I brief;
you leak;
he/she commits a criminal offence
by divulging classified information.

— British Civil Service Verb

They constantly try to escape
From the darkness outside and within
By dreaming of systems so perfect that no one will need to be good

— TS Eliot

8.1   Introduction

I mentioned in the introduction that military database systems, which can hold information at a number of different levels of classification (Confidential, Secret, Top Secret, . . .), have to ensure that data can only be read by a principal whose level is at least as high as the data's classification. The policies they implement are known as *multilevel secure* or alternatively as *mandatory access control* or MAC.

Multilevel secure systems are important because:

1. a huge amount of research has been done on them, thanks to military funding for computer science in the USA. So the military model of protection has been worked out in much more detail than any other, and it gives us a lot of examples of the second-order and even third-order effects of implementing a security policy rigorously;

2. although multilevel concepts were originally developed to support confidentiality in military systems, many commercial systems now use multilevel integrity policies. For example, telecomms operators want their billing system to be able to see what's happening in their switching system, but not affect it;

3. recently, products such as Microsoft Vista and Red Hat Linux have started to incorporate mandatory access control mechanisms, and they have also appeared in disguise in digital rights management systems. For example, Red Hat uses SELinux mechanisms developed by the NSA to isolate different servers running on a machine — so that even if your web server is hacked, it doesn't necessarily follow that your DNS server gets taken over too. Vista has a multilevel integrity policy under which Internet Explorer runs by default at 'Low' — which means that even if it gets taken over, the attacker should not be able to change system files, or anything else with a higher integrity level. These mechanisms are still largely invisible to the domestic computer user, but their professional use is increasing;

4. multilevel confidentiality ideas are often applied in environments where they're ineffective or even harmful, because of the huge vested interests and momentum behind them. This can be a contributory factor in the failure of large system projects, especially in the public sector.

Sir Isiah Berlin famously described thinkers as either foxes or hedgehogs: a fox knows many little things, while a hedgehog knows one big thing. The multilevel philosophy is the hedgehog approach to security engineering.

8.2   What Is a Security Policy Model?

Where a top-down approach to security engineering is possible, it will typically take the form of *threat model — security policy — security mechanisms*. The critical, and often neglected, part of this process is the security policy.

By a security policy, we mean a document that expresses clearly and concisely what the protection mechanisms are to achieve. It is driven by our understanding of threats, and in turn drives our system design. It will often take the form of statements about which users may access which data. It plays the same role in specifying the system's protection requirements, and evaluating whether they have been met, that the system specification does for general functionality. Indeed, a security policy may be part of a system specification, and like the specification its primary function is to communicate.

Many organizations use the phrase 'security policy' to mean a collection of vapid statements. Figure 8.1 gives a simple example:

Megacorp Inc security policy

1. This policy is approved by Management.

2. All staff shall obey this security policy.

3. Data shall be available only to those with a 'need-to-know'.

4. All breaches of this policy shall be reported at once to Security.

Figure 8.1: A typical corporate information security policy

This sort of waffle is very common but is useless to the security engineer.

Its first failing is it dodges the central issue, namely 'Who determines "need-to-know" and how?' Second, it mixes statements at a number of different levels (organizational approval of a policy should logically not be part of the policy itself). Third, there is a mechanism but it's implied rather than explicit: 'staff shall obey' — but what does this mean they actually have to do? Must the obedience be enforced by the system, or are users 'on their honour'? Fourth, how are breaches to be detected and who has a specific duty to report them?

We must do better than this. In fact, because the term 'security policy' is widely abused to mean a collection of managerialist platitudes, there are three more precise terms which have come into use to describe the specification of protection requirements.

A *security policy model* is a succinct statement of the protection properties which a system, or generic type of system, must have. Its key points can typically be written down in a page or less. It is the document in which the protection goals of the system are agreed with an entire community, or with the top management of a customer. It may also be the basis of formal mathematical analysis.

A *security target* is a more detailed description of the protection mechanisms that a specific implementation provides, and how they relate to a list of control objectives (some but not all of which are typically derived from the policy model). The security target forms the basis for testing and evaluation of a product.

A *protection profile* is like a security target but expressed in an implementation-independent way to enable comparable evaluations across products and versions. This can involve the use of a semi-formal language, or at least of suitable security jargon. A protection profile is a requirement for products that are to be evaluated under the *Common Criteria* [935]. (I discuss the Common

Criteria in Part III; they are associated with a scheme used by many governments for mutual recognition of security evaluations of defense information systems.)

When I don't have to be so precise, I may use the phrase 'security policy' to refer to either a security policy model or a security target. I will never use it to refer to a collection of platitudes.

Sometimes, we are confronted with a completely new application and have to design a security policy model from scratch. More commonly, there already exists a model; we just have to choose the right one, and develop it into a security target. Neither of these steps is easy. Indeed one of the purposes of this section of the book is to provide a number of security policy models, describe them in the context of real systems, and examine the engineering mechanisms (and associated constraints) which a security target can use to meet them.

Finally, you may come across a third usage of the phrase 'security policy' — as a list of specific configuration settings for some protection product. We will refer to this as *configuration management*, or occasionally as *trusted configuration management*, in what follows.

8.3   The Bell-LaPadula Security Policy Model

The classic example of a security policy model was proposed by Bell and LaPadula in 1973, in response to US Air Force concerns over the security of time-sharing mainframe systems[1]. By the early 1970's, people had realised that the protection offered by many commercial operating systems was poor, and was not getting any better. As soon as one operating system bug was fixed, some other vulnerability would be discovered. (Modern reliability growth models can quantify this and confirm that the pessimism was justified; I discuss them further in section 26.2.4.) There was the constant worry that even unskilled users would discover loopholes and use them opportunistically; there was also a keen and growing awareness of the threat from malicious code. (Viruses were not invented until the following decade; the 70's concern was about Trojans.) There was a serious scare when it was discovered that the Pentagon's World Wide Military Command and Control System was vulnerable to Trojan Horse attacks; this had the effect of restricting its use to people with a 'Top Secret' clearance, which was inconvenient. Finally, academic and industrial researchers were coming up with some interesting new ideas on protection, which I discuss below.

A study by James Anderson led the US government to conclude that a secure system should do one or two things well; and that these protection

---

[1] This built on the work of a number of other researchers; see section 9.2.1 below for a sketch of the technical history.

properties should be enforced by mechanisms which were simple enough to verify and that would change only rarely [29]. It introduced the concept of a *reference monitor* — a component of the operating system which would mediate access control decisions and be small enough to be subject to analysis and tests, the completeness of which could be assured. In modern parlance, such components — together with their associated operating procedures — make up the *Trusted Computing Base* (TCB). More formally, the TCB is defined as the set of components (hardware, software, human, . . .) whose correct functioning is sufficient to ensure that the security policy is enforced, or, more vividly, whose failure could cause a breach of the security policy. The Anderson report's goal was to make the security policy simple enough for the TCB to be amenable to careful verification.

But what are these core security properties that should be enforced above all others?

8.3.1 Classifications and Clearances

The Second World War, and the Cold War which followed, led NATO governments to move to a common protective marking scheme for labelling the sensitivity of documents. *Classifications* are labels, which run upwards from *Unclassified* through *Confidential*, *Secret* and *Top Secret* (see Figure 8.2.). The details change from time to time. The original idea was that information whose compromise could cost lives was marked 'Secret' while information whose compromise could cost many lives was 'Top Secret'. Government employees have *clearances* depending on the care with which they've been vetted; in the USA, for example, a 'Secret' clearance involves checking FBI fingerprint files, while 'Top Secret' also involves background checks for the previous five to fifteen years' employment [379].

The access control policy was simple: an official could read a document only if his clearance was at least as high as the document's classification. So an official cleared to 'Top Secret' could read a 'Secret' document, but not vice versa. The effect is that information may only flow upwards, from confidential to secret to top secret, but it may never flow downwards unless an authorized person takes a deliberate decision to declassify it.

There are also document handling rules; thus a 'Confidential' document might be kept in a locked filing cabinet in an ordinary government office,

TOP SECRET
SECRET
CONFIDENTIAL
UNCLASSIFIED

Figure 8.2: Multilevel security

while higher levels may require safes of an approved type, guarded rooms with control over photocopiers, and so on. (The NSA security manual [952] gives a summary of the procedures used with 'top secret' intelligence data.)

The system rapidly became more complicated. The damage criteria for classifying documents were expanded from possible military consequences to economic harm and even political embarrassment. The UK has an extra level, 'Restricted', between 'Unclassified' and 'Confidential'; the USA used to have this too but abolished it after the Freedom of Information Act was introduced. America now has two more specific markings: 'For Official Use only' (FOUO) refers to unclassified data that can't be released under FOIA, while 'Unclassified but Sensitive' includes FOUO plus material which might be released in response to a FOIA request. In the UK, 'Restricted' information is in practice shared freely, but marking everything 'Restricted' allows journalists and others involved in leaks to be prosecuted under Official Secrets law. (Its other main practical effect is that an unclassified US document which is sent across the Atlantic automatically becomes 'Restricted' in the UK and then 'Confidential' when shipped back to the USA. American military system builders complain that the UK policy breaks the US classification scheme!)

There is also a system of codewords whereby information, especially at Secret and above, can be further restricted. For example, information which might reveal intelligence sources or methods — such as the identities of agents or decrypts of foreign government traffic — is typically classified 'Top Secret Special Compartmented Intelligence' or TS/SCI, which means that so-called *need to know* restrictions are imposed as well, with one or more codewords attached to a file. Some of the codewords relate to a particular military operation or intelligence source and are available only to a group of named users. To read a document, a user must have all the codewords that are attached to it. A classification label, plus a set of codewords, makes up a *security category* or (if there's at least one codeword) a *compartment*, which is a set of records with the same access control policy. I discuss compartmentation in more detail in the chapter on multilateral security.

There are also *descriptors*, *caveats* and *IDO markings*. Descriptors are words such as 'Management', 'Budget', and 'Appointments': they do not invoke any special handling requirements, so we can deal with a file marked 'Confidential — Management' as if it were simply marked 'Confidential'. Caveats are warnings such as 'UK Eyes Only', or the US equivalent, 'NOFORN'; there are also *International Defence Organisation* markings such as *NATO*. The lack of obvious differences between codewords, descriptors, caveats and IDO marking is one of the things that can make the system confusing. A more detailed explanation can be found in [1051].

The final generic comment about access control doctrine is that allowing upward-only flow of information also models what happens in wiretapping. In the old days, tapping someone's telephone meant adding a physical wire at the exchange; nowadays, it's all done in the telephone exchange software and the effect is somewhat like making the target calls into conference calls with an extra participant. The usual security requirement is that the target of investigation should not know he is being wiretapped, so the third party should be silent — and its very presence must remain unknown to the target. For example, now that wiretaps are implemented as silent conference calls, care has to be taken to ensure that the charge for the conference call facility goes to the wiretapper, not to the target. Wiretapping requires an information flow policy in which the 'High' principal can see 'Low' data, but a 'Low' principal can't tell whether 'High' is reading any data at all, let alone what data.

8.3.2   Information Flow Control

It was in this context of the classification of government data that the *Bell-LaPadula* or *BLP* model of computer security was formulated in 1973 [146]. It is also known as *multilevel security* and systems which implement it are often called *multilevel secure* or *MLS* systems. Their basic property is that information cannot flow downwards.

More formally, the Bell-LaPadula model enforces two properties:

- The *simple security property*: no process may read data at a higher level. This is also known as *no read up (NRU)*;

- The **-property*: no process may write data to a lower level. This is also known as *no write down (NWD)*.

The *-property was Bell and LaPadula's critical innovation. It was driven by the fear of attacks using malicious code. An uncleared user might write a Trojan and leave it around where a system administrator cleared to 'Secret' might execute it; it could then copy itself into the 'Secret' part of the system, read the data there and try to signal it down somehow. It's also quite possible that an enemy agent could get a job at a commercial software house and embed some code in a product which would look for secret documents to copy. If it could then write them down to where its creator could read it, the security policy would have been violated. Information might also be leaked as a result of a bug, if applications could write down.

Vulnerabilities such as malicious and buggy code are assumed to be given. It is also assumed that most staff are careless, and some are dishonest; extensive operational security measures have long been used, especially in defence environments, to prevent people leaking paper documents. (When I worked in defense avionics as a youngster, all copies of circuit diagrams, blueprints etc were numbered and had to be accounted for.) So there was a pre-existing culture that security policy was enforced independently of user actions; the move to computers didn't change this. It had to be clarified, which is what Bell-LaPadula does: the security policy must be enforced not just independently of users' direct actions, but of their indirect actions (such as the actions taken by programs they run).

So we must prevent programs running at 'Secret' from writing to files at 'Unclassified', or more generally prevent any process at High from signalling to any object (or subject) at Low. In general, when systems enforce a security policy independently of user actions, they are described as having *mandatory access control*, as opposed to the *discretionary access control* in systems like Unix where users can take their own access decisions about their files.

The Bell-LaPadula model makes it relatively straightforward to verify claims about the protection provided by a design. Given both the simple security property (no read up), and the star property (no write down), various results can be proved about the machine states which can be reached from a given starting state, and this simplifies formal analysis. There are some elaborations, such as a *trusted subject* — a principal who is allowed to declassify files. To keep things simple, we'll ignore this; we'll also ignore the possibility of incompatible security levels for the time being, and return to them in the next chapter; and finally, in order to simplify matters still further, we will assume from now on that the system has only two levels, High and Low (unless there is some particular reason to name individual compartments).

Multilevel security can be implemented in a number of ways. The original idea was to implement a reference monitor by beefing up the part of an operating system which supervises all operating system calls and checks access permissions to decide whether the call can be serviced or not. However in practice things get much more complex as it's often hard to build systems whose trusted computing base is substantially less than the whole operating system kernel (plus quite a number of its utilities).

Another approach that has been gaining ground as hardware has got cheaper and faster is to replicate systems. This replication was often physical in the 1990s, and since about 2005 it may use virtual machines; some promising recent work builds on virtualization products such as VMware and Xen to provide multiple systems at different security levels on the same PC. One might, for example, have one database running at Low and another at High, on separate instances of Windows XP, with a *pump* that constantly copies information from Low up to High, all running on VMware on top of SELinux. I'll discuss pumps in more detail later.

8.3.3 The Standard Criticisms of Bell-LaPadula

The introduction of BLP caused a lot of excitement: here was a straightforward security policy which was clear to the intuitive understanding yet still allowed people to prove theorems. But John McLean showed that the BLP rules were not in themselves enough. He introduced *System Z*, defined as a BLP system with the added feature that a user can ask the system administrator to temporarily declassify any file from High to Low. In this way, Low users can read any High file without breaking the BLP assumptions.

Bell's argument was that System Z cheats by doing something the model doesn't allow (changing labels isn't a valid operation on the state), and McLean's argument was that it didn't explicitly tell him so. The issue is dealt with by introducing a *tranquility property*. The strong tranquility property says that security labels never change during system operation, while the weak tranquility property says that labels never change in such a way as to violate a defined security policy.

The motivation for the weak property is that in a real system we often want to observe the principle of least privilege and start off a process at the uncleared level, even if the owner of the process were cleared to 'Top Secret'. If she then accesses a confidential email, her session is automatically upgraded to 'Confidential'; and in general, her process is upgraded each time it accesses data at a higher level (this is known as the *high water mark* principle). As subjects are usually an abstraction of the memory management sub-system and file handles, rather than processes, this means that state changes when access rights change, rather than when data actually moves.

The practical implication is that a process acquires the security labels of all the files it reads, and these become the default label set of every file that it writes. So a process which has read files at 'Secret' and 'Crypto' will thereafter create files marked (at least) 'Secret Crypto'. This will include temporary copies made of other files. If it then reads a file at 'Top Secret Daffodil' then all files it creates after that will be labelled 'Top Secret Crypto Daffodil', and it will not be able to write to any temporary files at 'Secret Crypto'. The effect this has on applications is one of the serious complexities of multilevel security; most application software needs to be rewritten (or at least modified) to run on MLS platforms. Read-time changes in security level introduce the problem that access to resources can be revoked at any time, including in the middle of a transaction. Now the revocation problem is generally unsolvable in modern operating systems, at least in any complete form, which means that the applications have to cope somehow. Unless you invest some care and effort, you can easily find that everything ends up in the highest compartment — or that the system fragments into thousands of tiny compartments that don't communicate at all with each other. I'll discuss this in more detail in the next chapter.

Another problem with BLP, and indeed with all mandatory access control systems, is that separating users and processes is relatively straightforward; the hard part is when some controlled interaction is needed. Most real applications need some kind of 'trusted subject' that can break the security policy; an example is a trusted word processor that helps an intelligence analyst scrub a Top Secret document when she's editing it down to Secret [861]. BLP is silent on how the system should protect such an application. Does it become part of the Trusted Computing Base? I'll discuss this in more detail below.

Finally it's worth noting that even with the high-water-mark refinement, BLP still doesn't deal with the creation or destruction of subjects or objects (which is one of the hard problems of building a real MLS system).

8.3.4 Alternative Formulations

Multilevel security properties have been expressed in several other ways.

The first multilevel security policy was a version of high water mark written in 1967–8 for the ADEPT-50, a mandatory access control system developed for the IBM S/360 mainframe [1334]. This used triples of level, compartment and group, with the groups being files, users, terminals and jobs. As programs (rather than processes) were subjects, it was vulnerable to Trojan horse compromises, and it was more complex than need be. Nonetheless, it laid the foundation for BLP, and also led to the current IBM S/390 mainframe hardware security architecture [632].

Shortly after that, a number of teams produced primitive versions of the lattice model, which I'll discuss in more detail in the next chapter. These also made a significant contribution to the Bell-LaPadula work, as did engineers working on Multics. Multics had started as an MIT project in 1965 and developed into a Honeywell product; it became the template for the 'trusted systems' specified in the Orange Book, being the inspirational example of the B2 level operating system. The evaluation that was carried out on it by Paul Karger and Roger Schell was hugely influential and was the first appearance of the idea that malware could be hidden in the compiler [693] — which led to Ken Thompson's famous paper 'On Trusting Trust' ten years later. Multics itself developed into a system called SCOMP that I'll discuss in section 8.4.1 below.

Noninterference was introduced by Joseph Goguen and Jose Meseguer in 1982 [532]. In a system with this property, High's actions have no effect on what Low can see. *Nondeducibility* is less restrictive and was introduced by David Sutherland in 1986 [1233]. Here the idea is to try and prove that Low cannot deduce anything with 100 percent certainty about High's input. Low users can see High actions, just not understand them; a more formal definition is that any legal string of high level inputs is compatible with every string of low level events. So for every trace Low can see, there's a similar trace that didn't involve High input. But different low-level event streams may require changes to high-level outputs or reordering of high-level/low-level event sequences.

The motive for nondeducibility is to find a model that can deal with applications such as a LAN on which there are machines at both Low and High, with the High machines encrypting their LAN traffic. (Quite a lot else is needed to do this right, from padding the High traffic with nulls so that Low users can't do traffic analysis, and even ensuring that the packets are the same size — see [1096] for an early example of such a system.)

Nondeducibility has historical importance since it was the first nondeterministic version of Goguen and Messeguer's ideas. But it is hopelessly weak. There's nothing to stop Low making deductions about High input with 99% certainty. There's also a whole lot of problems when we are trying to prove results about databases, and have to take into account any information which can be inferred from data structures (such as from partial views of data with redundancy) as well as considering the traces of executing programs. I'll discuss these problems further in the next chapter.

Improved models include *Generalized Noninterference* and *restrictiveness*. The former is the requirement that if one alters a high level input event in a legal sequence of system events, the resulting sequence can be made legal by, at most, altering one or more subsequent high-level output events. The latter adds a further restriction on the part of the trace where the alteration of the high-level outputs can take place. This is needed for technical reasons to ensure that two systems satisfying the restrictiveness property can be composed into a third which also does. See [864] which explains these issues.

The *Harrison-Ruzzo-Ullman* model tackles the problem of how to deal with the creation and deletion of files, an issue on which BLP is silent. It operates on access matrices and verifies whether there is a sequence of instructions which causes an access right to leak to somewhere it was initially not present [584]. This is more expressive than BLP, but is more complex and thus less tractable as an aid to verification.

John Woodward proposed a *Compartmented Mode Workstation* (CMW) policy, which attempted to model the classification of information using floating labels, as opposed to the fixed labels associated with BLP [1357, 552]. It was ultimately unsuccessful, because labels tend to either float up too far too fast (if done correctly), or they float up more slowly (but don't block all the opportunities for malicious information flow). However, CMW ideas have led to real products — albeit products that provide separation more than information sharing.

The *type enforcement* model, due to Earl Boebert and Dick Kain [198], assigns subjects to *domains* and objects to *types*, with matrices defining permitted domain-domain and domain-type interactions. This is used in a popular and important mandatory access control system, SELinux, which simplifies it by putting both subjects and objects in types and having a matrix of allowed type pairs [813]. In effect this is a second access-control matrix; in addition to having a user ID and group ID, each process has a security ID. The Linux Security Modules framework provides pluggable security modules with rules operating on SIDs.

Type enforcement was later extended by Badger and others to *Domain and Type Enforcement* [106]. They introduced their own language for configuration (DTEL), and implicit typing of files based on pathname; for example, all objects in a given subdirectory may be declared to be in a given domain. TE and DTE are more general than simple MLS policies such as BLP, as they start to deal with integrity as well as confidentiality concerns. One of their early uses, starting in the LOCK system, was to enforce trusted pipelines: the idea is to confine a set of trusted processes in a pipeline so that each can only talk to previous stage and the next stage. This can be used to assemble guards and firewalls which cannot be bypassed unless at least two stages are compromised [963]. Type-enforcement mechanisms are used, for example, in the Sidewinder firewall. A further advantage of type enforcement mechanisms is that they can be aware of code versus data, and privileges can be bound to code; in consequence the tranquility problem can be dealt with at execute time rather than as data are read. This can make things much more tractable.

The downside of the greater flexibility and expressiveness of TE/DTE is that it is not always straightforward to implement BLP, because of the state explosion; when writing a security policy you have to consider all the possible interactions between different types. (For this reason, SELinux also implements a simple MLS policy. I'll discuss SELinux in more detail below.)

Finally, a policy model getting much attention from researchers in recent years is *role-based access control* (RBAC), introduced by David Ferraiolo and Richard Kuhn [466, 467]. This provides a more general framework for mandatory access control than BLP in which access decisions don't depend on users' names but on the functions which they are currently performing within the organization. Transactions which may be performed by holders of a given role are specified, then mechanisms for granting membership of a role (including delegation). Roles, or groups, had for years been the mechanism used in practice in organizations such as banks to manage access control; the RBAC model starts to formalize this. It can be used to give finer-grained control, for example by granting different access rights to 'Ross as Professor', 'Ross as member of the Planning and Resources Committee' and 'Ross reading private email'. Implementations vary; the banking systems of twenty years ago kept the controls in middleware, and some modern RBAC products do control at the application layer where it's easy to bypass. SELinux builds it on top of TE, so that users are mapped to roles at login time, roles are authorized for domains and domains are given permissions to types. On such a platform, RBAC can usefully deal with integrity issues as well as confidentiality, by allowing role membership to be revised when certain programs are invoked. Thus, for example, a process calling untrusted software that had been downloaded from the net might lose the role membership required to write to sensitive system files.

8.3.5   The Biba Model and Vista

The incorporation into Windows Vista of a multilevel integrity model has revived interest in a security model devised in 1975 by Ken Biba [168], which textbooks often refer to as 'Bell-LaPadula upside down'. The Biba model deals with integrity alone and ignores confidentiality. The key observation is that confidentiality and integrity are in some sense dual concepts — confidentiality is a constraint on who can read a message, while integrity is a constraint on who can write or alter it.

As a concrete application, an electronic medical device such as an ECG may have two separate modes: calibration and use. Calibration data must be protected from corruption by normal users, who will therefore be able to read it but not write to it; when a normal user resets the device, it will lose its current user state (i.e., any patient data in memory) but the calibration will remain unchanged.

To model such a system, we can use a multilevel integrity policy with the rules that we can read data at higher levels (i.e., a user process can read the calibration data) and write to lower levels (i.e., a calibration process can write to a buffer in a user process); but we must never read down or write up, as either could allow High integrity objects to become contaminated with Low — that is potentially unreliable — data. The Biba model is often formulated in terms of the *low water mark* principle, which is the dual of the high water mark principle discussed above: the integrity of an object is the lowest level of all the objects that contributed to its creation.

This was the first formal model of integrity. A surprisingly large number of real systems work along Biba lines. For example, the passenger information system in a railroad may get information from the signalling system, but certainly shouldn't be able to affect it (other than through a trusted interface, such as one of the control staff). However, few of the people who build such systems are aware of the Biba model or what it might teach them.

Vista marks file objects with an integrity level, which can be Low, Medium, High or System, and implements a default policy of NoWriteUp. Critical Vista files are at System and other objects are at Medium by default — except for Internet Explorer which is at Low. The effect is that things downloaded using IE can read most files in a Vista system, but cannot write them. The idea is to limit the damage that can be done by viruses and other malware. I'll describe Vista's mechanisms in more detail below.

An interesting precursor to Vista was LOMAC, a Linux extension that implemented a low water mark policy [494]. It provided two levels — high and low integrity — with system files at High and the network at Low. As soon as a program (such as a daemon) received traffic from the network, it was automatically downgraded to Low. Thus even if the traffic contains an attack that forks a root shell, this shell could not write to the password file as a normal root shell would. As one might expect, a number of system tasks (such as logging) became tricky and required trusted code.

As you might expect, Biba has the same fundamental problems as Bell-LaPadula. It cannot accommodate real-world operation very well without numerous exceptions. For example, a real system will usually require 'trusted' subjects that can override the security model, but Biba on its own fails to provide effective mechanisms to protect and confine them; and in general it doesn't work so well with modern software environments. In the end, Vista dropped the NoReadDown restriction and did not end up using its integrity model to protect the base system from users.

Biba also cannot express many real integrity goals, like assured pipelines. In fact, the Type Enforcement model was introduced by Boebert and Kain as an alternative to Biba. It is unfortunate that Vista didn't incorporate TE.

I will consider more complex models when I discuss banking and book-keeping systems in Chapter 10; these are more complex in that they retain security state in the form of dual control mechanisms, audit trails and so on.

8.4   Historical Examples of MLS Systems

Following some research products in the late 1970's (such as KSOS [166], a kernelised secure version of Unix), products that implemented multilevel security policies started arriving in dribs and drabs in the early 1980's. By about 1988, a number of companies started implementing MLS versions of their operating systems. MLS concepts were extended to all sorts of products.

8.4.1   SCOMP

One of the most important products was the *secure communications processor* (SCOMP), a derivative of Multics launched in 1983 [491]. This was a no-expense-spared implementation of what the US Department of Defense believed it wanted for handling messaging at multiple levels of classification. It had formally verified hardware and software, with a minimal kernel and four rings of protection (rather than Multics' seven) to keep things simple. Its operating system, STOP, used these rings to maintain up to 32 separate compartments, and to allow appropriate one-way information flows between them.

SCOMP was used in applications such as military *mail guards*. These are specialised firewalls which typically allow mail to pass from Low to High but not vice versa [369]. (In general, a device which does this is known as a *data diode*.) SCOMP's successor, XTS-300, supported C2G, the Command and Control Guard. This was used in the time phased force deployment data (TPFDD) system whose function was to plan US troop movements and associated logistics. Military plans are developed as TPFDDs at a high classification level, and then distributed at the appropriate times as commands to lower levels for implementation. (The issue of how high information is deliberately downgraded raises a number of issues, some of which I'll deal with below. In the case of TPFDD, the guard examines the content of each record before deciding whether to release it.)

SCOMP's most significant contribution was to serve as a model for the *Orange Book* [375] — the US Trusted Computer Systems Evaluation Criteria. This was the first systematic set of standards for secure computer systems, being introduced in 1985 and finally retired in December 2000. The Orange Book was enormously influential not just in the USA but among allied powers; countries such as the UK, Germany, and Canada based their own national standards on it, until these national standards were finally subsumed into the Common Criteria [935].

The Orange Book allowed systems to be evaluated at a number of levels with A1 being the highest, and moving downwards through B3, B2, B1 and C2 to C1. SCOMP was the first system to be rated A1. It was also extensively documented in the open literature. Being first, and being fairly public, it set the standard for the next generation of military systems. This standard has rarely been met since; in fact, the XTS-300 was only evaluated to B3 (the formal proofs of correctness required for an A1 evaluation were dropped).

8.4.2   Blacker

Blacker was a series of encryption devices designed to incorporate MLS technology. Previously, encryption devices were built with separate processors for the ciphertext, or *Black*, end and the cleartext, or *Red*, end. Various possible failures can be prevented if one can coordinate the Red and Black processing. One can also make the device simpler, and provide greater operational flexibility: the device isn't limited to separating two logical networks, but can provide encryption and integrity assurance selectively, and interact in useful ways with routers. But then a high level of assurance is required that the 'Red' data won't leak out via the 'Black'.

Blacker entered service in 1989, and the main lesson learned from it was the extreme difficulty of accommodating administrative traffic within a model of classification levels [1335]. As late as 1994, it was the only communications security device with an A1 evaluation [161]. So it too had an effect on later systems. It was not widely used though, and its successor (the Motorola Network Encryption System), had only a B2 evaluation.

8.4.3   MLS Unix and Compartmented Mode Workstations

MLS versions of Unix started to appear in the late 1980's, such as AT&T's System V/MLS [27]. This added security levels and labels, initially by using some of the bits in the group id record and later by using this to point to a more elaborate structure. This enabled MLS properties to be introduced with minimal changes to the system kernel. Other products of this kind included (and its derivatives, such as SCO and HP VirtualVault), and Addamax. By the time of writing (2007), Sun's Solaris has emerged as the clear market leader, being the platform of choice for high-assurance server systems and for many clients as well. Trusted Solaris 8 gave way to Solaris trusted Extensions 10, which has now been folded into Solaris, so that every copy of Solaris contains MLS mechanisms, for those knowledgeable enough to use them.

Comparted Mode Workstations (CMWs) are an example of MLS clients. They allow data at different levels to be viewed and modified at the same time by a human operator, and ensure that labels attached to the information are updated appropriately. The initial demand came from the intelligence community, whose analysts may have access to 'Top Secret' data, such as decrypts and agent reports, and produce reports at the 'Secret' level for users such as political leaders and officers in the field. As these reports are vulnerable to capture, they must not contain any information which would compromise intelligence sources and methods.

CMWs allow an analyst to view the 'Top Secret' data in one window, compose a report in another, and have mechanisms to prevent the accidental copying of the former into the latter (i.e., cut-and-paste works from 'Secret' to 'Top Secret' but not vice versa). CMWs have proved useful in operations, logistics and drug enforcement as well [631]. For the engineering issues involved in doing mandatory access control in windowing systems, see [437, 438] which describe a prototype for Trusted X, a system implementing MLS but not information labelling. It runs one instance of X Windows per sensitivity level, and has a small amount of trusted code which allows users to cut and paste from a lower level to a higher one. For the specific architectural issues with Sun's CMW product, see [451].

8.4.4   The NRL Pump

It was soon realised that simple mail guards and crypto boxes were too restrictive, as many more networked services were developed besides mail. Traditional MLS mechanisms (such as blind write-ups and periodic read-downs) are inefficient for real-time services.

The US Naval Research Laboratory (NRL) therefore developed the *Pump* — a one-way data transfer device (a data diode) to allow secure one-way information flow (Figure 8.3). The main problem is that while sending data from Low to High is easy, the need for assured transmission reliability means that acknowledgement messages must be sent back from High to Low. The Pump limits the bandwidth of possible backward leakage using a number of mechanisms such as using buffering and randomizing the timing of acknowledgements [685, 687, 688]. The attraction of this approach is that one can build MLS systems by using pumps to connect separate systems at different security levels. As these systems don't process data at more than one level, they can be

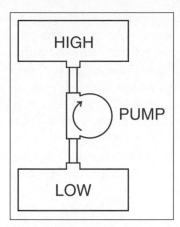

Figure 8.3: The NRL pump

built from cheap commercial-off-the-shelf (COTS) components [689]. As the cost of hardware falls, this is often the preferred option where it's possible. The pump's story is told in [691].

The Australian government developed a product called *Starlight* that uses pump-type technology married with a keyboard switch to provide a nice MLS-type windowing system (albeit without any visible labels) using a bit of trusted hardware which connects the keyboard and mouse with High and Low systems [30]. There is no trusted software. It's been integrated with the NRL Pump [689]. A number of semi-commercial data diode products have also been introduced.

8.4.5 Logistics Systems

Military stores, like government documents, can have different classification levels. Some signals intelligence equipment is 'Top Secret', while things like jet fuel and bootlaces are not; but even such simple commodities may become 'Secret' when their quantities or movements might leak information about tactical intentions. There are also some peculiarities: for example, an inertial navigation system classified 'Confidential' in the peacetime inventory might contain a laser gyro platform classified 'Secret' (thus security levels are *nonmonotonic*).

The systems needed to manage all this seem to be hard to build, as MLS logistics projects in both the USA and UK have ended up as expensive disasters. In the UK, the Royal Air Force's Logistics Information Technology System (LITS) was a 10 year (1989–99), £500m project to provide a single stores management system for the RAF's 80 bases [932]. It was designed to operate on two levels: 'Restricted' for the jet fuel and boot polish, and 'Secret' for special stores such as nuclear bombs. It was initially implemented as two separate database systems connected by a pump to enforce the MLS property. The project became a classic tale of escalating costs driven by creeping requirements changes. One of these changes was the easing of classification rules with the end of the Cold War. As a result, it was found that almost all the 'Secret' information was now static (e.g., operating manuals for air-drop nuclear bombs which are now kept in strategic stockpiles rather than at airbases). In order to save money, the 'Secret' information is now kept on a CD and locked up in a safe.

Logistics systems often have application security features too. The classic example is that ordnance control systems alert users who are about to breach safety rules by putting explosives and detonators in the same truck or magazine [910].

8.4.6   Sybard Suite

Most governments' information security agencies have been unable to resist user demands to run standard applications (such as MS Office) which are not available for multilevel secure platforms. One response was the 'Purple Penelope' software, from Qinetiq in the UK, now sold as Sybard Suite. This puts an MLS wrapper round a Windows workstation, implementing the high water mark version of BLP. It displays in the background the current security level of the device and upgrades it when necessary as more sensitive resources are read. It ensures that the resulting work product is labelled correctly.

Rather than preventing users from downgrading, as a classical BLP system might do, it allows them to assign any security label they like to their output. However, if this involves a downgrade, the user must confirm the release of the data using a trusted path interface, thus ensuring no Trojan Horse or virus can release anything completely unnoticed. Of course, a really clever malicious program can piggy-back classified material on stuff that the user does wish to release, so there are other tricks to make that harder. There is also an audit trail to provide a record of all downgrades, so that errors and attacks (whether by users, or by malware) can be traced after the fact [1032]. The security policy was described to me by one of its authors as 'we accept that we can't stop people leaking the order of battle to the Guardian newspaper if they really want to; we just want to make sure we arrest the right person for it.'

8.4.7   Wiretap Systems

One of the large applications of MLS is in wiretapping systems. Communications intelligence is generally fragile; once a target knows his traffic is being read he can usually do something to frustrate it. Traditional wiretap kit, based on 'loop extenders' spliced into the line, could often be detected by competent targets; modern digital systems try to avoid these problems, and provide a multilevel model in which multiple agencies at different levels can monitor a target, and each other; the police might be tapping a drug dealer, and an anti-corruption unit watching the police, and so on. Wiretaps are commonly implemented as conference calls with a silent third party, and the main protection goal is to eliminate any covert channels that might disclose the existence of surveillance. This is not always met. For a survey, see [1161], which also points out that the pure MLS security policy is insufficient: suspects can confuse wiretapping equipment by introducing bogus signalling tones. The policy should thus have included resistance against online tampering.

Another secondary protection goal should have been to protect against software tampering. In a recent notorious case, a wiretap was discovered on the mobile phones of the Greek Prime Minister and his senior colleagues; this involved unauthorised software in the mobile phone company's switchgear that abused the lawful intercept facility. It was detected when the buggers' modifications caused some text messages not to be delivered [1042]. The phone company was fined 76 million Euros (almost $100m). Perhaps phone companies will be less willing to report unauthorized wiretaps in future.

8.5 Future MLS Systems

In the first edition of this book, I wrote that the MLS industry's attempts to market its products as platforms for firewalls, web servers and other exposed systems were failing because 'the BLP controls do not provide enough of a protection benefit in many commercial environments to justify their large development costs, and widely fielded products are often better because of the evolution that results from large-scale user feedback'. I also noted research on using mandatory access controls to accommodate both confidentiality and integrity in environments such as smartcards [692], and to provide real-time performance guarantees to prevent service denial attacks [889]. I ventured that 'perhaps the real future of multilevel systems is not in confidentiality, but integrity'.

The last seven years appear to have proved this right.

8.5.1 Vista

Multilevel integrity is coming to the mass market in Vista. As I already mentioned, Vista essentially uses the Biba model. All processes do, and all securable objects (including directories, files and registry keys) may, have an integrity-level label. File objects are labelled at 'Medium' by default, while Internet Explorer (and everything downloaded using it) is labelled 'Low'. User action is therefore needed to upgrade downloaded content before it can modify existing files. This may not be a panacea: it may become so routine a demand from all installed software that users will be trained to meekly upgrade viruses too on request. And it must be borne in mind that much of the spyware infesting the average home PC was installed there deliberately (albeit carelessly and with incomplete knowledge of the consequences) after visiting some commercial website. This overlap between desired and undesired software sets a limit on how much can be achieved against downloaded malware. We will have to wait and see.

It is also possible to implement a crude BLP policy using Vista, as you can also set 'NoReadUp' and 'NoExecuteUp' policies. These are not installed as default; the reason appears to be that Microsoft was principally concerned about malware installing itself in the system and then hiding. Keeping the browser 'Low' makes installation harder, and allowing all processes (even Low ones) to inspect the rest of the system makes hiding harder. But it does mean that malware running at Low can steal all your data; so some users might care to set 'NoReadUp' for sensitive directories. No doubt this will break a number of applications, so a cautious user might care to have separate accounts for web browsing, email and sensitive projects. This is all discussed by Joanna Rutkowska in [1099]; she also describes some interesting potential attacks based on virtualization. A further problem is that Vista, in protected mode, does still write to high-integrity parts of the registry, even though Microsoft says it shouldn't [555].

In passing, it's also worth mentioning rights management, whether of the classical DRM kind or the more recent IRM (Information Rights Management) variety, as a case of mandatory access control. Vista, for example, tries to ensure that no high definition video content is ever available to an untrusted process. I will discuss it in more detail later, but for now I'll just remark that many of the things that go wrong with multilevel systems might also become vulnerabilities in, or impediments to the use of, rights-management systems. Conversely, the efforts expended by opponents of rights management in trying to hack the Vista DRM mechanisms may also open up holes in its integrity protection.

8.5.2   Linux

The case of SELinux and Red Hat is somewhat similar to Vista in that the immediate goal of the new mandatory access control mechanisms is also to limit the effects of a compromise. SELinux [813] is based on the Flask security architecture [1209], which separates the policy from the enforcement mechanism; a security context contains all of the security attributes associated with a subject or object in Flask, where one of those attributes includes the Type Enforcement type attribute. A security identifier is a handle to a security context, mapped by the security server. It has a security server where policy decisions are made, this resides in-kernel since Linux has a monolithic kernel and the designers did not want to require a kernel-userspace call for security decisions (especially as some occur on critical paths where the kernel is holding locks) [557]). The server provides a general security API to the rest of the kernel, with the security model hidden behind that API. The server internally implements RBAC, TE, and MLS (or to be precise, a general constraints engine that can express MLS or any other model you like). SELinux is included in a number of Linux distributions, and Red Hat's use is typical. There its function is to separate various services. Thus an attacker who takes over your web server does not thereby acquire your DNS server as well.

Suse Linux has taken a different path to the same goal. It uses AppArmor, a monitoring mechanism maintained by Novell, which keeps a list of all the paths each protected application uses and prevents it accessing any new ones. It is claimed to be easier to use than the SELinux model; but operating-system experts distrust it as it relies on pathnames as the basis for its decisions. In consequence, it has ambiguous and mutable identifiers; no system view of subjects and objects; no uniform abstraction for handling non-file objects; and no useful information for runtime files (such as /tmp). By forcing policy to be written in terms of individual objects and filesystem layout rather than security equivalence classes, it makes policy harder to analyze. However, in practice, with either AppArmor or SELinux, you instrument the code you plan to protect, watch for some months what it does, and work out a policy that allows it to do just what it needs. Even so, after you have fielded it, you will still have to observe and act on bug reports for a year or so. Modern software components tend to be so complex that figuring out what access they need is an empirical and iterative process[2].

It's also worth bearing in mind that simple integrity controls merely stop malware taking over the machine — they don't stop it infecting a Low compartment and using that as a springboard from which to spread elsewhere.

Integrity protection is not the only use of SELinux. At present there is considerable excitement about it in some sections of government, who are excited at the prospect of 'cross department access to data . . . and a common trust infrastructure for shared services' (UK Cabinet Office) and allowing 'users to access multiple independent sessions at varying classification levels' (US Coast Guard) [505]. Replacing multiple terminals with single ones, and moving from proprietary systems to open ones, is attractive for many reasons — and providing simple separation between multiple terminal emulators or browsers running on the same PC is straightforward. However, traditional MAC might not be the only way to do it.

---

[2]Indeed, some of the mandatory access control mechanisms promised in Vista — such as remote attestation — did not ship in the first version, and there have been many papers from folks at Microsoft Research on ways of managing access control and security policy in complex middleware. Draw your own conclusions.

8.5.3   Virtualization

Another technological approach is virtualization. Products such as VMware and Xen are being used to provide multiple virtual machines at different levels. Indeed, the NSA has produced a hardened version of VMware, called NetTop, which is optimised for running several Windows virtual machines on top of an SELinux platform. This holds out the prospect of giving the users what they want — computers that have the look and feel of ordinary windows boxes — while simultaneously giving the security folks what they want, namely high-assurance separation between material at different levels of classification. So far, there is little information available on NetTop, but it appears to do separation rather than sharing.

A current limit is the sheer technical complexity of modern PCs; it's very difficult to find out what things like graphics cards actually do, and thus to get high assurance that they don't contain huge covert channels. It can also be quite difficult to ensure that a device such as a microphone or camera is really connected to the Secret virtual machine rather than the Unclassified one. However, given the effort being put by Microsoft into assurance for high-definition video content, there's at least the prospect that some COTS machines might eventually offer reasonable assurance on I/O eventually.

The next question must be whether mandatory access control for confidentiality, as opposed to integrity, will make its way out of the government sector and into the corporate world. The simplest application might be for a company to provide its employees with separate virtual laptops for corporate and home use (whether with virtualisation or with mandatory access controls). From the engineering viewpoint, virtualization might preferable, as it's not clear that corporate security managers will want much information flow between the two virtual laptops: flows from 'home' to 'work' could introduce malware while flow from 'work' to 'home' could leak corporate secrets. From the business viewpoint, it's less clear that virtualization will take off. Many corporates would rather pretend that company laptops don't get used for anything else, and as the software industry generally charges per virtual machine rather than per machine, there could be nontrivial costs involved. I expect most companies will continue to ignore the problem and just fire people whose machines cause visible trouble.

The hardest problem is often managing the interfaces between levels, as people usually end up having to get material from one level to another in order to get their work done. If the information flows are limited and easy to model, as with the Pump and the CMW, well and good; the way forward may well be Pump or CMW functionality also hosted on virtual machines. (Virtualisation per se doesn't give you CMW — you need a trusted client for that, or an app running on a trusted server — but it's possible to envisage a trusted thin client plus VMs at two different levels all running on the same box.

So virtualization should probably be seen as complementary to mandatory access control, rather than a competitor.

But many things can go wrong, as I will discuss in the next session.

8.5.4   Embedded Systems

There are more and more fielded systems which implement some variant of the Biba model. As well as the medical-device and railroad signalling applications already mentioned, there are utilities. In an electricity utility, for example, operational systems such as power dispatching should not be affected by any others. The metering systems can be observed by, but not influenced by, the billing system. Both billing and power dispatching feed information into fraud detection, and at the end of the chain the executive information systems can observe everything while having no direct effect on operations. These one-way information flows can be implemented using mandatory access controls and there are signs that, given growing concerns about the vulnerability of critical infrastructure, some utilities are starting to look at SELinux.

There are many military embedded systems too. The primitive mail guards of 20 years ago have by now been supplanted by guards that pass not just email but chat, web services and streaming media, often based on SELinux; an example is described in [478]. There are many more esoteric applications: for example, some US radars won't display the velocity of a US aircraft whose performance is classified, unless the operator has the appropriate clearance. (This has always struck me as overkill, as he can just use a stopwatch.)

Anyway, it's now clear that many of the lessons learned in the early multilevel systems go across to a number of applications of much wider interest. So do a number of the failure modes, which I'll now discuss.

8.6   What Goes Wrong

As I've frequently pointed out, engineers learn more from the systems that fail than from those that succeed, and MLS systems have certainly been an effective teacher. The large effort expended in building systems to follow a simple policy with a high level of assurance has led to the elucidation of many second- and third-order consequences of information flow controls. I'll start with the more theoretical and work through to the business and engineering end.

8.6.1   Composability

Consider a simple device that accepts two 'High' inputs H_1 and H_2; multiplexes them; encrypts them by xor'ing them with a one-time pad (i.e., a random generator); outputs the other copy of the pad on H_3; and outputs the

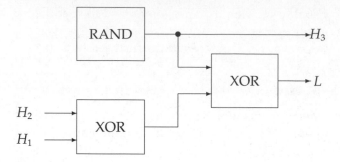

Figure 8.4: Insecure composition of secure systems with feedback

ciphertext, which being encrypted with a cipher system giving perfect secrecy, is considered to be low (output L), as in Figure 8.4.

In isolation, this device is provably secure. However, if feedback is permitted, then the output from H_3 can be fed back into H_2, with the result that the high input H_1 now appears at the low output L. Timing inconsistencies can also lead to the composition of two secure systems being insecure (see for example McCullough [854]). Simple information flow doesn't compose; neither does noninterference or nondeducibility.

In general, the problem of how to compose two or more secure components into a secure system is hard, even at the relatively uncluttered level of proving results about ideal components. Most of the low-level problems arise when some sort of feedback is introduced into the system; without it, composition can be achieved under a number of formal models [865]. However, in real life, feedback is pervasive, and composition of security properties can be made even harder by detailed interface issues, feature interactions and so on. For example, one system might produce data at such a rate as to perform a service-denial attack on another. (I'll discuss some of the interface problems with reference monitors in detail in Chapter 18, 'API Attacks'.)

Finally, the composition of secure components or systems is very often frustrated by higher-level incompatibilities. Components might have been designed in accordance with two different security policies, or designed according to requirements that are inconsistent or even incompatible. This is bad enough for different variants on the BLP theme but even worse when one of the policies is of a non-BLP type, as we will encounter in the following two chapters. Composability is a long-standing and very serious problem with trustworthy systems; a good recent survey is the final report of the CHATS project [963].

8.6.2 The Cascade Problem

An example of the difficulty of composing multilevel secure systems is given by the cascade problem (Figure 8.5). After the Orange book introduced a series

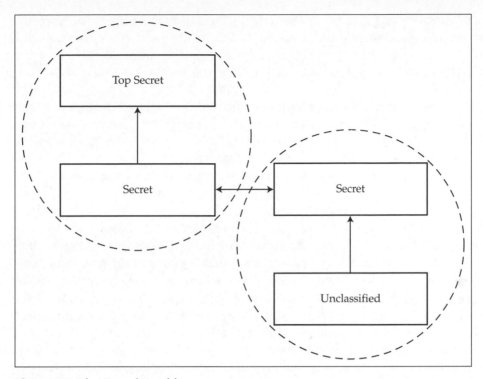

Figure 8.5: The cascade problem

of graduated evaluation levels, this led to rules about the number of levels which a system can span [379]. For example, a system evaluated to B3 was in general allowed to process information at Unclassified, Confidential and Secret, or at Confidential, Secret and Top Secret; there was no system permitted to process Unclassified and Top Secret data simultaneously [379].

As the diagram shows, it is straightforward to connect together two B3 systems in such a way that this security policy is broken. The first system connects together Unclassified, Confidential and Secret, and its Confidential and Secret levels communicate with the second system which also processes Top Secret information. (The problem's discussed in more detail in [622].) This illustrates another kind of danger which formal models of security (and practical implementations) must take into account.

8.6.3 Covert Channels

One of the reasons why these span limits are imposed on multilevel systems emerges from a famous — and extensively studied — problem: the *covert channel*. First pointed out by Lampson in 1973 [768], a covert channel is a mechanism that was not designed for communication but which can nonetheless be abused to allow information to be communicated down from High to Low.

A typical covert channel arises when a high process can signal to a low one by affecting some shared resource. For example, it could position the disk head at the outside of the drive at time t_i to signal that the i-th bit in a Top Secret file was a 1, and position it at the inside to signal that the bit was a 0.

All systems with shared resources must find a balance between covert channel capacity, resource utilization, and fairness. If a machine is shared between high and low, and resources are not allocated in fixed slices, then the high process can signal by filling up the disk drive, or by using a lot of CPU or bus cycles (some people call the former case a *storage channel* and the latter a *timing channel*, though in practice they can often be converted into each other). There are many others such as sequential process IDs, shared file locks and last access times on files — reimplementing all of these in a multilevel secure way is an enormous task. Various strategies have been adopted to minimize their bandwidth; for example, we can arrange that the scheduler assigns a fixed disk quota to each level, and reads the boot sector each time control is passed downwards; and we might also allocate a fixed proportion of the available time slices to processes at each level, and change these proportions infrequently. Each change might allow one or more bits to be signalled, but such strategies can enormously reduce the available bandwidth. (A more complex multilevel design, which uses local schedulers at each level plus a global scheduler to maintain overall consistency, is described in [686].)

It is also possible to limit the covert channel capacity by introducing noise. Some machines have had randomised system clocks for this purpose. But some covert channel capacity almost always remains. (Techniques to analyze the trade-offs between covert channel capacity and system performance are discussed in [554].)

Many covert channels occur at the application layer, and are a real concern to security engineers (especially as they are often overlooked). An example from social care is a UK proposal to create a national database of all children, for child-protection and welfare purposes, containing a list of all professionals with which each child has contact. Now it may be innocuous that child X is registered with family doctor Y, but the fact of a child's registration with a social work department is not innocuous at all — it's well known to be stigmatizing. For example, teachers will have lower expectations of children whom they know to have been in contact with social workers. So it is quite reasonable for parents (and children) to want to keep any record of such contact private [66].

A more subtle example is that in general personal health information derived from visits to genitourinary medicine clinics is High in the sense that it can't be shared with the patient's normal doctor and thus appear in their normal medical record (Low) unless the patient consents. In one case, a woman's visit to a GUM clinic leaked when the insurer failed to recall her for a smear test which her normal doctor knew was due [886]. The insurer knew that a smear test had been done already by the clinic, and didn't want to pay twice.

Another case of general interest arises in multilevel integrity systems such as banking and utility billing, where a programmer who has inserted Trojan code in a bookkeeping system can turn off the billing to an account by a certain pattern of behavior (in a phone system he might call three numbers in succession, for example). Code review is the only real way to block such attacks, though balancing controls can also help in the specific case of bookkeeping.

The highest-bandwidth covert channel of which I'm aware is also a feature of a specific application. It occurs in large early warning radar systems, where High — the radar processor — controls hundreds of antenna elements that illuminate Low — the target — with high speed pulse trains that are modulated with pseudorandom noise to make jamming harder. In this case, the radar code must be trusted as the covert channel bandwidth is many megabits per second.

The best that developers have been able to do consistently with BLP confidentiality protection in regular time-sharing operating systems is to limit it to 1 bit per second or so. (That is a DoD target [376], and techniques for doing a systematic analysis may be found in Kemmerer [706].) One bit per second may be tolerable in an environment where we wish to prevent large TS/SCI files — such as satellite photographs — leaking down from TS/SCI users to 'Secret' users. It is much less than the rate at which malicious code might hide data in outgoing traffic that would be approved by a guard. However, it is inadequate if we want to prevent the leakage of a cryptographic key. This is one of the reasons for the military doctrine of doing crypto in special purpose hardware rather than in software.

8.6.4 The Threat from Viruses

The vast majority of viruses are found on mass-market products such as PCs. However, the defense computer community was shocked when Cohen used viruses to penetrate multilevel secure systems easily in 1983. In his first experiment, a file virus which took only eight hours to write managed to penetrate a system previously believed to be multilevel secure [311].

There are a number of ways in which viruses and other malicious code can be used to perform such attacks. If the reference monitor (or other TCB components) can be corrupted, then a virus could deliver the entire system to the attacker, for example by issuing him with an unauthorised clearance. For this reason, slightly looser rules apply to so-called *closed security environments* which are defined to be those where 'system applications are adequately protected against the insertion of malicious logic' [379]. But even if the TCB remains intact, the virus could still use any available covert channel to signal information down.

So in many cases a TCB will provide some protection against viral attacks, as well as against careless disclosure by users or application software — which is often more important than malicious disclosure. However, the main effect of viruses on military doctrine has been to strengthen the perceived case for multilevel security. The argument goes that even if personnel can be trusted, one cannot rely on technical measures short of total isolation to prevent viruses moving up the system, so one must do whatever reasonably possible to stop them signalling back down.

8.6.5   Polyinstantiation

Another problem that has much exercised the research community is *polyinstantiation*. Suppose that our High user has created a file named `agents`, and our Low user now tries to do the same. If the MLS operating system prohibits him, it will have leaked information — namely that there is a file called `agents` at High. But if it lets him, it will now have two files with the same name.

Often we can solve the problem by a naming convention, which could be as simple as giving Low and High users different directories. But the problem remains a hard one for databases [1112]. Suppose that a High user allocates a classified cargo to a ship. The system will not divulge this information to a Low user, who might think the ship is empty, and try to allocate it another cargo or even to change its destination.

The solution favoured in the USA for such systems is that the High user allocates a Low cover story at the same time as the real High cargo. Thus the underlying data will look something like Figure 8.6.

In the UK, the theory is simpler — the system will automatically reply 'classified' to a Low user who tries to see or alter a High record. The two available views would be as in Figure 8.7.

Level	Cargo	Destination
Secret	Missiles	Iran
Restricted	—	—
Unclassified	Engine spares	Cyprus

Figure 8.6: How the USA deals with classified data

Level	Cargo	Destination
Secret	Missiles	Iran
Restricted	Classified	Classified
Unclassified	—	—

Figure 8.7: How the UK deals with classified data

This makes the system engineering simpler. It also prevents the mistakes and covert channels which can still arise with cover stories (e.g., a Low user tries to add a container of ammunition for Cyprus). The drawback is that everyone tends to need the highest available clearance in order to get their work done. (In practice, of course, cover stories still get used in order not to advertise the existence of a covert mission any more than need be.)

There may be an interesting new application to the world of online gaming. Different countries have different rules about online content; for example, the USA limits online gambling, while Germany has strict prohibitions on the display of swastikas and other insignia of the Third Reich. Now suppose a second-world-war reenactment society wants to operate in Second Life. If a German resident sees flags with swastikas, an offence is committed there. Linden Labs, the operator of Second Life, has suggested authenticating users' jurisdictions; but it's not enough just to exclude Germans, as one of them might look over the fence. An alternative proposal is to tag alternative objects for visibility, so that a German looking at the Battle of Kursk would see only inoffensive symbols. Similarly, an American looking at an online casino might just see a church instead. Here too the lie has its limits; when the American tries to visit that church he'll find that he can't get through the door.

8.6.6   Other Practical Problems

Multilevel secure systems are surprisingly expensive and difficult to build and deploy. There are many sources of cost and confusion.

1. MLS systems are built in small volumes, and often to high standards of physical robustness, using elaborate documentation, testing and other quality control measures driven by military purchasing bureaucracies.

2. MLS systems have idiosyncratic administration tools and procedures. A trained Unix administrator can't just take on an MLS installation without significant further training. A USAF survey showed that many MLS systems were installed without their features being used [1044].

3. Many applications need to be rewritten or at least greatly modified to run under MLS operating systems [1092]. For example, compartmented mode workstations that display information at different levels in different windows, and prevent the user from doing cut-and-paste operations from high to low, often have problems with code which tries to manipulate the colour map. Access to files might be quite different, as well as the format of things like access control lists. Another source of conflict with commercial software is the licence server; if a High user invokes an application, which goes to a licence server for permission to execute, then an MLS operating system will promptly reclassify the server High and deny access to Low users. So in practice, you usually end up (a) running two separate

license servers, thus violating the license terms, or (b) you have an MLS license server which tracks licenses at all levels (this restricts your choice of platforms), or (c) you only access the licensed software at one of the levels.

4. Because processes are automatically upgraded as they see new labels, the files they use have to be too. New files default to the highest label belonging to any possible input. The result of all this is a chronic tendency for things to be overclassified.

5. It is often inconvenient to deal with 'blind write-up' — when a low level application sends data to a higher level one, BLP prevents any acknowledgment being sent. The effect is that information vanishes into a 'black hole'. The answer to this is varied. Some organizations accept the problem as a fact of life; in the words of a former NSA chief scientist 'When you pray to God, you do not expect an individual acknowledgement of each prayer before saying the next one'. Others use pumps rather than prayer, and accept a residual covert bandwidth as a fact of life.

6. The classification of data can get complex:

   ▪ in the run-up to a military operation, the location of 'innocuous' stores such as food could reveal tactical intentions, and so may be suddenly upgraded. It follows that the tranquility property cannot simply be assumed;

   ▪ classifications are not necessarily monotone. Equipment classified at 'confidential' in the peacetime inventory may easily contain components classified 'secret';

   ▪ information may need to be downgraded. An intelligence analyst might need to take a satellite photo classified at TS/SCI, and paste it into an assessment for field commanders at 'secret'. However, information could have been covertly hidden in the image by a virus, and retrieved later once the file is downgraded. So downgrading procedures may involve all sorts of special filters, such as lossy compression of images and word processors which scrub and reformat text, in the hope that the only information remaining is that which lies in plain sight. (I will discuss information hiding in more detail in the context of copyright marking.)

   ▪ we may need to worry about the volume of information available to an attacker. For example, we might be happy to declassify any single satellite photo, but declassifying the whole collection would reveal our surveillance capability and the history of our intelligence priorities. Similarly, the government payroll may not be very sensitive per se, but it is well known that journalists can often identify intelligence personnel working under civilian cover from studying the evolution of departmental staff lists over a period of a few years. (I will look at this issue — the 'aggregation problem' — in more detail in section 9.3.2.)

- a related problem is that the output of an unclassified program acting on unclassified data may be classified. This is also related to the aggregation problem.

7. There are always system components — such as memory management — that must be able to read and write at all levels. This objection is dealt with by abstracting it away, and assuming that memory management is part of the trusted computing base which enforces our mandatory access control policy. The practical outcome is that often a quite uncomfortably large part of the operating system (plus utilities, plus windowing system software, plus middleware such as database software) ends up part of the trusted computing base. 'TCB bloat' constantly pushes up the cost of evaluation and reduces assurance.

8. Finally, although MLS systems can prevent undesired things (such as information leakage) from happening, they also prevent desired things from happening too (such as efficient ways of enabling data to be downgraded from High to Low, which are essential if many systems are to be useful). So even in military environments, the benefits they provide can be very questionable. The associated doctrine also sets all sorts of traps for government systems builders. A recent example comes from the debate over a UK law to extend wiretaps to Internet Service Providers (ISPs). (I'll discuss wiretapping in Part III). Opponents of the bill forced the government to declare that information on the existence of an interception operation against an identified target would be classified 'Secret'. This would have made wiretaps on Internet traffic impossible without redeveloping all the systems used by Internet Service Providers to support an MLS security policy — which would have been totally impractical. So the UK government had to declare that it wouldn't apply the laid down standards in this case because of cost.

8.7   Broader Implications of MLS

The reader's reaction by this point may well be that mandatory access control is too hard to do properly; there are just too many complications. This may be true, and we are about to see the technology seriously tested as it's deployed in hundreds of millions of Vista PCs and Linux boxes. We will see to what extent mandatory access control really helps contain the malware threat, whether to commodity PCs or to servers in hosting centres. We'll also see whether variants of the problems described here cause serious or even fatal problems for the DRM vision.

However it's also true that Bell-LaPadula and Biba are the simplest security policy models we know of, and everything else is even harder. We'll look at other models in the next few chapters.

Anyway, although the MLS program has not delivered what was expected, it has spun off a lot of useful ideas and know-how. Worrying about not just the direct ways in which a secure system could be defeated but also about the second- and third-order consequences of the protection mechanisms has been important in developing the underlying science. Practical work on building MLS systems also led people to work through many other aspects of computer security, such as *Trusted Path* (how does a user know he's talking to a genuine copy of the operating system?), *Trusted Distribution* (how does a user know he's installing a genuine copy of the operating system?) and *Trusted Facility Management* (how can we be sure it's all administered correctly?). In effect, tackling one simplified example of protection in great detail led to many things being highlighted which previously were glossed over. The resulting lessons can be applied to systems with quite different policies.

These lessons were set out in the 'Rainbow Series' of books on computer security, produced by the NSA following the development of SCOMP and the publication of the Orange Book which it inspired. These books are so called because of the different coloured covers by which they're known. The series did a lot to raise consciousness of operational and evaluation issues that are otherwise easy to ignore (or to dismiss as boring matters best left to the end purchasers). In fact, the integration of technical protection mechanisms with operational and procedural controls is one of the most critical, and neglected, aspects of security engineering. I will have much more to say on this topic in Part III, and in the context of a number of case studies throughout this book.

Apart from the official 'lessons learned' from MLS, there have been other effects noticed over the years. In particular, the MLS program has had negative effects on many of the government institutions that used it. There is a tactical problem, and a strategic one.

The tactical problem is that the existence of trusted system components plus a large set of bureaucratic guidelines has a strong tendency to displace critical thought. Instead of working out a system's security requirements in a methodical way, designers just choose what they think is the appropriate security class of component and then regurgitate the description of this class as the security specification of the overall system [1044].

One should never lose sight of the human motivations which drive a system design, and the costs which it imposes. Moynihan's book [907] provides a critical study of the real purposes and huge costs of obsessive secrecy in US foreign and military affairs. Following a Senate enquiry, he discovered that President Truman was never told of the Venona decrypts because the material was considered 'Army Property' — despite its being the main motivation for the prosecution of Alger Hiss. As his book puts it: 'Departments and agencies hoard information, and the government becomes a kind of market. Secrets become organizational assets, never to be shared save in exchange for another organization's assets.' He reports, for example, that in 1996 the number of original classification authorities decreased by 959 to 4,420 (following post-Cold-War budget cuts) but that the total of all classification actions reported for fiscal year 1996 increased by 62 percent to 5,789,625.

I wrote in the first edition in 2001: 'Yet despite the huge increase in secrecy, the quality of intelligence made available to the political leadership appears to have declined over time. Effectiveness is undermined by inter-agency feuding and refusal to share information, and by the lack of effective external critique[3]. So a strong case can be made that MLS systems, by making the classification process easier and controlled data sharing harder, actually impair operational effectiveness'. A few months after the book was published, the attacks of 9/11 drove home the lesson that the US intelligence community, with its resources fragmented into more than twenty agencies and over a million compartments, was failing to join up the dots into an overall picture. Since then, massive efforts have been made to get the agencies to share data. It's not clear that this is working; some barriers are torn down, others are erected, and bureaucratic empire building games continue as always. There have, however, been leaks of information that the old rules should have prevented. For example, a Bin Laden video obtained prior to its official release by Al-Qaida in September 2007 spread rapidly through U.S. intelligence agencies and was leaked by officials to TV news, compromising the source [1322].

In the UK, the system of classification is pretty much the same as the U.S. system described in this chapter, but the system itself is secret, with the full manual being available only to senior officials. This was a contributory factor in a public scandal in which a junior official at the tax office wrote a file containing the personal information of all the nation's children and their families to two CDs, which proceeded to get lost in the post. He simply was not aware that data this sensitive should have been handled with more care [591]. I'll describe this scandal and discuss its implications in more detail in the next chapter.

So multilevel security can be a double-edged sword. It has become entrenched in government, and in the security-industrial complex generally, and is often used in inappropriate ways. Even long-time intelligence insiders have documented this [671]. There are many problems which we need to be a 'fox' rather than a 'hedgehog' to solve. Even where a simple, mandatory, access control system could be appropriate, we often need to control information flows across, rather than information flows down. Medical systems are a good example of this, and we will look at them next.

---

[3]Although senior people follow the official line when speaking on the record, once in private they rail at the penalties imposed by the bureaucracy. My favorite quip is from an exasperated British general: 'What's the difference between Jurassic Park and the Ministry of Defence? One's a theme park full of dinosaurs, and the other's a movie!'

8.8   Summary

Mandatory access control was developed for military applications, most notably specialized kinds of firewalls (guards and pumps). They are being incorporated into commodity platforms such as Vista and Linux. They have even broader importance in that they have been the main subject of computer security research since the mid-1970's, and their assumptions underlie many of the schemes used for security evaluation. It is important for the practitioner to understand both their strengths and limitations, so that you can draw on the considerable research literature when it's appropriate, and avoid being dragged into error when it's not.

Research Problems

Multilevel confidentiality appears to have been comprehensively done to death by generations of DARPA-funded research students. The opportunity now is to explore what can be done with the second-generation mandatory access control systems shipped with Vista and SELinux, and with virtualization products such as VMware and Xen; what can be done to make it easier to devise policies for these systems that enable them to do useful work; in better mechanisms for controlling information flow between compartments; the interaction which multilevel systems have with other security policies; and in ways to make mandatory access control systems usable.

An ever broader challenge, sketched out by Earl Boebert after the NSA launched SELinux, is to adapt mandatory access control mechanisms to safety-critical systems (see the quote at the head of this chapter, and [197]). As a tool for building high-assurance, special-purpose devices where the consequences of errors and failures can be limited, mechanisms such as type enforcement and role-based access control look like they will be useful outside the world of security. By locking down intended information flows, designers can reduce the likelihood of unanticipated interactions.

Further Reading

The report on the Walker spy ring is essential reading for anyone interested in the system of classifications and clearances [587]: this describes in great detail the system's most spectacular known failure. It brings home the sheer complexity of running a system in which maybe three million people have a current SECRET or TOP SECRET clearance at any one time, with a million applications being processed each year — especially when the system was designed on the basis of how people should behave, rather than on how they actually do behave. And the classic on the abuse of the classification process to cover up waste, fraud and mismanagement in the public sector was written by Chapman [282].

On the technical side, one of the better introductions to MLS systems, and especially the problems of databases, is Gollmann's *Computer Security* [537]. Amoroso's *'Fundamentals of Computer Security Technology'* [27] is the best introduction to the formal mathematics underlying the Bell-LaPadula, noninterference and nondeducibility security models.

The bulk of the published papers on engineering actual MLS systems can be found in the annual proceedings of three conferences: the *IEEE Symposium on Security & Privacy* (known as 'Oakland' as that's where it's held), the *National Computer Security Conference* (renamed the *National Information Systems Security Conference* in 1995), whose proceedings were published by NIST until the conference ended in 1999, and the *Computer Security Applications Conference* whose proceedings are (like Oakland's) published by the IEEE. Fred Cohen's experiments on breaking MLS systems using viruses are described in his book, *'A Short Course on Computer Viruses'* [311]. Many of the classic early papers in the field can be found at the NIST archive [934].

Multilateral Security

9.1 Introduction

Often our goal is not to prevent information flowing 'down' a hierarchy but to prevent it flowing 'across' between departments. Relevant applications range from healthcare to national intelligence, and include most applications where the privacy of individual customers', citizens' or patients' data is at stake. They account for a significant proportion of information processing systems but their protection is often poorly designed and implemented. This has led to a number of expensive fiascos.

The basic problem is that if you centralise systems containing sensitive information, you risk creating a more valuable asset and simultaneously giving more people access to it. This is now a pressing problem in the world of 'Web 2.0' as online applications amass petabytes of people's private information. And it's not just Google Documents; a number of organisations plan to warehouse your medical records online. Microsoft has announced HealthVault, which will let your doctors store your medical records online in a data centre and give you some control over access; other IT firms have broadly similar plans. Yet privacy activists point out that however convenient this may be in an emergency, it gives access to insurance companies, government agencies and anyone else who comes along with a court order [1332]. So what are the real issues with such systems, should they be built, if so how should we protect them, and are there any precedents from which we can learn?

One lesson comes from banking. In the old days, a private investigator who wanted copies of your bank statements had to subvert someone at the branch where your account was kept. But after banks hooked all their branches up online in the 1980s, they typically let any teller enquire about any customer's account. This brought the convenience of being able to cash a check when you are out of town; but it's also meant that private eyes buy and sell your bank statements for a few hundred dollars. They only have to corrupt one employee at each bank, rather than one at each branch. Another example comes from the UK Inland Revenue, the tax collection office; staff were caught making improper access to the records of celebrities, selling data to outsiders, and leaking income details in alimony cases [129].

In such systems, a typical requirement will be to stop users looking at records belonging to a different branch, or a different geographical region, or a different partner in the firm — except under strict controls. Thus instead of the information flow control boundaries being horizontal as we saw in the Bell-LaPadula model as in Figure 9.1, we instead need the boundaries to be mostly vertical, as shown in Figure 9.2.

These lateral information flow controls may be organizational, as in an intelligence organization which wants to keep the names of agents working in one foreign country secret from the department responsible for spying on another. They may be privilege-based, as in a law firm where different clients' affairs, and the clients of different partners, must be kept separate. They may even be a mixture of the two, as in medicine where patient confidentiality

TOP SECRET
SECRET
CONFIDENTIAL
OPEN

Figure 9.1: Multilevel security

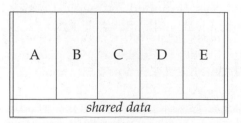

Figure 9.2: Multilateral security

is based in law on the rights of the patient but usually enforced by limiting medical record access to a particular hospital department.

The control of lateral information flows is a very general problem, of which we'll use medicine as a clear and well-studied example. The problems of medical systems are readily understandable by the nonspecialist and have considerable economic and social importance. Much of what we have to say about them goes across with little or no change to the practice of other professions, and to government applications where access to particular kinds of classified data are restricted to particular teams or departments.

One minor problem we face is one of terminology. Information flow controls of the type we're interested in are known by a number of different names; in the U.S. intelligence community, for example, they are known as *compartmented security* or *compartmentation*. We will use the European term *multilateral security* as the healthcare application is bigger than intelligence, and as the term also covers the use of techniques such as anonymity — the classic case being de-identified research databases of medical records. This is an important part of multilateral security. As well as preventing overt information flows, we also have to prevent information leakage through, for example, statistical and billing data which get released.

The use of de-identified data has wider applicability. Another example is the processing of census data. In general, the relevant protection techniques are known as *inference control*. Despite occasional differences in terminology, the problems facing the operators of census databases and medical research databases are very much the same.

9.2   Compartmentation, the Chinese Wall and the BMA Model

There are (at least) three different models of how to implement access controls and information flow controls in a multilateral security model. These are compartmentation, used by the intelligence community; the *Chinese Wall* model, which describes the mechanisms used to prevent conflicts of interest in professional practice; and the *BMA model*, developed by the British Medical Association to describe the information flows permitted by medical ethics. Each of these has potential applications outside its initial field.

9.2.1   Compartmentation and the Lattice Model

For many years, it has been standard practice in the United States and allied governments to restrict access to information by the use of codewords as well as classifications. The best documented example is the codeword *Ultra* in World

War 2, which referred to British and American decrypts of German messages enciphered using the Enigma cipher machine. The fact that the Enigma had been broken was so important that it was worth protecting at almost any cost. So Ultra clearances were given to only a small number of people — in addition to the cryptanalysts and their support staff, the list included the Allied leaders, their senior generals, and hand-picked analysts. No-one who had ever held an Ultra clearance could be placed at risk of capture; and the intelligence could never be used in such a way as to let Hitler suspect that his principal cipher had been broken. Thus when Ultra told of a target, such as an Italian convoy to North Africa, the Allies would send over a plane to 'spot' it and report its position by radio an hour or so before the attack. This policy was enforced by special handling rules; for example, Churchill got his Ultra summaries in a special dispatch box to which he had a key but his staff did not. Because such special rules may apply, access to a codeword is sometimes referred to as an *indoctrination* rather than simply a clearance. (Ultra security is described in Kahn [677] and in Welchman [1336].)

Much the same precautions are in place today to protect information whose compromise could expose intelligence sources or methods, such as agent names, cryptanalytic successes, the capabilities of equipment used for electronic eavesdropping, and the performance of surveillance satellites. The proliferation of codewords results in a large number of compartments, especially at classification levels above Top Secret.

One reason for this is that classifications are inherited by derived work; so a report written using sources from 'Secret Desert Storm' and 'Top Secret Umbra' can in theory only be read by someone with a clearance of 'Top Secret' and membership of the groups 'Umbra' and 'Desert Storm'. Each combination of codewords gives a compartment, and some intelligence agencies have over a million active compartments. Managing them is a significant problem. Other agencies let people with high level clearances have relatively wide access. But when the control mechanisms fail, the result can be disastrous. Aldritch Ames, a CIA officer who had accumulated access to a large number of compartments by virtue of long service and seniority, and because he worked in counterintelligence, was able to betray almost the entire U.S. agent network in Russia.

Codewords are in effect a pre-computer way of expressing access control groups, and can be dealt with using a variant of Bell-LaPadula, called the *lattice model*. Classifications together with codewords form a lattice — a mathematical structure in which any two objects A and B can be in a dominance relation $A > B$ or $B > A$. They don't have to be: A and B could simply be incomparable (but in this case, for the structure to be a lattice, they will have a least upper bound and a greatest lower bound). As an illustration, suppose we have a codeword, say 'Crypto'. Then someone cleared to 'Top Secret' would be entitled to read files classified 'Top Secret' and 'Secret', but would have no access to files classified 'Secret Crypto' unless he also had a crypto clearance. This can be expressed as shown in Figure 9.3.

In order for information systems to support this, we need to distill the essence of classifications, clearances and labels into a security policy that we can then use to drive security targets, implementation, and evaluation. As it happens, the Bell-LaPadula model goes across more or less unchanged. We still have information flows between High and Low as before, where High is a compartment that dominates Low. If two nodes in a lattice are incompatible — as with 'Top Secret' and 'Secret Crypto' in the above diagram — then there should be no information flow between them at all.

In fact, the lattice and Bell-LaPadula models are essentially equivalent, and were developed at the same time.

- Roger Schell, Peter Downey, and Gerald Popek of the U.S. Air Force produced an early lattice model in 1972 [1119].

- A Cambridge PhD thesis by Jeffrey Fenton included a representation in which labels were managed using a matrix [464].

- About this time, the Pentagon's World Wide Military Command and Control System (WWMCCS) used a primitive lattice model, but without the *-property. The demonstration that a fielded, critical, system handling Top Secret data was vulnerable to attack by Trojans caused some consternation [1118]. It meant that all users had to be cleared to the highest level of data in the machine.

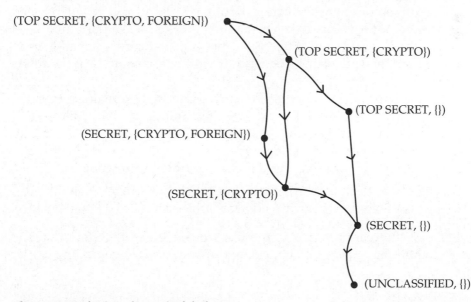

Figure 9.3: A lattice of security labels

- Kenneth Walter, Walter Ogden, William Rounds, Frank Bradshaw, Stan Ames, and David Shumway of Case Western University produced a more advanced lattice model as well as working out a lot of the problems with file and directory attributes, which they fed to Bell and LaPadula [1312, 1313][1].

- Finally, the lattice model was systematized and popularized by Denning [368].

Most products built for the multilevel secure market can be reused in compartmented mode. But, in practice, these products are not as effective as one might like. It is easy to use a multilevel operating system to keep data in different compartments separate — just give them incompatible labels ('Secret Tulip', 'Secret Daffodil', 'Secret Crocus', ...). But the operating system has now become an isolation mechanism, rather than a sharing mechanism; the real problem is how to control information sharing.

One solution is to impose least upper bounds in the lattice using some algorithm. An example comes from the system used by the government of Saudi Arabia to manage the Haj, the annual pilgrimage to Mecca [606]. While most compartments are by default Confidential, the combination of data from different compartments is Secret. Thus 'Haj-visas' and 'Gov-guest' are confidential, but their combination is Secret.

In many intelligence systems, where the users are already operating at the highest level of clearance, data owners don't want a further classification level at which everything is visible. So data derived from two compartments effectively creates a third compartment using the lattice model. The proliferation of millions of compartments is complex to manage and can be intertwined with applications. So a more common solution is to use a standard multilevel product, such as a mail guard, to ensure that 'untrustworthy' email goes to filters. But now the core of the trusted computing base consists of the filters rather than the guard.

Worse, the guard may lose some of the more important functionality of the underlying operating system. For example, the Standard Mail Guard [1193] was built on top of an operating system called LOCK whose basic mechanism is type enforcement, as described in the previous chapter. Later versions of LOCK support role-based access control, which would be a more appropriate mechanism to manage the relationships between compartments directly [612]. Using it merely as a platform to support BLP may have been wasteful.

In general, the real problems facing users of intelligence systems have to do with combining data in different compartments, and downgrading it after

---

[1]Walter and his colleagues deserve more credit than history has given them. They had the main results first [1312] but Bell and LaPadula had their work heavily promoted by the U.S. Air Force. Fenton has also been largely ignored, not being an American.

sanitization. Multilevel and lattice security models offer little help here. Indeed one of the biggest problems facing the U.S. intelligence community since 9/11 is how to handle search over systems with many compartments. A search done over many agencies' databases can throw up results with many codewords attached; if this were to be aggregated in one place, then that place would in effect possess all clearances. What new systems do is to send out search queries bound with the clearance of the user: 'Show me everything that matches Uzbek and Peshawar and weapons and motorcycle, and can be seen by someone with a clearance of Top Secret Umbra'. Here, local labels just get in the way; but without them, how do you forestall a future Aldritch Ames?

There's a also sobering precedent in the Walker spy case. There, an attempt to keep naval vessels in compartments just didn't work, as a ship could be sent anywhere on no notice, and for a ship to be isolated with no local key material was operationally unacceptable. So the U.S. Navy's 800 ships all ended up with the same set of cipher keys, which got sold to the Russians [587].

9.2.2   The Chinese Wall

The second model of multilateral security is the Chinese Wall model, developed by Brewer and Nash [224]. Its name comes from the fact that financial services firms from investment banks to accountants have internal rules designed to prevent conflicts of interest, which they call Chinese Walls.

The model's scope is wider than just finance. There are many professional and services firms whose clients may be in competition with each other: software vendors and advertising agencies are other examples. A typical rule is that 'a partner who has worked recently for one company in a business sector may not see the papers of any other company in that sector'. So once an advertising copywriter has worked on (say) the Shell account, he will not be allowed to work on any other oil company's account for some fixed period of time.

The Chinese Wall model thus features a mix of free choice and mandatory access control: a partner can choose which oil company to work for, but once that decision is taken his actions in that sector are completely constrained. It also introduces the concept of *separation of duty* into access control; a given user may perform transaction A or transaction B, but not both.

Part of the attraction of the Chinese Wall model to the security research community comes from the fact that it can be expressed in a way that is fairly similar to Bell-LaPadula. If we write, for each object c, $y(c)$ for c's company and $x(c)$ for c's conflict-of-interest class, then like BLP it can be expressed in two properties:

- The *simple security property*: a subject s has access to c if and only if, for all c' which s can read, either $y(c) \notin x(c')$ or $y(c) = y(c')$

■ The **-property*: a subject s can write to c only if s cannot read any c' with $x(c') \neq \oslash$ and $y(c) \neq y(c')$.

The Chinese Wall model made a seminal contribution to the theory of access control. It also sparked a debate about the extent to which it is consistent with the BLP tranquility properties, and some work on the formal semantics of such systems (see, for example, Foley [480] on the relationship with non-interference). There are also some interesting new questions about covert channels. For example, could an oil company find out whether a competitor which used the same investment bank was planning a bid for a third oil company, by asking which specialists were available for consultation and noticing that their number had dropped suddenly?

In practice, however, Chinese Walls still get implemented using manual methods. One large software consultancy has each of its staff maintain an 'unclassified' curriculum vitae containing entries that have been sanitized and agreed with the customer. A typical entry might be:

> **Sep 97 — Apr 98**: consulted on security requirements for a new branch accounting system for a major U.S. retail bank

This is not the only control. A consultant's manager should be aware of possible conflicts and not forward the CV to the client if in doubt; if this fails the client can spot potential conflicts himself from the CV; and if this also fails then the consultant is duty bound to report any potential conflicts as soon as they appear.

9.2.3 The BMA Model

Perhaps the most important, interesting and instructive example of multilateral security is found in medical information systems. The healthcare sector spends a much larger share of national income than the military in developed countries, and although hospitals are still less automated, they are catching up fast. A 2006 study for the U.S. Department of Health and Human Services (DHHS) showed that investments in health IT were recouped in from three to thirteen years, and could make health care safer as well as more efficient [1160].

Healthcare safety and (especially) privacy have become hot-button issues in many countries. In the USA, the Health Insurance Portability and Accountability Act (HIPAA) was passed by Congress in 1996 following a number of privacy failures. In one notorious case, Mark Farley, a convicted child rapist working as an orthopedic technician at Newton-Wellesley Hospital in Newton, Massachusetts, was caught using a former employee's password to go through the records of 954 patients (mostly young females) to get the phone numbers of girls to whom he then made obscene phone calls [??]. He ended up doing jail time, and the Massachusetts senator Edward Kennedy was one of HIPAA's sponsors. There are many more incidents of a less dramatic nature. Also in 1995–96, the UK government attempted to centralise all medical records, which led to a confrontation with the British Medical Association (BMA). The BMA hired me to devise a policy for safety and privacy of clinical information, which I'll discuss below.

The controversy continued. In the late 1990s, a project in Iceland to build a national medical database incorporating not just medical records but also genetic and genealogical data, so that inherited diseases can be tracked across generations, caused an uproar. Eleven percent of the population opted out; eventually the Icelandic Supreme Court decided that the database had to be opt-in rather than opt-out, and now about half the population participate.

In 2002, President Bush rewrote and relaxed the HIPAA regulations, known as the 'Privacy Rule'; this was followed by further 'administrative simplification' in 2006. The U.S. situation is now that, although medical data must still be protected in hospitals, clinics and insurers, its use outside the immediate care setting (for example, by researchers, employers and welfare agencies) is outside the regulations and so much less controlled. No-one's completely happy: health privacy advocates consider the regime to be quite inadequate; hospitals complain that it adds unnecessarily to their costs; and patient advocates note that HIPAA is often used by hospital staff as an excuse to be unhelpful [560]. At the time of writing (2007), Atlanta's Piedmont Hospital has just become the first institution in the USA to be audited for compliance with the security and privacy regulations, which came into force in 2005. This audit covered topics from physical and logical access to systems and data through Internet usage to violations of security rules by employees, and helped many other healthcare providers decide to invest in encryption and other protection technologies [1295]. In addition, the Government Accountability Office (GAO) has just reported that the DHHS needs to do a lot more to ensure patient privacy, particularly by defining an overall strategy for privacy and by adopting milestones for dealing with nationwide health data exchange (which is not just a matter of inadequate technical protection but also of varying state laws) [735].

In various European countries, there have been debates about the safety and privacy tradeoffs involved with emergency medical information. The Germans put data such as current prescriptions and allergies on the medical insurance card that residents carry; other countries have held back from this, reasoning that if data currently held on a human-readable MedAlert bracelet, such as allergies, are moved to a machine-readable device such as a smartcard, then there is a risk to patients who fall ill in locations where there is no reader available, such as on an airplane or a foreign holiday. In the UK, the government is creating a 'summary care record' of prescriptions and allergies that will be kept on a central database and will be available to many health-care workers, from emergency room clinicians to paramedics and the operators of out-of-hours medical helpline services. One problem is that a patient's current medications often reveal highly sensitive information — such as treatment for HIV, depression or alcoholism — and making such information available to hundreds of thousands of people carries substantial risks of abuse. Patients have been offered the right to opt out of this system.

There have also been debates about privacy and ethical issues relating to secondary uses of medical information, such as in research. First, there are worries about privacy failures, for example, when a research professor loses a laptop containing the records of millions of patients. Although records used in research often have names and addresses removed, it is a seriously hard job to de-identify records properly; I'll discuss this in detail below. Second, there are ethics issues related to consent. For example, a devout Catholic woman might object to her gynaecological data being used to develop a better morning-after pill. Third, there are economic issues; if my data get used to develop a drug from which a company makes billions of dollars, shouldn't I get a share?

The protection of medical information is thus an interesting case history for the security engineer. It has a lot of rich and complex tradeoffs; it's important to all of us; and it's frequently in the news.

Medical privacy is also a model for protecting personal information of other kinds, such as the information held on individual customers by companies and government agencies. In all European countries (and in many others, such as Canada and Australia) there are *data protection* laws that restrict the dissemination of such data. I'll discuss data protection law in Part III; for present purposes, it's enough to note that some classes of data (affecting health, sexual behavior, political activity and religious belief) the *data subject* must either consent to information sharing, or have a right of veto, or there must be a specific law that permits sharing for the public interest in circumstances that are well enough defined for the data subject to predict them. This raises the issue of how one can construct a security policy in which the access control decisions are taken not by a central authority (as in Bell-LaPadula) or by the system's users (as in discretionary access control) but by the data subjects.

Let's look first at the access control aspects.

9.2.3.1 *The Threat Model*

The main threat to medical privacy is abuse of authorised access by insiders, and the most common threat vector is social engineering. The typical attack comes from a private detective who phones a doctor's office or health insurer with a plausible tale:

> Hello, this is Dr Burnett of the cardiology department at the Conquest Hospital in Hastings. Your patient Sam Simmonds has just been admitted here in a coma, and he has a funny looking ventricular arrhythmia. Can you tell me if there's anything relevant in his record?

This kind of attack is usually so successful that in both the USA and the UK there are people who earn their living doing it [411]. (It's not restricted to health records — in June 2000, Tony Blair's fundraiser Lord Levy was acutely embarrassed after someone called the tax office pretending to be him and found out that he'd only paid £5000 in tax the previous year [1064]. But the medical context is a good one in which to discuss it.)

As I mentioned briefly in Chapter 2, an experiment was done in the UK in 1996 whereby the staff at a health authority (a government-owned insurer that purchases health care for a district of several hundred thousand people) were trained to screen out false-pretext telephone calls. The advice they were given is described in [36] but the most important element of it was that they were to always call back — and not to a number given by the caller, but to the number in the phone book for the hospital or other institution where the caller claimed to work. It turned out that some thirty telephone enquiries a week were bogus.

Such *operational security* measures are much more important than most technical protection measures, but they are difficult. If everyone was as unhelpful as intelligence-agency staff are trained to be, the world would grind to a halt. And the best staff training in the world won't protect a system where too many people see too much data. There will always be staff who are careless or even crooked; and the more records they can get, the more harm they can do. Also, organisations have established cultures; we have been simply unable to embed even lightweight operational-security measures on any scale in healthcare, simply because that's not how people work. Staff are focussed on delivering care rather than questioning each other. The few real operational improvements in the last few years have all followed scares; for example, maternity units in Britain now have reasonable entry controls, following incidents in which babies were stolen from nurseries. Also, geriatric wards are often locked to stop demented patients from wandering off. However, most hospital wards are completely open; anyone can wander in off the street to visit their relatives, and the clinical benefits of frequent visits outweigh the occasional violent incidents. PCs are left unattended and logged on to the hospital network. Recently, a health IT investment programme in the UK has tried to standardise access control and issued clinical staff with smartcards to log on to hospital systems; but since logging off as Nurse Jones and on again as Nurse Smith takes several seconds, staff don't bother.

A more general problem is that even where staff behave ethically, a lack of technical understanding — or, as we might more properly describe it, poor security usability — causes leaks of personal information. Old PCs sold on the second hand market or given to schools often have recoverable data on the hard disk; most people are unaware that the usual 'delete' command does not remove the file, but merely marks the space it occupies as re-usable. A PC sold on the second hand market by investment bank Morgan Grenfell

Asset Management had recoverable files containing the financial dealings of ex-Beatle Paul McCartney [254]: there have been similar problems with old health records. Equipment also gets stolen: some 11% of UK family doctors have experienced the theft of a practice PC, and in one case two prominent society ladies were blackmailed over terminations of pregnancy following such a theft [37]. The UK government response to this threat is to try to persuade family doctors to move to 'hosted' systems, where the practice data are kept on regional server farms; but it's quite unclear that there's a net privacy gain. Data theft may be harder, but once data are centralised you can expect access creep; more and more public agencies will come up with arguments why they need access to the data. Even if all the access cases are individually sound, the net effect over time can be quite destructive of privacy.

The fundamental problem is this. The likelihood that a resource will be abused depends on its value and on the number of people who have access to it. Aggregating personal information into large databases increases both these risk factors at the same time. Put simply, we can live with a situation in which a doctor's receptionist has access to 2,000 patients' records: there will be abuse from time to time, but at a tolerably low level. However, if the receptionists of the 5,000 family doctors who might work with a large American HMO, or in one of the five regions of England's National Health Service, all have access to the records of maybe ten million patients, then abuse becomes likely. It only takes one insider who learns to walk up to a PC that's logged on using someone else's smartcard, read a file, and pass the information on to a private eye in exchange for cash. It's not just doctors; in England, each region has tens of thousands of people with access, from nurses and programmers and receptionists to drivers and caterers and cleaners. Many of the staff are temporary, many are foreign, and many are earning close to the minimum wage. And privacy issues aren't limited to organizations that treat patients directly: some of the largest collections of personal health information are in the hands of health insurers and research organizations. I'll discuss their special problems below in section 9.3.

In such an environment, lateral information flow controls are required. A good example of what can go wrong without them comes from an early UK hospital system whose designers believed that for reasons of safety, all staff should have access to all records. This decision was influenced by lobbying from geriatricians and pediatricians, whose patients are often treated by a number of specialist departments in the hospital. They were frustrated by the incompatibilities between different departmental systems. The system was fielded in 1995 in Hampshire, where the then health minister Gerry Malone had his parliamentary seat. The system made all lab tests performed for local doctors at the hospital's pathology lab visible to most of the hospital's staff. A nurse who had had a test done by her family doctor complained to him after she found the result on the hospital system at Basingstoke where she worked; this caused outrage among local medics, and Malone lost his seat in Parliament at the 1997 election (by two votes) [46].

So how can we avoid letting everyone see every record? There are many ad-hoc things you can do: one fairly effective measure is to keep the records of former patients in a separate archive, and give only a small number of admissions staff the power to move records from there to the main system. Another is to introduce a *honey trap*: one Boston hospital has on its system some bogus 'medical records' with the names of Kennedy family members, so it can identify and discipline staff who browse them. A particularly ingenious proposal, due to Gus Simmons, is to investigate all staff who consult a patient record but do not submit a payment claim to the insurer within thirty days; this aligns the patient's interest in privacy with the hospital's interest in maximizing its income.

However, a patchwork of ad-hoc measures isn't a good way to secure a system. We need a proper access control policy, thought through from first principles and driven by a realistic model of the threats. What policy is appropriate for healthcare?

9.2.3.2   *The Security Policy*

This question faced the BMA in 1995. The UK government had introduced an IT strategy for the National Health Service which involved centralizing a lot of data on central servers and whose security policy was multilevel: the idea was that AIDS databases would be at a level corresponding to Secret, normal patient records at Confidential and administrative data such as drug prescriptions and bills for treatment at Restricted. It was soon realised that this wasn't going to work. For example, how should a prescription for AZT be classified? As it's a drug prescription, it should be Restricted; but as it identifies a person as HIV positive, it must be Secret. So all the 'Secret' AZT prescriptions must be removed from the 'Restricted' file of drug prescriptions. But then so must almost all the other prescriptions as they identify treatments for named individuals and so should be 'Confidential'. But then what use will the file of prescriptions be to anybody?

A second problem is that the strategy was based on the idea of a single *electronic patient record* (EPR) that would follow the patient around from conception to autopsy, rather than the traditional system of having different records on the same patient at different hospitals and doctors' offices, with information flowing between them in the form of referral and discharge letters. An attempt to devise a security policy for the EPR, which would observe existing ethical norms, quickly became unmanageably complex [558].

In a project for which I was responsible, the BMA developed a security policy to fill the gap. The critical innovation was to define the medical record not as the total of all clinical facts relating to a patient, but as the maximum set of facts relating to a patient and to which the same staff had access. So an individual patient will have more than one record, and this offended the 'purist' advocates of the EPR. But multiple records are dictated anyway by law and practice. Depending on the country (and even the state) that you're in, you may have to keep separate medical records for human fertilization, sexually transmitted diseases, prison medical services, and even birth records (as they pertain to the health of the mother as well as the child, and can't simply be released to the child later without violating the mother's confidentiality). This situation is likely to get more complex still as genetic data start being used more widely.

In many countries, including all signatories to the European Convention on Human Rights, a special status is given to patient consent in law as well as in medical ethics. Records can only be shared with third parties if the patient approves, or in a limited range of statutory exceptions, such as tracing contacts of people with infectious diseases like TB. Definitions are slightly fluid; in some countries, HIV infection is notifiable, in others it isn't, and in others the data are collected stealthily.

The goals of the BMA security policy were therefore to enforce the principle of patient consent, and to prevent too many people getting access to too many identifiable records. It did not try to do anything new, but merely to codify existing best practice. It also sought to express other security features of medical record management such as safety and accountability. For example, it must be possible to reconstruct the contents of the record at any time in the past, so that for example if a malpractice suit is brought the court can determine what information was available to the doctor at the time. The details of the requirements analysis are in [37].

The policy consists of nine principles.

1. Access control: each identifiable clinical record shall be marked with an access control list naming the people or groups of people who may read it and append data to it. The system shall prevent anyone not on the access control list from accessing the record in any way.

2. Record opening: a clinician may open a record with herself and the patient on the access control list. Where a patient has been referred, she may open a record with herself, the patient and the referring clinician(s) on the access control list.

3. Control: One of the clinicians on the access control list must be marked as being responsible. Only she may alter the access control list, and she may only add other health care professionals to it.

4. Consent and notification: the responsible clinician must notify the patient of the names on his record's access control list when it is opened, of all subsequent additions, and whenever responsibility is transferred. His

consent must also be obtained, except in emergency or in the case of statutory exemptions.

5. Persistence: no-one shall have the ability to delete clinical information until the appropriate time period has expired.

6. Attribution: all accesses to clinical records shall be marked on the record with the subject's name, as well as the date and time. An audit trail must also be kept of all deletions.

7. Information flow: Information derived from record A may be appended to record B if and only if B's access control list is contained in A's.

8. Aggregation control: there shall be effective measures to prevent the aggregation of personal health information. In particular, patients must receive special notification if any person whom it is proposed to add to their access control list already has access to personal health information on a large number of people.

9. Trusted computing base: computer systems that handle personal health information shall have a subsystem that enforces the above principles in an effective way. Its effectiveness shall be subject to evaluation by independent experts.

This policy may seem to be just common sense, but is surprisingly comprehensive and radical in technical terms. For example, it is strictly more expressive than the Bell-LaPadula model of the last chapter; it contains a BLP-type information flow control mechanism in principle 7, but also contains state. (A fuller discussion from the point of view of access control, and for a technical audience, can be found at [38].)

Similar policies were developed by other medical bodies including the Swedish and German medical associations; the Health Informatics Association of Canada, and an EU project (these are surveyed in [732]). However the BMA model is the most detailed and has been subjected to the most rigorous review; it was adopted by the Union of European Medical Organisations (UEMO) in 1996. Feedback from public consultation on the policy can be found in [39].

9.2.3.3 *Pilot Implementations*

In a top-down approach to security engineering, one should first determine the threat model, then write the policy, and then finally test the policy by observing whether it works in real life.

BMA-compliant systems have now been implemented both in general practice [585], and in a hospital system developed in Hastings, England, that enforces similar access rules using a mixture of roles and capabilities. It has rules such as 'a ward nurse can see the records of all patients who have within the previous 90 days been on her ward', 'a doctor can see the records of all patients who have been treated in her department', and 'a senior doctor can see the records of all patients, but if she accesses the record of a patient who has never been treated in her department, then the senior doctor responsible for that patient's care will be notified'. (The hospital system was initially designed independently of the BMA project. When we learned of each other we were surprised at how much our approaches coincided, and reassured that we had captured the profession's expectations in a reasonably accurate way.)

The lessons learned are discussed in [366, 367, 585]. One was the difficulty of constructing a small trusted computing base. The hospital records system has to rely on the patient administrative system to tell it which patients, and which nurses, are on which ward. A different prototype system at a hospital in Cambridge, England, furnished staff with certificates in smartcards which they used to log on.

9.2.4   Current Privacy Issues

In 2002, Prime Minister Tony Blair was persuaded to allocate £6bn to modernise health service computing in England. This led to a scramble for contracts with security being something of an afterthought. The original vision was for much improved communications in each local health community; so that if a diabetic patient was being seen by a family doctor, a hospital diabetologist, a community nurse and an optician, they would all be able to see each others' notes and test results. The patient herself would also be able to upload data such as blood glucose levels, see her medical notes, and participate in her care. This vision had been pioneered in the Wirral near Liverpool.

When the dust of the contracting process had settled, the local empowerment vision had been replaced with a much more central approach. Contracts were let for five regions, each with about 10 million people, calling for all hospital systems to be replaced during 2004–2010 with standard ones. The number of system suppliers has been whittled down to two — Cerner and iSoft — and the security policy has been the subject of much debate. The current policy is for three main mechanisms.

1. The workhorse of access control will be role-based access controls, similar to those pioneered at Hastings, but much more complex; rather than a dozen or so roles the plan is now for there to be over three hundred.

2. In order to access patient data, a staff member will also need a *legitimate relationship*. This is an abstraction of the Hastings idea of 'her department'.

3. By default each patient has a single electronic patient record. However, patients will also be able to declare that certain parts of their records are either 'sealed' or 'sealed and locked'. In the latter case, the records will only be visible to a particular care team. In the former, their existence will

be visible to other staff who look at the patient record, and who will be able to break the seal in an emergency.

Initial implementations have thrown up a whole host of detailed problems. For example, patients receiving outpatient psychiatric care at a hospital used to have their notes kept in paper in the psychiatrist's filing cabinet; all the receptionist got to know was that Mrs Smith was seen once a month by Dr Jones. Now, however, the receptionist can see the notes too. Her role had to be given access to patient records so that she could see and amend administrative data such as appointment times; and if she's working reception in the hospital wing where Dr Jones has his office, then she has a legitimate relationship. Record sealing and locking aren't implemented yet. Thus she gets access to everything. This is a good example of why the 'EPR' doctrine of one record per patient was a bad idea, and the BMA vision of multiple linked records was better; it now looks like all records in psychiatry, sexual health etc may have to be sealed (or even sealed-and-locked) by default. Then the care of such patients across different departments will start to cause problems. As with multilevel secure systems, the hard thing isn't so much separating systems, but managing information flows across levels, or across compartments.

Perhaps the toughest problems with the new English systems, however, concern patient consent. The health service is allowing people to opt out of the summary care record — the central database of emergency medical information, containing things like medications, allergies and major medical history. This is not such a big deal; most people have nothing stigmatising in there. (Indeed, most people under the retirement age have no significant chronic conditions and could do perfectly well without a summary record.) The bigger deal is that the new hospital systems will make detailed records available to third parties as never before, for research, health service management and even law enforcement.

Previously, your medical privacy was protected by the fact that a hospital might have had over seventy different departmental record systems, while your records at your family doctor were protected by being partly on paper and partly on a PC that was switched off at six every evening and to which outsiders had no access. Once everything sits in standard systems on a regional health server farm, the game changes. Previously, a policeman who wanted to see your medical records needed to persuade a judge that he had reasonable grounds to believe he would find actual evidence of a crime; he then had to take the warrant along to your family doctor, or your hospital's medical director. The costs of this procedure ensured that it was invoked only rarely, and in cases like terrorism, murder or rape. A server farm, though, is a much easier target — and if it contains data of everyone who's confessed illegal drug use to their doctor, it's a tempting target. Indeed, from June 2007 all UK doctors are supposed to complete a 'treatment outcomes profile' for drug users, asking them whether they've committed any crimes in the past four weeks, including theft, assault and selling drugs. It's hard to believe that this information won't eventually find its way into police hands. But what are the consequences for public health when people can no longer trust their doctors — especially the most vulnerable and marginalised members of society? We already have cases of immigrants with TB absconding, since health service demographic data started being used to find illegal immigrants.

Thus even if the security policy in centralised systems amounts to a faithful implementation of the BMA policy — with the exception of the eighth principle of non-aggregation — we may expect problems. There are some aspects of security policy that just don't scale. Creating large databases of sensitive personal information is intrinsically hazardous. It increases the motive for abuse, and the opportunity for abuse, at the same time. And even if the controls work perfectly to prevent unlawful abuse (whether by outsiders or insiders) the existence of such databases can lead to lawful abuse — powerful interests in society lobby for, and achieve, access to data on a scale and of a kind that sensible people would not permit.

There are some advantages to standard central systems. In the USA, the Veterans' Administration runs such systems for its hospital network; after Hurricane Katrina, veterans from Louisiana who'd ended up as refugees in Texas or Florida, or even Minnesota, could go straight to local VA hospitals and find their notes there at the doctor's fingertips. Patients of many other hospitals and clinics in New Orleans lost their notes altogether. But centralization can definitely harm privacy. In May 2006, the personal information on all 26.5 million U.S. veterans — including names, social security numbers and in some cases disabilities — was stolen from the residence of a Department of Veterans Affairs employee who had taken the data home without authorization. And it's not enough just to compartmentalise the medical records themselves: in the Netherlands, which has carefully avoided record centralization, there is still a 'Vecozo' database that contains medical insurance details on citizens, and almost 80,000 people had access to it, from doctors and pharmacists to alternative healers and even taxi firms. There was a scandal when journalists found it was easy to get the private addresses and ex-directory phone numbers of a number of famous politicians, criminals and personalities [126]. (After the scandal broke, the insurers and their database operator each tried to blame the other — neither would accept responsibility for the fact that it made too much information available to too many people.)

So if a political decision is taken to have a large centralised database, the aggregation issue will haunt the detailed design and continued operation: even if some people (or applications) are allowed to look at everything, it's an extremely bad idea not to control the principals that actually do so. If you find that most physicians at your hospital look at a few thousand out of the several million records in the database, and one looks at all of them, what does that tell you? You'd better find out[2]. But many fielded systems don't have rate controls, or effective alarms, and even where alarms exist they are often not acted on. Again in the UK, over 50 hospital staff looked at the records of a footballing personality in hospital, despite not being involved in his care, and none of them was disciplined.

And even apart from controversial uses of medical records, such as police access, there are serious problems in protecting relatively uncontroversial uses, such as research. I'll turn to that next.

9.3 Inference Control

Access control in medical record systems is hard enough in hospitals and clinics that care for patients directly. It is much harder to assure patient privacy in secondary applications such as databases for research, cost control and clinical audit. This is one respect in which doctors have a harder time protecting their data than lawyers; lawyers can lock up their confidential client files and never let any outsider see them at all, while doctors are under all sorts of pressures to share data with third parties.

9.3.1 Basic Problems of Inference Control in Medicine

The standard way of protecting medical records used in research is to remove patients' names and addresses and thus make them anonymous. Indeed, privacy advocates often talk about 'Privacy Enhancing Technologies' (PETs) and de-identification is a frequently cited example. But this is rarely bullet-proof. If a database allows detailed queries, then individuals can still usually be identified, and this is especially so if information about different clinical episodes can be linked. For example, if I am trying to find out whether a politician born on the 2nd June 1946 and treated for a broken collar bone after a college football game on the 8th May 1967, had since been treated for drug or alcohol problems, and I could make an enquiry on those two dates, then I could very probably pull out his record from a national database. Even if the date of birth is replaced by a year of birth, I am still likely to be able to compromise patient privacy if the records are detailed or if records of different individuals can be linked. For example, a query such as 'show me the records of all women aged 36 with daughters aged 14 and 16 such that the mother and exactly one daughter have psoriasis' is also likely to find one individual out of

---

[2]In November 2007, a former DuPont scientist was sentenced for theft of trade secrets after they noticed he was downloading more internal documents than almost anyone else in the firm, and investigated [294]. It's not just hospitals and spooks that need to keep an eye on data aggregation!

millions. And complex queries with lots of conditions are precisely the kind that researchers want to make.

For this reason, the U.S. Healthcare Finance Administration (HCFA), which pays doctors and hospitals for treatments provided under the Medicare program, maintains three sets of records. There are complete records, used for billing. There are *beneficiary-encrypted* records, with only patients' names and social security numbers obscured. These are still considered personal data (as they still have dates of birth, postal codes and so on) and so are only usable by trusted researchers. Finally there are *public-access* records which have been stripped of identifiers down to the level where patients are only identified is general terms such as 'a white female aged 70–74 living in Vermont'. Nonetheless, researchers have found that many patients can still be identified by cross-correlating the public access records with commercial databases, and following complaints by privacy advocates, a report from the General Accounting Office criticised HCFA for lax security [520].

U.S. law, which comes under the HIPAA privacy rule, now recognizes *de-identified information* as medical data that has been 'properly' de-identified. This means either that 18 specific identifiers have been removed and the database operator has no actual knowledge that the remaining information can be used alone or in combination with other data to identify the subject; or that a qualified statistician concludes that the risk is substantially limited. Where such data are inadequate for research, it also recognises *limited data sets* that contain more information, but where the users are bound by contractual and technical measures to protect the information and not to try to re-identify subjects.

Many other countries have healthcare monitoring systems that use similar approaches. Germany has very strict privacy laws and takes the 'de-identified information' route; the fall of the Berlin Wall forced the former East German cancer registries to install protection mechanisms rapidly [192]. New Zealand takes the 'limited data sets' approach with a national database of encrypted-beneficiary medical records; access is restricted to a small number of specially cleared medical statisticians, and no query is answered with respect to less than six records [955]. In Switzerland, some research systems were replaced at the insistence of privacy regulators [1137].

In other countries, protection has been less adequate. Britain's National Health Service built a number of centralized databases in the 1990s that make personal health information widely available within government and that led to confrontation with doctors. The government set up a committee to investigate under Dame Fiona Caldicott; her report identified over sixty illegal information flows within the health service [46, 252]. Some research datasets were de-identified; others (including data on people with HIV/AIDS) were re-identified afterwards, so that people and HIV charities whose data had been collected under a promise of anonymity were deceived. Parliament then passed a law giving ministers the power to regulate secondary uses of medical data. Data kept for secondary uses are kept with postcode plus date of birth, and as UK postcodes are shared by at most a few dozen houses, this means that most records are easily identifiable. This remains a cause of controversy. In 2007, Parliament's Health Select Committee conducted an inquiry into the Electronic Patient Record, and heard evidence from a wide range of viewpoints — from researchers who believed that the law should compel information sharing for research, through to physicians, human-rights lawyers and privacy advocates who argued that there should only be the narrowest exceptions to medical privacy[3]. The Committee made many recommendations, including that patients should be permitted to prevent the use of their data in research [624]. The Government rejected this.

The most controversial of all was a genetic database in Iceland, which I'll discuss in more detail below.

Stripping personal information is important in many other fields. Under the rubric of *Privacy Enhancing Technology* (PET) it has been promoted recently by regulators in Europe and Canada as a general privacy mechanism [447]. But, as the medical examples show, there can be serious tension between the desire of researchers for detailed data, and the right of patients (or other data subjects) to privacy. Anonymisation is much more fragile than it seems; and when it fails, companies and individuals that relied on it can suffer serious consequences.

AOL faced a storm of protest in 2006 when it released the supposedly anonymous records of 20 million search queries made over three months by 657,000 people. Searchers' names and IP addresses were replaced with numbers, but that didn't help. Investigative journalists looked through the searches and rapidly identifid some of the searchers, who were shocked at the privacy breach [116]. This data was released 'for research purposes': the leak led to complaints being filed with the FTC, following which the company's CTO resigned, and the firm fired both the employee who released the data and the employee's supervisor.

Another example is in movie privacy. The DVD rental firm Netflix ships over a million DVDs a day to over 6 million U.S. customers, has a rating system to match films to customers, and published the viewer ratings of 500,000 subscribers with their names removed. (They offered a $1m prize for a better recommender algorithm.) In November 2007, Arvind Narayanan and Vitaly Shmatikov showed that many subscribers could be reidentified by comparing the anonymous records with preferences publicly expressed in the Internet Movie Database [928]. This is partly due to the 'long tail' effect: once you disregard the 100 or so movies everyone watches, people's viewing preferences are pretty unique. Anyway, U.S. law protects movie rental privacy, and the attack was a serious embarrassment for Netflix.

---

[3]Declaration of interest: I was a Special Adviser to the Committee.

So it is important to understand what can, and what cannot, be achieved with this technology.

9.3.2   Other Applications of Inference Control

The inference control problem was first seriously studied in the context of census data. A census collects a vast amount of sensitive information about individuals, then makes statistical summaries of it available by geographical (and governmental) units such as regions, districts and wards. This information is used to determine electoral districts, to set levels of government funding for public services, and as inputs to all sorts of other policy decisions. The census problem is somewhat simpler than the medical record problem as the data are rather restricted and in a standard format (age, sex, race, income, number of children, highest educational attainment, and so on).

There are two broad approaches, depending on whether the data are de-identified before or during processing — or equivalently whether the software that will process the data is untrusted or trusted.

An example of the first kind of processing comes from the treatment of U.S. census data until the 1960's. The procedure then was that one record in a thousand was made available on tape — minus names, exact addresses and other sensitive data. There was also noise added to the data in order to prevent people with some extra knowledge (such as of the salaries paid by the employer in a company town) from tracing individuals. In addition to the sample records, local averages were also given for people selected by various attributes. But records with extreme values — such as very high incomes — were suppressed. The reason for this is that a wealthy family living in a small village might make a significant difference to the per-capita village income. So their income might be deduced by comparing the village's average income with that of other villages nearby.

In the second type of processing, identifiable data are retained in a database, and privacy protection comes from controlling the kind of queries that may be made. Early attempts at this were not very successful, and various attacks were proposed on the processing used at that time by the U.S. census. The question was whether it was possible to construct a number of enquiries about samples containing a target individual, and work back to obtain supposedly confidential information about that individual.

If our census system allows a wide range of statistical queries, such as 'tell me the number of households headed by a man earning between $50,000 and $55,000', 'tell me the proportion of households headed by a man aged 40–45 years earning between $50,000 and $55,000', 'tell me the proportion of households headed by a man earning between $50,000 and $55,000 whose children have grown up and left home', and so on, then an attacker can quickly home in on an individual. Such queries, in which we add additional circumstantial information in order to defeat averaging and other controls, are known as *trackers*. They are usually easy to construct.

A problem related to inference is that an opponent who gets hold of a number of unclassified files might deduce sensitive information from them. For example, a New Zealand journalist deduced the identities of many officers in GCSB (that country's equivalent of the NSA) by examining lists of service personnel and looking for patterns of postings over time [576]. Intelligence officers' cover postings might also be blown if an opponent gets hold of the internal phone book for the unit where the officer is supposed to be posted, and doesn't find his name there. The army list might be public, and the phone book 'Restricted'; but the fact that a given officer is involved in intelligence work might be 'Secret'. Combining low level sources to draw a high level conclusion is known as an *aggregation attack*. It is related to the increased risk to personal information that arises when databases are aggregated together, thus making more context available to the attacker and making tracker and other attacks easier. The techniques that can be used to counter aggregation threats are similar to those used for general inference attacks on databases, although there are some particularly difficult problems where we have a multilevel security policy and the inference or aggregation threats have the potential to subvert it.

9.3.3 The Theory of Inference Control

A theory of inference control was developed by Denning and others in late 1970s and early 1980s, largely in response to problems of census bureaux [369]. The developers of many modern privacy systems are often unaware of this work, and repeat many of the mistakes of the 1960s. (Inference control is not the only problem in computer security where this happens.) The following is an overview of the most important ideas.

A *characteristic formula* is the expression (in some database query language) that selects a set, known as the *query set*, of records. An example might be 'all female employees of the Computer Laboratory at the grade of professor'. The smallest query sets, obtained by the logical AND of all the attributes (or their negations) are known as *elementary sets* or *cells*. The statistics corresponding to query sets may be *sensitive statistics* if they meet criteria which I'll discuss below (such as the set size being too small). The objective of inference control is to prevent the disclosure of sensitive statistics.

If we let D be the set of statistics that are disclosed and P the set which are sensitive and must be protected, then we need $D \subseteq P'$ for privacy, where P' is the complement of P. If $D = P'$ then the protection is said to be *precise*. Protection which is not precise will usually carry some cost in terms of the range of queries which the database can answer and may thus degrade its usefulness to its owner.

9.3.3.1   Query Set Size Control

The simplest protection mechanism is to specify a minimum query size. As I mentioned, New Zealand's National Health Information System databases will reject statistical queries whose answers would be based on fewer than six patients' records. But this is not enough in itself. An obvious tracker attack is to make an enquiry on six patients' records, and then on those records plus the target's. Rather than reduce the effectiveness of the database by building in more restrictive query controls, the designers of this system opted to restrict access to a small number of specially cleared medical statisticians.

Even so, one extra control is needed, and is often forgotten. You must prevent the attacker from querying all but one of the records in the database. In general, if there are N records, query set size control with a threshold of t means that between t and $N - t$ of them must be the subject of a query for it to be allowed.

9.3.3.2   Trackers

Probably the most important attacks on statistical databases come from trackers. There are many simple examples. In our laboratory, only one of the full professors is female. So we can find out her salary with just two queries: 'Average salary professors?' and 'Average salary male professors?'.

This is an example of an *individual tracker*, a custom formula that allows us to calculate the answer to a forbidden query indirectly. There are also *general trackers* — sets of formulae which will enable any sensitive statistic to be revealed. A somewhat depressing discovery made in the late 1970s was that general trackers are usually easy to find. Provided the minimum query set size n is less than a quarter of the total number of statistics N, and there are no further restrictions on the type of queries that are allowed, then we can find formulae that provide general trackers [372]. So tracker attacks are easy, unless we place severe restrictions on the query set size or control the allowed queries in some other way. (In fact results like this caused the research community to largely lose interest in inference security as being 'too hard', and this is one of the reasons that many system designers are not aware of the problems and build databases vulnerable to trackers and other attacks.)

9.3.3.3   More Sophisticated Query Controls

There are a number of alternatives to simple query set size control. The U.S. census, for example, uses the 'n-respondent, k%-dominance rule': it will not release a statistic of which k% or more is contributed by n values or less. Other techniques include, as I mentioned, suppressing data with extreme values. A census bureau may deal with high-net-worth individuals in national statistics but not in the local figures, while some medical databases do the same for less common diseases. For example, a UK prescribing statistics system suppresses sales of the AIDS drug AZT from local statistics [847]. When it was designed in the late 1990s, there were counties with only one single patient receiving this drug.

9.3.3.4 Cell Suppression

The next question is how to deal with the side-effects of suppressing certain statistics. UK rules, for example, require that it be 'unlikely that any statistical unit, having identified themselves, could use that knowledge, by deduction, to identify other statistical units in National Statistics outputs' [953]. To make this concrete, suppose that a university wants to release average marks for various combinations of courses, so that people can check that the marking is fair across courses. Suppose now that the table in Figure 9.4 contains the number of students studying two science subjects, one as their major subject and one as their minor subject.

The UK rules imply that our minimum query set size is 3 (if we set it at 2, then either of the two students who studied 'geology-with-chemistry' could trivially work out the other's mark). Then we cannot release the average mark for 'geology-with-chemistry'. But if the average mark for chemistry is known, then this mark can easily be reconstructed from the averages for 'biology-with-chemistry' and 'physics-with-chemistry'. So we have to suppress at least one other mark in the chemistry row, and for similar reasons we need to suppress one in the geology column. But if we suppress 'geology-with-biology' and 'physics-with-chemistry', then we'd also better suppress 'physics-with-biology' to prevent these values being worked out in turn. Our table will now look like Figure 9.5.

This process is called *complementary cell suppression*. If there are further attributes in the database schema — for example, if figures are also broken down by race and sex, to show compliance with anti-discrimination laws — then even more information may be lost. Where a database scheme contains m-tuples, blanking a single cell generally means suppressing $2^m - 1$

Major:	Biology	Physics	Chemistry	Geology
Minor:				
Biology	–	16	17	11
Physics	7	–	32	18
Chemistry	33	41	–	2
Geology	9	13	6	–

Figure 9.4: Table containing data before cell suppression

Major:	Biology	Physics	Chemistry	Geology
Minor:				
Biology	–	blanked	17	blanked
Physics	7	–	32	18
Chemistry	33	blanked	–	blanked
Geology	9	13	6	–

Figure 9.5: Table after cell suppression

other cells, arranged in a hypercube with the sensitive statistic at one vertex. So even precise protection can rapidly make the database unusable.

Sometimes complementary cell suppression can be avoided, as when large incomes (or rare diseases) are tabulated nationally and excluded from local figures. But it is often necessary when we are publishing microstatistics, as in the above tables of exam marks. Where the database is open for online queries, we can get much of the same effect by *implied queries control*: we allow a query on m attribute values only if all of the 2^m implied query sets given by setting the m attributes to true or false, have at least k records.

9.3.3.5 Maximum Order Control and the Lattice Model

The next thing we might try in order to make it harder to construct trackers is to limit the type of inquiries that can be made. *Maximum order control* limits the number of attributes that any query can have. However, to be effective, the limit may have to be severe. One study found that of 1000 medical records, three attributes were safe while with four attributes, one individual record could be found and with 10 attributes most records could be isolated. A more thorough approach (where it is feasible) is to reject queries that would partition the sample population into too many sets.

We saw how lattices can be used in compartmented security to define a partial order to control permitted information flows between compartments with combinations of codewords. They can also be used in a slightly different way to systematize query controls in some databases. If we have, for example, three attributes A, B and C (say area of residence, birth year and medical condition), we may find that while enquiries on any one of these attributes are non-sensitive, as are enquiries on A and B and on B and C, the combination of A and C might be sensitive. It follows that an enquiry on all three would not be permissible either. So the lattice divides naturally into a 'top half' of prohibited queries and a 'bottom half' of allowable queries, as shown in Figure 9.6.

9.3.3.6 Audit Based Control

As mentioned, some systems try to get round the limits imposed by static query control by keeping track of who accessed what. Known as *query overlap control*,

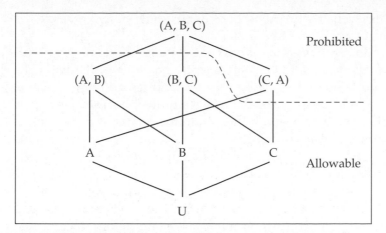

Figure 9.6: Table lattice for a database with three attributes

this involves rejecting any query from a user which, combined with what the user knows already, would disclose a sensitive statistic. This may sound perfect in theory but in practice it suffers from two usually unsurmountable drawbacks. First, the complexity of the processing involved increases over time, and often exponentially. Second, it's extremely hard to be sure that your users aren't in collusion, or that one user has registered under two different names. Even if your users are all honest and distinct persons today, it's always possible that one of them will take over another, or get taken over by a predator, tomorrow.

9.3.3.7 *Randomization*

Our cell suppression example shows that if various kinds of query control are the only protection mechanisms used in a statistical database, they can often have an unacceptable performance penalty. So query control is often used in conjunction with various kinds of randomization, designed to degrade the signal-to-noise ratio from the attacker's point of view while impairing that of the legitimate user as little as possible.

The simplest such technique is *perturbation*, or adding noise with zero mean and a known variance to the data. One way of doing this is to round or truncate the data by some deterministic rule; another is to swap some records. Perturbation is often not as effective as one would like, as it will tend to damage the legitimate user's results precisely when the sample set sizes are small, and leave them intact when the sample sets are large (where we might have been able to use simple query controls anyway). There is also the worry that suitable averaging techniques might be used to eliminate some of the added noise. A modern, sophisticated variant on the same theme is *controlled tabular adjustment* where you identify the sensitive cells and replace their values with 'safe' (sufficiently different) ones, then adjust other values in the table to restore additive relationships [330].

Often a good randomization technique is to use *random sample queries*. This is another of the methods used by census bureaux. The idea is that we make all the query sets the same size, selecting them at random from the available relevant statistics. Thus all the released data are computed from small samples rather than from the whole database. If this random selection is done using a pseudorandom number generator keyed to the input query, then the results will have the virtue of repeatability. Random sample queries are a natural protection mechanism for large medical databases, where the correlations being investigated are often such that a sample of a few hundred is sufficient. For example, when investigating the correlation between a given disease and some aspect of lifestyle, the correlation must be strong before doctors will advise patients to make radical changes to their way of life, or take other actions that might have undesirable side effects. If a teaching hospital has records on five million patients, and five thousand have the disease being investigated, then a randomly selected sample of two hundred sufferers might be all the researcher could use.

This doesn't work so well where the disease is rare, or where for other reasons there is only a small number of relevant statistics. A possible strategy here is *randomized response*, where we randomly restrict the data we collect (the subjects' responses). For example, if the three variables under investigation are obesity, smoking and AIDS, we might ask each subject with HIV infection to record whether they smoke or whether they are overweight, but not both. Of course, this can limit the value of the data.

9.3.4 Limitations of Generic Approaches

As with any protection technology, statistical security can only be evaluated in a particular environment and against a particular threat model. Whether it is adequate or not depends to an even greater extent than usual on the details of the application.

An instructive example is a system used for analyzing trends in drug prescribing. Here, prescriptions are collected (minus patient names) from pharmacies. A further stage of de-identification removes the doctors' identities, and the information is then sold to drug company marketing departments. The system has to protect the privacy of doctors as well as of patients: the last thing a busy family doctor wants is to be pestered by a drug rep for prescribing a competitor's brands.

One early prototype of this system merely replaced the names of doctors in a cell of four or five practices with 'doctor A', 'doctor B' and so on, as in Figure 9.7. We realised that an alert drug rep could identify doctors from prescribing patterns, by noticing, for example, ''Well, doctor B must be Susan

Week:	1	2	3	4
Doctor A	17	26	19	22
Doctor B	25	31	9	29
Doctor C	32	30	39	27
Doctor D	16	19	18	13

Figure 9.7: Sample of de-identified drug prescribing data

Jones because she went skiing in the third week in January and look at the fall-off in prescriptions here. And doctor C is probably her partner Mervyn Smith who'll have been covering for her'' The fix was to replace absolute numbers of prescriptions with the percentage of each doctor's prescribing which went on each particular drug, to drop some doctors at random, and to randomly perturb the timing by shifting the figures backwards or forwards a few weeks [847].

This is a good example of the sort of system where the inference control problem can have a robust solution. The application is well-defined, the database is not too rich, and the allowable queries are fairly simple. Indeed, this system was the subject of litigation; the UK government's Department of Health sued the database operator, alleging that the database might compromise privacy. Their motive was to maintain a monopoly on the supply of such information to industry. They lost, and this established the precedent that (in Britain at least) inference security controls may, if they are robust, exempt statistical data from being considered as 'personal information' for the purpose of privacy laws [1204].

In general, though, it's not so easy. For a start, de-identification doesn't compose: it's easy to have two separate applications, each of which provides the same results via anonymized versions of the same data, but where an attacker with access to both of them can easily identify individuals. In the general case, contextual knowledge is extremely hard to quantify, and is likely to grow over time. Latanya Sweeney has shown that even the HCFA's 'public-use' files can often be reidentified by cross-correlating them with commercial databases [1235]: for example, most U.S. citizens can be identified by their ZIP code plus their gender and date of birth. Such *data detective* work is an important part of assessing the level of protection which an actual statistical database gives, just as we only have confidence in cryptographic algorithms which have withstood extensive analysis by capable motivated opponents. The emergence of social networks since 2004 has made inference control much harder wherever they can be brought to bear; I will discuss this when we get to social networks in section 23.3.3. And even without cross-correlation, there may be contextual information available internally. Users of medical research databases are often doctors who have normal access to parts of the patient record databases from which the statistical data are drawn.

9.3.4.1 Active Attacks

Active attacks are particularly powerful. These are where users have the ability to insert or delete records into the database. A user might add records to create a group that contains the target's record plus those of a number of nonexistent subjects created by himself. One (imperfect) countermeasure is add or delete new records in batches. Taking this to an extreme gives *partitioning* — in which records are added in groups and any query must be answered with respect to all of them or none. However, this is once more equivalent to publishing tables of microstatistics.

Active attacks are not limited to data, but can also target metadata. A nice example, due to Whit Diffie, is the *chosen drug attack*. Suppose a drug company has access through a statistical system to the amounts of money spent on behalf of various groups of patients and wishes to find out which patients are receiving which drug, in order to direct its marketing better (there was a scandal in Quebec about just such an inference attack). A possible trick is to set the drug prices in such a way as to make the resulting equations easy to solve.

A prominent case at the turn of the century was a medical research database in Iceland. The plan was for three linked databases: one with the nation's medical records, a second with the genealogy of the whole population, and a third with genetic data acquired from sequencing. The rationale was that since Iceland's population is largely descended from a few founding families who settled there about a thousand years ago, there is much less genic variance than in the general human population and so genes for hereditary illnesses should be much easier to find. A Swiss drug company bankrolled the construction of the database, and the Reykjavik government embraced it as a means of modernising the country's health IT infrastructure and simultaneously creating a few hundred high-tech jobs in medical research. Iceland's doctors, however, mostly reacted negatively, seeing the system as a threat both to patient privacy and professional autonomy.

The privacy problem in the Icelandic database was more acute than in the general case. For example, by linking medical records to genealogies, which are in any case public (genealogy is a common Icelandic hobby), patients can be identified by such factors as the number of their uncles, aunts, great-uncles, great-aunts and so on — in effect by the shape of their family trees. There was much debate about whether the design could even theoretically meet legal privacy requirements [47], and European privacy officials expressed grave concern about the possible consequences for Europe's system of privacy laws [349]. The Icelandic government pressed ahead with it anyway, with a patient opt-out. Many doctors advised patients to opt out, and 11% of the population did so. Eventually, the Icelandic Supreme Court found that European privacy law required the database to be opt-in rather than opt-out. In addition, many Icelanders had invested in the database company, and lost money when its share value sank at the end of the dotcom boom. Nowadays about half the population have opted in to the system and the controversy is defused.

My own view, for what it's worth, is that patient consent is the key to effective medical research. This not only allows full access to data, without the problems we've been discussing in this section, but provides motivated subjects and much higher-quality clinical information than can be harvested simply as a byproduct of normal clinical activities. For example, a network of researchers into ALS (the motor-neurone disease from which Cambridge astronomer Stephen Hawking suffers) shares fully-identifiable information between doctors and other researchers in over a dozen countries with the full consent of the patients and their families. This network allows data sharing between Germany, with very strong privacy laws, and Japan, with almost none; and data continued to be shared between researchers in the USA and Serbia even when the USAF was bombing Serbia. The consent model is spreading. Britain's biggest medical charity is funding a 'Biobank' database in which several hundred thousand volunteers will be asked to give researchers not just answers to an extensive questionnaire and full access to their records for the rest of their lives, but also to lodge blood samples so that those who develop interesting diseases in later life can have their genetic and proteomic makeup analysed.

9.3.5   The Value of Imperfect Protection

So doing de-identification right is hard, and the issues can be politically fraught. The best way to solve the inference control problem is to avoid it, for example by recruiting volunteers for your medical research rather than recycling data collected for other purposes. But there are applications where it's used, and applications where it's all that's available. An example was the epidemic of HIV/AIDS; in the 1980s and 1990s researchers struggling to understand what was going on had little choice but to use medical data that had been originally collected for other purposes. Another example, of course, is the census. In such applications the protection you can provide will be imperfect. How do you cope with that?

Some kinds of security mechanism may be worse than useless if they can be compromised. Weak encryption is a good example. The main problem facing the world's signals intelligence agencies is *traffic selection* — how to filter out interesting nuggets from the mass of international phone, fax, email and other traffic. A terrorist who helpfully encrypts his important traffic does this part of the police's job for them. If the encryption algorithm used is breakable, or if the end systems can be hacked, then the net result is worse than if the traffic had been sent in clear.

Statistical security is not generally like this. The main threat to databases of personal information is often *mission creep*. Once an organization has access to potentially valuable data, then all sorts of ways of exploiting that value will be developed. Some of these are likely to be highly objectionable; one topical U.S. example is the resale of medical records to banks for use in filtering loan applications. However, even an imperfect de-identification system may destroy the value of medical data to a bank's loan department. If only five percent of the patients can be identified, and then only with effort, then the bank may decide that it's simpler to tell loan applicants to take out their own insurance and let the insurance companies send out medical questionnaires if they wish. So de-identification can help prevent mission creep, even if the main effect is prophylaxis against future harm rather than treatment of existing defects.

As well as harming privacy, mission creep can have safety implications. In the UK, diabetic registers were set up in the 1990s to monitor the quality of diabetes care; they were databases to which GPs, hospital consultants, nurses and opthalmologists could upload test results, so that important indicators would not be missed. As hospitals had no working email system, they were promptly abused to provide a rudimentary messaging system between hospitals and general practice. But as the diabetes registers were never designed as communications systems, they lacked the safety and other mechanisms that such systems should have had if they were to be used for clinical data. Even rudimentary de-identification would have prevented this abuse and motivated diabetologists to get email working instead.

So in statistical security, the question of whether one should let the best be the enemy of the good can require a finer judgment call than elsewhere.

9.4 The Residual Problem

The above two sections may have convinced you that the problem of managing medical record privacy in the context of immediate care (such as in a hospital) is reasonably straightforward, while in the context of secondary databases (such as for research, audit and cost control) there are statistical security techniques which, with care, can solve much of the problem. Somewhat similar techniques can be used to manage highly sensitive commercial data such as details of forthcoming mergers and acquisitions in an investment bank, and even intelligence information. (There was a lot of interest in the BMA model from people designing police intelligence systems.) In all cases, the underlying concept is that the really secret material is restricted to a compartment of a small number of identified individuals, and less secret versions of the data may be manufactured for wider use. This involves not just suppressing the names of the patients, or spies, or target companies, but also careful management of contextual and other information by which they might be re-identified.

But making such systems work well in real life is much harder than it looks. First, determining the sensitivity level of information is fiendishly difficult, and many initial expectations turn out to be wrong. You might expect, for example, that HIV status would be the most sensitive medical data there is; yet many HIV sufferers are quite open about their status. You might also expect that people would rather entrust sensitive personal health information to a healthcare professional such as a doctor or pharmacist rather than to a marketing database. Yet many women are so sensitive about the purchase of feminine hygiene products that, rather than going into a pharmacy and buying them for cash, they prefer to use an automatic checkout facility in a supermarket — even if this means they have to use their store card and credit card, so that the purchase is linked to their name and stays on the marketing database forever. The actual embarrassment of being seen with a packet of tampons is immediate, and outweighs the future embarrassment of being sent discount coupons for baby wear six months after the menopause.

Second, it is extraordinarily difficult to exclude single points of failure, no matter how hard you try to build watertight compartments. The CIA's Soviet assets were compromised by Aldritch Ames — who as a senior counterintelligence man had access to too many compartments. The KGB's overseas operations were similarly compromised by Vassily Mitrokhin — an officer who'd become disillusioned with communism after 1968 and who was sent to work in the archives while waiting for his pension [77]. And in March 2007, historians Margo Anderson and William Seltzer found, that contrary to decades of denials, census data was used in 1943 to round up Japanese-Americans for internment [1142]. The single point of failure there appears to have been Census Bureau director JC Capt, who unlawfully released the data to the Secret Service following a request from Treasury Secretary HC Morgenthau. The Bureau has since publicly apologised [893].

In medicine, many of the hard problems lie in the systems that process medical claims for payment. When a patient is treated and a request for payment sent to the insurer, it has not just full details of the illness, the treatment and the cost, but also the patient's name, insurance number and other details such as date of birth. There have been proposals for payment to be effected using anonymous credit cards [191], but as far as I am aware none of them has been fielded. Insurers want to know which patients, and which doctors, are the most expensive. In fact, during a debate on medical privacy at an IEEE conference in 1996 — just as HIPAA was being pushed through the U.S. Congress — a representative of a large systems house declared that the medical records of 8 million Americans were one of his company's strategic assets, which they would never give up. This holds whether the insurer is a private insurance company (or employer) or a government-owned health authority, such as HCFA, the VA, or Britain's National Health Service. Once an insurer possesses large quantities of personal health information, it becomes very reluctant to delete it. Its potential future value, in all sorts of applications from cost control through research to marketing, is immediate and obvious, while patients' privacy concerns are not.

In the USA, the retention of copies of medical records by insurers, employers and others is widely seen as a serious problem. Writers from such widely different political viewpoints as the communitarian Amitai Etzioni [441] and the libertarian Simson Garfinkel [515] agree on this point, if on little else. As mentioned, HIPAA only empowered the DHHS to regulate health plans, healthcare clearinghouses, and healthcare providers, leaving many organizations that process medical data (such as lawyers, employers and universities) outside its scope. In fact, Microsoft's recent announcement that it would set up a 'HealthVault' to guard your medical records was met with a sharp retort from privacy activists that since Microsoft isn't a 'covered entity' as specified by HIPAA, putting your medical data there would place it outside HIPAA's protection [81].

What lessons can be drawn from other countries?

Medical privacy is strongly conditioned by how people pay for healthcare. In Britain, the government pays for most healthcare, and the attempts of successive British governments to centralise medical records for cost control and management purposes have led to over a decade of conflict with doctors and with patients' associations. In Germany, the richer people use private insurers (who are bound by tight data protection laws), while the poor use state health insurers that are run by doctors, so non-doctors don't have access to records. Singapore residents pay into compulsory savings accounts from their wages and use them to pay for healthcare; the government steps in to insure expensive procedures, but most doctor visits are paid by the patient directly. Patients who stay healthy and accumulate a surplus can add some of it to their pension and pass the rest to their heirs. The most radical solution is in Japan, where costs are controlled by regulating fees: doctors are discouraged from performing expensive procedures such as heart transplants by pricing them below cost. In the mid-1990s, healthcare took up some 3% of GNP in Japan, versus 7–9% for the typical developed country and 15% for America; since then the figures have risen by a percent or so, but the general rankings remain the same. Japanese (and Singaporeans) pay less for healthcare than Europeans, and Americans pay more. The curious thing is that Japanese (and Singaporeans) live longer than Europeans, who live longer than Americans. Life expectancy and medical costs seem to be negatively correlated.

To sum up, the problem of health record privacy is not just a socio-technical one but socio-technico-political. Whether large quantities of medical records accumulate in one database depends on how the health care system is organized, and whether these are destroyed — or de-identified — after payment has been processed is more to do with institutional structures, incentives and regulation than technology. In such debates, one role of the security engineer is to get policymakers to understand the likely consequences of their actions.

Privacy is poorest in countries that fail to align incentives properly, and as a result have detailed cost oversight of individual treatments — whether by insurers / employers, as in the USA, or by bureaucrats as in Britain.

In the UK, a scandal broke in November 2007 when the tax authorities lost the records of 25 million people. The records of all the nation's children and their families — including names, addresses, phone numbers and tha parents' bank account details — were burned on two CDs for dispatch to the National Audit Office, and lost in the post. The Prime Minister had to apologise to Parliament and promised to make good any resulting 'identify theft' losses. In the aftermath, there has been wide public questioning of his government's programme to build ever-larger central databases of citizens' personal information — not just for taxation but for medical research, health-service administration, and child welfare. As I write in December 2007, the feeling in London is that plans for a national ID card are effectively dead, as is a proposal to build a database of all vehicle movements to facilitate road pricing. The National Health Service is continuing to build central health databases against growing medical resistance, but the opposition Conservative Party (which now has a clear lead in the polls) have promised to abolish not just the ID card system but proposed children's databases if they win the next election.

Other privacy problems also tend to have a serious political entanglement. Bank customer privacy can be tied up with the bank's internal politics; the strongest driver for privacy protection may come from branch managers' reluctance to let other branches learn about their customers. Access to criminal records and intelligence depends on how law enforcement agencies decide to share data with each other, and the choices they make internally about whether access to highly sensitive information about sources and methods should be decentralized (risking occasional losses), or centralized (bringing lower-probability but higher-cost exposure to a traitor at head office). The world since 9/11 has moved sharply towards centralisation; expect a high-profile traitor like Aldrich Ames to come along sometime soon.

9.5   Summary

In this chapter, we looked at the problem of assuring the privacy of medical records. This is typical of a number of information security problems, ranging from the protection of national intelligence data through professional practice in general to the protection of census data.

It turns out that with medical records there is an easy problem, a harder problem, and a really hard problem.

The easy problem is setting up systems of access controls so that access to a particular record is limited to a sensible number of staff. Such systems can be designed largely by automating existing working practices, and role-based access controls are currently the technology of choice. The harder problem is statistical security — how one designs databases of medical records (or census returns) so as to allow researchers to make statistical enquiries without compromising individuals' privacy. The hardest problem is how to manage the interface between the two, and in the specific case of medicine, how to prevent the spread of payment information. The only realistic solution for this lies in regulation.

Medical systems also teach us about the limits of some privacy enhancing technologies, such as de-identification. While making medical records anonymous in research databases can help mitigate the consequences of unauthorised access and prevent mission creep, it's by no means bulletproof. Rich data about real people can usually be re-identified. The mechanisms used in healthcare to deal with this problem are worth studying.

Research Problems

In the near future, a lot of medical treatment may involve genetic information. So your medical records may involve personal health information about your parents, siblings, cousins and so on. How can privacy models be extended to deal with multiple individuals? For example, in many countries you have the right not to know the outcome of a DNA test that a relative has for an inheritable disease such as Huntington's Chorea, as it may affect the odds that you have the disease too. Your relative does have a right to know, and may tell others. This is a problem not just for technology, but also for privacy law [1231]

Are there any ways of linking together access control policies for privacy with statistical security? Can there be such a thing as seamless privacy where everything fits neatly together? Or would you end up giving patients an extremely complex set of access control options — like Facebook's but worse — in which each patient had to wade through dozens of pages of options and approve or deny permission for her data to be used in each of dozens of secondary applications and research projects? In short, are there any useful and useable abstractions?

What other ways of writing privacy policies are there? For example, are there useful ways to combine BMA and Chinese Wall? Are there any ways, whether technical or economic, of aligning the data subject's interest with those of the system operator and other stakeholders?

Further Reading

The literature on compartmented-mode security is somewhat scattered: most of the public domain papers are in the proceedings of the NCSC/NISSC and

ACSAC conferences cited in detail at the end of Chapter 8. Standard textbooks such as Amoroso [27] and Gollmann [537] cover the basics of the lattice and Chinese Wall models.

For the BMA model see the policy document itself — the Blue Book [37], the shorter version at [38], and the proceedings of the conference on the policy [43]. See also the papers on the pilot system at Hastings [366, 367]. For more on Japanese healthcare, see [263]. For a National Research Council study of medical privacy issues in the USA, see [951]; there is also an HHS report on the use of de-identified data in research at [816].

As for inference control, this has become an active research field again in the last few years, with regular conferences on 'Privacy in Statistical Databases'; see the proceedings of these events to catch up with current frontiers. Denning's book [369] is the classic reference, and still worth a look; there's an update at [374]. A more modern textbook on database security is the one by Castano et al [276]. The most comprehensive resource, though, from the practical viewpoint — with links to a vast range of practical literature across a number of application areas — may be the website of the American Statistical Association [26]. The standard reference for people involved in government work is the Federal Committee on Statistical Methodology's *'Report on Statistical Disclosure Limitation Methodology'* which provides a good introduction to the standard tools and describes the methods used in various U.S. departments and agencies [455]. As an example of a quite different application, Mark Allman and Vern Paxson discuss the problems of anonymizing IP packet traces for network systems research in [23].

Finally, Margo Anderson and William Seltzer's papers on the abuses of census data in the USA, particularly during World War 2, can be found at [31].

CHAPTER 10

Banking and Bookkeeping

*The arguments of lawyers and engineers pass through one
another like angry ghosts.*

— **Nick Bohm, Brian Gladman and Ian Brown [201]**

*Computers are not (yet?) capable of being reasonable
any more than is a Second Lieutenant.*

— **Casey Schaufler**

Against stupidity, the Gods themselves contend in vain.

— **JC Friedrich von Schiller**

10.1   Introduction

Banking systems range from cash machine networks and credit card
processing, both online and offline, through high-value interbank money
transfer systems, to the back-end bookkeeping systems that keep track of it all
and settle up afterwards. There are specialised systems for everything from
stock trading to bills of lading; and large companies have internal bookkeeping and cash management systems that duplicate many of the functions of
a bank.

Such systems are important for a number of reasons. First, an understanding of transaction processing is a prerequisite for tackling the broader
problems of electronic commerce and fraud. Many dotcom firms fell down
badly on elementary bookkeeping; in the rush to raise money and build
web sites, traditional business discipline was ignored. The collapse of Enron
led to stiffened board-level accountability for internal control; laws such as

Sarbanes-Oxley and Gramm-Leach-Bliley now drive much of the investment in information security. When you propose protection mechanisms to a client, one of the first things you're likely to be asked is the extent to which they'll help directors of the company discharge their fiduciary responsibilities to shareholders.

Second, bookkeeping was for many years the mainstay of the computer industry, with banking its most intensive application area. Personal applications such as web browsers and Office might now run on more machines, but accounting is still the critical application for the average business. So the protection of bookkeeping systems is of great practical importance. It also gives us a well-understood model of protection in which confidentiality plays little role, but where the integrity of records (and their immutability once made) is of paramount importance.

Third, transaction processing systems — whether for small debits such as $50 cash machine withdrawals, or multimillion dollar wire transfers — were the application that launched commercial cryptology. Banking applications drove the development not just of encryption algorithms and protocols, but also of the supporting technology such as tamper-resistant cryptographic processors. These processors provide an important and interesting example of a trusted computing base that is quite different from the hardened operating systems discussed in the context of multilevel security. Many instructive mistakes were first made (or at least publicly documented) in the area of commercial cryptography. The problem of how to interface crypto with access control was studied by financial cryptographers before any others in the open research community.

Finally, banking systems provide another example of multilateral security — but aimed at authenticity rather than confidentiality. A banking system should prevent customers from cheating each other, or the bank; it should prevent bank employees from cheating the bank, or its customers; and the evidence it provides should be sufficiently strong that none of these principals can get away with falsely accusing another principal of cheating.

In this chapter, I'll first describe the bookkeeping systems used to keep track of assets despite occasional corrupt staff; these are fairly typical of accounting systems used by other companies too. I'll then describe the banks' principal international funds-transfer systems; similar systems are used to settle securities transactions and to manage trade documents such as bills of lading. Next, I'll describe ATM systems, which are increasingly the public face of banking, and whose technology has been adopted in applications such as utility meters; and then I'll tell the story of credit cards, which have become the main payment mechanism online. I'll then move on to more recent technical advances, including the smartcards recently introduced in Europe, RFID credit cards, and nonbank payment services such as PayPal. I'll wrap up with some points on money laundering, and what controls really work against fraud.

10.1.1 The Origins of Bookkeeping

Bookkeeping appears to have started in the Neolithic Middle East in about 8500 BC, just after the invention of agriculture [1122]. When people started to produce surplus food, they started to store and trade it. Suddenly they needed a way to keep track of which villager had put how much in the communal warehouse. To start with, each unit of food (sheep, wheat, oil, ...) was represented by a clay token, or *bulla*, which was placed inside a clay envelope and sealed by rolling it with the pattern of the warehouse keeper. (See Figure 10.1.) When the farmer wanted to get his food back, the seal was broken by the keeper in the presence of a witness. (This may be the oldest known security protocol.) By about 3000BC, this had led to the invention of writing [1018]; after another thousand years, we find equivalents of promissory notes, bills of lading, and so on. At about the same time, metal ingots started to be used as an intermediate commodity, often sealed inside a bulla by an assayer. In 700BC, Lydia's King Croesus started stamping the metal directly and thus invented coins [1045]; by the Athens of Pericles, there were a number of wealthy individuals in business as bankers [531].

Figure 10.1: Clay envelope and its content of tokens representing 7 jars of oil, from Uruk, present day Iraq, ca. 3300 BC (Courtesy Denise Schmandt-Besserat and the Louvre Museum)

The next significant innovation dates to late medieval times. As the dark ages came to a close and trade started to grow, some businesses became too large for a single family to manage. The earliest of the recognisably modern banks date to this period; by having branches in a number of cities, they could finance trade efficiently. But as the economy grew, it was necessary to hire managers from outside, and the owner's family could not supervise them closely. This brought with it an increased risk of fraud, and the mechanism that evolved to control it was *double-entry bookkeeping*. People used to think this was invented in Italy sometime in the 1300s, though the first book on it did not appear until 1494, after the printing press came along [355]. Recently, however, historians have found double-entry records created by Jewish merchants in twelfth-century Cairo, and it's now believed that the Italians learned the technique from them [1140].

10.1.2 Double-Entry Bookkeeping

The idea behind double-entry bookkeeping is extremely simple, as with most hugely influential ideas. Each transaction is posted to two separate books, as a credit in one and a debit in the other. For example, when a firm sells a customer $100 worth of goods on credit, it posts a $100 credit on the Sales account, and a $100 debit onto the Receivables account. When the customer pays the money, it will credit the Receivables account (thereby reducing the asset of money receivable), and debit the Cash account. (The principle taught in accountancy school is 'debit the receiver, credit the giver'.) At the end of the day, the books should *balance*, that is, add up to zero; the assets and the liabilities should be equal. (If the firm has made some profit, then this is a liability to the shareholders.) In all but the smallest firms, the books will be kept by different clerks, and have to balance at the end of every month (at banks, every day).

By suitable design of the ledger system, we can see to it that each shop, or branch, can be balanced separately. Thus each cashier will balance her cash tray before locking it in the vault overnight; the debits in the cash legder should exactly balance the physical banknotes she's collected. So most frauds need the collusion of two or more members of staff; and this principle of *split responsibility*, also known as *dual control*, is complemented by audit. Not only are the books audited at year end, but there are random audits too; a team of inspectors may descend on a branch at no notice and insist that all the books are balanced before the staff go home.

10.1.3 A Telegraphic History of E-commerce

Many of the problems afflicting e-businesses stem from the popular notion that e-commerce is something completely new, invented in the mid 1990s. This is simply untrue.

Various kinds of visual signalling were deployed from classical times, including heliographs (which used mirrors to flash sunlight at the receiver), semaphones (which used the positions of moving arms to signal letters and numbers) and flags. Land-based systems sent messages along chains of beacon towers, and naval systems relayed them between ships. To begin with, their use was military, but after the Napoleonic War the French government opened its heliograph network to commercial use. Very soon the first frauds were carried out. For two years up till they were discovered in 1836, two bankers bribed an operator to signal the movements of the stock market to them covertly by making errors in transmissions that they could observe from a safe distance. Other techniques were devised to signal the results of horseraces. Various laws were passed to criminalise this kind of activity but they were ineffective. The only solution for the bookies was to 'call time' by a clock, rather than waiting for the result and hoping that they were the first to hear it.

From the 1760's to the 1840's, the electric telegraph was developed by a number of pioneers, of whom the most influential was Samuel Morse. He persuaded Congress in 1842 to fund an experimental line from Washington to Baltimore; this so impressed people that serious commercial investment started, and by the end of that decade there were 12,000 miles of line operated by 20 companies. This was remarkably like the Internet boom of the late 1990's.

Banks were the first big users of the telegraph, and they decided that they needed technical protection mechanisms to prevent transactions being altered by crooked operators en route. (I discussed the *test key* systems they developed for the purpose in section 5.2.4.) Telegrams were also used to create national markets. For the first time, commodity traders in New York could find out within minutes what prices had been set in auctions in Chicago, and fishing skippers arriving in Boston could find out the price of cod in Gloucester. The history of the period shows that most of the concepts and problems of e-commerce were familiar to the Victorians [1215]. How do you know who you're speaking to? How do you know if they're trustworthy? How do you know whether the goods will be delivered, and whether payments will arrive? The answers found in the nineteenth century involved intermediaries — principally banks who helped business manage risk using instruments such as references, guarantees and letters of credit.

10.2 How Bank Computer Systems Work

Banks were among the first large organizations to use computers for bookkeeping. They started in the late 1950s and early 1960s with applications such as check processing, and once they found that even the slow and expensive computers of that era were much cheaper than armies of clerks, they proceeded to automate most of the rest of their back-office operations during the

1960s and 1970s. The 1960s saw banks offering automated payroll services to their corporate customers, and by the 1970s they were supporting business-to-business e-commerce based on *electronic data interchange* (EDI), whereby firms from General Motors to Marks and Spencer built systems that enabled them to link up their computers to their suppliers' so that goods could be ordered automatically. Travel agents built similar systems to order tickets in real time from airlines. ATMs arrived en masse in the 1970s, and online banking systems in the 1980s; web-based banking followed in the 1990s. Yet the fancy front-end systems still rely on traditional back-office automation for maintaining account data and performing settlement.

Computer systems used for bookkeeping typically claim to implement variations on the double-entry theme. But the quality of control is highly variable. The double-entry features may be just a skin in the user interface, while the underlying file formats have no integrity controls. And if the ledgers are all kept on the same system, someone with root access — or with physical access and a debugging tool — may be able to change the records so that the balancing controls are bypassed. It may also be possible to evade the balancing controls in various ways; staff may notice bugs in the software and take advantage of them. Despite all these problems, the law in most developed countries requires companies to have effective internal controls, and makes the managers responsible for them. Such laws are the main drivers of investment in information security mechanisms, but they also a reason for much wasted investment. So we need to look at the mechanics of electronic bookkeeping in a more detail.

A typical banking system has a number of data structures. There is an *account master file* which contains each customer's current balance together with previous transactions for a period of perhaps ninety days; a number of *ledgers* which track cash and other assets on their way through the system; various *journals* which hold transactions that have been received from teller stations, cash machines, check sorters and so on, but not yet entered in the ledgers; and an *audit trail* that records which staff member did what and when.

The processing software that acts on these data structures will include a suite of overnight batch processing programs, which apply the transactions from the journals to the various ledgers and the account master file. The online processing will include a number of modules which post transactions to the relevant combinations of ledgers. So when a customer pays $100 into his savings account the teller will make a transaction which records a credit to the customer's savings account ledger of $100 while debiting the same amount to the cash ledger recording the amount of money in the drawer. The fact that all the ledgers should always add up to zero provides an important check; if the bank (or one of its branches) is ever out of balance, an alarm will go off and people will start looking for the cause.

The invariant provided by the ledger system is checked daily during the overnight batch run, and means that a programmer who wants to add to his own account balance will have to take the money from some other account, rather than just creating it out of thin air by tweaking the account master file. Just as in a traditional business one has different ledgers managed by different clerks, so in a banking data processing shop there are different programmers in charge of different subsystems. In addition, all code is subjected to scrutiny by an internal auditor, and to testing by a separate test department. Once it has been approved, it will be run on a production machine that does not have a development environment, but only approved object code and data.

10.2.1 The Clark-Wilson Security Policy Model

Although such systems had been in the field since the 1960s, a formal model of their security policy was only introduced in 1987, by Dave Clark and Dave Wilson (the former a computer scientist, and the latter an accountant) [295]. In their model, some data items are constrained so that they can only be acted on by a certain set of transformation procedures.

More formally, there are special procedures whereby data can be input — turned from an *unconstrained data item*, or UDI, into a *constrained data item*, or CDI; *integrity verification procedures* (IVP's) to check the validity of any CDI (e.g., that the books balance); and *transformation procedures* (TPs) which may be thought of in the banking case as transactions which preserve balance. In the general formulation, they maintain the integrity of CDIs; they also write enough information to an append-only CDI (the audit trail) for transactions to be reconstructed. Access control is by means of triples *(subject, TP, CDI)*, which are so structured that a dual control policy is enforced. In the formulation in [27]:

1. the system will have an IVP for validating the integrity of any CDI;

2. the application of a TP to any CDI must maintain its integrity;

3. a CDI can only be changed by a TP;

4. subjects can only initiate certain TPs on certain CDIs;

5. triples must enforce an appropriate separation-of-duty policy on subjects;

6. certain special TPs on UDIs can produce CDIs as output;

7. each application of a TP must cause enough information to reconstruct it to be written to a special append-only CDI;

8. the system must authenticate subjects attempting to initiate a TP;

9. the system must let only special subjects (i.e., security officers) make changes to authorization-related lists.

A number of things bear saying about Clark-Wilson.

First, unlike Bell-LaPadula, Clark-Wilson involves maintaining state. Even disregarding the audit trail, this is usually necessary for dual control as you have to keep track of which transactions have been partially approved — such as those approved by only one manager when two are needed. If dual control is implemented using access control mechanisms, it typically means holding partially approved transactions in a special journal file. This means that some of the user state is actually security state, which in turn makes the trusted computing base harder to define. If it is implemented using crypto instead, such as by having managers attach digital signatures to transactions of which they approve, then there can be problems managing all the partially approved transactions so that they get to a second approver in time.

Second, the model doesn't do everything. It captures the idea that state transitions should preserve an invariant such as balance, but not that state transitions should be correct. Incorrect transitions, such as paying into the wrong bank account, are not prevented by this model.

Third, Clark-Wilson ducks the hardest question, namely: how do we control the risks from dishonest staff? Rule 5 says that 'an appropriate separation of duty policy' must be supported, but nothing about what this means. Indeed, it's very hard to find any systematic description in the accounting literature of how you design internal controls — it's something that auditors tend to learn on the job. Companies' internal controls tend to evolve over time in response to real or feared incidents, whether in the company's own experience or its auditors'. In the next section, I try to distill into a few principles the experience gained from several years working at the coalface in banking and consultancy, and more recently on our university's finance and other committees.

10.2.2   Designing Internal Controls

Over the years, a number of standards have been put forward by the accountancy profession, by stock markets and by banking regulators, about how bookkeeping and internal control systems should be designed. In the USA, for example, there is the *Committee of Sponsoring Organizations* (COSO), a group of U.S. accounting and auditing bodies [318]. This self-regulation failed to stop the excesses of the dotcom era, and following the collapse of Enron there was intervention from U.S. lawmakers in the form of the Sarbanes-Oxley Act of 2002. It protects whistleblowers (the main source of information on serious insider fraud), and its section 404 makes managers responsible for maintaining 'adequate internal control structure and procedures for financial reporting'. It also demands that auditors attest to the management's assessment of these controls and disclose any 'material weaknesses'. CEOs also have to certify the truthfulness of financial statements. There was also the Gramm-Leach-Bliley Act of 1999, which liberalised bank regulation in many respects but which obliged banks to have security mechanisms to protect information from foreseeable threats in security and integrity. Along with HIPAA in the medical sector, Gramm-Leach-Bliley and Sarbanes-Oxley have driven much of the investment in information security and internal control over the early years of the 21st century. (Other countries have equivalents; in the UK it's the Turnbull Guidance from the Financial Reporting Council.) I'll return to them and look in more detail at the policy aspects in Part III.

In this section, my concern is with the technical aspects. Modern risk management systems typically require a company to identify and assess its risks, and then build controls to mitigate them. A company's risk register might contain many pages of items such as 'insider makes large unauthorised bank transaction'. Some of these will be mitigated using non-technical measures such as insurance, but others will end up in your lap. So how do you engineer away a problem like this?

There are basically two kinds of separation of duty policy: dual control and functional separation.

In dual control, two or more staff members must act together to authorize a transaction. The classic military example is in nuclear command systems, which may require two officers to turn their keys simultaneously in consoles that are too far apart for any single person to reach both locks. I'll discuss nuclear command and control further in a later chapter. The classic civilian example is when a bank issues a letter of guarantee, which will typically undertake to carry the losses should a loan made by another bank go sour. Guarantees are particularly prone to fraud; if you can get bank A to guarantee a loan to your business from bank B, then bank B is supervising your account while bank A's money is at risk. A dishonest businessmen with a forged or corruptly-obtained guarantee can take his time to plunder the loan account at bank B, with the alarm only being raised when he absconds and bank B asks bank A for the money. If a single manager could issue such an instrument, the temptation would be strong. I'll discuss this further in section 10.3.2.

With functional separation of duties, two or more different staff members act on a transaction at different points in its path. The classic example is corporate purchasing. A manager takes a purchase decision and tells the purchasing department; a clerk there raises a purchase order; the store clerk records the goods' arrival; an invoice arrives at accounts; the accounts clerk correlates it with the purchase order and the stores receipt and raises a check; and the accounts manager signs the check.

However, it doesn't stop there. The manager now gets a debit on her monthly statement for that internal account, her boss reviews the accounts to make sure the division's profit targets are likely to be met, the internal audit department can descend at any time to audit the division's books, and when the external auditors come in once a year they will check the books of a randomly selected sample of departments. Finally, when frauds are discovered, the company's lawyers may make vigorous efforts to get the money back.

So the model can be described as *prevent — detect — recover*. The level of reliance placed on each of these three legs will depend on the application. Where detection may be delayed for months or years, and recovery may therefore be very difficult — as with corrupt bank guarantees — it is prudent to put extra effort into prevention, using techniques such as dual control. Where prevention is hard, you should see to it that detection is fast enough, and recovery vigorous enough, to provide a deterrent effect. The classic example here is that bank tellers can quite easily take cash, so you need to count the money every day and catch them afterwards.

Bookkeeping and management control are not only one of the earliest security systems; they also have given rise to much of management science and civil law. They are entwined with a company's business processes, and exist in its cultural context. In Swiss banks, there are two managers' signatures on almost everything, while Americans are much more relaxed. In most countries' banks, staff get background checks, can be moved randomly from one task to another, and are forced to take holidays at least once a year. This would not be acceptable in the typical university — but in academia the opportunities for fraud are much less.

Designing an internal control system is hard because it's a highly interdisciplinary problem. The financial controllers, the personnel department, the lawyers, the auditors and the systems people all come at the problem from different directions, offer partial solutions, fail to understand each other's control objectives, and things fall down the hole in the middle. Human factors are very often neglected, and systems end up being vulnerable to helpful subordinates or authoritarian managers who can cause dual control to fail. It's important not just to match the controls to the culture, but also motivate people to use them; for example, in the better run banks, management controls are marketed to staff as a means of protecting them against blackmail and kidnapping.

Security researchers have so far focused on the small part of the problem which pertains to creating dual control (or in general, where there are more than two principals, *shared control*) systems. Even this is not at all easy. For example, rule 9 in Clark-Wilson says that security officers can change access rights — so what's to stop a security officer creating logons for two managers and using them to send all the bank's money to Switzerland?

In theory you could use cryptography, and split the signing key between two or more principals. In a Windows network, the obvious way to manage things is to put users in separately administered domains. With a traditional banking system using the mainframe operating system MVS, you can separate duties between the sysadmin and the auditor; the former can do anything he wishes, except finding out which of his activities the latter is monitoring [159]. But in real life, dual control is hard to do end-to-end because there are many system interfaces that provide single points of failure, and in any case split-responsibility systems administration is tedious.

So the practical answer is that most bank sysadmins are in a position to do just this type of fraud. Some have tried, and where they fall down is when the back-office balancing controls set off the alarm after a day or two and money laundering controls stop him getting away with very much. I'll discuss this further in section 10.3.2. The point to bear in mind here is that serial controls along the *prevent — detect — recover* model are usually more important than shared control. They depend ultimately on some persistent state in the system and are in tension with programmers' desire to keep things simple by making transactions atomic.

There are also tranquility issues. For example, could an accountant knowing that he was due to be promoted to manager tomorrow end up doing both authorizations on a large transfer? A technical fix for this might involve a Chinese Wall mechanism supporting a primitive 'X may do Y only if he hasn't done Z' ('A manager can confirm a payment only if his name doesn't appear on it as the creator'). So we would end up with a number of exclusion and other rules involving individuals, groups and object labels; once the number of rules becomes large (as it will in a real bank) we would need a systematic way of examining this rule set and verifying that it doesn't have any horrible loopholes.

In the medium term, banking security policy — like medical security policy — may find its most convenient expression in using role based access control, although this will typically be implemented in banking middleware rather than in an underlying platform such as Windows or Linux. Real systems will need to manage separation-of-duty policies with both parallel elements, such as dual control, and serial elements such as functional separation along a transaction's path. This argues for the access control mechanisms being near to the application. But then, of course, they are likely to be more complex, proprietary, and not so well studied as the mechanisms that come with the operating system.

One really important aspect of internal control in banking — and in systems generally — is to minimise the number of 'sysadmins', that is, of people with complete access to the whole system and the ability to change it. For decades now, the standard approach has been to keep development staff quite separate from live production systems. A traditional bank in the old days would have two mainframes, one to run the live systems, with the other being a backup machine that was normally used for development and testing. Programmers would create new software that would be tested by a test department and subject to source code review by internal auditors; once approved this would be handed off to a change management department that would install it in the live system at the next upgrade. The live system would be run by an operations team with no access to compilers, debuggers or other tools that would let them alter live code or data.

In theory this prevents abuse by programmers, and in practice it can work fairly well. However there are leaks. First, there are always some sysadmins who need full access in order to do their jobs; and second, there are always emergencies. The ATM system goes down at the weekend, and the ATM team's duty programmer is given access to the live system from home so she can fix the bug. You audit such accesses as well as you can, but it's still inevitable that your top sysadmins will be so much more knowledgeable than your auditors that they could do bad things if they really wanted to. Indeed, at banks I've helped with security, you might find that there are thirty or forty people whom you just have to trust — the CEO, the chief dealer, the top sysadmins and a number of others. It's important to know who these people are, and to minimise their numbers. Pay them well — and watch discreetly to see if they start spending even more.

A final remark on dual control is that it's often not adequate for transactions involving more than one organization, because of the difficulties of dispute resolution: 'My two managers say the money was sent!' 'But my two say it wasn't!'

10.2.3   What Goes Wrong

Theft can take a variety of forms, from the purely opportunist to clever insider frauds; but the experience is that most thefts from the average company are due to insiders. There are many surveys; a typical one, by accountants Ernst and Young, reports that 82% of the worst frauds were committed by employees; nearly half of the perpetrators had been there over five years and a third of them were managers [1162].

Typical computer crime cases include:

- Paul Stubbs, a password reset clerk at HSBC, conspired with persons unknown to change the password used by AT&T to access their bank account with HSBC. The new password was used to transfer £11.8 million — over $20 million — to offshore companies, from which it was not recovered. Stubbs was a vulnerable young man who had been employed as a password reset clerk after failing internal exams; the court took mercy on him and he got away with five years [975]. It was alleged that an AT&T employee had conspired to cover up the transactions, but that gentleman was acquitted.

- A bank had a system of suspense accounts, which would be used temporarily if one of the parties to a transaction could not be identified (such as when an account number was entered wrongly on a funds transfer). This was a workaround added to the dual control system to deal with transactions that got lost or otherwise couldn't be balanced immediately. As it was a potential vulnerability, the bank had a rule that suspense accounts would be investigated if they were not cleared within three days. One of the clerks exploited this by setting up a scheme whereby she would post a debit to a suspense account and an equal credit to her boyfriend's account; after three days, she would raise another debit to pay off the first. In almost two years she netted hundreds of thousands of dollars. (The bank negligently ignored a regulatory requirement that all staff take at least ten consecutive days' vacation no more than fifteen months from the last such vacation.) In the end, she was caught when she could no longer keep track of the growing mountain of bogus transactions.

- A clerk at an education authority wanted to visit relatives in Australia, and in order to get some money she created a fictitious school, complete with staff whose salaries were paid into her own bank account. It was only discovered by accident when someone noticed that different records gave the authority different numbers of schools.

- A bank clerk in Hastings, England, noticed that the branch computer system did not audit address changes. He picked a customer who had a lot of money in her account and got a statement only once a year; he then changed her address to his, issued a new ATM card and PIN, and changed her address back to its original value. He stole £8,600 from her account, and when she complained she was not believed: the bank maintained that its computer systems were infallible, and so the withdrawals must have been her fault. The matter was only cleared up when the clerk got an attack of conscience and started stuffing the cash he'd stolen in brown envelopes through the branch's letter box at night. As people don't normally give money to banks, the branch manager finally realized that something was seriously wrong.

Volume crime — such as card fraud — often depends on liability rules. Where banks can tell customers who complain of fraud to get lost (as in much of Europe), bank staff know that complaints won't be investigated properly or at all, and get careless. Things are better in the USA where Regulation E places the onus of proof in disputed transaction cases squarely on the bank. I'll discuss this in detail in section 10.4 below.

All the really large frauds — the cases over a billion dollars — have involved lax internal controls. The collapse of Barings Bank is a good example: managers failed to control rogue trader Nick Leeson, blinded by greed for the bonuses his apparent trading profits earned them. The same holds true for other financial sector frauds, such as the Equity Funding scandal, in which an insurance company's management created thousands of fake people on their computer system, insured them, and sold the policies on to reinsurers; and frauds in other sectors such as Robert Maxwell's looting of the Daily Mirror newspaper pension funds in Britain. (For a collection of computer crime case histories, see Parker [1005].) Either the victim's top management were grossly negligent, as in the case of Barings, or perpetrated the scam, as with Equity Funding and Maxwell.

The auditors are also a problem. On the one hand, they are appointed by the company's managers and are thus extremely bad at detecting frauds in which the managers are involved; so the assurance that shareholders get is less than many might have thought. (The legal infighting following the collapse of Enron destroyed its auditors Arthur Andersen and thus reduced the 'big five' audit firms to the 'big four'; now auditors go out of their way to avoid liability for fraud.) Second, there were for many years huge conflicts of interest, as accountants offered cheap audits in order to get their foot in the door, whereupon they made their real money from systems consultancy. (This has been greatly restricted since Enron.) Third, the big audit firms have their own list of favourite controls, which often bear little relationship to the client's real risks, and may even make matters worse. For example, our university's auditors nag us every year to get all our staff to change their passwords every month. This advice is wrong, for reasons explained in Chapter 2 — so every year we point this out and challenge them to justify their advice. But they seem incapable of learning, and they have no incentive to: they can be expected to nitpick, and to ignore any evidence that a particular nit is unhelpful until long after the evidence has become overwhelming. While failing to disclose a material weakness could get them into trouble, at least in the USA, the nitpicking has turned into a bonanza for them. It's reckoned that the auditors' gold-plating of the Sarbanes-Oxley requirements is costing the average U.S. listed company \$2.4m a year in audit fees, plus 70,000 hours of internal work to ensure compliance; the total cost of SOX could be as much as \$1.4 trillion [412]. (My own advice, for what it's worth, is to never use a big-four accountant; smaller firms are cheaper, and a study done by my student Tyler Moore failed to find any evidence that companies audited by the Big Four performed better on the stock market.)

Changing technology also has a habit of eroding controls, which therefore need constant attention and maintenance. For example, thanks to new systems for high-speed processing of bank checks, banks in California stopped a few years ago from honoring requests by depositors that checks have two signatures. Even when a check has imprinted on it 'Two Signatures Required', banks will honor that check with only one signature [1086]. This might seem to be a problem for the customer's security rather than the bank's, but bank checks can also be at risk and if something goes wrong even with a merchant transaction then the bank might still get sued.

The lessons to be learned include:

- it's not always obvious which transactions are security sensitive;
- maintaining a working security system can be hard in the face of a changing environment;
- if you rely on customer complaints to alert you to fraud, you had better listen to them;
- there will always be people in positions of relative trust who can get away with a scam for a while;
- no security policy will ever be completely rigid. There will always have to be workarounds for people to cope with real life;
- these workarounds naturally create vulnerabilities. So the lower the transaction error rate, the better.

There will always be residual risks. Managing these residual risks remains one of the hardest and most neglected of jobs. It means not just technical measures, such as involving knowledgeable industry experts, auditors and insurance people in the detailed design, and iterating the design once some loss history is available. It also means training managers, auditors and others to detect problems and react to them appropriately. I'll revisit this in Part III.

The general experience of banks in the English-speaking world is that some 1% of staff are sacked each year. The typical offence is minor embezzlement with a loss of a few thousand dollars. No-one has found an effective way of predicting which staff will go bad; previously loyal staff can be thrown off the rails by shocks such as divorce, or may over time develop a gambling or alcohol habit. Losing a few hundred tellers a year is simply seen as a cost of doing business. What banks find very much harder to cope with are incidents in which senior people go wrong — indeed, in several cases within my experience, banks have gone to great lengths to avoid admitting that a senior insider was bent. And risks that managers are unwilling to confront, they are often unable to control. No-one at Barings even wanted to think that their star dealer Leeson might be a crook; and pop went the bank.

Finally, it's not enough, when doing an audit or a security investigation, to merely check that the books are internally consistent. It's also important to check that they correspond to external reality. This was brought home to the accounting profession in 1938 with the collapse of McKesson and Robbins, a large, well-known drug and chemical company with reported assets of $100m[1]. It turned out that 20% of the recorded assets and inventory were nonexistent. The president, Philip Musica, turned out to be an impostor with

---

[1]In 2007 dollars, that's $1.4bn if you deflate by prices, $3bn if you deflate by unskilled wages and over $15bn by share of GDP.

a previous fraud conviction; with his three brothers, he inflated the firm's figures using a fake foreign drug business involving a bogus shipping agent and a fake Montreal bank. The auditors, who had accepted the McKesson account without making enquiries about the company's bosses, had failed to check inventories, verify accounts receivable with customers, or think about separation of duties within the company [1082]. The lessons from that incident clearly weren't learned well enough, as the same general things continue to happen regularly and on all sorts of scales from small firms and small branches of big ones, to the likes of Enron.

So if you ever have responsibility for security in a financial (or other) firm, you should think hard about which of your managers could defraud your company by colluding with customers or suppliers. Could a branch manager be lending money to a dodgy business run by his cousin against forged collateral? Could he have sold life-insurance policies to nonexistent people and forged their death certificates? Could an operations manager be taking bribes from a supplier? Could one of your call-center staff be selling customer passwords to the Mafia? Lots of things can and do go wrong; you have to figure out which of them matter, and how you get to find out. Remember: a trusted person is one who can damage you. Who can damage you, and how? This is the basic question that a designer of internal controls must be constantly asking.

10.3   Wholesale Payment Systems

When people think of electronic bank fraud, they often envisage a Hollywood scene in which crafty Russian hackers break a bank's codes and send multi-million dollar wire transfers to tax havens. Systems for transferring money electronically are indeed an occasional target of sophisticated crime, and have been for a century and a half, as I noted earlier in section 5.2.4 when I discussed test key systems.

By the early 1970s, bankers started to realise that this worthy old Victorian system was due for an overhaul.

First, most test-key systems were vulnerable in theory at least to cryptanalysis; someone who observed a number of transactions could gradually work out the key material.

Second, although the test key tables were kept in the safe, there was nothing really to stop staff members working out tests for unauthorised messages at the same time as a test for an authorised message. In theory, you might require that two staff members retrieve the tables from the safe, sit down at a table facing each other and perform the calculation. However, in practice people would work sequentially in a corner (the tables were secret, after all) and even if you could compel them to work together, a bent employee might mentally compute the test on an unauthorized message while overtly computing the test on an authorized one. So, in reality, test key schemes didn't support dual control. Having tests computed by one staff member and checked by another doubled the risk rather than reducing it. (There are ways to do dual control with manual authenticators, such as by getting the two staff members to work out different codes using different tables; and there are other techniques, used in the control of nuclear weapons, which I'll discuss in 13.4.)

Third, there was a big concern with cost and efficiency. There seemed little point in having the bank's computer print out a transaction in the telex room, having a test computed manually, then composing a telex to the other bank, then checking the test, and then entering it into the other bank's computer. Errors were much more of a problem than frauds, as the telex operators introduced typing errors. Customers who got large payments into their accounts in error sometimes just spent the money, and in one case an erroneous recipient spent some of his windfall on clever lawyers, who helped him keep it. This shocked the industry. Surely the payments could flow directly from one bank's computer to another?

10.3.1 SWIFT

The Society for Worldwide International Financial Telecommunications (SWIFT) was set up in the 1970s by a consortium of banks to provide a more secure and efficient means than telex of sending payment instructions between member banks. It can be thought of as an email system with built-in encryption, authentication and non-repudiation services. It's important not just because it's used to ship trillions of dollars round the world daily, but because its design has been copied in systems processing many other kinds of intangible asset, from equities to bills of lading.

The design constraints are interesting. The banks did not wish to trust SWIFT, in the sense of enabling dishonest employees there to forge transactions. The authenticity mechanisms had to be independent of the confidentiality mechanisms, since at the time a number of countries (such as France) forbade the civilian use of cryptography for confidentiality. The non-repudiation functions had to be provided without the use of digital signatures, as these hadn't been invented yet. Finally, the banks had to be able to enforce Clark-Wilson type controls over interbank transactions. (Clark-Wilson also hadn't been invented yet but its components, dual control, balancing, audit and so on, were well enough established.)

The SWIFT design is summarized in Figure 10.2. Authenticity of messages was assured by computing a message authentication code (MAC) at the sending bank and checking it at the receiving bank. The keys for this MAC used to be managed end-to-end: whenever a bank set up a relationship overseas, the senior manager who negotiated it would exchange keys with his opposite number, whether in a face-to-face meeting or afterwards by post to each others' home addresses. There would typically be two key components to minimize the risk of compromise, with one sent in each direction (since even if a bank manager's mail is read in his mailbox by a criminal at one end, it's not likely to happen at both). The key was not enabled until both banks confirmed that it had been safely received and installed.

This way, SWIFT had no part in the message authentication; so long as the authentication algorithm in use was sound, none of their staff could forge a transaction. The authentication algorithm used is supposed to be a trade secret; but as banks like their security mechanisms to be international standards, a natural place to look might be the algorithm described in ISO 8731 [1094]. In this way, they got the worst of all possible worlds: the algorithm was fielded without the benefit of public analysis but got it later once it was expensive to change! An attack was found on the ISO 8731 message authentication algorithm and published in [1040] but, fortunately for the industry, it takes over 100,000 messages to recover a key — which is too large for a practical attack on a typical system that is used prudently.

Although SWIFT itself was largely outside the trust perimeter for message authentication, it did provide a non-repudiation service. Banks in each country sent their messages to a *Regional General Processor* (RGP) which logged them and forwarded them to SWIFT, which also logged them and sent them on to the recipient via the RGP in his country, which also logged them. The RGPs were generally run by different facilities management firms. Thus a bank (or a crooked bank employee) wishing to dishonestly repudiate a done transaction would have to subvert not just the local SWIFT application and its surrounding controls, but also two independent contractors in different countries. Note that the repudiation control from multiple logging is better than the integrity control. A bent bank wanting to claim that a transaction had been done when it hadn't could always try to insert the message between the other bank and their RGP; while a bent bank employee would probably just insert a bogus incoming message directly into a local system. So logs can be a powerful way of making repudiation difficult, and are much easier for judges to understand than cryptography.

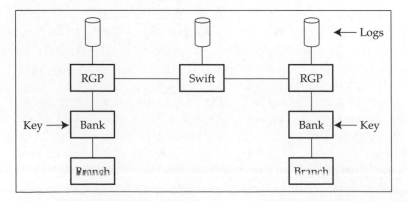

Figure 10.2: Architecture of SWIFT

Confidentiality depended on line encryption devices between the banks and the RGP node, and between these nodes and the main SWIFT processing sites. Key management was straightforward at first. Keys were hand carried in EEPROM cartridges between the devices at either end of a leased line. In countries where confidentiality was illegal, these devices could be omitted without impairing the authenticity and non-repudiation mechanisms.

Dual control was provided either by the use of specialized terminals (in small banks) or by mainframe software packages which could be integrated with a bank's main production system. The usual method of operation is to have three separate staff to do a SWIFT transaction: one to enter it, one to check it, and one to authorize it. (As the checker can modify any aspect of the message, this really only gives dual control, not triple control — and the programmers who maintain the interface can always attack the system there). Reconciliation was provided by checking transactions against daily statements received electronically from correspondent banks. This meant that someone who managed to get a bogus message into the system would sound an alarm within two or three days.

10.3.2 What Goes Wrong

SWIFT I ran for twenty years without a single report of external fraud. In the mid 1990s, it was enhanced by adding public key mechanisms; MAC keys are now shared between correspondent banks using public key cryptography and the MACs themselves may be further protected by a digital signature. The key management mechanisms have been ensconced as ISO standard 11166, which in turn has been used in other systems (such as CREST, which is used by banks and stockbrokers to register and transfer UK stocks and shares). There has been some debate over the security of this architecture [73, 1094]. Quite apart from the centralization of trust brought about by the adoption of public key cryptography — in that the central certification authority can falsely certify a key as belonging to a bank when it doesn't — CREST adopted 512-bit public keys, and these are too short: as I mentioned in the chapter on cryptology, at least one RSA public key of this length has been factored surreptitiously by a group of students [24].

However the main practical attacks on such systems have not involved the payment mechanisms themselves. The typical attack comes from a bank programmer inserting a bogus message into the processing queue. It usually fails because he does not understand the other controls in the system, or the procedural controls surrounding large transfers. For example, banks maintain accounts with each other, so when bank A sends money to a customer of bank B it actually sends an instruction 'please pay this customer the following sum out of our account with you'. As these accounts have both balances and credit limits, large payments aren't processed entirely automatically but need intervention from the dealing room to ensure that the needed currency or credit line is made available. So transfers over a million dollars or so tend to need managerial interventions of which technical staff are ignorant; and there are also filters that look for large transactions so that the bank can report them to the money-laundering authorities if need be. There is also the common-sense factor, in that anyone who opens a bank account, receives a large incoming wire transfer and then starts frantically moving money out again used to need a very convincing excuse. (Common sense has become less of a backstop since 9/11 as customer due diligence and anti-money-laundering rules have become both formalised and onerous; bank staff rely more on box-ticking, which has made life easier for the bad guys [55].) In any case, the programmer who inserts a bogus transaction into the system usually gets arrested when he turns up to collect the cash. If your life's goal is a career in bank fraud, you're better off getting an accounting or law degree and working in a loans office rather than messing about with computers.

Other possible technical attacks, such as inserting Trojan software into the PCs used by bank managers to initiate transactions, wiretapping the link from the branch to the bank mainframe, subverting the authentication protocol used by bank managers to log on, and even inserting a bogus transaction in the branch LAN causing it to appear on the relevant printer — would also run up against the business-process controls. In fact, most large scale bank frauds which 'worked' have not used technical attacks but exploited procedural vulnerabilities.

- The classic example is a letter of guarantee. It is common enough for a company in one country to guarantee a loan to a company in another. This can be set up as a SWIFT message, or even a paper letter. But as no cash changes hands at the time, the balancing controls are inoperative. If a forged guarantee is accepted as genuine, the 'beneficiary' can take his time borrowing money from the accepting bank, laundering it, and disappearing. Only when the victim bank realises that the loan has gone sour and tries to call in the guarantee is the forgery discovered.

- An interesting fraud of a slightly different type took place in 1986 between London and Johannesburg. At that time, the South African government operated two exchange rates, and in one bank the manager responsible for deciding which rate applied to each transaction conspired with a rich man in London. They sent money out to Johannesburg at an exchange rate of seven Rand to the Pound, and back again the following day at four. After two weeks of this, the authorities became suspicious, and the police came round. On seeing them in the dealing room, the manager fled without stopping to collect his jacket, drove over the border to Swaziland, and flew via Nairobi to London. There, he boasted to the press about how he had defrauded the wicked apartheid system. As the UK has no exchange control, exchange control fraud isn't an offence and so he couldn't be extradited. The conspirators got away with millions, and the bank couldn't even sue them.

■ Perhaps the best known money transfer fraud occurred in 1979 when Stanley Rifkin, a computer consultant, embezzled over ten million dollars from Security Pacific National Bank. He got round the money laundering controls by agreeing to buy a large shipment of diamonds from a Russian government agency in Switzerland. He got the transfer into the system by observing an authorization code used internally when dictating transfers to the wire transfer department, and simply used it over the telephone (a classic example of dual control breakdown at a system interface). He even gave himself extra time to escape by doing the deal just before a U.S. bank holiday. Where he went wrong was in not planning what to do after he collected the stones. If he'd hid them in Europe, gone back to the USA and helped investigate the fraud, he might well have got away with it; as it was, he ended up on the run and got caught.

The system design lesson is unchanged: one must always be alert to things which defeat the dual control philosophy. However, as time goes on we have to see it in a broader context. Even if we can solve the technical problems of systems administration, interfaces and so on, there's still the business process problem of what we control — quite often critical transactions don't appear as such at a casual inspection.

10.4   Automatic Teller Machines

Another set of lessons about the difficulties and limitations of dual control emerges from studying the security of *automatic teller machines* (ATMs). ATMs, also known as cash machines, have been one of the most influential technological innovations of the 20th century.

ATMs were the first large-scale retail transaction processing systems. They were devised in 1938 by the inventor Luther Simjian, who also thought up the teleprompter and the self-focussing camera. He persuaded Citicorp to install his 'Bankamat' machine in New York in 1939; they withdrew it after six months, saying 'the only people using the machines were a small number of prostitutes and gamblers who didn't want to deal with tellers face to face' [1168]. Its commercial introduction dates to 1967, when a machine made by De La Rue was installed by Barclays Bank in Enfield, London. The world installed base is now thought to be about 1,500,000 machines. The technology developed for them is now also used in card payment terminals in shops. Modern block ciphers were first used on a large scale in ATM networks: they are used to generate and verify PINs in secure hardware devices located within the ATMs and at bank computer centres. This technology, including block ciphers, tamper-resistant hardware and the supporting protocols, ended up being used in many other applications from postal franking machines to lottery ticket terminals. In short, ATMs were the 'killer app' that got modern commercial cryptology and retail payment technology off the ground.

10.4.1   ATM Basics

Most ATMs operate using some variant of a system developed by IBM for its 3624 series cash machines in the late 1970s. The card contains the customer's primary account number, *PAN*. A secret key, called the 'PIN key', is used to encrypt the account number, then decriminalize it and truncate it. The result of this operation is called the 'natural PIN'; an offset can be added to it in order to give the PIN which the customer must enter. The offset has no real cryptographic function; it just enables customers to choose their own PIN. An example of the process is shown in Figure 10.3.

In the first ATMs to use PINs, each ATM contained a copy of the PIN key and each card contained the offset as well as the primary account number. Each ATM could thus verify all customer PINs. Early ATMs also operated offline; if your cash withdrawal limit was $500 per week, a counter was kept on the card. In recent years networks have become more dependable and ATMs have tended to operate online only, which simplifies the design; the cash counters and offsets have vanished from magnetic strips and are now kept on servers. In the last few years, magnetic strips have been supplemented with smartcard chips in some countries, especially in Europe; I will describe the smartcard systems later. However the basic principle remains: PINs are generated and protected using cryptography.

Dual control is implemented in this system using tamper-resistant hardware. A cryptographic processor, also known as a *security module*, is kept in the bank's server room and will perform a number of defined operations on customer PINs and on related keys in ways that enforce a dual-control policy. This includes the following.

1. Operations on the clear values of customer PINs, and on the keys needed to compute them or used to protect them, are all done in tamper-resistant

Account number PAN:	8807012345691715
PIN key KP:	FEFEFEFEFEFEFEFE
Result of DES $\{PAN\}_{KP}$:	A2CE126C69AEC82D
$\{N\}_{KP}$ decimalized:	0224126269042823
Natural PIN:	0224
Offset:	6565
Customer PIN:	6789

Figure 10.3: IBM method for generating bank card PINs

hardware and the clear values are never made available to any single member of the bank's staff.

2. Thus, for example, the cards and PINs are sent to the customer via separate channels. The cards are personalized in a facility with embossing and mag strip printing machinery, and the PIN mailers are printed in a separate facility containing a printer attached to a security module.

3. A *terminal master key* is supplied to each ATM in the form of two printed components, which are carried to the branch by two separate officials, input at the ATM keyboard, and combined to form the key. Similar procedures (but with three officials) are used to set up master keys between banks and network switches such as VISA.

4. If ATMs are to perform PIN verification locally, then the PIN key is encrypted under the terminal master key and then sent to the ATM.

5. If the PIN verification is to be done centrally over the network, the PIN is encrypted under a key set up using the terminal master key. It will then be sent from the ATM to a central security module for checking.

6. If the bank's ATMs are to accept other banks' cards, then its security modules use transactions that take a PIN encrypted under an ATM key, decrypt it and re-encrypt it for its destination, such as using a key shared with VISA. This *PIN translation* function is done entirely within the hardware security module, so that clear values of PINs are never available to the bank's programmers. VISA will similarly decrypt the PIN and re-encrypt it using a key shared with the bank that issued the card, so that the PIN can be verified by the security module that knows the relevant PIN key.

During the 1980s and 1990s, hardware security modules became more and more complex, as ever more functionality got added to support more complex financial applications from online transactions to smartcards. An example of a leading product is the IBM 4758 — this also has the virtue of having its documentation available publicly online for study (see [641] for the command set and [1195] for the architecture and hardware design). We'll discuss this later in the chapter on tamper resistance.

But extending the dual control security policy from a single bank to tens of thousands of banks worldwide, as modern ATM networks do, was not completely straightforward.

■ When people started building ATM networks in the mid 1980s, many banks used software encryption rather than hardware security modules to support ATMs. So in theory, any bank's programmers might get access to the PINs of any other bank's customers. The remedy was to push through standards for security module use. In many countries (such as the USA), these standards were largely ignored; but even where they were respected, some banks continued using software for transactions involving their own customers. So some keys (such as those used to communicate with ATMs) had to be available in software too, and knowledge of these keys could be used to compromise the PINs of other banks' customers. (I'll explain this in more detail later.) So the protection given by the hardware TCB was rarely complete.

▪ It is not feasible for 10,000 banks to share keys in pairs, so each bank connects to a switch provided by an organization such as VISA or Cirrus, and the security modules in these switches translate the traffic. The switches also do accounting, and enable banks to settle their accounts for each day's transactions with all the other banks in the system by means of a single electronic debit or credit. The switch is highly trusted, and if something goes wrong there the consequences can be severe. In one case, there turned out to be not just security problems but also dishonest staff. The switch manager ended up a fugitive from justice, and the bill for remediation was in the millions. In another case, a Y2K-related software upgrade at a switch was bungled, with the result that cardholders in one country found that for a day or two they could withdraw money even if their accounts were empty. This also led to a very large bill.

▪ Corners are cut to reduce the cost of dealing with huge transaction volumes. For example, it is common for authentication of authorization responses to be turned off. So anyone with access to the network can cause a given ATM to accept any card presented to it, by simply replaying a positive authorization response. Network managers claim that should a fraud ever start, then the authentication can always be turned back on. This might seem reasonable; attacks involving manipulated authorization responses are very rare. Similarly, after UK banks put smartcard chips into bank cards, some of them kept on accepting magnetic-strip transactions, so that a card with a broken chip would still work so long as the magnetic strip could be read. But such shortcuts — even when apparently reasonable on grounds of risk and cost — mean that a bank which stonewalls customer complaints by saying its ATM network is secure, and so the transaction must be the customer's fault, is not telling the truth. This may lay the bank and its directors open to fraud charges. What's more, changing the network's modus operandi suddenly in response to a fraud can be difficult; it can unmask serious dependability problems or lead to unacceptable congestion. This brings home the late Roger Needham's saying that 'optimization is the process of taking something which works, and replacing it by something which doesn't quite but is cheaper'.

There are many other ways in which ATM networks can be attacked in theory, and I'll discuss a number of them later in the context of interface security: the design of the hardware security modules that were in use for decades was so poor that programmers could extract PINs and keys simply by issuing suitable sequences of commands to the device's interface with the server, without having to break either the cryptographic algorithms or the hardware tamper-resistance. However, one of the interesting things about these systems is that they have now been around long enough, and have been attacked enough by both insiders and outsiders, to give us a lot of data points on how such systems fail in practice.

10.4.2   What Goes Wrong

ATM fraud is an interesting study as this is a mature system with huge volumes and a wide diversity of operators. There have been successive waves of ATM fraud, which have been significant since the early 1990s. In each wave, a set of vulnerabilities was exploited and then eventually fixed; but the rapidly growing scale of payment card operations opened up new vulnerabilities. There is a fascinating interplay between the technical and regulatory aspects of protection.

The first large wave of fraud lasted from perhaps 1990–96 and exploited the poor implementation and management of early systems. In the UK, one prolific fraudster, Andrew Stone, was convicted three times of ATM fraud, the last time getting five and a half years in prison. He got involved in fraud when he discovered by chance the 'encryption replacement' trick I discussed in the chapter on protocols: he changed the account number on his bank card to his wife's and found by chance that he could take money out of her account using his PIN. In fact, he could take money out of any account at that bank using his PIN. This happened because his bank (and at least two others) wrote the encrypted PIN to the card's magnetic strip without linking it to the account number in any robust way (for example, by using the 'offset' method described above). His second method was 'shoulder surfing': he'd stand in line behind a victim, observe the entered PIN, and pick up the discarded ATM slip. Most banks at the time printed the full account number on the slip, and a card would work with no other correct information on it.

Stone's methods spread via people he trained as his accomplices, and via a 'Howto' manual he wrote in prison. Some two thousand victims of his (and other) frauds banded together to bring a class action against thirteen banks to get their money back; the banks beat this on the technical legal argument that the facts in each case were different. I was an expert in this case, and used it to write a survey of what went wrong [33] (there is further material in [34]). The fraud spread to the Netherlands, Italy and eventually worldwide, as criminals learned a number of simple hacks. Here I'll summarize the more important and interesting lessons we learned.

The engineers who designed ATM security systems in the 1970s and 1980s (of whom I was one) had assumed that criminals would be relatively sophisticated, fairly well-informed about the system design, and rational in their choice of attack methods. In addition to worrying about the many banks which were slow to buy security modules and implementation loopholes such as omitting authentication codes on authorization responses, we agonized over whether the encryption algorithms were strong enough, whether the tamper-resistant boxes were tamper-resistant enough, and whether the random number generators used to manufacture keys were random enough. We knew we just couldn't enforce dual control properly: bank managers considered it beneath their dignity to touch a keyboard, so rather than entering the ATM master key components themselves after a maintenance visit, most of them would just give both key components to the ATM engineer. We wondered whether a repairman would get his hands on a bank's PIN key, forge cards in industrial quantities, close down the whole system, and wreck public confidence in electronic banking.

The great bulk of the actual 'phantom withdrawals', however, appeared to have one of the following three causes:

▪ Simple processing errors account for a lot of disputes. With U.S. customers making something like 5 billion ATM withdrawals a year, even a system that only makes one error per hundred thousand transactions will give rise to 50,000 disputes a year. In practice the error rate seems to lie somewhere between 1 in 10,000 and 1 in 100,000. One source of errors we tracked down was that a large bank's ATMs would send a transaction again if the network went down before a confirmation message was received from the mainframe; periodically, the mainframe itself crashed and forgot about open transactions. We also found customers whose accounts were debited with other customers' transactions, and other customers who were never debited at all for their card transactions. (We used to call these cards 'directors' cards' and joked that they were issued to bank directors.)

▪ Thefts from the mail were also huge. They are reckoned to account for 30% of all UK payment card losses, but most banks' postal control procedures have always been dismal. For example, when I moved to Cambridge in February 1992 I asked my bank for an increased card limit: the bank sent not one, but two, cards and PINs through the post. These cards arrived only a few days after intruders had got hold of our apartment block's mail and torn it up looking for valuables. It turned out that this bank did not have the systems to deliver a card by registered post. (I'd asked them to send the card to the branch for me to collect but the branch staff had simply re-addressed the envelope to me.) Many banks now make you phone a call center to activate a card before you can use it. This made a dent in the fraud rates.

■ Frauds by bank staff appeared to be the third big cause of phantoms. We mentioned the Hastings case in section 10.2.3 above; there are many others. For example, in Paisley, Scotland, an ATM repairman installed a portable computer inside an ATM to record customer card and PIN data and then went on a spending spree with forged cards. In London, England, a bank stupidly used the same cryptographic keys in its live and test systems; maintenance staff found out that they could work out customer PINs using their test equipment, and started offering this as a service to local criminals at £50 a card. Insider frauds were particularly common in countries like Britain where the law generally made the customer pay for fraud, and rarer in countries like the USA where the bank paid; British bank staff knew that customer complaints wouldn't be investigated carefully, so they got lazy, careless, and sometimes bent.

These failures are all very much simpler and more straightforward than the ones we'd worried about. In fact, the only fraud we had worried about and that actually happened to any great extent was on offline processing. In the 1980s, many ATMs would process transactions while the network was down, so as to give 24-hour service; criminals — especially in Italy and later in England too — learned to open bank accounts, duplicate the cards and then 'jackpot' a lot of ATMs overnight when the network was down [775]. This forced most ATM operations to be online-only by 1994.

However, there were plenty of frauds that happened in quite unexpected ways. I already mentioned the Utrecht case in section 3.5, where a tap on a garage point-of-sale terminal was used to harvest card and PIN data; and Stone's 'encryption replacement' trick. There were plenty more.

■ Stone's shoulder-surfing trick of standing in an ATM queue, observing a customer's PIN, picking up the discarded ticket and copying the data to a blank card, was not in fact invented by him. It was first reported in New York in the mid 1980s; and it was still working in the Bay Area in the mid 1990s. By then it had been automated; Stone (and Bay area criminals) used video cameras with motion sensors to snoop on PINs, whether by renting an apartment overlooking an ATM or even parking a rented van there. Visual copying is easy to stop: the standard technique nowadays is to print only the last four digits of the account number on the ticket, and there's also a three-digit 'card verification value' (CVV) on the magnetic strip that should never be printed. Thus even if the villain's camera is good enough to read the account number and expiry date from the front of the card, a working copy can't be made. (The CVV is like the three-digit security code on the signature strip, but different digits; each is computed from the account number and expiry date by encrypting them with a suitable key). Surprisingly, it still happens; I have a letter from a UK bank dated May 2007 claiming that a series of terrorist-related ATM frauds were perpetrated using closed-circuit TV. This amounts to an admission that the CVV is not always checked.

■ There were some losses due to programming errors by banks. One small institution issued the same PIN to all its customers; another bank's cash machines had the feature that when a telephone card was entered at an ATM, it believed that the previous card had been inserted again. Crooks stood in line, observed customers' PINs, and helped themselves.

■ There were losses due to design errors by ATM vendors. One model, common in the 1980s, would output ten banknotes from the lowest denomination non-empty cash drawer, whenever a certain fourteen digit sequence was entered at the keyboard. One bank printed this sequence in its branch manual, and three years later there was a sudden spate of losses. All the banks using the machine had to rush out a patch to disable the test transaction. And despite the fact that I documented this in 1993, and again in the first edition of this book in 2001, similar incidents are still reported in 2007. Some makes of ATM used in stores can be reprogrammed into thinking that they are dispensing $1 bills when in fact they're dispensing twenties; it just takes a default master password that is printed in widely-available online manuals. Any passer-by who knows this can stroll up to the machine, reset the bill value, withdraw $400, and have his account debited with $20. The store owners who lease the machines are not told of the vulnerability, and are left to pick up the tab [1037].

■ Several banks thought up check-digit schemes to enable PINs to be checked by offline ATMs without having to give them the bank's PIN key. For example, customers of one British bank get a credit card PIN with digit one plus digit four equal to digit two plus digit three, and a debit card PIN with one plus three equals two plus four. Crooks found they could use stolen cards in offline devices by entering a PIN such as 4455.

■ Many banks' operational security procedures were simply dire. In August 1993, my wife went into a branch of our bank with a witness and told them she'd forgotten her PIN. The teller helpfully printed her a new PIN mailer from a printer attached to a PC behind the counter — just like that! It was not the branch where our account is kept. Nobody knew her and all the identification she offered was our bank card and her checkbook. When anyone who's snatched a handbag can walk in off the street and get a PIN for the card in it at any branch, no amount of encryption technology will do much good. (The bank in question has since fallen victim to a takeover.)

- A rapidly growing modus operandi in the early 1990s was to use false terminals to collect card and PIN data. The first report was from the USA in 1988; there, crooks built a vending machine which would accept any card and PIN, and dispense a packet of cigarettes. In 1993, two villains installed a bogus ATM in the Buckland Hills Mall in Connecticut [667, 962]. They had managed to get a proper ATM and a software development kit for it — all bought on credit. Unfortunately for them, they decided to use the forged cards in New York, where cash machines have hidden video cameras, and as they'd crossed a state line they ended up getting long stretches in Club Fed.

So the first thing we did wrong when designing ATM security systems in the early to mid 1980s was to worry about criminals being clever, when we should rather have worried about our customers — the banks' system designers, implementers and testers — being stupid. Crypto is usually only part of a very much larger system. It gets a lot of attention because it's mathematically interesting; but as correspondingly little attention is paid to the 'boring' bits such as training, usability, standards and audit, it's rare that the bad guys have to break the crypto to compromise a system. It's also worth bearing in mind that there are so many users for large systems such as ATM networks that we must expect the chance discovery and exploitation of accidental vulnerabilities which were simply too obscure to be caught in testing.

The second thing we did wrong was to not figure out what attacks could be industrialised, and focus on those. In the case of ATMs, the false-terminal attack is the one that made the big time. The first hint of organised crime involvement was in 1999 in Canada, where dozens of alleged Eastern European organized-crime figures were arrested in the Toronto area for deploying doctored point-of-sale terminals [85, 152]. The technology has since become much more sophisticated; 'skimmers' made in Eastern Europe are attached to the throats of cash machines to read the magnetic strip and also capture the PIN using a tiny camera. I'll discuss these in more detail in the next section. Despite attempts to deal with false-terminal attacks by moving from magnetic strip cards to smartcards, they have become pervasive. They will be difficult and expensive to eliminate.

10.4.3   Incentives and Injustices

In the USA, the banks have to carry the risks associated with new technology. This was decided in a historic precedent, Judd versus Citibank, in which bank customer Dorothy Judd claimed that she had not made some disputed withdrawals and Citibank said that as its systems were secure, she must have done.

The judge ruled that Citibank's claim to infallibility was wrong in law, as it put an unmeetable burden of proof on her, and gave her her money back [674]. The U.S. Federal Reserve incorporated this into 'Regulation E', which requires banks to refund all disputed transactions unless they can prove fraud by the customer [440]. This has led to some minor abuse — misrepresentations by customers are estimated to cost the average U.S. bank about $15,000 a year — but this is an acceptable cost (especially as losses from vandalism are typically three times as much) [1362].

In other countries — such as the UK, Germany, the Netherlands and Norway — the banks got away for many years with claiming that their ATM systems were infallible. Phantom withdrawals, they maintained, could not possibly exist and a customer who complained of one must be mistaken or lying. This position was demolished in the UK when Stone and a number of others started being jailed for ATM fraud, as the problem couldn't be denied any more. Until that happened, however, there were some rather unpleasant incidents which got banks a lot of bad publicity [34]. The worst was maybe the Munden case.

John Munden was one of our local police constables, based in Bottisham, Cambridgeshire; his beat included the village of Lode where I lived at the time. He came home from holiday in September 1992 to find his bank account empty. He asked for a statement, found six withdrawals for a total of £460 which he did not recall making, and complained. His bank responded by having him prosecuted for attempting to obtain money by deception. It came out during the trial that the bank's system had been implemented and managed in a ramshackle way; the disputed transactions had not been properly investigated; and all sorts of wild claims were made by the bank, such as that their ATM system couldn't suffer from bugs as its software was written in assembler. Nonetheless, it was his word against the bank's. He was convicted in February 1994 and sacked from the police force.

This miscarriage of justice was overturned on appeal, and in an interesting way. Just before the appeal was due to be heard, the prosecution served up a fat report from the bank's auditors claiming that the system was secure. The defense demanded equal access to the bank's systems for its own expert. The bank refused and the court therefore disallowed all its computer evidence — including even its bank statements. The appeal succeeded, and John got reinstated. But this was only in July 1996 — he'd spent the best part of four years in limbo and his family had suffered terrible stress. Had the incident happened in California, he could have won enormous punitive damages — a point bankers should ponder as their systems become global and their customers can be anywhere.[2]

[2]Recently the same drama played itself out again when Jane Badger, of Burton-on-Trent, England, was prosecuted for complaining about phantom withdrawals. The case against her collapsed in January 2008. The bank, which is called Egg, is a subsidiary of Citicorp.

The lesson to be drawn from such cases is that dual control is not enough. If a system is to provide evidence, then it must be able to withstand examination by hostile experts. In effect, the bank had used the wrong security policy. What they really needed wasn't dual control but *non-repudiation*: the ability for the principals in a transaction to prove afterwards what happened. This could have been provided by installing ATM cameras; although these were available (and are used in some U.S. states), they were not used in Britain. Indeed, during the 1992–4 wave of ATM frauds, the few banks who had installed ATM cameras were pressured by the other banks into withdrawing them; camera evidence could have undermined the stance that the banks took in the class action that their systems were infallible.

One curious thing that emerged from this whole episode was that although U.S. banks faced a much fiercer liability regime, they actually spent less on security than UK banks did, and UK banks suffered more fraud. This appears to have been a moral-hazard effect, and was one of the anomalies that sparked interest in security economics. Secure systems need properly aligned incentives.

10.5   Credit Cards

The second theme in consumer payment systems is the credit card. For many years after their invention in the 1950s, credit cards were treated by most banks as a loss leader with which to attract high-value customers. Eventually, in most countries, the number of merchants and cardholders reached critical mass and the transaction volume suddenly took off. In Britain, it took almost twenty years before most banks found the business profitable; then all of a sudden it was extremely profitable. Payment systems have strong network externalities, just like communications technologies or computer platforms: they are two-sided markets in which the service provider must recruit enough merchants to appeal to cardholders, and vice versa. Because of this, and the huge investment involved in rolling out a new payment system to tens of thousands of banks, millions of merchants and billions of customers worldwide, any new payment mechanism is likely to take some time to get established. (The potentially interesting exceptions are where payment is bundled with some other service, such as with Google Checkout.)

Anyway, when you use a credit card to pay for a purchase in a store, the transaction flows from the merchant to his bank (the acquiring bank) which pays him after deducting a *merchant discount* of typically 4–5%. If the card was issued by a different bank, the transaction now flows to a switching center run by the brand (such as VISA) which takes a commission and passes it to the issuing bank for payment. Daily payments between the banks and the brands settle the net cash flows. The issuer also gets a slice of the merchant discount, but makes most of its money from extending credit to cardholders at rates that are usually much higher than the interbank rate.

10.5.1 Fraud

The risk of fraud using stolen cards was traditionally managed by a system of *hot card lists* and merchant *floor limits*. Each merchant gets a local hot card list — formerly on paper, now stored in his terminal — plus a limit set by their acquiring bank above which they have to call for authorization. The call center, or online service, which he uses for this has access to a national hot card list; above a higher limit, they will contact VISA or MasterCard which has a complete list of all hot cards being used internationally; and above a still higher limit, the transaction will be checked all the way back to the card issuer. Recently, the falling cost of communications has led to many transactions being authorised all the way back to the issuer, but there are still extensive fallback processing capabilities. This is because maintaining 99.9999% availability on a network, plus the capacity to handle peak transaction volumes on the Wednesday before Thanksgiving and the Saturday just before Christmas, still costs a whole lot more than the fraud from occasional offline and stand-in processing.

The introduction of *mail order and telephone order* (MOTO) transactions in the 1970s meant that the merchant did not have the customer present, and was not able to inspect the card. What was to stop someone ordering goods using a credit card number he'd picked up from a discarded receipt?

Banks managed the risk by using the expiry date as a password, lowering the floor limits, increasing the merchant discount and insisting on delivery to a cardholder address, which is supposed to be checked during authorization. But the main change was to shift liability so that the merchant bore the full risk of disputes. If you challenge an online credit card transaction (or in fact any transaction made under MOTO rules) then the full amount is immediately debited back to the merchant, together with a significant handling fee. The same procedure applies whether the debit is a fraud, a dispute or a return.

A recent development has been the 'Verified by VISA' program under which merchants can refer online credit-card transactions directly to the issuing bank, which can then authenticate the cardholder using its preferred method. The incentive for the merchant is that the transaction is then treated as a cardholder-present one, so the merchant is no longer at risk. The problem with this is that the quality of authentication offered by participating banks varies wildly. At the top of the scale are banks that use two-channel authentication: when you buy online you get a text message saying something like 'If you really want to pay Amazon.com $76.23, enter the code 4697 in your browser now'. At the bottom end are banks that ask you to enter your ATM PIN into the browser directly — thereby making their customers wide-open targets for particularly severe phishing attacks. There is a clear disincentive for the cardholder, who may now be held liable in many countries regardless of the quality of the local authentication methods.

Of course, even if you have the cardholder physically present, this doesn't guarantee that fraud will be rare. For many years, most fraud was done in person with stolen cards, and stores which got badly hit tended to be those selling goods that can be easily fenced, such as jewelry and consumer electronics. Banks responded by lowering their floor limits. More recently, as technical protection mechanisms have improved, there has been an increase in scams involving cards that were never received by genuine customers. This *pre-issue fraud* can involve thefts from the mail of the many 'pre-approved' cards which arrive in junk mail, or even applications made in the names of people who exist and are creditworthy, but are not aware of the application ('identity theft'). These attacks on the system are intrinsically hard to tackle using purely technical means.

10.5.2 Forgery

In the early 1980's, electronic terminals were introduced through which a sales clerk could swipe a card and get an authorization automatically. But the sales draft was still captured from the embossing, so crooks figured out how to re-encode the magnetic strip of a stolen card with the account number and expiry date of a valid card, which they often got by fishing out discarded receipts from the trash cans of expensive restaurants. A re-encoded card would authorize perfectly, but when the merchant submitted the draft for payment, the account number didn't match the authorization code (a six digit number typically generated by encrypting the account number, date and amount). So the merchants didn't get paid and raised hell.

Banks then introduced *terminal draft capture* where a sales draft is printed automatically using the data on the card strip. The crooks' response was a flood of forged cards, many produced by Triad gangs: between 1989 and 1992, magnetic strip counterfeiting grew from an occasional nuisance into half the total fraud losses [7]. VISA's response was *card verification values* (CVVs) — these are three-digit MACs computed on the card strip contents (account number, version number, expiry date) and written at the end of the strip. They worked well initially; in the first quarter of 1994, VISA International's fraud losses dropped by 15.5% while Mastercard's rose 67% [269]. So Mastercard adopted similar checksums too.

The crooks moved to *skimming* — operating businesses where genuine customer cards were swiped through an extra, unauthorized, terminal to grab a copy of the magnetic strip, which would then be re-encoded on a genuine card. The banks' response was intrusion detection systems, which in the first instance tried to identify criminal businesses by correlating the previous purchase histories of customers who complained.

In the late 1990's, credit card fraud rose sharply due to another simple innovation in criminal technology: the operators of the crooked businesses which skim card data absorb the cost of the customer's transaction rather than billing it. You have a meal at a Mafia-owned restaurant, offer a card, sign the voucher, and fail to notice when the charge doesn't appear on your bill. Perhaps a year later, there is suddenly a huge bill for jewelry, electrical goods or even casino chips. By then you've completely forgotten about the meal, and the bank never had a record of it [501].

In the early 2000's, high-tech criminals became better organised as electronic crime became specialised. Phishing involved malware writers, botnet herders, phishing site operators and cash-out specialists, linked by black markets organised in chat rooms. This has spilled over from targeting online transactions to attacks on retail terminals. Fake terminals, and terminal tapping devices, used in the USA and Canada simply record mag-strip card and PIN data, which are used to make card clones for use in ATMs. In the Far East, wiretaps have been used to harvest card data wholesale [792]. Things are more complex in Europe which has introduced smartcards, but there are now plenty of devices that copy the EMV standard smartcards to mag-strip cards that are used in terminals that accept mag-strip transactions. Some of them use vulnerabilities in the EMV protocol, and so I'll come back to discuss them after I've described bank smartcard use in the next section.

10.5.3 Automatic Fraud Detection

There has been a lot of work since the mid-1990s on more sophisticated financial intrusion detection. Some generic systems do abuse detection using techniques such as neural networks, but it's unclear how effective they are. When fraud is down one year, it's hailed as a success for the latest fraud spotting system [101], while when the figures are up a few years later the vendors let the matter pass quietly [1191].

More convincing are projects undertaken by specific store chains that look for known patterns of misuse. For example, an electrical goods chain in the New York area observed that offender profiling (by age, sex, race and so on) was ineffective, and used purchase profiling instead to cut fraud by 82% in a year. Their technique involved not just being suspicious of high value purchases, but training staff to be careful when customers were careless about purchases and spent less than the usual amount of time discussing options and features. These factors can be monitored online too, but one important aspect of the New York success is harder for a web site: employee rewarding. Banks give a $50 reward per bad card captured, which many stores just keep — so their employees won't make an effort to spot cards or risk embarrassment by confronting a customer. In New York, some store staff were regularly earning a weekly bonus of $150 or more [840].

With online shopping, the only psychology the site designer can leverage is that of the villain. It has been suggested that an e-commerce site should have an unreasonably expensive 'platinum' option that few genuine customers will want to buy. This performs two functions. First, it helps you to do basic purchase profiling. Second, it fits with the model of *Goldilocks pricing* developed by economists Hal Shapiro and Carl Varian, who point out that the real effect of airlines' offering first class fares is to boost sales of business class seats to travelers who can now convince their bosses (or themselves) that they are being 'economical' [1159]. Another idea is to have a carefully engineered response to suspect transactions: if you just say 'bad card, try another one' then the fraudster probably will. You may even end up being used by the crooks as an online service that tells them which of their stolen cards are on the hot list, and this can upset your bank (even though the banks are to blame for the system design). A better approach is claim that you're out of stock, so the bad guy will go elsewhere [1199].

As for electronic banking, it has recently become important to make intrusion detection systems work better with lower-level mechanisms. A good example is the real-time man-in-the-middle attack. After banks in the Netherlands handed out password calculators to their online banking customers, the response of the phishermen was to phish in real time: the mark would log on to the phishing site, which would then log on to the bank site and relay the challenge for the mark to enter into his calculator. The quick fix for this is to look out for large numbers of logons coming from the same IP address. It's likely to be a long struggle, of course; by next year, the bad guys may be using botnets to host the middleman software.

10.5.4 The Economics of Fraud

There's a lot of misinformation about credit card fraud, with statistics quoted selectively to make points. In one beautiful example, VISA was reported to have claimed that card fraud was up, and that card fraud was down, on the same day [598].

But a consistent pattern of figures can be dug out of the trade publications. The actual cost of credit card fraud during the 1990s was about 0.15% of all international transactions processed by VISA and Mastercard [1087], while national rates varied from 1% in America through 0.2% in UK to under 0.1% in France and Spain. The prevailing business culture has a large effect on the rate. U.S. banks, for example, are much more willing to send out huge junk mailings of pre-approved cards to increase their customer base, and write off the inevitable pre-issue fraud as a cost of doing business. In other countries, banks are more risk-averse.

The case of France is interesting, as it seems at first sight to be an exceptional case in which a particular technology has brought real benefits. French banks introduced chip cards for all domestic transactions in the late 1980's, and this reduced losses from 0.269% of turnover in 1987 to 0.04% in 1993 and 0.028%

in 1995. However, there is now an increasing amount of cross-border fraud. French villains use foreign magnetic stripe cards — particularly from the UK [498, 1087] — while French chip cards are used at merchants in non-chip countries [270]. But the biggest reduction in Europe was not in France but in Spain, where the policy was to reduce all merchant floor limits to zero and make all transactions online. This cut their losses from 0.21% of turnover in 1988 to 0.008% in 1991 [110].

The lessons appear to be that first, card fraud is cyclical as new defences are introduced and the villains learn to defeat them; and second, that the most complicated and expensive technological solution doesn't necessarily work best in the field. In fact, villains get smarter all the time. After the UK moved from magnetic strip cards to chipcards in 2005, it took less than eighteen months for the crooks to industrialise the process of moving stolen card data abroad: by 2007, as I'll discuss shortly.

10.5.5 Online Credit Card Fraud — the Hype and the Reality

Turning now from traditional credit card fraud to the online variety, I first helped the police investigate an online credit card fraud in 1987. In that case, the bad guy got a list of hot credit card numbers from his girlfriend who worked in a supermarket, and used them to buy software from companies in California, which he downloaded to order for his customers. This worked because hot card lists at the time carried only those cards which were being used fraudulently in that country; it also guaranteed that the bank would not be able to debit an innocent customer. As it happens, the criminal quit before there was enough evidence to nail him. A rainstorm washed away the riverbank opposite his house and exposed a hide which the police had built to stake him out.

From about 1995, there was great anxiety at the start of the dotcom boom that the use of credit cards on the Internet would lead to an avalanche of fraud, as 'evil hackers' intercepted emails and web forms and harvested credit card numbers by the million. These fears drove Microsoft and Netscape to introduce SSL/TLS to encrypt credit card transactions en route from browsers to web servers. (There was also a more secure protocol, SET, in which the browser would get a certificate from the card-issuing bank and would actually sign the transaction; this failed to take off as the designers didn't get the incentives right.)

The hype about risks to credit card numbers was overdone. Intercepting email is indeed possible but it's surprisingly difficult in practice — so much so that governments had to bully ISPs to install snooping devices on their networks to make court-authorized wiretaps easier [187]. I'll discuss this further in Part III. The actual threat is twofold. First, there's the growth of phishing since 2004; there (as I remarked in Chapter 2) the issue is much more psychology than cryptography. TLS per se doesn't help, as the bad guys can also get certificates and encrypt the traffic.

Second, most of the credit card numbers that are traded online got into bad hands because someone hacked a merchant's computer. VISA had had rules for many years prohibiting merchants from storing credit card data once the transaction had been processed, but many merchants simply ignored them. From 2000, VISA added new rules that merchants had to install a firewall, keep security patches up-to-date, encrypt stored and transmitted data and regularly update antivirus software [1262]. These were also not enforced. The latest set of rules, the Payment Card Industry Data Security Standard, are a joint effort by VISA and Mastercard, and supported by the other brands too; they say much the same things, and we'll have to wait and see whether the enforcement is any better. 'PCI', as the new system's called, certainly seems to be causing some pain; in October 2007, the U.S. National Retail Federation asked credit card companies to stop forcing retailers to store credit card data at all (at present they are supposed to store card numbers temporarily in case of chargebacks) [1296].

The real incentives facing merchants are, first, the cost of disputes, and second, the security-breach disclosure laws that are (in 2007) in force in 34 U.S. states and that are contemplated as a European Directive. Disclosure laws have had a very definite effect in the USA as the stock prices of companies suffering a breach can fall several percent. As for disputes, consumer protection laws in many countries make it easy to repudiate a transaction. Basically all the customer has to do is call the credit card company and say 'I didn't authorize that' and the merchant is saddled with the bill. This was workable in the days when almost all credit card transactions took place locally and most were for significant amounts. If a customer fraudulently repudiated a transaction, the merchant would pursue them through the courts and harrass them using local credit reference agencies. In addition, the banks' systems are often quite capable of verifying local cardholder addresses.

But the Internet differs from the old mail order/telephone order regime in that many transactions are international, amounts are small, and verifying overseas addresses via the credit card system is problematic. Often all the call center operator can do is check that the merchant seems confident when reading an address in the right country. So the opportunity for repudiating transactions — and getting away with it — is hugely increased. There are particularly high rates of repudiation of payment to porn sites. No doubt some of these disputes happen when a transaction made under the influence of a flush of hormones turns up on the family credit card bill and the cardholder has to repudiate it to save his marriage; but many are the result of blatant fraud by operators. A common scam was to offer a 'free tour' of the site and demand a credit card number, supposedly to verify that the user was over 18, and then bill him anyway. Some sites billed other consumers who have never visited them at all [620]. Even apparently large and 'respectable' web sites like playboy.com were criticised for such practices, and at the bottom end of the porn industry, things are atrocious.

The main brake on wicked websites is the credit-card chargeback. A bank will typically charge the merchant $100–200 in fees for each of them, as well as debiting the transaction amount from his account. So if more than a small percentage of the transactions on your site are challenged by customers, your margins will be eroded. If chargebacks go over perhaps 10%, your bank may withdraw your card acquisition service. This has happened to a number of porn sites; a more prosaic example was the collapse of sportswear merchant boo.com because they had too many returns: their business model assumed a no-quibble exchange or refund policy, similar to those operated by high-street discount clothing stores. Yet more of their shipments than they'd expected were the wrong size, or the wrong colour, or just didn't appeal to the customers. Refunds are cheaper than chargebacks, but still, the credit card penalties broke the company [1199]. Chargebacks also motivate merchants to take case — to beware of odd orders (e.g. for four watches), orders from dodgy countries, customers using free email services, requests for expedited delivery, and so on. But leaving the bulk of the liability for mail-order transactions with them is suboptimal: the banks know much more about fraud patterns.

This history suggests that purely technological fixes may not be easy, and that the most effective controls will be at least partly procedural. Some card issuers offer credit card numbers that can be used once only; as they issue them one at a time to customers via their web site, this also helps drive lots of traffic to their advertisers [324]. Other banks have found that they get better results by investing in address verification [102]. However the big investment in the last few years has been in new card technologies, with Europe replacing both credit cards and debit cards with smartcards complying with the EMV 'chip and PIN' standard, while U.S. banks are starting to roll out bank cards based on RFID.

10.6   Smartcard-Based Banking

In the 1960s and 70s, various people proposed putting integrated circuits in bank cards. The Germans consider the smartcard to have been invented by Helmut Gröttrup and Jürgen Dethloff in 1968, when they proposed and patented putting a custom IC in a card 1968; the French credit Roland Moreno, who proposed putting memory chips in cards in 1973, and Michel Ugon who proposed adding a microprocessor in 1977. The French company Honeywell-Bull patented a chip containing memory, a microcontroller and everything else needed to do transactions in 1982; they started being used in French pay phones in 1983; and in banking from the mid-1980s, as discussed in section 10.5.4 above.

Smartcards were marketed from the beginning as the French contribution to the information age, and the nascent industry got huge government subsidies. In the rest of the world, progress was slower. There were numerous pilot projects in which smartcards were tried out with different protocols, and in different applications. I already mentioned the COPAC system at 3.8.1; we developed this in 1991–2 for use in countries with poor telecommunications, and it sold best in Russia. Norway's commercial banks started issuing smartcards in 1986 but its savings banks refused to; when the central bank pressured the banks to unite on a common technology, mag stripe won and smartcards were withdrawn in 1995. Britain's NatWest Bank developed the Mondex electronic purse system in the early 90s, piloted it in Swindon, then sold it to Mastercard. There was a patent fight between VISA (which had bought the COPAC rights) and Mastercard. The Belgian banks implemented an electronic purse called 'Proton' for low-value payments to devices like parking meters; the Germans followed with 'Geldkarte' which became the European standard EN1546 and is now also available as the 'Moneo' electronic purse in France.

Offline systems such as Mondex had problems dealing with broken cards. If the back-end system doesn't do full balancing, then when a customer complains that a card has stopped working, all the bank can do is either to refund the amount the customer claims was on the card, or tell her to get lost; so most modern systems do balancing, which means they aren't as cheap to operate as one might have hoped. All this was good learning experience. But for a payment card to be truly useful, it has to work internationally — and especially so in Europe with many small countries jammed up close together, where even a one-hour shopping trip in the car may involve international travel. So the banks finally got together with their suppliers and hammered out a standard.

10.6.1 EMV

The EMV standards are named after the participating institutions Europay, Mastercard and VISA (Europay developed the Belgian Proton card). As of 2007, several hundred million European cardholders now have debit and credit cards that conform to this standard, and can be used more or less interoperably in the UK, Ireland, France, Germany and other participating countries. In English speaking countries such as the UK and Ireland, EMV has been branded as 'chip and PIN' (although the standards do also support signature-based transactions). The standards' proponents hope that they will become the worldwide norm for card payments, although this is not quite a done deal: Japan and increasingly the USA are adopting RFID standards for contactless payment, which I'll discuss in the next section. Anyway, in much of the world, the EMV standards act as a 'fraud bulldozer', moving around the payment-systems landscape so that some types of fraud become less common and others more so.

The EMV protocol documents [429] are not so much a single protocol as a suite of protocols. The VISA version of the protocols alone come to more than 3,600 pages, and these are only the compatibility aspects — there are further documents specific to individual banks. Specifications this complex cannot be expected to be bug-free, and I'll describe some of the bugs in the following sections. The most obvious problem is that the documents allow many options, some of which are dangerous, either individually or in combination. So EMV can be thought of as a construction kit for building payment systems, with which one can build systems that are quite secure, or very insecure, depending on how various parameters are set, what sort of fallback modes are invoked on failure, and what other systems are hooked up.

In order to understand this, we need to look briefly at the EMV mechanisms. Each customer card contains a smartcard chip with the capability to verify a PIN and authenticate a transaction. The cards come in two types: low-cost cards that do only symmetric cryptography and use a set of protocols known as static data authentication (SDA); and more expensive cards that can generate digital signatures, supporting protocols called dynamic data authentication (DDA) and combined data authentication (CDA).

10.6.1.1 Static Data Authentication

SDA is the default EMV protocol, and it works as follows. The customer puts her card into the 'chip and PIN' terminal to which it sends a digital certificate, account number and the other data found on the old-fashioned magnetic strip, plus a digital signature from the card-issuing bank (the bank chooses which data items to sign). The terminal verifies the signature and the merchant enters the payment amount; the terminal solicits the PIN; the customer enters it; and it's sent in clear to the card. If the PIN is accepted, the card tells the terminal that all's well and generates a MAC, called an 'application data cryptogram', on the supplied data (merchant ID, amount, serial number, nonce and so on). The key used to compute this MAC is shared between the card and the customer's bank, and so it can only be verified by the issuing bank. (The bank could thus use any algorithm it liked, but the default is DES-CBC-MAC with triple-DES for the last block.) Also, the only way the terminal can check that the transaction is genuine is by going online and getting an acknowledgement. As this isn't always convenient, some merchants have a 'floor limit' below which offline transactions are permitted.

This protocol has a number of vulnerabilities that are by now well known. The most commonly-exploited one is backwards compatibility with magnetic strip cards: as the certificate contains all the information needed to forge a mag-strip card, and as the introduction of chip and PIN means that people now enter PINs everywhere rather than just at ATMs, a number of gangs have used assorted sniffers to collect card data from terminals and collected money using mag-strip forgeries. Many ATMs and merchant terminals even in the EMV adopter countries will fall back to mag-strip processing for reliability reasons, and there are many countries — from the USA to Thailand — that haven't adopted EMV at all. There are two flavours of attack: where the PIN is harvested along with the card details, and where it's harvested separately.

First, where the card reader and the PIN pad are separate devices, then a wiretap between them will get PINs as well as card data. Since 2005 there have been reports of sniffing devices, made in Eastern Europe, that have been found in stores in Italy; they harvest the card and PIN data and send it by SMS to the villains who installed them. This may be done under cover of a false-pretext 'maintenance' visit or by corrupt store staff. There have also been reports of card cloning at petrol stations after PIN pads were replaced with tampered ones; although these cases are waiting to come to trial as I write, I investigated the tamper-resistance of PIN pads with two colleagues and we found that the leading makes were very easy to compromise.

For example, the Ingenico i3300, one of the most widely-deployed terminals in the UK in 2007, suffers from a series of design flaws. Its rear has a user-accessible compartment, shown in Figure 10.4, for the insertion of optional extra components. This space is not designed to be tamper-proof, and when covered it cannot be inspected by the cardholder even if she handles the device. This compartment gives access to the bottom layer of the circuit board. This does not give direct access to sensitive data — but, curiously, the designers opted to provide the attacker 1 mm diameter holes (used for positioning the optional components) and vias through the circuit board. From there, a simple metal hook can tap the serial data line. We found that a 1 mm diameter via, carrying the serial data signal, is easily accessed using a bent paperclip. This can be inserted through a hole in the plastic surrounding the internal compartment, and does not leave any external marks. The effect is that the attacker can design a small wiretap circuit that sits invisibly inside the terminal and gathers both card and PIN data. This circuit can be powered from the terminal itself and could contain a small mobile phone to SMS the booty to its makers.

Britain had an epidemic of fraud in 2006–7 apparently involving sniffer devices inserted into the wiring between card terminals and branch servers in petrol stations in the UK. As the card readers generally have integral PIN pads in this application, the PINs may be harvested by eye by petrol-station staff, many of whom are Tamils who arrived as refugees from the civil war in Sri Lanka. It's said that the Tamil Tigers — a terrorist group — intimidates them into participating. This was discovered when Thai police caught men in Phuket with 5,000 forged UK debit and credit cards, copied on to 'white plastic'.

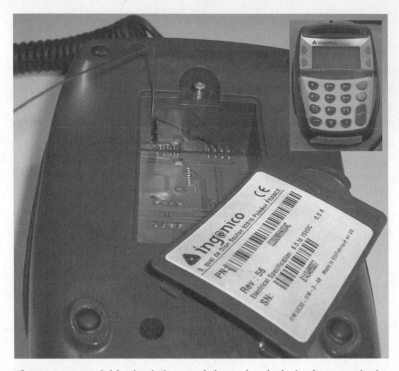

Figure 10.4: A rigid wire is inserted through a hole in the Ingenico's concealed compartment wall to intercept the smartcard data. The front of the device is shown on the top right.

Attacks exploiting the fact that the MAC can't be read by the merchant include 'yescards'. These are cards programmed to accept any PIN (hence the name) and to participate in the EMV protocol using an externally-supplied certificate, returning random values for the MAC. A villain with a yescard and access to genuine card certificates — perhaps through a wiretap on a merchant terminal — can copy a cert to a yescard, take it to a merchant with a reasonable floor limit, and do a transaction using any PIN. This attack has been reported in France and suspected in the UK [122]; it's pushing France towards a move from SDA to DDA. However, most such frauds in Britain still use magnetic strip fallback: many ATMs and merchants use the strip if the chip is not working.

Another family of problems with EMV has to do with authentication methods. Each card, and each terminal, has a list of preferred methods, which might say in effect: 'first try online PIN verification, and if that's not supported use local cleartext PIN verification, and if that's not possible then you don't need to authenticate the customer at all'. It might at first sight be surprising that 'no authentication' is ever an option, but it's frequently there, in order to support devices such as parking ticket vending machines that don't have

PIN pads. One glitch is that the list of authentication methods isn't itself authenticated, so a bad man might manipulate it in a false-terminal or relay attack. Another possibility is to have two cards: your own card, for which you know the PIN, and a stolen card for which you don't, slotted into a device that lets you switch between them. You present the first card to the terminal and verify the PIN; you then present the transaction to the stolen card with the verification method changed to 'no authentication'. The stolen card computes the MAC and gets debited. The bank then maintains to the victim that as his chip was read and a PIN was used, he's liable for the money.

One countermeasure being contemplated is to insert the verification method into the transaction data; another is to reprogram cards to remove 'no authentication' from the list of acceptable options. If your bank takes the latter option, you'd better keep some change in your car ashtray! Yet another is to reprogram customer cards so that 'no authentication' works only up to some limit, say $200.

The fact that banks can now reprogram customers' cards in the field is also novel. The mechanism uses the shared key material and kicks in when the card's at an online terminal such as an ATM. One serious bug we discovered is that the encryption used to protect these messages is so poorly implemented that bank insiders can easily extract the keys from the hardware security modules [12]. I'll discuss this kind of vulnerability at greater length when we dive into the thicket of API security. Remote reprogrammability was pioneered by the pay-TV stations in their wars against pirates who cloned their smartcards; it can be a powerful tool, but it can also be badly misused. For example, it opens the possibility of a disgruntled insider launching a service-denial attack that rapidly wipes out all a bank's customers' cards.

However, such bankers' nightmares aside, the practical security of EMV depends to a great extent on implementation details such as the extent to which fallback magnetic-strip processing is available in local ATMs, the proportion of local shops open to various kinds of skimmer attacks (whether because of personnel vulnerability factors or because there are many store chains using separate card readers and PIN pads), and — as always — incentives. Do the banks carry the can for fraud as in the USA, which makes them take care, or are they able to dump the costs on merchants and cardholders, as in much of Europe, which blunts their motivation to insist on high standards? Indeed, in some countries — notably the UK — banks appear to have seen EMV not so much as a fraud-reduction technology but a liability-engineering one. In the old days they generally paid for fraud in signature-based transactions but often blamed the customer for the PIN-based ones ('your PIN was used so you must have been negligent'). The attractions of changing most in-store transactions from signatures to PINs were obvious.

The bottom-line question is, of course, whether it paid for itself. In Britain it hasn't. Fraud rose initially, thanks to the much larger number of cards stolen from the mail during the changeover period; local fraud has been said to fall since, though this has been achieved with the help of some fairly blatant manipulation of the numbers. For example, bank customers were stopped from reporting card fraud to the police from April 2007; frauds must be reported to the bank. Oh, and the banks have taken over much of the financing of the small police unit that does still investigate card fraud. This helps the government massage the crime statistics downward, and lets the banking industry control such prosecutions as do happen. Meanwhile overseas fraud has rocketed, thanks to the Tamil Tigers and to the vigorous international trade in stolen card numbers. The net effect was that by October 2007 fraud was up 26% on the previous year [83].

10.6.1.2 Dynamic Data Authentication

DDA is a more complex EMV protocol, used in Germany. It differs from SDA in that the cards are capable of doing public-key cryptography: each has an RSA public-private keypair, with the public part embedded in the card certificate. The cryptography is used for two functions. First, when the card is first inserted into the terminal, it's sent a nonce, which it signs. This assures the terminal that the card is present (somewhere). The terminal then sends the transaction data plus the PIN encrypted using the card's public key, and the card returns the application data cryptogram as before.

This provides a small amount of extra protection (though at the cost of a more expensive card — perhaps $1 each in volume rather than 50c). In particular, the PIN doesn't travel in the clear between the PIN pad and the terminal, so the Hungarian skimmer won't work. (The Tamil Tiger attack still works as in that case the shop assistant collected the PIN using the mark 1 eyeball.)

There are still significant vulnerabilities though. Even assuming that the cryptography is sound, that the software's properly written, that the interfaces are well-designed, and that the cards are too expensive to clone, the lack of any hard link between the public-key operation of proving freshness and accepting the PIN, and the shared-key operation of computing the MAC, means that the two-card attack could still be perpetrated.

10.6.1.3 Combined Data Authentication

CDA is the Rolls-Royce of EMV protocols. it's like DDA except that the card also computes a signature on the MAC. This ties the transaction data to the public key and to the fact that a PIN verification was performed (assuming, that is, the bank selected the option of including a PIN-verification flag in in the transaction data).

But the protocol still isn't bulletproof, as the customer has no trustworthy user interface. A wicked merchant could mount a false front over a payment terminal so that the customer would think she was paying $5 for a box of chocolates when in reality she was authorising a payment of $2500. (With over 200 approved terminal types, it's unreasonable to expect customers to tell a genuine terminal from a bogus one.) A bad merchant can also mount a *relay* attack. Two students of mine implemented this as a proof-of-concept for a TV program; a bogus terminal in a café was hooked up via WiFi and a laptop to a bogus card. When a sucker in the café went to pay £5 for his cake to a till operated by one student, his card was connected up to the false card carried by the other, who was lingering in a bookstore waiting to buy a book for £50. The £50 transaction went through successfully [401, 915].

An interesting possibility for relay attacks is to provide deniability in money-laundering. EMV transactions are now routinely used for high-value transactions, such as buying cars and yachts, and as they're between bank accounts directly they attract little attention from the authorities. So a bad man in London wanting to pay $100,000 to a crook in Moscow could simply arrange to buy him a BMW. With relaying, he could get an alibi by making this transaction just after a local one with witnesses; he might take his Member of Parliament out to a meal. If challenged he could claim that the car purchase was a fraud, and the police could have a hard time proving a transaction relay in the face of bank denials that such things happen.

There also are the usual 'social engineering' attacks; for example, a dishonest merchant observes the customer entering the PIN and then steals the card, whether by palming it and giving her back a previously-stolen card issued by the same bank, or by following her and stealing it from her bag (or snatching her bag). Such attacks have happened since the early days of bank cards. They can be automated: a bogus vending machine might retain a card and give back a previously-stolen one; or more pernicious still, use a card in its temporary possession to make a large online purchase. There is a nasty variant for systems that use the same card for online banking: the wicked parking meter goes online and sends all your money to Russia in the few seconds when you thought it was simply debiting you $2.50.

10.6.2 RFID

In the USA, where thanks to the Federal Reserve the incentives facing banks and merchants are less perverted, the banking industry has remained unconvinced that the multibillion-dollar costs of moving to EMV would be justified by any reductions in losses. Rather than moving to EMV, the industry has preferred to skip a generation and wait for the next payment method — so-called 'RFID' or 'contactless' payment cards.

Contactless payment has been a reality for a few years in a number of transport systems from London to Tokyo. When you buy a season ticket you get a 'contactless' smartcard — a device using short-range radio or magnetic signals to communicate with a terminal embedded in the turnstile. The automation allows a greater variety of deals to be sold than the traditional season ticket too; you can pay as you go and top up your credit as you need it. Turning this technology into a general-purpose payment instrument has a number of advantages.

One interesting new development is NFC — near-field communications. NFC is a means of building contactless/RFID communications capability into devices such as mobile phones. This means that your phone can double as your season ticket; at Japanese subway turnstiles, you can just touch your phone on the payment pad in order to get through. Small payments can be processed quickly and automatically, while for larger payments the phone can provide the trustworthy use interface whose lack is such a serious problem for EMV-style payment systems.

There are quite a few problems to be tackled. First, if RFID payment cards can also be used in traditional credit-card systems, then a bad man can harvest credit card numbers, security codes and expiry dates by doing RFID transactions with victims' cards as he brushes past them in the street — or by reading cards that have been sent to customers in the mail, without opening the envelopes [601].

Second, there are practical problems to do with RF propagation: if you have three cards in your wallet and you wave the wallet over a subway turnstile, which of them gets debited? (All of them?)

Third, our old friend the middleperson attack (and his evil twin the forwarding attack) return with a vengeance. When my students implemented the forwarding attack on EMV, they had to spend several weeks building custom electronics for the wicked reader and the bogus card. Once RFID and NFC become pervasive, making equipment is just a programming task, and not even a very tricky one. Any two NFC phones should be able to act in concert as the false terminal and the wicked card. And it appears that no-one's taking ownership of the problem of securing RFID payments; each of the players in the business appears to be hoping that someone else will solve the problem [56].

10.7   Home Banking and Money Laundering

After credit and debit cards, the third thread of electronic banking at the consumer-level is home banking. In 1985, the first such service in the world was offered by the Bank of Scotland, whose customers could use Prestel, a proprietary email system operated by British Telecom, to make payments.

When Steve Gold and Robert Schifreen hacked Prestel — as described in the chapter on passwords — it initially terrified the press and the bankers. They realised that the hackers could easily have captured and altered transactions. But once the dust settled and people thought through the detail, they realised there was little real risk. The system allowed only payments between your own accounts and to accounts you'd previously notified to the bank, such as you gas and electricity suppliers.

This pattern, of high-profile hacks — which caused great consternation but which on sober reflection turned out to be not really a big deal — has continued ever since.

To resume this brief history, the late 1980's and early 1990's saw the rapid growth of call centers, which — despite all the hoopla about the web — still probably remain in 2007 the largest delivery channel for business-to-consumer electronic commerce[3]. The driver was cost cutting: call centres are cheaper than bank branches. Round about 1999, banks rushed to build websites in order to cut costs still further, and in so doing they also cut corners. The bank-end controls, which limited who you could pay and how much, were abolished amid the general euphoria, and as we've seen, the phishermen arrived in earnest from 2004. Phishermen are not the only threat, although they appear to be the main one in the English-speaking world; in Continental Europe, there is some suspicion that keyloggers may be responsible for more account takeovers.

As I mentioned in the chapter on passwords, the main change is the increasing specialisation of gangs involved in financial crime. One firm writes the malware, another herds the botnet; another does the 'Madison Avenue' job of writing the spam; and there are specialists who will accept hot money and launder it. (Note that if it becomes too easy for bent programmers to make contact with capable money launderers, this could have a material effect on the fraud risk faced by systems such as SWIFT. It would undermine our current implicit separation-of-duty policy in that the techies who know how to hack the message queue don't understand how to get money out of the system.)

The hot topic in 2007 is how to stop phishermen getting away with money stolen from compromised bank accounts, and a phisherman faces essentially the same money-laundering problem as a bent bank programmer. Until May 2007, the preferred route was eGold, a company operated from Florida but with a legal domicile in the Caribbean, which offered unregulated electronic payment services. The attraction to the villains was that eGold payments were irreversible; their staff would stonewall bank investigators who were hot on the trail of stolen money. eGold duly got raided by the FBI and indicted.

---

[3]I'm not aware of any global figures, but, to get some indication, the UK has 6000 call centres employing half a million people; and Lloyds TSB, a large high-street bank, had 16 million accounts of whom most use telephone banking but under 2 million used online banking regularly in 2005.

The villains' second recourse was to send money through banks in Finland to their subsidiaries in the Baltic states and on to Russia; no doubt the Finnish regulators will have cleaned this up by the time this book appears. The third choice was wire-transfer firms like Western Union, and various electronic money services in Russia and the Middle East. I wrote a survey of this for the U.S. Federal Reserve; see [55].

At the time of writing, the favourite modus operandi of the folks who launder money for the phishermen is to recruit *mules* to act as cut-outs when sending money from compromised accounts to Western Union [545]. Mules are attracted by spam offering jobs in which they work from home and earn a commission. They're told they will be an agent for a foreign company; their work is to receive several payments a week, deduct their own commission, and then send the balance onward via Western Union. Money duly arrives in their account and they pay most of it onwards. After a few days, the bank from whose customer the money was stolen notices and reverses out the credit. The poor mule is left with a huge overdraft and finds that he can't get the money back from Western Union. In the English-speaking world, that's just about it; in Germany, mules are also prosecuted and jailed. (Even some German bankers consider this to be harsh, as the typical mule is an elderly working-class person who grew up under the communists in East Germany and doesn't even understand capitalism, let alone the Internet.) As the word gets round, mule recruitment appears to be getting more and more difficult — if we can judge from the rapidly increasing quantities of mule-recruitment spam during the middle of 2007. Note in passing that as the real victims of many phishing attacks are the poor mules, this implies that phishing losses as reported by the banks may be a significant underestimate.

Another thing we've learned from watching the phishermen over the past few years is that the most effective countermeasure isn't improving authentication, but sharpening up asset recovery. Of the £35m lost by UK banks in 2006, over £33m was lost by one bank. Its competitors assure me that the secret of their success is that they spot account takeovers quickly and follow them up aggressively; if money's sent to a mule's account, he may find his account frozen before he can get to Western Union. So the phishermen avoid them. This emphasises once more the importance of sound back-end controls. The authentication mechanisms alone can't do the job; you need to make the audit and intrusion-detection mechanisms work together with them.

Another thing we've learned is that liability dumping is not just pervasive but bad for security. The rush to online banking led many financial institutions to adopt terms and conditions under which their records of an electronic transaction are definitive; this conflicts with consumer law and traditional banking practice [201]. Unfortunately, the EU's 2007 Payment Services Directive allows all European banks to set dispute resolution procedures in their terms and conditions, and undermines the incentive to deal with the problems. The ability of banks to blame their customers for fraud has also led to many sloppy practices. In the UK, when it turned out that people who'd accessed electronic services at Barclays Bank via a public terminal could be hacked by the next user pressing the 'back' button on the browser, they tried to blame customers for not clearing their web caches [1249]. (If opposing that in court, I'd have great fun finding out how many of Barclays' branch managers knew what a cache is, and the precise date on which the bank's directors had it brought to their attention that such knowledge is now essential to the proper conduct of retail banking business.)

10.8 Summary

Banking systems are interesting in a number of ways.

Bookkeeping applications give us a mature example of systems whose security is oriented towards authenticity and accountability rather than confidentiality. Their protection goal is to prevent and detect frauds being committed by dishonest insiders. The Clark-Wilson security policy provides a model of how they operate. It can be summarized as: *'all transactions must preserve an invariant of the system, namely that the books must balance (so a negative entry in one ledger must be balanced by a positive entry in another one); some transactions must be performed by two or more staff members; and records of transactions cannot be destroyed after they are committed'*. This was based on time-honoured bookkeeping procedures, and led the research community to consider systems other than variants of Bell-LaPadula.

But manual bookkeeping systems use more than just dual control. Although some systems do need transactions to be authorised in parallel by two or more staff, a separation of duty policy more often works in series, in that different people do different things to each transaction as it passes through the system. Designing bookkeeping systems to do this well is a hard and often neglected problem, that involves input from many disciplines. Another common requirement is non-repudiation — that principals should be able to generate, retain and use evidence about the relevant actions of other principals.

The other major banking application, remote payment, is increasingly critical to commerce of all kinds. In fact, wire transfers of money go back to the middle of the Victorian era. Because there is an obvious motive to attack these systems, and villains who steal large amounts and get caught are generally prosecuted, payment systems are a valuable source of information about what goes wrong. Their loss history teaches us the importance of minimizing the background error rate, preventing procedural attacks that defeat technical controls (such as thefts of ATM cards from the mail), and having adequate controls to deter and detect internal fraud.

Payment systems have also played a significant role in the development and application of cryptology. One innovation was the idea that cryptography could be used to confine the critical part of the application to a trusted computing base consisting of tamper-resistant processors — an approach since used in many other applications.

The recent adoption of various kinds of smartcard-based payment mechanism - EMV in Europe, RFID in the USA and Japan — is changing the fraud landscape. It opens up the possibility of more secure payment systems, but this is not at all guaranteed. In each case, the platform merely provides a toolkit, with which banks and merchants can implement good systems, or awful ones.

Finally, the recent history of attacks on electronic banking systems by means of account takeover — by phishermen, and to a lesser extent using keyloggers — presents a challenge that may over time become deeper and more pervasive than previous challenges. Up till now, banking folks — from the operations guys up to the regulators and down to the system designers — saw the mission as maintaining the integrity of the financial system. We may have to come to terms with a world in which perhaps one customer account in ten thousand or so has been compromised at any given time. Instead, we will have to talk about the resilience of the financial system.

Research Problems

Designing internal controls is still pre-scientific; we could do with tools to help us do it in a more systematic, less error-prone way. Accountants, lawyers, financial market regulators and system engineers all seem to feel that this is someone else's responsibility. This is a striking opportunity to do multidisciplinary research that has the potential to be outstandingly useful.

At a more techie level, we don't even fully understand stateful access control systems, such as Clark-Wilson and Chinese Wall. To what extent does one do more than the other on the separation-of-duty front? How should dual control systems be designed anyway? How much of the authorization logic can we abstract out of application code into middleware? Can we separate policy and implementation to make enterprise-wide policies easier to administer?

As for robustness of cryptographic systems, the usability of security mechanisms, and assurance generally, these are huge topics and still only partially mapped. Robustness and assurance are partially understood, but usability is still a very grey area. There are many more mathematicians active in security research than applied psychologists, and it shows.

Finally, if account takeover is going to become pervasive, and a typical bank has 0.01% of its customer accounts under the control of the Russian mafia at any one time, what are the implications? I said that instead of talking about the integrity of the financial system, we have to talk about its resilience. But what does this mean? No-one's quite sure what resilience implies in this context. Recent experience suggests that extending the principles of internal control and combining them with aggressive fraud detection and asset recovery could be a good place for engineers to start. But what are the broader implications? Personally I suspect that our regulatory approach to money laundering needs a thorough overhaul. The measures introduced in a panic after the passage of the U.S. Patriot Act have been counterproductive, and perhaps emotions have subsided now to the point that governments can be more rational. But what should we do? Should Western Union be closed down by the Feds, as eGold was? That's probably excessive — but I believe that laundering controls should be less obsessive about identity, and more concerned about asset recovery.

Further Reading

I don't know of any comprehensive book on banking computer systems, although there are many papers on specific payment systems available from the Bank for International Settlements [114]. When it comes to developing robust management controls and business processes that limit the amount of damage that any one staff member could do, there is a striking lack of hard material (especially given the demands of Gramm-Leach-Bliley and Sarbanes-Oxley). There was one academic conference in 1997 [657], and the best book I know of on the design and evolution of internal controls, by Steven Root, predates the Enron saga [1082]. As the interpretation put on these new laws by the big four accountancy firms makes the weather on internal controls, and as their gold-plating costs the economy so much, it is certainly in the public interest for more to be published and discussed. I'll revisit this topic in Part III.

For the specifics of financial transaction processing systems, the cited articles [33, 34] provide a basic introduction. More comprehensive, if somewhat dated, is [354] while [525] describes the CIRRUS network as of the mid-80s. The transcript of Paul Stubbs' trial gives a snapshot of the internal controls in the better electronic banking systems in 2004 [975]; for conspicuous internal control failure, see for example [1038]. The most informative public domain source on the technology — though somewhat heavy going — may be the huge online manuals for standards such as EMV [429] and the equipment that supports it, such as the IBM 4758 and CCA [641].

CHAPTER 11

Physical Protection

For if a man watch too long, it is odds he will fall asleepe.
— Francis Bacon

*The greatest of faults, I should say,
is to be conscious of none.*
— Thomas Carlyle

11.1 Introduction

Most security engineers nowadays are largely concerned with electronic systems, but there are several reasons why physical protection cannot be entirely neglected. First, if you're advising on a company's overall risk management strategy, then walls and locks are a factor. Second, as it's easier to teach someone with an electrical engineering/computer science background the basics of physical security than the other way round, interactions between physical and logical protection will be up to the systems person to manage. Third, you will often be asked for your opinion on your client's installations — which will often have been installed by local contractors who are well known to your client but have rather narrow horizons as far as system issues are concerned. You'll need to be able to give informed, but diplomatic, answers. Fourth, many security mechanisms can be defeated if a bad man has physical access to them, whether at the factory, or during shipment, or before installation. Fifth, many locks have recently been completely compromised by 'bumping', an easy covert-entry technique; their manufacturers (even those selling 'high-security' devices) seemed to be unaware of vulnerabilities that enable their products to be quickly bypassed. Finally, your client's hosting centres will usually be its most hardened facilities, and will be the responsibility of the systems managers who will most often seek your advice.

Much of physical security is just common sense, but there are some non-obvious twists and there have been significant recent advances in technology, notably in lock-picking and other forms of covert entry. There are ideas from criminology and architecture on how you can reduce the incidence of crime around your facilities. And perhaps most importantly, there are burglar alarms — which have a number of interesting system aspects.

For example, in order to defeat a burglar alarm it is sufficient to make it stop working, or — in many cases — to persuade its operators that it has become unreliable. This raises the spectre of *denial of service attacks*, which are increasingly important yet often difficult to deal with. Just as we have seen military messaging systems designed to enforce confidentiality and book-keeping systems whose goal is preserving record authenticity, monitoring applications give us the classic example of systems designed to be dependably available. If there is a burglar in my bank vault, then I do not care very much who else gets to know (so I'm not worried about confidentiality), or who it was who told me (so authenticity isn't a major concern); but I do care very much that an attempt to tell me is not thwarted. Now, historically, about 90% of computer security research was about confidentiality, about 9% about authenticity and 1% about availability. But actual attacks — and companies' expenditures — tend to be the other way round: more is spent on availability than on authenticity and confidentiality combined. And it's alarm systems, above all else, that can teach us about availability.

11.2   Threats and Barriers

Physical protection is no different at heart from computer security: you perform a threat analysis, then design a system that involves equipment and procedures, then test it. The system itself typically has a number of elements:

Deter—detect—alarm—delay—respond

A facility can deter intruders using hard methods such as guards and razor-wire fences, or softer methods such as being inconspicuous. It will then have one or more layers of barriers and sensors whose job is to keep out casual intruders, detect deliberate intruders, and make it difficult for them to defeat your security too quickly. This defense-in-depth will be complemented by an alarm system designed to bring a response to the scene in time. The barriers will have doors in them for authorized staff to go in and out; this means some kind of entry control system that could be anything from metal keys to biometric scanners. Finally, these measures will be supported by operational controls. How do you cope, for example, with your facility manager having his family taken hostage by villains?

As I noted earlier, one of the ways in which you get your staff to accept dual controls and integrate them into their work culture is that these controls protect them, as well as protecting the assets. Unless the operational aspects of security are embedded in the firm's culture, they won't work well, and this applies to physical security as much as to the computer variety. It's also vital to get unified operational security across the physical, business and information domains: there's little point in spending $10m to protect a vault containing $100m of diamonds if a bad man can sneak a false delivery order into your system, and send a DHL van to pick up the diamonds from reception. That is another reason why, as the information security guy, you have to pay attention to the physical side too or you won't get joined-up protection.

11.2.1 Threat Model

An important design consideration is the level of skill, equipment and motivation that the attacker might have. Movies like 'Entrapment' might be good entertainment, but don't give a realistic view of the world of theft. As we have seen in one context after another, 'security' isn't a scalar. It doesn't make sense to ask 'Is device X secure?' without a context: 'secure against whom and in what environment?'

In the absence of an 'international standard burglar', the nearest I know to a working classification is one developed by a U.S. Army expert [118].

■ *Derek* is a 19-year old addict. He's looking for a low-risk opportunity to steal something he can sell for his next fix.

■ *Charlie* is a 40-year old inadequate with seven convictions for burglary. He's spent seventeen of the last twenty-five years in prison. Although not very intelligent he is cunning and experienced; he has picked up a lot of 'lore' during his spells inside. He steals from small shops and suburban houses, taking whatever he thinks he can sell to local fences.

■ *Bruno* is a 'gentleman criminal'. His business is mostly stealing art. As a cover, he runs a small art gallery. He has a (forged) university degree in art history on the wall, and one conviction for robbery eighteen years ago. After two years in jail, he changed his name and moved to a different part of the country. He has done occasional 'black bag' jobs for intelligence agencies who know his past. He'd like to get into computer crime, but the most he's done so far is stripping $100,000 worth of memory chips from a university's PCs back in the mid-1990s when there was a memory famine.

■ *Abdurrahman* heads a cell of a dozen militants, most with military training. They have infantry weapons and explosives, with PhD-grade technical support provided by a disreputable country. Abdurrahman himself came third out of a class of 280 at the military academy of that country but was not promoted because he's from the wrong ethnic group. He thinks of himself as a good man rather than a bad man. His mission is to steal plutonium.

So Derek is unskilled, Charlie is skilled, Bruno is highly skilled and may have the help of an unskilled insider such as a cleaner, while Abdurrahman is not only highly skilled but has substantial resources. He may even have the help of a technician or other skilled insider who has been suborned. (It's true that many terrorists these days aren't even as skilled as Charlie, but it would not be prudent to design a nuclear power station on the assumption that Charlie would be the highest grade of attacker.)

While the sociologists focus on Derek, the criminologists on Charlie and the military on Abdurrahman, our concern is mainly with Bruno. He isn't the highest available grade of 'civilian' criminal: that distinction probably goes to the bent bankers and lawyers who launder money for drug gangs. (I'll talk about them in a later chapter.) But the physical defenses of banks and computer rooms tend to be designed with someone like Bruno in mind. (Whether this is rational, or an overplay, will depend on the business your client is in.)

11.2.2   Deterrence

The first consideration is whether you can prevent bad people ever trying to break in. It's a good idea to make your asset anonymous and inconspicuous if you can. It might be a nondescript building in the suburbs; in somewhere like Hong Kong, with astronomical property prices, it might be half a floor of an undistinguished skyscraper.

Location matters; some neighbourhoods have much less crime than others. Part of this has to do with whether other property nearby is protected vigorously, and how easy it is for a crook to tell which properties are protected. If some owners just install visible alarms, they may redistribute crime to their neighbours; but invisible alarms that get criminals caught rather than just sent next door can have strongly positive externalities. For example, Ian Ayres and Steven Levitt studied the effect on auto thefts of Lojack, a radio tag that's embedded invisibly in cars and lets the police find them if they're stolen. In towns where a lot of cars have Lojack, car thieves are caught quickly and 'chop-shops' that break up stolen cars for parts are closed down. Ayres and Levitt found that although a motorist who installs Lojack pays about $100 a year, the social benefit from his doing this — the reduced car crime suffered by others — is $1500 [100]. One implication is that good alarm services may be undersupplied by the free market, as many people will free ride off their neighbours: only rich people, or people with newer cars, or who are particularly loss-averse, will install alarms. The same principle applies to real estate; an upper-class neighbourhood in which a fair number of houses have high-grade alarms that quietly call the police is a dangerous place for a burglar to work.

However, that is by no means all. Since the 1960s, there has arisen a substantial literature on using environmental design to deflect and deter threats. Much of this evolved in the context of low-income housing, as criminologists and architects learned which designs made crime more or less likely. In 1961, Elizabeth Wood urged architects to improve the visibility of apartment units by residents, and create communal spaces where people would gather and keep apartment entrances in view, thus fostering social surveillance; areas that are out of sight are more vulnerable [1355]. In 1972, Oscar Newman developed this into the concept of 'Defensible Space': buildings should be designed 'to release the latent sense of territoriality and community' of residents [968]. Small courtyards are better than large parks, as intruders are more likely to be identified, and residents are more likely to challenge them. At the same time, Ray Jeffery developed a model that is based on psychology rather than sociology and thus takes account of the wide differences between individual offenders; it is reflected in our four 'model' villains. Intruders are not all the same, and not all rational [1079].

Jeffery's 'Crime Prevention Through Environmental Design' has been influential and challenges a number of old-fashioned ideas about deterrence. Old timers liked bright security lights; but they create glare, and pools of shadow in which villains can lurk. It's better to have a civilised front, with windows overlooking sidewalks and car parks. In the old days, cyclone fences with barbed wire were thought to be a good thing; but they communicate an absence of personal control. A communal area with picnic seating, in which activities happen frequently, has a greater deterrent effect. Trees also help, as they make shared areas feel safer (perhaps a throwback to an ancestral environment where grassland with some trees helped us see predators coming and take refuge from them). Access matters too; defensible spaces should have single egress points, so that potential intruders are afraid of being trapped. It's been found, for example, that CCTV cameras only deter crime in facilities such as car parks where there's a single exit [527]. There are also many tricks developed over the years, from using passing vehicles to enhance site visibility to planting low thorn bushes under windows. Advice on these can be found in the more modern standards such as [229].

Another influential idea is the broken windows theory of George Kelling and Catherine Coles [700]. They noted that if a building has a broken window that's not repaired, then soon vandals will break more, and perhaps squatters or drug dealers will move in; if litter is left on a sidewalk then eventually people will start dumping their trash there. The moral is that problems should be fixed when they're still small. Kelling was hired as a consultant to help

New York clean up its vandalised subways, and inspired the zero-tolerance policing movement of police chief William Bratton, who cracked down on public drinkers, squeegee men and other nuisances. Both petty crime and serious crime in New York fell sharply. Criminologists still arguing about whether the fall was due to zero tolerance, or to other simultaneous changes such as demographics [787] and right-to-carry laws [814].

A related set of ideas can be found in the situational crime prevention theory of Ronald Clarke. This builds on the work of Jeffery and Newman, and is broader than just property crime; it proposes a number of principles for reducing crime generally by increasing the risks and effort, reducing the rewards and provocations, and removing excuses. Its focus is largely on designing crime out of products and out of the routines of everyday life; it's pragmatic and driven by applications rather than drawing on theories of psychology and sociology [298]. It involves detailed study of specific threats; for example, car theft is considered to be a number of different problems, such as joyriding by juveniles, theft to get home at night, theft of parts, and theft by professional gangs of car thieves for dismantling or sale abroad — and these threats can be countered by quite different measures. Such empirical studies are often criticised by criminologists who have a sociology background as lacking 'theory', but are gaining influence and are not far from what security engineers do. Many of the mechanisms discussed in this book fit easily within a framework of application-level opportunity reduction.

This framework naturally accommodates the extension of environmental controls to other topics when needed. Thus, for example, if you're planning on anonymity of your premises as a defence against targeted attack, you have to think about how you limit the number of people who know that the basement of your Norwich sales office actually contains your main hosting centre. This brings in internal control, culture and even information security policy. Governments often use multilevel policies for this; there may be a rule that the location of all public-sector hosting centres is 'Restricted'. Even in a commercial firm that doesn't burden itself with all the overhead of multilevel security, some of the ideas I discussed in that context in Chapter 8 may be useful.

11.2.3 Walls and Barriers

Anyway, once you've decided what environmental features you'll use to deter Derek or Charlie from trying to break into your site, and how you make it harder for Bruno to find out which of your sites he should break into, you then have the problem of designing the physical barriers.

The first task is to figure out what you're really trying to protect. In the old days, banks used to go to great lengths to make life really tough for robbers, but this has its limits: a robber can always threaten to shoot a customer. So by a generation ago, the philosophy had shifted to 'give him all the cash he can see'. This philosophy has spread to the rest of retail. In 1997, Starbucks reviewed physical security following an incident in which three employees were shot dead in a bungled robbery. They decided to move the safes from the manager's office to the front of the store, and made these safes highly visible not just to staff, customers and passers-by, but also to the control room via CCTV. A side-benefit was improved customer service. The new design was tested at a number of U.S. locations, where increased sales and loss reductions gave a good return on investment [341]. Indeed, I notice that young people increasingly leave their car keys by the front door at home; if someone breaks into your house in order to steal a car, do you really want to engage them in hand-to-hand combat?

Second, having settled your protection goals, you have to decide what security perimeters or boundaries there will be for what purposes, and where they'll be located. A growth industry recently has been the provision of vehicle traps to prevent car bombs being brought close to iconic terrorist targets. However a common failing is to focus on rare but 'exciting' threats at the expense of mundane ones. It's common to find buildings with stout walls but whose roofs are easy to penetrate, for example; perhaps a terrorist would blow himself up at your main gate to no effect, but an environmental protester could cripple your fab and cost you hundreds of millions in lost production by climbing on the roof, cutting a hole and dropping some burning newspaper.

For this reason, organisations such as NIST, the Builders' Hardware Manufacturers' Association, Underwriters' Laboratories, and their equivalents in other countries have a plethora of test results and standards for walls, roofs, safes and so on. The basic idea is to assess how long a barrier will resist an attacker who has certain resources — typically hand tools or power tools. Normal building materials don't offer much delay at all; a man can get through a cavity brick wall in less than a minute using a sledgehammer, and regardless of how good a lock you put on your front door, a police unit raiding your house will typically break the door off its hinges with a battering-ram. So could a robber. Thus for many years the designers of data centres, bank vaults and the like have favoured reinforced concrete walls, floors and roofs, with steel doorframes. Of course, if the bad guys can work undisturbed all weekend, then even eight inches of concrete won't keep them out.

There's a further problem in that the organisations that certify locks, safes and vaults often place unrealistic constraints on the tools available to an attacker. The lock on your car steering wheel is certified to resist a man putting his weight on it; car thieves just use a scaffolding pole, which gives them enough leverage to break it. The typical bank vault is certified to resist attack for ten minutes, yet your local Fire Department can get in there in two minutes using an abrasive wheel. And if the bad guys have access to proper explosives such as shaped charges, they can get through almost anything in seconds. Another issue is the thermic lance, or burning bar, which will cut through most barrier materials quickly: safe engineers use them to get into a vault whose combination has been lost. Robbers can get them too. So barriers can't be seen in isolation. You have to evaluate them in the context of assumptions about the threats, and about the intrusion detection and response on which you can rely.

11.2.4 Mechanical Locks

The locksmithing industry has been seriously upset in the last couple of years by a couple of developments that have exposed the vulnerability of many low-cost mechanical locks.

The first of these is *bumping*. This technique enables many locks to be opened quickly and without damage by unskilled people using tools that are now readily available. Its main target is the pin-tumbler lock originally patented by Linus Yale in 1860 (see Figure 11.1). This was actually used in ancient Egypt, but Yale rediscovered it and it's often known as a 'Yale lock', although many firms make versions nowadays.

These locks have a cylindrical plug set inside a shell, and prevented from rotating by a number of *pin stacks*. Each stack usually consists of two or three pins, one on top of the other. The *bottom pin* or *key pin* makes direct contact with the key; behind it is a spring-loaded *top pin* or *driver pin* that forces the bottom pin as far down as possible in the keyway. When the correct key is inserted, the gaps between the top pin and the bottom pin align with the edge of the plug, creating a *shear line*; the plug can now be turned. A typical house or office lock might have five or six pins each of which could have the gap in ten different positions, giving a theoretical key diversity of 10^5 or 10^6 possible *key*

Figure 11.1: A cutaway pin-tumbler lock (Courtesy of Marc Weber Tobias)

differs. The actual number will be less because of mechanical tolerances and key-cutting restrictions.

It had been known for years that such locks can be picked, given special tools. You can find details in the MIT Lock Picking Manual [1258] or in treatises such as that by Marc Weber Tobias [1253]: the basic idea is that you twist the plug slightly using a tension wrench, and then manipulate the pins with a lockpick until they all line up along the shear line. Such techniques are used by intelligence agencies, locksmiths and high-grade crooks; but they take a lot of practice, and it's unlawful to possess the tools in many jurisdictions (for the laws in the USA, see [1255]. Until recently, lockpicking was generally thought to be a threat only to high-value targets where covert entry was of particular value to an attacker, such as investment banks and embassies.

The new discovery is that an attacker can insert a specially made *bump key* each of whose teeth is set at the lowest pin position and whose shoulder is slightly rounded. (Such keys are also known as '999' keys as all the teeth are at the lowest position, or *bitting*, namely number 9.) He can then place the key under slight torsion with his fingertips and tap the key head with a rubber mallet. The shock causes the pins to bounce upwards; the applied torsion causes them to stick as the spring pushes them back down, but with the gap at the cylinder edge. The net effect is that with a few taps of the mallet, the lock can be opened.

This trick had been known for years, but recently became much more effective because of better tools and techniques. It was publicised by a 2005 white paper written by Barry Wels and Rop Gonggrijp of The Open Organization Of Lockpickers (TOOOL), a Dutch 'lock sports' group (as the pastime of amateur locksmithing is starting to be known [1337]). TV coverage spread the message to a wide audience. There followed a technical analysis by lock expert Marc Weber Tobias [1254]; in his view, the main threat from bumping is that it deskills lockpicking. The consequences are potentially serious. It's been found, for example, that the locks in U.S. mailboxes can be opened easily, as can the pin-tumbler locks with 70% of the U.S. domestic market. The Dutch paper, and the subsequent publicity, have kicked off an arms race, with vendors producing more complex designs and amateur locksmiths reporting bumping attacks on many of them.

Until recently, locks from Medeco were thought to be unpickable (as well as being certified as such), and the company had a dominant position in the high-security lock market. Medeco uses secondary keying not in the form of a sidebar but in the angle at which cuts are made in the key. In this 'biaxial' system, angled cuts rotate the pins to engage sliders. In 2005, Medeco introduced the m3 which also has a simple sidebar in the form of a slider cut into the side of the key. In 2007, Tobias reported an attack on the m3 and biaxial locks, using a bent paperclip to set the slider and then a combination of bumping and picking to rotate the plug [1256].

What can a householder do? As an experiment, I replaced my own front door lock. The only high-security product I could find in a store within an hour's drive turned out to be a rebranded Mul-T-Lock device from Israel. It took two attempts to install, jamming the first time; it then took about a week for family members to learn to use the more complex deadbolt, which can easily fail open if operated carelessly. And the next time we were visited by someone with an intelligence background, he remarked that in the UK only drug dealers fitted such locks; so if the police ever pass by, I might end up on their database as a suspected pusher. This dubious improvement to my home security cost me $200 as opposed to under $20 for a standard product; and as in practice a burglar could always break a window, our actual protection still depends more on our location and our dogs than on any hardware. Indeed, Yochanan Shachmurove and colleagues surveyed the residents of Greenwich, Connecticut, and built a model of how domestic burglaries varied as a function of the precautions taken; locks and deadbolts had essentially no effect, as there were always alternative means of entry such as windows. The most effective deterrents were alarms and visible signs of occupancy such as cars in the drive [1154].

The situation for commercial firms is slightly better (but not much). The usual standards for high-security locks in the USA, UL 437 and ANSI 156.30, specify resistance to picking and drilling, but not to bumping; and although pick-resistant locks are generally more difficult to bump, this is no guarantee. Knowledge does exist about which lock designs resist bumping, but you have to look for it. (Tobias' paper, and www.toool.org, are good starting points.) UL has just recently taken up the issue of bumping and has formed a task force to determine whether this method of attack should be included in their testing of high security locks. BHMA/ANSI are also looking at the issue.

Purchasers therefore face a lemons market — as one might suspect anyway from the glossiness and lack of technical content of many lock vendors' marketing literature. And even expensive pick-resistant locks are often poorly installed by builders or OEMs; when I once had to break into a cryptographic processor with a really expensive lock, I found it could be levered open easily as the lock turned a cam that was made of soft metal. Indeed a recent security alert by Tobias disclosed that one of the most popular high security deadbolts could be mechanically bypassed by sliding a narrow screwdriver down the keyway, catching the bolt at the end and turning it, even without defeating the extensive security protections within the lock. This design had existed for more than twenty years and the vulnerability was unknown to the manufacturer before the disclosure. Many high security installations employ this or similar hardware.

The second recent class of problems are *master key attacks*. These have also been known to locksmiths for some time but have recently been improved and published, in this case by Matt Blaze. Master key systems are designed so that in addition to the individual key for each door in a building, there can be a top-level master key that opens them all — say, for use by the cleaners. More complex schemes are common; in our building, for example, I can open my students' doors while the system administrators and cleaners can open mine. In pin-tumbler locks, such schemes are implemented by having extra cuts in some of the pin stacks. Thus instead of having a top pin and a bottom pin with a single cut between them, some of the pin stacks will have a middle pin as well.

The master-key attack is to search for the extra cuts one at a time. Suppose my key bitting is 557346, and the master key for my corridor is 232346. I make a key with the bitting 157346, and try it in the lock. It doesn't work. I then file the first position down to 257346. As 2 is a valid bitting for the first pin, this opens the lock, and as it's different from my user bitting of 5, I know it is the master key bitting for that pin. I will have to try on average four bittings for each pin, and if three pins are master-keyed then I will have a master key after about twelve tests. So master keying allows much greater convenience not just to the building occupants but also to the burglar. This is really important, as most large commercial premises use master keying. There are master-keying systems that resist this attack — for example, the Austrian lockmaker Evva has a system involving magnets embedded in metal keys which are much harder to duplicate. But most fielded systems appear vulnerable.

Another thing to worry about is, as always, revocation. Keyholders leave, and may become hostile. They may have made a copy of their key, and sell it to an attacker. Mechanical locks are easy to change singly but locking systems generally cope very poorly with revocation. Master-key attacks are important here, and so is bumping. Indeed, many expensive, pick-resistant locks actually make the problem worse. They often depend on a secondary keying mechanism such as a sidebar: the keys look like two normal pin-tumbler keys welded together, as in Figure 11.2. The sidebar is often the same for all the locks in the building (master-keyed systems generally require common sidebars in locks that share master keys). So if a bad man can get hold of a genuine key belonging to one of my students, he may be able to turn it into a bump key that will open my door, and indeed every door in the building, as in Figure 11.3. This may not be a problem in normal commercial premises, but it definitely is for banks, bullion dealers and wholesale jewelers where

Figure 11.2: Key for a sidebar lock

Figure 11.3: Bump key for a sidebar lock

attackers might spend two years planning a raid. Indeed, if such a facility had a master-keying system using sidebar locks, and a staff member were even suspected of having leaked a key, the prudent course of action would be to replace every single lock.

The combined effect of bumping, bad deadbolts, master-key attacks and other recent discoveries might be summarised as follows. Within a few years — as the tools and knowledge spread — a career criminal like Charlie will be able to open almost any house lock quickly and without leaving any forensic trace, while more professional attackers like Bruno and Abdurrahman will be able to open the locks in most commercial premises too. House locks may not matter all that much, as Charlie will just go through the window anyway; but the vulnerability of most mechanical locks in commercial premises could have much more complex and serious implications. If your responsibilities include the physical protection of computer or other assets, it's time to start thinking about them.

11.2.5 Electronic Locks

The difficulty of revocation is just one reason why electronic locks are starting to gain market share. They have been around for a long time — hotels have been using card locks since the 1970s. There's an enormous diversity of product offerings, using all sorts of mechanisms from contactless smartcards through PIN pads to biometrics. Many of these can be bypassed in various ways, and most of the chapters of this book can be applied in one way or another to their design, evaluation and assurance. There are also some electromechanical locks that combine mechanical and electronic (or magnetic) components; some of these we just don't know how to attack short of physical destruction. But, from the viewpoint of a company using locks to protect sensitive premises, the big problem is not so much the locks themselves but how you hook up dozens or hundreds of locks in a building. Think of a research laboratory some of whose rooms contain valuable inventions that haven't been patented yet, or a law firm where the offices might contain highly sensitive documents on forthcoming takeovers. Here you worry about insiders as well as outsiders.

In the long run, buildings may become aware of who is where, using multiple sensors, and integrate physical with logical access control. Knowing who went through which door in real time enables interesting security policies to be enforced; for example, if classified material is being handled, you can sound an alarm if there's anyone in the room without the right clearance. Buildings can monitor objects as well as people; in an experiment at our lab, both people and devices carried active badges for location tracking [1318]. Electronic systems can be fully, or almost always, online, making revocation easy. As well as enforcing security policy, smart buildings could provide other benefits, such as saving energy by turning lights off and by tailoring airconditioning to the presence of occupants. But we're not there yet.

One practical problem, as we found when we built our new lab building, is that only a few firms sell turnkey entry control systems. We initially wanted to have biometric entry control based on iris scanners, as they were invented by one of my faculty colleagues, John Daugman. But back in 2000, we couldn't do that. The vendors' protocols didn't support the kit and we didn't have the time and the people to build our own entry control system from scratch. (And if a computer science department can't do that, the average customer has no chance.) We learned that the existing vendors operate just as other systems houses do: they make their money from lockin (in the economic, rather than locksmithing sense). However, the systems you buy can be extraordinarily troublesome, dysfunctional and expensive. You end up paying $2000 for a door lock that cost maybe $10 to manufacture, because of proprietary cabling systems and card designs. The main limit to the lockin is the cost of ripping and replacing the whole system — hence the vendors' love of proprietary cabling.

Our lab is now moving to a more open system based on standard contactless smartcards that are available from multiple vendors. The experience has taught us that an entry control system should be managed like any other computer system purchase, with very careful attention to maintenance costs, standards, extensibility, and total cost of ownership. We are keen to get a system we can install and maintain ourselves, and that allows us to specify security policies at a decent level of abstraction. (Our old system just has a matrix specifying which key opens which lock.) We are just starting to see the sort of components that will make decent systems integration possible — such as reasonably-priced door locks that run off the building's standard Ethernet. In short, the locksmithing industry is ripe for competition and modernisation. It's going to go digital, like most other industries.

It reminds me of the long conflict between phone companies and computer companies. The phone companies had their solid, established ways of doing things and assumed they could dictate to the computer industry how data would be sent along their lines. They lost; computer firms were nimbler and more entrepreneurial, and understood the technology better. I expect the same will happen with locks. Within ten years, commercial entry control systems will just be computer systems, albeit with some specialised peripherals. They will be run by your systems administrator rather than by the retired policeman who now controls your site guards. They will finally integrate with environmental controls, personnel systems and alarms, making the smart building practical. The entry control industry will resist for a while, and use all the complex government and insurance certification requirements that have accreted over the years, just as the phone companies used their own regulators to try to strangle almost every innovation from the early data networks to VOIP. And just as computer firms have had to learn about dependability as they got into online systems, so there are other dependability lessons to be learned when doing physical security. This brings us to the most automated and sophisticated aspect of physical security, namely alarms.

11.3 Alarms

Alarms are used to deal with much more than burglary. Their applications range from monitoring freezer temperatures in supermarkets (so staff don't 'accidentally' switch off freezer cabinets in the hope of being given food to take home), right through to improvised explosive devices in Iraq and elsewhere that are sometimes booby-trapped. However, it's convenient to discuss them in the context of burglary and of protecting rooms where computer equipment and other assets are kept. Alarms also give us a good grounding in the wider problem of service denial attacks, which dominate the business of electronic warfare and are a problem elsewhere too.

Standards and requirements for alarms vary between countries and between different types of risk. You will normally use a local specialist firm for this kind of work; but as a security engineer you must be aware of the issues. Alarms often affect larger system designs: in my own professional practice this has ranged from the alarms built into automatic teller machines, through the evaluation of the security of the communications used by an alarm system for large risks such as wholesale jewelers, to continually staffed systems used to protect bank computer rooms.

An alarm in a bank vault is very well protected from tampering (at least by outsiders), so is a rather simple case. In order to look at the problem more generally, I'll consider the task of designing an alarm system for an art gallery. This is more interesting, because attackers can come in during the day as members of the public and get up to mischief. We'll imagine that the attacker is Bruno — the educated professional art thief. The common view of Bruno is that he organizes cunning attacks on alarm systems, having spent days poring over the building plans in the local town hall. You probably read about this kind of crime several times a year in the papers.

How to steal a painting (1)

A Picasso is stolen from a gallery with supposedly 'state-of-the-art' alarm systems by a thief who removes a dozen roofing tiles and lowers himself down a rope so as not to activate the pressure mats under the carpet. He grabs the painting, climbs back out without touching the floor, and probably sells the thing for a quarter of a million dollars to a wealthy cocaine dealer.

The press loves this kind of stuff, and it does happen from time to time. Reality is both simpler and stranger. Let's work through the threat scenarios systematically.

11.3.1   How not to Protect a Painting

A common mistake when designing alarm systems is to be captivated by the latest sensor technology. There's a lot of impressive stuff on the market, such as a fiber optic cable which you can loop round protected objects and which will alarm if the cable is stretched or relaxed by less than 100nm — a ten-thousandth of a millimeter. Isn't modern science marvellous? So the naive art gallery owner will buy a few feet of this magic cable, glue it to the back of his prize Picasso and connect it to an alarm company.

How to steal a painting (2)

Bruno's attack is to visit as a tourist and hide in a broom cupboard. At one in the morning, he emerges, snatches the painting and heads for the fire exit. Off goes the alarm, but so what! In less than a minute, Bruno will be on his motorbike. By the time the cops arrive twelve minutes later he has vanished.

This sort of theft is much more likely than a bosun's chair through the roof. It's often easy because alarms are rarely integrated well with building entry controls. Many designers don't realise that unless you can positively account for all the people who've entered the premises during the day, it may be prudent to take some precautions against the 'stay-behind' villain — even if this is only an inspection tour after the gallery has closed. So serious physical security means serious controls on people. In fact, the first recorded use of the RSA cryptosystem — in 1978 — was not to encrypt communications but to provide digital signatures on credentials used by staff to get past the entry barrier to a plutonium reactor at Idaho Falls. The credentials contained data such as body weight and hand geometry [1170, 1174]. But I'm still amazed by the ease with which building entry controls are defeated at most secure sites I visit — whether by mildly technical means, such as sitting on somebody else's shoulders to go through an entry booth, or even just by helpful people holding the door open.

In addition, the alarm response process often hasn't been thought through carefully. (The *Titanic Effect* of over-reliance on the latest gee-whiz technology often blinds people to common sense.) As we'll see below, this leads to still simpler attacks on most systems.

So we mustn't think of the alarm mechanism in isolation. As I mentioned above, a physical protection system has several steps: *deter — detect — alarm — delay — respond*, and the emphasis will vary from one application to another. If our opponent is Derek or Charlie, we will mostly be concerned with deterrence. At the sort of targets Abdurrahman's interested in, an attack will almost certainly be detected; the main problem is to delay him long enough for the Marines to arrive. Bruno is the most interesting case as we won't have the military budget to spend on keeping him out, and there are many more premises whose defenders worry about Bruno than about Abdurrahman. So you have to look carefully at the circumstances, and decide whether the bigger problem is with detection, with delay or with response.

11.3.2 Sensor Defeats

Burglar alarms use a wide range of *sensors*, including:

- vibration detectors, to sense fence disturbance, footsteps, breaking glass or other attacks on buildings or perimeters;
- switches on doors and windows;
- passive infrared devices to detect body heat;
- motion detectors using ultrasonics or microwave;
- invisible barriers of microwave or infrared beams;
- pressure pads under the carpet, which in extreme cases may extend to instrumenting the entire floor with pressure transducers under each tile;
- video cameras, maybe with movement detectors, to alarm automatically or provide a live video feed to a monitoring center;
- movement sensors on equipment, ranging from simple tie-down cables through seismometers to loops of optical fiber.

Most sensors can be circumvented one way or another. Fence disturbance sensors can be defeated by vaulting the fence; motion sensors by moving very slowly; door and window switches by breaking through a wall. Designing a good combination of sensors comes down to skill and experience (with the latter not always guaranteeing the former). A standard, if slightly dated, reference on sensor installation is [283].

The main problem is limiting the number of false alarms. Ultrasonics don't perform well near moving air such as central heating inlets, while vibration detectors can be rendered useless by traffic. Severe weather, such as lightning, will trigger most systems, and a hurricane can increase the number of calls per day on a town's police force from dozens to thousands. In some places, even normal weather can make protection difficult: a site where the intruder might be able to ski over your sensors (and even over your fence) is an interesting challenge for the security engineer. (For an instructive worked example of intruder detection for a nuclear power station in a snow zone see [118]).

But regardless of whether you're in Alaska or Arizona, the principal dilemma is that the closer you get to the object being protected, the more tightly you can control the environment and so the lower the achievable false alarm rate. Conversely, at the perimeter it's hard to keep the false alarm rate down. But to delay an intruder long enough for the guards to get there, the outer perimeter is exactly where you need reliable sensors.

How to steal a painting (3)

So Bruno's next attack is to wait for a dark and stormy night. He sets off the alarm somehow, taking care not to get caught on CCTV or otherwise leave any hard evidence that the alarm was a real one. He retires a few hundred yards and hides in the bushes. The guards come out and find nothing. He waits half an hour and sets off the alarm again. This time the guards don't bother, so in he goes.

False alarms — whether induced deliberately or not — are the bane of the industry. They provide a direct denial-of-service attack on the alarm response force. Experience from the world of electronic warfare is that a false alarm rate of greater than about 15% degrades the performance of radar operators; and most intruder alarm responders are operating well above this threshold. Deliberately induced false alarms are especially effective against sites that don't have round-the-clock guards. Many police forces have a policy that after a certain number of false alarms from a given site (typically three to five in a year), they will no longer send a squad car there until the alarm company, or another keyholder, has been there to check.

False alarms degrade systems in other ways. The rate at which they are caused by environmental stimuli such as weather conditions and traffic noise limits the sensitivity of the sensors that can usefully be deployed. Also, the very success of the alarm industry has greatly increased the total number of alarms and thus decreased police tolerance of false alarms. A common strategy is to have remote video surveillance as a second line of defense, so the customer's premises can be inspected by the alarm company's dispatcher; and many police forces prioritize alarms confirmed by such means [661]. But even online video links are not a panacea. The attacker can disable the lighting, or start a fire. He can set off alarms in other buildings in the same street. The failure of a telephone exchange, as a result of a flood or hurricane, may well lead to opportunistic looting.

After environmental constraints such as traffic and weather, Bruno's next ally is time. Vegetation grows into the path of sensor beams, fences become slack so the vibration sensors don't work so well, the criminal community learns new tricks, and meanwhile the sentries become complacent.

For this reason, sites with a serious physical protection requirement typically have several concentric perimeters. The traditional approach was an outer fence to keep out drunks, wildlife and other low-grade intruders; then level grass with buried sensors, then an inner fence with an infrared barrier, and finally a building of sufficiently massive construction to delay the bad guys until the cavalry gets there. The regulations laid down by the International Atomic Energy Agency for sites that hold more than 15g of plutonium are an instructive read [640]. A modern hosting centre might follow the same strategy; it may be in a nondescript building whose walls keep out the drunks and the rats, but with more serious internal walls and sensors protecting the machine room.

At most sites this kind of protection won't be possible. It will be too expensive. And even if you have loads of money, you may be in a city like Hong Kong where real estate's in really short supply: like it or not, your bank computer room will just be a floor of an office building and you'll have to protect it as best you can.

Anyway, the combination of sensors and physical barriers which you select and install are still less than half the story.

11.3.3 Feature Interactions

Intruder alarms and barriers interact in a number of ways with other services. The most obvious of these is electricity. A power cut will leave many sites dark and unprotected, so a serious alarm installation needs backup power. A less obvious interaction is with fire alarms and firefighting.

How to steal a painting (4)

Bruno visits the gallery as a tourist and leaves a smoke grenade on a timer. It goes off at one in the morning and sets off the fire alarm, which in turn causes the burglar alarm to ignore signals from its passive infrared sensors. (If it doesn't, the alarm dispatcher will ignore them anyway as he concentrates on getting the fire trucks to the scene.) Bruno smashes his way in through a fire exit and grabs the Picasso. He'll probably manage to escape in the general chaos, but if he doesn't he has a cunning plan: to claim he was a public-spirited bystander who saw the fire and risked his life to save the town's priceless cultural heritage. The police might not believe him, but they'll have a hard time prosecuting him.

The interaction between fire and intrusion works in a number of ways. At nuclear reactors, there's typically a security rule that if a bomb is discovered, the site's locked down, with no-one allowed in or out; and a fire safety rule that in the event of a blaze, much of the staff have to be evacuated (plus perhaps some of the local population too). This raises the interesting question of which rule prevails should a bomb ever go off. And there are fire precautions that can only be used if there are effective means of keeping out innocent intruders. Many computer rooms have automatic fire extinguishers, and since fears over the ozone layer made Halon unavailable, this means carbon dioxide flooding. A CO_2 dump is lethal to untrained personnel. Getting out of a room on the air you have in your lungs is much harder than it looks when visibility drops to a few inches and you are disoriented by the terrible shrieking noise of the dump. A malfunctioning intruder alarm that let a drunk into your computer room, where he lit up a cigarette and was promptly executed by your fire extinguisher, might raise a few chuckles among the anti-smoking militants but is unlikely to make your lawyers very happy.

In any case, the most severe feature interactions are between alarm and communication systems.

11.3.4   Attacks on Communications

A sophisticated attacker is at least as likely to attack the communications as the sensors. Sometimes this will mean the cabling between the sensors and the alarm controller.

How to steal a painting (5)

Bruno goes into an art gallery and, while the staff are distracted, he cuts the wire from a window switch. He goes back that evening and helps himself.

It's also quite possible that one of your staff, or a cleaner, will be bribed, seduced or coerced into creating a vulnerability (attacks on really high-value targets such as bank cash processing centres and diamond exchanges commonly involve insiders). So frequent operational testing is a good idea, along with sensor overlap, means to detect equipment substitution (such as seals), strict configuration management and tamper-resistant cabling. High-value sites that take seriously the possibility of suborned insiders insist that alarm maintenance and testing be done by two people rather than one; another edge case is the prison system, where attacks on sensors, cabling and indeed the very fabric of the building are so frequent that a continuing program of test and inspection is essential. It can be useful to ask yourself, 'How would I do this differently if half my staff were convicts on day release?'

The old-fashioned way of protecting the communications between the alarm sensors and the controller was physical: lay multiple wires to each sensor and bury them in concrete, or use armored gas-pressurized cables. The more modern way is to encrypt the communications. An example is Argus, a system originally developed for nuclear labs [483].

But the more usual attack on communications is to go for the link between the alarm controller and the security company which provides or organizes the response force.

How to steal a painting (6)

Bruno phones up his rival gallery claiming to be from the security company that handles their alarms. He says that they're updating their computers so could *they please tell him the serial number on their alarm controller unit? An office junior helpfully does so — not realising that the serial number on the box is also the cryptographic key that secures the communications. Bruno buys an identical controller for $200 and, after half an hour learning how to use an EEPROM programmer, he has a functionally identical unit which he splices into his rival's phone line. This continues to report 'all's well' even when it isn't.*

Substituting bogus alarm equipment, or a computer that mimics it, is known as 'spoofing'. There have been reports for many years of 'black boxes' that spoof various alarm controllers. As early as 1981, thieves made off with $1.5 million in jade statuary and gold jewelry imported from China, driving the importer into bankruptcy. The alarm system protecting its warehouse in Hackensack, New Jersey, was cut off. Normally that would trigger an alarm at a security company, but the burglars attached a homemade electronic device to an external cable to ensure continuous voltage [581].

With the better modern systems, either the alarm controller in the vault sends a cryptographic pseudorandom sequence to the alarm company, which will assume the worst if it's interrupted, or the alarm company sends periodic random challenges to the controller which are encrypted and returned, just as with IFF. However, the design is often faulty, having been done by engineers with no training in security protocols. The crypto algorithm may be weak, or its key may be too short (whether because of incompetence or export regulations). Even if not, Bruno might be able to record the pseudorandom sequence and replay it slightly more slowly, so that by early Monday morning he might have accumulated five minutes of 'slack' to cover a lightning raid.

An even more frequent cause of failure is the gross design blunder. One typical example is having a dial-up modem port for remote maintenance, with a default password that most users never change. Another is making the crypto key equal to the device serial number. As well as being vulnerable to social engineering, the serial number often appears in the purchase order, invoice, and other paperwork which lots of people get to see. (In general, it's a good idea to buy your alarm controller for cash. This also makes it less likely that you'll get one that's been 'spiked'. But big firms often have difficulty doing this.)

By now you've probably decided not to go into the art gallery business. But I've saved the best for last. Here is the most powerful attack on burglar alarm systems. It's a variant on (3) but rather than targeting the sensors, it goes for the communications.

How to steal a painting (7)

Bruno cuts the telephone line to his rival's gallery and hides a few hundred yards away in the bushes. He counts the number of men in blue uniforms who arrive, and the number who depart. If the two numbers are equal, then it's a fair guess the custodian has said, 'Oh bother, we'll fix it in the morning', or words to that effect. He now knows he has several hours to work.

This is more or less the standard way to attack a bank vault, and it's also been used on computer installations. The modus operandi can vary from simply reversing a truck into the phone company's kerbside junction box, to more sophisticated attempts to cause multiple simultaneous alarms in different premises and thus swamp the local police force. (This is why it's so much more powerful than just rattling the fence.)

In one case, thieves in New Jersey cut three main telephone cables, knocking out phones and alarm apparatus in three police stations and thousands of homes and businesses in the Hackensack Meadowlands. They used this opportunity to steal Lucien Piccard wristwatches from the American distributor, with a value of $2.1 million wholesale and perhaps $8 million retail [581]. In another, an Oklahoma deputy sheriff cut the phone lines to 50,000 homes in Tulsa before burgling a narcotics warehouse [1275]. In a third, a villain blew up a telephone exchange, interrupting service to dozens of shops in London's jewelry quarter. Blanket service denial attacks of this kind, which saturate the response force's capacity, are the burglarious equivalent of a nuclear strike.

In future they might not involve explosives but a software-based distributed denial-of-service attack on network facilities, as computers and communications converge. Rather than causing all the alarms to go off in a neighborhood (which could be protected to some extent by swamping it with police) it might be possible to set off several thousand alarms all over New York, creating an effect similar to that of a hurricane or a power cut but at a time convenient for the crooks. Another possibility might be to run a service-denial attack against the alarm company's control centre.

An angle which seriously concerns insurers is that phone company staff might be bribed to create false alarms. So insurance companies would prefer it if alarm communications consisted of anonymous packets, which most of the phone company's staff could not relate to any particular alarm. This would make targeted service denial attacks harder. But phone companies — who carry most of the alarm signal traffic — prefer to concentrate it in exchanges, which makes targeted service denial attacks easier. The police are also generally suspicious of anonymous communications. These tensions are discussed in [957].

For these reasons, the rule in the London insurance market (which does most of the world's major reinsurance business) is that alarm controllers in places insured for over £20 million must have two independent means of communication. One option is a leased line and a packet radio service. Another is a radio system with two antennas, each of which will send an alarm if the other is tampered with.[1] In the nuclear world, IAEA regulations stipulate that sites containing more than 500g of plutonium or 2Kg of U-235 must have their alarm control center and response force on the premises [640].

Where the asset you're protecting isn't a vault but a hosting center, the network is also critical to your operations. There's little point in having eight-inch concrete walls and roofs if the single fibre connecting you to the net runs through a kerbside junction box. You'll want two buried fibres going to two different telcos — and do you want them to be using switches and routers from different vendors? Even so, the simplest way for a knowledgeable opponent to take out a hosting centre is usually to cut its communications. That's why firms have two, three or even four centres. But it would still only take four, six or eight holes in the ground to close down your operations. Who wants to dig, who knows where to, and would you detect them in time?

Finally, it's worth bearing in mind that many physical security incidents arise from angry people coming into the workplace — whether spouses, former employees or customers. Alarm systems should be able to cope with incidents that arise during the day as well as at night.

11.3.5 Lessons Learned

The reader might still ask why a book that's essentially about security in computer systems should spend several pages describing walls, locks and alarm systems. There are many reasons.

- Dealing with service denial attacks is the hardest part of many secure system designs. As the bad guys come to understand system level vulnerabilities, it's also often the most important. Intruder alarms give us one of the largest available bodies of applicable knowledge and experience.

- The lesson that one must look at the overall system — from intrusion through detection, alarm, delay and response — is widely applicable, yet increasingly hard to follow in general purpose distributed systems.

- The observation that the outermost perimeter defenses are the ones that you'd most like to rely on, but also the ones on which the least reliance can be placed, is also quite general.

- The trade-off between the missed alarm rate and the false alarm rate — the receiver operating characteristic — is a pervasive problem in security engineering.

---

[1]I used to wonder, back in the days when I was a banker, whether two bad men who practised a bit could cut both cables simultaneously. I concluded that the threat wasn't worth bothering about for bank branches with a mere $100,000 or so in the vault. Our large cash processing centers were staffed 24 by 7, so the threat model there focused on dishonest insiders, hostage taking and so on.

- There are some lessons we can learn from the alarm business. For example, the U.S. Transportation Security Administration inserts false alarms into airport luggage to ensure that screeners stay alert; there are X-ray machines whose software inserts an image of a gun or bomb about once per shift, and there are also penetration teams who insert real objects into real suitcases. This still doesn't work very well — a 2006 report showed that 75% of the threats got through at Los Angeles and 60% at O'Hare where the screening is done once per checkpoint per shift. But it may be fixable: at San Francisco, where screeners work for a private company and are tested several times per shift, only 20% of threats get through [492].

- Failure to understand the threat model — designing for Charlie and hoping to keep out Bruno — causes many real life failures. It's necessary to know what actually goes wrong, not just what crime writers think goes wrong.

- And finally, you can't just leave the technical aspects of a security engineering project to specialist subcontractors, as critical stuff will always fall down between the cracks.

As well as these system-level lessons, there are a number of other applications where the experience of the burglar alarm industry is relevant. I already mentioned improvised explosive devices; in a later chapter, I'll discuss tamper-resistant processors that are designed to detect attempts to dismantle them and respond by destroying all their cryptographic key material.

11.4 Summary

Like it or not, security engineers have to deal with physical protection as well as with computers and cipher systems. Indeed, just as the confluence of computers and telecomms saw computer-industry standards and methods of working displace the old phone company ways of doing things, so the increasing automation of physical protection systems will bring the world of barriers, locks and alarms within our orbit. Future buildings are likely to have much more integrated entry controls, alarms and system security. Their management will be the job of systems administrators rather than retired policemen.

In this chapter, I highlighted a few things worth noting. First, environmental protection matters; things like architecture, landscaping and lighting can make a difference, and quite a lot is known about them.

Second, physical locks are not as secure as you might think. Recent developments in covert entry technology have led to wide publication of attacks that compromise the most widely-used mechanical locks and even the most widely-used high-security locks. The bump keys and other tools needed for such attacks on many locks are easily available online.

Third, there's quite a lot to learn from the one aspect of physical security that is already fairly well automated, namely alarms. Alarms provide us with a good example of a system whose security policy hinges on availability rather than on confidentiality or integrity. They can give us some useful insights when dealing with service-denial attacks in other contexts.

Research Problems

At the strategic level, the confluence of physical security and systems security is bound to throw up all sorts of new problems. I expect that novel research challenges will be found by those who first explore the information / physical security boundary in new applications. From the viewpoint of security economics, I'm eager to see whether the locksmithing industry will be disrupted by its collision with digital systems, or whether the incumbents will manage to adapt. I suspect it will be disrupted — but what does this teach us about the strategies existing industries should adopt as the world goes digital?

At the technical level, we will probably need better middleware, in the sense of mechanisms for specifying and implementing policy engines that can manage both physical and other forms of protection. And as for low-level mechanisms, we could do with better tools to manage keys in embedded systems. As one engineer from Philips put it to me, will the smart building mean that I have to perform a security protocol every time I change a lightbulb?

Further Reading

The best all round reference I know of on alarm systems is [118] while the system issues are discussed succinctly in [957]. Resources for specific countries are often available through trade societies such as the American Society for Industrial Security [25], and though the local insurance industry; many countries have a not-for-profit body such as Underwriters' Laboratories [1268] in the USA, and schemes to certify products, installations or both. For progress on lock bumping and related topics, I'd monitor troublemakers like the Toool group, Marc Weber Tobias, and Matt Blaze; Matt has also written on safecracking [186]. Research papers on the latest sensor technologies appear at the IEEE Carnahan conferences [643]. Finally, the systems used to monitor compliance with nuclear arms control treaties are written up in [1171].

CHAPTER 12

Monitoring and Metering

The market is not an invention of capitalism. It has existed for centuries. It is an
invention of civilization.
— **Mikhail Gorbachev**

12.1 Introduction

Many secure systems are concerned with monitoring and metering the environment. They go back a long way. James Watt, the inventor of the steam engine, licensed his patents using a sealed counter that measured the number of revolutions an engine had made; his inspectors read these from time to time and billed the licensee for royalties.

Electronic systems that use cryptography and tamper-resistance are rapidly displacing older mechanical systems, and also opening up all sorts of new applications. Ticketing is a huge application, from transport tickets through sports tickets to theatre tickets; my case study for ticketing is the meters used for utilities such as gas and electricity. Then I'll turn to vehicle systems; the most familiar of these may be taxi meters but I'll mainly discuss tachographs — devices used in Europe to record the speed and working hours of truck and coach drivers, and in the USA to record the comings and goings of bank trucks. My third case study is the electronic postage meter used to frank letters.

You will recall that in order to defeat a burglar alarm it is sufficient to make it appear unreliable. Such service-denial attacks can be tricky enough to deal with; meters add further subtleties.

When we discussed an alarm in a bank vault, we were largely concerned with attacks on communications (though sensor defeats also matter).

But many metering systems are much more exposed physically. A taxi driver (or owner) may want the meter to read more miles or more minutes than were actually worked, so he may manipulate its inputs or try to disrupt it so that it over-measures. With tachographs, it's the reverse: the truck driver usually wants to drive above the speed limit, or work dangerously long hours, so he wants to tachograph to ignore some of the driving. Utility consumers similarly have a motive to cause their meters to ignore some of the passing electricity. In these the attacker can either cause the device to make false readings, or simply to fail. There are also markets for bad people who can sell exploits, whether by forging tickets for electricity meters or selling devices that can be installed in vehicles to deceive a taxi meter or tachograph.

In many metering and vehicle monitoring systems (as indeed with nuclear verification) we are also concerned with evidence. An opponent could get an advantage either by manipulating communications (such as by replaying old messages) or by falsely claiming that someone else had done so. As for postal franking systems, it's not sufficient for the attacker to cause a failure (as then he can't post his letters) but the threat model has some interesting twists; the post office is mostly concerned with stopping wholesale fraud, such as crooked direct marketers who bribe postal employees to slip a truckload of mail into the system. It's thus directed internally more than externally.

Metering systems also have quite a lot in common with systems designed to enforce the copyright of software and other digital media, which I will discuss in a later chapter.

12.2 Prepayment Meters

Our first case study comes from prepayment metering. There are many systems where the user pays in one place for a token — whether a magic number, or a cardboard ticket with a magnetic strip, or even a rechargeable token such as a smartcard — and uses this stored value in some other place.

Examples include the stored-value cards that operate photocopiers in libraries, lift passes at ski resorts, and washing machine tokens in university halls of residence. Many transport tickets are similar — especially if the terminals which validate the tickets are mounted on buses or trains and so are not usually online.

The main protection goal in these systems is to prevent the stored-value tokens being duplicated or forged en masse. Duplicating a single subway ticket is not too hard, and repeating a magic number a second time is trivial. This can be made irrelevant if we make all the tokens unique and log their use at both ends. But things get more complicated when the device that accepts the token does not have a channel of communication back to the ticket issuer, so all the replay and forgery detection must be done offline — in a terminal that is often vulnerable to physical attack. So if we simply encipher all our tokens using a universal master key, a villain could extract it from a stolen terminal and set up in businesses selling tokens.

There are also attacks on the server end of things. One neat attack on a vending card system used in the staff canteen of one of our local supermarkets exploited the fact that when a card was recharged, the vending machine first read the old amount, then asked for money, and then wrote the amended amount. The attack was to insert a card with some money in it, say £49, on top of a blank card. The top card would then be removed and a £1 coin inserted in the machine, which would duly write £50 to the blank card. This left the perpetrator with two cards, with a total value of £99. This kind of attack was supposed to be prevented by two levers that extended to grip the card in the machine. However, by cutting the corners off the top card, this precaution could easily be defeated (see Figure 12.1) [749]. This attack is interesting because no amount of encryption of the card contents will make any difference. Although it could in theory be stopped by keeping logs at both ends, they would have to be designed a bit more carefully than is usual.

But we mustn't get carried away with neat tricks like this, or we risk getting so involved with even more clever countermeasures that we fall prey to the Titanic Effect again by ignoring the system level issues. In most ticketing systems, petty fraud is easy. A free rider can jump the barrier at a subway station; an electricity meter can have a bypass switch wired across it; things like barcoded ski lift passes and parking lot tickets can be forged with a

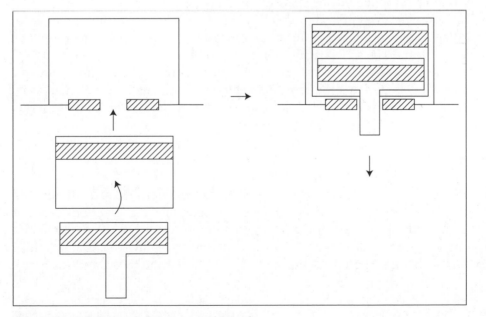

Figure 12.1: Superposing two payment cards

scanner and printer. The goal is to prevent fraud becoming systematic. So petty fraud should be at least slightly inconvenient and — more importantly — there should be more serious mechanisms to prevent anyone forging tickets on a large enough scale to develop a black market that could affect your client's business.

The first example I'll discuss in detail is the prepayment electricity meter. I chose this because I was lucky enough to consult on a project to electrify three million households in South Africa (a central election pledge made by Nelson Mandela when he took power). This work is described in some detail in [59]. Most of the lessons learned apply directly to other ticketing systems.

12.2.1 Utility Metering

In a number of European countries, householders who can't get credit (because they are on welfare, have court judgements against them, or whatever) buy gas and electricity services using prepayment meters (Figure 2.2). In the old days they were coin-operated, but the costs of coin collection led vendors to develop token-based meters instead. The UK now has 3.6 million electricity meters and 2 million gas meters. In South Africa, development was particularly rapid because of a national priority project to electrify the townships; as many of the houses were informally constructed, and the owners did not even have addresses (let alone credit ratings), prepayment was the only way to go. There are now 5.5 million of these meters in use in South Africa, which has exported 1.5 million to other countries in Africa, Latin America and elsewhere.

The customer goes to a shop and buys a token, which may be a smartcard, or a disposable cardboard ticket with a magnetic strip, or even just a magic number. Of the UK's electricity meters, 2.4 million use smartcards[1] and 1.2 million use magnetic tickets. Most of South Africa's meters use a magic number. This is perhaps the most convenient for the customer, as no special vending apparatus is required: a ticket can be dispensed at a supermarket checkout, at an ATM, or even over the phone.

The token is really just a string of bits containing one or more instructions, encrypted using a key unique to the meter, which decodes them and acts on them. Most tokens say something like 'meter 12345 — dispense 50KWh of electricity!' The idea is that the meter will dispense the purchased amount and then interrupt the supply. Some tokens have engineering functions too. For example, if the power company charges different rates for the daytime and evening, the meter may have to know the relative prices and the times at which the tariffs change. Special tokens may be used to change these, and to change

---

[1]1.6 million of these smartcards are repackaged in plastic keys; the other 0.8 are normal smartcards. The packaging may improve usability, especially in a darkened house, but does not affect the cryptographic security.

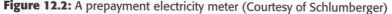

Figure 12.2: A prepayment electricity meter (Courtesy of Schlumberger)

keys. The meters that use smartcards are able to report consumption patterns, tampering attempts and so on back to the power company; however the magnetic-ticket and magic-number meters do not have such a back channel.

The manufacture of these meters has become big business. Growth in the third world is strong: prepayment metering was the only way the government in South Africa could meet its election pledge to electrify millions of homes quickly. In the developed world, the main impetus for prepayment metering is reducing administrative costs. Electric utilities find that billing systems can devour 20 percent of retail customer revenue, when you add up the costs of meter reading, billing, credit control, bad debts and so on. Prepayment systems typically cost under 10 percent: the shop that sells the tokens gets five percent, while the meters and the infrastructure cost about the same again.

12.2.2   How the System Works

The security requirements for prepayment meters seem straightforward. Tokens should not be easy to forge, while genuine tokens should not work in the wrong meter, or in the right meter twice. One strategy is to make tokens tamper-resistant, by using smartcard chips of some kind or another;

the alternative is to tie each token to a unique meter, so that someone can't use the same magic number in two different meters, and also make each token unique using serial numbers or random numbers, so that the same token can't be used twice in the same meter. But it has taken a surprising amount of field experience to develop the idea into a robust system.

The meter needs a cryptographic key to authenticate its instructions from the vending station. The original system had a single vending machine for each neighbourhood, usually located in a local store. The machine has a vend key K_V which acts as the master key for a neighborhood and derives the device key when needed by encrypting the meter ID under the vend key:

$$K_{ID} = \{ID\}_{K_V}$$

This is the same key diversification technique described for parking lot access devices in Chapter 3. Diversifying the vend key K_V to a group of meter keys K_{ID} provides a very simple solution where all the tokens are bought locally. However, once the system rolled out, we found that real life was less straightforward. In Britain, deregulation of the electricity industry led to a multitude of electricity companies who buy power from generators and sell it onward to households through a common infrastructure, so metering systems must support multiple power companies with different tariff structures. In South Africa, many people commute long distances from townships or home-lands to their places of work, so they are never at home during business hours and want to buy tickets where they work. So we had to support multiple retailers, by letting customers register at an out-of-area vending station. This meant protocols to send a customer meter key from the vending station that 'owns' the meter to another station, and to pass sales data in the opposite direction for balancing and settlement, somewhat like in ATM networks. The most recent development (2007) is online vending; a customer can buy a magic number over the Internet or via their mobile phone from a central token server. This server can deal directly with four million customers and also about 10,000 online vend points such as ATMs.

Statistical balancing is used to detect what are euphemistically known as *non-technical losses*, that is, theft of power through meter tampering or unauthorized direct connections to mains cables. The mechanism is to compare the readings on a feeder meter, which might supply 30 houses, with token sales to those houses. This turns out to be harder than it looks. Customers hoard tickets, meter readers lie about the date when they read the meter, and many other things go wrong. Vending statistics are also used in conventional balancing systems, like those discussed in Chapter 10.

There have been a few cases where vending machines were stolen and used to sell tokens in competition with the utility. These 'ghost vendors' are extremely difficult to track down, and the early ones generally stayed in business until the keys in all the meters were changed. The countermeasure has been to get the vending machines to maintain a credit balance in the tamper-resistant security processor that also protects vend keys and foreign meter keys. The balance is decremented with each sale and only credited again when cash is banked with the local operating company; the company then sends a magic number that reloads the vending machine with credit. The operating company in turn has to account to the next level up in the distribution network, and so on. So here we have an accounting system enforced by a value counter at the point of sale, rather than just by ledger data kept on servers in a vault. Subversion of value counters can in theory be picked up by statistical and balancing checks at higher layers.

This distribution of security state is seen in other applications too, such as in some smartcard-based electronic purse schemes. However, the strategic direction for power vending is now believed to be centralisation. Now that the communications infrastructure is more dependable, many of the original 1200 vending machines will be replaced by online vending points that get their tokens in real time from the central service. (In banking, too, there is a move away from offline operation as communications get more dependable.)

So what can go wrong?

12.2.3 What Goes Wrong

Service denial remains an important issue. Where there is no return channel from the meter to the vending station, the only evidence of how much electricity has been sold resides in the vending equipment itself. The agents who operate the vending machines are typically small shopkeepers or other township entrepreneurs who have little capital so are allowed to sell electricity on credit. In some cases, agents who couldn't pay the electricity bill to the operating company at the end of the month just dumped their equipment and claimed that it had been stolen. This is manageable with small agents, but when an organization such as a local government is allowed to sell large amounts of electricity through multiple outlets, there is definitely an exposure. A lot of the complexity was needed to deal with untrustworthy (and mutually mistrustful) principals.

As with burglar alarms, environmental robustness is critical. Apart from the huge range of temperatures (as variable in South Africa as in the continental United States) many areas have severe thunderstorms: the meter is in effect a microprocessor with a 3-kilometer lightning conductor attached.

When meters were destroyed by lightning, the customers complained and got credit for the value they said was still unused. So their next step was to poke live mains wires into the meter to try to emulate the effects of the lightning. It turned out that one make of meter would give unlimited credit if a particular part of the circuitry (that lay under the token slot) was destroyed. So service denial attacks worked well enough to become popular.

It was to get worse. The most expensive security failure in the program came when kids in Soweto observed that when there was a brown-out — a fall in voltage from 220 to 180 volts — then a particular make of meter went to maximum credit. Soon kids were throwing steel chains over the 11KV feeders and crediting all the meters in the neighborhood. This was the fault of a simple bug in the meter ROM, which wasn't picked up because brown-out testing hadn't been specified. The underlying problem was that developed-country environmental standards were inadequate for use in Africa and had to be rewritten. The effect on the business was that 100,000 meters had to be pulled out and re-ROMmed; the responsible company almost went bust.

There were numerous other bugs. One make of meter didn't vend a specified quantity of electricity, but so much worth of electricity at such-and-such a rate. It turned out that the tariff could be set to a minute amount by vending staff, so that it would operate almost for ever. Another allowed refunds, but a copy of the refunded token could still be used (blacklisting the serial numbers of refunded tokens in subsequent token commands is hard, as tokens are hoarded and used out of order). Another remembered only the last token serial number entered, so by alternately entering duplicates of two tokens it could be charged up indefinitely.

As with cash machines, the real security breaches resulted from bugs and blunders, which could be quite obscure, but were discovered by accident and exploited in quite opportunistic ways. These exploits were sometimes on a large scale, costing millions to fix.

Other lessons learned, which we wrote up in [59], were:

- prepayment may be cheap so long as you control the marketing channel, but when you try to make it even cheaper by selling prepayment tokens through third parties (such as banks and supermarkets) it can rapidly become expensive, complicated and risky. This is largely because of the security engineering problems created by mutual mistrust between the various organizations involved;

- changes to a business process can be very expensive if they affect the security infrastructure. For example, the requirement to sell meter tokens at distant shops, to support commuters, was not anticipated and was costly to implement;

- recycle technology if you can, as it's likely to have fewer bugs than something designed on a blank sheet of paper. Much of what we needed for prepayment metering was borrowed from the world of cash machines;

- use multiple experts. One expert alone can not usually span all the issues, and even the best will miss things;

- no matter what is done, small mistakes with large consequences will still creep in. So you absolutely need prolonged field testing. This is where many errors and impracticalities will first make themselves known.

Meters are a good case study for ticketing. Transport ticketing, theater ticketing and sports ticketing may be larger applications, but I don't know of any serious and publicly available studies of their failure modes. In general the end systems — such as the meters or turnstiles — are fairly soft, so the main concern is to prevent large scale fraud. This means paying a lot of attention to the intermediate servers such as vending machines, and hardening them to ensure they will resist manipulation and tampering. In the case of London transport tickets, deregulation of the railways led to reports of problems with train companies manipulating ticket sales by booking them at stations where they got a larger percentage of the takings, and clearly if you're designing a system that shares revenue between multiple vendors, you should try to think of how arbitrage opportunities can be minimised. One still does what one economically can to prevent the end users developing systematic attacks on the end systems that are too hard to detect.

I'll now look at a class of applications where there are severe and prolonged attacks on end systems which must therefore be made much more tamper resistant than electricity meters. The threat model includes sensor manipulation, service denial, accounting fiddles, procedural defeats and the corruption of operating staff. This exemplary field of study is vehicle monitoring systems.

12.3 Taxi Meters, Tachographs and Truck Speed Limiters

A number of systems are used to monitor and control vehicles. The most familiar is probably the odometer in your car. When buying a used car you'll be concerned that the car has been *clocked*, that is, had its indicated mileage reduced. As odometers become digital, clocking is becoming a type of computer fraud; a conviction has already been reported [274]. A related problem is *chipping*, that is, replacing or reprogramming the engine controller. This can be done for two basic reasons. First, the engine controller acts as the server for the remote key-entry systems that protect most modern cars from theft, as described in Chapter 3; so if you want to steal a car without stealing the key, the engine controller is the natural target (you might replace the controller in the street, or else tow the car and replace or reprogram the controller later). Second, people reprogram their cars' engine controllers to make them go faster, and the manufacturers dislike this because of the increased warranty claims from burned-out engines. So they try to make the controllers more tamper resistant, or at least tamper-evident.

This fascinating arms race is described in [426]. Some vehicles now keep logs that are uploaded to the manufacturer during servicing. General Motors started equipping some vehicles with black boxes to record crash data in 1990. By the time the logging became public in 1999, some six million vehicles had been instrumented, and the disclosure caused protests from privacy activists [1282]. Indeed, there's now a whole conference, ESCAR, devoted to electronic security in cars.

There are a number of monitoring systems separate from those provided by the engine manufacturer, and the most familiar may be the taxi meter. A taxi driver has an incentive to manipulate the meter to show more miles travelled (or minutes waited) if he can get away with it. There are various other kinds of 'black box' used to record the movement of vehicles from aircraft through fishing vessels to armored bank trucks, and their operators have differing levels of motive for tampering with them. A recent development is the black boxes supplied by insurers who sell 'pay-as-you-drive' insurance to young and high-risk drivers; these boxes contain satellite navigation devices that let the insurer charge a couple of pennies a mile for driving along a country road in the afternoon but a couple of dollars a mile for evening driving in an inner city [1264]. It's conceivable that within a few years this will be the only type of insurance available to many youngsters; if the dangerous drivers flock to any flat-rate contracts still on offer, they may become unaffordable. In that case, any young man who wants to impress girls by driving around town on a Saturday night will have a strong incentive to beat the black box.

12.3.1 The Tachograph

The case study I'm going to use here is the tachograph. These are devices used to monitor truck drivers' speed and working hours; they have recently been the subject of a huge experiment in Europe, in which old analogue devices are being replaced by digital ones. This gives us some interesting data on how such equipment works, and can fail; and it's an example of how a move to digital technology didn't necessarily make things better. It contains useful warnings for engineers trying to modernise systems that do analogue monitoring in hostile environments.

Vehicle accidents resulting from a driver falling asleep at the wheel cause several times more accidents than drunkenness (20 percent versus 3 percent of accidents in the UK, for example). Accidents involving trucks are more likely to lead to fatal injuries because of the truck's mass. So most countries regulate truck drivers' working hours. While these laws are enforced in the USA using weigh stations and drivers' log books, countries in Europe use tachographs that record a 24-hour history of the vehicle's speed. Until 2005–6, this was recorded on a circular waxed paper chart (Figure 12.3); since then,

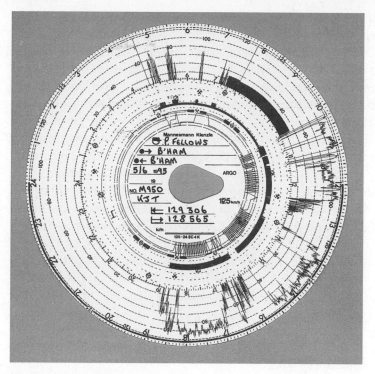

Figure 12.3: A tachograph chart

digital tachographs have been introduced and the two systems are currently running side-by-side[2]. Eventually the analogue systems will be phased out; in the meantime they provide an interesting study of the relative strengths and weaknesses of analogue and digital systems. First let's look at the old analogue system, which is still used in most trucks on Europe's roads.

The chart is loaded into the tachograph, which is part of the vehicle's speedometer/odometer unit. It turns slowly on a turntable inside the instrument and a speed history is inscribed by a fine stylus connected to the speedometer. With some exceptions that needn't concern us, it is an offence to drive a truck in Europe unless you have a tachograph; if it's analogue you must have a chart installed, and have written on it your starting time and location. You must also keep several days' charts with you to establish that you've complied with the relevant driving hours regulations (typically 8.5 hours per day with rules for rest breaks per day and rest days per week). If it's digital you have to have a driver card plugged into it; the card and the vehicle unit both keep records.

---

[2]Vehicles registered since August 2004 in the UK have had to have digital systems fitted, cards have been issued since June 2005 and since August 2006 the use of digital systems in new vehicles has been mandatory; the dates vary slightly for other EU countries.

European law also restricts trucks to 100 Km/h (62 mph) on freeways and less on other roads. This is enforced not just by police speed traps and the tachograph record, but directly by a speed limiter that is also driven by the tachograph. Tachograph charts are also used to investigate other offences, such as unlicensed toxic waste dumping, and by fleet operators to detect fuel theft. So there are plenty reasons why a truck driver might want to fiddle his tachograph. Indeed, it's a general principle in security engineering that one shouldn't aggregate targets. So NATO rules prohibit money or other valuables being carried in a container for classified information — you don't want someone who set out to steal your regiment's payroll getting away with your spy satellite photographs too. Forcing a truck driver to defeat his tachograph in order to circumvent his speed limiter, and vice versa, was a serious design error — but one that's now too entrenched to change easily.

Most of what we have to say applies just as well to taxi meters and other monitoring devices. While the truck driver wants his vehicle to appear to have gone less distance, the taxi driver wants the opposite. This has little effect on the actual tampering techniques.

12.3.2 What Goes Wrong

According to a 1998 survey of 1060 convictions of drivers and operators [45], the offences were distributed as follows.

12.3.2.1 How Most Tachograph Manipulation Is Done

About 70% of offences that result in conviction do not involve tampering but exploit procedural weaknesses. For example, a company with premises in Dundee and Southampton should have four drivers in order to operate one vehicle per day in each direction, as the distance is about 500 miles and the journey takes about 10 hours — which is illegal for a single driver to do every day. The standard fiddle is to have two drivers who meet at an intermediate point such as Penrith, change trucks, and insert new paper charts into the tachographs. So the driver who had come from Southampton now returns home with the vehicle from Dundee. When stopped and asked for his charts, he shows the current chart from Penrith to Southampton, the previous day's for Southampton to Penrith, the day before's for Penrith to Southampton, and so on. In this way he can give the false impression that he spent every other night in Penrith and was thus legal. This (widespread) practice, of swapping vehicles halfway through the working day, is called *ghosting*. It's even harder to detect in mainland Europe, where a driver might be operating out of a depot in France on Monday, in Belgium on Tuesday and in Holland on Wednesday.

Simpler frauds include setting the clock wrongly, pretending that a hitch-hiker is a relief driver, and recording the start point as a village with a very common name — such as 'Milton' in England or 'La Hoya' in Spain. If stopped, the driver can claim he started from a nearby Milton or La Hoya.

Such tricks often involve collusion between the driver and the operator. When the operator is ordered to produce charts and supporting documents such as pay records, weigh station slips and ferry tickets, his office may well conveniently burn down. (It's remarkable how many truck companies operate out of small cheap wooden sheds that are located a safe distance from the trucks in their yard.)

12.3.2.2 *Tampering with the Supply*

The next largest category of fraud, amounting to about 20% of the total, involves tampering with the supply to the tachograph instrument, including interference with the power and impulse supply, cables and seals.

Old-fashioned tachographs used a rotating wire cable — as did the speedometers in cars up until the early 1980s — that was hard to fiddle with; if you jammed the truck's odometer it was quite likely that you'd shear off the cable. More recent analogue tachographs are 'electronic', in that they use electric cables rather than rotating wire. The input comes from a sensor in the gearbox, which sends electrical impulses as the prop shaft rotates. This has made fiddling much easier! A common attack is to unscrew the sensor about a tenth of an inch, which causes the impulses to cease, as if the vehicle were stationary. To prevent this, sensors are fixed in place with a wire and lead seal. Fitters are bribed to wrap the wire anticlockwise rather than clockwise, which causes it to loosen rather than break when the sensor is unscrewed. The fact that seals are issued to workshops rather than to individual fitters complicates prosecution.

But most of the fiddles are much simpler still. Drivers short out the cable or replace the tachograph fuse with a blown one. (One manufacturer tried to stop this trick by putting the truck's anti-lock braking system on the same fuse. Many drivers preferred to get home sooner than to drive a safe vehicle.) Again, there is evidence of a power supply interruption on the chart in Figure 12.3: around 11 A.M., there are several places where the speed indicated in the outside trace goes suddenly from zero to over 100 km/h. These indicate power interruptions, except where there's also a discontinuity in the distance trace. There, the unit was open.

12.3.2.3 *Tampering with the Instrument*

The third category of fraud is tampering with the tachograph unit itself. This amounts for some 6% of offences, but declined through the 1990s as tampering with digital communications is much easier than tampering with a rotating wire cable used to be. The typical offence in this category is miscalibration, usually done in cahoots with the fitter but sometimes by the driver defeating the seal on the device.

12.3.2.4 High-Tech Attacks

The state of the tampering art at the time of the 1998 survey was the equipment in Figure 12.4. The plastic cylinder on the left of the photo is marked 'Voltage Regulator — Made in Japan' and is certainly not a voltage regulator. (It actually appears to be made in Italy.) It is spliced into the tachograph cable and controlled by the driver using the remote control key fob. A first press causes the indicated speed to drop by 10%, a second press causes a drop of 20%, a third press causes it to fall to zero, and a fourth causes the device to return to proper operation.

This kind of device accounted for under 1% of convictions but its use is believed to be much more widespread. It's extremely hard to find as it can be hidden at many different places in the truck's cable harness. Police officers who stop a speeding truck equipped with such a device, and can't find it, have difficulty getting a conviction: the sealed and apparently correctly calibrated tachograph contradicts the evidence from their radar or camera.

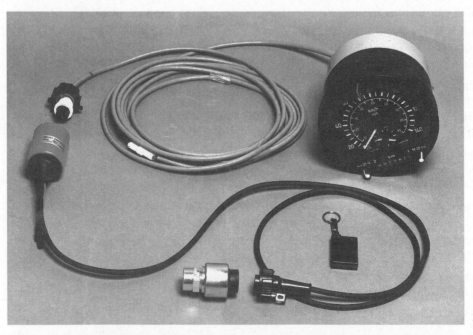

Figure 12.4: A tachograph with an interruptor controlled by the driver using a radio key fob. (Courtesy of Hampshire Constabulary, England)

12.3.3 The Digital Tachograph Project

The countermeasures taken against tachograph manipulation vary by country. In Britain, trucks are stopped at the roadside for random checks by vehicle inspectors, and particularly suspect trucks may be shadowed across the country. In the Netherlands, inspectors prefer to descend on a trucking company and go through their delivery documents, drivers' timesheets, fuel records etc. In Italy, data from the toll booths on the freeways are used to prosecute drivers who've averaged more than the speed limit (you can often see trucks parked just in front of Italian toll booths). But such measures are only partially effective, and drivers can arbitrage between the differing control regimes. For example, a truck driver operating between France and Holland can keep his documents at a depot in France where the Dutch vehicle inspectors can't get at them.

So the European Union took the initiative to design a unified electronic tachograph system to replace the existing paper-based charts with smartcards. Each driver can now get a 'driver card' that contains a record of his driving hours over the last 28 days. Every new vehicle has a vehicle unit that can hold a year's history. There are two further types of credential: workshop cards used by mechanics to calibrate devices, and control cards used by law enforcement officers to read them out at the roadside. In 1998, I was hired by the UK Department of Transport to look at the new scheme and try to figure out what would go wrong. After talking to a wide range of people from policemen and vehicle inspectors to tachograph vendors and accident investigators, I wrote a report [45]. I revisited the field in 2007 when writing the second edition of this book; it was simultaneously pleasing and depressing to find that I'd mostly predicted the problems correctly. However a few interesting new twists also emerged.

The most substantial objection raised to the project was that it was not clear how going digital will help combat the procedural frauds that make up 70% of the current total. Indeed, our pair of drivers 'ghosting' between Dundee and Southampton will have their lives made even easier. It will take maybe ten years — the lifetime of a truck — to change over to the new system and meantime a crooked company can run one new digital truck and one old analogue one. Each driver will now have one chart and one card, with five hours a day on each, rather than two charts which they might accidentally mix up when stopped. This has turned out to be well-founded. In the UK, it's now estimated that 20% of the vehicle fleet has digital tachographs — somewhat more than would be expected — which suggests that operators have been installing digital devices before they need to as they're easier to fiddle. (So, in the short term at least, the equipment vendors appear to be profiting from the poor design of the system: in the medium term they may well profit even more, if European governments decide on yet another technology change.)

Another objection was that enforcement would be made harder by the loss of detailed speed and driving hours information. Back in 1998, the Germans had wanted the driver card to be a memory device so it could contain detailed records; the French insisted on a smartcard, as they're proud of their smartcard industry. So the driver card has only 32K of memory, and can only contain a limited number of alarm events. (Indeed until a late change in the regulations it didn't contain data on rest periods at all.) The choice of a smartcard rather than a memory card was probably the most critical wrong decision in the whole programme.

12.3.3.1 *System Level Problems*

The response to this problem varies by country. Germany has gone for an infrastructure of fleet management systems that accept digital tachograph data, digitized versions of the analog data from the existing paper charts, fuel data, delivery data and even payroll, and reconcile them all to provide not just management information for the trucking company but surveillance data for the police. Britain has something similar, although it's up to the police to decide which companies to inspect; unless they do so, data on driving infringements is only available to the employer. Germany has also introduced a system of road pricing for heavy goods vehicles that gives further inputs into fleet management systems.

Britain thought initially of road pricing, with tachograph data correlated with GPS location sensors in the trucks, and of using the country's network of automatic number plate reader (ANPR) cameras. The nationwide road-charging plan has become bogged down, as initial plans involved road charging for cars too and drew heavy resistance from motoring organisations. So in the UK ANPR has become the main means of complementary surveillance. It was initially installed around London to make IRA bombing attacks harder, and has now been extended nationwide. It was initially justified on the basis of detecting car tax evaders, but has turned out to be useful in many other policing tasks. We see ANPR data adduced in more and more prosecutions, for everything from terrorism down to burglary. 'Denying criminals the use of the roads' has now become an element in UK police doctrine. In the case of drivers' hours enforcement, the strategy is to verify a sample of logged journeys against the ANPR database; where discrepancies are found, the company's operations are then scrutinised more closely.

However, disagreements about privacy issues and about national economic interests have prevented any EU-wide standardization. It's up to individual countries whether they require truck companies to download and analyze the data from their trucks. And even among countries that require this, fleet management systems aren't a panacea, because of arbitrage. For example, the German police are much more vigorous at enforcing drivers' hours regulations than their Italian counterparts. So, under the analogue system, an Italian driver who normally doesn't bother to put a chart in his machine will do so while driving over the Alps. Meanwhile, the driver of the German truck going the other way takes his chart out. The net effect is that all drivers in a given country are subject to the same level of law enforcement. But if the driving data get regularly uploaded from the Italian driver's card and kept on a PC at a truck company in Rome then they'll be subject to Italian levels of enforcement (or even less if the Italian police decide they don't care about accidents in Germany). The fix to this was extraterritoriality; an Italian truck driver stopped in Germany can be prosecuted there if he can't show satisfactory records of his driving in Italy for the week before he crossed the border.

12.3.3.2 *Other Problems*

So the move from analogue to digital isn't always an improvement. As well as the lower tamper-resistance of electronic versus mechanical signalling, and the system level problem that the location of the security state can't be tackled in a uniform way, there are several further interesting problems with tachographs being digital.

A curious problem for the policy folks is that digital tachographs have for the first time caused digital signatures to turn up in court in large numbers. For many years, security researchers have been writing academic papers with punchlines like 'the judge then raises X to the power Y, finds it's equal to Z, and sends Bob to jail'. The reality is very different. Apparently judges find digital signatures too 'difficult' as they're all in hex. The police, always eager to please, have resolved the problem by applying standard procedures for 'securing' digital evidence. When they raid a dodgy trucking company, they image the PC's disk drive and take copies on DVDs that are sealed in evidence bags. One gets given to the defence and one kept for appeal. The paper logs documenting the copying are available for Their Worships to inspect. Everyone's happy, and truckers duly get fined as before.

From the operational viewpoint, the main emerging problem is that many drivers have more than one driver card. This is an offence everywhere but that doesn't stop it! One source of cards is to borrow them from drivers who use them only occasionally — for example because they usually drive analogue trucks, or trucks under 3.5 tonnes. Another is that many drivers have more than one address; the Jean Moulin of Toulouse may also be Jean Moulin of Antwerp. A database, 'Tachonet', was set up to try to catch duplicate applications across European countries but it doesn't seem to work very well. For example, drivers may forget their middle name in one of their countries of residence.

Second, there will be new kinds of service denial attacks (as well as the traditional ones involving gearbox sensors, fuses and so on). A truck driver can easily destroy his smartcard by feeding it with mains electricity (in fact, even a truck's 24 volts will do fine). Under the regulations he is allowed to drive for 15 days while waiting for a replacement. As static electricity destroys maybe 1% of cards a year anyway, it is hard to prosecute drivers for doing this occasionally. Similar card-destruction attacks have been perpetrated on bank smartcard systems in order to force a merchant back into less robust fallback modes of operation.

Third, I mentioned that the loss of detailed, redundant data on the tachograph chart makes enforcement harder. At present, experienced vehicle inspectors have a 'feel' for when a chart isn't right, but the analogue trace is replaced by a binary signal saying either that the driver infringed the regulations or that he didn't. This spills over into other enforcement tasks; analogue charts were often used to collect evidence of illegal toxic waste dumping, for example, as the recorded speed patterns often give a knowledgeable inspector a good idea of the truck's route.

Next, some of the cards in the system (notably the workshop cards used to set up the instruments, and the control cards used by police and vehicle inspectors) are very powerful. They can be used to erase evidence of wrongdoing. For example, if you use a workshop card to wind back the clock in a vehicle unit from 10th July to 8th July, then the entries for July 9th and 10th become unreadable. (Of course the vendors should have implemented a proper append-only file system, but they had only 32Kb smartcards to work with not 32Mb memory cards.) Some countries have therefore gone to great lengths to minimise the number of workshop cards that fall into bad hands. In the UK, for example, truck mechanics have to pass a criminal records check to get one; yet this isn't foolproof as it's often companies that get convicted, and the wealthy owners of crooked truck-maintenance firms just set up new firms. There's no company licensing scheme, and although wrongdoers can be blacklisted from acting as directors of licensed firms, crooks just hide behind nominee directors.

Various technical attacks are possible. When assessing the security of the proposed design in the late 1990s, I was concerned that villains might physically reverse-engineer a card, extracting its master key and enabling a powerful workshop or police card to be forged. Since then, tamper-resistance has got better, so attacks are more expensive; and my 1998 critique helped move the design from shared-key to public-key crypto, limiting the damage from a single card compromise. But the most recent attacks on smartcard systems are definitely a concern. Consider for example relay attacks, in which a bogus card, connected to a bogus reader using mobile phones, enables a smartcard in country A to appear to be in country B [401]. In Chapter 10, I discussed this as a means of bank fraud. In the tachograph world, its implications are different. If any police card, or workshop card, can be used to erase evidence of a crime, then what's to stop a corrupt mechanic or policeman in Sicily or in Romania from using his card to destroy evidence in London or in Berlin? This really is arbitrage with a vengeance. It's no longer enough for British coppers or the German Polizei to be honest, if officials from less well governed countries can indulge in telepresence. Perhaps we'll need region coding for policemen just as we have for DVDs.

This helps illustrate that key management is, as always, difficult. This is a pervasive problem with security systems in vehicles — not just tachographs and taxi meters, but even such simple devices as card door locks and the PIN codes used to protect car radios against theft. If the garage must always be able to override the security mechanisms, and a third of garage mechanics have criminal records, then what sort of protection are you buying? (In my own experience, PIN-protected radios are just a protection racket for the garages — you end up paying a garage £20 to tell you the PIN after you get a flat battery.)

12.3.3.3 *The Resurrecting Duckling*

In the late 1990s, a European Union regulation decreed that, in order to frustrate the use of interruptors of the kind shown in Figure 12.4 above, all digital tachographs had to encrypt the pulse train from the gearbox sensor to the vehicle unit. As both of these devices contain a microcontroller, and the data rate is fairly low, this shouldn't in theory have been a problem. But how on earth could we distribute the keys? If we just set up a hotline that garages could call, it is likely to be abused. There's a long history of fitters conspiring with truck drivers to defeat the system, and of garage staff abusing helplines to get unlocking data for stolen cars and even PIN codes for stolen radios.

One solution is given by the *resurrecting duckling* security policy model. This is named after the fact that a duckling emerging from its egg will recognize as its mother the first moving object it sees that makes a sound: this is called imprinting. Similarly, a 'newborn' vehicle unit, just removed from the shrink wrap, can recognize as its owner the first gearbox sensor that sends it a secret key. The sensor does this on power-up. As soon as this key is received, the vehicle unit is no longer a newborn and will stay faithful to the gearbox sensor for the rest of its 'life'. If the sensor fails and has to be replaced, a workshop card can be used to 'kill' the vehicle unit's key store and resurrect it as a newborn, whereupon it can imprint on the new sensor. Each act of resurrection is indelibly logged in the vehicle unit to make abuse harder. (This at least was the theory — the implementation fell somewhat short in that in one unit the error code for sensor rekeying is the same as the error code for a power outage.)

The resurrecting duckling model of key management was originally developed to deal with the secure imprinting of a digital thermometer or other piece of medical equipment to a doctor's PDA or a bedside monitor. It can also be used to imprint consumer electronics to a remote control in such a way as to make it more difficult for a thief who steals the device but not the controller to make use of it [1218].

Another possible application is weapon security. Many of the police officers who are shot dead on duty are killed with their own guns, so there has been some interest in safety mechanisms. One approach is to design the gun so it will fire only when within a foot or so of a signet ring the officer wears. The problem is managing the relationship between rings and guns, and a possible solution is to let the gun imprint on any ring, but with a delay of a minute or so. This is not a big deal for the policeman signing a gun out of the armory, but is a problem for the crook who snatches it. (One may assume that if the policeman can't either overpower the crook or run for it within a minute, then he's a goner in any case.) Such mechanisms might also mitigate the effects of battlefield capture of military weapons, for which passwords are often unacceptable [175].

However, one last problem with the idea of a secure sensor has emerged in the last two years, since digital tachographs started shipping. The folks in Italy who brought you the interruptor now have a new product. This is a black box containing electromagnets and electronics to simulate a gearbox. The errant truck driver unscrews his gearbox sensor and places it in this virtual gearbox. The box comes with its own cable and a sensor that he plugs into his actual gearbox. The system now operates as before; on command it will either relay impulses faithfully, or discard them, or filter some of them out. The dodgy pulse-train arrives at the tachograph as before, but this time beautifully encrypted using triple-DES. Secure sensing is harder than it looks!

12.4   Postage Meters

My third case history of metering is the postage meter. Postage stamps were introduced in Britain 1840 by Sir Rowland Hill to simplify charging for post, and developed into a special currency that could be used for certain purposes, from paying for postage to paying certain taxes and topping up the value of postal money orders. Bulk users of the postal system started to find stamps unsatisfactory by the late 19th century, and the postage meter was invented in 1889 by Josef Baumann. Its first commercial use was in Norway in 1903; in the USA Arthur Pitney and Walter Bowes had a meter approved for use in 1920 and built a large business on it. Early postal meters were analogue, and would print a stamp (known as an indicium) on a letter, or on a tape to stick on a parcel. The indicium had a date so that old indicia couldn't be peeled off and reused. Each meter had a mechanical value counter, protected by a physical seal; every so often you'd take your meter into the post office to be read and reset. Fraud prevention relied on users taking their mail to the local post office, which knew them; the clerk could check the date and the meter serial number.

In 1979, Pitney Bowes introduced a 'reset-by-phone' service, which enabled firms to buy an extra $500 worth of credit over the phone; the implementation involved a mechanical one-time pad, with the meter containing a tape with successive recharge codes [328]. In 1981, this was upgraded to a DES-based system that enabled a meter to be recharged with any sum of money. The recharge codes were calculated in part from the value counter — so if the firm lied about how much postage they'd used, they couldn't recharge the device. However, these meters still produced inked indicia.

In 1990, José Pastor of Pitney Bowes suggested replacing stamps and indicia with digital marks protected by digital signatures [1007]. This caught the attention of the U.S. Postal Service, which started a program to investigate whether cryptography could help produce better postage meters. One concern was whether the availability of color scanners and copiers would make stamps and indicia too easy to forge. A threat analysis done for them by Doug Tygar, Bennett Yee and Nevin Heintze revealed that the big problem was not so much the forging or copying of stamps, or even tampering with meters to get extra postage. It was bulk mailers corrupting Postal Service employees so as to insert truckloads of junk mail into the system without paying for them [1265]. As a bulk mailer who was fiddling his meter seriously would risk arousing the suspicion of alert staff, there was a temptation to cut them in on the deal; and then it was natural to forge a meter plate whose inducting post office was elsewhere. By 1990 U.S. Postal service losses were in nine figures, and through the 1990s there were a number of high-profile convictions of bulk mailers who had manipulated their meters, and got away with millions of dollars of free postage [190].

This led to a development programme to produce a design based on digital signatures, generated by tamper-resistant processors in the postage meters, that were developed from Pastor's ideas into an open standard available to multiple competing manufacturers. The basic idea is that the indicium, which is machine-readable, contains both the sender and recipient postal codes, the meter number, the date, the postage rate, the amount of postage ever sold by the meter and the amount of credit remaining in it, all protected with a digital signature. The private signature key is kept in the meter's processor while its corresponding public signature verification key is kept in a Postal Service directory, indexed by the meter serial number. In this way, postal inspectors can sample mail in bulk at sorting offices, checking that each item is not only franked but on a logical route from its ostensible source to its destination.

The USA introduced the technology in 2000, with Germany next in 2004 and Canada in 2006; other countries are moving to follow suit. By 2006, the USA had about 450,000 digital meters out of a total market of 1.6 million, and it's expected that digital devices will have taken over completely by 2012. Also, by 2006, all U.S. postal facilities had the scanners needed to read the new indicia, of which an example is illustrated in Figure 12.5 below.

Such indicia can be produced by postage meters that are drop-in replacements for the old-fashioned devices; you weigh a letter, frank it, and get billed at the end of the month. You don't have to take the meter in to be read though, as that can be done over the Internet for a credit meter, while if you buy a prepayment meter you replenish it by phoning a call center and buying a magic number with your credit card. This works in much the same way as the prepayment electricity meters discussed earlier in this chapter. The tamper-resistance is used to implement what's in effect prepaid digital cash (or preauthorized digital credit) that's kept in the meter on the customer's premises.

Indicia can also be produced without any special equipment locally; you can buy a stamp over the Internet by simply specifying the sender and destination postal codes. This facility, 'online postage', is aimed at small businesses and people working from home who don't send enough mail for it to be worth their while buying a meter. Both metered and online postage are cheaper than stamps to distribute. Also, it becomes possible to manage the system much better, by tracking volumes and profitability of mail down to local level. This matters as many countries' postal systems are deregulated and open up to competition. And despite predictions that email would displace physical mail, post volumes continue to grow by 1% a year, and it turns out that households with broadband actually receive more post.

Figure 12.5: One of the new formats for U.S. postal meters (courtesy of Symbol Technologies)

So, all told, digital postal meters offer more flexibility to both users and postal services than the old analogue ones. But what about security?

One way of looking at postage meters is that they're a slight extension of the utility metering model. There is a tamper-resistant processor, either in the meter itself, or attached to a web server in the case of online postage; this has a value counter and a crypto key. It dispenses value, by creating indicia in the requested denominations, until the value counter is exhausted. It then requires replenishment via a cryptographically-protected message from a control unit higher up in the chain. There are some additional features in each case. Many postage meters include a 'Clark-Wilson' feature whereby the value counter actually consist of two counters, an Ascending Register (AR) containing the total value ever dispensed by the meter, and a Descending Register (DR) indicating the remaining credit. The balancing control is $AR + DR = TS$, the 'total setting', that is, the total of all the sales made by or authorised for that device. If the balance fails, the meter locks up and can only be accessed by inspectors.

An alternative way of looking at postage meters is that they constitute a distributed mint. In Sir Rowland Hill's original British postage system, the penny black stamps were printed at the mint; and postage engineers to this day refer to the step of generating an indicium as 'minting', whether it's done in a tamper-resistant processor in a meter or in an online server. These systems can provide a lot of useful experience for anyone wanting to design novel payment and e-money protocols.

The full threat model includes stolen postage meters, meters that have been tampered with to provide free postage, genuine meters used by unauthorised people, mail pieces with indicia of insufficient value to cover the weight and service class, and straightforward copies of valid indicia. Various sampling and other tests are used to control these risks. Subtleties include how you deal with features like certified mail and reply mail. There are also national differences on matters ranging from which authentication algorithms are used to what sort of usage data the meters have to upload back to the postal service.

One interesting development is that, as operators get real experience of digital postal metering, the industry is moving away from the initial design of using digital signatures to one of using message authentication codes. Signatures appealed because they were elegant; but in real life, signature verification is expensive, and has also turned out to be unnecessary. Equipment at major sorting offices must process thousands of mail pieces a minute, and even using low-exponent RSA, this entails a lot of computation. One argument for signatures was that indicia could be verified even when central servers are offline; but in real operations, postal services usually verify indicia as an offline batch operation. This means that forged mail pieces go through initially and are only intercepted once a pattern of abuse emerges. Once the verification is done offline, this can just as easily be MAC verification as signature verification. (The central servers have hardware security modules with master keys that were diversified to a MAC key in each meter.) It turns out that only two digits of the MAC are needed, as this is enough to detect any systematic abuse before it becomes significant [328].

The most recent optimisation is for the postal service not to do any cryptography at all, but to contract it out to the meter vendors. This in turn means that indicia are verified only in the home postal system, as overseas systems will often use different vendors. (So if you want to bribe a postal employee to let a few tons of junk mail into the system, the place to do it is now at a border crossing.) The upshot of the move away from public-key cryptography is a diversity of architectures, and sometimes multiple architectures in one country. Canada, for example, uses both signatures and MACs on its indicia.

How stuff actually breaks in real life is — as always — instructive. In the German post office's 'Stampit' scheme, a user buys 'smart pdf' files that contact the post office to say they're being printed, without any interaction with the user or her software. If the paper jams, or the printer is out of toner, then tough. So users arrange to photocopy the stamp, or to copy it to a file from which it can be printed again if need be. The UK system has learnt from this: although a stamp is grey-listed when a user PC phones home and says it's been printed, the grey doesn't turn to black until the stamp appears at the sorting office. The difference in syntax is subtle: the German system tried to stop you printing the stamp more than once, while the British system more realistically tries to stop you using it more than once [592].

All told, moving to digital postal meters involves a nontrivial investment, but enables much better control than was possible in the old days, when postal inspectors had to refer to paper records of mechanical meter readings. The hardware tamper-resistance also facilitates prepayment business models that extend the service's scope to many more customers and that also improve a service's cash flow and credit control. Unlike the case of digital tachographs, digital postal meters appear to be a success story.

12.5   Summary

Many security systems are concerned one way or another with monitoring or metering some aspect of the environment. They range from utility meters to taxi meters, tachographs, and postal meters. We'll come across further metering and payment systems in later chapters, ranging from the mechanisms used to stop printer cartridges working once they have printed a certain number of pages, to prepay scratch cards for mobile phone use, which may be the world's largest application-specific payment mechanism.

Many monitoring, metering and payment systems are being redesigned as the world moves from analogue to digital technology. Some of the redesigns are a success, and others aren't. The new digital prepayment electricity meters have been a success, and are being introduced around the developing world as an enabling technology that lets utility companies sell power to people who don't even have addresses, let alone credit ratings. Digital tachographs have been much less impressive; they just do what the old analogue systems did, but less well. Our third example, postage meters, appear to be a success.

As with burglar alarms, the protection of these systems is tied up with dependability; if you're designing such a thing, you have to think long and hard about what sort of service denial attacks are possible on system components. Key management can be an issue, especially in low cost widely distributed systems where a central key management facility can't be justified or an adequate base of trustworthy personnel doesn't exist. Systems may have to deal with numerous mutually suspicious parties, and must often be implemented on the cheapest possible microcontrollers. Many of them are routinely in the hands of the opponent. And there are all sorts of application-level subtleties that had better be understood if you want your design to succeed.

Research Problems

We're gradually acquiring a set of worked examples of secure embedded metering, thanks to the kinds of systems described here. We don't yet have a really general set of tools for building them. At the component level, we have crypto algorithms as seen in Chapter 5, protocols as described in Chapter 3, security policies like Clark-Wilson which I described in Chapter 10, and tamper resistant processors, which I'll describe later. However we don't have many concepts, abstractions, or middleware that help us pull these components together into larger building blocks. Although the mechanisms (and products) developed for automatic teller machine networks can be adapted (and are), much of the design work has to be redone and the end result often has vulnerabilities. Top level standards for ways in which crypto and other mechanisms can be built into a range of monitoring and ticketing systems might save engineers a lot of effort. Meanwhile we have to rely on case histories like those presented here. Metering applications are particularly useful because of the pervasive mutual mistrust caused not just by competing commercial entities but by the presence of dishonest staff at every level, as well as dishonest customers; and the fact that most of the equipment is in the custody of the attackers.

Again, there are questions for the security economist, and the business school researchers. Why did some digitisations of existing metering systems work well (utilities, postage) while others were much less impressive (tachographs)? Why were some disruptive, in that new entrants successfully challenged the previous incumbent suppliers, while in other cases (such as postage) the existing suppliers managed the transition to better digital systems and largely saw off competition from dotcom startups?

Further Reading

Prepayment electricity meters are described in [59]. Tachographs are written up in [45]; other papers relevant to transport appear in the annual ESCAR conference on electronic security in cars. The early work on postal meters is in [1265] and the U.S. regulations can be found in [894]. However by far the most detailed exposition of postage meter security is in a book written by Gerrit Bleumer, a scientist at Francotyp-Postalia that took a leading role in the program [190].

CHAPTER 13

Nuclear Command and Control

In Germany and Turkey they viewed scenes that were particularly distressing. On the runway stood a German (or Turkish) quick-reaction alert airplane loaded with nuclear weapons and with a foreign pilot in the cockpit. The airplane was ready to take off at the earliest warning, and the nuclear weapons were fully operational. The only evidence of U.S. control was a lonely 18-year-old sentry armed with a carbine and standing on the tarmac. When the sentry at the German airfield was asked how he intended to maintain control of the nuclear weapons should the pilot suddenly decide to scramble (either through personal caprice or through an order from the German command circumventing U.S. command), the sentry replied that he would shoot the pilot; Agnew directed him to shoot the bomb.

— Jerome Wiesner, reporting to President
Kennedy on nuclear arms command
and control after the cuban crisis

13.1 Introduction

The catastrophic harm that could result from the unauthorized use of a nuclear weapon, or from the proliferation of nuclear technology to unsuitable states or substate groups, has led the U.S. and other nuclear powers to spend colossal amounts of money protecting not just nuclear warheads but also the supporting infrastructure, industry and materials. The growing concern about global warming makes nuclear protection all the more critical: how do we build new nuclear power stations without greatly increasing the risk that bad people get hold of weapons or fissile materials?

A surprising amount of nuclear security know-how has been published. In fact, severe limits have been placed on how much could be kept secret even if this was thought desirable. Many countries are capable of producing nuclear weapons but have decided not to (Japan, Australia, Switzerland, . . .) and so maintain controls on nuclear materials in a civilian context. Much of the real force of nonproliferation is cultural, built over the years through diplomacy and through the restraint of nuclear powers who since 1945 forebore use of these weapons even when facing defeat at the hands of non-nuclear states. The culture is backed by international nonproliferation agreements, such as the Convention on the Physical Protection of Nuclear Material [640], enforced by the International Atomic Energy Agency (IAEA).

Eleven tons of plutonium are produced by civil reactors each year, and if the human race is to rely on nuclear power long-term then we'll be burning it in reactors as well as just making it as a side-effect of burning uranium. So ways have to be found to guard the stuff, and these have to inspire international confidence — not just between governments but from an increasingly sceptical public[1].

So a vast range of security technology has spun off from the nuclear program. The U.S. Department of Energy weapons laboratories — Sandia, Lawrence Livermore and Los Alamos — have worked for two generations to make nuclear weapons and materials as safe as can be achieved, using almost unlimited budgets. I've already mentioned some of their more pedestrian spin-offs, from the discovery that passwords of more than twelve digits were not usable under battlefield conditions to high-end burglar alarm systems. The trick of wrapping an optical fiber round the devices to be protected and using interference effects to detect a change in length of less than a micron, is also one of theirs — it was designed to loop round the warheads in an armoury and alarm without fail if any of them are moved.

In later chapters, we'll see still more technology of nuclear origin. For example, iris recognition — the most accurate system known for biometric identification of individuals — was developed using U.S. Department of Energy funds to control entry to the plutonium store, and much of the expertise in tamper-resistance and tamper-sensing technology originally evolved to prevent the abuse of stolen weapons or control devices. The increased tension since 9/11 has led to further spread of controls, especially once it was realised that for terrorist purposes it isn't necessary to get fissile materials like plutonium or uranium-235. A 'dirty bomb' — a device that would disperse radioactive material over a city block — is also a real threat, and one that jihadists have talked about. It might not kill anyone but it could lead to panic, and in a financial center it could cause great economic damage. For example, in March 2007, GAO investigators set up a bogus company and got a license from the Nuclear Regulatory Commission authorizing them to buy isotopes with which they could have built such a radiological dispersion device. What's

---

[1]For example, the British government was seriously embarrassed in 2007 when its safety arrangements for its 100-ton plutonium stockpile were criticised by eminent scientists [1089].

more, the license was printed on ordinary paper; the investigators altered it to change the quantity of material they were allowed to buy, then used it to order dozens of moisture density gauges containing americium-241 and cesium-137 [757]. This incident suggests that materials control may spread quite widely in the economy, and it may involve the wider deployment of many of the technologies described in this book.

Nuclear safety continually teaches us lessons about the limits of assurance. For example, it's tempting to assume that if a certain action that you don't want to happen has a probability of 1 in 10 of happening through human error, then by getting five different people to check, you can reduce the probability to 1 in 100,000. The U.S. Air Force thought so too. Yet in October 2007, six U.S. hydrogen bombs went missing for 36 hours after a plane taking cruise missiles from Minot Air Force Base in North Dakota to Barksdale in Louisiana was mistakenly loaded with six missiles armed with live warheads. This was supposed to be prevented by the handlers inspecting all the missiles in the storage area and checking them against a schedule (which was out of date), by ground crew waiting for the inspection to finish before moving any missiles, (they didn't), by ground crew inspecting the missiles (they didn't look in little glass portholes to see whether the warheads were real or dummy), by the driver calling in the identification numbers to a control center (nobody there bothered to check), and finally by the navigator during his preflight check (he didn't look at the wing with the live missiles). The plane took off, flew to Louisiana, landed, and sat unguarded on the runway for nine hours before the ground crew there arrived to unload the missiles and discovered they were live [127, 380]. This illustrates one of the limits to shared control. People will rely on others and slack off — a lesson also known in the world of medical safety. Indeed, in the USAF case it turned out that the airmen had replaced the official procedures with an 'informal' schedule of their own. So how can you design systems that don't fail in this way?

In this chapter I'm going to describe the nuclear safety environment and some of the tricks that might still find applications (or pose threats) elsewhere. This chapter has been assembled from public sources — but even from the available material there are useful lessons to be drawn.

13.2   The Evolution of Command and Control

The first atomic bomb to be used in combat was the 'Little Boy' dropped on Hiroshima. It came with three detonators, and the weapons officer was supposed to replace green dummy ones with red live ones once the plane was airborne. However, a number of heavily loaded B-29s had crashed on takeoff from Tinian, the base that was used. The Enola Gay weapon officer, Navy Captain Deak Parsons, reckoned that if the Enola Gay, crashed, the primer might explode, detonating the bomb and wiping out the island. So he spent the day before the raid practicing removing and reinstalling the primer — a gunpowder charge about the size of a loaf of bread — so he could install it after takeoff instead.

Doctrine has rather moved away from improvization of weapon safety procedures in the field. If anything we're at the other extreme now, with mechanisms and procedures tested and drilled and exercised and analysed by multiple experts from different agencies. It has of course been an evolutionary process. When weapons started being carried in single-seat tactical aircraft in the 1950s, and also started being slung under the wings rather than in a bomb bay, it was no longer possible for someone to manually insert a bag of gunpowder. There was a move to combination locks: the pilot would arm the bomb after takeoff by entering a 6-digit code into a special keypad with a wired-seal lid. This enabled some measure of control; the pilot might only receive the code once airborne. However both the technical and procedural controls in early strategic systems were primitive.

13.2.1 The Kennedy Memorandum

The Cuban missile crisis changed all that. U.S. policymakers (and many others) suddenly became very concerned that a world war might start by accident. Hundreds of U.S. nuclear weapons were kept in allied countries such as Greece and Turkey, which were not particularly stable and occasionally fought with each other. These weapons were protected by only token U.S. custodial forces, so there was no physical reason why the weapons couldn't be seized in time of crisis. There was also some worry about possible unauthorized use of nuclear weapons by U.S. commanders — for example, if a local commander under pressure felt that 'if only they knew in Washington how bad things were here, they would let us use the bomb.' These worries were confirmed by three emergency studies carried out by presidential science adviser Jerome Wiesner. In [1223] we find the passage quoted at the head of this chapter.

President Kennedy's response was National Security Action Memo no. 160 [153]. This ordered that America's 7,000 nuclear weapons then dispersed to NATO commands should be got under positive U.S. control using technical means, whether they were in the custody of U.S. or allied forces. Although this policy was sold to Congress as protecting U.S. nuclear weapons from foreigners, the worries about a psychotic 'Dr Strangelove' were also real: they were actually at the top of Wiesner's list, although of course they were downplayed politically.

The Department of Energy was already working on safety devices for nuclear weapons. The basic principle was that a unique aspect of the environment had to be sensed before the weapon would arm. For example, missile warheads and some free-fall bombs had to experience zero gravity, while artillery shells had to experience an acceleration of thousands of G. There was one exception:

atomic demolition munitions. These are designed to be taken to their targets by ground troops and detonated using time fuses. There appears to be no scope for a unique environmental sensor to prevent accidental or malicious detonation.

The solution then under development was a secret arming code that activated a solenoid safe lock buried deep in the plutonium pit at the heart of the weapon. The main engineering problem was maintenance. When the lock was exposed, for example to replace the power supply, the code might become known. So it was not acceptable to have the same code in every weapon. Group codes were one possibility — firing codes shared by only a small batch of warheads.

Following the Kennedy memo, it was proposed that all nuclear bombs should be protected using code locks, and that there should be a 'universal unlock' action message that only the president or his legal successors could give. The problem was to find a way to translate this code securely to a large number of individual firing codes, each of which enabled a small batch of weapons. The problem became worse in the 1960s and 1970s when the doctrine changed from massive retaliation to 'measured response'. Instead of arming all nuclear weapons or none, the President now needed to be able to arm selected batches (such as 'all nuclear artillery in Germany'). This clearly starts to lead us to a system of some complexity, especially when we realise that we need disarming codes too, for maintenance purposes, and that we need some means of navigating the trade-offs between weapons safety and effective command.

13.2.2   Authorization, Environment, Intent

So the deep question was the security policy that nuclear safety systems, and command systems, should enforce. What emerged was the rule of 'authorization, environment, intent'. For a warhead to detonate, three conditions must be met.

Authorization: the use of the weapon in question must have been authorized by the *national command authority* (i.e., the President and his lawful successors in office).

Environment: the weapon must have sensed the appropriate aspect of the environment. (With atomic demolition munitions, this requirement is replaced by the use of a special container.)

Intent: the officer commanding the aircraft, ship or other unit must unambiguously command the weapon's use.

In early systems, 'authorization' meant the entry into the device of a four-digit authorization code.

The means of signalling 'intent' depended on the platform. Aircraft typically use a six-digit arming or 'use control' code. The command consoles for intercontinental ballistic missiles are operated by two officers, each of whom must enter and turn a key to launch the rocket. Whatever the implementation, the common concept is that there must be a unique signal; the effectively 22 bits derived from a six-digit code is believed to be a good tradeoff between a number of factors from usability to minimising the risk of accidental arming [908].

13.3   Unconditionally Secure Authentication

Nuclear command and control led to the development of a theory of one-time authentication codes. These are similar in concept to the test keys which were invented to protect telegraphic money transfers, in that a keyed transformation is applied to the message in order to yield a short authentication code, also known as an *authenticator* or *tag*. As the keys are only used once, authentication codes can be made unconditionally secure. So they do for authentication what the one-time pad does for confidentiality.

Recall from Chapter 5, 'Cryptography', that while a computationally secure system could be broken by some known computation and depends on this being too hard, the perfect security provided by the one-time pad is independent of the computational resources available to the attacker.

There are differences though between authentication codes and the one-time pad. As the authentication code is of finite length, it's always possible for the opponent to guess it, and the probability of a successful guess might be different depending on whether the opponent was trying to guess a valid message from scratch (*impersonation*) or modify an existing valid message so as to get another one (*substitution*).

An example should make this clear. Suppose a commander has agreed an authentication scheme with a subordinate under which an instruction is to be encoded as a three digit number from 000 to 999. The instruction may have two values: 'Attack Russia' and 'Attack China'. One of these will be encoded as an even number, and the other by an odd number: which is which will be part of the secret key. The authenticity of the message will be vouched for by making its remainder, when divided by 337, equal to a secret number which is the second part of the key.

Suppose the key is that:

■ 'Attack Russia' codes to even numbers, and 'Attack China' to odd

■ an authentic message is one which has the remainder 12 when divided by 337.

So 'Attack Russia' is '686' (or '12') and 'Attack China' is '349'.

An enemy who has taken over the communications channel between the commander and the subordinate, and who knows the scheme but not the key, has a probability of only 1 in 337 of successfully impersonating the commander.

However, once he sees a valid message (say '12' for 'Attack Russia'), then he can easily change it to the other by adding 337, and so (provided he understood what it meant) he can send the missiles to the other country. So the probability of a successful substitution attack in this case is 1.

As with computationally secure authentication, the unconditional variety can provide message secrecy or not: it might work like a block cipher, or like a MAC on a plaintext message. Similarly, it can use an arbitrator or not. One might even want multiple arbitrators, so that they don't have to be trusted individually. If the first arbitrator wrongfully finds in favor of the cheated party, then a multi-arbitrator scheme lets his victim denounce him. Schemes may combine unconditional with computational security. For example, an unconditional code without secrecy could have computationally secure secrecy added by simply enciphering the message and the authenticator using a conventional cipher system.

Authentication is in some sense the dual of coding in that in the latter, given an incorrect message, we want to find the nearest correct message efficiently; in the former, we want finding a correct message to be impossible unless you've seen it already or are authorized to construct it. And just as the designer of an error-correcting code wants the shortest length of code for a given error recovery capability, so the designer of an authentication code wants to minimize the key length required to achieve a given bound on the deception probabilities.

One application that's worth noting is the new GCM mode of operation for block ciphers, described briefly in Chapter 5, 'Cryptography'. In effect this uses the user-supplied key to generate an unconditionally-secure authentication code on the plaintext; it's just a polynomial function of the key and the plaintext. Combined with the counter-mode encryption of the plaintext, this gives an authenticated encryption mode that requires only one pass through the block cipher, rather than the two passes required for CBC plus MAC.

The authentication terminology used in civil and military applications is slightly different [1172]. More importantly, the threat models are different. Soldiers are in general not too worried about non-repudiation — except when enforcing treaties with other countries, which might later repudiate a message claiming that the key had been leaked by a 'defector'. In business, the majority of frauds are carried out by insiders, so shared control systems are the main issue when designing authentication mechanisms.

Quite a few more details have to be fixed before you have a fully-functioning command and control system. You have to work out ways to build the key control mechanisms into warheads in ways that will resist disarming or dismantling by people without disarming keys. You need mechanisms for generating keys and embedding them in weapons and control devices. You have to think of all the ways an attacker might social-engineer maintenance staff, and what you'll do to forestall this. And there is one element of cryptographic complexity. How do you introduce an element of one-wayness, so that a maintenance man who disarms a bomb to change the battery doesn't end up knowing the universal unlock code? You need to be able to derive the code to unlock this one specific device from the universal unlock, but not vice-versa. What's more, you need serviceable mechanisms for recovery and re-keying in the event that a crisis causes you to authorize some weapons, that thankfully are stood down rather than used. U.S. systems now use public-key cryptography to implement this one-wayness, but you could also use one-way functions. In either case, you will end up with an interesting mix of unconditional and computational security.

13.4   Shared Control Schemes

The nuclear command and control business became even more complex with the concern, from the late 1970s, that a Soviet decapitation strike against the U.S. national command authority might leave the arsenal intact but useless. There was also concern that past a certain threshold of readiness, it wasn't sensible to assume that communications between the authority and field commanders could be maintained, because of the damage that electromagnetic pulse could do (and other possible attacks on communications).

The solution was found in another branch of cryptomathematics known as *secret sharing*, whose development it helped to inspire. The idea is that in time of tension a backup control system will be activated in which combinations of office holders or field commanders can jointly allow a weapon to be armed. Otherwise the problems of maintaining detailed central control of a large number of weapons would likely become insoluble. There was some precedent for this in submarine-launched ballistic missiles. These exist in part to provide a second-strike capability — that is, to take vengeance on a country that has destroyed your country with a first strike. In such circumstances it is impossible for the submarine commander to be left unable to arm his weapons unless he gets a code from the President. So arming material is kept in safes under the control of the boat's officers, along with orders from the command authority on the circumstances in which weapons are to be used.

Now there is an obvious way to do shared control — just give half of the authentication key to each of two people. The drawback is that you need twice the length of key, assuming that the original security parameter must apply even if one of them is suborned. An alternative approach is to give each of them a number and have the two of them add up to the key. This is how keys for automatic teller machines are managed[2]. But this still may not be

---

[2]Combining keys using addition or exclusive-or turns out to be a bad idea for ATMs as it opens up the system to attacks that I'll discuss later under the rubric of 'API security'. However in the context of unconditionally-secure authentication codes, addition is often OK.

enough in command applications, as one cannot be sure that the personnel operating the equipment will consent, without discussion or query, to unleash Armageddon. So a more general approach was invented independently by Blakley and Shamir in 1979 [181, 1146]. Their basic idea is illustrated in the following diagram (Figure 13.1).

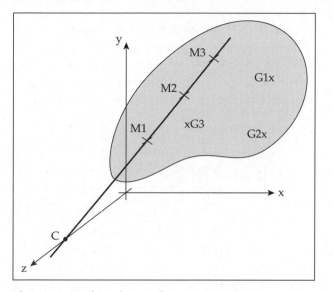

Figure 13.1: Shared control using geometry

Suppose the rule Britain wants to enforce if the Prime Minister is assassinated is that a weapon can be armed either by any two cabinet ministers, or by any three generals, or by a cabinet minister and two generals. To implement this, let the point C on the z axis be the unlock code that has to be supplied to the weapon. We now draw a line at random through C and give each cabinet minister a random point on the line. Now any two of them can together work out the coordinates of the line and find the point C where it meets the z axis. Similarly, we embed the line in a random plane and give each general a random point on the plane. Now any three generals, or two generals plus a minister, can reconstruct the plane and thence the firing code C.

By generalizing this simple construction to geometries of n dimensions, or to general algebraic structures rather than lines and planes, this technique enables weapons, commanders and options to be linked together with a complexity limited only by the available bandwidth. An introduction to secret sharing can be found in [1226] and a more detailed exposition in [1173]. This inspired the development of threshold signature schemes, as described in Chapter 5, 'Cryptography', and can be used in products that enforce a rule such as 'Any two vice-presidents of the company may sign a check'.

As with authentication codes, there is a difference between civil and military views of shared secrets. In the typical military application, two-out-of-n control is used; n must be large enough that at least two of the keyholders will be ready and able to do the job, despite combat losses. Many details need attention. For example, the death of a commander shouldn't give his deputy both halves of the key, and there are all sorts of nitty-gritty issues such as who shoots whom when (on the same side).

In many civilian applications, however, many insiders may conspire to break your system. The classic example is pay-TV where a pirate may buy several dozen subscriber cards and reverse engineer them for their secrets. So the pay-TV operator wants a system that's robust against multiple compromised subscribers. I'll talk about this *traitor tracing* problem more in the chapter on copyright.

13.5   Tamper Resistance and PALs

In modern weapons the solenoid safe locks have been superseded by *prescribed action links*, more recently renamed *permissive action links* (either way, PALs), which are used to protect most U.S. nuclear devices. A summary of the published information about PALs can be found in [153]. PAL development started in about 1961, but deployment was slow. Even twenty years later, about half the U.S. nuclear warheads in Europe still used four-digit code locks[3]. As more complex arming options were introduced, the codes increased in length from 4 to 6 and finally to 12 digits. Devices started to have multiple codes, with separate 'enable' and 'authorize' commands and also the ability to change codes in the field (to recover from false alarms).

The PAL system is supplemented by various coded switch systems and operational procedures, and in the case of weapons such as atomic demolition munitions, which are not complex enough for the PAL to be made inaccessible in the core of the device, the weapon is also stored in tamper sensing containers called PAPS (for *prescribed action protective system*). Other mechanisms used to prevent accidental detonation include the deliberate weakening of critical parts of the detonator system, so that they will fail if exposed to certain abnormal environments.

Whatever combination of systems is used, there are penalty mechanisms to deny a thief the ability to obtain a nuclear yield from a stolen weapon. These mechanisms vary from one weapon type to another but include gas bottles

---

[3]Bruce Blair says that Strategic Air Command resisted the new doctrine and kept Minuteman authorization codes at '00000000' until 1977, lying to a succession of Presidents and Defense Secretaries [180]. Other researchers have claimed this was not the authorization code but just the use control code.

to deform the pit and hydride the plutonium in it, shaped charges to destroy components such as neutron generators and the tritium boost, and asymmetric detonation that results in plutonium dispersal rather than yield. Indeed most weapons have a self-destruct procedure that will render them permanently inoperative, without yield, if enemy capture is threatened. It is always a priority to destroy the code. It is assumed that a renegade government prepared to deploy 'terrorists' to steal a shipment of bombs would be prepared to sacrifice some of the bombs (and some technical personnel) to obtain a single serviceable weapon.

To perform authorized maintenance, the tamper protection must be disabled, and this requires a separate unlock code. The devices that hold the various unlock codes — for servicing and firing — are themselves protected in similar ways to the weapons.

The assurance target is summarized in [1223]:

> It is currently believed that even someone who gained possession of such a weapon, had a set of drawings, and enjoyed the technical capability of one of the national laboratories would be unable to successfully cause a detonation without knowing the code.

Meeting such an ambitious goal requires a very substantial effort. There are several examples of the level of care needed:

- after tests showed that 1 mm chip fragments survived the protective detonation of a control device carried aboard airborne command posts, the software was rewritten so that all key material was stored as two separate components, which were kept at addresses more than 1 mm apart on the chip surface;

- the 'football', the command device carried around behind the President, is said to be as thick as it is because of fear that shaped charges might be used to disable its protective mechanisms. (This may or may not be an urban myth.) Shaped charges can generate a plasma jet with a velocity of 8000m/s, which could in theory be used to disable tamper sensing circuitry. So some distance may be needed to give the alarm circuit enough time to zeroize the code memory.

This care must extend to many details of implementation and operation. The weapons testing process includes not just independent verification and validation, but hostile 'black hat' penetration attempts by competing agencies. Even then, all practical measures are taken to prevent access by possible opponents. The devices (both munition and control) are defended in depth by armed forces; there are frequent zero-notice challenge inspections; and staff may be made to re-sit the relevant examinations at any time of the day or night.

I'll discuss tamper resistance in much more detail in a later chapter, as it's becoming rather widely used in applications from pay-TV to bank cards. However, tamper resistance, secret sharing and one-time authenticators aren't the only technologies to have benefitted from the nuclear industry's interest. There are more subtle system lessons too.

13.6   Treaty Verification

A variety of verification systems are used to monitor compliance with nuclear nonproliferation treaties. For example, the IAEA and the U.S. Nuclear Regulatory Commission (NRC) monitor fissile materials in licensed civilian power reactors and other facilities.

An interesting example comes from the tamper resistant seismic sensor devices designed to monitor the Comprehensive Test Ban Treaty [1170]. The goal in this application was to have sufficiently sensitive sensors emplaced in each signatory's test sites that any violation of the treaty (such as by testing too large a device) can be detected with high probability. The tamper sensing here is fairly straightforward: the seismic sensors are fitted in a steel tube and inserted into a drill hole that is backfilled with concrete. The whole assembly is so solid that the seismometers themselves can be relied upon to detect tampering events with a fairly high probability. This physical protection is reinforced by random challenge inspections.

The authentication process becomes somewhat more complex because one has to make an assumption of pervasive deceit. Because of the lack of a third party trusted by both sides, and because the quantity of seismic data being transmitted is of the order of 10^8 bits per day, a digital signature scheme (RSA) was used instead of one-time authentication tags. But this is only part of the answer. One party might, for example, disavow a signed message by saying that the official responsible for generating it had defected, and so the signature was forged. So it is necessary for keys to be generated within the seismic package itself once it has been sealed by both sides. Also, if one side builds the equipment, the other will suspect it of having hidden functionality. Several protocols were proposed of the *cut and choose* variety, in which one party would produce several devices of which the other party would dismantle a sample for inspection. A number of these issues have since resurfaced in electronic commerce. (Many system designers since could have saved themselves a lot of grief if they'd read Gus Simmons' account of these treaty monitoring systems in [1170].)

13.7   What Goes Wrong

Despite the huge amounts of money invested in developing high-tech protection mechanisms, nuclear control and safety systems appear to suffer from just the same kind of design bugs, implementation blunders and careless operations as any others.

Britain's main waste reprocessing plant at Sellafield, which handles plutonium in multiple-ton quantities, has been plagued with a series of scandals. Waste documentation has been forged; radiation leaks have been covered up; workers altered entry passes so they could bring their cars into restricted areas; and there have been reports of sabotage. The nuclear police force only managed to clear up 17 out of 158 thefts and 3 out of 20 cases of criminal damage [776]. The situation in the former Soviet Union appears to be very much worse. A survey of nuclear safekeeping describes how dilapidated their security mechanisms have become following the collapse of the USSR, with fissile materials occasionally appearing on the black market and whistleblowers being prosecuted [644].

There are also a number of problems relating to the reliability of communications and other systems under attack. How can communication between the President and many sites round the world be assured? I'll discuss these later in the chapter on 'Electronic and Information Warfare'.

There have also been a number of interesting high-tech security failures. One example is a possible attack discovered on a nuclear arms reduction treaty which led to the development of a new branch of cryptomathematics — the study of subliminal channels — and is relevant to later discussions of copyright marking and steganography.

The story is told in [1176]. During the Carter administration, the USA proposed a deal with the USSR under which each side would cooperate with the other to verify the number of intercontinental ballistic missiles. In order to protect U.S. Minuteman missiles against a possible Soviet first strike, it was proposed that 100 missiles be moved randomly around a field of 1000 silos by giant trucks, which were designed so that observers couldn't determine whether they were moving a missile or not. So the Soviets would have had to destroy all 1,000 silos to make a successful first strike, and in the context of the proposed arms controls this was thought impractical.

This raised the interesting problem of how to assure the Soviets that there were at most 100 missiles in the silo field, but without letting them find out which silos were occupied. The proposed solution was that the silos would have a Russian sensor package that would detect the presence or absence of a missile, sign this single bit of information, and send it via a U.S. monitoring facility to Moscow. The sensors would be packaged and randomly shuffled by the USA before emplacement, so that the Russians could not correlate 'full' or 'empty' signals with particular silos. The catch was that only this single bit of information could be sent; if the Russians could smuggle any more information into the message, they could quickly locate the full silos — as it would take only ten bits of address information to specify a single silo in the field. (There were many other security requirements to prevent either side cheating, or falsely accusing the other of cheating: for more details, see [1175].)

To see how subliminal channels work, consider the Digital Signature Algorithm described in the chapter on cryptography. The system-wide values are a prime number p, a prime number q dividing $p - 1$, and a generator g of a subgroup of F_p^* of order q. The signature on the message M is r, s where $r = (g^k$ (mod p)) (mod q), and k is a random session key. The mapping from k to r is fairly random, so a signer who wishes to hide ten bits of information in this signature for covert transmission to an accomplice can firstly agree a convention about how the bits will be hidden (such as 'bits 72–81') and secondly, try out one value of k after another until the resulting value r has the desired value in the agreed place.

This could have caused a disastrous failure of the security protocol as there had been an agreement that the monitoring messages would be authenticated first with a Russian scheme, using Russian equipment, and then by an American scheme using American equipment. Had the Russians specified a signature scheme like DSA then they could have leaked the location of the occupied silos and acquired the capability to make a first strike against the Minuteman force.

In the end, the 'missile shell game', as it had become known in the popular press, wasn't used. The cooling of relations following the 1980 election put things on hold. Eventually with the medium range ballistic missile treaty (MRBM) statistical methods were used. The Russians could say 'we'd like to look at the following 20 silos' and they would be uncapped for the Soviet satellites to take a look. With the end of the Cold War, inspections have become much more intimate with inspection flights in manned aircraft, with observers from both sides, rather than satellites.

Still, the discovery of subliminal channels was significant. Ways in which they might be abused include putting HIV status, or the fact of a felony conviction, into a digital passport or identity card. Where this is unacceptable, and the card issuer isn't sufficiently trusted not to do it, then the remedy is to use a completely deterministic signature scheme such as RSA instead of one that uses a random session key like DSA.

13.8   Secrecy or Openness?

Finally, the nuclear industry provides a nice case history of secrecy. In the 1930s, physicists from many countries had freely shared the scientific ideas that led to the development of the bomb, but after the 'atomic spies' (Fuchs, the Rosenbergs and others) had leaked the designs of the Hiroshima and Nagasaki devices to the Soviet Union, things swung to the other extreme. The U.S. adopted a policy that atomic knowledge was *born classified*. That meant that if you were within U.S. jurisdiction and had an idea relevant to nuclear weapons, you had to keep it secret regardless of whether you held a security clearance or even worked in the nuclear industry. This was clearly in tension with the Constitution. Things have greatly relaxed since then, as the protection issues were thought through in detail.

'We've a database in New Mexico that records the physical and chemical properties of plutonium at very high temperatures and pressures', a former head of U.S. nuclear security once told me. 'At what level should I classify that? Who's going to steal it, and will it do them any good? The Russians, they've got that data for themselves. The Israelis can figure it out. Gaddafi? What the hell will he do with it?'

As issues like this got worked though, a surprising amount of the technology has been declassified and sometimes published, at least in outline. Starting from early publication at scientific conferences of results on authentication codes and subliminal channels in the early 1980s, the benefits of public design review have been found to outweigh the possible advantage to an opponent of knowing broadly the system in use.

Many implementation details are kept secret, though; information that could facilitate sabotage, such as which of a facility's fifty buildings contains the alarm response force, gets marked *unclassified controlled nuclear information* (UCNI) adding yet another layer of complexity to the security policy model.

Yet the big picture is open (or so we're assured), and command and control technologies used to be explicitly offered to other states, including hostile ones like the USSR. The benefits of reducing the likelihood of an accidental war were considered to outweigh the possible benefits of secrecy. Post-9/11, it's clear that we'd rather have decent nuclear command and control systems in Pakistan rather than risk having one of their weapons used against us by some mid-level officer suffering from an attack of religious zealotry. This is a modern reincarnation of Kerckhoffs' doctrine, first put forward in the nineteenth century, that the security of a system must depend on its key, not on its design remaining obscure [713].

Indeed, the nuclear lessons should be learned more widely. Post-9/11, a number of governments (including those of the UK and the European Union) are talking up the possibility of terrorists using biological weapons, and imposing various controls on research and teaching in bacteriology, virology, toxicology and indeed medicine. My faculty colleagues in these disciplines are deeply unimpressed. 'You just shouldn't worry about anthrax', one of the UK's top virologists told me. 'The real nasties are the things Mother Nature dreams up like HIV and SARS and bird flu. If these policies mean that there aren't any capable public health people in Khartoum next time a virus comes down the Nile, we'll be sorry'.

13.9   Summary

The control of nuclear weapons, and subsidiary activities from protecting the integrity of the national command system through physical security of nuclear facilities to monitoring international arms control treaties, has made a huge contribution to the development of security technology.

The rational decision that weapons and fissile material had to be protected almost regardless of the cost drove the development of a lot of mathematics and science that has found application elsewhere. The particular examples we've looked at in this chapter are authentication codes, shared control schemes and subliminal channels. There are other examples scattered through the rest of this book, from alarms to iris biometrics and from tamper-resistant electronic devices to seals.

Research Problems

The research problem I set at the end of this chapter in the first edition in 2001 was 'Find interesting applications for technologies developed in this area, such as authentication codes.' The recently standardised Galois Counter mode of operation is a pretty good response to that challenge. What else might there be?

Further Reading

As my own experience of this subject is rather indirect, being limited to working in the 1970s on the avionics of nuclear-capable aircraft, this chapter has been assembled from published sources. One of the best sources of public information on nuclear weapons is the Federation of American Scientists [460]. The rationale for the recent declassification of many nuclear arms technologies is presented in detail at [460]. Declassification issues are discussed in [1361], and the publicly available material on PALs has been assembled by Bellovin [153].

Simmons was a pioneer of authentication codes, shared control schemes and subliminal channels. His book [1172] remains the best reference for most of the technical material discussed in this chapter. A more concise introduction to both authentication and secret sharing can be found in Doug Stinson's textbook [1226].

Control failures in nuclear installations are documented in many places. The problems with Russian installations are discussed in [644]; U.S. nuclear safety is overseen by the Nuclear Regulatory Commission [976]; and shortcomings with UK installations are documented in the quarterly reports posted by the Health and Safety Executive [586].

CHAPTER 14

Security Printing and Seals

A seal is only as good as the man in whose briefcase it's carried.

— **Karen Spärck Jones**

*You can't make something secure if you don't
know how to break it.*

— **Marc Weber Tobias**

14.1   Introduction

Many computer systems rely to some extent on secure printing, packaging and seals to guarantee important aspects of their protection.

- Most security products can be defeated if a bad man can get at them — whether to patch them, damage them, or substitute them — before you install them. Seals, and tamper-evident packaging generally, can help with *trusted distribution*, that is, assuring the user that the product hasn't been tampered with since leaving the factory.

- Many software products get some protection against forgery using seals and packaging. They can at least raise the costs of large-scale forgery somewhat.

- We saw how monitoring systems, such as taxi meters, often use seals to make it harder for users to tamper with input. No matter how sophisticated the cryptography, a defeat for the seals can be a defeat for the system.

- I also discussed how contactless systems such as those used in the chips in passports and identity cards can be vulnerable to man-in-the-middle attacks. If you're scrutinising the ID of an engineer from one of your suppliers before you let him into your hosting centre, it can be a good idea to eyeball the ID as well as reading it electronically. If all you do is the latter, he might be relaying the transaction to somewhere else. So even with electronic ID cards, the security printing can still matter.

■ Many security tokens, such as smartcards, are difficult to make truly tamper proof. It may be feasible for the opponent to dismantle the device and probe out the content. A more realistic goal may be *tamper evidence* rather than tamper proofness: if someone dismantles their smartcard and gets the keys out, they should not be able to reassemble it into something that will pass close examination. Security printing can help here. If a bank smartcard really is tamper-evident, then the bank might tell its customers that disputes will only be entertained if they can produce the card intact. (Banks might not get away with this though, because consumer protection lawyers will demand that they deal fairly with honest customers who lose their cards or have them stolen).

Quite apart from these direct applications of printing and sealing technology, the ease with which modern color scanners and printers can be used to make passable forgeries has opened up another front. Banknote printers are now promoting digital protection techniques [178]. These include invisible copyright marks that can enable forgeries to be detected, can help vending machines recognise genuine currency, and set off alarms in image processing software if you try to scan or copy them [562]. Meanwhile, vendors of color copiers and printers embed forensic tracking codes in printout that contain the machine serial number, date and time [425]. So the digital world and the world of 'funny inks' are growing rapidly closer together.

14.2   History

Seals have a long and interesting history. In the chapter on banking systems, I discussed how bookkeeping systems had their origin in the clay tablets, or bullae, used by neolithic warehouse keepers in Mesopotamia as receipts for produce. Over 5000 years ago, the bulla system was adapted to resolve disputes by having the warehouse keeper bake the bulla in a clay envelope with his mark on it.

Seals were commonly used to authenticate documents in classical times and in ancient China. They were used in medieval Europe as a means of social control before paper came along; a carter would be given a lead seal at one tollbooth and hand it in at the next, while pilgrims would get lead tokens from shrines to prove that they had gone on pilgrimage (indeed, the young Gutenberg got his first break in business by inventing a way of embedding slivers of mirror in lead seals to prevent forgery and protect church revenues) [559]. Even after handwritten signatures had taken over as the principal authentication mechanism for letters, they lingered on as a secondary mechanism. Until the nineteenth century, letters were not placed in envelopes, but folded over several times and sealed using hot wax and a signet ring.

Seals are still the preferred authentication mechanism for important documents in China, Japan and Korea. Elsewhere, traces of their former importance survive in the company seals and notaries' seals affixed to important documents, and the national seals that some countries' heads of state apply to archival copies of legislation.

However, by the middle of the last century, their use with documents had become less important in the West than their use to authenticate packaging. The move from loose goods to packaged goods, and the growing importance of brands, created not just the potential for greater quality control but also the vulnerability that bad people might tamper with products. The USA suffered an epidemic of tampering incidents, particularly of soft drinks and medical products, leading to a peak of 235 reported cases in 1993 [699]. This helped push many manufacturers towards making products tamper-evident.

The ease with which software can be copied, and consumer resistance to technical copy-protection mechanisms from the mid 1980s, led software companies to rely increasingly on packaging to deter counterfeiters. That was just part of a much larger market in preventing the forgery of high value branded goods ranging from perfume and cigarettes through aircraft spares to pharmaceuticals. In short, huge amounts of money have poured into seals and other kinds of secure packaging. Unfortunately, most seals are still fairly easy to defeat.

Now the typical seal consists of a substrate with security printing, which is then glued or tied round the object being sealed. So we must first look at security printing. If the whole seal can be forged easily then no amount of glue or string is going to help.

14.3 Security Printing

The introduction of paper money into Europe by Napoleon in the early 1800s, and of other valuable documents such as bearer securities and passports, kicked off a battle between security printers and counterfeiters that exhibits many of the characteristics of a coevolution of predators and prey. Photography (1839) helped the attackers, then color printing and steel etching (1850s) the defenders. In recent years, the color copier and the cheap scanner have been countered by holograms and other optically variable devices. Sometimes the same people were involved on both sides, as when a government's intelligence services try to forge another government's passports — or even its currency, as both sides did in World War Two.

On occasion, the banknote designers succumb to the Titanic Effect, of believing too much in the latest technology, and place too much faith in some particular trick. An example comes from the forgery of British banknotes in the 1990s. These notes have a *window thread* — a metal strip through the paper that is about 1 mm wide and comes to the paper surface every 8 mm. So when you look at the note in reflected light, it appears to have a dotted metallic line running across it, but when you hold it up and view it through transmitted light, the metal strip is dark and solid. Duplicating this was thought to be hard. Yet a criminal gang came up with a beautiful hack. They used a cheap hot stamping process to lay down a metal strip on the surface of the paper, and then printed a pattern of solid bars over it using white ink to leave the expected metal pattern visible. They were found at their trial to have forged tens of millions of pounds' worth of notes over a period of several years [477]. (There was also a complacency issue; European bankers believe that forgers would go for the US dollar as it only had three colors at the time.)

14.3.1 Threat Model

As always we have to evaluate a protection technology in the context of a model of the threats. Broadly speaking, the threat can be from a properly funded organization (such as a government trying to forge another nation's banknotes), from a medium sized organization (whether a criminal gang forging several million dollars a month or a distributor forging labels on vintage wines), to amateurs using equipment they have at home or in the office.

In the banknote business, the big growth area in the last years of the twentieth century was amateur forgery. Knowledge had spread in the printing trade of how to manufacture high-quality forgeries of many banknotes, which one might have thought would increase the level of professional forgery. But the spread of high quality color scanners and printers has put temptation in the way of many people who would never have dreamed of getting into forgery in the days when it required messy wet inks. Amateurs used to be thought a minor nuisance, but since about 1997 or 1998 they have accounted for most of the forgeries detected in the USA (it varies from one country to another; most UK forgers use traditional litho printing while in Spain, like the USA, the inkjet printer has taken over [628]). Amateur forgers are hard to combat as there are many of them; they mostly work on such a small scale that their product takes a long time to come to the attention of authority; and they are less likely to have criminal records. The notes they produce are often not good enough to pass a bank teller, but are uttered in places such as dark and noisy nightclubs.

The industry distinguishes three different levels of inspection which a forged banknote or document may or may not pass [1279]:

1. a *primary* inspection is one performed by an untrained inexperienced person, such as a member of the public or a new cashier at a store. Often the primary inspector has no motivation, or even a negative motivation. If he gets a banknote that feels slightly dodgy, he may try to pass it on without looking at it closely enough to have to decide between becoming an accomplice or going to the hassle of reporting it;

2. a *secondary* inspection is one performed in the field by a competent and motivated person, such as an experienced bank teller in the case of banknotes or a trained manufacturer's inspector in the case of product labels. This person may have some special equipment such as an ultra-violet lamp, a pen with a chemical reagent, or even a scanner and a PC. However the equipment will be limited in both cost and bulk, and will be completely understood by serious counterfeiters;

3. a *tertiary* inspection is one performed at the laboratory of the manufacturer or the note issuing bank. The experts who designed the security printing (and perhaps even the underlying industrial processes) will be on hand, with substantial equipment and support.

The state of the security printing art can be summarised as follows. Getting a counterfeit past a primary inspection is usually easy, while getting it past tertiary inspection is usually impossible if the product and the inspection process have been competently designed. So secondary inspection is the battleground — except in a few applications such as banknote printing where attention is now being paid to the primary level. (There, the incentives are wrong, in that if I look closely at a banknote and find it's a forgery I'm legally bound to hand it in and lose the value.) The main limits on what sort of counterfeits can be detected by the secondary inspector in the field have to do with the bulk and the cost of the equipment needed.

14.3.2 Security Printing Techniques

Traditional security documents utilize a number of printing processes, including:

- *intaglio*, a process where an engraved pattern is used to press the ink on to the paper with great force, leaving a raised ink impression with high definition. This is often used for scroll work on banknotes and passports;

- *letterpress* in which the ink is rolled on raised type that is then pressed on to the page, leaving a depression. The numbers on banknotes are usually printed this way, often with numbers of different sizes and using different inks to prevent off-the-shelf numbering equipment being used;

- special printing presses, called *Simultan presses*, which transfer all the inks, for both front and back, to the paper simultaneously. The printing on front and back can therefore be accurately aligned; patterns can be printed partly on the front and partly on the back so that they match up perfectly when the note is held up to the light (*see-through register*). Reproducing this is believed to be hard on cheap color printing equipment. The Simultan presses also have the special ducting to make ink colors vary along the line (*rainbowing*);

- rubber stamps that are used to endorse documents, or to seal photographs to them;

- embossing and laminates that are also used to seal photographs, and on bank cards to push up the cost of forgery. Embossing can be physical, or use laser engraving techniques to burn a photo into an ID card;

- *watermarks* are an example of putting protection features in the paper. They are more translucent areas inserted into the paper by varying its thickness when it is manufactured. Many other special materials, such as fluorescent threads, are used for similar purposes. An extreme example is the Australian $10 note, which is printed on plastic and has a see-through window.

More modern techniques include:

- optically variable inks, such as the patches on Canadian $20 bills that change color from green to gold depending on the viewing angle;

- inks with magnetic, photochromic or thermochromic properties;

- printing features visible only with special equipment, such as the micro-printing on US bills which requires a magnifying glass to see, and printing in ultraviolet, infrared or magnetic inks (the last of these being used in the black printing on US bills);

- metal threads and foils, from simple iridescent features to foil color copying through to foils with optically variable effects such as *holograms* and *kinegrams*, as found on the latest issue of British banknotes. Holograms are typically produced optically, and look like a solid object behind the film, while kinegrams are produced by computer and may show a number of startlingly different views from slightly different angles;

- *screen traps* such as details too faint to scan properly, and *alias band structures* which contain detail at the correct size to form interference effects with the dot separation of common scanners and copiers;

- *digital copyright marks* which may vary from images hidden by microprinting their Fourier transforms directly, to spread spectrum signals that will be recognized by a color copier, scanner or printer and cause it to stop;

- unique stock, such as paper with magnetic fibers randomly spread through it during manufacture so that each sheet has a characteristic pattern that can be digitally signed and printed on the document using a barcode.

For the design of the new US $100 bill, see [921]; and for a study of counterfeit banknotes, with an analysis of which features provide what evidence, see [1280]. In general, banknotes' genuineness cannot readily be confirmed by the inspection of a single security feature. Many of the older techniques, and some of the newer, can be mimicked in ways that will pass primary inspection. The tactile effects of intaglio and letterpress printing wear off, so crumpling and dirtying a forged note is standard practice, and skilled banknote forgers mimic watermarks with faint grey printing (though watermarks remain surprisingly effective against amateurs). Holograms and kinegrams can be vulnerable to people using electrochemical techniques to make mechanical copies, and if not then villains may originate their own master copies from scratch.

When a hologram of Shakespeare was introduced on UK bank cards in 1988, I visited the factory as the representative of a bank and was told proudly that, as the industry had demanded a second source of supply, they had given a spare set of plates to a large security printing firm — and this competitor of theirs had been quite unable to manufacture acceptable foils. (The Shakespeare foil was the first commercially used diffraction hologram to be in full color and to move as the viewing angle changed). Surely a device which couldn't be forged, even by a major security printing company with access to genuine printing plates, must give total protection? But when I visited Singapore seven years later, I bought a similar (but larger) hologram of Shakespeare in the flea market. This was clearly a boast by the maker that he could forge UK bank cards if he wished to. By then, a police expert estimated that there were over 100 forgers in China with the skill to produce passable forgeries [969].

So the technology constantly moves on, and inventions that aid the villains come from such unexpected directions that technology controls are of little use. For example, ion beam workstations — machines which can be used to create the masters for kinegrams — used to cost many millions of dollars in the mid-1990's but have turned out to be so useful in metallurgical lab work that sales have shot up, prices have plummeted and there are now many bureaus which rent out machine time for a few hundred dollars an hour. Scanning electron microscopes, which are even more widely available, can be used with home-made add-ons to create new kinegrams using electron beam lithography. So it is imprudent to rely on a single protection technology. Even if one defense is completely defeated (such as if it becomes easy to make mechanical copies of metal foils), you have at least one completely different trick to fall back on (such as optically variable ink).

But designing a security document is much harder than this. There are complex trade-offs between protection, aesthetics and robustness, and the business focus can also change. For many years, banknote designers aimed at preventing forgeries passing secondary or tertiary inspection rather than on the more common primary inspection. Much time was spent handwringing about the difficulty of training people to examine documents properly, and not enough attention was paid to studying how the typical user of a product such as a banknote actually decides subconsciously whether it's acceptable. In other words, the technological focus had usurped the business focus. This defect is now receiving serious attention.

The lessons drawn so far are [1279]:

- security features should convey a message relevant to the product. So it's better to use iridescent ink to print the denomination of a banknote than some obscure feature of it;

- they should obviously belong where they are, so that they become embedded in the user's cognitive model of the object;

- their effects should be obvious, distinct and intelligible;

- they should not have existing competitors that can provide a basis for imitations;

- they should be standardized.

This work deserves much wider attention, as the banknote community is one of the few subdisciplines of our trade to have devoted a lot of thought to security usability. (We've seen over and over again that one of the main failings of security products is that usability gets ignored.) When it comes to documents other than banknotes, such as passports, there are also issues relating to political environment of the country and the mores of the society in which they will be used [874].

Usability also matters during second-line inspection, but here the issues are more subtle and focus on the process which the inspector has to follow to distinguish genuine from fake.

With banknotes, the theory is that you design a note with perhaps twenty features that are not advertised to the public. A number of features are made known to secondary inspectors such as bank staff. In due course these become known to the forgers. As time goes on, more and more features are revealed. Eventually, when they are all exposed, the note is retired from circulation and replaced. This process may become harder as the emphasis switches from manual to automatic verification. A thief who steals a vending machine, dismantles it, and reads out the software, gains a complete and accurate description of the checks currently in use. Having once spent several weeks or months doing this, he will find it much easier the second time round. So when the central bank tells manufacturers the secret polynomial for the second level digital watermark (or whatever), and this gets fielded, he can steal another machine and get the new data within days. So failures can be more sudden and complete than with manual systems, and the cycle of discovery could turn more quickly than in the past.

With product packaging, the typical business model is that samples of forgeries are found and taken to the laboratory, where the scientists find some way in which they are different — perhaps the hologram is not quite right. Kits are then produced for field inspectors to go out and track down the source. If these kits are bulky and expensive, fewer of them can be fielded. If there are many different forgery detection devices from different companies, then it is hard to persuade customs officers to use any of them. Ideas such as printing individual microscopic ultraviolet barcodes on plastic product shrinkwrap often fail because of the cost of the microscope, laptop and online connection needed to do the verification. As with banknotes, you can get a much more robust system with multiple features but this pushes the cost and bulk of the reading device up still further. There is now a substantial research effort towards developing unique marks, such as special chemical coatings containing proteins or even DNA molecules which encode hidden serial numbers, and which might enable one type of verification equipment to check many different products.

With financial instruments, and especially checks, alteration is a much bigger problem than copying or forgery from scratch. In numerous scams, villains got genuine checks from businesses by tricks such as by prepaying deposits or making reservations in cash and then cancelling the order. The victim duly sends out a check, which is altered to a much larger amount, often using readily available domestic solvents. The standard countermeasure is background printing using inks which discolor and run in the presence of solvents. But the protection isn't complete because of tricks for removing laser printer toner (and even simple things like typewriter correction ribbon). One enterprising villain even presented his victims with pens that had been specially selected to have easily removable ink [5].

While the security literature says a lot about debit card fraud (as the encryption systems ATMs use are interesting to techies), and a little about credit card fraud (as there's a lot of talk about credit card fraud on the net), there is very little about check fraud. Yet check fraud is many times greater in value than credit card fraud, and debit cards are almost insignificant by comparison. Although check fraud is critically important, the research community considers it to be boring.

The practical problem for the banks is the huge volume of checks processed daily. This makes scrutiny impossible except for very large amounts — and the sums stolen by small-time check fiddlers may be small by the standards of the victim organization (say, in the thousands to tens of thousands of dollars). In the Far East, where people use a personal *chop* or signature stamp to sign checks instead of a manuscript signature, low-cost automatic chop verification is possible [630]. However, with handwritten signatures, automated verification with acceptable error rates is still beyond the state of the art (I'll discuss it in section 15.2). In some countries, such as Germany, check frauds have been largely suppressed by businesses making most payments using bank transfers rather than checks (even for small customer refunds). Such a change means overcoming huge cultural inertia, but the move to the Euro is pushing this along in Europe. Although about two dozen countries now use a common currency, their national banking systems survive, with the result that electronic payments are much quicker and cheaper than check payments in the Euro zone. Presumably the lower costs of online payments will also persuade US businesses to make the switch eventually.

Alterations are also a big problem for the typical bank's credit card department. It is much simpler to alter the magnetic strip on a card than to re-originate the hologram. Up till the early 1980s, card transactions were recorded mechanically using zip-zap machines; then banks started to save on authorisation costs at their call centres by verifying the card's magnetic strip data using an online terminal. This meant that the authorization was done against the card number on the strip, while the transaction was booked against the card number on the embossing. Villains started to take stolen cards and reencode them with the account details of people with high credit limits — captured, for example, from waste carbons in the bins outside fancy restaurants. The bank would then repudiate the transaction, as the authorization code didn't match the recorded account number. So banks started fighting with their corporate customers over liability, and the system was changed so that drafts were captured electronically from the magnetic strip. Now the hologram really doesn't serve any useful purpose, at least against competent villains.

It's important to pay attention to whether partial alterations like these can be made to documents or tokens in ways that interact unpleasantly with other parts of the system. Of course, alterations aren't just a banking problem.

Most fake travel documents are altered rather than counterfeited from scratch. Names are changed, photographs are replaced, or pages are added and removed.

14.4   Packaging and Seals

This brings us on to the added problems of packaging and seals. A seal, in the definition of the Los Alamos vulnerability assessment team, is 'a tamper-indicating device designed to leave non-erasable, unambiguous evidence of unauthorized entry or tampering.'

Not all seals work by gluing a substrate with security printing to the object being sealed. I mentioned the lead and wire seals used to prevent tampering with truck speed sensors, and there are many products following the same general philosophy but using different materials, such as plastic straps that are easy to tighten but are supposed to be hard to loosen without cutting. We also mentioned the special chemical coatings, microscopic bar codes and other tricks used to make products or product batches traceable.

However, most of the seals in use work by applying some kind of security printing to a substrate to get a tag, and then fixing this tag to the material to be protected. The most important application in financial terms may be the protection of pharmaceutical products against both counterfeiting and tampering, though it's useful to bear in mind others, from nuclear nonproliferation through cargo containers to ballot boxes.

14.4.1   Substrate Properties

Some systems add random variability to the substrate material. We mentioned the trick of loading paper with magnetic fibers; there are also *watermark magnetics* in which a random high-coercivity signal is embedded in a card strip which can subsequently be read and written using standard low-coercivity equipment without the unique random pattern being disturbed. They are used in bank cards in Sweden, telephone cards in Korea, and entry control cards in some of the buildings in my university.

A similar idea is used in arms control. Many weapons and materials have surfaces that are unique; see for example Figure 14.1 for the surface of paper. Other material surfaces can be made unique; for example, a patch can be eroded on a tank gun barrel using a small explosive charge. The pattern is measured using laser speckle techniques, and either recorded in a log or attached to the device as a machine-readable digital signature [1172]. This makes it easy to identify capital equipment such as heavy artillery where identifying each gun barrel is enough to prevent either side from cheating.

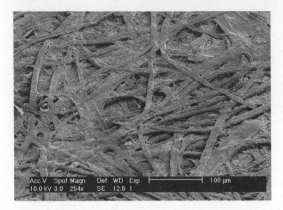

Figure 14.1: Scanning electron micrograph of paper (courtesy Ingenia Technology Ltd)

Recently there have been significant improvements in the technology for reading and recording the microscale randomness of materials. One system is Laser Surface Authentication, developed by Russell Cowburn and his colleagues [236]. They scan the surface of a document or package and use laser speckle to encode its surface roughness into a 256-byte code that is very robust to creasing, drying, scribbling and even scorching. (Declaration of interest: I worked with Russell on the security of this technique.) A typical application is to register all the cartons of a fast-moving consumer good as they come off the production line. Inspectors with hand-held laser scanners and a link to an online database of LSA codes can then not just verify whether a package is genuine, but also identify it uniquely. This is cheaper than RFID, and is also more controllable in that you can restrict access to the database. It thus may be particularly attractive to companies who are worried about internal control, or who want to crack down on grey market trading. In the long term, I'd not be surprised to see this technique used on banknotes.

14.4.2   The Problems of Glue

Although a tag's uniqueness can be a side-effect of its manufacture, most seals still work by fixing a security-printed tag on to the target object. This raises the question of how the beautiful piece of iridescent printed art can be attached to a crude physical object in a way that is very hard to remove.

In the particular case of tamper-evident packaging, the attachment is part of an industrial process; it could be a pressurized container with a pop-up button or a break-off lid. The usual answer is to use a glue which is stronger than the seal substrate itself, so that the seal will tear or at least deform noticeably if pulled away. This is the case with foil seals under drink caps, many blister packs, and of course the seals you find on software packages.

However, in most products, the implementation is rather poor. Many seals are vulnerable to direct removal using only hand tools and a little patience. Take a sharp knife and experiment with the next few letters that arrive in self-seal envelopes. Many of these envelopes are supposed to tear, rather than peel open; the flap may have a few vertical slots cut into it for this purpose. But this hoped-for tamper evidence usually assumes that people will open them by pulling the envelope flap back from the body. By raising the flap slightly and working the knife back and forth, it is often possible to cut the glue without damaging the flap and thus open the envelope without leaving suspicious marks. (Some glues should be softened first using a hairdryer, or made more fragile by freezing.) Or open the envelope at the other end, where the glue is not designed to be mildly tamper-evident. Either way you'll probably get an envelope that looks slightly crumpled on careful examination. If it's noticeable, iron out the crumples. This attack usually works against a primary inspection, probably fails a tertiary inspection, and may well pass secondary inspection: crumples happen in the post anyway.

Many of the seals on the market can be defeated using similarly simple tricks. For example, there is a colored adhesive tape that when ripped off leaves behind a warning such as 'Danger' or 'Do not use'. The warning is printed between two layers of glue, the bottom of which is stronger, and is supposed to remain behind if the seal is tampered with. But the tape only behaves in this way if it is pulled from above. By cutting from the side, one can remove it intact and re-use it [749].

14.4.3 PIN Mailers

An interesting recent development is the appearance of special print stocks on which banks laser-print customer PINs. In the old days, PIN mailers used multipart stationery and impact printers; you got the PIN by ripping the envelope open and pulling out a slip on which the PIN had been impressed. The move from impact to laser technology led to a number of companies inventing letter stationery from which you pull a tab to read the PIN. The idea is that just as a seal can't be moved without leaving visible evidence, with this stationery the secret can't be extracted without leaving visible evidence. A typical mechanism is to have a patch on the paper that's printed with an obscuring pattern and that also has an adhesive film over it, on which the PIN is printed. behind the film is a die-cut tab in the paper that can be pulled away, thus removing the obscuring background and making the PIN visible.

My students Mike Bond, Steven Murdoch and Jolyon Clulow had some fun finding vulnerabilities with successive versions of these products. The early products could be read by holding them up to the light, so that the light glanced off the surface at about 10 degrees; the opaque toner showed up clearly against the shiny adhesive film. The next attack was to scan the printing into Photoshop and filter out the dense black of the toner from the grey of the underlying printing. Another was thermal transfer; put a blank sheet of paper on top of the mailer and run an iron over it. Yet another was chemical transfer using blotting paper and organic solvents. This work was reported to the banking industry in 2004, and finally published in 2005 [205]. The banks have now issued test standards for mailers. Yet to this day we keep getting mailers on which the PIN is easy to read: the latest ones have inks that change color when you pull the tab, and come in an envelope with a leaflet saying 'if the dots are blue, reject this PIN mailer and call us'; but an attacker would just swap this for a leaflet saying 'if the dots aren't blue, reject this PIN mailer and call us'.

This is an example of a system that doesn't work, and yet no-one cares. Come to think of it, if a bad man knows I'm getting a new bank card, and can steal from my mail, he'll just take both the card and the PIN. It's hard to think of any real attacks that the 'tamper-evident' PIN mailer prevents. It might occasionally prevent a family member learning a PIN by accident; equally, there might be an occasional customer who reads the PIN without tearing the tab, withdraws a lot of money, then claims he didn't do it, in which case the bank has to disown its own mailer. But the threats are vestigial compared with the amount that's being spent on all this fancy stationery. Perhaps the banks treat it as 'security theater'; or perhaps the managers involved just don't want to abandon the system and send out PINs printed on plain paper as they're embarrassed at having wasted all this money.

14.5 Systemic Vulnerabilities

We turn now from the specific threats against particular printing tricks and glues to the system level threats, of which there are many.

A possibly useful example is in Figure 14.2. At our local swimming pool, congestion is managed by issuing swimmers with wristbands during busy periods. A different color is issued every twenty minutes or so, and from time to time all people with bands of a certain color are asked to leave. The band is made of waxed paper. At one end it has a printed pattern and serial number on one side and glue on the other; the paper is cross-cut with the result that it is completely destroyed if you tear it off carelessly. (It's very similar to the luggage seals used at some airports.)

The simplest attack is to phone up the supplier; boxes of 100 wristbands cost about $8. If you don't want to spend money, you can use each band once, then ease it off gently by pulling it alternately from different directions, giving the result shown in the photo. The printing is crumpled, though intact; the damage isn't such as to be visible by a poolside attendant, and could in fact have been caused by careless application. The point is that the damage done

Figure 14.2: A wristband seal from our local swimming pool

to the seal by fixing it twice, carefully, is not easily distinguishable from the effects of a naive user fixing it once. (An even more powerful attack is to not remove the backing tape from the seal at all, but use some other means — a safety pin, or your own glue — to fix it.)

Despite this, the wristband seal is perfectly fit for purpose. There is little incentive to cheat: the Olympic hopefuls who swim for two hours at a stretch use the pool when it's not congested. They also buy a season ticket, so they can go out at any time to get a band of the current color. But it illustrates many of the things that can go wrong. The customer is the enemy; it's the customer who applies the seal; the effects of seal re-use are indistinguishable from those of random failure; unused seals can be bought in the marketplace; counterfeit seals could also be manufactured at little cost; and effective inspection is infeasible. (And yet this swimming pool seal is still harder to defeat than many sealing products sold for high-value industrial applications.)

14.5.1 Peculiarities of the Threat Model

We've seen systems where your customer is your enemy, as in banking. In military systems the enemy is the single disloyal soldier, or the other side's special forces trying to sabotage your equipment. In nuclear monitoring systems it can be the host government trying to divert fissile materials from a licensed civilian reactor.

But some of the most difficult sealing tasks arise in commerce. Again, it's often the enemy who will apply the seal. A typical application is where a company subcontracts the manufacture of some of its products and is afraid that the contractor will produce more of the goods than agreed. Overproduction is the main source by value of counterfeit goods worldwide; the perpetrators have access to the authorized manufacturing process and raw materials, and grey markets provide natural distribution channels. Even detecting such frauds — let alone proving them to a court — can be hard.

A typical solution for high-value goods such as cosmetics may involve sourcing packaging materials from a number of different companies, whose identities are kept secret from the firm operating the final assembly plant. Some of these materials may have serial numbers embedded in various ways (such as by laser engraving in bottle glass, or printing on cellophane using inks visible only under UV light). There may be an online service whereby the manufacturer's field agents can verify the serial numbers of samples purchased randomly in shops, or there might be a digital signature on the packaging that links all the various serial numbers together for offline checking.

There are limits on what seals can achieve in isolation. Sometimes the brand owner himself is the villain, as when a vineyard falsely labels as vintage an extra thousand cases of wine that were actually made from bought-in blended grapes. So bottles of South African wine all carry a government regulated seal with a unique serial number; here, the seal doesn't prove the fraud but makes it harder for a dishonest vintner to evade the other controls such as inspection and audit. So sealing mechanisms usually must be designed with the audit, testing and inspection process in mind.

Inspection can be harder than one would think. The distributor who has bought counterfeit goods on the grey market, believing them to be genuine, may set out to deceive the inspectors without any criminal intent. Where grey markets are an issue, the products bought from 'Fred' will be pushed out rapidly to the customers, ensuring that the inspectors see only authorized products in his stockroom. Also, the distributor may be completely in the dark; it could be his staff who are peddling the counterfeits. A well-known scam is for airline staff to buy counterfeit perfumes, watches and the like in the Far East, sell them in-flight to customers, and trouser the proceeds [783]. The stocks in the airline's warehouses (and in the duty-free carts after the planes land) will all be completely genuine. So it is usually essential to have agents go out and make sample purchases, and the sealing mechanisms must support this.

14.5.2   Anti-Gundecking Measures

Whether the seal adheres properly to the object being sealed may also depend on the honesty and diligence of low-level staff. I mentioned in section 12.3.2.2 how in truck speed limiter systems, the gearbox sensor is secured using a piece of wire that the calibrating garage seals with a lead disc that is crimped in place with special tongs. The defeat is to bribe the garage mechanic to wrap the wire the wrong way, so that when the sensor is unscrewed from the gearbox the wire will loosen, instead of tightening and breaking the seal. There is absolutely no need to go to amateur sculptor classes so that you can take a cast of the seal and forge a pair of sealing tongs out of bronze (unless you want to save on bribes, or frame the garage).

The people who apply seals can be careless as well as corrupt. In the last few years, some airports have taken to applying tape seals to passengers' checked bags after X-raying them using a machine near the check-in queue. On about half of the occasions this has been done to my baggage, the tape has been poorly fixed; either it didn't cross the fastener between the suitcase and the lid, or it came off at one end, or the case had several compartments big enough to hold a bomb but only one of their fasteners was sealed.

Much of the interesting recent research in seals has focussed on usability. One huge problem is checking whether staff who're supposed to inspect seals have actually done so. *Gundecking* is a naval term used to refer to people who pretend to have done their duty, but were actually down on the gun deck having a smoke. So if your task is to inspect the seals on thousands of shipping containers arriving at a port, how do you ensure that your staff actually look at each one?

The vulnerability assessment team at Los Alamos has come up with a number of anti-gundecking designs for seals. One approach is to include in each container seal a small processor with a cryptographic keystream generator that produces a new number every minute or so, just like the password generators I discussed in Chapter 3. Then the inspector's task is to visit all the inbound containers and record the numbers they display. If a tampering event is detected, the device erases its key, and can generate no more numbers. If your inspector doesn't bring back a valid seal code from one of the containers, you know something's wrong, whether with it or with him. Such seals are also known as 'anti-evidence' seals: the idea is that you store information that a device hasn't been tampered with, and destroy it when tampering occurs, leaving nothing for an adversary to counterfeit.

Carelessness and corruption interact. If enough of the staff applying or verifying a seal are careless, then if I bribe one of them the resulting defect doesn't of itself prove dishonesty.

14.5.3 The Effect of Random Failure

There are similar effects when seals can break for completely innocent reasons. For example, speed limiter seals often break when a truck engine is steam-cleaned, so a driver will not be prosecuted for tampering if a broken seal is all the evidence the traffic policeman can find. (Truck drivers know this.)

There are other consequences too. For example, after opening a too-well-sealed envelope, a villain can close it again with a sticker saying 'Opened by customs' or 'Burst in transit — sealed by the Post Office'. He could even just tape it shut and scrawl 'delivered to wrong address try again' on the front.

The consequences of such failures and attacks have to be thought through carefully. If the protection goal is to prevent large-scale forgery of a product, occasional breakages may not matter; but if it is to support prosecutions, spontaneous seal failure can be a serious problem. In extreme cases, placing too much trust in the robustness of a seal might lead to a miscarriage of justice and completely undermine the sealing product's evidential (and thus commercial) value.

14.5.4   Materials Control

Another common vulnerability is that supplies of sealing materials are uncontrolled. Corporate seals are a nice example. In the UK, these typically consist of two metal embossing plates that are inserted into special pliers and were used to crimp important documents. Several suppliers manufacture the plates, and a lawyer who has ordered hundreds of them tells me that no check was ever made. Although it might be slightly risky to order a seal for 'Microsoft Corporation', it should be easy to have a seal made for almost any less well known target: all you have to do is write a letter that looks like it came from a law firm.

A more serious example is the reliance of the pharmaceutical industry on blister packs, sometimes supplemented with holograms and color-shifting inks. All these technologies are freely available to anyone who cares to buy them, and they are not particularly expensive either. Or consider the plastic envelopes used by some courier companies, which are designed to stretch and tear when opened. So long as you can walk in off the street and pick up virgin envelopes at the depot, they are unlikely to deter anyone who invests some time and thought in planning an attack; he can substitute the packaging either before, of after, a parcel's trip through the courier's network.

It is also an 'urban myth' that the police and security services cannot open envelopes tracelessly if the flaps have been reinforced with sticky tape that has been burnished down by rubbing it with a thumbnail (I recently received some paperwork from a bank that had been sealed in just this way). This is not entirely believable — even if no police lab has invented a magic solvent for sellotape glue, the nineteenth century Tsarist police already used forked sticks to wind up letters inside a sealed envelope so that they could be pulled out, read, and then put back [676].

Even if sellotape were guaranteed to leave a visible mark on an envelope, one would have to assume that the police's envelope-steaming department have no stock of comparable envelopes, and that the recipient would be observant enough to spot a forged envelope. Given the ease with which an envelope with a company logo can be scanned and then duplicated using a cheap color printer, these assumptions are fairly ambitious. In any case, the arrival of desktop color printers has caused a lot of organizations to stop using preprinted stationery. This makes the forger's job much easier.

14.5.5   Not Protecting the Right Things

I mentioned how credit cards were vulnerable in the late 1980's as the authorization terminals read the magnetic strip while the payment draft capture equipment used the embossing. Crooks who changed the mag strip but not the embossing defeated the system. There are also attacks involving partial alterations. For example, as the hologram on a credit card covers only the last four digits, the attacker could always change the other twelve. When the algorithm the bank used to generate credit card numbers was known, this involved only flattening, reprinting and re-embossing the rest of the card, which could be done with cheap equipment.

Such attacks are now rare, because villains now realize that very few shop staff check that the account number printed on the slip is the same as that embossed on the card. So the account number on the strip need bear no resemblance at all to the numbers embossed on the face. In effect, all the hologram says is 'This was once a valid card'.

Finally, food and drug producers often use shrink-wrap or blister packaging, which if well designed can be moderately difficult for amateurs to forge well enough to withstand close inspection. However when selecting protective measures you have to be very clear about the threat model — is it counterfeiting, alteration, duplication, simulation, diversion, dilution, substitution or something else? [1025] If the threat model is a psychotic with a syringe full of poison, then simple blister or shrink-wrap packaging is not quite enough. What's really needed is a tamper sensing membrane, which will react visibly and irreversibly to even a tiny penetration. (Such membranes exist but are still too expensive for consumer products. I'll discuss one of them in the chapter on tamper resistance.)

14.5.6   The Cost and Nature of Inspection

There are many stories in the industry of villains replacing the hologram on a bank card with something else — say a rabbit instead of a dove — whereupon the response of shopkeepers is just to say: 'Oh, look, they changed the hologram!' This isn't a criticism of holograms but is a much deeper issue of applied psychology and public education. It's a worry for bankers when new notes are being introduced — the few weeks during which everyone is getting familiar with the new notes can be a bonanza for forgers.

A related problem is the huge variety of passports, driver's licenses, letterheads, corporate seals, and variations in packaging. Without samples of genuine articles for comparison, inspection is more or less limited to the primary level and so forgery is easy. Even though bank clerks have books with pictures of foreign banknotes, and immigration officers similarly have pictures of foreign passports, there is often only a small amount of information on security features, and in any case the absence of real physical samples means that the tactile aspects of the product go unexamined.

A somewhat shocking experiment was performed by Sonia Trujillo at the 7th Security Seals Symposium in Santa Barbara in March 2006. She tampered with nine out of thirty different food and drug products, using only low-tech attacks, and invited 71 tamper-detection experts to tell them apart. Each subject was asked to pick exactly three out of ten products that they thought had been tampered. The experts did no better than random, even though most of them took significantly longer than the four seconds per product that they were directed to. If even the experts can't detect tampering, even when they're told it has been happening, what chance does the average consumer have?

So the seal that can be checked by the public or by staff with minimal training, and without access to an online database, remains an ideal. The main purpose of tamper-evident packaging is to reassure the customer; secondary purposes include minimising product returns, due diligence and reducing the size of jury awards. Deterring incompetent tamperers might just about be in there somewhere.

Firms that take forgery seriously, like large software companies, have adopted many of the techniques pioneered by banknote printers. But high-value product packages are harder to protect than banknotes. Familiarity is important: people get a 'feel' for things they handle frequently such as local money, but are much less likely to notice something wrong with a package they see only rarely — such as the latest version of Microsoft Office, which they may purchase every five years or so. For this reason, much of the work in protecting software products against forgery has been shifting over the past few years to online registration mechanisms.

One of the possibilities is to enlist the public as inspectors, not so much of the packaging, but of unique serial numbers. Instead of having these numbers hidden from view in RFID chips, vendors can print them on product labels, and people who're concerned about whether they got a genuine product could call in to verify. This may often get the incentives aligned better, but can be harder than it looks. For example, when Microsoft first shipped its antispyware beta, I installed it on a family PC — whose copy of Windows was immediately denounced as evil. Now that PC was bought at a regular store, and I simply did not need the hassle of explaining this to the Empire. I particularly did not like their initial negotiating position, namely that the remedy was for me to send them more money. The remedy eventually agreed on was that they gave me another copy of Windows XP. But how many people are able to negotiate that?

14.6   Evaluation Methodology

This discussion suggests a systematic way to evaluate a seal product for a given application. Rather than just asking, 'Can you remove the seal in ways other than the obvious one?' we need to follow it from design and field test through manufacture, application, use, checking, destruction and finally retirement from service. Here are some of the questions that should be asked:

- If a seal is forged, who's supposed to spot it? If it's the public, then how often will they see genuine seals? Has the vendor done experiments, that pass muster by the standards of applied psychology, to establish the likely false accept and false reject rates? If it's your inspectors in the field, how much will their equipment and training cost? And how well are these inspectors — public or professional — really motivated to find and report defects?

- Has anybody who really knows what they're doing tried hard to defeat the system? And what's a defeat anyway — tampering, forgery, alteration, erosion of evidential value or a 'PR' attack on your commercial credibility?

- What is the reputation of the team that designed it — did they have a history of successfully defeating opponents' products?

- How long has it been in the field, and how likely is it that progress will make a defeat significantly easier?

- How widely available are the sealing materials — who else can buy, forge or steal supplies?

- Will the person who applies the seal be careless or corrupt, and if so, how will you cope with that?

- Does the way the seal will be used protect the right part (or enough) of the product?

- What are the quality issues? What about the effects of dirt, oil, noise, vibration, cleaning, and manufacturing defects? Will the product have to survive outdoor weather, petrol splashes, being carried next to the skin or being dropped in a glass of beer? Or is it supposed to respond visibly if such a thing happens? How often will there be random seal failures and what effect will they have?

- Are there any evidential issues? If you're going to end up in court, are there experts other than your own (or the vendor's) on whom the other side can rely? If the answer is no, then is this a good thing or a bad thing? Why should the jury believe you, the system's inventor, rather than the sweet little old lady in the dock? Will the judge let her off on fair trial grounds — because rebutting your technical claims would be an impossible burden of proof for her to discharge? (This is exactly what happened in Judd vs Citibank, the case which settled US law on 'phantom withdrawals' from cash machines [674].)

■ Once the product is used, how will the seals be disposed of — are you bothered if someone recovers a few old seals from the trash?

Remember that defeating seals is about fooling people, not beating hardware. So think hard whether the people who apply and check the seals will perform their tasks faithfully and effectively; analyze motive, opportunity, skills, audit and accountability. Be particularly cautious where the seal is applied by the enemy (as in the case of contract manufacture) or by someone open to corruption (such as the garage eager to win the truck company's business). Finally, think through the likely consequences of seal failure and inspection error rates not just from the point of view of the client company and its opponents, but also from the points of view of innocent system users and of legal evidence.

Of course, this whole-life-cycle assurance process should also be applied to computer systems in general. I'll talk about that some more in Part III.

14.7 Summary

Most commercially available sealing products are relatively easy to defeat, and this is particularly true when seal inspection is performed casually by untrained personnel. Sealing has to be evaluated over the whole lifetime of the seal from manufacture through materials control, application, verification and eventual destruction; hostile testing is highly advisable in critical applications. Seals often depend on security printing, about which broadly similar comments may be made.

Research Problems

A lot of money is already being spent on research and product development in this area. But much of it isn't spent effectively, and it has all the characteristics of a lemons market which third rate products dominate because of low cost and user ignorance. No doubt lots of fancy new technologies will be touted for product safety and counterfeit detection, from nanoparticles through ferrofluids to DNA; but so long as the markets are broken, and people ignore the system-level issues, what good will they do? Do any of them have novel properties that enable us to tackle the hard problems of primary inspectability and the prevention of gundecking?

Automatic inspection systems may be one way forward; perhaps in the future a product's RFID tag will deactivate itself if the container is tampered. At present such devices cost dollars; within a few years they might cost cents. But which vendors would deploy them, and for what applications? Where will the incentives be? And, hardest of all, how does this help the consumer? Most of the counterfeits and poisoned products are introduced at the retail level, and protecting the retailer doesn't help here.

Further Reading

The definitive textbook on security printing is van Renesse [1279] which goes into not just the technical tricks such as holograms and kinegrams, but how they work in a variety of applications from banknote printing through passports to packaging. This is very important background reading.

The essential writing on seals can be found in the many publications by Roger Johnston's seal vulnerability assessment team at Los Alamos National Laboratory (e.g., [668]).

The history of counterfeiting is fascinating. From Independence to the Civil War, Americans used banknotes issued by private banks rather than by the government, and counterfeiting was pervasive. Banks could act against local forgers, but by about 1800 there had arisen a network of engravers, papermakers, printers, wholesalers, retailers and passers, with safe havens in the badlands on the border between Vermont and Canada; neither the U.S. nor the Canadian government wanted to take ownership of the problem [887]. It was in many ways reminiscent of the current struggle against phishing.

Biometrics

And the Gileadites took the passages of Jordan before the Ephraimites: and it was so, that when those Ephraimites which were escaped said, Let me go over; that the men of Gilead said unto him, Art thou an Ephraimite? If he said, Nay; Then said they unto him, Say now Shibboleth: and he said Sibboleth: for he could not frame to pronounce it right. Then they took him, and slew him at the passages of the Jordan: and there fell at that time of the Ephraimites forty and two thousand.

— Judges 12:5–6

15.1 Introduction

The above quotation may be the first recorded military use of a security protocol in which the authentication relies on a property of the human being — in this case his accent. (There had been less formal uses before this, as when Isaac tried to identify Esau by his bodily hair but got deceived by Jacob, or indeed when people recognized each other by their faces — which I'll discuss later.)

Biometrics identify people by measuring some aspect of individual anatomy or physiology (such as your hand geometry or fingerprint), some deeply ingrained skill or behavior (such as your handwritten signature), or some combination of the two (such as your voice).

Over the last quarter century or so, people have developed a large number of biometric devices. Since 9/11 the market has really taken off, with a number of large-scale programs including the international standards for biometric travel documents, the US-VISIT program which fingerprints visitors to the USA, Europe's Schengen visa, assorted ID card initiatives, and various registered traveler programs. Some large systems already existed, such as the FBI's fingerprint database, which is now being expanded to contain a range of biometric data for both identification and forensic purposes. The Biometric systems market was reportedly worth over \$1.5bn in 2005 [675], a massive increase from \$50 m in 1998 [655]. I already mentioned the use of hand geometry to identify staff at a nuclear reactor in the late 1970s. But the best established biometric techniques predate the computer age altogether — namely the use of handwritten signatures, facial features and fingerprints. I will look at these first, then go on to the fancier, more 'high-tech' techniques.

15.2   Handwritten Signatures

Handwritten signatures had been used in classical China, but carved personal seals came to be considered higher status; they are still used for serious transactions in China, Japan and Korea. Europe was the other way round: seals had been used in medieval times, but as writing spread after the Renaissance people increasingly just wrote their names to signify assent to documents. Over time the signature became accepted as the standard. Every day, billions of dollars' worth of contracts are concluded by handwritten signatures on documents; how these will be replaced by electronic mechanisms remains a hot policy and technology issue.

Handwritten signatures are a very weak authentication mechanism by themselves (in that they're easy to forge) but have worked well for centuries because of the context of their use. An important factor is the liability for forgery. UK law provides that a forged handwritten signature is completely null and void, and this has survived in the laws of many countries that were part of the British Empire at the time. It means that the risk from a forged signature falls on the party who relies on it, and it's not possible for a bank to use its standard terms and conditions to dump the risk on the customer. So manuscript signatures are better for the customer, while the PINs and electronic tokens that are now replacing them can be better for the bank. This is not the case everywhere; some Swiss banks make customers liable for forged cheques. In the USA, Regulation E makes banks liable for the electronic systems they deploy, so the introduction of electronics doesn't change the game much. Needless to say, European banks have moved much further than U.S. banks in moving customers away from handwritten signatures.

Now the probability that a forged signature will be accepted as genuine mainly depends on the amount of care taken when examining it. Many bank card transactions in stores are accepted without even a glance at the specimen signature on the card — so much so that many Americans do not even bother to sign their credit cards[1]. But even diligent signature checking

---

[1]Indeed it's not in the cardholder's interest to give a specimen signature to a thief — if the thief makes a random signature on a voucher, it's easier for the real cardholder to disown it. Signing the card is in the bank's interest but not the customer's.

doesn't reduce the risk of fraud to zero. An experiment showed that 105 professional document examiners, who each did 144 pairwise comparisons, misattributed 6.5% of documents. Meanwhile, a control group of 34 untrained people of the same educational level got it wrong 38.3% of the time [682], and the nonprofessionals' performance couldn't be improved by giving them monetary incentives [683]. Errors made by professionals are a subject of continuing discussion in the industry but are thought to reflect the examiner's preconceptions [137] and context [403]. As the participants in these tests were given reasonable handwriting samples rather than just a signature, it seems fair to assume that the results for verifying signatures on checks or credit card vouchers would be even worse.

So handwritten signatures are surrounded by a number of conventions and special rules that vary from one country to another, and these extend well beyond banking. For example, to buy a house in England using money borrowed from a bank of which you're not an established customer, the procedure is to go to a lawyer's office with a document such as a passport, sign the property transfer and loan contract, and get the contract countersigned by the lawyer. The requirement for government issued photo-ID is imposed by the mortgage lender to keep its insurers happy, while the requirement that a purchase of real estate be in writing was imposed by the government some centuries ago in order to collect tax on property transactions. Other types of document (such as expert testimony) may have to be notarized in particular ways. Many curious anomalies go back to the nineteenth century, and the invention of the typewriter. Some countries require that machine written contracts be initialled on each page, while some don't, and these differences have sometimes persisted for over a century. Clashes in conventions still cause serious problems. In one case, a real estate transaction in Spain was held to be invalid because the deal had been concluded by fax, and a UK company went bust as a result.

In most of the English speaking world, however, most documents do not need to be authenticated by special measures. The essence of a signature is the intent of the signer, so an illiterate's 'X' on a document is just as valid as the flourish of an educated man. In fact, a plaintext name at the bottom of an email message also has just as much legal force [1358], except where there are specific regulations to the contrary. There may be many obscure signature regulations scattered through each country's laws.

It's actually very rare for signatures to be disputed in court cases, as the context mostly makes it clear who did what. So we have a very weak biometric mechanism that works fairly well in practice — except that it's choked by procedural rules and liability traps that vary by country and by application. Sorting out this mess, and imposing reasonably uniform rules for electronic documents, is a subject of much international activity. A summary of the issues can be found in [1359], with an analysis by country in [109]. I'll discuss some of the issues further in Part III. Meanwhile, note that the form of a signature, the ease with which it can be forged, and whether it has legal validity in a given context, are largely independent questions.

There is one application where better automatic recognition of handwritten signatures could be valuable. This is check clearing.

A bank's check processing center will typically only verify signatures on checks over a certain amount — perhaps $1,000, perhaps $10,000, perhaps a percentage of the last three months' movement on the account. The signature verification is done by an operator who is simultaneously presented on screen with the check image and the customer's reference signature. Verifying checks for small amounts is not economic unless it could be automated.

So a number of researchers have worked on systems to compare handwritten signatures automatically. This turns out to be a very difficult image processing task because of the variability between one genuine signature and another. A much easier option is to use a *signature tablet*. This is a sensor surface on which the user does a signature; it records not just the shape of the curve but also its dynamics (the velocity of the hand, where the pen was lifted off the paper, and so on). Tablets are used by delivery drivers to collect receipts for goods; there have been products since the early 1990s that will compare captured signatures against specimens enrolled previously.

Like alarm systems, most biometric systems have a trade-off between false accept and false reject rates, often referred to in the banking industry as the *fraud* and *insult* rates and in the biometric literature as *type 1* and *type 2* errors. Many systems can be tuned to favor one over the other. The trade-off is known as the *receiver operating characteristic*, a term first used by radar operators; if you turn up the gain on your radar set too high, you can't see the target for clutter, while if it's too low you can't see it at all. It's up to the operator to select a suitable point on this curve. The *equal error rate* is when the system is tuned so that the probabilities of false accept and false reject are equal. For tablet-based signature recognition systems, the equal error rate is at best 1%; for purely optical comparison it's several percent. This is not fatal in an operation such as a check processing center, as the automated comparison is used as a filter to preselect dubious checks for scrutiny by a human operator. However, it is a show-stopper in a customer-facing application such as a retail store. If one transaction in a hundred fails, the aggravation to customers would be unacceptable. So UK banks set a target for biometrics of a fraud rate of 1% and an insult rate of 0.01%, which is beyond the current state of the art in signature verification and indeed fingerprint scanning [500].

What can be done to bridge the gap? An interesting experiment was conducted by the University of Kent, England, to cut fraud by welfare claimants who were drawing their benefits at a post office near Southampton. The novel feature of this system is that, just as in a check processing center, it was used to screen signatures and support human decisions rather than to take decisions itself. So instead of being tuned for a low insult rate, with a correspondingly high fraud rate, it had fraud and insult rates approximately equal. When a signature is rejected, this merely tells the staff to look more closely, and ask for a driver's license or other photo-ID. With 8500 samples taken from 343 customers, 98.2% were verified correctly at the first attempt, rising to 99.15% after three attempts [452]. But this rate was achieved by excluding *goats* — a term used by the biometric community for people whose templates don't classify well. With them included, the false reject rate was 6.9% [453]. Because of this disappointing performance, sales of signature recognition technology are only 1.7% of the total biometric market; automation has cost it its leadership of the biometric market.

In general, biometric mechanisms tend to be much more robust in attended operations where they assist a guard rather than replacing him. The false alarm rate may then actually help by keeping the guard alert.

15.3   Face Recognition

Recognizing people by their facial features is the oldest identification mechanism of all, going back at least to our early primate ancestors. Biologists believe that a significant part of our cognitive function evolved to provide efficient ways of recognizing other people's facial features and expressions [1076]. For example, we are extremely good at detecting whether another person is looking at us or not. In normal social applications, humans' ability to identify people by their faces appears to be very much better than any automatic facial-recognition system produced to date.

The human ability to recognize faces is important to the security engineer because of the widespread reliance placed on photo ID. Drivers' licenses, passports and other kinds of identity card are not only used to control entry to computer rooms directly, they are also used to bootstrap most other systems. The issue of a password, or a smartcard, or the registration of a user for a biometric system using some other technique such as iris recognition, is often the end point of a process which was started by that person presenting photo ID when applying for a job, opening a bank account or whatever.

But even if we are good at recognising friends in the flesh, how good are we at identifying strangers by photo ID?

The simple answer is that we're not. Psychologists at the University of Westminster conducted a fascinating experiment with the help of a supermarket chain and a bank [705]. They recruited 44 students and issued each of them with four credit cards each with a different photograph on it:

- one of the photos was a 'good, good' one. It was genuine and recent;
- the second was a 'bad, good one'. It was genuine but a bit old, and the student now had different clothing, hairstyle or whatever. In other

words, it was typical of the photo that most people have on their photo ID;

■ the third was a 'good, bad one'. From a pile of a hundred or so random photographs of different people, investigators chose the one which most looked like the subject. In other words, it was typical of the match that criminals could get if they had a stack of stolen cards;

■ the fourth was a 'bad, bad' one. It was chosen at random except that it had the same sex and race as the subject. In other words, it was typical of the match that really lazy, careless criminals would get.

The experiment was conducted in a supermarket after normal business hours, but with experienced cashiers on duty, and aware of the purpose of the experiment. Each student made several trips past the checkout using different cards. It transpired that none of the checkout staff could tell the difference between 'good, bad' photos and 'bad, good' photos. In fact, some of them could not even tell the difference between 'good, good' and 'bad, bad'. Now this experiment was done under optimum conditions, with experienced staff, plenty of time, and no threat of embarrassment or violence if a card was rejected. Real life performance can be expected to be worse. In fact, many stores do not pass on to their checkout staff the reward offered by credit card companies for capturing stolen cards. So even the most basic incentive is absent.

The response of the banking industry to this experiment was ambivalent. At least two banks who had experimented with photos on credit cards had experienced a substantial drop in fraud — to less than one percent of the expected amount in the case of one Scottish bank [107]. The overall conclusion was that the benefit to be had from photo ID is essentially its deterrent effect [471].

So maybe people won't use their facial recognition skills effectively in identification contexts, or maybe the information we use to identify people in social contexts is stored differently in our brains from information we get by looking at a single photo. (Recognising passing strangers is in any case much harder than recognising people you know. It's reckoned that misidentifications are the main cause of false imprisonment, with 20% of witnesses making mistakes in identity parades [1360] — not as bad as the near-random outcomes when comparing faces with photos, but still not good.)

But in any case, photo-ID doesn't seem to work, and this is one of the reasons for trying to automate the process. Attempts go back to the nineteenth century, when Francis Galton devised a series of spring-loaded 'mechanical selectors' for facial measurements [510]. But automated face recognition actually subsumes a number of separate problems, and in most of them we don't have the luxury of taking careful 3-d measurements of the subject. In a typical identity verification application, the subject looks straight at the camera under controlled lighting conditions, and his face is compared with the one on file. A related but harder problem is found in forensics, where we may be trying to establish whether a suspect's face fits a low-quality recording on a security video. The hardest of all is surveillance, where the goal may be to scan a moving crowd of people at an airport and try to pick out anyone who is on a list of thousands of known suspects. Yet automatic face recognition was one of the technologies most hyped by the security-industrial complex after 9/11 [1084].

Even picking out faces from an image of a crowd is a non-trivial computational task [798]. An academic study of the robustness of different facial feature extraction methods found that given reasonable variations in lighting, viewpoint and expression, no method was sufficient by itself and error rates were up to 20% [13]. Systems that use a combination of techniques can get the error rate down but not to the levels possible with many other biometrics [898, 1370]. Field trials by the U.S. Department of Defense in 2002 found that a leading face-recognition product correctly recognized one individual out of 270 only 51% of the time, and identified one person correctly to within a range of 10 participants 81% of the time [852]. (The vendor in question had put out a press release on the afternoon of September 11th and seen a huge rise in its stock price in the week after trading resumed [782].) By 2003, the technology had improved somewhat, with one vendor recognising 64% of subjects against a database of over 30,000, although performance outdoors was poorer. Tests done in 2001 by the UK National Physical Laboratory (NPL) of a number of biometric technologies found that face recognition was almost the worst, outperforming only vein patterns; its single-attempt equal-error rate was almost ten percent [834]. A UK Passport Office trial in 2005, that was a better approximation to field conditions, found it recognised only 69% of users (though this fell to 48% for disabled participants) [1274].

So the technology still does not work very well in engineering terms. But there are applications where it can have an effect. For example, the Illinois Department of Motor Vehicles uses it to detect people who apply for extra drivers' licenses in false names [454]. Where wrongdoers can be punished, it may be worthwhile to try to detect them even if you only catch a quarter of them (that's still better than the 8% or so of house burglars we catch).

Face recognition has also been used as what Bruce Schneier calls 'security theater'. In 1998, the London borough of Newham placed video cameras prominently in the high street and ran a PR campaign about how their new computer system constantly scanned the faces in the crowd for several hundred known local criminals. They managed to get a significant reduction in burglary, shoplifting and street crime. The system even worries civil libertarians — but it worked entirely by the placebo effect [1227]. The police have since admitted that they only ever had 20 or 25 villains' faces on the system, and it never recognised any of them [871]. In Tampa, Florida, a similar system was abandoned after an ACLU freedom of information request discovered that it had recognised no villains [1072]. The ACLU welcomed its demise, remarking that 'every person who walked down the street was subjected to an electronic police line-up without their consent'. (Given that the technology just didn't work, this was maybe a tad zealous.) Face recognition was also tried at Boston's Logan airport; passengers passing through security screening were observed and matched. The system was found to be impractical, with no useful balance between false matches and false alarms [222].

Yet facial recognition is already the second largest-selling biometric with a nominal 19% of the market. However, much of this relates to the automated storage of facial images that are compared by humans — for example, the photos stored in the chips on the new biometric passports. The market for automated recognition is much smaller. Maybe as time passes and technology improves, both its potential (and the privacy worries) will increase.

15.4   Bertillonage

Inventors in the nineteenth century spent quite a lot of effort trying to identify people by their bodily measurements. The most famous of these, Alphonse Bertillon, started out as a clerk in the police records department in Paris, where an important task was to identify serial offenders. In 1882 he published a system based on bodily measurements, such as height standing and sitting, the length and width of the face, and the size and angle of the ear. These were principally used to index a collection of record cards that also held mugshots and thumbprints, which could be used to confirm an identification. This system was known as 'anthropometry', and also as 'Bertillonage' in honour of its creator. Eventually it fell out of favour, once police forces understood how to index and search for fingerprints.

This technique has made a comeback in the form of hand-geometry readers. In addition to its use since the 1970s in nuclear premises entry control, hand geometry is now used at airports by the U.S. Immigration and Naturalization Service to provide a 'fast track' for frequent flyers. It is simple to implement and fairly robust, and the NPL trials found a single-attempt equal error rate of about one percent [834]. (Passport inspection is a less critical application than one might initially think, as airline staff also check passports against passenger lists and provide these lists to the homeland security folks.) Hand geometry is now reported to have 8.8% of the biometric market.

15.5   Fingerprints

Automatic fingerprint identification systems (AFIS) are by far the biggest single technology. In 1998, AFIS products accounted for a whopping 78%

of the \$50 m sales of biometric technology; the huge growth of the industry since then has cut this in percentage terms to 43.5% of \$1,539m by 2005, but it leads all other automated recognition options. AFIS products look at the friction ridges that cover the fingertips and classify patterns of *minutiae* such as branches and end points of the ridges. Some also look at the pores in the skin of the ridges. A recent technical reference book on automatic fingerprint identification systems is [832].

The use of fingerprints to identify people was discovered independently a number of times. Mark Twain mentions thumbprints in 1883 in *Life on the Mississippi* where he claims to have learned about them from an old Frenchman who had been a prison-keeper; his 1894 novel *Pudd'nhead Wilson* made the idea popular in the States. Long before that, fingerprints were accepted in a seventh century Chinese legal code as an alternative to a seal or a signature, and required by an eighth century Japanese code when an illiterate man wished to divorce his wife. They were also used in India centuries ago. Following the invention of the microscope, they were mentioned by the English botanist Nathaniel Grew in 1684, by Marcello Malpighi in Italy in 1686; in 1691, 225 citizens of Londonderry in Ireland used their fingerprints to sign a petition asking for reparations following the siege of the city by King William.

The first modern systematic use was in India from 1858, by William Herschel, grandson of the astronomer and a colonial magistrate. He introduced handprints and then fingerprints to sign contracts, stop impersonation of pensioners who had died, and prevent rich criminals paying poor people to serve their jail sentences for them. Henry Faulds, a medical missionary in Japan, discovered them independently in the 1870s, and came up with the idea of using latent prints from crime scenes to identify criminals. Faulds brought fingerprints to the attention of Charles Darwin, who in turn motivated Francis Galton to study them. Galton wrote an article in *Nature* [510]; this got him in touch with the retired Herschel, whose data convinced Galton that fingerprints persisted throughout a person's life. Galton went on to collect many more prints and devise a scheme for classifying their patterns [511]. The Indian history is told by Chandak Sengoopta, whose book also makes the point that fingerprinting saved two somewhat questionable Imperial institutions, namely the indentured labor system and the opium trade [1145].

The practical introduction of the technique owes a lot to Sir Edward Henry, who had been a policeman in Bengal. He wrote a book in 1900 describing a simpler and more robust classification, of *loops*, *whorls*, *arches* and *tents*, that he had developed with his assistants Azizul Haque and Hem Chandra Bose, and that is still in use today. In the same year he became Commissioner of the Metropilitan Police in London from where the technique spread round the world[2]. Henry's real scientific contribution was to develop Galton's classification into an indexing system. By assigning one bit to whether or not each of a suspect's ten fingers had a whorl — a type of circular pattern — he divided the fingerprint files into 1024 bins. In this way, it was possible to reduce the number of records that have to be searched by orders of magnitude. Meanwhile, as Britain had stopped sending convicted felons to Australia, there was a perceived need to identify previous offenders, so that they could be given longer jail sentences.

Fingerprints are now used by the world's police forces for essentially two different purposes: identifying people (the main use in the USA), and crime scene forensics (their main use in Europe).

I'll now look at these two technologies in turn.

15.5.1 Verifying Positive or Negative Identity Claims

In America nowadays — as in nineteenth-century England — quite a few criminals change their names and move somewhere new on release from prison. This is fine when offenders go straight, but what about fugitives and recidivists? American police forces have historically used fingerprints to identify arrested suspects to determine whether they're currently wanted by other agencies, whether they have criminal records and whether they've previously come to attention under other names. The FBI maintains a large online system for this purpose; it identifies about eight thousand fugitives a month [1208]. It is also used to screen job applicants; for example, anyone wanting a U.S. government clearance at Secret or above must have an FBI fingerprint check, and checks are also run on some people applying to work with children or the elderly. Up to 100,000 fingerprint checks are made a day, and 900,000 federal, local and state law enforcement officers have access. There's now a project to expand this to contain other biometrics, to hold data on foreign nationals, and to provide a 'rap-back' service that will alert the employer of anyone with a clearance who gets into trouble with the law — all of which disturbs civil-rights groups [927]. Since 9/11, fingerprints are also used in immigration. The US-VISIT program fingerprints all aliens arriving at U.S. ports and matches them against a watch list of bad guys, compiled with the help of other police forces and intelligence services worldwide.

These are examples of one type of identity verification — checking an (implicit) claim not to be on a blacklist. The other type is where the system

---

[2]In the Spanish version of history, they were first used in Argentina where they secured a murder conviction in 1892; while Cuba, which set up its fingerprint bureau in 1907, beat the USA whose first conviction was in Illinois in 1911. The Croation version notes that the Argentinian system was developed by one Juan Vucetich, who had emigrated from Dalmatia. The German version refers to Professor Purkinje of Breslau, who wrote about fingerprints in 1828. Success truly has many fathers!

checks a claim to have a certain known identity. Fingerprints are used for this purpose in the USA for building entry control and welfare payment [405]; and banks use them to identify customers in countries such as India and Saudi Arabia, where the use of ink fingerprints was already common thanks to high levels of illiteracy.

Fingerprints have not really taken off in banking systems in North America or Europe because of the association with crime, though a few U.S. banks do ask for fingerprints if you cash a check there and are not a customer. They find this cuts check fraud by about a half. Some have gone as far as fingerprinting new customers, and found that customer resistance is less than expected, especially if they use scanners rather than ink and paper [497]. These applications are not routine identity verification, though, so much as an attempt to identify customers who later turn out to be bad — another example being the large British van-hire company that demands a thumbprint when you rent a van. If the vehicle isn't returned, or if it's used in a crime and then turns out to have been rented with a stolen credit card, the thumbprint is given to the police. They are thus really a 'crime scene forensics' application, which I'll discuss in the following section.

So how good are automatic fingerprint identification systems? A good rule of thumb (if one might call it that) is that to verify a claim to identity, it may be enough to scan a single finger, while to check someone against a blacklist of millions of felons, you had better scan all ten. In fact, the US-VISIT program set out to scan just the two index fingers of each arriving visitor, and has been overwhelmed by false matches. With 6,000,000 bad guys on the database, the false match rate in 2004 was 0.31% and the missed match rate 4% [1347]. Although these numbers could be improved somewhat by using the best algorithms we have now in 2007, the program is now moving to '10-prints', as they're called, where each visitor will present the four fingers of each hand, and then both thumbs, in three successive scans.

This is all about the trade-off between false negatives and false positives — the receiver operating characteristic, described in the previous section. In 2001, the NPL study found a 1% false match and 8% false accept rate for common products; by now, the better ones have an equal error rate of slightly below 1% per finger. False accepts happen because of features incorporated to reduce the false reject rate — such as allowance for distortion and flexibility in feature selection [1080]. Spotting returning fugitives with high enough probability to deter them and high enough certainty to detain them (which means keeping false alarms at manageable levels) will require several fingers to be matched — perhaps eight out of ten. But requiring every finger of every passenger to be scanned properly at immigration may cause delays; a UK Passport Office study found that about 20% of participants failed to register properly when taking a 10-print, and that 10-print verification took over a minute [1274]. This will come down with time, but with even an extra

30 seconds per passenger, an airport getting a planeload of 300 international arrivals every 15 minutes would need an extra 10 working immigration lanes. The extra building and staffing costs could swamp anything spent on hardware and software. (For more on algorithms and systems, see [832, 656, 831].)

Errors are not uniformly distributed. A number of people such as manual workers and pipe smokers damage their fingerprints frequently, and both the young and the old have faint prints [275]. Automated systems also have problems with amputees, people with birth defects such as extra fingers, and the (rare) people born without conventional fingerprint patterns at all [764]. Fingerprint damage can also impair recognition. When I was a kid, I slashed my left middle finger while cutting an apple, and this left a scar about half an inch long. When I presented this finger to the system used in 1989 by the FBI for building entry control, my scar crashed the scanner. (It worked OK with the successor system from the same company when I tried again ten years later.) Even where scars don't cause gross system malfunctions, they still increase the error rate.

Fingerprint identification systems can be attacked in a number of ways. An old trick was for a crook to distract (or bribe) the officer fingerprinting him, so that instead of the hand being indexed under the Henry system as '01101' it becomes perhaps '01011', so his record isn't found and he gets the lighter sentence due a first offender [764]. The most recent batch of headlines was in 2002, when Tsutomu Matsumoto caused much alarm in the industry; he and his colleagues showed that fingerprints could be molded and cloned quickly and cheaply using cooking gelatin [845]. He tested eleven commercially available fingerprint readers and easily fooled all of them. This prompted the German computer magazine C'T to test a number of biometric devices that were offered for sale at the CeBIT electronic fair in Hamburg — nine fingerprint readers, one face-recognition system and one iris scanner. They were all easy to fool — the low-cost capacitative sensors often by such simple tricks as breathing on a finger scanner to reactivate a latent print left there by a previous, authorized, user [1246]. Latent fingerprints can also be reactivated — or transferred — using adhesive tape. The more expensive thermal scanners could still be defeated by rubber molded fingers.

However, fingerprint systems still dominate the biometric market, and are rapidly expanding into relatively low-assurance applications, from entry into golf club car parks to automatic book borrowing in school libraries. (Most European countries' privacy authorities have banned the use of fingerprint scanners in schools; Britain allows it, subject to government guidelines, with the rationale that fingerprints can't be reverse engineered from templates and thus privacy is protected [132]. As I'll discuss later, this reasoning is bogus.)

An important aspect of the success of fingerprint identification systems is not so much their error rate, as measured under laboratory conditions, but their deterrent effect. This is particularly pronounced in welfare payment systems. Even though the cheap fingerprint readers used to authenticate welfare claimants have an error rate as much as 5% [267], they have turned out to be such an effective way of reducing the welfare rolls that they have been adopted in one place after another [890].

15.5.2 Crime Scene Forensics

The second use of fingerprint recognition is in crime scene forensics. In Europe, forensics are the main application. Prints found at a crime scene are matched against database records, and any that match to more than a certain level are taken as hard evidence that a suspect visited the crime scene. They are often enough to secure a conviction on their own. In some countries, fingerprints are required from all citizens and all resident foreigners.

The error rate in forensic applications has become extremely controversial in recent years, the critical limitation being the size and quality of the image taken from the crime scene. The quality and procedure rules vary from one country to another. The UK used to require that fingerprints match in sixteen *points* (corresponding minutiae), and a UK police expert estimated that this will only happen by chance somewhere between one in four billion and one in ten billion matches [764]. Greece accepts 10, Turkey 8, while the USA has no set limit (it certifies examiners instead). This means that in the USA, matches can be found with poorer quality prints but they can be open to doubt.

In the UK, fingerprint evidence went for almost a century without a successful challenge; a 16-point fingerprint match was considered to be incontrovertible evidence. The courts' confidence in this was shattered by the notorious McKie case [867]. Shirley McKie, a Scottish policewoman, was prosecuted on the basis of a fingerprint match on the required sixteen points, verified by four examiners of the Scottish Criminal Records Office. She denied that it was her fingerprint, and found that she could not get an independent expert in Britain to support her; the profession closed ranks. She called two American examiners who presented testimony that it is not an identification. The crime scene print is in Figure 15.1, and her file print is at Figure 15.2.

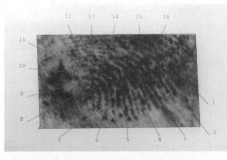

Figure 15.1: Crime scene print

Figure 15.2: Inked print

She was acquitted [866], which led to a political drama that ran on for years. The first problem was the nature of the case against her [867]. A number of senior police officers had tried to persuade her to make a false statement in order to explain the presence, at the scene of a gruesome murder, of the misidentified print. Her refusal to do so led to her being prosecuted for perjury, as a means of discrediting her. Her acquittal said in effect that Glasgow police officers were not reliable witnesses. An immediate effect was that the man convicted of the murder, David Asbury, was acquitted on appeal and sued the police for compensation. A longer term effect was to undermine confidence in fingerprints as forensic evidence. The government then prosecuted its four fingerprint experts for perjury, but this didn't get anywhere either. The issue went back to the Scottish parliament again and again. The police refused to reinstate Shirley, the officers involved got promoted, and the row got ever more acrimonious. Eventually she won £750,000 compensation from the government [130].

The McKie case led to wide discussion among experts of the value of fingerprint identification [522]. It also led to fingerprint evidence being successfully challenged in a number of other countries. Two high-profile cases in the USA were Stephan Cowans and Brandon Mayfield. Cowans had been convicted of shooting a police officer in 1997 following a robbery, but was acquitted on appeal six years later after he argued that his print was a misidentification and saved up enough money to have the evidence tested for DNA. The DNA didn't match, which got the Boston and State police to reanalyze the fingerprint, whereupon they realised it was not a match after all. Brandon Mayfield was an Oregon lawyer who was mistakenly identified by the FBI as one of the perpetrators of the Madrid bombing, and held for two weeks until the Madrid police arrested another man whose fingerprint was a better match. The FBI, which had called their match 'absolutely incontrovertible', agreed to pay Mayfield $2 m in 2006.

In a subsequent study, psychologist Itiel Dror showed five fingerprint examiners a pair of prints, told them they were from the Mayfield case, and asked them where the FBI had gone wrong. Three of the examiners decided that the prints did not match and pointed out why; one was unsure; and one maintained that they did match. He alone was right. The prints weren't the Mayfield set, but were in each case a pair that the examiner himself had matched in a recent criminal case [402]. Dror repeated this with six experts who each looked at eight prints, all of which they had examined for real in the previous few years. Only two of the experts remained consistent; the other four made six inconsistent decisions between them. The prints had a range of difficulty, and in only half of the cases was misleading contextual information supplied [403].

How did we get to a point where law enforcement agencies insist to juries that forensic results are error-free when FBI proficiency exams have long had an error rate of about one percent [141], and misleading contextual information can push this up to ten percent or more?

Four comments are in order.

- As Figure 15.1 should make clear, fingerprint impressions are often very noisy, being obscured by dirt. So mistakes are quite possible, and the skill (and prejudices) of the examiner enter into the equation in a much bigger way than was accepted until the McKie case, the Mayfield case, and the general uproar that they have caused. Dror's work confirmed that the cases in which misidentifications occur tend to be the difficult ones [403]. Yet the forensic culture was such that only certainty was acceptable; the International Association for Identification, the largest forensic group, held that testifying about "possible, probable or likely identification shall be deemed . . . conduct unbecoming." [141]

- Even if the probability of a false match on sixteen points were one in ten billion (10^{-10}) as claimed by police optimists, once many prints are compared against each other, probability theory starts to bite. A system that worked fine in the old days as a crime scene print would be compared manually with the records of a hundred and fifty-seven known local burglars, breaks down once thousands of prints are compared every year with an online database of millions. It was inevitable that sooner or later, enough matches would have been done to find a 16-point mismatch. Indeed, as most people on the fingerprint database are petty criminals who will not be able to muster the resolute defence that Shirley McKie did, I would be surprised if there hadn't already been other wrongful convictions. Indeed, things may get worse, because of a 2007 agreement between European police forces that they will link up their biometric databases (both fingerprints and DNA) so that police forces can search for matches across all EU member states [1261]. I expect they will find they need to develop a better understanding of probability, and much more robust ways of handling false positives.

- The belief that any security mechanism is infallible creates the complacency and carelessness needed to undermine its proper use. No consideration appears to have been given to increasing the number of points required from sixteen to (say) twenty with the introduction of computer matching. Sixteen was tradition, the system was infallible, and there was certainly no reason to make public funds available for defendants' experts. In the UK, all the experts were policemen or former policemen, so there were no independents available for hire. Even so, it would have been possible to use randomised matching with multiple experts; but if the fingerprint bureau had had to tell the defence in the perhaps 5–10% of cases when (say) one of four experts disagreed, then many more defendants would have been acquitted and the fingerprint service would have been seen as less valuable.

▪ A belief of infallibility ensures that the consequences of the eventual failure will be severe. As with the Munden case described in section 10.4.3, which helped torpedo claims about cash machine security, an assumption that a security mechanism is infallible causes procedures, cultural assumptions and even laws to spring up which ensure that its eventual failure will be denied for as long as possible, and will thus have serious effects when it can no longer be postponed. In the Scottish case, there appears to have arisen a hierarchical risk-averse culture in which no-one wanted to rock the boat, so examiners were predisposed to confirm identifications made by colleagues (especially senior colleagues). This risk aversion backfired when four of them were tried for perjury.

However, even when we do have a correct match its implications are not always entirely obvious. It is possible for fingerprints to be transferred using adhesive tape, or for molds to be made — even without the knowledge of the target — using techniques originally devised for police use. So it is possible that the suspect whose print is found at the crime scene was framed by another criminal (or by the police — most fingerprint fabrication cases involve law enforcement personnel rather than other suspects [179]). Of course, even if the villain wasn't framed, he can always claim that he was and the jury might believe him.

In the USA, the Supreme Court's Daubert judgment [350] ruled that trial judges should screen the principles and methodology behind forensic evidence to ensure it is relevant and reliable. The judge ought to consider the refereed scientific literature — and in the case of fingerprints this has been somewhat lacking, as law enforcement agencies have been generally unwilling to submit their examination procedures to rigorous double-blind testing. A number of Daubert hearings relating to forensic fingerprint evidence have recently been held in U.S. trials, and the FBI has generally prevailed [523]. However, the bureau's former line that fingerprint examination has a zero error rate is now widely ridiculed [1208].

15.6   Iris Codes

We turn now from the traditional ways of identifying people to the modern and innovative. Recognizing people by the patterns in the irises of their eyes is far and away the technique with the best error rates of automated systems when measured under lab conditions. Research on the subject was funded by the Department of Energy, which wanted the most secure possible way of controlling entry to premises such as plutonium stores, and the technology is now being used in applications such as immigration. The latest international standards for machine-readable travel documents mandate the use of photographs, and permit both fingerprints and irises.

So far as is known, every human iris is measurably unique. It is fairly easy to detect in a video picture, it does not wear out, and it is isolated from the external environment by the cornea (which in turn has its own cleaning mechanism). The iris pattern contains a large amount of randomness, and appears to have many times the number of degrees of freedom of a fingerprint. It is formed between the third and eighth month of gestation, and (like the fingerprint pattern) is *phenotypic* in that there appears to be limited genetic influence; the mechanisms that form it appear to be chaotic. So the patterns are different even for identical twins (and for the two eyes of a single individual), and they appear to be stable throughout life.

John Daugman found signal processing techniques that extract the information from an image of the iris into a 256 byte *iris code*. This involves a circular wavelet transform taken at a number of concentric rings between the pupil and the outside of the iris (Figure 15.3). The resulting iris codes have the neat property that two codes computed from the same iris will typically match in 90% of their bits [351]. This is much simpler than in fingerprint scanners where orienting and classifying the minutiae is a hard task. The speed and accuracy of iris coding has led to a number of commercial iris recognition products [1327]. Iris codes provide the lowest false accept rates of any known verification system — zero, in tests conducted by both the U.S. Department of

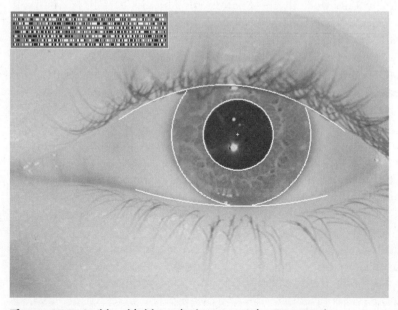

Figure 15.3: An iris with iris code (courtesy John Daugman)

Energy and the NPL [834]. The equal error rate has been shown to be better than one in a million, and if one is prepared to tolerate a false reject rate of one in ten thousand then the theoretical false accept rate would be less than one in a trillion. In practice, the false reject rate is significantly higher than this; many things, from eyelashes to hangovers, can cause the camera to not see enough of the iris. The U.S. Department of Defense found a 6% false reject rate in its 2002 field trials [852]; the Passport Office trial found 4% for normal users and 9% for disabled users [1274]. A further problem is failure to enrol; the Passport Office trial failed to enrol 10% of participants, and the rate was higher among black users, the over-60s and the disabled.

One practical problem with iris scanning used to be getting the picture cheaply without being too intrusive. The iris is small (less than half an inch) and an image including several hundred pixels of iris is needed. A cooperative subject can place his eye within a few inches of a video camera, and the best standard equipment will work up to a distance of two or three feet. Cooperation can be assumed with entry control to computer rooms. But it is less acceptable in general retail applications as some people find being so close to a camera uncomfortable. All current iris scanning systems use infrared light, and some people feel uncomfortable when this is shone in their eyes. (The Chinese government gave this as an excuse for rejecting iris scanning for the latest Hong Kong identity cards, going for a thumbprint instead [771].) Given more sophisticated cameras, with automatic facial feature recognition, pan and zoom, it is now possible to capture iris codes from airline passengers covertly as they walk along a corridor [841], and no doubt the cost will come down in time (especially once the key patent runs out in 2011). This is likely to make overt uses less objectionable; but covert identification of passers-by has Orwellian overtones, and in Europe, data protection law could be a show-stopper.

Possible attacks on iris recognition systems include — in unattended operation at least — a simple photograph of the target's iris. This may not be a problem in entry control to supervised premises, but if everyone starts to use iris codes to authenticate bank card transactions, then your code will become known to many organizations. There are terminals available that will detect such simple fakes, for example by measuring *hippus* — a natural fluctuation in the diameter of the pupil that happens at about 0.5 Hz. But the widely-sold cheap terminals don't do this, and if liveness detection became widespread then no doubt attackers would try more sophisticated tricks, such as printing the target's iris patterns on a contact lens.

As iris recognition is fairly new, we don't have as much experience with it as we have with fingerprints. The biggest deployment so far is in the United Arab Emirates where it's used to screen incoming travelers against a blacklist of people previously deported for illegal working. The blacklist has 595,000 people as of July 2007 — 1.19 million irises — and so far 150,000 deportees have been caught trying to re-enter the country. The typical arrestee is a lady with a previous conviction for prostitution, who returns with a genuine (but corruptly issued) passport, in a new name, from a low or middle income Asian country. A typical attack was for the returning deportee to take atropine eyedrops on the plane, dilating her pupils; nowadays such travelers are held in custody until their eyes return to normal. Nonetheless, the atropine trick might be a problem for blacklist applications in developed countries. There might also be evidentiary problems, as iris recognition depends on computer processing; there are no 'experts' at recognising eyes, and it's doubtful whether humans could do so reliably, as the information that John Daugman's algorithms depend on is mostly phase information, to which the human eye is insensitive. (In developed countries, however, the typical application is a frequent-traveler program that allows enrolees to bypass passport control at an airport; there the users want to be recognised, rather than wanting not to be. The UK, for example, has such a scheme with 200,000 enrolees. Here, evidence isn't really an issue.)

Despite the difficulties, iris codes remain a very strong contender as they can, in the correct circumstances, provide much greater certainty than any other method that the individual in front of you is the same human as the one who was initially registered on the system. They alone can meet the goal of automatic recognition with zero false acceptances.

15.7 Voice Recognition

Voice recognition — also known as *speaker recognition* — is the problem of identifying a speaker from a short utterance. While *speech recognition* systems are concerned with transcribing speech and need to ignore speech idiosyncrasies, voice recognition systems need to amplify and classify them. There are many subproblems, such as whether the recognition is text dependent or not, whether the environment is noisy, whether operation must be real time and whether one needs only to verify speakers or to recognize them from a large set.

As with fingerprints, the technology is used for both identification and forensics. In *forensic phonology*, the task is usually to match a recorded telephone conversation, such as a bomb threat, to speech samples from a number of suspects. Typical techniques involve filtering and extracting features from the spectrum; for more details see [721]. A more straightforward biometric authentication objective is to verify a claim to identity in some telephone systems. These range from telephone banking to the identification of military personnel, with over a dozen systems on the market. Campbell describes a system that can be used with the U.S. government STU-III encrypting telephone and that achieves an equal error rate of about 1% [264]; and the NSA maintains a standard corpus of test data for evaluating speaker recognition systems [655]. A recent application is the use of voice recognition to track asylum seekers in the UK; they will be required to ring in several times every week [1260]. Such systems tend to use caller-ID to establish where people are, and are also used for people like football hooligans who're under court orders not to go to certain places at certain times.

There are some interesting attacks on these systems, quite apart from the possibility that a villain might somehow manage to train himself to imitate your voice in a manner that the equipment finds acceptable. In [506] there is a brief description of a system fielded in U.S. EP-3 aircraft that breaks up intercepted messages from enemy aircraft and ground controllers into quarter second segments that are then cut and pasted to provide new, deceptive messages. This is primitive compared with what can now be done with digital signal processing. Some informed observers expect that within a few years, there will be products available that support real-time voice and image forgery. Crude voice morphing systems already exist, and enable female victims of telephone sex pests to answer the phone with a male sounding voice. There has been research aimed at improving them to the point that call centers can have the same 'person' always greet you when you phone; and audio remixing products improve all the time. Remote voice biometrics look less and less able to withstand a capable motivated opponent.

15.8   Other Systems

Many other biometric technologies have been proposed [890]. Typing patterns, were used in products in the 1980s but don't appear to have been successful (typing patterns, also known as keystroke dynamics, had a famous precursor in the wartime technique of identifying wireless telegraphy operators by their *fist*, the way in which they used a Morse key). Vein patterns have been used in one or two systems but don't seem to have been widely sold (in the NPL trials, the vein recognition ROC curve was almost all outside the other curves; it was the worst of the lot) [834].

There has been growing interest recently in identifying anonymous authors from their writing styles. Literary analysis of course goes back many years; as a young man, the famous cryptologist William Friedman was hired by an eccentric millionaire to study whether Bacon wrote Shakespeare. (He eventually debunked this idea but got interested in cryptography in the process.) Computers make it possible to run ever more subtle statistical tests; applications range from trying to identify people who post to extremist web fora to such mundane matters as plagiarism detection [3]. It's possible that such software will move from forensic applications to real-time monitoring, in which case it would become a biometric identification technology.

Other proposals include *facial thermograms* (maps of the surface temperature of the face, derived from infrared images), the shape of the ear, gait, lip prints and the patterns of veins in the hand. Bertillon used the shape of the ear in nineteenth century Paris, but most of the rest of these exotica don't seem to have been marketed as products. Other technologies may provide opportunities in the future. For example, the huge investment in developing digital noses for quality control in the food and drink industries may lead to a 'digital doggie' which recognizes its master by scent.

One final biometric deserves passing mention — DNA typing. This has become a valuable tool for crime scene forensics and for determining parenthood in child support cases, but it is still too slow for applications like building entry control. Being genotypic rather than phenotypic, its accuracy is also limited by the incidence of monozygotic twins: about one white person in 120 has an identical twin. There's also a privacy problem in that it should soon be possible to reconstruct a large amount of information about an individual from his DNA sample. There have been major procedural problems, with false matches resulting from sloppy lab procedure. And there are also major data quality problems; the UK police have the biggest DNA database in the world, with records on about four million people, but have got the names misspelled or even wrong for about half a million of them [588]. The processes that work for local policing don't always scale nationally — small errors from mistyped records, to suspects giving false names that were never discovered because they weren't prosecuted, accumulate along with lab errors until the false-positive rate becomes a serious operational and political issue. For a survey of forensic DNA analysis, and suggestions of how to make national DNA databases consistent with privacy law, see [1124].

15.9   What Goes Wrong

As with other aspects of security, we find the usual crop of failures due to bugs, blunders and complacency. The main problem faced by DNA typing, for example, was an initially high rate of false positives, due to careless laboratory procedure. This scared off some police forces which sent in samples from different volunteers and got back false matches, but also led to disputed court cases and miscarriages of justice. This is reminiscent of the fingerprint story, and brings to mind the quote from Lars Knudsen at the head of Chapter 5: *'if it's provably secure, it probably isn't'*. Any protection measure that's believed to be infallible will make its operators careless enough to break it.

Biometrics are also like many other physical protection mechanisms (alarms, seals, tamper sensing enclosures, . . .) in that environmental conditions can cause havoc. Noise, dirt, vibration and unreliable lighting conditions all take their toll. Some systems, like speaker recognition, are vulnerable to alcohol intake and stress. Changes in environmental assumptions, such as from closed to open systems, from small systems to large ones, from attended to stand-alone, from cooperative to recalcitrant subjects, and from verification to identification, can all undermine a system's viability.

There are a number of interesting attacks that are more specific to biometric systems and that apply to more than one type of biometric.

■ Forensic biometrics often don't tell as much as one might assume. Apart from the possibility that a fingerprint or DNA sample might have been planted by the police, it may just be old. The age of a fingerprint can't be determined directly, and prints on areas with public access say little. A print on a bank door says much less than a print in a robbed vault. So in premises vulnerable to robbery, cleaning procedures may be critical for evidence. If a suspect's prints are found on a bank counter, and he claims that he had gone there three days previously, he may be convicted by evidence that the branch counter is polished every evening. Putting this in system terms, freshness is often a critical issue, and some quite unexpected things can find themselves inside the 'trusted computing base'.

■ Another aspect of freshness is that most biometric systems can, at least in theory, be attacked using suitable recordings. We mentioned direct attacks on voice recognition, attacks on iris scanners by photos on a contact lens, and moulds of fingerprints. Even simpler still, in countries like South Africa where fingerprints are used to pay pensions, there are persistent tales of 'Granny's finger in the pickle jar' being the most valuable property she bequeathed to her family. The lesson to be learned here is that unattended operation of biometric authentication devices is tricky. Attacks aren't always straightforward; although it's easy to make a mold from a good fingerprint [281], the forensic-grade prints that people leave lying around on doorknobs, beer glasses and so on are often too smudged and fragmentary to pass an identification system. However, attacks are definitely possible, and definitely happen.

■ Most biometrics are not as accurate for all people, and some of the population can't be identified as reliably as the rest (or even at all). The elderly, and manual workers, often have damaged or abraded fingerprints. People with dark eyes, and large pupils, give poorer iris codes. Disabled people with no fingers, or no eyes, risk exclusion if such systems become widespread. Illiterates who make an 'X' are more at risk from signature forgery.

Biometric engineers sometimes refer to such subjects dismissively as goats, but this is foolish and offensive. A biometric system that is (or is seen to be) socially regressive — that puts the disabled, the poor, the old and ethnic minorities at greater risk of impersonation — may meet with principled resistance. In fact a biometric system might be defeated by legal challenges on a number of grounds [1046]. It may also be vulnerable to villains who are (or pretend to be) disabled. Fallback modes of operation will have to be provided. If these are less secure, then forcing their use may yield an attack, and if they are at least as secure, then why use biometrics at all?

- A point that follows from this is that systems may be vulnerable to collusion. Alice opens a bank account and her accomplice Betty withdraws money from it; Alice then complains of theft and produces a watertight alibi. Quite apart from simply letting Betty take a rubber impression of her fingertip, Alice might voluntarily decrease handwriting ability; by giving several slightly different childish sample signatures, she can force the machine to accept a lower threshold than usual. She can spend a couple of weeks as a bricklayer, building a wall round her garden, and wear her fingerprints flat, so as to degrade registration in a fingerprint system. She might register for a voice recognition system when drunk.

- The statistics are often not understood by system designers, and the birthday theorem is particularly poorly appreciated. With 10,000 biometrics in a database, for example, there are about 50,000,000 pairs. So even with a false accept rate of only one in a million, the likelihood of there being at least one false match will rise above one-half as soon as there are somewhat over a thousand people (in fact, 1609 people) enrolled. So identification is a tougher task than verification [352]. The practical consequence is that a system designed for authentication may fail when you try to rely on it for evidence.

- Another aspect of statistics comes into play when designers assume that by combining biometrics they can get a lower error rate. The curious and perhaps counter-intuitive result is that a combination will typically result in improving either the false accept or the false reject rate, while making the other worse. One way to look at this is that if you install two different burglar alarm systems at your home, then the probability that they will be simultaneously defeated goes down while the number of false alarms goes up. In some cases, such as when a very good biometric is combined with a very imprecise one, the effect can be worse overall [352].

- Many vendors have claimed that their products protect privacy, as what's stored is not the image of your face or fingerprint or iris, but rather a template that's derived from it, somewhat like a one-way hash, and from which you can't be identified. It's been argued from this that biometric data are not personal data, in terms of privacy law, and can thus be passed around without restriction. These claims were exploded by Andy Adler who came up with an interesting *hill-climbing attack* on face recognition systems. Given a recogniser that outputs how close an input image is to a target template, the input face is successively altered to increase the match. With the tested systems, this led rapidly to a recognizable image of the target — a printout of which would be accepted as the target's face [14]. He then showed how this hill-climbing technique could be used to attack other biometrics, including some based on fingerprints [15].

▪ Automating biometrics can subtly change the way in which security protocols work, so that stuff that used to work now doesn't. An example is the biometric passport or identity card that contains your digital photo, and perhaps your fingerprint and iris data, on an RFID chip. The chip can be cloned by copying the contents to another RFID chip (or replaying them through a phone with an NFC interface.) The world's passport offices took the view that this wasn't a big deal as the data are signed and so the chip can't be altered. However, the police have another use for passports — if you're on bail they insist that you leave your passport with them. That protocol now breaks if you can leave the country via the fast track channel by replaying your iris data through your mobile phone. There was also some embarrassment when researchers discovered that despite the digital signature, they could modify the RFID contents after all — by replacing the JPEG facial image with a bitstring that crashed the reader [1374]. This in turn raises the question of whether a more cunningly designed bitstring could modify the reader's behaviour so that it accepted forged passports. I suppose the moral is that when passport offices digitized their systems they should have read all of this book, not just the chapters on biometrics and crypto.

▪ It's worth thinking what happens when humans and computers disagree. Iris data can't be matched by unaided humans at all; that technology is automatic-only. But what happens when a guard and a program disagree on whether a subject's face matches a file photo, or handwriting-recognition software says a bank manager's writing looks like a scrawled ransom note when they look quite different to the human eye? Psychologists advise that biometric systems should be used in ways that support and empower human cognition and that work within our social norms [404]. Yet we engineers often find it easier to treat the users as a nuisance that must adapt to our technology. This may degrade the performance of the humans. For example when an automated fingerprint database pulls out what it thinks is the most likely print and presents it to the examiner: is he not likely to be biased in its favour? Yet if the computer constantly tested the examiner's alertness by giving him the three best matches plus two poor matches, would that work any better?

- Finally, Christian fundamentalists are uneasy about biometric technology. They find written of the Antichrist in Revelation 13:16-18: 'And he causes all, both small and great, rich and poor, free and slave, to receive a mark on their right hand or on their foreheads, and that no one may buy or sell except one who has the mark or the name of the beast, or the number of his name.' So biometrics may arouse political opposition on the right as well as the left.

So there are some non-trivial problems to be overcome as biometrics tiptoe towards mass-market use. But despite the cost and the error rates, they have proved their worth in a number of applications — most notably where their deterrent effect is useful.

15.10   Summary

Biometric measures of one kind or another have been used to identify people since ancient times, with handwritten signatures, facial features and fingerprints being the traditional methods. Systems have been built that automate the task of recognition, using these methods and newer ones such as iris patterns and voiceprints. These systems have different strengths and weaknesses. In automatic operation, most have error rates of the order of 1% (though iris recognition is better, hand geometry slightly better, and face recognition much worse). There is always a trade-off between the false accept rate (the fraud rate) and the false reject rate (the insult rate). The statistics of error rates are deceptively difficult.

If any biometric becomes very widely used, there is increased risk of forgery in unattended operation: voice synthesisers, photographs of irises, fingerprint moulds and even good old-fashioned forged signatures must all be thought of in system design. These do not rule out the use of biometrics, as traditional methods such as handwritten signatures are usable in practice despite very large error rates. That particular case teaches us that context matters; even a weak biometric can be effective if its use is well embedded in the social and legal matrix.

Biometrics are usually more powerful in attended operation, where with good system design the relative strengths and weaknesses of the human guard and the machine recognition system may complement one another. Forensic uses are problematic, and courts are much less blindly trusting of even fingerprint evidence than they were ten years ago. Finally, many biometric systems achieve most or all of their result by deterring criminals rather than actually identifying them.

Research Problems

Many practical research problems relate to the design, or improvement, of biometric systems. Is it possible to build a system — other than iris scanning — which will meet the banks' goal of a 1% fraud rate and a 0.01% insult rate? Is it possible to build a static signature verification system which has a good enough error rate (say 1%) for it to be used for screening images of all checks, rather than just as a pre-screening stage to human inspection of high-value checks? Are there any completely new biometrics that might be useful in some circumstances?

One I thought up while writing this chapter for the first edition in 2000, in a conversation with William Clocksin and Alan Blackwell, was instrumenting a car so as to identify a driver by the way in which he operated the gears and the clutch. If your car thinks it's been stolen, it phones a GPS fix to a control center which then calls you to check. Recently this has come to pass; there is now research showing that users of haptic systems can be recognised by the way in which they use tools [990].

Further Reading

The history of fingerprints is good reading. The standard reference is Lambourne [764], while Block has a good collection of U.S. case histories [195] and the history of fingerprints in India is told by Sengoopta [1145]. The McKie case is described in a book by Ian McKie and Michael Russella [867]. A good technical reference on automated fingerprint identification systems is the book by Maltoni, Maio, Jain and Prabhakar [832]; there's also an earlier book by Jain, Bolle and Pankanti [655]. As for facial and handwriting recognition in the text, there's also an IBM experimental system described at [684] and a survey of the literature at [288]. The standard work on iris codes is Daugman [351]. For voice recognition, there is a tutorial in [264] which focuses on speaker identification while for the forensic aspects, see Klevans and Rodman [721]. Snapshots of the state of the technical art can be found in two journal special issues of the *Proceedings of the IEEE* on biometric systems — volume 85 no 9 (September 1997) and volume 94 no 11 (November 2006).

CHAPTER 16

Physical Tamper Resistance

It is relatively easy to build an encryption system that is secure if it is working as intended and is used correctly but it is still very hard to build a system that does not compromise its security in situations in which it is either misused or one or more of its sub-components fails (or is 'encouraged' to misbehave) . . . this is now the only area where the closed world is still a long way ahead of the open world and the many failures we see in commercial cryptographic systems provide some evidence for this.

— Brian Gladman

The amount of careful, critical security thinking that has gone into a given security device, system or program is inversely proportional to the amount of high-technology it uses.

— Roger Johnston

16.1   Introduction

Low-cost tamper-resistant devices are becoming almost ubiquitous. Examples I've discussed so far include:

- smartcards used as SIMs in mobile phones and as bank cards in Europe;
- accessory control chips used in printer toner cartridges, mobile phone batteries and games-console memory modules;
- the TPM chips being shipped in PCs and Macs to support hard-disk encryption, DRM and software registration;
- security modules used to manage bank PINs, not just in bank server farms but in ATMs and point-of-sale terminals;

- security modules buried in vending machines that sell everything from railway tickets through postage stamps to the magic numbers that activate your electricity meter.

Many of the devices on the market are simply pathetic, like the banking terminals whose failures I described in section 10.6.1.1: those terminals could be trivially compromised in under a minute using simple tools, despite having been evaluated by VISA and also using the Common Criteria framework.

Yet some tamper-resistant processors are getting pretty good. For example, I know of one firm that spent half a million dollars trying, and failing, to reverse-engineer the protocol used by a games console vendor to stop competitors making memory modules compatible with its equipment[1]. But a few years ago this was not the case. Serious tamper resistance emerged out of an arms race between firms that wanted to lock down their products, and others who wanted to unlock them. Some of the attackers were respectable companies exercising their legal rights to reverse engineer for compatibility. Others were lawyers, reverse engineering products to prove patent infringements. There are half a dozen specialist firms that work for the lawyers, and the legal reverse engineers. There are academics who hack systems for glory, and to push forward the state of the art. There are bad guys like the pay-TV pirates who clone subscriber cards. And finally there are lots of grey areas. If you find a way to unlock a particular make of mobile phone, so that it can be used on any network, is that a crime? The answer is, it depends what country you're in.

There are now many products on the market that claim to be tamper-resistant, from cheap microcontrollers through smartcards to expensive cryptoprocessors. Some of them are good; many are indifferent; and some are downright awful. It is increasingly important for the security engineer to understand what tamper resistance is, and what it can and can't do. In this chapter I'm going to take you through the past fifteen years or so, as ever more clever attacks have been met with successively more sophisticated defenses.

It has long been important to make computers resist physical tampering, as an attacker who can get access can in principle change the software and get the machine to do what he wants. While computers were massive objects, this involved the techniques discussed in the previous few chapters — physical barriers, sensors and alarms. In some applications, a computer is still made into a massive object: an ATM is basically a PC in a safe with banknote dispensers and alarm sensors, while the sensor packages used to detect unlawful nuclear tests may be at the bottom of a borehole several hundred feet deep and backfilled with concrete.

Where tamper resistance is needed purely for integrity and availability, it can sometimes be implemented using replication instead of physical protection. A

---

[1]Eventually the memory module was cracked, but it took a custom lab with chip testing equipment and a seven figure budget.

service may be implemented on different servers in different sites that perform transactions simultaneously and vote on the result; and the threshold schemes discussed in section 13.4 can also provide confidentiality for key material. But tamper-resistant devices can provide confidentiality for the data too. This is one respect in which the principle that many things can be done either with mathematics or with metal, breaks down.

16.2   History

The use of tamper resistance in cryptography goes back centuries [676]. Naval codebooks were weighted so they could be thrown overboard if capture was imminent; to this day, the dispatch boxes used by British government ministers' aides to carry state papers are lead lined so they will sink. Codes and, more recently, the keys for wartime cipher machines have been printed in water soluble ink; Russian one-time pads were printed on cellulose nitrate, so that they would burn furiously if lit; and one U.S. wartime cipher machine came with self-destruct thermite charges so it could be destroyed quickly.

But such mechanisms depended on the vigilance of the operator, and key material was often captured in surprise attacks. So attempts were made to automate the process. Early electronic devices, as well as some mechanical ciphers, were built so that opening the case erased the key settings.

Following a number of cases in which key material was sold to the other side by cipher staff — such as the notorious Walker family in the USA, who sold U.S. Navy key material to the Russians for over 20 years [587] — engineers paid more attention to the question of how to protect keys in transit too. The goal was 'to reduce the street value of key material to zero', and this can be achieved either by *tamper resistant* devices from which the key cannot be extracted, or *tamper evident* ones from which key extraction would be obvious.

Paper keys were once carried in 'tattle-tale containers', designed to show evidence of tampering. When electronic key distribution came along, a typical solution was the 'fill gun': a portable device that dispenses crypto keys in a controlled way. Nowadays this function is usually performed using a small security processor such as a smartcard; as with electricity meters, it may be packaged as a 'crypto ignition key'. Control protocols range from a limit on the number of times a key can be dispensed, to mechanisms using public key cryptography to ensure that keys are only loaded into authorized equipment. The control of key material also acquired broader purposes. In both the USA and the UK, it was centralized and used to enforce the use of properly approved computer and communications products. Live key material would only be supplied to a system once it had been properly accredited.

Once initial keys have been loaded, further keys may be distributed using various authentication and key agreement protocols. I already talked about many of the basic tools, such as key diversification, in the chapter on protocols in Part I, and I'll have more to say on protocols later in the chapter in API attacks. Here, I'm going to look first at the physical defenses against tampering.

16.3   High-End Physically Secure Processors

An example worth studying is the IBM 4758 (Figures 16.1 and 16.2). This is important for three reasons. First, it was the first commercially available processor to have been successfully evaluated to the highest level of tamper resistance (FIPS 140-1 level 4) [938] then set by the U.S. government. Second, there is an extensive public literature about it, including the history of its design evolution, its protection mechanisms, and the transaction set it supports [1195, 1328, 1330]. Third, as it was the first level-4-evaluated product, it was the highest profile target in the world of tamper resistance, and from 2000–2005 my students and I put some effort into attacking it.

Figure 16.1: The IBM 4758 cryptoprocessor (courtesy of Steve Weingart)

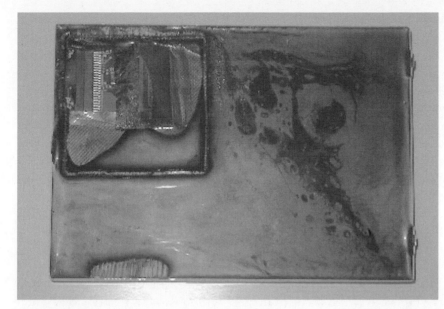

Figure 16.2: The 4758 partially opened showing (from top left downward) the circuitry, aluminium electromagnetic shielding, tamper sensing mesh and potting material (courtesy of Frank Stajano)

The evolution that led to this product is briefly as follows. The spread of multi-user operating systems, and the regularity with which bugs were found in their protection mechanisms, meant that large numbers of people might potentially have access to the data being processed. The reaction of the military computing community, which I described in Chapter 9, was the Anderson report and multilevel security. The reaction of the banking community was to focus on particularly sensitive data — and specifically on long-term cryptographic keys and the personal identification numbers (PINs) used by bank customers to identify themselves to cash machines. It was realized in the early 1980s that the level of protection available from commercial operating systems was likely to remain insufficient for these 'crown jewels'.

This led to the development of standalone *security modules* of which the first to be commercially successful were the IBM 3848 and the VISA security module. Both of these were microcomputers encased in robust metal enclosures, with encryption hardware and special *key memory*, which was static RAM designed to be zeroized when the enclosure was opened. This was accomplished by wiring the power supply to the key memory through a number of lid switches. So whenever the maintenance crew came to replace batteries, they'd open the lid and destroy the keys. Once they'd finished, the device operators would then reload the key material. In this way, the device's owner could be happy that its keys were under the unique control of its own staff.

How to hack a cryptoprocessor (1)

The obvious attack on such a device is for the operator to steal the keys. In early banking security modules, the master keys were kept in PROMs that were loaded into a special socket in the device to be read during initialization, or as strings of numbers which were typed in at a console. The PROMs could easily be pocketed, taken home and read out using hobbyist equipment. Cleartext paper keys were even easier to steal.

The fix was shared control — to have two or three PROMs with master key components, and make the device master keys the exclusive-or of all the components. The PROMs can then be kept in different safes under the control of different departments. (With the virtue of hindsight, the use of exclusive-or for this purpose was an error, and a hash function should have been used instead. I'll explain why shortly.)

However, this procedure is tedious and such procedures tend to degrade. In theory, when a device is maintained, its custodians should open the lid to erase the live keys, let the maintenance engineer load test keys, and then re-load live keys afterwards. The managers with custodial responsibility will often give their PROMs to the engineer rather than bothering with them. I've even come across cases of the master keys for an automatic teller machine being kept in the correspondence file in a bank branch, where any of the staff could look them up.

Prudent cryptography designers try to minimize the number of times that a key reload will be necessary, whether because of maintenance or power failure. So modern security modules typically have batteries to back up the mains power supply (at least to the key memory). Thus, in practice, the custodians have to load the keys only when the device is first installed, and after occasional maintenance visits after that.

It has been debated whether frequent or infrequent key loading is best. If key loading is very infrequent, then the responsible personnel will likely never have performed the task before, and may either delegate it out of ignorance, or be hoodwinked by a more technically astute member of staff into doing it in an insecure way (see [33] for a case history of this). The modern trend is toward devices that generate master keys (or have them loaded) in a secure facility after manufacture but before distribution. But not all keys can be embedded in the processor at the factory. Some keys may be kept on smartcards and used to bootstrap key sharing and backup between processors; others may be generated after distribution, especially signature keys that for legal reasons should always be under the customer's unique control.

How to hack a cryptoprocessor (2)

Early devices were vulnerable to attackers cutting through the casing, and to maintenance engineers who could disable the lid switches on one visit and extract the keys on the next. Second generation devices dealt with the easier of these problems, namely physical attack, by adding further sensors such as photocells and tilt switches. These may be enough for a device kept in a secure area to which access is controlled. But the hard problem is to prevent attacks by the maintenance man.

The strategy adopted by many of the better products is to separate all the components that can be serviced (such as batteries) from the core of the device (such as the tamper sensors, crypto, processor, key memory and alarm circuits). The core is then 'potted' into a solid block of a hard, opaque substance such as epoxy. The idea is that any physical attack will be 'obvious' in that it involves an action such as cutting or drilling, which can be detected by the guard who accompanies the maintenance engineer into the bank computer room. (That at least was the theory; my own experience suggests that it's a bit much to ask a minimum-wage guard to ensure that a specialist in some exotic piece equipment repairs it using some tools but not others.) At least it should leave evidence of tampering after the fact. This is the level of protection needed for medium-level evaluations under the FIPS standard.

How to hack a cryptoprocessor (3)

However, if a competent person can get unsupervised access to the device for even a short period of time — and, to be realistic, that's what the maintenance engineer probably has, even if the guard is breathing down his neck — then potting the device core is inadequate. For example, it is often possible to scrape away the potting with a knife and drop the probe from a logic analyzer on to one of the bus lines in the core. Most common cryptographic algorithms, such as RSA and DES, have the property that an attacker who can monitor any bitplane during the computation can recover the key [580]. So an attacker who can get a probe anywhere into the device while it is operating can likely extract secret key material.

So the high-end products have a tamper-sensing barrier whose penetration triggers destruction of the secrets inside. An early example appeared in IBM's μABYSS system in the mid 1980s. This used loops of 40-gauge nichrome wire that were wound loosely around the device as it was embedded in epoxy, and then connected to a sensing circuit [1328]. Bulk removal techniques such as milling, etching and laser ablation break the wire, which erases the keys. But the wire-in-epoxy technique can be vulnerable to slow erosion using sand blasting; when the sensing wires become visible at the surface of the potting, shunts can be connected round them. So the next major product from IBM, the 4753, used a metal shield combined with a membrane printed with a pattern of conductive ink and surrounded by a more durable material of similar chemistry. The idea was that any attack would break the membrane with high probability.

How to hack a cryptoprocessor (4)

The next class of methods an attacker can try involve the exploitation of *memory remanence*, the fact that many kinds of computer memory retain some trace of data that have been stored there. Sometimes all that is necessary is that the same data were stored for a long time. An attacker might bribe the garbage truck operator to obtain a bank's discarded security modules: as reported in [69], once a certain security module had been operated for some years using the same master keys, the values of these keys were *burned in* to the device's static RAM. On power-up, about 90% of the relevant bits would assume the values of the corresponding keybits, which was more than enough to recover the keys.

Memory remanence affects not just static and dynamic RAM, but other storage media as well. For example, the heads of a disk drive change alignment over time, so that it may be impossible to completely overwrite data that were first written some time ago. The relevant engineering and physics issues are discussed in [566] and [568], while [1184] explains how to extract data from Flash memory in microcontrollers, even after it has been 'erased' several times. The NSA has published guidelines (the 'Forest Green Book') on preventing remanence attacks by precautions such as careful degaussing of media that are to be reused [378].

The better third generation devices have *RAM savers* which function in much the same way as screen savers; they move data around the RAM to prevent it being burned in anywhere.

How to hack a cryptoprocessor (5)

A further problem is that computer memory can be frozen by low temperatures. By the 1980s it was realized that below about $-20°$ C, static RAM contents can persist for several seconds after power is removed. This extends to minutes at the temperatures of liquid nitrogen. So an attacker might freeze a device, remove the power, cut through the tamper sensing barrier, extract the RAM chips containing the keys and power them up again in a test rig. RAM contents can also be *burned in* by ionising radiation. (For the memory chips of the 1980s, this required a serious industrial X-ray machine; but as far as I'm aware, no-one has tested the current, much smaller, memory chip designs.)

So the better devices have temperature and radiation alarms. These can be difficult to implement properly, as modern RAM chips exhibit a wide variety of memory remanence behaviors, with some of them keeping data for several seconds even at room temperature. What's worse, remanence seems to have got longer as feature sizes have shrunk, and in unpredictable ways even within standard product lines. The upshot is that although your security module might pass a remanence test using a given make of SRAM chip, it might fail the same test if fitted with the same make of chip purchased a year later [1182]. This shows the dangers of relying on a property of some component to whose manufacturer the control of this property is unimportant.

Temperature sensors are also a real bugbear to security module vendors, as a device that self-destructs if frozen can't be sent reliably through normal distribution channels. (We've bought cryptoprocessors on eBay and found them dead on arrival.)

How to hack a cryptoprocessor (6)

The next set of attacks on cryptographic hardware involve either monitoring the RF and other electromagnetic signals emitted by the device, or even injecting signals into it and measuring their externally visible effects. This technique, which is variously known as 'Tempest', 'power analysis,' 'side-channel attacks' or 'emission security', is such a large subject that I devote the next chapter to it. As far as the 4758 is concerned, the strategy is to have solid aluminium shielding and to low-pass filter the power supply to block the egress of any signals at the frequencies used internally for computation.

The 4758 also has an improved tamper sensing membrane in which four overlapping zig-zag conducting patterns are doped into a urethane sheet, which is potted in a chemically similar substance so that an attacker cutting into the device has difficulty even detecting the conductive path, let alone connecting to it. This potting surrounds the metal shielding which in turn contains the cryptographic core. The design is described in more detail in [1195].

How to hack a cryptoprocessor (7)

I don't know how to attack the hardware of the 4758. My students and I found a number of novel software vulnerabilities, which I'll describe later in the chapter on API Attacks. But here are a few ideas for keen grad students who want to have a go at the hardware:

- The straightforward approach would be to devise some way to erode the protective potting, detect mesh lines, and connect shunts round them. A magnetic force microscope might be worth a try.

- One could invent a means of drilling holes eight millimeters long and only 0.1 millimeters wide (that is, much less than the mesh line diameter). This isn't straightforward with standard mechanical drills, and the same holds for laser ablation and ion milling. However I speculate that some combination of nanotechnology and ideas from the oil industry might make such a drill possible eventually. Then one could drill right through the protective mesh with a fair probability of not breaking the circuit.

- Having dismantled a few instances of the device and understood its hardware, the attacker might attempt to destroy the tamper responding circuitry before it has time to react. One possibility is to use an industrial X-ray machine; another would be to use shaped explosive charges to send plasma jets of the kind discussed in section 13.5 into the device.

The success of such attacks is uncertain, and they are likely to remain beyond the resources of the average villain for some time.

So by far the attacks on 4758-based systems involve the exploitation of logical rather than physical flaws. The device's operating system has been subjected to formal verification, so the main risk resides in application design errors that allow an opponent to manipulate the transactions provided by the device to authorized users. Most users of the 4758 use an application called CCA that is described in [619] and contains many features that make it difficult to use properly (these are largely the legacy of previous encryption devices with which 4758 users wished to be backward compatible.) Starting in 2000, we discovered that the application programming interface (API) which the 4758 exposed to the host contained a number of serious flaws. (Most of the other security modules on the market were worse.) The effect was that a programmer with access to the host could send the security module a series of commands that would cause it to leak PINs or keys. I'll discuss these API attacks in Chapter 18.

Finally, it should be mentioned that the main constraints on the design and manufacture of security processors are remarkably similar to those we encountered with more general alarms. There is a trade-off between the false alarm rate and the missed alarm rate, and thus between security and robustness. Vibration, power transients and electromagnetic interference can be a problem, but temperature is the worst. I mentioned the difficulty of passing security processors that self-destruct at $-20°$ C through normal shipping channels, where goods are often subjected to $-40°$ C in aircraft holds. Military equipment makers have the converse problem: their kit must be rated from $-55°$ to $+155°$ C. Some military devices use protective detonation; memory chips are potted in steel cans with a thermite charge precisely calculated to destroy the chip without causing gas release from the can. Meeting simultaneous targets for tamper resistance, temperature tolerance, radiation hardening and weight can be expensive.

16.4   Evaluation

A few comments about the evaluation of tamper-resistant devices are in order before I go on to discuss cheaper devices.

The IBM paper which describes the design of the 4753 [6] proposed the following classification of attackers, which has been widely used since:

1. Class 1 attackers — 'clever outsiders' — are often very intelligent but may have insufficient knowledge of the system. They may have access to only moderately sophisticated equipment. They often try to take advantage of an existing weakness in the system, rather than try to create one.

2. Class 2 attackers — 'knowledgeable insiders' — have substantial specialized technical education and experience. They have varying degrees of understanding of parts of the system but potential access to most of it. They often have highly sophisticated tools and instruments for analysis.

3. Class 3 attackers — 'funded organizations' — are able to assemble teams of specialists with related and complementary skills backed by great funding resources. They are capable of in-depth analysis of the system, designing sophisticated attacks, and using the most advanced analysis tools. They may use Class 2 adversaries as part of the attack team.

Within this scheme, the typical SSL accelerator card is aimed at blocking clever outsiders; the early 4753 aimed at stopping clever insiders, and the 4758 was aimed at (and certified for) blocking funded organizations. (By the way, this classification is becoming a bit dated; we see class 1 attackers renting access to class 3 equipment and so on. It's better to create an attacker profile for your application, rather than try to reuse one of these old industry standard ones.)

The FIPS certification scheme is operated by laboratories licenced by the U.S. government. The original standard, FIPS 140-1, set out four levels of protection, with level 4 being the highest, and this remained in the next version, FIPS 140-2, which was introduced in 2001. At the time of writing, only three vendors — IBM, AEP and Thales — have managed to get products certified at level 4. There is a large gap between level 4 and the next one down, level 3, where only potting is required and attacks that exploit electromagnetic leakage, memory remanence, drilling, sandblasting and so on may still be possible. (I have handled a level-3 certified device from which I could scrape off the potting with my Swiss army knife.) So while FIPS 140-1 level 3 devices can be (and have been) defeated by class 1 attackers in the IBM sense, the next step up — FIPS 140-1 level 4 — is expected to keep out an IBM class 3 opponent. There is no FIPS level corresponding to a defence against IBM's class 2.

In fact, the original paper on levels of evaluation was written by IBM engineers and proposed six levels [1330]; the FIPS standard adopted the first three of these as its levels 1–3, and the proposed level 6 as its level 4 (the 4758 designer Steve Weingart tells the story in [1329]). The gap, commonly referred to as 'level 3.5', is where many of the better commercial systems are aimed. Such equipment certainly attempts to keep out the class 1 attack community, while making life hard for class 2 and expensive for class 3.

At the time of writing (2007) there is a revised Federal standard, FIPS 140-3, out from NIST for consultation. This increases the number of levels from four to five, by adding a fifth level with additional testing required. However the standard does not deal with the problem of API attacks, and indeed neither did FIPS 140-1 or 140-2. The FIPS standard unfortunately covers only the device's resistance against direct invasive and semi-invasive hardware attacks, of the kind discussed in this chapter, and against noninvasive attacks using techniques like power analysis, which I discuss in the next.

16.5   Medium Security Processors

Good examples of 'level 3.5' products are the *iButton* and 5002 security processors from Dallas Semiconductor, and the *Capstone* chip used to protect U.S. military communications up to 'Secret'. While the 4758 costs $2000, these products cost of the order of $10–20. Yet mounting an attack on them is far from trivial.

16.5.1   The iButton

The original iButton from Dallas Semiconductor was designed to be a minimal, self-contained cryptographic processor for use in applications such as postal meters. It has a microcontroller, static RAM for keys and software, a clock and tamper sensors encased in a steel can with a lithium battery that can maintain keys in the RAM for a design life of ten years (see Figure 16.3). It is small enough to be worn in a signet ring or carried as a key fob. An early application was as an access token for the 'Electronic Red Box', a secure laptop system designed for use by UK government ministers. To access secret documents, the minister had to press his signet ring into a reader at the side of the laptop. (One of the design criteria had been: 'Ministers shall not have to use passwords'.) Other applications include ticketing for the İstanbul mass transit system, parking meters in Argentina, and tokens used by bar staff to logon rapidly to tills.

The iButton was a pure security product when I wrote the first edition in 2000 and some versions even had a cryptoprocessor to do public-key operations. In December 1999 the first break of an iButton took place; the printer vendor Lexmark had started incorporating iButtons in some of its printer cartridges in 1998, to stop aftermarket vendors selling compatible ones, and Static Control Components finally broke the system and produced a compatible chip for the aftermarket in December 1999 [1221]. Since then Dallas has become a subsidiary of Maxim and the iButton has evolved into a broader product range. There are now versions containing temperature sensors that provide a dependable temperature history of perishable goods in transit, simple versions that are in effect just RFID tokens, and complex versions that contain a JVM. So it's no longer the case that all iButtons are 'secure': any given device might not be designed to be, or it might have been programmed (deliberately or otherwise) not to be. However the range still does include tamper-resistant devices that use SHA-1 to support cryptographic authentication, and it's still widely used in security applications.

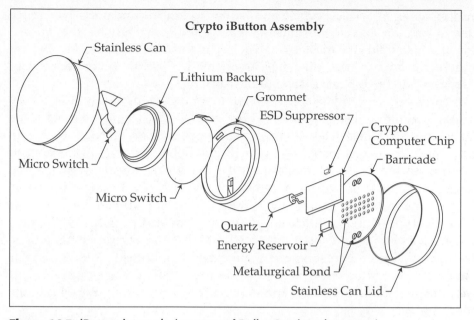

Figure 16.3: iButton internals (courtesy of Dallas Semiconductor Inc.)

How might a secure iButton be attacked? The most obvious difference from the 4758 is the lack of a tamper-sensing barrier. So one might try drilling in through the side and then either probing the device in operation, or disabling the tamper sensing circuitry. As the iButton has lid switches to detect the can being opened, and as the processor is mounted upside-down on the circuit board and is also protected by a mesh in the top metal layer of the chip, this is unlikely to be a trivial exercise and might well involve building custom jigs and tools. I wrote in the first edition, 'it's a tempting target for the next bright graduate student who wants to win his spurs as a hardware hacker', and SCC appear to have risen to the challenge. (Lexmark then sued them under the DMCA and lost; I'll discuss this further in section 22.6 on accessory control.)

16.5.2 The Dallas 5000 Series

Another medium-grade security device from Maxim / Dallas is the 5000 series secure microcontroller, which is widely used in devices such as point-of-sale terminals where it holds the keys used to encrypt customer PINs.

The ingenious idea behind this device is *bus encryption*. The chip has added hardware which encrypts memory addresses and contents on the fly as data are loaded and stored. This means that the device can operate with external memory and is not limited to the small amount of RAM that can be fitted into a low-cost tamper-sensing package. Each device has a unique master key, which is generated at random when it is powered up. The software is then loaded through the serial port, encrypted and written to external memory. The device is then ready for use. Power must be maintained constantly, or the internal register which holds the master key will lose it; this also happens if a physical tampering event is sensed (like the iButton, the DS5002 has a tamper-sensing mesh built into the top metal layer of the chip).

An early version of the 5002 (1995) fell to an ingenious protocol attack by Markus Kuhn, the *cipher instruction search attack* [748]. The idea is that some of the processor's instructions have a visible external effect, such as I/O. In particular, there is one instruction which causes the next byte in memory to be output to the device's parallel port. So the trick is to intercept the bus between the processor and memory using a test clip, and feed in all possible 8-bit instruction bytes at some point in the instruction stream. One of them should decrypt to the parallel output instruction, and output the plaintext version of the next 'encrypted memory' byte. By varying this byte, a table could be built up of corresponding plaintext and ciphertext. After using this technique to learn the encryption function for a sequence of seven or eight bytes, the attacker could encipher and execute a short program to dump the entire memory contents.

The full details are a bit more intricate. The problem has since been fixed, and Dallas is selling successor products such as the 5250. However, the attack on bus encryption is a good example of the completely unexpected things that go wrong when trying to implement a clever new security concept for the first time.

16.5.3   FPGA Security, and the Clipper Chip

In 1993, the security world was convulsed when the US government introduced the *Clipper chip* as a proposed replacement for DES. Clipper, also known as the *Escrowed Encryption Standard* (EES), was a tamper-resistant chip that implemented the Skipjack block cipher in a protocol designed to allow the U.S. government to decrypt any traffic encrypted using Clipper. The idea was that when a user supplied Clipper with a string of data and a key with which to encrypt it, the chip returned not just the ciphertext but also a 'Law Enforcement Access Field', or LEAF, which contained the user-supplied key encrypted under a key embedded in the device and known to the government. To prevent people cheating and sending along the wrong LEAF with a message, the LEAF has a cryptographic checksum computed with a 'family key' shared by all interoperable Clipper chips. This functionality was continued into the next generation chips, called Capstone, which incorporate ARM processors to do public key encryption and digital signature operations.

Almost as soon as Capstone chips hit the market, a protocol vulnerability was found [183]. As the cryptographic checksum used to bind the LEAF to the message was only 16 bits long, it was possible to feed message keys into the device until you got one with a given LEAF, thus enabling a message to be sent with a LEAF that would remain impenetrable to the government. The Clipper initiative was abandoned and replaced with other policies aimed at controlling the 'proliferation' of cryptography, but Capstone quietly entered government service and is now widely used in the Fortezza card, a PCMCIA card used in PCs to encrypt data at levels up to Secret. The Skipjack block cipher, which was initially classified, has since been placed in the public domain [939].

Of more interest here are the tamper protection mechanisms used, which were perhaps the most sophisticated in any single-chip device at the time, and were claimed at the time to be sufficient to withstand a 'very sophisticated, well funded adversary' [937]. Although it was claimed that the Clipper chip would be unclassified and exportable, I was never able to get hold of one for dismantling despite repeated attempts.

Its successor is the QuickLogic military FPGA. This is designed to enable its users to conceal proprietary algorithms from their customers, and it is advertised as being 'virtually impossible to reverse engineer'. Like Clipper, it uses *Vialink read only memory* (VROM) in which bits are set by blowing antifuses between the metal 1 and metal 2 layers on the chip. A programming pulse at a sufficiently high voltage is used to melt a conducting path through the polysilicon which separates the two metal layers. Further details and micrographs can be found in a paper in the relevant data book [547].

FPGA security has since become a thriving research field. There are basically four approaches to reverse engineering an antifuse device.

- The easiest way to read out an FPGA is usually to use the test circuit that's provided in order to read back and verify the bitstream during programming. Until recently, many chips disabled this by melting a single fuse after programming. If you could get sample devices and a programmer, you could find out where this fuse was located, for example by differential optical probing [1186]. You could then use a focussed ion beam workstation to repair the fuse. Once you have re-enabled the test circuit you can read out the bitstream. Turning this into a netlist isn't entirely straightforward but it's not impossible given patience. This attack technique works not just for antifuse FPGAs but also for the Flash and EEPROM varieties.

- With antifuse FPGAs, it's sometimes possible to abuse the programming circuit. This circuit is designed to send a pulse to melt the fuse, but stop once the resistance drops, as this means the metal has melted and established contact. If the pulse weren't stopped then the metal might vaporise and go open circuit again. So the programming circuit has sensors to detect whether a fuse is open or short, and if these aren't sufficiently disabled after programming they can be used to read the bitstream out.

■ The brute-force approach is to determine the presence of blown anti-fuses using optical or electron microscopy, for example by removing the top metal layer of the chip and looking at the vias directly. This can be extremely tedious, but brute force attacks have been done on some security processors.

■ Where the device implements a cryptographic algorithm, or some other piece of logic with a relatively compact description, an inference attack using side-channel data may be the fastest way in. Most devices manufactured before about 2000 are rather vulnerable to power analysis, which can be used to reconstruct not just the keys of block ciphers but also the block cipher design by studying the device's power consumption. I'll describe this in more detail in the next chapter. A more direct attack is to drop microprobes directly on the gate array's bus lines and look at the signals. Other possible sensors include optical probing, electromagnetic coils, voltage contrast microscopy and a growing number of other chip testing techniques. In any case, the point is that it may be faster to reconstruct an algorithm from observing on-chip signals than from doing a full circuit reconstruction.

So this technology isn't infallible, but used intelligently it certainly has potential. Its main use nowadays is in FPGAs that are used to protect designs from reverse engineering.

In recent years, most FPGAs sold have had conventional memory rather than antifuse, which means that they can be made reprogrammable. They also have a higher memory density, albeit at some cost in power, size and performance compared to ASICs or antifuse devices. The current market leaders are volatile FPGAs that use SRAM, and many chips don't really have any protection beyond the obscurity of the bitstream encoding; you can read the unencrypted bitstream in transit to the FPGA on power-up. Others have one or more embedded keys kept in nonvolatile memory, and the bitstream is uploaded and then decrypted on power-up. Non-volatile devices generally use Flash for the bitstream, and reprogramming involves sending the device an encrypted bitstream with a message authentication code to guarantee integrity. In both cases, there may be a few fuses to protect the key material and the protection state. The better designs are so arranged that an attacker would have to find several fuses and antifuses and wire them in a particular way in order to extract the bitstream. Saar Drimer has a survey of FPGA design security [400].

Such FPGAs are used in equipment from routers through printers to cameras, and the main threat models are that a manufacturing subcontractor may try to overbuild the design so as to sell the extra products on the grey market, or that a competitor will try to make compatible accessories. In the former case, the vendor can separate programming from assembly, and also use the upgrade cycle to undermine the value of any black-market copies. In the latter case the FPGA logic typically implements an authentication mechanism of some kind.

One trap to watch out for when designing a field-upgradeable product using an FPGA is to prevent service denial attacks via the upgrade mechanism. For example, a Flash FPGA usually only has enough memory for one copy of the bitstream, not two; so the usual drill is to read in the bitstream once to decrypt it and verify the MAC, and then a second time to actually reprogram the part. If the bitstream supplied the second time is corrupt, then the likely outcome is a dead product. The typical SRAM-based FPGAs doesn't have bitstream authentication, so people could usually replay old bitstreams and thus escape an upgrade if they wish. It's also possible that if an attacker gets your products to load a random encrypted bitstream, this could cause short circuits and do permanent damage. So it's worth thinking whether anyone might be malicious enough to try to destroy your installed product base via a corrupt upgrade, and if so you might consider whether your product needs a secure bitstream loader.

16.6   Smartcards and Microcontrollers

In volume terms, the most common secure processors nowadays are self-contained one-ship security processors containing nonvolatile memory, I/O, usually a CPU, often some specialised logic, and some mechanisms to prevent memory contents from being read out. They range from microcontrollers with a memory-protect bit at the low end, up to smartcards and the TPMs that now ship with most computer motherboards. Smartcards have quite a range of capabilities. At the low end are phone cards costing under a dollar; then there are bank cards that will do conventional crypto, with 8/16 bit processors; at the top end there are bank cards that will do public-key crypto and often have 32-bit processors. There are also 'contactless' smartcards — essentially RFID devices that can perform cryptographic protocols rather than just emitting static data — that are used in applications such as transport ticketing.

As these devices are cheap and sold in large volumes, an opponent can often obtain many samples and take them away to probe at her leisure. So many attacks on them have been developed[2]. Pay-TV subscriber cards in particular have been subjected to many cloning attacks and nowadays have a lot of special protection mechanisms. In this section, I'll tell the story of how smartcard security evolved with successive attacks and defenses.

---

[2]As this book was about to go to press at the end of 2007, there was an announcement at the Chaos Computer Club conference in Berlin that the widely-used Mifare contactless system had been reverse engineered and turned out to use a weak 48-bit stream cipher.

16.6.1   History

Although smartcards are marketed as a 'new' security solution, they actually go back a long way, with the early patents (which date from the late 1960s through mid 1970s) having long since expired [383]. For a history of the development of smartcards, see [563]. For many years, they were mostly used in France, where much of the original development work was done with government support. In the late 1980s and early 1990s, they started to be used on a large scale outside France, principally as the *subscriber identity modules* (SIMs) in GSM mobile phones, and as subscriber cards for pay-TV stations. They started being used as bank cards in France in 1994, and in the rest of Europe from about 2005.

A smartcard is a self-contained microcontroller, with a microprocessor, memory and a serial interface integrated in a single chip and packaged in a plastic card. Smartcards used in banking use a standard size bank card, while in most mobile phones a much smaller size is used. Smartcard chips are also packaged in other ways. For example, many UK prepayment electricity meters use them packaged in a plastic key, as do Nagravision pay-TV set-top boxes. In the STU-III secure telephones used in the U.S. government, each user has a 'crypto ignition key' which is also packaged to look and feel like a physical key. The TPM chips built into computer motherboards to support 'Trusted Computing' are in effect public-key smartcard chips but with added parallel ports. Contactless smartcards contain a smartcard chip plus a wire-loop antenna. In what follows I'll mostly disregard the packaging form factor and just refer to these products as 'smartcards' or 'chipcards'.

Their single most widespread application is the GSM mobile phone system, the standard in some U.S. networks and in almost all countries outside the U.S. The telephone handsets are commodity items, and are personalized for each user by the SIM, a smartcard that contains not just your personal phone book, call history and so on, but also a cryptographic key with which you authenticate yourself to the network.

The strategy of using a cheap smartcard to provide the personalisation and authentication functions of a more expensive consumer electronic device has a number of advantages. The expensive device can be manufactured in bulk, with each unit being exactly the same, while the smartcard can be replaced relatively quickly and cheaply in the event of a successful attack. This has led many pay-TV operators to adopt smartcards. The satellite TV dish and decoder become commodity consumer durables, while each subscriber gets a personalized smartcard containing the key material needed to decrypt the channels to which he has subscribed.

Chipcards are also used in a range of other applications ranging from hotel keys to public payphones — though in such applications it's still common to find low-cost devices that contain no microprocessor but just some EEPROM memory to store a counter or certificate, and some logic to perform a simple authentication protocol.

Devices such as prepayment electricity meters are typically built around a microcontroller — a chip that performs the same kind of functions as a smartcard but has less sophisticated protection. Typically, this consists of setting a single 'memory protection' bit that prevents the EEPROM contents being read out easily by an attacker. There have been many design defects in particular products; for example, a computer authentication token called iKey had a master password which was hashed using MD5 and stored on an EEPROM external to the processor, so a user could overwrite it with the hash of a known password and assume complete control of the device [719]. For more details of attacks specific to microcontrollers, see [68, 1181, 1183].

16.6.2 Architecture

The typical smartcard consists of a single die of up to 25 square millimeters of silicon containing a microprocessor (larger dies are more likely to break as the card is flexed). Cheap products have an 8-bit processor such as an 8051 or 6805, and the more expensive products either have a 32-bit processor such as an ARM, or else a dedicated modular multiplication circuit to do public-key cryptography. It also has serial I/O circuitry and a hierarchy of three classes of memory — ROM or Flash to hold the program and immutable data, EEPROM to hold customer-specific data such as the registered user's name and account number as well as crypto keys, value counters and the like; and RAM registers to hold transient data during computation.

The memory is very limited by the standards of normal computers. A typical card on sale in 2007 might have 64 Kbytes of ROM, 8–32 Kbytes of EEPROM and 2K bytes of RAM. The bus is not available outside the device; the only connections supplied are for power, reset, a clock and a serial port. The physical, electrical and low-level logical connections, together with a file-system-like access protocol, are specified in ISO 7816. These specifications have not changed much since 2000; prices for volumes of a few hundred cards haven't changed much either (maybe $3 for an 8-bit card that will do DES and AES, $7 for a card with a cryptoprocessor to do elliptic curve crypto, and $12 for one beefy enough for RSA). Large-volume users pay much less. The main change over the past seven years is that development kits are now widely available, whereas in 2000 most vendors screened purchasers and imposed NDAs. The implication is of course that if an opponent can reverse engineer your smartcard application, she has no difficulty buying and programming cards.

16.6.3 Security Evolution

When I first heard a sales pitch from a smartcard vendor — in 1986 when I was working as a banker — I asked how come the device was secure. I was assured that since the machinery needed to make the card cost $20m, just as for making banknotes, the system must be secure. I didn't believe this but didn't then have the time or the tools to prove the claim wrong. I later learned from industry executives that none of their customers were prepared to pay for serious security until about 1995, and so until then they relied on the small size of the devices, the obscurity of their design, and the rarity of chip testing tools to make attacks more difficult.

The application that changed all this was satellite TV. TV operators broadcast their signals over a large footprint — such as all of Europe — and give each subscriber a card that will compute the keys needed to decipher the channels they've paid for. Since the operators had usually only purchased the rights to the movies for one or two countries, they couldn't sell the subscriber cards elsewhere. This created a black market in pay-TV cards, into which forged cards could be sold. A critical factor was that 'Star Trek', which people in Europe had picked up from UK satellite broadcasts for years, was suddenly encrypted in 1993. In some countries, such as Germany, it simply wasn't available legally at any price. This motivated a lot of keen young computer science and engineering students to look for vulnerabilities.

There have since been large financial frauds carried out with cloned cards. The first to be reported involved a smartcard used to give Portuguese farmers rebates on fuel. The villain conspired with petrol stations that registered other fuel sales to the bogus cards in return for a share of the proceeds. The fraud, which took place in February/March 1995, is reported to have netted about thirty million dollars [900].

How to hack a smartcard (1)

The earliest hacks targeted the protocols in which the cards were used. For example, some early pay-TV systems gave each customer a card with access to all channels, and then sent messages over the air to cancel those channels to which the customer hadn't subscribed after an introductory period. This opened an attack in which a device was inserted between the smartcard and the decoder which would intercept and discard any messages addressed to the card. Subscribers could then cancel their subscription without the vendor being able to cancel their service.

The same kind of attack was launched on the German phone card system. A hacker tipped off Deutsche Telekom that it was possible to make phone cards that gave unlimited free calls. He had discovered this by putting a laptop between a card and a phone to analyze the traffic. Telekom's experts refused to believe him, so he exploited his knowledge by selling handmade chip cards in brothels and in hostels for asylum seekers [1210]. Such low-cost attacks were particularly distressing to the phone companies as the main reason for moving to smartcards was to cut the cost of having to validate cheaper tokens online [124]. I'll discuss these protocol failures further in the chapter on copyright enforcement systems. There has also been a fairly full range of standard computer attacks; such as stack overwriting by sending too long a string of parameters. In what follows, we'll concentrate on the attacks that are peculiar to smartcards.

How to hack a smartcard (2)

As smartcards use an external power supply, and store security state such as crypto keys and value counters in EEPROM, an attacker could freeze the EEPROM contents by removing the programming voltage, V_{PP}. Early smartcards received V_{PP} on a dedicated connection from the host interface. This led to very simple attacks: by covering the V_{PP} contact with sticky tape, cardholders could prevent cancellation signals from affecting their card. The same trick could be used with some payphone chipcards; a card with tape over the appropriate contact had 'infinite units'.

The fix was to generate V_{PP} internally from the supply voltage V_{CC} using a voltage multiplier circuit. However, this isn't entirely foolproof as the circuit can be destroyed by an attacker. So a prudent programmer, having (for example) decremented the retry counter after a user enters an incorrect PIN, will read it back and check it. She will also check that memory writing actually works each time the card is reset, as otherwise the bad guy who has shot away the voltage multiplier can just repeatedly reset the card and try every possible PIN, one after another.

How to hack a smartcard (3)

Another early attack was to slow down the card's execution, or even single-step it through a transaction by repeatedly resetting it and clocking it n times, then $n+1$ times, and so on. In one card, it was possible to read out RAM contents with a suitable transaction after reset, as working memory wasn't zeroized. With very many cards, it was possible to read the voltages on the chip surface using an electron microscope. (The low-cost scanning electron microscopes generally available in universities can't do voltage contrast microscopy at more than a few tens of kilohertz, hence the need to slow down the execution.)

So many smartcard processors have a circuit to detect low clock frequency and either freeze or reset the card; others use dynamic logic to achieve the same effect. But, as with burglar alarms, there is a trade-off between the false alarm rate and the missed alarm rate. This leads to many of the alarm features provided by smartcard chip makers simply not being used by the OEMs or application developers. For example, with cheap card readers, there can be wild fluctuations in clock frequency when a card is powered up, causing so many false alarms that some developers do not use the feature. So low clock frequency detectors need careful design.

How to hack a smartcard (4)

Once pay-TV operators had fixed most of the simple attacks, pirates turned to attacks using physical probing. Until a few years ago, most smartcards had no protection against physical tampering except the microscopic scale of the circuit, a thin glass *passivation layer* on the surface of the chip, and potting which is typically some kind of epoxy. Techniques for depackaging chips are well known, and discussed in detail in standard works on semiconductor testing, such as [136]. In most cases, a few milliliters of fuming nitric acid are all that's required to dissolve the epoxy, and the passivation layer is removed where required for probing.

Probing stations consist of microscopes with micromanipulators attached for landing fine probes on the surface of the chip. They are widely used in the semiconductor manufacturing industry for manual testing of production line samples, and can be obtained second hand for under $10,000 (see Figure 16.4). They may have specialized accessories, such as a laser to shoot holes in the chip's passivation layer.

Figure 16.4: Low-cost probing station

The usual target of a probing attack is the processor's bus. If the bus traffic can be recorded, this gives a trace of the program's operation with both code and data. If the attacker is lucky, the card designer will have computed a checksum on memory immediately after reset (a recommended defense industry practice) which will give him a complete listing of the card memory contents. So the attacker will identify the bus and expose the bus lines for probing (see Figure 16.5). Indeed, if the chip is performing a known cryptographic protocol with well understood algorithms, then unless there's some defense mechanism such as lots of dummy instructions, a trace from a single bus line is likely to give away the key [580].

The first defense used by the pay-TV card industry against attacks of this kind was to endow each card with multiple keys and/or algorithms, and arrange things so that only those in current use would appear on the processor bus. Whenever pirate cards appeared on the market, a command would be issued over the air to cause legitimate cards to activate new keys or algorithms from a previously unused area of memory. In this way, the pirates' customers would suffer a loss of service until the probing attack could be repeated and either new pirate cards, or updates to the existing ones, could somehow be distributed.

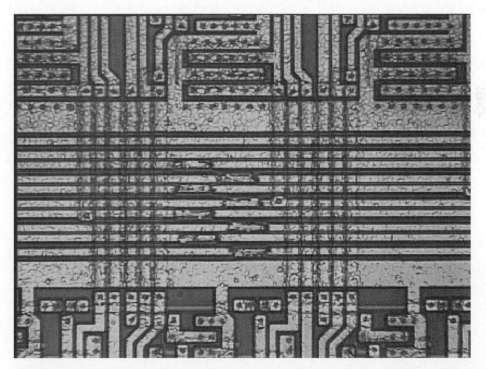

Figure 16.5: The data bus of an ST16 smartcard prepared for probing by excavating eight trenches through the passivation layer with laser shots (Photo courtesy Oliver Kömmerling)

How to hack a smartcard (5)

The defeat for this strategy was Oliver Kömmerling's *memory linearization attack* in which the analyst damages the chip's instruction decoder in such a way that instructions which change the program address other than by incrementing it — such as jumps and calls — become inoperable [733]. One way to do this is to drop a grounded microprobe needle on the control line to the instruction latch, so that whatever instruction happens to be there on power-up is executed repeatedly. The memory contents can now be read off the bus. In fact, once some of the device's ROM and EEPROM is understood, the attacker can skip over unwanted instructions and cause the device to execute only instructions of his choice. So with a single probing needle, he can get the card to execute arbitrary code, and in theory could get it to output its secret key material on the serial port. But probing the memory contents off the bus is usually more convenient.

In practice, there are often several places in the instruction decoder where a grounded needle will have the effect of preventing programmed changes in the control flow. So even if the processor isn't fully understood, memory linearization can often be achieved by trial and error. Some of the more modern processors have traps which prevent memory linearization, such as hardware access control matrices which prevent particular areas of memory being read unless some specific sequence of commands is presented. But such circuits can often be defeated by shooting away carefully chosen gates using a laser or an ion beam.

Memory linearization is an example of a *fault induction attack*. There are quite a few examples of this; faults can be injected into smartcards and other security processors in a number of ways, from hardware probing through power transients to our old friend, the stack overflow. A variant on the theme is given by attacks on the card's test circuitry. A typical smartcard chip has a self-test routine in ROM that is executed in the factory and allows all the memory contents to be read and verified. As with FPGAs, a fuse is then blown in the chip to stop an attacker using the same facility. All that the attacker had to do was to cause a fault in this mechanism — by finding the fuse and repairing it. This could be as simple as bridging it with two probing needles [212]. A more careful design might put the test circuitry on the part of the silicon that is sawn away when the wafer is diced into individual chips.

It's also possible to exploit already existing hardware bugs. For example, Adi Shamir pointed out that if a CPU has an error in its multiply unit — even just a single computation $ab = c$ whose result is returned consistently wrong in a single bit — then it's possible to send it an RSA ciphertext for decryption (or an RSA plaintext for signature) constructed so that the computation will be done correctly mod p but incorrectly mod q; if this result is returned to the attacker, he can instantly work out the private key [1148]. For this reason, a careful programmer will check the results of critical computations.

How to hack a smartcard (6)

The next thing the pay-TV card industry tried was to incorporate hardware cryptographic processors, in order to force attackers to reconstruct hardware circuits rather than simply clone software, and to force them to use more expensive processors in their pirate cards. In the first such implementation, the crypto processor was a separate chip packaged into the card, and it had an interesting protocol failure: it would always work out the key needed to decrypt the current video stream, and then pass it to the CPU which would decide whether or not to pass it on to the outside world. Hackers broke this by developing a way to tap into the wiring between the two chips.

Later implementations have the crypto hardware built into the CPU itself. Where this consists of just a few thousand gates, it is feasible for an attacker to reconstruct the circuit manually from micrographs of the chip. But with larger gate counts and deep submicron processes, a successful attack may require automatic layout reconstruction: successively etching away the layers of the chip, taking electron micrographs and using image processing software to reconstruct a 3-d map of the chip, or at least identify its component cells [196]. However, assembling all the equipment, writing the software and integrating the systems involves huge effort and expense.

A much simpler, and common, attack is for pirates to ask one of the half dozen or so existing commercial reverse engineering labs to reconstruct the relevant area of the chip. Such labs get much of their business from analyzing integrated circuits on behalf of the chip maker's competitors, looking for patent infringements. They also reverse engineer chips used for accessory control in consumer electronic devices, as doing this for compatibility rather than piracy is quite lawful. So they are used to operating in conditions of some secrecy, and there's been at least one case in which a pirate had a pay-TV card reverse engineered by an above-board company by pretending to be a bona fide business.

How to hack a smartcard (7)

The next defense the card industry thought up was to furnish the chip with protective surface mesh, implemented in a top metal layer as a serpentine pattern of ground, power and sensor lines. The idea was that any break or short in the pattern would be sensed as soon as the chip was powered up and trigger a self destruct mechanism.

We mentioned such meshes in connection with the Dallas processors; after the usual initial crop of implementation blunders, they proved to be an effective way of pushing up the cost of an attack. The appropriate tool to defeat them is the *Focused Ion Beam Workstation* or FIB. For a detailed description of FIBs and other semiconductor test equipment that can be used in reverse engineering, see Martin [837]; in brief, a FIB is a device similar to a scanning electron microscope but uses a beam of ions instead of electrons. By varying the beam current, it can be used either as a microscope or as a milling machine, with a useful resolution under 10 nanometers. By introducing a suitable gas which is broken down by the ion beam, it is possible to lay down either conductors or insulators with a precision of a few tens of nanometers.

FIBs are such extremely useful devices in all sorts of applications, from semiconductor testing through metallurgy and forensics to nanotechnology, that they are rapidly becoming widely available and the prices are tumbling. Many universities and industrial labs now have one, and time on them can be rented from a number of agencies for a few hundred dollars an hour.

Given a FIB, it is straightforward to attack a sensor mesh that is not powered up. One simply drills a hole through the mesh to the metal line that carries the desired signal, fills it up with insulator, drills another hole through the center of the insulator, fills it with metal, and plates a contact on top — typically a platinum 'L' or 'X' a few microns wide, which is easy to contact with a needle from the probing station (see Figure 16.6).

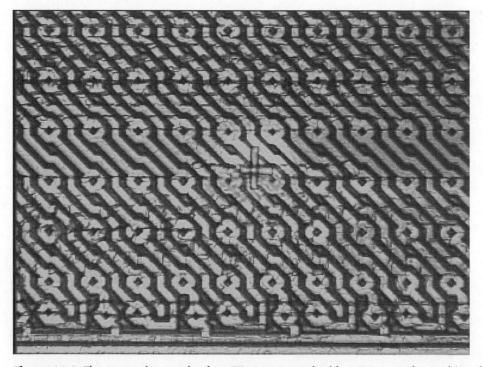

Figure 16.6: The protective mesh of an ST16 smartcard with a FIB cross for probing the bus line visible underneath (Photo courtesy Oliver Kömmerling)

Defeating a sensor mesh that is continually powered up is much harder, but some tools exist. For example, there are techniques to mill through the back side of a chip with a suitably equipped FIB and make contact directly to the electronics without disturbing the sensor mesh at all.

Many other defensive techniques can force the attacker to do more work. Some chips are packaged in much thicker glass than in a normal passivation layer. The idea is that the obvious ways of removing this (such as hydrofluoric acid) are likely to damage the chip. Other chips have protective coatings of substances such as silicon carbide or boron nitride. (Chips with protective coatings are on display at the NSA Museum at Fort Meade, Md). Such coatings can force the FIB operator to go slowly rather than damage the chip through a build-up of electrical charge.

How to hack a smartcard (8)

In 1998, the smartcard industry was shaken when Paul Kocher announced a new attack known as *differential power analysis*. This relied on the fact that different instructions consumed different amounts of power, so by measuring the power consumed by a smartcard chip it was possible to extract the key. This had always been known to be theoretically possible, but Kocher came up with efficient signal processing techniques that made it easy, and which I'll describe in the following chapter on emission security. He came up with even simpler attacks based on timing; if cryptographic operations don't take the same number of clock cycles, this can leak key material too. On larger processors, it can be even worse; a number of researchers have developed attacks on crypto algorithms based on cache misses. Power and timing attacks are examples of *side-channel attacks*, where the opponent can obtain and exploit some extra information about the processor's state while a cryptographic computation is going on. Essentially all the smartcards on the market at that time turned out to be vulnerable to power analysis or other side-channel attacks, and this held up the industry's development for a couple of years while countermeasures were developed.

We classify mechanical probing as an *invasive attack* as it involves penetrating the passivation layer, and power analysis as a *noninvasive attack* as the smartcard is left untouched; the attacker merely observes its operation. Noninvasive attacks can be further classified into local attacks, where the opponent needs access to the device, as with power analysis; and remote noninvasive attacks, where she could be anywhere. Timing attacks, and protocol attacks, are examples of the latter.

A lot of engineering effort was invested in the late 1990s and early 2000s in making noninvasive attacks more difficult. This is actually more complex than it might seem, as the measures one can take to make one noninvasive attack more difficult often turn out to make another one easier. I'll discuss the problems in more detail in the next chapter.

How to hack a smartcard (9)

Mechanical probing techniques worked until the early 2000s, but since then they have been increasingly difficult because of shrinking feature sizes. The next attack technology to develop was optical probing. There was a first report from Sandia National Laboratories in 1995 of a way to read out a voltage directly using a laser [17]. Since 2001 optical probing has been developed into an effective and low-cost technology, largely by my colleague Sergei Skorobogatov at Cambridge. In 2002 we reported using a photographic flashgun, mounted on the microscope of a probing station, to induce transient faults in selected transistors of an IC [1187]. The light ionises the silicon, causing transistors to conduct. Once you can focus the light on single transistors, whether by using a metal mask or by upgrading from a flashgun to a laser, this enables direct attacks on many chips. For example, microcontrollers can be opened by zapping the flip-flop that latches their protection state.

Later that year, Sergei reported using a laser mounted on the same cheap microscope to read out the memory contents of a microcontroller directly [1111]. The basic idea is simple: if you use a laser to make a transistor conduct, this will increase the device's power consumption unless it was conducting already. By scanning the laser across the device, it is possible to make a map of which transistors are off and which are on. We developed this into a reasonably dependable way of reading out memory cells [1111].

How to hack a smartcard (10)

At the time of writing (2007), smartcard vendors are using 0.18 and 0.13 micron processes which typically have seven metal layers. Direct optical probe attacks on the logic from the surface of the chip are now difficult because of the feature size and because the metal layers get in the way, dispersing the laser light. The faults that are induced are thus more random and less targeted. In addition, the sheer size and complexity of the chips makes it difficult to know where to aim. This is made worse by the use of *glue logic* — essentially randomised place-and-route.

As you can see in Figure 16.7, the older MC68 device has clearly distinguishable blocks, and quite a lot can be learned about its structure and organisation just by looking at it. Bus lines can be picked out and targeted for attack. However, the SX28 in Figure 16.8 just looks like a random sea of gates. The only easily distinguishable features are the EEPROM (at top left) and the RAM (at top right). And the SX28 is a relatively old design; more modern chips are planarised by chemical mechanical polishing so that even fewer details are visible, unless infrared light is used.

Figure 16.7: MC68HC705P6A microcontroller (courtesy of Sergei Skorobogatov)

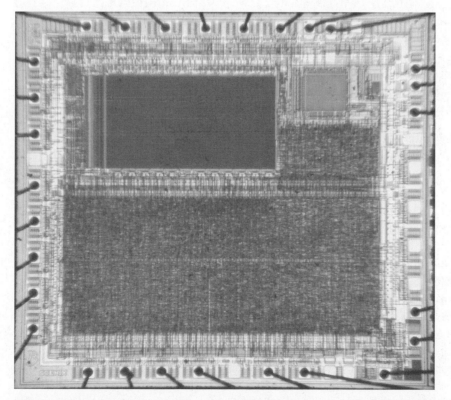

Figure 16.8: SX28 microcontroller with 'glue logic' (courtesy of Sergei Skorobogatov)

The two current windows of vulnerability are the memory and the rear side. Static RAM cells are still fairly large; even with 0.13 micron process an SRAM cell is about 1.2 by 1.7 microns and can thus be individually targeted, whether for fault induction or for read-out of its contents. Rear-side optical attacks use the fact that silicon is transparent at wavelengths greater than 1.1 microns, while rear-side probing attacks use FIBs with special equipment for the purpose.

16.6.4   The State of the Art

The levels of physical tamper-resistance available from the best vendors has improved significantly over the last few years. Much of this comes from the smaller features, more metal layers, and greater design complexity of the latest devices. In the 2001 edition of this book, I wrote, 'there isn't any technology, or combination of technologies, known to me which can make a smartcard resistant to penetration by a skilled and determined attacker'. This is still almost true, but nowadays, it can take a lot of time and money to penetrate a good design. If you can't find an easier way in and have to reverse engineer the entire chip, you'll have to cope with hundreds of thousands of transistors laid out in randomized glue logic with perhaps seven metal layers. One approach is to have sophisticated layout-reconstruction software; another is to send micrographs to a subcontractor in China that just throws a lot of people at the problem. Either way, you can be looking at a year's delay, a budget of over a million dollars, and no certainty of success.

I know of one case where companies spent a huge amount of money (and several years) trying to reverse an authentication chip. That was the Sony MagicGate, a chip found in Playstation accessories and which is recognised by security logic in the Playstation's graphics chip. This used some interesting protection tricks, and an authentication protocol that was both simple (so protocol attacks couldn't be found) and randomised (so that attackers couldn't learn anything from repeating transactions). Most designs aren't that good. Many chips remain vulnerable to side-channel attacks such as power analysis, which I'll discuss in Chapter 17. Many are too complex, or become complex over time, leading to logical vulnerabilities; I will discuss API attacks in Chapter 18.

A final problem is our old friend, the market for lemons. There are smartcard products out there that give very high levels of protection, and others that don't. Needless to say, the vendors all claim that their products are secure. Some of them have Common Criteria evaluations, but these are difficult to interpret; there was at least one case of a chip advertised with a very high rating, that was easy to probe (a careful reading of the evaluation certificate would have revealed that it applied only to the card's operating system, not to its hardware).

So although, at the silicon level, smartcards are usually much harder to copy than magnetic stripe cards, the level of protection they give in an actual application will depend critically on what products you select and how cleverly you use them.

So what sort of strategies are available to you if you are designing a system which depends on smartcards?

16.6.4.1 Defense in Depth

The first, used by pay-TV companies, is defense in depth. Smartcards may use nonstandard processors with custom instruction sets, hardware crypto-processors, registers that use dynamic rather than static RAM to prevent single-stepping, and obscure proprietary encryption algorithms. Normally, using home-brewed encryption schemes is a bad thing: Kerckhoffs' principle almost always wins in the end, and a bad scheme, once published, can be fatal. Defense in depth of pay-TV provides an interesting exception. The goal is to minimize, insofar as possible, the likelihood of a shortcut attack, and to force the attacker to go to the trouble of reverse engineering substantially the whole system. If you are prepared to spend serious money on revenue protection, and you have access to serious expertise, the full-custom route is the way to go.

Technical measures on their own are not enough, though. It's important to think through the business model. Over the last few years of the 20th century, the pay-TV industry managed to reduce piracy losses from over 5% of revenue to an almost negligible proportion. More complex smartcards played a role, but much of the improvement came from legal action against pirates, and from making technical and legal measures work together efficiently. (I'll discuss this further in the chapter on copyright.) And if you can be sure that the opponent has to reconstruct your chip fully before he can threaten your revenue, and you're confident that will take him a year and a million dollars, then you can keep him perpetutally a year behind, and this may be enough. If you also have the ability to refresh your security quickly — say by sending your subscribers a new smartcard — then you can undermine his revenue expectations still further and deter him from entering into the game.

16.6.4.2 Stop Loss

Whether you go for the defense-in-depth approach will often depend on the extent to which you can limit the losses that result from a single card's being successfully probed. In early pay-TV systems, the system architecture forced all customer cards to contain the same master secret. Once this secret became known, pirate cards can be manufactured at will, and the card base had to be replaced. The pay-TV systems currently being deployed for digital broadcasting use crypto protocols in which cards have different keys, so that cloned cards can be revoked. I'll describe these protocols in section 22.2.4.3. This makes the cards less attractive targets.

In other systems, such telephone SIM cards and EMV bank cards, each device contains a key to authorise transactions — whether calls or debits — on a single customer's account. Probing a key out of a card is thus pretty well equivalent to stealing a card, or setting up an account in the target's name and getting a genuine card issued against his credit rating. Attacks that cost millions to research and many thousands per card to carry out are not usually the real problem here. The main threat rather comes from noninvasive attacks, where people are duped into putting their cards into wicked terminals. Although it is conceivable that such a terminal could do a power analysis attack, in practice it's the protocol vulnerabilities that provide the weakest link. So it is quite logical for banks and phone companies to use cheap commodity cards. The system of merchant floor limits, random online authorizations, lists of hot cards and so on, limits the possible damage. (It's still objectionable, though, for the banks to say 'We use smartcards which are secure, therefore any disputed transaction is your fault.')

16.7   What Goes Wrong

There are failure modes of systems involving tamper-resistant processors that are more or less independent of whether the device is a low-cost smartcard or a high-end banking security module.

16.7.1   The Trusted Interface Problem

None of the devices described in the above sections has a really trustworthy user interface. Some of the bank security modules have a physical lock (or two) on the front to ensure that only the person with a given metal key (or smartcard) can perform certain privileged transactions. But whether you use a $2000 4758 or a $2 smartcard to do digital signatures, you still trust the PC that drives them. If it shows you a text saying 'Please pay amazon.com $37.99 for a copy of Anderson's *Security Engineering*' while the message it actually sends for signature is 'Please remortgage my house at 13 Acacia Avenue and pay the proceeds to Mafia Real Estate Inc', then the tamper resistance has not bought you much. Indeed, it may even make your situation worse. Banks in many countries used to move to electronic systems as an opportunity to change their contract terms and conditions, so as to undermine consumer protection [201]. In the UK in particular, smartcards have been more a liability engineering technology than a protective one, complaints are answered with a standard refrain of 'your chip and PIN card was used, so it's your fault.'

This is usually a user interface issue, though not always. Recall the digital tachographs we discussed in Chapter 12; after vendors made the sensor in the truck's gearbox into a secure processor, with its own unique crypto key, the attackers build a gearbox emulator that surrounded it and fed tampered data into the sensor. Even where you put some effort into building a user interface into a tamper-resistant device, it may be compromised via the environment; the classic example here is the skimmer that is fitted to the card slot of an ATM, reads your card on the way in, and captures your PIN using a tiny camera.

Tamper-resistant processors are often able to add more value where they do not have to authenticate users or sense the environment (beyond detecting tampering attempts). Recall the example of prepayment electricity metering, in Chapter 13: there, tamper-resistant processors are used to limit the loss when a token vending machine is stolen. Tokens are generated using keys kept in a cryptoprocessor that maintains and decrypts a value counter, enforcing a credit limit on each vending machine. Postal meters work in exactly the same way.

The critical difference is that the banking application needs to authenticate the customer, while the electricity and postal metering applications don't. Other applications that use crypto chips but don't care who uses them range from accessory control in printer ink cartridges and games consoles to prepaid phone cards. There, the vendor only cares that only one person uses the product and often that they only use it so much.

16.7.2 Conflicts

A further set of issues is that where an application is implemented on a number of devices, under the control of different parties, you have to consider what happens when each party attacks the others. In banking, the card issuer, the terminal owner and the customer are different; all the interactions of cloned cards, bogus terminals and cheating banks need to be thought through. This is quite different from a building entry control application, where one firm owns the cards and the terminals; phone cards are somewhere in the middle.

Bruce Schneier and Adam Shostack suggest a framework for analysing this in [1136]. Imagine that the customer started off with a secure PC; say something like a palmtop computer with software to generate digital signatures. Now consider what happens when you split this up, for example by requiring her to use a remote keyboard and screen controlled by somebody else, or by requiring her to have the crypto done using a smartcard whose software is controlled by somebody else. Then think of what happens when any one of these components is temporarily subverted: the customer's card is stolen, or her computer gets infected. This gives a lot of abuse cases to consider, and designers habitually miss some of them (especially the cases that are hard to solve with their product, or that are embarrassing to their client). And every time you introduce a split into a system, the interface creates new possibilities for mayhem; a survey of flaws found by a commercial evaluation laboratory showed that most of them were at the interfaces between physical, logical and organisational measures [213]. I'll discuss this at greater length in the chapter on API attacks.

There are further problems with displacement. It's common for designers to think that, just because their product contains a security processor, its protection needs have somehow been taken care of. The security box has been ticked. But because of interface and other issues, this is rarely so.

A further source of conflict and vulnerability is that many of the users of tamper resistance are firms implementing business models that restrict their customers' use of their product — such as rights management and accessory control. Their customers are therefore in some sense their enemies. They have not only access to the product, but the incentive to tamper with it if they can.

16.7.3   The Lemons Market, Risk Dumping and Evaluation

Each of the product categories discussed here, from hardware security modules down through smartcards to microcontrollers, has a wide range of offerings with an extremely wide variability in the quality of protection provided. Although quite a few products have evaluations, these don't really mean very much.

First, there are very few offerings at the highest protection level — FIPS-140 level 4 or Common Criteria levels above 4. There are very many at lower levels, where the tests are fairly easy to pass, and where vendors can also shop around for a lab that will give them an easy ride. This leads to a lemons market in which all but the best informed and motivated players will be tempted to go for the cheapest level 3 product, or even an unevaluated offering.

Second, evaluation certificates don't mean what they seem. Someone buying a 4758 in 2001 might have interpreted its level 4 evaluation to mean that it was unbreakable — and then been startled when we broke it. In fact, the FIPS certificate referred only to the hardware, and we found vulnerabilities in the software. It's happened the other way too: there's been a smartcard with a Common criteria level 6 evaluation, but that referred only to the operating system — which ran on a chip with no real defences against microprobing. I'll discuss the failings of our evaluation systems at greater length in Part III.

Third, many firms aim at using secure processors to dump risk rather than minimise it. The banks who say 'your chip and PIN card was used, so it's your fault' are by no means alone. There are many environments, from medicine to defense, where what's sought is often a certificate of security rather than real protection, and this interacts in many ways with the flaws in the evaluation system. Indeed, the main users of security evaluation are precisely those system operators whose focus is on due diligence rather than risk reduction, and they are also disproportionate users of tamper-resistant processors.

16.7.4   Security-By-Obscurity

Until very recently, the designers of cryptoprocessors tried hard to keep their products' design obscure. You had to sign an NDA to get smartcard development tools, and until the mid-1990s there was just no serious information available on how smartcards could be attacked. Their vendors just did not imagine that attackers might buy semiconductor lab tools second-hand and find ingenious ways to use them to probe data out. The security target still used for evaluating many smartcards under the Common Criteria focuses on maintaining obscurity of the design. Chip masks have to be secret, staff have to be vetted, developers have to sign NDAs — there were many requirements that pushed up industry's costs [448]. Obscurity was also a common requirement for export approval, leading to a suspicion that it covers up deliberately inserted vulnerabilities. For example, a card we tested would always produce the same value when instructed to generate a private / public keypair and output the public part.

In short, the industry's security culture was inappropriate. Almost none of the actual attacks on fielded smartcard systems used inside information. Most of them started out with a probing attack or side-channel attack on a card bought at retail. The industry did not do hostile attacks on its own products, so the products were weak and were eventually subjected to hostile attack by others. The culture is now changing and some organisations, such as VISA, specify penetration testing [1300]. However, the incentives are still wrong; a sensible vendor will go to whatever evaluation lab gives him the easiest ride, rather than to an ace attack team that'll find dozens of extra vulnerabilities in the product and destroy its chances of launching on time. We'll return to this subject to discuss the underlying economics and politics of evaluation in section 26.3.3.1.

16.7.5   Interaction with Policy

There are many other unexpected interactions with the world of policy. A good example was the drive that started during the dotcom boom to have smartcards adopted as the preferred device for digital signatures where people interact with government. The European Union passed a law that gave a strong presumption of validity to electronic signatures made using approved smartcards. This was irrational, given the lack of a trusted user interface; for signing documents it would be better to use something like a PDA, where at least the customer can at least see what she's signing and protect the device using common sense [111]. Yet the smartcard vendors lobbied hard and got their law. Thankfully, this was completely counterproductive: the law moved the liability for forged signatures from the relying party to the party whose key was apparently used. By accepting such a device, you were in effect saying, 'I agree to be bound by any signature that appears to have been made by this device, regardless of whether or not I actually made it'. This is unattractive and has helped limit the use of digital signatures to niche applications.

16.7.6 Function Creep

We've already seen numerous examples of how function creep, and changes in environmental conditions, have broken secure systems by undermining their design assumptions. I mentioned, for example, how replacing paper passports (that are unique) with electronic passports (that are easy to copy) undermines the bail system; criminals awaiting trial could flee the country using copies of their passports. A more general problem is when multiple applications are put on the same card. If you deploy a phone banking system, then the SIM card that was previously just a means of identifying people to the phone company now becomes a token that controls access to their bank accounts. It follows that it may attract a much higher grade of attacker. Does this matter? In the present (2007) environment of growing phishing attacks, I'd say it probably doesn't; using text messages to confirm bank transactions gives a valuable second authentication channel (the main risk, as described in Chapter 2, is probably that a fraudster talks the phone company into issuing a SIM to the wrong person).

But what will happen in five or ten years' time, once everyone is doing it? What if the iPhone takes off as Apple hopes, so that everyone uses an iPhone not just as their phone, but as their web browser? All of a sudden the two authentication channels have shrunk to one; both the SMS messages and the IP traffic to the bank web site go through the same operating system, which is now deployed on a large enough scale to attract attention from the gentlemen in Russia.

16.8   So What Should One Protect?

It's common enough that the purpose for which a technology was first invented or marketed isn't the one for which it takes off. The steam engine was invented for pumping water out of coal mines, and the telephone to enable post office clerks to read text to telegraph operators rather than sending it through a pneumatic tube. Similarly, the inventors of smartcards thought they would be a hit in banking; yet they first took off in phone cards, then pay-TV. Despite their use in banking in Europe, they have yet to catch on in markets like the USA where bank customers have better legal protection. The largest sales volumes of the lowest cost crypto chips are in accessory control applications such as printer cartridges and console games.

So what value can tamper-resistant devices actually add?

First, they can control information processing by linking it to a single physical token. A pay-TV subscriber card can be bought and sold in a grey market, but so long as it isn't copied the station operator isn't too concerned. Another example comes from accessory control chips such as the Sony MagicGate; any PlayStation should work with any PlayStation memory cartridge, but not with a cheap Korean competitor. Yet another is the use of crypto to enforce evaluation standards in government networks: if you only get key material once your system has been inspected and accredited, then it's inconvenient to connect an unlicensed system of any size to the classified government network. This enables you to link information protection with physical and operational protection.

Second, they can be used to control value counters, as with the electricity prepayment and postal metering discussed in Chapter 12 and in section 16.7.1 above. These typically use devices such as the iButton to hold keys and also a credit counter. Even if the device is stolen, the total value of the service it can vend is limited. A related application is in printers where ink cartridges are often programmed to dispense only so much ink and then declare themselves to be dry.

Third, they can reduce the need to trust human operators. Their main purpose in some government systems was 'reducing the street value of key material to zero'. A crypto ignition key for a STU-III should allow a thief only to masquerade as the rightful owner, and only if he has access to an actual STU-III device, and only so long as neither the key nor the phone have been reported stolen. The same general considerations applied in ATM networks: no bank wanted to make its own customers' security depend on the trustworthiness of the staff of another bank. In effect, they not only implement a separation of duty policy, but transfer a good portion of the trust from people to things. If these things can be physically controlled — whether by their classification or their sheer mass — that reduces the exposure from both treachery and carelessness.

This is an incomplete list. But what these applications, and their underlying principles, have in common is that a security property can be provided independently of the trustworthiness of the surrounding environment. In other words, be careful when using tamper resistant devices to try to offset the lack of a trustworthy interface. This doesn't mean that no value at all can be added where the interface is problematic. For example, the tamper-resistant crypto modules used in ATM networks cannot prevent small-scale theft using bogus ATMs; but they can prevent large-scale PIN compromise if used properly. In general, tamper-resistant devices are often a useful component, but only very rarely provide a fully engineered solution.

16.9   Summary

Tamper resistant devices and systems have a long history, and predate the development of electronic computing. Computers can be protected against physical tampering in a number of ways, such as by keeping them locked up in a guarded room. There are also several cheaper and more portable options, from hardware security modules that cost thousands of dollars and are certified to resist all currently known attacks, through smartcards whose hardware can now be quite difficult to penetrate, down to low-cost security microcontrollers that can often be defeated with a few hours to days of work.

I've told the story of how hardware tamper-resistance developed through the 1990s through a series of cycles of attack and improved defence, and given many examples of applications. Almost regardless of their price point, security processors are typically vulnerable to attacks on interfaces (human, sensor or system) but can often deliver value in applications where we need to link processing to physical objects and to keep track of value in the absence of a dependable online service.

Research Problems

There are basically two strands of research in tamper resistant processor design. The first concerns itself with making 'faster, better, cheaper' processors: how can the protection offered by a high end device be brought to products with mid-range prices and sizes, and how mid-range protection can be brought to smartcards. The second concerns itself with pushing forward the state of the attack art. How can the latest chip testing technologies be used to make 'faster, better, cheaper' attacks?

These are intertwined with research into emission security and into the protection of application programming interfaces, which I'll discuss in the next two chapters.

Further Reading

Colleagues and I wrote a survey of security processors [65] and I'd recommend that if you're looking for a more detailed treatment of the material in this chapter. Beyond that, there's a tutorial by Sergei Skorobogatov at [1186]. The best current research in the field usually appears in the proceedings of CHES — the workshop on Cryptographic Hardware and Embedded Systems. FPGA security is reviewed at [400], and the other good reads include Bunnie Huang's book on hacking the Xbox [629].

For the early history of crypto, including things like weighted codebooks and water-soluble inks, the source is of course Kahn [676]. For a handbook on the chip card technology of the mid-to-late 1990s, see [1056], while the gory details of tampering attacks on those generations of cards can be found in [68, 69, 733]. The IBM and Dallas products mentioned have extensive documentation online [641], where you can also find the U.S. FIPS documents [936].

CHAPTER 17

Emission Security

The hum of either army stilly sounds,
That the fixed sentinels almost receive
The secret whispers of each others' watch;
Fire answers fire, and through their paly flames
Each battle sees the other's umbred face.

— William Shakespeare, King Henry V, Act IV

17.1   Introduction

Emission security, or Emsec, is about preventing attacks using *compromising emanations*, namely conducted or radiated electromagnetic signals. It has many aspects. Military organizations are greatly concerned with *Tempest* defenses, which prevent the stray RF emitted by computers and other electronic equipment from being picked up by an opponent and used to reconstruct the data being processed. Tempest has recently become an issue for electronic voting too, after a Dutch group found they could tell at a distance which party a voter had selected on a voting machine. The smartcard industry has been greatly exercised by *power analysis*, in which a computation being performed by a smartcard — such as a digital signature — is observed by measuring the current drawn by the CPU and the measurements used to reconstruct the key. These threats are closely related, and have a number of common countermeasures. Researchers have also discovered attacks that exploit stray optical, thermal and acoustic emanations from various kinds of equipment. Such techniques are also referred to as *side channel* attacks as the information is leaking through a channel other than those deliberately engineered for communication.

People often underestimate the importance of Emsec. However, it seems that the world's military organizations spent as much on it as on cryptography during the last quarter of the twentieth century. In the commercial world, the uptake of smartcards was materially set back in the last few years of that century by the realization that all the smartcards then on the market were extremely vulnerable to simple attacks which required the attacker only to trick the customer into using a specially adapted terminal that would analyze the current it drew during a small number of transactions. These attacks did not involve penetrating the card and thus might leave no trace. Once fielded, they were very much cheaper than probing attacks, and potentially allowed large-scale card-cloning attacks against an unsuspecting cardholder population.

Electromagnetic eavesdropping attacks have been demonstrated against other commercial systems, including automatic teller machines. They can interact with malware, in that rogue software can cause a computer to emit a stronger signal than it normally would, and even modulate the signal so as to get stolen data past a corporate firewall. There has also been alarm about disruptive electromagnetic attacks, in which a terrorist group might use a high-energy microwave source to destroy the computers in a target organization without killing people. (I'll discuss these in more detail in the chapter on electronic warfare.)

Both active and passive Emsec measures are closely related to *electromagnetic compatibility* (EMC) and *radio frequency interference* (RFI), which can disrupt systems accidentally. If you fly regularly, you'll be familiar with the captain saying something like 'All electronic devices must be switched off now, and not switched on again until I turn off the seat belt sign'. This problem is getting worse as everything becomes electronic and clock frequencies go up. And how do you obey the captain now that more and more devices are 'always on' — so that the 'off' switch only turns off the green tell-tale light?

As more and more everyday devices get hooked up to wireless networks, and as processor speeds head up into the gigahertz range, all these problems — RFI/EMC, Emsec and various electronic warfare threats — are set to get worse.

17.2   History

Crosstalk between telephone wires was well known to the pioneers of telephony in the 19th century, whose two-wire circuits were stacked on tiers of crosstrees on supporting poles. One way of dealing with it was to use 'transpositions', in which the wires were crossed over at intervals to make the circuit a twisted pair. This problem appears to have first come to the attention of the military during the British Army expedition to the Nile and Suakin in 1884–85 [923].

The first known exploitation of compromising emanations in warfare was in 1914. Field telephone wires were laid to connect the troops bogged down in the mud of Flanders with their headquarters, and these often ran for miles, parallel to enemy trenches that were only a few hundred yards away. A phone circuit was a single-core insulated cable, which used earth return in order to halve the weight and bulk of the cable. It was soon discovered that earth leakage caused a lot of crosstalk, including messages from the enemy side. Listening posts were quickly established and protective measures were introduced, including the use of twisted pair cable. By 1915, valve amplifiers had extended the earth leakage listening range to 100 yards for telephony and 300 yards for Morse code. It was found that the tangle of abandoned telegraph wire in no-man's land provided such a good communications channel, and leaked so much traffic to the Germans, that clearing it away become a task for which lives were spent. By 1916, earth return circuits had been abolished within 3000 yards of the front. When the USA joined the war, the techniques were passed on to them [869, 923].

The Second World War brought advances in radar, passive direction finding and low-probability-of-intercept techniques, which I'll discuss in the chapter on Electronic Warfare. By the 1960s, the stray RF leaking from the local oscillator signals in domestic television sets was being targeted by direction-finding equipment in 'TV detector vans' in Britain, where TV owners must pay an annual license fee to support public broadcast services. Some people in the computer security community were also aware that information could leak from cross-coupling and stray RF. The earliest published reference appears to be a 1970 Rand Corporation report written by Willis Ware [1319].

The intelligence community also started to exploit side channel attacks. During the Suez crisis in 1956, the British figured out the settings of the Egyptian embassy's Hagelin cipher machine using a phone bug. In 1960, after the Prime Minister ordered surveillance on the French embassy during negotiations about joining the European Economic Community, his security service's scientists noticed that the enciphered traffic from the embassy carried a faint secondary signal, and constructed equipment to recover it. It turned out to be the plaintext, which somehow leaked through the cipher machine [1363]. This is more common than one might suppose; there has been more than one case of a cipher machine broadcasting in clear on radio frequencies (though often there is reason to suspect that the vendor's government was aware of this).

During the 1970s, emission security became a highly classified topic and vanished from the open literature. It came back to public attention in 1985 when Wim van Eck, a Dutch researcher, published an article describing how he had managed to reconstruct the picture on a VDU at a distance using a modified TV set [408]. The revelation that Tempest attacks were not just feasible, but could be mounted with simple home-built equipment, sent a shudder through the computer security industry.

Published research in emission security and related topics took off in the second half of the 1990s. In 1996 Markus Kuhn and I reported that many smartcards could be broken by inserting transients, or *glitches*, in their power or clock lines [68]. Paul Kocher also showed that many common implementations of cryptosystems could be broken by making precise measurements of the time taken [727]. In 1998 Kuhn and I showed that many of the compromising emanations from a PC could be made better, or worse, by appropriate software measures [753]. In 1998–9, Kocher showed that crypto keys used in smartcards could be recovered by appropriate processing of precise measurements of the current drawn by the card [728]. Although smartcard vendors had been aware of a possible problem from the late 1980s, Kocher's *differential power analysis* provided a simple and powerful signal processing technique for recovering data that completely overwhelmed the somewhat primitive defences that the industry had seen fit to provide.

In recent years, results have followed steadily. 2002 brought results on optical leakage: Markus Kuhn showed that a VDU's screen contents can be recovered optically, even from diffuse light reflected off room walls or the operator's face [750], while Joe Loughry and David Umphress also found serial port data in many of the LED status indicators on data serial lines [815]. In 2004, Dmitri Asonov and Rakesh Agrawal showed that the different keys on a keyboard made sufficiently different sounds that someone's typing could be picked up from acoustic emanations [91]; in 2005, Li Zhuang, Feng Zhou, and Doug Tygar improved this to use keyboard characteristics and text statistics to decipher a recording of text typed for ten minutes on a random keyboard, to which there had been no previous access to train the recognition software [1376]. In 2006, Steven Murdoch showed that many computers reveal their CPU load via thermal leakage; clock skew is a function of ambient temperature, and can be measured remotely. He hypothesised that it might even be used to work out a target machine's latitude and longitude [914]. These results just seem to keep on coming.

17.3   Technical Surveillance and Countermeasures

Before getting carried away with high-tech toys such as Tempest monitoring receivers, we ought to stop and think about bugs. The simplest and most widespread attacks that use the electromagnetic spectrum are not those exploiting some unintended feature of innocuous equipment, but those in which a custom-designed device is introduced by the attacker.

No matter how well it is protected by encryption and access controls while in transit or storage, most highly confidential information originally comes into being either as speech or as keystrokes on a PC. If it can be captured by the opponent at this stage, then no subsequent protective measures are likely to help very much.

So an extraordinary range of bugs is available on the market:

- At the low end, a few tens of dollars will buy a simple radio microphone that you can stick under a table when visiting the target. Battery life is the main constraint on these devices. They typically have a range of only a few hundred yards, and a lifetime of days to weeks.

- At the next step up are devices that draw their power from the mains, a telephone cable or some other external electricity supply, and so can last indefinitely once emplaced. Some are simple microphones, which can be installed quickly in cable ducting by an adversary who can get a few minutes alone in a room. Others are inserted from a neighboring building or apartment by drilling most of the way through a wall or floor. Yet others look like electrical adaptors but actually contain a microphone, a radio transmitter and a TV camera. Others monitor data — for example a Trojan computer keyboard with bugging hardware contained in the cable connector.

- Many modern bugs use off-the-shelf mobile phone technology. They can be seen as slightly modified cellphone handsets that go off-hook silently when called. This gives them worldwide range; whether they last more than a week or so depends on whether they can be connected to a power source when installed.

- One exotic device, on show at the NSA Museum in Fort Meade, Md., was presented to the U.S. ambassador in Moscow in 1946 by a class of schoolchildren. It was a wooden replica of the Great Seal of the United States, and the ambassador hung it on the wall of the office in his residence. In 1952, it was discovered to contain a resonant cavity that acted as a microphone when illuminated by microwaves from outside the building, and retransmitted the conversations that took place in his office. Right up to the end of the Cold War, embassies in Moscow were regularly irradiated with microwaves, so variants of the technique presumably remained in use.

- Laser microphones work by shining a laser beam at a reflective or partially reflective surface, such as a window pane, in the room where the target conversation is taking place. The sound waves modulate the reflected light, which can be picked up and decoded at a distance.

- High-end devices used today by governments, which can cost upwards of $10,000, use low-probability-of-intercept radio techniques such as frequency hopping and burst transmission. They can also be turned on and off remotely. These features can make them much harder to find.

■ People constantly come up with creative new ideas. A recent one is the *jitterbug* which you put in a keyboard cable. It modulates keystroke data, such as passwords, into sub-perceptible keystroke delays. This means that a password you type can be more easily guessed by an attacker who wiretaps your connection, even if it's encrypted [1155].

A number of countermeasures can give a fair degree of protection against such attacks, provided they are used by skilled and experienced experts.

■ The *nonlinear junction detector* is a device that can find hidden electronic equipment at close range. It works because the transistors, diodes and other nonlinear junctions in electronic equipment rectify incident RF signals. The nonlinear junction detector broadcasts a weak radio signal and listens for odd harmonics. It can detect unshielded electronics at a range of a few feet. However, if the bug has been planted in or near existing electronic equipment, then the nonlinear junction detector is not much help. There are also expensive bugs designed not to re-radiate at all. A variant was invented by the investigative journalist Duncan Campbell in the early 1970s to detect telephone taps: the amplifier used at that time by the security services re-radiated harmonics down the line. Following a raid on his house, the plans for this device were seized; it was then 'invented' in a government laboratory, and credited to a government scientist.

■ There are a number of *surveillance receivers* on the market. The better ones sweep the radio spectrum from about 10 KHz to 3 GHz every few tens of seconds, and look for signals that can't be explained as broadcast, police, air traffic control and so on. (Above 3GHz, signals are so attenuated by building materials, and device antennas can be so directional, that general spectrum search is no longer as effective as nonlinear junction detectors and physical searching.) Contrary to popular belief, some low-probability-of-intercept techniques do not give complete protection. Direct sequence spread spectrum can be spotted from its power spectrum, and frequency hoppers will typically be observed at different frequencies on successive sweeps. Burst transmission does better. But the effectiveness of survcillance receivers is increasingly limited by the availability of bugs that use the same frequencies and protocols as legitimate mobile or cordless phones. Security conscious organizations can always try to forbid the use of mobiles, but this tends not to last long outside the military. For example, Britain's parliament forbade mobiles until 1997, but the rule was overturned when the government changed.

■ Breaking the line of sight, such as by planting trees around your laboratory, can be effective against laser microphones but is often impractical.

- Some facilities at military organizations are placed in completely shielded buildings, or underground, so that even if bugs are introduced their signals can't be heard outside [87]. This is very expensive; but if you can confine your secret conversations to a single room, then there are vendors who sell prefabricated rooms with acoustic and electro-magnetic shielding. Another option is to ensure that devices such as wire-line microphones aren't installed in the building when it's con-structed, that there are frequent sweeps, and that untrusted visitors (and contractors such as cleaning staff) are kept out of the most sensitive areas. But this is harder than it looks. A new U.S. embassy building in Moscow had to be abandoned after large numbers of microphones were found in the structure, and Britain's counterintelligence service had to tear down and rebuild a large part of a new headquarters building, at a cost of about $50m, after an employee of one of the building contrac-tors was found to have past associations with the Provisional IRA.

The tension here is between technological defenses, which can be effective but very expensive, and procedural controls, which are cheap but tedious.

All that said, technological developments are steadily making life easier for the bugger and harder for the defense. As more and more devices acquire intelligence and short-range radio or infrared communications — as 'things that think' become 'things that chatter' — there is ever more scope for attacks via equipment that's already in place rather than stuff that needs to emplaced for the purpose. For example:

- The risks associated with telephones are much more than many people would like to believe. More and more people use cordless phones for convenience, and forget that they're easy to eavesdrop. Phones can be doctored so that they'll go off-hook under remote control; some digital phones have such a facility already built into them (and it's said that some countries make this a condition of import licensing). Also, some makes of PBX can be reprogrammed to support this kind of surveillance.

- The typical laptop computer has a microphone that can be switched on under software control, and is increasingly likely to be online from time to time. An attacker can infect it with malware that listens to conversa-tions in the room, compresses them, encrypts them and mails them back to its creator.

- The NSA banned Furby toys in its buildings, as the Furby remembers (and randomly repeats) things said in its presence.

But there are many more ways in which existing electronic equipment can be exploited by an adversary.

17.4   Passive Attacks

We'll first consider passive attacks, that is, attacks in which the opponent makes use of whatever electromagnetic signals are presented to him without any effort on his part to create them. I'll exclude optical signals for now, although light is electromagnetic; I'll discuss them along with acoustic attacks later.

Broadly speaking, there are two categories of electromagnetic attack. The signal can either be conducted over some kind of circuit (such as a power line or phone line), or it may be radiated as radio frequency energy. These two types of threat are referred to by the military as 'Hijack' and 'Tempest' respectively. They are not mutually exclusive; RF threats often have a conducted component. For example, radio signals emitted by a computer can be picked up by the mains power circuits and conducted into neighboring buildings. However it's a reasonable working classification most of the time.

17.4.1   Leakage Through Power and Signal Cables

Since the nineteenth century, engineers have been aware that high-frequency signals leak everywhere and that care is needed to stop them causing problems, and, as I noted, the leakage has been exploited for military purposes since 1914. Conducted leakage of information can be largely suppressed by careful design, with power supplies and signal cables suitably filtered and suppressed. This makes up a significant part of the cost difference between otherwise comparable military and civilian electronics.

17.4.1.1   Red/Black Separation

Red equipment (carrying confidential data such as plaintext) has to be isolated by filters and shields from *black* equipment (that can send signals directly to the outside world). Equipment with both 'red' and 'black' connections, such as cipher machines, is particularly difficult to get right. It's made more expensive by the fact that the standards for emission security, such as the NACSIM 5100A that specifies the test requirements for Tempest protected equipment, and its NATO equivalent AMSG 720B, are classified [1098] (though they've leaked, as I'll discuss in section 17.4.2 later).

So properly shielded equipment tends to be available only in small quantities, and made specifically for defense markets. This makes it extremely expensive. However, the costs don't stop there. The operations room at an air base can have thousands of cables leading from it; filtering them all, and imposing strict enough configuration management to preserve red/black separation, can cost millions.

17.4.1.2 Timing Analysis

In 1996, Paul Kocher showed that many implementations of public-key algorithms such as RSA and DSA leaked key information through the amount of time they took [727]. His idea was that when doing exponentiation, software typically steps through the secret exponent one bit at a time, and if the next bit is a one it does a multiply. This enables an opponent who knows the first b bits of an exponent to work out the $b + 1$-st bit by observing a number of exponentiations. Attack and defence coevolved for a while, and many people thought their implementations were secure if they used the Chinese Remainder Theorem. But in 2003, David Brumley and Dan Boneh implemented a timing attack against Apache using OpenSSL, and showed how to extract the private key from a remote server by timing about a million decryptions [233]. Good implementations of public-key algorithms now use blinding to prevent such attacks (OpenSSL did offer blinding as an option, but Apache didn't use it).

John Kelsey, Bruce Schneier, David Wagner and Chris Hall pointed out in 1998 that block ciphers using large S-boxes, such as AES, could be vulnerable to timing attacks based on cache misses [704]. The attacker can verify guesses about the output of the first round of the cipher by predicting whether the guessed value would cause a cache miss on S-box lookup, and verifying this against observation. A number of researchers have improved this attack since then, and nowadays a naive implementation of AES can be broken by observing a few hundred encryptions [999, 164, 994].

17.4.1.3 Power Analysis

Often people aren't aware of the need to filter signals until an exploit is found. A very important example comes from the discovery of power attacks on smartcards. As a smartcard is usually a single silicon chip in a very thin carrier, there is little scope for filtering the power supply using extra components such as chokes and capacitors — and given that a smartcard costs 50¢–$1 in bulk, while a capacitor would cost 10¢ to fit, it's rarely economic. The power supply may also be under the control of the enemy. If you use your bank smartcard to make a purchase in a Mafia-owned store, then the terminal might have extra electronics built into it to cheat you.

By the early 1990s, it appears to have been known to pay-TV hackers and to some government agencies that a lot of information could be gathered about the computations being performed in a smartcard by simply measuring the current it drew from its power supply. This attack, known as *power analysis* or *rail noise analysis*, may involve as little as inserting a 10Ω resistor in the ground line and connecting a digital storage oscilloscope across it to observe fluctuations in the current drawn by the device. An example of the resulting power trace can be seen in Figure 17.1. This shows how a password can be extracted from a microcontroller by guessing it a byte at a time and looking for a different power trace when the correct byte is guessed.

Different instructions have quite different power consumption profiles, and, as you can see, the power consumption also depends on the data being processed. The main data-dependent contribution in many circumstances is from the bus driver transistors, which are quite large (see the top of Figure 16.6). Depending on the design, the current may vary by several hundred microamps over a period of several hundred nanoseconds for each bit of the bus whose state is changed [877]. Thus the Hamming weight of the difference between each data byte and the preceding byte on the bus (the *transition count*) is available to an attacker. In some devices, the Hamming weight of each data byte is available too [881]. EEPROM reads and writes can give even more substantial signals.

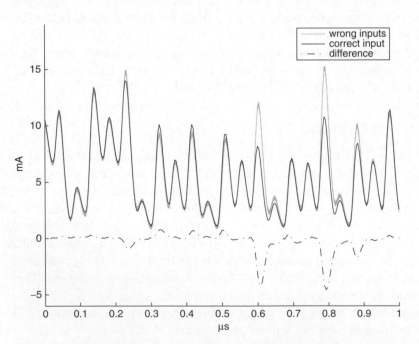

Figure 17.1: Plot of the current measured during 256 single attempts to guess the first byte of a service password stored in the microcontroller at the heart of a car immobilizer (courtesy of Markus Kuhn and Sergei Skorobogatov).

The effect of this leakage is not limited to password extraction. An attacker who understands (or guesses) how a cipher is implemented can obtain significant information about the card's secrets and in many cases deduce the value of the key in use. It is particularly significant because it is a noninvasive attack, and can be carried out by suitably modified terminal equipment on a smartcard carried by an unsuspecting customer. This means that once the attacker has taken the trouble to understand a card and design the attack, a very large number of cards may be compromised at little marginal cost.

The threat posed to smartcards by power analysis was brought forcefully to the industry's attention in 1998 with the development of an efficient signal processing technique to extract the key bits used in a block cipher such as DES from a collection of power curves, without knowing any implementation details of the card software. This technique, Paul Kocher's *differential power analysis*, works as follows [728].

The attacker first collects a number of curves (typically several hundred) by performing known transactions with the target card — transactions for which the encryption algorithm and either the plaintext or the ciphertext is known. She then guesses some of the internal state of the cipher. In the case of DES, each round of the cipher has eight table look-ups in which six bits of the current input is exclusive-or'ed with six bits of key material, and then used to look up a four-bit output from an S-box. So if it's the ciphertext to which the attacker has access, she will guess the six input bits to an S-box in the last round. The power curves are then sorted into two sets based on this guess and synchronized. Average curves are then computed and compared. The difference between the two average curves is called a *differential trace*.

The process is repeated for each of the 64 possible six-bit inputs to the target S-box. It is generally found that the correct input value — which separates the power curves into two sets each with a different S-box output value — will result in a differential trace with a noticeable peak. Wrong guesses of input values, however, generally result in randomly sorted curves and thus in a differential trace that looks like random noise. In this way, the six keybits which go to the S-box in question can be found, followed by the others used in the last round of the cipher. In the case of DES, this gives 48 of the 56 keybits, and the remainder can be found trivially by exhaustive search. If the cipher has many more keybits, then the attacker can unroll it a round at a time.

The effect is that, even if a card could be constructed that resisted probing attacks, it is likely to be vulnerable unless specific power analysis defenses are built in. (In fact, all smartcards then on the market appeared to be vulnerable [728].) Furthermore, even attackers without access to probing equipment could mount attacks cheaply and quickly.

This discovery got wide publicity and held up the deployment of smartcards while people worked on defenses. In some cases, protocol level defenses are possible; the EMV protocol for bank cards mandates (from version 4.1) that the key used to compute the MAC on a transaction be a session key derived from an on-card master key by encrypting a counter. In this way, no two ciphertexts that are visible outside the card should ever be generated using the same key. But most existing protocols are too well entrenched to be changed radically. Another idea was to insert randomness into the way the cryptography was done. One (bad) idea was that, at each round of DES, one might look up the eight S-boxes in a random order; all this achieves is that instead of one large spike in the differential trace, one gets eight spikes each with an eighth the amplitude, so the attacker has merely to collect some more power curves. A better idea was to mask the computation by introducing some offsets in each round and recalculating the S-boxes to compensate for them. This way, the implementation of the cipher changes every time it's invoked.

The defenses now being fielded against power analysis in the better devices depend on special hardware. One of the market-leading cards has hardware that inserts a dummy operation about every 64 machine instructions; another has an internal clock that is only loosely coupled to the external one and that changes frequency about every 64 cycles. Neither of these is foolproof, as an attacker might use signal processing techniques to realign the power curves for averaging. Testing a device for DPA resistance is not straightforward; there is a discussion by Paul Kocher at [729].

There are many variants on power analysis. Attacks based on cache misses can be carried out by measuring power as well as the time taken to encrypt, as a miss activates a lot of circuitry to read nonvolatile memory; so you can't stop cache attacks on AES just by ensuring that each encryption takes a constant number of clock cycles. Another variant is to use different sensors: David Samyde and Jean-Jacques Quisquater created *electromagnetic analysis*, in which they move a tiny pickup coil over the surface of the chip to pick up local signals rather than relying simply on the device's power supply [1054]. The latest twist was invented by Sergei Skorobogatov, who uses a laser to illuminate a single target transistor in the device under test for half of the test runs [1185]. This gives access not just to a Hamming weight of a computation, but a single bit; even if the device is constructed using glue logic, the attacker can still target the sense amplifiers of memory structures.

17.4.2 Leakage Through RF Signals

When I first learned to program in 1972 at the Glasgow Schools' Computer Centre, we had an early IBM machine with a 1.5 MHz clock. A radio tuned to this frequency in the machine room would emit a loud whistle, which varied depending on the data being processed. This phenomenon was noted by many people, some of whom used it as a debugging aid. A school colleague of mine had a better idea: he wrote a set of subroutines of different lengths such that by calling them in sequence, the computer could be made to play a tune. We didn't think of the security implications at the time.

Moving now to more modern equipment, all VDUs emit a weak TV signal — a VHF or UHF radio signal modulated with a distorted version of the image currently being displayed — unless they have been carefully designed not to. The video signal is available at a number of places in the equipment, notably in the beam current which is modulated with it. This signal contains many harmonics of the dot rate, some of which radiate better than others because cables and other components resonate at their wavelength. Given a suitable broadband receiver, these emissions can be picked up and reconstituted as video. The design of suitable equipment is discussed in [408, 753]. Contrary to popular belief, LCD displays are also generally easy for the eavesdropper; a typical laptop has a serial line going through the hinge from the system unit to the display and this carries the video signal (Figure 17.2).

Other researchers quickly established the possibility of remote snooping on everything from fax machines through shielded RS-232 cables to ethernet [365, 1196]. A few companies sprang up to sell 'jammers' but this is hard to do properly [98]: they can interfere with TV and other services. The military use 'Tempest' shielded equipment, but this has generally remained unavailable to the commercial sector. In any case, it is usually a generation out of date and five times as expensive as off-the-shelf PCs. The view taken in the banking industry was 'well, we don't do it to our competitors, so they probably don't do it to us, and we don't know where to get effective countermeasures anyway — so

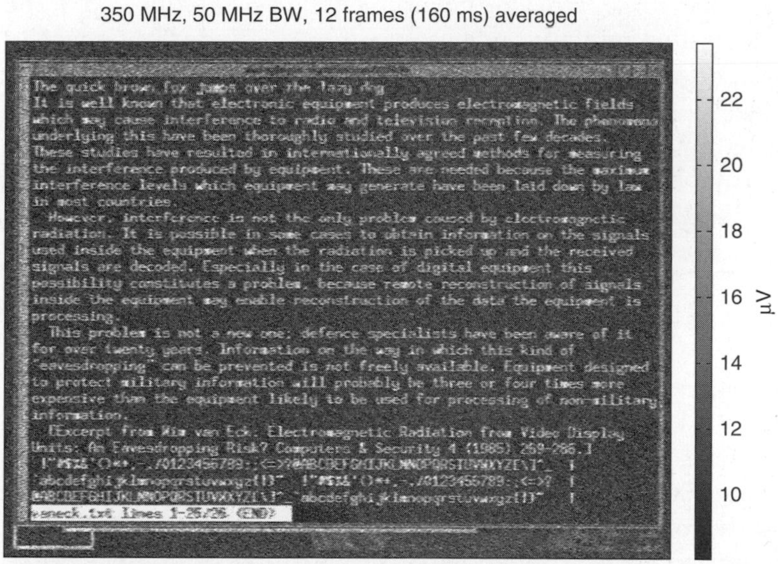

350 MHz, 50 MHz BW, 12 frames (160 ms) averaged

Figure 17.2: RF signal from a Toshiba laptop reconstructed several rooms away, through three plasterboard walls (courtesy of Markus Kuhn [752]).

put it in the "too hard" file'. This view got shaken somewhat in the late 1990s when Hans-Georg Wolf demonstrated a Tempest attack that could recover card and PIN data from a cash machine at a distance of eight meters [744].

Tempest precautions remain a rarity outside the defense sector, but one recent exception comes from the world of voting machines. In October 2006, a Dutch group opposed to electronic voting machines demonstrated that the voting machine used to collect 90% of the election ballots in the Netherlands could be eavesdropped from a distance of several tens of meters [541]. This has led to a Dutch government requirement that voting equipment be Tempest-tested to a level of 'Zone 1–12 dB'.

The *zone* system works as follows. Equipment certified as Zone 0 should not emit any signals that are exploitable at a distance of one meter; it should protect data from electronic eavesdropping even if the opponent is in the next room, and the wall is something flimsy like plasterboard. Zone 1 equipment should be safe from opponents at a distance of 20 meters, and thus the Dutch 'Zone 1–12 dB' criterion means that a voting machine should not leak any data on what vote was cast to an eavesdropper 5 meters away. Zone 2 and Zone 3 mean 120 and 1200 meters respectively. Technical details of zoning were briefly published in 2007, as [243]. (This document was then withdrawn, perhaps because the Americans objected to the Germans releasing it. However everything in it was already in the public domain except the zone limit curves, which are worst-case relative attenuations between distances of 20 m, 120 m and 1200 m from a small dipole or loop antenna, taking into account the difference between nearfield and farfield dropoff.)

The zone system has come into wide governmental use since the end of the Cold War, which slashed military budgets and forced government agencies to use commercial off-the-shelf equipment rather than developing hardware exclusively for their own use. Commercial off-the-shelf equipment tends to be zone 2 when tested, with some particularly noisy pieces of kit in zone 3. By knowing which equipment radiates what, you can keep most sensitive data on equipment furthest from the facility perimeter, and shield stuff only when you really have to. The most sensitive systems (such as national intelligence) and those exposed to the highest threats (such as in embassies overseas) are still either shielded, or kept in shielded rooms. Zoning has greatly cut the costs of emission security, but the overall bill in NATO government agencies comes to over a billion dollars a year.

Markus Kuhn and I developed a lower-cost protection technology, called 'Soft Tempest', which has been deployed in some products, from the email encryption package PGP to the latest Dutch election machines [753]. Soft Tempest uses software techniques to filter, mask or render incomprehensible the information bearing electromagnetic emanations from a computer system. We discovered that most of the information bearing RF energy from a VDU was concentrated in the top of the spectrum, so filtering out this component is a logical first step. We removed the top 30% of the Fourier transform of a standard font by convolving it with a suitable low-pass filter (see Figures 17.3 and 17.4).

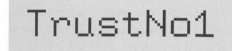

Figure 17.3: Normal text

Figure 17.4: Text low-pass filtered

This turns out to have an almost imperceptible effect on the screen contents as seen by the user. Figures 17.5 and 17.6 display photographs of the screen with the two video signals from Figures 17.3 and 17.4.

Figure 17.5: Screen, normal text

Figure 17.6: Screen, filtered text

However, the difference in the emitted RF is dramatic, as illustrated in the photographs in Figures 17.7 and 17.8. These show the potentially compromising emanations, as seen by a Tempest monitoring receiver.

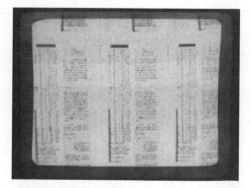

Figure 17.7: Page of normal text

Figure 17.8: Page of filtered text

While the level of protection which Soft Tempest techniques can provide for VDUs is only of the order of 10–20 dB, this translates to a difference of a zone — which in an organization the size of a government, can save a lot of money [70].

There are other attacks that software tricks can block completely. For example, computer keyboards can be snooped on while the microcontroller goes through a loop that scans all the keys until it encounters one that is pressed. The currently pressed key is modulated on to the RF emissions from the keyboard. By encrypting the order in which the keys are scanned, this kind of attack can be completely blocked.

17.5 Active Attacks

However, it's not enough to simply encrypt a keyboard scan pattern to protect it, as the attacker can use active as well as passive techniques. Against a keyboard, the technique is to irradiate the cable with a radio wave at its resonant frequency. Thanks to the nonlinear junction effect, the keypress codes are modulated into the return signal which is reradiated by the cable. This can be picked up at a distance of 50–100 yards. To prevent it, one must also encrypt the signal from the keyboard to the PC [753].

17.5.1 Tempest Viruses

There are quite a few other active attacks possible on various systems. The phenomenon that we observed with the IBM 1401 — that a suitable program would cause a computer to play a tune on the radio, in effect turning it into a low-grade radio transmitter — is easy enough to reimplement on a modern PC. Figures 17.9 and 17.10 show what the screen on a PC looks like when the video signal is an RF carrier at 2 MHz, modulated with pure tones of 300 and 1200 Hz.

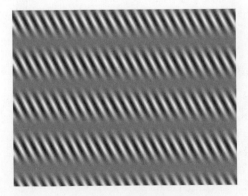

Figure 17.9: 300 Hz AM signal

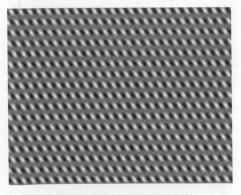

Figure 17.10: 1200 Hz AM signal

Using phenomena like this, it is possible to write a *Tempest virus* that will infect a target computer and transmit the secret data it steals to a radio receiver hidden nearby. This can happen even if the machine is not connected to the net. The receiver need not be expensive; a short wave radio with a cassette recorder will do, and exploit code has already been published. With more sophisticated techniques, such as spread-spectrum modulation, it's possible for an attacker with more expensive equipment to get much better ranges [753].

Some of these methods were already known to the intelligence community. There have been reports of the CIA using software-based RF exploits in economic espionage against certain European countries (for example, in a TV documentary accompanying the release of [725]). Material recently declassified by the NSA in response to a FOIA request [869, 666] reveals the use of the codeword *Teapot* to refer to 'the investigation, study, and control of intentional compromising emanations (i.e., those that are hostilely induced or provoked) from telecommunications and automated information systems equipment'. A further example is to attack equipment that's been shielded and Tempest-certified up to a certain frequency (say, 3 GHz) by irradiating it through the ventilation slots using microwaves of a much higher frequency (say 10GHz) at which these slots become transparent [753].

The possibility of attacks using malicious code is one reason why Tempest testing involves not just listening passively to the emanations from the device under test, but injecting into it signals such as long linear feedback shift register sequences. These create a spread-spectrum signal which will likely be detectable outside the device and thus simulate the worst-case attack in which the opponent has used a software exploit to take over the device [177]. I understand that normal Tempest certification does not take account of the process gain that can be obtained by such techniques.

17.5.2 Nonstop

Another class of active methods, called *Nonstop* by the U.S. military [87], is the exploitation of RF emanations that are accidentally induced by nearby radio transmitters and other RF sources. If equipment processing sensitive data is used near a mobile phone, then the phone's transmitter may induce currents in the equipment that get modulated with sensitive data by the nonlinear junction effect and reradiated.

For this reason, it used to be forbidden to use a mobile phone within 5 meters of classified equipment. Nonstop attacks are also the main Emsec concern for ships and aircraft; here, an attacker who can get close enough to do a passive Tempest attack can probably do much more serious harm than eavesdropping, but as military ships and aircraft often carry very powerful radios and radars, one must be careful that their signals don't get modulated accidentally with something useful to the enemy.

17.5.3 Glitching

Active Emsec threats are also significant in the smartcard world, where perhaps the best known is the *glitch attack* [68]. Here, the opponent inserts transients into the power or clock supply to the card in the hope of inducing a useful error.

For example, one smartcard used in early banking applications had the feature that an unacceptably high clock frequency only triggered a reset after a number of cycles, so that transients would be less likely to cause false alarms. So it was possible to replace a single clock pulse with two much narrower pulses without causing an alarm that would reset the card. This reliably caused the processor to execute a NOP regardless of what instruction it was supposed to execute. This gives rise to a *selective code execution* attack that can be extraordinarily powerful. For example, the attacker can step over jump instructions and thus bypass access controls.

17.5.4 Differential Fault Analysis

Even where the attacker does not know the card's software in detail, glitch attacks can still be a knockout. Dan Boneh, Richard DeMillo and Richard Lipton noticed that a number of public key cryptographic algorithms break if a random error can be induced [206]. For example, when doing an RSA signature the secret computation $S = h(m)^d \pmod{pq}$ is carried out mod p, then mod q, and the results are then combined, as this is much faster. But if the card returns a defective signature S_p which is correct modulo p but incorrect modulo q, then we will have

$$p = \gcd(pq, S_p^e - h(m))$$

which breaks the system at once. These attacks can easily be implemented if the card isn't protected against glitches, and can also be easily extended to many symmetric algorithms and protocols. For example, Eli Biham and Adi Shamir pointed out that if we have the power to set a given bit of memory to zero (or one), and we know where in memory a key is kept, we can find out the key by just doing an encryption, zeroising the leading bit, doing another encryption and seeing if the result's different, then zeroising the next bit and so on [171]. Optical probing may be just the tool for this.

Our subsequent discovery of the power of optical probing means that such attacks can be implemented routinely by an attacker who can get access to the chip surface and identify the relevant memory structures [1111].

17.5.5 Combination Attacks

Other attacks use a combination of active and passive methods. I mentioned in passing in Part I a trick that could be used to find the PIN in a stolen smartcard. Early card systems would ask the customer for a PIN and if it was incorrect they would decrement a retry counter. As this involved writing a byte to EEPROM, the current consumed by the card rose measurably as the capacitors in the circuit that boosts the supply voltage V_{cc} to the programming voltage V_{pp} were charged up. On noticing this, the attacker could simply reset the card and try the next candidate PIN.

The leading active-passive method at the time of writing is Sergei Skorobogatov's optically enhanced position-locked power analysis [1185], which uses a laser to partially ionise a target transistor while power analysis is carried out, and which I discussed in section 17.4 above. This can be extended to an active attack by increasing the laser power so as to make the target transistor conduct.

17.5.6 Commercial Exploitation

Not all Emsec attacks involve covert military surveillance or lab attacks on tamper-resistant devices. I already mentioned the TV detector vans used in Britain to catch TV license defaulters, and the uproar over voting machines in Holland. There are also marketing applications. U.S. venue operator SFX Entertainment monitors what customers are playing on their car radios as they drive into venue parking lots by picking up the stray RF from the radio's local oscillator. Although legal, this annoys privacy advocates [1212]. The same equipment has been sold to car dealers, mall operators and radio stations.

17.5.7 Defenses

The techniques that can be used to defend smartcards against active Emsec threats are similar to those used in the passive case, but not quite the same.

The use of timing randomness — jitter — is still useful, as a naive opponent might no longer know precisely when to insert the glitch. However, a clever opponent may well be able to analyze the power curve from the processor in real time and compare it against the code so as to spot the critical target instructions. In addition, fault attacks are hard to stop with jitter, as the precise location of the fault in the code is not usually critical.

In some cases, defensive programming is enough. For example, the PIN search described above in section 17.5.5 is prevented in more modern cards by decrementing the counter, soliciting the PIN, and then increasing the counter again if it's correct. Fault attacks on public key protocols can be made a lot harder if you just check the result.

Other systems use specific protective hardware, such as a circuit that integrates the card reset with the circuit that detects clock frequencies that are too high or too low. Normal resets involve halving the clock frequency for a few cycles, so an attacker who found some means of disabling the monitoring function would quite likely find himself unable to reset the card at all on power up [733].

So we know in principle how to defend ourselves against glitch attacks (though extensive device testing is always advisable). Optical probing is harder; the sort of attack a card can face nowadays is from an opponent who puts it in a test rig, initiates a cryptographic operation, and fires a laser at the chip to cause a single device upset at a precisely measured time. With a motorised stage, hundreds of different targets can be tried per hour.

Colleagues and I at Cambridge designed and prototyped a defence technology that can resist such an onslaught, using dual-rail self-timed logic. In such logic, rather than signaling '1' by High and '0' by Low on a single line, we have two lines for each logic bit. We signal '1' by 'HighLow' and '0' by 'LowHigh'; the end of a logic operation is 'LowLow'. Such logic has been known for some years, and has the property that if the 'HighHigh' state somehow enters the system, it tends to propagate across the chip, locking it up and rendering the device inoperable until it's reset. We made a virtue of this by defining 'HighHigh' to be the 'alarm' state, and redesigning the gates so that a single-event upset would cause an alarm to propagate. We also salted the chip with a number of alarm sensors. And because the logic is balanced, the power consumption is much less dependent on the data; the signals potentially exploitable by power analysis were reduced by about 20 dB [903]. A number of other researchers have recently started looking at such exotic design styles, and some have started to appear in products. Redundant design can be fairly expensive, costing at least three times as much as standard CMOS, but the cost per transistor may now have fallen to the point where it makes sense.

17.6   Optical, Acoustic and Thermal Side Channels

In recent years, there has been a stream of interesting new results on novel side-channel attacks. Have you ever looked across a city at night, and seen someone working late in their office, their face and shirt lit up by the diffuse reflected glow from their computer monitor? Did you ever stop to wonder whether any information might be recovered from the glow? In 2002 Markus Kuhn showed that the answer was pretty well 'everything': he hooked up a high-performance photomultiplier tube to an oscilloscope, and found that the light from the blue and green phosphors used in common VDU tubes decays after a few microseconds. As a result, the diffuse reflected glow contains much of the screen information, encoded in the time domain. Thus, given a telescope, a photomultiplier tube and suitable image-processing software, it was possible to read the computer screen at which a banker was looking by decoding the light scattered from his face or his shirt [750].

The next headline was from Joe Loughry and David Umphress, who looked at the LED status indicators found on the data serial lines of PCs, modems, routers and other communications equipment. They found that a significant number of them were transmitting the serial data optically: 11 out of 12 modems tested, 2 out of 7 routers, and one data storage device. The designers were just driving the tell-tale light off the serial data line, without stopping to realise that the LED had sufficient bandwidth to transmit the data to a waiting telescope [815].

Acoustics came next. There had always been a 'folk rumour' that the spooks were able to tell what someone was typing on the old IBM Selectric typewriter by just recording the sound they made, and it had been reported that data could be recovered from the noise made by dot matrix printers [228]. In 2004, Dmitri Asonov and Rakesh Agrawal showed that the different keys on a keyboard made different enough sounds. They trained a neural network to recognise the clicks made by key presses on a target keyboard and concluded that someone's typing could be picked up from acoustic emanations with an error rate of only a few percent [91]. Now Dawn Song, David Wagner and XuQing Tian had also shown that SSH encrypted sessions leak a considerable amount of information as the keystrokes are sent in individual packets, the time-delays between which are visible to an attacker; they noted that this would enable an attacker about a factor of 50 advantage in guessing a password whose encrypted value he'd observed [1203].

In 2005, Li Zhuang, Feng Zhou, and Doug Tygar combined these threads to come up with an even more powerful attack. Given a recording of someone typing text in English for about ten minutes on an unknown keyboard, they recognised the individual keys, then used the inter-keypress times and the known statistics of English to figure out which key was which. Thus they could decode text from a recording of a keyboard to which they had never had access [1376].

In 2004, Eran Tromer and Adi Shamir took the acoustic analysis idea down to a much lower level: they showed that keys leak via the acoustic emanations from a PC, generated mostly at frequencies above 10KHz by capacitors on the motherboard [1263].

The latest development has been thermal covert channels. In 2006, Steven Murdoch discovered that a typical computer's clock skew, which can be measured remotely, showed diurnal variation, and realised this was a function of ambient temperature. His experiments showed that unless a machine's owner takes countermeasures, then anyone who can extract accurate timestamps from it can measure its CPU load; and this raises the question of whether an attacker can find where in the world a hidden machine is located. The longitude comes from the time zone, and the latitude (more slowly) from the seasons. So hiding behind an anonymity service such as Tor might not be as easy as it looks [914, 916].

17.7   How Serious are Emsec Attacks?

Technical surveillance and its countermeasures — bugs — are the most important aspect of Emsec, in both government and industry. They are likely to remain so. The range of bugs and other surveillance devices that can be bought easily is large and growing. The motivation for people to spy on their rivals, employees and lovers will continue. If anything, the move to a wired world will make electronic surveillance more important, and countermeasures will take up more of security budgets.

Those aspects of Emsec which concern equipment not designed for surveillance — Tempest, Teapot, Hijack, Nonstop and the various types of power and glitch attack — are set to become another of the many technologies which got their initial development in the government sector but which become important in the design of commercial products.

17.7.1   Governments

The Emsec threats to embassies in hostile countries are real. If your country is forced by the President of Lower Slobovia to place its embassy in the second floor of an office block whose first and third floors are occupied by the local secret police, then security is a hard problem. Shielding all electronic equipment (except that used for deception) will be part of the solution. It won't be all of it; your cleaning ladies will no doubt be in the pay of the Slobovian security forces and will helpfully loosen your equipment's Tempest gaskets, just as they change the batteries in the room bugs.

In less threatening environments, the cost-effectiveness of hardware Tempest shielding is more doubtful. Despite the hype with which the Tempest industry maintained itself during the Cold War, there is a growing scepticism about whether any actual Tempest attacks had ever been mounted by foreign agents in the USA. Anecdotes abound. It's said, for example, that the only known use of such surveillance techniques against U.S. interests in the whole of North America was by Canadian intelligence personnel, who overheard U.S. diplomats discussing the U.S. bottom line in grain sales to China.

There was a scandal in April 2007 when it emerged that Lockheed-Martin had ignored Tempest standards when installing equipment in U.S. Coast Guard vessels. Documents were left on the web site of the Coast Guard's Deepwater project and ended up an activist website, cryptome.org, which was closed down for a while. The documents tell a story not just of emission security defects — wrong cable types, violations of cable separation rules, incorrect grounding, missing filters, red/black violations, and so on — but of a more generally botched job. The ships also had hull cracks, outdoor radios that were not waterproof, a security CCTV installation that did not provide the specified 360 degree coverage, and much more [338]. This led to a Congressional inquiry. The documents at least provide some insight into the otherwise classified Tempest and Nonstop accreditation procedures.

I must confess I might have some sympathy if Coast Guard personnel had simply placed a low priority on Tempest defences. Having been driven around an English town looking for Tempest signals, I can testify that doing such attacks is much harder in practice than it might seem in theory, and the kind of opponents we face nowadays are rather different from the old Soviet intelligence machine. Governments are rightly more relaxed about Tempest risks than twenty years ago.

17.7.2 Businesses

In the private sector, the reverse is the case. The discovery of fault attacks and then power attacks was a big deal for the smartcard industry, and held up for probably two years the deployment of smartcards in banking applications in those countries that hadn't already committed to them. The currently deployed devices are still not perfect; attacks are kept at bay by a mishmash of ad-hoc mechanisms whose effectiveness depends on there being capable designers who understand the problem and whose managers remain worried about it. As the 'DPA' scare recedes, and equipment becomes ever more complex, expect the residual vulnerabilities to reassert themselves. Building chip-scale devices that really block side-channel attacks is hard, and few customers are prepared to pay for it.

And what about the future?

The 'non-security' aspects of emission management, namely RFI/EMC, are becoming steadily more important. Ever higher clock speeds, plus the introduction of all sorts of wireless devices and networks and the proliferation of digital electronics into many devices which were previously analogue or mechanical, are making electromagnetic compatibility a steadily harder and yet more important problem. A host of incompatible standards are managed by different industry groups, many of which are rapidly becoming obsolete — for example, by not requiring testing above 1 GHz, or by assuming protection distances that are no longer reasonable [715].

On the 'security' side, attacks are likely to become easier. The advent of *software radios* — radios that digitize a signal at the intermediate frequency stage and do all the demodulation and subsequent processing in software — will be important. These were until recently an expensive military curiosity [761] but are now finding applications in places like cellular radio base stations. The next generation may be consumer devices, designed to function as GPS receivers, GSM phones, wireless LAN basestations, and support whatever other radio based services have been licensed locally — all with only a change in software.

Once people learn how to program them, they may well use them for Tempest attacks.

Finally, Emsec issues are not entirely divorced from electronic warfare. As society becomes more and more dependent on devices that are vulnerable to strong radio frequency signals — such as the high power microwaves generated by military radars — so the temptation to mount attacks will increase. I'll discuss high energy radio frequency attacks in the next chapter but one.

17.8   Summary

Emission security covers a whole range of threats in which the security of systems can be subverted by compromising emanations, whether from implanted bugs, from unintentional radio frequency or conducted electromagnetic leakage, to emanations that are induced in some way. Although originally a concern in the national intelligence community, Emsec is now a real issue for companies that build security products such as smartcards and cash machines. Many of these products can be defeated by observing stray RF or conducted signals. Protecting against such threats isn't as straightforward as it might seem.

Research Problems

We need a comprehensive set of emission security standards for commercial use. The military standards — NATO SDIP-27 and USA NSTISSAM — are classified, although they've leaked as described in section 17.4.2. RFI/EMC standards — the civilian IEC/CISPR 22 and the stricter MIL-STD-461E — were simply not designed to protect information. The recent panic in Holland about Tempest snooping on voting machines shows that standards are needed, so that equipment purchasers and vendors can take a view on whether they're needed in any given application.

Further Reading

There is a shortage of open literature on Emsec. The classic van Eck article [408] is still worth a read, and the only book on computer security (until this one) to have a chapter on the subject is Russell and Gangemi [1098]. Our work on Soft Tempest, Teapot and related topics can be found in [753]. For power analysis, see the papers by Kocher [728] and by Messergues et al. [877]; more papers appearing regularly at the CHES workshop. Joel McNamara runs an unofficial Tempest Web site at [869]. For timing and power analysis, the original papers by Paul Kocher and colleagues are the classic references [727, 728]; there's also a book by Stefan Mangard, Elisabeth Oswald and Thomas Popp [833].

CHAPTER 18

API Attacks

One is happenstance; twice is coincidence; but three times is enemy action.
— Goldfinger

Simplicity is the ultimate sophistication.
— Leonardo Da Vinci

18.1 Introduction

Many supposedly secure devices have some kind of application programming interface, or API, that untrustworthy people and processes can call in order to get some task performed.

- A bank's server will ask an attached hardware security module 'Here's a customer account number and PIN, with the PIN encrypted using the key we share with VISA. Is the PIN correct?'

- If you enable javascript, then your browser exposes an application programming interface — javascript — which the owners of websites you visit can use to do various things.

- A secure operating system may limit the calls that an application program can make, using a reference monitor or other wrapper to enforce a policy such as preventing information flow from High to Low.

The natural question to ask is whether it's safe to separate tasks into a trusted component and a less trusted one, and it's recently been realised that the answer is very often no. Designing security APIs is a very hard problem indeed.

API security is related to some of the problems I've already discussed. For example, multilevel secure systems impose flow controls on static data, while a security API is often trying to prevent some information flow in the presence of tight and dynamic interaction — a much harder problem. It's also related to protocol security: as I will discuss shortly, bank security modules are often insecure because of interactions between a number of different protocols that they support. It touches on software security: the javascript implementation in Firefox lets calling programs scan all variables set by existing plugins — which may compromise your privacy by leaking information about your browsing habits and web mail usage [543]. The javascript developers just didn't think to have a separate sandbox for each visited website. Indeed, the most common API failure mode is that transactions that are secure in isolation become insecure in combination, whether because of application syntax, feature interaction, slow information leakage or concurrency problems.

There are many other examples. In the context of embedded systems, for example, I discussed prepayment electricity meters; the token vending machines use tamper-resistant security modules to protect keys and value counters. There, an attack was to change the electricity tariff to the lowest possible value and issue tokens that entitled recipients to power for much less than its market value. The design error was to not bind in tariff reporting into the end-to-end protocol design.

A potentially critical example is 'Trusted Computing'. This initiative has put a TPM chip for secure crypto key storage on most of the PC and Mac motherboards shipping today. The plan, according to Microsoft, is that future applications will have a traditional 'insecure' part running on top of Windows as before, and also a 'secure' part or NCA that will run on top of a new security kernel known as the Nexus, which will be formally verified and thus much more resistant to software attacks. The Nexus and the NCA will guard crypto keys and other critical variables for applications. The question this then raises is how the interface between the application and the NCA is to be protected.

In short, whenever a trusted computer talks to a less trusted one, the language they use is critical. You have to expect that the less trusted device will try out all sorts of unexpected combinations of commands in order to trick the more trusted one. How can we analyse this systematically?

18.2   API Attacks on Security Modules

We have learned a lot about API security from failures of the hardware security modules used by banks to protect PINs and crypto keys for ATM networks. In 1988, Longley and Rigby identified the importance of separating key types while doing work for security module vendor Eracom [811]. In 1993, we reported a security flaw that arose from a custom transaction added to a security module [69]. However the subject really got going in 2000 when I started to think systematically about whether there might be a series of transactions that one could call from a security module that would break its security [52]. I asked: 'So how can you be sure that there isn't some chain of 17 transactions which will leak a clear key?' Looking through the manuals, I discovered the following vulnerability.

18.2.1   The XOR-To-Null-Key Attack

Hardware security modules are driven by transactions sent to them by the host computers to which they are attached. Each transaction typically consists of a command, a serial number, and several data items. The response contains the serial number and several other data items. The security module contains a number of master keys that are kept in tamper-responding memory, which is zeroized if the device is opened. However, there is often not enough storage in the device for all the keys it might have to use, so instead keys are stored encrypted outside the device. Furthermore, the way in which these working keys are encrypted provides them with a type system. For example, in the security modules provided by VISA, a key used to derive a PIN from an account number (as described in section 10.4.1) is stored encrypted under a particular pair of master DES keys.

Among the VISA security module's transactions can be found support for generating a *Terminal Master Key* for an ATM. You'll recall from Chapter 10 that ATM security is based on dual control, so a way had to be found to generate two separate keys that could be carried from the bank to the ATM, say by the branch manager and the branch accountant, and entered into it at a keypad. The VISA device thus had a transaction to generate a key component and print out its clear value on an attached security printer. It also returned its value to the calling program, encrypted under the relevant master key KM, which was kept in the tamper-resistant hardware:

$$\text{VSM} \rightarrow \text{printer: } KMT_i$$
$$\text{VSM} \rightarrow \text{host: } \{KMT_i\}_{KM}$$

It also had another transaction that will combine two such components to produce a terminal key:

$$\text{Host} \rightarrow \text{VSM: } \{KMT_1\}_{KM}, \{KMT_2\}_{KM}$$
$$\text{VSM} \rightarrow \text{host: } \{KMT_1 \oplus KMT_2\}_{KM}$$

The idea was that to generate a terminal key for the first time, you'd use the first of these transactions twice followed by the second. Then you'd have $KMT = KMT_1$ exclusive-or KMT_2. However, there was nothing to stop the programmer taking any old encrypted key and supplying it twice in the second transaction, resulting in a known terminal key (the key of all zeroes, as the key is exclusive-or'ed with itself):

$$\text{Host} \longrightarrow \text{VSM: } \{KMT_1\}_{KM}, \{KMT_1\}_{KM}$$
$$\text{VSM} \longrightarrow \text{host: } \{KMT_1 \oplus KMT_1\}_{KM}$$

So now we have managed to insert a known key into the system. What can be done with it? Well, the module also had a transaction to encrypt any key supplied encrypted under KM, under any other key that itself is encrypted under KM. Sounds complicated? Well, that's where things break. The purpose of this odd transaction was to enable a bank to encrypt its PIN verification key under a terminal master key, so it could be sent out to an ATM for offline PIN verification. What's more, the key type 'terminal master key' and the key type 'PIN verification key' were the same. The effect of this was drastic. A programmer can retrieve the bank's PIN verification key — which is also kept outside the security module, encrypted with KM, and have it encrypted under the zero key that he now has inserted into the system:

$$\text{Host} \longrightarrow \text{VSM: } \{0\}_{KM}, \{PIN\}_{KM}$$
$$\text{VSM} \longrightarrow \text{host: } \{PIN\}_0$$

The programmer can now decrypt the PIN verification key — the bank's crown jewels — and can work out the PIN for any customer account. The purpose of the security module has been completely defeated; the bank might as well have just worked out PINs using encryption software, or kept them in clear on its database.

The above attack went undiscovered for a long time because it's a bit hard to understand the implications of *'a transaction to encrypt any key supplied encrypted under KM, under any other key that itself is encrypted under KM'*. It was just not clear what the various types of key in the device were suppose to do, and what security properties the type system had to have in order to achieve its goals. In fact, there seemed to be no formal statement of the protection goals at all; the module had simply evolved from earlier, simpler designs as banks asked for more features.

The next attack was found using formal methods. My student Mike Bond built a formal model of the key types used in the device and immediately discovered another flaw. The key type 'communications key' is used for MAC keys, which have the property that you can input a MAC key in the clear and get it encrypted by — you guessed it — 'any key that itself is encrypted under KM'. So here was another way in which you could get a known key into the system. You could put in an account number into the system, pretending it's a MAC key, and get it encrypted with the PIN verification key — this gives you the customer PIN directly. (Confused? Initially everyone was — modern APIs are just too complicated for bugs to be evident on casual inspection. Anyway, the full details are at [65].)

18.2.2 The Attack on the 4758

We next found a number of cryptographic attacks on the API of the VISA module and on its IBM equivalent, the 4758 [641]. For example, they both generate 'check values' for keys — a key identifier calculated by encrypting a string of zeroes under the key. This opens up a birthday attack, also known as a time-memory tradeoff attack. Suppose you want to crack a DES key of a type that you can't extract from the device. Now DES keys can be broken with about 2^{55} effort, but that's a lot of work. However, in the security module architecture it's generally enough to crack any key of a given type, as data can be converted back and forth between them. You're also able to generate large numbers of keys of any given type — several hundred a second.

The attack therefore goes as follows.

1. Generate a large number of terminal master keys, and collect the check value of each.

2. Store all the check values in a hash table.

3. Perform a brute force search, by guessing a key and encrypting the fixed test pattern with it.

4. Compare the resulting check value against all the stored check values by looking it up in the hash table (an $O(1)$ operation).

With a 2^{56} keyspace, an attacker who can generate 2^{16} target keys (which can be done over lunchtime), a target key should be hit by luck with roughly $2^{56}/2^{16} = 2^{40}$ effort (which you can do in a week or so on your PC). This is also called a 'meet-in-the-middle' attack, reflecting the meeting of effort spent by the HSM generating keys and effort spent by the brute-force search checking keys.

Within a short space of time, Mike Bond had come up with an actual attack on the 4758. This really shook the industry, as the device had been certified to FIPS 140-1 level 4; in effect the US government had said it was unbreakable. In addition to the meet-in-the-middle attack, he used a further obscure design error, key replication.

As DES became vulnerable to keysearch during the 1980s, financial institutions started migrating systems to two-key triple-DES: the block was encrypted with the left key, decrypted with the right key and then encrypted with the left key once more. This piece of cleverness gave a backward compatibility mode: set the left key equal to the right key, and the encryption reverts to single-DES. The 4758 compounded the cleverness by storing left keys and right keys separately. IBM took precautions to stop them being confused — left keys and right keys were encrypted differently, giving them different types — but failed to bind together the two halves.

So an attacker could use the meet-in-the-middle trick to get two single DES keys with known values inside a 4758, then swap the left and right halves to get a known true triple-DES key. This could then be used to export other valuable keys. Several variants of this attack are described in [202]; the attack was actually implemented and demonstrated on prime-time television [306].

18.2.3   Multiparty Computation, and Differential Protocol Attacks

The next set of attacks on security module APIs was initiated by Jolyon Clulow in 2003 [309], and they depend on manipulating the details of the application logic so as to leak information.

His first attack exploited error messages. One of the PIN block formats in common use combines the PIN and the account number by exclusive-or and then encrypts them; this is to prevent attacks such as the one I described in section 10.4.2 where the encrypted PIN isn't linked to the customer account number. However (as with combining keys) it turned out that exclusive-or was a bad way to do this. The reason was this: if the wrong account number was sent along with the PIN block, the device would decrypt the PIN block, xor in the account number, discover (with reasonable probability) that the result was not a decimal number, and return an error message. The upshot was that by sending a series of transactions to the security module that had the wrong account number, you could quickly work out the PIN.

An even simpler attack was then found by Mike Bond and Piotr Zielinski. Recall the method used by IBM (and most of the industry) to generate PINs, as in Figure 18.1:

Account number PAN:	8807012345691715
PIN key KP:	FEFEFEFEFEFEFEFE
Result of DES $\{PAN\}_{KP}$:	A2CE126C69AEC82D
$\{N\}_{KP}$ decimalized:	0224126269042823
Natural PIN:	0224
Offset:	6565
Customer PIN:	6789

Figure 18.1: IBM method for generating bank card PINs

The customer account number is encrypted using the PIN verification key, yielding a string of 16 hex digits. The first four are converted to decimal digits for use as the PIN using a user-supplied function: the *decimalisation table*. This gives the natural PIN; an offset is then added whose function is to enable the customer to select a memorable PIN. The customer PIN is the natural PIN plus the offset. The most common decimalisation table is 012345689012345, which just takes the DES output modulo 10.

The problem is that the decimalisation table can be manipulated. If we set the table to all zeros (i.e., 0000000000000000) then a PIN of '0000' will be generated and returned in encrypted form. We then repeat the call using the table 1000000000000000. If the encrypted result changes, we know that the DES output contained a 0 in its first four digits. Given a few dozen suitably-chosen queries, the value of the PIN can be found. Since the method compares repeated, but slightly modified, runs of the same protocol, we called this attack *differential protocol analysis*.

The industry's initial response was to impose rules on allowable decimalisation tables. One vendor decreed, for example, that a table would have to have at least eight different values, with no value occurring more than four times. This doesn't actually cut it (try 0123456789012345, then 1123456789012345, and so on). The only real solution is to rip out the decimalisation table altogether; you can pay your security-module vendor extra money to sell you a machine that's got your own bank's decimalisation table hard-coded.

At a philosophical level, this neatly illustrates the difficulty of designing a device that will perform a secure multiparty computation — where a computation has to be performed using secret information from one party, and some inputs that can be manipulated by a hostile party [64][1]. Even in this extremely simple case, it's so hard that you end up having to abandon the IBM method of PIN generation, or at least nail down its parameters so hard that you might as well not have made those parameters tweakable in the first place.

At a practical level, it illustrates one of the main reasons APIs fail. They get made more and more complex, to accommodate the needs of more and more diverse customers, until suddenly there's an attack.

18.2.4   The EMV Attack

You'd have thought that after the initial batch of API attacks were published in 2001, security module designers would have started being careful about adding new transactions. Not so! Again and again, the banking industry has demanded the addition of new transactions that add to the insecurity.

---

[1]We came across this problem in Chapter 9 where we discussed active attacks on inference control mechanisms.

An interesting recent example is a transaction ordered by the EMV consortium to support secure messaging between a smartcard and a bank security module. The goal is that when a bank card appears in an online transaction, the bank can order it to change some parameter, such as a new key. So far so good. However, the specification had a serious error, which has appeared in a number of implementations [12].

The transaction `Secure Messaging For Keys` allows the server to command the security module to encrypt a text message, followed by a key, with a key of a type for sharing with bank smartcards. The encryption can be in CBC or ECB mode, and the text message can be of variable length. This lets an attacker choose a message length so that just one byte of the target key crosses the boundary of an encryption block. That byte can then be determined by sending a series of messages that are one byte longer, where the extra byte cycles through all possible values until the key byte is found. The attacker can then attack each of the other key bytes, one after another. Any exportable key can be extracted from the module in this way. (There is also a transaction `Secure Messaging For PINs`, but who needs to extract PINs one by one if you can rip off all the master keys?)

To sum up: the security modules sold to the banking industry over the last quarter century were almost completely insecure, because the APIs were very badly designed. At one time or another, we found an attack on at least one version of every security module on the market. In time the vendors stopped or mitigated most of these attacks by shipping software upgrades. However, the customers — the banking industry — keep on thinking up cool new things to do with payment networks, and these keep on breaking the APIs all over again. The typical attacks involve multiple transactions, with the technical cause being feature interaction (with particularly carelessly designed application features) or slow information leakage. The root cause, as with many areas of our field, is featuritis. People make APIs so complex that they break, and the breaks aren't at all obvious.

18.3   API Attacks on Operating Systems

A second class of API attacks involve concurrency, and are well illustrated by vulnerabilities found by Robert Watson in system call wrappers [1325].

System call wrappers are used to beef up operating systems security; the reference monitors discussed in Chapter 8 are an example, and anti-virus software is another. Wrappers intercept calls made by applications to the operating system, parse them, audit them, and may pass them on with some modification: for example, a Low process that attempts to access High data may get diverted to dummy data or given an error message. There are various frameworks available, including Systrace, the Generic Software

Wrapper Toolkit (GSWTK) and CerbNG, that enable you to write wrappers for common operating systems. They typically execute in the kernel's address space, inspect the enter and exit state on all system calls, and encapsulate only security logic.

When John Anderson proposed the concept of the reference monitor in 1972, he stipulated that it should be tamper-proof, nonbypassable, and small enough to verify. On the face of it, today's wrappers are so — until you start to think of time. Wrappers generally assume that system calls are atomic, but they're not; modern operating system kernels are very highly concurrent. System calls are not atomic with respect to each other, nor are they so with respect to wrappers. There are many possibilities for two system calls to race each other for access to shared memory, and this gives rise to *time-of-check-to-time-of-use* (TOCTTOU) attacks of the kind briefly mentioned in Chapter 6.

A typical attack is to race on user-process memory by getting the kernel to sleep at an inconvenient time, for example by a page fault. In an attack on GSWTK, Watson calls a path whose name spills over a page boundary by one byte, causing the kernel to sleep while the page is fetched; he then replaces the path in memory. It turns out that the race windows are large and reliable.

Processors are steadily getting more concurrent, with more processors shipped in each CPU chip as time passes, and operating systems are optimised to take advantage of them. This sort of attack may become more and more of a problem; indeed, as code analysis tools make stack overflows rarer, it may well be that race conditions will become the attack of choice.

What can be done to limit them? The only real solution is to rewrite the API. In an ideal world, operating systems would move to a message-passing model, which would eliminate (or at least greatly reduce) concurrency issues. That's hardly practical for operating system vendors whose business models depend on backwards compatibility. A pragmatic compromise is to build features into the operating system specifically to deal with concurrency attacks; Linux Security Modules do this, as does Mac OS/X 10.5 (based on TrustedBSD, on which Watson worked).

In short, the APIs exposed by standard operating systems have a number of known weaknesses, but the wrapper solution, of interposing another API in front of the vulnerable API, looks extremely fragile in a highly concurrent environment. The wrapper would have to understand the memory layout fairly completely to be fully effective, and this would make it as complex (and vulnerable) as the operating system it was trying to protect.

18.4   Summary

Interfaces get richer, and dirtier, and nastier, over time. Interface design flaws are widespread, from the world of cryptoprocessors through sundry embedded systems right through to antivirus software and the operating system itself. Wherever trusted software talks to less trusted software, the interface is likely to leak more than the designer of the trusted software intended.

Failures tend to arise from complexity. I've discussed two main case histories — cryptoprocessors, which accumulated transactions beyond the designers' ability to understand their interactions, and system call wrappers, which try to audit and filter the calls made to an operating system's API. At the level of pure computer science, we could see the former as instances of the composition problem or the secure multiparty computation problem, and the latter as concurrency failures. However, these are industrial-scale systems rather than blackboard systems. A security module may have hundreds of transactions, with a fresh batch being added at each upgrade. At the application level, many of the failures can be seen as feature interactions. There are also specific failures such as the slow leakage of information from poorly designed cryptosystems, which would not be serious in the case of a single transaction but which become fatal when an opponent can commandeer a server and inject hundreds of transactions a second.

API security is already important, and becoming more so as computers become more complex, more diverse and more concurrent. If Microsoft ships the original mechanisms promised for Trusted Computing with a future release of Vista, then APIs will become more critical still — application developers will be encouraged to write code that contains a 'more trusted' NCA and a 'less trusted' normal application. Even professionals who work for security module companies ship APIs with serious bugs; what chance is there that NCAs will provide value, if everyone starts designing their security APIs?

What can be done? Well, one of the lessons learned is that a 'secure' processor isn't, unless the API is simple enough to understand and verify. If you're responsible for a bank's cryptography, the prudent thing to do is to have a security module adapted for your needs so that it contains only the transactions you actually need. If this is too inconvenient or expensive, filter the transactions and throw away all but the essential ones. (Do read the research literature carefully before deciding which transactions are essential!)

As Watson's work shows, complex APIs for highly-concurrent systems probably cannot be fixed in this way. If you've got critical applications that depend on such a platform, then maybe you should be making migration plans.

Finally, there will probably be a whole host of API issues with interacting applications. As the world moves to web services that start to talk to each other, their APIs are opened up to third-party developers — as has just happened, for example, with Facebook. Complexity alone is bad enough; I'll discuss in Chapter 23 how social-networking sites in particular are pushing complexity limits in security policy as they try to capture a significant subset of human social behaviour. And managing the evolution of an API is one of the toughest jobs in security engineering (I'll come to this in Chapter 25). Combine this with the fact that economic pressures push web applications toward unsafe defaults, such as making everything searchable, and the strong likelihood that not all third-party developers will be benevolent — and it should be clear that we can expect problems.

Research Problems

The computer science approach to the API security problem has been to try to adapt formal-methods tools to prove that interfaces are safe. There is a growing literature on this, but the methods can still only tackle fairly simple APIs. Verifying an individual protocol is difficult enough, and the research community spent much the 1990s learning how to do it. Yet a protocol might consist of perhaps 2–5 messages, while a cryptoprocessor might have hundreds of transactions.

An alternative approach, as in the world on protocols, is to try to come up with robustness principles to guide the designer. As in that field, robustness is to some extent about explicitness. Checking that there isn't some obscure sequence of transactions that breaks your security policy is hard enough; when your policy isn't even precisely stated it looks impossible.

Robustness isn't everything, though. At the tactical level, the API security story has taught us a number of things. Atomicity really does matter (together with consistency, isolation and durability, the other desirable attributes of transaction-processing systems). At an even lower level, we've seen a couple of good reasons why it's a really dumb idea to use exclusive-or to combine keys or PINs; no-one understood this before. What other common design practices should we unlearn?

Further Reading

To learn more about API security, you should first read our survey papers [63, 64, 65] as well as Robert Watson's paper on concurrency attacks [1325]. There is now an annual conference, the International Workshop on Analysis of Security APIs, where you can catch up with the latest research.

CHAPTER 19

Electronic and Information Warfare

All warfare is based on deception . . . hold out baits to entice the enemy. Feign disorder, and crush him.

— Sun Tzu, *The Art of War*, 1.18–20

Force, and Fraud, are in warre the two Cardinal Virtues.

— Thomas Hobbes

19.1   Introduction

For decades, electronic warfare has been a separate subject from computer security, even though they use some common technologies (such as cryptography). This is starting to change as elements of the two disciplines fuse to form the new subject of information warfare. The Pentagon's embrace of information warfare as a slogan in the last years of the twentieth century established its importance — even if its concepts, theory and doctrine are still underdeveloped. The Russian denial-of-service attacks on Estonia in 2007 have put it firmly on many policy agendas — even though it's not clear that these attacks were conducted by the Russian government; as far as we know, it may have been just a bunch of Russian hackers.

There are other reasons why a knowledge of electronic warfare is important to the security engineer. Many technologies originally developed for the warrior have been adapted for commercial use, and instructive parallels abound. The struggle for control of the electromagnetic spectrum has consumed so many clever people and so many tens of billions of dollars that we find deception strategies and tactics of a unique depth and subtlety. It is the one area of electronic security to have experienced a lengthy period of coevolution of attack and defense involving capable motivated opponents.

Electronic warfare is also our main teacher when it comes to service-denial attacks, a topic that computer security people ignored for years. It suddenly took center stage a few years ago thanks to denial-of-service attacks on commercial web sites, and when blackmailers started taking down Internet gambling sites and demanding to be paid off, it got serious.

As I develop this discussion, I'll try to draw out the parallels between electronic warfare and other information security problems. In general, while people say that computer security is about confidentiality, integrity and availability, electronic warfare has this reversed and back-to-front. The priorities are:

1. denial of service, which includes jamming, mimicry and physical attack;

2. deception, which may be targeted at automated systems or at people; and

3. exploitation, which includes not just eavesdropping but obtaining any operationally valuable information from the enemy's use of his electronic systems.

19.2 Basics

The goal of electronic warfare is to control the electromagnetic spectrum. It is generally considered to consist of

- *electronic attack*, such as jamming enemy communications or radar, and disrupting enemy equipment using high-power microwaves;

- *electronic protection*, which ranges from designing systems resistant to jamming, through hardening equipment to resist high-power microwave attack, to the destruction of enemy jammers using anti-radiation missiles; and

- *electronic support*, which supplies the necessary intelligence and threat recognition to allow effective attack and protection. It allows commanders to search for, identify and locate sources of intentional and unintentional electromagnetic energy.

These definitions are taken from Schleher [1121]. The traditional topic of cryptography, namely *communications security* (Comsec), is only a small part of electronic protection, just as it is becoming only a small part of information protection in more general systems. Electronic support includes *signals intelligence*, or Sigint, which consists of *communications intelligence* (Comint) and *electronic intelligence* (Elint). The former collects enemy communications, including both message content and traffic data about which units are communicating, while the latter concerns itself with recognizing hostile radars and other non-communicating sources of electromagnetic energy.

Deception is central to electronic attack. The goal is to mislead the enemy by manipulating his perceptions in order to degrade the accuracy of his intelligence and target acquisition. Its effective use depends on clarity about who (or what) is to be deceived, about what and how long, and — where the targets of deception are human — the exploitation of pride, greed, laziness and other vices. Deception can be extremely cost effective and is increasingly relevant to commercial systems.

Physical destruction is an important part of the mix; while some enemy sensors and communications links may be neutralized by jamming (so-called *soft kill*), others will often be destroyed (*hard kill*). Successful electronic warfare depends on using the available tools in a coordinated way.

Electronic weapon systems are like other weapons in that there are *sensors*, such as radar, infrared and sonar; a *communications* links which take sensor data to the command and control center; and output devices such as jammers, lasers, missiles, bombs and so on. I'll discuss the communications system issues first, as they are the most self-contained, then the sensors and associated jammers, and finally other devices such as electromagnetic pulse generators. Once we're done with e-war, we'll look at the lessons we might take over to i-war.

19.3   Communications Systems

Military communications were dominated by physical dispatch until about 1860, then by the telegraph until 1915, and then by the telephone until recently [923]. Nowadays, a typical command and control structure is made up of various tactical and strategic radio networks supporting data, voice and images, operating over point-to-point links and broadcast. Without situational awareness and the means to direct forces, the commander is likely to be ineffective. But the need to secure communications is much more pervasive than one might at first realize, and the threats are much more diverse.

- One obvious type of traffic is the communications between fixed sites such as army headquarters and the political leadership. A significant historical threat here was that the cipher security might be penetrated and the orders, situation reports and so on compromised, whether as a result of cryptanalysis or — more likely — equipment sabotage, subversion of personnel or theft of key material. The insertion of deceptive messages may also be a threat in some circumstances. But cipher security will often include protection against traffic analysis (such as by link encryption) as well as of the transmitted message confidentiality and authenticity. The secondary threat is that the link might be disrupted, such as by destruction of cables or relay stations.

■ There are more stringent requirements for communications with covert assets such as agents in the field. Here, in addition to cipher security issues, location security is important. The agent will have to take steps to minimize the risk of being caught as a result of communications monitoring. If he sends messages using a medium which the enemy can monitor, such as the public telephone network or radio, then much of his effort may go into frustrating traffic analysis and radio direction finding.

■ Tactical communications, such as between HQ and a platoon in the field, also have more stringent (but slightly different) needs. Radio direction finding is still an issue, but jamming may be at least as important, and deliberately deceptive messages may also be a problem. For example, there is equipment that enables an enemy air controller's voice commands to be captured, cut into phonemes and spliced back together into deceptive commands, in order to gain a tactical advantage in air combat [506]. As voice morphing techniques are developed for commercial use, the risk of spoofing attacks on unprotected communications will increase. So cipher security may include authenticity as well as confidentiality and covertness.

■ Control and telemetry communications, such as signals sent from an aircraft to a missile it has just launched, must be protected against jamming and modification. It would also be desirable if they could be covert (so as not to trigger a target's warning receiver) but that is in tension with the power levels needed to defeat defensive jamming systems. One solution is to make the communications adaptive — to start off in a low-probability-of-intercept mode and ramp up the power if needed in response to jamming.

So the protection of communications will require some mix, depending on the circumstances, of content secrecy, authenticity, resistance to traffic analysis and radio direction finding, and resistance to various kinds of jamming. These interact in some rather unobvious ways. For example, one radio designed for use by dissident organizations in Eastern Europe in the early 1980s operated in the radio bands normally occupied by the Voice of America and the BBC World Service — which were routinely jammed by the Russians. The idea was that unless the Russians were prepared to turn off their jammers, they would have difficulty doing direction finding.

Attack also generally requires a combination of techniques — even where the objective is not analysis or direction finding but simply denial of service.

Owen Lewis sums it up succinctly: according to Soviet doctrine, a comprehensive and successful attack on a military communications infrastructure would involve destroying one third of it physically, denying effective use of a second third through techniques such as jamming, trojans or deception, and then allowing the adversary to disable the remaining third by attempting to pass all his traffic over a third of his installed capacity [789]. This applies even in guerilla wars; in Malaya, Kenya and Cyprus the rebels managed to degrade the telephone system enough to force the police to set up radio nets [923].

NATO developed a comparable doctrine, called *Counter-Command, Control and Communications* operations (C-C3, pronounced C C cubed), in the 80s. It achieved its first flowering in the Gulf War. Of course, attacking an army's command structures is much older than that; it's a basic principle to shoot at an officer before shooting at his men.

19.3.1 Signals Intelligence Techniques

Before communications can be attacked, the enemy's network must be mapped. The most expensive and critical task in signals intelligence is identifying and extracting the interesting material from the cacophony of radio signals and the huge mass of traffic on systems such as the telephone network and the Internet. The technologies in use are extensive and largely classified, but some aspects are public.

In the case of radio signals, communications intelligence agencies use receiving equipment, that can recognize a huge variety of signal types, to maintain extensive databases of signals — which stations or services use which frequencies. In many cases, it is possible to identify individual equipment by signal analysis. The components can include any unintentional frequency modulation, the shape of the transmitter turn-on transient, the precise center frequency and the final-stage amplifier harmonics. This *RF fingerprinting*, or RFID, technology was declassified in the mid-1990s for use in identifying cloned cellular telephones, where its makers claim a 95% success rate [534, 1121]. It is the direct descendant of the World War 2 technique of recognizing a wireless operator by his *fist* — the way he used Morse Code [836].

Radio Direction Finding (RDF) is also critical. In the old days, this involved triangulating the signal of interest using directional antennas at two monitoring stations. So spies might have several minutes to send a message home before having to move. Modern monitoring stations use *time difference of arrival* (TDOA) to locate a suspect signal rapidly, accurately and automatically by comparing the phase of the signals received at two sites; anything more than a second or so of transmission can be a giveaway.

Traffic analysis — looking at the number of messages by source and destination — can also give very valuable information, not just about imminent attacks (which were signalled in World War 1 by a greatly increased volume of radio messages) but also about unit movements and other more routine matters. However, traffic analysis really comes into its own when sifting through traffic on public networks, where its importance (both for national intelligence and police purposes) is difficult to overstate. Until a few years ago, traffic analysis was the domain of intelligence agencies — when NSA men referred to themselves as 'hunter-gatherers', traffic analysis was much of the 'hunting'. In the last few years, however, traffic analysis has come out of the shadows and become a major subject of study.

One of the basic techniques is the *snowball search*. If you suspect Alice of espionage (or drug dealing, or whatever), you note everyone she calls, and everyone who calls her. This gives you a list of dozens of suspects. You eliminate the likes of banks and doctors, who receive calls from too many people to analyze (your *whitelist*), and repeat the procedure on each remaining number. Having done this procedure recursively several times, you have a mass of thousands of contacts — they accumulate like a snowball rolling downhill. You now sift the snowball you've collected — for example, for people already on one of your blacklists, and for telephone numbers that appear more than once. So if Bob, Camilla and Donald are Alice's contacts, with Bob and Camilla in contact with Eve and Donald and Eve in touch with Farquhar, then all of these people may be considered suspects. You now draw a *friendship tree* which gives a first approximation to Alice's network, and refine it by collating it with other intelligence sources. *Covert community detection* has become a very hot topic since 9/11, and researchers have tried all sorts of hierarchical clustering and graph partitioning methods to the problem. As of 2007, the leading algorithm is by Mark Newman [966]; it uses spectral methods to partition a network into its natural communities so as to maximise modularity.

But even given good mathematical tools for analysing abstract networks, reality is messier. People can have several numbers, and people share numbers. When conspirators take active countermeasures, it gets harder still; Bob might get a call from Alice at his work number and then call Eve from a phone box. (If you're running a terrorist cell, your signals officer should get a job at a dentist's or a doctor's or some other place that's likely to be whitelisted.) Also, you will need some means of correlating telephone numbers to people. Even if you have access to the phone company's database of unlisted numbers, prepaid mobile phones can be a serious headache, as can cloned phones and hacked PBXs. Tying IP addresses to people is even harder; ISPs don't always keep the Radius logs for long. I'll discuss all these issues in more detail in later chapters; for now, I'll just remark that anonymous communications aren't new. There have been letter boxes and public phone booths for generations. But they are not a universal answer for the crook as the discipline needed to use anonymous communications properly is beyond most criminals. It's reported, for example, that the 9/11 mastermind Khalid Sheikh Mohammed was caught after he used in his mobile phone in Pakistan a prepaid SIM card that had been bought in Switzerland in the same batch as a SIM that had been used in another Al-Qaida operation.

Signals collection is not restricted to getting phone companies to give access to the content of phone calls and the itemised billing records. It also involves a wide range of specialized facilities ranging from expensive fixed installations that copy international satellite links, down to temporary tactical arrangements. A book by Nicky Hagar [576] describes the main fixed collection network operated by the USA, Canada, the UK, Australia and New Zealand. Known as *Echelon*, this consists of a number of fixed collection stations that monitor international phone, fax and data traffic with computers called *dictionaries* which search passing traffic for interesting phone numbers, network addresses and machine-readable content; this is driven by search strings entered by intelligence analysts. One can think of this as a kind of Google for the world's phone system (though given the data volumes nowadays, content generally has to be selected in real time; not even the NSA can afford to store all the data on the Internet and the phone networks).

This fixed network is supplemented by tactical collection facilities as needed; Hagar describes, for example, the dispatch of Australian and New Zealand navy frigates to monitor domestic communications in Fiji during military coups in the 1980s. Koch and Sperber discuss U.S. and German installations in Germany in [725]; Fulghum describes airborne signals collection in [506]; satellites are also used to collect signals, and there are covert collection facilities too that are not known to the host country.

But despite all this huge capital investment, the most difficult and expensive part of the whole operation is traffic selection rather than collection [770]. Thus, contrary to one's initial expectations, cryptography can make communications more vulnerable rather than less (if used incompetently, as it usually is). If you just encipher all the traffic you consider to be important, you have thereby marked it for collection by the enemy. And if your cryptosecurity were perfect, you've just helped the enemy map your network, which means he can collect all the unencrypted traffic that you share with third parties.

Now if everyone encrypted all their traffic, then hiding traffic could be much easier (hence the push by signals intelligence agencies to prevent the widespread use of cryptography, even if it's freely available to individuals). This brings us to the topic of attacks.

19.3.2 Attacks on Communications

Once you have mapped the enemy network, you may wish to attack it. People often talk in terms of 'codebreaking' but this is a gross oversimplification.

First, although some systems have been broken by pure cryptanalysis, this is fairly rare. Most production attacks have involved theft of key material, as when the State Department code book was stolen during World War 2 by the valet of the American ambassador to Rome, or errors in the manufacture and distribution of key material, as in the 'Venona' attacks on Soviet diplomatic traffic [676]. Even where attacks based on cryptanalysis have been possible, they have often been made much easier by operational errors, an example being the attacks on the German Enigma traffic during World War 2 [677]. The pattern continues to this day. The history of Soviet intelligence during the Cold War reveals that the USA's technological advantage was largely nullified by Soviet skills in 'using Humint in Sigint support' — which largely consisted of recruiting traitors who sold key material, such as the Walker family [77].

Second, access to content is often not the desired result. In tactical situations, the goal is often to detect and destroy nodes, or to jam the traffic. Jamming can involve not just noise insertion but active deception. In World War 2, the Allies used German speakers as bogus controllers to send German nightfighters confusing instructions, and there was a battle of wits as authentication techniques were invented and defeated. More recently, as I noted in the chapter on biometrics, the U.S. Air Force has deployed more sophisticated systems based on voice morphing. I mentioned in an earlier chapter the tension between intelligence and operational units: the former want to listen to the other side's traffic, and the latter to deny them its use [103]. Compromises between these goals can be hard to find. It's not enough to jam the traffic you can't read as that tells the enemy what you can read!

Matters can be simplified if the opponent uses cryptography — especially if they're competent and you can't read their encrypted traffic. This removes the ops/intel tension, and you switch to RDF or the destruction of protected links as appropriate. This can involve the hard-kill approach of digging up cables or bombing telephone exchanges (both of which the Allies did during the Gulf War), the soft-kill approach of jamming, or whatever combination of the two is economic. Jamming is useful where a link is to be disrupted for a short period, but is often expensive; not only does it tie up facilities, but the jammer itself becomes a target. Cases where it is more effective than physical attack include satellite links, where the uplink can often be jammed using a tight beam from a hidden location using only a modest amount of power.

The increasing use of civilian infrastructure, and in particular the Internet, raises the question of whether systematic denial-of-service attacks might be used to jam traffic. (There were anecdotes during the Bosnian war of Serbian information warfare cells attempting to DDoS NATO web sites.) This threat is still considered real enough that many Western countries have separate intranets for government and military use.

19.3.3   Protection Techniques

As should be clear from the above, communications security techniques involve not just protecting the authenticity and confidentiality of the content — which can be achieved in a relatively straightforward way by encryption and authentication protocols — but also preventing traffic analysis, direction finding, jamming and physical destruction. Encryption can stretch to the first of these if applied at the link layer, so that all links appear to have a constant-rate pseudorandom bitstream on them at all times, regardless of whether there is any message traffic. But link layer encryption alone is not always enough, as enemy capture of a single node might put the whole network at risk.

Encryption alone cannot protect against RDF, jamming, and the destruction of links or nodes. For this, different technologies are needed. The obvious solutions are:

- redundant dedicated lines or optical fibers;
- highly directional transmission links, such as optical links using infrared lasers or microwave links using highly directional antennas and extremely high frequencies;
- *low-probability-of-intercept* (LPI), *low-probability-of-position-fix* (LPPF) and anti-jam radio techniques.

The first two of these options are fairly straightforward to understand, and where they are feasible they are usually the best. Cabled networks are very hard to destroy completely, unless the enemy knows where the cables are and has physical access to cut them. Even with massive artillery bombardment, the telephone network in Stalingrad remained in use (by both sides) all through the siege.

The third option is a substantial subject in itself, which I will now describe (albeit only briefly).

A number of LPI/LPPF/antijam techniques go under the generic name of *spread spectrum* communications. They include *frequency hoppers*, *direct sequence spread spectrum* (DSSS) and *burst transmission*. From beginnings around World War 2, spread spectrum has spawned a substantial industry and the technology (especially DSSS) has been applied to numerous other problems, ranging from high resolution ranging (in the GPS system) through copyright marks in digital images (which I'll discuss later). I'll look at each of these three approaches in turn.

19.3.3.1 Frequency Hopping

Frequency hoppers are the simplest spread spectrum systems to understand and to implement. They do exactly as their name suggests — they hop rapidly from one frequency to another, with the sequence of frequencies determined by a pseudorandom sequence known to the authorized principals. They were invented, famously, over dinner in 1940 by actress Hedy Lamarr and screenwriter George Antheil, who devised the technique as a means of controlling torpedos without the enemy detecting them or jamming their transmissions [763]. A frequency hopping radar was independently developed at about the same time by the Germans [1138].

Hoppers are resistant to jamming by an opponent who doesn't know the hop sequence. If the hopping is slow and a nearby opponent has capable equipment, then an option might be *follower jamming* — observing the signal and following it around the band, typically jamming each successive frequency with a single tone. However if the hopping is fast enough, or propagation delays are excessive, the opponent may have to jam much of the band, which requires much more power. The ratio of the input signal's bandwidth to that of the transmitted signal is called the *process gain* of the system; thus a 100 bit/sec signal spread over 10MHz has a process gain of $10^7/10^2 = 10^5 = 50$dB. The *jamming margin*, which is defined as the maximum tolerable ratio of jamming power to signal power, is essentially the process gain modulo implementation and other losses (strictly speaking, process gain divided by the minimum bit energy-to-noise density ratio). The optimal jamming strategy, for an opponent who can't predict or effectively follow the hop sequence, is *partial band jamming* — to jam enough of the band to introduce an unacceptable error rate in the signal.

Frequency hopping is used in some civilian applications, such as Bluetooth, where it gives a decent level of interference robustness at low cost. On the military side of things, although hoppers can give a large jamming margin, they give little protection against direction finding. A signal analysis receiver that sweeps across the frequency band of interest will usually intercept them (and depending on the relevant bandwidths, sweep rate and dwell time, it might intercept a hopping signal several times).

Since frequency hoppers are simple to implement and give a useful level of jam-resistance, they are often used in combat networks, such as man pack radios, with hop rates of 50–500 per second. To disrupt these communications, the enemy will need a fast or powerful jammer, which is inconvenient for the battlefield. Fast hoppers (defined in theory as having hop rates exceeding the bit rate; in practice, with hop rates of 10,000 per second or more) can pass the limit of even large jammers. Hoppers are less 'LPI' than the techniques I'll describe next, as an opponent with a sweep receiver can detect the presence of a signal; and slow hoppers have some vulnerability to eavesdropping and direction finding, as an opponent with suitable wideband receiving equipment can often follow the signal.

19.3.3.2 DSSS

In direct sequence spread spectrum, we multiply the information-bearing sequence by a much higher rate pseudorandom sequence, usually generated by some kind of stream cipher (see Figures 19.1 and 19.2). This spreads the spectrum by increasing the bandwidth. The technique was first described by a Swiss engineer, Gustav Guanella, in a 1938 patent application [1138], and developed extensively in the USA in the 1950s. Its first deployment in anger was in Berlin in 1959.

Like hopping, DSSS can give substantial jamming margin (the two systems have the same theoretical performance). But it can also make the signal significantly harder to intercept. The trick is to arrange things so that at the intercept location, the signal strength is so low that it is lost in the noise floor unless the opponent knows the spreading sequence with which to recover it. Of course, it's harder to do both at the same time, since an antijam signal should be high power and an LPI/LPPF signal low power; the usual tactic is to work in LPI mode until detected by the enemy (for example, when coming within radar range) and then boost transmitter power into antijam mode.

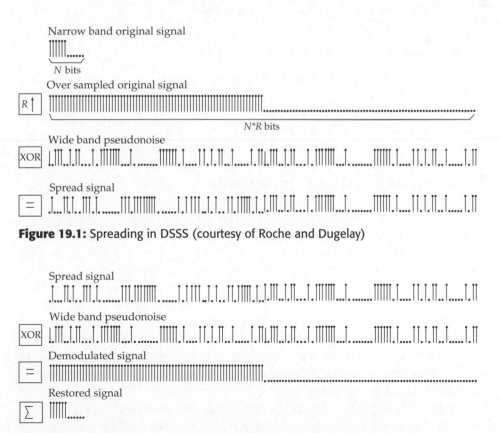

Figure 19.1: Spreading in DSSS (courtesy of Roche and Dugelay)

Figure 19.2: Unspreading in DSSS (courtesy of Roche and Dugelay)

There is a large literature on DSSS, and the techniques have now been taken up by the commercial world as *code division multiple access* (CDMA) in various mobile radio and phone systems. Third-generation mobile phones in particular rely on CDMA for their performance.

DSSS is sometimes referred to as 'encrypting the RF' and it comes in a number of variants. For example, when the underlying modulation scheme is FM rather than AM it's called *chirp*. The classic introduction to the underlying mathematics and technology is [1026]; the engineering complexity is higher than with frequency hop for various reasons. For example, synchronization is particularly critical. One strategy is to have your users take turns at providing a reference signal. If your users have access to a reference time signal (such as GPS, or an atomic clock) you might rely on this; but if you don't control GPS, you may be open to synchronization attacks, and even if you do the GPS signal might be jammed. It was reported in 2000 that the French jammed GPS in Greece in an attempt to sabotage a British bid to sell 250 tanks to the Greek government, a deal for which France was a competitor. This caused the British tanks to get lost during trials. When the ruse was discovered, the Greeks found it all rather amusing [1269]. Now GPS jammers are commodity items, and I'll discuss them in more detail below.

19.3.3.3   *Burst Communications*

Burst communications, as their name suggests, involve compressing the data and transmitting it in short bursts at times unpredictable by the enemy. They are also known as *time-hop*. They are usually not so jam-resistant (except insofar as the higher data rate spreads the spectrum) but can be even more difficult to detect than DSSS; if the duty cycle is low, a sweep receiver can easily miss them. They are often used in radios for special forces and intelligence agents. Really high-grade room bugs often use burst.

An interesting variant is *meteor burst* transmission (also known as *meteor scatter*). This relies on the billions of micrometeorites that strike the Earth's atmosphere each day, each leaving a long ionization trail that persists for typically a third of a second and provides a temporary transmission path between a mother station and an area of maybe a hundred miles long and a few miles wide. The mother station transmits continuously; whenever one of the daughters is within such an area, it hears mother and starts to send packets of data at high speed, to which mother replies. With the low power levels used in covert operations one can achieve an average data rate of about 50 bps, with an average latency of about 5 minutes and a range of 500–1500 miles. With higher power levels, and in higher latitudes, average data rates can rise into the tens of kilobits per second.

As well as special forces, the USAF in Alaska uses meteor scatter as backup communications for early warning radars. It's also used in civilian applications such as monitoring rainfall in remote parts of the third world. In niche markets where low bit rates and high latency can be tolerated, but where equipment size and cost are important, meteor scatter can be hard to beat. The technology is described in [1120].

19.3.3.4 *Combining Covertness and Jam Resistance*

There are some rather complex tradeoffs between different LPI, LPPF and jam resistance features, and other aspects of performance such as resistance to fading and multipath, and the number of users that can be accommodated simultaneously. They also behave differently in the face of specialized jamming techniques such as *swept-frequency jamming* (where the jammer sweeps repeatedly through the target frequency band) and follower. Some types of jamming translate between different modes: for example, an opponent with insufficient power to block a signal completely can do *partial time jamming* on DSSS by emitting pulses that cover a part of its utilized spectrum, and on frequency hop by *partial band jamming*.

There are also engineering tradeoffs. For example, DSSS tends to be about twice as efficient as frequency hop in power terms, but frequency hop gives much more jamming margin for a given complexity of equipment. On the other hand, DSSS signals are much harder to locate using direction finding techniques [461].

System survivability requirements can impose further constraints. It may be essential to prevent an opponent who has captured one radio and extracted its current key material from using this to jam a whole network.

So a typical modern military system will use some combination of tight beams, DSSS, hopping and burst.

- The Jaguar tactical radio used by UK armed forces hops over one of nine 6.4 MHz bands, and also has an antenna with a steerable null which can be pointed at a jammer or at a hostile intercept station.

- Both DSSS and hopping are used with TDMA in *Joint Tactical Information Distribution System* (JTIDS) — a U.S. data link system used by AWACS to communicate with fighters [1121]. TDMA separates transmission from reception and lets users know when to expect their slot. It has a DSSS signal with a 57.6 KHz data rate and a 10 MHz chip rate (and so a jamming margin of 36.5 dB), which hops around in a 255 MHz band with minimum jump of 30 MHz. The hopping code is available to all users, while the spreading code is limited to individual circuits. The rationale is that if an equipment capture leads to the compromise of the spreading code, this would allow jamming of only a single 10MHz band, not the full 255 MHz.

- MILSTAR is a U.S. satellite communications system with 1 degree beams from a geostationary orbit (20 GHz down, 44 GHz up). The effect of the narrow beam is that users can operate within three miles of the enemy without being detected. Jam protection is from hopping: its channels hop several thousand times a second in bands of 2 GHz.

- A system designed to control MX missiles is described in [530] and gives an example of extreme survivability engineering. To be able to withstand a nuclear first strike, the system had to withstand significant levels of node destruction, jamming and atmospheric noise. The design adopted was a frequency hopper at 450 KHz with a dynamically reconfigurable network. It was not in the end deployed.

- French tactical radios have remote controls. The soldier can use the handset a hundred yards from the radio. This means that attacks on the high-power emitter don't have to endanger the troops so much [348].

There are also some system level tricks, such as *interference cancellation* — here the idea is to communicate in a band which you are jamming and whose jamming waveform is known to your own radios, so they can cancel it out or hop around it. This can make jamming harder for the enemy by forcing him to spread his available power over a larger bandwidth, and can make signals intelligence harder too [1074].

19.3.4 Interaction Between Civil and Military Uses

Civil and military uses of communications are increasingly intertwined. Operation Desert Storm (the First Gulf War against Iraq) made extensive use of the Gulf States' civilian infrastructure: a huge tactical communications network was created in a short space of time using satellites, radio links and leased lines, and experts from various U.S. armed services claim that the effect of communications capability on the war was absolutely decisive [634]. It can be expected that both military and substate groups will attack civilian infrastructure to deny it to their opponents. Already, as I noted, satellite links are vulnerable to uplink jamming.

Another example of growing interdependency is given by the Global Positioning System, GPS. This started off as a U.S. military navigation system and had a *selective availability* feature that limited the accuracy to about a hundred yards unless the user had the relevant cryptographic key. This had to be turned off during Desert Storm as there weren't enough military GPS sets to go round and civilian equipment had to be used instead. As time went on, GPS turned out to be so useful, particularly in civil aviation, that the FAA helped find ways to defeat selective availability that give an accuracy of about 3 yards compared with a claimed 8 yards for the standard military receiver [431]. Finally, in May 2000, President Clinton announced the end of selective availability. Various people have experimented with jamming GPS, which turns out to be not that difficult, and there has been some discussion of the systemic vulnerabilities that result from overreliance on it [490].

The U.S. government still reserves the right to switch off GPS, or to introduce errors into it, for example if terrorists were thought to be using it. But many diverse systems now depend on GPS, and many of them have motivated opponents; some countries are starting to use GPS to do road pricing, or to enforce parole terms on released prisoners via electronic ankle bracelets. As a result, GPS jammers appeared in car magazines in 2007 for $700; the price is bound to come down as truck drivers try to cheat road toll systems and car drivers try to beat pay-as-you-drive insurance schemes. Once their use becomes widespread, the consequences could be startling for other GPS users. Perhaps the solution lies in diversity: Russia has a separate navigation satellite system, and Europe's thinking of building one. Anyway, the security of navigation signals is starting to become a topic of research [751].

The civilian infrastructure also provides some defensive systems that government organizations (especially in the intelligence field) use. I mentioned the prepaid mobile phone, which provides a fair degree of anonymity; secure web servers offer some possibilities; and another example is the *anonymous remailer* — a device that accepts encrypted email, decrypts it, and sends it on to a destination contained within the outer encrypted envelope. The Tor network, pioneered by the U.S. Navy, does much the same for web pages, providing a low-latency way to browse the web via a network of proxies. I'll discuss this technology in more detail in section 23.4.2; the Navy makes it available to everyone on the Internet so as to generate lots of cover traffic to hide its own communications [1062]. Indeed, many future military applications are likely to use the Internet, and this will raise many interesting questions — ranging from the ethics of attacking the information infrastructure of hostile or neutral countries, to the details of how military traffic of various kinds can be hidden among civilian packets and bistreams.

There may indeed be some convergence. Although communications security on the net has until now been interpreted largely in terms of message confidentiality and authentication, the future may become much more like military communications in that jamming, service denial, anonymity, and deception will become increasingly important. I'll return to this theme later.

Next, let's look at the aspects of electronic warfare that have to do with target acquisition and weapon guidance, as these are where the arts of jamming and deception have been most highly developed. (In fact, although there is much more in the open literature on the application of electronic attack and defense to radar than to communications, much of the same material applies to both.)

19.4   Surveillance and Target Acquisition

Although some sensor systems use passive direction finding, the main methods used to detect hostile targets and guide weapons to them are sonar, radar and infrared. The first of these to be developed was sonar, which was invented and deployed in World War 1 (under the name of 'Asdic') [574]. Except in submarine warfare, the key sensor is radar. Although radar was invented in 1904 as a maritime anti-collision device, its serious development only occurred in the 1930s and it was used by all major participants in World War 2 [578, 670]. The electronic attack and protection techniques developed for it tend to be better developed than, and often go over to, systems using other sensors. In the context of radar, 'electronic attack' usually means jamming (though in theory it also includes stealth technology), and 'electronic protection' refers to the techniques used to preserve at least some radar capability.

19.4.1   Types of Radar

A wide range of systems is in use, including search radars, fire-control radars, terrain-following radars, counter-bombardment radars and weather radars. They have a wide variety of signal characteristics. For example, radars with a low RF and a low *pulse repetition frequency* (PRF) are better for search while high frequency, high PRF devices are better for tracking. A good textbook on the technology is by Schleher [1121].

Simple radar designs for search applications may have a rotating antenna that emits a sequence of pulses and detects echos. This was an easy way to implement radar in the days before digital electronics; the sweep in the display tube could be mechanically rotated in synch with the antenna. Fire control radars often used *conical scan*: the beam would be tracked in a circle around the target's position, and the amplitude of the returns could drive positioning servos (and weapon controls) directly. Now the beams are often generated electronically using multiple antenna elements, but tracking loops remain central. Many radars have a *range gate*, circuitry which focuses on targets within a certain range of distances from the antenna; if the radar had to track all objects between (say) zero and 100 miles, then its pulse repetition frequency would be limited by the time it takes radio waves to travel 200 miles. This would have consequences for angular resolution and tracking performance generally.

Doppler radar measures the velocity of the target by the change in frequency in the return signal. It is very important in distinguishing moving targets from *clutter*, the returns reflected from the ground. Doppler radars may have *velocity gates* that restrict attention to targets whose radial speed with respect to the antenna is within certain limits.

19.4.2 Jamming Techniques

Electronic attack techniques can be passive or active.

The earliest countermeasure to be widely used was *chaff* — thin strips of conducting foil that are cut to a half the wavelength of the target signal and then dispersed to provide a false return. Toward the end of World War 2, allied aircraft were dropping 2000 tons of chaff a day to degrade German air defenses. Chaff can be dropped directly by the aircraft attempting to penetrate the defenses (which isn't ideal as they will then be at the apex of an elongated signal), or by support aircraft, or fired forward into a suitable pattern using rockets or shells. The main counter-countermeasure against chaff is the use of Doppler radars; as the chaff is very light it comes to rest almost at once and can be distinguished fairly easily from moving targets.

Other decoy techniques include small decoys with active repeaters that retransmit radar signals and larger decoys that simply reflect them; sometimes one vehicle (such as a helicopter) acts as a decoy for another more valuable one (such as an aircraft carrier). These principles are quite general. Weapons that home in on their targets using RDF are decoyed by special drones that emit seduction RF signals, while infrared guided missiles are diverted using flares.

The passive countermeasure in which the most money has been invested is *stealth* — reducing the *radar cross-section* (RCS) of a vehicle so that it can be detected only at very much shorter range. This means, for example, that the enemy has to place his air defense radars closer together, so he has to buy a lot more of them. Stealth includes a wide range of techniques and a proper discussion is well beyond the scope of this book. Some people think of it as 'extremely expensive black paint' but there's more to it than that; as an aircraft's RCS is typically a function of its aspect, it may have a fly-by-wire system that continually exhibits an aspect with a low RCS to identified hostile emitters.

Active countermeasures are much more diverse. Early jammers simply generated a lot of noise in the range of frequencies used by the target radar; this technique is known as *noise jamming* or *barrage jamming*. Some systems used systematic frequency patterns, such as pulse jammers, or swept jammers that traversed the frequency range of interest (also known as *squidging oscillators*). But such a signal is fairly easy to block — one trick is to use a *guard band* receiver, a receiver on a frequency adjacent to the one in use, and to blank the signal when this receiver shows a jamming signal. It should also be noted that jamming isn't restricted to one side; as well as being used by the radar's opponent, the radar itself can also send suitable spurious signals from an auxiliary antenna to mask the real signal or simply overload the defenses.

At the other end of the scale lie hard-kill techniques such as *anti-radiation missiles* (ARMs), often fired by support aircraft, which home in on the sources of hostile signals. Defenses against such weapons include the use of decoy transmitters, and blinking transmitters on and off.

In the middle lies a large toolkit of *deception jamming* techniques. Most jammers used for self-protection are deception jammers of one kind or another; barrage and ARM techniques tend to be more suited to use by support vehicles.

The usual goal with a self-protection jammer is to deny range and bearing information to attackers. The basic trick is *inverse gain jamming* or *inverse gain amplitude modulation*. This is based on the observation that the directionality of the attacker's antenna is usually not perfect; as well as the main beam it has *sidelobes* through which energy is also transmitted and received, albeit much less efficiently. The sidelobe response can be mapped by observing the transmitted signal, and a jamming signal can be generated so that the net emission is the inverse of the antenna's directional response. The effect, as far as the attacker's radar is concerned, is that the signal seems to come from everywhere; instead of a 'blip' on the radar screen you see a circle centered on your own antenna. Inverse gain jamming is very effective against the older conical-scan fire-control systems.

More generally, the technique is to retransmit the radar signal with a systematic change in delay and/or frequency. This can be non-coherent, in which case the jammer's called a *transponder*, or coherent — that is, with the right waveform — when it's a *repeater*. (It is now common to store received waveforms in *digital radio frequency memory* (DRFM) and manipulate them using signal processing chips.)

An elementary countermeasure is *burn-through*. By lowering the pulse repetition frequency, the dwell time is increased and so the return signal is stronger — at the cost of less precision. A more sophisticated countermeasure is *range gate pull-off* (RGPO). Here, the jammer transmits a number of fake pulses that are stronger than the real ones, thus capturing the receiver, and then moving them out of phase so that the target is no longer in the receiver's range gate. Similarly, with Doppler radars the basic trick is *velocity gate pull-off* (VGPO). With older radars, successful RGPO would cause the radar to break lock and the target to disappear from the screen. Modern radars can reacquire lock very quickly, and so RGPO must either be performed repeatedly or combined with another technique — commonly, with inverse gain jamming to break angle tracking at the same time.

An elementary counter-countermeasure is to jitter the pulse repetition frequency. Each outgoing pulse is either delayed or not depending on a *lag sequence* generated by a stream cipher or random number generator. This means that the jammer cannot anticipate when the next pulse will arrive and has to follow it. Such *follower jamming* can only make false targets that appear to be further away. So the counter-counter-countermeasure, or (counter)[3]-measure, is for the radar to have a *leading edge tracker*, which responds only to the first return pulse; and the (counter)[4]-measures can include jamming at such a high power that the receiver's automatic gain control circuit is captured. An alternative is *cover jamming* in which the jamming pulse is long enough to cover the maximum jitter period.

The next twist of the screw may involve tactics. Chaff is often used to force a radar into Doppler mode, which makes PRF jitter difficult (as continuous waveforms are better than pulsed for Doppler), while leading edge trackers may be combined with frequency agility and smart signal processing. For example, true target returns fluctuate, and have realistic accelerations, while simple transponders and repeaters give out a more or less steady signal. Of course, it's always possible for designers to be too clever; the Mig-29 could decelerate more rapidly in level flight by a rapid pull-up than some radar designers had anticipated, so pilots could use this manoeuvre to break radar lock. And now of course, CPUs are powerful enough to manufacture realistic false returns.

19.4.3   Advanced Radars and Countermeasures

A number of advanced techniques are used to give an edge on the jammer.

Pulse compression was first developed in Germany in World War 2, and uses a kind of direct sequence spread spectrum pulse, filtered on return by a matched filter to compress it again. This can give processing gains of 10–1000. Pulse compression radars are resistant to transponder jammers, but are vulnerable to repeater jammers, especially those with digital radio frequency memory. However, the use of LPI waveforms is important if you do not wish the target to detect you long before you detect him.

Pulsed Doppler is much the same as Doppler, and sends a series of phase stable pulses. It has come to dominate many high end markets, and is widely used, for example, in *look-down shoot-down* systems for air defense against low-flying intruders. As with elementary pulsed tracking radars, different RF and pulse repetition frequencies give different characteristics: we want low frequency/PRF for unambiguous range/velocity and also to reduce clutter — but this can leave many blind spots. Airborne radars that have to deal with many threats use high PRF and look only for velocities above some threshold, say 100 knots — but are weak in tail chases. The usual compromise is medium PRF — but this suffers from severe range ambiguities in airborne operations. Also, search radar requires long, diverse bursts but tracking needs only short, tuned ones. An advantage is that pulsed Doppler can discriminate some very specific signals, such as modulation provided by turbine blades in jet engines. The main deception strategy used against pulsed Doppler is velocity gate pull-off, although a new variant is to excite multiple velocity gates with deceptive returns.

Monopulse is becoming one of the most popular techniques. It is used, for example, in the Exocet missiles that proved so difficult to jam in the Falklands war. The idea is to have four linked antennas so that azimuth and elevation data can be computed from each return pulse using interferometric techniques. Monopulse radars are difficult and expensive to jam, unless a design defect can be exploited; the usual techniques involve tricks such as formation jamming and terrain bounce. Often the preferred defensive strategy is just to use towed decoys.

One of the more recent tricks is *passive coherent location*. Lockheed's 'Silent Sentry' system has no emitters at all, but rather utilizes reflections of commercial radio and television broadcast signals to detect and track airborne objects [807], and the UK 'Celldar' project aims to use the signals from mobile-phone masts for the same purpose [246]. The receivers, being passive, are hard to locate and attack; knocking out the system entails destroying major civilian infrastructure, which opponents will often prefer not to do for legal and propaganda reasons. Passive coherent location is effective against some kinds of stealth technology, particularly those that entail steering the aircraft so that it presents the nulls in its radar cross-section to visible emitters.

Attack and defence could become much more complex given the arrival of digital radio frequency memory and other software radio techniques. Both radar and jammer waveforms may be adapted to the tactical situation with much greater flexibility than before. But fancy combinations of spectral, temporal and spatial characteristics will not be the whole story. Effective electronic attack is likely to continue to require the effective coordination of different passive and active tools with weapons and tactics. The importance of intelligence, and of careful deception planning, is likely to increase.

19.4.4 Other Sensors and Multisensor Issues

Much of what I've said about radar applies to sonar as well, and a fair amount to infrared. Passive decoys — flares — worked very well against early heat-seeking missiles which used a mechanically spun detector, but are less effective against modern detectors that incorporate signal processing. Flares are like chaff in that they decelerate rapidly with respect to the target, so the attacker can filter on velocity or acceleration. They are also like repeater jammers in that their signals are relatively stable and strong compared with real targets.

Active infrared jamming is harder and thus less widespread than radar jamming; it tends to exploit features of the hostile sensor by pulsing at a rate or in a pattern which causes confusion. Some infrared defense systems are starting to employ lasers to disable the sensors of incoming weapons; and it's been admitted that a number of 'UFO' sightings were actually due to various kinds of jamming (both radar and infrared) [119].

One growth area is *multisensor data fusion* whereby inputs from radars, infrared sensors, video cameras and even humans are combined to give better target identification and tracking than any could individually. The Rapier air defense missile, for example, uses radar to acquire azimuth while tracking is carried out optically in visual conditions. Data fusion can be harder than it seems. As I discussed in section 15.9, combining two alarm systems will generally result in improving either the false alarm or the missed alarm rate, while making the other worse. If you scramble your fighters when you see a blip on either the radar or the infrared, there will be more false alarms; but if you scramble only when you see both then it will be easier for the enemy to jam you or sneak through.

System issues become more complex where the attacker himself is on a platform that's vulnerable to counter-attack, such as a fighter bomber. He will have systems for threat recognition, direction finding and missile approach warning, and the receivers in these will be deafened by his jammer. The usual trick is to turn the jammer off for a short 'look-through' period at random times.

With multiple friendly and hostile platforms, things get more complex still. Each side might have specialist support vehicles with high power dedicated equipment, which makes it to some extent an energy battle — 'he with the most watts wins'. A SAM belt may have multiple radars at different frequencies to make jamming harder. The overall effect of jamming (as of stealth) is to reduce the effective range of radar. But jamming margin also matters, and who has the most vehicles, and the tactics employed.

With multiple vehicles engaged, it's also necessary to have a reliable way of distinguishing friend from foe.

19.5 IFF Systems

Identify-Friend-or-Foe (IFF) systems are both critical and controversial, with a significant number of 'blue-on-blue' incidents in Iraq being due to equipment incompatibility between U.S. and allied forces. Incidents in which U.S. aircraft bombed British soldiers have contributed significantly to loss of UK public support for the war, especially after the authorities in both countries tried and failed to cover up such incidents out of a wish to both preserve technical security and also to minimise political embarrassment.

IFF goes back in its non-technical forms to antiquity; see for example the quote from Judges 12:5–6 at the head of Chapter 15 on identifying soldiers by whether they could pronounce 'Shibboleth'. World War 2 demonstrated the need for systems that could cope with radar; the Japanese aircraft heading toward Pearl Harbour were seen by a radar operator at Diamond Head but assumed to be an incoming flight of U.S. planes. Initial measures were procedural; returning bombers would be expected to arrive at particular times and cross the coast at particular places, while stragglers would announce their lack of hostile intent by some pre-arranged manoeuvre such as flying in an equilateral triangle before crossing the coast. (German planes would roll over when the radio operator challenged them, so as to create a 'blip' in their radar cross-section.) There were also some early attempts at automation, with the 'Mark 1' system being mechanically tuned and not very usable. There were also early attempts at spoofing.

The Korean war saw the arrival on both sides of jet aircraft and missiles, which made it impractical to identify targets visually and imperative to have automatic IFF. Early systems simply used a vehicle serial number or 'code of the day', but this was wide open to spoofing, and the world's air forces started work on cryptographic authentication.

Since the 1960s, U.S. and other NATO aircraft have used the Mark XII system. This uses a crypto unit with a block cipher that is a DES precursor, and is available for export to non-NATO customers with alternative block ciphers. However, it isn't the cryptography that's the hard part, but rather the protocol problems discussed in Chapter 3. The Mark XII has four modes of which the secure mode uses a 32-bit challenge and a 4-bit response. This is a precedent set by its predecessor, the Mark X; if challenges or responses were too long, then the radar's pulse repetition frequency (and thus it accuracy) would be degraded. So it's necessary to use short challenge-response pairs for radar security reasons, and many of them for cryptosecurity reasons. The Mark 12 sends 12–20 challenges in a series, and in the original implementation the responses were displayed on a screen at a position offset by the arithmetic difference between the actual response and the expected one. The effect was that while a foe had a null or random response, a 'friend' would have responses at or near the center screen, which would light up. Reflection attacks are prevented, and MIG-in-the-middle attacks made much harder, because the challenge uses a focussed antenna, while the receiver is omnidirectional. (In fact, the antenna used for the challenge is typically the fire control radar, which in older systems was conically scanned.)

This mechanism still doesn't completely stop 'ack wars' when two squadrons (or naval flotillas) meet each other. Meanwhile systems are becoming ever more complex. There's a program to create a NATO Mark XIIA that will be backwards-compatible with the existing Mark X/XII systems, and a U.S. Mark XV, both of which use spread-spectrum waveforms. The systems used in military aircraft also have compatibility modes with the civil systems used by aircraft to 'squawk' their ID to secondary surveillance radar. However, that's only for air-to-air IFF, and the real problems are now air-to-ground. NATO's IFF systems evolved for a Cold War scenario of thousands of tactical aircraft on each side of the Iron Curtain; how do they fare in a modern conflict like Iraq or Afghanistan?

Historically, about 10–15% of casualties were due to 'friendly fire' but in the First Gulf War this rose to 25%. Such casualties are more likely at the interfaces between air and land battle, and between sea and land, because of the different services' way of doing things; joint operations are thus particularly risky. Coalition operations also increase the risk because of different national systems. Following this experience, several experimental systems were developed to extend IFF to ground troops. One U.S. system combines laser and RF components. Shooters have lasers, and soldiers have transponders; when the soldier is illuminated with a suitable challenge his equipment broadcasts a 'don't shoot me' message using frequency-hopping radio [1372]. An extension allows aircraft to broadcast targeting intentions on millimeter wave radio. The UK started developing a cheaper system in which friendly vehicles carry an LPI millimeter-wave transmitter, and shooters carry a directional receiver [599]. (Dismounted British foot soldiers, unlike their American counterparts, were not deemed worthy of protection.) A prototype system was ready in 2001 but not put into production. Other countries started developing yet other systems.

But when Gulf War 2 came along, nothing decent had been deployed. A report from Britain's National Audit Office from 2002 describes what went wrong [930]. In a world where defence is purchased not just by nation states, and not just by services, but by factions within these services, and where legislators try to signal their 'patriotism' to less-educated voters by blocking technical collaboration with allies ('to stop them stealing our jobs and our secrets'), it's hard. The institutional and political structures just aren't conducive to providing defense 'public goods' such as a decent IFF system that would work across NATO. And NATO is a broad alliance; as one insider told me, "Trying to evolve a solution that met the aspirations of both the U.S. at one extreme and Greece (for example) at the other was a near hopeless task."

Project complexity is one issue: it's not too hard to stop your air force planes shooting each other, it's a lot more complex to stop them shooting at your ships or tanks, and it's much harder still when a dozen nations are involved. Technical fixes are still being sought; for example, the latest U.S. software radio project, the Joint Tactial Radio System (JTRS, or 'jitters'), may eventually equip all services with radios that interoperate and do at least two IFF modes. However, it's late, over budget, and fragmented into subprojects managed by the different services. There are also some sexy systems used by a small number of units in Iraq that let all soldiers see each others' positions superimposed in real time on a map display on a helmet-mounted monocle. They greatly increase force capability in mobile warfare, allowing units to execute perilous manoevres like driving through each others' kill zones, but are not a panacea in complex warfare such as Iraq in 2007: there, the key networks are social, not electronic, and it's hard to automate networks with nodes of unknown trustworthiness [1116].

In any case, experience so far has taught us that even with 'hard-core' IFF, such as where ships and planes identify each other, the hardest issues weren't technical but to do with economics, politics and doctrine. Over more than a decade of wrangling within NATO, America wanted an expensive high-tech system, for which its defense industry was lobbying hard, while European countries wanted something simpler and cheaper that they could also build themselves, for example by tracking units through the normal command-and-control system and having decent interfaces between nations. But the USA refused to release the location of its units to anyone else for 'security' reasons. America spends more on defense than its allies combined and believed it should lead; the allies didn't want their own capability further marginalised by yet more dependence on U.S. suppliers.

Underlying doctrinal tensions added to this. U.S. doctrine, the so-called 'Revolution in Military Affairs' (RMA) promoted by Donald Rumsfeld and based on an electronic system-of-systems, was not only beyond the allies' budget but was distrusted, based as it is on minimising one's own casualties through vast material and technological supremacy. The Europeans argued that one shouldn't automatically react to sniper fire from a village by bombing the village; as well as killing ten insurgents, you kill a hundred civilians and recruit several hundred of their relatives to the other side. The American retort to this was that Europe was too weak and divided to even deal with genocide in Bosnia. The result was deadlock; countries decided to pursue national solutions, and no real progress has been made on interoperability in twenty years. Allied forces in Iraq and Afghanistan were reduced to painting large color patches on the roofs of their vehicles and hoping the air strikes would pass them by. U.S. aircraft duly bombed and killed a number of allied servicemen, which weakened the alliance. Perhaps we'll have convergence in the long run, as European countries try to catch up with U.S. military systems, and U.S. troops revert to a more traditional combat mode as they discover the virtues of winning local tribal allies in the fight against Al-Qaida in Iraq. However, for a converged solution to be stable, we may well need some institutional redesign.

19.6   Improvised Explosive Devices

A significant effort has been invested in 2004–7 in electronic-warfare measures to counter the improvised explosive devices (IEDs) that are the weapon of choice of insurgents in Iraq and, increasingly, Afghanistan. Since the first IED attack on U.S. forces in March 2003, there have been 81,000 attacks, with 25,000 in 2007 alone. These bombs have become the 'signature weapon' of the Iraq war, as the machine-gun was of World War 1 and the laser-guided bomb of Gulf War I. (And now that unmanned aerial vehicles are built by hobbyists for about $1000, using model-aircraft parts, a GPS receiver and a Lego Mindstorms robotics kit, we might even see improvised cruise missiles.)

Anyway, over 33,000 jammers have been made and shipped to coalition forces. The Department of Defense spent over $1bn on them in 2006, in an operation that, according to insiders, 'proved the largest technological challenge for DOD in the war, on a scale last experienced in World War 2' [94]. The overall budget for the Pentagon's Joint IED Defeat Organization was claimed to almost $4bn by the end of 2006. Between early 2006 and late 2007, the proportion of radio-controlled IEDs dropped from as much as 70% to 10%; the proportion triggered by command wires increased to 40%.

Rebels have been building bombs since at least Guy Fawkes, who tried to blow up Britain's Houses of Parliament in 1605. Many other nationalist and insurgent groups have used IEDs, from anarchists through the Russian resistance in World War 2, the Irgun, ETA and the Viet Cong to Irish nationalists. The IRA got so expert at hiding IEDs in drains and culverts that the British Army had to use helicopters instead of road vehicles in the 'bandit country' near the Irish border. They also ran bombing campaigns against the UK on a number of occasions in the twentieth century. In the last of these, from 1970–94, they blew up the Grand Hotel in Brighton when Margaret Thatcher was staying there for a party conference, killing several of her colleagues; later, London suffered two incidents in which the IRA set off truckloads of home-made explosive causing widespread devastation. The fight against the IRA involved 7,000 IEDs, and gave UK defense scientists much experience in jamming: barrage jammers were fitted in VIP cars that would cause IEDs to go off either too early or too late. These were made available to allies; such a jammer saved the life of President Musharraf of Pakistan when Al-Qaida tried to blow up his convoy in 2005.

The electronic environment in Iraq turned out to be much more difficult than either Belfast or the North-West Frontier. Bombers can use any device that will flip a switch at a distance, and employed everything from key fobs to cellphones. Meanwhile the RF environment in Iraq had become complex and chaotic. Millions of Iraqis used unregulated cellphones, walkie-talkies and satellite phones, as most of the optical-fibre and copper infrastructure had been destroyed in the 2003 war or looted afterwards. 150,000 coalition troops also sent out a huge variety of radio emissions, which changed all the time as units rotated. Over 80,000 radio frequencies were in use, and monitored using 300 databases — many of them not interoperable. Allied forces only started to get on top of the problem when hundreds of Navy electronic warfare specialists were deployed in Baghdad; after that, coalition jamming efforts were better coordinated and started to cut the proportion of IEDs detonated by radio.

But the 'success' in electronic warfare hasn't translated into a reduction in allied casualties. The IED makers have simply switched from radio-controlled bombs to devices detonated by pressure plates, command wires, passive infrared or volunteers. The focus is now shifting to a mix of tactics: 'right of boom' measures such as better vehicle armor, and 'left of boom' measures such as disrupting the bomb-making networks (Britain and Israel had for years targeted bombmakers in Ireland and Lebanon respectively). Better armor at least is having some effect: while in 2003 almost every IED caused a coalition casualty, now it takes four devices on average [94]. Armored vehicles were also a key tactic in other insurgencies. Network disruption, though, is a longer-term play as it depends largely on building up good sources of human intelligence.

19.7   Directed Energy Weapons

In the late 1930s, there was panic in Britain and America on rumors that the Nazis had developed a high-power radio beam that would burn out vehicle ignition systems. British scientists studied the problem and concluded that this was infeasible [670]. They were correct — given the relatively low-powered radio transmitters, and the simple but robust vehicle electronics, of the 1930s.

Things started to change with the arrival of the atomic bomb. The detonation of a nuclear device creates a large pulse of gamma-ray photons, which in turn displace electrons from air molecules by Compton scattering. The large induced currents give rise to an electromagnetic pulse (EMP), which may be thought of as a very high amplitude pulse of radio waves with a very short rise time.

Where a nuclear explosion occurs within the earth's atmosphere, the EMP energy is predominantly in the VHF and UHF bands, though there is enough energy at lower frequencies for a radio flash to be observable thousands of miles away. Within a few tens of miles of the explosion, the radio frequency energy may induce currents large enough to damage most electronic equipment that has not been hardened. The effects of a blast outside the earth's atmosphere are believed to be much worse (although there has never been a test). The gamma photons can travel thousands of miles before they strike the earth's atmosphere, which could ionize to form an antenna on a continental scale. It is reckoned that most electronic equipment in Northern Europe could be burned out by a one megaton blast at a height of 250 miles above the North Sea. For this reason, critical military systems are carefully shielded.

Western concern about EMP grew after the Soviet Union started a research program on non-nuclear EMP weapons in the mid-80s. At the time, the United States was deploying 'neutron bombs' in Europe — enhanced radiation weapons that could kill people without demolishing buildings. The Soviets portrayed this as a 'capitalist bomb' which would destroy people while leaving property intact, and responded by threatening a 'socialist bomb' to destroy property (in the form of electronics) while leaving the surrounding people intact.

By the end of World War 2, the invention of the cavity magnetron had made it possible to build radars powerful enough to damage unprotected electronic circuitry at a range of several hundred yards. The move from valves to transistors and integrated circuits has increased the vulnerability of most commercial electronic equipment. A terrorist group could in theory mount a radar in a truck and drive around a city's financial sector wiping out the banks. In fact, the banks' underground server farms would likely be unaffected; the real damage would be to everyday electronic devices. For example, some electronic car keys are so susceptible to RF that they can be destroyed if left next to a cell phone [1073]. Replacing the millions of gadgets on which a city's life depends would be extremely tiresome.

For battlefield use, it's useful if the weapon can be built into a standard bomb or shell casing rather than having to be truck-mounted. The Soviets are said to have built high-energy RF (HERF) devices, and the U.S. responded with its own arsenal: a device called Blow Torch was tried in Iraq as a means of frying the electronics in IEDs, but it didn't work well [94]. There's a survey of usable technologies at [737] that describes how power pulses in the Terawatt range can be generated using explosively-pumped flux compression generators and magnetohydrodynamic devices, as well as by more conventional high-power microwave devices.

By the mid 1990s, the concern that terrorists might get hold of these weapons from the former Soviet Union led the agencies to try to sell commerce and industry on the idea of electromagnetic shielding. These efforts were dismissed as hype. Personally, I tend to agree. Physics suggests that EMP is limited by the dielectric strength of air and the cross-section of the antenna. In nuclear EMP, the effective antenna size could be a few hundred meters for an endoatmospheric blast, up to several thousand kilometers for an exoatmospheric one. But in 'ordinary' EMP/HERF, the antenna will usually just be a few meters. According to the cited paper, EMP bombs need to be dropped from aircraft and deploy antennas before detonation in order to get decent coupling, and even so are lethal to ordinary electronic equipment for a radius of only a few hundred meters. NATO planners concluded that military command and control systems that were already hardened for nuclear EMP should be unaffected.

And as far as terrorists are concerned, I wrote here in the first edition of this book: 'As for the civilian infrastructure, I suspect that a terrorist can do a lot more damage with an old-fashioned truck bomb made with a ton of fertilizer and fuel oil, and he doesn't need a PhD in physics to design one!' That was published a few months before 9/11. Of course, a Boeing 767 will do more damage than a truck bomb, but a truck bomb still does plenty, as we see regularly in Iraq, and even small IEDs of the kind used by Al-Qaida in London in 2005 can kill enough people to have a serious political effect. In addition, studies of the psychology of terror support the view that lethal attacks are much more terrifying than nonlethal ones almost regardless of the economic damage they do (I'll come back to this in Part III). So I expect that terrorists will continue to prefer a truckload of fertiliser to a truckload of magnetrons.

There remains one serious concern: that the EMP from a single nuclear explosion at an altitude of 250 miles would do colossal economic damage, while killing few people directly [80]. This gives a blackmail weapon to countries such as Iran and North Korea with nuclear ambitions but primitive technology otherwise. North Korea recently fired a missile into the sea near Japan, which together with their nuclear test sent a clear signal: 'We can switch off your economy any time we like, and without directly killing a single Japanese civilian either'. And how would Japan respond? (They're hurriedly testing anti-missile defences.) What, for that matter, would the USA do if Kim Jong-Il mounted a missile on a ship, sailed it towards the Panama Canal, and fired a nuke 250 miles above the central United States? That could knock out computers and communications from coast to coast. A massive attack on electronic communications is more of a threat to countries such as the USA and Japan that depend on them, than on countries such as North Korea (or Iran) that don't.

This observation goes across to attacks on the Internet as well, so let's now turn to 'Information Warfare'.

19.8   Information Warfare

From about 1995, the phrase *Information warfare* came into wide use. Its popularity was boosted by operational experience in Desert Storm. There, air power was used to degrade the Iraqi defenses before the land attack was launched, and one goal of NSA personnel supporting the allies was to enable the initial attack to be made without casualties — even though the Iraqi air defenses were at that time intact and alert. The attack involved a mixture of standard e-war techniques such as jammers and antiradiation missiles; cruise missile attacks on command centers; attacks by special forces who sneaked into Iraq and dug up lengths of communications cabling from the desert; and, allegedly, the use of hacking tricks to disable computers and telephone exchanges. (By 1990, the U.S. Army was already calling for bids for virus production [825].) The operation successfully achieved its mission of ensuring zero allied casualties on the first night of the aerial bombardment. Military planners and think tanks started to consider how the success could be built on.

After 9/11, information warfare was somewhat eclipsed as the security-industrial complex focussed on topics from airport screening to the detection of improvised explosive devices. But in April 2007, it was thrust back on the agenda by events in Estonia. There, the government had angered Russia by moving an old Soviet war memorial, and shortly afterwards the country was subjected to a number of distributed denial-of-service attacks that appeared to originate from Russia [359]. Estonia's computer emergency response team tackled the problem with cool professionalism, but their national leadership didn't. Their panicky reaction got world headlines [413]; they even thought of invoking the NATO treaty and calling for U.S. military help against Russia.

Fortunately common sense prevailed. It seems that the packet storms were simply launched by Russian botnet herders, reacting to the news from Estonia and egging each other on via chat rooms, rather than being an act of state aggression; the one man convicted of the attacks was an ethnic Russian teenager in Estonia itself. There have been similar tussles between Israeli and Palestinian hackers, and between Indians and Pakistanis. Estonia also had some minor street disturbances caused by rowdy ethnic Russians objecting to the statue's removal; 'Web War 1' seems to have been the digital equivalent. Since then, however, there have been press reports alleging Chinese attacks on government systems in both the USA and the UK, including service-denial attacks and attempted intrusions, causing 'minor administrative disruptions' [973]. Defense insiders leak reports saying that China has a massive capability to attack the West [1063]. Is this serious, or is it just the agencies shaking the tin for more money?

But what's information warfare anyway? There is little agreement on definitions. The conventional view, arising out of Desert Storm, was expressed by Whitehead [1314]:

> The strategist ... should employ (the information weapon) as a precursor weapon to blind the enemy prior to conventional attacks and operations.

Meanwhile, the more aggressive view is that properly conducted information operations should encompass everything from signals intelligence to propaganda, and given the reliance that modern societies place on information, it should suffice to break the enemy's will without fighting.

19.8.1   Definitions

In fact, there are roughly three views on what information warfare means:

- that it is just 'a remarketing of the stuff that the agencies have been doing for decades anyway', in an attempt to maintain the agencies' budgets post-Cold-War;

- that it consists of the use of 'hacking' in a broad sense — network attack tools, computer viruses and so on — in conflict between states or substate groups, in order to deny critical military and other services whether for operational or propaganda purposes. It is observed, for example, that the Internet was designed to withstand thermonuclear bombardment, but was knocked out by the Morris worm;

- that it extends the electronic warfare doctrine of controlling the electromagnetic spectrum to control all information relevant to the conflict. It thus extends traditional e-war techniques such as radar jammers by adding assorted hacking techniques, but also incorporates propaganda and news management.

The first of these views was the one taken by some cynical defense insiders. The second is the popular view found in newspaper articles, and also Whitehead's. It's the one I'll use as a guide in this section, but without taking a position on whether it actually contains anything really new either technically or doctrinally.

The third finds expression by Dorothy Denning [370] whose definition of information warfare is 'operations that target or exploit information media in order to win some advantage over an adversary'. Its interpretation is so broad that it includes not just hacking but all of electronic warfare and all existing intelligence gathering techniques (from Sigint through satellite imagery to spies), but propaganda too. In a later article she discussed the role of the net in the propaganda and activism surrounding the Kosovo war [371]. However the bulk of her book is given over to computer security and related topics.

A similar view of information warfare, and from a writer whose background is defense planning rather than computer security, is given by Edward Waltz [1314]. He defines *information superiority* as 'the capability to collect, process and disseminate an uninterrupted flow of information while exploiting or denying an adversary's ability to do the same'. The theory is that such superiority will allow the conduct of operations without effective opposition. The book has less technical detail on computer security matters than Denning but set forth a first attempt to formulate a military doctrine of information operations.

19.8.2 Doctrine

When writers such as Denning and Waltz include propaganda operations in information warfare, the cynical defense insider will remark that nothing has changed. From Roman and Mongol efforts to promote a myth of invincibility, through the use of propaganda radio stations by both sides in World War 2 and the Cold War, to the bombing of Serbian TV during the Kosovo campaign and denial-of-service attacks on Chechen web sites by Russian agencies [320] — the tools may change but the game remains the same.

But there is a twist, perhaps thanks to government and military leaders' lack of familiarity with the Internet. When teenage kids deface a U.S. government department web site, an experienced computer security professional is likely to see it as the equivalent of graffiti scrawled on the wall of a public building. After all, it's easy enough to do, and easy enough to remove. But the information warfare community can paint it as undermining the posture of information dominance that a country must project in order to deter aggression.

So there is a fair amount of debunking to be done before the political and military leadership can start to think clearly about the issues. For example, it's often stated that information warfare provides a casualty-free way to win wars: 'just hack the Iranian power grid and watch them sue for peace'. The three obvious comments are as follows.

- The denial-of-service attacks that have so far been conducted on information systems without the use of physical force have mostly had a transient effect. A computer comes down; the operators find out what happened; they restore the system from backup and restart it. An outage of a few hours may be enough to let a bomber aircraft get through unscathed, but is unlikely to bring a country to its knees. In this context, the failure of the Millennium Bug to cause the expected damage may be a useful warning.

- Insofar as there is a vulnerability, more developed countries are more exposed. The power grid in the USA or the UK is likely to be much more computerized than that in a developing country.

- Finally, if such an attack causes the deaths of several dozen people in hospitals, the Iranians aren't likely to see the matter as being much different from a conventional military attack that killed the same number of people. Indeed, if information war targets civilians to an even greater extent than the alternatives, then the attackers' leaders are likely to be portrayed as war criminals. The Pinochet case, in which a former head of government only escaped extradition on health grounds, should give pause for thought.

Having made these points, I will restrict discussion in the rest of this section to technical matters.

19.8.3 Potentially Useful Lessons from Electronic Warfare

Perhaps the most important policy lesson from the world of electronic warfare is that conducting operations that involve more than one service is very much harder than it looks. Things are bad enough when army, navy and air force units have to be coordinated — during the U.S. invasion of Grenada, a ground commander had to go to a pay phone and call home using his credit card in order to call down an air strike, as the different services' radios were incompatible. (Indeed, this was the spur for the development of software radios [761].) Things are even worse when intelligence services are involved, as they don't train with warfighters in peacetime and thus take a long time to become productive once the fighting starts. Turf fights also get in the way: under current U.S. rules, the air force can decide to bomb an enemy telephone exchange but has to get permission from the NSA and/or CIA to hack it [103]. The U.S. Army's communications strategy is now taking account of the need to communicate across the traditional command hierarchy, and to make extensive use of the existing civilian infrastructure [1115].

At the technical level, there are many concepts which may go across from electronic warfare to information protection in general.

- The electronic warfare community uses guard band receivers to detect jamming, so it can be filtered out (for example, by blanking receivers at the precise time a sweep jammer passes through their frequency). The use of bait addresses to detect spam is essentially the same concept.

- There is also an analogy between virus recognition and radar signal recognition. Virus writers may make their code *polymorphic*, in that it changes its form as it propagates, in order to make life harder for the virus scanner vendors; similarly, radar designers use very diverse waveforms in order to make it harder to store enough of the waveform in digital radio frequency memory to do coherent jamming effectively.

- Our old friends, the false accept and false reject rate, continue to dominate tactics and strategy. As with burglar alarms or radar jamming, the ability to cause many false alarms (however crudely) will always be worth something: as soon as the false alarm rate exceeds about 15%, operator performance is degraded. As for filtering, it can usually be cheated.

- The limiting economic factor in both attack and defense will increasingly be the software cost, and the speed with which new tools can be created and deployed.

- It is useful, when subjected to jamming, not to let the jammer know whether, or how, his attack is succeeding. In military communications, it's usually better to respond to jamming by dropping the bit rate rather than boosting power; similarly, when a non-existent credit card number is presented at your web site, you might say 'Sorry, bad card number, try again', but the second time it happens you want a different line (or the attacker will keep on trying). Something like 'Sorry, the items you have requested are temporarily out of stock and should be dispatched within five working days' may do the trick.

- Although defense in depth is in general a good idea, you have to be careful of interactions between the different defenses. The classic case in e-war is when chaff dispensed to defend against an incoming cruise missile knocks out the anti-aircraft gun. The side-effects of defenses can also be exploited. The most common case on the net is the mail bomb in which an attacker forges offensive newsgroup messages that appear to come from the victim, who then gets subjected to a barrage of abuse and attacks.

■ Finally, some perspective can be drawn from the differing roles of hard kill and soft kill in electronic warfare. Jamming and other soft-kill attacks are cheaper, can be used against multiple threats, and have reduced political consequences. But damage assessment is hard, and you may just divert the weapon to another target. As most information war is soft-kill, these comments can be expected to go across too.

19.8.4 Differences Between E-war and I-war

As well as similarities, there are differences between traditional electronic warfare and the kinds of attack that can potentially be run over the net.

■ There are roughly two kinds of war — open war and guerilla war. Electronic warfare comes into its own in the first of these: in air combat, most naval engagements, and the desert. In forests, mountains and cities, the man with the AK47 can still get a result against mechanized forces. Guerilla war has largely been ignored by the e-war community, except insofar as they make and sell radars to detect snipers and concealed mortar batteries.

In cyberspace, the 'forests, mountains and cities' are the large numbers of insecure hosts belonging to friendly or neutral civilians and organizations. The distributed denial of service attack, in which millions of innocent machines are subverted and used to bombard a target website with traffic, has no real analogue in the world of electronic warfare: yet it is the likely platform for launching attacks even on 'open' targets such as large commercial web sites. So it's unclear where the open countryside in cyberspace actually is.

■ Another possible source of asymmetric advantage for the guerilla is complexity. Large countries have many incompatible systems, which makes little difference when fighting another large country with similarly incompatible systems, but can leave them at a disadvantage to a small group with simple coherent systems.

■ Anyone trying to attack the USA in future is unlikely to repeat Saddam Hussein's mistake of taking on the West in a tank battle. Asymmetric conflict is now the norm, and although cyberspace has some potential here, physical attacks have so far got much more traction — whether at the Al-Qaida level of murderous attacks, or at the lower level of (say) animal rights activists, who set out to harass people rather than murder them and thus stay just below the threshold at which a drastic state response would be invoked. A group that wants to stay at this level — so that its operatives risk short prison sentences rather than execution — can have more impact if it uses physical as well as electronic harassment.

As a member of Cambridge University's governing body, the Council, I was subjected for some months to this kind of hassle, as animal rights fanatics protested at our psychology department's plans to construct a new building to house its monkeys. I also watched the harassment's effects on colleagues. Spam floods were easily enough dealt with; people got much more upset when protesters woke them and their families in the small hours, by throwing rocks on their house roofs and screaming abuse. I'll discuss this later in Part III.

■ There is no electronic-warfare analogue of script kiddies — people who download attack scripts and launch them without really understanding how they work. That such tools are available universally, and for free, has few analogues in meatspace. You might draw a comparison with the lawless areas of countries such as Afghanistan where all men go about armed. But the damage done by Russian script kiddies to Estonia was nothing like the damage done to allied troops by Afghan tribesmen — whether in the present Afghan war or in its nineteenth century predecessors.

19.9 Summary

Electronic warfare is much more developed than most other areas of information security. There are many lessons to be learned, from the technical level up through the tactical level to matters of planning and strategy. We can expect that if information warfare takes off, and turns from a fashionable concept into established doctrine and practice, these lessons will become important for engineers.

Research Problems

An interesting research problem is how to port techniques and experience from the world of electronic warfare to the Internet. This chapter is only a sketchy first attempt at setting down the possible parallels and differences.

Further Reading

A good (although non-technical) introduction to radar is by P. S. Hall [578]. The best all-round reference for the technical aspects of electronic warfare, from radar through stealth to EMP weapons, is by Curtis Schleher [1121]; a good summary was written by Doug Richardson [1074]. The classic introduction to the anti-jam properties of spread spectrum sequences is by Andrew Viterbi [1301]; the history of spread spectrum is ably told by Robert Scholtz [1138]; the classic introduction to the mathematics of spread spectrum is by Raymond Pickholtz, Donald Schilling and Lawrence Milstein [1026]; while the standard textbook is by Robert Dixon [393]. The most thorough reference on communications jamming is by Richard Poisel [1029]. An overall history of British electronic warfare and scientific intelligence, which was written by a true insider and gives a lot of insight not just into how the technology developed but also into strategic and tactical deception, is by R. V. Jones [670, 671].

CHAPTER 20

Telecom System Security

*I rarely had to resort to a technical attack. Companies can spend
millions of dollars toward technological protections and that's
wasted if somebody can basically call someone on the telephone and
either convince them to do something on the computer that lowers
the computer's defenses or reveals the information they were seeking.*

— Kevin Mitnick

*There are two kinds of fools. One says, "This is old, therefore it is
good." The other one says, "This is new, therefore it is better".*

— Dean William Inge

20.1   Introduction

The protection of telecommunications systems is an important case study for a
number of reasons. First, many distributed systems rely on the fixed or mobile
phone network in ways that are often not obvious, and the dependability of
these networks is declining. For example, POTS — the 'plain old telephone
system' — typically required exchanges to have backup generators with
enough diesel to survive a six-week outage in the electricity supply, while
cellular systems typically use batteries that will last at most 48 hours. What's
worse, the electricity companies rely on mobile phones to direct their engineers when repairing faults. When people realised that this could cause serious
problems where outages lasted more than two days, the electricity companies
started buying satellite phones as a backup.

Second, the history of telecomms security failures is very instructive.
Early attacks were carried out on phone companies by enthusiasts ('phone
phreaks') to get free calls; then the phone system's vulnerabilities started to be

exploited by crooks to evade police wiretapping; then premium rate calls were introduced, which created the motive for large-scale fraud; then when telecomms markets were liberalized, some phone companies started conducting attacks on each other's customers; and some phone companies have even attacked each other. At each stage the defensive measures undertaken were not only very expensive but also tended to be inadequate for various reasons. The same pattern is repeating with the Internet — only with history much speeded up. A number of the policy issues that arose with wireline phones, such as wiretapping, have played themselves out again on the Internet.

Finally, the latest developments in telecomms, from VOIP at the consumer level to the adoption of IP networks as the underlying technology by telecomms providers, create further interactions. Skype's two-day failure in August 2007 following Microsoft's Patch Tuesday is just one case in point. Systems are becoming much more complex and interdependent, and are generally not being engineered to the old standards.

20.2 Phone Phreaking

The abuse of communication services goes back centuries. Before Sir Rowland Hill invented the postage stamp, postage was paid by the recipient. Unsolicited mail became a huge problem — especially for famous people — so recipients were allowed to inspect a letter and reject it rather than paying for it. People soon worked out schemes to send short messages on the covers of letters which their correspondents rejected. Regulations were brought in to stop this, but were never really effective [979].

A second set of abuses developed with the telegraph. The early optical telegraphs, which worked using semaphores or heliographs, were abused by people to place foreknowledge bets on races; if you could learn which horse had won before the bookmaker did, you were well away. People would bribe operators, or 'hack the local loop' by observing the last heliograph station through a telescope. Here too, attempts to legislate the problem away were a failure [1215]. The problems got even more widespread when the electric telegraph brought costs down; the greater volumes of communication, and the greater flexibility that got built into and on top of the service, led to greater complexity and volume of abuse.

The telephone was to be no different.

20.2.1 Attacks on Metering

Early metering systems were wide open to abuse.

- In the 1950's, the operator in some systems had to listen for the sound of coins dropping on a metal plate to tell that a callbox customer had paid, so some people acquired the knack of hitting the coinbox with a piece of metal that struck the right note.

- Initially, the operator had no way of knowing which phone a call had come from, so she had to ask the caller his number. He could give the number of someone else — who would be charged. This was risky to do from your own phone, so people did it from call boxes. Operators started calling back to verify the number for international calls, so people worked out social engineering attacks ('This is IBM here, we'd like to book a call to San Francisco and because of the time difference can our Managing Director take it at home tonight? His number's xxx-yyyy'). So call box lines had a feature added to alert the operator. But in the UK implementation, there was a bug: a customer who had called the operator from a callbox could depress the rest for a quarter second or so, whereupon he'd be disconnected and reconnected (often to a different operator), with no signal this time that the call was from a callbox. He could then place a call to anywhere and bill it to any local number.

- Early systems also signalled the entry of a coin by one or more pulses, each of which consisted of the insertion of a resistance in the line followed by a brief open circuit. At a number of colleges, enterprising students installed 'magic buttons' which could simulate this in a callbox in the student union so people could phone for free. (The bill in this case went to the student union, for which the magic button was not quite so amusing.)

Attacks on metering mechanisms continue. Many countries have moved their payphones to chip cards in order to cut the costs of coin collection and vandalism. Some of the implementations have been poor (as I remarked in the chapter on tamper resistance) and villains have manufactured large quantities of bogus phone cards. Other attacks involve what's called *clip-on*: physically attaching a phone to someone else's line to steal their service.

In the 1970's, when international phone calls were very expensive, foreign students would clip their own phone on to a residential line in order to call home; an unsuspecting home owner could get a huge bill. Despite the fact that in most countries the cable was the phone company's legal responsibility up to the service socket in the house, phone companies were mostly adamant that householders should pay and could threaten to blacklist them if they didn't. Now that long distance calls are cheap, the financial incentive for clip-on fraud has largely disappeared. But it's still enough of a problem that the Norwegian phone company designed a system whereby a challenge and response are exchanged between a wall-socket mounted authentication device and the exchange software before a dial tone is given [673].

Clip-on fraud had a catastrophic effect on a family in Cramlington, a town in the North East of England. The first sign they had of trouble was hearing a conversation on their line. The next was a visit from the police who said there'd been complaints of nuisance phone calls. The complainants were three ladies, all of whom had a number one digit different from a number to which this family had supposedly made a huge number of calls. When the family's bill was examined, there were also calls to clusters of numbers that turned out to be payphones; these had started quite suddenly at the same time as the nuisance calls. When the family had complained later to the phone company about a fault, their connection was rerouted and this had solved the problem.

But the phone company denied the possibility of a tap, despite the report from their maintenance person which noted that the family's line had been tampered with at the distribution cabinet. (The phone company later claimed this report was in error.) It turned out that a drug dealer had lived close by, and it seemed a reasonable inference that he'd tapped their line in order to call his couriers at the payphones. By using an innocent family's phone line instead of his own, he not only saved on the phone bill, but also had a better chance of evading police surveillance. But both the police and the local phone company refused to go into the house where the dealer had lived, claiming it was too dangerous — even though the dealer had by now got six years in jail. The Norwegian phone company declined an invitation to testify about clip-on for the defence. The upshot was that the subscriber was convicted of making harassing phone calls, in a case widely believed to have been a miscarriage of justice. There was discussion at the time about whether the closing of ranks between the phone company and the police was a bureaucratic reflex — or something more sinister. Since 9/11, it's emerged that many phone companies have been giving the police easy access to systems for years, often without warrants, in return for favours. The logical consequence was a policy of covering up anything that could stray into this territory — even if the coverup caused collateral damage. I'll discuss all this later in the third part of this book.

Stealing dial tone from cordless phones is another variant on the theme. In the 1990s, this became so widespread in Paris that France Telecom broke with phone company tradition and announced that it was happening, claiming that the victims were using illegally imported cordless phones which were easy to spoof [745]. Yet to this day I am unaware of any cordless phones — authorised or not — with decent air link authentication. The new digital cordless phones use the DECT standard which allows for challenge-response mechanisms [1283] but the equipment sold so far seems to simply send a handset serial number to the base station.

Social engineering is also widespread. A crook calls you pretending to be from AT&T security and asks whether you made a large number of calls to Peru on your calling card. When you deny this, he says that they were obviously fake and, in order to reverse out the charges, can he confirm that your card number is 123-456-7890-6543? No, you say (if you're not really alert), it's 123-456-7890-5678. Now 123-456-7890 is your phone number and 5678 your password, so you've just given that caller the ability to bill calls to you.

The growth of premium rate phone services during the 1990s also led to scamsters developing all sorts of tricks to get people to call them: pager messages, job ads, fake emergency messages about relatives, 'low cost' calling cards with 0900 access numbers, you name it. (In fact, the whole business of tricking people into calling expensive premium numbers enabled crooks to develop a lot of the techniques we now see used in email as part of phishing attacks.) The 809 area code for the Caribbean used to be a favourite cover for crooks targeting U.S. subscribers; many people weren't aware that 'domestic' numbers (numbers within the USA's +1 international direct dialling code) extend outside the relatively cheap USA (and Canada). Even though many people have now learned that +1 809 is 'foreign' and more expensive, the introduction of still more Caribbean area codes, such as +1 345 for the Cayman Islands, has made it even harder to spot premium rate numbers.

Phone companies advised their customers 'Do not return calls to unfamiliar telephone numbers' and 'Beware of faxes, e-mail, voice mail and pages requesting a return call to an unfamiliar number' [22] — but how practical is that? Just as banks now train their customers to click on links in marketing emails and thus make them vulnerable to phishing attacks, so I've had junk marketing calls from my phone company — even though I'm on the do-not-call list. And as for governments, they have tended to set up weak regulators to oversee phone system abuses at home, and avoid anything that might get them involved in trying to regulate premium rate scams overseas. For example, they let phone companies harass their customers into paying bills for overseas services even when they knew that the overseas traffic was fraudulent.

Indeed, by no means all premium-rate scams involved obviously dodgy companies running sex lines; as I write in 2007, the British press are full of stores about how TV companies rip off their customers by getting them to call premium lines in order to compete, and vote, in all sorts of shows. It's turned out that many of these are recorded, so the calls are totally futile; and even the live ones are managed so that people who live in the wrong part of the country or speak with the wrong accent have no chance. The authorities tried to leave this to 'self-regulation' and on-air apologies from TV bosses, until a public outcry (whipped up by their competitors) led to the file being sent to the police in October 2007. It's a recurring pattern that the biggest scams are often run by 'respectable' companies rather than by Russian gangsters.

20.2.2 Attacks on Signaling

The term 'phone phreaking' refers to attacks on signaling as well as pure toll fraud. Until the 1980s, phone companies used signalling systems that worked *in-band* by sending tone pulses in the same circuit that carried the speech. The first attack I've heard of dates back to 1952, and by the mid-to-late 1960s many enthusiasts in both America and Britain had worked out ways of rerouting calls. One of the pioneers, Joe Engresia, had perfect pitch and discovered as a child that he could make free phone calls by whistling a tone he'd heard in the background of a long-distance call. His less gifted colleagues typically used home-made tone generators, of which the most common were called *blue boxes*. The trick was to call an 0800 number and then send a 2600Hz tone that would *clear down* the line at the far end — that is, disconnect the called party while leaving the caller with a trunk line connected to the exchange. The caller could now enter the number he really wanted and be connected without paying. Phone phreaking was one of the roots of the computer hacker culture that took root in the Bay Area and was formative in the development and evolution of personal computers [835]. For example, Steve Jobs and Steve Wozniak first built blue boxes before they diversified into computers [502].

Phone phreaking started out with a strong ideological element. In those days most phone companies had monopolies. They were large, faceless and unresponsive. In America, AT&T was such an abusive monopoly that the courts eventually broke it up; most phone companies in Europe were government departments. People whose domestic phone lines had been involved in a service theft found they were stuck with the charges. If the young man who had courted your daughter was (unknown to you) a phone phreak who hadn't paid for the calls he made to her, you would suddenly find the company trying to extort either the young man's name or a payment. Phone companies were also aligned with state security. Phone phreaks in many countries discovered signalling codes or switch features that would enable the police or the spooks to tap your phone from the comfort of their desks, without having to send out a lineman to install a wiretap. Back in the days of Vietnam and student protests, this was inflammatory stuff. Phone phreaks were counterculture heroes, while phone companies were hand-in-hand with the forces of darkness.

As there was no way to stop blue-box type attacks so long as telephone signalling was carried in-band, the phone companies spent years and many billions of dollars upgrading exchanges so that the signaling was moved out-of-band, in separate channels to which the subscribers had no easy access. Gradually, region by region, the world was closed off to blue box attacks. There are still a few places left. For example, the first time that USAF operations were disrupted by an 'information warfare' attack by noncombatants was in 1994 when two British hackers broke into the Rome Air Force Base via an analog link through an ancient phone system in Argentina which they used to hold up investigators [1202]. There's also an interesting legacy vulnerability in wiretapping systems: common phone-tapping equipment was designed to be backwards compatible with in-band signalling, with the result that you can evade surveillance by using a blue box to convince the police equipment that you've hung up. The telephone exchange ignores this signal, so you remain on the phone but with the police recording stopped [1151].

But to defeat a modern telephone network — as opposed to its law-enforcement add-ons — different techniques are needed.

20.2.3   Attacks on Switching and Configuration

The second wave of attacks targeted the computers that did the switching. Typically these were Unix machines on a LAN in the exchange, which also had machines with administrative functions such as scheduling maintenance. By hacking one of these less well guarded machines, a phreak could go across the LAN and break into the switching equipment — or in to other secondary systems such as subscriber databases. For a survey of PacBell's experience of this, see [271]; for Bellcore's, see [722].

Using these techniques, unlisted phone numbers could be found, calls could be forwarded without a subscriber's knowledge, and all sorts of mischief became possible. A Californian phone phreak called Kevin Poulsen got root access to many of PacBel's switches and other systems in 1985–88: this apparently involved burglary as much as hacking (he was eventually convicted of conspiring to possess fifteen or more counterfeit, unauthorized and stolen access devices.) He did petty things like obtaining unlisted phone numbers for celebrities and winning a Porsche from Los Angeles radio station KIIS-FM. Each week KIIS would give a Porsche to the 102nd caller, so Poulsen and his accomplices blocked out all calls to the radio station's 25 phone lines save their own, made the 102nd call and collected the Porsche. He was also accused of unlawful wiretapping and espionage; these charges were dismissed. In fact, the FBI came down on him so heavily that there were allegations of an improper relationship between the agency and the phone companies, along the lines of 'you scratch our backs with wiretaps when needed, and we'll investigate your hacker problems' [472].

Although the unauthorized wiretapping charges against Poulsen were dismissed, the FBI's sensitivity does highlight the possibility that attacks on phone company computers can be used by foreign intelligence agencies to conduct remote wiretaps. Some of the attacks mentioned in [271] were from overseas, and the possibility that such tricks might be used to crash the whole phone system in the context of an information warfare attack has for some years worried the NSA [495, 754]. Countries that import their telephone exchanges rather than building their own are in an even worse position; a prudent nations will assume that its telephone switchgear has vulnerabilities known to the government of the country from which they bought it. (It was notable that during the invasion of Afghanistan in 2001, Kabul had two exchanges: an old electromechanical one and a new electronic one. The USAF bombed only the first of these.)

But although high-tech attacks do happen, and newspaper articles on phone phreaking tend to play up the 'evil hacker' aspects, most real attacks are much simpler. Many involve insiders, who deliberately misconfigure systems to provide free calls from (or through) favored numbers. This didn't matter all that much when the phone company's marginal cost of servicing an extra phone call was near zero, but with the modern proliferation of value-added services, people with access to the systems can be tempted to place (or forge) large numbers of calls to accomplices' sex lines. Deregulation, and the advent of mobile phones, have also made fraud serious as they give rise to cash payments between phone companies [317]. Insiders also get up to mischief with services that depend on the security of the phone network. In a hack reminiscent of Poulsen, two staff at British Telecom were dismissed after they each won ten tickets for Concorde from a phone-in offer at which only one randomly selected call in a thousand was supposed to get through [1266].

As for outsiders, the other 'arch-hacker' apart from Poulsen was Kevin Mitnick, who got arrested and convicted following a series of break-ins, many of which involved phone systems and which made him the target of an FBI manhunt. They initially thought that he was a foreign agent who was abusing the U.S. phone system in order to wiretap sensitive U.S. targets. As I mentioned in Chapter 2, he testified after his release from prison that almost all of his exploits had involved social engineering. He came out with the quote at the head of this chapter: 'Companies can spend millions of dollars toward technological protections and that's wasted if somebody can basically call someone on the telephone and either convince them to do something on the computer that lowers the computer's defenses or reveals the information they were seeking' [895]. So phone company systems are vulnerable to careless insiders as well as malicious insiders — just like hospital systems and many others we've discussed.

A worrying recent development is the emergence of switching exploits by organisations. The protocols used between phone companies to switch calls — notably 5ESS — aren't particularly secure, as the move from in-band to out-of-band signaling was supposed to restrict access to trusted parties. But once again, changing environments undermine security assumptions. Now that there are many entrepreneurial phone companies rather than a handful of large ones, all sorts of people have access to the switching. An example is location service. This is provided for a fee by mobile networks; you can register your child's mobile, or your employees' mobiles, and trace them through a website. One entrepreneur undercut this service in the UK by using the switching interface exported by a local telco. While such issues can generally be resolved by contracts, litigation and regulation, there remains a lingering worry that attackers might bring down a telco by exploiting access to its switching and network management. This worry increases as telcos migrate their networks to IP, and they start to converge with VOIP services that give users access to the IP layer. I'll return to VOIP later.

20.2.4   Insecure End Systems

After direct attacks on the systems kept on phone company premises, the next major vulnerabilities of modern phone systems are insecure terminal equipment and feature interaction.

There have been a number of cases where villains exploited people's answering machines. The same technique can be used for at least two different purposes: the relatively innocuous one of tricking someone into dialling a premium rate number, or the somewhat more sinister one of using their answering machine as a covert remailer for a voicemail message. The problem arises from phone company switches that give you dial tone twelve seconds after the other party hangs up. So a terrorist who wants to send an untraceable instruction to a colleague can record on your answering machine thirteen blank seconds, followed by the tones needed to dial his colleague's number and the secret message. He then calls again, gets the machine to play back its messages, and hangs up on it.

But the really big frauds using insecure end systems are directed against companies and government departments. Attacks on corporate *private branch exchange* systems (PBXes) had become big business by the mid-1990's and cost business billions of dollars a year [322]. PBXes are usually supplied with facilities for *refiling* calls, also known as *direct inward system access* (DISA). The typical application is that the company's sales force can call in to an 0800 number, enter a PIN or password, and then call out again taking advantage of the low rates a large company can get for long distance calls. As you'd expect, these PINs become known and get traded by villains [911]. The result is known as *dial-through* fraud.

In many cases, the PINs are set to a default by the manufacturer, and never changed by the customer. In other cases, PINs are captured by crooks who monitor telephone traffic in hotels anyway in order to steal credit card numbers; phone card numbers and PBX PINs are a useful sideline. Many PBX designs have fixed engineering passwords that allow remote maintenance access, and prudent people reckon that any PBX will have at least one back door installed by the manufacturer to give easy access to law enforcement and intelligence agencies (it's said, as a condition of export licensing). Of course such features get discovered and abused. In one case, the PBX at Scotland Yard was compromised and used by villains to refile calls, costing the Yard a million pounds, for which they sued their telephone installer. The crooks were never caught [1244]. This was particularly poignant, as one of the criminals' motivations in such cases is to get access to communications that will not be tapped. Businesses who're the victims of such crimes nevertheless find the police reluctant to investigate, and one reason for this is that the phone companies aren't particularly helpful — presumably as they don't like having their bills disputed [1088].

In another case, Chinese gangsters involved in labor market racketeering — smuggling illegal immigrants from Fujian, China, into Britain where they were put to work in sweatshops, on farms and so on — hacked the PBX of an English district council and used it to refile over a million pounds' worth of calls to China. The gang was tackled by the police after a number of its labourers died; they were picking shellfish in Morecambe Bay when the tide came in and drowned them. The council had by now discovered the discrepancy in its phone bills and sued the phone company for its money back. The phone company argued that it wasn't to blame, even although it had supplied the insecure PBX. Here, too, the gangsters were interested not just in saving money but in evading surveillance. (Indeed, they routed their calls to China via a compromised PBX in Albania, so that the cross-border segment of the call, which is most likely to be monitored by the agencies, was between whitelisted numbers; the same trick seems to have been used in the Scotland Yard case, where the crooks made their calls via the USA.)

Such cases apart, dial-through fraud is mostly driven by premium rate services: the main culprits are crooks who are in cahoots with premium line owners. Most companies don't understand the need to guard their 'dial tone' and don't know how to even if they wanted to. PBXes are typically run by company telecomms managers who know little about security, while the security manager often knows little about phones. This is changing, albeit slowly, as VOIP technologies take over and the company phone network merges with the data network.

Exploits of insecure end-systems sometimes affect domestic subscribers too. A notorious case was the Moldova scam. In 1997, customers of a porn site were told to download a 'viewer' program that dropped their phone line and connected them to a phone number in Moldova (having turned off their modem speakers so they wouldn't notice). The new connection stayed up until they turned off their computers; thousands of subscribers incurred hundreds of thousands of dollars in international long distance charges at over $2 per minute. Their phone companies tried to collect this money but there was an outcry. Eventually the subscribers got their money back, and the Federal Trade Commission enjoined and prosecuted the perpetrators [456]. Since then there have been a number of copycat scams [870]; but as more and more people move to cable modems or broadband, and their PCs are no longer able to dial out on the plain old telephone system, this kind of abuse is getting less common. The latest twist is premium-rate mobile malware: in 2006, for example, the Red Browser worm cashed out by sending $5 SMSs to Russia [633].

Premium rate scams and anonymous calling are not the only motives. Now that phones are used more and more for tasks such as voting, securing entry into apartment buildings, checking that offenders are observing their parole terms, and authenticating financial transactions, more motives are created for ever more creative kinds of mischief, and especially for hacks that defeat caller line ID. For example, caller-line ID hacks make middleperson attacks on payment systems easier; SMS spoofing and attacks on the SS7 signaling in the underlying network can have similar effects [897].

And sometimes attacks are conducted by upstanding citizens for perfectly honorable motives. A neat example, due to Udi Manber, is as follows. Suppose you have bought something which breaks, and the manufacturer's helpline only has an answering machine. To get service, you have to take the answering machine out of service. This can often be done by recording its message, and playing it back so that it appears as the customer message. With luck the machine's owner will think it's broken and it'll be sent off for maintenance.

20.2.5 Feature Interaction

More and more cases of telephone manipulation involve feature interaction.

- Inmates at the Clallam Bay Correctional Center in Washington state, who were only allowed to make collect calls, found an interesting exploit of a system which the phone company ('Fone America') introduced to handle collect calls automatically. The system would call the dialled number and a synthesised voice would say: 'If you will accept a collect call from . . . (name of caller) . . . please press the number 3 on your telephone twice'. Prisoners were supposed to state their name for the machine to record and insert. The system had, as an additional feature, the ability to have the greeting delivered in Spanish. Inmates did so, and when asked to identify themselves, said 'If you want to hear this message in English, press 33'. This worked often enough that they could get through to corporate PBXes and talk the operator into giving them an outside line. The University of Washington was hit several times by this scam [476].

- A number of directory-enquiry services will connect you to the number they've just given you, as a service to motorists who can't dial while driving. But this can often be used to defeat mechanisms that depend on endpoint identification. Adulterers use it to prevent their spouses seeing lovers' numbers on the family phone bill, and naughty children use it to call sex lines despite call barring [977].

- Call forwarding is a source of many scams. In the old days, it was used for pranks, such as kids social-engineering a phone company operator to forward calls for someone they didn't like to a sex line. Nowadays, it's quite often both professional and nasty. For example, a fraudster may tell a victim to confirm her phone number with the bank by dialing a sequence of digits — which forwards her incoming calls to a number controlled by the attacker. So the bank's callback machanisms are defeated when the customer isn't aware that a certain sequence of dialed numbers can alter the behavior of her phone.

- British Telecom launched a feature called 'Ringback'. If you dial an engaged number, you can then enter a short code and as soon as the called number is free, both your phone and theirs will ring. The resulting call is billed to you. However, when you used ringback used from a pay phone, it was the phone's owner who ended up with the bill. People with private pay phones, such as pub landlords and shopkeepers, lost a lot of money, which the phone company was eventually obliged to refund [652].

- Conference calls also cause a lot of trouble. For example, football hooligans in some countries are placed under a curfew that requires them to be at home during a match, and to prove this by calling the probation service, which verifies their number using caller ID. The trick is to get one of your kids to set up a conference call with the probation service and the mobile you've taken to the match. If the probation officer asks about the crowd noise, you tell him it's the TV and you can't turn it down or your mates will kill you. (And if he wants to call you back, you get your kids to forward the call.)

This brings us to the many problems with mobile phones.

20.3   Mobile Phones

Since their beginnings as an expensive luxury in the early 1980s, mobile phones have become one of the big technological success stories. By 2007, we now have over a billion subscribers; it's said that over a billion phones will be sold this year and the total subscriber base may rise to two billion. In developed countries, most people have at least one mobile, and many new electronic services are being built on top of them. Scandinavia has led here: you get a ferry ticket in Helsinki by sending a text message to the vending machine, and you get a can of Coke the same way. You can also scan a bar code at a bus stop with your phone camera, and get sent a text message 90 seconds before the next bus arrives; that way you don't have to stand out in the snow.

Growth is rapid in developing countries too, where the wireline network is often dilapidated and people used to wait years for phone service to be installed. In some places it's the arrival of mobile phone service that's connected villages to the world. Criminals also make heavy use of mobiles, and not just for communications: and in large tracts of the third world, mobile phone units have become a de facto currency. If you get kidnapped in Katanga, the kidnappers will tell your relatives in Kinshasa to buy mobile phone units and text them the magic numbers. In developed countries, the criminal interest is largely in communications, and most police wiretaps are now on mobile numbers.

So mobile phones are very important to the security engineer, both as part of the underlying infrastructure and as a channel for service delivery. They can also teach us a lot about fraud techniques and countermeasures.

20.3.1 Mobile Phone Cloning

The first generation of mobile phones used analog signals with no real authentication. The handset simply sent its serial numbers in clear over the air link. (In the U.S. system, there were two of them: one for the equipment, and one for the subscriber.) So villains built devices to capture these numbers from calls in the neighborhood. (I've even seen a phone that a student had reprogrammed to do this by a simple software hack.) One of the main customers was the *call-sell operation* that would steal phone service and resell it cheaply, often to immigrants or students who wanted to call home. The call-sell operators would hang out at known pitches with cloned mobiles, and their customers would queue up to phone home for a few dollars.

So a black market developed in phone serial numbers. The call-sell market was complemented by the market for anonymous communications for criminals: enterprising engineers built mobile phones which used a different identity for each call. Known as *tumblers*, these were particularly hard for the police to track [636]. The demand for serial numbers grew rapidly and satisfying it was increasingly difficult, even by snooping at places like airports where lots of mobiles were turned on. So prices rose, and as well as passive listening, active methods started to get used.

Modern mobile phones are cellular, in that the operator divides the service area up into cells, each covered by a base station. The mobile uses whichever base station has the strongest signal, and there are protocols for handing off calls from one cell to another as the customer roams. (For a survey of mobile phone technology, see [1061].) The active attack consists of a fake base station, typically at a place with a lot of passing traffic such as a freeway bridge. As phones pass by, they hear a stronger base station signal and attempt to register by sending their serial numbers.

A number of mechanisms were tried to cut the volume of fraud. Most operators developed or bought intrusion detection systems, which watch out for suspicious patterns of activity. A number of heuristics were developed. For example, genuine mobiles which roam and call home regularly, but then stop calling home, have usually been stolen; other indicators include too-rapid movement (such as calls being made from New York and LA within an hour of each other) and even just a rapid increase in call volume or duration.

In the chapter on electronic warfare, I mentioned RF fingerprinting — a formerly classified military technology in which signal characteristics that arise from manufacturing variability in the handset's radio transmitter are used to identify individual devices and tie them to the claimed serial numbers [534]. Although this technique works — it was used by Vodafone in the UK to almost eliminate cloning fraud from analogue mobiles — it is expensive as it involves modifying the base stations. (Vodafone also used an intrusion detection system that tracked customer call patterns and mobility, described in [1283]; their competitor Cellnet simply blocked international calls from analogue mobiles, which helped move its high value customers to its more modern digital network.) Another proposed solution was to adopt a cryptographic authentication protocol, but there are limits on how much can be done without changing the whole network. For example, one can use a challenge-response protocol to modify the serial number [485]. But many of the mechanisms people proposed to fortify the security of analog cellular phones have turned out to be weak [1305].

Eventually the industry decided to upgrade to a new digital system. Revenue protection was an issue, but far from the only one; digital systems offered more efficient use of bandwidth, and a whole host of new features — including easier international roaming (important in Europe with lots of small countries jammed close together), and the ability to send and receive short text messages. (Text messages were almost an afterthought; the designers didn't realise they'd be hugely popular.) From the operators' viewpoint, the move to standard digital equipment cut costs and enabled rapid, wide-scale deployment.

20.3.2   GSM Security Mechanisms

The second generation of mobile phones adopted digital technology. Most handsets worldwide use the *Global System for Mobile Communications*, or GSM, which was designed from the start to facilitate international roaming; it was founded when 15 companies signed up to the GSM Association in 1987, and service was launched in 1992. As of 2007, the GSM system extends to over two billion handsets in over 200 countries; a typical developed country has more handsets in service than it has people [133]. The USA, Japan, Korea and Israel had different second-generation digital standards (although the USA has GSM service too). Since about 2001, most countries also have a third-generation service, which I'll describe in the next section.

The designers of GSM set out to secure the system against cloning and other attacks: their goal was that GSM should be at least as secure as the wireline system. What they did, how they succeeded and where they failed, make an interesting case history.

The authentication protocols are described in a number of places, such as [232] (which also describes the mechanisms in an incompatible U.S. system). The industry initially tried to keep secret the cryptographic and other protection mechanisms which form the core of the GSM protocols. This didn't work: some eventually leaked and the rest were discovered by reverse engineering. I'll describe them briefly here.

Each network has two databases, a *home location register* (HLR) that contains the location of its own mobiles, and a *visitor location register* (VLR) for the location of mobiles which have roamed in from other networks. These databases enable incoming calls to be forwarded to the correct cell.

The handsets are commodity items. They are personalised using a *subscriber identity module* (SIM) — a smartcard you get when you sign up for a network service, and which you load into your handset. The SIM can be thought of as containing three numbers:

1. there may be a personal identification number that you use to unlock the card. In theory, this stops stolen mobiles being used. In practice, many networks set an initial PIN of 0000, and most users never change it or even use it;

2. there's an *international mobile subscriber identification* (IMSI), a unique number that maps on to your mobile phone number;

3. finally there is a *subscriber authentication key* K_i, a 128-bit number that serves to authenticate that IMSI and is known to your home network.

Unlike the banks, which used master keys to generate PINs, the phone companies decided that master keys were too dangerous. So instead of diversifying a master key KM to manufacture the authentication keys as $K_i = \{IMSI\}_{KM}$, the keys are generated randomly and kept in an authentication database attached to the HLR.

The protocol used to authenticate the handset to the network runs as follows (see Figure 20.1). On power-up, the SIM may request the customer's PIN; if this isn't configured, or once it's entered correctly, the SIM emits the IMSI, which the handset sends to the nearest base station. It's relayed to the subscriber's HLR, which generates five *triplets*. Each triplet consists of:

- RAND, a random challenge;
- SRES, a response; and
- K_c, a ciphering key.

The relationship between these values is that RAND, encrypted under the SIM's authentication key K_i, gives an output which is SRES concatenated with K_c:

$$\{RAND\}_{K_i} = (SRES|K_c)$$

The standard way to do this encryption is using a one-way function called Comp128, or A3/A8. (A3 refers to the SRES output and A8 to the K_c output). Comp128 is a hash function with 40 rounds, described in detail in [226], and like most proprietary algorithms that were designed in the shadows and fielded quietly in the 1980s and 90s, it turns out to be vulnerable to cryptanalysis. The basic design of the function is much like in Figure 5.10 — each round consists of table lookups followed by mixing. There are five tables, with 512, 256, 128, 64 and 32 byte entries each, and the hash function uses them successively in each block of five rounds; there are eight of these blocks. This may seem very complex, but once its design became public, a vulnerability was soon noticed. Four of the bytes at the output of the second round depend only on the value of the same bytes of the input. This four-byte to four-byte channel is called a *narrow pipe* and it's possible to probe it by tweaking input bytes until you detect a collision. Once all the details have been worked out, it turns out that you need about 150,000 suitably chosen challenges to extract the key [1306, 1307]. The effect is that given access to a SIM issued by a network that uses Comp128, the authentication key can be extracted in several hours using software that is now freely available.

This attack is yet another example of the dangers of using a secret crypto primitive that has been evaluated by only a few friends; the cryptanalytic techniques necessary to find the flaw were well known [1287] and if Comp128 had been open to hostile public scrutiny, the flaw would most probably have been found. Thankfully, a phone company can replace Comp128 with a proper hash function such as SHA-256 without affecting anyone else; the hash function is present only in the SIM cards it issues to its customers and the software at its HLR. In any case, there don't seem to be any industrial-scale attacks based on a vulnerable hash function; the normal user doesn't have any incentive to crack his K_i out from his SIM as it doesn't let him bill calls to (or steal calls from) anyone else.

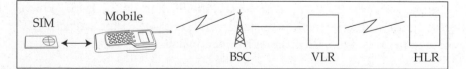

Figure 20.1: GSM authentication system components

Anyway, the triplets are sent to the base station, which now presents the first RAND to the mobile. It passes this to the SIM, which computes SRES. The mobile returns this to the base station and if it's correct the mobile and the base station can now communicate using the ciphering key K_c. So the whole authentication protocol runs as in Figure 20.2.

SIM → HLR	IMSI
HLR → BSC	$(RAND, SRES, K_c), \dots$
BSC → SIM	RAND
SIM → BSC	SRES
BSC → mobile	$\{traffic\}_{K_c}$

Figure 20.2: GSM authentication protocol

There are several vulnerabilities in this protocol. In most countries the communications between base stations and the VLR pass unencrypted on microwave links[1]. So an attacker could send out an IMSI of his choice and then intercept the triplet on the microwave link back to the local base station. A German mobile operator, which offered a reward of 100,000 Deutschmarks to anyone who could bill a call to a mobile number whose SIM card was held in their lawyer's office, backed down when asked for the IMSI [44].

Second, triples can be replayed. An unscrupulous foreign network can get five triples while you are roaming on it and then keep on reusing them to allow you to phone as much as you want. (Home networks could stop this by contract but they don't.) So the visited network doesn't have to refer back to your home network for further authorisation — and even if they do, it doesn't protect you as the visited network might not bill you for a week or more. So your home network can't reliably shut you down while you roam and it may still be liable to pay the roamed network the money. Dishonest networks also defraud roaming customers by *cramming* — by creating false billing records, a practice I'll describe in more detail later. So even if you thought you'd limited your liability by using a pre-paid SIM, you might still end up with your network trying to collect money from you. This is why, to enable roaming with a pre-paid SIM, you're normally asked for a credit card number. You can end up being billed for more than you expected.

---

[1]The equipment can encrypt traffic, but the average phone company has no incentive to switch the cryptography on. Indeed, as intelligence agencies often monitor the backhaul near major switching nodes as an efficient means of getting warrantless access to traffic, a phone company that did switch on the crypto might find that persons unknown started jamming the link to make them stop.

The introduction of GSM caused significant shifts in patterns of crime generally. The authentication mechanisms made phone cloning difficult, so the villains switched their modus operandi to buying phones using stolen credit cards, using stolen identities or bribing insiders [1352]. Robbery was another issue. We've had a spate of media stories in Britain about kids being mugged for their phones. Mobile phone crime did indeed increase 190% between 1995 and 2002, but to keep this in context, the number of subscribers went up 600% in the same period [583]. Some of the theft is bullying — kids taking smaller kids' phones; some is insurance fraud by subscribers who've dropped their phones in the toilet and report them as stolen as their insurance doesn't cover accidental damage; but there is a hard core of theft where muggers take phones and sell them to fences. Many of the fences either work at mobile phone shops that have authorised access to tools for reprogramming the International Mobile Equipment Identifier (IMEI), the serial number in the handset, or else have links to organised criminals who ship the handsets abroad. Things are worse in Brazil, where kidnapping is endemic: there are now fake kidnappings in which a child's phone is snatched by a criminal who phones its parents to demand a ransom[2].

From about 1997, prepaid mobile phones were introduced. This kicked off a period of rapid growth in the industry as the technology became available to people without credit ratings. For example, prepaids make up 90% of the market in Mexico but 15% in the USA. Worldwide, they're over half, and growing. They also made anonymous communication much more practical, and many criminals have started using them. The issues include not just evading police wiretapping but stalking, extortion, bullying and other kinds of harassment. Prepaids also facilitate simple frauds; if your identity isn't checked when you buy a phone, there's little risk to you if you recharge it with a stolen credit card [343].

It must be said though that most people who use prepaid phones for crime are only getting lightweight anonymity, and remain undetected only because the police don't put serious effort into catching petty crooks. If a really serious crime is committed, traffic analysis will be used, and most criminals don't have any clue of the level of operational discipline needed to stop this. As I already remarked, the alleged 9/11 mastermind Khalid Shaikh Mohammed was caught when he used a prepaid SIM from the same batch as one that had been used by another Al-Qaida member; and after the failed 21/7 London bombings, the would-be bomber Husein Osman fled to Rome, where he was promptly caught. He had changed the SIM in his mobile phone en route; but

---

[2]There are also completely fake kidnappings in which the bad guys just lie: they say they've snatched the child, and if they call its phone it will be killed. The perpetrators of these crimes are often in prison and have little to lose. 20% of parents still pay up rather than take the risk.

call records show not just the IMSI from the SIM, but also the IMEI from the handset. If you've got all the world's police after you, just changing the SIM isn't anything like enough. Operational security requires a detailed technical understanding of how networks operate, and levels of training and discipline that are most unusual outside national intelligence agencies.

Finally, prepaid mobiles were a gift to crooked call-sell operators. As the billing infrastructure is only invoked when a phone goes on-hook, it's possible for a bad guy to make a call last all day: the numbers called by each of his clients are simply added to a long conference call one after the other. At the end of the day, the phone goes on-hook, a bill for thousands of dollars is generated, the alarm goes off, and the crook tosses the phone in the river. The following day he buys another. That's why network operators typically tear down any call that lasts more than a few hours.

In addition to authentication, the GSM system is supposed to provide two further kinds of protection — location security and call content confidentiality.

The location security mechanism is that once a mobile is registered to a network, it is issued with a *temporary mobile subscriber identification* (TMSI), which acts as its address as it roams through the network. The attack on this mechanism uses a device called an *IMSI-catcher*, which is sold to police forces [488]. The IMSI-catcher, which is typically operated in a police car tailing a suspect, pretends to be a GSM base station. Being closer than the genuine article, its signal is stronger and the mobile tries to register with it. The IMSI catcher claims not to understand the TMSI, so the handset helpfully sends it the cleartext IMSI. This feature is needed if mobiles are to be able to roam from one network to another without the call being dropped, and to recover from failures at the VLR [1283]. The police can now get a warrant to intercept the traffic to that mobile or — if they're in a hurry — just do a middleperson attack in which they pretend to be the network to the mobile and the mobile to the network.

The GSM system is supposed to provide call content confidentiality by encrypting the traffic between the handset and the base station once the authentication and registration are completed. The speech is digitized, compressed and chopped into packets; each packet is encrypted by xor-ing it with a pseudorandom sequence generated from the ciphering key K_c and the packet number. The algorithm commonly used in Europe is A5/1.

A5/1, like Comp128, was originally secret; like Comp128, it was leaked and attacks were quickly found on it. The algorithm is shown in Figure 20.3. There are three linear feedback shift registers of lengths 19, 22 and 23 and their outputs are combined using exclusive-or to form the output keystream. The nonlinearity in this generator comes from a majority-clocking arrangement whereby the middle bits c_i of the three shift registers are compared and the two or three shift registers whose middle bits agree are clocked.

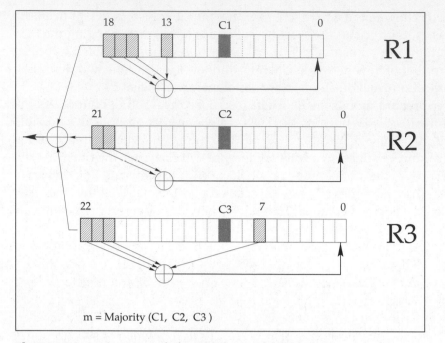

Figure 20.3: A5 (courtesy of Alex Biryukov and Adi Shamir)

The obvious attack on this arrangement is to guess the two shorter registers and then work out the value of the third. As there are 41 bits to guess, one might think that about 2^{40} computations would be needed on average. It's slightly more complex than this, as the generator loses state; many states have more than one possible precursor, so more guesses are needed. This led to an attack using a lot of FPGAs that is sold for about $1m[3]. Then Biryukov and Shamir found some optimizations and tradeoffs that let A5 be broken with much less effort. Their basic idea is to compute a large file of special points to which the state of the algorithm converges, and then look for a match with the observed traffic. Given this precomputed file, the attack can use several seconds of traffic and several minutes' work on a PC, or several minutes of traffic and several seconds' work [173]. Reverse engineering actual systems also showed that the keying of A5 was deliberately weakened. Although in theory A5 has a 64-bit key (the initial loads for the shift registers) the actual implementations set the ten least significant key bits to zero. Anyway, the response of the GSM vendors to these disclosures was to introduce a third cipher, A5/3, which is based on a strong block cipher known as Kasumi that's also used in third-generation mobile phones.

---

[3] A system of 15 boxes, each with 20 cards, each with 18 ICs, each with 32 cores, each running at 150MHz, checking one key per Hz, takes 7.5 sec per key and burns 15KW.

However, this attempt to fix the content-confidentiality problem has been undermined by an attack that exploits the underlying authentication protocol and that is now coming into widespread use by police and surveillance folks. It relies on the fact that phone companies in many countries use a weakened version of A5/1, called A5/2. Mobile phones are generally able to use either algorithm, so that they can roam freely. The attack was invented by Elad Barkan, Eli Biham and Nathan Keller [117], and runs as follows. If you're following a suspect who uses his mobile, you record the call, including the initial protocol exchange of challenge and response. Once he's finished, you switch on your IMSI-catcher and cause him to register with your bogus base station. The IMSI-catcher tells his phone to use A5/2 rather than A5/1, and a key is duly set up — with the IMSI-catcher sending the challenge that was used before. So the mobile phone generates the same key K_c as before. As this is now being used in a weak cipher, it can be cracked quickly, giving access to the target conversation recorded previously. In fact it doesn't matter whether that was protected using the medium-security A5/1 or the high-security A5/3. The facts that there's a low-security algorithm, that keys are determined by one of the two principals, and that keys are shared between algorithms, together make the whole system weak.

The A5/1 vulnerability was introduced following pressure from Europe's intelligence agencies, and the ostensible justification was that they didn't want even halfways decent security exported to potentially hostile countries, as it would be harder to spy on them. The conspiracy theorists had a field day with all this — for example, there was a political row in Australia when it turned out that A5/2 was being used there, as it was seen as implying that European governments saw Australia as an intelligence target rather than an ally.

The truth is, as always, more subtle. Weak ciphers can definitely help in some tactical situations. Consider the case I mentioned in the chapter on electronic warfare, where the New Zealand navy sent a frigate to monitor a coup in Fiji. If the Fijian phone company had been allowed to use A5/1 rather than A5/2, this would not have frustrated the mission: the sigint officers could snatch the triplets off the microwave links, hack the location register, and if all else fails, brute force a key. But being able to break traffic quickly is very convenient.

On the other hand, imposing weak cipher security on less developed countries can also have operational costs. In 2007, the Taleban started tapping mobile phone calls made by British soldiers to friends and relatives back home, whom they then called. The wife of one RAF officer was told: 'You'll never see your husband alive — we have just killed him'. It was some hours before she could confirm that he was still safe and well [603]. British troops have now been banned from using mobile phones — which doesn't exactly help morale.

In domestic or friendly-country operations, it's even more complex. The agencies can get lawful access to cleartext from phone companies, but sometimes the warrantry procedures are (or are felt to be) too cumbersome. Hence the sweetheart deals with some phone companies to get access without warrants; this has led to a number of scandals recently. For example, it emerged that AT&T had been giving the US authorities access to itemised billing data for years. Sweetheart deals were common with companies that used to be monopolies, but are becoming less common as most countries have now deregulated telecomms and have hundreds of phone companies, not just one. Some phone companies are distrusted by the authorities because they're owned by foreigners or even by gangsters. Others are tiny, have never been tapped before, the police just don't know who to talk to. Other companies are respectable and willing to comply with warrants, but unable to do so. One of Britain's most closely guarded law-enforcement and intelligence secrets for several years was that one of the mobile phone networks couldn't be conveniently tapped. Engineers tried to hook up their complex, messy systems to the intelligence community's complex, messy systems but the project went off the rails and they just could not get the thing to work. The police were really scared that crooks might find this out, and migrate en masse to that network.

How are we to make sense of this mess? It's as well to admit that there are many reasons, some honourable and some less so, why government employees may want to get access to traffic by technical means rather than by using the lawful interfaces provided for the purpose. But that doesn't mean that such access should be allowed. The huge improvements in liberty, prosperity and quality of life that the West has enjoyed since the Enlightenment and the Industrial Revolution are due in large part to our replacing the divine right of kings with freedom under the law in a democracy. We elect legislators to make the rules, and if we decide through them that the police can't torture suspects any more, then they'd better not try. Similarly, if our legislators decide that police and intelligence agencies should get warrants to wiretap, then the agencies must obey the law like anyone else. The GSM security story provides a good example of how the deliberate insertion of vulnerabilities can have wide-ranging and unforeseen engineering consequences. It must also be said that the facilities that phone companies and ISPs are now being compelled to provide for properly warranted law-enforcement access are often so poorly engineered that they can be abused [1151]. In 2004–5, persons unknown tapped the mobile phones of the Greek Prime Minister and about a hundred of that country's political, law enforcement and military elite, by subverting the wiretapping facilities built into Vodafone's Greek network. Both Vodafone, and their equipment supplier Ericsson, were heavily fined [1042]. Colleagues and I warned about this problem years ago [4] and I expect it to get worse. I'll discuss it at greater length in Part III.

There are further policy issues with location privacy. There was a storm in Switzerland in 1997 when the press found that the phone company was routinely giving location data to the police [1030], while in the USA, the FCC ordered mobile phone companies to be able to locate people 'so that 911 calls could be dispatched to the right place'. This was imposed on every user of mobile phone service, rather than letting users decide whether to buy mobile location services or not. Privacy activists were not happy with this.

Anyway, the net effect is that the initial GSM security mechanisms provided slightly better protection than the wireline network in countries allowed to use A5/1, and slightly worse protection elsewhere, until the protocol attacks were discovered and exploited. Now privacy is slightly worse everywhere, as people with the right equipment can get fairly straightforward access to traffic. But it's probably not a big deal. Relatively few people ever get followed around by an investigator with professional snooping equipment — and if you're such a person, then ways to detect and prevent semi-active attacks on your mobile phone are just a small part of the tradecraft you need to know. If you're an average subscriber, the privacy threat comes from possible abuse of data collected by the phone company, such as itemized billing data. From that viewpoint, the vulnerabilities in the communications security mechanisms neither expose you to additional wiretapping, nor prevent the frauds that are likely to cause you the most grief.

20.3.3   Third Generation Mobiles – 3gpp

The third generation of digital mobile phones was initially known as the *Universal Mobile Telecommunications System* (UMTS) and now as the *Third Generation Partnership Project* (3gpp, or just 3g). These systems are now available almost everywhere, the exception being in China which is working on its own proprietary variant. Elsewhere, the security is much the same as GSM, but upgraded to deal with a number of GSM's known vulnerabilities. Third generation systems entered service in 2003–2004; the main advantage of 3g over GSM is higher data rates; instead of the 9.6kb/s of GSM and the tens of kilobits per second of GPRS, third-generation data rates are in the hundreds of thousands to millions of bits per second. The vision is that 3g will enable all sorts of mobile services, from mobile TV to laptops that just go online anywhere.

The overall security strategy is described in [1310], and the security architecture is at [1298]. The crypto algorithms A5/1, A5/2 and Comp128 are replaced by various modes of operation of a block cipher called Kasumi [696]. Kasumi is public and is based on a design by Mitsuru Matsui called Misty, which was properly peer-reviewed and has now withstood public scrutiny for a decade [844]. All keys are now 128 bits. Cryptography is used to protect the integrity and confidentiality of both message content and signalling data, rather than just content confidentiality, and the protection at least runs from the handset to a fairly central node, rather than simply to the local base station. This means the picking up the triples, or the plaintext, from the microwave backhaul is no longer an attack. The authentication is now two-way rather than one-way, ending the vulnerability to rogue base stations; so IMSI-catchers don't work against third generation mobiles. Instead, there is a properly engineered interface for lawful interception [1299]. This can supply key material as well as plaintext, so that if the police follow a suspect, record a call and identify the mobile in the process, they can decrypt that call later, rather than being limited to the plaintext of calls recorded by the phone company after they get their warrant approved.

The protocol mechanics work as follows (see Figure 20.4). In the basic 3gpp protocol, the authentication is pushed back from the base station controller to the visitor location register. The home location register is now known as the *home environment* (HE) and the SIM as the *UMTS SIM* (USIM). The home environment chooses a random challenge RAND as before and enciphers it with the USIM authentication key K to generate a response RES, a confidentiality key CK, and integrity key IK, and an anonymity key AK.

$$\{RAND\}_K = (RES|CK|IK|AK)$$

There is also a sequence number SEQ known to the HE and the USIM. A MAC is computed on RAND and SEQ, and then the sequence number is masked by exclusive-or'ing it with the anonymity key. The challenge, the expected response, the confidentiality key, the integrity key, and the masked sequence number made up into an *authentication vector AV* which is sent from the HE to the VLR. The VLR then sends the USIM the challenge, the masked sequence number and the MAC; the USIM computes the response and the keys, unmasks the sequence number, verifies the MAC, and if it's correct returns the response to the VLR.

USIM → HE	IMSI (this can optionally be encrypted)
HE → VLR	RAND, XRES, CK, IK, $SEQ \oplus AK$, MAC
VLR → USIM	RAND, $SEQ \oplus AK$, MAC
USIM → VLR	RES

Figure 20.4: 3gpp authentication protocol

The UMTS standards set out are many other features, including details of sequence number generation, identity and location privacy mechanisms, backwards compatibility with GSM, mechanisms for public-key encryption of authentication vectors in transit from HEs to VLRs, and negotiation of various optional cryptographic mechanisms.

The net effect is that confidentiality will be improved over GSM: eavesdropping on the air link is prevented by higher-quality mechanisms, and the current attacks on the backbone network, or by bogus base stations, are excluded. Police wiretaps are done at the VLR. In a number of countries, third-generation mobiles were hard for the police to tap in the first few years, as they had to learn to operate through formal channels and also to integrate their systems with those of the network operators. In the second phase, it's proposed to have end-to-end encryption, so that the call content and some of the associated signaling will be protected from one handset to another. This led to government demands for a *key escrow protocol* — a protocol to make keys available to police and intelligence services on demand. The catch is that if a mobile phone call takes place from a British phone company's subscriber using a U.S. handset, roaming in France, to a German company's subscriber roaming in Switzerland using a Finnish handset, and the call goes via a long distance service based in Canada and using Swedish exchange equipment, then which of these countries' intelligence agencies will have access to the keys? [1299] (Traditionally, most of them would have had access to the call content one way or another.)

One solution pushed by the agencies in Britain and France is the so-called Royal Holloway protocol [663], designed largely by Vodafone, which gives access to the countries where the subscribers are based (so in this case, Britain and Germany). This is achieved by using a variant of Diffie-Hellman key exchange in which the users' private keys are obtained by encrypting their names under a super-secret master key known to the local phone company and/or intelligence agency. Although this protocol has been adopted in the British civil service and the French health service, it is at odds with the phone company security philosophy that master keys are a bad thing. The protocol is also clunky and inefficient [76].

So 3gpp won't provide a revolution in confidentiality, merely a modest improvement. As with GSM, its design goal is that security should be comparable with that of the wired network [621] and this looks like being achieved.

20.3.4   Platform Security

The final point I need to make here is that as mobile phones become more widespread and more programmable, they may suffer from the malware problems that have plagued the PC. They have followed the pattern predicted by security economics. At first, the platform vendors — the firms selling operating systems, such as Symbian, Microsoft and Linux — didn't incorporate much security, as it would have got in application developers' way and appealing to complementers is vital when building share in a new market with network externalities. Then, as one platform pulled ahead of the others, the malware writers targeted it. In 2007, viruses and worms are being detected at the rate of about 300 per annum for Symbian phones, and one or two a year for the others. Symbian has started a program of hardening their platform, with progressively more sophisticated access controls, code signing, and so on.

Mobile phone platforms have also acquired DRM mechanisms. The Open Mobile Alliance DRM version 1 supports the download of ringtones, while version 2 supports music and video download with more general mechanisms. Version 1 is widely used, but version 2 has been held up by an interesting dispute. The main OMA promoter, Nokia, would like to become the distribution channel of choice for mobile music, just as Apple has become for PCs with iTunes. However the network operators are extremely reluctant to let Nokia have a business relationship with their customers directly, and this has held up deployment.

In general, security is made more difficult by the long and complex supply chain that delivers mobile phone service to customers. IP companies like ARM own the chip designs; foundries such as Infineon make the chips; handset designers like Samsung manufacture the actual mobiles; Symbian provides the operating system; Nokia may provide some more software for a download interface; a network operator such as Vodafone provides the national infrastructure; and a local operating company then bills the customer. There has been a tendency for everyone in this chain to see security as a problem to be tossed over the fence to the companies on either side. On top of this there might be apps provided by games vendors, and corporate apps such as fleet management that are provided by third-party software houses. Add the next generation of location-based services and offerings from the likes of Google and eBay, and the whole thing becomes complex beyond belief.

One final aspect of mobile phone platforms is locking. In many countries, handsets are subsidised out of future call revenue: you get a cheap phone in return for a year's contract with a network. The downside is that your phone is locked to the network. Even some prepaid phones are locked, and carry an implicit subsidy from expected future token sales. However, in some countries, this business model isn't permitted. There has thus arisen a brisk trade in unlocking tools and services, some of which are devised by finding exploits in the phone software, and others using the kind of hardware reverse-engineering techniques I described in Chapter 16. Legal skirmishing between the phone companies and the unlocking services came to a head after Apple launched the iPhone, which had a twist on this business model: the networks for which you could buy it were those that had paid Apple the most for the privilege. This annoyed iPhone purchasers as the U.S. network of choice, AT&T, was fairly slow. The iPhone was duly hacked, and AT&T sent its lawyers after the unlockers. It also shipped a software upgrade that disabled unlocked phones.

Laws on locking and unlocking vary widely. In the USA, the Digital Millennium Copyright Act (DMCA), which prohibits interference with any technical mechanism that enforces copyright, has a specific exemption for cellphone unlocking, in order that copyright law shouldn't be abused to stifle competition in the mobile phone market. It's now being argued that this exemption covers only people who unlock their own phones, but doesn't extend to the sale of unlocking tools or services [821]. So in America, unlocking is legal if you're a customer (though the provider may brick your phone), and may be open to challenge if you do it commercially. At the other end of the scale, courts in France and Germany have held mobile phone locking to be illegal: Apple will have to offer unlocked models for sale there if it offers the product at all. Such variations in law and business practice have led to the development of a thriving grey market whereby phones are shipped from one country to another; this in turn has driven secondary markets for unlocking tools and even for assorted frauds.

20.3.5 So Was Mobile Security a Success or a Failure?

Whether mobile-phone security has been a success or a failure depends on whom you ask.

From the point of view of cryptography, it was a failure. Both the Comp128 hash function and the A5 encryption algorithm were broken once they became public. In fact, GSM is often cited as an object lesson in Kerckhoffs' Principle — that cryptographic security should reside in the choice of the key, rather than in the obscurity of the mechanism. The mechanism will leak sooner or later and it's better to subject it to public review before, rather than after, a hundred million units have been manufactured. (GSM security wasn't a disaster for most cryptographers, of course, as it provided plenty opportunities to write research papers.)

From the phone companies' point of view, GSM was a success. The shareholders of GSM operators such as Vodafone have made vast amounts of money, and a (small) part of this is due to the challenge-response mechanism in GSM stopping cloning. The crypto weaknesses were irrelevant as they were never exploited (at least not in ways that did significant harm to call revenue). There are one or two frauds that persist, such as the long conference call trick; but on balance the GSM design has been good to the phone companies.

From the criminals' point of view, GSM was also fine. It did not stop them stealing phone service: the modus operandi merely changed, with the cost falling on credit card companies or on individual victims of 'identity theft' or street robbery. It did not stop calls from anonymous phones; the rise of the prepaid phone industry made them even easier. (The phone companies were happy with both of these changes.) And of course GSM did nothing about dial-through fraud.

From the point of view of the large-country intelligence agencies, GSM was fine. They have access to local and international traffic in the clear anyway, and the weakened version of A5 facilitates tactical signint against developing countries. And the second wave of GSM equipment is bringing some juicy features, such as remote control of handsets by the operator [1061]. If you can subvert (or masquerade as) the operator, then there seems to be nothing to stop you quietly turning on a target's mobile phone without his knowledge and listening to the conversation in the room.

From the point of view of the police and low-resource intelligence agencies, things are not quite so bright. The problem isn't the added technical complexity of GSM networks: court-ordered wiretaps can be left to the phone company (although finding the number to tap can be a hassle if the suspect is mobile). The problem is the introduction of prepaid mobile phones. This not only decreases the signal to noise ratio of traffic analysis algorithms and makes it harder to target wiretaps, but also encourages crimes such as extortion and stalking.

From the customer's point of view, GSM was originally sold as being completely secure. Was this accurate? The encryption of the air link certainly did stop casual eavesdropping, which was an occasional nuisance with analog phones. (There had been some high-profile cases of celebrities being embarrassed, including one case in Britain where Prince Charles was overheard talking to his mistress Camilla Parker-Bowles before his divorce from Princess Diana, and one in the USA involving Newt Gingrich.) But almost all the phone tapping in the world is done by large intelligence agencies, to whom the encryption doesn't make much difference.

Things are even less positive for the subscriber when we look at billing. Cryptographic authentication of handsets can't stop the many frauds perpetrated by premium rate operators and phone companies. If anything it makes it harder to wriggle out of bogus charges, as the phone company can say in court that your smartcard and your PIN must have been used in the handset that made the call. The same will apply to 3rd generation phones. The one minor compensation is that GSM facilitated the spread of prepaid phones, which can limit the exposure.

So the security features designed into GSM don't help the subscriber much. They were designed to provide 'security' from the phone company's point of view: they dump much of the toll fraud risk, while not interrupting the flow of premium rate business — whether genuine or fraudulent.

In the medium term, the one ray of comfort for the poor subscriber is that the increasing complexity of both handsets and services may create regulatory pressure for transparent mechanisms that enable the customer to control the amount she's billed. There are a number of factors pushing for this, such as the growing vulnerability of platforms to malware; and a number of factors pushing in the other direction, such as the phone companies' desire to keep pricing opaque so that they can rip customers off. I mean this not just in the strict sense that phone companies often defraud their customers, but also in the colloquial sense that confusion pricing is a mainstay of phone company economics. I'll go into this in more detail in the next section, where I'll look at the economics of telecomms and how they relate to fraud and abuse.

20.3.6 VOIP

The latest development in telephone is voice over IP (VOIP), in which voice traffic is digitised, compressed and routed over the Internet. This had experimental beginnings in the 1970s; products started appearing in the 1990s; but decent call quality requires bandwidth of about 80 kbit/sec, more than can be got from a dial-up modem. As a result, VOIP only really took off once a critical mass of households had broadband connections. Since about 2005, it has become big business, with eBay purchasing Skype in 2006 for $2.6bn. In fact, most normal phone calls are digitized and sent over IP networks belonging to the phone companies, so in a technical sense almost all phone calls are 'VOIP', but in line with common usage I'll use the term only for those calls made by customers over an IP service that they access directly, via their ISP.

The VOIP market is still fragmented, and suffers many of the problems you'd expect. Most products were shipped quickly in a race to market, with security an afterthought at best. There was the usual crop of stack overflows and other vulnerabilities at the implementation level. The most popular VOIP protocol, the Session Initiation Protocol (SIP), turns out to have vulnerabilities that enable third parties to wrongly bill calls to subscribers [1375]. These could give rise to difficult disputes between VOIP services and their customers.

There are many issues with VOIP as the market shakes down. The leading system, Skype, is a closed system using proprietary protocols while its many competitors are fragmented. One business opportunity is 'click-to-call' whereby an advertisement could contain a VOIP link enabling a prospective customer to click to speak to a representative; early efforts have run up against compatibility problems. Technical problems range from differing protocols through how to deal with the jitter (time delay variation) caused by the variable quality of service on the Internet, and how to deal with network address translation at firewalls.

The interaction with security is complex. Corporate security policies can result in firewalls refusing to pass VOIP traffic. Phone calls can be more secure if made over VOIP, as encryption is easy to add and with some services (such as Skype) it comes turned on by default. For some time at least, it may be more difficult for police and intelligence services to get access to call contents and to records of who called whom; many services have not yet got round to engineering a law-enforcement interface, and in the case of Skype, its peer-to-peer nature might make that difficult. The FBI is currently pushing for the CALEA regulations to be applied rigorously to VOIP providers, while the industry and civil liberties groups are resisting. (I'll have more to say about this in Part III.) Wiretaps are not the only issue; click-to-call clearly will have other security, privacy and safety issues in the context of social networking sites, especially those used by minors.

A more high-profile regulatory issue is that governments want emergency calls made through VOIP services to work reliably, and provide information about the location of the caller. This is hard; an IP packet stream can be coming from anywhere, and no-one owns enough of the Internet to guarantee quality of service. At a deeper level than that, the dispute over dependability is just the latest tussle in the forty years' war between computer companies and phone companies, which I've alluded to from time to time. Computer companies are innovative and entrepreneurial, racing to market with products that are just about good enough; phone companies are slow-moving and heavily regulated, with a fifteen-year product cycle and services engineered for 99.999% availability. Ever since people started using modems on a large scale in the 1960s, there has been one battle after another — which the computer companies pretty well always win. A glimpse into the future may have been provided by a two-day Skype outage in August 2007, caused by poorly-engineered protocols. After a large number of computers rebooted following Microsoft's 'patch Tuesday' security update, tens of millions of Skype clients simultaneously tried to contact the network. The congestion caused the network to fail, yet the clients kept on trying. We can probably expect a lot more failures. Although a VOIP handset looks like a phone and works like a phone, it's more like email in terms of reliability. If the power goes off, so does your service.

The main problems beyond that have to do with the incompatibility of the phone companies' business model and the nature of the Internet. Phone companies make their money by charging you vastly different rates for different types of content: their typical rates work out at a hundredth of a cent per megabyte for cable TV, eight cents per megabyte for wireline phone, three dollars a megabyte for mobile phone, and a whopping three thousand dollars a megabyte for text messages. The opportunity exploited by VOIP is to arbitrage these, and it's hardly surprising that the phone companies do what they can to get in the way. ISPs who are also phone companies deliberately cause problems for VOIP to stop it competing with their phone service; this is particularly pronounced with mobile IP service. For these reasons, we'd better look at the economics of phone companies and the interaction with security.

20.4   Security Economics of Telecomms

Phone companies are classic examples of a business with extremely high fixed costs and very low marginal costs. Building a nationwide network costs billions and yet the cost of handling an additional phone call is essentially zero. As I discussed in Chapter 7 on Economics, this has a couple of implications.

First, there's a tendency towards dominant-firm markets in which the winner takes all. Indeed for many years telephone service was considered in most countries to be a 'natural monopoly' and operated by the government; the main exception was the USA where the old AT&T system was heavily regulated. After the breakup of AT&T following an antitrust case, and Margaret Thatcher's privatisation of BT, the world moved to a different model, of regulated competition. The details vary from one country to another but, in general, some sectors (such as mobile phones) had a fixed number of allowed competitors; others (such as long-distance provision) were free for companies to compete in; and others (such as local loop provision) remained de facto monopolies but were regulated.

Second, because the marginal cost of service provision is zero, the competitive sectors (such as long-distance calling) saw prices drop quickly to a very low level — in many cases below the level needed to recoup the investment. (The large investments made during the dotcom bubble end up being treated as sunk costs.)

In such a market, firms will try to maintain price discrimination by whatever means they can. In many telecomms markets, the outcome is *confusion pricing* — products are continually churned, with new offerings giving generous introductory discounts to compete with the low-cost providers, but with rates sneakily raised afterwards. The effect is to discriminate between 'people who will spend money to save time, and people who will spend time to save money'. If you can be bothered to continually check prices, you can get really good deals, but often at the cost of indifferent service. If you don't have the time to keep scrutinising your phone bills, and the latest emails you get from your ISP advising you of the latest service changes, you can find that the call home you made from your mobile while on business in France just ate up all that month's savings. In the end, you can end up paying about the same amount per month that you did in the past. Andrew Odlyzko, a scholar of phone-company economics, suggests the eventual way forward will be fixed-price contracts: for a certain amount per month you'll get a home phone, ISP service, a couple of mobiles and a decent allowance of air minutes and texts [982]. In the meantime, telecomms pricing remains murky, contentious and far from transparent. This leads directly to abuse.

20.4.1 Frauds by Phone Companies

One of the steadily growing scams is the unscrupulous phone company that bills lots of small sums to unwitting users. It collects phone numbers in various ways. (For example, if you call an 800 number, then your own number will be passed to the far end regardless of whether you tried to block caller line ID.) The wicked phone company then bills you a few dollars. Your own phone company passes on this charge and you find there's no effective way to dispute it. Sometimes the scam uses a legal loophole: if you call an 800 number in the USA, the company may say 'Can we call you right back?' and if you agree then you're deemed to have accepted the charges, which are likely to be at a high premium rate. The same can happen if you respond to voice prompts as the call progresses. These practices are known as *cramming*.

I was myself the victim on an attempt at cramming. On holiday in Barcelona, my wife's bag was snatched, so we called up and cancelled the phone that she'd had in it. Several months later, we got a demand from our mobile provider to pay a few tens of dollars roaming charges recently incurred by that SIM card in Spain. In all probability, the Spanish phone company was simply putting through a few charges to a number that they'd seen previously, in the knowledge that they'd usually get away with it. My mobile service provider initially insisted that even though I'd cancelled the number, I was still liable for calls billed to it months afterwards and had to pay up. I got out of the charges only because I'd met the company's CEO at an academic seminar and was able to get his private office to fix the problem. Customers without such access usually get the short end of the stick. Indeed, UK phone companies' response to complaints has been to offer its customers 'insurance' against fraudulent charges. That they can get away with this is a clear regulatory (and indeed policing) failure.

Another problem is *slamming* — the unauthorized change of a subscriber's long distance telephone service provider without their consent. The slammers tell your local phone company that you have opted for their service; your phone company routes your long distance calls through them; they hope you don't notice the change and dispute the bill; and the telephone charges can then be jacked up. Some local phone companies, such as Bell Atlantic, allow their customers to freeze their chosen long distance carrier [22].

It would be a mistake to assume that cramming and slamming are just done by small fly-by-night operators. AT&T is one of the worst offenders, having been fined $300,000 not only for slamming, but for actually using forged signatures of subscribers to make it look as if they had agreed to switch to their service. They got caught when they forged a signature of the deceased spouse of a subscriber in Texas [390]. As for the UK, slamming wasn't even made illegal until 2005.

Another problem is the fly-by-night phone company. As anyone in the USA is legally entitled to set up a phone company, it is straightforward to set one up, collect some cash from subscribers, and then vanish once the invoices for interconnect fees come in. Companies also advertise sex lines with normal phone numbers to trap the unwary, then send huge bills to the subscriber at his residential addresses and try to intimidate him into paying. The regulation of premium-rate providers and their business practices is a widespread problem.

And it's not just the small operators that indulge in sharp practice. An example that affects even some large phone companies is the short termination of international calls.

Although premium-rate numbers are used for a number of more or less legitimate purposes such as software support, many of them exploit minors or people with compulsive behaviour disorders. So regulators have forced phone companies in many countries to offer premium-rate number blocking to subscribers. Phone companies get round this by disguising premium rate numbers as international ones. I mentioned scams with Caribbean numbers in section 20.2.1 above. Now many other phone companies from small countries with lax regulators have got into the act, and offer sex line operators a range of numbers on which they share the revenue.

Often a call made to a small-country phone company doesn't go anywhere near its ostensible destination. One of the hacks used to do this is called *short termination*, and here's an example that surfaced a few years ago. Normally calls for the small Pacific country of Tuvalu went via Telstra in Perth, Australia, where they were forwarded by satellite. However, the sex line numbers were marked as invalid in Telstra's system, so they were automatically sent via the second-choice operator — a company in New Zealand. (The girls — or to be more precise, the elderly retired hookers who pretend to be young girls — were actually in Manchester, England.) Technically, this is an interesting case of a fallback mechanism being used as an attack vehicle. Legally, it is hard to challenge as there is an international agreement (the Nairobi Convention) that stops phone companies selectively blocking international destinations. So if you want to stop your kids phoning the sex line in Tuvalu, you have to block all international calls, which makes it harder for you to phone that important client in Germany.

Problems like these are ultimately regulatory failures, and they are increasingly common. (For example, in the Moldova scam I mentioned earlier, the calls didn't go to Moldova but to Canada [251].) They are continuing to get worse as technology makes new, complex services possible and the regulators fail to keep up.

20.4.2 Billing Mechanisms

Billing mechanisms are a growing source of problems, as the economic forces discussed above lead to ever-more-complex rate cards. Even the phone companies themselves sometimes fall foul of the growing complexity. Sometimes their rates get so complex that people can arbitrage against them; there has been more than one case in which an entrepreneur found he could set up an international premium-rate service and be paid more per minute for calling it, than it cost him to call it using the best discount rate. Phone companies have tried to recover such trading profits through the courts, claiming fraud — with mixed success.

The security of the billing mechanisms covers a much wider range of issues. Present arrangements are inadequate for a number of reasons.

■ A *call detail record* (CDR) is only generated once the calling phone goes on-hook. This was a long-established feature of wireline networks, but once the environment changed to mobile it became a serious problem. As I mentioned above, someone running a call-sell operation can set up a long conference call using a stolen or prepaid mobile, which clients join and leave one after the other. The phone stays off-hook continuously for hours. As soon as it goes on-hook, a CDR for several thousand dollars is generated, and the alarm goes off. The operator throws the phone in the river and starts using the next one. By 1996, this had become so serious that Vodafone introduced a six hour limit on all mobile calls. But it won't be acceptable to just drop all 3gpp calls after six hours. Many users are expected to have always-on internet connections (such as from their laptops) with relatively light packet traffic most of the time.

■ More seriously, the back-end accounting system was designed in the days when phone companies were sleepy government departments or national monopolies, and there were no premium-rate services through which real money could be extracted from the system. So it has little in the way of audit and non-repudiation. In effect, phone company A tells phone company B, 'please debit your customer no. X the sum of $Y and send me the money' — and it does. Even when these debits are mistaken or fraudulent, phone company B has no incentive to quibble, as it gets a cut. The result, as we saw with the cramming cases above, is that fraud slowly rises as insiders abuse the system. This is no longer fit for purpose in a world with many phone companies, quite a few of which are unscrupulous. The regulators aren't effective, and the only real backward pressure comes from the growing number of prepay customers.

■ The phone companies also want to be able to charge for relatively high-value product and service delivery, extending the current premium services through location-based services ('give me a map showing me how to drive to the nearest McDonalds') to music and video downloads and extra services such as the Finnish ferry tickets, cans of coke from vending machines, and (most recently) parking meters in London. The accounting system will have to become a lot more robust, and dispute resolution mechanisms fairer and more transparent, if this potential is to be realised.

■ All this interacts with platform security. If malware becomes widespread on mobile phones, then the botnet herders who control subverted phones will be able to pay for all sorts of goods and services by getting infected machines to send text messages. Recent history suggests that any exploits that can be industrialised to make money on a large scale, will be.

So how can phone payment systems be improved?

One proposed way of implementing this is to incorporate a micropayment mechanism [92]. The idea is that the phone will send regular *tick payments* to each of the networks or service providers which are due to be paid for the call. The tick payments can be thought of as electronic coins and are cryptographically protected against forgery. At the start of the call, the handset will compute a number of phone ticks by repeated hashing: $t_1 = h(t_0)$, $t_2 = h(t_1)$, and so on, with t_k (for some credit limit k, typically 2^{10} units) being signed by the phone company. The phone will then release ticks regularly in order to pay for the services as the call progresses. It starts by releasing t_k, then t_{k-1}, then t_{k-2} and so on. If a charge is subsequently disputed — whether by a subscriber or a network operator — the party claiming an amount of (say) j ticks must exhibit the ticks t_{k-j} and t_k, the latter with a certificate. As the hash function h is one-way, this should be hard to do unless the handset actually released that many ticks. The tick t_{k-j} can how be checked by applying the hash function to it j times and verifying that the result is t_k[4]. One advantage of tick payments is that as well as protecting the phone companies from conference call frauds, it could protect the subscriber from many more. It could enable phone application designers to empower users in new ways: for example, you might by default decide to accept calls, or play games, or do other functions, only so long as they cost less than a dollar, and require user intervention for anything more expensive. At present, that kind of functionality just isn't available, except via the rather clunky mechanism of only loading so much airtime into your phone.

The industry's proposed solution is to redesign the call data record to contain a lot more information. In addition to time, duration and called number, it will have fields for data quantity, location and quality-of-service. This is not just to support possible future differential charging for quality of service, but also to help with emergency call tracking, and to comply with a 2002 European directive on telecomms requires all mobile operators retain location information on mobile phones for at least a year, for law enforcement purposes. There was a proposal for an online cost-control mechanism to limit the charges incurred for each user [901], but this appears to have stalled. The cost-control mechanisms are not being standardized but can involve forwarding charging data from either the local network or the gateway to the home environment which will be able to have the call terminated if the available credit is exhausted (as with a prepaid SIM card) or if the use appears to be fraudulent. It's tempting to draw a parallel with NATO's failure to make IFF work properly across different countries' armed forces, which I discussed in Chapter 19. The public good (in this case, transparent and dependable cost

---

[4]This protocol is an example of multiple simultaneous discovery, having been invented by our group at Cambridge, by Pedersen, and by Rivest and Shamir, independently in 1995 [40, 1013, 1077].

control) isn't high on the agendas of the stakeholders who'd have to work together to make it happen. Indeed, it's even worse. It would be hard to find a general anywhere in North America or Europe who didn't agree that decent IFF would be a Good Thing; but many of the major stakeholders depend for their existence on confusion pricing and would see a decent charging system as a serious threat.

The extreme difficulty of engineering a global solution has left the market open to a variety of local ones. In the USA, there is a move to integrate RFID-based credit cards with NFC-compatible mobile phones. In the UK, a scheme called PayForIt was launched in 2007 by the main mobile operators that aims to replace premium SMS services with a WAP-based protocol that 'provides a uniform payment experience' and requires 'clear pricing, access to terms and conditions and merchant contact details before a purchase is confirmed'. O2, one of the big networks, required all its users to switch from June 2007. They said there would be 'reduced customer care issues'.

Personally, I am sceptical, because of the lack of bankable guarantees for the customer; the terms and conditions state that 'any queries or complaints regarding Goods and Services must be referred to the Supplier,' while firms advertising PayForIt transaction acquisition quote fixed prices and seem ready to accept all comers, respectable or otherwise. Perhaps the scheme will simply hold up the growth of phone-based payments by making them more fiddly and restricting them to more capable handsets, while not resolving the underlying trust problem. A law that enforced customer rights would be better for all. In its absence, the phone companies appear to be setting up a banking system but without the regulations and controls that long and bitter experience has shown necessary for bank stability and trustworthiness. In civilised countries, mafiosi are not allowed to run banks. But gangsters have a basic human right (in America at least) to own a phone company. So phone companies should not run banks.

20.5 Summary

Phone fraud is a fascinating case study. People have been cheating phone companies for decades, and recently the phone companies have been vigorously returning the compliment. To start off with, systems were not really protected at all, and it was easy to evade charges and redirect calls. The mechanism adopted to prevent this — out-of-band signalling — proved inadequate as the rapidly growing complexity of the system opened up many more vulnerabilities. These range from social engineering attacks on users through poor design and management of terminal equipment such as PBXes to the exploitation of various hard-to-predict feature interactions.

On the mobile front, the attempts to secure GSM and its third generation successor make an interesting case study. Their engineers concentrated on communications security threats rather than computer security threats, and they concentrated on the phone companies' interests at the expense of the customers'. Their efforts were not entirely in vain but did not give a definitive solution.

Overall, the security problems in telecomms are the result of environmental changes, including deregulation, which brought in many new phone companies. But the main change was the introduction of premium rate numbers. While previously phone companies sold a service with a negligible marginal cost of provision, suddenly real money was involved; and while previously about the only serious benefit to be had from manipulating the system was free calls, or calls that were hard for the police to tap, suddenly serious money could be earned. The existing protection mechanisms were unable to cope with this evolution. However, the major phone companies are so threatened by price competition that their business models are now predicated on confusion pricing. So the incentives for an overhaul of the billing mechanisms are just not there.

Ultimately, I suspect, the regulator will have to step in. The best solution in the USA could be the extension of Regulation E, which governs electronic banking, to phone companies — as they have become de facto banks. When you can use your mobile phone to buy ferry tickets and songs, and feed parking meters, it's performing all the functions of an electronic purse, which if issued by a traditional payment service provider such as VISA or Mastercard would fall squarely under Reg E. Also, I believe that either the FCC or the Federal Reserve should have the right to ban known criminals from owning or managing regulated phone companies. Europe is even further behind, but there is some action in the regulatory pipeline: a draft Directive that will impose a Europe-wide duty on companies to disclose security breaches in telecomms to affected customers, similar to the breach notification laws in force in over 30 U.S states in 2007. This at least will be a start.

Research Problems

Relatively little research is done outside phone company and intelligence agency labs on issues related specifically to phone fraud and wiretapping. There is growing interest in traffic analysis, which I'll discuss later; and in the likely effects of next-generation value added services, which are bound to introduce new feature interactions and other vulnerabilities. The interaction between all communications (especially mobile), platform security, and the mechanisms used to protect distributed systems security, also looks like fertile ground for both interesting research and expensive engineering errors. Society expects greater resilience and availability from the phone system than from the Internet — for example, to get through to emergency services — and as the two systems converge there will be some interesting assurance problems.

Further Reading

There are a lot of scattered articles about phone fraud, but nothing I know of that brings everything together. The underlying technologies are described in a number of reference books, such as [1061] on GSM, and more can be found on websites such as [1190]. An overview of UMTS can be found in [642], and a number of relevant research papers at [92]. To keep up with phone fraud, a useful resource is the Discount Long Distance Digest [390]. NIST has a guide on how to evaluate your PBX for vulnerabilities [943]. Finally, there's a survey of threats to mobile payment systems by the Mobile Payment Forum that gives a summary of the state of play as of 2002 [897].

CHAPTER 21

Network Attack and Defense

*Whoever thinks his problem can be solved using cryptography,
doesn't understand his problem and doesn't understand cryptography.*
— **Attributed by Roger Needham and Butler Lampson to Each Other**

*If you spend more on coffee than on IT security, then you will be hacked.
What's more, you deserve to be hacked.*
— **Richard Clarke, Former U.S. Cybersecurity Tsar**

21.1   Introduction

So far we've seen a large number of attacks against individual computers and
other devices. But attacks increasingly depend on connectivity. Consider the
following examples.

1. An office worker clicks on an attachment in email. This infects her PC
   with malware that compromises other machines in her office by snooping passwords that travel across the LAN.

2. The reason she clicked on the attachment is that the email came from her
   mother. The malware had infected her mother's machine and then sent
   out a copy of a recent email, with itself attached, to everyone in mum's
   address book.

3. Her mother in turn got infected by an old friend who chose a common
   password for his ISP account. When there are many machines on a network, the bad guys don't have to be choosy; rather than trying to guess
   the password for a particular account, they just try one password over
   and over for millions of accounts. Given a webmail account, they can
   send out bad email to the whole contact list.

4. Another attack technique that makes sense only in a network context is *Google hacking*. Here, the bad guys use search engines to find web servers that are running vulnerable applications.

5. The malware writers infect a whole lot of PCs more or less at random using a set of tricks like these. They then look for choice pickings, such as machines in companies from which large numbers of credit card numbers can be stolen, or web servers that can be used to host phishing web pages as well. These may be auctioned off to specialists to exploit. Finally they sell on the residual infected machines for under a dollar a time to a *botnet herder* — who operates a large network of compromised machines that he rents out to spammers, phishermen and extortionists.

6. One of the applications is *fast-flux*. This changes the IP address of a web site perhaps once every 20 minutes, so that it's much more difficult to take down. A different machine in the botnet acts as the host (or as a proxy to the real host) with each change of IP address, so blocking such an address has at most a temporary effect. Fast-flux hosting is used by the better phishing gangs for their bogus bank websites.

There are many attacks, and defenses, that emerge once we have large numbers of machines networked together. These depend on a number of factors, the most important of which are the protocols the network uses. A second set of factors relate to the *topology of the network*: is every machine able to contact every other machine, or does it only have direct access to a handful of others? In our example above, a virus spreads itself via a social network — from one friend to another, just like the flu virus.

I've touched on network aspects of attack and defense before, notably in the chapters on telecomms and electronic warfare. However in this chapter I'm going to try to draw together the network aspects of security in a coherent framework. First I'm going to discuss networking protocols, then malware; then defensive technologies, from filtering and intrusion detection to the widely-used crypto protocols TLS, SSH, IPsec and wireless LAN encryption. Finally I'll discuss network topology. The most immediate application of this bundle of technologies is the defence of networks of PCs against malware; however as other devices go online the lessons will apply there too. In addition, many network security techniques can be used for multiple purposes. If you invent a better firewall, then — like it or not — you've also invented a better machine for online censorship and a better police wiretap device as well. Conversely, if mobility and virtual private networks make life tough for the firewall designer, they can give the censor and the police wiretap department a hard time, too.

21.2   Vulnerabilities in Network Protocols

This book isn't an appropriate place to explain basic network protocols. The telegraphic summary is as follows. The *Internet Protocol* (IP) is a stateless protocol that transfers packet data from one machine to another; IP version 4 uses 32-bit *IP addresses*, often written as four decimal numbers in the range 0–255, such as 172.16.8.93. People have started to migrate to IP version 6, as the 4 billion possible IPv4 addresses will have been allocated sometime between 2010 and 2015; IPv6 uses 128-bit addresses. Most modern kit is ready to use IPv6 but the changeover, which companies will probably do one LAN at a time, will no doubt throw up some interesting problems. The *Domain Name System* (DNS) allows mnemonic names such as www.ross-anderson.com to be mapped to IP addresses of either kind; there's a hierarchy of DNS servers that do this, ranging from thirteen top-level servers down through machines at ISPs and on local networks, which cache DNS records for performance and reliability.

The core routing protocol of the Internet is the *Border Gateway Protocol* (BGP). The Internet consists of a large number of *Autonomous Systems* (ASs) such as ISPs, telcos and large companies, each of which controls a range of IP addresses. The routers — the specialized computers that ship packets on the Internet — use BGP to exchange information about what routes are available to get to particular blocks of IP addresses, and to maintain routing tables so they can select efficient routes.

Most Internet services use a protocol called *transmission control protocol* (TCP) that is layered on top of IP and provides virtual circuits. It does this by splitting up the data stream into IP packets and reassembling it at the far end, automatically retransmitting any packets whose receipt is not acknowledged. IP addresses are translated into the familiar Internet host addresses using the *domain name system* (DNS), a worldwide distributed service in which higher-level name servers point to local name servers for particular domains. Local networks mostly use ethernet, in which devices have unique ethernet addresses (also called MAC addresses) that are mapped to IP addresses using the *address resolution protocol* (ARP). Because of the growing shortage of IP addresses, most organisations and ISPs now use the *Dynamic Host Configuration Protocol* (DHCP) to allocate IP addresses to machines as needed and to ensure that each IP address is unique. So if you want to track down a machine that has done something wicked, you will often have to get the logs that map MAC addresses to IP addresses.

There are many other components in the protocol suite for managing communications and providing higher-level services. Most of them were developed in the good old days when the net had only trusted hosts and security wasn't a concern. So there is little authentication built in. This is a particular problem with DNS and with BGP. For example, if a small ISP mistakenly advertises to a large neighbour that it has good routes to a large part of the Internet, it may be swamped by the traffic. Here at least there are sound economic incentives, in that ISPs either swap, or pay for, routes with their peers; BGP security is in effect bodged up using manual intervention. DNS is trickier, in that disruptions are often malicious rather than mistaken. A DNS server may be fed wrong information to drive clients to a wicked website. This can be done either wholesale, by an attack on the DNS servers of a large ISP, or at the local level. For example, many homes have a wireless router attached to a broadband connection, and the router contains the address of the DNS server the customer uses. In an attack called *Drive-By Pharming*, the villain lures you to view a web page containing javascript code that sets your router's DNS server to one under his control [1213]. The effect is that next time you try to go to www.citibank.com, you may be directed to a phishing site that emulates it. For this reason it's a really good idea to change the default password on your home router.

21.2.1 Attacks on Local Networks

Suppose the attacker controls one of your PCs. Perhaps one of your employees was careless; or maybe he's gone bad, and wants to take over an account in someone else's name to defraud you, or to do some other bad thing such as downloading child porn in the hope of framing someone. There are several possibilities open to him.

1. He can install packet sniffer software to harvest passwords, get the root password, and thus take over a suitable account. Password-sniffing attacks can be blocked if you use challenge-response password generators, or a protocol such as Kerberos or ssh to ensure that clear text passwords don't go over the LAN. I described Kerberos in Chapter 3, and I'll describe SSH later.

2. Another approach is to masquerade as a machine where the target user — say the sysadmin — has already logged on. It is often possible for the attacker simply to set his MAC address and IP address to those of the target. In theory, the target machine should send 'reset' packets when it sees traffic to its IP address that's not in response to its own packets; but many machines nowadays have personal firewalls, which throw away 'suspicious' packets. As a result, the alarm doesn't get raised [300].

3. There's a whole host of technical address-hijacking attacks that work fine against old-fashioned LANs. An example I gave in the first edition of my book was that the attacker gives wrong answers to ARP messages, claiming to be the target, and may stop the target machine noticing and

raising the alarm by sending it a false subnet mask. Another possibility is to send bogus DHCP messages. Attacks like this may or may not work against a modern switched ethernet, depending on how it's configured.

4. A further set of attacks target particular platforms. For example, if the target company uses Linux or Unix servers, they are likely to use Sun's *Network File System* (NFS) for file sharing. This allows workstations to use a network disk drive as if it were a local disk, and has a number of well-known vulnerabilities to attackers on the same LAN. When a volume is first mounted, the client gets a *root filehandle* from the server. This is in effect an access ticket that refers to the root directory of the mounted filesystem, but that doesn't depend on the time, or the server generation number, and can't be revoked. There is no mechanism for per-user authentication: the server must trust a client completely or not at all. Also, NFS servers often reply to requests from a different network interface to the one on which the request arrived. So it's possible to wait until an administrator is using a file server and then masquerade as him to overwrite the password file. Filehandles can also be intercepted by network sniffing, though again, switched ethernet makes this harder. Kerberos can be used to authenticate clients and servers, but many firms don't use it; getting it to work in a heterogeneous environment can be difficult.

So the ease with which a bad machine on your network can take over other machines depends on how tightly you have the network locked down, and the damage that a bad machine can do will depend on the size of the local network. There are limits to how far a sysadmin can go; your firm might need to run a complex mixture of legacy systems for which Kerberos just can't be got to work. Also, a security-conscious system administrator can impose real costs. At our lab we argued with our sysadmins for years, trying to get access to the Internet for visiting guests, while they resisted on both technical protection and policy grounds (our academic network shouldn't be made available to commercial users). In the end, we solved the problem by setting up a separate guest network that is connected to a commercial ISP rather than to the University's backbone.

This raises a wider problem: where's the network boundary? In the old days, many companies had a single internal network, connected to the Internet via a firewall of some kind. But compartmentation often makes sense, as I discussed in Chapter 9: separate networks for each department can limit the damage that a compromised machine can do. There may be particularly strong arguments for this if some of your departments may have high protection requirements, while others need great flexibility. In our university, for example, we don't want the students on the same LAN that the payroll folks use; in fact we separate student, staff and administrative networks, and the first two of these are also separated by college and department. Recently, mobility and virtual networks have made definition of clear network boundaries even harder. This debate goes by the buzz-word of *deperimiterisation* and I'll return to it later.

One final attack is worth mentioning under the heading of attacks on local networks, and that's the *rogue access point*. Occasionally one finds WiFi access points in public areas, such as airports, that have been deployed maliciously. The operator might sit in the airport lounge with a laptop that accesses the Internet via a paid WiFi service and advertises a free one; if you use it, he'll be able to sniff any plaintext passwords you enter, for example to your webmail or Amazon account, and if you tried to do online banking he might conceivably send you to a malicious site. So the effects can be somewhat like drive-by pharming, although more reliable and less scalable. In addition, rogue access points may also be devices that employees have installed for their own convenience in defiance of corporate policy, or even official nodes that have been misconfigured so that they don't encrypt the traffic. Whether unencrypted WiFi traffic is a big deal will depend on the circumstances; I'll discuss this in more detail later when we come to encryption.

21.2.2 Attacks Using Internet Protocols and Mechanisms

Moving up now to the Internet protocol suite, the basic problem is similar: there is no real authenticity protection in the default mechanisms. This is particularly manifest at the lower level TCP/IP protocols, and has given rise to many attacks.

Consider for example the 3-way handshake used by Alice to initiate a TCP connection to Bob and set up sequence numbers.

This protocol can be exploited in a surprising number of different ways. Now that service denial is becoming really important, let's start off with the simplest service denial attack: the *SYN flood*.

21.2.2.1 SYN Flooding

The attack is quite simply to send a large number of SYN packets and never acknowledge any of the replies. This leads the recipient (Bob, in Figure 21.1) to accumulate more records of SYN packets than his software can handle. This attack had been known to be theoretically possible since the 1980s but came to public attention when it was used to bring down Panix, a New York ISP, for several days in 1996.

A technical fix has been incorporated in Linux and some other systems. This is the so-called 'SYNcookie'. Rather than keeping a copy of the incoming SYN packet, B simply sends out as Y an encrypted version of X. That way, it's

A → B: SYN; my number is X
B → A: ACK; now X+1
        SYN; my number is Y
A → B: ACK; now Y+1
        (start talking)

Figure 21.1: TCP/IP handshake

not necessary to retain state about sessions which are half-open. Despite this, SYN floods are still a big deal, accounting for the largest number of reported attacks (27%) in 2006, although they were only the third-largest in terms of traffic volume (18%, behind UDP floods and application-layer attacks) [86].

There is an important general principle here: when you're designing a protocol that anyone can invoke, don't make it easy for malicious users to make honest ones consume resources. Don't let anyone in the world force your software to allocate memory, or do a lot of computation. In the online world, that's just asking for trouble.

21.2.2.2 Smurfing

A common way of bringing down a host in the 90s was *smurfing*. This exploited the *Internet control message protocol* (ICMP), which enables users to send an echo packet to a remote host to check whether it's alive. The problem was with broadcast addresses that are shared by a number of hosts. Some implementations of the Internet protocols responded to pings to both the broadcast address as well as the local address — so you could test a LAN to see what was alive. A collection of such hosts at a broadcast address is called a *smurf amplifier*. Bad guys would construct a packet with the source address forged to be that of the victim, and send it to a number of smurf amplifiers. These would then send a flurry of packets to the target, which could swamp it. Smurfing was typically used by kids to take over an *Internet relay chat* (IRC) server, so they could assume control of the chatroom. For a while this was a big deal, and the protocol standards were changed in August 1999 so that ping packets sent to a broadcast address are no longer answered [1144]. Another part of the fix was socio-economic: vigilante sites produced lists of smurf amplifiers. Diligent administrators spotted their networks on there and fixed them; the lazy ones then found that the bad guys used more and more of their bandwidth, and thus got pressured into fixing the problem too. By now (2007), smurfing is more or less fixed; it's no longer an attack that many people use.

But there's a useful moral: *don't create amplifiers*. When you design a network protocol, be extremely careful to ensure that no-one who puts one packet in can get two packets out. It's also important to avoid feedback and loops. A classic example was *source routing*. A feature of early IP that enabled the sender of a packet to specify not just its destination but the route that it should take. This made attacks too easy: you'd just send a packet from A to B to C to B to C and so on, before going to its final destination. Most ISPs now throw away all packets with source routing set. (There was an alarm in early 2007 when it turned out that source routing had found its way back into the specification for IPv6, but that's now been fixed [417].)

21.2.2.3 *Distributed Denial of Service Attacks*

As the clever ways of creating service-denial attacks have been closed off one by one, the bad guys have turned increasingly to brute force, for example by sending floods of UDP packets from infected machines. The *distributed denial of service* (DDoS) attack made its appearance in October 1999 with the attack already mentioned on a New York ISP, Panix. In DDoS, the attacker subverts a large number of machines over a period of time and, on a given signal, these machines all start to bombard the target with traffic [391]. Curiously, most of the machines in the first botnets around 1999–2000 were U.S. medical sites. The FDA insisted that medical Unix machines which were certified for certain clinical uses have a known configuration. Once bugs were found in this, there was a guaranteed supply of vulnerable machines; an object lesson in the dangers of monoculture.

Nowadays, botnets are assembled using all sorts of vulnerabilities, and a market has arisen whereby people who specialise in hacking machines can sell their product to people who specialise in herding them and extracting value. Compromised machines typically pass down a kind of value chain; they are first used for targeted attacks, then for sending spam, then (once they get known to spam filters) for applications like fast flux, and then finally (once they're on all the blacklists) for DDoS.

DDoS attacks have been launched at a number of high-profile web sites, including Amazon and Yahoo, but nowadays the major sites have so much bandwidth that they're very hard to dent. The next development was extortionists taking out online horserace-betting sites just before popular race meetings that would have generated a lot of business, and demanding ransoms not to do it again. Some bookmakers moved their operations to high-bandwidth hosting services such as Akamai that are highly distributed and can cope with large packet volumes, and others to specialist ISPs with packet-washing equipment that filters out bad packets at high speed. However the real fix for extortion wasn't technical. First, the bookmakers got together, compared notes, and resolved that in future none of them would pay any ransom. Second, the Russian government was leant on to deal with the main gang; three men were arrested in 2004 and sent to prison for eight years in 2006 [791].

For a while, there was a technical arms race. Attackers started to spoof source IP addresses, and to reflecting packets off innocuous hosts [1011]. One countermeasure was traceback: the idea was that whenever a router forwards a packet, it would also send an ICMP packet to the destination, with a probability of about 1 in 20,000, containing details of the previous hop, the next hop, and as much of the packet as will fit. Large-scale flooding attacks could thus be traced back to the responsible machines, even despite forged source IP addresses [154]. However, this arms race has largely fizzled out, and for a number of reasons. First, Microsoft changed their network stack to make it much harder for an infected machine to send a packet with a spoofed IP address; you now need to hack the operating system, not just any old application. Second, more and more equipment at the edges of the network won't accept spoofed packets, and now about half of broadband ISPs filter them out [86].

However, the main reasons for the arms race stopping had to do with economics. Tracing back packets didn't work across different autonomous systems; if you were a large telco, for example, you would not give network access to your competitors' technical staff. So the bad guys found that in practice nobody came after them, and stopped using spoofing. Also, once markets emerged round about 2004 for botnet machines to be bought and sold (along with credit card numbers, spam contracts and other criminal services), the price of compromised machines fell so low, and botnets started to become so large, that the whole game changed. Instead of using a handful of compromised machines to send out clever attacks via amplifiers using spoofed source addresses, the bad guys simply burn thousands of end-of-life botnet machines to send the bad packets directly. The rapier has been replaced with the Kalashnikov.

Most recently, in 2005–7, there have been attempts to target core services such as DNS and thus take down the whole Internet. DNS has now been expanded to thirteen servers (the maximum the protocol will support), and many of them use *anycast* — a protocol whereby when you ask to resolve the domain name of a host into an IP address, the result that you get depends on where you are. The net effect is that DNS has become a massively distributed system using a lot of very fast machines connected to very high-capacity networks. In the end, the brute force of the modern DDoS attack was simply answered by even more brute force. If a hundred peasants with Kalashnikovs are going to shoot at you, you'd better buy a tank with good enough armor to absorb the fire.

Large-scale DDoS attacks on critical services seem quiescent at present. There are a few residual worries, though.

- There's a rising tide of DDoS attacks that happen by accident rather than as a result of malice. For example, in 2003 the University of Wisconsin-Madison found itself receiving hundreds of thousands of packets per second requesting the time. It turned out that Netgear had sold some 700,000 routers that were hard-coded to ask their time server what time it was, and to ask again a second later if no response was received. Netgear ended up paying the university to maintain a high-bandwidth time server for them. There have been dozens of similar incidents [303].

■ There's a steady stream of DDoS attacks by spammers and phishermen on the websites of organisations that try to hinder their activities, such as Artists Against 419 and Spamhaus.

■ There are continuing worries that DDoS attacks might come back on an even larger scale. As of September 2007, there are several botnets with over half a million machines [742]. The operators of such networks can send out packet floods that will disable all but the biggest sites. These worries have been amplified in some quarters by the 2007 attacks on Estonia (even although that attack would not have harmed a large commercial target like Microsoft or Google). The highest attack rate seen in 2006 was 24 Gbit/sec, compared with 10 Gbit/sec in 2004 and 1.2 Gbit/sec in 2002 [86]. A further order-of-magnitude increase could put all but the most distributed targets at risk.

■ Even if we never see the Internet taken down by a monster botnet, attacks can still be carried out on smaller targets. Prior to the Estonia incident, there had been a DDoS attack on the servers of an opposition party in Kyrgyzstan, and these followed the site when it was relocated to North America [1081]. Certainly, DDoS puts a weapon in the hands of gangsters that can be rented out to various unsavoury people.

■ That said, one mustn't forget online activism. If a hundred thousand people send email to the White House protesting against some policy or other, is this a DDoS attack? Protesters should not be treated as felons; but drawing legislative distinctions can be hard.

21.2.2.4 *Spam*

Spam is in some respects similar to a DDoS attack: floods of generally unwanted traffic sent out for the most part by botnets, and often with clear criminal intent. The technical aspects are related, in that both email and the web protocols (smtp and http) assume wrongly that the lower levels are secure. Just as DDoS bots may forge IP addresses, spam bots may forge the sender's email address.

Spam differs in a various ways, though, from packet-level DDoS. First, it's enough of an annoyance and a cost for there to be real pressure on ISPs to send less of it. If you're a medium-sized ISP you will typically peer with other ISPs as much as you can, and buy routes from large telcos only where you can't trade for them; if other ISPs see you as a source of spam they may drop your peering arrangements, which costs real money. As a result, some ISPs are starting to do *egress filtering*: they monitor spam coming out of their own networks and then quarantine the infected PCs into a 'walled garden' from which they have access to antivirus software but little else [300].

Second, unlike DDoS, spam does not seem to be tailing off. It does appear that spammers are consolidating, in that most spam comes from several dozen large gangs. This is apparent from the 'lumpiness' of spam statistics: if there were hundreds of thousands of mom-and-pop spam operations, you'd expect to see spam volumes pretty constant, but this is no longer what we see [305]. So rather than spending more money on spam filters, it might be cheaper to get the police to arrest the gangs. Trends do change over time, though. Between 2006 and 2007, we've seen a drop in *backscatter* — in messages sent to the people whose email addresses were forged by spammers. Quite a lot of this came from anti-virus products, and it was pointed that the vendors were often breaking the antispam laws by sending messages saying 'Product X found worm Y in the message you sent'. If worm Y was known to use address forgery, the only conceivable purpose of sending such a message to the party who hadn't sent the offending message was to advertise product X. At the same time, there's been a huge increase in mule recruitment spam.

21.2.2.5   DNS Security and Pharming

I've given two examples so far of attacks in which a user is duped by being directed to a malicious DNS server, with the result that when he tries to go to his bank website he ends up entering his password into a fake one instead. This is generally referred to as *pharming*. I mentioned drive-by pharming, in which people's home routers are reconfigured by malicious javascript in web pages they download, and rogue access points in which the attacker offers a WiFi service to the victim and then has complete control over all his unprotected traffic.

There are a number of other variants on this theme, including feeding false DNS records to genuine servers. Older DNS servers would accept additional records without checking; if they asked your server where X was, you could volunteer an IP address for Y as well. This has been fixed but there are still older servers in use that are vulnerable. Such attacks are often referred to as *DNS cache poisoning* as they basically affect users who trust the information about the target that's cached by the attacked machine. They've been used not just for pharming but also for simple vandalism, such as replacing the web site of a target company with something offensive. They can also be used for censorship; China has used DNS spoofing against dissident websites for years, and by 2007 was also using it to make Voice of America news unavailable [1297].

A number of researchers have worked on a proposed upgrade to the security of DNS, but they have turned out to be hard to deploy for economic reasons; most of the things that secure DNS would do can be done by TLS without the need for new infrastructure, and individual network operators don't get enough benefit from DNS security until enough other operators have adopted them first [997].

21.3 Trojans, Viruses, Worms and Rootkits

Computer security experts have long been aware of the threat from malicious code. The first such programs were *Trojan Horses*, named after the horse the Greeks left supposedly as a gift for the Trojans but which contained soldiers who opened the gates of Troy to the Greek army. The use of the term for malicious code goes back many years (see the discussion in [774] p 7). There are also *viruses* and *worms*, which are self-propagating malicious programs, and to which I've referred in earlier chapters. There is debate about their precise definitions; the common usage is that a Trojan is a program that does something malicious (such as capturing passwords) when run by an unsuspecting user, while a worm is something that replicates and a virus is a worm which replicates by attaching itself to other programs.

Finally, the most rapidly-growing problem is the *rootkit* — a piece of software that once installed on a machine surreptitiously places it under remote control. Rootkits can be used for targeted attacks (law enforcement agencies use them to turn suspects' laptops into listening devices) or for financial fraud (they may come with keyloggers that capture passwords). One of the most salient features of rootkits nowadays is stealth; they try to hide from the operating system so that they can't be located and removed using standard tools. But sooner or later rootkits are identified and tools to remove them are written. On the other side of the coin, most PCs infected in this way end up in botnets, so another way of framing the problem is how botnets are set up, maintained and used. The rootkit vendors now do after-sales-service, supplying their customers the botnet herders with the tools to upgrade rootkits for which removal tools are becoming available.

21.3.1 Early History of Malicious Code

Malicious code, or *malware*, seems likely to appear whenever a large enough number of users share a computing platform. It goes back at least to the early 1960's, when machines were slow and their CPU cycles were carefully rationed between different groups of users — with students often at the tail of the queue. Students invented tricks such as writing computer games with a Trojan inside to check if the program is running as root, and if so to create an extra privileged account with a known password. By the 1970s, large time-sharing systems at universities were the target of more and more pranks involving Trojans. All sorts of tricks were developed. In 1978, John Shoch and Jon Hupp of Xerox PARC wrote a program they called a *worm*, which replicated itself across a network looking for idle processors so it could assign them tasks. They discussed this in a paper in 1982 [1164].

In 1984, Ken Thompson wrote a classic paper 'On Trusting Trust', in which he showed that even if the source code for a system were carefully inspected and known to be free of vulnerabilities, a trapdoor could still be inserted [1247]. Thompson's trick was to build the trapdoor into the compiler. If this recognized that it was compiling the login program, it would insert a trapdoor such as a master password that would work on any account. (This developed an idea first floated by Paul Karger and Robert Schell during the Multics evaluation in 1974 [693].) Of course, someone might try to stop this by examining the source code for the compiler, and then compiling it again from scratch. So the next step is to see to it that, if the compiler recognizes that it's compiling itself, it inserts the vulnerability even if it's not present in the source. So even if you can buy a system with verifiably secure software for the operating system, applications and tools, the compiler binary can still contain a Trojan. The moral is that vulnerabilities can be inserted at any point in the tool chain, so you can't trust a system you didn't build completely yourself.

1984 was also the year when computer viruses appeared in public following the thesis work of Fred Cohen. He performed a series of experiments with different operating systems in which he showed how code could propagate itself from one machine to another, and (as I mentioned in Chapter 8) from one compartment of a multilevel system to another. This caused alarm and consternation, and within about three years we started to see the first real live viruses in the wild[1]. Almost all of them were PC viruses as DOS was the predominant operating system. They spread from one user to another when users shared programs on diskettes or via bulletin boards.

One early innovation was the 'Christma' virus, which spread round IBM mainframes in December 1987. It was a program written in the mainframe command language REXX that had a header saying 'Don't read me, EXEC me' and code that, if executed, drew a Christmas tree on the screen — then sent itself to everyone in the user's contacts file. It was written as a prank, rather than out of malice; and by using the network (IBM's BITNET) to spread, it was ahead of its time.

The next year came the Internet worm, which alerted the press and the general public to the problem.

21.3.2   The Internet Worm

The first famous case of a service denial-attack was the Internet worm of November 1988 [421]. This was a program written by Robert Morris Jr that exploited a number of vulnerabilities to spread from one machine to another. Some of these were general (e.g. 432 common passwords were used in a guessing attack, and opportunistic use was made of .rhosts files), and others

---

[1]That's when I first came across them, as a security guy working in a bank; we now learn that the first ever computer virus in the wild was written for the Apple II by a 9th-grader in 1981 [1101].

were system specific (problems with sendmail, and the fingerd bug mentioned in section 4.4.1). The worm took steps to camouflage itself; it was called sh and it encrypted its data strings (albeit with a Caesar cipher).

Its author claimed that this code was not a deliberate attack on the Internet — merely an experiment to see whether code could replicate from one machine to another. It was successful. It also had a bug. It should have recognised already infected machines, and not infected them again, but this feature didn't work. The result was a huge volume of communications traffic that completely clogged up the Internet.

Given that the Internet (or more accurately, its predecessor the Arpanet) had been designed to provide a very high degree of resilience against attacks — up to and including a strategic nuclear strike — it was remarkable that a program written by a student could disable it completely.

What's less often remarked on is that the mess was cleaned up and normal service restored within a day or two; that it only affected Berkeley Unix and its derivatives (which may say something about the dangers of the Microsoft monoculture today); and that sites that kept their nerve and didn't pull their network connection recovered more quickly as they could find out what was happening and get the fixes.

21.3.3 How Viruses and Worms Work

A virus or worm typically has two components — a replication mechanism and a payload. A worm simply makes a copy of itself somewhere else when it's run, perhaps by breaking into another system (as the Internet worm did) or mailing itself as an attachment to the addresses on the infected system's address list (as many recent worms have done). In the days of DOS viruses, the commonest way for a virus to replicate was to append itself to an executable file and patch itself in, so that the execution path jumps to the virus code and then back to the original program.

Given a specific platform, there are usually additional tricks available to the virus writer. For example, if the target system was a DOS PC with a file called ACCOUNTS.EXE, one could introduce a file called ACCOUNTS.COM, which DOS will execute in preference. DOS viruses could also attack the boot sector or the partition table, and there are even printable viruses — viruses all of whose opcodes are printable ASCII characters, so that they can even propagate on paper. A number of DOS viruses are examined in detail in [817].

The second component of a virus is the payload. This will usually be activated by a trigger, such as a date, and may then do one or more of a number of bad things:

■ make selective or random changes to the machine's protection state (this is what we worried about with multilevel secure systems);

- make changes to user data (some early viruses would trash your hard disk while some recent ones encrypt your disk and ask you to pay a ransom for the decryption key);

- lock the network (e.g., start replicating at maximum speed);

- perform some nefarious task (e.g. use the CPU for DES keysearch);

- get your modem to phone a premium-rate number in order to transfer money from you to a telephone scamster;

- install spyware or adware in your machine. This might just tell marketers what you do online — but it might steal your bank passwords and extract money from your account;

- install a *rootkit* — software that hides in your machine having taken it over. This is typically used to recruit your machine into a botnet, so that it can be used later for spam, phishing and distributed denial of service attacks at the botnet herder's pleasure.

The history of malware, and of countermeasures, has some interesting twists and turns.

21.3.4   The History of Malware

By the late 1980s and early 1990s, PC viruses had become such a problem that they gave rise to a whole industry of anti-virus software writers and consultants. Many people thought that this couldn't last, and that the move from DOS to 'proper' operating systems such as Windows would solve the problem. Some of the anti-virus pioneers even sold their companies; one of them tells his story in [1198].

However, the move to 32-bit operating systems gave only temporary respite. Soon, the spread of interpreted languages provided fertile soil for mischief. Bad Java applets flourished in the late 1990s as people found ways of penetrating Java implementations in browsers [859]. By the start of the 21st century, the main vector was the macro languages in products such as Word, and the main transmission mechanism had become the Internet [95, 209]; by 2000, macro viruses accounted for almost all incidents of mobile malicious code. Indeed, an insider says that the net 'saved' the antivirus industry [669]. A more cynical view is that the industry was never really under threat, as people will always want to share code and data, and in the absence of trustworthy computing platforms one can expect malware to exploit whichever sharing mechanisms they use. Another view is that Microsoft is responsible as they were reckless in incorporating such powerful scripting capabilities in all sorts of products. As they say, your mileage may vary.

In passing, it's worth noting that malicious data can also be a problem. An interesting example is related by David Mazières and Frans Kaashoek who operated an anonymous remailer at MIT. This device decrypted incoming messages from anywhere on the net, uncompressed them and acted on them. Someone sent them a series of 25 Mbyte messages consisting of a single line of text repeated over and over; these compressed very well and so were only small ciphertexts when input, but when uncompressed they quickly filled up the spool file and crashed the system [849]. There are similar attacks on other programs that do decompression such as MPEG decoders. However, the most egregious cases involve not malicious data but malicious code.

Anyway, the next phase of malware evolution may have been the 'Love Bug' virus in 2000. This was actually a self-propagating worm; it propagated by sending itself to everyone in the victim's address book, and the subject line 'I love you' was calculated to get people to open it. In theory, companies can defend themselves against such things by filtering out Microsoft executables; in practice, life isn't so simple. A large Canadian company with 85,000 staff did just this, but many of their staff had personal accounts at web-based email services, and so the Love Bug virus got into the company without going through the mail filter at the firewall. The company had configured its employees' mail clients so that each of them had the entire corporate directory in her personal address book. The result was meltdown as 85,000 mail clients each tried to send an email to each of 85,000 addresses. The Love Bug was followed by a number of similar worms, which persuaded people to click on them by offering pictures of celebs such as Anna Kournikova, Britney Spears and Paris Hilton. There were also 'flash worms' that propagated by scanning the whole Internet for machines that were vulnerable to some exploit or other, and taking them over; worms of this type, such as Code Red and Slammer, infected all vulnerable machines within hours or even minutes, and caused some alarm about what sort of defences might possibly react in time [1220].

At about the same time, in the early 2000s, we saw a significant rise in the amount of *spyware* and *adware*. Spyware is technology that collects and forwards information about computer use without the owner's authorization, or with at best a a popup box that asks users to agree to perform some obscure function, so that even those who don't just reflexively click it away will not really know what they're agreeing to. This doesn't pass muster as 'consent' under European data-protection and unfair-contracts laws, but enforcement is weak. Adware may bombard the user with advertising popups and can be bundled with spyware. The vendors of this tiresome crud have even sued antivirus companies who blacklisted their wares. This all complicates everything.

A large change came about in 2004 or so. Until then, we saw a huge range of different viruses and payloads. Most virus writers did so for fun, for bragging rights, to impress their girlfriends — basically, they were amateurs. Since then, the emergence of an organised criminal economy in information goods has made the whole business much more professional. The goal of the malware writers is to recruit machines that can be sold on for cash to botnet herders and for other exploits.

Most viruses in the 1980s and 1990s were very flaky; although tens of thousands of different viruses were reported, very few actually spread in the wild. It's actually rather difficult to write a virus that spreads properly; if it's not infectious enough it won't spread, while if you make it too infectious then it gets noticed quickly and dealt with. However, those viruses that did spread often spread very widely and infected millions of machines.

A widespread self-replicating worm may bring a huge ego boost to a teenage programmer, but for the Mafia it's not optimal. Such a worm becomes headline news and within a few hours the world's anti-virus vendors are upgrading their products to detect and remove it. Even the mass media get in on the act, telling the public not to click on any link in such-and-such an email. Now that the writers are focussed on money rather than bragging rights, they release more attacks but limited ones. Furthermore, rather than using self-replicating worms — which attract attention by clogging up the Internet — the modern trend is towards manually-controlled exploit campaigns.

In September 2007 the largest botnet was perhaps the Storm network, with around a million machines. Its herders are constantly recruiting more machines to it, using one theme after another. For example, following the start of the National Football League season on September 6th, they sent out spam on September 9th saying simply 'Football ... Need we say more? Know all the games, what time, what channel and all the stats. Never be in the dark again with this online game tracker', following by a link to a URL from which the gullible download a file called tracker.exe that installs a rootkit in their machine. Using techniques like this — essentially, professional online marketing — they constantly grow their network. And although the media refer to Storm as a 'worm', it isn't really: it's a Trojan and a rootkit. Victims have to click away several warnings before they install it; Windows warns them that it isn't signed and asks them if they really want to install it. However, Windows pops up so many annoying dialog boxes that most people are well trained to click them away. In the case of Storm, it was targeted by Microsoft's malicious software removal tool on September 11th, and Redmond reported that over a quarter of a million machines had been cleaned; they also estimated that Storm had half a million active machines, with perhaps a few hundred thousand that were not being actively used. The network — the most powerful supercomputer on the planet — earned its living by being rented out to pump-and-dump operators and pharmacy scammers [742]. Two other networks were also identified as having over half a million bots; Gozi and Nugache use the same peer-to-peer architecture as Storm, and by the end of 2007 these networks were getting increasingly sophisticated and exploring new criminal business models [1134].

So the malware business now operates on an industrial scale, with the top botnet herders controlling roughly the same number of machines as Google. Big business has been built on the fact that users have been trained to click on stuff. As malware goes industrial, Trojans are becoming more common than viruses; when the latter email themselves out from an infected machine, they draw attention to themselves and the machine's more likely to get cleaned up, while with Trojans the botnet herder sends the infectious traffic directly, which also gives him better control [1239]. And once you install something, there's no telling whether it's a rootkit, or malicious spyware that will use a keystroke logger to steal your banking passwords, or a 'normal' piece of spyware that will simply collect your personal data for sale to the highest bidder. Truth to tell, the categories are hard to separate cleanly.

21.3.5 Countermeasures

Within a few months of the first PC viruses appearing in the wild in 1987, companies had set up to sell antivirus software. This led to an arms race in which each tried to outwit the other. Early software came in basically two flavours — *scanners* and *checksummers*.

Scanners are programs that search executable files for a string of bytes known to be from an identified virus. Virus writers responded in various ways, such as specific counterattacks on popular antivirus programs; the most general technique is *polymorphism*. The idea here is to change the code each time the virus or worm replicates, to make it harder to write effective scanners. The usual technique is to encrypt the code using a simple cipher, and have a small header that contains decryption code. With each replication, the virus re-encrypts itself under a different key, and tweaks the decryption code by substituting equivalent sequences of instructions.

Checksummers keep a list of all the authorised executables on the system, together with checksums of the original versions, typically computed using a hash function. The main countermeasure is *stealth*, which in this context means that the virus watches out for operating system calls of the kind used by the checksummer and hides itself whenever a check is being done.

Researchers have also looked into the theory of malware replication. In order for a virus infestation to be self-sustaining, it needs to pass an *epidemic threshold* — at which its rate of replication exceeds the rate at which it's removed [711]. This depends not just on the infectivity of the virus itself but on the number (and proportion) of connected machines that are vulnerable. Epidemic models from medicine go over to some extent, though they are limited by the different topology of software intercourse (sharing of software is highly localised) and so predict higher infection rates than are actually observed. (I'll return to topology later.) People have also tried to use immune-system models to develop distributed strategies for malware detection [482].

One medical lesson which does seem to apply is that the most effective organisational countermeasure is centralised reporting and response using selective vaccination [712].

In the practical world, antivirus software and managerial discipline are to a certain extent substitutes, but to be really effective, you have to combine tools, incentives and management. In the old days of DOS-based file viruses, this came down to providing a central reporting point for all incidents, and controlling all software loaded on the organisation's machines. The main risks were files coming in via PCs used at home both for work and for other things (such as kids playing games), and files coming in from other organisations. But how do you get staff to sweep all incoming email and diskettes for viruses? One effective strategy, adopted at a London law firm, was to reward whoever found a virus with a box of chocolates — which would then be invoiced to the company that had sent the infected file.

Now that malware arrives mostly in email attachments or in web pages, things are often more technical, with automatic screening and central reporting. A company may filter executables out at the firewall, and see to it that users have prudent default settings on their systems — such as disabling active content on browsers and macros in word processing documents. Of course, this creates a clash with usability. People will also create all sorts of unauthorized communications channels, so you have to assume that screening can't be perfect; staff must still be trained not to open suspicious email attachments, and in recovery procedures so they can deal with infected backups. In short, the issues are more complex and diffuse. But as with the organic kind of disease, prevention is better than cure; and software hygiene can be integrated with controls on illegal software copying and unauthorised private use of equipment.

Recently, antivirus software seems to be getting steadily less effective. The commercialisation of botnets and of machine exploitation has meant that malware writers have decent tools and training. Almost all Trojans and other exploits are undetectable by the current antivirus products when first launched — as their writers test them properly — and many of them run their course (by recruiting their target number of machines) without coming to the attention of the antivirus industry. The net effect is that while antivirus software might have detected almost all of the exploits in circulation in the early 2000s, by 2007 the typical product might detect only a third of them.

And as for the rootkits that the exploits leave behind, they are also much better written than a few years ago, and rarely cause trouble for the owner of the machine on which they're installed. Some rootkits even install up-to-date antivirus software to stop any competing botnet from taking the machine over. They also use all sorts of stealth techniques to hide from detectors. What's more, the specialists who sell the rootkits provide after-sales service; if a removal kit is shipped, the rootkit vendor will rapidly ship countermeasures.

It's not at all clear that technical defences are keeping up with malware. On the global scale, police action against the large gangs is needed, and although it's starting to ramp up, there's a long way to go. Well-run firms can use managerial discipline to contain the threat, but for private users of Windows machines, the outlook isn't particularly rosy. One survey suggested that 8% of sales of new PCs are to people who've simply given up on machines that have become so infested with adware and other crud as to become unusable [325]; and there is a growing threat from *keyloggers* that capture everything the user does at his machine. Some of these are simply spyware that sells information to marketers; others look out for bank passwords and other key data that can be used to commit fraud directly.

21.4   Defense Against Network Attack

In defending against network attack, there are broadly speaking four sets of available tools.

1. First is management — keeping your systems up-to-date and configured in ways that will minimise the attack surface;

2. Next is filtering — the use of firewalls to stop bad things like Trojans and network exploits, and to detect signs of attack and compromise if anything gets through;

3. Next is intrusion detection — having programs monitoring your networks and machines for signs of malicious behaviour;

4. Finally there's encryption — protocols such as TLS and SSH that enable you to protect specific parts of the network against particular attacks.

Let's work through these in turn.

21.4.1   Configuration Management and Operational Security

The great majority of technical attacks on systems in the period 2000–07 exploited already known vulnerabilities. The typical cycle is that Microsoft announces a set of security patches once a month; as soon as they come out, the attackers start reverse engineering them; within a few days, the vulnerabilities that they fixed are understood and exploits appear. A well-run firm will test its operational systems quickly on Patch Tuesday and apply the patches, provided they don't break anything important. If they do break something, that will be fixed as quickly as reasonably possible.

Tight configuration management is not just about patches, though. Many software products ship with unsafe defaults, such as well-known default passwords. It's a good idea to have someone whose job it is to understand and deal with such problems. It's also common to remove unnecessary services from machines; there is usually no reason for every workstation in your company to be running a mail server, and ftp server and DNS, and stripping things down can greatly reduce the attack surface. Frequent reinstallation is another powerful tool: when this was first tried at MIT during Project Athena, a policy of overnight reinstallation of all software greatly cut the number of sysadmins needed to look after student machines. Operations like call centres often do the same; that way if anyone wants to install unauthorised software they have to do it again every shift, and are more likely to get caught. There are also network configuration issues: you want to know your network's topology, and have some means of hunting down things like rogue access points. If all this is done competently, then you can deal with most of the common technical attacks. (You'll need separate procedures to deal with bugs that arise in your own code, but as most software is bought rather than written these days, configuration management is most of the battle.)

There are many tools to help the sysadmin in these tasks. Some enable you to do centralized version control so that patches can be applied overnight and everything kept in synch; others look for vulnerabilities in your network. When the first such tool came out (Satan [503]) there was quite a lot of controversy; this has led to some countries passing laws against 'hacking tools'. Now there are dozens of such tools, but they have to be used with care.

However, a strategy of having your system administrators stop all vulnerabilities at source is harder than it looks; even diligent organisations may find it's just too expensive to fix all the security holes at once. Patches may break critical applications, and it seems to be a general rule that an organisation's most critical systems run on the least secure machines, as administrators have not dared to apply upgrades and patches for fear of losing service.

This leads us to operational security, and the use of filtering tools such as firewalls.

Operational security, as mentioned in Chapter 2 and Chapter 8, is about training staff to not expose systems by foolish actions. There we were largely interested in social engineering attacks involving the telephone; the main way of getting unauthorised access to information is still to phone up and pretend to be someone who's entitled to know.

Now the main way machines get compromised in 2007 is because people click on links in email that cause them to download and install rootkits. Of course you must train your staff to not click on links in mail, but don't expect that this alone will fix the problem; many banks and other businesses expect their customers to click on links, and many of your staff will have to do some clicking to get their work done. You can shield low-grade staff by not giving them administrator access to their machines, and you can shield your creative staff by letting them buy Macs; but there is still going to be a residual risk. One common way of dealing with it is to strip out all executables at your firewall.

21.4.2　Filtering: Firewalls, Spam Filters, Censorware and Wiretaps

The most widely sold solution to the 'problems of Internet security' is the *firewall*. This is a machine which stands between a local system and the Internet and filters out traffic that might be harmful. The idea of a 'solution in a box' has great appeal to many organisations, and is now so widely accepted that it's seen as an essential part of corporate due diligence. (This in itself creates a risk — many firms prefer expensive firewalls to good ones.)

Firewalls are just one example of systems that examine streams of packets and perform filtering operations. Bad packets may be thrown away, or modified in such a way as to make them harmless. They may also be copied to a log or audit trail. Very similar systems are also used for Internet censorship and for law-enforcement wiretapping; almost everything I'll discuss in this section goes across to those applications too. Developments in any of these fields potentially affect the others; and actual systems may have overlapping functions. For example, many corporate firewalls or mail filters screen out pornography, and some even block bad language, while ISP systems that censor child pornography or dissenting political speech may report the perpetrators automatically to the authorities.

Filters come in basically three flavours, depending on whether they operate at the IP packet level, at the TCP session level or at the application level.

21.4.2.1　*Packet Filtering*

The simplest kind of filter merely inspects packet addresses and port numbers. This functionality is also available in routers, in Linux and indeed in Windows. A firewall can block IP spoofing by ensuring that only 'local' packets leave a network, and only 'foreign' ones enter. It can also stop denial-of-service attacks in which malformed packets are sent to a host. It's also easy to block traffic to or from 'known bad' IP addresses. For example, IP filtering is a major component of the censorship mechanisms in the Great Firewall of China; a list of bad IP addresses can be kept in router hardware, which enables packet filtering to be done at great speed.

Basic packet filtering is also available as standard on most machines and can be used for more mundane firewalling tasks. For example, packet filters can be configured to block all traffic except that arriving on specific port numbers. The configuration might be initially to allow the ports used by common services such as email and web traffic, and then open up ports as the protected machine or subnet uses them.

However, packet filters can be defeated by a number of tricks. For example, a packet can be fragmented in such a way that the initial fragment (which passes the firewall's inspection) is overwritten by a subsequent fragment, thereby replacing the source address with one that violates the firewall's security policy. Another limitation is that maintaining a blacklist is difficult, and especially so when it's not the IP address specifically you want to block, but something that resolves into an IP address, especially on a transient basis. For example, the phishermen are starting to use tricks like fast-flux in which a site's IP address changes several times an hour.

21.4.2.2 *Circuit Gateways*

The next step up is a more complex arrangement, a *circuit gateway*, that operates at level 4, typically by reassembling and examining all the packets in each TCP session. This is more expensive than simple packet filtering; its main advantage is that it can also provide the added functionality of a *virtual private network* whereby corporate traffic passed over the Internet is encrypted from firewall to firewall. I'll discuss the IPSEC protocol that's used for this in the last section of this chapter.

TCP-level filtering can be used to do a few more things, such as DNS filtering. However, it can't screen out bad things at the application level, such as malicious code, image spam and unlawful images of child abuse. Thus it may often be programmed to direct certain types of traffic to specific application filters. An example is British Telecom's CleanFeed system, which tries to prevent its customers getting access to child pornography. As some bad sites are hosted on public web services and blocking all the web pages at the service would be excessive, TCP/IP filtering is used to redirect traffic with such sites to a proxy that can examine it in detail.

21.4.2.3 *Application Relays*

The third type of firewall is the *application relay*, which acts as a proxy for one or more services. Examples are mail filters that try to weed out spam, and web proxies that block or remove undesirable content. The classic example is a corporate rule about stripping out code, be it straightforward executables, active content in web pages, macros from incoming Word documents. Over the period 2000–07, this has been a constant arms race between the firewall vendors, the spammers, and people trying to circumvent controls to get their work done.

The flood of Word macro viruses around 2000 led many firms to strip out Word macros (or even all Word documents) from email. Workers got round this by zipping documents first. Firewalls started unzipping them to inspect them, whereupon people started encrypting them using zip's password feature, and putting the password in the email plaintext. Once firewalls started to cope with this, the spammers started putting zip passwords in images attached to the mail along with the zip file. Eventually, many companies started adopting a policy of not sending out Word documents, but Pdf documents instead; this not only made it easier to get past firewalls, but also stopped people carelessly sending out documents containing the last few dozen edits. Needless to say, the spammers now send out Pdf attachments — and their botnets have the power to make all the attachments different, for example by combining text, and image, and a number of random color blocks for background. Rootkit executables are now often distributed as web links; August 2007 saw floods of messages telling people they'd got a card, while in September it was links to a bogus NFL site. For complete protection, you have to filter executables in your web proxy too (but this would really get in the way of users who wish to run the latest applications). There is no sign of this arms race abating.

An application relay can also turn out to be a serious bottleneck. This applies not just to the corporate application, but in censorship. An example is the Great Firewall of China, which tries to block mail and web content that refers to banned subjects. Although the firewall can block 'known bad' sites by simple IP filtering, finding forbidden words involves deep packet inspection — which needs much more horsepower. An investigation by Richard Clayton, Steven Murdoch and Robert Watson showed bad content wasn't in fact blocked; machines in China simply sent 'reset' packets to both ends of a connection on which a bad word had appeared. This was almost certainly because they needed a number of extra machines for the filtering, rather than doing it in the router; one side-effect was that you could defeat the firewall by ignoring these reset packets [308]. (Of course, someone within China who did that might eventually get a visit from the authorities.)

At the application level in particular, the pace of innovation leaves the firewall vendors (and the censors and the wiretappers) trailing behind. A good example is the move to edge-based computing. Google's word processor — Google Documents — is used by many people to edit documents online, simply to save them the cost of buying Microsoft Word. As a side-effect, its users can instantly share documents with each other, creating a new communications channel of which classical filters are unaware. So the service might be used to smuggle confidential documents out of a company, to defeat political censors, or to communicate covertly. (It even blurs the distinction between traffic and content, which is central to the legal regulation of wiretapping in most countries.) Even more esoteric communications channels are readily available — conspirators could join an online multi-user game, and pass their messages via the silver dragon in the sixth dungeon.

Another problem is that application-level filtering can be very expensive, especially of high-bandwidth web content. That's why a number of web filtering systems are hybrids, such as the CleanFeed mechanism mentioned above where only those domains that contain at least some objectionable content are sent to full http proxy filtering. Application proxies can also interact with other protection mechanisms. Not only can spammers (and others) use encryption to defeat content inspection; but some corporate web proxies are set up to break encryption by doing middleperson attacks on TLS. Even if you think you're giving an encrypted credit card number to Amazon, your encrypted session may just be with your employer's web proxy, while it runs another encrypted session with Amazon's web server. I'll discuss TLS later in this chapter.

21.4.2.4 *Ingress Versus Egress Filtering*

At present, most firewalls look outwards and try to keep bad things out, but a growing number look inwards and try to stop bad things leaving. The pioneers were military mail systems that monitor outgoing traffic to ensure that nothing classified goes out in the clear; around 2005 some ISPs started looking at outgoing mail traffic to try to detect spam. The reason is that ISPs which host lots of infected machines and thus pump out lots of spam damage their peering relationships with other ISPs, which costs real money; so various systems have been developed to help them spot infected machines, that can then be restricted to a 'walled garden' from which they can access anti-virus software but not much else [300].

If companies whose machines get used in service denial attacks start getting sued, as has been proposed in [1285], then egress filtering can at least in principle be used to detect and stop such attacks. However, at present the incentives just aren't there, and so although people care about spam floods, almost nobody at the ISP level bothers about packet floods. This might of course change as attacks get worse or if the regulatory environment changes.

Another possible development is egress filtering for privacy, given the rising tide of spyware. Software that 'phones home', whether for copyright enforcement or marketing purposes, can disclose highly sensitive material such as local hard disk directories. Prudent organizations will increasingly wish to monitor and control this kind of traffic. In the long term we expect that 'pervasive computing' will fill our homes with all sorts of gadgets that communicate, so I wouldn't be surprised to see home firewalls that enable the householder to control which of them 'phone home', and for what purpose.

21.4.2.5 *Architecture*

Many firms just buy a firewall because it's on the tick-list of due-diligence things their auditors want to see. In that case, the sensible choice is a simple filtering router, which won't need much maintenance and won't get in the way. Where security's taken seriously, one possible approach is to invest in a really serious firewall system, which might consist of a packet filter connecting the outside world to a screened subnet, also known as a *demilitarized zone*

(DMZ), which in turn contains a number of application servers or proxies to filter mail, web and other services. The DMZ may then be connected to the internal network via a further filter that does network address translation.

In [323], there is a case study of how a firewall was deployed at Hanscom Air Force Base. The work involved surveying the user community to find what network services were needed; devising a network security policy; using network monitors to discover unexpected services that were in use; and lab testing prior to installation. Once it was up and running, the problems included ongoing maintenance (due to personnel turnover), the presence of (unmonitored) communications to other military bases, and the presence of modem pools. Few non-military organizations are likely to take this much care.

An alternative approach is to have more networks, but smaller ones. At our university, we have firewalls to separate departments, although we've got a shared network backbone and there are some shared central services. There's no reason why the students and the finance department should be on the same network, and a computer science department has got quite different requirements (and users) from a department of theology — so the network security policies should be different too. In any case keeping each network small limits the scope of any compromise.

You may even find both a big corporate firewall and departmental boundaries. At defense contractors, you may expect to find not just a fancy firewall at the perimeter, but also pumps separating networks operating at different clearance levels, with filters to ensure that classified information doesn't escape either outwards or downwards (Figure 21.2).

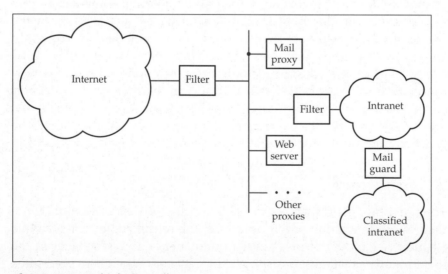

Figure 21.2: Multiple firewalls

Which is better? Well, it depends. Factors to consider when designing a network security architecture are simplicity, usability, maintainability, deperimeterisation, underblocking versus overblocking, and incentives.

First, since firewalls do only a small number of things, it's possible to make them very simple and remove many of the complex components from the underlying operating system, removing a lot of sources of vulnerability and error. If your organization has a large heterogeneous population of machines, then loading as much of the security management task as possible on a small number of simple boxes makes sense. On the other hand, if you're running something like a call centre, with a thousand identically-configured PCs, it makes sense to put your effort into keeping this configuration tight.

Second, elaborate central installations not only impose greater operational costs, but can get in the way so much that people install back doors, such as cable modems that bypass your firewall, to get their work done. In the 1990s, UK diplomats got fed up waiting for a 'secure' email system from government suppliers; they needed access to email so they could talk to people who preferred to use it. Some of them simply bought PCs from local stores and got accounts on AOL, thus exposing sensitive data to anyone who tapped the network or indeed guessed an AOL password. In fact, the diplomats of over a hundred countries had webmail accounts compromised when they were foolish enough to rely on Tor for message confidentiality, and got attacked by a malicious Tor exit node (an incident I'll discuss in section 23.4.2.) So a prudent system administrator will ensure that he knows the actual network configuration rather than just the one stated by 'policy'.

Third, firewalls (like other filtering products) tend only to work for a while until people find ways round them. Early firewalls tended to let only mail and web traffic through; so writers of applications from computer games to anonymity proxies redesigned their protocols to make the client-server traffic look as much like normal web traffic as possible. Now, of course, in the world of Web 2.0, more and more applications are actually web-based; so we can expect the same games to be played out again in the web proxy. There are particular issues with software products that insist on calling home. For example, the first time you use Windows Media Player, it tells you you need a 'security upgrade'. What's actually happening is that it 'individualizes' itself by generating a public-private keypair and sending the public key to Microsoft. If your firewall doesn't allow this, then WMP won't play protected content. Microsoft suggests you use their ISA firewall product, which will pass WMP traffic automatically. Quite a few issues of trust, transparency and competition may be raised by this!

Next, there's *deperimiterization* — the latest buzzword. Progress is making it steadily harder to put all the protection at the perimeter. The very technical ability to maintain a perimeter is undermined by the proliferation of memory sticks, of laptops, of PDAs being used for functions that used to be done on desktop computers, and by changing business methods that involve more outsourcing of functions — whether formally to subcontractors or informally to advertising-supported web apps. If some parts of your organisation can't be controlled well (e.g. the sales force and the R&D lab) while others must be (the finance office) then separate networks are needed. The crumbling of the perimeter will be made even worse by mobility, and by the proliferation of web applications. This is complemented by a blunting of the incentive to do things at the perimeter, as useful things become harder to do. The difference between code and data is steadily eroded by new scripting languages; a determination to not allow javascript in the firm is quickly eroded by popular web sites that require it; and so on.

And then there's our old friend the Receiver Operating Characteristic or ROC curve. No filtering mechanism has complete precision, so there's inevitably a trade-off between underblocking and overblocking. If you're running a censorship system to stop kids accessing pornography in public libraries, do you underblock, and annoy parents and churches when some pictures get through, or do you overblock and get sued for infringing free-speech rights? Things are made worse by the fact that the firewall systems used to filter web content for sex, violence and bad language also tend to block free-speech sites (as many of these criticise the firewall vendors — and some offer technical advice on how to circumvent blocking.)

Finally, security depends at least as much on incentives as on technology. A sysadmin who's looking after a departmental network used by a hundred people he knows, and who will personally have to clear up any mess caused by an intrusion or a configuration error, is much more motivated than someone who's merely one member of a large team looking after thousands of machines.

21.4.3 Intrusion Detection

It's a good idea to assume that attacks will happen, and it's often cheaper to prevent some attacks and detect the rest than it is to try to prevent everything. The systems used to detect bad things happening are referred to generically as *intrusion detection systems*. The antivirus software products I discussed earlier are one example; but the term is most usually applied to boxes that sit on your network and look for signs of an attack in progress or a compromised machine [1100]. Examples include:

■ spam coming from a machine in your network;

■ packets with forged source addresses — such as packets that claim to be from outside a subnet coming from it, or packets that claim to be from inside arriving at it;

■ a machine trying to contact a 'known bad' service such as an IRC channel that's being used to control a botnet.

In cases like this, the IDS essentially tells the sysadmin that a particular machine needs to be scrubbed and have its software reinstalled.

Other examples of intrusion detection, that we've seen in earlier chapters, are the mechanisms for detecting mobile phone cloning and fraud by bank tellers. There are also bank systems that look at customer complaints of credit card fraud to try to figure out which merchants have been leaking card data, and stock market systems that try to detect insider trading by looking for increases in trading volume prior to a price-sensitive announcement and other suspicious patterns of activity. And there are 'suspect' lists kept by airport screeners; if your name is down there, you'll be selected 'at random' for extra screening. Although these intrusion detection systems are all performing very similar tasks, their developers don't talk to each other much. One sees the same old wheels being re-invented again and again. But it's starting slowly to become a more coherent discipline, as the U.S. government has thrown hundreds of millions at the problem.

The research program actually started in the mid-1990s and was prompted by the realisation that many systems make no effective use of log and audit data. In the case of Sun's operating system Solaris, for example, we found in 1996 that the audit formats were not documented and tools to read them were not available. The audit facility seemed to have been installed to satisfy the formal checklist requirements of government systems buyers rather than to perform any useful function. There was at least the hope that improving this would help system administrators detect attacks, whether after the fact or even when they were still in progress. Since 9/11, of course, there has been a great switch of emphasis to doing data mining on large corpora of both government and commercial data, looking for conspiracies.

21.4.3.1 *Types of Intrusion Detection*

The simplest intrusion detection method is to sound an alarm when a threshold is passed. Three or more failed logons, a credit card expenditure of more than twice the moving average of the last three months, or a mobile phone call lasting more than six hours, might all flag the account in question for attention. More sophisticated systems generally fall into two categories.

Misuse detection systems operate using a model of the likely behaviour of an intruder. A banking system may alarm if a user draws the maximum permitted amount from a cash machine on three successive days; and a Unix intrusion detection system may look for user account takeover by alarming if a previously naive user suddenly started to use sophisticated tools like compilers. Indeed, most misuse detection systems, like antivirus scanners, look for a *signature* — a known characteristic of a particular attack.

Anomaly detection systems attempt the much harder job of looking for anomalous patterns of behaviour in the absence of a clear model of the attacker's modus operandi. The hope is to detect attacks that have not been previously recognized and cataloged. Systems of this type often use AI techniques — neural networks have been fashionable from time to time.

The dividing line between misuse and anomaly detection is somewhat blurred. A good borderline case is Benford's law, which describes the distribution of digits in random numbers. One might expect that numbers beginning with the digits '1', '2', ... '9' would be equally common. But in fact with numbers that come from random natural sources, so that their distribution is independent of the number system in which they're expressed, the distribution is logarithmic: about 30% of decimal numbers start with '1'. Crooked clerks who think up numbers to cook the books, or even use random number generators without knowing Benford's law, are often caught using it [846]. Another borderline case is the *honey trap* — something enticing left to attract attention. I mentioned, for example, that some hospitals have dummy records with celebrities' names in order to entrap staff who don't respect medical confidentiality.

21.4.3.2 *General Limitations of Intrusion Detection*

Some intrusions are really obvious. If what you're worried about is a script kiddie vandalizing your corporate web site, then the obvious defence is to have a machine somewhere that fetches the page regularly, inspects it, and rings a really loud alarm when it changes. (Make sure you do this via an outside proxy, and don't forget that it's not just your own systems at risk. The kiddie could replace your advertisers' pictures with porn, for example, and then you'd want to pull the links to them pretty fast.)

But in the general case, intrusion detection is hard. Cohen proved that detecting viruses (in the sense of deciding whether a program is going to do something bad) is as hard as the halting problem, so we can't ever expect a complete solution [311].

Another fundamental limitation comes from the fact that there are basically two different types of security failure — those which cause an error (which we defined in 6.3 to be an incorrect state) and those which don't. An example of the former is a theft from a bank which leaves traces on the audit trail. An example of the latter is an undetected confidentiality failure caused by a radio microphone placed by a foreign intelligence service in your room. The former can be detected (at least in principle, and forgetting for now about the halting problem) by suitable processing of the data available to you. But the latter can't be. It's a good idea to design systems so that as many failures as possible fall into the former category, but it's not always practicable [289].

There's also the matter of definitions. Some intrusion detection systems are configured to block any instances of suspicious behaviour and in extreme cases to take down the affected systems. Quite apart from opening the door to service denial attacks, this turns the intrusion detection system into firewall or an access control mechanism; and as we've already seen, access control is in general a hard problem and incorporates all sorts of issues of security policy which people often disagree on or simply get wrong.

I prefer to define an intrusion detection system as one that monitors the logs and draws the attention of authority to suspicious occurrences. This is closer to the way mobile phone operators work. It's also critical in financial investigations; see [1095] for a discussion by a special agent with the U.S. Internal Revenue Service, of what he looks for when trying to trace hidden assets and income streams. A lot hangs on educated suspicion based on long experience. For example, a $25 utility bill may lead to a $250,000 second house hidden behind a nominee. Building an effective system means having the people, and the machines, each do the part of the job they're best at; and this means getting the machine to do the preliminary filtering.

Then there's the cost of false alarms. For example, I used to go to San Francisco every May, and I got used to the fact that after I'd used my UK debit card in an ATM five days in a row, it would stop working. This not only upsets the customer, but the villains quickly learn to exploit it. (So do the customers — I just started making sure I got enough dollars out in the first five days to last me the whole trip.) As in so many security engineering problems, the trade-off between the fraud rate and the insult rate is the critical one — and, as discussed in section 15.9, you can't expect to improve this trade-off simply by looking at lots of different indicators. In general, you must expect that an opponent will always get past the threshold if he's patient enough and either does the attack very slowly, or does a large number of small attacks.

A difficult policy problem with commercial intrusion detection systems is *redlining*. When insurance companies used claim statistics on postcodes to decide the level of premiums to charge, it was found that many poor and black areas suffered high premiums or were excluded altogether from cover. In a number of jurisdictions this is now illegal. In general, if you build an intrusion detection system based on data mining techniques, you are at serious risk of discriminating. If you use neural network techniques, you'll have no way of explaining to a court what the rules underlying your decisions are, so defending yourself could be hard. Opaque rules can also contravene European data protection law, which entitles citizens to know the algorithms used to process their personal data.

Already in 1997, systems introduced to profile U.S. airline passengers for terrorism risk, so they could be subjected to more stringent screening, were denounced by the American-Arab Anti-Discrimination Committee [823]. Since 9/11 such problems have become much worse. How do we judge the balance point beyond which we just radicalize people and breed more attacks? I'll come back to this in Part III.

21.4.4   Specific Problems Detecting Network Attacks

Turning now to the specific problem of detecting network intrusion, the problem is much harder than (say) detecting mobile phone cloning for a number of reasons. Network intrusion detection products still don't work very well, with both high missed alarm and false alarm rates. It's common not to detect actual intrusions until afterwards — although once one is detected by other means, the traces can be found on the logs.

The reasons for the poor performance include the following, in no particular order.

- The Internet is a very noisy environment — not just at the level of content but also at the packet level. A large amount of random crud arrives at any substantial site, and enough of it can be interpreted as hostile to provide a significant false alarm rate. A survey by Bellovin [149] reports that many bad packets result from software bugs; others are the fault of out-of-date or corrupt DNS data; and some are local packets that escaped, travelled the world and returned.

- There are 'too few attacks'. If there are ten real attacks per million sessions — which is almost certainly an overestimate — then even if the system has a false alarm rate as low as 0.1%, the ratio of false to real alarms will be 100. We talked about similar problems with burglar alarms; it's also a well known problem for medics running screening programs for diseases like HIV where the test error exceeds the organism's prevalence. In general, where the signal is far below the noise, the guards get tired and even the genuine alarms get missed.

- Many network attacks are specific to particular versions of software, so a general misuse detection tool must have a large and constantly changing library of attack signatures.

- In many cases, commercial organisations appear to buy intrusion detection systems simply in order to tick a 'due diligence' box to satisfy insurers or consultants. That means the products aren't always kept up to date.

- Encrypted traffic can't easily be subjected to content analysis any more than it can be filtered for malicious code.

- The issues we discussed in the context of firewalls largely apply to intrusion detection too. You can filter at the packet layer, which is fast but can be defeated by packet fragmentation; or you can reconstruct each session, which takes more computation and so is not really suitable for network backbones; or you can examine application data, which is more expensive still — and needs to be constantly updated to cope with the arrival of new applications and attacks.

- You may have to do intrusion detection both locally and globally. The antivirus side of things may have to be done on local machines, especially if the malware arrives on encrypted web sessions; on the other hand, some attacks are *stealthy* — the opponent sends 1–2 packets per day to each of maybe 100,000 hosts. Such attacks are unlikely to be found by local monitoring; you need a central monitor that keeps histograms of packets by source and destination address and by port.

So it appears unlikely that a single-product solution will do the trick. Future intrusion detection systems are likely to involve the coordination of a number of monitoring mechanisms at different levels both in the network (backbone, LAN, individual machine) and in the protocol stack (packet, session and application).

21.4.5   Encryption

In the context of preventing network attacks, many people have been conditioned to think of encryption. Encryption usually does a lot less than you might hope, as the quote from Butler Lampson and Roger Needham at the head of this chapter suggests. But it can sometimes be useful. Here I'm going to describe briefly the four most relevant network encryption scenarios: SSH; the local link protection offered by WiFi, Bluetooth and HomePlug; IPSec; and TLS. Finally I'll briefly discuss public key infrastructures (PKI), which are used to support the last two of these.

21.4.5.1   SSH

When I use my laptop to read email on my desktop machine, or do anything with any other machine in our lab for that matter, I use a protocol called *secure shell* (SSH) which provides encrypted links between Unix and Windows hosts [1369, 1, 988]. So when I come in from home over the net, my traffic is protected, and when I log on from the PC at my desk to another machine in the lab, the password I use doesn't go across the LAN in the clear.

SSH was initially written in 1995 by Tatu Ylönen, a researcher at Helsinki University of Technology in Finland, following a password-sniffing attack there. It not only sets up encrypted connections between machines, so that logon passwords don't travel across the network in the clear; it also supports other useful features, such as forwarding X sessions, which led to its rapid adoption. (In fact it's a classic case study in how to get a security product accepted in the marketplace; see [1083] for an analysis. Normally people don't want to use encryption products until a lot of other people are using them too, because of network effects; so the trick is to bundle some real other benefits with the product.)

There is a proprietary SSH product from Ylönen's company, and a number of open implementations such as OpenSSH and Putty; there's also an associated file transfer protocol SCP ('secure copy'). There are various configuration options, but in the most straightforward one, each machine has a public-private keypair. The private key is protected by a passphrase that the user types at the keyboard. To connect from (say) my laptop to a server at the lab, I ensure that my public key is loaded on, and trusted by, the server. Manual key installation is at once a strength and a weakness; it's strong in that management is intuitive, and weak as it doesn't scale particularly well. In any case, when I wish to log on to the server I'm prompted for my passphrase; a key is then set up; and the traffic is both encrypted and authenticated. Fresh keys are set up after an hour, or after a Gigabyte of traffic has been exchanged.

Possible problems with the use of SSH include the fact that the earliest version, SSH 1.0, is vulnerable to middleperson attacks because of a poor key-exchange protocol; and that if you're typing at the keyboard one character at a time, then each character gets sent in its own packet. The packet inter-arrival times can leak a surprising amount of information about what you're typing [1203]. However, the worst is probably that most SSH keys are stored in the clear, without being protected by a password at all. The consequence is that if a machine is compromised, the same can happen to every other machine that trusts an SSH key installed on it.

21.4.5.2 *WiFi*

WiFi is a technology used for wireless local area networks, and is very widely used: people use it at home to connect PCs to a home router, and businesses use it too, connecting devices such as tills and payment terminals as well as PCs. Games consoles and even mobile phones make increasing use of wireless LANs.

Wifi has come with a series of encryption protocols since its launch in 1997. The first widely-used one, WEP (for *wired equivalent privacy*), was shown to be fairly easily broken, even when configured correctly. Standardised with IEEE 802.11 in 1999, WEP uses the RC4 stream cipher to encrypt data with only a cyclic redundancy check for integrity. Nikita Borisov, Ian Goldberg and David Wagner showed that this led to attacks in depth [210]. Known plaintext allows keystream to be stripped off and reused; in addition, the initial values used in encryption were only 24 bits, which enabled IV collisions to be found leading to further depth attacks. False messages could be encrypted and injected into a wireless LAN, opening it to other attacks. What's more, the key was only 40 bits long in early implementations, because of U.S. export rules; so keys could be brute-forced.

That merely whetted cryptanalysts' appetite. Shortly afterwards, Scott Fluhrer, Itzhak Mantin and Adi Shamir found a really devastating attack.

It is an initialisation weakness in the RC4 stream cipher that interacts with the way in which WEP set up its initialization vectors [479]; in short order, Adam Stubblefield, John Ioannidis and Avi Rubin turned this into a working attack on WEP [1230]. Vendors bodged up their products so they would not use the specific weak keys exploited in the initial attack programs; later programs used a wider range of weak keys, and the attacks steadily improved. The history of the attack evolution is told in [993]; the latest attack, by Erik Tews, Ralf-Philipp Weinmann and Andrei Pyshkin, recovers 95% of all keys within 85,000 packets [1245]. Now there are publicly-available tools that will extract WEP keys after observing a few minutes' traffic.

Stronger encryption systems, known as Wi-Fi Protected Access (WPA), aim to solve this problem and are available on most new products. WPA shipped in 2003, and was an intermediate solution that still uses RC4. WPA2 shipped in 2004; it is also called the Robust Security Network (RSN) and uses the AES block cipher in counter mode with CBC-MAC. Within a few years, as older machines become obsolete, WPA2 should solve the cipher security problem.

So what are we to make of WiFi security? There has been a lot of noise in the press about how people should set passwords on their home routers, in case a bad man stops outside your house and uses your network to download child porn. However, a straw poll of security experts at WEIS 2006 showed that most did not bother to encrypt their home networks; drive-by downloads are a fairly remote threat. For most people in the UK or America, it's just convenient to have an open network for your guests to use, and so that you and your neighbours can use each others' networks as backups. Things are different in countries where you pay for download bandwidth; there, home router passwords are mostly set.

Things are different for businesses because of the possibility of targeted attacks. If you use a Windows machine with Windows shares open, then someone on your LAN can probably use that to infect you with malware. A random home owner may not be at much risk — with botnets trading at about a dollar a machine, it's not worth someone's while to drive around town infecting machines by hand. But if you're a high-value target, then the odds change significantly. In March 2007, retail chain TJ Maxx reported that some 45.7 million credit card numbers had been stolen from its systems; these card numbers largely related to sales in 2003 and 2004, and had been stolen from 2005 but discovered only in December 2006. The Wall Street Journal reported that an insecure WiFi connection in St Paul, Mn., was to blame [1014]; the company's SEC filing about the incident is at [1252], and the Canadian Privacy Commissioner concluded that 'The company collected too much personal information, kept it too long and relied on weak encryption technology to protect it — putting the privacy of millions of its customers at risk' [1047]. Banks sued the company, with VISA claiming fraud losses of over $68m from the compromise of 65 million accounts; the banks eventually settled for damages of $41m [544]. Since June 2007, the banking industry's Payment Card Industry Data Security Standard (PCI DSS) requires companies processing credit card data to meet certain data security standards, and VISA or Mastercard can fine member banks whose merchants don't comply with it. (However, enforcement has historically been weak: it turned out that VISA had known about TJX's compliance problems, and had allowed them an extension until 2009 [1349].)

The latest implementations of WiFi are coming with mechanisms that encourage users to set up WPA encryption, and usability is a big deal for the other local connectivity protocols too.

21.4.5.3   Bluetooth

Bluetooth is another protocol used for short-range wireless communication. It's aimed at *personal area networks*, such as linking a headset to a mobile phone, or linking a mobile phone in your pocket to a hands-free phone interface in your car. It's also used to connect cameras and phones to laptops, keyboards to PCs and so on. Like WiFi, the initially deployed security protocol turned out to have flaws. In the original version, devices discover each other, and the users confirm that they wish two devices to pair by entering the same PIN at their keyboards. An attacker who's present during this pairing process can observe the traffic and then brute-force the PIN. Worse, Ollie Whitehouse, Yaniv Shaked and Avishai Wool figured out how to force two devices to rerun the pairing protocol, so that PIN-cracking attacks could be performed even on devices that were already paired [1341, 1156]. Denis Kügler also showed how to manipulate the frequency hopping so as to do a man-in-the-middle attack [747]. It's possible to mitigate these vulnerabilities by only doing pairing in a secure place and refusing requests to rekey.

Now, from version 2.1 (released in 2007), Bluetooth supports Secure Simple Pairing, an improved protocol [802]. This uses elliptic curve Diffie-Hellmann key exchange to thwart passive eavesdropping attacks, but man-in-the-middle attacks are harder; they are dealt with by generating a six digit number for numerical comparison, with a view to reducing the chance of an attack succeeding to one in a million. However, because one or both of the devices might lack a keyboard or screen (or both), it's also possible for the six-digit number to be generated at one device and entered as a passkey at another; and there's a 'just works' mode that's fully vulnerable to a middleperson attack. Finally, there's a capability to load keys out of band, such as from some other protocol that the devices use.

21.4.5.4   HomePlug

HomePlug is a protocol used for communication over the mains power line. An early version had a low bitrate, but HomePlug AV, available from 2007, supports broadband. (Declaration of interest: I was one of the protocol's designers.) It aims to allow TVs, set-top boxes, personal video recorders, DSL and cable modems and other such devices to communicate in the home without additional cabling. We were faced with the same design constraints as the Bluetooth team: not all devices have keyboards or screens, and we needed to keep costs low. After much thought we decided to offer only two modes of operation: secure mode, in which the user manually enters into her network controller a unique AES key that's printed on the label of every device, and robust or 'simple connect' mode in which the keys are exchanged without authentication. In fact, the keys aren't even encrypted in this mode; its purpose is not to provide security but to prevent wrong associations, such as when your speakers wrongly get their audio signal from the apartment next door.

We considered offering a public-key exchange protocol, as with Bluetooth, but came to the conclusion that it didn't achieve much. If there's a middleperson attack going on where the attacker knocks out your set-top box using a jammer and connects a bogus box of the same type to your mains, then the chances are that you'll go to your network controller (some software on your PC) and see a message 'Set-top box type Philips 123 seeks admission to network. Certificate hash = 12345678. Admit/deny?' In such a circumstance, most people will press 'admit' and allow the attacker in. The only way to prevent them is to get them to read the certificate hash from the device label and type it in — and if they're going to do that, they might as well type in the key directly [967]. In short, our design was driven by usability, and we weren't convinced that public-key crypto actually bought us anything.

Time will tell which approach was best. And if we turn out to have been wrong, HomePlug (like Bluetooth and the latest versions of WiFi) lets keys be set up from other protocols by out-of-band mechanisms. So all devices in the office or home could end up with their keys managed by a single mechanism or device; and this could be convenient, or a source of vulnerabilities, depending on how future security engineers build it.

21.4.5.5   IPsec

Another approach is to do encryption and/or authentication at the IP layer using a protocol suite known as IPsec. IPsec defines a *security association* as the combination of keys, algorithms and parameters used to protect a particular packet stream. Protected packets are either encrypted or authenticated (or both); in the latter case, an authentication header is added that protects data integrity using HMAC-SHA1, while in the former the packet is encrypted and encapsulated in other packets. (The use of encryption without authentication is discouraged as it's insecure [151].) There's also an *Internet Key Exchange* (IKE) protocol to set up keys and negotiate parameters. IKE has been through a number of versions (some of the bugs that were fixed are discussed in [465]).

IPsec is widely used by firewall vendors who offer a *virtual private network* facility with their products; that is, by installing one of their boxes in each branch between the local LAN and the router, all the internal traffic can pass encrypted over the Internet. Individual PCs, such as workers' laptops and home PCs, can in theory join a VPN given a firewall that supports IPsec, but this is harder than it looks. Compatibility has been a major problem with different manufacturers' offerings just not working with each other; although firewall-to-firewall compatibility has improved recently, getting random PCs to work with a given VPN is still very much a hit-or-miss affair.

IPsec has the potential to stop some network attacks, and be a useful component in designing robust distributed systems. But it isn't a panacea. Indeed, virtual private networks exacerbate the 'deperimeterization' problem already discussed. If you have thousands of machines sitting in your employee's homes that are both in the network (as they connect via a VPN) and connected to the Internet (as their browser talks to the Internet directly via the home's cable modem) then they become a potential weak point. (Indeed, the U.S. Department of Justice ruled in 2007 that employees can't use their own PCs or PDAs for work purposes; all mobile devices used for departmental business must be centrally managed [108].)

21.4.5.6 TLS

Recall that when discussing public key encryption, I remarked that a server could publish a public key KS and any web browser could then send a message M containing a credit card number to it encrypted using KS: $\{M\}_{KS}$. This is in essence what the TLS protocol (formerly known as SSL) does, although in practice it is more complicated. It was developed to support encryption and authentication in both directions, so that both http requests and responses can be protected against both eavesdropping and manipulation. It's the protocol that's activated when you see the padlock on your browser toolbar.

Here is a simplified description of the version as used to protect web pages that solicit credit card numbers:

1. the client sends the server a *client hello* message that contains its name C, a transaction serial number $C\#$, and a random nonce N_C;

2. the server replies with a *server hello* message that contains its name S, a transaction serial number $S\#$, a random nonce N_S, and a certificate CS containing its public key KS. The client now checks the certificate CS back to a root certificate issued by a company such as Verisign and stored in the browser;

3. the client sends a *key exchange* message containing a *pre-master-secret* key, K_0, encrypted under the server public key KS. It also sends a *finished* message with a message authentication code (MAC) computed on all the

the messages to date. The key for this MAC is the *master-secret*, K_1. This key is computed by hashing the pre-master-secret key with the nonces sent by the client and server: $K_1 = h(K_0, N_C, N_S)$. From this point onward, all the traffic is encrypted; we'll write this as $\{...\}_{KCS}$ in the client-server direction and $\{...\}_{KSC}$ from the server to the client. These keys are generated in turn by hashing the nonces with K_1.

4. The server also sends a *finished* message with a MAC computed on all the messages to date. It then finally starts sending the data.

$$C \rightarrow S: \ C, C\#, N_C$$
$$S \rightarrow C: \ S, S\#, N_S, CS$$
$$C \rightarrow S: \ \{K_0\}_{KS}$$
$$C \rightarrow S: \ \{\textit{finished}, MAC(K_1, \textit{everythingtodate})\}_{KCS}$$
$$S \rightarrow C: \ \{\textit{finished}, MAC(K_1, \textit{everythingtodate})\}_{KSC}, \{\textit{data}\}_{KSC}$$

The design goals included minimising the load on the browser, and then minimising the load on the server. Thus the public key encryption operation is done by the client, and the decryption by the server; the standard encryption method (*ciphersuite*) uses RSA for which encryption can be arranged to be very much faster than decryption. (This was a wrong design decision as browsers generally have a lot more compute cycles to spare than servers; it has created a brisk aftermarket for crypto accelerator boards for web servers.) Also, once a client and server have established a pre-master-secret, no more public key operations are needed as further master secrets can be obtained by hashing it with new nonces.

The full protocol is more complex than this, and has gone through a number of versions. It supports a number of different ciphersuites, so that export versions of browsers for example can be limited to 40 bit keys — a condition of export licensing that was imposed for many years by the U.S. government. Other ciphersuites support signed Diffie-Hellman key exchanges for transient keys, to provide forward and backward secrecy. TLS also has options for bidirectional authentication so that if the client also has a certificate, this can be checked by the server. In addition, the working keys *KCS* and *KSC* can contain separate subkeys for encryption and authentication. For example, the most commonly used ciphersuite uses the stream cipher RC4 for the former and HMAC for the latter, and these need separate keys.

Although early versions of SSL had a number of bugs [1308], version 3 and later (called TLS since version 3.1) appear to be sound (but they have to be implemented carefully [189]). They are being used for much more than electronic commerce — an example being medical privacy [280]. In our local teaching hospital, clinical personnel were issued with smartcards containing TLS certificates enabling them to log on to systems containing patient records. This meant, for example, that researchers could access clinical data from home during an emergency, or from their university offices if doing research. TLS has also been available as an authentication option in Windows from Windows 2000 onwards; you can use it instead of Kerberos if you wish.

Another application is in mail, where more and more mail servers now use TLS opportunistically when exchanging emails with another mail server that's also prepared to use it. This stops passive eavesdropping, although it leaves open the possibility of middleperson attacks. To stop them too, you need some means of authenticating the public keys you use, and that brings us to the topic of public-key certificates.

21.4.5.7   PKI

During the dotcom boom, a number of companies achieved astronomical valuations by cornering the market in public-key certificates. The leading European certificate provider, Baltimore, achieved an eleven-figure market cap before crashing and burning in 2001. Investors believed that every device would need a public-key certificate in order to connect to other devices; you'd need to pay Baltimore (or Thawte, or Verisign) ten bucks every two years to renew the certificate on your toaster, or it wouldn't talk to your fridge.

As I discussed above, the keys in devices like fridges and toasters are best set up by local mechanisms such as the Bluetooth and HomePlug pairing mechanisms. But public key infrastructures are still used in a number of applications. First, there are the certificates that web sites use with TLS and that activate the security icon in your browser. Second, there are private infrastructures, such as those used by banks to set up keys for SWIFT, by mobile phone companies to exchange messages between Home Location Registers, and by companies that use TLS to authenticate users of their networks.

There is frequent semantic confusion between 'public (key infrastructure)' and '(public key) infrastructure'. In the first, the infrastructure can be used by whatever new applications come along; I'll call this an *open PKI*. In the second, it can't; I'll call this a *closed PKI*.

PKI has a number of intrinsic limitations, many of which have to do with the first interpretation — namely that the infrastructure is provided as a public service that anyone can use. I discussed many of the underlying problems in Chapter 7. Naming is difficult, and a certificate saying 'Ross Anderson has the right to administer the machine foo.com' means little in a world with dozens of people (and machines) of that name. Also, there's Kent's law: the more applications rely on a certificate, the shorter its useful life will be.

This is the 'one key or many' debate. As the world goes digital, should I expect to have a single digital key to replace each of the metal keys, credit cards, swipe access cards and other tokens that I currently carry around? Or should each of them be replaced by a different digital key? Multiple keys protect the customer: I don't want to have to use a key with which I can remortgage my house to make calls from a payphone. It's just too easy to dupe people into signing a message by having the equipment display another, innocuous, one[2].

However, the killer turned out to be business needs. Multiple keys are more convenient for business, as sharing access tokens can lead to greater administrative costs and liability issues. There were many attempts to share keys; the smartcard industry tried to market 'multifunction smartcards' through the 1990s that could work as bank cards, electricity meter cards and even building access cards. Singapore even implemented such a scheme, in which even military ID doubled as bank cards. However, such schemes have pretty well died out. In one that I worked on — to reuse bank cards in electricity meters — the issues were control of the customer base and of the process of developing, upgrading and reissuing cards. In other cases, projects foundered because no-one could agree which company's logo would go on the smartcard.

Now the standard PKI machinery (the X.509 protocol suite) was largely developed to provide an electronic replacement for the telephone book, so it tends to assume that everyone will have a unique name and a unique key in an open PKI architecture. Governments hoped for a 'one key fits all' model of the world, so they could license and control the keys. But, in most applications, the natural solution is for each business to run its own closed PKI, which might be thought of at the system level as giving customers a unique account number which isn't shared with anyone else. Since then, the CA market has fractured; whereas in the late 1990s, Internet Explorer shipped with only a handful of CA keys (giving huge if temporary fortunes to the firms that controlled them), now the version in Windows XP contains hundreds.

This in turn leads to issues of trust. You don't really know who controls a key whose signature is accepted by a typical browser. Further issues include

- If you remove one of the 200-plus root certificates from Windows XP Service Pack 2, then Windows silently replaces it — unless you've got the skill to dissect out the software that does this [613]. Vista comes with fewer root certificates — but you can't delete them at all. This could be bad news for a company that doesn't want to trust a competitor, or a government that doesn't want to trust foreigners. For example, the large CA Verisign also does wiretap work for the U.S. government; so if I were running China, I wouldn't want any Chinese PC to trust their certificates (as Verisign could not just sign bad web pages — they could also sign code that Chinese machines would install and run).

- Usability is dreadful, as many sites use out-of-date certs, or certs that correspond to the wrong company. As a result, users are well trained to ignore security warnings. For example, when a New Zealand bank

---

[2]I just don't know how to be confident of a digital signature I make even on my own PC — and I've worked in security for over fifteen years. Checking all the software in the critical path between the display and the signature software is way beyond my patience.

messed up its certificate with the result that users got warned it didn't correspond to the bank, only one user out of 300 stopped — the rest just went ahead with their business [569].

■ It's bad enough that the users don't care whether certificates work; yet the CAs don't seem to care, either. The UK certifier Tscheme was set up by industry as a self-regulatory scheme under the Electronic Communications Act as *'a source of independent assurance for all types of e-business and e-government transactions — especially for those transactions that depend on reliable, secure online identities.'* It was noticed in July 2006 that `https://www.tscheme.org/` had its certification path misconfigured: there was a certificate missing in the middle of the chain, so verification failed unless you manually added the missing cert. By December 2007, it still wasn't properly fixed. According to the documentation, the 'HMG Root CA' should certify everything, yet it doesn't certify the Tscheme 'Trustis FPS Root CA', and neither is included in the standard Firefox distribution. In the CA world, it seems, everyone wants to be root, and no-one wants anyone else's signature on their keys, as then they'd have no reason to exist. So stuff still doesn't work.

■ Many users disable security features on their browsers, even if these weren't disabled by default when the software shipped. Recall that the third step of the TLS protocol was for the client browser to check the cert against its stored root certificates. If the check fails, the browser may ask the client for permission to proceed; but many browsers are configured to just proceed anyway.

■ Certs bind a company name to a DNS name, but their vendors are usually not authorities on either; they hand out certificates after cursory due diligence, and in their 'certification practice statements' they go out of their way to deny all liability.

■ There are still technical shortcomings. For example, the dominant certificate format (X.509) does not have the kind of flexible and scalable 'hot card' system which the credit card industry has evolved, but rather assumes that anyone relying on a cert can download a *certificate revocation list* from the issuing authority. Also, certs are designed to certify names, when for most purposes one wants to certify an authorization.

Behind all this mess lies, as usual, security economics. During the dotcom boom in the 1990s, the SSL protocol (as TLS then was) won out over a more complex and heavyweight protocol called SET, because it placed less of a burden on developers [72]. This is exactly the same reason that operating systems such as Windows and Symbian were initially developed with too little security — they were competing for pole position in a two-sided market.

The downside in this case was that the costs of compliance were dumped on the users — who are unable to cope [357].

In short, while public key infrastructures can be useful in some applications, they are not the universal solution to security problems that their advocates claimed in the late 1990s. It's a shame some governments still think they can use PKI as a mechanism for empire-building and social control.

21.5   Topology

The topology of a network is the pattern in which its nodes are connected. The Internet classically is thought of as a cloud to which all machines are attached, so in effect every machine is (potentially) in contact with every other one. So from the viewpoint of a flash worm that propagates from one machine to another directly, without human intervention, and by choosing the next machine to attack at random, the network can be thought of as a fully connected graph. However, in many networks each node communicates with only a limited number of others. This may result from physical connectivity, as with PCs on an isolated LAN, or with a camera and a laptop that are communicating via Bluetooth; or it may come from logical connectivity. For example, when a virus spreads by mailing itself to everyone in an infected machine's address book, the network that it's infecting is one whose nodes are users of the vulnerable email client and whose edges are their presence in each others' address books.

We can bring other ideas and tools to bear when the network is in effect a *social network* like this. In recent years, physicists and sociologists have collaborated in applying thermodynamic models to the analysis of complex networks of social interactions; the emerging discipline of network analysis is reviewed in [965], and has been applied to disciplines from criminology to the study of how new technologies diffuse.

Network topology turns out to be important in service denial attacks. Rulers have known for centuries that when crushing dissidents, it's best to focus on the ringleaders; and when music industry enforcers try to close down peer-to-peer file-sharing networks they similarly go after the most prominent nodes. There's now a solid scientific basis for this. It turns out that social networks can be modelled by a type of graph in which there's a power-law distribution of vertex order; in other words, a small number of nodes have a large number of edges ending at them. These well-connected nodes help make the network resilient against random failure, and easy to navigate. Yet Reka Albert, Hawoong Jeong and Albert-László Barabási showed that they also make such networks vulnerable to targeted attack. Remove the well-connected nodes, and the network is easily disconnected [20].

This has prompted further work on how topology interacts with conflict. For example, Shishir Nagaraja and I extended Albert, Jeong and Barabási's work to the dynamic case in which, at each round, the attacker gets to destroy some nodes according to an attack strategy, and the defender then gets to replace a similar number of nodes using a defense strategy. We played attack and defense strategies off against each other; against a decapitation attack, the best defense we found was a cell structure. This helps explain why peer-to-peer systems with ring architectures turned out to be rather fragile — and why revolutionaries have tended to organise themselves in cells [924]. George Danezis and Bettina Wittneben applied these network analysis ideas to privacy, and found that by doing traffic analysis against just a few well-connected organisers, a police force can identify a surprising number of members of a dissident organisation. The reason is that if you monitor everyone who calls, or is called by, the main organisers of a typical social network, you get most of the members — unless effort was expended in organising it in a cell structure in the first place [345].

These techniques may well become even more relevant to network attack and defence for a number of reasons. First, early social-network techniques have produced real results; the capture of Saddam Hussein used a layered social network analysis [623]. Second, as people try to attack (and defend) local networks organised on an ad-hoc basis using technologies like WiFi and Bluetooth, topology will matter more. Third, social networking sites — and more conventional services like Google mail that use introductions to acquire new customers — have a lot of social network information that can be used to track people; if a phisherman uses Google mail, the police can look for the people who introduced him, and then for everyone else they introduced, when searching for contacts. Fourth, as social structure starts to be used against wrongdoers (and against citizens by repressive regimes) people will invest in cell-structured organisations and in other stealth techniques to defeat it. Finally, there are all sorts of useful things that can potentially be done with topological information. For example, people may be more able to take a view on whether devices that are 'nearby' are trustworthy, and you may not need to filter traffic so assiduously if it can come from only a few sources rather than the whole Internet. This isn't entirely straightforward, as systems change over time in ways that undermine their builders' trust assumptions, but it can still be worth thinking about.

21.6   Summary

Preventing and detecting attacks that are launched over networks, and particularly over the Internet, is probably the most newsworthy aspect of security engineering. The problem is unlikely to be solved any time soon, as many different kinds of vulnerability contribute to the attacker's toolkit. Ideally, people would run carefully written code on trustworthy platforms. In real life, this won't happen always, or even often. In the corporate world, there are grounds for hope that firewalls can keep out the worst of the attacks, careful configuration management can block most of the rest, and intrusion detection can catch most of the residue that make it through. Home users are less well placed, and most of the machines being recruited to the vast botnets we see in action today are home machines attached to DSL or cable modems.

Hacking techniques depend partly on the opportunistic exploitation of vulnerabilities introduced accidentally by the major vendors, and partly on techniques to social-engineer people into running untrustworthy code. Most of the bad things that result are just the same bad things that happened a generation ago, but moved online, on a larger scale, and with a speed, level of automation and global dispersion that leaves law enforcement wrong-footed.

Despite all this, the Internet is not a disaster. It's always possible for a security engineer, when contemplating the problems we've discussed in this chapter, to sink into doom and gloom. Yet the Internet has brought huge benefits to billions of people, and levels of online crime are well below the levels of real-world crime. I'll discuss this in more detail when we get to policy in Part III; for now, note that the $200 m–$1 bn lost in the USA to phishing in 2006 was way below ordinary fraud involving things like checks, not to mention the drug trade or even the trade in stolen cars.

Herd effects matter. A useful analogy for the millions of insecure computers is given by the herds of millions of gnu that once roamed the plains of Africa. The lions could make life hard for any one gnu, but most of them survived for years by taking shelter in numbers. The Internet's much the same. There are analogues of the White Hunter, who'll carefully stalk a prime trophy animal; so you need to take special care if anyone might see you in these terms. And if you think that the alarms in the press about 'Evil Hackers Bringing Down the Internet' are somehow equivalent to a hungry African peasant poaching the game, then do bear in mind the much greater destruction done by colonial ranching companies who had the capital to fence off the veld in 100,000-acre lots. Economics matters, and we are still feeling our way towards the kinds of regulation that will give us a reasonably stable equilibrium. In fact, colleagues and I wrote a report for the European Network and Information Security Agency on the sort of policy incentives that might help [62]. I'll return to policy in Part III.

Research Problems

Seven years ago, the centre of gravity in network security research was technical: we were busy looking for new attacks on protocols and applications as the potential for denial-of-service attacks started to become clear. Now, in 2007, there are more threads of research. Getting protocols right still matters and it's unfortunate (though understandable in business terms) that many firms still ship products quickly and get them right later. This has led to calls for vendor liability, for example from a committee of the UK Parliament [625]. On the security-economics front, there is much interesting work to be done on decent metrics: on measuring the actual wickedness that goes on, and feeding this not just into the policy debate but also into law enforcement.

Systems people do a lot of work on measuring the Internet to understand how it's evolving as more and more devices, people and applications join in. And at the level of theory, more and more computer scientists are looking at ways in which network protocols could be aligned with stakeholder interests, so that participants have less incentive to cheat [971].

Further Reading

The early classic on Internet security was written by Steve Bellovin and Bill Cheswick [157]; other solid books are by Simson Garfinkel and Eugene Spafford on Unix and Internet security [517], and by Terry Escamilla on intrusion detection [439]. These give good introductions to network attacks (though like any print work in this fast-moving field, they are all slightly dated). The seminal work on viruses is by Fred Cohen [311], while Java security is discussed by Gary McGraw and Ed Felten [859] as well as by LiGong (who designed it) [539]. Eric Rescorla has a book on the details of TLS [1070]; another useful description — shorter than Eric's but longer than the one I gave above — is by Larry Paulson [1010]. Our policy paper for ENISA can be found at [62].

It's important to know a bit about the history of attacks — as they recur — and to keep up to date with what's going on. A survey of security incidents on the Internet in the late 1990s can be found in John Howard's thesis [626]. Advisories from CERT [321] and bugtraq [239] are one way of keeping up with events, and hacker sites such as `www.phrack.com` bear watching. However, as malware becomes commercial, I'd suggest you also keep up with the people who measure botnets, spam and phishing. As of 2007, I'd recommend Team Cymru at `http://www.cymru.com/`, the Anti-Phishing Working Group at `http://www.antiphishing.org/`, the Shadowserver Foundation at `http://www.shadowserver.org/`, Symantec's half-yearly threat report at `www.symantec.com/threatreport/`, and our blog at `www.lightbluetouchpaper.net`.

CHAPTER 22

Copyright and DRM

The DeCSS case is almost certainly a harbinger of what I would consider to be the defining battle of censorship in cyberspace. In my opinion, this will not be fought over pornography, neo-Nazism, bomb design, blasphemy, or political dissent. Instead, the Armageddon of digital control, the real death match between the Party of the Past and Party of the Future, will be fought over copyright.

— John Perry Barlow

Be very glad that your PC is insecure — it means that after you buy it, you can break into it and install whatever software you want. What YOU want, not what Sony or Warner or AOL wants.

— John Gilmore

22.1 Introduction

Copyright, and digital rights management (DRM), have been among the most contentious issues of the digital age. At the political level, there is the conflict alluded to by Barlow in the above quotation. The control of information has been near the centre of government concerns since before William Tyndale (one of the founders of the Cambridge University Press) was burned at the stake for printing the Bible in English. The sensitivity continued through the establishment of modern copyright law starting with the Statute of Anne in 1709, through the eighteenth century battles over press censorship, to the Enlightenment and the framing of the U.S. Constitution. The link between copyright and censorship is obscured by technology from time to time, but has a habit of reappearing. Copyright mechanisms exist to keep information out of the hands of people who haven't paid for it, while censors keep information out of the hands of people who satisfy some other criterion. If ISPs are ever compelled to install filters that will prevent their customers from downloading copyrighted content, these filters could also be used to prevent the download of seditious content.

In the last few generations, the great wealth accruing to the owners of literary copyright, films and music has created another powerful interest in control. As the music and film industries in particular feared loss of sales to digital copying, they lobbied for sweetheart laws — the DMCA in America, and a series of IP Directives in Europe — that give special legal protection to mechanisms that enforce copyright. These laws are now being used and abused for all sorts of other purposes, from taking down phishing websites to stopping people from refilling printer cartridges.

The ostensible target of these laws, though, remains the DRM mechanisms that are used in products such as Windows Media Player and Apple's iTunes to control copying of music and videos that have been purchased online. I'll describe how DRM works. The basic mechanism is to make available an encrypted media file, and then to sell separately a 'license' which is the key to the media file encrypted using a key unique to the user, plus some statements in a 'rights management language' about what the user can do with the content. I'll also describe some interesting variants such as satellite TV encryption systems, copyright marking, traitor tracing, and Blu-Ray. And, of course, no discussion of copyright would be complete these days without some mention of file-sharing systems, and the mechanisms used by Hollywood to try to close them down.

Finally, there are some thorny policy issues tied up in all this. Economists pointed out that stronger DRM would help the platform industry more than the music industry, and their warnings have come true: Apple is making more money and the music majors are making less. The possible implications for video are interesting. And finally there are some serious privacy issues with rights management systems. Do you really want a license management server, whether in Redmond or Cupertino, to know every music track you've ever listened to, and every movie you've ever watched?

22.2   Copyright

The protection of copyright has for years been an obsession of the film, music and book publishing industries (often referred to collectively — and perjoratively — by computer industry people as *Hollywood*). But this didn't start with the Internet. There were long and acrimonious disputes in many countries about whether blank audio- or videocassettes should be subjected to a tax whose proceeds would be distributed to copyright owners; and the issue isn't confined to electronic media. In the UK, several million pounds a year are distributed to authors whose books are borrowed from public lending libraries [1050]. Going back to the nineteenth century, there was alarm that the invention of photography would destroy the book publishing trade; and in the sixteenth, the invention of movable type printing was considered to be highly subversive by most of the powers that were, including princes, bishops and craft guilds.

There's a lot we can learn from historical examples such as book publishing, and pay-TV. But I'm going to start by looking at software protection — as most of the current copyright issues have been played out in the PC and games software markets over the last twenty years or so. Also, the music industry forced the computer industry to introduce DRM, saying that without it they'd be ruined — and the computer industry for years retorted that the music industry should just change its business model, so it's interesting to use software as the baseline. Finally, the computer industry frequently argued in its tussles with the music majors that in an open platform such as the PC it's intrinsically hard to stop people copying bitstreams — so how did they themselves cope?

22.2.1 Software

Software for early computers was given away free by the hardware vendors or by users who'd written it. IBM even set up a scheme in the 1960's whereby its users could share programs they had written. (Most of them were useless as they were too specialised, too poorly documented, or just too hard to adapt.) So protecting software copyright was not an issue. Almost all organizations that owned computers were large and respectable; the software tended to require skilled maintenance; and so they often had full-time system engineers employed by the hardware vendor on site. There are still sectors which operate on this business model. For example, one supplier of bank dealing room software takes the view that anyone who pirates their code is welcome, as using it without skilled technical support would be a fast way for a bank to lose millions.

But when minicomputers arrived in the 1960's, software costs started to become significant. Hardware vendors started to charge extra for their operating system, and third party system houses sprang up. To begin with, they mostly sold you a complete bespoke system — hardware, software and maintenance — so piracy was still not much of an issue. By the mid-1970's, some of them had turned bespoke systems into packages: software originally written for one bakery would be parametrized and sold to many bakeries. The most common copyright dispute in those days was when a programmer left your company to join a competitor, and their code suddenly acquired a number of your features; the question then was whether he'd taken code with him, or reimplemented it.

The standard way to resolve such a problem is to look at *software birthmarks* — features of how a particular implementation was done, such as the order in which registers are pushed and popped. This continues to be important, and there are various code comparison tools available — many of them developed in universities to detect students cheating on programming assignments. (This thread of research leads to general purpose plagiarism detection tools, which can trawl through natural language as well as code and typically recognise a passage of text by indexing it according to the least common words which appear in it [589], on to systems used by humanities scholars to figure out whether Bacon wrote Shakespeare, and back to tools which try to identify the authors of viruses from their coding style [746].)

With time, people invented lots of useful things to do with software. So a firm that had bought a minicomputer for stock control (or contracted for time on a bureau service) might be tempted to run a statistical program as well to prepare management reports. Meanwhile, the installed base of machines got large enough for software sharing to happen more than just occasionally. So some system houses started to put in copyright enforcement mechanisms. A common one was to check the processor serial number; another was the *time bomb*. When I worked in 1981 for a company selling retail stock control systems, we caused a message to come up every few months saying something like 'Fault no. WXYZ — please call technical support'. WXYZ was an encrypted version of the license serial number, and if the caller claimed to be from that customer we'd give them a password to re-enable the system for the next few months. (If not, we'd send round a salesman.) This mechanism could have been defeated easily if the 'customer' understood it, but in practice it worked fine: most of the time it was a low-level clerk who encountered the fault message and called our office.

Software piracy really started to become an issue when the arrival of microcomputers in the late 1970's and early 80's created a mass market, and software houses started to ship products that didn't need support to install and run. Initial responses varied. There was a famous open letter from Bill Gates in 1976, a year after Microsoft was founded, in which he complained that less than 10% of all microcomputer users had paid them for BASIC [502]. 'Who cares if the people who worked on it get paid?' he asked. 'Is this fair?' His letter concluded: 'Nothing would please me more than being able to hire ten programmers and deluge the hobby market with good software'.

Appeals to people's sense of fair play only got so far, and the industry next seized on the obvious difference between minis and micros — the latter had no processor serial numbers. There were three general approaches tried: to add uniqueness on to the machine, to create uniqueness in it, or to use whatever uniqueness happened to exist already by chance.

1. The standard way to add hardware uniqueness was a *dongle* — a device, typically attached to the PC's parallel port, which could be interrogated by the software. The simplest just had a serial number; the most common executed a simple challenge-response protocol; while some top-end devices actually performed some critical part of the computation.

2. A cheaper and very common strategy was for the software to install itself on the PC's hard disk in a way that was resistant to naive copying. For example, a sector of the hard disk would be marked as bad, and a critical part of the code or data written there. Now if the product were copied from the hard disk using the utilities provided by the operating system for the purpose, the data hidden in the bad sector wouldn't be copied and so the copy wouldn't work. A variant on the same theme was to require the presence of a master diskette which had been customized in some way, such as by formatting it in a strange way or even burning holes in it with a laser. In general, though, a distinction should be drawn between protecting the copy and protecting the master; it's often a requirement that people should be able to make copies for backup if they wish, but not to make copies of the copies (this is called *copy generation control*).

3. A product I worked on stored the PC's configuration — what cards were present, how much memory, what type of printer — and if this changed too radically, it would ask the user to phone the helpline. It's actually quite surprising how many unique identifiers there are in the average PC; ethernet addresses and serial numbers of disk controllers are only the more obvious ones. Provided you have some means of dealing with upgrades, you can use component details to tie software to a given machine.

A generic attack that works against most of these defenses is to go through the software with a debugger and remove all the calls made to the copy protection routines. Many hobbyists did this for sport, and competed to put unprotected versions of software products online as soon as possible after their launch. Even people with licensed copies of the software often got hold of unprotected versions as they were easier to back up and often more reliable generally. You can stop this by having critical code somewhere really uncopiable, such as in a dongle, but the lesson from this arms race was that the kids with the debuggers would always break your scheme eventually.

The vendors also used psychological techniques.

- The installation routine for many business programs would embed the registered user's name and company on the screen, for example, in the toolbar. This wouldn't stop a pirate distributing copies registered in a false name, but it will discourage legitimate users from giving casual copies to colleagues.

- Industry publicists retailed stories of organizations that had come unstuck when they failed to get a critical upgrade of software they hadn't paid for. One of the favourite stories was of the U.S. army bases in Germany that didn't pay for the VAX VMS operating system and got hacked after they didn't get a security patch (described above in section 2.5.4).

- If early Microsoft software (Multiplan, Word or Chart) thought you were running it under a debugger, trying to trace through it, it would put up the message 'The tree of evil bears bitter fruit. Now trashing program disk.' It would then seek to track zero on the floppy and go 'rrnt, rrnt, rrnt'.

In the mid- to late-1980s, the market split. The games market moved in the direction of hardware protection, and ended up dominated by games console products with closed architectures where the software is sold in proprietary cartridges. The driver for this was that consumers are more sensitive about the sticker price of a product than about its total cost of ownership, so it makes sense to subsidise the cost of the console out of later sales of software for it (a strategy since adopted by printer makers who subsidise the printers from the ink cartridges). This strategy led to strict *accessory control* in which hardware protection was used to prevent competitors selling software or other add-ons unless they had paid the appropriate royalty.

Business software vendors, however, generally stopped trying to protect mass market products using predominantly technical means. There were several reasons.

- Unless you're prepared to spend money on seriously tamper resistant dongle hardware which executes some of your critical code, the mechanisms will be defeated by people for whom it's an intellectual challenge, and unprotected code will be anonymously published. Code that isn't protected in the first place is less of a challenge.

- As processors got faster and code got more complex, operating system interfaces became higher level, and software protection routines of the 'bad disk sector' variety became harder to write. And now that it's possible to run a Windows NT system on top of Linux using VMware or Xen, application software can be completely shielded from machine specifics such as ethernet addresses. The net effect is an increase in the cost and complexity of both protection and piracy.

- Protection is a nuisance. Multiple dongles get in the way or even interfere with each other. Software protection techniques tend to make a product less robust and cause you problems — as when their hard disk fails and they recover from backup to a new disk. Protection mechanisms can also cause software from different vendors to be unnecessarily incompatible and in some cases unable to reside on the same machine.

- Technical support became more and more important as software products became more complex, and you only get it if you pay for the software.

- The arrival of computer viruses was great for the industry. It forced corporate customers to invest in software hygiene, which in turn meant that casual copying couldn't be condoned so easily. Within a few years, antivirus programs made life much harder for copy protection designers in any case, as non-standard operating system usage tended to set off virus alarms.

- There was not much money to be made out of harassing personal users as they often made only casual use of the product and would throw it away rather than pay.

- A certain level of piracy was good for business. People who got a pirate copy of a tool and liked it would often buy a regular copy, or persuade their employer to buy one.

- In Microsoft's case, customer reaction to their scare message was pretty negative.

- Many vendors preferred not to have to worry about whether the software was licensed to the user (in which case he could migrate it to a new machine) or to the machine (in which case he could sell the computer second-hand with the software installed). As both practices were common, mechanisms that made one or the other very much harder caused problems. Mechanisms that could easily deal with both (such as dongles) tended to be expensive, either to implement, or in call-centre support costs.

- Finally, Borland shook up the industry with its launch of Turbo Pascal. Before then a typical language compiler cost about $500 and came with such poor documentation that you had to spend a further $50 on a book to tell you how to use it. Borland's product cost $49.95, was technically superior to the competition, and came with a manual that was just as good as a third party product. (So, like many other people, once I'd heard of it, borowed a copy from a friend, tried it and liked it, I went out and bought it.) 'Pile it high and sell it cheap' simply proved to be a more profitable business model — even for speciality products such as compilers.

The industry then swung to legal solutions. The main initiative was to establish anti-piracy trade organizations in most countries (in the USA, the Software Publishers' Association) that brought high-profile prosecutions of large companies that had been condoning widespread use of pirate PC software. This was followed up by harassing medium and even small businesses with threatening letters demanding details of the company's policy on enforcing copyright — holding out a carrot of approved software audit schemes and a stick of possible raids by enforcement squads. All sorts of tricks were used to get pirates to incriminate themselves. A typical ruse was the *salted list*; for example, one trade directory product I worked on contained details of a number of bogus companies with phone numbers directed to the publisher's help desk, whose staff would ask for the caller's company and check it off against the list of paid subscribers.

Eventually, the industry discovered that the law not only provides tools for enforcement, but sets limits too. The time-honoured technique of using timebombs has now been found to be illegal in a number of jurisdictions. In 1993, for example, a software company director in Scunthorpe, England, received a criminal conviction under Britain's Computer Misuse Act for 'making an unauthorized modification' to a system after he used a time-bomb to enforce payment of an disputed invoice [313]. Many jurisdictions now consider time bombs unacceptable unless the customer is adequately notified of their existence at the time of purchase.

The emphasis is now swinging somewhat back in the direction of technical mechanisms. Site licence agreements are enforced using *license servers*, which are somewhat like dongles but are implemented on PCs which sit on a corporate network and limit the number of copies of an application that can run simultaneously. They can still be defeated by disassembling the application code, but as code becomes larger this gets harder, and combined with the threat of legal action they are often adequate.

The model to which the software industry is converging is thus one that combines technical and legal measures, understanding the limits of both, and accepting that a certain amount of copying will take place (with which you try to leverage fully-paid sales). One of Bill's more revealing sayings is:

> Although about three million computers get sold every year in China, people don't pay for the software. Someday they will, though. And as long as they're going to steal it, we want them to steal ours. They'll get sort of addicted, and then we'll somehow figure out how to collect sometime in the next decade [518].

The latest emphasis is on online registration. If you design your product so that customers interact with your web site — for example, to download the latest exchange rates, virus signatures or security patches, then you can keep a log of everyone who uses your software. But this can be dangerous. When Microsoft tried it with Registration Wizard in Windows 95, it caused a storm of protest. Also, a colleague found that he couldn't upgrade Windows 98 on a machine on his yacht since it was always offline. And when I first tried Microsoft Antispyware Beta on a machine we had at home with Windows XP, it was denounced as a pirate copy — despite the fact that the PC had been bought legally in a local store. Microsoft did sort that out for me, but having flaky registration mechanisms clearly costs money, and building robust ones is not trivial if you're selling large volumes of many products through complex supply chains. (In fact, it's against the public interest for security patches to be limited to registered licensees; a security-economics analysis we did of the problem recommended that the practice be outlawed [62].)

It's also worth noting that different methods are used to counter different threats. Large-scale commercial counterfeiting may be detected by monitoring product serial numbers registered online, but such operations are found and closed down by using investigative agencies to trace their product back through the supply chains. For example, once they got their product registration sorted out, Microsoft found that a third of the copies of Office sold in Germany were counterfeit, and traced them to a small factory a few miles up the road from us in Cambridge. Almost all the factory's staff were unaware of the scam — they believed the company was a bona fide Microsoft supplier. They were even proud of it and their salesmen used it to try to get disk duplication business from other software vendors.

That is more or less what's done with the personal and small business sectors, but with medium sized and large businesses the main risk is that fewer legal copies will be purchased than there are machines which run them. The usual countermeasure is to combine legal pressure from software trade associations with site licences and rewards for whistleblowers. It's significant that companies such as Microsoft make the vast bulk of their sales from business rather than personal customers. Many large businesses prefer not to have machines registered online individually, as they want to keep their staff numbers and structures confidential from the vendors; many vendors respect this, but the downside is that an 'unprotected' binary originally issued to a large company is often the standard 'warez' that people swap. Many firms still hold back from using online registration to enforce copyright aggressively against personal users; the potential extra revenues are small given the possible costs of a public backlash. Other considerations include the difficulty of tracing people who change addresses or trade PCs secondhand. It is just very expensive to maintain a high-quality database of millions of small customers.

For companies that do have deep pockets, such as Google, one option is to provide not just the software but also the processor to run it. It's worth noting that software-as-a-service may be the ultimate copyright protection or DRM for software (or any other content that can live online): you can't buy it, freeze the version you're running, or use it offline. You may also get to control all your customers' data too, giving you impressive lockin. (I will discuss web services in the next chapter.)

With that exception, none of the mass-market protection technologies available at the beginning of the 21st century is foolproof, especially against a determined opponent. But by using the right combination of them a large software vendor can usually get a tolerable result — especially if prices aren't too extortionate and the vendor isn't too unpopular. Small software companies are under less pressure, as their products tend to be more specialised and the risk of copying is lower, so they can often get away with making little or no effort to control copying. (And if they have only a few customers, it may even be economic for them to supply software as a service.)

There are also many alternative business models. One is to give away a limited version of the product, and sell online a password which unlocks its full functionality. Unix was popularized by giving it away free to universities, while companies had to pay; a variant on this theme is to give basic software away free to individuals but charge companies, as Netscape did. An even more radical model is to give your software away completely free, and make your money from selling services. The Linux industry makes its money from consultancy and support, while Web applications such as Google Documents make their money from advertising.

This experience has led many computer people to believe that the solution for Hollywood's problem lies in a change of business model. But before we dive into the world of protecting multimedia content, let's look briefly at a few historical precedents.

22.2.2 Books

Carl Shapiro and Hal Varian present a useful historical lesson in the rise of book publishing [1159]. In 1800, there were only 80,000 frequent readers in England; most of the books up till then were serious philosophical or theological tomes. After the invention of the novel, a mass market appeared for books, and circulating libraries sprung up to service it. The educated classes were appalled, and the printers were frightened that the libraries would deprive them of sales.

But the libraries so whetted people's appetite for books that the number of readers grew to 5,000,000 by 1850. Sales of books soared as people bought books they'd first borrowed from a library. The library movement turned out to have been the printers' greatest ally and helped create a whole new market for mass-market books.

22.2.3 Audio

Pirates have also been copying music and other audio much longer than software. Paganini was so worried that people would copy his violin concertos that he distributed the scores himself to the orchestra just before rehearsals and performances, and collected them again afterwards. (As a result, many of his works were lost to posterity.)

In recent years, there have been several flurries of industry concern. When the cassette recorder came along in the 1960's, the record industry lobbied for (and in some countries got) a tax on audiocassettes, to be distributed to copyright holders. Technical measures were also tried. The Beatles' record Sergeant Pepper contained a 20 KHz spoiler tone that should in theory have combined with the 21 KHz bias frequency of the tape to produce a 1 KHz whistle that would spoil the sound. In practice it didn't work, as many record players didn't have the bandwidth to pick up the spoiler tone. But in practice this didn't matter. Cassettes turned out not to be a huge problem because the degradation in quality is noticeable on home equipment; many people just used them to record music to listen to in their cars. Then, in the 1980s, the arrival of the Sony Walkman made cassettes into big business, and although there was some copying, there were huge sales of pre-recorded cassettes and the music industry cleaned up.

The introduction of *digital audio tape* (DAT) caused the next worry, because a perfect copy of the contents of a CD could be made. The eventual response was to introduce a *serial copy management system* (SCMS) — a single bit in the tape header that said whether a track could be copied or not [648]. The idea was that copies made from a CD would be marked as uncopiable, so people could copy CDs they already owned, to listen to on the move, but couldn't make copies of the copies. This didn't work well, as the no-more-copies bit is ignored by many recorders and can be defeated by simple filtering. Again, this didn't matter as DAT didn't become widely used. (CDROMs also have a no-copy bit in the track header but this is almost universally ignored.)

Audio copying has become a headline concern again, thanks to the MP3 format for compressing audio. Previously, digital audio was protected by its size: a CD full of uncompressed music can take 650 Mb. However, MP3 enables people to squeeze an audio CD track into a few megabytes, and universal broadband enables files of this size to be shared easily. Usage in universities is particularly heavy; by 1998, some 40% of the network traffic at MIT was MP3 traffic. Some students became underground disc jockeys and relayed audio streams around campus — without paying royalties to the copyright owners.

The initial response of the industry was to push for technical fixes. This led to the growth of the rights-management industry. It had its origins in work on digital publishing and in the mechanisms used to protect pay-TV and DVDs, so let's look at those first.

22.2.4   Video and Pay-TV

The early history of videocassettes was just like that of audio cassettes. At first Hollywood was terrified, and refused to release movies for home viewing. Again, there were technical measures taken to prevent copying — such as the Macrovision system which adds spurious synchronization pulses to confuse the recording circuitry of domestic VCRs — but again these turned out to be straightforward for technically savvy users to defeat. Then Hollywood became paranoid about video rental stores, just as book publishers had been about libraries: but being able to rent videos greatly increased the number of VCRs and whetted people's desire to own their favorite movies. VCRs and videocassettes became mass market products rather than rock stars' toys, and now sales of prerecorded cassettes make up most of the income of firms like Disney. The business model has changed so that the cinema release is really just advertising for the sales of the video.

And now that many of the world's pre-teens demand that their parents build them a collection of Disney cassettes, just like their friends have, a videocassette pirate must make the packaging look original. This reduces the problem to an industrial counterfeiting one. As with mass market software before the onset of online registration, or with perfumes and Swiss watches today, enforcement involves sending out field agents to buy cassettes, look for forgeries, trace the supply chain and bring prosecutions.

Much more interesting technical protection mechanisms have been built into the last few generations of pay-TV equipment.

The advent of pay-TV, whether delivered by cable or satellite, created a need for *conditional access* mechanisms which would allow a station operator to restrict reception of a channel in various ways. If he'd only bought the rights to screen a movie in Poland, then he'd have to block German or Russian viewers within the satellite footprint from watching. Porn channel operators needed to prevent reception in countries like Britain and Ireland with strict censorship laws. Most operators also wanted to be able to charge extra for specific events such as boxing matches.

22.2.4.1   Typical System Architecture

The evolution of early systems was determined largely by the hardware cost of deciphering video (for a history of set-top boxes, see [293]). The first generation of systems, available since the 1970's, were crude analog devices which used tricks such as inverting the video signal from time to time, interfering with the synchronization, and inserting spikes to confuse the TV's automatic gain control. They were easy enough to implement, but also easy to defeat; breaking them didn't involve cryptanalysis, just an oscilloscope and persistence.

The second generation of systems appeared in the late 1980's and employed a hybrid of analog and digital technologies: the broadcast was analogue, the subscriber control was digital. These included systems such as Videocrypt and Nagravision, and typically have three components:

- a subscription management service at the station enciphers the outgoing video, embeds various *entitlement management messages* (EMMs) and *entitlement control messages* (ECMs) in it, and issues access tokens such as smartcards to subscribers;

- a *set-top box* converts the cable or satellite signal into one the TV can deal with. This includes descrambling it;

- the subscriber smartcard personalises the device and controls what programmes the set-top box is allowed to descramble. It does this by interpreting the ECMs and providing keys to the descrambling circuit in the set-top box.

This arrangement means that the complex, expensive processes such as bulk video scrambling can be done in a mass-produced custom chip with a long product life, while security-critical functions that may need to be replaced in a hurry after a hack can be sold to the customer in a low-cost token that is easy to replace. If the set-top box itself had to replaced every time the system was hacked, the economics would be much less attractive.

The basic mechanism is that the set-top box decodes the ECMs from the input datastream and passes them to the card. The card deciphers the ECMs to get both control messages (such as 'smartcard number 123356, your subscriber hasn't paid, stop working until further notice') and keys, known as *control words*, that are passed to the set-top box. The set-top box then uses the control words to descramble the video and audio streams. There's a detailed description in a patent filed in 1991 by NDS [314].

22.2.4.2 *Video Scrambling Techniques*

Because of the limitations on the chips available at low cost in the early 1990s, hybrid systems typically scramble video by applying a transposition cipher to picture elements. A typical scheme was the *cut-and-rotate* algorithm used in

Videocrypt. This scrambles one line of video at a time by cutting it at a point determined by a control byte and swapping the left and right halves (Figure 22.1):

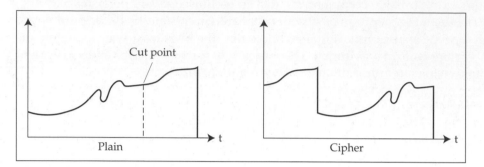

Figure 22.1: Cut-and-rotate scrambling

This involved analog-to-digital conversion of the video signal, storage in a buffer, and digital-to-analog conversion after rotation — a process which could just about be shoehorned into a low-cost custom VLSI chip by 1990. However, a systemic vulnerability of such systems is that video is highly redundant, so it may be possible to reconstruct the image using signal processing techniques. This was first done by Markus Kuhn in 1995 and required the use of a supercomputer at the University of Erlangen to do in real time. Figure 22.2 shows a frame of enciphered video, and Figure 22.3 the same frame after processing. By now, it's possible to do this on a PC [1222]. If this attack had been feasible earlier, it would have given a complete break of the system, as regardless of how well the smartcard managed the keys, the video signal could be retrieved without them. Hybrid systems are still used by some stations, particularly in less developed countries, together with frequent key changes to make life inconvenient for the pirates — whose problem is to somehow distribute the keys to their customers as they crack them.

Figure 22.2: Scrambled video frame

Figure 22.3: Processed video frame

As for major developed-world operators, they moved to digital systems in the early 2000s. These digital systems work on the same principle — a set-top box with the crypto hardware and a smartcard to hold the personal keys that in turn decipher the content keys from ECMs. However the crypto now typically uses a block cipher to protect the entire digital video stream. I'll describe the current digital video broadcast systems in the next section.

The hybrid scrambling techniques lasted (just) long enough. However, they have some interesting lessons to teach, as they were subjected to quite determined attack in decade after 1995, so I'll spend a page or two going through what went wrong.

22.2.4.3 *Attacks on Hybrid Scrambling Systems*

Given a population of set-top boxes that will unscramble broadcast video given a stream of control words, the next problem is to see to it that only paying customers can generate the control words. In general, this can be done with white lists or black lists. But the bandwidth available to last-generation pay-TV systems was low — typically of the order of ten ECMs per second could be sent, or a bit over half a million a day. So the blacklist approach was the main one. With a subscriber base of five million customers, sending an individual message to each customer would take over a week.

The basic protocol is that the customer smartcard interprets the ECMs. If the current programme is one the subscriber is allowed to watch, then a keyed hash — essentially a message authentication code (MAC) — is computed on a series of ECMs using a master key held in the card and supplied to the set-top box as the control word:

$$CW = MAC(K; ECM_1, ECM_2, ECM_3, ECM_4)$$

So if a subscriber stops paying his subscription, his card can be inactivated by sending an ECM ordering it to stop issuing control words; and it needs access to the ECM stream in order to compute the control words at all. So provided the cards can be made tamper-resistant, only compliant devices should have access to the master key K, and they should commit suicide on demand. So what could go wrong?

Well, the first attacks were on the protocol. Since the control word sent from the smartcard to the set-top box is the same for every set-top box currently unscrambling the program, one person can record the stream of control words, by placing a PC between the smartcard and the set-top box, and post them to the Internet. Other people can video-record the scrambled program, and unscramble it later after downloading the control word stream [850]. Servers sprung up for this key-log attack exist, but were only a minor nuisance to the pay-TV industry; not many viewers were prepared to get a special adapter to connect their PC to their set-top box.

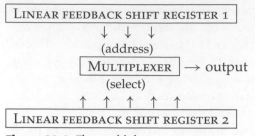

Figure 22.4: The multiplexer generator

Cryptanalysis also gave opportunities to the hackers. Every half-second or so the smartcard supplies the set-top box with a new control word, and this is loaded into a keystream generator which works as follows. There are two linear feedback shift registers, of lengths 31 and 29 in the Eurocrypt system, which generate long linear sequences. Some of the bits of register 1 are used as address lines to a multiplexer, which selects a bit from register 2; this bit becomes the next bit of the keystream sequence. Each successive byte of output becomes a control byte for the scrambler (Figure 22.4).

The designers intended that breaking this cipher should involve guessing the key, and as this is 60 bits long a guess would take on average 2^{59} trials which is uneconomic — as it has to be done about twice a second. But it turns out that the cipher has a shortcut attack. The trick is to guess the contents of register 1, use this address information to place bits of the observed keystream in register 2, and if this causes a clash, reject the current guess for register 1. (I discovered this attack in 1985 and it's what got me interested in cryptography.) The effect of this is that as the high order four bits or so of each control word are easy to deduce from inter-line correlations — it's the least significant bits you really have to work hard for. So you can easily get about half the bits from a segment of keystream, and reconstruct the control word using cryptanalysis. But this computation is still comparable with the full signal processing attack, and of interest to hobbyists rather than the mass market.

Other hobbyist attacks included *blockers*, which would prevent ECMs addressed to your card from being delivered to it; this way, you could cancel your subscription without the station operator being able to cancel your service [850]. Perhaps the most powerful of the 'amateur' attacks exploited a master key leakage: someone bought a second-hand PC, looked out of curiosity to see if there were any interesting deleted files on the hard disk, and managed to undelete a complete subscriber management system for one pay-TV operator, including embedded master keys. This enabled software to be written that would completely emulate a subscriber smartcard — in fact, it could be 'improved' in that it would not turn itself off when ordered to do so by an ECM.

Anyway, once this 'low-hanging fruit' had been picked, the commercial pirates turned to reverse engineering smartcards using microprobing techniques. In Chapter 16 I described the arms race between attackers and defenders. But hardware level fixes were limited to new card issues, and the operators didn't want to issue a new card more than once a year as it cost several dollars per subscriber, and the subscriptions were usually less than $20 a month. So other defensive techniques had to be found.

Litigation was tried, but it took time. A lawsuit was lost against a pirate in Ireland, which for a while became a haven from which pirates sold cards by mail order all over Europe. The industry's lobbying muscle was deployed to bring in European law to override Dublin, but this took years. By the middle of 1995, for example, the main UK satellite TV station (Sky-TV) was losing 5% of its revenue to pirate cards.

So all through the mid 1990s, pirates and the operators engaged in a war of countermeasures and counter-countermeasures. The operators would buy pirate cards, analyze them, and develop all sorts of tricks to cause them to fail. The problem faced by the operators was this: when all the secrets in your system are compromised, how can you still fight back against the pirates?

The operators came up with all sorts of cunning tricks. One of their more effective ones was an ECM whose packet contents were executed as code by the smartcard; in this way, the existing card base could be upgraded on the fly and implementation differences between the genuine and pirate cards could be exploited. Any computation that would give a different answer on the two platforms — even if only as a result of an unintentional timing condition — could be fed into the MAC algorithm and used to make the pirate cards deliver invalid control words.

One of the systems (Eurocrypt) had an efficient revocation scheme designed in from the start, and it's worth looking at briefly. Each of the subscriber smartcards contains a subscriber key k_i, and there is a binary tree of intermediate group keys $KGij$ linking the subscriber keys to the currently active master key K_M. Each operational card knows all the group keys in the path between it and the master key, as in Figure 22.5.

In this scheme, if (say) key k_2 appears in pirate cards and has to be revoked, then the operator will send out a stream of packets that let all the other subscriber cards compute a new master key K_M. The first packet will be $\{K'_M\}_{KG12}$ which will let half the subscribers compute K'_M at once; then there will be a K'_M encrypted under an updated version of $KG11$: $\{K'_M\}_{KG'11}$; then this new group key $KG'11$ encrypted under $GK22$; and so on. The effect is that even with ten million customers the operator has to transmit less than fifty ECMs in order to do a complete key change. Of course, this isn't a complete solution: one also needs to think about how to deal with pirate cards that contain several subscriber keys, and hopefully how leaked keys can by identified without having to go to the trouble of breaking into pirate cards. But it's a useful tool in the countermeasures war.

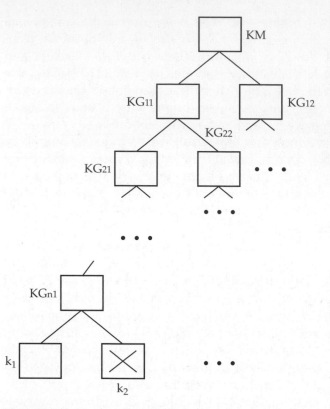

Figure 22.5: Binary revocation tree

Psychological measures were also used. For example, one cable TV station broadcast a special offer for a free T-shirt, and stopped legitimate viewers from seeing the 0800 number to call; this got them a list of the pirates' customers. Economic factors also matter here, as everywhere. Pay-TV pirates depend for their success on time-to-market as much as conventional software firms: a pirate who could produce a 99% correct forgery in three weeks would wipe out a competitor who produced a 99.9% forgery after three months. So pirates race to market just as legitimate vendors do, and pirate cards have bugs just as Windows does. An understanding of economics helps you exploit them effectively: it's best to let a pirate build up a substantial user base before you pull the plug on him, as this gives him time to wipe out his competitors, and also as switching off his cards once he's established will destroy his credibility with more potential customers than an immediate response would. But if you leave him too long, he may acquire both the financial and technical resources to become a persistent problem.

The pay-TV industry learned to plan in advance for security recovery, and to hide a number of features in their products that weren't used initially but could be activated later. (As usual, the same lesson had been learned years previously by another industry — in this particular case the banknote printers.)

Eventually, the smartcards were made much harder to forge by including proprietary encryption algorithms in the processor hardware. As the attacker couldn't simply read out the algorithm with a probing station but had to reverse engineer thousands of gates in the chip, they reduced to a few dozen the number of laboratories with the technical capability to do attacks. Many of these laboratories were drawn into the industry's orbit by consultancy deals or other kinds of sponsorship. Those who remained outside the tent, and appeared to pose a threat, were watched carefully. Vigorous legal enforcement provided the last link in the chain. The industry hunted down the main commercial pirates and put them out of business, whether by having them jailed or by drowning them in litigation.

In the last big pay-TV piracy case in the 20th century, British pirate Chris Cary was convicted of forging Sky-TV smartcards whose design he had had reverse engineered by a company in Canada for $105,000. He then sold forgeries through a front company in Ireland, where counterfeit cards were not illegal at the time [922]. So Sky TV's security consultants infiltrated a spy into his Dublin sales office, and she quietly photocopied enough documents to prove that the operation was really being run from the UK [645]. The British authorities didn't want to prosecute, so Sky brought a private prosecution and had him convicted. When he later escaped from jail, Sky's private detectives relentlessly hunted him down and eventually caught him in New Zealand, where he'd fled using a passport in a dead person's name [575].

So pay-TV history reinforces the lesson that one must make the engineering and legal aspects of copyright protection work together. Neither is likely to be adequate on its own.

22.2.4.4 DVB

Digital video broadcasting (DVB) largely operates using a set of standards that have evolved over the ten years since 1996 and that are controlled by the DVB Consortium, and industry group of over 250 members. The standards are many and complex, relating to IPTV and digital terrestrial TV as well as satellite TV, and to free-to-air services as well as pay-TV.

The protection mechanisms are still a work in progress, and some of them are covered by nondisclosure agreements, but here is a telegraphic summary. The conditional access mechanisms for pay-TV are similar to the hybrid system: the content encryption is digital, but the keys are generated by subscriber smartcards operating on EMMs and ECMs as before. The encryption uses the DVB Common Scrambling Algorithm, which is available only under NDA. The smartcards are not standardised (except at the interface level) so each broadcaster can use his favorite crypto tricks and suppliers; the piracy to date seems to have involved smartcard cloning, but none of the major systems appear to have been broken since 2005 (the relentless viciousness shown by NDS in the Cary case may have had a deterrent effect).

Current standardization work focusses on Content Protection & Copy Management (CPCM), a set of mechanisms for protecting digital content after it's been descrambled and made available within the home. The aim is to enable set-top boxes and other consumer electronic devices to work together so that a customer who's bought a film from pay-TV can store it on a personal video recorder or PC and watch it later at his leisure. (At present, pay-TV operators that offer this do it by selling a more expensive set-top box that contains an extra tuner and a built-in PVR). The basic idea is that all the CPCM-compliant devices in a home will join an 'authorized domain' within which media can be shared and usage information will be logged. This work is still at the proof-of-concept stage. Established DRM vendors, such as Microsoft, already have mechanisms whereby protected content can be moved between compliant devices within their proprietary ecosystem, and there are strong economic incentives on DRM vendors to keep their systems incompatible, so as to maximise the lockin and thus the switching costs. There are also incentive issues with suppliers: how do you stop each individual equipment vendor from making his protection as weak as he can get away with, so that the resulting 'race to the bottom' undermines protection completely?

A good example of 'how not to do it' comes from the world of DVD.

22.2.5 DVD

The consumer electronics industry introduced the *digital video disk* (DVD), later renamed the *digital versatile disk*, in 1996. As usual, Hollywood took fright and said that unless DVD had a decent copy protection mechanism, first-class movies wouldn't be released for it. So a mechanism called the *content scrambling system* (CSS) was built in at the last minute; arguments over this held up the launch of DVD and it was designed in a rush. (The story of how the DVD standards evolved is told in Jim Taylor's standard reference [1242], which also describes most of them.)

DVD has *region coding*: it divides the world into five regions, and disks are supposed to run only on players from some designated list of regions. The goal was to support the traditional practice of releasing a movie in the USA first, then in Europe and so on, in order to minimise the cost of producing physical film prints for use in movie theatres, and the financial loss if the film bombs. But a strong implementation of region coding was not in the vendors' interests; it became clear that users preferred to buy DVD players in which region coding could be turned off, so the vendors raced to ensure that everyone knew how to turn it off in their products. Region coding is less important now, as the Internet has pushed the studios towards near-simultaneous global release of films; but the failure of region coding is yet another example of what happens when the people who have to implement some protection measure are not the people who suffer the costs of failure.

This left CSS, which was known to be vulnerable by the time that DVD was launched [1004]. I heard that the designers were told to come up with a copy protection scheme in two weeks, to use no more than 3,000 gates, and to limit the keylength to 40 bits so the equipment wouldn't fall foul of U.S. expert regulations; another story was that they only ever wanted to compel DVD player manufacturers to licence the CSS patent, so that makers could be compelled to implement other copy protection mechanisms as a condition of the license [193]. No matter whose fault the design was, it's actually quite curious that their system held up for three years. The detailed description of CSS is the subject of much litigation, with numerous injunctions issued in the USA against web sites that have published it. (In fact the hated Digital Millennium Copyright Act, under which U.S. actions are often brought, was introduced in anticipation of the DVD to reinforce its technical protection.)

The flood of legal threats was counterproductive, as Hollywood just got everybody's back up. In 1999, a California court enjoined the posting of DeCSS, one of the CSS decryption programs, but not links pointing to implementations of it; a New York court added a prohibition of links in a case against the hacker magazine 2600 the next year. Such injunctions were seen as censorship, and software to decrypt CSS started appearing on websites outside the USA, on T-shirts, in songs, and in other forms of speech that more traditionally enjoy constitutional protection. This just got the software distributed ever more widely, and made Hollywood look foolish [772]. Their lawyers blundered on, persuading the government of Norway to prosecute a teenager, Jon Lech Johansen, who was one of the authors of DeCSS. He released the code in October 1999; was acquitted on appeal in 2003; and finally in 2004 the Norwegian government decided not to attempt a retrial.

Here's an abbreviated description of CSS[1]. It is based on a stream cipher similar to that in Figure 22.4 except that the multiplexer is replaced with a full adder: each successive keystream bit is obtained by adding together the next two outputs from the shift registers with carry. Combining the xor operations of the shift registers with the add-with-carry of the combiner can actually give a strong cipher if there are (say) five shift registers with coprime lengths greater than 70 [1093]; but in CSS there are only two registers, with lengths 17 and 25, so there is a 2^{16} shortcut attack of exactly the same kind as the one discussed above. Where the cipher is used to protect keys rather than data, there is a further mangling step; but this only increases the complexity to 2^{25}.

Each player has one or more keys specific to the manufacturer, and each DVD disk has a disk key kd encrypted under each of the manufacturer keys

---

[1]Lawyers note: this was published in the first edition of this book in 2001.

(409 of them in 1999) kmi: $\{kd\}_{km1}$, $\{kd\}_{km2}$, $\{kd\}_{km3}$, $\ldots$, $\{kd\}_{km409}$. There is also a hash of kd computed by encrypting it with itself: $\{kd\}_{kd}$. The actual content is protected under sector keys derived from kd. Of course, given that the cipher can be broken with 2^{25} effort, any disk key can be found from a single disk hash.

The DVD consortium hoped to keep enough of the manufacturer keys secret by economic pressure: the idea was that if any manufacturer's master key got leaked, then it wouldn't be used on future disks, so his players wouldn't be able to play new releases. So manufacturers would implement decent tamper resistance — or so it was hoped. But the design of CSS doesn't support this: given any key in the system, all the others can be found at once. Also, the economics of mass-produced consumer electronics just don't allow a few dollars more for a tamper-resistant processor. In effect, CSS contravened Kerckhoffs' principle, in that it depended for its protection on remaining secret, which was never realistic. I also don't think it was realistic for the consortium to think it could blacklist a large electronics firm, as this would not only have sparked off vicious litigation; it would also have meant that the millions of honest consumers who'd bought that company's products would then find they had to go out and buy a new DVD player. The outcry would have been too much; had this nuclear button ever been pressed, I expect governments could have rushed through laws demanding that all DVDs have all master keys. (I'll discuss later how the industry hopes to manage revocation better with the new Blu-Ray standard.)

Another set of problems came from the fact that the PC is an open platform. The DVD consortium required people producing DVD player software to obfuscate their code so that it would be hard to reverse engineer. Papers duly appeared on tricks for systematic software obfuscation [96]. These tricks may have pushed up the cost of reverse engineering from a few days of effort to a few weeks, but once the CSS design was out, that was it.

An even more serious problem with came from Linux, the open source PC operating system used by millions of people. The DVD consortium's philosophy and architecture were not consistent with making DVD drivers available to the Linux community. So as PCs with CD drives started being replaced in the shops with PCs fitted with DVD drives, the Linux user community either had to break CSS, or give up using Linux in favour of Windows. Under the circumstances, it was only a matter of time before someone figured out CSS and DeCSS appeared.

Anyway, DVD followed the usual pattern: Hollywood terrified, and refusing to release their best movies; technical measures taken to prevent copying, which got broken; then litigation. I wrote in 2001: 'A reasonable person might hope that once again the studios will see sense in the end, and make a lot of money from selling DVDs. There will be copying, of course, but it's not entirely trivial yet — even a DSL modem takes hours to send a 4Gb DVD movie to a friend, and PC disk space is also an issue'. This has come true; although some studios held out for a year or two, they all climbed on the DVD bandwagon within a few years, and Disney now makes most of its money from DVD sales. Peer-to-peer sharing is an issue, but because of the bandwidth and disk space constraints it's less so for films than with music.

So will we see the same pattern repeated with high-definition video? Let's look next at the new generation of DVD formats which are being introduced in the hope of grabbing the market for recordings made for high-definition TV, as well as for longer video recordings and larger mass storage of other data.

22.2.6 HD-DVD and Blu-ray

As I was writing this chapter in 2007, a format war was raging between two proposed successors to DVDs, each backed by a large industrial consortium. HD-DVD and Blu-ray are in many respects similar; they both use shorter wavelength lasers to encode information more densely than an old-fashioned DVD does, so a standard disk will store 25 Gb and a double-layered one 50 Gb. Both of them use a content encryption system called AACS, while Blu-ray adds an interesting extra mechanism called SPDC. (As I was correcting the proofs in early 2008, it became clear that Blu-ray had won.)

22.2.6.1 AACS — Broadcast Encryption and Traitor Tracing

The Advanced Access Content System (AACS) has an open design, documented in [647]. Its design goals included the provision of robust, renewable protection on both embedded and general-purpose computers so as to limit output and recording of protected material to approved methods. The encryption is done using AES.

Key management is based on a *broadcast encryption scheme*. The basic idea, due to Li Gong and David Wheeler, is that you can give each user a number of different keys, chosen from a large pool, and arrange things so that any two of them will find some subset of keys that they have in common [540]. So a large number of people can talk to each other without needing a unique key for every other user (or public-key certificates, or a Kerberos server). Amos Fiat and Moni Naor applied this to pay-TV: the broadcaster gives each decoder a small set of keys from the pool, and sets up content keys so that each decoder can compute them using a subset of its keys [469]. When a decoder's compromised, its keys are no longer used, and many researchers have worked on optimising things (so that decoders don't need to hold too many keys, and quite a few of them can be revoked before key material has to be updated).

AACS gives each decoder 256 device keys, and information bundled with the disk tells the decoder which keys to use and how in order to create a *Processing Key*. The idea was that each processing key would be used only for a set of disks. The mechanism is a *Media Key Block* that tells the decoder how to combine its existing media keys to get the Processing Key. The goal is to be able to remove single devices, as with the revocation tree in Figure 22.5, although the details are somewhat different; AACS basically uses a subset-difference tree that enables each decoder to arrive at the same result (for details, see the specification [647]). When a decoder is revoked, a new MKB can be distributed which won't work for that decoder. The processing key in turn protects a Volume Unique Key (VUK), that in turn protects a title key, that encrypts the content.

This creates a less catastrophic way to revoke a player whose keys have been incorporated in unlicensed ripping software. While with a traditional DVD the studios would have had to revoke all players by that manufacturer, AACS lets them revoke an individual machine; the broadcast encryption scheme lets them target one player out of billions, rather than one vendor out of several hundred.

Has it worked? Well, at present a steady stream of keys are being extracted from software DVD players, essentially by reading them from memory, and published. To begin with, these were VUKs, and that was bad enough: once a VUK is known, anyone can decrypt that disk's content. But recently processing keys have been published too. In theory, publishers should have used many different processing keys, but it now appears that many were using a single processing key for all disks. When it's compromised, they change it, but hackers don't seem to have too much difficulty digging out the processing keys from DVD player software — and each of these lets people decrypt all the content published up till the next key change. There has been the usual circus of lawyers issuing threatening letters, injunctions and takedown notices to websites where processing keys appear, while people who don't like Hollywood have delighted in publishing these keys in all sorts of innovative ways. The first processing key to be published appeared on T-shirts and registered in domain names; it appeared on Digg.com, and when the administrators removed it, Digg's users revolted and forced them to climb down. It's been déja vu all over again.

So broadcast encryption, although a neat idea, doesn't seem to have been enough on its own to stop people decrypting movies.

There are features in AACS that don't seem to have been used yet. For example, there's a *traitor tracing* scheme. The idea behind traitor tracing is that you add some unique marks to each copy, so if decrypted content fetches up on a peer-to-peer network, the studios know who to sue. Such methods have been used with the electronic distribution of films to movie theatres, where the goal is to identify theatres that let the pirates record new films on camcorders. Another application is in the Oscars, where Academy members are given 'screeners' — DVDs of candidate films. These used to leak regularly; but in 2004, after the studios started to individualize them, the actor Carmine Caridi was ordered to pay $300,000 after forensics identified him as the source of leaked screeners that ended up providing masters for illegal copies in 21 countries [1250]. Since then, Academy members have been more careful.

With a small distribution, it's possible to mark copies at production, but this is not feasible when mass-producing disks. A method is therefore needed to add uniqueness during the decryption process. How AACS supports this is as follows. Each cell (time segment) is usually decrypted by a title key, but issuers can insert a *sequence key cell* — of which there will be up to eight, each encrypted with a different segment key, and there can be up to 32 sequence key cells in a disk. The key management mechanism is arranged so that different players will derive different sets of segment keys. So if decrypted content appears somewhere, the content owner can see which segment keys were used and from that work out which player was used. The actual marking of each segment might be something overt from the production process, such as the color of shirt an actor's wearing, or more likely a robust hidden mark (which I'll describe later). However, the traitor-tracing mechanisms in AACS do not seem to have been deployed so far.

22.2.6.2 *Blu-ray and SPDC*

So the content protection in HD-DVD was starting to look slightly shaky, which helped the competing format, Blu-ray, as it also supports a novel protection mechanism called *Self-Protecting Digital Content* (SPDC).

SPDC is a very neat idea that tries to tackle the underlying incentive problem — that while it's the studios that want to protect the content, it's the equipment makers that provide the protection. The innovation is that each player contains a virtual machine that can run content-protection code that's unique to each title. The studios write this code and can change it from one disk to the next, or even between versions of the same disk. This gives the studios a number of options for responding to a compromise, and they can do so directly rather than having to work through trade associations, standards bodies or the vendors themselves.

If a particular player is seen to be leaking content, they can blacklist it in future discs; if a particular type of player is leaking, they can arrange that it only outputs low-resolution video. When it comes to tracing they can do their own; content can be marked after decoding. This not only avoids relying on the AACS mechanisms to identify compromised players or player types, but is potentially much more flexible as marks can be embedded much more pervasively in audio and video (I'll discuss marking technology below). For these reasons, SPDC provides more resilient protection than the key-management and device-revocation mechanisms in AACS alone; it's described in an evaluation report [637]. As of the beginning of 2008, the studios have been struggling with teething problems with movies using SPDC, but have decided to favor it; it now looks like SPDC has helped Blu-ray win the format war.

There are two engineering challenges facing rights-management engineers. First, people increasingly expect to move content they've purchased from one device to another. If you buy and download the latest recording of Mahler's fifth, you expect to play it not just on your laptop and iPod, but also on your home audio system; and if you buy and download a baseball game, you'll want to see it on your wide-screen TV. Second, as you make content, and the keys that protect it, available on more and more platforms, so the risk of leakage rises — and the incentives can potentially drift ever more out of alignment.

In any case, as more and more digital content is distributed online using DRM, we need to look at that next.

22.3 General Platforms

In the mid-1990s, a number of researchers started work on ways to control the sale and distribution of digital goods over the Internet to customers with personal computers. The original applications included the distribution of newspapers and articles from scientific journals [221], although it was always understood that music and video would follow once networks had enough bandwidth.

The basic problem is that a PC, being a general-purpose computer, can in principle copy any file and send it to any other computer; unlike with analogue copying, copies are perfect, so millions of copies might be made from one original. The problem is compounded by the fact that, from the viewpoint of the content vendor, the PC owner is the 'enemy'. The music industry believed that unlimited copying would destroy their business; the computer industry told them that DRM was intrinsically impossible on a general-purpose computer, so they'd better get a new business model. The music and film industries, despite being a tenth of the computer industry's size, had much more clout in Congress (a Microsoft guy told me this was because the average Congressman was much keener to be photographed with Madonna than with Bill). So Hollywood got its way. The result is a number of products generally referred to as *digital rights management* or DRM.

Curiously, despite the acrimony of the argument between computer people and Hollywood in the 1990s about whether DRM was possible or desirable, it now seems that both of them may have been taking the wrong side in the argument! Stronger DRM has turned out to benefit the platform vendors, such as Apple, more than the content companies (and economists had predicted this). And although all DRM mechanisms seem to get broken sooner or later, the existence of a modest bar to copying does have effects on the business. But as download sites move to selling unprotected MP3s, it's not clear that it's strictly necessary. However, I'll come back to the policy issues later. First let's look at the most common DRM mechanism, Windows Media Player.

22.3.1   Windows Media Rights Management

At the time of writing, Windows Media Player (WMP) comes bundled with every copy of Windows sold on general-purpose PCs. This will change, as the European Court has found the bundling to be an anticompetitive practice and ordered Microsoft to make Windows available without it. However, people will still be able to download it for free, and given the large number of websites that use Windows Media file formats, it is bound to remain an important platform.

WMP replaced an earlier media player application when Windows 98 was released. It enables a user to play music, watch video and view photos, and has all sorts of features from MP3 player support to synchronisation of lyrics for Karaoke. However our main interest here is its ability to play files protected using *Windows Media Rights Management* (WMRM). This works as follows.

A store wanting to sell digital media encrypts each item using a content key and puts the encrypted files on a streaming media server that is typically linked to their web site. In order to access a media object, the customer must get hold of a license, which consists of the object identifier, the license key seed, and a set of instructions in a *rights management language* which state what she can do with it; how many times she may play it, whether she's allowed to burn it to a CD, and so on. The license is generated by a license server and encrypted using her public key. The license acquisition may involve her going to a registration or payment page, or it may happen silently in the background [1049].

In order to use this system, the customer must first personalize her media player, which is done automatically the first time she accesses protected content. The player generates a public/private keypair (WMP uses elliptic curve cryptography) and the public key is sent to the license server.

The architecture is very similar to pay-TV conditional access, in that the bulk encryption task of protecting the music or video is separated from the personal task of key management, so the video doesn't have to be encrypted anew for each customer. And just as pay-TV smartcards can be replaced when keys are leaked or the key management mechanism compromised, so the key management functions of WMRM are performed in an 'individualized blackbox' (IBX) component of the software, which gets replaced as needed.

The IBX internals are not documented publicly by Microsoft, but according to a description by people who reverse-engineered WMP version 2 in 2001, the basic components are elliptic curve cryptography for public-key encryption; DES, RC4 and a proprietary cipher for symmetric crypto; and SHA-1 for hashing [1141]. The customer's private key is obscured by the blackbox and hidden in a file. Licenses the customer has previously acquired are kept in a license store; when a new object is encountered, the software looks up the object ID and key ID, and if a license isn't already stored for them, it sends a session key encrypted under the license server's public key. The session key is used to encrypt the license that's sent back. Once the client software has used the session key to decrypt the license, it's added to the license store. Stored licenses have a further layer of encryption, presumably to stop people reading clear keys or manipulating permissions: the content key is encrypted using the customer's public key, and there's also a digital signature. By now, of course, the protocol may have been tweaked — as Microsoft has had to recover several times from hacks, and because WMP has now acquired many more features.

WMRM is used at its most basic to provide a streaming media service, to make it slightly harder for people to record music and video from news sites and Internet radio. (Vendors seem to have given up on audio, as it's very easy to record audio after decryption as it's passed to the sound card; but Microsoft is making a serious effort in Vista to stop people grabbing video in this way [570].) More sophisticated uses of WMRM include music subscription services, where you can download as many songs as you wish, but they will all become unplayable if you stop paying; and geographically-linked services, such as MLB.com which makes Major League baseball games available everywhere except in the team's home area — for which the rights have usually been sold for megabucks to local TV stations.

22.3.2   Other Online Rights-Management Systems

The Microsoft offering is fairly typical of rights-management systems. Apple's FairPlay, which is used in the iPod and in its media player QuickTime, also has tunes encrypted under master keys, and when a tune is bought the user is sent the master key encrypted under a random session key, plus the session key encrypted under his iTunes player's RSA public key. Session keys are backed up online on Apple's servers. As with Windows, a number of programs appeared that unlocked protected content, and Apple duly upgraded iTunes to stop these programs working in September 2006.

In the mid-2000s there were growing calls from consumer and industry groups for DRM systems to become more interoperable. Real Networks is the other major supplier of media player software for PCs, and its RealPlayer uses its own proprietary DRM. In a tussle reminiscent of the word-processing file-format wars of the 1980s, Real made their music tracks readable by iTunes in 2004; Apple responded by threatening litigation, and ended the compatibility in a 2006 upgrade. This should surprise no-one: recall the discussion in section 7.3.2 of how the value of a software company depends on the total lock-in of its customers. In 2007, Steve Jobs of Apple called on the music industry to sell music without DRM; this was surprising, given the incentives facing Apple. However, the gamble seems to be paying off, in that some music labels are now starting to make unprotected music available, but at higher prices and not on a large enough scale to threaten Apple's lock-in of its iTunes customer base. Apple's revenues continue to soar, while the music majors see sales tumbling.

The Open Mobile Alliance (OMA) is a consortium that promotes standards for interoperable DRM on mobile devices. Its OMA DRM Version 1.0 is widely used to protect mobile phone ringtones; it mostly consists of a simple rights management language whose most important feature is 'forward lock': a way of marking content so that the phone knows it must not forward the object to any other device. Download protection is typically using standard TLS mechanisms. Version 2.0 is similar in its expressive power to WMRM or FairPlay, but is still not widely used. Network operators have objected to the idea that anyone else should have direct access to their customer base.

22.3.3   Peer-to-Peer Systems

Peer-to-peer file-sharing has become one of the main ways in which music is distributed online. After Napster's initial music-sharing service was closed down by music industry lawyers, systems such as Gnutella and Freenet borrowed ideas from the world of censorship-resistant systems to set up networks with no central node that could be closed down using legal attacks.

I was the designer of an early censorship-resistant system, the Eternity Service. I had been alarmed when an early anonymous remailer, `anon.penet.fi`, was closed down following legal action brought by the Scientologists [590]. It had been used to post a message that upset them. This contained an affidavit by a former minister of their church, the gist of which was reported to be an allegation that once members had been fully initiated they were told that the rest of the human race was suffering from false consciousness; that, in reality, Jesus was the bad guy and Lucifer was the good guy. Well, history has many examples of religions that denounced their competitors as both deluded and wicked; the Scientologists' innovation was to claim that the details were their copyright. They were successful in bringing lawsuits in a number of jurisdictions.

The Eternity Service was designed to provide long-term file storage by distributing file fragments across the net, encrypted so that the people hosting them would not be able to tell which fragments they had, and so that reconstruction could only be performed via remailer mechanisms [41]. A later version of this was Publius[2], which also provided a censor-resistant anonymous publishing mechanism [1309].

In 1999, Shawn Fanning, a 18-year-old drop-out, revolutionised the music business by creating the Napster service, which enabled people to share MP3

---

[2]For non-U.S. readers: the revolutionaries Alexander Hamilton, John Jay, and James Madison used the pen name Publius when they wrote the Federalist Papers, a collection of 85 articles published in New York State newspapers in 1787–8 and which helped convince New York voters to ratify the United States constitution.

audio files with each other [931]. Rather than keeping the files centrally, which would invite legal action, Napster just provided an index so that someone wanting a given track can find out who else has got it and is prepared to share or trade. It attracted tens of millions of users, and then lawsuits from Hollywood that closed it down in 2001. The gap that it left behind was promptly filled by peer-to-peer networks such as Gnutella and Freenet [297] that were in turn inspired by the earlier censorship resistant systems. These were followed by commercial systems such as Kazaa and eMule, which were also targeted by music industry lawyers (and many of which acquired a reputation for being full of spyware).

The United States Copyright Office defines peer-to-peer networks as networks where computers are linked to one another directly rather than through a central server. The absence of a server that can be closed down by court order creates an interesting problem for music industry enforcers. They have tried persuasion, by playing up stories of people who'd carelessly set a P2P program to share all their hard disk, rather than just their music files. But the two tactics on which the music industry has relied are suing uploaders and technical attacks on the systems.

In section 21.5 I explained how social networks are often vulnerable to decapitation attack, as they rely for their connectivity on a small number of particularly well-connected nodes. Taking down these nodes will disconnect the network. Similarly, peer-to-peer networks have well-connected nodes, and in filesharing systems there are also nodes whose owners contribute more than their share of the uploaded content. The music industry has for some years been targeting key nodes for legal action, having filed over 20,000 lawsuits since 2003. In many cases people agree to cease and desist and pay a small penalty rather than fight a case; but in October 2007 a federal jury in Duluth, MN., convicted 30-year-old Jammie Thomas of copyright infringement for sharing material on Kazaa and ordered her to pay $9,250 for each of the 24 songs involved in the case.

On the technical-countermeasures side, it was long known that firms working for the music industry were uploading damaged music files to spam out systems (which will usually be legal), and it was suspected that they were also conducting denial-of-service attacks (which in many jurisdictions isn't). But there was no evidence. Then in September 2007, a company called Media Defender that worked for the music industry on 'file-sharing mitigation' suffered the embarrassment of having several thousand of its internal emails leaked, after an employee forwarded his email to Gmail and his password was compromised. The emails not only disclosed many details of the 'mitigation' tactics, but also revealed that the company worked closely with the New York Attorney General's office — potentially embarrassing in view of the industry's possibly illegal attacks on computers and invasions of privacy. It turned out that Media Defender's business model was to charge $4,000 per album per month, and \$2,000 per track per month, for 'protection' that involved attacks on twelve million users of fifteen P2P networks [1009].

Peer-to-peer systems have also allegedly been attacked by Comcast, which is said to have disrupted its customers' use of BitTorrent by sending forged reset packets to tear down connections. Comcast might prefer its customers to watch TV over its cable network, so they see its ads, rather than via filesharing; but the allegations raise some public policy issues if true: BitTorrent partners with content owners such as Fox and MGM, while Comcast is not a law-enforcement agency [155]. In any case, this harassment of file sharers is fuelling an arms race; the proportion of BitTorrent traffic that's encrypted rose from 4% to 40% during 2006–7 [1346].

22.3.4   Rights Management of Semiconductor IP

Another live problem is the protection of designs licensed for use in semi-conductors. Companies like ARM make their living by designing processors and other components that they sell to firms making custom chips, whether by designing application-specific integrated circuits (ASICs) or by using Field-Programmable Gate Arrays (FPGAs).

The first problem is overrun production. A camera company licenses a circuit that they integrate into a bitstream that's loaded into an FPGA, that then becomes a key component in a new camera that they have made in a factory in China. They pay for 100,000 licenses, yet 200,000 cameras arrive on the market. There are two failure modes: the camera company could have ordered the extra production and lied to the IP owner, or the Chinese factory could be cheating the camera company. In fact, they could both be cheating, each having decided to make an extra 50,000 units. Now there are technical mechanisms that the camera company could use, such as personalising each camera with a serial number and so on after manufacture — but these could make it harder to cheat.

The second problem is knowing when a product contains a particular circuit. The camera company might have licensed a processor, or a filter, for one model, then built it into another cheaper model too without declaring it.

These risks cause a partial market failure, in that large IP vendors often prefer to license their best designs only to other large firms that they trust, so small startups can find it difficult to compete on equal terms [1348]. They also depress sales of FPGAs, whose manufacturers would dearly love a rights management system for design IP. The best that's been done so far are mechanisms to tackle the first problem by distributing encrypted bitstreams and updates for whole chips; the second problem is a lot harder, because the chip design tools would be squarely within the trust boundary. Customers would need to be able to evaluate designs, and debug designs, while maintaining some control on dissemination. At present, the best that can often be done is to use side-channels for forensics. Owners of semiconductor IP can buy up samples of suspect goods, operate them, and observe the chips' precise power consumption, electromagnetic emissions, thermal signature and so on, which can often reveal the presence of a given functional component.

This brings us to the question of copyright marking, which has blossomed into a large and complex research area.

22.4   Information Hiding

Hollywood's interest in finding new mechanisms for protecting copyright came together in the mid-1990's with the military's interest in unobtrusive communications and public concerns over government efforts to control cryptography, and started to drive rapid developments in the field of *information hiding*. This largely refers to techniques which enable data to be hidden in other data, such as when a secret message is hidden in an MP3 audio file, or a program's serial number is embedded in the order in which certain instructions are executed.

The Hollywood interest is in *copyright marks* which can be hidden unobtrusively in digital audio, video and artwork. These are generally either *watermarks*, which are hidden copyright messages, or *fingerprints* which are hidden serial numbers. For example, when you download an MP3 file from Apple's iTunes music store, it contains a fingerprint embedded in the audio that identifies you. The idea is that if you then upload your copy to a filesharing system, the copyright owner can sue you. (This isn't universal: some people believe that fingerprinting depresses sales overall because of the legal hazards it creates for honest purchasers. Amazon, for example, does not mark MP3 downloads [577].)

The privacy interest is in *steganography* whose purpose is to embed a message in some cover medium in such a way that its very existence remains undetectable. The conceptual model, proposed by Gus Simmons [1169, 1176], is as follows. Alice and Bob are in jail and wish to hatch an escape plan; all their communications pass through the warden, Willie; and if Willie detects any encrypted messages, he will frustrate their plan by throwing them into solitary confinement. So they must find some way of hiding their secret messages in an innocuous-looking covertext. As in the related field of cryptography, we assume that the mechanism in use is known to the warden, and so the security must depend solely on a secret key that Alice and Bob have somehow managed to share.

There is some similarity with electronic warfare. First, if steganography is seen as a low-probability-of-intercept communication, then copyright marking is like the related jam-resistant communication technique: it may use much the same methods but in order to resist focussed attacks it is likely to have a much lower bit rate. We can think of Willie as the pirate who tries to mangle the audio or video signal in such a way as to cause the copyright mark detector to fail. Second, techniques such as direct sequence spread spectrum that were originally developed for electronic warfare are finding wide use in the information hiding community.

Of course, copyright marks don't have to be hidden to be effective. Some TV stations embed their logo in a visible but unobtrusive manner in the corner of the picture, and many DRM systems have control tags bundled quite visibly with the content. In many cases this will be the appropriate technology. However, in what follows we'll concentrate on hidden copyright marks.

22.4.1 Watermarks and Copy Generation Management

The DVD consortium became concerned that digital video or audio could be decoded to analog format and then redistributed (the so-called 'analog hole'). They set out to invent a *copy generation management system* that would work even with analog signals. The idea was that a video or music track might be unmarked, or marked 'never copy', or marked 'copy once only'; compliant players would not record a video marked 'never copy' and when recording one marked 'copy once only' would change its mark to 'never copy'. Commercially sold videos would be marked 'never copy', while TV broadcasts and similar material would be marked 'copy once only'. In this way, the DVD players available to consumers would allow unlimited copying of home videos and time-shifted viewing of TV programmes, but could not easily be abused for commercial piracy.

The proposed mechanisms depended on hiding one or more copyright marks in the content, and are reviewed in [193, 800]. For each disk, choose a *ticket X*, which can be a random number, plus copy control information, plus possibly some information unique to the physical medium such as the wobble in the lead-in track. Use a one-way hash function h to compute $h(X)$ and then $h(h(X))$. Embed $h(h(X))$ in the video as a hidden copyright mark. See to it that compliant machines look for a watermark, and if they find one will refuse to play a track unless they are supplied with $h(X)$ which they check by hashing it and comparing it with the mark. Finally, arrange things so that a compliant device will only record a marked track if given X, in which case only a $h(X)$ is written to the new disc. In this way, a 'copy once only' track in the original medium becomes a 'copy no more' track in the new medium. DVD-audio uses such a marking mechanism; SDMI also uses a *fragile watermark* that's damaged by unauthorised processing. (I'll discuss mark removal techniques in the next section.)

The main use of marking with video content will be if Blu-ray wins the standards war with HD-DVD. Then the SPDC processor will be able to embed unique fingerprints into decrypted content in real time. Each plaintext copy of a video derived from a decoder can be unique, and the studios can use forensic techniques to determine which decoder it came from. Unless the decoder itself is compromised, the marking mechanism can give a much more resilient way of identifying subscribers who're leaking content. This raises a number of questions. First, how well does marking work? Second, how well does it scale? And third, what about the policy aspects?

Quality brings us back to our old friend, the ROC. It's not enough for a marking mechanism, whether used for copy management or for traitor tracing, to have a low missed alarm rate; it needs a low false alarm rate [892] too. If your legitimate DVD player were to detect a 'no-copy' mark in your wedding video by mistake, then you'd have to buy a pirate player to watch it. So what sort of marks are possible, and how robust are they against forgery, spoofing and other attacks?

22.4.2 General Information Hiding Techniques

Information hiding goes back even further than cryptology, having its roots in camouflage. Herodotus records tricks used during the wars between the Greeks and the Persians, including hiding a message in the belly of a hare carried by a hunter, tattooing it on the shaven head of a slave whose hair was then allowed to grow back, and writing it on the wooden base under the wax of a writing tablet [595]. Francis Bacon proposed a system which embedded a binary message in a book at one bit per letter by alternating between two different fonts [1016]. Until quite modern times, most writers considered hiding confidential information much more important than enciphering it [1345]. Military organizations still largely hold this view and have used all sorts of technologies from the microdots used by spies in much of the twentieth century to low-probability-of-intercept radios.

When it comes to hiding data in other data, the modern terminology of the subject is as follows [1023]. The copyright mark, or in the case of steganography, the *embedded text*, is hidden in the *cover-text* producing the *marked text* or in the case of steganography the *stego-text*. In most cases, additional secret information is used during this process; this is the *marking key* or *stego-key*, and some function of it is typically needed to recover the mark or embedded text. Here, the word 'text' can be replaced by 'audio', 'video' and so on, as appropriate.

A wide variety of embedding schemes has been proposed.

▪ Many people have proposed hiding mark or secret message in the least significant bits of an audio or video signal. This isn't usually a very good strategy, as the hidden data is easy to detect statistically (the least significant bits are no longer correlated with the rest of the image), and it's trivial to remove or replace. It's also severely damaged by lossy compression techniques.

■ A better technique is to hide the mark at a location determined by a secret key. This was first invented in classical China. The sender and receiver had copies of a paper mask with holes cut out of it at random locations. The sender would place his mask over a blank sheet of paper, write his message in the holes, then remove it and compose a cover message including the characters of the secret embedded message. This trick was reinvented in the 16th century by the Italian mathematician Cardan and is now known to cryptographers as the Cardan grille [676].

■ A modern version of this hides a mark in a `.gif` format image as follows. A secret key is expanded to a keystream which selects an appropriate number of pixels. The embedded message is the parity of the color codes for these pixels. In practice even a quite large number of the pixels in an image can have their color changed to that of a similar one in the palette without any visible effects [654]. However, if all the pixels are tweaked in this way, then again the hidden data is easy to remove by just tweaking them again. A better result is obtained if the cover image and embedding method are such that (say) only 10% of the pixels can safely be tweaked. Then, if the warden repeats the process but with a different key, a different 10% of the pixels will be tweaked and only 10% of the bits of the hidden data will be corrupted.

■ In general, the introduction of noise or distortion — as happens with lossy compression — will introduce errors into the hidden data almost regardless of the embedding method unless some kind of error correcting code is added. A system proposed for banknote marking, Patchwork, uses a repetition code — the key selects two subsets of pixels, one of which is marked by increasing the luminosity and the other by decreasing it. This embeds a single bit; the note is either watermarked using that key, or it isn't [160, 562]. You can think of this as like differential power analysis: the key tells you how to sort your input data into two piles, and if the key was right they're noticeably different.

■ In the general case, one may want to embed more than one bit, and have the embedded data to survive very high levels of induced errors. So a common technique is to use direct-sequence spread-spectrum techniques borrowed from electronic warfare [1251]. You have a number of secret sequences, each coding a particular symbol, and you add one of them to the content to mark it.

■ Spread spectrum encoding is often done in a transform space to make its effects less perceptible and more robust against common forms of compression. These techniques are also commonly used in conjunction with perceptual filtering, which emphasises the encoding in the noisiest or perceptually most significant parts of the image or music track, where it will be least obtrusive, and de-emphasises it in quiet passages of music or large expanses of color [208].

▪ Some schemes use the characteristics of particular media, such as a scheme for marking print media by moving text lines up or down by a three-hundredth of an inch [221], or adding extra echoes to music below the threshold of perception [160]. So far, such techniques don't seem to have become as robust, or as widely used, as generic techniques based on keyed embedding using transform spaces, spread spectrum and perceptual filtering.

Progress in copyright marking and steganography was very rapid in the late 1990s: people invented marking schemes which other people broke, until eventually the technology became more mature and robust.

22.4.3   Attacks on Copyright Marking Schemes

Throughout this book, we've seen attacks on cryptographic systems that occasionally involved cryptanalysis but more often relied on mistaken assumptions, protecting the wrong things, protocol failures and implementation bugs. And in the history of technology as a whole, inventions tend to end up being used to solve problems somewhat different from the problems the inventor was originally thinking about. Copyright marking has been no different on either count.

▪ In the beginning, many people assumed that the main market would be embedding hidden copyright messages so that ownership of a work could be proved in court. This was mistaken. Intellectual property lawyers almost never have any difficulty in proving ownership of an exhibit; they don't rely on technical measures which might confuse a jury, but on documents such as contracts with bands and model release forms.

▪ As usual, many designers ignored Kerckhoffs' principle — that the security of a system should reside in the choice of key, not in the algorithm in use. But this principle applies with greater than usual force when marks are to be used in evidence, as this means disclosing them in court. In fact, as even the marking keys may need to be disclosed, it may be necessary to protect objects with multiple marks. For example, one can have a mark with a secret key that is system-wide and which serves to identify which customer re-sold protected content in violation of his licence, and a second mark with a unique key that can be disclosed in court when he's prosecuted.

- Many marks are simply additive. This opens a whole series of possible vulnerabilities. For example, if all the frames in a video carry the same mark, you can average them to get the mark and then subtract it out. An even simpler attack is to supply some known content to a marking system, and compare its input and output. Even if this isn't possible — say the mark is applied in a tamper-resistant processor immediately after decryption and every device adds a different mark — then if the mark consists of small signals added at discrete points in the content, an opponent can just decrypt the content with several different devices and compare them to remove the marks.

- There have been various attempts to develop a marking equivalent of public key cryptography, so that (for example) anyone could insert a mark which only one principal could detect, or anyone could detect a mark that only one principal could have inserted. The former seems just about feasible if the mark can be inserted as the cover audio or video is being manufactured [334]. The latter is the case of particular interest to Hollywood. However, it seems a lot harder than it looks as there is a very general attack. Given a device that will detect the mark, an attacker can remove a mark by applying small changes to the image until the decoder cannot find it anymore [1015, 803]. Hence the drive to have mechanisms that enable you to put a different mark in each instance of the content, as the content is decrypted.

- Some neat steganalysis techniques were developed to break particular embedding schemes. For example, where the mark was added by either increasing or decreasing the luminosity of the image by a small fixed amount, the caused the peaks in the luminosity graph to become twin peaks, which meant that the mark could be filtered out over much of many images [826].

- The first large vendor of marking systems — Digimarc — set up a service to track intellectual property on the web. They supplied tools to let picture owners embed invisible fingerprints, but their initial implementation could be easily defeated by guessing the master password, or by modifying the marking software so that it would overwrite existing marks. They also had a 'Marc spider', a bot which crawled the web looking for marked pictures and reporting them to the copyright owner, but there were many ways to defeat this. For example, the typical web browser when presented with a series of graphics images will display them one after another without any gaps; so a marked image can often be chopped up into smaller images which will together look just like the original when displayed on a web page but in which a copyright mark won't be detected (Figure 22.6) [1019].

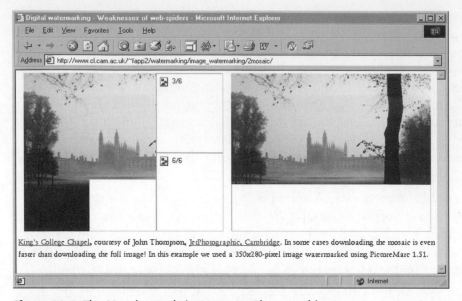

Figure 22.6: The Mosaic attack (courtesy Jet Photographic, `www.jetphotographic .com`)

Digimarc has now fixed the bugs and concentrates on monitoring broadcast streams; this enables advertisers, for example, to check whether the ads they've paid for have actually gone out. But they've found that a larger business is to move digital technology into the world of security printing: they put watermarks in ID documents to prevent them being copied, and licensed their marking technology to central banks as a counterfeit detection measure. For example, it's found in the new Euro banknotes, which it prevents from being scanned or copied using the latest equipment [1373]. Software packages such as Photoshop and Paintshop Pro now refuse to handle marked images.

■ However, the most general known attacks on copyright marking schemes involve suitably chosen distortions. Audio marks can be removed by randomly duplicating or deleting sound samples to introduce inaudible jitter; techniques used for click removal and resampling are also powerful mark removers. For images, a tool my students developed, called Stirmark, introduces the same kind of errors into an image as printing it on a high quality printer and then scanning it again with a high quality scanner. It applies a minor geometric distortion: the image is slightly stretched, sheared, shifted, and/or rotated by an unnoticeable random amount (see Figure 22.7). This defeated almost all the marking schemes in existence when it was developed and is now a standard benchmark for copyright mark robustness [1019]. In general, it's not clear how to design marking schemes that will resist a *chosen distortion attack* in which the attacker who understands the marking scheme mangles the content in such a way as to cause maximum damage to the mark while doing minimal damage to the marked content.

For a fuller account of attacks on copyright marking schemes, see [1019, 1020]. The technology's improving slowly but the limiting factor appears to be the difficulty of designing marking schemes that remain robust once the mark detection algorithm is known. If any copy control scheme based on marking is implemented in PC software or low-cost tamper-resistant processors, it's only a matter of time before the algorithm gets out; then expect to see people writing quite effective unmarking software.

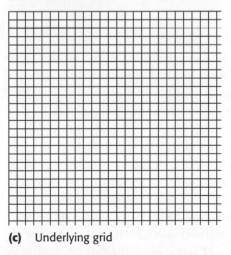

(a)   Picture of Lena

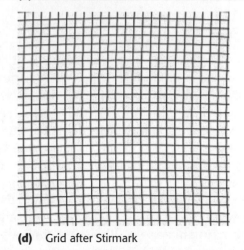

(b)   Lena after Stirmark

(c)   Underlying grid

(d)   Grid after Stirmark

Figure 22.7: *The effect of Stirmark*

The security-by-obscurity issue has led to at least one political row. The Digimarc software used in commercial graphics packages to prevent them loading images of currency is only available under NDA. Thus proposed legislation to compel its use will place open-source graphics packages such as Gimp in danger.

22.4.4   Applications of Copyright Marking Schemes

The applications of marking techniques are much broader than just DVDs and banknotes. Color copiers sold in the U.S. have hidden their serial number in the bit patterns of copies, for example, as an extra means of detecting currency forgers [1331]. Another technique is to embed fragile marks in still pictures as they are taken, so that alterations are readily detected by forensic labs [769].

A further class of proposed applications have to do with convenience or safety rather than preventing malicious behaviour. It's been proposed that music broadcast over the radio should be marked with the CD's number so that someone who likes it could order the CD automatically by pressing a button. And in medicine, digital versions of X-rays often get separated from the patient's details, as the various proprietary file formats get mangled through numerous protocol conversions; this safety problem might be solved by embedding patient details directly in the image.

Finally, a fair proportion of information hiding research doesn't aim at Hollywood's requirements, or those of the Bureau of Engraving and Printing, but at hiding information for privacy purposes. I'll discuss such applications in the next chapter.

22.5   Policy

The IP policy debate got heated in the 1990s are early 2000s, as a series of laws from copyright term extension to America's Digital Millennium Copyright Act (DMCA) shifted power to the owners of 'intellectual property' — copyrights, patents and trademarks — in ways that many people in the computer industry and elsewhere felt to be threatening. Stricter copyright enforcement impinges on free-speech rights, for example: the law used to provide 'fair use' or 'fair dealing' exemptions that enable you to parody or criticise a work by someone else, but these exemptions weren't respected in all countries during the rush to update copyright laws. In addition, the DMCA gives copyright owners the power ('Notice and Take Down') to compel ISPs to take down websites with infringing material. Although there is also a provision ('Notice and Put Back') for the subscriber to file a counter notice and have his stuff put back within 14 days unless the copyright owner files suit, in practice many ISPs will just terminate a customer's service rather than get involved in litigation.

There are continuing concerns about the effect of DMCA on libraries, especially as more and more material becomes electronic: the legal controls that allowed, for example, library lending are being replaced by technical controls that don't [730]. For example, when I applied for planning permission to extend my kitchen, I had to file four copies of a local plan; and the map software at our university library only lets you print three copies. This is of course quite deliberate. Legal controls are supplemented by access controls, and the legal privilege given to those access controls by the DMCA creates a new bundle of de-facto rights, criticised by many legal scholars as 'paracopyright' [364]. In effect, copyright regulations are no longer made by lawmakers in Washington or Brussels, but on the hoof by programmers working for Microsoft or Apple. The result, according to copyright law critics such as Larry Lessig and Pamela Samuelson, has been to greatly decrease the rights of copyright users.

At the same time, copyright law has suddenly become relevant to millions of people. Whereas in the past it was only a concern of specialists such as publishers, it now touches the lives of everyone who downloads music, time-shifts movies using a TiVo, or maintains a personal web page. As the law has failed to keep up with technology, the gap between what it permits and what people actually do has become wider. In the UK, for example, it's technically illegal to rip a CD on to an iPod, yet as this is one of the main reasons that people buy CDs nowadays, the British Phonographic Industry (the trade body) graciously says it won't sue anybody. The law-norm gap can only become wider as we move increasingly to a remix culture, and as the many minor infringements that used to take place in private, or undocumented public, spaces (such as singing a song in a pub) go online (as when a phone video clip of the song gets on someone's social-network page). John Tehranian calculates that a typical law professor commits over 80 copyright infringements a day, carrying statutory penalties of over $10 m [1243].

On the other side of the coin, there are the privacy concerns. In the old days, people would buy a book or a record for cash; the move to down-loads means that DRM license servers run by firms such as Microsoft and Apple have a record of what people watch and listen to, and this can be subpoena'ed. (It's equally true that the move to online bookselling has created similar records at Amazon.) These records are also used for marketing. A survey for the Privacy Commissioner of Canada found many examples of intrusive behavior, including e-book software profiling individuals, Double-Click advertising in a library service, systems tracking individuals via IP addresses, and contradictions between vendors' started privacy policies and observed behaviour — including undisclosed communications to third parties [468]. Not one of the organisations whose products and services were tested complied with requests from the testers to disclose personal information held about them. It looks inevitable that such DRM systems break European privacy law too, as it's based on the same principles. A particularly extreme case arose in 2005 when Microsoft decided that Sony's XCP system was 'spyware' and and 'rootkit', and would thus be removed by Windows Defender and the Malcicious Software Removal Tool [884]. So next time you hear a large company bellyaching about how its users break the law by copying its music or its software, bear in mind that it may well be a lawbreaker too.

Where will it all lead? Until recently, the copyright law debate was a straight fight between corporate lobbyists on the one hand, and activists such as academics and the free software community on the other; the latter had the arguments, but the former always got their way with legislatures. This has now changed, and in two interesting ways. First, the IP lobby started to run out of steam, and second, Hollywood started to realise that stronger DRM was likely to shift power away from content owners towards the platform vendors.

22.5.1   The IP Lobby

First, the IP lobby. This has its modern origins in an effort by the drug company Pfizer to extend patent protection on its drugs from the USA to less developed countries like Brazil and India in the 1970s. The story is told in a history by Peter Drahos and John Braithwaite [398]; in summary, Pfizer and the other drug companies allied themselves with the music and film industry (who wanted to cut bootlegging and copying), the luxury-goods industry (who wanted to reduce the number of cheap knock-offs), and a number of other U.S. players (including, it should be said, the Business Software Alliance), and persuaded the U.S. government to start applying pressure to less developed countries to bring their patent, copyright and trade-mark laws in line with America's. From the mid-1980s onwards this was largely a matter of bilateral action, but in 1994 the a treaty on Trade-Relates Aspects of Intellectual Property Rights (TRIPS) was signed, followed by two treaties of the World Intellectual Property Organisation (WIPO) in 1996. Essentially the USA and the EU got together and bullied holdouts like India and Brazil.

The implementation of these treaties stirred up a lot of opposition in developed countries as people began to realise how they might be affected. In the USA, the Digital Millennium Copyright Act of 1998 made it an offence to circumvent a copyright-protection mechanism, as required by WIPO, while in the European Union the Copyright Directive of 2001 had a similar effect. This was seen as enabling vendors to create closed platforms and control competition; it was also seen as a threat by the free and open source software movement, and by security researchers — especially after the Russian researcher Dmitri Sklyarov was arrested at a U.S. conference at the request of Adobe after his employer had sold tools circumventing password protection on pdf documents.

There were many other high-profile incidents; for example, I was on the program committee of the 2001 Information Hiding Workshop when an attempt was made by the Recording Industry Association of America (RIAA) to force the program chair to pull a paper by Ed Felten and his students describing vulnerabilities in a copyright marking scheme being touted for a digital music standard [335]. This led to a lawsuit in which Ed sued RIAA, which became a landmark academic-freedom case [424]. The irony is that the promoters of this challenge had issued a public challenge to academics and others to break their scheme. The next case was Bunnie Huang's book 'Hacking the Xbox': this described in detail how, as an MIT student, he'd overcome the protection mechanisms in the first version of Microsoft's games console [629]. The book he wrote caused his publisher to take fright, but he found another one and the publicity can't have done his sales any harm. In any case, the encroachment on liberties threatened by rights-management mechanisms and anti-hacking laws led to the growth of digital rights NGOs in a number of countries (others had them already as a result of the 'Crypto Wars'; I'll discuss all this in more detail in Part III).

The turning point appears to have come in 2003–4, as the IP lobby was trying to steer a further measure through Brussels, the IP Enforcement Directive. This would have further ratcheted up the penalties on infringers and removed the prospects for public-interest defences based on free speech or fair use. This time opponents of the measure managed to assemble a sufficiently strong coalition of interests opposed to stronger IP enforcement that the measure was substantially amended. By then there were the beginnings of decent economic arguments, such as the first result mentioned in section 7.5.5 that downloading doesn't actually harm music sales; and meanwhile the IP lobby had seriously overreached.

For example, the IP folks tried to compel every country in Europe to make patent infringement a crime, rather than just a civil matter. This was designed by the leading drugs companies to undermine firms who manufacture and sell generic versions of drugs once they have come off patent. At present, drug companies try to prolong their patents by 'evergreening' — filing subsidiary, later patents, with often dubious derivative claims — which the generic drug-makers deal with by offering their distributors indemnities against having to pay damages. Making infringement a criminal matter would have upset these arrangements. This caused the generic drugmakers to oppose the directive vigorously, along with supermarkets, car parts dealers and consumer groups. Even the software industry started to get nervous: we pointed out to Microsoft that thousands of companies believe that Microsoft is infringing their patents, but don't have the money to go the distance in a civil court. If patent infringement became a crime, surely they would take their grievances to the police? Would Bill risk arrest on some future trip to Europe?

With hindsight, this was bound to be the eventual fate of the IP movement. A rich, powerful lobby isn't stopped by fine words, or by outrage from university professors and free-software activists (such as the words of John

Perry Barlow at the head of this chapter). It's stopped when it comes up against another rich, powerful lobby pushing in the opposite direction. That point now appears to have been passed; for example, in June 2007 WIPO abandoned the attempt by the IP lobby to conclude a new treaty on broadcasting.

The IP movement have have passed its high water mark, but it is not quite dead yet; following the election of Nicholas Sarkozy as President of France, they persuaded him to back a law that would make ISPs responsible for copyright enforcement — which would push up their costs and make them less competitive [115]. It will be interesting to see whether French ISPs — or the European Commission — manage to push back on this one; even though the tide is no longer flowing in the IP lobby's direction, there are bound to be a lot of skirmishes like this before the law finally stabilises.

There are some other problems with copyright that people will have to worry about eventually. Some copyright activists have assumed that once copyright expires — or assuming that lots of material can be made available under a Creative Commons license — then everything will be hunky-dory. I doubt it. Curating old bits costs money, just as curating old manuscripts does; indeed the film industry has recently discovered that archiving digital productions actually costs more than they used to pay in the old days, when they just locked away the master copies in an old salt mine. There's just an awful lot of bits generated during digital production, and copying them to new disks every few years isn't cheap. In the long term, once bitstrings belong to nobody, who will pay for their upkeep? Some lawyers would like to extend copyright term indefinitely, but that violates the social contract on which copyright is based and it also doesn't solve the problem properly: many publishers have failed to look after their own back catalogue properly and had to retrieve copies from national deposit collections. When NGO colleagues and I considered this problem the best solution we could come up with was a digital preservation law plus a taxpayer-funded digital deposit library [418].

22.5.2   Who Benefits?

As I discussed in section 7.5.5, a further important development came in 2005. In January of that year, Google's chief economist Hal Varian addressed a DRM conference in Berlin and asked who would benefit from stronger DRM. He pointed out that, in classical economic theory, a technical link between two industries would usually benefit the more concentrated industry (for example, car makers and car parts). Now the platform industry is concentrated (Apple, Microsoft) while the music industry is less so (four majors and many independents): so why should the music industry expect to be the winners from better DRM? Economic theory says that platform vendors should win more.

The music industry scoffed, and yet by the end of that year they were hurting — lobbying governments and the European Commission to 'do something' about Apple, such as forcing it to open its FairPlay DRM scheme. It's now becoming clear that music downloading — with or without DRM — is changing the structure and dynamics of the music industry. Bands used to rely on the majors to promote them, but now they can do that themselves by giving away their albums on their websites; they always made most of their money from performances, and now they make more than ever.

In the first edition of this book, I predicted that big bands might follow the Linux business model: 'it may make sense to give the "product" away free and make money on the "maintenance" (tours, T-shirts, fan club ...)', while for more specialised acts 'the trick may be slightly keener pricing and/or packaging that appeals to the collector'. So far, that was called right. I also wrote 'I also expect that Hollywood will follow the software industry and adopt a somewhat more mature attitude to copying. After all, 70% of a market worth $100 billion is better than 98% of a market worth $50 billion. And just as a certain amount of copying helped market software, it can help music sales too: the Grateful Dead encouraged bootleg taping because they had learned it didn't harm their sales'. On that one, the current state of play is that CD sales are declining steadily, and while download sales are starting to rise, they're not rising fast enough yet to compensate. We shall have to wait and see.

22.6 Accessory Control

There was concern in the late 1990s and early 2000s that the prohibitions against reverse engineering introduced at Hollywood's request via the DMCA would have evil effects on competition. Indeed, one of the most important and rapidly-growing uses of cryptographic mechanisms and of rights-management technology generally since the DMCA was passed is in accessory control. The familiar example is the printer cartridge.

The practice started in 1996 with the Xerox N24 (see [1221] for the history of cartridge chips). In a typical system, if the printer senses a third-party cartridge, or a refilled cartridge, it may silently downgrade from 1200 dpi to 300 dpi, or even refuse to work at all. In 2003, expiry dates and ink usage controls were added: cartridges for the HP BusinessJet 2200C expire after being in the printer for 30 months, or 4.5 years after manufacture [827]; and modern cartridges now limit the amount of ink dispensed electronically rather than waiting for it to run out physically. The latest development is region coding: you can't use U.S. ink cartidges in a recently UK-purchased HP printer.

All this has caused grumbling; the European Parliament approved a 'Directive on waste electrical and electronic equipment' designed to force member states to outlaw the circumvention of EU recycling rules by companies who design products with chips to ensure that they cannot be recycled [230, 332]. But by the time this was translated into actual regulation, the authorities had relented. The printer companies lobbied hard and the regulations eventually said that so long as the vendors accept empty cartridges back for disposal, they will have discharged their obligations to the environment [1323], while the UK government has said that as cartridges are consumables, the law won't apply [1097].

In the USA, the matter was decided in court. The printer maker Lexmark sued SCC, which (as I recounted in the chapter on tamper resistance at 16.5.1) had reverse-engineered their print-cartridge crypto, alleging violation of the Digital Millennium Copyright Act. Although they won at first instance, they lost on appeal in 2004 [790]. In a similar case, Chamberlain (who make garage door openers) sued Skylink (who made compatible openers) and also lost, losing the appeal too in 2004. This appears to settle U.S. law in favour of a free market for cryptologists, which was always the position before the DMCA came along [1110]. A firm wanting to control its aftermarket using crypto chips is free to hire the smartest cryptographers it can find to build authentication chips that are really hard to hack, and its competitors are free to hire the smartest cryptanalysts they can find to try to reverse-engineer them. Other fields in which crypto is used for accessory control include games console software and add-ons, and mobile phone batteries[3].

Other industries are eyeing up the technology. For example, the carmaker Volkswagen makes a range of models at different prices, and this is reflected in the price of spares; you can pay $12 for an air filter for a Skoda, $40 for the same air filter for a Volkswagen, and over $100 for the same air filter for an Audi. Will we in future see cars authenticating their major spare parts, to prevent arbitrage? (If the motor industry's smart it will be marketed as a 'safety measure' to stop unsafe foreign parts — this is the line Motorola took when it introduced authentication chips into phone batteries.)

Is accessory control objectionable? The economist Hal Varian analyses it as follows [1286]:

> The answer depends on how competitive the markets are. Take the inkjet printer market. If cartridges have a high profit margin but the market for printers is competitive, competition will push down the price of printers to compensate for the high-priced cartridges. Restricting after-purchase use makes the monopoly in cartridges stronger (since it inhibits refills), but that just makes sellers compete more intensely to sell printers, leading to lower prices in that

---

[3]There are limits to the freedom to reverse engineer. In the UK, a man was convicted in October 2007 of selling modchips that allowed people to run programs on games consoles without their being signed by the vendor. This relies on a 2003 law implementing the EU Copyright Directive that made Member States prohibit the sale of devices designed to circumvent copy protection. He is appealing [879]. However, a court in Helsinki made a possibly conflicting ruling [1216] — so it's not clear that we have a consistent law in Europe.

market. This is just the old story of "give away the razor and sell the blades."

However, in many other industries it might be anticompetitive; it just depends on how concentrated the industry is, and in winner-take-all platform markets it could be particularly objectionable [53]. So it's a good job that early fears of a legal prohibition against reverse engineering for compatibility have proved largely unfounded. Of course, the right to reverse engineer is not the same as the right to succeed at reverse engineering, and so there may be cases in the future — as shrinking feature sizes and growing complexity make reverse engineering harder — where firms locked out of a market will have to use antitrust law to get access.

22.7 Summary

The technical protection of digital content against unauthorised copying is a difficult problem both technically and politically. It's difficult technically because general-purpose computers can copy bitstrings at no cost, and it's difficult politically because Hollywood's attempts to impose rights-management technology on a reluctant computer industry have done a lot of collateral damage. Some of problems people agonised about — including the effects on reverse engineering for compatibility — have failed to materialise, but there is still real complexity. At the technical level, compatibility between DRM systems is a big issue, and it's not at all clear how DRM will work in the home of the future where people will expect to play music and videos that they've bought on multiple devices. At the political level, it appears that the music industry has brought down grief on itself by insisting on stronger DRM, as this simply shifted power in the supply chain from itself to the platform vendors (and specifically Apple). It remains to be seen whether the same will happen to Hollywood: will the move to high-definition video result in Microsoft stealing their lunch? At least there's one strategy for them to fight back — by using the SPDC mechanisms to assume part of the role of platform owner.

At any rate, the development of copyright and rights-management systems over the last ten years has been a fascinating if bumpy ride, and its evolution over the next ten will surely be too.

Research Problems

There are many interesting research problems in copyright management. Some of them we've already touched on, such as how to build cheaper tamper-proof hardware tokens, and better ways of embedding copyright marks in digital pictures and sound. But a huge amount of research was done on these topics from the mid-90s until about 2005; there are many competing proposals, and lawyers are fighting through patent thickets. Novel ideas would surely be of interest to many stakeholders, but the low-hanging fruit may have been plucked by now.

Further Reading

Software copy protection techniques are discussed at length in [561]; there's a brief history of technical protection mechanisms for audio and video in [487]; and a racy account of the coevolution of attack and defense in pay-TV systems in [850]. More information about pay-TV, and the available information on DVD, can be found at various web sites (which may move because of legal harassment), while there's a lawyer's view at [565].

There is an overview of information hiding techniques, including steganography and information hiding, in a special issue of the Proceedings of the IEEE [822]; for attacks on marking schemes in particular, see [1019, 1020]. For more detail there's a recent book on the subject [697]. Kahn is, as usual, good historical background reading [676]. A useful guided tour of U.S. copyright law is by Gordon [546]. Ongoing research work can be found in the proceedings of the workshops on information hiding [42, 97, 1022]. And finally, no chapter on copyright would be complete without a reference to Larry Lessig's books on the subject [784, 785] and Pam Samuelson's writings [1107, 1108, 1109, 1110].

CHAPTER 23

The Bleeding Edge

What information consumes is rather obvious: it consumes the attention of its recipients. Hence a wealth of information creates a poverty of attention, and a need to allocate that attention efficiently among the overabundance of information sources that might consume it.

— Herb Simon

Voting machine software is a special case because the biggest danger to security comes from the people who are supposed to be responsible for it.

— Richard Stallman

23.1 Introduction

Our security group at Cambridge runs a blog, www.lightbluetouchpaper.org, where we discuss the latest hacks and cracks. We even found some vulnerabilities in the Wordpress blog software we use and reported them to the maintainers. But we weren't alone in finding flaws, and in October 2007, the blog itself was compromised by a Russian script kiddie who tried to put on some drug ads. The attack itself was only an inconvenience, as we spotted it quickly and recovered from backup, but it brought home how dependent we've all become on a vast range of applications that we just don't have time to evaluate. And the blog posts themselves show that many of the attacks, and much of the cutting-edge work in security research, hinge on specific applications. There will still be exploits against platforms like Windows and Symbian, but there are many more vulnerabilities out there in apps. As Microsoft cleans up its act, and as search engines make it easier to find machines running specific apps, that's where the action may well shift.

In the case of blog software, the Wordpress security engineering was not very impressive, but its competitors are even worse; and this one application alone exposes thousands of machines to compromise. There are many, many applications, and their developers usually don't care about security until they get hacked. The same learning process that Microsoft's gone through since 2000 will be repeated in one domain after another. But not all applications are the same; while some (like blog software) simply open up PCs to botnet recruitment, there are others from which money can be extracted directly, others that people rely on for privacy, and others that mediate power.

I've already discussed a number of more or less 'embedded' apps, from banking through alarms to prepayment meters. In this chapter I'm going to briefly describe four types of application that make up the bleeding edge of security research. They are where we find innovative attacks, novel protection problems, and thorny policy issues. They are: online games; web applications such as auction, social networking and search; privacy technologies such as anonymizing proxies; and, finally, electronic elections.

Games and Web 2.0 highlight the fact that the real 'killer application' of the Internet is other people. As more people come online in ever more contexts, we're creating complex socio-technical systems of a kind that never existed before. That means quite novel attacks, exploits, tussles and disputes. We've already seen several examples, such as click fraud and impression spam, as well as new variants on old scams.

Anonymity systems follow naturally: if you want to reap some of the benefits of web applications but not end up exposing your privacy to them, you may wish to play under a pseudonym. Mechanisms to do this have been discussed for decades and real systems have emerged; but as you'd expect from our discussion of inference control in Chapter 9, anonymity is much harder than it looks.

Finally, elections are a classic example of an application where anonymity is required, but coupled with accountability: you want voters in an election to be able to satisfy themselves that their vote was counted, yet not to be able to prove to anyone else who they voted for (so they can't be bribed or bullied). Elections are also the key interface between social computing and power.

23.2 Computer Games

Games were one of the first applications of all — pretty well as soon as the world's first proper computer, the EDSAC, was operational, research students were writing games for it. The early AI researchers started writing chess programs, believing that when this problem was solved, computers would be able to function more or less as people. And in my own spotty youth, the first cryptanalysis program I wrote was to let me peek ahead into the rooms of a dungeon game.

There are limited opportunities for cheating at games of perfect information like chess, especially when playing against a computer. But there are many ways to cheat in other games, and they're becoming a big deal. Millions of people play online games, many of them bright and a lot of them poor; the large online worlds have a turnover larger than some small countries; and thousands of people make a living from online games, from the developers who create and maintain them to Chinese gold farmers. So the motives for cheating exist; and as games are software, and software has bugs, the means for cheating exist too. Yet if cheating becomes pervasive it spoils the fun. People don't enjoy an unfair fight — and in the long run even successful cheaters get bored (unless cheating and counter-cheating become the new game). Even the perception of cheating destroys players' enjoyment, so they go elsewhere and the game vendor loses a ton of money. So vendors make a serious effort to stop it. All told, online games provide a first-class social laboratory for the study of hacking, and game security has become the subject of serious study.

Computer games are also big business, as they have been for decades. They drove the home-computer boom of the 1970s that in turn spawned the PC industry; games consoles have been a huge market for microprocessors and memory chips; and gaming — whether on consoles or PCs — has largely driven the development of computer graphics [1367]. By 2001, game sales in the USA hit $9.4 billion, outperforming movie box-office sales of $8.35 billion. Comparing the two industries isn't straightforward, as movie stars have other sources of income too, and the industries are getting entangled with more and more movies being made with computer graphics effects. But in order-of-magnitude terms, computer games are probably of comparable economic importance to movies. Certainly a blockbuster online game grosses much more nowadays than a blockbuster movie; as games go online, you're selling subscriptions, not just one-off tickets [203].

'Security' in games has meant different things down through the years. The early arcade games of the 1970s concentrated on protecting the coin box against robbers. When Nintendo moved console games into the home, they subsidised the consoles from later sales of software cartridges and other add-ons, so a lot of effort was put into controlling which accessories could be used, as I discussed in section 22.6; their later competitors from Sega to Sony and Microsoft ended up fighting both legal and technical battles against reverse-engineers. Copy-protection of game software for PCs has also been a big deal, and there have been pre-release leaks of standalone games, just like prerelease leaks of movies. However the move to online computer games has trimmed the concerns. As a critical part of the game logic runs on a server, the client software can be given away, and the residual issue is whether players can get an unfair advantage. That's what I'll focus on now.

23.2.1   Types of Cheating

There are basically three types of cheating.

The first is where the original game has a known vulnerability that goes across into the online world and may be made worse. For example, a hand of contract bridge starts with players taking turns to bid how many tricks they think they can take. Each hand has four players, in two teams, and during the bidding no-one may communicate any information about the cards in their hand to their partner other than their public bids. In competitive play, a screen is placed diagonally across the table during bidding so that no-one can see their partner. Yet there are still occasional suspicions that some covert communication has taken place, for example in the players' tone of voice. In the real world, allegations of cheating are heard by a jury of experienced players, who take a view on whether the outcome was better than could have been expected in honest play. Even so, some decisions remain controversial for years: players may be exceptionally skilful, or lucky, and partners who've played together for years may communicate subconsciously without trying to.

Bridge is an example of two much more general problems, namely exploiting game rules, and cheating by collusion, both of which existed long before computers. Moving to online play creates both an opportunity and a problem. The opportunity is that if players are honest, all the bids can be mediated through the system: there's no tone of voice to give rise to a dispute. The problem is that if four people are playing online bridge together from their own homes, then there's nothing to stop a pair setting up a separate communications channel — a single text message of the cards in a hand is all it takes. Can technology help? Well, online bridge means online records, so you can mine the records of large numbers of games to determine whether a suspect pair do better over the long run than they should. It also makes it easier to run tournaments where each match is played simultaneously by many players using the same deal of cards — which makes a cheat easier to spot. Finally, it facilitates new ways of organising play: if you have an online game server available 24 by 7, people can turn up singly to play and start a game whenever four have arrived. So people play with many partners rather than just one; both the motive to cheat and the means are reduced, while the risks are increased.

Where's there's a single forum, such as a single dominant server, you can also construct global controls. For example, a problem in some games is *escaping*, where someone who's losing simply drops the connection. With a global service, you can remove the incentive for this by recording an escape as a loss (but only so long as your service is reliable — some game servers end a quarter of sessions in crashes, and this strategy wouldn't be popular there). Other exploits that are also found in real-world games include pretending to be less skilled than you are, losing a few games, but then winning once the other player gets confident and plays for more money; pool-room and poker sharks have used such strategies for ages, and there are many team variants too. In some games, you can get an advantage by having multiple players, and get some to kill off others to accumulate points. The susceptibility of online games to this sort of rigging depends to a great extent on whether identity is durable. If people can easily create, or cheaply buy, new identities, then rigging games using multiple front identities becomes simpler. (This is known as a *Sybil attack* and is also a problem in peer-to-peer systems [396].) One way to deal with this is a reputation system — a topic to which I'll return when we discuss auctions. In others, rather than having many characters operated by one human player, you use the reverse trick of having one character operated by shifts of successive human operators; this is typically done in online mulitplayer games where the goal is to accumulate online time and points.

The second type of cheating is where known computer-security issues apply straight off to the world of gaming. Five percent of the badware measured by Symantec in the first half of 2007 was aimed at online games, with the two most common items being Trojans designed to steal account information from players of Gampass and Lineage [1239]. There's a great variety of other attacks, from straightforward phishing to denial-of-service attacks that push up the network latency of your opponent so you can beat him at blitz chess. A lot of the material in this book applies one way or another to gaming: cheaters hack servers, eavesdrop on communications, and tamper with client memory to make walls invisible (there's a survey and taxonomy at [1368]). Policy issues such as privacy turn out to matter here too: a lot of people in Second Life were annoyed when an enterprising company built a search engine that went through their homes and indexed their stuff. And just as in other applications, a lot of exploits arise because of the chance discovery of bugs — such as in one game where you could drive up to a wall in a jeep, hit the 'disembark' button, and appear instantly on the other side of the wall [203]. Many games have glitches of this kind, and knowledge of them spreads quickly.

The third type are the new cheating tactics that emerge because of the nature of computer games, and the online variety in particular. In tactical shooters, for example, success should depend on the player's tactics and shooting skill, not on the game mechanics. Yet there are always shortcomings in the game's physics model, often introduced by network latency and by the optimisations game designers use to deal with it. In effect, the developers try to deceive you into believing that their world is consistent with itself and with Newton's laws, when it isn't really. For example, you'd normally expect that in a shooting duel, you'd have an advantage if you have the lowest network latency, or if you move first. Yet the prediction algorithms used in many game clients can twist this or into an exclusive-or: a high-latency player has an advantage if he moves first. This is because clients cache information about nearby players, so if you leap round a corner, see your enemy and shoot, then the slower your network connection is, the longer it will take before he can see you and respond. (There's a wide range of such tactics: see [203] for a discussion.)

There are many interesting borderline cases where an activity can be skill or cheating depending on the circumstances. Mike Bond coined the term 'neo-tactic' to refer to players subliminally exploiting network effects, such as the latency advantage for first movers. Are neotactics genius, or cheating? As in Bridge, the one can easily be mistaken for the other. But most people would say it's definitely cheating if you use mechanical assistance, such as a proxy server that slows down your packet stream just before you launch an attack.

23.2.2 Aimbots and Other Unauthorized Software

That brings us on to one of the classic game cheats, namely bots. One of the persistent cheating strategies is to have code of your own to provide you with automation and support. People have written a huge variety of tools, from simple routines that repeatedly click a fire button (to hack the games where the rate at which you can physically fire is a factor) through proxies that intercept the incoming network packets, identify the bad guys, examine your outgoing shots, and optimise their aim. These *aimbots* come with different levels of sophistication, from code that does all the target acquisition and shooting, to human-controlled versions that merely improve your aim. They can hook into the packet stream as proxies, into the graphics card, or even into the client code. Another variant on the same theme is the *wall hack*, where a player modifies his software to see through walls — for example, by changing the graphics software to make them translucent rather than opaque.

Game companies who sell first-person shooters reckon that aimbots seri-ously spoil other players' fun, so they use encryption and authentication mechanisms to protect the packet stream. (These are usually proprietary and hackable but that will no doubt get fixed in time.) They also use guard software, such as Punkbuster, that uses anti-virus techniques to detect attempts to hook into game code or the drivers on which it relies. A recent innovation, found in Call of Duty 4, is to offer action replays of kills, seen from the viewpoint of the player who makes the kill: this enables the killed player to see whether he was killed 'fairly' or not. This may not only reduce cheating, but also the perception of cheating — which is almost as damaging to the game operator [204].

Inappropriate software can also be run on game servers. A common hack is to get an object such as a gun to run multiple copies of a script in parallel — a trick that could have been prevented by proper resource accounting at the server. However, servers face critical real-time demands and their designers try to keep them as simple as possible. Self-replicating objects are used to run service-denial attacks, or to create temporary buildings that escape the resource controls on permanent structures. And people program magic swords to do unexpected tricks.

It must be said, though, that the relatively uncontrolled game scripting languages which make this possible have also been turned to creative use. People have realised that game engines can be used to render whole movies in 3-d; the quality may not be as good as on Pixar's rendering farms, but it works, and it's essentially free. This has led to the growth of a whole new art form of *machinima* (machine cinema). As they say, it's a rare wind that blows nobody any good.

23.2.3   Virtual Worlds, Virtual Economies

Bots are also used in farming, where entrepreneurs do the boring legwork of accumulating game objects such as gold coins or magic swords for sale to impatient players. However, most of the farming is done by real people in low-wage countries from Romania to China. 'Gold farming' is now a significant export that's creating new economic opportunities for young people in remote villages that have few other employers [384]. The economy of a large online community, such as World of Warcraft — with 8 million subscribers, of whom half a million are online at any time — is larger than that of some countries.

This means in turn that macroeconomic effects, such as exchange rates and rents, start to matter. Second Life, for example, is essentially a 3-d chat room run by Linden Labs, which rents out space to third parties, who can then customise their property as they want. It has a local currency of Linden dollars, that can be bought for U.S. dollars using a credit card, either through Linden Labs or via third-party brokers. The currency enables in-game entrepreneurs to sell value-added items such as clothes, artwork, pornography and services. After the FBI cracked down on online casinos, there was a surge of interest in gambling in Second Life; so in April 2007 the Feds visited Linden Labs [1006]. Just before the visit, 26% of announcements were about gambling; after it, commercial rents fell. And the world of anti-money-laundering controls made its appearance when Linden Labs started discriminating between 'verified' and 'unverified' accounts (the former being those where the player had used a credit card to subscribe)[1].

Markets for game goods are also getting better organised. For several years, magic swords and gold coins were traded in grey markets on eBay, but starting with Sony's 'Station Exchange' in 2005, game operators began running proper auction sites where players can trade game goods for real money. In 2006, we had reports of the first serious fraud: crooks used stolen identities to set up hundreds of thousands of accounts on the South Korean game Lineage, with

---

[1]The Financial Action Task Force — an international body that bullies countries into asking people who open bank accounts to provide government-issue photo-ID and two utility bills — wants payment systems that don't participate in their 'identity circus' to impose limits on payment amounts and velocity. That's why accounts at PayPal or even African mobile-phone payment systems restrict what you can do if you're unverified.

allegedly some inside help, and cashed out by selling some $15 m in game goods [758]. This all helps to raise the stakes in gaming, and to make stability more important. It also brings us naturally to eBay and to other 'real-world' web applications.

23.3   Web Applications

While online computer games are partly implemented in servers and partly in client software, an increasing number of services are entirely online and accessed via a standard web browser. They range from auction services like eBay through search engines such as Google and Yahoo, online mail services like Hotmail and AOL, online word processors such as Google documents, and e-commerce sites selling all kinds of good things (and bad things). Some industries — travel, entertainment, insurance and bookselling — have moved much of their sales online. And the recent trend to social networking brings in all sorts of new angles.

There are many problems common to all manner of web sites. One is that web servers are often insufficiently careful about the input they accept from users, leading for example to the SQL insertion attacks I discussed in section 4.4.2. Another increasingly common vulnerability is *cross-site scripting* (XSS). Scripting languages such as javascript are supposed to observe a *same origin policy* in that scripts will only act on data from the same domain; you don't want a script from a Mafia-run porn site acting on your electronic banking data. But this policy has been repeatedly circumvented, exploiting everything from carelessly-written web services that let users upload html containing scripts that other users can then read and execute, to errors in the design of virtual machines — such as the Firefox javascript bug discussed in Chapter 18. Web services as diverse as Hotmail, Orkut, Myspace and even PayPal have been hacked using XSS exploits, and removing them completely from your site involves very careful processing of all user-supplied html code. However, even if your own site is clean, your customers may still be vulnerable. The latest tricks involve using web services to launder origin: for example, the attacker makes a mash-up of the target site plus some evil scripts of his own, and then gets the victim to view it through a proxy such as Google Translate [1239].

The problems are compounded when a single firm provides a wide range of services. Google, for example, offers everything from search through maps to mail and word-processing, and other large service companies also have broad offerings. Where many services live at the same domain, the same origin policy doesn't do much work, and there have indeed been a number of XSS-type vulnerabilities between applications at Google and elsewhere. There are also privacy consequences of service aggregation, which I'll come to later.

A further bundle of problems with web services is that their structure is usually at least partially open to inspection. A user is passed from one page to another as he goes through a process such as browsing, search, product selection and payment; the attacker can read the html and javascript source, observe how parameters are passed, and look for nuggets such as SQL queries that can be manipulated [78]. He can also look to see whether input choices are screened by javascript, and try bypassing this to see if interesting things can be done (this needn't mean buffer overflows, but even just such simple hacks as ordering stuff at a discount). He can also monkey with hidden fields to see if they're used to pass interesting data. A prudent developer will assume that clients are malicious — but most developers don't; the rush online by millions of businesses has totally outpaced the available security skills (and tools). As a result, many services are not only buggy but open to manipulation.

So much personal information is now stored on web-based applications that a successful attacker can make off with large amounts of exploitable data. In November 2007, Salesforce.com admitted that it had lost the contact lists of a number of its customers after an employee got phished; for example, its customer SunTrust had 40,000 of its own customers compromised of whom 500 complained of bad emails that seemed to come from SunTrust [743]. These emails tried to install malware on their machines. In an earlier incident, Monster.com's resume database was breached, compromising 1.3 million job seekers. (These incidents raise a question about the adequacy of current breach disclosure laws, many of which don't consider someone's email address and the name of one of their business contacts to be 'personal information' whose loss is notifiable — but clearly such losses should be notified.)

So much for general vulnerabilities. Let's now look at the specific problems of some common web services.

23.3.1   eBay

The leading auction site, together with its payment service company PayPal, are significant to the security engineer for quite a number of reasons. For starters, they're the phishermens' largest target by far, as well as being the platform for lots of old-fashioned fraud. Phishing attacks against PayPal directly are not much different from the attacks against banks that I discussed in Chapter 2 (except in that as PayPal isn't a bank, its customers don't have the protection of banking law, such as the U.S. Regulation E, and rely on PayPal's good will to make good their losses). Many other frauds are variants of old commercial scams. For example, hucksters email the underbidders in an auction, offering goods similar to those that were on sale — but which turn out to be shoddy or nonexistent. And one of the biggest scams on eBay was run by a trader in Salt Lake City who sold laptops online. First he traded honestly, selling 750 laptops legitimately and accumulating a good reputation; then he took money for 1000 more that he didn't deliver. That sort of trading strategy has been around as long as commerce has.

But the auction site adds another twist. It provides a reputation service whereby honest traders accumulate good references from their trading partners, and many small-time occasional sellers have acquired high trust ratings. So an increasingly common attack is to hijack one of their accounts — whether by password guessing, phishing or something more technical — and use this for fraud. Account takeovers have been reported to be growing rapidly from the start of 2007 [542].

The easy way to exploit a hijacked account is to sell nonexistent goods, take the money and run, but there are many variants. A trick that's growing in popularity in 2007 is the fake escrow site. The bad guy offers a car for sale; you win the auction; he then suggests that you use an escrow service to which he'll ship the car and you'll pay the money. Real escrow services do actually exist, such as escrow.com, but so do many dodgy services set up by fraud gangs [57]; if you wire them the money that's the last you'll see of it.

Escrow scams are an example of reputation theft, which brings us to Google.

23.3.2   Google

Google's security manager looks set to have one of the most interesting jobs in the business over the next five years, just as her counterparts at Microsoft have had over the last five. The sheer scale of Google's activities make it both a target and a conduit for all sorts of wickedness. Again, some of it's as old as sin, but other attacks are quite novel.

A good example is *Google hacking*, where people use a search engine to look for vulnerable machines. The online Google Hacking Database has hundreds of examples of search strings that turn up everything from unpatched servers to files containing passwords [810]. Suitable searches can also be used against human targets: these can be searches for anyone who's exposed themselves in some specific way, such as by leaving their social security number visible online, or searches for usable data on some specific person. If you're a possible target, it's a good idea to do the search first. For example, I was a target for a while of an animal-rights terror group[2], so I used the main search engines to find out where my home address could be found. Companies and governments regularly search for their own secrets too. Search has simply changed the world since Altavista burst on the world a little over a decade ago; inquiries that previously would have taken the resources of a major government can now be conducted from anyone's laptop or mobile phone in seconds. And although the benefits of this revolution greatly outweigh the costs, the costs aren't zero.

---

[2]I was an elected member of the governing body of Cambridge University, which was thinking of building a monkey house.

The two main innovations that enabled Google to pull away from the other search engines were the Pagerank algorithm, which ranks a page based on the number of other pages that link to it, and the idea of linking search to targeted advertising, rather than the banner ads used by earlier engines like Altavista. A number of small text ads are placed on the search result page, and advertisers bid against each other for specific search terms in a continuous auction. Advertisers are charged when a user clicks on one of their ads. Google also lets publishers put links on their web pages in which it serves ads relevant to the page content, and pays them a percentage of the click-through revenue. This has turned out to be hugely popular and profitable, and has revolutionised classified advertising.

Yet it's brought wave after wave of attacks. The big problem in 2006 was *click-fraud*; your firm's competitors click repeatedly on your ads, thereby burning up your ad budget. Click-fraud can also be done by publishers who want to maximise their commissions. Google added various algorithms to try to detect click fraud: repeated clicks from one IP address, for example, are discounted when it comes to billing. Attackers then figured out that the order in which ads appeared depends on the click-through rate, as Google optimises its own revenue by ranking popular ads higher. This led to a further service-denial attack, *impression spam*, in which your competitor repeatedly calls up the results pages in which your ads appear but doesn't click on them. This causes your click-through rate to plummet, so your ads get downgraded.

In 2007, one of the big problems was *Google arbitrage*. A publisher buys cheap ads to drive traffic to his site, where he writes about topics that attract more expensive ads. If customers who arrive at his site cheaply leave via a more expensive route, he makes a profit. Attitudes to this are mixed. Buying ads in order to sell ads has a long enough history; your local paper probably lives from classified advertising, and may also have posters all over town. Some advertisers think it's fraud: they pay for clicks from people fresh off searches, and instead get second-hand traffic from people escaping boring web pages that they didn't really want to go to. Google acts from time to time against the arbitrageurs, whose profits were dwindling by year end.

But this is just a small part of a larger problem, namely 'Made for Adsense' (MFA) sites. One pattern we've detected is the fake institution: the scamster copies an existing charitable or educational website with only minor changes to the content and uses the knock-off to host something with a high cost-per-click such as job ads. The idea is that where websites are highly ranked, copies of them will be too: and some of the bogus charities even set out to exchange links with real ones to further confuse the issue[3].

---

[3]That's how we stumbled across the network, when they offered an ad exchange with the Foundation for Information Policy Research, which I chair.

Another series of sites is run by a firm that buys up abandoned domain names, writes relevant editorial content, and fills them with ads. (The content is written for free by journalism students who look for places at which to 'intern' as part of their course). When I presented an analysis of such sites at Google, the reaction was mixed. There's a serious policy question here: although one might not think very much of the content, this is in some sense a new literary genre that's emerged on the back of the Adsense model, just as soap operas emerged once TV stations started being funded by adverts for fast-moving consumer goods. Googlers' view on balance was that such sites should be left to market forces. But there are clearly some close judgment calls between what's abuse and what's merely tiresome.

There are many interesting research problems here, such as how one goes about identifying and mapping bogus communities, where links have been manufactured to create a semblance of real social or economic activity in order to fool the Pagerank algorithm, and hidden communities, such as the network of sites based on abandoned domain names. The latter, at least, is similar to the problems faced by police and intelligence agencies searching for insurgent groups, while distinguishing bogus communities from genuine ones may also come to depend on increasingly sophisticated traffic analysis and social-network analysis of the sort discussed in sections 19.3.1, 21.5 and 24.3.2.

This brings us inevitably to the issue that most observers consider to be Google's Achilles heel: privacy. Privacy concerns operate at many levels.

- First, there's unauthorized access to data. When a firm with tens of thousands of employees holds personal data on hundreds of millions of people, there's a clear risk that information will leak — perhaps via a disgruntled insider, or perhaps via an exploit of some kind. These are basically the issues I discussed in Chapter 9, although on a much larger scale than ever before.

- Second, there's privacy law. For example, the European Commission is in dispute about how long clickstream data should be kept: Google's agreed to 'de-identify' clickstreams after 18 months, but this doesn't really satisfy the Commission. In section 9.3.1 I discussed how AOL released anonymised search histories for 'research', and some users were promptly identified from their search patterns; from the technical point of view, achieving privacy via anonymity requires frequent changes of pseudonym. (I'll return to privacy later when I deal with policy.)

- Third, there's lawful access to authorised data, as when the FBI (or a divorce lawyer) turns up in Mountain View with a subpoena.

Various people, for various reasons, will want to limit the possible damage resulting from one of more of these possible types of privacy exposure.

And the tensions look set to become steadily more serious as more information about us becomes available and searchable.

But before we go on to examine privacy technology, there's a third type of web service that can collect even more intimate and pervasive information: the social-networking site.

23.3.3   Social Networking Sites

Social networking sites such as MySpace and Facebook have taken off rapidly since about 2004, and are now used by large numbers of young people to organise their social lives. Other sites aim at organising professionals. The field is developing rapidly, but as I write in January 2008, the main users are still the young, and the typical site offers not just a place to store a home page but ways to link to your friends' pages too. The key idea is that the site mirrors the underlying social network: the added value is that it enhances your social network by helping you communicate with friends more conveniently and by making new friends. The access-control mechanisms typically let your friends see more of your stuff; there are messaging services such as forums, chat rooms and instant messenger, to support social interaction; and there are various structured methods of getting to know people. On some sites, you have to be introduced by mutual acquaintances; on others, you can search for people who meet given criteria such as age, location, musical tastes, hobbies, sex and sexual orientation. Society always had such mechanisms, of course, in the form of clubs, and some people see social networking merely as a kind of online cocktail party. However, the social-networking revolution enables rapid innovation of the mechanisms that people use to form friendships, look for partners and set up professional and business relationships.

The putative business model is, first, that the huge amount of information subscribers make available to the operators of these sites will enable even better targeted advertisement than on Google; and second, that friendship networks can create massive lockin, which is the source of value in the information industries. It's hard not to have a page on Facebook if all your friends do, and having a hundred million people keeping their address books and message archives on your servers rather than on their own PCs may seem like a license to print money[4].

So what problems should you anticipate when designing a social-networking site? Much government advice centres on the fearmongering aspects: young people reveal a lot about themselves on social sites, and can attract sex predators. It's certainly true that the Internet has had an effect on sex crimes, while

[4]Don't forget fashion though: in England everyone seems to have had a MySpace page in 2006, and most people have a Facebook page now in 2007 — but Brazilians use Orkut, and who can tell what will be cool in 2012?

no significant impact has been detected on any other category of offense. Its uptake across U.S. states and other countries was associated with a small rise in 'runaways', that is, under-18s leaving home without their parents' permission. Some runaways were no doubt kids escaping unsatisfactory homes or simply heading off to seek their fortunes; the key question is how many of them were abused. The figures show that Internet uptake was correlated with a drop in reported cases of rape, and that there was no increase in the murder rate [709]. One might worry about whether runaway teens turn to sex work, but prostitution also fell as the Internet spread. It might still be argued that a small increase in sexual abuse of runaway teens was masked by a larger fall in sex crimes overall, caused in turn by the greater availability of pornography; but the drop in sex crimes was significant only among male offenders aged 15–24 and there was no corresponding increase of older offenders. And young people I've talked to take the view that fending off unwanted advances from older men is just part of life anyway, whether offline or online.

The view you take of all this, if you're building such a system, may depend on whether your site is aimed at distance networking — as with photographers from different continents trading pictures and tips on Flickr — or at networks involving physical relationships. In the second case, the next question is whether you restrict membership to teens and above, as Facebook does, or let anyone join, as MySpace does. There's a reasonable discussion of the policy and technical issues from ENISA [615]. As for younger children, it's clearly prudent for parents to keep an eye on online activities; the junior members of our family get to use the computer in the kitchen, which also helps get across the message that the Internet is public space rather than private space. ENISA also recommends that schools should encourage rather than prohibit social network use, so that bullying can be reported and dealt with. Bullying has always been a low-grade problem for schools, erupting into very occasional tragedy with suicides or killings. Before the Internet, bullied children could escape for long periods of time at home and with friends; nowadays the taunting can follow them to their bedrooms. This can make it all the more miserable if their Internet use is secret and furtive. The cure is to bring things into the open.

These are, of course, broad issues that apply to Internet use generally, not just to social networking sites. And on the face of it, you might expect social networking sites to be less dangerous than random online chat rooms, as the service operator has an incentive to limit egregious abuse because of the associated reputation risk. But what are the interesting security engineering issues?

One emerging property of social networking systems is the sheer complexity of security policy. In Chapter 4, I discussed how access controls are simple close to the hardware, but get more complex as you move up the stack through the operating system and middleware to the application. Social networking applications attempt to encapsulate a significant subset of human behaviour in groups; the result is ever-more complicated sets of rules, which are very difficult for users to manage.

For example, setting privacy policy on Facebook in October 2007 means wading through no less than six screens of access options — essentially a set of access control lists to different parts of your profile. And the controls aren't linear; photos, for example, have a policy of opt-in and opt-out. If I recognise you in a photo on someone's page, I can tag that photo with your name, but the tag won't be publicly visible until the photo owner agrees (the opt-in). If you're a Facebook member you'll be notified, and you can remove the tag if you want (the opt-out) [450]. However you might not notice the tag, and this could have consequences if the photo were embarrassing — say, a drunken party. For example, on New Year's day 2008, following the assassination of Benazir Bhutto in Pakistan, the UK press published a photo of her son and political heir Bilawal Bhutto, dressed up in a devil's costume with red horns for a Halloween party, which was found on the Facebook site of one of his student friends.

Many people just don't understand what the terms used in the access controls mean. For example, if you make photos available to the 'community', that means by default anyone with an email address within your institution — which has led to campus police having discussions with people who've uploaded photos of assorted kinds of rulebreaking activities [463]. Facebook also doesn't deal with multiple personae; for example, I'm Ross the computer scientist, Ross the technology-policy guy, Ross the musician, Ross the family man, and so on — and as I can't separate them, I've 'friended' only people I know from the first two communities on Facebook.

There are also some quite subtle policy issues: for example, you'd think it was alright to publish information that was already public? Wrong! There was a huge row when Facebook added a news feed feature that notified all your status changes to all your friends. Previously, if you'd broken up with your girlfriend, this would be publicly visible anyway (assuming you made partnership data public). Suddenly, such a change was automatically and instantly broadcast to your entire social circle — which upset a lot of people. It's not just that the site had automated some of the social aspects of gossip; it suddenly made social faux pas very visible [216]. This feature can now be turned off, but the extra complexity just makes it even harder for people to manage their privacy.

Another example is search. Most web services firms are tempted to use private data in public searches in order to make them more precise. Back in the early days (2004), it turned out that search on Friendster leaked private data: a chain of suitably-chosen searches could infer a user's surname and zip code even where this data had been set as private [902]. The moral was that public searches should never be allowed to return results based on private data. Another lesson that should have been more widely learned is that once the social network is known, inference control becomes much harder. Friendster duly fixed its systems. Yet the bug was rediscovered in Facebook in 2007: Facebook had simply left it to users to decide whether they wanted to turn off search on private terms, and essentially none of them had done so [1197]. That's now fixed, but the issue arose yet again when Facebook made available stripped-down versions of user profiles to Google. Once more, it had been left to users to become aware of this risk and turn off the relevant feature; once more, almost nobody did so [694]. Facebook appears to have a strategy of dumping all the really hard security decisions on the users — so they can respond to criticism by blaming users for not turning off features X and Y. Searchability by default may be in their short-term financial interest, but the end result can too easily be unusable security plus unsafe defaults.

Another tension between corporate growth and security usability was a recent decision to allow third-party application developers access to profile data. When someone builds an app that allows people to export photos (say) from Flickr to Facebook, then how on earth are we to evaluate that? Even if the two systems are secure in isolation, there's no guarantee that this will compose — especially where systems have complex and ever-changing APIs, and complex hard-to-use privacy policies. Then, in late 2007, Facebook faced a revolt of its users after it introduced 'Beacon', an advertising system that told users' friends about what they'd just purchased on other websites, and made the feature opt-out rather than opt-in. Mark Zuckerberg, founder and chief executive, apologized to the site's users for handling the matter badly. (It remains to be seen whether future marketing ideas will be opt-in.)

There are both 'soft' and 'hard' issues bundled up here. At the soft end, people present different personae at different sites; for example, by placing different kinds of photos on Flickr and Facebook [1276]. At the nastier end, not all applications are written by large, respectable companies. Yet once you authorise a third-party application to access your profile, it can do most anything you can — including spamming your friends and selling their personal information to third parties. There's a sense in which making a 'friend' on Facebook is the digital equivalent of unprotected sex — you're exposed to everything they've got.

All the usual tussles between free speech and censorship pop up too. For example, in Flickr, you're not supposed to upload photos you wouldn't show your mum unless you tag them as 'restricted' (i.e. adult). You're not allowed to view such material if you're in Germany, or search for it in Singapore. Yet a colleague who uploaded art nudes had his account blacklisted as 'unsafe', even though he's quite happy to show his mum his work. And as far as data protection law is concerned, Facebook tends to reveal the data subject's race, sex life, health, religion, political beliefs and whether he belongs to a trade union — precisely those 'sensitive' types of data that get special protection under European privacy law [235].

There's a further bunch of problems at the interface between technical and social mechanisms. For example, you make confidential information available to your friends, one of whom gets his account compromised, and your data ends up public. When this was first reported (in 2003), pioneers expected that social pressures would make users more careful [961], but this hasn't happened. The underlying reasons may be familiar: in a world of strong network externalities, systems start off insecure in order to grow as quickly as possible. But while Windows and Symbian were insecure in order to appeal to complementers while building a dominant position in a two-sided market, social-network site operators bias their algorithms and their presentation to get people to enrol as many friends as possible. This undermines any possible social discipline.

Other socio-technical attacks include cross-site scripting vulnerabilities, of which there have been plenty [902]. Spam is rising fast, and a particularly ominous problem may be phishing. A recent experiment at Indiana University sent phish to a sample of students, asking them to check out an off-campus website that solicited entry of their university password. The success rate with the control group was 16% but a group targeted using data harvested from social networks were much more vulnerable — 72% of them were hooked by the phish [653]. Already there's a significant amount of phishing being reported on MySpace [796].

I'll finish up this section by making two more general points. The first is that, as the social-networking sites learn rapidly from experience and clean up their act, the largest medium-term problems may well be, first, the migration online of real-world social problems such as bullying; and second, that many teens put stuff online that they'll later regret, such as boasts of experiments with drink, drugs and sex that get dug up when they apply for jobs. In Seoul, a girl was asked to pick up some poo left by her dog, and refused; a bystander filmed this, she became known as 'dog poo girl', and she was hounded from university [1201]. Although that's an extreme case, the principle is not really new: people who posted immoderately on the old network news system sometimes found themselves haunted by 'the Ghost of Usenet Postings Past' [507]; and there are tales going back centuries of social faux pas that ruined lives, families and fortunes. But while in olden times it would most likely be a lapse of manners at court that got you in bad trouble, now it can be a lapse of manners on the subway.

The world is steadily becoming more documented — more like the villages most of us lived in until the eighteenth century, where everyone's doings were known. Back then, the village gossips would serve up a mèlange of assorted factoids about anyone local — some true, and some false — which people would use when forming opinions. Nowadays, Google has taken over that role, and it's much less susceptible to social pressure to correct errors, or forgive the occasional blunders of otherwise decent people. Also, much of the anonymity that people got from moving into towns during the industrial revolution is being lost. The effect of persistent social memory on social problems will be mixed. Bullying may be mitigated because of the record left behind, while the embarrassment problem may be resolved by some combination of a more relaxed attitude to youthful indiscretions, plus greater discretion on the part of youth. We'll have to wait and see which dominates, but early signs are that people are becoming more relaxed: the Pew Internet & American Life Project found that 60% of Americans are unconcerned in 2007 about the 'digital footprint' they leave behind, while in a survey in 2000, 84% were worried. So we're learning to cope [1229]. (Discretion is part of coping, and that may involve the use of a pseudonym or nickname that isn't too easy for outsiders to link to your real person, but I'll discuss all that in the next section.)

Second, social network systems have the potential to do an awful lot of good. The Harvard sociologist Robert Putnam documented, in his influential book 'Bowling Alone', how social networks in America and elsewhere were damaged by the advent of television, the move to the suburbs and even the move by women into work (though TV did by far the most damage) [1052]. The baby-boom generation, who were the first to be raised with TV, are much less likely to join clubs, know our neighbours, meet frequently with friends or participate in team sports than our parents did, and the succeeding 'generation X' are less likely still. Now it seems that sociability is ticking upwards once more. What TV and mass consumer culture took away, the PC and the mobile phone may be giving back. Easier communication not only makes people communicate more but in different ways; the old communities based on geography are being supplemented by communities of shared interest. We academics were among the first to benefit; the communities of people interested in cryptography, or protocols, or number theory, have been held together as much by the Internet as by the conference circuit for many years. Now these benefits are spreading to everybody, and that's great.

Social-networking sites also provide a platform for rapid experimentation and innovation in new ways of making and maintaining friendships. And they may be brilliant for the geeky, the shy, the ugly, and people with borderline Asperger's. But to the extent that they try to encapsulate more and more of the complexity of real social life, their policies will become ever more complex. And just as we're limited in our ability to build large software systems by technical complexity, so social-networking systems may explore a new space in which policy complexity — security usability, in a new guise — may provide one of the ultimate limits to growth. It will be interesting to watch.

23.4 Privacy Technology

As business moves online, vast amounts of information start to get collected. In the old days, you walked into a record store and bought an album for cash; now you download a track from a server, which downloads a license to your PC. The central license server knows exactly who bought access to what, and when. Marketers think this is magnificent; privacy advocates are appalled [410]. The move to pervasive computing is also greatly increasing the amount of information held on us by others — for example, if people start using applications in their mobile phones to track their social networks and help them manage their time better [407]. There will no doubt be all sorts of 'must have' applications in the future that collect data about us, which means growing uncertainty about what will be available to whom.

Technology is already putting some social conventions under strain. In pre-technological societies, two people could walk a short distance away from everyone else and have a conversation that left no hard evidence of what was said. If Alice claimed that Bob had tried to recruit her for an insurrection, then Bob could always claim the converse — that it was Alice who'd proposed to overthrow the king and he who'd refused out of loyalty. In other words, many communications were *deniable*. Plausible deniability remains an important feature of some communications today, from everyday life up to the highest reaches of intelligence and diplomacy. It can sometimes be fixed by convention: for example, a litigant in England can write a letter marked 'without prejudice' to another proposing a settlement, and this letter cannot be used in evidence. But most circumstances lack such clear and convenient rules, and the electronic nature of communication often means that 'just stepping outside for a minute' isn't an option. What then?

Another issue is anonymity. Until the industrial revolution, most people lived in small villages, and it was a relief — in fact a revolution — to move into a town. You could change your religion, or vote for a land-reform candidate, without your landlord throwing you off your farm. Nowadays, the phrase 'electronic village' not only captures the way in which electronic communications have shrunk distance, but also the fear that they will shrink our freedom too.

Can technology do anything to help? Let's consider some 'users' — some people with specific privacy problems.

1. Andrew is a missionary in Texas whose website has attracted a number of converts in Saudi Arabia. That country executes citizens who change their religion. He suspects that some of the people who've

contacted him aren't real converts, but religious policemen hunting for apostates. He can't tell policemen apart from real converts. What sort of technology should he use to communicate privately with them?

2. Betty is your ten-year-old daughter, who's been warned by her teacher to remain anonymous online. What sort of training and tools should you give her to help her manage this?

3. Charles is an engineer at a Silicon Valley startup that's still in stealth mode, and he's running a blog — in contravention of his company's rules. How can he avoid getting caught and fired?

4. Dai is a human-rights worker in Vietnam, in contact with people trying to set up independent trade unions, microfinance cooperatives and the like. The police harass her frequently. How should she communicate with co-workers?

5. Elizabeth works as an analyst for an investment bank that's advising on a merger. She wants ways of investigating a takeover target without letting the target get wind of her interest — or even learn that anybody at all is interested.

6. Firoz is a gay man who lives in Teheran, where being gay is a capital offence. He'd like some way to download porn without getting hanged.

7. Graziano is a magistrate in Palermo setting up a hotline to let people tip off the authorities about Mafia activity. He knows that some of the cops who staff the office in future will be in the Mafia's pay — and that potential informants know this too. How does he limit the damage that future corrupt cops can do?

This helps to illustrate that privacy isn't just about encrypting phone calls or web traffic. For example, if Andrew tells his converts to download and use a particular cryptography program, then so will the police spies; and the national firewall will be set to detect anyone who sends or receives messages using that program. Andrew has to make his traffic look innocuous — so that the religious police can't spot converts even when they have full knowledge of what apostate traffic looks like.

And while suitable technical measures may solve part of Andrew's problem, they won't be much use with Betty's. The risk to her is largely that she will give out information carelessly that might come back to haunt her. Filtering software can help — if she's not allowed to give out her home address over the Internet, a filter can look for it, and beep if she gets careless — but most of the effort will have to go into training her.

There's also wide variation in the level at which the protection is provided. Betty's protection has to be provided mostly at the application layer, as the main problem is unintentional leaks via content; the same applies to Charles.

However, Charles might face more sophisticated analysis, perhaps at the hands of someone like Elizabeth: she might trawl through his postings looking for metadata from camera serial numbers in the images to names of workgroups or even printers embedded in documents, so that she can figure out who he's working with on his secret project.

The intensity of attacks will also vary. Charles and Firoz might face only sporadic interest, while Dai is subjected to constant surveillance. She'll use anonymous communications not so much to protect herself, but to protect others who haven't yet come to the police's attention. There are huge differences in protection incentives: Andrew may go to a lot of trouble to make his website as harmless as possible to its visitors (for example, by hosting it on the same machine as many innocuous services), while the sites in which Firoz is interested don't care much about his safety. Andrew, Dai and Graziano all have to think hard about dishonest insiders. Different probability thresholds mark the difference between success and failure; plausible deniability of an association might be enough to get Charles off the hook, while mere suspicion would frustrate Elizabeth's plans. And there are different costs of failure: Elizabeth may lose some money if she's caught, while Firoz could lose his life.

We've come across anonymity mechanisms before, when we discussed how people who don't want their phone calls traced buy prepaid mobile phones, use them for a while, and throw them away. Even that's hard; and even Al-Qaida couldn't do it right. So what are the prospects for hard privacy online?

23.4.1 Anonymous Email – The Dining Cryptographers and Mixes

As we remarked in several contexts, the opponent often gets most of his information from traffic analysis. Even if the communications between Alice and Bob are encrypted and the ciphertext hidden in MP3 files, and even if on inspection neither Alice's laptop nor Bob's contains any suspicious material, the mere fact that Alice communicated with Bob may give the game away.

This is why criminals set much more store by anonymous communication (such as using prepaid mobile phones) than by encryption. There are many legitimate uses too, from the folks on our list above through anonymous helplines for abuse victims; corporate whistleblowers; protest groups who wish to dig an elephant trap for the government; anonymous student feedback on professors; anonymous refereeing of conference paper submissions, and anonymous HIV tests where you get the results online using a one-time password that came with a test kit you bought for cash. You may want to apply for a job without your current employer finding out, to exchange private email with people who don't use encryption, or fight a harmful and vengeful cult.

There are two basic mechanisms, both invented by David Chaum in the 1980's. The first is the *dining cryptographers problem*, inspired by the 'dining philosophers' problem discussed in section 6.2.4. Several cryptographers are gathered around a table for dinner, and the waiter informs them that the meal has already been paid for by an anonymous benefactor, who could be one of the participants or the NSA. The cryptographers would like to know which. So pairs of principals share one time pads, after which each principal outputs a function of her 'I paid/I didn't pay' bit and everyone can later work out the total parity of all such bits. As long as not more than one of the cryptographers says 'I paid', even parity means that the NSA paid, while odd parity means that one of the diners paid, even if nobody can figure out who [286]. This mechanism can be considered the anonymity equivalent of the one-time pad; it gives 'unconditional anonymity', albeit at the cost of a laborious protocol and a lot of key material. Various extensions have been proposed, including one in which 'dining drug dealers' can auction a consignment of cocaine without the bidders' identities being revealed to the other bidders or to the seller. Nobody except buyer and seller know who won the auction; and even the seller is not able to find out the identity of the highest bidder before committing to the sale [1219].

However, for practical anonymity applications, the pioneering innovation was another idea of Chaum's, the *mix* or *anonymous remailer* [284]. This accepts encrypted messages, strips off the encryption, and then remails them to the address that it finds inside. In its simplest form, if Alice wants to send anonymous email to Bob via Charlie and David, she sends them the message:

$$A \rightarrow C : \{D, \{B, \{M\}_{KB}\}_{KD}\}_{KC}$$

Charlie now strips off the outer wrapper, finds David's address plus a ciphertext, and sends the ciphertext to David. David decrypts it and finds Bob's address plus a ciphertext, so he sends the ciphertext to Bob. Bob decrypts this and gets the message M.

Anonymous remailers came into use in the 1990s. To start off with, people used single remailers, but, as I mentioned in section 22.3.3, an early remailer was closed down following court action by the Scientologists, after it was used to post material critical of them. A lot of people still rely on services such as Hotmail and Hushmail that provide simple, low-cost anonymity, but if you might be subjected to legal compulsion (or sophisticated technical attack) it's wise not to have a single point of failure[5]. Chainable remailers were initially developed by the cypherpunks; they not only did nested encryption of outgoing traffic but also supported a *reply block* — a set of nested public keys and email addresses that lets the recipient reply to you. There are also *nymservers* that will store reply blocks and handle anonymous return mail automatically. The most common design at present is the Mixmaster remailer, which also

---

[5]'Wired' was surprised in November 2007 when it turned out that Hushmail responded to warrants [1177] — which itself is surprising.

protects against basic traffic analysis by padding messages and subjecting them to random delays [899].

A common application is anonymous posting to mailing lists with sensitive content — applications range from reporting security vulnerabilities through abuse support to anonymous political speech. Of course, an anonymous remailer could be an attractive honey trap for an intelligence agency to operate, and so it's common to send messages through a number of successive remailers and arrange things so that most of them would have to conspire to break the traffic. Even so, selective service-denial attacks are possible; if the NSA runs remailers X and Y, and you try a path through X and Z, they can cause that to not work; so you then try X and Y, which 'works', and you're happy (as are they). Remailer operators can also be subjected to all sorts of attacks, ranging from subpoenas and litigation to spam floods that aim get the operator blacklisted; David Mazières and Frans Kaashoek have a paper on their experiences running such a service [849]. The technology is still evolving, with the latest proposals incorporating not just more robust mechanisms for fixed-length packets and single-use reply blocks, but also directory and reputation services that will allow users to monitor selective service-denial attacks [344].

23.4.2 Anonymous Web Browsing – Tor

Anonymous connections aren't limited to email, but can include any communications service. As the web has come to dominate online applications, The Onion Router (Tor) has become the most widely-used anonymous communication system, with over 200,000 users. Tor began its life as an experimental US Navy Labs system, called Onion Routing because the messages are nested like the layers of an onion [1062]. The Navy opened it up to the world, presumably because you can usually only be anonymous in a crowd. If Tor had been restricted to the U.S. intelligence community, then any website getting Tor traffic could draw an obvious conclusion. U.S. Naval personnel in the Middle East use Tor to connect back to their servers in Maryland. They don't think of it as an anonymity system but as a personal safety system: they don't want anyone watching the house they're in to learn their affiliation, and they don't want anyone watching the servers in Maryland to learn where they are. In effect, they hide among local (Iraqi and Maryland) men looking for porn; and porn traffic also conceals human-rights workers in the third world. Tor may be a part of the solution adopted by several of our representative privacy users (Charles, Dai, Elizabeth, Firoz and maybe even Graziano), so I'll now discuss its design and its limitations[6].

---

[6]By way of declaration of interest, I hold a grant from the Tor Project that pays one of my postdocs to help develop their software. There are also commercial services, such as Anonymizer [79], that let you browse the web anonymously, but they're routinely blocked by repressive governments.

The Tor software consists of the Tor client, which forwards TCP traffic, a web proxy through which it talks to your browser, and optionally a 'Tor Button' that acts as an extension to the Firefox browser and lets you switch rapidly between normal and anonymous browsing. In the latter mode, the Tor button disables cookies, javascript and all other plugins. Volunteers with high-bandwidth connections enable the Tor client to also act as a server, of which there may be a few thousand active at any time. When you turn on a Tor client, it opens a circuit by finding three Tor servers through which it connects to the outside world. It negotiates an encrypted session with the first server, then through this it negotiates another encrypted session to the second server, through which it then sets up a third encrypted session to the exit node. Your web browser traffic flows in the clear from the exit node to your destination.

This brings us immediately to one widely-publicised Tor vulnerability — the *malicious exit node*. In September 2007, someone set up five Tor exit nodes, monitored the traffic that went through them, and published the interesting stuff [917]. This included logons and passwords for a number of webmail accounts used by embassies, including missions from Iran, India, Japan and Russia. (This gave an insight into password robustness policy: Uzbekistan came top with passwords like 's1e7u0l7c' while Tunisia just used 'Tunisia' and an Indian embassy '1234'.) Yet the Tor documentation and website make clear that exit traffic can be read, so clueful people would have either used a webmail service that supports TLS encryption, like Gmail, or else used email encryption software such as PGP (which I'll mention later).

The second problem with anonymous web browsing is the many side-channels by which modern content calls home. This is why the proxy distributed with the Tor client kills off cookies and javascript, but that's just the beginning. If Firoz downloads a porn movie, and his Windows Media Player then calls the porn server directly to get a license, the packet traffic from his IP address to a 'known Satanic' site may be a giveaway; but then, if he blocks the license request, he won't be able to watch the film. ActiveX controls, Flash and other browser add-ons can also open connections outside the proxy. For surveys of ways in which websites can defeat anonymising services, see [1091, 1194].

Third, while the Mixmaster and later remailers can make traffic analysis harder by dicing, padding and delaying traffic, this introduces latency that would not be acceptable in most web applications. Low-latency, high-bandwidth systems such as Tor are intrinsically more exposed to traffic analysis. A global adversary such as the NSA, that taps traffic at many points in the Internet, can certainly recover information about some Tor circuits by correlating their activity; in fact, they only need to tap a small number of key exchange points to get a good sample of the traffic [920] (so if the U.S. government figures in your threat model, it may be prudent to set up new Tor circuits frequently).

Finally, many applications get users to identify themselves explicitly, and others get them to leak information about who they are without realising it. In section 9.3.1 I discussed how supposedly anonymous search histories from AOL identified many users: a combination of local searches (that tell where you live) and special-interest searches (that reveal your hobbies) may be enough to identify you. So if you're using Tor to do anonymous search, and there is even the slightest possibility that your opponent might be able to serve a subpoena on the search engine, you had better set up new circuits, and thus new pseudonyms, frequently.

If your opponent is less capable, then traffic patterns may still give the game away. First, suppose you want to browse a forbidden website that has a known and stable structure; a modern commercial web page might contain some 30 objects ranging in site from a few hundred bytes to a few tens of kilobytes. This pattern is usually unique and is clearly visible even after TLS encryption. Even although Tor traffic (as seen by a wiretap close to the user) lies under three layes of Tor encryption, and even though cells are padded to 512 bytes, random web pages still leak a lot of information about their identity. So if Andrew wants his converts to view his website through Tor, and there's a real risk that they'll be killed if they're caught, he should think hard. Should he pad his webpages so that, encrypted, they will be the same size as a popular and innocuous site? Should be put short sermons on YouTube, of the same length as popular music tracks? Or should he use a different technology entirely?

An opponent who can occasionally get control of the forbidden website can play yet more tricks. Graziano, who's worried about Mafia takeover of the police's Mafia tip-off site, should consider the following attack. The Mafia technicians make a number of probes to all the Tor servers as the page is loaded, and from the effects on server load they can identify the path along which the download was made. They then go to the local ISP, which thcy bribe or coerce into handing over the traffic logs that show who established a connection with the entry node at the relevant time [919]. (So from Graziano's point of view, at least, the recent European directive compelling ISPs to retain traffic logs may not always help the police.)

There's no doubt that Tor is an extremely useful privacy tool, but it has to be used with care. It's more effective when browsing websites that try to respect users' privacy than when browsing sites that try to compromise them; and it's often used in combination with other tools. For example, human-rights workers in less developed countries commonly use it along with Skype and PGP.

23.4.3 Confidential and Anonymous Phone Calls

I discussed in Chapter 20 how criminals looking for anonymous communications often just buy prepaid mobiles, use them for a while, and throw them away. They are a useful tool for others too; among our representative privacy users, Andrew might think of telling his converts to use them. But they are not the only option, and they don't provide protection against wiretapping. If your opponent has the technology to do automatic keyword search or speaker recognition on phone traffic, as the NSA does, or the manpower to run a large number of wiretaps, as a typical third-world despot does, then you might want to consider voice over IP.

In theory, you can run VOIP communications through proxies like Tor [665]; but in practice, not many people do; and as anonymity usually means hiding in a crowd, that brings us to Skype. Skype is not only the largest VOIP operator, which gives safety in numbers; it's got a peer-to-peer architecture, so your calls go end-to-end; and the traffic's encrypted, with mechanisms that have undergone an independent evaluation [165].

So what can go wrong? Well, if Andrew were to use Skype to talk to his converts then he'd better not use the same username to talk to all of them; otherwise the religious police will learn this username from their bogus convert and search for everyone who calls it. Fortunately, you can get multiple, throwaway Skype usernames, and provided Andrew uses a different username for each contact Skype may be a suitable mechanism. The next problem, for some applications at least, is that Skype being owned by a large U.S. company is likely to respond to warrants[7] So if your threat model includes the U.S. Government, you'd better assume that the call content can be decrypted once the NSA identifies your traffic as of interest. You might be at risk if you're opposing a government, such as that of Uzbekistan, with which the USA has intelligence-sharing agreements; and you might also be at risk if Skype's parent company, eBay, has an office in the country whose police you're trying to hide your traffic from. So if Andrew's unsure about whether eBay would help out the Saudi government, he might use Skype largely as an anonymity mechanism, and use it to mask the transfer of files that are encrypted using a product such as PGP.

Human-rights workers such as Dai do in fact use Skype plus PGP plus Tor to protect their traffic, and the attacks to which they're subjected are the stuff of intelligence tradecraft. The police enter their homes covertly to implant rootkits that sniff passwords, and room bugs to listen to conversations. When you encrypt a phone call, you have to wonder whether the secret police are getting one side of it (or both) from a hidden microphone. Countering such attacks requires tradecraft in turn. Some of this is just like in spy movies: leaving telltales to detect covert entry, keeping your laptop with you at all times, and holding sensitive conversations in places that are hard to bug. Other aspects of it are different: as human-rights workers (like journalists but unlike

---

[7]Skype itself is actually a Luxembourg company, and its officers who respond to law enforcement are based there: so an FBI National Security Letter may not be effective, but a judicial warrant should be.

spies) are known to the host government, they need to avoid breaking the law and they need to nurture support structures, including overt support from overseas NGOs and governments. They also need — while under intermittent observation — to make covert contact with people who aren't themselves under suspicion.

23.4.4 Email Encryption

During the 'Crypto Wars' on the 1990s, cyber-activists fought their governments for the right to encrypt email, while governments pushed for laws restricting encryption. I'll discuss the politics in the next chapter. However one focus of that struggle, the encryption product *Pretty Good Privacy* (PGP), along with compatible free products such as GPG, have become fairly widely used among geeks. A typical use is by Computer Emergency Response Teams (CERTs) who encrypt information about attacks and vulnerabilities when they share it with each other. Many private individuals also have PGP encryption keys and some encrypt traffic to each other by default.

PGP has a number of features but in its most basic form, each user generates a private/public keypair. To protect a message, you sign a hash of it using your private key, encrypt both the message and the signature with a randomly chosen session key, and then encrypt the session key using the public key of each of the intended recipients. Thus, if Alice wants to send an encrypted email to Bob and Charlie, she forms the message

$$\{KS\}_{KB}, \{KS\}_{KC}, \{M, \{h(M)\}_{KA}^{-1}\}_{KS}$$

The management of keys is left to the user, the rationale being that a single centralized certification authority would become such an attractive target that it would likely be cracked or come under legal coercion. So the intended mode of operation is that each user collects the public keys of people she intends to correspond with and bundles them into a *public keyring* that she keeps on her system. The public keys can be authenticated by any convenient method such as by printing them on her business card; to make this easier, PGP supports a *key fingerprint* which is a one-way hash of the public key, presented as a hexadecimal string. Another mechanism is for users to sign each others' keys. This may simply be used as an integrity-protection mechanism on their public keyrings, but becomes more interesting if the signatures are exported. The set of publicly visible PGP signatures makes up the *web of trust*, which may be thought of as an early form of social network of people interested in cryptography. Yet another mechanism was to establish key servers; yet as anyone could upload any key, we ended up with keys for addresses such as `president@whitehouse.gov` not controlled by the people you might think. Colleagues and I also published a book of important public keys [67].

Many things were learned from the deployment and use of PGP during the 1990s. One of the most significant was usability. In a seminal paper, Alma Whitten and Doug Tygar did a cognitive walkthrough analysis of PGP 5.0 followed by a lab test, to assess whether motivated but cryptologically unsophisticated users could understand what was going on well enough to drive the program safely — to understand the need to generate a public/private keypair, figure out how to do so, encrypt messages and sign keys as needed, and not make gross errors such as accidentally failing to encrypt, or trusting the wrong public keys. The analysis showed unsafe design decisions and defaults, such as downloading keys from the MIT server without making clear that this was happening. The actual test threw up much worse horrors. Only four of twelve subjects were able to correctly send encrypted email to the other subjects, and only three of them expressed any doubt about keys from the key server. Every subject made at least one significant error [1342]. The moral is that if you're going to get people without degrees in math or computer science to use encryption, you have to bury it transparently in another product (such as an online computer game) or you have to train them — and test them afterwards. So PGP and similar products can be an option for human-rights workers (and are used by them); but for lonely converts in a hostile country, encryption alone is questionable.

There may be other reasons why encrypting email is only part of the solution. In some countries, including Russia, Zimbabwe and the UK, the police have the power to require you to decrypt ciphertext they seize, or even hand over the key. This power is also available to the civil courts in many more countries, and to many tax authorities. Other situations in which coercion may be a problem include where soldiers or intelligence agents could be captured; where police power is abused, for example to seize a key on the grounds of a supposed criminal investigation but where in reality they've been bribed to obtain commercially confidential information; and even in private homes (kids can be abused by parents, as I noted in the chapter on medical privacy, and householders are sometimes tortured by robbers to get bank card PINs and to open safes [1326]).

Making encryption resistant to *rubber hose cryptanalysis*, as it's called, is hard, but it's possible at least to block access to old messages. For example, the U.S. Defense Messaging System supports the use of public encryption keys only once. Each user has a key server that will provide a fresh public encryption key on demand, signed by the user's signing key, and once the user receives and decrypts the message he destroys the decryption key. This forward secrecy property is also found in Skype; beating someone's passphrase out of them doesn't let you decipher old conversations. As for stored data, making that coercion-resistant brings us to the topic of steganography.

23.4.5   Steganography and Forensics Countermeasures

When your threat model includes coercion, simply destroying old keys may not always be enough, as the very existence of protected material can be sufficient to cause harm. In such circumstances, more complete plausible deniability can be provided by the use of *steganography*, which is about hiding data in other data. As an example, Fabien Petitcolas wrote a program called MP3stego, which will take some information you want to hide (such as an encrypted message) and hide it in audio: it takes an audio track and compresses it using the MP3 algorithm, and wherever it can make a random choice about the compression it uses this to hide the next bit of message. And the CIA is reported to have had a camera that hid data in the least significant bits of randomly-selected pixels [1020]. There are many steganography programs floating around on the net, but most of them are easy to break: they simply hide your message in the least-significant bits of an audio or video file, and that's easy to detect. Recall our discussion of steganography theory in section 22.4: the two participants, Alice and Bob, have to communicate via a warden, Willie, who wins the game if he can detect even the existence of a hidden message.

The classic use of steganography is hiding sensitive data (such as ciphertext, where that arouses suspicion) in innocuous communications, though increasingly nowadays people worry about protecting stored data. Most customs authorities have the power to require travellers to decrypt any material found on the hard disk of their laptop in order to check for subversive material, pornography and the like. There are many crude ways to hide the existence of files; at most borders it's still enough to have an Apple laptop, or a separate Linux partition on your hard disk which runs Linux, as the normal customs tools don't deal with these. But that problem will be fixed eventually, and against a capable opponent such low-level tricks are likely to be ineffective. Files can be hidden using steganography tools in larger multimedia files, but this is inefficient.

Adi Shamir, Roger Needham and I invented the *steganographic file system*, which has the property that a user may provide it with the name of an object, such as a file or directory, together with a password; and if these are correct for an object in the system, access to it will be provided. However, an attacker who does not have the matching object name and password, and lacks the computational power to guess it, can get no information about whether the named object even exists. This is an even stronger property than Bell-LaPadula; Low cannot even demonstrate the existence of High. In our initial design, the whole disk was encrypted, and fragments of the files are scattered through it at places that depend on the password, with some redundancy to recover from cases where High data is accidentally overwritten by a Low user [75, 856].

In recent years, file-encryption programs such as TrueCrypt have adopted this idea although in TrueCrypt's case the implementation is simpler: each encrypted volume has its free space overwritten with random data, and there may or may not be a hidden volume in there that can be revealed to a user with the right password.

Now TrueCrypt is one of the tools commonly used by human-rights workers; would it be sensible for Firoz to use it too? The answer is, as usual, 'it depends'. If the Iranian religious police normally only find TrueCrypt installed by human-rights workers there, he's likely to be treated as one of them if he's raided and it's found. In general, if the existence of a product is in itself incriminating, he might want to hide that too.

The fundamental problem facing forensic investigators, as I'll discuss in detail later in section 24.5, is the sheer volume of data found when searching a house nowadays: there can be terabytes of data scattered over laptops, mobile phones, cameras, iPods and memory sticks. If you don't want a needle to be found, build a larger haystack. So Firoz might have a lot of electronic junk scattered around his apartment, as cover for the memory stick that actually contains the forbidden pictures stashed in a hidden TrueCrypt container. He might even have some straight porn in the ordinary encrypted volume, so he's got something to give the police if they torture him. And there are many ad-hoc ways in which content can be made inaccessible to the casual searcher; he might damage the memory stick in some repairable way. If he had a forbidden movie in WMV format, he might delete its license from the WMP store — so the license store had to be restored from backup before the movie could be played. (A movie for which a license is no longer available is a much less suspicious kind of ciphertext than a TrueCrypt volume.)

In short, as the world adapts to the digital age, people adopt ways of doing things, and these procedures in turn have weak points, which leads us back to tradecraft. What works will vary from one place and time to another, as it depends on what the local opponents actually do. But there are some principles. For example, anonymity loves company; it's much easier to hide in a crowd than in the middle of a desert. And in some applications, deniability may be enough: *Crowds* was a system in which users group together and do web page forwarding for each other, so that if one of them downloaded a subversive web page, the secret police have several hundred suspects to deal with [1067]. A similar scheme was devised by a well-known company CEO who, each morning, used to borrow at random one of the mobile phones of his managers, and have his switchboard forward his calls.

Forensics are subtly different: cops tend only to have tools for the most popular products. They can usually search for 'obvious' wickedness in Windows PCs but often can't search Macs at all; they have tools to extract address books from the three or four most popular mobile phones, but not obscure makes; they can wiretap the large ISPs but often not the mom-and-pop outfits.

They're also usually a bit behind the curve. They may know how to deal with Facebook now, but they probably didn't in 2004. Cool kids and gadget freaks may always be a few steps ahead.

23.4.6 Putting It All Together

Returning now to our list of typical privacy technology users, what can we say?

1. The missionary, Andrew, has one of the hardest secure communication tasks. He can't meet his converts to train them to use Tor and PGP properly, and religious factors might prevent them communicating covertly by joining an online computer game in which they played the roles of dragons, wizards and so on. Perhaps the simplest solution for him is Skype.

2. In the case of your daughter Betty, all the evidence is that parental concerns over the Internet are grossly over-inflated. Rather than trying to get her to surf the net using Tor (which she'd just consider to be creepy if her friends don't use it too), you'd be better to make scams, phishing and other abuses into a regular but not obsessive topic of conversation round the dinner table. (Once she gets the confidence to join in the conversation, she may turn out to have better tales than you do.)

3. The corporate engineer, Charles, may find his main risk is that if he posts from a work machine, then even if he's using a throwaway webmail address, he might inadvertently include material in documents such as local printer or workgroup names or a camera serial number that the corporate security guy then finds on Google. The simplest solution is to use home equipment that isn't cross-contaminated with work material. Essentially this is a multilevel policy of the sort discussed in Chapter 8.

4. The human-rights activist Dai has one of the hardest jobs of all, but as she's being regularly shaken down by the police and is in contact with a network of other activists with whom she can share experiences, she at least has an opportunity to evolve good tradecraft over time.

5. The M&A analyst Elizabeth may well find that Tor does pretty well what she needs. Her main problem will be using it properly (even I once found that I'd misconfigured my system so that I thought I was browsing through Tor when I wasn't — and I'm supposed to be a security expert).

6. Firoz is in a pretty bad way, and quite frankly were I in his situation I'd emigrate. If that's not possible then he should not just use Tor, but get a Mac or Linux box so he's less exposed to porn-site malware. Some combination of cryptographic hiding, camouflage and deception may save

his life if he gets raided by the police; and perhaps he should join the Revolutionary Guard so the police won't dare raid him in the first place.

7. Graziano also has an extremely hard job. It's bad enough defending a covert network against one or two traitors at the client end (as Andrew must); defending against occasional treachery at the server side is even harder. Were I designing such a system I'd establish clear public policies and expectations on how informers' identity would be protected, so that any attempt by a future corrupt webmaster to subvert the procedures would be visible. I'd also test the system regularly by having undercover policemen call in as informers, and track their revelations, to spot bent cops who lose information. Where informers did identify themselves — deliberately or accidentally — I'd ensure that only one handler and his supervisor know this.

Wicked people use anonymity too, of course, and the many tales of how they fail underline the difficulty of finding true anonymity in the modern world. In a child-custody case in Taunton, England, the wife's lawyer emailed a bogus legal judgment to the father, pretending the email was from a fathers' rights charity. When the father read this out in court, the lawyer stood up and accused him of forgery. Outraged, the father tracked the email to a shop in London's Tottenham Court Road, where the staff remembered someone coming in to use their service and dug out still images from their CCTV camera which identified the lawyer, Bruce Hyman [397]. Mr Hyman was sent to prison for twelve months at Bristol Crown Court. He was an expert on evidence — and the first British barrister to be imprisoned in modern times for perverting the course of justice.

Richard Clayton wrote a thesis on anonymity and traceability in cyberspace, which Mr Hyman should perhaps have read [300]. There are many ways in which people who try to be anonymous, fail; and there are also many ways in which even people who made no particular effort to hide themselves end up not being traceable. It's hard to establish responsibility when abusive traffic comes from a phone line in a multi-occupied student house, or when someone accesses a dial-up account on a free ISP from a phone whose calling line ID has been blocked. ISPs also often keep quite inadequate logs and can't trace abusive traffic afterwards. So in practice, as opposed to theory, anonymity is already pretty widespread. This may gradually contract over time, because pressure over peer-to-peer traffic, spam and phishing may make ISPs manage things more tightly and respond better to complaints. The view of UK ISPs, for example, is that 'Anonymity should be explicitly supported by relevant tools, rather than being present as a blanket status quo, open to use and misuse' [307].

As privacy technology evolves, it may modify the shape of the trade-off between privacy and surveillance that is conditioned by the much larger-scale development of online technology in general. Privacy technology will be driven to some extent by the desire to evade copyright, by various political liberation agendas, and by criminal innovation. Tools invented to protect the privacy of the law-abiding, and of foreign lawbreakers whose subversion we support, will be used occasionally by criminals in our countries too. So far, there's little sign of it, but it's bound to happen eventually. For this reason a number of people have proposed *identity escrow* schemes in which net users have pseudonyms which normally provide identity protection but which can be removed by order of a court [255]. But such systems would put most of the privacy users we discussed in this section directly in harm's way. What's more, escrow mechanisms tend to be expensive and fragile, and cause unforeseen side-effects [4].

In the next chapter I'll describe the 'Crypto Wars' — the long struggle through the 1990s by governments to control cryptography, by demanding that keys be escrowed. Eventually they gave up on that; and the same arguments apply to anonymity systems. I believe we just have to accept that providing privacy to people we approve of means that occasionally some people we don't approve of will use it too. As Whit Diffie, the inventor of digital signatures and a leading crypto warrior, put it: 'If you campaign for liberty you're likely to find yourself drinking in bad company at the wrong end of the bar'.

23.5   Elections

One application of which all democracies by definition approve, and in which almost all mandate anonymity, is the election. However, the move to electronic voting has been highly controversial. In the USA, Congress voted almost four billion dollars to upgrade states' election systems following the Florida fiasco in 2000, and a lot of this money's been wasted on voting machines that turned out to be insecure. There have been similar scandals elsewhere, including the UK and the Netherlands.

Research into electronic election mechanisms goes back to the early 1980s, when David Chaum invented *digital cash* — a payment medium that is anonymous, untraceable and unlinkable [285, 287]. In section 5.7.3 I described the mechanism: a customer presents a banknote to a bank, blinded by a random factor so that the bank can't see the serial number; the bank signs the note; the customer then unblinds it; and she now has an electronic banknote with a serial number the bank doesn't know. There are a few more details you have to fix to get a viable system, such as arranging that the customer's anonymity fails if she spends the banknote twice [287]. Digital cash hasn't succeeded, as it's not really compatible either with the anti-money-laundering regime or the banks' business models[8]. However the application on which a number of research teams are still working is the digital election. The voter can be given a ballot paper manufactured using the same general techniques as a digital coin; she can spend it with the candidate of his choice; and she can get caught if she cheats by double-spending.

There are a number of further requirements on electronic voting systems, of which perhaps the two most difficult to satisfy simultaneously are that the voter should be able to satisfy herself that her vote has been properly counted and that she should not be able to prove to anybody else how she voted. If she can, then the doors are opened to vote-buying and intimidation. Getting the anonymity and auditability right simultaneously depends on a good combination of physical security and computer-security mechanisms.

Digital elections remained something of an academic backwater until 2000, when the outcome of the U.S. Presidential election turned on a handful of disputed votes in Florida. At the time, I was attending the Applications Security conference in New Orleans, and we organised a debate; it rapidly became clear that, even though politicians thought that mechanical or paper voting systems should be replaced with electronic ones as quickly as possible, security experts didn't agree. A large majority of the attendees — including many NSA and defense contractor staff — voted (on an old-fashioned show of hands) they didn't trust electronic elections[9]. Nonetheless Congress went ahead and passed the Help America Vote Act in 2002, which provided $3.8 billion for states to update their voting equipment.

By the following year, this particular barrel of pork had degenerated into a national scandal. Many problems were reported in the 2002 elections [551]; then, the following summer, the leading voting-machine supplier Diebold left its voting system files on an open web site, a stunning security lapse. Avi Rubin and colleagues at Johns Hopkins trawled through them found that the equipment was far below even minimal standards of security expected in other contexts. Voters could cast unlimited votes, insiders could identify voters, and outsiders could also hack the system [731]. Almost on cue, Diebold CEO Walden O'Dell, who was active in the campaign to re-elect President Bush, wrote 'I am committed to helping Ohio deliver its electoral votes to the president next year' [1320]. This led to uproar.

Electronic equipment had actually been used for some time to count ballots in a number of U.S. districts, but there are a number of different ways to do

---

[8]A variant may be used for pseudonymous credentials in Trusted Computing [220].

[9]One of the strongest arguments was a simple question: do you know how to clear the Internet Explorer cache? As the hotel didn't have an Internet connection, we all had to check our email at a café in Bourbon Street that had two PCs, one with Netscape and the other with IE. The attendees preferred Netscape as it was easy to stop the next user retrieving your password from the cache.

this. One option is optical scanning, where paper ballots are used but fed into a system that recognises votes, gets an operator to adjudicate difficult cases, and outputs the tally. This has the advantage that, if the count is challenged, officials (or a court) can send for the original ballots and count them by hand. Another alternative is the ballotmarking machine: the voter makes her choices on a touch screen, after which the machine prints out a voting form that she can inspect visually and drop into a ballot box. Many (but not all) of the problems arose from 'Direct-recording electronic' (DRE) voting systems, in which the voter's choice is entered directly into a terminal that tallies the votes and outputs the result at the end of the day. If the software in such a device is buggy, or open to manipulation, it can give the wrong result; and unless the result is wildly out of kilter with common sense, there's simply no way to tell. The only verification procedure available on many models was to press the 'count' button again to get it to print out the tally again. Even although voting machines are certified by the Federal Election Commission (FEC), the FEC rules don't require that a tally be independently auditable. This is wrong, according to the majority of experts, who now believe that all voting systems should have a voter-verifiable audit trail. This happens automatically with scanning systems; Rebecca Mercuri advocates that DRE equipment should display the voter's choice on a paper roll behind a window and get them to validate it prior to casting. (That was in 1992, and was reiterated in her thesis on electronic voting in 2000 [875, 876].)

The latest round in the U.S. voting saga comes from California, Florida and Ohio. The Californian Secretary of State Debra Bowen authorized and paid for a large team of computer scientists, led by University of California professors David Wagner and Matt Bishop, to do a top-to-bottom evaluation of the state's voting systems, including source code reviews and red-team attacks, in order to decide what equipment could be used in the 2008 elections. The reports, published in May 2007, make depressing reading [215]. All of the voting systems examined contained serious design flaws that led directly to specific vulnerabilities that attackers could exploit to affect election outcomes. All of the previously approved voting machines — by Diebold, Hart and Sequoia — had their certification withdrawn, and were informed they would need to undertake substantial remediation before recertification. A late-submitted system from ES&S was also decertified. California could still take such radical action, as perhaps three-quarters of the 9 million people who voted in 2004 did so using a paper or optical-scan ballot. As this book went to press in December 2007, Ms Bowen had just said that electronic voting systems were still not good enough to be trusted with state elections. 'When the government finds a car is unsafe, it orders a recall', she said. 'Here we're talking about systems used to cast and tally votes, the most basic tool of democracy'. [1343].

A similar inspection of Florida equipment was carried out by scientists at Florida State University; they reported a bundle of new vulnerabilities in the Diebold equipment in July 2007 [514]. Ohio followed suit; their evaluation of election equipment and standards came to similar conclusions. All the evaluated equipment had serious security failings: data that should have been encrypted wasn't; encryption done badly (for example, the key stored in the clear next to the ciphertext); buffer overflows; useless (and misapplied) physical security; SQL injection; audit logs that could be tampered with; and undocumented back doors [855]. Interestingly, the Florida and Ohio teams found plenty of new vulnerabilities that the California team missed, and all were working quickly; this raises interesting questions about the total number of security flaws in these systems.

Our experience in the UK is broadly similar, although the detail is different. Tony Blair's government progressively expanded the use of postal and other absentee forms of ballot, which was criticised by opposition parties as it made vote-buying and intimidation easier. Party workers (of which Blair's Labour party had more) could pressure voters into opting for a postal ballot, then collect their ballot forms, fill them out, and submit them. Plans to extend voting from the post to email and text were criticised for making this existing low-grade abuse easier and potentially open to automation. Finally, in the May 2007 local government elections, electronic voting pilots were held in eleven areas around the UK. Two of my postdocs acted as scrutineers in the Bedford election, and observed the same kind of shambles that had been reported at various U.S. elections. The counting was slower than with paper; the system (optical-scan software bought from Spain) had a high error rate, resulting in many more ballots than expected being sent to human adjudicators for decision. (This was because the printers had changed the ink halfway through the print run, and half the ballot papers were the wrong shade of black.) Even worse, the software sometimes sent the same ballot paper to multiple adjudicators, and it wasn't clear which of their decisions were counted. In the end, so that everyone could go home, the returning officer accepted a letter of assurance (written on the spot by the vendor) saying that no vote would have been miscounted as a result. Yet the exercise left the representatives from the various parties with serious misgivings. The Open Rights Group, which organised the volunteers, reported that it could not express confidence in the results for the areas observed [987].

There was an interesting twist in the Netherlands. DRE voting machines had been introduced progressively during the 1990s, and cyber-rights activists were worried about the possibility of tampering and fraud along the lines observed in the USA. They discovered that the machines from the leading vendor, Nedap, were vulnerable to a Tempest attack: using simple equipment, an observer sitting outside the polling station could see what party a voter had selected [541]. From the security engineer's perspective this was great stuff, as it led to the declassification by the German intelligence folks of a lot of Cold War tempest material, as I discussed in section 17.4.2 (the Nedap machines are also used in Germany). The activists also got a result: on October 1 2007 the District Court in Amsterdam decertified all the Nedap machines.

As for other countries, the picture is mixed. The OpenNet Initiative (of which I've been a member since 2006) monitors election abuses in the third world. We have found that in some less-developed country elections, the state has systematically censored opposition parties' websites and run denial-of-service attacks; in others (typically the most backward), elections are rigged by more traditional methods such as kidnapping and murdering opposition candidates. The evidence of electronic cheating is less clear-cut but is often suspected. Take for example Russia. I wrote in the first edition in 2001: 'I sincerely hope that the election of Vladimir Putin as the president of Russia had nothing to do with the fact that the national electoral reporting system is run by FAPSI, a Russian signals intelligence agency formed in 1991 as the successor to the KGB's 8th and 16th directorates. Its head, General Starovoitov, was reported to be an old KGB type; his agency reported directly to President Yeltsin, who chose Putin as his successor' [509, 678]. Yet by the time Putin's party was re-elected in 2007, the cheating had become so blatant — with gross media bias and state employees ordered to vote for the ruling party — that the international community would not accept the result as free and fair.

Wherever you go, electronic abuses at election time, and abuses of electronic election equipment, are just one of many tools used by the powerful to hang on to power. It's worth remembering that in Florida in 2000, more voters were disenfranchised as a result of registration abuses than there were ballots disputed because of hanging chads. And just as the government can bias an election by making it harder to vote if you haven't got a car, it could conceivably make it harder to vote if you haven't got a computer. It's not unknown for the ballot to be made so complex as to disenfranchise the less educated. And large-scale abuses can defeat even technical ballot privacy; for example, in a number of less-developed countries, districts that elected the 'wrong' candidate have been punished. (And although we shake our heads in sorrow when that happens in Zimbabwe, we just shrug when a British government channels extra money to schools and hospitals in marginal constituences.) In fact, it has struck me that if an incumbent wants to change not 1% of the votes, but 10% — say to turn a 40–60 defeat into a 60–40 victory — then bribing or bullying voters may provide a more robust result than tinkering with the vote-tallying computer. Voters who've been bribed or bullied are less likely to riot than voters who've been cheated. The bullied voters in Russia didn't riot; the cheated voters in Kenya did.

So high-technology cheating shouldn't get all, or even most, of an election monitor's attention. But it needs to get some. And it behoves citizens to be more sceptical than usual about the latest wizzo technology when it's being sold to us by politicians who hope to get reelected using it. Finally, even where politicians have comfortable majorities and aren't consciously trying to cheat, they are often vulnerable to computer salesmen, as they're scared of being accused of technophobia. It takes geeks to have the confidence to say stop!

23.6   Summary

Some of the most challenging security engineering problems at the beginning of the twenty-first century have to do with the new online applications that are sweeping the world, from online games through search and auctions to social networking. This chapter was really just a helicopter tour of new services and the new cheating strategies they've spawned.

Much of what goes wrong with online services, as with anonymity services and digital elections, is just the same as we've seen elsewhere — the usual sad litany of bugs and blunders, of protection requirements ignored in the rush to market or just not understood by the developers of the early systems. Elections in particular provide a sobering case history of proprietary systems developed for an application that was known to be sensitive, and by developers who made all sorts of security claims; yet once their products were exposed to fresh air and sunlight, they turned out to be terrible.

What's also starting to become clear is that as more and more of human life moves online, so the criticality and the complexity of online applications grow at the same time. Many of the familiar problems come back again and again, in ever less tractable forms. Enforcing privacy is difficult enough in a large hospital, but just about doable. How do you enforce privacy in something as big as Google, or as complex as Facebook? And how do you do security architecture when ever more functionality is provided to ever more people by ever more code written by constantly growing armies of inexperienced programmers? Traditional software engineering tools helped developers get ever further up the complexity mountain before they fell off. How do you see to it that you don't fall off, or if you do, you don't fall too hard?

Research Problems

This leads me to suggest that one of the critical research problems between now and the third edition of this book (if there is one) will be how protection mechanisms scale.

The hard mechanism-design problem may be how one goes about evolving 'security' (or any other emergent property) in a socio-technical system with billions of users. In the simple, million-user government applications of yesteryear, a central authority could impose some elementary rules — a 'Secret' document had to be locked in a filing cabinet when you went to the toilet, and a 'Secret' computer system needed an Orange book evaluation. But such rules were never natural, and people always had to break them to get their work done. Trying to scale access-control rules to social networking sites like Facebook is probably already beyond the complexity limit, and the revolution has only just started.

In a truly complex socio-technical system you can expect that the rules will evolve in a process whereby the technology and the behaviour continually adapt to each other. But at present the incentives faced by the system developers are also wrong; site operators want search while users want privacy. Governments will want to get in on the act, but they're an order of magnitude too slow and have perverse incentives of their own. So what sorts of mechanisms can be evolved for rule negotiation? Will it simply be survival of the fittest, spiced with the drives of fashion, as one social-networking site replaces another? Or is there some legal framework that might help?

Further Reading

The standard reference on game security at present is Greg Hoglund and Gary McGraw's book [617]. For the history of computer games, and cheating, read Jeff Yan and Brian Randell in [1367]; Jeff's thesis discusses online bridge [1364]. There's an annual conference, NetGames, which usually has a number of papers on cheating, and the Terra Nova blog on virtual worlds has regular articles on cheating.

The best general work I know of on security in web services is Mike Andrews and James Whitaker's 'How to Break Web Software' [78]. There are many books on specific services, such as John Battelle's book on Google [125] and Adam Cohen's of eBay [310]; and if you need to explain the problem to management, read (or give them) the article by Jeremy Epstein, Scott Matsumoto and Gary McGraw about how web-service developers get software security wrong [436]. As for social networking, I don't think the definitive book has come out yet.

As for privacy technology, the best introduction to anonymous remailers is probably [849]. I don't know of a good treatment of privacy and anonymity technology in real-world contexts; the above vignettes of Andrew and others are my own modest attempt to fill that gap. To go into this subject in depth, look through the anonymity bibliography maintained by Roger Dingledine, Nick Matthewson and George Danezis [82], and the survey of anonymity systems by George Danezis and Claudia Diaz [347]. For traffic analysis, you might start with the survey by Richard Clayton and George Danezis [346].

There's now quite a literature on electronic voting. The issues are largely the same as with voting by mail or by phone, but not quite. An early survey of the requirements, and of the things that can go wrong, was written by Mike

Shamos [1149], who is also a prominent defender of electronic voting [1150]; while Roy Saltzman (for many years the authority at NIST) discusses things that have gone wrong in the USA, and various NIST recommendations, in [1103]. The leading critics of current electronic voting arrangements include David Dill's Verified Voting Foundation, and Rebecca Mercuri, whose 2000 thesis on 'Electronic Vote Tabulation — Checks & Balances' [876] might perhaps have been heeded more, along with an early report on the feasibility of Internet voting from the State of California [253]. Certainly, the recent evaluation reports from California [215], Florida [514], Ohio [855] and Britain [987] lend strong confirmation to the sceptical viewpoint.

PART

III

In the final part of the book I cover three themes: politics, management and assurance. Given that we now have some idea how to provide protection, the three big questions are: what are you allowed to do? How do you go about organizing it? And how do you know when you're done?

Since 9/11, we've seen the growth of a security-industrial complex that has consumed billions of dollars and caused great inconvenience to the public, for often negligible gains in actual protection. Politicians scare up the vote, and vendors help them with systems that are best described as 'security theater'. This gives rise to many difficult political issues for the security engineer. Are our societies vulnerable to terrorism because we overreact, and if so, how can we avoid becoming part of the problem rather than part of the solution? Can we find ways to make more rational decisions about allocating protective resources, or at least stop security arguments being used to bolster bad policy? And how do these issues interact with the more traditional security policy issues we already worried about in the 1990s, such as surveillance, wiretapping, the rules of digital evidence, censorship, export control and privacy law?

Our next chapter is about management. This has become a dirty word in the information security world; there are endless vapid articles written in managementese which manage to say nothing at great length. But management issues are important: organisational and economic incentives often determine whether secure systems get built or not. The growth of security economics as a discipline over the last six years enables us to discuss these problems in a much more mature way than previously, and the insights help us tackle the critical problem of how you go about managing a team to develop a predictably dependable system.

Assurance is a huge political can of worms. On the face of it, it's just an engineering issue: how do you go about finding convincing answers to the questions: are we building the right system? and, are we building it right? These questions are familiar from software engineering (which can teach us a lot), but they acquire new meaning when systems are exposed to hostile attack. Also, most of the organisational structures within which assurance claims can be made, or certified, are poisoned one way or another. Claims about system security properties are often thinly veiled assertions of power and control, so it should surprise no-one if the results of evaluation by equipment makers, insurers' laboratories, military agencies and academic attackers are very different. So it's really important for the security engineer to set out at the start of a project not just what the objective is, but the criteria by which it will be judged a success or a failure.

CHAPTER 24

Terror, Justice and Freedom

Al-Qaida spent $500,000 on the event, while America, in the incident and its aftermath, lost — according to the lowest estimate — more than $500 billion.

— Osama bin Laden

Experience should teach us to be most on our guard to protect liberty when the government's purposes are beneficient . . . The greatest dangers to liberty lurk in insidious encroachment by men of zeal, well meaning but without understanding.

— Supreme Court Justice Louis Brandeis

They that can give up essential liberty to obtain a little temporary safety deserve neither liberty nor safety.

— Benjamin Franklin

24.1 Introduction

The attacks of September 11, 2001, on New York and Washington have had a huge impact on the world of security engineering, and this impact has been deepened by the later attacks on Madrid, London and elsewhere. As everyone has surely realised by now — and as the quote from Osama bin Laden bluntly spells out — modern terrorism works largely by provoking overreaction.

There are many thorny issues. First, there's the political question: are Western societies uniquely vulnerable — because we're open societies with democracy and a free press, whose interaction facilitates fearmongering — and if so what (if anything) should we do about it? The attacks challenged our core values — expressed in the USA as the Constitution, and in Europe as the Convention on Human Rights. Our common heritage of democracy and the rule of law, built slowly and painfully since the eighteenth century, might have been thought well entrenched, especially after we defended it successfully in the Cold War. Yet the aftermath of 9/11 saw one government after another introducing authoritarian measures ranging from fingerprinting at airports through ID cards and large-scale surveillance to detention without trial and even torture. Scant heed has been given to whether these measures would actually be effective: we saw in Chapter 15 that the US-VISIT fingerprinting program didn't work, and that given the false alarm rate of the underlying technology it could never reasonably have been expected to work. We've not merely compromised our principles; we've wasted billions on bad engineering, and damaged whole industries. Can't we find better ways to defend freedom?

Second, there's the economic question: why are such vast amounts of money spent on security measures of little or no value? America alone has spent over \$14 bn on screening airline passengers without catching a single terrorist — and it's rather doubtful that the 9/11 tactics would ever work again, as neither flight crew nor passengers will ever be as passive again (indeed, on 9/11, the tactics only worked for the first 71 minutes). As I noted in Chapter 1, well-known vulnerabilities in screening ground staff, reinforcing cockpit doors and guarding aircraft on the ground overnight have been ignored by the political leadership. Never mind that they could be fixed for a fraction of the cost of passenger screening: invisible measures don't have the political impact and can't compete for budget dollars. So we spend a fortune on measures that annoy passengers but make flying no safer, and according to a Harvard study don't even meet the basic quality standards for other, less-political, screening programs [801]. Is there any way — short of waiting for more attacks — to establish protection priorities more sensibly?

Third, there are the effects on our industry. President Eisenhower warned in his valedictory speech that 'we must guard against the acquisition of unwarranted influence, whether sought or unsought, by the military industrial complex. The potential for the disastrous rise of misplaced power exists and will persist'. In the wake of 9/11, we saw a frantic stampede by security vendors, consultancy companies, and intelligence agencies hustling for publicity, money and power. We're seeing the emergence of a security-industrial complex that's capturing policy in the same ways that the defense industry did at the start of the Cold War. One might have thought that technological progress would have a positive effect on trade-offs between freedom and security; that better sensors and smarter processing would shift the ROC curve towards greater precision. Yet the real-world outcome seems often to be the reverse. How is the civic-minded engineer to deal with this?

Fourth, technical security arguments are often used to bolster the case for bad policy. All through the Irish terrorist campaign, the British police had to charge arrested terrorist suspects within four days. But after 9/11, this was quickly raised to 28 days; then the government said it needed 90 days, claiming they might have difficulty decrypting data on PCs seized from suspects. That argument turned out to be misleading: the real problem was police inefficiency at managing forensics. Now if the police had just said 'we need to hold suspects for 90 days because we don't have enough Somali interpreters' then common sense could have kicked in; Parliament might well have told them to use staff from commercial translation agencies. But security technology arguments are repeatedly used to bamboozle legislators, and engineers who work for firms with lucrative government contracts may find it difficult to speak out.

Finally, there is the spillover into public policy on topics such as wiretapping, surveillance and export control, that affect security engineers directly, and the corresponding neglect of the more 'civilian' policy issues such as consumer protection and liability. Even before 9/11, governments were struggling to find a role in cyberspace, and not doing a particularly good job of it. The attacks and their aftermath have skewed their efforts in ways that raise pervasive and sometimes quite difficult issues of freedom and justice. Authoritarian behaviour by Western governments also provides an excuse for rules in places from Burma to Zimbabwe to censor communications and spy on their citizens. Now the falling costs of storage may have made increased surveillance inevitable; but the 'war on terror' is exacerbating this and may be catalysing deeper and faster changes that we'd have seen otherwise.

In this chapter, I'm going to look at terrorism, then discuss the directly related questions of surveillance and control, before discussing some other IT policy matters and trying to put the whole in context.

24.2 Terrorism

Political violence is nothing new; anthropologists have found that tribal warfare was endemic among early humans, as indeed it is among chimpanzees [777]. Terror has long been used to cow subject populations — by the Maya, by the Inca, by William the Conqueror. Terrorism of the 'modern' sort goes back centuries: Guy Fawkes tried to blow up Britain's Houses of Parliament in 1605; his successors, the Irish Republican Army, ran a number of campaigns against the UK. In the latest, from 1970–94, some three thousand people died, and the IRA even blew up a hotel where Margaret Thatcher was staying for a party conference, killing several of her colleagues. During the Cold War the Russians supported not just the IRA but the Baader Meinhof Gang in Germany and many others; the West armed and supported partisans from France in World War 2, and jihadists fighting the Soviets in Afghanistan in the 1980s. Some terrorists, like Baader and Meinhof, ended up in jail, while others — such as the IRA leaders Gerry Adams and Martin McGuinness, the Irgun leader Menachim Begin, the French resistance leader Charles de Gaulle and the African anti-colonial leaders Jomo Kenyatta, Robert Mugabe and Nelson Mandela — ended up in office.

What general lessons can be drawn from this history? Well, there's good news and bad news.

24.2.1   Causes of Political Violence

The first piece of good news is that the trend in terrorist violence has been steadily downward [909]. There were many insurgencies in the 1960s and 70s, some ethnic, some anti-colonial, and some ideological. Many were financed by the Soviet Union or its allies as proxy conflicts in the Cold War, although a handful (notably the Nicaraguan Contras and the resistance to the Soviets in Afghanistan) were financed by the West. The end of the Cold War removed the motive and the money.

The second (and related) point is that the causes of civil conflict are mostly economic. An influential study by Paul Collier and Anke Hoeffler for the World Bank looked at wars from 1960-1999 to see whether they were caused largely by grievances (such as high inequality, a lack of political rights, or ethnic and religious divisions), or by greed (some rebellions are more economically viable than others) [315]. The data show convincingly that grievances play little role; the incidence of rebellion was largely determined by whether it could be sustained. (Indeed, Cicero said two thousand years ago that 'Endless money forms the sinews of war'.) Thus the IRA campaign continued largely because of support from the Soviet bloc and from Irish-Americans; when the former vanished and the latter decided that terror was no longer acceptable, the guns were put beyond use. Similarly, the conflict in Sierra Leone was driven by conflict diamonds, the Tamil revolt in Sri Lanka by funds from ethnic Tamils in the USA and India, and Al-Qaida was financed by rich donors in the Gulf states. So the economic analysis gives clear advice on how to deal with an insurgency: cut off their money supply.

24.2.2   The Psychology of Political Violence

Less encouraging findings come from scholars of psychology, politics and the media. I mentioned the affect heuristic in section 2.3.2: where people rely on affect, or emotion, calculations of probability tend to be disregarded. The prospect of a happy event, such as winning the lottery, will blind most people to the long odds and the low expected return; similarly, a dreadful event, such as a terrorist attack, will make most people disregard the fact that such events are exceedingly rare [1189]. Most of the Americans who died as a result of 9/11 did so since then in car crashes, after deciding to drive rather than fly.

There are other effects, too, at the border between psychology and culture. A study of the psychology of terror by Tom Pyszczynski, Sheldon Solomon and Jeff Greenberg looked at how people cope with the fear of death. They got 22 municipal court judges in Tucson, Arizona, to participate in an experiment in which they were asked to set bail for a drug-addicted prostitute [1053]. They were all given a personality questionnaire first, in which half were asked questions such as 'Please briefly describe the emotions that the thought of your own death arouses in you' to remind them that we all die one day. The judges for whom mortality had become salient set an average bail of $455 while the control group set an average bond of $50 — a huge effect for such an experiment. Further experiments showed that the mortality-salience group had not become mean: they were prepared to give larger rewards to citizens who performed some public act. It turns out that the fear of death makes people adhere more strongly to cultural norms and defend their worldview much more vigorously.

Thinkers have long known that, given the transience of human existence in such a large and strange cosmos, people search for meaning and permanence through religion, through their children, through their creative works, through their tribe and their nation. Different generations of philosophers theorised about this in different languages, from the medieval 'memento mori' through psychonalysis to more recent writings on our need to assuage existential anxiety. Pyszczynski and his colleagues now provide an experimental methodology to study this; it turns out, for example, that mortality salience intensifies altruism and the need for heroes. The 9/11 attacks brought mortality to the forefront of people's minds, and were also an assault on symbols of national and cultural pride. It was natural that the response included religion (the highest level of church attendance since the 1950s), patriotism (in the form of a high approval rating for the President), and intensified bigotry. It was also natural that, as the memory of the attacks receded, society would repolarise because of divergent core values. The analysis can also support constructive suggestions: for example, a future national leader trying to keep a country together following an attack could do well to constantly remind people what they're fighting for. It turns out that, when they're reminded that they'll die one day, both conservatives and liberals take a more polarised view of an anti-American essay written by a foreign student — except in experiments where they are first reminded of the Constitution [1053].

Some countries have taken a bipartisan approach to terrorism — as when Germany faced the Baader-Meinhof Gang, and Britain the IRA. In other countries, politicians have given in to the temptation to use fearmongering to get re-elected. The American political scientist John Mueller has documented the Bush administration's hyping of the terror threat in the campaign against John Kerry [909]; here in the UK we saw Tony Blair proposing the introduction of ID cards, in a move that brilliantly split the opposition Conservative party in the run-up to the 2005 election (the authoritarian Tory leader Michael Howard was in favour, but the libertarian majority in his shadow cabinet forced a U-turn). How can we make sense of a world in which critical decisions, with huge costs and impact, are made on such a basis?

24.2.3   The Role of Political Institutions

In fact, there's a whole academic subject — *public-choice economics* — devoted to explaining why governments act the way they do, and for which its founder James Buchanan won the Nobel Prize in 1986. As he put it in his prize lecture, 'Economists should cease proffering policy advice as if they were employed by a benevolent despot, and they should look to the structure within which political decisions are made'. Much government behaviour is easily explained by the incentives facing individual public-sector decision makers. It's natural for officials to build empires as they are ranked by their span of control rather than, as in industry, by the profits they generate. Similarly, politicians maximise their chances of reelection rather than the abstract welfare of the public. Understanding their decisions requires methodological individualism — considering the incentives facing individual presidents, congressmen, generals, police chiefs and newspaper editors, rather than the potential gains or losses of a nation. We know it's prudent to design institutions so that their leaders' incentives are aligned with its goals — we give company managers stock options to make them act like shareholders. But this is harder in a polity. How is the national interest to be defined?

Public-choice scholars argue that both markets and politics are instruments of exchange. In the former we seek to optimise our utility individually, while in the latter we do the same but using collective actions to achieve goals that we cannot attain in markets because of externalities or other failures. The political process in turn is thus prone to specific types of failure, such as deficit financing. Intergenerational bargaining is hard: it's easy for politicians to borrow money to buy votes now, and leave the bill with the next generation. But then why do some countries have much worse public debt than others? The short answer is that institutions matter. Political results depend critically on the rules that constrain political action.

Although public-choice economics emerged in response to problems in public finance in the 1960s, it has some clear lessons. Constitutions matter, as they set the ground rules of the political game. So do administrative structures, as officials are self-interested agents too. In the UK, for example, the initial response to 9/11 was to increase the budget for the security service; but this hundred million dollars or so didn't offer real pork to the security-industrial complex. So all the pet projects got dusted off, and the political beauty contest was won by a national ID card, a grandiose project that in its original form would have cost £20 billion ($40 billion [809]). Observers of the Washington scene have remarked that a similar dynamic may have been involved in the decision to invade Iraq: although the 2001 invasion of Afghanistan had been successful, it had not given much of a role to the Pentagon barons who'd spent careers assembling fleets of tanks, capital ships and fighter-bombers. Cynics remarked that it didn't give much of a payoff to the defense industry either.

Similar things were said in the aftermath of World War 1, which was blamed on the 'merchants of death'. I suppose we will have to wait for the verdict of the historians.

24.2.4 The Role of the Press

The third locus of concern must surely be the press. 'If it bleeds, it leads', as the saying goes; bad news sells more papers than good. Editors want to sell more papers, so they listen to the scariest versions of the story of the day. For example, in 1997, I got some news coverage when I remarked that British Telecom was spending hundreds of millions more on bug-fixing than its Korean counterpart: was BT wasting money, I asked, or was the infrastructure in middle-income countries at risk? In 1999, after we'd checked out all the university systems, I concluded that although some stuff would break, none of it really mattered. I wrote up a paper and got the University to send out a press release telling people not to worry. There was an almost total lack of interest. There were doomsayers on TV right up till the last midnight of 1999; but 'We're not all going to die' just isn't a story.

The self-interest of media owners combines with that of politicians who want to get re-elected, officials who want to build empires, and vendors who want to sell security stuff. They pick up on, and amplify, the temporary blip in patriotism and the need for heroes that terrorist attacks naturally instil. Fearmongering gets politicians on the front page and helps them control the agenda so that their opponents are always off-balance and following along behind.

24.2.5 The Democratic Response

Is this a counsel of despair? I don't think so: people learn over time. On the 7th July 2005, four suicide bombers killed 52 people on London's public transport and injured about 700. The initial response of the public was one of gritty resignation: 'Oh, well, we knew something like this was going to happen — bad luck if you were there, but life goes on.'[1] The psychological effect on the population was much less than that of the 9/11 bombings on America — which must surely be due to a quarter-century of IRA bombings. Both bombers and fearmongers lose their impact over time.

And as populations learn, so will political elites. John Mueller has written a history of the attitudes to terrorism of successive U.S. administrations [909]. Presidents Kennedy, Johnson, Nixon and Ford ignored terrorism. President

---

[1]One curious thing was that the press went along with this for a couple of days: then there was an explosion of fearmongering. It seems that ministers needed a day or two of meetings to sort out their shopping lists and decide what they would try to shake out of Parliament.

Carter made a big deal of the Iran hostage crisis, and like 9/11 it gave him a huge boost in the polls at the beginning, but later it ended his presidency. His Secretary of State Cyrus Vance later admitted they should have played down the crisis rather than giving undeserved credibility to the 'students' who'd kidnapped U.S. diplomats. President Reagan mostly ignored provocations, but succumbed to temptation over the Lebanese hostages and shipped arms to Iran to secure their release. However, once he'd distanced himself from this error, his ratings recovered quickly. Now President Bush's fear-based policies have led to serious problems round the world and tumbling popularity; the contenders for the 2008 election all propose policy changes of various kinds. Much the same has happened in the U.K., where Tony Blair's departure from office was met with a great sigh of relief and a rebound in the polls for the ruling Labour Party. His successor Gordon Brown has forbidden ministers to use the phrase 'war on terror'. The message is getting through: fearmongering can bring spectacular short-term political gains, but the voters eventually see through it. And just as this book went to press, in early January 2008, the voters of Iowa selected a Republican candidate who says 'The quickest way to get out of Iraq is to win', and a Democract who promises to end the war in Iraq and be a President 'who understands that 9/11 is not a way to scare up votes but a challenge that should unite America and the world against the common threats of the 21st century'. So it looks like the voters will get their say.

24.3   Surveillance

One of the side-effects of 9/11 has been a huge increase in technical surveillance, both by wiretapping and through the mining of commercial data sources by government agencies. Recent disclosures of unlawful surveillance in a number of countries, together with differing U.S. and European views on privacy, have politicised matters. Wiretapping was already an issue in the 1990s, and millions of words have been written about it. In this section, all I can reasonably try to provide is a helicopter tour: to place the debate in context, sketch what's going on, and provide pointers to primary sources.

24.3.1   The History of Government Wiretapping

Rulers have always tried to control communications. In classical times, couriers were checked at customs posts, and from the Middle Ages, many kings either operated a postal monopoly or granted it to a crony. The letter opening and codebreaking facilities of early modern states, the so-called *Black Chambers*, are described in David Kahn's history [676].

The invention of electronic communications brought forth a defensive response. In most of Europe, the telegraph service was set up as part of the

Post Office and was always owned by the government. Even where it wasn't, regulation was usually so tight that the industry's growth was severely hampered, leaving America with a clear competitive advantage. A profusion of national rules, which sometimes clashed with each other, so exasperated everyone that the *International Telegraph Union* (ITU) was set up in 1865 [1215]. This didn't satisfy everyone. In Britain, the telegraph industry was nationalized by Gladstone in 1869.

The invention of the telephone further increased both government interest in surveillance and resistance to it, both legal and technical. In the USA, the Supreme Court ruled in 1928 in *Olmstead vs United States* that wiretapping didn't violate the fourth amendment provisions on search and seizure as there was no physical breach of a dwelling; Judge Brandeis famously dissented. In 1967, the Court reversed itself in *Katz vs United States*, ruling that the amendment protects people, not places. The following year, Congress legalized Federal wiretapping (in 'title III' of the Omnibus Crime Control and Safe Streets Act) following testimony on the scale of organized crime. In 1978, following an investigation into the Nixon administration's abuses, Congress passed the Federal Intelligence Surveillance Act (FISA), which controls wiretapping for national security. In 1986, the Electronic Communications Protection Act (ECPA) relaxed the Title III warrant provisions. By the early 1990s, the spread of deregulated services from mobile phones to call forwarding had started to undermine the authorities' ability to implement wiretaps, as did technical developments such as out-of-band signaling and adaptive echo cancellation in modems.

So in 1994 the Communications Assistance for Law Enforcement Act (CALEA) required all communications companies to make their networks tappable in ways approved by the FBI. By 1999, over 2,450,000 telephone conversations were legally tapped following 1,350 court orders [434, 851]. The relevant law is 18 USC (U.S. Code) 2510–2521 for telco services, while FISA's regulation of foreign intelligence gathering is now codified in U.S. law as 50 USC 1801–1811 [1272].

Even before 9/11, some serious analysts believed that there were at least as many unauthorized wiretaps as authorized ones [387]. First, there's phone company collusion: while a phone company must give the police access if they present a warrant, in many countries they are also allowed to give access otherwise — and there have been many reports over the years of phone companies being cosy with the government. Second, there's intelligence-agency collusion: if the NSA wants to wiretap an American citizen without a warrant they can get an ally to do it, and return the favour later (it's said that Margaret Thatcher used the Canadian intelligence services to wiretap ministers who were suspected of disloyalty) [496]. Third, in some countries, wiretapping is uncontrolled if one of the subscribers consents — so that calls from phone boxes are free to tap (the owner of the phone box is considered to be the legal subscriber). Finally, in many countries, the police get hold of email and other stored communications by subpoena rather than warrant (they used to do this in America too before a court stopped the practice in June 2007 [795]).

But even if the official figures had to be doubled or tripled, democratic regimes used wiretapping very much less than authoritarian ones. For example, lawful wiretapping amounted to 63,243 line-days in the USA in 1999, or an average of just over 173 taps in operation on an average day. The former East Germany had some 25,000 telephone taps in place, despite having a fraction of the U.S. population [474]. There was also extensive use of technical surveillance measures such as room bugs and body wires. (It's hardly surprising that nudist resorts became extremely popular in that sad country.)

The incidence of wiretapping was also highly variable within and between democracies. In the USA, for example, only about half the states used it, and for many years the bulk of the taps were in the 'Mafia' states of New York, New Jersey and Florida (though recently, Pennsylvania and California have caught up) [582]. There is similar variation in Europe. Wiretaps are very common in the Netherlands, despite Dutch liberalism on other issues [248]: they have up to 1,000 taps on the go at once with a tenth of America's population. In a homicide investigation, for example, it's routine to tap everyone in the victim's address book for a week to monitor how they react to the news of the death. The developed country with the most wiretaps is Italy, thanks to its tradition of organised crime [794]. In the UK, wiretaps are supposed to need a ministerial warrant, and are rarer; but police use room bugs and similar techniques (including computer exploits) quite a lot in serious cases. To some extent, the technologies are interchangeable: if you can mount a rootkit in a gangster's laptop you can record, and mail home, everything said nearby, whether it's said to someone in the same room, or over a phone.

The cost of wiretapping is an issue. Before CALEA was introduced, in 1993, U.S. police agencies spent only $51.7 million on wiretaps — perhaps a good estimate of their value before the issue became politicised [582]. The implementation of CALEA has supposedly cost over $500 m, even though it doesn't cover ISPs. The FCC has recently (2006–7) extended the CALEA rules to VOIP, which has provoked much grumbling from the industry about the added costs of compliance, loss of some of the flexibility which IP-based services offer, loss of opportunities to innovate, and potential security problems with VOIP services. Certainly it's a lot harder to wiretap VOIP calls: as the critics point out, 'The paradigm of VoIP intercept difficulty is a call between two road warriors who constantly change locations and who, for example, may call from a cafe in Boston to a hotel room in Paris and an hour later from an office in Cambridge to a giftshop at the Louvre' [156]. So how can policymarkers figure out whether it's worth it? If the agencies had to face the full economic costs of wiretapping, would they cut back and spend the money on more gumshoes instead? Once you start molding an infrastructure to meet requirements other than cost and efficiency, someone has to pay: and as the infrastructure gets more complex, the bills keep on mounting. If other people have to pay them, the incentives are perverted and inefficiency can become structural.

Since 9/11, though, economic arguments about surveillance have been more or less suspended. 43 days after the attacks, Congress passed the Patriot Act, which facilitated electronic surveillance in a number of ways; for example, it allowed increased access by law enforcement to stored records (including financial, medical and government records), 'sneak-and-peek' searches of homes and businesses without the owner's knowledge, and the use by the FBI of National Security Letters to get access to financial, email and telephone records. While access to email is often wiretapping, access to call records is really traffic analysis, which I'll deal with in the next section, and may account for most of the actual volume of interception.

The result has been a steady increase in wiretapping rather than a step change. The 1350 wiretaps authorized by State and Federal courts in 1999 fell to 1190 in 2000, rose to 1491 in 2001, fell to 1358 in 2002, and then rose to 1,442 in 2003, 1,710 in 2004 and 1,773 in 2005. There has been a sharper increase in FISA warrants, from 934 in 2001 to 1228 in 2002, 1724 in 2003 and eventually 2176 in 2006 [435]. This reflects the greater interest in foreign nationals and the Patriot Act's provision that FISA warrants could be used in national-security cases. (These used to be extremely rare: in 1998, for example, only 45 of the FBI's 12,730 convictions involved what the Justice Department classified as internal security or terrorism matters [1259]).

In December 2005, the New York Times revealed that the NSA had been illegally wiretapping people in the U.S. without a warrant. The Administration proposed a rewrite of FISA to legalise this activity, the result was the recently enacted 'Protect America Act', which amends the FISA and sunsets early in 2008. Under this Act, the NSA no longer needs even a FISA warrant to tap a call if one party's believed to be outside the USA or a non-U.S. person. This in effect allowed warrantless surveillance of large numbers of U.S. calls. However, due to the very visible dispute between the President and the Congress over U.S. wiretap law, it's not clear whether and how Congress will revise this when it comes up for renewal. The current action (October 2007) is about granting retrospective immunity to phone companies who cooperated with unlawful wiretapping activities.

24.3.2 The Growing Controversy about Traffic Analysis

However the great bulk of police communications intelligence in developed countries does not come from the surveillance of content, but the analysis of telephone toll records and other communications data. I examined in the chapter on telecomms security how criminals go to great lengths to bury their signals in innocuous traffic using techniques such as pre-paid mobile phones and PBX hacking; and the techniques used by the police to trace networks of criminal contacts nonetheless.

Again, this is nothing new. Rulers have long used their control over postal services to track the correspondents of suspects, even when the letters weren't opened. The introduction of postage stamps in 1840 was an advance for privacy as it made it much easier to send a letter anonymously. Some countries got so worried about the threat of sedition and libel that they passed laws requiring a return address to be written on the back of the envelope. The development of the telegraph, on the other hand, was an advance for surveillance; as messages were logged by sender, receiver and word count, traffic totals could be compiled and were found to be an effective indicator of economic activity [1215]. The First World War brought home to the combatants the value of the intelligence that could be gleaned from listening to the volume of enemy radio traffic, even when it couldn't conveniently be deciphered [676, 923]. Later conflicts reinforced this.

Traffic analysis continues to provide the bulk of police communications intelligence. For example, in the USA, there were 1,329 wiretap applications approved in 1998 (the last year for which comparable statistics were available when I wrote the first edition of this book) while there were 4886 subpoenas (plus 4621 extensions) for *pen registers* (devices which record all the numbers dialed from a particular phone line) and 2437 subpoenas (plus 2770 extensions) for *trap-and-trace* devices (which record the calling line ID of incoming calls, even if the caller tries to block it). In other words, there were more than ten times as many warrants for communications data as for content. What's more, these data were even more incomplete than for wiretapping. The trend in recent years — even before 9/11 — was to switch to using subpoenas for the call-detail records in the phone companies' databases, rather than getting pen-register data directly from the switch (a move facilitated by CALEA). Bell Atlantic, for example, indicated that for the years 1989 through 1992, it had responded to 25,453 subpoenas or court orders for toll billing records of 213,821 of its customers, while NYNEX reported that it had processed 25,510 subpoenas covering an unrecorded number of customers in 1992 alone [279]. Scaled up across the country, this suggests perhaps half a million customers are having their records seized every year, and that traffic data are collected on perhaps a hundred times as many people as are subjected to wiretapping. Statistics have become much more patchy and sporadic since 9/11, but there's no reason to believe that traffic data have become less important: they have been more important for years, and across many countries. (Indeed, recently we're getting indications of further qualitative increases in traffic surveillance, which I'll discuss below.) Why should this be?

Wiretaps are so expensive to listen to and transcribe that most police forces use them only as a weapon of last resort. In contrast, the numbers a suspect calls, and that call him, give a rapid overview of his pattern of contacts. Also, while wiretaps usually have fairly strict warrantry requirements, most countries impose little or no restrictions on the police use of communications data. In the USA, no paperwork was required until ECPA. Even after that, they have been easy to get: under 18 USC 3123 [1272], the investigative officer merely had to certify to a magistrate 'that the information likely to be obtained by such installation and use is relevant to an ongoing criminal investigation'. This can be any crime — felony or misdemeanour — and under either Federal or State law. Unlike with wiretaps, the court has no power to deny a subpoena once a formally correct application has been made, and there is no court supervision once the order has been granted. Since the passage of CALEA, warrants are still required for such communications data as the addresses to which a subscriber has sent e-mail messages, but basic toll records could be obtained under subpoena — and the subscriber need not be notified.

The most controversial current issue may be access to multiple generations of call data and indeed to whole phone-company databases. In section 19.3.1, I described the snowball search, in which the investigator not only looks at who the target calls, but who they call, and so on recursively, accumulating n-th generation contacts like a snowball rolling downhill, and then eventually sifting the snowball for known suspects or suspicious patterns. If a pen-register, trap-and-trace, or call-detail subpoena is needed for every node in the search, the administrative costs mount up. There were thus rumours in many countries for years that the phone companies simply give the intelligence services access to (or even copies of) their databases.

24.3.3   Unlawful Surveillance

In 2006, it emerged that the rumours were correct. AT&T had indeed given the NSA the call records of millions of Americans; the agency's goal is 'to create a database of every call ever made within the nation's borders' so it can map the entire U.S. social network for the War on Terror [277]. Apparently this data has now been collected for the 200 m customers of AT&T, Verizon and BellSouth, the nation's three biggest phone companies. The program started just after 9/11. Qwest did not cooperate, because its CEO at the time, Joe Nacchio, did not believe the NSA's claim that Qwest didn't need a court order (or approval under FISA). The NSA put pressure on Qwest by threatening to withhold classified contracts, and Qwest's lawyers asked NSA to take its proposal to the FISA court. The NSA refused, saying the court might not agree with them. It's since emerged that the NSA had put pressure on Qwest to hand over data even before 9/11 [528]. In October 2007, further confirmation was obtained by Democrat senators when Verizon admitted to them that it had given the FBI second-generation call data on its customers against national security letters on 720 occasions since 2005 [925]; and in November 2007, the Washington Post revealed that the NSA had tapped a lot of purely domestic phone calls and traffic data, and had also tapped AT&T's peering centre in San Francisco to get access to Internet traffic as well [926].

Both phone and computer service records can be provided to bodies other than law enforcement agencies under 18 USC 2703(c); thus, for example, we find Virginia and Maryland planning to use mobile phone tracking data to monitor congestion on the Capital Beltway [1179]. Toll data use for marketing purposes was also expressly envisioned by Congress when this law was passed. However, the growing availability of mobile phone records has now made them available to criminals too, enabling gangsters to track targets and find out if any of their colleagues have been calling the police [830].

In the UK, files of telephone toll tickets were provided to the police without any control whatsoever until European law forced the government to regulate the practice in the Regulation of Investigatory Powers Act in 2000. It was long rumoured that the large phone companies gave the spooks copies of their itemised billing databases as a matter of course. Since then, communications data requires only a notice from a senior police officer to the phone company or ISP, not a warrant; and data can be provided to a wide range of public-sector bodies, just as in the USA. (There was a public outcry when the Government published regulations under the Act, which made clear that your mobile phone records could be seized by anyone from your parish council to the Egg Marketing Board.)

24.3.4   Access to Search Terms and Location Data

One problem is that communications data and content are becoming inter-mixed, as what's content at one level of abstraction is often communications data at the next. People might think of a URL is just the address of a page to be fetched, but a URL such as `http://www.google.com/search?q=marijuana+cultivation+UK` contains the terms entered into a search engine as well as the search engine's name. Clearly some policemen would like a list of everyone who submitted such an enquiry. Equally clearly, giving this sort of data to the police on a large scale would have a chilling effect on online discourse.

In the USA, the Department of Justice issued a subpoena to a number of search engines to hand over two full months' worth of search queries, as well as all the URLs in their index, claiming it needed the data to bolster its claims that the Child Online Protection Act did not violate the constitution and that filtering could be effective against child pornography. (Recall we discussed in section 9.3.1 how when AOL released some search histories, a number of them were easily identifiable to individuals.) AOL, Microsoft and Yahoo quietly complied, but Google resisted. A judge ruled that the Department would get no search queries, and only a random sample of 50,000 of the URLs it had originally sought [1353].

In the UK, the government tried to define URLs as traffic data when it was pushing the RIP bill through parliament, and the news that the police would have unrestricted access to the URLs each user enters — their *click-stream* — caused a public outcry against 'Big Browser', and the definition of communications data was trimmed. For general Internet traffic, it means IP addresses, but it also includes email addresses. All this can be demanded with only a notice from a senior policeman.

More subtleties arise with the phone system. In Britain, all information about the location of mobile phones counts as traffic data, and officials get it easily; but in the USA, the Court of Appeals ruled in 2000 that when the police get a warrant for the location of a mobile, the cell in which it is active is sufficient, and that to require triangulation on the device (an interpretation the police had wanted) would invade privacy [1273]. Also, even cell-granularity location information would not be available under the lower standards applied to pen-register subpoenas. Subpoenas were also found insufficient for *post-cut-through* dialed digits as there is no way to distinguish in advance from digits dialed to route calls and digits dialed to access or give information. What this means in practice is that if a target goes down a 7–11 store and buys a phone card for a few dollars, the police can't get a list of who he calls without a full wiretap warrant. All they can get by subpoena are the digits he dials to contact the phone card operator, not the digits he dials afterwards to be connected.

24.3.5   Data Mining

The analysis of call data is only one aspect of a much wider issue: law enforcement *data matching*, namely the processing of data from numerous sources. The earliest serious use of multiple source data appears to have been in Germany in the late 1970s to track down safe houses used by the Baader Meinhof terrorist group. Investigators looked for rented apartments with irregular peaks in utility usage, and for which the rent and electricity bills were paid by remote credit transfer from a series of different locations. This worked: it yielded a list of several hundred apartments among which were several safe houses. The tools to do this kind of analysis are now shipped with a number of the products used for traffic analysis and for the management of major police investigations. The extent to which they're used depends on the local regulatory climate; there have been rows in the UK over police access to databases of the prescriptions filled by pharmacists, while in the USA doctors are alarmed at the frequency with which personal health information is subpoenaed from health insurance companies by investigators. There are also practical limits imposed by the cost of understanding the many proprietary data formats used by commercial and government data processors. But it's common for police to have access at least to utility data, such as electricity bills which get trawled to find marijuana growers.

However, there are many indications that the combination of more aggressive searches and mounting data volumes are making data-mining operations since 9/11 less productive. Terrorists are just so rare as a percentage of the population that any tests you use to 'detect' them would require extraordinary sensitivity if you're not to drown in false positives. Adding more data doesn't necessarily help; as I explained in section 15.9, combining multiple sensors is hard and you're unlikely to improve both the false positive and false negative error rates at the same time. Simply put, if you're looking for a needle in a haystack, the last thing you need to do is to build a bigger haystack. As Jeff Jonas, the chief scientist at IBM's data-mining operation, put it, 'techniques that look at people's behavior to predict terrorist intent are so far from reaching the level of accuracy that's necessary that I see them as nothing but civil liberty infringement engines' [519].

Finally, policemen (and even divorce lawyers) are increasingly using subpoenas to get hold of email from service providers once the recipient has read it. The legal reasoning is that whereas it takes an interception warrant to get the postman to hand over physical mail, a simple search warrant will do once the letter lands on your doormat; and so although a proper warrant is needed to seize email on its way through an ISP to you, once it's sitting in your mail folder at AOL or Google it's just stored data. You might think it prudent to use a mail service provider that deletes mail once you've read it; but in the UK at least, a court found that police who ordered an ISP to preserve email that they'd normally overwritten were acting lawfully [974], and in March 2006 the European Union adopted a Directive compelling Member States to enact laws compelling communication services to retain traffic data for between six months and two years. It's unclear how many ISPs will go to the trouble of deleting email contents; if they have to retain the headers anyway, they might as well keep the lot. And in the long term, absolutely anything that gets monitored and logged is potentially liable to be subpoenaed.

24.3.6 Surveillance via ISPs – Carnivore and its Offspring

One big recent development is intrusive surveillance at Internet Service Providers (ISPs). Tapping data traffic is harder than voice used to be; there are many obstacles, such as transient IP addresses given to most customers and the increasingly distributed nature of traffic. In the old days (say 2002), an ISP might have had modem racks, and a LAN where a wiretap device could be located; nowadays many customers come in via DSL, and providers use switched networks that often don't have any obvious place to put a tap.

Many countries have laws requiring ISPs to facilitate wiretapping, and the usual way to do it at a large ISP is to have equipment already installed that will split a target network so that copies of packets of interest go to a separate classified network with wiretap equipment. Small ISPs tend not to have such facilities. In the late 1990s, the FBI developed a system called Carnivore that they could lug around to smaller ISPs when a wiretap was needed; it was a PC with software that could be configured to record a suspect's email, or web browsing, or whatever traffic a warrant or subpoena specified. It became controversial in 2000 when an ISP challenged it in court; it was being used to record email headers as traffic data, without a wiretap warrant. Congress legalized this practice in the Patriot Act in 2001, and in about 2002 Carnivore was retired in favour of more modern equipment. We have recent FOI revelations about the FBI's current wiretapping network, DCSNet, which is very slick −allowing agents remote and near-instantaneous access to traffic and content from participating phone companies [1178].

Access by the police and intelligence services to ISPs is patchy for a number of reasons. No-one bothers about small ISPs, but they can grow quickly; large ISPs' systems can be hard to integrate with law-enforcement kit, and the project can remain stuck in the development backlog for years as it brings no revenue; ISPs coming into contact with the world of surveillance for the first time usually don't have cleared staff to operate government equipment; and the wiretap equipment is very often poorly engineered [1151]. As a result, it's often not practical for the police to tap particular ISPs for months or even years on end, and the information about which providers are wiretap-resistant is rather closely held. (Smart bad guys still use small ISPs.) In addition, it is often difficult for the authorities to get IP traffic data without a full wiretap warrant; for assorted technical reasons, all the traffic data that it's usually convenient to provide against a subpoena are extracts from those logs that the ISP keeps anyway. And things often go wrong because the police don't understand ISPs; they subpoena the wrong things, or provide inaccurate timestamps so that the wrong user is associated with an IP address. For an analysis of failure modes, see Clayton [300].

24.3.7 Communications Intelligence on Foreign Targets

I discussed the technical aspects of signals intelligence in Chapter 19; now let's look briefly at the political and organizational aspects.

The bulk of communications intelligence, whether involving wiretaps, traffic analysis or other techniques, is not conducted for law enforcement purposes but for foreign intelligence. In the U.S. the main agency responsible for this is the National Security Agency, which has huge facilities and tens of thousands of employees. While law enforcement agencies have 150–200 active wiretaps at any one time, the NSA utterly dwarfs this. The situation is similar in other countries; Britain's Government Communications Headquarters (GCHQ) has thousands of employees and a budget of about a billion dollars, while for many years one single police officer at New Scotland Yard handled the administration of all the police wiretaps in London (and did other things too).

Information has steadily trickled out about the scale and effectiveness of modern signals intelligence operations. David Kahn's influential history of cryptography laid the groundwork by describing much of what happened up till the start of World War Two [676]; an anonymous former NSA analyst, later identified as Perry Fellwock, revealed the scale of NSA operations in 1972 [462]. 'Information gathering by NSA is complete', he wrote. 'It covers what foreign governments are doing, planning to do, have done in the past: what armies are moving where and against whom; what air forces are moving where, and what their capabilities are. There really aren't any limits on NSA. Its mission goes all the way from calling in the B-52s in Vietnam to monitoring every aspect of the Soviet space program'.

While Fellwock's motive was opposition to Vietnam, the next major whistle-blower was a British wartime codebreaker, Frederick Winterbotham, who wanted to write a memoir of his wartime achievements and, as he was dying, was not bothered about prosecution. In 1974, he revealed the Allies' success in breaking German and Japanese cipher systems during that war [1350], which led to many further books on World War 2 sigint [296, 677, 1336]. Thereafter there was a slow drip of revelations by investigative journalists, quite of few of whose sources were concerned about corruption or abuse of the facilities by officials monitoring targets they should not have, such as domestic political groups. For example, whistleblower Peg Newsham revealed that the NSA had illegally tapped a phone call made by Senator Strom Thurmond [258, 259]. James Bamford pieced together a fair amount of information on the NSA from open sources and by talking to former employees [112], while the most substantial recent source on the organization and methods of U.S. and allied signals intelligence was put together by New Zealand journalist Nicky Hager [576] following the New Zealand intelligence community's failure to obey an order from their Prime Minister to downgrade intelligence cooperation with the USA.

The end of the Cold War forced the agencies to find new reasons to justify their budgets, and a common theme was developing economic intelligence operations against competitor countries. This accelerated the flow of information about sources and methods. The most high-profile exposé of US economic espionage was made in a 1999 report to the European parliament [443], which was concerned that after the collapse of the USSR, European Union member nations were becoming the NSA's main targets [262].

The picture that emerged from these sources was of a worldwide signals intelligence collection system, *Echelon*, run jointly by the USA, the UK, Canada, Australia and New Zealand. Data, faxes and phone calls get collected at a large number of nodes which range from international communications cables that land in member countries (or are tapped clandestinely underwater), through observation of traffic to and from commercial communications satellites and special sigint satellites that collect traffic over hostile countries, to listening posts in member states' embassies [443]. The collected traffic is searched in real time by computers known as *dictionaries* according to criteria such as the phone numbers or IP addresses of the sender or receiver, plus keyword search on the contents of email. These search criteria are entered by member countries' intelligence analysts; the dictionaries then collect traffic satisfying them and ship them back to the analyst. Echelon appears to work very much like Google, except that instead of searching web pages it searches through the world's phone and data network traffic in real time.

24.3.8 Intelligence Strengths and Weaknesses

Echelon seems impressive — if scary. But several points are worth bearing in mind.

First, the network built up by the NSA and its allies was mainly aimed at the old USSR, where human intelligence was difficult, and hoovering up vast quantities of phone calls gave at least some idea of what was going on. But the resulting political and economic intelligence turned out to be poor; the West thought that Russia's economy was about twice as large as it actually was, and was surprised by its collapse post-1989. (The agencies' incentives to talk up the threat are clear.) In any case, much of the effort was military, aimed at understanding Soviet radar and communications, and at gaining a decisive advantage in location, jamming and deception. Without an ability to conduct electronic warfare, a modern state is not competitive in air or naval warfare or in tank battles on the ground. So it's not surprising that most of the personnel at NSA are military, and its director has always been a serving general. There is still a lot of effort put into understanding the signals of potential adversaries.

Second, there have been some successes against terrorists — notably the arrest of the alleged 9/11 mastermind Khalid Shaikh Mohammed after he used a mobile phone SIM from a batch bought by a known terrorist in Switzerland. But electronic warfare against insurgents in Iraq has proved to be unproductive, as I discussed in Chapter 19. And it's long been clear that much more effort should have been put into human intelligence. In an article published just before 9/11, an analyst wrote 'The CIA probably doesn't have a single truly qualified Arabic-speaking officer of Middle Eastern background who can play a believable Muslim fundamentalist who would volunteer to spend years of his life with shitty food and no women in the mountains of Afghanistan. For Christ's sake, most case officers live in the suburbs of Virginia. We don't do that kind of thing'. Another put it even more bluntly: 'Operations that include diarrhea as a way of life don't happen' [521]. The combination of stand-off technical intelligence plus massive firepower suits the private interests of bureaucrats and equipment vendors, but it makes allied forces ineffective at counterinsurgency, where the enemy blends with the civilian population. Similar perverse incentives hamper the military. For example, Britain is spending billions on two new aircraft carriers and on modernising the nuclear deterrent, but even six years after 9/11 we haven't trained enough soldiers to carry a basic conversation in Arabic. The big debate now brewing in the Pentagon is not just about intelligence, but how to evolve a smarter approach to counterinsurgency across the board [414].

Third, while the proliferation of mobile phones, wireless LANs and online services presents the agencies with a cornucopia of new information sources, the volume is a huge problem. Even with a budget of billions of dollars a year and tens of thousands of staff, not even the NSA can collect all the electronic communications everywhere in the world. The days in which they could record all transatlantic phone calls with a rack of 16-track tape recorders are no more. Equipment for tapping high-speed backbone links does exist [167], but it's expensive. Sprint's budget is bigger than the NSA's, and is spent on low-cost commercial products rather than high-cost classified ones, so they can put in lines much faster than the NSA can tap them. Data volumes force most traffic selection to be done locally, and in real time [770]. Suppose, for example, that the NSA got interested in the UK university system — let's call it a hundred institutions at 2 Gbit/sec each. They couldn't ship all the bits across the Atlantic to Fort Meade as there just isn't enough transatlantic bandwidth. Tapping all the data streams of all the corporations in Japan would be an order of magnitude harder.

Fourth, although other countries may complain about U.S. sigint collection, for them to moralize about it is hypocritical. Other countries also run intelligence operations, and are often much more aggressive in conducting economic and other non-military espionage. The real difference between the WASP countries and the others is that no-one else has built the Echelon 'system-of-systems'. Indeed, there may be network effects at work in sigint as elsewhere: the value of a network grows faster than its size, and the more you tap, the cheaper it gets. There have thus been moves to construct a 'European Echelon' involving the police and intelligence agencies of continental European countries [430, 445].

The mature view, I think, is that signals intelligence is necessary for a nation's survival but potentially dangerous — just like the armed forces it serves. An army can be a good servant but is likely to be an intolerable master. The issue is not whether such resources should exist, but how they are held accountable. In the USA, hearings by Senator Church in 1975 detailed a number of abuses such as the illegal monitoring of U.S. citizens [292]. Foreign intelligence gathering is now regulated by U.S. law in the form of 50 USC 1801–1811 [1272], which codifies FISA. This isn't perfect; as already noted, it's the subject of fierce tussles between the executive and the legislature about the recent provision that the NSA can wiretap U.S. calls so long as one of the parties is believed not to be a U.S. person. Even before this, the number of FISA warrants has risen steadily since 9/11 to exceed the number of ordinary (title III) wiretap warrants. But at least Congress has got interested. And the USA is lucky: in most countries, the oversight of intelligence isn't even discussed.

Finally, poor accountability costs more than just erosion of liberty and occasional political abuse. There is also a real operational cost in the proliferation of intelligence bureaucracies that turn out to be largely useless once the shooting starts. In Washington during the Cold War, the agencies hated each other much more than they hated the Russians. In the UK, one of the most vicious intelligence battles was not against the IRA, but between the police and MI5 over who would be the lead in the fight against the IRA. There are numerous accounts of intelligence inefficiency and infighting by well-placed insiders, such as R.V. Jones [671]. It is in this context of bureaucratic turf wars that I'll now describe the 'Crypto Wars' of the 1990s, which were a formative experience for many governments (and NGOs) on issues of surveillance and technology policy.

24.3.9 The Crypto Wars

Technology policy during the 1990s was dominated by acrimonious debates about *key escrow* — the doctrine that anyone who encrypted data should give the government a copy of the key, so that the civilian use of cryptography would not interfere with intelligence gathering by the NSA and others.

Although some restrictions on cryptography had existed for years and irritated both academic researchers and civilian users, they shot to the headlines in 1993 when President Clinton astonished the IT industry with the *Escrowed Encryption Standard*, more popularly known as the *Clipper chip*. This was a proposed replacement for DES, with a built-in back door key so that government agencies could decipher any traffic. The NSA had tried to sell the program to the cabinet of President Bush senior and failed; but the new administration was happy to help.

American opinion polarized. The government argued that since cryptography is about keeping messages secret, it could be used by criminals to prevent the police gathering evidence from wiretaps; the IT industry (with a few exceptions) took the conflicting view that cryptography was the only means of protecting electronic commerce and was thus vital to the future development of the net. Civil liberties groups lined up with the industry, and claimed that cryptography would be the critical technology for privacy. By 1994, the NSA had concluded that they faced a war with Microsoft that Bill would win, so they handed off the policy lead to the FBI while continuing to direct matters from behind the scenes.

The debate got rapidly tangled up with export controls on weapons, the means by which cryptography was traditionally controlled. U.S. software firms were not allowed to export products containing cryptography which was too hard to break (usually meaning a keylength of over 40 bits). A U.S. software author, Phil Zimmermann, was hauled up before a grand jury for arms trafficking after a program he wrote — PGP — 'escaped' on to the Internet. He immediately became a folk hero and made a fortune as his product grabbed market leadership. The conflict became international: the U.S. State Department tried hard to persuade other countries to control cryptography too. It became one of the personal missions of Vice-President Gore (a reason why many in Redmond and the Valley contributed to the Bush campaign in 2000).

The results were mixed. Some countries with memories of oppressive regimes, such as Germany and Japan, resisted American blandishments. Others, such as Russia, seized the excuse to pass harsh crypto control laws. France thumbed its nose by relaxing a traditional prohibition on non-government use of crypto; Britain obediently changed from a liberal, laissez-faire policy under John Major in the mid 1990s to a draconian law under Tony Blair. The *Regulation of Investigatory Powers* (RIP) Act of 2000 enables the police to demand that I hand over a key or password in my possession, and the Export Control Act of 2002 instructs me to get an export license if I send any cryptographic software outside Europe that uses keys longer than 56 bits. Oh, and the government has also taken powers to vet foreign research students studying dangerous subjects like computer science, and to refuse visas to those they consider a proliferation risk.

I was involved in all this as one of the academics whose research and teaching was under threat from the proposed controls, and in 1998 I was one of the people who set up the Foundation for Information Policy Research, the UK's leading internet-policy think-tank, which wrestled with crypto policy, export policy, copyright and related issues. In the next few sections I'll lay out a brief background to the crypto wars, and then describe the consequences for export controls today, and for what we can learn about the way governments have failed to get to grips with the Internet.

24.3.9.1 *The Back Story to Crypto Policy*

Many countries made laws in the mid-19th century banning the use of cryptography in telegraph messages, and some even forbade the use of languages other than those on an approved list. Prussia went as far as to require telegraph operators to keep copies of the plaintext of all messages [1215]. Sometimes the excuse was law enforcement — preventing people obtaining horse race results or stock prices in advance of the 'official' transmissions — but the real concern was national security. This pattern was to repeat itself again in the twentieth century.

After the immense success that the Allies had during World War 2 with cryptanalysis and signals intelligence in general, the UK and US governments agreed in 1957 to continue intelligence cooperation. This is known as the UKUSA agreement, although Canada, Australia and New Zealand quickly joined. The member nations operated a crypto policy whose main goal was to prevent the proliferation of cryptographic equipment and know-how. Until the 1980s, about the only makers of cryptographic equipment were companies selling into government markets. They could mostly be trusted not to sell anything overseas which would upset their major customers at home. This was reinforced by export controls which were operated 'in as covert a way as possible, with the minimum of open guidance to anyone wanting, for example, an export licence. Most things were done in behind-the-scenes negotiation between the officials and a trusted representative of the would-be exporter'. [142]

In these negotiations, the authorities would try to steer applicants towards using weak cryptography where possible, and where confronted with a more sophisticated user would try to see to it that systems had a 'back door' (known in the trade as a *red thread*) which would give access to traffic. Anyone who tried to sell decent crypto domestically could be dissuaded by various means. If they were a large company, they would be threatened with loss of government contracts; if a small one, they could be strangled with red tape as they tried to get telecomms and other product approvals.

The 'nonproliferation' controls were much wider than cryptography, as computers also fell within their scope. By the mid-1980s, the home computers kids had in their bedrooms were considered to be munitions, and manufacturers ended up doing lots of paperwork for export orders. This pleased the bureaucrats as it gave them jobs and power. The power was often abused: in one case, an export order for a large number of British-made home computers to the school system in Yugoslavia was blocked at the insistence of the U.S. authorities, on the grounds that it contained a U.S. microprocessor; a U.S. firm was promptly granted a license to export into this market. Although incidents like this brought the system into disrepute, it persists to this day.

Crypto policy was run in these years along the same lines as controls on missile technology exports: to let just enough out to prevent companies in other countries developing viable markets. Whenever crypto controls got so onerous that banks in somewhere like Brazil or South Africa started having crypto equipment custom built by local electronics firms, export licensing would ease up until the threat had passed. And, as I described in the chapter on API security, the hardware security modules sold to banks throughout this period had such poor interface designs that compromising them was trivial anyway.

Vulnerabilities in bank crypto merely increased the risk of fraud slightly, but bad crypto elsewhere exposed its users to surveillance. The Swedish government got upset when they learned that the 'export version' of Lotus Notes which they used widely in public service had its cryptography deliberately weakened to allow NSA access; and at least one (U.S. export approved) cipher machine has broadcast its plaintext in the clear in the VHF band. But the most notorious example was the Bühler case.

Hans Bühler worked as a salesman for the Swiss firm Crypto AG, which was a leading supplier of cryptographic equipment to governments without the technical capability to build their own. He was arrested in 1992 in Iran and the authorities accused him of selling them cipher machines which had been tampered with so that the NSA could get at the plaintext. After he had spent some time in prison, Crypto AG paid 1.44 billion Rials — about a million U.S. dollars — to bail him, but then fired him once he got back to Switzerland. Bühler then alleged on Swiss radio and TV that the firm was secretly controlled by the German intelligence services and that it had been involved in intelligence work for years [238]. The interpretation commonly put on this was that ultimate control resided with the NSA (the founder of Crypto, Boris Hagelin, had been a lifelong friend of William Friedman, the NSA's chief scientist) and that equipment was routinely red threaded [824]. A competing interpretation is that these allegations were concocted by the NSA to undermine the company, as it was one of the third world's few sources of cryptographic equipment. Bühler's story is told in [1228].

24.3.9.2   DES and Crypto Research

Despite the very poor implementation quality of early banking cryptosystems, the NSA still worried in the seventies that the banking sector might evolve good algorithms that would escape into the wild. Many countries were still using rotor machines or other equipment that could be broken using the techniques developed in World War 2. How could the banking industry's thirst for a respectable cipher be slaked, not just in the U.S. but overseas, without this cipher being adopted by foreign governments and thus adding to the costs of intelligence collection?

The solution was the Data Encryption Standard (DES). At the time, as I mentioned in section 5.4.3.2, there was controversy about whether 56 bits were enough. We now know that this was deliberate. The NSA did not at the time have the machinery to do DES keysearch; that came later. But by giving the impression that they did, they managed to stop most foreign governments adopting it. The rotor machines continued in service, in many cases reimplemented using microcontrollers, and the traffic continued to be harvested. Foreigners who encrypted their important data with such ciphers merely solved the NSA's traffic selection problem.

A second initiative was to undermine academic research in cryptology. In the 1970s this was done directly by harassing the people involved; by the 1980s it had evolved into the subtler strategy of claiming that published research work was all old hat. The agencies opposed crypto research funding by saying 'we did all that stuff thirty years ago; why should the taxpayer pay for it twice?' The insinuation that DES may have had a 'trapdoor' inserted into it fitted well with this play. A side effect we still live with is that the crypto and computer security communities got separated from each other in the early 1980s as the NSA worked to suppress one and build up the other.

By the mid 1990s this line had become exhausted. Agency blunders in the design of various key escrow systems showed that they have no special expertise in cryptology compared with the open research community, and as attempts to influence the direction of academic research by interfering with funding have become less effective they have become much less common.

24.3.9.3   *The Clipper Chip*

Crypto policy came into the open in 1993 with the launch of the Clipper chip. The immediate stimulus was the proposed introduction by AT&T to the U.S. domestic market of a high-grade encrypting telephone that would have used Diffie-Hellman key exchange and triple-DES to protect traffic. The NSA thought that the government could use its huge buying power to ensure the success of a different standard in which spare keys would be available to the agencies to decrypt traffic. This led to a public outcry; an AT&T computer scientist, Matt Blaze, found a protocol vulnerability in Clipper [183] and the proposal was withdrawn.

Several more attempts were made to promote the use of cryptography with government access to keys in various guises. Key escrow acquired various new names, such as *key recovery*; certification authorities which kept copies of their clients' private decryption keys became known as *Trusted Third Parties* (TTPs) — somewhat emphasising the NSA definition of a trusted component as one which can break security. In the UK, a key escrow protocol was introduced for the public sector, and this was used to try to get the private sector to adopt it to; but a number of vulnerabilities were found in it too [76].

Much of the real policy leverage had to do with export licensing. As the typical U.S. software firm exports most of its product, and as maintaining a separate product line for export is expensive, many firms could be dissuaded from offering strong cryptography by prohibiting its export. Products with 'approved' key escrow functionality were then granted preferential U.S. export license treatment. The history of this struggle is still to be fully written, but a first draft is available from Diffie and Landau [387] and many of the U.S. source documents, obtained under FOIA, have been published in [1135].

One of the engineering lessons from this whole process is that doing key escrow properly is hard. Making two-party security protocols into three-party protocols increases the complexity and the risk of serious design errors, and centralizing the escrow databases creates huge targets [4]. Where escrow is required it's usually better done with simple local mechanisms. In one army, the elegant solution is that every officer must write down his passphrase on a piece of paper, put it into an envelope, stamp it 'Secret' and hand it to his commanding officer, who puts it in his office safe. That way the keys are kept in the same place as the documents whose electronic versions they protect, and there's no central database for an airplane to bomb or a spy to steal.

24.3.10   Did the Crypto Wars Matter?

When the key escrow debate got going in the UK in 1994–5, I took a line that was unpopular at the time with both the pro-escrow and the anti-escrow lobbies. The pro-escrow people said that as crypto provided confidentiality, and confidentiality could help criminals, there needed to be some way to defeat it. The anti-escrow lobby said that since crypto was necessary for privacy, there must not be a way to defeat it. I argued in [35] that essentially all the premises behind these arguments were wrong. Most crypto applications (in the real world, as opposed to academia) are about authentication rather than confidentiality; they help the police rather than hindering them. As for criminals, they require unobtrusive communications — and encrypting a phone call is a good way to bring yourself to the attention of the agencies. As for privacy, most violations result from abuse of authorized access by insiders. Finally, a much more severe problem for policemen investigating electronic crimes is to find acceptable evidence, for which decent authentication can be helpful.

This is not to say that the police have no use for wiretaps. Although many police forces get by quite happily without them, and many of the figures put forward by the pro-wiretap lobby are dishonest [387], there are some occasions where wiretapping can be economic as an investigative tool. The Walsh report — by a senior Australian intelligence officer — gives a reasonably balanced examination of the issues [1311]. Walsh compared the operational merits of wiretaps, bugs and physical surveillance, and pointed out that wiretaps were either the cheapest or the only investigative technique in some circumstances. He nonetheless found that there is 'no compelling reason or virtue to move early on regulation or legislation concerning cryptography', but he did recommend that police and intelligence agencies be allowed to hack into target computers to obtain access or evidence[2]. It took the view that although there will be some policing costs associated with technological advances, there will also be opportunities: for example, to infect a suspect's computer with software that will turn it into a listening device. This hit the nail on the head. The police — like the intelligence services — are reaping a rich harvest from modern technology.

We all knew, of course, that the police forces who argued in favour of key escrow did so under orders and as a front for the spooks[3]. Now the aims and objectives of policemen and spies are not quite identical, and confusing them has clouded matters. It is perhaps an oversimplification that the former try to prevent crimes at home, while the latter try to commit them abroad; but such aphorisms bring out some of the underlying tension. For example, policemen want to preserve evidence while spies like to be able to forge or repudiate documents at will. During the discussions on a European policy toward key escrow ('Euroclipper') that led up to the Electronic Signature Directive, the German government demanded that only confidentiality keys should be escrowed, not signature keys; while Britain wanted signature keys to be escrowed as well. The British view followed the military doctrine that deception is at least as important as eavesdropping, while the Germans supported the police doctrine of avoiding investigative techniques that undermine the value of any evidence subsequently seized.

The key goal of the intelligence community in the 1990s, as we later learned, was to minimise the number of systems that used crypto by default. If a significant proportion of data traffic were encrypted, then the automated keyword searching done by systems such as Echelon would be largely frustrated. The NSA was quite aware that many new network systems were being built rapidly during the dotcom boom, and if cryptography wasn't built in at the start, it should usually be too expensive to retrofit it later. So each year the NSA held the line on crypto controls meant dozens of systems open to surveillance for decades in the future. In these terms, the policy was successful: little of the world's network traffic is encrypted, the main exceptions being DRM-protected content, Skype, the few web pages that are protected by TLS, opportunistic TLS encryption between mail servers, SSH traffic, corporate VPNs and online computer games. Everything else is pretty much open to interception — including masses of highly sensitive email between companies.

---

[2]The Walsh report has an interesting publishing history. Originally released in 1997 as an unclassified document, it was withdrawn three weeks later after people asked why it wasn't yet on sale in the shops. It was then republished in redacted form. Then researchers found unexpurgated copies in a number of libraries. So these were published on the web, and the redacted parts drew attention at once to the issues the government considered sensitive. As late as 1999, the Australian government was still trying to suppress the report [1311].

[3]This was admitted in an unguarded moment in 1996 by the UK representative on the European body responsible for crypto policy [596].

In the end, the crypto wars ended in the USA because Al Gore felt he needed to woo Silicon Valley in 2000 and gave up on the initiative (too late — many software millionaires supported the Republicans that year), and in Europe because the European Commission felt that it was getting in the way of building confidence in online banking and commerce — so they passed an Electronic Signature Directive that said in effect that signature keys couldn't be escrowed or they would lose their legal effectiveness. The Germans had won the argument. As for whether it mattered, U.S. government reports of Title III wiretaps since then disclose only one case in which cryptography prevented the authorities from recovering the plaintext [435].

24.3.11   Export Control

The main spillover from the crypto wars was the imposition of much more stringent export controls than before, particularly in Europe. There is a survey of cryptography law at [736]; here's a quick summary.

International arms control agreements (COCOM and Wassenaar) bind most governments to implement export controls on cryptographic equipment, and the latter is implemented in the European Union by an EU regulation compelling Member States to control and license the export of *dual-use goods* — goods which have both civilian and military uses. Cryptanalytic products fall under the military regime, whereas the great bulk of software that just uses cryptography for protection falls under dual-use.

But national implementations vary. UK law didn't control the export of intangibles until 2002, so crypto software could be exported electronically; the Belgian government grants licences for almost anything; and Switzerland remains a large exporter of crypto equipment. Domestic controls also varied. The French government started off from a position of prohibiting almost all civilian cryptography and moved to almost complete liberalisation, while Britain went the other way.

What this meant in practice during the 1990s was that European researchers like me could write crypto software and publish it on our web pages, while our counterparts in the USA were prevented from doing that by the U.S. International Trafficking in Arms Regulations (ITAR). Non-U.S. companies started to get a competitive advantage because they could export software in intangible form. The U.S. government got annoyed and in 1997, Al Gore persuaded the incoming British Prime Minister Tony Blair to get Europe to extend export control to intangibles. Meanwhile the USA relaxed its own controls, so now the positions are reversed, and Europe has the fiercest rules. Tens of thousands of small software companies are breaking the law without knowing it by exporting products (or even by giving away software) containing crypto with keys longer than 56 bits.

There are several ways to deal with this. In many countries people will just ignore the law and just pay a bribe if, by misfortune, they are targeted for enforcement. In Northern Europe, one course of action is to try to use various Open General Export Licenses (OGELs) that provide specific exemptions for particular products and activities, but these require a cumbersome registration process and will often be unsuited to an innovative company. Another is to use the exemption in export law for material being put in the public domain; make your software (or the relevant parts of it) free or open-source and make your money on support and services. Another, in the UK, at least, is to use the fact that placing something on a web server isn't export; the exporter, in law, is any person outside Europe who downloads it. So a developer can leave material online for download without committing an offence. Yet another is of course to actually apply for an export license, but the licensing system is geared to small numbers of large companies that export military hardware and are known to the licensing authorities. If large numbers of small software firms were to deluge them with applications for licenses, the system would break down. At present some officials are trying to empire-build by 'raising awareness' of export controls among academics (who ignore them); thankfully there are no signs of the controls being marketed to the software industry.

24.4 Censorship

I wrote in the first edition that 'the 1990s debate on crypto policy is likely to be a test run for an even bigger battle, which will be over anonymity, censorship and copyright'. Although (as I discussed in Chapter 22) copyright law has largely stabilised, there is still pressure from Hollywood for ISPs to filter out file-sharing traffic. However censorship has become a much bigger issue over the past few years.

Censorship is done for a variety of motives. China blocks not just dissident websites, but even emails mentioning forbidden movements. Some countries switch censorship on during elections, or after crises; Burma imposed curfews after suppressing a wave of demonstrations. The live debate in the USA is about whether ISPs who are also phone companies should be able to block VOIP, and whether ISPs who also run cable channels should be able to block P2P: the principle of *net neutrality* says that ISPs should treat all packets equally. Net neutrality isn't as much of an issue in Europe where there's more competition between ISPs; the issue is that different European countries ban different types of content (France and Germany, for example, ban the sale of Nazi memorabilia, and won't let Amazon sell copies of Mein Kampf). Many countries have made attempts to introduce some kind of controls on child pornography — it's become a standard excuse for politicians who want to 'do something' about the Internet — and as I write there's a European initiative to ban radical

Islamist websites. Finally, censorship is sometimes imposed by courts in the context of civil disputes, such as the ban on publishing the DeCSS code that I mentioned in Chapter 22.

Censorship also takes a number of forms, from blocking certain types of traffic to IP address filtering, DNS poisoning, content inspection, and out-of-band mechanisms such as the punishment of individuals who downloaded (or were alleged to have downloaded) discountenanced material. I'll look now at a number of cases. (Declaration of interest: I've been funded by the Open Net Initiative as a result of which my students and postdocs have been busy measuring censorship in a number of countries.)

24.4.1 Censorship by Authoritarian Regimes

Rulers have long censored books, although the invention of the printing press made their job a whole lot harder. For example, John Wycliffe translated the Bible into English in 1380–1, but the Lollard movement he started was suppressed along with the Peasants' Revolt. When William Tyndale had another go in 1524–5, the technology now let him spread the word so quickly that the princes and bishops could not suppress it. They had him burned at the stake, but too late; over 50,000 copies of the New Testament had been printed, and the Reformation got under way. After that upset, printers were closely licensed and controlled; things only eased up in the eighteenth century.

The invention of the Internet has made the censors' job easier in some ways and harder in others. It's easier for the authorities to order changes in material that not many people care about: for example, courts that find a newspaper guilty of libel order the offending material to be removed, and changing the historical record wasn't possible when it consisted of physical copies in libraries rather than, as now, the online archive. It's easier for the authorities to observe the transmission of disapproved material, as they can monitor the content of electronic communications much more easily than physical packages. But mostly it's harder for them, as nowadays everyone can be a publisher; governments can still crack down on mainstream publishers, but have to contend with thousands of bloggers. A good reason for hope comes from observation of countries that try hard to censor content, such as China.

China had 137 million Internet users at the end of 2006, including a quarter of the population in the big cities. The government of Hu Jintao is committed to control and has invested hugely in filtering technology. People refer to 'the Great Firewall of China' although in fact the controls in that country are a complex socio-technical system that gives defence in depth against a range of material, from pornography to religious material to political dissent [984].

First, there are the perimeter defences. Most of China's Internet traffic flows through routers in Shenzhen near Hong Kong which filter on IP addresses to block access to known 'bad' sites like the Voice of America and the BBC;

they also use DNS cache poisoning. In addition, deep packet inspection at the TCP level is used to identify emails and web pages containing forbidden words such as 'Falun Gong': TCP reset packets are sent to both ends of such connections to tear them down. (I described the mechanisms in section 21.4.2.3 and noted there that while they can be fairly easily circumvented, anyone who did so regularly might expect a visit from the police.) Keyword filtering based on about 1000 wicked words is also implemented in Chinese search engines and blogs, while some individual Internet service providers also implement their own blocking and Internet cafés are required to by law.

Second, there are application-level defences. Some services are blocked and some aren't, depending on the extent to which the service provider plays along with the regime. There was a huge row when Google agreed to censor its search results in China (what they actually do is to populate their China index using spiders that search from within China, and thus only see material that's visible there anyway). The incentives created by China's rapidly growing markets enable its government to bully large international firms into compliance. One effect is that, as more and more of the online action moves to server farms run by transnational firms, the borders that matter are those of firms rather than of nations [918] (this is still probably an improvement, as new companies are easier to start than new countries).

Third, there are social defences. These range from 30,000 online police, through trials of cyber-dissidents and laws requiring cyber-cafés to identify customers, to a pair of Internet police cartoon mascots (Jingjing and Chacha) who pop up everywhere online to remind users that they're in social space rather than private space.

Yet the controls appear to be falling behind. There are more than 20 million blogs in China, and although the online police are vigorous at taking down openly seditious material, the online discussion of local news events has led to the emergence of a proper 'public opinion' that for the first time is not in thrall to media managers [985]. This is not just a function of email and blogs but also the rapid growth in mobile phone use. Local events such as land seizures by corrupt officials can now rapidly climb the news agenda, exposing the government to pressures from which it was previously insulated. It will be interesting to see how things go as China hosts the Olympics in 2008 and continues to develop beyond that.

A somewhat different example is Burma. There, a sudden increase in fuel prices in August 2007 led to mass protests and a violent crackdown by the army from September 26th that left perhaps several hundred people dead. During the protests and at the start of the crackdown, Burmese citizens used the Internet and mobile phone services to send photos, videos and other information to the outside world, with the result that their insurrection grabbed world headlines and the crackdown brought widespread condemnation on the ruling junta.

This happened despite the fact that Burma is one of only 30 countries in the world with less than 1% of its population online.

Other authoritarian states — such as Belarus, Uganda and the Yemen — had imposed Internet censorship around elections and other political events, and initially the Burmese junta concentrated on filtering political information arriving from overseas. But the world headlines clearly caused pain, and an Internet closedown started on September 29th, the third day of the crackdown. This was the first time wholesale Internet blocking was used to stop news getting out [986]. Service was resumed patchily after October 4; from the 4th to the 12th there was a curfew, with connectivity available only from 10pm until 4am; and in the third phase, some Internet cafés were allowed to reopen on October 11th, but speeds were limited to 256 kbit/sec; others were closed down and had equipment confiscated. It seems that most Burmese had been using censorship-circumvention tools such as proxies. In fact the uprising was called 'the g-lite revolution' after a popular Gmail proxy, `http://glite.sayni.net`.

If the lesson to learn from this sad incident is that even 1% Internet use can destabilise a dictatorship, and that even dictatorships have a hard time getting by without the Internet, then that's rather encouraging.

24.4.2   Network Neutrality

A number of less developed countries block voice-over-IP (VOIP) services to make phone tapping easier, and to keep the state phone company profitable. LDC phone companies often get much of their revenue from their share of the charges paid by foreigners to call that country, and VOIP lets expats escape these charges.

However, most of the problems experienced by VOIP operators are in the developed world, and particularly in America. A number of ISPs are also phone companies, and use technical mechanisms to disrupt VOIP services — such as introducing jitter or short outages into the packet stream. This affects not just wireline providers but also mobile firms. As a result, a fierce debate has erupted in Washington about *network neutrality*. On one side, the VOIP industry argues in favour of a law that would compel ISPs to treat all traffic equally; on the other, the phone companies retort 'Don't regulate the Internet'.

The issue is wider than just VOIP. Phone companies always charged widely different rates for different types of traffic: given that they have high fixed costs and low marginal costs, they have every incentive to price discriminate. Ed Whitacre, the AT&T chairman, kicked off the debate in 2005 when he argued that for companies like Google, Yahoo or Vonage to use 'his' broadband pipes for free to make money for themselves was 'nuts' [1340]. This has split Congress broadly on party lines, with Democrats favouring net neutrality and Republicans favoring the phone companies.

In Europe, net neutrality is less of an issue, as we have more competition in the ISP market. Regulators tend to take the view that if some ISPs indulge in traffic shaping (as it's politely called), then that doesn't matter so long as customers can switch to other ISPs that don't. There are some residual issues to do with mobile operators, as international calls from mobiles are expensive, but regulators are trying to tackle high charges directly rather than worrying about whether people can use Skype over GPRS.

24.4.3 Peer-to-Peer, Hate Speech and Child Porn

The three horses being flogged by the advocates of Internet censorship in the developed countries are file sharing, hate speech and child pornography.

File-sharing systems raise some of the net neutrality issues; for example, Comcast has been disrupting BitTorrent, using the same forged-reset packet techniques observed in the Great Firewall of China [409]. In Comcast's case, being a cable operator, they want their customers to watch TV on their cable channel, rather than as downloads, to maximise their ad revenue. Other ISPs have different incentives; many people sign up to broadband service specifically so they can download stuff. Whether this makes a profit for the ISP or not will depend on how much traffic new customers generate and whether the backhaul costs more than their subscriptions. In general, ISPs make money from P2P, though often they have to restrict bandwidth use.

The main players arguing for filtering of peer-to-peer traffic are the music companies. Many universities have been bullied by the threat of litigation into restricting such traffic on student LANs; others have cut it simply to save on bandwidth charges. And despite all the economic evidence I discussed in Chapter 22, about the modest effect that file-sharing has on music sales, the music industry believes its interests would be served by imposing this censorship more widely. ISPs resist cenorship citing the high costs of filtering. It's therefore going to be interesting to see whether countries introduce mandatory filtering for 'moral' purposes, which the music industry can then have used for its purposes too.

There was a recent attempt in Europe to introduce a duty on ISPs to filter hate speech, and specifically jihadist websites. Europe has a history of such restrictions: France and Germany both prohibit the sale of Nazi memorabilia. (I recall one German justice minister telling a policy conference that her greatest achievement in office was to stop Amazon selling 'Mein Kampf' in Germany, and her greatest ambition was to stop them selling it in Arizona too.) I'm very sceptical about whether such a law would make Europe any safer; banning the writings of the militant Deobandi Muslim sect, to which perhaps a third of Britain's Muslims belong, is likely to aggravate community tensions more than anything else. Furthermore, research shows that most of the hate literature distributed inside and outside Britain's mosques is produced or funded by religious institutions from Saudi Arabia [857]. The response of our government is not to stand up to King Abdullah, but to invite him for a state visit. Internet censorship here (as elsewhere) appears to be a displacement activity; it lets the government claim it's doing something. It's also likely to encourage all the third-world despots and Asian strongmen who denounce the freedom of speech on the Internet. Better, I'd think, to leave this material in the open, as America does, and let the police monitor the traffic to the worst of the sites, rather than driving Muslim youth to acquire the skills of the Chinese and Burmese at using proxies. In the end, the policy advice to the European Commission was along these lines: they should train the police to use the existing laws better [442]. And while they're at it, let law enforcement be technology-neutral: the cops should also monitor the young men who sell the hate tracts in the mosques (and if they ever pluck up the courage to prosecute them for breaking the existing laws on incitement to murder, so much the better).

The third horseman is child pornography. During the 1990s, as governments were looking for some handle on the Internet, a view arose that explicit images of child sex abuse were about the one thing that all states could agree should be banned. When arguing in favour of the latest repressive measure — such as key escrow — governments trotted out people from children's charities who would argue passionately that the Stalinism du jour was vital to save children from harm [272]. Needless to say, those of us on the liberal side of the argument would have preferred the charities to spend their money campaigning about more serious and potentially fixable child-protection problems, such as the abuse of children in local authority care homes, and under-age prostitution; and when a really serious problem arose at the boundary between IT policy and child protection — a proposal to construct a national child-welfare database that will expose the personal information of millions of children to hundreds of thousands of public-sector workers [66] — these worthy child-protectors remained silent.

The child-porn debate has subsided in most countries[4], as terrorism has taken the place of kiddieporn as the executive's ace of trumps –the argument that no-one's supposed to gainsay. But the hysteria did have some evil effects. They were severe in the UK where it was used to justify not only more pervasive online surveillance, but also a National High-Tech Crime Unit. This unit ran Operation Ore, in which some eight thousand UK citizens got raided by the police on suspicion of purchasing child pornography. It turned out that most of them were probably victims of card fraud. The porn squad didn't understand card fraud, and didn't want to know; they were fixated on getting porn convictions, and didn't ask their experts to even consider the possibility

---

[4]Russia's a notable exception; Putin uses kiddieporn as the leading excuse for censorship directed at political opponents, while his police take little action against the many pornographers and other online criminals in that country.

of fraud. Several thousand men had their lives disrupted for months or even years following wrongful arrest for highly stigmatised offences of which they were innocent, and at the time of writing (2007) there's a steady stream of acquittals, of civil lawsuits for compensation against police forces, and calls for public inquiries. The sad story of police bungling and cover-up is told by Duncan Campbell in [260, 261]. For some, the revelation that the police had screwed up came too late; over thirty men, faced with the prospect of a public prosecution that would probably destroy their families, killed themselves. At least one, Commodore David White, commander of British forces in Gibraltar, appears to have been innocent [594].

The cause of all this was that operators of illegal porn sites bought up lists of credit card numbers and then booked them through the portals that they used to collect payment — presumably in the belief that many people would not dare to report debits for such services to the police. And although the police justified their operations by claiming they would reduce harm to children, the child-porn purveyors in the Ore case escaped prosecution. (The operator of the main portal, Thomas Reedy, did get convicted and sentenced to over 1000 years in a Texas jail, but he was just the fall guy who collected the credit card payments. The gangsters in Indonesia and Brazil who organised and photographed the child abuse do not seem to have been seriously pursued.)

America actually handled this case much better than Britain. Some 300,000 U.S. credit card numbers were found on Reedy's servers; the police used the names for intelligence rather than evidence, matching the names against their databases, identifying suspects of concern — such as people working with children — and quietly investigating them. Over a hundred convictions for actual child abuse followed, and no wrongful convictions of which I'm aware. As with jihadist websites, a pragmatic emphasis on good old-fashioned policing is much preferable to fearmongering and grand political gestures.

24.5   Forensics and Rules of Evidence

This leads us naturally to the last main topic in the justice space, namely how information can be recovered from computers, mobile phones and other electronic devices for use in evidence. The three big changes in recent years have been, first, the sheer volumes of data; second, the growth of search engines and other tools to find relevant material; and third, that courts are becoming gradually more relaxed and competent.

24.5.1   Forensics

When the police raid even a small-time drug dealer nowadays, they can get well over a Terabyte of data: several laptops, half-a-dozen mobile phones, a couple of iPods and perhaps a box of memory sticks. The suspect may also have dozens of accounts online for webmail services, social-networking sites and other services. He may have interesting gadgets — such as navigators that hold his location history (much of which is also available, with less resolution, via his mobile phone records). Security researchers have found all sorts of clever ways of extracting information from the data — for example, you can identify which camera took a picture from the pattern noise of the CCD array [818], and the number of such tricks can only increase.

The use of all this material in evidence depends, in most countries, on following certain procedures. Material has to be lawfully collected, whether with a search warrant or equivalent powers; and the forensic officer has to maintain a *chain of custody*, which means being able to satisfy a court that evidence wasn't tampered with afterwards. The details can vary from one jurisdiction to another, and I'll describe them in the next section.

The basic procedure is to use tools that have been appropriately tested and evaluated to make trustworthy copies of data, which may mean computing a one-way hash of the data so as to establish its authenticity later; to document everything that's done; and to have means of dealing appropriately with any private material that's found (such as privileged attorney-client emails, or the trade secrets of the suspect's employer). The details can be found in standard forensics textbooks such as Sammes and Jenkinson [1105], and much of the technical complexity comes from the proliferation of mobile phones, organisers, iPods and other storage devices, which the practitioner should be able to deal with. Indeed, as time goes on, specialist firms are springing up that deal with phones and other less common types of kit.

Computer forensics pose increasingly complex engineering problems. A recent example is that many police forces adopted a rigid procedure of always turning PCs off, so that hard disks could be mirrored and multiple copies made for prosecution and defence lawyers. The Rockphish gang exploited this by making their phishing software memory-resident. The police would arrive at a house containing a phishing server, inform the startled householder that his PC was being used for wicked purposes, switch the machine off — and lose all the information that would have let them trace the real server for which the seized machine had been acting as a proxy.

A related problem is that Windows Vista ships with Bitlocker, a disc encryption utility that stores keys in the TPM chip on the motherboard, and thus makes files unusable after the machine's switched off unless you know the password. While the UK now has a law enabling courts to jail people for failing to supply a password, most countries don't; so thoughtful police forces now operate a rule whereby a decision on whether to switch the machine off is at the officer's discretion. It's a judgment call whether to risk losing data by turning the machine off, or to image it when it's running and risk the defence lawyers arguing that it was tampered with. Truth to tell, however, the forensic folks are still not discovering any great technical sophistication among normal criminals.

Another issue is that it may be important to minimise the disruption caused by forensic copying, especially where the machine belongs to someone other than an arrested suspect. Even where a machine is confiscated from a suspect, it can be problematic if you take too long to examine it. For example, in the Operation Ore cases I mentioned in the last section, many people who later turned out to be innocent had their PCs taken away and stored for months or even years because the police didn't have the forensic capacity to cope. As a result they remained under a cloud of suspicion for much longer than was reasonable; this had an adverse effect on people in regulated professions, leading to litigation against the police.

There's also the issue of loss of access to data, which for an individual or small business can be catastrophic. I reckon it's prudent practice nowadays for a student to have seizure-proof offsite backup, for example by getting a Gmail account and emailing copies of your thesis there regularly as you write it. Otherwise your house might be raided and both your PC and backups removed to the police forensic lab for months or even years. And it needn't be your fault; perhaps the guy on the second floor is smoking dope, or running a supernode in a music file-sharing system. You can just never tell.

Another forensic pitfall is relying on evidence extracted from the systems of one party to a dispute, without applying enough scepticism about claims made for its dependability. Recall the Munden case I described in section 10.4.3. A man was falsely accused and wrongly convicted of attempted fraud after he complained of unauthorized withdrawals from his bank account. On appeal, his defence team got an order from the court that the bank open its systems to the defence expert as it had done to the prosecution. The bank refused, the bank statements were ruled inadmissible and the case collapsed. So it's worthwhile when relying on forensic evidence supplied by a disputant to think in advance about whether it will have to withstand examination by hostile experts.

In general, when designing a system you should stop and think about the forensic aspects. You may want it not to provide evidence; an example is the policy adopted by Microsoft after their antitrust battles with the U.S. government, at which embarrassing emails came out. The firm reacted with a policy that all emails should be discarded after a fixed period of time unless someone took positive action to save them. In other circumstances you may want your system to provide evidence. Then there's not just the matter of whether the relevant data are preserved, and for how long (if your local statute of limitations for civil claims is seven years, you'll probably want to keep business data for at least this long), but also how the data are to be extracted. In many jurisdictions, court rules admit evidence only if it passes certain tests, for example that it was generated in the normal course of business operations. So we need to look at such requirements next.

24.5.2   Admissibility of Evidence

When courts were first confronted with computer evidence in the 1960s there were many concerns about its reliability. There was not just the engineering issue of whether the data were accurate, but the legal issue of whether computer-generated data were inadmissible on the grounds that they were hearsay. Different legislatures tackled this differently. In the U.S. most of the law is found in the Federal Rules of Evidence where computer records are usually introduced as business records. We find at 803(6):

> *Records of regularly conducted activity. A memorandum, report, record, or data compilation, in any form, of acts, events, conditions, opinions, or diagnoses, made at or near the time by, or from information transmitted by, a person with knowledge, if kept in the course of a regularly conducted business activity, and if it was the regular practice of that business activity to make the memorandum, report, record, or data compilation, all as shown by the testimony of the custodian or other qualified witness, unless the source of information or the method or circumstances of preparation indicate lack of trustworthiness. The term 'business' as used in this paragraph includes business, institution, association, profession, occupation, and calling of every kind, whether or not conducted for profit.*

The UK is similar: the Civil Evidence Act 1995 covers civil litigation while the Police and Criminal Evidence Act 1984 deals with criminal matters[5]. The requirement that the machine be operated in the normal course of business can cause problems when machines have to be operated in abnormal ways to extract information. In one case in my own experience, a woman was accused of stealing a debit card from the mail and the police wished to ascertain whether a torn-off corner of a PIN mailer found in her purse would activate the stolen card. So they got the branch manager to put the card into a statement printer in the branch, entered the PIN, and the card was confiscated. The manager testified that the way the card was confiscated showed that it was because the account had been closed rather than because the PIN was wrong. However, the court ruled this evidence to be inadmissible. The rules of electronic evidence in the common-law countries (England, the USA, Canada, Australia, South Africa and Singapore) are analysed in detail by Stephen Mason [838]; for a summary of relevant U.S. cases, read Orin Kerr [714].

There are some special legal provisions for particular technologies, many of them enacted during or shortly after the dotcom boom as legislators sought to smooth the path for e-commerce without really understanding the problems.

---

[5]The latter used to require a certificate from the machine operator to the effect that the equipment was working normally, but this was dropped as it caused problems with evidence from hacked machines.

Many industry lobbyists claimed that e-commerce was held up by uncertainty about whether electronic documents would be accepted as 'writing' for those laws that required certain transactions to be written (typical examples are real-estate transfers and patent licenses). Legislatures, starting with Utah's, therefore introduced laws granting special status to digital signatures. In most cases these had no effect, as courts took the sensible view that an email is writing just as a letter is: the essence of a signature is the signer's intent, and courts had long decided cases this way. For example, a farm worker who was crushed to death by a tractor and had managed to scrawl 'all to mum' on the tyre was held to have made a legal will [1358, 1359]. For surveys of digital signature laws, see [109, 524].

However there's one case in which eager legislators got it completely wrong, and that's Europe. The Electronic Signature Directive, which came into force in 2000, compels all Member States to give special force to an *advanced electronic signature*, which basically means a digital signature generated with a smartcard. Europe's smartcard industry thought this would earn them lots of money. However, it had the opposite effect. At present, the risk that a paper check will be forged is borne by the relying party: if someone forges a check on my account, then it's not my signature, and I have not given the bank my mandate to debit my account; so if they negligently rely on a forged signature and do so, that's their lookout[6]. However, if I were foolish enough to ever accept an advanced electronic signature device, then there would be a presumption of the validity of any signature that appeared to have been made with it. All of a sudden, the risk shifts from the bank to me. I become liable to anyone in the world for any signature that appears to have been made by this infernal device, regardless of whether or not I actually made it! This, coupled with the facts that smartcards don't have a trusted user interface and that the PCs which most people would use to provide this interface are easily and frequently subverted, made electronic signatures instantly unattractive.

Finally, a word on click-wrap. In 2000, the U.S. Congress enacted the Electronic Signatures in Global and National Commerce ('ESIGN') Act, which gives legal force to any 'sound, symbol, or process' by which a consumer assents to something. So pressing a telephone keypad ('press 0 to agree or 9 to terminate this transaction'), clicking a hyper-link to enter a web site, or clicking 'continue' on a software installer, the consumer consents to be bound to a contract [457]. This makes click-wrap licenses work in America. The general view of lawyers in Europe is that they probably don't work here, but no-one's eager to bring the first case.

---

[6]Some countries, like Switzerland, let their banks shift the fraud risk to the account holder using their terms and conditions, but Britain always prohibited this, first by common law and then by the Bills of Exchange Act 1886.

24.6   Privacy and Data Protection

Data protection is a term used in Europe to mean the protection of personal information from inappropriate use. Personal information generally means any data kept on an identifiable human being, or *data subject*, such as bank account details and credit card purchasing patterns. It corresponds roughly to the U.S. term *computer privacy*. The difference in terminology is accompanied by a huge difference in law and in attitudes. This is likely to remain a problem for global business, and may get worse.

European law gives data subjects the right to inspect personal data held on them, have them changed if inaccurate, understand how they're processed, and in many cases prevent them being passed on to other organizations without their consent. There are exemptions for national security, but they are not as complete as the spooks would like: there was a big row when it turned out that data from SWIFT, which processes interbank payments, were being copied to the Department of Homeland Security without the knowledge of data subjects. European privacy authorities ruled that SWIFT had broken European, Belgian and Swiss privacy law, and it agreed to stop processing European data in the USA by the end of 2009 [995, 996].

Almost all commercial data are covered, and there are particularly stringent controls on data relating to intimate matters such as health, religion, race, sexual life and political affiliations. Finally, recent law prescribes that personal data may not be sent to organizations in countries whose laws do not provide comparable protection. In practice that means America and India, where legal protections on privacy are fragmentary. The resolution so far is the *safe harbour agreement* whereby a data processor in America or India promises to their European customer to abide by European law. Many firms do this, pioneered by Citibank which set up such an arrangement to process German cardholder data in South Dakota. But this creates practical enforcement problems for EU citizens who feel that their rights have been violated; they aren't privy to the contract, and may have a hard time persuading the U.S. Department of Commerce to take action against a U.S. firm that is quite possibly obeying local laws perfectly well. So the safe harbour provisions may well fail when tested in court. For a discussion, see [1339]. We'll have to wait until test cases find their way to the European Court.

If safe harbour fails, the cynical fix may be to put the servers in a European country with very lax enforcement, such as Britain, but even so there are problems: the UK is currently in dispute with the European Commission, which claims that British law falls short of European requirements on eleven separate points [406]. Another is to insist that customers agree to their personal data being shared before you do business with them. This works to some extent at present (it's how U.S. medical insurers get away with their abuses), but it doesn't work for data protection as coercive consent is specifically disallowed [66].

European privacy law didn't spring full-formed from the brow of Zeus though, and it may be helpful to look at its origins.

24.6.1 European Data Protection

Technofear isn't a late twentieth century invention. As early as 1890, Justices Warren and Brandeis warned of the threat to privacy posed by 'recent inventions and business methods' — specifically photography and investigative journalism [1321]. Years later, after large retail businesses started using computers in the 1950s and banks followed in the early 1960s, people started to worry about the social implications if all a citizen's transactions could be collected, consolidated and analyzed. In Europe, big business escaped censure by making the case that only government could afford enough computers to be a serious privacy threat. Once people realised it was both economic and rational for government to extend its grasp by using the personal data of all citizens as a basis for prognosis, this became a human rights issue — given the recent memory of the Gestapo in most European countries.

A patchwork of data protection laws started to appear starting with the German state of Hesse in 1969. Because of the rate at which technology changes, the successful laws have been technology neutral. Their common theme was a regulator (whether at national or state level) to whom users of personal data had to report and who could instruct them to cease and desist from inappropriate processing. The practical effect was usually that the general law became expressed through a plethora of domain-specific codes of practice.

Over time, processing by multinational businesses became an issue too, and people realised that purely local or national initiatives were likely to be ineffective against them. Following a voluntary code of conduct promulgated by the OECD in 1980 [991], data protection was entrenched by a Council of Europe convention in January 1981, which entered into force in October 1985 [327]. Although strictly speaking this convention was voluntary, many states signed up to it for fear of losing access to data processing markets. It required signatory states to pass domestic legislation to implement at least certain minimum safeguards. Data had to be obtained lawfully and processed fairly, and states had to ensure that legal remedies were available when breaches occurred.

The quality of implementation varied widely. In the UK, for example, Margaret Thatcher unashamedly did the least possible to comply with European law; a data protection body was established but starved of funds and technical expertise, and many exemptions were provided for favored constituencies[7]. In hard-line privacy countries, such as Germany, the data protection bodies became serious law-enforcement agencies. Many other countries, such as Australia, Canada, New Zealand and Switzerland passed comparable privacy laws in the 1980s and early 1990s: some, like Switzerland, went for the German model while others, like Iceland, followed the British one.

By the early 1990s it was clear that the difference between national laws was creating barriers to trade. Many businesses avoided controls altogether by moving their data processing to the USA. So data protection was finally elevated to the status of full-blown European law in 1995 with a Data Protection Directive [444]. This sets higher minimum standards than most countries had required before, with particularly stringent controls on highly sensitive data such as health, religion, race and political affiliation. It also prevents personal information being shipped to 'data havens' such as the USA unless there are comparable controls enforced by contract.

24.6.2   Differences between Europe and the USA

The history in the USA is surveyed in [933]; basically business managed to persuade government to leave privacy largely to 'self-regulation'. Although there is a patchwork of state and federal laws, they are application-specific and highly fragmented. In general, privacy in federal government records and in communications is fairly heavily regulated, while business data are largely uncontrolled. There are a few islands of regulation, such as the Fair Credit Reporting Act of 1970, which governs disclosure of credit information and is broadly similar to European rules; the Video Privacy Protection Act or 'Bork Bill', enacted after a Washington newspaper published Judge Robert Bork's video rental history following his nomination to the U.S. Supreme Court; the Drivers' Privacy Protection Act, enacted to protect privacy of DMV records after the actress Rebecca Schaeffer was murdered by an obsessed fan who hired a private eye to find her address; and the Health Insurance Portability and Accountability Act which protects medical records and which I discussed in Chapter 9. However U.S. privacy law also includes several torts that provide a basis for civil action, and they cover a surprising number of circumstances; for a survey, see Daniel Solove [1200]. There was also a landmark case in 2006, when Choicepoint paid $10 m to settle a lawsuit brought by the FTC after it failed to vet subscribers properly and let crooks buy the personal information of over 160,000 Americans, leading to at least 800 cases of 'identity theft' [459].

---

[7]In one case where you'd expect there to be an exemption, there wasn't; journalists who kept notes on their laptops or PCs which identified people were formally liable to give copies of this information to the data subjects on demand.

That may have started to put privacy on CEOs' radar. Yet, overall, privacy regulation in the USA is slack compared with Europe.

Attitudes also differ. Some researchers report a growing feeling in the USA that people have lost control of the uses to which their personal information is put, while in some European countries privacy is seen as a fundamental human right that requires vigorous legislative support; in Germany, it's entrenched in the constitution [1339]. But it must be said that there's a persistent problem here. As I discussed in section 7.5.4, people say that they value privacy, yet act otherwise. The great majority of people, whether in the USA or Europe, will trade their privacy for very small advantages. Privacy-enhancing technologies have been offered for sale, yet most have failed in the marketplace.

There's simply no telling how the gulf between the USA and Europe on privacy laws will evolve over time. In recent years, Europe has been getting less coherent: the UK in particular has been drifting towards the U.S. model, with ever more relaxed enforcement; and the new Member States that used to be part of the Soviet Union or Yugoslavia are not rocking the boat. Commerce is certainly pulling in the U.S. direction. As I discussed in section 7.5.4, technology simultaneously creates the incentive for greater price discrimination and the means to do it by collecting ever more personal data. Yet in other countries, courts have become more protective of citizens' rights post-9/11. In Germany, which generally takes the hardest line, privacy trumps even the 'war on terror': the highest court found unconstitutional a 2001 police action to create a file on over 30,000 male students or former students aged 18 to 40 from Muslim-majority countries — even though no-one was arrested as a result. It decided that such exercises could be performed only in response to concrete threats, not as a precautionary measure [244].

The flip side of the privacy-law coin is freedom-of-information law. A radical version of this is proposed by David Brin [227]. He reasons that the falling costs of data acquisition, transmission and storage will make pervasive surveillance technologies available to the authorities, so the only real question is whether they are available to the rest of us too. He paints a choice between two futures — one in which the citizens live in fear of an East German–style police force and one in which officials are held to account by public scrutiny. The cameras will exist: will they be surveillance cams or webcams? He argues that essentially all information should be open — including, for example, all our bank accounts. Weaker versions of this have been tried: tax returns are published in Iceland and in some Swiss cantons, and the practice cuts evasion, as rich men fear the loss of social status that an artificially low declared income would bring. Still weaker versions, such as the U.S. and U.K. Freedom of Information Acts, still give some useful benefit in ensuring that the flow of information between the citizen and the state isn't all one-way. As technology continues to develop, the privacy and freedom-of-information boundaries will no doubt involve a lot of pushing and shoving.

There are some interesting engineering questions. For example, while U.S. felony convictions remain on the record for ever, many European countries have offender-rehabilitation laws, under which most convictions disappear after a period of time that depends on the severity of the offence. But how can such laws be enforced now that web search engines exist? The German response is that if you want to cite a criminal case, you're supposed to get an officially de-identified transcript from the court. In Italy, a convicted business person got a court to order the removal from a government website of a record of his conviction, after the conviction had expired. But if electronic newspaper archives are searchable online, what good will this do — unless the identities of all offenders are blocked from electronic reporting? There has recently, for example, been much debate over the monitoring of former child sex offenders, with laws in some states requiring that registers of offenders be publicly available, and riots in the UK following the naming of some former offenders by a Sunday newspaper. How can you rehabilitate offenders in a world with Google? For example, do you tag the names of offenders in newspaper accounts of trials with an expiration date, and pass laws compelling search and archive services to respect them?

The upshot is that even if data is public, its use can still cause offences under European privacy law. This causes peculiar difficulties in the USA, where courts have consistently interpreted the First Amendment to mean that you can't stop the repetition of true statements in peacetime except in a small number of cases[8]. So it's hardly surprising that the current flashpoint between Europe and America over privacy concerns Google. The immediate casus belli is that EU law requires personal data to be deleted once it's no longer needed, while Google built its systems to keep data such as clickstreams indefinitely. During 2007, the European data-protection folks brought this to Google's attention; the search engine has offered to de-identify clickstreams after 18 months. Given the difficulty of doing inference control properly — as I discussed in Chapter 9 — this claim will no doubt be examined closely by the European authorities. No doubt this saga will run and run. Even in America, there's been a call from CDT and EFF for a 'Do Not Track' list, similar to the Do Not Call list, so that people could opt out; other activists disagree, saying this would undermine the paid-by-ads model of useful web services [1333]. In any case, less than a percent of people bother to use ad-blocking software. We'll have to wait and see.

24.7 Summary

Governments and public policy are entangled more and more with the work of the security engineer. The 'crypto wars' were a harbinger of this, as were the

---

[8]The classic example is a regulated profession such as securities trading.

struggles over copyright, DRM and Trusted Computing. Current problems also include surveillance, privacy, the admissibility and quality of evidence, and the strains between U.S. and European ways of dealing with these problems. In less developed countries, censorship is a big issue, although from the data we have to date the Internet still works as a definite force for good there.

Perhaps the biggest set of issues, though, hinge on the climate of fear whipped up since the 9/11 attacks. This has led to the growth of a security-industrial complex which makes billions selling counterproductive measures that erode our liberty, our quality of life and even our security. Understanding and pushing back on this folly is the highest priority for security engineers who have the ability to get involved in public life — whether directly, or via our writing and teaching. And research also helps. Individual academics can't hope to compete with national leaders in the mass media, but the slow, careful accumulation of knowledge over the years can and will undermine their excuses. I don't mean just knowledge about why extreme airport screening measures are a waste of money; we also must disseminate knowledge about the economics and psychology that underlie maladaptive government behaviour. The more people understand 'what's going on', the sooner it will stop.

Research Problems

Technopolicy involves a complex interplay between science, engineering, psychology, law and economics. There is altogether too little serious cross-disciplinary research, and initiatives which speed up this process are almost certainly a good thing. Bringing in psychologists, anthropologists and historians would also be positive. Since 2002 I've helped to build up the security-economics research community; we now have to broaden this.

Further Reading

It's extraordinarily easy for technopolicy arguments to get detached at one or more corners from reality, and many of the nightmares conjured up to get attention and money (such as 'credit card transactions being intercepted on the Internet') are really the modern equivalent of the monsters that appeared on medieval maps to cover up the cartographer's ignorance. An engineer who wants to build things that work and last has a duty not to get carried away. For this reason, it's particularly important to dig out primary sources — material written by experienced insiders such as R.V. Jones [671] and Gerard Walsh [1311].

There's a good book on the history of wiretapping and crypto policy by Whit Diffie and Susan Landau, who had a long involvement in the policy process [387], an NRC study on cryptography policy was also influential [950]; and there's a compilation of primary materials at [1135]. There's also useful stuff at the web sites of organizations such as EPIC [432], EFF [422], FIPR [484], CDT [278], the Privacy Exchange [1048] and on mailing lists such as politech [1031] and ukcrypto [1267].

There are many resources on online censorship, starting perhaps with the OpenNet Initiative; and Reporters without Borders publish a 'Handbook for bloggers and cyber-dissidents' that not only contains guides on how to circumvent censorship, but a number of case histories of how blogging has helped open up the media in less liberal countries [1069].

The standard work on computer forensics is by Tony Sammes and Brian Jenkinson [1105], and there's a nice article by Peter Sommer on the forensics and evidential issues that arose when prosecuting some UK youngsters who hacked the USAF Rome airbase [1202]. The Department of Justice's 'Guidelines for Searching and Seizing Computers' also bear some attention [381]. For collections of computer crime case histories, see Peter Neumann [962], Dorothy Denning [370] and Donn Parker [1005]. The standard work on computer evidence in the common law countries is by Stephen Mason [838].

On the topic of data protection, there is a huge literature but no concise guide that I know of. [1339] provides a good historical overview, with a perspective on the coming collision between Europe and the USA. Simson Garfinkel [515] and Michael Froomkin [504] survey privacy and surveillance issues with special relevance to the USA.

CHAPTER 25

Managing the Development of Secure Systems

My own experience is that developers with a clean, expressive set of specific security requirements can build a very tight machine. They don't have to be security gurus, but they have to understand what they're trying to build and how it should work.

— **Rick Smith**

One of the most important problems we face today, as techniques and systems become more and more pervasive, is the risk of missing that fine, human point that may well make the difference between success and failure, fair and unfair, right and wrong . . . no IBM computer has an education in the humanities.

— **Tom Watson**

Management is that for which there is no algorithm. Where there is an algorithm, it's administration.

— **Roger Needham**

25.1 Introduction

So far we've discussed a great variety of security applications, techniques and concerns. If you're a working IT manager or consultant, paid to build a secure system, you will by now be looking for a systematic way to select protection aims and mechanisms. This brings us to the topics of system engineering, risk analysis and, finally, the secret sauce: how you manage a team to write secure code.

Business schools reckon that management training should be conducted largely through case histories, stiffened with focussed courses on basic topics such as law, economics and accounting. I have broadly followed their model in this book. We went over the fundamentals, such as protocols, access control and crypto, and then looked at a lot of different applications with a lot of case histories.

Now we have to pull the threads together and discuss how to go about solving a general security engineering problem. Organizational issues matter here as well as technical ones. It's important to understand the capabilities of the staff who'll operate your control systems, such as guards and auditors, to take account of the managerial and work-group pressures on them, and get feedback from them as the system evolves. You also have to instil suitable ways of thinking and working into your development team. Success is about attitudes and work practices as well as skills. There are tensions: how do you get people to think like criminals, yet work enthusiastically for the good of the product?

25.2   Managing a Security Project

The hardest part of the project manager's job is usually figuring out what to protect and how. Threat modelling and requirements engineering are what separate out the star teams from the also-rans.

The first killer problem is understanding the tradeoff between risk and reward. Security people naturally focus too much on the former and neglect the latter. If the client has a turnover of $10 m, profits of $1 m and theft losses of $150,000, the security consultant may make a loss-reduction pitch about 'how to increase your profits by 15%'; but it could well be in the shareholders' interests to double the turnover to $20 m, even if this triples the losses to $450,000. Assuming the margins stay the same, the profit is now $1.85 m, up 85%.

So if you're the owner of the company, don't fall into the trap of believing that the only possible response to a vulnerability is to fix it, and distrust the sort of consultant who can only talk about 'tightening security'. Often it's too tight already, and what you really need to do is just focus it slightly differently. But the security team — whether internal developers or external consultants — usually has an incentive to play up the threats, and as it has more expertise on the subject it's hard to gainsay. The same mechanisms that drive national overreaction to terrorist incidents are at work in the corporation too.

25.2.1   A Tale of Three Supermarkets

My thumbnail case history to illustrate this point concerns three supermarkets. Among the large operational costs of running a retail chain are the salaries of the checkout and security staff, and the stock shrinkage due to theft. Checkout queues aggravate your customers, so cutting staff isn't always an option, and working them harder might mean more shrinkage. So what might technology do to help?

One supermarket in South Africa decided to automate completely. All produce would carry an RFID tag, so that an entire trolley-load could be scanned automatically. If this had worked, it could have killed both birds with one stone; the same RFID tags could have cut staff numbers and made theft harder. There was a pilot, but the idea couldn't compete with barcodes. Customers had to use a special trolley, which was large and ugly — and the RF tags also cost money. There has been a lot of investment in RFID, but there's still a problem: tags fixed to goods that conduct electricity, such as canned drinks, are hard to read reliably.

Another supermarket in a European country believed that much of their losses were due to a hard core of professional thieves, and wanted to use RFID to cut this. When they eventually realized this wouldn't work, they then talked of building a face-recognition system to alert the guards whenever a known villain came into a store. But current technology can't do that with low enough error rates. In the end, the chosen route was civil recovery. When a shoplifter is caught, then even after the local magistrates have fined her a few bucks, the supermarket sues her in the civil courts for wasted time, lost earnings, attorneys' fees and everything else they can think of; and then armed with a judgement for a few thousand bucks they go round to her house and seize all the furniture. So far so good. But their management spent their time and energy getting vengeance on petty thieves rather than increasing sales. Soon they started losing market share and saw their stock price slide. Diverting effort from marketing to security was probably a symptom of their decline rather than a cause, but may have contributed to it.

The supermarket that seemed to be doing best when I wrote the first edition in 2001 was Waitrose in England, which had just introduced self-service scanning. When you go into their store you swipe your store card in a machine that dispenses a portable barcode scanner. You scan the goods as you pick them off the shelves and drop them into your shopping bag. At the exit you check in the scanner, get a printed list of everything you've bought, swipe your credit card and head for the car park. This might seem rather risky — but then so did the self-service supermarket back in the days when traditional grocers' shops had all the goods behind the counter. In fact, there are several subtle control mechanisms at work. Limiting the service to store card holders not only lets you exclude known shoplifters, but also helps market the store card. By having one you acquire a trusted status visible to any neighbors you meet while shopping — so losing your card (whether by getting caught stealing, or more likely falling behind on your payments) could be embarrassing. And trusting people removes much of the motive for cheating as there's no kudos in beating the system. Of course, should the guard at the video screen see someone lingering suspiciously near the racks of hundred-dollar wines, it can always be arranged for the system to 'break' as the suspect gets to the checkout, which gives the staff a non-confrontational way to recheck the bag's contents.

Since then, the other supermarkets in the UK have adopted self-service, but the quality of the implementation varies hugely. The most defensive stores — where the security folks have had too much say in the design — force you to scan at specially-designed self-service checkout lanes, and weigh each item as you place it on the packing stand after scanning, in an attempt to detect anyone packing an item without scanning it first. These systems are flaky and frequently interrupt the shopper with complaints, which communicate distrust. Waitrose seems to be going from strength to strength, while the most defensive store (with the most offensive systems) is facing a takeover bid as I write.

25.2.2   Risk Management

Security policies tend to come from a company's risk management mechanisms. Risk management is one of the world's largest industries: it includes not just security engineers but also fire and casualty services, insurers, the road safety industry and much of the legal profession. Yet it is startling how little is really known about the subject. Engineers, economists, actuaries and lawyers all come at the problem from different directions, use different language and arrive at quite incompatible conclusions. There are also strong cultural factors at work. For example, if we distinguish risk as being where the odds are known but the outcome isn't, from uncertainty where even the odds are unknown, then most people are more uncertainty-averse than risk-averse. Where the odds are directly perceptible, a risk is often dealt with intuitively; but even there, our reactions are colored by the various cognitive biases discussed in Chapter 2. Where the science is unknown or inconclusive, people are free to project all sorts of fears and prejudices. But risk management is not just a matter of actuarial science colored by psychology. Organisations matter too, whether governments or businesses.

The purpose of business is profit, and profit is the reward for risk. Security mechanisms can often make a real difference to the risk/reward equation but ultimately it's the duty of a company's board of directors to get the balance right. In this *risk management* task, they may draw on all sorts of advice — lawyers, actuaries, security engineers — as well as listening to their marketing, operations and financial teams. A sound corporate risk management strategy involves much more than attacks on information systems; there are non-IT operational risks such as fires and floods as well as legal risks, exchange rate risks, political risks, and many more. Company bosses need the big picture view to take sensible decisions, and a difficult part of their task is to ensure that advisers from different disciplines work together closely enough, but without succumbing to groupthink.

In the culture that's grown up since Enron and Sarbanes-Oxley, risk management is supposed to drive internal control. The theory and practice of this are somewhat divergent. In theory, internal controls are about mitigating and managing the tensions between employees' duty to maximise shareholder utility, and their natural tendency to maximise their own personal utility instead. At the criminal end of things this encompasses theft and fraud from the company; I discussed in Chapter 10 how to control that. However, internal controls are also about softer conflicts of interest. Managers build empires; researchers tackle interesting problems rather than profitable ones; programmers choose tools and platforms that will look good on their CVs, rather than those best suited to the company's tasks. A large body of organizational theory applies microeconomic analysis to behaviour in firms in an attempt to get a handle on this. One of its effects is the growing use of stock options and bonus schemes to try to align employees' interests with shareholders'.

The practice of risk management has been largely determined by the rules evolved by the Big Four audit firms in response to Sarbanes-Oxley. A typical firm will show that it's discharging its responsibilities by keeping a risk register that identifies the main risks to its financial performance and ranks them in some kind of order. Risks then get 'owners', senior managers who are responsible for monitoring them and deciding on any specific countermeasures. Thus the finance director might be allocated exchange-rate and interest-rate risks, some of which he'll hedge; operational risks like fires and floods will be managed by insurance; and the IT director might end up with the system risks. The actual controls tend to evolve over time, and I'll discuss the process in more detail in section 25.4.1.2 later.

25.2.3 Organizational Issues

It goes without saying that advisers should understand each others' roles and work together rather than trying to undermine each other. But, human nature being what it is, the advisers may cosy up with each other and entrench a consensus view that steadily drifts away from reality. So the CEO, or other responsible manager, has to ask hard questions and stir the cauldron a bit. It's also important to have a variety of experts, and to constantly bring in new people. One of the most important changes post-Enron is the expectation that companies should change their auditors from time to time; and one of the most valuable tasks the security engineer gets called on to perform is when you're brought in, as an independent outsider, to challenge groupthink. On perhaps a third of the consulting assignments I've done, there's at least one person at the client company who knows exactly what the problem is and how to fix it — they just need a credible mercenary to beat up on the majority of their colleagues who've got stuck in a rut. (This is one reason why famous consulting firms that exude an air of quality and certainty may have a competitive advantage over specialists, but a generalist consultant may have difficulty telling which of the ten different dissenting views from insiders is the one that must be listened to.)

Although the goals and management structures in government may be slightly different, exactly the same principles apply. Risk management is often harder because people are more used to compliance with standards rather than case-by-case requirements engineering. Empire-building is a particular problem in the public sector. James Coyne and Normal Kluksdahl present in [331] a classic case study of information security run amok at NASA. There, the end of military involvement in Space Shuttle operations led to a security team being set up at the Mission Control Center in Houston to fill the vacuum left by the DoD's departure. This team was given an ambitious charter; it became independent of both development and operations; its impositions became increasingly unrelated to budget and operational constraints; and its relations with the rest of the organization became increasingly adversarial. In the end, it had to be overthrown or nothing would have got done.

The main point is that it's not enough, when doing a security requirements analysis, to understand the education, training and capabilities of the guards (and the auditors, and the checkout staff, and everyone else within the trust perimeter). Motivation is critical, and many systems fail because their designers make unrealistic assumptions about it. Organizational structures matter. There are also risk dynamics that can introduce instability. For example, an initially low rate of fraud can make people complacent and careless, until suddenly things explode. Also, an externally induced change in the organization — such as a merger, political uncertainty — can undermine morale and thus control. (Part of my younger life as a security consultant was spent travelling to places where local traumas were causing bank fraud to rocket, such as Hong Kong in 1989.)

So you have to make allowance in your designs for the ways in which human frailties express themselves through the way people behave in organizations.

25.2.3.1 *The Complacency Cycle and the Risk Thermostat*

Phone fraud in the USA has a seven year cycle: in any one year, one of the 'Baby Bells' is usually getting badly hurt. They hire experts, clean things up and get everything under control — at which point another of them becomes the favored target. Over the next six years, things gradually slacken off, then it's back to square one. This is a classic example of organizational complacency. How does it come about?

Some interesting and relevant work has been done on how people manage their exposure to risk. John Adams studied mandatory seat belt laws, and established that they don't actually save lives: they just transfer casualties from vehicle occupants to pedestrians and cyclists. Seat belts make drivers feel safer, so they drive faster in order to bring their perceived risk back up to its previous level. He calls this a *risk thermostat* and the model is borne out in other applications too [10, 11]. The complacency cycle can be thought of as the risk thermostat's corporate manifestation. Firms where managers move every two years and the business gets reorganised every five just can't maintain a long corporate memory of anything that wasn't widespread knowledge among the whole management; and problems that have been 'solved' tend to be forgotten. But risk management is an interactive business that involves all sorts of feedback and compensating behavior. The resulting system may be stable, as with road traffic fatalities; or it may oscillate, as with the Baby Bells.

Feedback mechanisms can also limit the performance of risk reduction systems. The incidence of attacks, or accidents, or whatever the organization is trying to prevent, will be reduced to the point at which there are not enough of them — as with the alarm systems described in Chapter 10 or the intrusion detection systems described in section 21.4.4. Then the sentries fall asleep, or real alarms are swamped by false ones, or organizational budgets are eroded to (and past) the point of danger. I mentioned in Chapter 12 how for 50 years the U.S. Air Force never lost a nuclear weapon. Then the five people who were supposed to check independently whether a cruise missile carried a live warhead or a blank failed to do so — each relied on the others. Six warheads were duly lost for 36 hours. Colonels will be court-martialled, and bombs will be counted carefully for a while. But eventually the courts martial will be forgotten. (How would you organize it differently?)

25.2.3.2 *Interaction with Reliability*

Poor internal control often results from systems where lots of transactions are always going wrong and have to be corrected manually. Just as in electronic warfare, noise degrades the receiver operating characteristic. A high tolerance of chaos undermines control, as it creates a high false alarm rate for many of the protection mechanisms at once. It also tempts staff: when they see that errors aren't spotted they conclude that theft won't be either.

The correlation between quality and security is a recurring theme in the literature. For example, it has been shown that investment in software quality will reduce the incidence of computer security problems, regardless of whether security was a target of the quality program or not; and that the most effective quality measure from the security point of view is the code walk-through [470]. The knowledge that one's output will be read and criticized has a salutary effect on many programmers.

Reliability can be one of your biggest selling points when trying to get a client's board of directors to agree on protective measures. Mistakes cost money; no-one really understands what software does; if mistakes are found then the frauds should be much more obvious; and all this can be communicated to top management without embarrassment on either side.

25.2.3.3 Solving the Wrong Problem

Faced with an intractable problem, it is common for people to furiously attack a related but easier one; we saw the effects of this in the public policy context earlier in section 24.3.10. Displacement activity is also common in the private sector, where an example comes from the smartcard industry. As discussed in section 16.7.4, the difficulty of protecting smartcards against probing and power-analysis attacks led the industry to concentrate on securing the chip mask instead. Technical manuals are available only under NDA; plant visitors have to sign an NDA at reception; much technical material isn't available at all; and vendor facilities have almost nuclear-grade physical security. Physical security overkill may impress naive customers — but almost all of the real attacks on fielded smartcard systems used technical attacks that didn't depend on design information.

One organizational driver for this is an inability to deal with uncertainty. Managers prefer approaches that they can implement by box-ticking their way down a checklist. So if an organization needs to deal with an actual risk, then some way needs to be found to keep it as a process, and stop it turning into a due-diligence checklist item. But there is constant pressure to replace processes with checklists, as they are less demanding of management attention and effort. The quality bureaucracy gets in the way here; firms wanting quality-assurance certification are prodded to document their business processes and make them repeatable. I noted in section 8.7 that bureaucratic guidelines had a strong tendency to displace critical thought; instead of thinking through a system's protection requirements, designers just reached for their checklists.

Another organizational issue is that when exposures are politically sensitive, some camouflage may be used. The classic example is the question of whether attacks come from insiders or outsiders. We've seen in system after system that the insiders are the main problem, whether because some of them are malicious or because most of them are careless. But it's often hard to enforce controls too overtly against line managers and IT staff, as this will alienate them, and it's also hard to get them to manage such controls themselves. It's not easy to sell a typical company's board of directors on the need for proper defences against insider attack, as this impugns the integrity and reliability of the staff who report to them. Most company boards are (quite rightly) full of entrepreneurial, positive, people with confidence in their staff and big plans for the future, rather than dyspeptic bean-counters who'd like to control everyone even more closely. So the complaint of information security managers down the years — that the board doesn't care — may not actually be a bug, but a feature.

Often a security manager will ask for, and get, money to defend against nonexistent 'evil hackers' so that he can spend most of it on controls to manage the real threat, namely dishonest or careless staff. I would be cautious about this strategy because protection mechanisms without clear justifications are likely to be eroded under operational pressure — especially if they are seen as bureaucratic impositions. Often it will take a certain amount of subtlety and negotiating skill, and controls will have to be marketed as a way of reducing errors and protecting staff. Bank managers love dual-control safe locks because they understand that it reduces the risk of their families being taken hostage; and requiring two signatures on transactions over a certain limit means extra shoulders to take the burden when something goes wrong. But such consensus on the need for protective measures is often lacking elsewhere.

25.2.3.4 *Incompetent and Inexperienced Security Managers*

Things are bad enough when even a competent IT security manager has to use guile to raise money for an activity that many of his management colleagues regard as a pure cost. In real life, things are even worse. In many traditional companies, promotions to top management jobs are a matter of seniority and contacts; so if you want to get to be the CEO you'll have to spend maybe 20 or 30 years in the company without offending too many people. Being a security manager is absolutely the last thing you want to do, as it will mean saying no to people all the time. It's hardly surprising that the average tenure of computer security managers at U.S. government agencies is only seven months [605].

Matters are complicated by reorganizations in which central computer security departments may be created and destroyed every few years, while the IT audit function oscillates between the IT department, an internal audit department and outside auditors or consultants. The security function is even less likely than other business processes to receive sustained attention and analytic thought, and more likely to succumb to a box-ticking due diligence mentality. Also, the loss of institutional memory is often a serious problem.

25.2.3.5 *Moral Hazard*

Companies often design systems so that the risk gets dumped on third parties. This can easily create a *moral hazard* by removing the incentives for people to take care, and for the company to invest in risk management techniques. I mentioned in Chapter 10 how banks in some countries claimed that their ATMs could not possibly make mistakes, so that any disputes must be the customer's fault. This led to a rise in fraud as staff got lazy and even crooked. So, quite in addition to the public policy aspects, risk denial can often make the problem worse: a company can leave itself open to staff who defraud it knowing that a prosecution would be too embarrassing.

Another kind of moral hazard is created when people who take system design decisions are unlikely to be held accountable for their actions. This can happen for many reasons. IT staff turnover could be high, with much reliance placed on contract staff; a rising management star with whom nobody wishes to argue can be involved as a user in the design team; imminent business process re-engineering may turn loyal staff into surreptitious job-seekers. In any case, when you are involved in designing a secure system, it's a good idea to look round your colleagues and ask yourself which of them will shoulder the blame three years later when things go wrong.

Another common incentive failure occurs when one part of an organization takes the credit for the profit generated by some activity, while another part picks up the bills when things go wrong. Very often the marketing department gets the praise for increased sales, while the finance department is left with the bad debts. A rational firm would strike a balance between risk and reward, but internal politics can make firms behave irrationally. The case of the three supermarkets, mentioned above, is just one example. Companies may swing wildly over a period of years from being risk takers to being excessively risk averse, and (less often) back again. John Adams found that risk taking and risk aversion are strongly associated with different personality types: the former tend to be individualists, a company's entrepreneurs, while the latter tend to be hierarchists. As the latter usually come to dominate bureaucracies, it is not surprising that stable, established organizations tend to be much more risk averse than rational economics would dictate.

So what tools and concepts can help us cut through the fog of bureaucratic infighting and determine a system's protection requirements from first principles?

The rest of this chapter will be organized as follows. The next section will look at basic methodological issues such as top-down versus iterative development. After that, I'll discuss how these apply to the specific problem of security requirements engineering. Having set the scene, I'll then return to risk management and look at technical tools. Then I'll come back and discuss how you manage people. That's really critical. How do you get people to care about vulnerabilities and bugs? This is partly incentives and partly culture; the two reinforce each other, and many companies get it wrong.

25.3   Methodology

Software projects usually take longer than planned, cost more than budgeted for and have more bugs than expected. (This is sometimes known as 'Cheops' law' after the builder of the Great Pyramid.) By the 1960s, this had become known as the *software crisis*, although the word 'crisis' is hardly appropriate for a state of affairs that has now lasted (like computer insecurity) for two generations. Anyway, the term *software engineering* was proposed by Brian Randall in 1968 and defined to be:

> *Software engineering is the establishment and use of sound engineering principles in order to obtain economically software that is reliable and works efficiently on real machines.*

This encompassed the hope that the problem could be solved in the same way that one builds ships and aircraft, with a proven scientific foundation and a set of design rules [954]. Since then much progress has been made. However, the results of the progress have been unexpected. Back in the late 1960s, people hoped that we'd cut the number of large software projects failing from the 30% or so that was observed at the time. Now, we still see about 30% of large projects failing — but the failures are much bigger. The tools get us farther up the complexity mountain before we fall off, but the rate of failure appears to be exogenous, set by such factors as company managers' appetite for risk[1].

Anyway, software engineering is about managing complexity, of which there are two kinds. There is the *incidental complexity* involved in programming using inappropriate tools, such as the assembly languages which were all that some early machines supported; programming a modern application with a graphical user interface in such a language would be impossibly tedious and error-prone. There is also the *intrinsic complexity* of dealing with large and complex problems. A bank's administrative systems, for example, may involve tens of millions of lines of code and be too complex for any one person to understand.

Incidental complexity is largely dealt with using technical tools. The most important of these are high-level languages that hide much of the drudgery of dealing with machine-specific detail and enable the programmer to develop code at an appropriate level of abstraction. There are also formal methods that enable particularly error-prone design and programming tasks to be checked. The obvious security engineering example is provided by the BAN logic for verifying cryptographic protocols, described in section 3.8.

Intrinsic complexity usually requires methodological tools that help divide up the problem into manageable subproblems and restrict the extent to which these subproblems can interact. There are many tools on the market to help you do this, and which you use may well be a matter of your client's policy. But there are basically two approaches — top-down and iterative.

---

[1] A related, and serious, problem is that while 30% of large projects fail in industry, perhaps only 30% of large projects in the public sector succeed; for a topical case history, see the National Academies' report on the collapse of the FBI's attempt to modernise its case file system [860].

25.3.1   Top-Down Design

The classical model of system development is the *waterfall model* developed by Win Royce in the 1960s for the U.S. Air Force [1090]. The idea is that you start from a concise statement of the system's requirements; elaborate this into a specification; implement and test the system's components; then integrate them together and test them as a system; then roll out the system for live operation (see Figure 25.1). Until recently, this was how all systems for the U.S. Department of Defense had to be developed.

The idea is that the requirements are written in the user language, the specification is written in technical language, the unit testing checks the units against the specification and the system testing checks whether the requirements are met. At the first two steps in this chain there is feedback on whether we're building the right system (*validation*) and at the next two on whether we're building it right (*verification*). There may be more than four steps: a common elaboration is to have a sequence of *refinement* steps as the requirements are developed into ever more detailed specifications. But that's by the way.

The critical thing about the waterfall model is that development flows inexorably downwards from the first statement of the requirements to the deployment of the system in the field. Although there is feedback from each stage to its predecessor, there is no system-level feedback from (say) system testing to the requirements. Therein lie the waterfall model's strengths, and also its weaknesses.

The strengths of the waterfall model are that it compels early clarification of system goals, architecture, and interfaces; it makes the project manager's

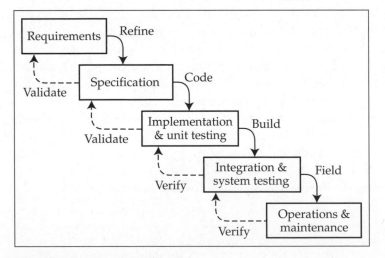

Figure 25.1: The waterfall model

task easier by providing definite milestones to aim at; it may increase cost transparency by enabling separate charges to be made for each step, and for any late specification changes; and it's compatible with a wide range of tools. Where it can be made to work, it's often the best approach. The critical question is whether the requirements are known in detail in advance of any development or prototyping work. Sometimes this is the case, such as when writing a compiler or (in the security world) designing a cryptographic processor to implement a known transaction set and pass a certain level of evaluation.

But very often the detailed requirements aren't known in advance and then an iterative approach is necessary. There are quite a few possible reasons for this. Perhaps the requirements aren't understood yet by the customer, and a prototype is necessary to clarify them rather than more discussion; the technology may be changing; the environment could be changing; or a critical part of the project may involve the design of a human-computer interface, which will probably involve several prototypes. In fact, very often the designer's most important task is to help the customer decide what he wants, and although this can sometimes be done by discussion, there will often be a need for some prototyping[2].

The most common reason of all for using an iterative development is that we're starting from an existing product which we want to improve. Even in the early days of computing, most programmer effort was always expended on maintaining and enhancing existing programs rather than developing new ones. Nowadays, as software becomes ever more packaged and the packages become ever more complex, the reality in many software firms is that 'the maintenance is the product'. The only way to write something as complex as Office is to start off from an existing version and enhance it. That does not mean that the waterfall model is obsolete; on the contrary, it may be used to manage a project to develop a major new feature. However, we also need to think of the overall management of the product, and that's likely to be based on iteration.

25.3.2 Iterative Design

So many development projects need iteration, whether to firm up the specification by prototyping, or to manage the complexity of enhancing an already large system.

---

[2]The Waterfall Model had a precursor in a methodology developed by Gerhard Pahl and Wolfgang Beitz in Germany just after World War 2 for the design and construction of mechanical equipment such as machine tools [1001]; apparently one of Pahl's students later recounted that it was originally designed as a means of getting the engineering student started, rather than as an accurate description of what experienced designers actually do. Win Royce also saw his model as a means of starting to get order out of chaos, rather than as a totally prescriptive system it developed into.

In the first case, a common approach is Barry Boehm's *spiral model* in which development proceeds through a pre-agreed number of iterations in which a prototype is built and tested, with managers being able to evaluate the risk at each stage so they can decide whether to proceed with the next iteration or to cut their losses. It's called the spiral model because the process is often depicted as in Figure 25.2.

In the second case, the standard model is *evolutionary development*. An early advocate for this approach was Harlan Mills, who taught that one should build the smallest system that works, try it out on real users, and then add functionality in small increments. This is how the packaged software industry works: software products nowadays quickly become so complex that they could not be economically developed (or redeveloped) from scratch. Indeed, Microsoft has tried more than once to rewrite Word, but gave up each time. Perhaps the best book on the evolutionary development model is by Maguire, a Microsoft author [829]. In this view of the world, products aren't the result of a project but of a process that involves continually modifying previous versions.

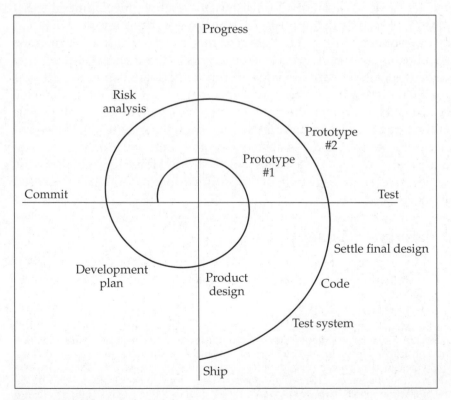

Figure 25.2: The spiral model

Unfortunately, evolutionary development tends to be neglected in academic courses and books on software engineering, and it can cause some particular problems for the security engineer.

The critical thing about evolutionary development is that just as each generation of a biological species has to be viable for the species to continue, so each generation of an evolving software product must be viable. The core technology is *regression testing*. At regular intervals — typically once a day — all the teams working on different features of a product check in their code, which gets compiled to a *build* that is then tested automatically against a large set of inputs. The regression test checks whether things that used to work still work, and that old bugs haven't found their way back. Of course, it's always possible that a build just doesn't work at all, and there may be quite long disruptions as a major change is implemented. So we consider the current 'generation' of the product to be the last build that worked. One way or another, we always have viable code that we can ship out for beta testing or whatever our next stage is.

The technology of testing is probably the biggest practical improvement in software engineering during the 1990s. Before automated regression tests were widely used, engineers used to reckon that 15% of bug fixes either introduced new bugs or reintroduced old ones [9]. But automated testing is less useful for the security engineer for a number of reasons. Security properties are more diverse, and security engineers are fewer in number, so we haven't had as much investment in tools and the available tools are much more fragmentary and primitive than those available to the general software engineering community. Many of the flaws that we want to find and fix — such as stack overflow attacks — tend to appear in new features rather than to reappear in old ones. Specific types of attack are also often easier to fix using specific remedies — such as the canary in the case of stack overflow. And many security flaws cross a system's levels of abstraction, such as when specification errors interact with user interface features — the sort of problem for which it's difficult to devise automated tests. But regression testing is still really important. It finds functionality that has been affected by a change but not fully understood.

Much the same applies to safety critical systems, which are similar in many respects to secure systems. Some useful lessons can be drawn from them.

25.3.3 Lessons from Safety-Critical Systems

Critical computer systems can be defined as those in which a certain class of failure is to be avoided if at all possible. Depending on the class of failure, they may be safety-critical, business-critical, security-critical, critical to the environment or whatever. Obvious examples of the safety-critical variety include flight controls and automatic braking systems. There is a large literature on this subject, and a lot of methodologies have been developed to help manage risk intelligently.

Overall, these methodologies tend to follow the waterfall view of the universe. The usual procedure is to identify hazards and assess risks; decide on a strategy to cope with them (avoidance, constraint, redundancy . . .); to trace the hazards down to hardware and software components which are thereby identified as critical; to identify the operator procedures which are also critical and study the various applied psychology and operations research issues; and finally to decide on a test plan and get on with the task of testing. The outcome of the testing is not just a system you're confident to run live, but a *safety case* to justify running it.

The safety case will provide the evidence, if something does go wrong, that you exercised due care; it will typically consist of the hazard analysis, the documentation linking this to component reliability and human factor issues, and the results of tests (both at component level and system level) which show that the required failure rates have been achieved.

The ideal system design avoids hazards entirely. A good illustration comes from the motor reversing circuits in Figure 25.3. In the first design on the left, a double-pole double-throw switch reverses the current passing from the battery through the motor. However, this has a potential problem: if only one of the two poles of the switch moves, the battery will be short circuited and a fire may result. The solution is to exchange the battery and the motor, as in the modified circuit on the right. Here, a switch failure will only short out the motor, not the battery.

Hazard elimination is useful in security engineering too. We saw an example in the early design of SWIFT in section 10.3.1: there, the keys used to authenticate transactions between one bank and another were exchanged between the banks directly. In this way, SWIFT personnel and systems did not have the means to forge a valid transaction and had to be trusted much less. In general, minimizing the trusted computing base is to a large extent an exercise in hazard elimination.

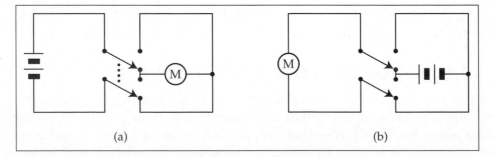

Figure 25.3: Hazard elimination in motor reversing circuit

Once as many hazards have been eliminated as possible, the next step is to identify failures that could cause accidents. A common top-down way of identifying the things that can go wrong is *fault tree analysis* as a tree is constructed whose root is the undesired behavior and whose successive nodes are its possible causes. This carries over in a fairly obvious way to security engineering, and here's an example of a fault tree (or *threat tree*, as it's often called in security engineering) for fraud from automatic teller machines (see Figure 25.4).

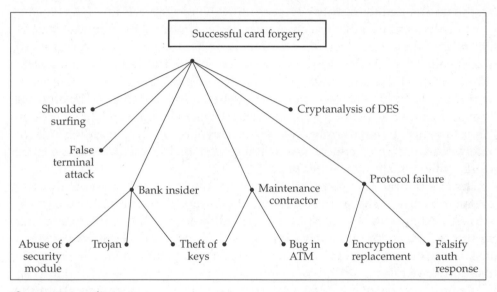

Figure 25.4: A threat tree

Threat trees are used in the U.S. Department of Defense. You start out from each undesirable outcome, and work backwards by writing down each possible immediate cause. You then work backwards by adding each precursor condition, and recurse. Then by working round the tree's leaves you should be able to see each combination of technical attack, operational blunder, physical penetration and so on which would break security. This can amount to an attack manual for the system, and so it may be highly classified. Nonetheless, it must exist, and if the system evaluators or accreditors can find any significant extra attacks, then they may fail the product.

Returning to the safety-critical world, another way of doing the hazard analysis is *failure modes and effects analysis* (FMEA), pioneered by NASA, which is bottom-up rather than top-down. This involves tracing the consequences of a failure of each of the system's components all the way up to the effect on the mission. This is often useful in security engineering; it's a good idea to understand the consequences of a failure of any one of your protection mechanisms.

A really thorough analysis of failure modes may combine top-down and bottom-up approaches. There are various ways to manage the resulting mass of data. For example, one can construct a matrix of hazards against safety mechanisms, and if the safety policy is that each serious hazard must be constrained by at least two independent mechanisms, then we can check that there are two entries in each of the relevant columns. In this way, we can demonstrate graphically that in the presence of the hazard in question, at least two failures will be required to cause an accident. This methodology goes across unchanged to security engineering, as I'll discuss below.

The safety-critical systems community has a number of techniques for dealing with failure and error rates. Component failure rates can be measured statistically; the number of bugs in software can be tracked by various techniques which I'll discuss in the next chapter; and there is a lot of experience with the probability of operator error at different types of activity. The bible for human-factors engineering in safety-critical systems is James Reason's book *'Human Error'*; I would probably consider anyone who was building human interfaces to security-critical systems and who hadn't read this book to be negligent if something went wrong.

The telegraphic summary is that the error rate depends on the familiarity and complexity of the task, the amount of pressure and the number of cues to success. Where a task is simple, performed often and there are strong cues to success, the error rate might be 1 in 100,000 operations. However, when a task is performed for the first time in a confusing environment where logical thought is required and the operator is under pressure, then the odds can be against successful completion of the task. Quite a lot is known about the cognitive biases and other psychological factors that make particular types of error more common, and a prudent engineer will understand and avoid these. Nonetheless, designers of things like nuclear reactors are well aware (at least since Three Mile Island) that no matter how many design walkthroughs you do, it's when the red lights go on for the first time that the worst mistakes get made.

Similarly, in security systems, it tends to be important but rarely performed tasks such as getting senior managers to set up master crypto keys where the most egregious blunders can be expected. A classic example from [34] was when a bank wished to create a set of three master keys to link their cash machine network to VISA and needed a terminal to drive the security module. A contractor obligingly lent them a laptop PC, together with software which emulated the desired type of terminal. With this the senior managers duly created the required keys and posted them off to VISA. None of them realized that most PC terminal emulation software packages can be set to log all the transactions passing through, and this is precisely what the contractor did. He captured the clear zone key as it was created, and later used it to decrypt the bank's master PIN key. The lesson to take from this is that security usability isn't just about presenting a nice intuitive interface to the end-user that accords with common mental models of threat and protection in the application area, as discussed in Chapter 2. It's pervasive, and extends all the way through the system's operations, at the back end as well as the front.

So when doing security requirements engineering, special care has to be paid to the skill level of the staff who will perform each critical task and estimates made of the likelihood of error. Be cautious here: an airplane designer can rely on a fairly predictable skill level from anyone with a commercial pilot's licence, and even a shipbuilder knows the strengths and weaknesses of a sailor in the Navy. Usability testing can (and should) be integrated with staff training: when pilots go for their six-monthly refresher courses in the simulator, instructors throw all sorts of combinations of equipment failure, bad weather, cabin crisis and air-traffic-control confusion at them. They observe what combinations of stress result in fatal accidents, and how these differ across cockpit types. This in turn provides valuable feedback to the cockpit designers.

The security engineer usually has no such luck. Many security failures remind me of a remark made by a ranger at Yosemite about the devices provided to keep bears from getting at campers' food supplies: that it's an impossible engineering problem because the brighter bears are smarter than the dumber campers.

As well as the problem of testing usability, there are also technical testability issues. A common problem with redundant systems is *fault masking*: if the output is determined by majority voting between three processors, and one of them fails, then the system will continue to work fine — but its safety margin will have been eroded. Several air crashes have resulted from flying an airliner with one of the flight control systems dysfunctional; although pilots may be intellectually aware that one of the cockpit displays is unreliable, their training may lead them to rely on it under pressure rather than checking with other instruments. So a further failure can be catastrophic. In such cases, it's better to arrange things so that displays give no reading at all rather than an inaccurate one. A security example is the ATM problem mentioned in section 10.4.2 where a bank issued all its customers with the same PIN. In such cases, the problem often isn't detected until much later. The fault gets masked by the handling precautions applied to PINs, which ensure that even the bank's security and audit staff only get hold of the PIN mailer for their own personal account. So some thought is needed about how faults can remain visible and testable even when their immediate effects are masked.

Our final lesson from safety critical systems is that although there will be a safety requirements specification and safety test criteria as part of the safety case for the lawyers or regulators, it is good practice to integrate this with the general requirements and test documentation. If the safety case is a separate set of documents, then it's easy to sideline it after approval is obtained and thus fail to maintain it properly. If, on the other hand, it's an integral part of the product's management, then not only will it likely get upgraded as the product is, but it is also much more likely to be taken heed of by experts from other domains who might be designing features with possible interactions.

As a general rule, safety must be built in as a system is developed, not retrofitted; the same goes for security. The main difference is in the failure model. Rather than the effects of random failure, we're dealing with a hostile opponent who can cause some of the components of our system to fail at the least convenient time and in the most damaging way possible. In effect, our task is to program a computer which gives answers which are subtly and maliciously wrong at the most inconvenient moment possible. I've described this as 'programming Satan's computer' to distinguish it from the more common problem of programming Murphy's [74]. This provides an insight into one of the reasons security engineering is hard: Satan's computer is hard to test [1126].

25.4   Security Requirements Engineering

In Chapter 8, I defined a *security policy model* to be a concise statement of the protection properties that a system, or generic type of system, must have. This was driven by the *threat model*, which sets out the attacks and failures with which the system must be able to cope. The security policy model is further refined into a *security target*, which is a more detailed description of the protection mechanisms a specific implementation provides, and how they relate to the control objectives. The security target forms the basis for testing and evaluation of a product. The policy model and the target together may be referred to loosely as the *security policy*, and the process of developing a security policy and obtaining agreement on it from the system owner is the process of *requirements engineering*.

Security requirements engineering is often the most critical task of managing secure system development, and can also be the hardest. It's where 'the rubber hits the road'. It's at the intersection of the most difficult technical issues, the most acute bureaucratic power struggles, and the most determined efforts at blame avoidance.

The available methodologies have consistently lagged behind those available to the rest of the system engineering world [123]. In my view, the critical insight is that the process of generating a security policy and a security target is not essentially different from the process of producing code. Depending on the application, you can use a top-down, waterfall approach; a limited iterative approach such as the spiral model; or a continuing iterative process such as the evolutionary model. In each case, we need to build in the means to manage risk, and have the risk assessment drive the development or evolution of the security policy.

Risk management must also continue once the system is deployed. It's rather hard to tell what a new invention will be useful for, and this applies to the dark side too: novel attacks are just as difficult to predict as anything else about the future. Phone companies spent the 1970s figuring out ways to stop phone phreaks getting free calls, but once premium-rate numbers appeared the real problem became stopping fraud. We worried about crooks hacking bank smartcards, and put in lots of back-end protection for the early electronic purses; the attacks came on pay-TV smartcards instead, while the bank fraud folks concentrated on mag-stripe fallback and on phishing. People worried about the security of credit card numbers used in transactions on the net, but it turned out that the main threat to online businesses was refunds and disputes. As they say, 'The street finds its own uses for things.' So you can't expect to get the protection requirements completely right at the first attempt. We've also seen many cases where the policy and mechanisms were set when a system was first built, and then undermined as the environment (and the product) evolved, but the protection did not.

If you're running a company, it's futile to spend a lot of money on trying to think up new attacks; that's research, and best left to university folks like me. What you do need is twofold: a mechanism for stopping your developers building systems that are vulnerable to known bugs like stack overflows and weak cryptography; and a mechanism for monitoring, and acting on, changing protection requirements.

Unlike in the previous section, we'll look at the case of evolving protection requirements first, as it is more common.

25.4.1 Managing Requirements Evolution

Most of the time, security requirements have to be tweaked for one of four reasons. First, we might need to fix a bug. Second, we may want to improve the system; as we get more experience of the kind of attacks that happen, we will want to tune some aspect of the controls. Third, we may want to deal with an evolving environment. For example, if an online ordering system that was previously limited to a handful of major suppliers is to be extended to all a firm's suppliers then the controls are likely to need review. Finally, there may be a change in the organization. Firms are continually undergoing mergers, management buyouts, business process re-engineering, you name it.

Of course, any of these could result in such a radical change that we would consider it to be a redevelopment rather than an evolution. The dividing line between the two is inevitably vague, but many evolutionary ideas carry over into one-off projects, and many systems' evolution contains occasional large leaps that are engineered in specific projects.

25.4.1.1   Bug Fixing

Most security enhancements fall into the category of bug fixes or product tuning. Fortunately, they are usually the easiest to cope with provided you have the right mechanisms for getting information about bugs, testing fixes and shipping upgrades.

If you sell software that's at all security critical — and most anything that can communicate with the outside world is potentially so — then the day will come when you hear of a vulnerability or even an attack. In the old days, vendors could take months to respond with a new version of the product, and would often do nothing at all but issue a warning (or even a denial). That doesn't work any more: public expectations are higher now. With mass market products you can expect press publicity; even with more specialized products there is a risk of it. Expectations are backed by laws. By 2007, most U.S. states had security breach notification laws, obliging firms to notify attacks to all individuals whose privacy could have thereby been compromised, and the European Union had such a law in the pipeline too. Now it's not inevitable that a vulnerability report will trigger such a law — if you're lucky the alarm won't be raised because of an exploit, but from one of your customers' technical staff noticing a problem and reporting it to stop it becoming an exploit. But, either way, you need a plan to deal with it. This will have four components: monitoring, repair, distribution and reassurance.

First, you need to be sure that you learn of vulnerabilities as soon as you can — and preferably no later than the press (or the bad guys) do. Listening to customers is important: you need an efficient way for them to report bugs. It may be an idea to provide some incentive, such as points towards their next upgrade, lottery tickets or even cash. The idea of vulnerability markets was first suggested by Jean Camp and Catherine Wolfram in 2000 [256]; two firms, iDefense and Tipping Point, are now openly buying vulnerabilities, so the market actually exists. Unfortunately, the prices are not published and they only trade in bugs in the major platforms; but this shouldn't stop you setting up a reward scheme. Then, however you get the bug reports in, you then need to make someone responsible for monitoring them, and also for reading relevant mailing lists, such as bugtraq [239].

Second, you need to be able to respond appropriately. In organizations such as banks with time-critical processing requirements, it's normal for one member of each product team to be 'on call' with a pager in case something goes wrong at three in the morning and needs fixing at once. This might be excessive for a small software company, but you should still know the home phone numbers of everyone who might be needed urgently; see to it that there's more than one person with each critical skill; and have supporting procedures. For example, emergency bug fixes must be run through the full testing process as soon as possible, and the documentation's got to be upgraded too. This is critical for evolutionary security improvement, but too often ignored: where the bug fix changes the requirements, you need to fix their documentation too (and perhaps your threat model, and even top level risk management paperwork).

Third, you need to be able to distribute the patch to your customers rapidly. So it needs to be planned in advance. The details will vary depending on your product: if you only have a few dozen customers running your code on servers at data centers that are staffed 24 x 7, then it may be very easy, but if it involves patching millions of copies of consumer software then a lot of care is needed. It may seem simple enough to get your customers to visit your website once a day and check for upgrades, but this just doesn't work. There is a serious tension between the desire to patch quickly to forestall attacks, and the desire to delay so as to test the patch properly [135]: pioneers who apply patches quickly end up discovering problems that break their systems, but laggards are more vulnerable to attack. There are also two quite different tensions between the vendor and the customer. First, the vendor would usually like to patch more quickly than the customer at the operational level, and second, the customer would probably want the threat of eventual breach disclosure, because without it the vendor would be less likely to issue patches at all [89].

Considerations like these led Microsoft to 'patch Tuesday', the policy of releasing a whole set of patches on the second Tuesday of every month. A monthly cycle seems a reasonable compromise between security, dependability and manageability. Individual customers usually patch automatically, while firms know to schedule testing of their enterprise systems for then so they can patch as quickly as possible thereafter. Most recent malware exploits have targeted vulnerabilities that were already patched — the bad guys reverse-engineer the patches to find the vulns and then get the machines that were patched late or not at all. So once a patch cycle is set up, it can become a treadmill. There are also quite a lot of details you have to get right to set up such a scheme — coping with traffic volumes, giving customers adequate legal notification of the effects of changes, and securing the mechanism against abuse. But as time goes on, I expect that more and more firms will have to introduce patch cycle management, as software gets more complex (and thus buggy), and as it spreads into more and more devices.

Finally, you need a plan to deal with the press. The last thing you need is for dozens of journalists to phone up and be stonewalled by your switchboard operator as you struggle madly to fix the bug. Have a set of press releases for incidents of varying severity ready to roll, so that you only have to pick the right one and fill in the details. The release can then ship as soon as the first (or perhaps the second) journalist calls.

25.4.1.2 Control Tuning and Corporate Governance

The main process by which organizations like banks develop their bookkeeping systems and their other internal controls is by tuning them in the light of experience. A bank with 25,000 staff might be sacking about one staff member a day for petty theft or embezzlement, and it's traditionally the internal audit department that will review the loss reports and recommend system changes to reduce the incidence of the most common scams. I gave some examples in section 10.2.3.

It is important for the security engineer to have some knowledge of internal controls. There is a shortage of books on this subject: audit is largely learned on the job, but know-how is also transmitted by courses and through accounting standards documents. There is a survey of internal audit standards by Janet Colbert and Paul Bowen [312]; the most influential is the Risk Management Framework from the *Committee of Sponsoring Organizations* (COSO), a group of U.S. accounting and auditing bodies [318]. This is the yardstick by which your system will be judged if it's used in the U.S. public sector or by companies quoted on U.S. equity markets. The standard reference on COSO is a book by Steven Root [1082], who also tells the story of how U.S. accounting standards evolved in the years prior to Enron.

The COSO model is targeted not just on internal control but on the reliability of financial reporting and compliance with laws and regulations. Its basic process is an evolutionary cycle: in a given environment, you assess the risks, design controls, monitor their performance, and then go round the loop again. COSO emphasizes soft aspects of corporate culture more than hard system design issues so may be seen as a guide to managing and documenting the process by which your system evolves. However, its core consists of the internal control procedures whereby senior management check that their control policies are being implemented and achieving their objectives, and modify them if not.

It is also worthwhile for the security engineer to learn about the more specialized information systems audit function. The IS auditor should not have line responsibility for security but should monitor how it's done, look into things that are substandard or appear suspicious, and suggest improvements. Much of the technical material is common with security engineering; if you have read and understood this book so far, you should be able to get well over 50% on the Certified Information Systems Auditor (CISA) exam (details are at [639]). The Information Systems Audit and Control Association, which administers CISA, has a refinement of COSO known as the *Control Objectives for Information and related Technology* (CobiT) which is more attuned to IT needs, more international and more accessible than COSO (it can be downloaded from [638]). It covers much more than engineering requirements, as issues such as personnel management, change control and project management are also the internal auditor's staples. (The working security engineer needs some familiarity with this material too.)

These general standards are necessarily rather vague. They provide the engineer with a context and a top-level checklist, but rarely with any clear guidance on specific measures. For example, CobiT 5.19 states: 'Regarding malicious software, such as computer viruses or trojan horses, management should establish a framework of adequate preventative, detective and corrective control measures'. More concrete standards are often developed to apply such general principles to specific application areas. For example, when I was working in banking security in the 1980's, I relied on guidelines from the Bank for International Settlements [113]. Where such standards exist, they are often the ultimate fulcrum of security evolutionary activity.

Further important drivers will be your auditors' interpretation of specific accounting laws, such as Sarbanes-Oxley for U.S. publicly-listed companies, Gramm-Leach-Bliley for U.S. financial-sector firms, and HIPAA for U.S. health-care providers. Sarbanes-Oxley, for example, requires information security measures to be documented, which fits well enough with CobiT. In Europe some comparable pressure comes from privacy laws. Recently the spread of security-breach disclosure laws has created much greater sensitivity about the protection of personal information about customers (and in particular about their credit card numbers, dates of birth or any other data that could be used in financial fraud). There are now breach disclosure laws in most U.S. states, and they're in the pipeline for Europe. If you have to disclose that your systems have been hacked and millions of customer credit card numbers compromised, you can expect to be sued and to see your stock fall by several percent. If it happens to you more than once, you can expect to lose customers: customer churn might only be 2% after one notified breach, but 30% after two and near 100% after three [1356]. The silver lining in this cloud is that, for the first time ever, information security has become a CEO issue; this means that you'll occasionally have access to the boss to make your case for investment.

It's also a good idea to have good channels of communication to your internal audit department. But it's not a good idea to rely on them completely for feedback. Usually the people who know most about how to break the system are the ordinary staff who actually use it. Ask them.

25.4.1.3 Evolving Environments and the Tragedy of the Commons

I've discussed a lot of systems that broke after their environment changed and appropriate changes to the protection mechanisms were skimped, avoided or forgotten. Card-and-PIN technology that worked fine with ATMs became vulnerable to false-terminal attacks when used with retail point-of-sale terminals; smartcards that were perfectly good for managing credit card numbers and PINs were inadequate to keep out the pay-TV pirates; and even very basic mechanisms such as authentication protocols had to be redesigned once they started to be used by systems where the main threat was internal rather than external. Military environments evolve particularly rapidly in wartime, as attack and defence coevolve; R. V. Jones attributes much of the UK's relative success in electronic warfare in World War 2 to the fact that the Germans used a rigid top-down development methodology, which resulted in beautifully engineered equipment that was always six months too late [670].

Changes in the application aren't the only problem. An operating system upgrade may introduce a whole new set of bugs into the underlying platform. Changes of scale as businesses go online can alter the cost-benefit equation, as can the fact that many system users may be in foreign jurisdictions with ineffective computer crime laws (or none at all). Also, attacks that were known by experts for many years to be possible, but which were ignored because they didn't happen in practice, can suddenly start to happen — good examples being phishing and the distributed denial-of-service attack.

Where you own the system, things are merely difficult. You manage risk by ensuring that someone in the organization has responsibility for maintaining its security rating; this may involve an annual review driven by your internal audit bureaucracy, or be an aspect of change control. Maintaining organizational memory is hard, thanks to the high turnover of both IT and security staff which we discussed in section 25.2.3.4 above. Keeping developer teams interested and up-to-date in security can be a hard problem, and I'll return to it towards the end of this chapter.

That's tough enough, but where many of the really intractable problems arise is where no-one owns the system at all. The responsibility for established standards, such as how ATMs check PINs, is diffuse. In that case, the company which developed most of the standards (IBM) lost its leading industry role and its successor, Microsoft, is not interested in the ATM market. Cryptographic equipment is sold by many specialist firms; although VISA used to certify equipment, they stopped in about 1990 and Mastercard never got into that business. The EMV consortium got going later, but for a while there was no one person or company in charge, and responsibility for standards outside the world of EMV smartcards is not always clear. So each player — equipment maker or bank — had a motive to push the boundaries just a little bit further, in the hope that when eventually something did go wrong, it would happen to somebody else.

This problem is familiar to economists, who call it the *tragedy of the commons* [806]. If a hundred peasants are allowed to graze their sheep on the village common, where the grass is finite, then whenever another sheep is added its owner gets almost the full benefit, while the other ninety-nine suffer only a very small disadvantage from the decline in the quality of the grazing. So they aren't motivated to object, but rather to add another sheep of their own and get as much of the declining resource as they can. The result is a dustbowl. In the world of agriculture, this problem is tackled by community mechanisms, such as getting the parish council set up a grazing control committee. One of the challenges facing the world of computer security is to devise the appropriate mix of technical and organizational mechanisms to achieve the same sort of result that was already achieved by a tenth-century Saxon village, only on the much larger and more diffuse scale of the Internet.

25.4.1.4 *Organizational Change*

Organizational issues are not just a contributory factor in security failure, as with the loss of organizational memory and the lack of community mechanisms for monitoring changing threat environments. They can often be a primary cause.

The early 1990s saw a management fashion for *business process re-engineering* which often meant using changes in business computer systems to compel changes in the way people worked. There have been some well-documented cases in which poorly designed systems interacted with resentful staff to cause a disaster.

Perhaps the best known case is that of the London Ambulance Service. They had a manual system in which incoming emergency calls were written on forms and sent by conveyer belt to three controllers who allocated vehicles and passed the form to a radio dispatcher. Industrial relations were poor, and there was pressure to cut costs: managers got the idea of solving all these problems by automating. Lots of things went wrong, and as the system was phased in it became clear that it couldn't cope with established working practices, such as crew taking the 'wrong' ambulance (staff had favorite vehicles with long-serving staff getting the better ones). Managers didn't want to know and forced the system into use on the 26th October 1992 by reorganizing the room so that controllers and dispatchers had to use terminals rather than paper.

The result was meltdown. A number of positive feedback loops became established which caused the system progressively to lose track of vehicles. Exception messages built up, scrolled off screen and were lost; incidents were held as allocators searched for vehicles; as the response time stretched, callbacks from patients increased (the average ring time for emergency callers went over ten minutes); as congestion increased, the ambulance crews got frustrated, pressed the wrong buttons on their new data terminals, couldn't get a result, tried calling on the voice channel, and increased the congestion; as more and more crews fell back on the methods they understood, they took the wrong vehicles even more; many vehicles were sent to an emergency, or none; and finally the whole service collapsed. It's reckoned that perhaps twenty people died as a direct result of not getting paramedic assistance in time. By the afternoon it was the major news item, the government intervened, and on the following day the system was switched back to semi-manual operation.

This is only one of many such disasters, but it's particularly valuable to the engineer as it was extremely well documented by the resulting public enquiry [1205]. In my own professional experience I've seen cases where similar attempts to force through changes in corporate culture by replacing computer systems have so undermined morale that honesty became a worry. (Much of my consulting work has had to do with environments placed under stress by corporate reorganization or even national political crises.)

In extreme cases, a step change in the environment brought on by a savage corporate restructuring will be more like a one-off project than an evolutionary change. There will often be some useful base to fall back on, such as an understanding of external threats; but the internal threat environment may become radically different. This is particularly clear in banking. Fifteen years ago, bank branches were run by avuncular managers and staffed by respectable middle-aged ladies who expected to spend their entire working lives there. Nowadays the managers have been replaced by product sales specialists and the teller staff are youngsters on near-minimum wages who turn over every year or so. It's simply not the same business.

25.4.2 Managing Project Requirements

This brings us to the much harder problem of how to do security requirements engineering for a one-off project. A common example in the 1990s was building an e-commerce application from scratch, whether for a start-up or for an established business desperate to create new online distribution channels. A common example in the next ten years might be an established application going online as critical components acquire the ability to communicate: examples I've discussed in Part II include postage meters, burglar alarms and door locks. There will be many more.

Building things from scratch is an accident-prone business; many large development projects have crashed and burned. The problems appear to be very much the same whether the disaster is a matter of safety, of security or of the software simply never working at all; so security people can learn a lot from the general software engineering literature, and indeed the broader engineering literature. For example, according to Herb Simon's classic model of engineering design, you start off from a goal, desiderata, a utility function and budget constraints; then work through a design tree of decisions until you find a design that's 'good enough'; then iterate the search until you find the best design or run out of time [1153].

At least as important as guidance on 'how to do it' are warnings about how not to. The classic study of large software project disasters was written by Bill Curtis, Herb Krasner, and Neil Iscoe [339]: they found that failure to understand the requirements was mostly to blame: a thin spread of application domain knowledge typically led to fluctuating and conflicting requirements which in turn caused a breakdown in communication. They suggested that the solution was to find an 'exceptional designer' with a deep understanding of the problem who would assume overall responsibility.

The millennium bug gives another useful data point, which many writers on software engineering still have to digest. If one accepts that many large commercial and government systems needed extensive repair work, and the conventional wisdom that a significant proportion of large development projects are late or never delivered at all, then the prediction of widespread chaos at the end of 1999 was inescapable. It didn't happen. Certainly, the risks to the systems used by small and medium sized firms were overstated [50]; nevertheless, the systems of some large firms whose operations are critical to the economy, such as banks and utilities, did need substantial fixing. But despite the conventional wisdom, there have been no reports of significant organizations going belly-up. This appears to support Curtis, Krasner, and Iscoe's thesis. The requirement for Y2K bug fixes was known completely: 'I want this system to keep on working, just as it is now, through into 2000 and beyond'.

So the requirements engineer needs to acquire a deep knowledge of the application as well as of the people who might attack it and the kind of tools they might use. If domain experts are available, well and good. When interviewing them try to distinguish things that are done for a purpose from those which are just 'how things are done around here'. Probe constantly for the reasons why things are done, and be sensitive to after-the-fact rationalizations. Focus particularly on the things that are going to change. For example, if dealing with customer complaints depends on whether the customer is presentable or not, and your job is to take this business online, then ask the experts what alternative controls might work in a world where it's much harder to tell a customer's age, sex and social class. (This should probably have been done round about the time of the civil rights movement in the 1960's, but better late than never.)

When tackling a new application, dig into its history. I've tried to do that throughout this book, and bring out the way in which problems repeat. To find out what electronic banking will be like in the twenty-first century, it's a good idea to know what it was like in the nineteenth; human nature doesn't change much. Historical parallels will also make it much easier for you to sell your proposal to your client's board of directors.

An influential recent publication is a book on threat modelling by Frank Swiderski and Window Snyder [1236]. This describes the methodology adopted by Microsoft following its big security push. The basic idea is that you list the assets you're trying to protect (ability to do transactions, access to classified data, whatever) and also the assets available to an attacker (perhaps the ability to subscribe to your system, or to manipulate inputs to the smartcard you supply him, or to get a job at your call center). You then trace through the system, from one module to another. You try to figure out what the trust levels are and where the attack paths might be; where the barriers are; and what techniques, such as spoofing, tampering, repudiation, information disclosure, service denial and elevation of privilege, might be used to overcome particular barriers. The threat model can be used for various purposes at different points in the security development lifecycle, from architecture reviews through targeting code reviews and penetration tests. What you're likely to find is that in order to make the complexity manageable, you have to impose a security policy — as an abstraction, or even just a rule of thumb that enables you to focus on the exceptions. Hopefully the security policies discussed in Part II of this book will give you some guidance and inspiration.

You will likely find that a security requirements specification for a new project requires iteration, so it's more likely to be spiral model than waterfall model. In the first pass, you'll describe the new application and how it differs from any existing applications for which loss histories are available, set out a model of the risks as you perceive them, and draft a security policy (I'll have more to say on risk analysis and management in the next section). In the second pass, you might get comments from your client's middle management and internal auditors, while meantime you scour the literature for useful checklist items and ideas you can recycle. The outcome of this will be a revised, more quantitative threat model; a security policy; and a security target which sketches how the policy will be implemented in real life. It will also set out how a system can be evaluated against these criteria. In the third pass, the documentation will circulate to a wider group of people including your client's senior management, external auditors, insurers and perhaps an external evaluator. The Microsoft model does indeed support iteration, and its authors advise that it be used even at the level of features when a product is undergoing evolution.

25.4.3 Parallelizing the Process

Often there isn't an expert to hand, as when something is being done for the first time, or when we're building a competitor to a proprietary system whose owners won't share their loss history with us. An interesting question here is how to brainstorm a specification by just trying to think of all the things that could go wrong. The common industry practice is to hire a single consulting firm to draw up a security target; but the experience described in 12.2.3 suggested that using several experts in parallel would be better. People with backgrounds in crypto, access control, internal audit and so on will see a problem from different angles. There is also an interesting analogy with the world of software testing where it is more cost efficient to test in parallel rather than series: each tester has a different focus in the testing space and will find some subset of flaws faster than the others. (I'll look at a more quantitative model of this in the next chapter.)

This all motivated me to carry out an experiment in 1999 to see if a high-quality requirements specification could be assembled quickly by getting a lot of different people to contribute drafts. The idea was that most of the possible attacks would be considered in at least one of them. So in one of our University exam questions, I asked what would be a suitable security policy for a company planning to bid for the licence for a public lottery.

The results are described in [49]. The model answer was that attackers, possibly in cahoots with insiders, would try to place bets once the result of the draw is known, whether by altering bet records or forging tickets; or place bets without paying for them; or operate bogus vending stations which would pay small claims but disappear if a client won a big prize. The security policy that follows logically from this is that bets should be registered online with a server which is secured prior to the draw, both against tampering and against the extraction of sufficient information to forge a winning ticket; that there should be credit limits for genuine vendors; and that there should be ways of identifying bogus vendors.

Valuable and original contributions from the students came at a number of levels, including policy goal statements, discussions of particular attacks, and arguments about the merits of particular protection mechanisms. At the policy level, there were a number of shrewd observations on the need to maintain public confidence and the threat from senior managers in the operating company. At the level of technical detail, one student discussed threats from refund mechanisms, while another looked at attacks on secure time mechanisms and observed that the use of the radio time signal in lottery terminals would be vulnerable to jamming (this turned out to be a real vulnerability in one existing lottery).

The students also came up with quite a number of routine checklist items of the kind that designers often overlook — such as 'tickets must be associated with a particular draw'. This might seem obvious, but a protocol design which used a purchase date, ticket serial number and server-supplied random challenge as input to a MAC computation might appear plausible to a superficial inspection. Experienced designers appreciate the value of such checklists[3].

The lesson to be learned from this case study is that requirements engineering, like software testing, is susceptible to a useful degree of parallelization. So if your target system is something novel, then instead of paying a single consultant to think about it for twenty days, consider getting fifteen people

---

[3]They did miss one lottery fraud that actually happened — when a couple won about half a million dollars, the employee to whom they presented the winning ticket claimed it himself and absconded overseas with the cash. The lottery compounded the failure by contesting the claim in court, and losing [765]. One might have thought their auditors and lawyers could have advised them better.

with diverse backgrounds to think about it for a day each. Have brainstorming sessions with a variety of staff, from your client company, its suppliers, and industry bodies.

But beware — people will naturally think of the problems that might make their own lives difficult, and will care less about things that inconvenience others. We learned this the hard way at our university where a number of administrative systems were overseen by project boards made up largely of staff from administrative departments. This was simply because the professors were too busy doing research and teaching to bother. We ended up with systems that are convenient for a small number of administrators, and inconvenient for a much larger number of professors. When choosing the membership of your brainstorming sessions, focus groups and project boards, it's worth making some effort to match their membership to the costs and risks to which the firm is exposed. If a university has five times as many professors as clerks, you should have this proportion involved in design; and if you're designing a bank system that will be the target of attack, then don't let the marketing folks drive the design. Make sure you have plenty internal audit folks, customer helpline managers and other people whose lives will be made a misery if there's suddenly a lot more fraud.

25.5   Risk Management

That brings us to our next topic. Whether our threat model and security policy evolve or are developed in a one-off project, at their heart lie business decisions about priorities: how much to spend on protection against what. This is risk management, and it must be done within a broader framework of managing non-IT risks.

Many firms sell methodologies for this. Some come in the form of do-it-yourself PC software, while others are part of a package of consultancy services. Which one you use may be determined by your client's policies; for example, if you're selling anything to the UK government you're likely to have to use a system called CRAMM. The basic purpose of such systems is to prioritise security expenditure, while at the same time providing a financial case for it to senior management.

The most common technique is to calculate the *annual loss expectancy* (ALE) for each possible loss scenario. This is the expected loss multiplied by the number of incidents expected in an average year. A typical ALE analysis for a bank's computer systems might consist of several hundred entries, including items such as we see in Figure 25.5.

Note that accurate figures are likely to be available for common losses (such as 'teller takes cash'), while for the uncommon, high-risk losses such as a large funds transfer fraud, the incidence is largely guesswork.

Loss type	Amount	Incidence	ALE
SWIFT fraud	$50,000,000	.005	$250,000
ATM fraud (large)	$250,000	.2	$100,000
ATM fraud (small)	$20,000	.5	$10,000
Teller takes cash	$3,240	200	$648,000

Figure 25.5: Computing annualized loss expectancy (ALE)

ALEs have long been standardized by NIST as the technique to use in U.S. government procurements [1005], and the audit culture post-Enron is spreading them everywhere. But in real life, the process of producing such a table is all too often just iterative guesswork. The consultant lists all the threats he can think of, attaches notional probabilities, works out the ALEs, adds them all up, and gets a ludicrous result: perhaps the bank's ALE exceeds its income. He then tweaks the total down to whatever will justify the largest security budget he thinks the board of directors will stand (or which his client, the chief internal auditor, has told him is politically possible). The loss probabilities are then massaged to give the right answer. (Great invention, the spreadsheet.) I'm sorry if this sounds a bit cynical; but it's what seems to happen more often than not. The point is, ALEs may be of some value, but they should not be elevated into a religion.

Insurance can be of some help in managing large but unlikely risks. But the insurance business is not completely scientific either. For years the annual premium for bankers' blanket bond insurance, which covered both computer crime and employee disloyalty, was 0.5% of the sum insured. This represented pure profit for Lloyds, which wrote the policies; then there was a large claim, and the premium doubled to 1% per annum. Such policies may have a deductible of between $50,000,000 and $10,000,000 per incident, and so they only remove a small number of very large risks from the equation. As for nonbanks, business insurance used to cover computer risks up until about 1998, when underwriters started excluding it because of the worries about the millennium bug. When it became available again in 2001, the premiums were much higher than before. They have since come down, but insurance is historically a cyclical industry: companies compete with low premiums whenever rising stock-market values boost the value of their investment portfolios, and jack up prices when markets fall. Around 2000, the end of the dotcom boom created a downswing that coincided with the millennium bug scare. Even now that markets are returning to normal, some kinds of cover are still limited because of correlated risks. Insurers are happy to cover events of known probability and local effect, but where the risk are unknown and the effect could be global (for example, a worm that took down the Internet for several days) markets tend to fail [200].

Anyway, a very important reason for large companies to take out computer crime cover — and do many other things — is due diligence. The risks that are being tackled may seem on the surface to be operational risks but are actually legal, regulatory and PR risks. Often they are managed by 'following the herd' — being just another one of the millions of gnu on the African veld, to reuse our metaphor for Internet security. This is one reason why information security is such a fashion-driven business. During the mid 1980's, hackers were what everyone talked about (even if their numbers were tiny), and firms selling dial-back modems did a roaring business. From the late 80's, viruses took over the corporate imagination, and antivirus software made some people rich. In the mid-1990s, the firewall became the star product. The late 1990s saw a frenzy over PKI. These are the products that CFOs see on TV and in the financial press. Amidst all this hoopla, the security professional must retain a healthy scepticism and strive to understand what the real threats are.

25.6   Managing the Team

It's now time to pull all the threads together and discuss how you manage a team of developers who're trying to produce — or enhance — a product that does useful work, while at the same time not introduce vulnerabilities that turn out to be show-stoppers. For this, you need to build a team with the right culture, the right mix of skills, and above all the right incentives.

One of the hardest issues to get right is the balance between having everyone on the team responsible for securing their own code, and having a security guru on whom everyone relies.

There is a growing consensus that, in order to get high-quality software, you have to make programmers test their own code and fix their own bugs. An important case history is how Microsoft beat IBM in the PC operating systems market. During the late 1980s, Microsoft and IBM collaborated on OS/2, but the partnership broke up in 1990 after which Microsoft developed Windows into the dominant position it has today. An important reason was Microsoft's impatience at IBM's development process, which was slow and produced bloated code. IBM followed the waterfall model, being careful to specify modules properly before they were written; it also divided up its developers into analysts, programmers and testers. This created a moral hazard, especially when teams were working under pressure: programmers would write a lot of shoddy code and 'throw it over the wall' for the testers to fix up. As a result, the code base was often so broken that it wouldn't run, so it wasn't possible to use regression tests to start pulling the bugs out. Microsoft took the view that they did not have programmers or testers, only developers: each programmer was responsible for fixing his own software, and a lot of attention was paid to ensuring that the software would build every night for testing. One of the consequences was that people who wrote buggy software ended up spending most of their time hunting and fixing bugs in their code, so more of the code base ended up being written by the more careful programmers. Another consequence was Microsoft won the battle to rule the world of 32-bit operating systems; their better development methodology let them take a $100 bn market from IBM. The story is told by Steve Maguire in [829].

When engineering systems to be secure — as opposed to merely on time and on budget — you certainly need to educate all your developers to the point that they understand the basics, such as the need to sanitise input to prevent overflows, and the need to lock variables to prevent race conditions. But there is a strong case for some extra specialised knowledge and input, especially at the testing phase. You can lecture programmers about stack overflows until you're blue in the face, and they'll dutifully stare at their code until they've convinced themselves that it doesn't have any. It's only when someone knowledgeable runs a fuzzing tool on it, and it breaks, that the message really gets through. So how do you square the need for specialists, in order to acquire and maintain know-how and tools, with the need for developers to test their own code, in order to ensure that most of your code is written by the most careful coders?

A second, and equally hard, problem is how you maintain the security of a system in the face of incremental development. You might be lucky to start off with a product that's got a clean architecture tied to a well-understood protection profile, in which case the problem may be maintaining its coherence as repeated bug fixes and feature enhancements add complexity. The case history of cryptographic processors which I described in the chapter on API security shows how you can suddenly pass a point at which feature interactions fatally undermine your security architecture. An even worse (and more likely) case is where you start off with a product that's already messy, and you simultaneously have to fix security problems and provide new features. The former require the product to be made simpler, while the latter are simultaneously making it more complex.

A large part of the answer lies in how you recruit, train and manage your team of developers, and create a culture in which they get progressively better at writing secure code. Some useful insights come from the Capability Maturity Model developed by the Software Engineering Institute at Carnegie-Mellon University [873]. Although this is aimed at dependability and at delivering code on time rather than specifically at security, their research shows that capability is something that develops in groups; it's not just a purely individual thing. This is especially important if your job is to write (say) the software for a new mobile phone and you've got 20 people only one of whom has any real security background.

The trick lies in managing the amount of specialisation in the team, and the way in which the specialists (such as the security architect and the testing guru) interact with the other developers. Let's think first of all the stuff you need to keep track of to manage the development of secure code.

First, there are some things that everybody should know. Everyone must understand that security software and software security aren't the same thing; and that just about any application can have vulnerabilities. Every developer has to know about the bugs that most commonly lead to vulnerabilities — stack overflows, integer overflows, race conditions and off-by-one errors. They should even understand the more exotic stuff like double frees. Personally I'd ask questions about these topics when recruiting, to filter out the clueless. If you're stuck with an existing team then you just have to train them — get them to read Gary McGraw's book 'Software Security — Building Security In' [858], and Michael Howard and David LeBlanc's 'Writing Secure Code' [627]. (Getting them to read this book too is unlikely to do them any harm, though I say it myself.) Everyone on your team should also know about the specific problems relevant to your application. if you're developing web applications, they have to know about cross-site attacks; if you're doing an accounting system, they need to know about COSO and internal controls.

Second, you need to think hard about the tool support your team will need. If you want to prevent most stack overflows being written, you'll need static analysis tools — and these had better be tools that you can maintain and extend yourself. Bugs tend to be correlated: when you find one, you'd better look for similar ones elsewhere in your code base. Indeed, one of the big improvements Microsoft's made in its development process since Bill's security blitz is that when a bug is found, they update their tools to find all similar ones. You'd better be able to do this too. You also need fuzzers so you can check code modules for vulnerability to overflows of various kinds; these are often not obvious to visual inspection, and now that the bad guys have automated means of finding them, you need the same.

Third, you need to think about the libraries you'll use. Professional development teams avoid a large number of the problems described in this book by using libraries. You avoid crypto problems — timing attacks, weak keys, zero keys — by using good libraries, which you'll probably buy in. You avoid many buffer overflows by using your own standard libraries for I/O and for those functions that your chosen programming language does badly. Your libraries should enforce a type system, so that normal code just can't process wicked input.

Fourth, your tools and libraries have to support your architecture. The really critical thing here is that you need to be able to evolve APIs safely. A system's architecture is defined more than anything else by its interfaces, and it decays by a thousand small cuts: by a programmer needing a file handling routine that uses two more parameters than the existing one, and who therefore writes a new routine — which may be dangerous in itself, or may just add to complexity and thus contribute indirectly to an eventual failure. You need to use, and build on, whatever structures your programming language provides so that you can spot API violations using types.

This is already more than most developers could cope with individually. So how do you manage the inevitable specialisation? One approach is inspired by Fred Brooks' famous book, 'The Mythical Man-Month', in which he describes the lessons learned from developing the world's first large software product, the operating system for the IBM S/360 mainframe [231]. He describes the 'chief programmer team', a concept evolved by his colleague Harlan Mills, in which a chief programmer — a highly productive coder — is supported by a number of other staff including a toolsmith, a tester and a language lawyer. Modern development teams don't quite fit this vision, as there will be a number of developers, but a variant of it makes sense if you're trying to develop secure code.

Assume that there will be an architect — perhaps the lead developer, perhaps a specialist — who will act, as Brooks puts it, as the agent, the approver and the advocate for the user. Assume that you'll also have a toolsmith, a tester and a language lawyer. One of these should be your security guru. If the tough issue is evolving a security policy, or even just tidying up a messy product and giving it the logical coherence needed for customers to understand it and use it safely, then the security guy should probably be the architect. If the tough issue is pulling out lots of implementation errors that have crept into a legacy product over years — as with Microsoft's security jihad on buffer overflows in Windows XP — then it should probably be the tester, at least in the beginning. If the task then changes to one of evolving the static analysis tools so that these vulnerabilities don't creep back, the security mantle will naturally pass to the toolsmith. And if the APIs are everything, and there is constant pressure to add extra features that will break them — as in the crypto processor case history I discussed in the chapter on API security — then the language lawyer will have to pick up the burden of ensuring that the APIs retain whatever type-safety and other properties are required to prevent attacks.

So far so good. However, it's not enough to have the skills: you need to get people to work together. There are many ways to do this. One possibility is the 'bug lunch' where developers are encouraged to discuss the latest subtle errors that they managed to find and remove. Whatever format you use, the critical factor is to create a culture in which people are open about stuff that broke and got fixed. It's bad practice if people who find bugs (even bugs that they coded themselves) just fix them quietly; as bugs are correlated, there are likely to be more. An example of good practice is in air traffic control, where it's expected that controllers making an error should not only fix it but declare it at once by open outcry: 'I have Speedbird 123 at flight level eight zero in the terminal control area by mistake, am instructing to descend to six zero'. That way any other controller with potentially conflicting traffic can notice, shout out, and coordinate. Software is less dramatic, but is no different: you need to get your developers comfortable with sharing their experiences with each other, including their errors.

Another very useful team-building exercise is the adoption of a standard style. One of the chronic problems with poorly-managed teams is that the codebase is in a chaotic mixture of styles, with everybody doing his own thing. The result is that when a programmer checks out some code to work on it, he may well spend half an hour formatting it and tweaking it into his own style. For efficiency reasons alone, you want to stop this. However, if your goal is to write secure code, there's another reason. When you find a bug, you want to know whether it was a design error or an implementation error. If you have no idea what the programmer who wrote it was thinking about, this can be hard. So it's important to have comments in the code which tell what the programmer thought he was doing. But teams can easily fight about the 'right' quantity and style of comments: in the OS/2 saga, IBM used a lot more than Microsoft did, so the IBM folks saw the guys from Redmond as a bunch of hackers, and they responded by disdaining the men from Armonk as a bunch of bureaucrats. So for goodness' sake sit everyone down and let them spend an afternoon hammering out what your house style will be. Provided there's enough for understanding bugs, it doesn't matter hugely what the style is: but it does matter that there is a consistent style that people accept and that is fit for purpose. Creating this style is a far better team-building activity than spending the afternoon paintballing.

25.7   Summary

Managing a project to build, or enhance, a system that has to be secure is a hard problem. This used to be thought of as 'security software' — producing a product such as an antivirus monitor or encryption program using expert help. The reality nowadays is often that you're writing a system that has to do real work — a web application, for example, or a gadget that listens to network traffic — and you want to keep out any vulnerabilities that would make it a target for attack. In other words, you want software security — and that isn't the same as security software.

Understanding the requirements is often the hardest part of the whole process. Like developing the system itself, security requirements engineering can involve a one-off project; it can be a limited iterative process; or it can be a matter of continuous evolution. Evolution is becoming the commonest as systems get larger and longer-lived, whether as packaged software, online services or gadgets. Security requirements are complicated by changes of scale, of business structures and — above all — of the environment, where the changes might be in the platform you use, the legal environment you work in, or the threats you face. Systems are fielded, get popular, and then get attacked.

Writing secure code has to be seen in this context: the big problem is to know what you're trying to do. However, even given a tight specification, or constant feedback from people hacking your product, you're not home and dry. There are a number of challenges in hiring the right people, keeping them up to date with attacks, backing them up with expertise in the right places which they'll actually use, reinforcing this with the right tools and language conventions, and above all creating an environment in which they work to improve their security capability.

Research Problems

The issues discussed in this chapter are among the hardest and the most important of any on our field. However, they tend to receive little attention because they lie at the boundaries with software engineering, applied psychology, economics and management. Each of these interfaces appears to be a potentially productive area of research. Security economics in particular has made great strides in the last few years, and people are starting to work on psychology. There is a thriving research community in decision science, where behavioural economists, psychologists and marketing folks look at why people really take the decisions they do; this field is ripe for mining by security researchers.

Yet we have all too little work on how these disciplines can be applied to organisations. For a start, it would be useful if someone were to collect a library of case histories of security failures caused by unsatisfactory incentives in organisations, such as [587, 662]. What might follow given a decent empirical foundation? For example, if organisational theory is where microeconomic analysis is applied to organisations, with a little psychology thrown in, then what would be the shape of an organisational theory applied to security? The late Jack Hirshleifer took the view that we should try to design organizations in which managers were forced to learn from their mistakes: how could we do that? How might you set up institutional structures to monitor changes in the threat environment and feed them through into not just systems development but into supporting activities such as internal control? Even more basically, how can you design an organization that is 'incentive-compatible' in the sense that staff behave with an appropriate level of care? And what might the cultural anthropology of organisations have to say? We saw in the last chapter how the response of governments to the apparently novel threats posed by Al-Qaida was maladaptive in many ways: how can you do corporate governance so that the firm doesn't fall prey to similar problems?

Further Reading

Managing the development of information systems has a large, diffuse and multidisciplinary literature. There are classics which everyone should read, such as Fred Brooks' 'Mythical Man Month' [231] and Nancy Leveson's 'Safeware' [786]. Standard textbooks on software engineering such as Roger Pressman [1041] and Hans van Vliet [1281] cover the basics of project management and requirements engineering. The economics of the software life cycle are discussed by Brooks and by Barry Boehm [199]. The Microsoft approach to managing software evolution is described by Steve McGuire [829], while their doctrine on threat modelling is discussed in a book by Frank Swiderski and Window Snyder [1236].

There are useful parallels with other engineering disciplines. An interesting book by Henry Petroski discusses the history of bridge building, why bridges fall down, and how civil engineers learned to learn from the collapses: what tends to happen is that an established design paradigm is stretched and stretched until it suddenly fails for some unforeseen reason [1021]. For a survey of risk management methods and tools, see Richard Baskerville [123] or Donn Parker [1005]. Computer system failures are another necessary subject of study; a must-read fortnightly source is the comp.risks newsgroup of which a selection has been collated and published in print by Peter Neumann [962].

Organizational aspects are discussed at length in the business school literature, but this can be bewildering to the outsider. If you're only going to read one book, make it Lewis Pinault's 'Consulting Demons' — the confessions of a former insider about how the big consulting firms rip off their customers [1028]. John Micklethwait and Adrian Wooldridge provide a critical guide to the more academic literature and draw out a number of highly relevant tensions, such as the illogicality of management gurus who tell managers to make their organizations more flexible by sacking people, while at the same time preaching the virtues of trust [882]. As for the theory of internal control, such as it is, the best book is by Steven Root, who discusses its design and evolution [1082]. The best introductory book I know to the underlying microeconomics is by Carl Shapiro and Hal Varian [1159]: the new institutional school has written much more on the theory of the firm.

Finally, the business of managing secure software development is getting more attention (at last). Microsoft's security VP Mike Nash describes the background to the big security push and the adoption of the security development lifecycle at [929]. The standard books I'd get everyone to read are Michael

Howard and David LeBlanc's 'Writing Secure Code' [627], which sets out the Microsoft approach to managing the security lifecycle, and Gary McGraw's book 'Software Security — Building Security In' [858], which is a first-class resource on what goes wrong. As I wrote, Microsoft, Symantec, EMC, Juniper Networks and SAP have just announced the establishment of an industry body, SAFEcode. to develop best practices. And about time too!

CHAPTER 26

System Evaluation and Assurance

If it's provably secure, it probably isn't.
— **Lars Knudsen**

I think any time you expose vulnerabilities it's a good thing.
— **Attorney General Janet Reno [1068]**

Open source is good for security because it prevents you from even trying to violate Kerckhoffs's Law.
— **Eric Raymond**

26.1   Introduction

I've covered a lot of material in this book, some of it quite difficult. But I've left the hardest parts to the last. These are the questions of *assurance* — whether the system will work — and *evaluation* — how you convince other people of this. How do you make a decision to ship the product, and how do you sell the safety case to your insurers?

Assurance fundamentally comes down to the question of whether capable motivated people have beat up on the system enough. But how do you define 'enough'? And how do you define the 'system'? How do you deal with people who protect the wrong thing, because their model of the requirements is out-of-date or plain wrong? And how do you allow for human failures? There are many systems which can be operated just fine by alert experienced professionals, but are unfit for purpose because they're too tricky for ordinary folk to use or are intolerant of error.

But if assurance is hard, evaluation is even harder. It's about how you convince your boss, your clients — and, in extremis, a jury — that the system is indeed fit for purpose; that it does indeed work (or that it did work at some particular time in the past). The reason that evaluation is both necessary and hard is that, often, one principal carries the cost of protection while another carries the risk of failure. This creates an obvious tension, and third-party evaluation schemes such as the Common Criteria are often used to make it more transparent.

26.2 Assurance

A working definition of *assurance* could be 'our estimate of the likelihood that a system will fail in a particular way'. This estimate can be based on a number of factors, such as the process used to develop the system; the identity of the person or team who developed it; particular technical assessments, such as the use of formal methods or the deliberate introduction of a number of bugs to see how many of them are caught by the testing team; and experience — which ultimately depends on having a model of how reliability grows (or decays) over time as a system is subjected to testing, use and maintenance.

26.2.1 Perverse Economic Incentives

A good starting point is to look at the various principals' motives, and as a preliminary let's consider the things of which we may need assurance. Right at the start of this book, in Figure 1.1, I presented a framework for thinking rationally about security engineering based on incentives, policy, mechanism and assurance.

- *Incentives* are critical, as we've seen time and again. If people don't actually want to protect a system it's hard to make them. They fall somewhat outside the formal assurance process, but are the most critical part of the environment within which the security policy has to be defined.

- *Policy* is often neglected, as we've seen: people often end up protecting the wrong things, or protecting the right things in the wrong way. Recall from Chapter 9, for example, how the use of the Bell-LaPadula model in the healthcare environment caused more problems than it solved. We spent much of Part II of the book exploring security policies for different applications, and much of the previous chapter discussing how you'd go about developing a policy for a new application.

- *Mechanisms* have been in the news repeatedly. U.S. export controls on crypto led to products like DVD being shipped with 40-bit keys that were intrinsically vulnerable. Strength of mechanisms is independent of policy, but can interact with it. For example, I remarked how the difficulty of preventing probing attacks on smartcards led the industry to protect other, relatively unimportant things such as the secrecy of chip masks.

■ Assurance traditionally focussed on *implementation*, and was about whether, given the agreed functionality and strength of mechanisms, the product has been implemented correctly. As we've seen, most real-life technical security failures are due to programming bugs — stack overflows, race conditions and the like. Finding and fixing them absorbs most of the effort of the assurance community.

In the last few years, since the world moved from the Orange Book to the Common Criteria, policy has come within the overall framework of assurance, through the mechanism of protection profiles. Firms that do evaluations can be asked to assess a new protection profile, just as they can be asked to verify that a particular system meets an existing one. The mechanisms aren't quite satisfactory, though, for reasons I'll discuss later.

I should mention here that the big missing factor in the traditional approach to evaluation is usability. Most system-level (as opposed to purely technical) failures have a significant human component. Usability is a cross-cutting issue in the above framework: if done properly, it has a subtle effect on policy, a large effect on choice of mechanisms, and a huge effect on how systems are tested. However, designers often see assurance simply as an absence of obvious bugs, and tie up the technical protection mechanisms without stopping to consider human frailty. (There are some honourable exceptions: bookkeeping systems are designed from the start to cope with both error and sin, while security printing technologies are often optimized to make it easier for lay people to spot forgeries.) Usability is not purely a matter for end-users, but concerns developers too. We've seen how the access controls provided with commodity operating systems often aren't used, as it's so much simpler to make code run with administrator privilege.

The above factors are interdependent, and interact in many ways with the functionality of a product. The incentives are also often adrift in that the customers and the vendors want different things.

A rational PC user, for example, might want high usability, medium assurance (high would be expensive, and we can live with the odd virus), high strength of mechanisms (they don't cost much more), and simple functionality (usability is more important). But the market doesn't deliver this, and a moment's thought will indicate why.

Commercial platform vendors go for rich functionality (each feature benefits a more concentrated group of users than pay its costs, rapid product versioning prevents the market being commoditized, and complementary vendors who grab too much market share can be undermined), low strength of mechanisms (except for cryptography where the escrow debate led them to regard strong crypto as an essential marketing feature), low implementation assurance (so the military-grade crypto is easily defeated by Trojan horses), and low usability (application programmers matter much more than customers as they enhance network externalities).

In Chapter 7, we described why this won't change any time soon. Companies racing for dominance in platform markets start out by shipping too little security, as it gets in the way of complementers to whom they must appeal; and such security as they do ship is often of the wrong kind, as it's designed to dump costs on users even when these could be better borne by complementers. Once a firm has achieved dominance in a platform market, it will add security, but again of the wrong kind, as its incentive is now to lock its customers in. We've seen this not just with the PC platform but with mainframes, mobile phones and even with telephone switchgear. So the vendors provide less security than a rational customer would want; and, in turn, the customer wants less than would be socially optimal, as many of the costs of attaching an insecure machine to the Internet fall on others.

Government agencies' ideals are also frustrated by economics. They would like to be able to buy commercial off-the-shelf products, replace a small number of components (such as by plugging in crypto cards to replace the standard crypto with a classified version) and just be able to use the result on defense networks. So they want multilevel, or role-based, functionality, and high implementation assurance. There is little concern with usability as the agencies (wrongly) assume that their workforce is trainable and well-disciplined. This wish list is unrealistic given not just the cost of high assurance (which I'll discuss below), but also the primacy of time-to-market, the requirement to appease the developer community, and the need for frequent product versioning to prevent the commoditization of markets. Also, a million government computer users can't expect to impose their will on 500 million users of Windows and Office.

It's in this treacherous landscape with its many intractable political conflicts that the assurance game is played.

26.2.2 Project Assurance

Assurance as a process is very much like the development of code or of documents. Just as you will have bugs in your code, and in your specification, you will also have bugs in your test procedures. So assurance can be something that's done as a one-off project, or the subject of continuous evolution. An example of the latter is given by the huge databases of known malware which anti-virus software vendors accumulate over the years to do regression testing of their products. It can lie between the two, as with the spiral model where a fixed number of prototyping stages are used in a project to help generate a whole lot of test data which weren't clear at the start.

It can also be a combination, as when a step in an evolutionary development is managed using project techniques and is tested as a feature before being integrated and subjected to system level regression tests. Here, you also have to find ways of building feature tests into your regression test suite.

Nonetheless, it's helpful to look first at the project issues and then at the evolutionary issues.

26.2.2.1 Security Testing

In practice, security testing usually comes down to reading the product documentation, then reviewing the code, and then performing a number of tests. (This is known as *white-box* testing, as opposed to *black-box* testing in which the tester has the product but not the design documents or source code.) The process is:

- First look for any architectural flaws. Does the system use guessable or too-persistent session identifiers? Is there any way you can inject code, for example by sneaking SQL through a webserver into a back-end database? Is the security policy coherent, or are there gaps in between the assumptions? Do these lead to gaps in between the mechanisms where you can do wicked things?

- Then look for implementation flaws, such as stack overflows and integer overflows. This will usually involve not just looking at the code, but using specialist tools such as fuzzers.

- Then work down a list of less common flaws, such as those described in the various chapters of this book. If the product uses crypto, look for weak keys (or keys set to constant values) and poor random-number generators; if it has components with different trust assumptions, try to manipulate the APIs between them, looking for race conditions and other combinations of transactions that have evil effects.

This is an extremely telegraphic summary of one of the most fascinating and challenging jobs in the world. Many of the things the security tester needs to look for have been described at various places in this book; he should also be familiar with David Litchfield's *'Database Hacker's Handbook'*, Greg Hoglund and Gary McGraw's *'Exploiting Software'*, and Gary McGraw's *'Software Security'*, at a very minimum.

The process is usually structured by the requirements of a particular evaluation environment. For example, it might be necessary to show that each of a list of control objectives was assured by at least one protection mechanism; and in some industries, such as bank inspection, there are more or less established checklists (in banking, for example, there's [114]).

26.2.2.2 Formal Methods

In Chapter 3, I presented an example of a formal method — the BAN logic that can be used to verify certain properties of cryptographic protocols. The working engineer's take on formal methods may be that they're widely taught in universities, but not used anywhere in the real world. This isn't quite true in the security business. There are problems — such as designing crypto protocols — where intuition is often inadequate, and formal verification can be helpful. Military purchasers go further, and require their use as a condition of higher levels of evaluation under the Orange Book and the Common Criteria. (I'll discuss this further below.) For now, it's enough to say that this restricts high evaluation levels to relatively small and simple products such as line encryption devices and operating systems for primitive computers such as smartcards.

Even so, formal methods aren't infallible. Proofs can have errors too; and often the wrong thing gets proved [1117]. The quote by Lars Knudsen at the head of this chapter refers to the large number of breaks of cryptographic algorithms or protocols that had previously been proven secure. These breaks generally occur because one of the proof's assumptions is unrealistic, or has become so over time — as I discussed in the context of key management protocols in section 3.7.1.

26.2.2.3 Quis Custodiet?

Just as mistakes can be made by theorem provers and by testers, so they can also be made by people who draw up checklists of things for the testers to test (and by the security textbook writers from whose works the checklist writers draw). This is the old problem of *quis custodiet ipsos custodes*, as the Romans more succinctly put it — who shall watch the watchmen?

There are a number of things one can do, few of which are likely to appeal to the organization whose goal is a declaration that a product is free of faults. The obvious one is *fault injection*, in which a number of errors are deliberately introduced into the code at random. If there are a hundred such errors, and the tester finds seventy of them plus a further seventy that weren't deliberately introduced, then once the thirty remaining deliberate errors are removed you might expect that there are thirty bugs left that you don't know about. (This assumes that the errors you don't know about are distributed the same as the ones you do; reality will almost always be worse than this [219].)

Even in the absence of deliberate bug insertion, a rough estimate can be obtained by looking at which bugs are found by which testers. For example, I had Chapter 8 of the first edition of this book reviewed by a fairly large number of people, as I took a draft to a conference on the topic. Given the bugs they found, and the number of people who reviewed the other chapters,

I estimated that there are maybe three dozen errors of substance left in the book. Seven years and 25,000 copies later, readers had reported 99 errors (and I'd found a handful more myself while writing the second edition). Most were typos: the sixteen errors of substance discovered so far include 4 inaccurate definitions, 3 errors in formulae, one error in arithmetic, three things wrongly described, three acronyms incorrectly expanded, and two cryptographers' names wrong (Bruce Schneier, who wrote the foreword, miraculously became Prince Schneier). As the second edition adds about a third as much new material again, we might estimate that about fifteen bugs remain from the first edition and a further score have been introduced: a dozen in the new material and the rest in the course of rewriting existing chapters. (In the absence of automated regression tests, software engineers reckon that rewriting code will bring back about 20% of the old bugs.) So the second edition probably also has about three dozen bugs, but given that it's a couple of hundred pages longer I can call it a quality improvement.

So we get feedback from the rate at which instances of known bugs are discovered in products once they're fielded. Another factor is the rate at which new attacks are discovered. In the university system, we train graduate students by letting them attack stuff; new vulnerabilities and exploits end up in research papers that bring fame and ultimately promotion. The incentives in government agencies and corporate labs are slightly different but the overall effect is the same: a large group of capable motivated people looking for new exploits. Academics usually publish, government scientists usually don't, and corporate researchers sometimes do.

This all provides valuable input for reliability growth models. Once you have a mature product, you should have a good idea of the rate at which bugs will be discovered, the rate at which they're reported, the speed with which they're fixed, the proportion of your users who patch their systems quickly, and thus the likely vulnerability of your systems to attackers who either develop zero-day exploits of their own, or who reverse your patches looking for the holes you were trying to block.

26.2.3 Process Assurance

In recent years less emphasis has come to be placed on assurance measures focused on the product, such as testing, and more on process measures such as who developed the system. As anyone who's done system development knows, some programmers produce code with an order of magnitude fewer bugs than others. There are also some organizations that produce much better quality code than others. This is the subject of much attention in the industry.

As I remarked in the previous chapter, some of the differences between high-quality and low-quality developers are amenable to direct management intervention. A really important factor is whether people are responsible for correcting their own bugs. In the 1980s, many organizations interpreted the waterfall model of system development to mean that one team wrote the specification, another wrote the code, yet another did the testing (including some bug fixing), while yet another did the maintenance (including the rest of the bug fixing). They communicated with each other only via the project documentation. This was justified on the grounds that it is more efficient for people to concentrate on a single task at a time, so interrupting a programmer to ask him to fix a bug in code he wrote six months ago and had forgotten about could cost a day's productivity, while getting a maintenance programmer to do it might cost only an hour.

But the effect was that the coders produced megabytes of buggy code, and left it to the poor testers to clear up the mess. Over time, both quality and productivity sagged. Industry analysts ascribed IBM's near-death experience in the early 1990s, which cost over $100 billion in asset value, to this [273]. For its part, Microsoft considers that one of its most crucial lessons learned as it struggled with the problems of writing ever larger programs was to have a firm policy that 'if you wrote it, you fix it'. Bugs should be fixed as soon as possible; and even though they're as inevitable as death and taxes, programmers should never give up trying to write clean code.

Many other controllable aspects of the organization can have a significant effect on output quality, ranging from how bright your hires are through how you train them and the work habits you inculcate. (See Maguire for an extended discussion of the Microsoft policy [829].)

For some years, internal auditors have included process issues in evaluating the quality of security code. This is harder to do than you might think because a large part of an organization's quality culture is intangible. While some rules (such as 'fix your own bugs') seem to be fairly universal, imposing a large number of specific rules would induce a bureaucratic box-ticking culture rather than a dynamic competitive one. So recent work has striven for a more holistic assessment of a team's capability; a lead contender is the *Capability Maturity Model* (CMM) from the Software Engineering Institute at Carnegie-Mellon University.

CMM is based on the idea that competence is a function of teams rather than just individual developers. There's more to a band than just throwing together half-a-dozen competent musicians, and the same holds for software. Developers start off with different coding styles, different conventions for commenting and formatting code, different ways of managing APIs, and even different workflow rhythms. As I described in the last chapter, a capable project manager will bring them together as a team by securing agreement on conventions and ways of working, developing an understanding of different people's strengths, and matching them better to tasks. The Carnegie-Mellon research showed that newly-formed teams tended to underestimate the amount of work in a project, and also had a high variance in the amount of time they took; the teams that worked best together were much better able to predict how long they'd take, in terms of the mean development time, but reduced the variance as well.

Now one problem is that firms are forever reorganising for various reasons, and this disrupts established and capable teams. How can one push back on this, so as to maintain capability? Well, CMM offers a certification process whereby established teams may get themselves considered to be assets that are not to be lightly squandered. The details of the model are perhaps less important than this institutional role. But, in any case, it has five levels — initial, repeatable, defined, managed and optimizing — with a list of new things to be added as you go up hierarchy. Thus, for example, project planning must be introduced to move up from 'initial' to 'repeatable', and peer reviews to make the transition from 'repeatable' to 'defined'. For a fuller description and bibliography, see Hans van Vliet [1281]; there have been several attempts to adapt it to security work and a significant number of vendors have adopted it over the years [873, 1378].

An even more common process assurance approach is the ISO 9001 standard. The essence is that a company must document its processes for design, development, testing, documentation, audit and management control generally. For more detail, see [1281]; there is now a whole industry of consultants helping companies get ISO 9001 certification. At its best, this can provide a framework for incremental process improvement; companies can monitor what goes wrong, trace it back to its source, fix it, and prevent it happening again. But very often ISO 9001 is an exercise in ass-covering and box-ticking that merely replaces chaos by more bureaucratic chaos.

Many writers have remarked that organizations have a natural life cycle, just as people do; Joseph Schumpeter argued that economic depressions perform a valuable societal function of clearing out companies that are past it or just generally unfit, in much the same way fires rejuvenate forests. It's certainly true that successful companies become complacent and bureaucratic. Many insiders opt for an easy life, while other more ambitious ones leave: it used to be said that the only people who ever left IBM were the good ones. Too-rapid growth also brings problems: Microsoft insiders blame many of the security and other problems of Windows products on the influx of tens of thousands of new hires in the 1990s, many of whom were motivated more by the prospect of making millions from stock options than by the mission to write good code and get it running on every computer in the known universe.

The cycle of corporate birth, death and reincarnation turns much more quickly in the computer industry than elsewhere, thanks to the combination of Moore's law, network externalities and a freewheeling entrepreneurial culture. The telecomms industry suffered severe trauma as the two industries merged and the phone companies' fifteen year product cycles collided with the fifteen month cycles of Cisco, Microsoft and others. The information security industry is feeling the same pressures. Teams that worked steadily for decades on cost-plus contracts to develop encryptors or MLS systems for the NSA were suddenly exposed to ferocious technological and market forces, and told to build quite different things. Some succeeded: the MLS supplier TIS reinvented itself as a firewall and antivirus vendor. Others failed and disappeared. So management may question the value of a team of MLS greybeards. And expert teams may depend on one or two key gurus; when they go off to do a startup, the team's capability can evaporate overnight.

A frequently overlooked point is that assurance schemes, like crypto protocols, should support revocation. CMM would be more powerful if teams that had lost their stars, their sparkle or their relevance also lost their ranking. Perhaps we should rather have the sort of ranking system used in food guides, where you can't declare a new establishment to be 'the best Asian restaurant in San Francisco' unless you dislodge the incumbent. Of course, if certification were a more perishable asset, it would have to confer greater market advantage for companies to invest the same amount of effort in getting it. But by and large the restaurant guide system works, and academic peer review works somewhat along the same lines.

26.2.4   Assurance Growth

Another aspect of process-based assurance is that most customers are not so much interested in the development team as in its product. But most software nowadays is packaged rather than bespoke, and is developed by continual evolutionary enhancement rather than in a one-off project. So what can usefully be said about the assurance level of evolving products?

The quality of such a product can reach equilibrium if the rate at which new bugs are introduced by product enhancements equals the rate at which old bugs are found and removed. But there's no guarantee that this will happen. (There are second-order effects, such as *senescence* — when repeated enhancement makes code so complex that its underlying reliability and maintainability drop off — but I'll ignore them for the sake of simplicity.)

While controlling the bug-introduction rate depends on the kind of development controls already described, measuring the bug-removal rate requires different tools — models of how the reliability of software improves under testing.

There's quite a lot known about reliability growth as it's of interest to many more people than just software engineers. Where the tester is trying to find a single bug in a system, a reasonable model is the Poisson distribution: the probability p that the bug remains undetected after t statistically random tests is given by $p = e^{-Et}$ where E depends on the proportion of possible inputs that it affects [805]. So where the reliability of a system is dominated by a single bug — as when we're looking for the first bug in a system, or the last one — reliability growth can be exponential.

But extensive empirical investigations have shown that in large and complex systems, the likelihood that the t-th test fails is not proportional to e^{-Et} but to k/t for some constant k. So the system's reliability grows very much more slowly. This phenomenon was first documented in the bug history of IBM mainframe operating systems [9], and has been confirmed in many other studies [819]. As a failure probability of k/t means a mean time between failure (MTBF) of about t/k, reliability grows linearly with testing time. This result is often stated by the safety critical systems community as 'If you want a mean time between failure of a million hours, then you have to test for (at least) a million hours' [247]. This has been one of the main arguments against the development of complex, critical systems that can't be fully tested before use, such as ballistic missile defence.

The reason for the k/t behaviour emerged in [174]; colleagues and I then proved it under much more general assumptions in [219]. The model gives a number of other interesting results. Under assumptions which are often reasonable, it is the best possible: the rule that you need a million hours of testing to get a million hours MTBF is inescapable, up to some constant multiple which depends on the initial quality of the code and the scope of the testing. This amounts to a proof of a version of 'Murphy's Law': that the number of defects which survive a selection process is maximised.

The model is similar to mathematical models of the evolution of a biological species under selective pressure. The role of 'bugs' is played, roughly, by genes that reduce fitness. But some of the implications are markedly different. 'Murphy's Law', that the number of defects that survive a selection process is maximised, may be bad news for the engineer but it's good news for biological species. While software testing removes the minimum possible number of bugs, consistent with the tests applied, biological evolution enables a species to adapt to a changed environment at a minimum cost in early deaths, and meanwhile preserving as much diversity as possible. This diversity helps the species survive future environmental shocks.

For example, if a population of rabbits is preyed on by snakes then they will be selected for alertness rather than speed. The variability in speed will remain, so if foxes arrive in the neighbourhood the rabbit population's average running speed will rise sharply under selective predation. More formally, the *fundamental theorem of natural selection* says that a species with a high genic variance can adapt to a changing environment more quickly. But when Sir Ronald Fisher proved this in 1930 [475], he was also proving that complex software will exhibit the maximum possible number of bugs when you migrate it to a new environment.

The evolutionary model also points to fundamental limits on the reliability gains to be had from re-usable software components such as objects or libraries;

well-tested libraries simply mean that overall failure rates will be dominated by new code. It also explains the safety-critical systems community's observation that test results are often a poor performance indicator [805]: the failure time measured by a tester depends only on the initial quality of the program, the scope of the testing and the number of tests, so it gives virtually no further information about the program's likely performance in another environment. There are also some results that are unexpected, but obvious in retrospect: for example, each bug's contribution to the overall failure rate is independent of whether the code containing it is executed frequently or rarely — intuitively, code that is executed less is also tested less. Finally, as I mentioned in section 25.4.3, it is often more economic for different testers to work on a program in parallel rather than in series.

So complex systems only become reliable following prolonged testing. The wide use of mass market software enables thorough debugging in principle, but in practice the constant new versions dictated by network economics place severe limits on what may reasonably be expected.

26.2.5   Evolution and Security Assurance

Evolutionary growth of reliability may be much worse for the software engineer than for a biological species, but for the security engineer it's worse still.

Rather than going into the detailed mathematics, let's take a simplified example. Suppose a complex product such as Windows Vista has 1,000,000 bugs each with an MTBF of 1,000,000,000 hours. Suppose that Ahmed works in Bin Laden's cave where his job is to break into the U.S. Army's network to get the list of informers in Baghdad, while Brian is the army assurance guy whose job is to stop Ahmed. So he must learn of the bugs before Ahmed does.

Ahmed has to move around to avoid the Pakistani army, so he can only do 1000 hours of testing a year. Brian has full Vista source code, dozens of PhDs, control of the commercial evaluation labs, an inside track on CERT, an information sharing deal with other UKUSA member states, and also runs the government's scheme to send round consultants to critical industries such as power and telecomms to find out how to hack them (pardon me, to advise them how to protect their systems). So Brian does 10,000,000 hours a year of testing.

After a year, Ahmed finds a bug, while Brian has found 10,000. But the probability that Brian has found Ahmed's bug is only 1%. Even if Brian drafts 50,000 computer science graduates to Fort Meade and sets them trawling through the Windows source code, he'll still only get 100,000,000 hours of testing done each year. After ten years he will find Ahmed's bug. But by then Ahmed will have found nine more, and it's unlikely that Brian will know of all of them. Worse, Brian's bug reports will have become such a firehose that Bill will have stopped fixing them.

In other words, Ahmed has thermodynamics on his side. Even a very moderately resourced attacker can break anything that's large and complex. There is nothing that can be done to stop this, so long as there are enough different security vulnerabilities to do statistics. In real life, vulnerabilities are correlated rather than independent; if 90% of your vulnerabilities are stack overflows, and you introduce compiler technology to trap them, then for modelling purposes there was only a single vulnerability. However, it's taken many years to sort-of-not-quite fix that particular vulnerability, and new ones come along all the time. So if you are actually responsible for Army security, you can't just rely on a large complex commercial off-the-shelf product. You have to have mandatory access controls, implemented in something like a mail guard that's simple enough to verify. Simplicity is the key to escaping the statistical trap.

26.3 Evaluation

A working definition of *evaluation* is 'the process of assembling evidence that a system meets, or fails to meet, a prescribed assurance target'. (It overlaps with testing and is sometimes confused with it.) As I mentioned above, this evidence might only be needed to convince your boss that you've completed the job. But often it is needed to reassure principals who will rely on the system. The fundamental problem is the tension that arises when the party who implements the protection and the party who relies on it are different.

Sometimes the tension is simple and fairly manageable, as when you design a burglar alarm to standards set by insurance underwriters and have it certified by inspectors at their laboratories. Sometimes it's still visible but more complex, as when designing to government security standards which try to reconcile dozens of conflicting institutional interests, or when hiring your company's auditors to review a system and tell your boss that it's fit for purpose. It is harder when multiple principals are involved; for example, when a smartcard vendor wants an evaluation certificate from a government agency (which is trying to encourage the use of some feature such as key escrow that is in no-one else's interest), in order to sell the card to a bank, which in turn wants to use it to dump the liability for fraud on to its customers. That may seem all rather crooked; but there may be no clearly criminal conduct by any of the people involved. The crookedness can be an emergent property that arises from managers following their own personal and departmental incentives.

For example, managers often buy products and services that they know to be suboptimal or even defective, but which are from big name suppliers — just to minimize the likelihood of getting fired when things go wrong. (It used to be said 20 years ago that 'no-one ever got fired for buying IBM'.) Corporate lawyers don't condemn this as fraud, but praise it as due diligence. The end result may be that someone who relies on a system — in this case, the bank's customer — has no say, and will find it hard to get redress against the bank, the vendor, the evaluator or the government when things go wrong.

Another serious and pervasive problem is that the words 'assurance' and 'evaluation' are often interpreted to apply only to the narrow technical aspects of the system, and ignore system issues like usability — not to mention organizational issues such as appropriate internal control and good corporate governance. Company directors also want assurance: that the directed procedures are followed, that there are no material errors in the accounts, that applicable laws are being complied with, and dozens of other things. But many evaluation schemes (especially the Common Criteria) studiously ignore the human and organizational elements in the system. If any thought is paid to them at all, the evaluation of these elements is considered to be a matter for the client's IT auditors, or even a matter for a system administrator setting up configuration files.

That said, I'll focus on technical evaluation in what follows.

It is convenient to break evaluation into two cases. The first is where the evaluation is performed by the relying party; this includes insurance assessments, the independent verification and validation done by NASA on mission critical code, and the previous generation of military evaluation criteria such as the Orange Book. The second is where the evaluation is done by someone other than the relying party. Nowadays this often means the Common Criteria.

26.3.1 Evaluations by the Relying Party

In Chapter 11, I discussed the concerns insurers have with physical security systems, and how they go about approving equipment for use with certain sizes of risk. The approval process itself is simple enough; the insurance industry operates laboratories where tests are conducted. These might involve a fixed budget of effort (perhaps one person for two weeks, or a cost of $15,000). The evaluator starts off with a fairly clear idea of what a burglar alarm (for example) should and should not do, spends the budgeted amount of effort looking for flaws and writes a report. The laboratory then either approves the device, turns it down or demands some changes.

The main failure mode of this process is that it doesn't always respond well enough to progress in attack technology. In the case of high-security locks, a lab may demand ten minutes' resistance to picking and say nothing about bumping. Yet bumping tools have improved enough to be a major threat, and picks have got better too. A product that got its certificate ten years ago might now be easy to bump (so the standard's out of date) and also be vulnerable to picking within 2–3 minutes (so the test result is too). Insurance labs in some countries, such as Germany, have been prepared to withdraw certifications as attacks got better; in other countries, like the USA, they're reluctant to do so, perhaps for fear of being sued.

In section 8.4, I mentioned another model of evaluation — that are done from 1985–2000 at the U.S. National Computer Security Center on computer security products proposed for government use. These evaluations were conducted according to the *Orange Book* — the Trusted Computer Systems Evaluation Criteria [375]. The Orange Book and its supporting documents set out a number of evaluation classes:

C1: discretionary access control by groups of users. In effect, this is considered to be equal to no protection.

C2: discretionary access control by single users; object reuse; audit. C2 corresponds to carefully configured commercial systems; for example, C2 evaluations were given to IBM mainframe operating systems, and to Windows NT. (Both of these were conditional on a particular configuration; in NT's case, for example, it was restricted to diskless workstations.)

B1: mandatory access control — all objects carry security labels and the security policy (which means Bell-LaPadula or a variant) is enforced independently of user actions. Labelling is enforced for all input information.

B2: structured protection — as B1 but there must also be a formal model of the security policy that has been proved consistent with security axioms. Tools must be provided for system administration and configuration management. The TCB must be properly structured and its interface clearly defined. Covert channel analysis must be performed. A trusted path must be provided from the user to the TCB. Severe testing, including penetration testing, must be carried out.

B3: security domains — as B2 but the TCB must be minimal, it must mediate all access requests, it must be tamper-resistant, and it must withstand formal analysis and testing. There must be real-time monitoring and alerting mechanisms, and structured techniques must be used in implementation.

A1: verification design. As B3, but formal techniques must be used to prove the equivalence between the TCB specification and the security policy model.

The evaluation class of a system determined what spread of information could be processed on it. The example I gave in section 8.6.2 was that a system evaluated to B3 may process information at Unclassified, Confidential and

Secret, or at Confidential, Secret and Top Secret. The complete rule set can be found in [379].

When the Orange Book was written, the Department of Defense thought the real problem was that markets for defense computing equipment were too small, leading to high prices. The solution was to expand the market for high-assurance computing. So the goal was to develop protection measures that would be standard in all major operating systems, rather than an expensive add-on for captive government markets.

However, the business model of Orange Book evaluations followed traditional government work practices. A government user would want some product evaluated; the NSA would allocate people to do it; given traditional civil service caution and delay, this could take two or three years; the product, if successful, would join the evaluated products list; and the bill was picked up by the taxpayer. The process was driven and controlled by the government — the party that was going to rely on the results of the evaluation — while the vendor was the supplicant at the gate. Because of the time the process took, evaluated products were usually one or two generations behind current commercial products. This meant that evaluated products were just not acceptable in commercial markets. The defense computing market stayed small, and prices stayed high.

The Orange Book wasn't the only evaluation scheme running in America. I mentioned in section 16.4 the FIPS 140-1 scheme for assessing the tamper-resistance of cryptographic processors; this uses a number of independent laboratories as contractors. Contractors are also used for *Independent Verification and Validation* (IV&V), a scheme set up by the Department of Energy for systems to be used in nuclear weapons, and later adopted by NASA for manned space flight which has many similar components (at least at the rocketry end of things). In IV&V, there is a simple evaluation target — zero defects. The process is still driven and controlled by the relying party — the government. The IV&V contractor is a competitor of the company that built the system, and its payments are tied to the number of bugs found.

Other governments had similar schemes. The Canadians had the *Canadian Trusted Products Evaluation Criteria* (CTPEC) while a number of European countries developed the *Information Technology Security Evaluation Criteria* (ITSEC). The idea was that a shared evaluation scheme would help European defense contractors compete against U.S. suppliers with their larger economies of scale; they would no longer have to have separate certification in Britain, France, Germany. ITSEC combined ideas from the Orange Book and IV&V processes in that there were a number of different evaluation levels, and for all but the highest of these levels the work was contracted out. However, ITSEC introduced a pernicious innovation — that the evaluation was not paid for by the government but by the vendor seeking an evaluation on its product. This was an attempt to kill several birds with one stone: saving public money while promoting a more competitive market. However, the incentive issues were not properly thought through.

This change in the rules motivated the vendor to shop around for the evaluation contractor who would give his product the easiest ride, whether by asking fewer questions, charging less money, taking the least time, or all of the above[1]. To be fair, the potential for this was realized, and schemes were set up whereby contractors could obtain approval as a *commercial licensed evaluation facility* (CLEF). The threat that a CLEF might have its license withdrawn was supposed to offset the commercial pressures to cut corners.

26.3.2   The Common Criteria

This sets the stage for the Common Criteria. The Defense Department began to realise that the Orange Book wasn't making procurement any easier, and contractors detested having to obtain separate evaluations for their products in the USA, Canada and Europe. Following the collapse of the Soviet Union in 1989, budgets started being cut, and it wasn't clear where the capable motivated opponents of the future would come from. The mood was in favour of radical cost-cutting. Eventually agreement was reached to scrap the national evaluation schemes and replace them with a single standard; the Common Criteria for Information Technology Security Evaluation [935].

The work was substantially done in 1994–1995, and the European model won out over the U.S. and Canadian alternatives. As with ITSEC, evaluations at all but the highest levels are done by CLEFs and are supposed to be recognised in all participating countries (though any country can refuse to honor an evaluation if it says its national security is at stake); and vendors pay for the evaluations.

There are some differences. Most crucially, the Common Criteria have much more flexibility than the Orange Book. Rather than expecting all systems to conform to Bell-LaPadula, a product is evaluated against a *protection profile*. There are protection profiles for operating systems, access control systems, boundary control devices, intrusion detection systems, smartcards, key management systems, VPN clients, and even waste-bin identification systems — for transponders that identify when a domestic bin was last emptied. The tent is certainly a lot broader than with the Orange Book. However, anyone can propose a protection profile and have it evaluated by the lab of his choice, and so there are a lot of profiles. It's not that Department of Defense has abandoned multilevel security, so much as tried to get commercial IT vendors to use the system for other purposes too, and thus defeat the perverse incentives described above. The aspiration was to create a

---

[1]The same may happen with FIPS 140-1 now that commercial companies are starting to rely on it for third-party evaluations.

bandwagon effect that would result in the commercial world adapting itself somewhat to the government way of doing things.

Its success has been mixed. The only major case I can recall of a large firm using evaluations in its general marketing was Oracle, which started a marketing campaign after 9/11 describing its products as 'Unbreakable', claiming that each of its fourteen security evaluations 'represented an extra million dollars' investment in security [989]. (This campaign ran out of steam after a number of people found ways to break their products.) But there have been quite a few cases of evaluations being used in more specialised markets; I already discussed bank card terminals (which turned out to be easy to break) in Chapter 10. The smartcard industry has been a particular fan of evaluation: in 2007, there are no less than 26 smartcard protection profiles, and a number of derivative profiles for smartcard-based devices such as TPMs and electronic signature creation devices. But perhaps it's worked too well. There's a big choice and it's not easy to understand what an evaluation certificate actually means. (We came across this problem in Chapter 16: some cryptographic processors were certified secure as hardware devices but broken easily as they were used to run inappropriate software.)

To discuss the Common Criteria in detail, we need some more jargon. The product under test is known as the *target of evaluation* (TOE). The rigor with which the examination is carried out is the *evaluation assurance level* (EAL) and can range from EAL 1, for which functional testing is sufficient, all the way up to EAL7 for which not only thorough testing is required but a formally verified design. The highest evaluation level commonly obtained for commercial products is EAL4, although there was one smartcard operating system at EAL6.

A protection profile consists of security requirements, their rationale, and an EAL. It's supposed to be expressed in an implementation-independent way to enable comparable evaluations across products and versions. A *security target* (ST) is a refinement of a protection profile for a given target of evaluation. As well as evaluating a specific target, one can evaluate a protection profile (to ensure that it's complete, consistent and technically sound) and a security target (to check that it properly refines a given protection profile). When devising something from scratch, the idea is to first create a protection profile and evaluate it (if a suitable one doesn't exist already), then do the same for the security target, then finally evaluate the actual product. The end result of all this is a registry of protection profiles and a catalogue of evaluated products.

A protection profile should describe the environmental assumptions, the objectives, and the protection requirements (in terms of both function and assurance) and break them down into components. There is a stylized way of doing this. For example, FCO_NRO is a functionality component (hence F) relating to communications (CO) and it refers to non-repudiation of origin (NRO). Other classes include FAU (audit), FCS (crypto support), and FDP which means data protection (this isn't data protection as in European law, but means access control, Bell-LaPadula information flow controls, and related properties).

There are catalogues of

- *threats*, such as T.Load_Mal — 'Data loading malfunction: an attacker may maliciously generate errors in set-up data to compromise the security functions of the TOE'

- *assumptions*, such as A.Role_Man — 'Role management: management of roles for the TOE is performed in a secure manner' (in other words, the developers, operators and so on behave themselves)

- *organizational policies*, such as P.Crypt_Std — 'Cryptographic standards: cryptographic entities, data authentication, and approval functions must be in accordance with ISO and associated industry or organizational standards'

- *objectives*, such as O.Flt_Ins — 'Fault insertion: the TOE must be resistant to repeated probing through insertion of erroneous data'

- *assurance requirements*, such as ADO_DEL.2 — 'Detection of modification: the developer shall document procedures for delivery of the TOE or parts of it to the user'

I mentioned that a protection profile will contain a *rationale*. This typically consists of tables showing how each threat is controlled by one or more objectives and in the reverse direction how each objective is necessitated by some combination of threats or environmental assumptions, plus supporting explanations. It will also justify the selection of an assurance level and requirements for strength of mechanism.

The fastest way to get the hang of this is probably to read a few of the existing profiles. You will realise that the quality varies quite widely. For example, the Eurosmart protection profile for smartcards relates largely to maintaining confidentiality of the chip design by imposing NDAs on contractors, shredding waste and so on [448], while in practice most attacks on smartcards used probing or power-analysis attacks for which knowledge of the chip mask was not relevant. Another example of an unimpressive protection profile is that for automatic cash dispensers, which is written in management-speak, complete with clip art, 'has elected not to include any security policy' and misses even many of the problems that were well known and documented when it was written in 1999. Indeed it states that it relies on the developer to document vulnerabilities and demands that 'the evaluator shall determine that the TOE is resistant to penetration attacks performed by an attacker possessing a moderate attack potential' [240]. A better example is the more recent profile devised by the German government for health professional cards — the cards used by doctors and nurses to log on to hospital computer systems [241]. This goes into great detail about possible threats involving physical tampering, power analysis, functionality abuse, and so on, and ties the protection mechanisms systematically to the control objectives.

So the first question you should ask when told that some product has a Common Criteria Evaluation is: 'against what protection profile?' Is it a secret design that will resist a 'moderate attack', or has it been evaluated against something thorough that's been thought through by people who know what they're doing? The interesting thing is that all the three profiles I mentioned in the above paragraph are for evaluation to level EAL4+ — so it's not the nominal CC level that tells you anything, but the details of the PP.

The Criteria do say that 'the fact that an IT product has been evaluated has meaning only in the context of the security properties that were evaluated and the evaluation methods that were used', but it goes on to say both that 'Evaluation authorities should carefully check the products, properties and methods to determine that an evaluation will provide meaningful results' and 'purchasers of evaluated products should carefully consider this context to determine whether the evaluated product is useful and applicable to their specific situation and needs.' So who's actually liable? Well, we find that 'the CC does not address the administrative and legal framework under which the criteria may be applied by evaluation authorities' and that 'The procedures for use of evaluation results in accreditation are outside the scope of the CC'.

The Common Criteria can sometimes be useful to the security engineer in that they give you an extensive list of things to check, and the framework can also help in keeping track of all the various threats and ensuring that they're all dealt with systematically (otherwise it's very easy for one to be forgotten in the mass of detail and slip through). What people often do, though, is to find a protection profile that seems reasonably close to what they're trying to do and just use it as a checklist without further thought. If you pick a profile that's a poor match, or one of the older and vaguer ones, you're asking for trouble.

26.3.3 What the Common Criteria Don't Do

It's also important to understand the Criteria's limitations. The documents claim that they don't deal with administrative security measures, nor 'technical physical' aspects such as Emsec, nor crypto algorithms, nor the evaluation methodology (though there's a companion volume on this), nor how the standards are to be used. They claim not to assume any specific development methodology (but then go on to assume a waterfall approach). There is a nod in the direction of evolving the policy in response to experience but re-evaluation of products is declared to be outside the scope. Oh, and there is no requirement for evidence that a protection profile corresponds to the real world; and I've seen a few that studiously ignore published work on relevant vulnerabilities. In other words, the Criteria avoid all the hard and interesting bits of security engineering, and can easily become a cherry pickers' charter.

The most common specific criticism (apart from cost and bureaucracy) is that the Criteria are too focused on the technical aspects of design: things like usability are almost ignored, and the interaction of a firm's administrative procedures with the technical controls is glossed over as outside the scope.

Another common criticism is that the Criteria don't cope well with change. A lot of commercial products have an evaluation that's essentially meaningless: operating systems such as Windows and Linux have been evaluated, but in very restricted configurations (typically, a workstation with no network connection or removable media — where all the evaluation is saying is that there's a logon process and that filesystem access controls work). Products with updates, such as Windows with its monthly security patches, are outside the scope. This can lead to insecurity directly: I remarked that the first real distributed denial-of-service attack used hospital PCs, as the evaluation and accreditation process in use at the time compelled hospitals to use an obsolete and thus unsafe configuration.

It's actually very common, when you read the small print of the PP, to find that only some very basic features of the product have been evaluated. The vendor might have evaluated the boot code, but left most of the operating system outside the scope. This applies not just to CC evaluations, but to FIPS-140 as well; in the chapter on API Security I told how the IBM 4758 was evaluated by the U.S. government to the highest standard of physical tamper-resistance, and yet broken easily. The evaluators looked only at the tamper-resistant platform, while the attackers also looked at the software that ran on it.

Another fundamental problem is that the Criteria are technology-driven, when in most applications it's the business processes that should drive protection decisions. Technical mechanisms shouldn't be used where the exposure is less than the cost of controlling it, or where procedural controls are cheaper. Remember why Samuel Morse beat the dozens of other people who raced to build electric telegraphs in the early nineteenth century. They tried to build modems, so they could deliver text from one end to the other; Morse realized that given the technology then available, it was cheaper to train people to be modems.

Over the last decade, I must have been involved in half-dozen disputes about whether protection mechanisms were properly designed or implemented, and in which the Common Criteria were in some way engaged. In not one of these has their approach proved satisfactory. (Perhaps that's because I only get called in when things go wrong — but my experience still indicates a lack of robustness in the process.) There are not just the technical limitations, and scope limitations; there are also perverse incentives and political failures.

26.3.3.1   Corruption, Manipulation and Inertia

Common Criteria evaluations are done by CLEFS — contractors who are 'Commercial Licensed Evaluation Facilities'. They are licensed by the local signals intelligence agency (the NSA in America, or its counterparts in the UK, Canada, France, Germany, Spain, the Netherlands, Australia, New Zealand and Japan). One consequence is that their staff must all have clearances. As a result, the CLEFs are rather beholden to the local spooks.

One egregious example in my experience occurred in the British National Health Service. The service had agreed, under pressure from doctors, to encrypt traffic on the health service network; the signals intelligence service GCHQ made clear that it wanted key escrow products used. Trials were arranged; one of them used commercial encryption software from a Danish supplier that had no key escrow and cost £3,000, while the other used software from a UK defence contractor that had key escrow and cost £100,000. To GCHQ's embarrassment, the Danish software worked but the British supplier produced nothing that was usable. The situation was quickly retrieved by having a company with a CLEF license evaluate the trials. In their report, they claimed the exact reverse: that the escrow software worked fine while the foreign product had all sorts of problems. Perhaps the CLEF was simply told what to write; or perhaps the staff wrote what they knew GCHQ wanted to read.

A second problem is that, as it's the vendor who pays the CLEF, the vendor can shop around for a CLEF that will give it an easy ride technically, or that will follow its political line. In the context of the Icelandic health database I discussed in section 9.3.4.1 above, its promoters wished to defuse criticism from doctors about its privacy problems, so they engaged a British CLEF to write a protection profile for them. This simply repeated, in Criteria jargon, the promoters' original design and claims; it studiously avoided noticing flaws in this design which had already been documented and even discussed on Icelandic TV [51].

Sometimes the protection profiles might be sound, but the way they're mapped to the application isn't. For example, smartcard vendors lobbied European governments to pass laws forcing business to recognise digital signatures made using smartcards; a number of protection profiles were duly written for a smartcard to function as a 'Secure Signature-Creation Device'. But the main problem in such an application is the PC that displays to the citizen the material she thinks she's signing. As that problem's too hard, it's excluded, and the end result will be a 'secure' (in the sense of non-repudiable) signature on whatever the virus or Trojan in your PC sent to your smartcard.

Electronic signatures didn't take off; no sensible person would agree to be bound by any signature that appeared to have been made by her smartcard, regardless of whether she actually made it. (By comparison, in the world of paper, a forged manuscript signature is completely null and void, and it can't bind anyone.) In this case, the greed of the vendors and the naivete of the legislators destroyed the market they hoped to profit from.

Insiders figure out even more sophisticated ways to manipulate the system. A nice example here comes from how the French circumvented British and German opposition to the smartcard based electronic tachograph described in section 12.3. The French wrote a relaxed protection profile and sent it to a British CLEF to be evaluated. The CLEF was an army software company and, whatever their knowledge of MLS, they knew nothing about smartcards. But this didn't lead them to turn down the business. They also didn't know that the UK government was opposed to approval of the protection profile (if they had done, they'd have no doubt toed the line). So Britain was left with a choice between accepting defective road safety standards as a fait accompli, or undermining confidence in the Common Criteria. In the end, no-one in London had the stomach to challenge the evaluation; eight years later, the old paper tachographs started being replaced with the new, less secure, electronic ones.

As for the organizational aspects, I mentioned in section 26.2.3 that process-based assurance systems fail if accredited teams don't lose their accreditation when they lose their sparkle. This clearly applies to CLEFs. Even if CLEFs were licensed by a body independent of the intelligence community, many will deteriorate as key staff leave or as skills don't keep up with technology; and as clients shop around for easier evaluations there will inevitably be both corruption and grade inflation. In the first edition of this book in 2001, I wrote: 'Yet at present I can see no usable mechanism whereby a practitioner with very solid evidence of incompetence (or even dishonesty) can challenge a CLEF and have it removed from the list. In the absence of sanctions for misbehaviour, the incentive will be for CLEFs to race to the bottom and compete to give vendors an easy ride'.

I described in section 10.6.1.1 how, in late 2007, colleagues and I discovered that PIN entry devices certified as secure by both VISA and the Common Criteria were anything but secure; indeed, the protection profile against which they'd been evaluated was unmeetable. After reporting the vulnerability to the vendors, to VISA, to the bankers' trade association and to GCHQ, we pointed out that this was a failure not just of the labs that had evaluated those particular devices, but that there was a systemic failure. What, we demanded, did VISA and GCHQ propose to do about it? The answer, it turned out, was nothing. VISA refused to withdraw its certification, and the UK government told us that as the evaluation had not been registered with them, it wasn't their problem. The suppliers are free to continue describing a defective terminal as 'CC evaluated' and even 'CC Approved', so long as they don't call it 'CC certified' or 'certified under the Common Criteria Recognition Arrangement (CCRA)'. This strikes me as a major problem with the CC brand. It will continue to be stamped on lousy products for the foreseeable future.

So the best advice I can offer is this. When presented with a security product, you must always consider whether the salesman is lying or mistaken, and how. The Common Criteria were supposed to fix this problem, but they don't. When presented with an evaluated product, you have to demand what vulnerabilities have been reported or discovered since the evaluation took place. (Get it in writing.) Then look hard at the protection profile: check whether it maps to what you really need. (Usually it doesn't — it protects the vendor, not you.) Don't limit your scepticism to the purely technical aspects: ask how it was manipulated and by whom; whether the CLEF that evaluated the profile was dishonest or incompetent; and what pressure from which government might have been applied behind the scenes.

You should also consider how your rights are eroded by the certificate. For example, if you use an unevaluated product to generate digital signatures, and a forged signature turns up which someone tries to use against you, you might reasonably expect to challenge the evidence by persuading a court to order the release of full documentation to your expert witnesses. A Common Criteria certificate might make a court very much less ready to order disclosure, and thus could prejudice your rights.

A cynic might suggest that this is precisely why, in the commercial world, it's the vendors of products that are designed to transfer liability (such as smartcards), or to satisfy due diligence requirements (such as firewalls) who are most enthusiastic about the Common Criteria. A really hard-bitten cynic might point out that since the collapse of the Soviet Union, the agencies justify their existence by economic espionage, and the Common Criteria signatory countries provide most of the interesting targets. A false U.S. evaluation of a product which is sold worldwide may compromise 250 million Americans, but as it will also compromise 400 million Europeans the balance of advantage lies in deception. The balance is even stronger with small countries such as Britain and the Netherlands, who have fewer citizens to protect and more foreigners to attack. In addition, agencies get brownie points (and budget) for foreign secrets they steal, not for local secrets that foreigners didn't manage to steal.

So an economist is unlikely to trust a Common Criteria evaluation. Perhaps I'm just a cynic, but I tend to view them as being somewhat like a rubber crutch. Such a device has all sorts of uses, from winning a judge's sympathy through wheedling money out of a gullible government to whacking people round the head. (Just don't try to put serious weight on it!)

Fortunately, the economics discussed in section 26.2.1 should also limit the uptake of the Criteria to sectors where an official certification, however irrelevant, erroneous or mendacious, offers some competitive advantage.

26.4 Ways Forward

In his classic book 'The Mythical Man Month', Brooks argues compellingly that there is no 'silver bullet' to solve the problems of software projects that run late and over budget [231]. The easy parts of the problem, such as developing high-level languages in which programmers are more productive, have been done. That removes much of the accidental complexity of programming, leaving the intrinsic complexity of the application. I discussed this in the previous chapter in the general context of system development methodology; the above discussion should convince the reader that exactly the same applies to the problem of assurance and, especially, evaluation.

A more realistic approach to evaluation and assurance would look not just at the technical features of the product but at how it behaves in real use. Usability is ignored by the Common Criteria, but is in reality all important; a UK government email system that required users to reboot their PC whenever they changed compartments frustrated users so much that they made informal agreements to put everything in common compartments — in effect wasting a nine-figure investment. (Official secrecy will no doubt continue to protect the guilty parties from punishment.) The kind of features we described in the context of bookkeeping systems in Chapter 10, which are designed to limit the effects of human frailty, are also critical. In most applications, one must assume that people are always careless, usually incompetent and occasionally dishonest.

It's also necessary to confront the fact of large, feature-rich programs that are updated frequently. Economics cannot be wished away. Evaluation and assurance schemes such as the Common Criteria, ISO9001 and even CMM try to squeeze a very volatile and competitive industry into a bureaucratic straightjacket, in order to provide purchasers with the illusion of stability. But given the way the industry works, the best people can do is flock to brands, such as IBM in the 70s and 80s, and Microsoft now. The establishment and maintenance of these brands involves huge market forces, and security plays little role.

I've probably given you enough hints by now about how to cheat the system and pass off a lousy system as a secure one — at least long enough for the problem to become someone else's. In the remainder of this book, I'll assume that you're making an honest effort to protect a system and want risk reduction, rather than due diligence or some other kind of liability dumping. There are still many systems where the system owner loses if the security fails; we've seen a number of them above (nuclear command and control, pay-TV, prepayment utility meters, . . .) and they provide many interesting engineering examples.

26.4.1   Hostile Review

When you really want a protection property to hold it is vital that the design be subjected to hostile review. It will be eventually, and it's better if it's done before the system is fielded. As we've seen in one case history after another, the motivation of the attacker is almost all-important; friendly reviews, by people who want the system to pass, are essentially useless compared with contributions by people who are seriously trying to break it.

The classic ways of doing hostile review are contractual and conflictual. An example of the contractual approach was the Independent Validation and Verification (IV&V) program used by NASA for manned space flight; contractors were hired to trawl through the code and paid a bonus for every bug they found. An example of the conflictual approach was in the evaluation of nuclear command and control, where Sandia National Laboratories and the NSA vied to find bugs in each others' designs.

One way of combining the two is simply to hire multiple experts from different consultancy firms or universities, and give the repeat business to whoever most noticeably finds bugs and improves the design. Another is to have multiple different accreditation bodies: I mentioned in section 23.5 how voting systems in the USA are vetted independently in each state; and in the days before standards were imposed by organizations such as VISA and SWIFT, banks would build local payment networks with each of them having the design checked by its own auditors. Neither approach is infallible, though; there are some really awful legacy voting and banking systems.

26.4.2   Free and Open-Source Software

The free and open-source software movement extends the philosophy of openness from the architecture to the implementation detail. Many security products have publicly available source code, of which the first was probably the PGP email encryption program. The Linux operating system and the Apache web server are also open-source and are relied on by many people to protect information. There is also a drive to adopt open source in government.

Open-source software is not entirely a recent invention; in the early days of computing, most system software vendors published their source code. This openness started to recede in the early 1980s when pressure of litigation led IBM to adopt an 'object-code-only' policy for its mainframe software, despite bitter criticism from its user community. The pendulum has recently been swinging back, and IBM is one of the stalwarts of open source.

There are a number of strong arguments in favour of open software, and a few against. First, if everyone in the world can inspect and play with the software, then bugs are likely to be found and fixed; in Raymond's famous phrase, 'To many eyes, all bugs are shallow' [1058]. This is especially so if the software is maintained in a cooperative effort, as Linux and Apache are. It may also be more difficult to insert backdoors into such a product.

A standard defense-contractor argument against open source is that once software becomes large and complex, there may be few or no capable motivated people studying it, and major vulnerabilities may take years to be found. For example, a programming bug in PGP versions 5 and 6 allowed an attacker to add an extra escrow key without the key holder's knowledge [1143]; this was around for years before it was spotted. There have also been back door 'maintenance passwords' in products such as sendmail that persisted for years before they were removed.

The worry is that there may be attackers who are sufficiently motivated to spend more time finding bugs or exploitable features in the published code than the community of reviewers. First, there may not be enough reviewers for many open products, as the typical volunteer finds developing code more rewarding than finding exploits. A lot of open-source development is done by students who find it helps them get good jobs later if they can point to some component of an employer's systems which they helped develop; perhaps it wouldn't be so helpful if all they could point to was a collection of bug reports that forced security upgrades. Second, as I noted in section 26.2.4, different testers find different bugs as their test focus is different; so it's quite possible that even once a product had withstood 10,000 hours of community scrutiny, a foreign intelligence agency that invested a mere 1000 hours might find a new vulnerability. Given the cited reliability growth models, the probabilities are easy enough to work out.

Other arguments include the observation that active open source projects add functionality and features at dizzying speed compared to closed software, which can open up nasty feature interactions; that such projects can fail to achieve consensus about what the security is trying to achieve; and that there are special cases, such as when protecting smartcards against various attacks, where a proprietary encryption algorithm embedded in the chip hardware can force the attacker to spend significantly more effort in reverse engineering.

So where is the balance of benefit? Eric Raymond's influential analysis of the economics of open source software [1059] suggests that there are five criteria for whether a product would be likely to benefit from an open source approach: where it is based on common engineering knowledge rather than proprietary techniques; where it is sensitive to failure; where it needs peer review for verification; where it is sufficiently business-critical that users will cooperate in finding and removing bugs; and where its economics include strong network effects. Security passes all these tests.

Some people have argued that while openness helps the defenders find bugs so they can fix them, it will also help the attackers find bugs so they can exploit them. Will the attackers or the defenders be helped more? In 2002 I proved that, under the standard model of reliability growth, openness helps attack and defence equally [54]. Thus whether an open or proprietary approach works best in a given application will depend on whether and how that application departs from the standard assumptions, for example, of independent vulnerabilities. As an example, a study of security bugs found in the OpenBSD operating system revealed that these bugs were significantly correlated, which suggests that openness there was a good thing [998].

In fact there's a long history of security engineers in different disciplines being converted to openness. The long-standing wisdom of Auguste Kerckhoffs was that cryptographic systems should be designed in such a way that they are not compromised if the opponent learns the technique being used [713]. The debate about whether locksmiths should discuss vulnerabilities in locks started in Victorian times, as I discussed in the Chapter 11. The law-and-economics scholar Peter Swire has explained why governments are intrinsically less likely to embrace disclosure: although competitive forces drive even Microsoft to open up a lot of its software for interoperability and trust reasons, government agencies play different games (such as expanding their budgets and avoiding embarrassment) [1238]. Yet the security arguments have started to prevail in some quarters: from tentative beginnings in about 1999, the U.S. Department of Defense has started to embrace open source, notably through the SELinux project I discussed in Chapter 8.

So while an open design is neither necessary nor sufficient, it is often going to be helpful. The important questions are how much effort was expended by capable people in checking and testing what you built — and whether they tell you everything they find.

26.4.3 Semi-Open Design

Where a fully open design isn't possible, you can often still get benefits by opting for a partly-open one. For example, the architectural design could be published even although some of the implementation details are not. Examples that we've seen include the smartcard banking protocol from section 3.8.1, the nuclear command and control systems mentioned in Chapter 13 and the SPDC mechanism in Blu-Ray.

Another approach to semi-open design is to use an open platform and build proprietary components on top. The best-known example here may be Apple's OS/X which combines the OpenBSD operating system with proprietary multimedia components. In other applications, a proprietary but widely-used product such as Windows or Oracle may be 'open enough'. Suppose, for example, you're worried about a legal attack. If there's an argument in court about whether the system was secure at the time of a disputed transaction, then rather than having opposing experts trawling through code, you can rely on the history of disclosed vulnerabilities, patches and attacks. Thus we find that more and more ATMs are using Windows as a platform (although the version they use does have a lot of the unnecessary stuff stripped out).

26.4.4 Penetrate-and-Patch, CERTs, and Bugtraq

Penetrate-and-patch was the name given dismissively in the 1970s and 1980s to the evolutionary procedure of finding security bugs in systems and then fixing them; it was widely seen at that time as inadequate, as more bugs were always found. As I discussed in Chapter 8, the hope at that time was that formal methods would enable bug-free systems to be constructed. It's now well known that formal verification only works for systems that are too small and limited for most applications. Like it or not, most software development is iterative, based on the build cycle discussed in Chapter 25. Iterative approaches to assurance are thus necessary, and the question is how to manage them.

The interests of the various stakeholders in a system can diverge quite radically at this point.

1. The vendor would prefer that bugs weren't found, to spare the expense of patching.

2. The average customer might prefer the same; lazy customers often don't patch, and get infected as a result. (So long as their ISP doesn't cut them off for sending spam, they may not notice or care.)

3. The typical security researcher wants a responsible means of disclosing his discoveries, so he can give the vendors a reasonable period of time to ship a patch before he ships his conference paper; so he will typically send a report to a local *computer emergency response team* (CERT) which in turn will notify the vendor and publish the vulnerability after 45 days.

4. The intelligence agencies want to learn of vulnerabilities quickly, so that they can be exploited until a patch is shipped. (Many CERTs are funded by the agencies and have cleared personnel.)

5. Some hackers disclose vulnerabilities on mailing lists such as bug-traq which don't impose a delay; this can force software vendors to ship emergency patches out of the usual cycle.

6. The security software companies benefit from the existence of unpatched vulnerabilities in that they can use their firewalls to filter for attacks using them, and the anti-virus software on their customers' PCs can often try to intercept such attacks too. (Symantec hosts the bugtraq list.)

7. Large companies don't like emergency patches, and neither do most government departments, as the process of testing a new patch against the enterprise's critical systems and rolling it out is expensive.

During the 1990s, the debate was driven by people who were frustrated at the software vendors for leaving their products unpatched for months or even years. This was one of the reasons the bugtraq list was set up; it then led to a debate on 'responsible disclosure' with various proposals about how long a breathing space the researcher should give the vendor [1055]. The CERT system of a 45-day delay emerged from this. It gives vendors a strong incentive to have an attentive bug reporting facility; in return they get enough time to test a fix properly before releasing it; researchers get credits to put on their CVs; and users get bug fixes at the same time as bug reports; and the big companies have regular updates or service packs for which their corporate customers can plan.

Is this system the best we could get? Recently, the patch cycle has become a subject of study by security economists. There was a debate at the 2004 Workshop on the Economics of Information Security between Eric Rescorla, who argued that since bugs are many and uncorrelated, and since most exploits use vulnerabilities reverse-engineered from existing patches, there should be minimal disclosure. Ashish Arora argued that, from both theoretical and empirical perspectives, the threat of disclosure was needed to get vendors to patch. I discussed this argument in section 7.5.2. There has been some innovation, notably the introduction of essentially automatic upgrades for mass-market users, and the establishment of firms that make markets in vulnerabilities; and we have some more research data, notably the fact that bugs in OpenBSD and some other systems are correlated. By and large, the current way of doing things seems reasonable and stable.

26.4.5 Education

Perhaps as an academic I'm biased, but I feel that the problems and technologies of system protection need to be much more widely understood. I have described case after case in which the wrong mechanisms were used, or the right mechanisms were used in the wrong way. It has been the norm for protection to be got right only at the fifth or sixth attempt, when with a slightly more informed approach it might have been the second or third. Security professionals unfortunately tend to be either too specialized and focused on some tiny aspect of the technology, or else generalists who've never been exposed to many of the deeper technical issues. But blaming the problem on the training we currently give to students — whether of computer science, business administration or law — is too easy; the hard part is figuring out what to do about it. This book isn't the first step, and certainly won't be the last word — but I hope it will be useful.

26.5 Summary

Sometimes the hardest part of a security engineering project is knowing when you're done. A number of evaluation and assurance methodologies are available to help. In moderation they can be very useful, especially to the start-up firm whose development culture is still fluid and which is seeking to establish good work habits and build a reputation. But the assistance they can give has its limits, and overuse of bureaucratic quality control tools can do grave harm. I think of them as like salt; a few shakes on your fries can be a good thing, but a few ounces definitely aren't.

But although the picture is gloomy, it doesn't justify despondency. As people gradually acquire experience of what works, what gets attacked and how, and as protection requirements and mechanisms become more part of the working engineer's skill set, things gradually get better. Security may only be got right at the fourth pass, but that's better than never — which was typical fifteen years ago.

Life is complex. Success means coping with it. Complaining too much about it is the path to failure.

Research Problems

We could do with some new ideas on how to manage evaluation. At present, we use vastly different — and quite incompatible — tools to measure the level of protection that can be expected from cryptographic algorithms; from technical physical protection mechanisms; from complex software; from the internal controls in an organisation; and, via usability studies, from people. Is there any way we can join these up, so that stuff doesn't fall down between the gaps? Can we get better mechanisms than the Common Criteria, which vendors privately regard as pointless bureaucracy? Perhaps it's possible to apply some of the tools that economists use to deal with imperfect information, from risk-pricing models to the theory of the firm. It would even be helpful if we had better statistical tools to measure and predict failure. We should also tackle some taboo subjects. Why did the Millennium Bug not bite?

Further Reading

There is a whole industry devoted to promoting the assurance and evaluation biz, supported by mountains of your tax dollars. Their enthusiasm can even have the flavour of religion. Unfortunately, there are nowhere near enough people writing heresy.

CHAPTER 27

Conclusions

We are in the middle of a huge change in how security is done.

Ten years ago, the security manager of a large company was usually a retired soldier or policemen, for whom 'computer security' was an unimportant speciality he left to the computer department, with occasional help from outside specialists. In ten years' time, his job will be occupied by a systems person; she will consider locks and guards to be a relatively unimportant speciality that she'll farm out to a facilities management company, with an occasional review by outside specialists.

Ten years ago, security technology was an archipelago of mutually suspicious islands — the cryptologists, the operating system protection people, the burglar alarm industry, right through to the chemists who did funny banknote inks. We all thought the world ended at our shore. Security engineering is now on the way to becoming an established discipline; the islands are already being joined up by bridges, and practitioners now realise they have to be familiar with all of them. The banknote ink man who doesn't understand digital watermarks, and the cryptologist who's only interested in communications confidentiality mechanisms, are poor value as employees. In ten years' time, everyone will need to have a systems perspective and design components that can be integrated into a larger whole.

Ten years ago, information security was said to be about 'confidentiality, integrity and availability'. These priorities are already reversed in many applications. Security engineering is about ensuring that systems are predictably dependable in the face of all sorts of malice, from bombers to botnets. And as attacks shift from the hard technology to the people who operate it, systems must also be resilient to error, mischance and even coercion. So a realistic understanding of human stakeholders — both staff and customers — is critical; human, institutional and economic factors are already as important as technical ones. The ways in which real systems provide dependability will become ever more diverse, and tuning the security policy to the application will be as essential as avoiding technical exploits. In ten years' time, protection goals will not just be closer to the application, they will be more subtle: examples include privacy, safety, and accountability. Conflicts between goals will be more common; where one principal wants accountability and another wants deniability, it's hard to please them both.

Ten years ago, the better information security products were designed for governments in secret and manufactured in small quantities by cosseted cost-plus defence contractors. Already, commercial uses dwarf government ones, and the rough and tumble of the marketplace has taken over. In ten years' time it'll be interesting to see whether civil government uses any technologies different from standard commercial ones, and even the military will make increasing use of off-the-shelf hardware and software.

Ten years ago, government policy towards information security was devoted to maintaining the effectiveness of huge communications intelligence networks built up over the Cold War. Crypto controls turned out to be almost irrelevant to real policy needs and were largely abandoned in 2000. Surveillance is still an important policy issue, but privacy, DRM, consumer protection and even electronic voting are acquiring comparable importance.

The biggest technical challenge is likely to be systems integration and assurance. Ten years ago, the inhabitants of the different islands in the security archipelago all had huge confidence in their products. The cryptologists believed that certain ciphers couldn't be broken; the smartcard vendors claimed that probing out crypto keys held in their chips was absolutely physically impossible; and the security printing people said that holograms couldn't be forged without a physics PhD and $20 m worth of equipment. At the system level, too, there was much misplaced confidence. The banks claimed that their automatic teller machines could not even conceivably make a mistaken debit; the multilevel secure operating systems crowd sold their approach as the solution for all system protection problems; and people assumed that a security evaluation done by a laboratory licensed by a developed country's government would be both honest and competent. These comfortable old certainties have all evaporated. Instead, security has become part of the larger dependability problem. We build better and better tools, and these help the system builders to get a little bit further up the complexity mountain, but in the end they fall off. A proportion of large complex system projects fail, just like in the 1970s; but we build much bigger disasters nowadays.

Complexity is the real enemy of security. The distinction between outsiders and insiders used to simplify the business, but as everything gets connected up it's disappearing fast. Protection used to be predicated on a few big ideas and on propositions that could be stated precisely, while now the subject is much more diverse and includes a lot of inexact and heuristic knowledge. The system life-cycle is also changing: in the old days, a closed system was developed in a finite project, while now systems evolve and accumulate features without limit.

Changes in the nature of work are significant: while previously a bank's chief internal auditor would remember all the frauds of the previous thirty years and prevent the data processing department repeating the errors that caused them, the new corporate culture of transient employment and 'perpetual revolution' (as Mao described it) has trashed corporate memory. Economics will continue to ensure that insecure systems get built — and the liability will be dumped on others whenever possible. Governments will try to keep up, but they're too slow and they can often be bought off for a while. So there will be many regulatory failures too.

The net effect of all these changes is that the protection of information in computer systems is no longer a scientific discipline, but an engineering one.

The security engineer of the twenty-first century will be responsible for systems that evolve constantly and face a changing spectrum of threats. She will have a large and constantly growing toolbox. A significant part of her job will be keeping up to date technically: understanding the latest attacks, learning how to use new tools, and keeping up on the legal and policy fronts. Like any engineer, she'll need a solid intellectual foundation; she will have to understand the core disciplines such as cryptology, access control, information flow, networking and signal detection. She'll also need to understand the basics of management: how accounts work, the principles of finance and the business processes of her client. But most important of all will be the ability to manage technology and play an effective part in the process of evolving a system to meet changing business needs. The ability to communicate with business people, rather than just with other engineers, will be vital; and experience will matter hugely. I don't think anybody with this combination of skills is likely to be unemployed — or bored — anytime soon.

Finally, the rampant growth of the security-industrial complex since 9/11, and the blatant fearmongering of many governments, are a scar on the world and on our profession. We have a duty to help it heal, and we can do that in many different ways. My own path has been largely research — developing the disciplines of security engineering and security economics, so that we can tell not just what works in the lab but what can be made to work in the world. The dissemination of knowledge is important, too — that's what this book is about. Economic growth also helps, and education: it's the poor and the uneducated who are most swayed by fearmongering (whether from Western leaders, or from bin Laden). At least in countries with educated populations, the voters have started to recognise the excesses of the 'War on Terror' and to deal with them. Just as individuals learn through experience to compensate for our psychological biases and deal more rationally with risk, so our societies learn and adapt too. Democracy is the key mechanism for that. So the final way in which security engineers can contribute is by taking part in the policy debate. The more we can engage the people who lead the discussions on emerging threats, the faster our societies will adapt to deal with them.

Bibliography

[1] M Abadi, "Explicit Communications Revisited: Two New Attacks on Authentication Protocols", in *IEEE Transactions on Software Engineering* v 23 no 3 (Mar 97) pp 185–186

[2] M Abadi, RM Needham, "Prudent Engineering Practice for Cryptographic Protocols", *IEEE Transactions on Software Engineering* v 22 no 1 (Jan 96) pp 6–15; also as DEC SRC Research Report no 125 (June 1 1994) at `ftp://gatekeeper.pa.dec.com/pub/DEC/SRC/research-reports/SRC-125.pdf`

[3] A Abbasi, HC Chen, "Visualizing Authorship for Identification", in *ISI 2006*, LNCS 3975 pp 60–71

[4] H Abelson, RJ Anderson, SM Bellovin, J Benaloh, M Blaze, W Diffie, J Gilmore, PG Neumann, RL Rivest, JI Schiller, B Schneier, "The Risks of Key Recovery, Key Escrow, and Trusted Third-Party Encryption", in *World Wide Web Journal* v 2 no 3 (Summer 1997) pp 241–257

[5] A Abulafia, S Brown, S Abramovich-Bar, "A Fraudulent Case Involving Novel Ink Eradication Methods", in *Journal of Forensic Sciences* v 41 (1996) pp 300–302

[6] DG Abraham, GM Dolan, GP Double, JV Stevens, "Transaction Security System", in *IBM Systems Journal* v 30 no 2 (1991) pp 206–229

[7] N Achs, "VISA confronts the con men", *Cards International* (20 Oct 1992) pp 8–9

[8] A Acquisti, A Friedman, R Telang, "Is There a Cost to Privacy Breaches?", *Fifth Workshop on the Economics of Information Security* (2006)

[9] EN Adams, "Optimising preventive maintenance of software products", *lBM Journal of Research and Development*, v 28 no 1 (1984) pp 2–14

[10] J Adams, *'Risk'*, University College London Press (1995), ISBN 1-85728-067-9

[11] J Adams, "Cars, Cholera and Cows: the management of risk and uncertainty", in *Policy Analysis* no 335, Cato Institute, Washington, 1999; at http://www.cato.org/pubs/pas/pa-335es.html

[12] B Adida, M Bond, J Clulow, A Lin, RJ Anderson, RL Rivest, "A Note on EMV Secure Messaging in the IBM 4758 CCA", at www.ross-anderson.com

[13] Y Adini, Y Moses, S Ullman, "Face recognition: The Problem of Compensating for Changes in Illumination Direction", in *IEEE Transactions on Pattern Analysis and Machine Intelligence* v 19 no 7 (July 97) pp 721–732

[14] A Adler, "Sample images can be independently restored from face recognition templates", in *Proc. Can. Conf. Elec. Comp. Eng.* (2003) pp 1163–1166; at http://www.sce.carleton.ca/faculty/adler/publications/publications.html

[15] A Adler, "Vulnerabilities in biometric encryption systems", in *NATO RTA Workshop: Enhancing Information Systems Security–Biometrics* (IST-044-RWS-007), at http://www. sce.carleton.ca/faculty/adler/publications/publications.html

[16] The AES Lounge, http://www.iaik.tu-graz.ac.at/research/krypto/AES/

[17] C Ajluni, "Two New Imaging Techniques Promise To Improve IC Defect Identification", in *Electronic Design* v 43 no 14 (10 July 1995) pp 37–38

[18] Y Akdeniz, "Regulation of Child Pornography on the Internet" (Dec 1999), at http://www.cyber-rights.org/reports/child.htm

[19] G Akerlof, "The Market for 'Lemons: Quality Uncertainty and the Market Mechanism", in *The Quarterly Journal of Economics* v 84 no 3 (1970) pp 488–500

[20] R Albert, HW Jeong, AL Barabási, "Error and attack tolerance of complex networks", in *Nature* v 406 no 1 (2000) pp 387–482

[21] J Alfke, "Facebook and Decentralized Identifiers", in *Thought Palace* Dec 2 2007; at `http://mooseyard.com/Jens/2007/12/facebook-and-decentralized-identifiers`

[22] Alliance to Outfox Phone Fraud, hosted by Verizon at `http://www.bell-atl.com/security/fraud/` but now withdrawn; as of August 2007, Verizon had its own scam alert page at `http://www22.verizon.com/pages/securityalerts/`

[23] M Allman, V Paxson, "Issues and Etiquette Concerning Use of Shared Measurement Data", in *Internet Measurement Conference* (IMC 2007), at `http://www.imconf.net/imc-2007/papers/imc80.pdf`

[24] F Almgren, G Andersson, T Granlund, L Ivansson, S Ulfberg, "How We Cracked the Code Book Ciphers", at `http://codebook.org`

[25] American Society for Industrial Security, `http://www.asisonline.org`

[26] American Statistical Association, *Privacy, Confidentiality, and Data Security web site*, at `http://www.amstat.org/comm/cmtepc/`

[27] E Amoroso, 'Fundamentals of Computer Security Technology', Prentice Hall (1994); ISBN 0-13-10829-3

[28] B Andersen, M Frenz, "The Impact of Music Downloads and P2P File-Sharing on the Purchase of Music: A Study for Industry Canada", 2007, at `http://strategis.ic.gc.ca/epic/site/ippd-dppi.nsf/en/h_ip01456e.html`

[29] J Anderson, 'Computer Security Technology Planning Study', ESD-TR-73-51, US Air Force Electronic Systems Division (1973) `http://csrc.nist.gov/publications/history/index.html`

[30] M Anderson, C North, J Griffin, R Milner, J Yesberg, K Yiu, "Starlight: Interactive Link", in *12th Annual Computer Security Applications Conference* (1996) proceedings published by the IEEE, ISBN 0-8186-7606-XA, pp 55–63

[31] M Anderson, W Seltzer, *Official Statistics and Statistical Confidentiality: Recent Writings and Essential Documents*, at `http://www.uwm.edu/%7Emargo/govstat/integrity.htm`

[32] RJ Anderson, "Solving a Class of Stream Ciphers", in *Cryptologia* v XIV no 3 (July 1990) pp 285–288

[33] RJ Anderson, "Why Cryptosystems Fail" in *Communications of the ACM* v 37 no 11 (November 1994) pp 32–40; earlier version at `http://www.cl.cam.ac.uk/users/rja14/wcf.html`

[34] RJ Anderson, "Liability and Computer Security: Nine Principles", in *Computer Security–ESORICS 94*, Springer LNCS v 875 pp 231–245

[35] RJ Anderson, "Crypto in Europe–Markets, Law and Policy", in *Cryptography: Policy and Algorithms*, Springer LNCS v 1029 pp 75–89

[36] RJ Anderson, "Clinical System Security–Interim Guidelines", in *British Medical Journal* v 312 no 7023 (13th January 1996) pp 109–111; `http://www.cl.cam.ac.uk/ftp/users/rja14/guidelines.txt`

[37] RJ Anderson, '*Security in Clinical Information Systems*', published by the British Medical Association (1996); ISBN 0-7279-1048-5

[38] RJ Anderson, "A Security Policy Model for Clinical Information Systems", in *Proceedings of the 1996 IEEE Symposium on Security and Privacy* pp 30–43 `http://www.cl.cam.ac.uk/users/rja14/policy11/policy11.html`

[39] RJ Anderson, "An Update on the BMA Security Policy", in [43] pp 233–250; `http://www.cl.cam.ac.uk/ftp/users/rja14/bmaupdate.ps.gz`

[40] RJ Anderson, C Manifavas, C Sutherland, "NetCard — A Practical Electronic Cash Scheme" in *Security Protocols* (1996), Springer LNCS v 1189 pp 49–57

[41] RJ Anderson, "The Eternity Service", in *Proceedings of Pragocrypt 96* (GC UCMP, ISBN 80-01-01502-5) pp 242–252

[42] RJ Anderson (ed), *Proceedings of the First International Workshop on Information Hiding* (1996), Springer LNCS v 1174

[43] RJ Anderson (ed), '*Personal Medical Information–Security, Engineering and Ethics*', Springer-Verlag (1997) ISBN 3-540-63244-1

[44] RJ Anderson, "GSM hack–operator flunks the challenge", in `comp.risks` v 19.48: `http://catless.ncl.ac.uk/Risks/19.48.html`

[45] RJ Anderson, "On the Security of Digital Tachographs", in *Computer Security–ESORICS 98*, Springer LNCS v 1485 pp 111–125; `http://www.cl.cam.ac.uk/ftp/users/rja14/tacho5.ps.gz`

[46] RJ Anderson, "Safety and Privacy in Clinical Information Systems", in *'Rethinking IT and Health'*, J Lenaghan (ed), IPPR (Nov 98) (ISBN 1-86030-077-4) pp 140–160

[47] RJ Anderson, "The DeCODE Proposal for an Icelandic Health Database"; part of this was published in *Læknablaðið* (The Icelandic Medical Journal) v 84 no 11 (Nov 98) pp 874–5; full text available from `http://www.cl.cam.ac.uk/users/rja14/#Med`

[48] RJ Anderson, "The Formal Verification of a Payment System", in *Industrial Strength Formal Methods: A Practitioners Handbook*, MG Hinchey and JP Bowen (editors), Springer Verlag (Sep 1999, 1-85233-640-4) pp 43–52

[49] RJ Anderson, "How to Cheat at the Lottery (or, Massively Parallel Requirements Engineering)", in *15th Annual Computer Security Application Conference* (1997); proceedings published by IEEE Computer Society, ISBN 0-7695-0346-2, pp xix–xxvii; at `http://www.cl.cam.ac.uk/~rja14/lottery/lottery.html`

[50] RJ Anderson, "The Millennium Bug–Reasons not to Panic", at `http://www.ftp.cl.cam.ac.uk/ftp/users/rja14/y2k.html`

[51] RJ Anderson, "Comments on the Security Targets for the Icelandic Health Database", at `http://www.cl.cam.ac.uk/ftp/users/rja14/iceland-admiral.pdf`

[52] "The Correctness of Crypto Transaction Sets", in *Proceedings of Protocols 2000*, Springer LNCS v 2133 pp 125–141

[53] Ross Anderson, "Cryptography and Competition Policy–Issues with 'Trusted Computing' ", *Second Workshop on Economics and Information Security* (2003)

[54] Ross Anderson, "Open and Closed Systems are Equivalent (that is, in an ideal world)", in *Perspectives on Free and Open Source Software*, MIT Press 2005, pp 127–142

[55] RJ Anderson, "Closing the Phishing Hole–Fraud, Risk and Nonbanks", at *Nonbanks in the Payments System: Innovation, Competition, and Risk*, US Federal Reserve, Santa Fe, May 2–4 2007

[56] RJ Anderson, "RFID and the Middleman", in *Proceedings of the Eleventh International Conference on Financial Cryptography and Data Security*, February 2007

[57] RJ Anderson, "Searching for Evil", Tech talk given at Google, Aug 24 2007, at `http://video.google.com/videoplay?docid=-1380463341028815296`

[58] RJ Anderson, *'Security Economics Resource Page'*, at `http://www.cl.cam.ac.uk/~rja14/econsec.html`

[59] RJ Anderson, SJ Bezuidenhoudt, "On the Reliability of Electronic Payment Systems", in *IEEE Transactions on Software Engineering* v 22 no 5 (May 1996) pp 294–301; `http://www.cl.cam.ac.uk/ftp/users/rja14/prepay-meters.pdf`

[60] RJ Anderson, E Biham, LR Knudsen, "Serpent: A Proposal for the Advanced Encryption Standard", submitted to NIST as an AES candidate; a short version of the paper appeared at the AES conference, August 1998; both papers available at [61]

[61] RJ Anderson, E Biham, L Knudsen, *'The Serpent Home Page'*, `http://www.cl.cam.ac.uk/~rja14/serpent.html`

[62] RJ Anderson, R Böhme, R Clayton, T Moore, *'Security Economics and the Internal Market'*, ENISA, 2008

[63] RJ Anderson, M Bond, "API-Level Attacks on Embedded Systems", in *IEEE Computer* v 34 no 10 (October 2001) pp 67–75

[64] RJ Anderson, M Bond, "Protocol Analysis, Composability and Computation" in *Computer Systems: Theory, Technology and Applications*, Springer 2003, pp 7–10

[65] RJ Anderson, M Bond, J Clulow, S Skorobogatov, *'Cryptographic processors—a survey'*, Cambridge University Computer Laboratory Technical Report no 641 (July 2005); shortened version in *Proc. IEEE* v 94 no 2 (Feb 2006) pp 357–369

[66] RJ Anderson, I Brown, R Clayton, T Dowty, D Korff, E Munro, *'Children's Databases—Safety and Privacy'*, Information Commissioner's Office, UK, Nov 2006

[67] RJ Anderson, B Crispo, JH Lee, C Manifavas, V Matyás, FAP Petitcolas, *'The Global Internet Trust Register'*, MIT Press (1999) (ISBN 0-262-51105-3) `http://www.cl.cam.ac.uk/Research/Security/Trust-Register/`

[68] RJ Anderson, MG Kuhn, "Tamper Resistance—a Cautionary Note", in *Proceedings of the Second Usenix Workshop on Electronic Commerce* (Nov 96) pp 1–11; `http://www.cl.cam.ac.uk/users/rja14/tamper.html`

[69] RJ Anderson, MG Kuhn, "Low Cost Attacks on Tamper Resistant Devices", in *Security Protocols–Proceedings of the 5th International Workshop* (1997) Springer LNCS v 1361 pp 125–136

[70] RJ Anderson, MG Kuhn, "Soft Tempest–An Opportunity for NATO", at *Protecting NATO Information Systems In The 21st Century*, Washington DC, Oct 25–26, 1999

[71] RJ Anderson, JH Lee, "Jikzi: A New Framework for Secure Publishing", in *Security Protocols 99*, Springer LNCS v 1976 pp 21–36

[72] RJ Anderson, TW Moore, "Information Security Economics–and Beyond", in *Advances in Cryptology–Crypto 2007*, Springer LNCS 4622, pp 68–91

[73] RJ Anderson, RM Needham, "Robustness principles for public key protocols", in *Advances in Cryptology–Crypto 95* Springer LNCS v 963 pp 236–247; http://www.cl.cam.ac.uk/ftp/users/rja14/robust-ness.ps.gz

[74] RJ Anderson, RM Needham, "Programming Satan's Computer" in *'Computer Science Today'*, Springer Lecture Notes in Computer Science v 1000 (1995) pp 426–441; http://www.cl.cam.ac.uk/ftp/users/rja14/satan.ps.gz

[75] RJ Anderson, RM Needham, A Shamir, "The Steganographic File System", in *Proceedings of the Second International Workshop on Information Hiding*, Springer LNCS v 1525 pp 74–84

[76] RJ Anderson, MR Roe, "The GCHQ Protocol and Its Problems", in *Advances in Cryptology–Eurocrypt 97*, Springer LNCS v 1233 pp 134–148; http://www.cl.cam.ac.uk/ftp/users/rja14/euro-clipper.ps.gz

[77] CM Andrew, V Mitrokhin, *'The Sword and the Shield: The Mitrokhin Archive and the Secret History of the KGB'*, Basic Books (1999) ISBN 0-46500310-9

[78] M Andrews, JA Whitaker, *'How to Break Web Software'*, Addison-Wesley 2006

[79] http://www.anonymizer.com

[80] JC Anselmo, "US Seen More Vulnerable to Electromagnetic Attack", in *Aviation Week and Space Technology* v 146 no 4 (28/7/97) p 67

[81] A Antón, "Is That Vault Really Protecting Your Privacy?", at *theprivacy-place.org* Oct 9 2007; at `http://theprivacyplace.org/2007/10/09/is-that-vault-really-protecting-your-privacy/`

[82] *Anonymity Bibliography*, 2007, at `http://freehaven.net/anonbib/`

[83] APACS, "Fraud abroad drives up card fraud losses", October 3 2007; at `http://www.apacs.org.uk/media_centre/press/03.10.07.html`; see also *The Register*, `http://www.theregister.co.uk/2007/10/03/card_fraud_trends/`

[84] APACS, "Payment Advice–Protect Your PIN", Aug 16 2007; at `http://www.apacs.org.uk/media_centre/press/08_16_07.html` and `www.cardwatch.org.uk`

[85] T Appleby, "Chilling debit-card scam uncovered", in *The Globe and Mail* (10/12/1999) p 1

[86] Arbor Networks Inc., *'Infrastructure Security Report'*, 2007, at `http://www.arbornetworks.com/report`

[87] US Army, *'Electromagnetic Pulse (EMP) and Tempest Protection for Facilities'*, Corps of Engineers Publications Depot, Hyattsville (1990)

[88] A Arora, R Krishnan, A Nandkumar, R Telang, YB Yang, "Impact of Vulnerability Disclosure and Patch Availability–An Empirical Analysis", *Third Workshop on the Economics of Information Security* (2004)

[89] A Arora, CM Forman, A Nandkumar, R Telang, "Competitive and strategic effects in the timing of patch release", in *Workshop on the Economics of Information Security* (2006)

[90] SE Asch, *'Social Psychology'*, OUP 1952

[91] D Asonov, R Agrawal, "Keyboard Acoustic Emanations", IBM Almaden Research Center, 2004

[92] *'ASPECT–Advanced Security for Personal Communications Technologies'*, at `http://www.esat.kuleuven.ac.be/cosic/aspect/index.html`

[93] Associated Press, "Charges dropped against Ex-HP chairwoman–Three others charged in boardroom spying case receive no jail time", Mar 14 2007, at `http://www.msnbc.msn.com/id/17611695/`

[94] R Atkinson, "The single most effective weapon against our deployed forces" and "The IED problem is getting out of control. We've got to stop the bleeding", in the *Washington Post*, Sep 30 2007; "There was a two-year learning curve ... and a lot of people died in those two years", Oct 1 2007; "You can't armor your way out of this problem",

Oct 2 2007; "If you don't go after the network, you're never going to stop these guys. Never", Oct 3 2007; all linked from `http://smallwarsjournal.com/blog/2007/09/print/weapon-of-choice/`

[95] D Aubrey-Jones, "Internet — Virusnet?", in *Network Security* (Feb 97) pp 15–19

[96] D Aucsmith, "Tamper-Resistant Software: An Implementation", in [42] pp 317–333

[97] D Aucsmith (editor), *Proceedings of the Second International Workshop on Information Hiding* (Portland, Apr 98), Springer LNCS v 1525

[98] B Audone, F Bresciani, "Signal Processing in Active Shielding and Direction-Finding Techniques", *IEEE Transactions on Electromagnetic Compatibility* v 38 no 3 (August 1996) pp 334–340

[99] R Axelrod, *The Evolution of Cooperation*, Basic Books (1984)

[100] I Ayres, SD Levitt, "Measuring Positive Externalities from Unobservable Victim Precaution: An Empirical Analysis of Lojack", in *Quarterly Journal of Economics* v 108 no 1 (Feb 1998), `http://www.nber.org/papers/w5928`

[101] "Barclays winning card fraud war", D Austin, in *Banking Technology* (April 94) p 5

[102] D Austin, "Flood warnings", in *Banking Technology* (Jul–Aug 1999) pp 28–31

[103] "Computer Combat Rules Frustrate the Pentagon", in *Aviation Week and Space Technology* v 147 no 11 (15/9/97) pp 67–68

[104] J Bacon, 'Concurrent Systems', Addison-Wesley (1997); ISBN 0-201-17767-6

[105] J Bacon, K Moody, J Bates, R Hayton, CY Ma, A McNeil, O Seidel, M Spiteri, "Generic Support for Distributed Applications", in *IEEE Computer* (March 2000) pp 68–76

[106] L Badger, DF Sterne, DL Sherman, KM Walker, SA Haghighat, "Practical Domain and Type Enforcement for UNIX," in *Proceedings of the 1995 IEEE Symposium on Security and Privacy* pp 66–77

[107] M Baggott, "The smart way to fight fraud", *Scottish Banker* (Nov 95) pp 32–33

[108] B Bain, "Justice says no to private PCs for telework", in *FCW.com*, Sep 13 2007; at `http://www.fcw.com/article103746-09-13-07`

[109] SA Baker, PR Hurst, 'The Limits of Trust', Kluwer Law International (1998) ISBN 9-0411-0639-1

[110] "Card Fraud: Banking's Boom Sector", in *Banking Automation Bulletin for Europe* (Mar 92) pp 1–5

[111] D Balfanz, EW Felten, "Hand-Held Computers Can Be Better Smart Cards", in *Eighth USENIX Security Symposium* (1999), ISBN 1-880446-28-6, pp 15–23

[112] J Bamford, 'The Puzzle Palace: A Report on NSA, America's Most Secret Agency', Houghton, Mifflin (1982–3rd Printing–revised edition due out shortly), ISBN 0-395-31286-8

[113] Bank for International Settlements, 'Security and Reliability in Electronic Systems for Payments', British Computer Society (1982–no ISBN)

[114] Bank for International Settlements, `http://www.bis.org/`

[115] E Bangeman, "The insanity of France's anti-file-sharing plan: L'État, c'est IFPI", in *Ars Technica* Nov 25 2007; at `http://arstechnica.com/news.ars/post/20071125-the-insanity-and-genius-of-frances-anti-file-sharingplan.html`

[116] M Barbaro, T Zeller, "A Face Is Exposed for AOL Searcher No. 4417749", in *New York Times* Aug 9 2006, at `http://query.nytimes.com/gst/fullpage.html?res=9E0CE3DD1F3FF93AA3575BC0A9609C8B63`

[117] E Barkan, E Biham, N Keller, "Instant Ciphertext-Only Cryptanalysis of GSM Encrypted Communication" Technion Technical Report CS-2006-07, at `http://www.cs.technion.ac.il/~biham/`

[118] RL Barnard, 'Intrusion Detection Systems', Butterworths (1988) ISBN 0-409-90030-3

[119] A Barnett, "Britain's UFO secrets revealed", in *The Observer* (4/6/2000) at `http://www.observer.co.uk/uk_news/story/0,6903,328010,00.html`

[120] S Baron-Cohen, *The Essential Difference: Men, Women, and the Extreme Male Brain*, Penguin, 2003 ISBN 0141011017

[121] J Barr, "The Gates of Hades", in *Linux World* April 2000; at `http://www.linuxworld.com/linuxworld/lw-2000-04/lw-04-vcontrol_3.html`

[122] B Barrow, B Quinn, "Millions in danger from chip and pin fraudsters" in *Daily Mail* June 5th 2006

[123] R Baskerville, "Information Systems Security Design Methods: Implications for Information Systems Development", in *ACM Computing Surveys* v 265 (1993) pp 375–414

[124] PJ Bass, "Telephone Cards and Technology Development as Experienced by GPT Telephone Systems", in *GEC Review* v 10 no 1 (95) pp 14–19

[125] J Battelle, *'The Search: How Google and Its Rivals Rewrote the Rules of Business and Transformed Our Culture'*, Portfolio, 2005

[126] W Bax, V Dekker, "Met zijn allen meekijken in de medische kaartenbak", in *Trouw* Dec 11 2007, at `http://www.trouw.nl/deverdieping/overigeartikelen/article867144.ece/`

[127] S Baxter, "US hits panic button as air force 'loses' nuclear missiles", in *Sunday Times* Oct 21 2007; at `http://www.timesonline.co.uk/tol/news/world/us_and_americas/article2702800.ece`

[128] "Great Microprocessors of the Past and Present", at `http://www.cs.uregina.ca/~bayko/cpu.html`

[129] BBC News Online, "Tax records 'for sale' scandal", Jan 16 2003, at `http://news.bbc.co.uk/1/hi/business/2662491.stm`

[130] BBC News Online, " 'Relief' over fingerprint verdict", Feb 7 2006, at `http://news.bbc.co.uk/1/hi/scotland/4689218.stm`

[131] BBC News Online, "UN warns on password 'explosion' ", Dec 4 2006, at `http://news.bbc.co.uk/1/hi/technology/6199372.stm`

[132] BBC News Online, "Schools get rules on biometrics", July 23 2007, at `http://news.bbc.co.uk/1/hi/education/6912232.stm`

[133] BBC News Online, "Mobile phone technology turns 20", Sep 7 2007, at `http://news.bbc.co.uk/1/hi/technology/6983869.stm`

[134] BBC News Online, "PC stripper helps spam to spread", Oct 30 2007, at `http://news.bbc.co.uk/1/hi/technology/7067962.stm`

[135] S Beattie, S Arnold, C Cowan, P Wagle, C Wright, "Timing the Application of Security Patches for Optimal Uptime", in *LISA XVI* (2002) pp 101–110

[136] F Beck, *'Integrated Circuit Failure Analysis–A Guide to Preparation Techniques'*, Wiley (1998), ISBN 0-471-97401-3

[137] J Beck, "Sources of Error in Forensic Handwriting Examination", in *Journal of Forensic Sciences* v 40 (1995) pp 78–87

[138] GS Becker, "Crime and Punishment: An Economic Approach", in *Journal of Political Economy* v 76 no 2 (March/April 1968) pp 169–217

[139] L Beckwith, M Burnett, V Grigoreanu, S Weidenbeck, "Gender HCI: What About the Software?", in *Computer* (Nov 2006) pp 97–101

[140] L Beckwith, C Kissinger, M Burnett, S Weidenbeck, J Lowrance, A Blackwell, C Cook, "Tinkering and Gender in End-User Programmers' Debugging", in *CHI '06*, Montreal, April 2006; at `http://eusesconsor-tium.org/gender/`

[141] S Begley, "Fingerprint Matches Come Under More Fire As Potentially Fallible", *Wall Street Journal* Oct 7 2005 p B1; at `http://online.wsj .com/article_print/SB112864132376462238.html`

[142] HA Beker, C Amery, "Cryptography Policy", at `http:// www.baltimore.com/library/whitepapers/mn_cryptography.html`

[143] HJ Beker, JMK Friend, PW Halliden, "Simplifying key management in electronic fund transfer point of sale systems", in *Electronics Letters* v 19 (1983) pp 442–443

[144] H Beker, F Piper, *'Cipher Systems'*, Northwood (1982)

[145] H Beker, M Walker, "Key management for secure electronic funds transfer in a retail environment", in *Advances in Cryptology–Crypto 84* Springer LNCS v 196 pp 401–410

[146] DE Bell, L LaPadula, *'Secure Computer Systems'*, ESD-TR-73-278, Mitre Corporation; v I and II: November 1973, v III: Apr 1974

[147] M Bellare, J Kilian, P Rogaway, "The Security of Cipher Block Chaining" in *Advances in Cryptology–Crypto 94* Springer LNCS v 839 pp 341–358

[148] M Bellare, P Rogaway, "Optimal Asymmetric Encryption", in *Advances in Cryptology–Eurocrypt 94*, Springer LNCS v 950 pp 103–113; see also RFC 2437, `http://sunsite.auc.dk/RFC/rfc/ rfc2437.html`

[149] SM Bellovin, "Packets Found on an Internet", in *Computer Communications Review* v 23 no 3 (July 1993) pp 26–31

[150] SM Bellovin, "Defending Against Sequence Number Attacks", RFC 1948 (May 1996) at `http://sunsite.auc.dk/RFC/rfc/rfc1948.html`

[151] SM Bellovin, "Problem Areas for the IP Security Protocols," in *Proceedings of the Sixth Usenix Unix Security Symposium* (1996); at `http:// www.cs.columbia.edu/~smb/papers/badesp.pdf`

[152] SM Bellovin, "Debit-card fraud in Canada", in `comp.risks` v 20.69; at `http://catless.ncl.ac.uk/Risks/20.69.html`

[153] SM Bellovin, "Permissive Action Links", at `http://www.research.att.com/~smb/nsam-160/`

[154] SM Bellovin, *'ICMP Traceback Messages'*, Internet Draft, March 2000, at `http://search.ietf.org/internet-drafts/draft-bellovin-itrace-00.txt`

[155] SM Bellovin, "More on Comcast Blocking Peer-to-Peer Traffic", Oct 22 2007, at `http://www.cs.columbia.edu/~smb/blog/2007-10/2007-10-22.html`; and "Comcast Apparently Blocking Some Peer-to-Peer Traffic", Oct 19 2007, ibid.

[156] S Bellovin, M Blaze, E Brickell, C Brooks, V Cerf, W Diffie, S Landau, J Peterson, J Treichler, "Security Implications of Applying the Communications Assistance to Law Enforcement Act to Voice over IP" `http:// www.itaa.org/news/docs/CALEAVOIPreport.pdf`

[157] SM Bellovin, WR Cheswick, *'Firewalls and Internet Security: Repelling the Wily Hacker'*, Addison-Wesley (1994); ISBN: 0-201-63357-4

[158] SM Bellovin, M Merritt, "Encrypted Key Exchange: Password-Based Protocols Secure Against Dictionary Attacks", in *Proceedings of the IEEE Symposium on Security and Privacy* (1992) pp 72–84

[159] M Benantar, R Guski, KM Triodle, "Access control systems: From host-centric to network-centric computing", in *IBM Systems Journal* v 35 no 1 (96) pp 94–112

[160] W Bender, D Gruhl, N Morimoto, A Lu, "Techniques for Data Hiding", in *IBM Systems Journal* v 35 no 3–4 (96) pp 313–336

[161] T Benkart, D Bitzer, "BFE Applicability to LAN Environments", in *Seventeenth National Computer Security Conference* (1994); proceedings published by NIST, pp 227–236

[162] AD Biderman, H Zimmer, *'The Manipulation of Human Behavior'*, Wiley 1961; at `http://www.archive.org/details/TheManipulationOfHuman-Behavior`

[163] F Bergadano, B Crispo, G Ruffo, "Proactive Password Checking with Decision Trees", in *4th ACM Conference on Computer and Communications Security* (1997), proceedings published by the ACM, ISBN 0-89791-912-2, pp 67–77

[164] DJ Bernstein, *'Cache-Timing Attacks on AES'*, preprint, 2005

[165] T Berson, "Skype Security Evaluation", Oct 18 2005, from `http://share.skype.com/sites/security/2005/10/skype_security_and_encryption.html`

[166] T Berson, G Barksdale, "KSOS: Development Methodology for a Secure Operating System", *AFIPS Conference proceedings* (1979)

[167] Bewert, "All About NSA's and AT&T's Big Brother Machine, the Narus 6400", in *Dailykos* Apr 7 2006; at `http://www.dailykos.com/storyonly/2006/4/8/14724/28476/`

[168] K Biba, *'Integrity Considerations for Secure Computer Systems'*, Mitre Corporation MTR-3153 (1975)

[169] E Biham, A Biryukov, "Cryptanalysis of Skipjack Reduced to 31 Rounds Using Impossible Differentials" in *Advances in Cryptology–Eurocrypt 97*, Springer LNCS v 1592 pp 12–23

[170] E Biham, A Shamir, *'Differential Cryptanalysis of the Data Encryption Standard'*, Springer (1993) ISBN 0-387-97930-1

[171] E Biham, A Shamir, "Differential Fault Analysis of Secret Key Cryptosystems", in *Advances in Cryptology–Crypto 97* Springer LNCS v 1294 pp 513–525

[172] E Biham, O Dunkelman, S Indesteege, N Keller, B Preneel, "How To Steal Cars–A Practical Attack on KeeLoq", 2007, at `http://www.cosic.esat.kuleuven.be/keeloq/`

[173] A Biryukov, A Shamir, D Wagner, "Real Time Cryptanalysis of A5/1 on a PC", in *Fast Software Encryption* (2000)

[174] R Bishop, R Bloomfield, "A Conservative Theory for Long-Term Reliability-Growth Prediction", in *IEEE Transactions on Reliability* v 45 no 4 (Dec 96) pp 550–560

[175] DM Bishop, "Applying COMPUSEC to the battle field", in *17th Annual National Computer Security Conference* (1994) pp 318–326

[176] M Bishop, M Dilger, "Checking for Race Conditions in File Accesses", in *Computing Systems Usenix* v 9 no 2 (Spring 1996) pp 131–152

[177] Wolfgang Bitzer, Joachim Opfer *'Schaltungsanordnung zum Messen der Korrelationsfunktion zwischen zwei vorgegebenen Signalen'* [Circuit arrangement for measuring the correlation function between two provided signals]. German Patent DE 3911155 C2, Deutsches Patent amt, November 11, 1993

[178] J Blackledge, "Making Money from Fractals and Chaos: Microbar", in *Mathematics Today* v 35 no 6 (Dec 99) pp 170–173

[179] RD Blackledge, "DNA versus fingerprints", in *Journal of Forensic Sciences* v 40 (1995) p 534

[180] B Blair, "Keeping Presidents in the Nuclear Dark", in *Bruce Blair's Nuclear Column*, Feb 11 2004, at `http://www.cdi.org/blair/permissiveaction-links.cfm`

[181] GR Blakley, "Safeguarding cryptographic keys", in *Proceedings of NCC AFIPS* (1979), pp 313–317

[182] B Blakley, R Blakley, RM Soley, *'CORBA Security: An Introduction to Safe Computing with Objects'* Addison-Wesley (1999) ISBN 0-201-32565-9

[183] MA Blaze, "Protocol Failure in the Escrowed Encryption Standard", in *Second ACM Conference on Computer and Communications Security*, 2–4 November 1994, Fairfax, Va; proceedings published by the ACM ISBN 0-89791-732-4, pp 59–67; at `http://www.crypto.com/papers/`

[184] Matt Blaze, "Cryptology and Physical Security: Rights Amplification in Master-Keyed Mechanical Locks", at *IEEE Symposium on Security and Privacy* 2003, at `http://www.crypto.com/papers/mk.pdf`

[185] MA Blaze, "Toward a Broader View of Security Protocols", in *Security Protocols 2004*, Springer LNCS v 3957, pp 106–132

[186] MA Blaze, "Safecracking for the computer scientist", U. Penn Technical Report (2004), at `http://www.crypto.com/papers/`

[187] MA Blaze, SM Bellovin, "Tapping, Tapping On My Network Door", in *Communications of the ACM* (Oct 2000), *Inside Risks* 124; at `http://www.crypto.com/papers/carnivore-risks.html`

[188] MA Blaze, J Feigenbaum, J Lacy, "Decentralized Trust Management", in *Proceedings of the 1996 IEEE Symposium on Security and Privacy* pp 164–173

[189] D Bleichenbacher, "Chosen Ciphertext Attacks against Protocols Based on the RSA Encryption Standard PKCS #1", in *Advances in Cryptology–Crypto 98* Springer LNCS v 1462 pp 1–12

[190] G Bleumer, *'Electronic Postage Systems–Technology, Security, Economics'*, Springer 2006; ISBN 0-387-29313-2

[191] G Bleumer, M Schunter, "Digital patient assistants: privacy vs cost in compulsory health insurance", in *Health Informatics Journal* v 4 nos 3–4 (Dec 1998) pp 138–156

[192] B Blobel, "Clinical record Systems in Oncology. Experiences and Developments on Cancer Registers in Eastern Germany", in [43] pp 39–56

[193] JA Bloom, IJ Cox, T Kalker, JPMG Linnartz, ML Miller, CBS Traw, "Copy Protection for DVD Video", in *Proceedings of the IEEE* v 87 no 7 (July 1999) pp 1267–1276

[194] P Bloom, *'Descartes' Baby: How Child Development Explains What Makes Us Human'*, Arrow (2005)

[195] ER Block, *'Fingerprinting'*, Franklin Wells (1970), SBN 85166-435-0

[196] S Blythe, B Fraboni, S Lall, H Ahmed, U de Riu, "Layout Reconstruction of Complex Silicon Chips", in *IEEE Journal of Solid-State Circuits* v 28 no 2 (Feb 93) pp 138–145

[197] WE Boebert, "Some Thoughts on the Occasion of the NSA Linux Release", in *Linux Journal*, Jan 24 2001; at `http://www.linuxjournal.com/article/4963`

[198] WE Boebert, RY Kain, "A Practical Alternative to Hierarchical Integrity Policies", in *8th National Computer Security Conference* (1985), proceedings published by NIST p 18

[199] BW Boehm, *'Software Engineering Economics'*, Prentice Hall (1981), ISBN 0-13-822122-7

[200] Rainer Boehme and Gaurav Kataria, "Models and Measures for Correlation in Cyber-Insurance", at *WEIS 2006*

[201] N Bohm, I Brown, B Gladman, *'Electronic Commerce–Who Carries the Risk of Fraud?'*, Foundation for Information Policy Research (2000), available from `http://www.fipr.org`

[202] M Bond, *'Understanding Security APIs,'*, PhD Thesis, Cambridge, 2004

[203] M Bond, "BOOM! HEADSHOT! (Building Neo-Tactics on Network-Level Anomalies in Online Tactical First-Person Shooters)" (2006), at `http://www.lightbluetouchpaper.org/2006/10/02/`

[204] M Bond, "Action Replay Justice", Nov 22 2007, at `http://www.lightbluetouchpaper.org/2007/11/22/action-replay-justice/`

[205] M Bond, SJ Murdoch, J Clulow, *'Laser-printed PIN Mailer Vulnerability Report'*, 2005, at `http://www.cl.cam.ac.uk/~sjm217/`

[206] D Boneh, RA Demillo, RJ Lipton, "On the Importance of Checking Cryptographic Protocols for Faults", in *Advances in Cryptology–Eurocrypt 97*, Springer LNCS v 1233 pp 37–51

[207] D Boneh, M Franklin, "Identity-Based Encryption from the Weil Pairing", in *Advances in Cryptology–Proceedings of CRYPTO 2001*, Springer LNCS 2139 pp 213–29

[208] L Boney, AH Tewfik, KN Hamdy, "Digital Watermarks for Audio Signals", in *Proceedings of the 1996 IEEE International Conference on Multimedia Computing and Systems*, pp 473–480

[209] V Bontchev, "Possible macro virus attacks and how to prevent them", in *Computers and Security* v 15 no 7 (96) pp 595–626

[210] N Borisov, I Goldberg, D Wagner, "Intercepting Mobile Communications: The Insecurity of 802.11", at *Mobicom 2001*

[211] NS Borenstein, "Perils and Pitfalls of Practical Cybercommerce", in *Communications of the ACM* v 39 no 6 (June 96) pp 36–44

[212] E Bovenlander, invited talk on smartcard security, *Eurocrypt 97*, reported in [69]

[213] E Bovenlander, RL van Renesse, "Smartcards and Biometrics: An Overview", in *Computer Fraud and Security Bulletin* (Dec 95) pp 8–12

[214] C Bowden, Y Akdeniz, "Cryptography and Democracy: Dilemmas of Freedom", in *Liberating Cyberspace: Civil Liberties, Human Rights, and the Internet* Pluto Press (1999) pp 81–125

[215] D Bowen, *'Top-to-Bottom Review'*, Aug 2007, at http://www.sos.ca .gov/elections/elections_vsr.htm

[216] D Boyd "Facebook's 'Privacy Trainwreck': Exposure, Invasion, and Drama", in *Apophenia Blog* Sep 8th 2006, at http://www.danah.org/ papers/FacebookAndPrivacy.html

[217] M Brader, "Car-door lock remote control activates another car's alarm", in comp.risks 21.56 (Jul 2001)

[218] M Brader, "How to lose 10,000,000 pounds", in comp.risks v 24 no 25, Apr 19 2006, at http://archives.neohapsis.com/archives/ risks/2006/0012.html

[219] RM Brady, RJ Anderson, RC Ball, *'Murphy's law, the fitness of evolving species, and the limits of software reliability'*, Cambridge University Computer Laboratory Technical Report no 471 (1999)

[220] S Brands, *'Rethinking Public Key Infrastructures and Digital Certificates –Building in Privacy'*, MIT Press (2000) http://www.freetechbooks .com/about390.html

[221] JT Brassil, S Low, NF Maxemchuk, "Copyright Protection for the Electronic Distribution of Text Documents", in *Proceedings of the IEEE* v 87 no 7 (July 1999) pp 1181–1196

[222] H Bray, " 'Face testing' at Logan is found lacking", in *Boston Globe* July 17 2002

[223] M Brelis, "Patients' files allegedly used for obscene calls", in *Boston Globe* April 11, 1995; also in `comp.risks` v 17 no 7

[224] DFC Brewer, MJ Nash, "Chinese Wall model", in *Proceedings of the 1989 IEEE Computer Society Symposium on Security and Privacy* pp 215–228

[225] B Brewin, "CAC use nearly halves DOD network intrusions, Croom says", in *fcw.com*, Jan 25 2007, at `http://www.fcw.com/article97480-01-25-07`

[226] M Briceno, I Goldberg, D Wagner, "An implementation of the GSM A3A8 algorithm", at `http://www.scard.org/gsm/a3a8.txt`

[227] D Brin, *'The Transparent Society: Will Technology Force Us to Choose Between Privacy and Freedom?'*, Perseus Press (1999) ISBN: 0-73820144-8; magazine version in *Wired*, Dec 1996, at `http://www.wired.com/wired/archive/4.12/fftransparent.html`

[228] R Briol "Emanation: How to keep your data confidential", in *Symposium on Electromagnetic Security For Information Protection, SEPI 91*, Rome, 1991

[229] British Standard 8220-1.2000, *'Guide for Security of Buildings Against Crime—Part 1: Dwellings'*

[230] M Broersma, "Printer makers rapped over refill restrictions", *ZDnet* Dec 20 2002, at `http://news.zdnet.co.uk/story/0,,t269-s2127877,00.html`

[231] F Brooks, *'The Mythical Man-Month: Essays on Software Engineering'*, Addison-Wesley (1995 Anniversary Edition)

[232] D Brown, "Techniques for Privacy and Authentication in Personal Communications Systems", in *IEEE Personal Communications* v 2 no 4 (Aug 95) pp 6–10

[233] D Brumley, D Boneh, "Remote timing attacks are practical", in *Computer Networks* v 48 no 5 (Aug 2005) pp 701–716

[234] D Brown, "Unprovable Security of RSA-OAEP in the Standard Model", IACR eprint no 2006/223, at `http://eprint.iacr.org/2006/223`

[235] I Brown, L Edwards, C Marsden, "Stalking 2.0: privacy protection in a leading Social Networking Site", in *GikII 2–law, technology and popular culture* (2007); at http://www.law.ed.ac.uk/ahrc/gikii/docs2/edwards.pdf

[236] JDR Buchanan, RP Cowburn, AV Jausovec, D Petit, P Seem, XO Gang, D Atkinson, K Fenton DA Allwood, MT Bryan, " 'Fingerprinting' documents and packaging", in *Nature* v 436 no 28 (July 2005) p 475

[237] JM Buchanan, "The Constitution of Economic Policy", 1986 Nobel Prize Lecture, at http://nobelprize.org/nobel_prizes/economics/laureates/1986/buchanan-lecture.html

[238] H Buehler, interview with Swiss Radio International, 4/7/1994, at http://www.funet.fi/pub/crypt/mirrors/idea.sec.dsi.unimi.it/rpub.cl.msu.edu/crypt/docs/hans-buehler-crypto-spy.txt

[239] *Bug Traq* http://archives.neohapsis.com/archives/bugtraq/

[240] Bull, Dassault, Diebold, NCR, Siemens Nixdorf and Wang Global, *'Protection Profile: Automatic Cash Dispensers / Teller Machines'*, version 1.0 (1999), at http://www.commoncriteriaportal.org/

[241] Bundesamt für Sicherheit in der Informationstechnik (German Information Security Agency), *'Common Criteria Protection Profile–Health Professional Card (HPC)–Heilberufsausweis (HPA)'*, BSI-PP-0018, at http://www.commoncriteriaportal.org/

[242] Bundesamt für Sicherheit in der Informationstechnik (German Information Security Agency), *'Schutzmaßnahmen gegen Lauschangriffe'* [Protection against bugs], Faltblätter des BSI v 5, Bonn, 1997; http://www.bsi.bund.de/literat/faltbl/laus005.htm

[243] Bundesamt für Sicherheit in der Informationstechnik (German Information Security Agency), *'Elektromagnetische Schirmung von Gebäuden*, 2007, BSI TR-03209

[244] Bundesverfasngsgericht, "Beschluss des Ersten Senats", Apr 4 2006, 1 BvR 518/02 Absatz-Nr. (1–184), at http://www.bverfg.de/entscheidungen/rs20060404_1bvr051802.html

[245] J Bunnell, J Podd, R Henderson, R Napier, J Kennedy-Moffatt, "Cognitive, associative and conventional passwords: Recall and guessing rates", in *Computers and Security* v 16 no 7 (1997) pp 645–657

[246] J Burke, P Warren, "How mobile phones let spies see our every move", in *The Observer* Oct 13 2002; at `http://observer.guardian .co.uk/uk_news/story/0,6903,811027,00.html`

[247] RW Butler, GB Finelli, "The infeasibility of experimental quantification of life-critical software reliability", in *ACM Symposium on Software for Critical Systems* (1991), ISBN 0-89791-455-4, pp 66–76

[248] Buro Jansen & Janssen, *'Making up the rules: interception versus privacy'*, 8/8/2000, at `http://www.xs4all.nl/~respub/crypto/english/`

[249] M Burrows, M Abadi, RM Needham, "A Logic of Authentication", in *Proceedings of the Royal Society of London A* v 426 (1989) pp 233–271; earlier version published as DEC SRC Research Report 39, `ftp://gatekeeper.pa.dec.com/pub/DEC/SRC/research-reports/ SRC-039.pdf`

[250] RW Byrne, A Whiten, *'Machiavellian Intelligence—Social Expertise and the Evolution of Intellect in Monkeys, Apes and Humans'*, Oxford, 1988; see also A Whiten, RW Byrne, *'Machiavellian Intelligence II—Extensions and Evaluations'*, Cambridge 1997

[251] "Long Distance Phone Scam Hits Internet Surfers", in `business-knowhow.com`, at `http://www.businessknowhow.com/newlong.htm`

[252] F Caldicott, *'Report on the review of patient-identifiable information'*, Department of Health, 1997

[253] California Secretary of State, *'A Report on the Feasibility of Internet Voting'* (January 2000), at `http://www.ss.ca.gov/executive/ivote/`

[254] J Calvert, P Warren, "Secrets of McCartney bank cash are leaked", in *The Express*, February 9 2000, pp 1–2

[255] J Camenisch, JM Piveteau, M Stadler, "An Efficient Fair Payment System", in *3rd ACM Conference on Computer and Communications Security* (1996), proceedings published by the ACM, ISBN 0-89791-829-0, pp 88–94

[256] J Camp, C Wolfram, "Pricing Security", in *Proceedings of the CERT Information Survivability Workshop* (Oct 24–26 2000) pp 31–39

[257] J Camp, S Lewis, *'Economics of Information Security'*, Springer 2004

[258] D Campbell, "Somebody's listening", in *The New Statesman* (12 August 1988) pp 1, 10–12; at `http://jya.com/echelon-dc.htm`

[259] D Campbell, "Making history: the original source for the 1988 first Echelon report steps forward" (25 February 2000), at `http://cryptome.org/echelon-mndc.htm`

[260] D Campbell, "Operation Ore Exposed", *PC Pro,* July 2005, at `http://www.pcpro.co.uk/features/74690/operation-ore-exposed/page1.html`

[261] D Campbell, "Sex, Lies and the Missing Videotape", *PC Pro,* April 2007, at `http://ore-exposed.obu-investigators.com/PC_PRO_Operation_Ore_Exposed_2.html`

[262] D Campbell, P Lashmar, "The new Cold War: How America spies on us for its oldest friend–the Dollar", in *The Independent* (2 July 2000), at `http://www.independent.co.uk/news/World/Americas/2000-07/coldwar020700.shtml`

[263] JC Campbell, N Ikegami, *'The Art of Balance in Health Policy–Maintaining Japan's Low-Cost, Egalitarian System'*, Cambridge University Press (1998) ISBN 0-521-57122-7

[264] JP Campbell, "Speaker Recognition: A Tutorial", in *Proceedings of the IEEE* v 85 no 9 (Sep 97) pp 1437–1462

[265] K Campbell, L Gordon, M Loeb and L Zhou, "The economic cost of publicly announced information security breaches: empirical evidence from the stock market", in *Journal of Computer Security* v 11 no 3 (2003) pp 431–448

[266] C Cant, S Wiseman, "Simple Assured Bastion Hosts", in *13th Annual Computer Security Application Conference* (1997); proceedings published by IEEE Computer Society, ISBN 0-8186-8274-4 ACSAC, pp 24–33

[267] "Dark horse in lead for fingerprint ID card", *Card World Independent* (May 94) p 2

[268] "German A555 takes its toll", in *Card World International* (12/94–1/95) p 6

[269] "High tech helps card fraud decline" in *Cards International* no 117 (29 Sep 94)

[270] "Visa beefs up its anti-fraud technology", in *Cards International* no 189 (12/12/97) p 5

[271] JM Carlin, "UNIX Security Update", at *Usenix Security 93* pp 119–130

[272] J Carr, "Doing nothing is just not an option", in *The Observer* (18/6/2000),at `http://www.guardian.co.uk/technology/2000/jun/18/onlinesecurity.politics`

[273] J Carroll, *'Big Blues: The Unmaking of IBM'*, Crown Publishers (1993), ISBN 0-517-59197-9

[274] H Carter, "Car clock fixer jailed for nine months", in *The Guardian* (15/2/2000) p 13

[275] R Carter, "What You Are ... Not What You Have", in *International Security Review* Access Control Special Issue (Winter 93/94) pp 14–16

[276] S Castano, M Fugini, G Martella, P Samarati, *'Database Security'*, Addison-Wesley, 1994; ISBN 0-201-59375-0

[277] L Cauley, "NSA has massive database of Americans' phone calls", in *USA Today* Nov 11 2005, at `http://www.usatoday.com/news/washington/2006-05-10-nsa_x.htm`

[278] Center for Democracy and Technology, `http://www.cdt.org/`

[279] "The Nature and Scope of Governmental Electronic Surveillance Activity", Center for Democracy and Technology, July 2006, at `http://www.cdt.org/wiretap/wiretap_overview.html`

[280] DW Chadwick, PJ Crook, AJ Young, DM McDowell, TL Dornan, JP New, "Using the internet to access confidential patient records: a case study", in *British Medical Journal* v 321 (9 September 2000) pp 612–614; at `http://bmj.com/cgi/content/full/321/7261/612`

[281] Chaos Computer Club, *'How to fake fingerprints?'*, at `http://www.ccc.de/biometrie/fingerabdruck_kopieren.xml?language=en`

[282] L Chapman, *'Your disobedient servant'*, Penguin Books (1979)

[283] Chartered Institute of Building Services Engineers, *'Security Engineering'*, Applications Manual AM4 (1991)

[284] D Chaum, "Untraceable electronic mail, return addresses, and digital pseudonyms", in *Communications of the ACM* v 24 no 2 (Feb 1981)

[285] D Chaum, "Blind signatures for untraceable payments", in *Crypto 82*, Plenum Press (1983) pp 199–203

[286] D Chaum, "The Dining Cryptographers Problem: Unconditional Sender and Recipient Untraceability", in *Journal of Cryptology* v 1 (1989) pp 65–75

[287] D Chaum, A Fiat, M Naor, "Untraceable Electronic Cash", in *Advances in Cryptology — CRYPTO '88*, Springer LNCS v 403 pp 319–327

[288] R Chellappa, CL Wilcon, S Sirohey, "Human and Machine Recognition of Faces: A Survey", in *Proceedings of the IEEE* v 83 no 5 (May 95) pp 705–740

[289] HJ Choi, private discussion

[290] *'Security Protocols–5th International Workshop'*, B Christianson et al (ed), Springer LNCS v 1360 (1998)

[291] *'Security Protocols–6th International Workshop'*, B Christianson et al (ed), Springer LNCS v 1550 (1999). Later workshops had proceedings as follows: 2000, v 2133; 2001, v 2467; 2002, 2845; 2003, v 3364; 2004, v 3957.

[292] F Church (chairman), *'Intelligence Activities–Senate Resolution 21'*, US Senate, 94 Congress, First Session, at `http://cryptome.org/nsa-4th.htm`

[293] WS Ciciora, "Inside the set-top box", in *IEEE Spectrum* v 12 no 4 (Apr 95) pp 70–75

[294] T Claburn, "Former DuPont Scientist Sentenced For Trade Secret Theft", in *Information Week* Nov 8 2007; at `http://www.information-week.com/shared/printableArticle.jhtml?articleID=202804057`

[295] D Clark, D Wilson, "A Comparison of Commercial and Military Computer Security Policies", in *Proceedings of the 1987 IEEE Symposium on Security and Privacy* pp 184–194

[296] R Clark, *'The man who broke Purple'*, Little, Brown (1977) ISBN 0-316-14595-5

[297] I Clarke, *'The Free Network Project Homepage'*, at `http://freenet.source-forge.net/`

[298] RW Clarke, "The Theory of Crime prevention Though Environmental Design", at `www.cutr.usf.edu/security/documents%5CCPTED%5CTheory%20of%20CPTED.pdf`; see also *'Situational Crime Prevention: successful case studies'* (2nd edition), Harrow and Heston (1997) and "Situational Crime Prevention–Everybody's Business", ACPC95, at `http://www.acpc.org.au/CONF95/Clarke.htm`

[299] R Clayton, "Techno-Risk", at *Cambridge International Symposium on Economic Crime* (2003), at `http://www.cl.cam.ac.uk/~rnc1/talks/030910-TechnoRisk.pdf`

[300] R Clayton, *'Anonymity and traceability in cyberspace'*, PhD Thesis, 2005; Cambridge University Technical Report UCAM-CL-TR-653

[301] R Clayton, "Insecure Real-Word Authentication Protocols (or Why Phishing Is So Profitable)", at *Cambridge Security Protocols Workshop 2005*, at `http://www.cl.cam.ac.uk/~rnc1/phishproto.pdf`

[302] R Clayton, private conversation, 2006

[303] R Clayton, "The Rising Tide: DDoS by Defective Designs and Defaults", at SRUTI 06; at `http://www.cl.cam.ac.uk/~rnc1/rising-tide.pdf`

[304] R Clayton, "When firmware attacks! (DDoS by D-Link)", *Light Blue Touchpaper*, at `http://www.lightbluetouchpaper.org/2006/04/07/`

[305] R Clayton, "There aren't that many serious spammers any more", *Light Blue Touchpaper*, at `http://www.lightbluetouchpaper.org/2007/04/03/`

[306] R Clayton, M Bond, "Experience Using a Low-Cost FPGA Design to Crack DES Keys", *CHES Workshop* (2002), Springer LNCS 2523 pp 579–592

[307] R Clayton, G Davies, C Hall, A Hilborne, K Hartnett, D Jones, P Mansfield, K Mitchell, R Payne, N Titley, D Williams, '*LINX Best Current Practice– Traceability*', Version 1.0, 18/5/1999, at `http://www.linx.net/noncore/bcp/traceability-bcp.html`

[308] R Clayton, S Murdoch, R Watson, "Ignoring the Great Firewall of China", at *6th Workshop on Privacy Enhancing Technologies* (2006), at `http://www.cl.cam.ac.uk/~rnc1/ignoring.pdf`

[309] J Clulow, '*The Design and Analysis of Cryptographic APIs for Security Devices*', MSc Thesis, University of Natal 2003

[310] A Cohen, '*A Perfect Store*', Back Bay Books, 2003

[311] FB Cohen, '*A Short Course on Computer Viruses*', Wiley (1994) ISBN 0-471-00769-2

[312] JL Colbert, PL Bowen, '*A Comparison of Internal Controls: COBIT, SAC, COSO and SAS 55/78*', at `http://www.isaca.org/bkr_cbt3.htm`

[313] A Collins, "Court decides software time-locks are illegal", in *Computer Weekly* (19 August 93) p 1

[314] D Cohen, J Hashkes, "A system for controlling access to broadcast transmissions", European Patent no EP0428252

[315] P Collier, A Hoeffler, "Greed and grievance in civil war", in *Oxford Economic Papers* v 56 (2004) pp 563–595, at http://oep.oxfordjournals.org/cgi/content/abstract/56/4/563

[316] D Comer, "Cryptographic techniques — secure your wireless designs", in *EDN* (18/1/96) pp 57–68

[317] "Telecomms Fraud in the Cellular Market: How Much is Hype and How Much is Real?', in *Computer Fraud and Security Bulletin* (Jun 97) pp 11–14

[318] Committee of Sponsoring Organizations of the Treadway Commission (CSOTC),'*Internal Control–Integrated Framework*' (COSO Report, 1992); from http://www.coso.org/

[319] '*Communicating Britain's Future*', at http://www.fipr.org/polarch/labour.html

[320] "Kavkaz-Tsentr says Russians hacking Chechen web sites"; " 'Information war' waged on web sites over Chechnya", in *Communications Law in Transition Newsletter* v 1 no 4 (Feb 2000), at http://pcmlp.socleg.ox.ac.uk/transition/issue04/russia.htm

[321] Computer Emergency Response Team Coordination Center, at http://www.cert.org/

[322] JB Condat, "Toll fraud on French PBX systems", in *Computer Law and Security Report* v 10 no 2 (Mar/April 94) pp 89–91

[323] J Connolly, "Operation Chain Link: The Deployment of a Firewall at Hanscom Air Force Base", *Twelfth Annual Computer Security Applications Conference* (1996), proceedings published by the IEEE, ISBN 0-8186-7606-X, pp 170–177

[324] E Constable, "American Express to reduce the risk of online fraud"

[325] US Consumer Reports, '*State of the Net*', Sep 6 2007, reported in http://www.webknowhow.net/news/news/060831ConsumerReport-OnlineThreats.html

[326] D Coppersmith, '*The Data Encryption Standard (DES) and its Strength Against Attacks*', IBM report RC 18613 (81421)

[327] Council of Europe, '*Convention For the Protection of Individuals with Regard to Automatic Processing of Personal Data*', European Treaty Series no 108 (January 28, 1981): at http://www.privacy.org/pi/intl_orgs/coe/dp_convention_108.txt

[328] R Cordery, L Pintsov, "History and Role of Information Security in Postage Evidencing and Payment", in *Cryptologia* v XXIX no 3 (Jul 2005) pp 257–271

[329] C Cowan, C Pu, D Maier, H Hinton, J Walpole, P Bakke, S Beattie, A Grier, P Wagle, Q Zhang, "StackGuard: Automatic Adaptive Detection and Prevention of Buffer-Overflow Attacks", *7th Usenix Security Conference* (1998) pp 63–77

[330] LH Cox, JP Kelly, R Patil, "Balancing quality and confidentiality for multivariate tabular data" in *Privacy in Statistical Data Bases* (2004) Springer LNCS v 3050 pp 87–98

[331] JW Coyne, NC Kluksdahl, " 'Mainstreaming' Automated Information Systems Security Engineering (A Case Study in Security Run Amok)", in *Second ACM Conference on Computer and Communications Security* (1994) proceedings published by the ACM, ISBN 0-89791-732-4, pp 251–257; at http://www.acm.org/pubs/contents/proceedings/commsec/191177/

[332] J Cradden, "Printer-makers hit by new EU law", in *Electricnews.net* December 19 2002, at http://www.electricnews.net/news.html?code=8859027

[333] L Cranor, S Garfinkel, *'Security Usability'*, O'Reilly 2005, ISBN 0-596-80827-9

[334] S Craver, "On Public-key Steganography in the Presence of an Active Warden", in *Proceedings of the Second International Workshop on Information Hiding* (1998), Springer LNCS v 1525 pp 355–368

[335] SA Craver, M Wu, BD Liu, A Stubblefield, B Swartzlander, DS Wallach, D Dean, EW Felten, "Reading Between the Lines: Lessons from the SDMI Challenge", in *Usenix Security Symposium* (2000), at http://www.cs.princeton.edu/~felten

[336] RJ Creasy, "The origin of the VM/370 time-sharing system", in *IBM Journal of Research and Development* v 25 no 5 (Sep 1981) pp 483–490, at http://www.research.ibm.com/journal/rd/255/ibmrd2505M.pdf

[337] B Crispo, M Lomas, "A Certification Scheme for Electronic Commerce", in *Security Protocols* (1996), Springer LNCS v 1189 pp 19–32

[338] Cryptome.org, Deepwater documents, May 2007; at http://cryptome.org/deepwater/deepwater.htm

[339] W Curtis, H Krasner, N Iscoe, "A Field Study of the Software Design Process for Large Systems", in *Communications of the ACM* v 31 no 11 (Nov 88) pp 1268–87

[340] D Cvrcek, "Counters, Freshness, and Implementation", Oct 2 2007, at http://www.lightbluetouchpaper.org/

[341] F D'Addario, "Testing Security's Effectiveness", in *Security Management Online* October 2001, at http://www.securitymanagement.com/library/Security_D'Addario1001.html

[342] J Daemen, V Rijmen, *'The Design of Rijndael: AES–The Advanced Encryption Standard'*, Springer (2002) ISBN 3-540-42580-2

[343] "Beating the credit card telephone fraudsters", in *Daily Telegraph* (9 Oct 1999), at http://www.telegraph.co.uk:80/

[344] G Danezis, Roger Dingledine, N Mathewson, "Mixminion: Design of a Type III Anonymous Remailer Protocol", in *IEEE Symposium on Security and Privacy* (2003) pp 2–15; at http://mixminion.net/miniondesign.pdf

[345] G Danezis, B Wittneben, "The Economics of Mass Surveillance", *Fifth Workshop on the Economics of Information Security* (2006)

[346] G Danezis, R Clayton, "Introducing Traffic Analysis", Jan 2007, in *Digital Privacy: Theory, Technologies, and Practices*, Taylor and Francis 2007, at http://homes.esat.kuleuven.be/~gdanezis/TAIntro-book.pdf

[347] G Danezis, C Diaz, "Survey of Privacy Technology", 2007, at http://homes.esat.kuleuven.be/~gdanezis/anonSurvey.pdf

[348] M Darman, E le Roux, "A new generation of terrestrial and satellite microwave communication products for military networks", in *Electrical Communication* (Q4 94) pp 359–364

[349] Two statements, made by the Data Protection Commissioners of EU and EES countries and Switzerland, *20th International Conference on Data Protection*, Santiago de Compostela, 16–18 September 1998; available at http://www.dataprotection.gov.uk/20dpcom.html

[350] Daubert v. Merrell Dow Pharmaceuticals, 113 S. Ct. 2786 (1993)

[351] J Daugman, "High Confidence Visual Recognition of Persons by a Test of Statistical Independence", in *IEEE Transactions on Pattern Analysis and Machine Intelligence* v 15 no 11 (Nov 93) pp 1148–1161

[352] J Daugman, *'Biometric decision landscapes'*, Technical Report no TR482, University of Cambridge Computer Laboratory.

[353] C Davies, R Ganesan, "BApasswd: A New Proactive Password Checker", in *16th National Computer Security Conference* (1993), proceedings published by NIST, pp 1–15

[354] DW Davies, WL Price, *'Security for Computer Networks'* (John Wiley and Sons 1984)

[355] G Davies, *'A History of money from ancient times to the present day'*, University of Wales Press (1996) ISBN 0-7083-1351-5; related material at `http://www.ex.ac.uk/%7ERDavies/arian/llyfr.html`

[356] H Davies, "Physiognomic access control", in *Information Security Monitor* v 10 no 3 (Feb 95) pp 5–8

[357] D Davis, "Compliance Defects in Public-Key Cryptography", in *Sixth Usenix Security Symposium Proceedings* (July 1996) pp 171–178

[358] D Davis, R Ihaka, P Fenstermacher, "Cryptographic Randomness from Air Turbulence in Disk Drives" in *Advances in Cryptology–Crypto 94* Springer LNCS v 839 pp 114–120

[359] J Davis, "Hackers Take Down the Most Wired Country in Europe", in *Wired*, Aug 21 2007, at `http://www.wired.com/politics/security/magazine/15-09/ff_estonia`

[360] D Dean, EW Felten, DS Wallach, "Java Security: From HotJava to Netscape and Beyond", in *Proceedings of the 1996 IEEE Symposium on Security and Privacy*, IEEE Computer Society Press, pp 190–200

[361] C Deavours, D Kahn, L Kruh, G Mellen, B Winkel, *'Cryptology–Yesterday, Today and Tomorrow'*, Artech House (1987), ISBN 0-89006-253-6

[362] C Deavours, D Kahn, L Kruh, G Mellen, B Winkel, *'Selections from Cryptologia–History, People and Technology'*, Artech House (1997) ISBN 0-89006-862-3

[363] C Deavours, L Kruh, *'Machine Cryptography and Modern Cryptanalysis'*, Artech House (1985) ISBN 0-89006-161-0

[364] JF de Beer, "Constitutional Jurisdiction Over Paracopyright Laws", in *'The Public Interest: The Future of Canadian Copyright Law'*, Irwin Law (2005)

[365] B Demoulin, L Kone, C Poudroux, P Degauque, "Electromagnetic Radiation of Shielded Data Transmission Lines", in [481] pp 163–173

[366] I Denley, S Weston-Smith, "Implementing access control to protect the confidentiality of patient information in clinical information systems in the acute hospital", in *Health Informatics Journal* v 4 nos 3–4 (Dec 1998) pp 174–178

[367] I Denley, S Weston-Smith, "Privacy in clinical information systems in secondary care" in *British Medical Journal* v 318 (15 May 1999) pp 1328–1331

[368] DE Denning, "The Lattice Model of Secure Information Flow", in *Communications of the ACM* v 19 no 5 pp 236–248

[369] DE Denning, *'Cryptography and Data Security'*, Addison-Wesley (1982) ISBN 0-201-10150-5

[370] DE Denning, *'Information Warfare and Security'*, Addison-Wesley (1999) ISBN 0-201-43303-6

[371] DE Denning, "Activism, Hacktivism, and Cyberterrorism: The Internet as a Tool for Influencing Foreign Policy", InfowarCon 2000, at `http://www.nautilus.org/info-policy/workshop/papers/denning.html`

[372] DE Denning, PJ Denning, M Schwartz, "The tracker: a threat to statistical database security", in *ACM Transactions on Database Systems* v 4 no 1 (1979) pp 76–96

[373] DE Denning, PH MacDoran, "Location-Based Authentication: Grounding Cyberspace for Better Security", in *Computer Fraud and Security Bulletin* (Feb 96) pp 12–16

[374] DE Denning, J Schlorer, "Inference Controls for Statistical Databases", in *IEEE Computer* v 16 no 7 (July 1983) pp 69–82

[375] Department of Defense, *'Department of Defense Trusted Computer System Evaluation Criteria'*, DoD 5200.28-STD, December 1985

[376] Department of Defense, *'A Guide to Understanding Covert Channel Analysis of Trusted Systems'*, NCSC-TG-030 (Nov 1993)

[377] Department of Defense, *'Password Management Guideline'*, CSC-STD-002-85 (1985)

[378] Department of Defense, *'A Guide to Understanding Data Remanence in Automated Information Systems'*, NCSC-TG-025 (1991)

[379] Department of Defense, *'Technical Rationale behind CSC-STD-003-85: computer security requirements'*, CSC-STD-004-85 (1985)

[380] Department of Defense, News Transcript, Oct 20 2007, at `http://cryptome.org/af-squirm/af-squirm.htm`

[381] Department of Justice, *'Guidelines for Searching and Seizing Computers'*, 1994; at `http://www.epic.org/security/computer_search_guidelines.txt`

[382] Y Desmedt, Y Frankel, "Threshold cryptosystems", in *Advances in Cryptology–Proceedings of Crypto 89*, Springer LNCS v 435 pp 307–315

[383] J Dethloff, "Special Report: Intellectual Property Rights and Smart Card Patents: The Past–The Present–The Future", in *Smart Card News* (Feb 96) pp 36–38

[384] J Dibbell, "The Life of the Chinese Gold Farmer", in *New York Times* Jun 17 2007; at `http://www.nytimes.com/2007/06/17/magazine/17lootfarmers-t.html?ex=1340769600&en=87f96d5d8676cbad&ei=5124&partner=permalink&exprod=permalink`

[385] W Diffie, ME Hellman, "New Directions in Cryptography", in *IEEE Transactions on information theory* v 22 no 6 (Nov 76) pp 644–654

[386] W Diffie, ME Hellman, "Exhaustive cryptanalysis of the NBS Data Encryption Standard", in *Computer* v 10 no 6 (June 77) pp 74–84

[387] W Diffie, S Landau, *'Privacy on the Line–The Politics of Wiretapping and Encryption'*, MIT Press (1998) ISBN 0-262-04167-7

[388] E Dijkstra, "Solution of a problem in concurrent programming control", in *Communications of the ACM* v 8 no 9 (1965) p 569

[389] Allana Dion, "Rapper Verified?", on *Gridgrind* Dec 8 2007; at `http://www.gridgrind.com/?p=229`

[390] The Discount Long Distance Digest, at `http://www.thedigest.com/shame/`

[391] D Dittrich, *'Distributed Denial of Service (DDoS) Attacks/tools'*, at `http://staff.washington.edu/dittrich/`

[392] AK Dixit, *'Lawlessness and Economics'*, Princeton University Press, 2003

[393] RC Dixon, *'Spread Spectrum Systems with Commercial Applications'*, Wiley (1994) ISBN 0-471-59342-7

[394] H Dobbertin, "Cryptanalysis of MD4", *Journal of Cryptology* v 11 no 4 (1998) pp 253–270

[395] B Dole, S Lodin, E Spafford, "Misplaced Trust: Kerberos 4 Session Keys", in *Internet Society Symposium on Network and Distributed System Security*, proceedings published by the IEEE, ISBN 0-8186-7767-8, pp 60–70

[396] JR Douceur, "The Sybil Attack", IPTPS 2002, at www.cs.rice.edu/ Conferences/IPTPS02/101.pdf

[397] J Doward, "The friend of the stars who fell from grace", in *The Observer* Aug 26 2007; at http://www.guardian.co.uk/media/2007/aug/26/ radio.television

[398] P Drahos, J Braithwaite, *'Information Feudalism–Who Owns the Knowledge Economy?'*, Earthscan 2002

[399] S Drimer, "Banks don't help fight phishing", Mar 10 2006, *Light Blue Touchpaper*; at http://www.lightbluetouchpaper.org/2006/03/ 10/banks-dont-help-fight-phishing/

[400] S Drimer, *'Volatile FPGA design security–a survey'*, 2007, at http://www.cl.cam.ac.uk/~sd410/papers/fpga_security.pdf

[401] S Drimer, SJ Murdoch, "Keep your enemies close: Distance bounding against smartcard relay attacks", in *16th USENIX Security Symposium* (2007), at http://www.cl.cam.ac.uk/~sd410/papers/sc_relay.pdf

[402] IE Dror, D Charlton, AE Péron, "Contextual information renders experts vulnerable to making erroneous identifications", in *Forensic Science International* 156 (2006) 74–78

[403] IE Dror, D Charlton, "Why Experts Make Errors", in *Journal of Forensic Identification* v 56 no 4 (2006) pp 600–616; at http://users .ecs.soton.ac.uk/id/biometrics.html

[404] IE Dror, "Don't forget us humans", in *The Times*, July 31 2006; at http://users.ecs.soton.ac.uk/id/biometrics.html

[405] I Drury, "Pointing the finger", in *Security Surveyor* v 27 no 5 (Jan 97) pp 15–17; at http://users.ecs.soton.ac.uk/id/biometrics.html

[406] C Dyer, "Europe's concern over UK data protection 'defects' revealed", in *The Guardian* Oct 1 2007; at http://www.guardian .co.uk/uk_news/story/0,,2180729,00.html

[407] N Eagle, A Pentland, D Lazer, "Inferring Social Network Structure using Mobile Phone Data", 2007, at http://reality.media.mit.edu/ pdfs/network_structure.pdf

[408] W van Eck, "Electromagnetic Radiation from Video Display Units: An Eavesdropping Risk? in *Computers and Security* v 4 (1985) pp 269–286

[409] P Eckersley, "Comcast is also Jamming Gnutella (and Lotus Notes?)", *EFF Deeplinks Blog* Oct 20 2007, at `http://www.eff.org/deeplinks/2007/10/comcast-also-jamming-gnutella-and-lotus-notes`

[410] *The Economist*, "Digital rights and wrongs" (17/7/1999); see `www.economist.com`

[411] *The Economist*, "Living in the global goldfish bowl ", 18–24 Dec 1999, Christmas special; see `www.economist.com`

[412] *The Economist*, "A price worth paying?", May 19 2005

[413] *The Economist*, "Cyberwarfare–Newly nasty", May 24 2007

[414] *The Economist*, "After smart weapons, smart soldiers", Oct 25 2007

[415] *The Economist*, "Getting the message, at last", Dec 13 2007, at `http://www.economist.com/opinion/displaystory.cfm?story_id=10286400`

[416] B Edelman, "Adverse Selection in Online 'Trust' Certificates", at *Fifth Workshop on the Economics of Information Security* (2006); at `http://weis2006.econinfosec.org/`

[417] J Edge, "IPv6 source routing: history repeats itself", May 7, 2007; at `http://lwn.net/Articles/232781/`

[418] EDRI, FIPR and VOSN, *'Response to the European commission consultation on the review of the "acquis communautaire" in the field of copyright and related rights'*, Oct 2004, at `http://www.edri.org/campaigns/copyright`

[419] A Edwards, "BOLERO, a TTP project for the Shipping Industry", in *Information Security Technical Report* v 1 no 1 (1996) pp 40–45

[420] M van Eeten, JM Bauer, M de Bruijne, J Groenewegen, W Lenstra, *'The Economics of Malware: Security Decisions, Incentives and Externalities'* OECD Report, 2008

[421] M Eichin, J Rochlis, "With Microscope and Tweezers: An Analysis of the Internet Virus of November 1988", in *Proceedings of the 1989 IEEE Symposium on Security and Privacy* pp 326–343

[422] Electronic Frontier Foundation, `http://www.eff.org`

[423] Electronic Frontier Foundation, *'Cracking DES: Secrets of Encryption Research, Wiretap Politics, and Chip Design'*, EFF (1998); ISBN 1-56592-520-3; `http://cryptome.org/cracking-des.htm`

[424] Electronic Frontier Foundation, *Felten, et al., v. RIAA, et al.* at `http://www.eff.org/IP/DMCA/Felten_v_RIAA/`

[425] Electronic Frontier Foundation, ''DocuColor Tracking Dot Decoding Guide'', at `http://w2.eff.org/Privacy/printers/docucolor/`

[426] M Ellims, ''Is Security Necessary for Safety?'', in *ESCAR 2006*, at `http://www.pi-shurlok.com/uploads/documents/security_and_safety.pdf`

[427] JH Ellis, *The History of Non-secret Encryption*, 1987, at `http://www.jya.com/ellisdoc.htm`

[428] C Ellison, B Schneier, ''Ten Risks of PKI: What You're Not Being Told About Public Key Infrastructure'', in *Computer Security Journal* v XIII no 1 (2000); also at `http://www.counterpane.com/pki-risks.html`

[429] EMV documents available from EMVCo LLP at `http://www.emvco.com/`

[430] *'Enfopol Papiere'*, Telepolis archiv special 1998/9, at `http://www.heise.de/tp/deutsch/special/enfo/default.html`

[431] P Enge, T Walter, S Pullen, CD Kee, YC Chao, YJ Tsai, ''Wide Area Augmentation of the Global Positioning System'', in *Proceedings of the IEEE* v 84 no 8 (Aug 96) pp 1063–1088

[432] Electronic Privacy Information Center, `http://www.epic.org`

[433] EPIC, *'Approvals for Federal Pen Registers and Trap and Trace Devices 1987–1998'*, at `http://www.epic.org/privacy/wiretap/stats/penreg.html`

[434] EPIC, *'Report of the Director of the Administrative Office of the United States Courts'*, at `http://www.epic.org/privacy/wiretap/stats/1999-report/wiretap99.pdf`

[435] EPIC, *'Wiretapping'*, at `http://www.epic.org/privacy/wiretap/`

[436] J Epstein, S Matsumoto, G McGraw, ''Software Security and SOA: Danger, Will Robinson!'', in *IEEE Security and Privacy*, Jan/Feb 2006,

pp 80–83, at http://www.cigital.com/papers/download/bsi12-soa
.doc.pdf

[437] J Epstein, H Orman, J McHugh, R Pascale, M Branstad, A Marmor-Squires, "A High Assurance Window System Prototype", in *Journal of Computer Security* v 2 no 2–3 (1993) pp 159–190

[438] J Epstein, R Pascale, "User Interface for a High Assurance Windowing System", in *Ninth Annual Computer Security Applications Conference* (1993), proceedings published by the IEEE, ISBN 0-8186-4330-7, pp 256–264

[439] T Escamilla, *'Intrusion Detection–Network Security beyond the Firewall'*, Wiley (1998) ISBN 0-471-29000-9

[440] J Essinger, *'ATM Networks–Their Organisation, Security and Future'*, Elsevier 1987

[441] A Etzioni, *'The Limits of Privacy'*, Basic Books (1999) ISBN 0-465-04089-6

[442] European Commission, *'Impact assessment–amending Framework Decision 2002/475/JHA on combating terrorism'*, Brussels, Nov 6 2007, SEC (2007) 1424, at http://www.ipex.eu/ipex/webdav/site/myjahiasite/groups/CentralSupport/public/2007/SEC_2007_1424/COM_SEC (2007)1424_EN.pdf

[443] European Parliament, *'Development of surveillance technology and risk of abuse of economic information'*, Luxembourg (April 1999) PE 166.184/Part 3/4, at http://www.gn.apc.org/duncan/stoa.htm

[444] European Union, *'Directive on the protection of individuals with regard to the processing of personal data and on the free movement of such data'*, Directive 95/46/EC, at http://www.privacy.org/pi/intl_orgs/ec/eudp.html

[445] European Union, "Draft Council Resolution on the lawful interception of telecommunications in relation to new technologies" 6715/99 (15/3/1999), at http://www.fipr.org/polarch/enfopol19.html; for background see http://www.fipr.org/polarch/

[446] European Union, *'Directive on the retention of data generated or processed in connection with the provision of publicly available electronic communications services or of public communications networks'*, 2006/24/EC

[447] European Union, "Promoting Data Protection by Privacy Enhancing Technologies (PETs)", COM(2007) 228 final, Brussels, May 2nd 2007

[448] Eurosmart, *'Protection Profile–Smart Card Integrated Circuit With Embedded Software'*, 1999, at `http://www.commoncriteriaportal.org/`

[449] R Evans, D Leigh, "GM subsidiary paid conman for 'blagged' private data, court told", *The Guardian* Apr 24, 2007; at `http://www.guardian.co.uk/crime/article/0,,2064180,00.html`

[450] Facebook, *Photos*, at `http://www.facebook.com/help.php?page=7`

[451] G Faden, "Reconciling CMW Requirements with Those of X11 Applications", in *Proceedings of the 14th Annual National Computer Security Conference* (1991)

[452] M Fairhurst, "The Hedge End Experiment", in *International Security Review* no 85 (Summer 94) p 20

[453] M Fairhurst, "Signature verification revisited: promoting practical exploitation of biometric technology", in *Electronics and Communication Engineering Journal* v 9 no 6 (Dec 97) pp 273–280

[454] B Feder, "Face-Recognition Technology Improves", *New York Times* Mar 14 2003; at `http://www.nytimes.com/2003/03/14/technology/14FACE.html`

[455] Federal Committee on Statistical Methodology, *' Statistical Policy Working Paper 22'* (Revised 2005)–*'Report on Statistical Disclosure Limitation Methodology'*), at `http://www.fcsm.gov/working-papers/spwp22.html`

[456] Federal Trade Commission v Audiotex Connection, Inc., and others, at `http://www.ftc.gov/os/1997/9711/Adtxamdfcmp.htm`

[457] Federal Trade Commission and Department of Commerce, *'Electronic Signatures in Global and National Commerce Act–The Consumer Consent Provision in Section 101(c)(1)(C)(ii) '*, June 2001, at `http://www.ftc.gov/os/2001/06/esign7.htm`

[458] Federal Trade Commission, *'ID Theft: When Bad Things Happen to Your Good Name'*, at `http://www.consumer.gov/idtheft/`

[459] Federal Trade Commission, *' ChoicePoint Settles Data Security Breach Charges; to Pay 10MillioninCivilPenalties,5 Million for Consumer Redress'*, Jan 26 2006, at `http://www.ftc.gov/opa/2006/01/choicepoint.shtm`

[460] Federation of American Scientists, `http://www.fas.org`

[461] H Federrath, J Thees, "Schutz der Vertraulichkeit des Aufenthaltsorts von Mobilfunkteilnehmern", in *Datenschutz und Datensicherheit* (June 1995) pp 338–348

[462] P Fellwock (using pseudonym 'Winslow Peck'), "U.S. Electronic Espionage: A Memoir", in *Ramparts* v 11 no 2 (August 1972) pp 35–50; at `http://jya.com/nsa-elint.htm`

[463] E Felten, "Facebook and the Campus Cops", Mar 20 2006, at `http://www.freedom-to-tinker.com/?p=994`

[464] JS Fenton, *'Information Protection Systems'*, PhD Thesis, Cambridge University, 1973

[465] N Ferguson, B Schneier, "A Cryptographic Evaluation of IPSEC", at `http://www.counterpane.com/ipsec.html`

[466] D Ferraiolo, R Kuhn, "Role-Based Access Control", in *15th National Computer Security Conference* (1992), proceedings published by NIST, pp 554–563

[467] D Ferraiolo, R Kuhn, R Chandramouli, *'Role-Based Access Control'*, Artech House, 2007

[468] D Fewer, P Gauvin, A Cameron, *'Digital Rights Management Technologies and Consumer Privacy—An Assessment of DRM Applications Under Canadian Privacy Law'*, September 2007, at `www.cippic.ca`

[469] A Fiat, M Naor, "Broadcast Encryption", in *Crypto '93*, Springer LNCS v 773 pp 480–491

[470] PFJ Fillery, AN Chandler, "Is lack of quality software a password to information security problems?", in *IFIP SEC 94* paper C8

[471] "Psychologists and banks clash over merits of photographs on cards", in *Financial Technology International Bulletin* v 13 no 5 (Jan 96) pp 2–3

[472] D Fine, "Why is Kevin Lee Poulsen Really in Jail?", at `http://www.well.com/user/fine/journalism/jail.html`

[473] G Fiorentini, S Pelzman, *'The Economics of Organised Crime'*, Cambridge University Press 1995

[474] B Fischer, talk at Cryptologic History Symposium, NSA, October 1999; reported in *Cryptologia* v 24 no 2 (Apr 2000) pp 160–167

[475] RA Fisher, *'The Genetical Theory of Natural Selection'*, Clarendon Press, Oxford (1930); 2nd ed. Dover Publications, NY (1958)

[476] J Flanagan, "Prison Phone Phraud (or The RISKS of Spanish)", reporting *University of Washington staff newspaper*, in `comp.risks` v 12.47; at `http://catless.ncl.ac.uk/Risks/20.69.html`

[477] M Fleet, "Five face sentence over notes that passed ultraviolet tests", in *The Daily Telegraph* (23/12/1999), available at http://www.telegraph.co.uk:80/

[478] B Fletcher, C Roberts, K Risser, "The Design and Implementation of a Guard Installation and Administration Framework", in *Third Annual SElinux Symposium*, at http://selinux-symposium.org/

[479] S Fluhrer, I Mantin, A Shamir, "Weaknesses in the Key Scheduling Algorithm of RC4" in *SAC 2001*

[480] SN Foley, "Aggregation and separation as noninterference properties", in *Journal of Computer Security* v 1 no 2 (1992) pp 158–188

[481] Fondazione Ugo Bordoni, '*Symposium on Electromagnetic Security for Information Protection*', Rome, Italy, 21–22 November 1991

[482] S Forrest, SA Hofmeyr, A Somayaji, "Computer Immunology", in *Communications of the ACM* v 40 no 10 (Oct 97) pp 88–96

[483] DS Fortney, JJ Lim, "A technical approach for determining the importance of information in computerised alarm systems", in *Seventeenth National Computer Security Conference* (1994), proceedings published by NIST; pp 348–357

[484] The Foundation for Information Policy Research, http://www.fipr.org

[485] B Fox, "How to keep thieves guessing", in *New Scientist* (3rd June 95) p 18

[486] B Fox, "Do not adjust your set . . . we have assumed radio control", in *New Scientist* 8 Jan 2000, at http://www.newscientist.com/ns/20000108/newsstory6.html

[487] B Fox, "The pirate's tale", in *New Scientist* 18 Dec 1999, at http://www.newscientist.com/ns/19991218/thepirates.html

[488] D Fox, "IMSI-Catcher", in *Datenschutz und Datensicherheit* v 21 no 9 (9/97) p 539

[489] D Foxwell, "Off-the-shelf, on to sea", in *International Defense Review* v 30 (Jan 97) pp 33–38

[490] D Foxwell, M Hewish, "GPS: is it lulling the military into a false sense of security?", in *Jane's International Defense Review* (Sep 98) pp 32–41

[491] LJ Fraim, "SCOMP: A Solution to the Multilevel Security Problem", in *IEEE Computer* v 16 no 7 (July 83) pp 26–34

[492] T Frank, "Tougher TSA bomb tests raise stakes for screeners", in *USA Today* Oct 18 2007, at `http://www.usatoday.com/printedition/news/20071018/a_insidescreeners18.art.htm`

[493] J Franks, P Hallam-Baker, J Hostetler, S Lawrence, P Leach, A Luotonen, L Stewart, "HTTP Authentication: Basic and Digest Access Authentication", RFC 2617

[494] T Fraser, "LOMAC: Low Water-Mark Integrity Protection for COTS Environments", in *Proceedings of the 2000 IEEE Symposium on Security and Privacy*, IEEE Computer Society Press, pp 230–245

[495] J Frizell, T Phillips, T Groover, "The electronic intrusion threat to national security and emergency preparedness telecommunications: an awareness document", in *Seventeenth National Computer Security Conference* (1994); proceedings published by NIST, pp 378–399

[496] M Frost, *'Spyworld: Inside the Canadian & American Intelligence Establishments'*, Diane Publishing Co (1994), ISBN 0-78815791-4

[497] "Banks fingerprint customers to cut cheque fraud", in *Fraud Watch* (1997) no 1 p 9

[498] "Chip cards reduce fraud in France", in *Fraud Watch* (1996) no 1 p 8

[499] "Counterfeit and cross border fraud on increase warning', in *Fraud Watch* (1996) no 1 pp 6–7

[500] "Finger minutiae system leaps the 1:100,000 false refusal barrier", in *Fraud Watch* (1996) no 2 pp 6–9

[501] "Widespread card skimming causes European concern", in *Fraud Watch* (1997) v 3 pp 1–2

[502] P Freiberger, M Swaine, *'Fire in the Valley — the Making of the Personal Computer'*, McGraw-Hill (1999) ISBN 0-07-135892-7

[503] M Freiss, *'Protecting Networks with Satan'*, O'Reilly (1997) ISBN 1-56592-425-8

[504] AM Froomkin, "The Death of Privacy", in *Stanford Law Review* v 52 pp 1461–1543, at `http://www.law.miami.edu/~froomkin/articles/privacy-deathof.pdf`

[505] D Frye, "Open and Secure: Linux Today and Tomorrow", in *2007 Security Enhanced Linux Symposium*, at `http://selinux-symposium.org/2007/agenda.php`

[506] DA Fulghum, "Communications Intercepts Pace EP-3s", in *Aviation Week and Space Technology* v 146 no 19 (5/5/97) pp 53–54

[507] Dr Fun, 'Suddenly, just as Paul was about to clinch the job interview, he received a visit from the Ghost of Usenet Postings Past', 1996, at `http://www.ibiblio.org/Dave/Dr-Fun/df9601/df960124.jpg`

[508] S Furber, *'ARM System Architecture'*, Addison-Wesley (1996); ISBN 0-210-40352-8

[509] M Galecotti, "Russia's eavesdroppers come out of the shadows", in *Jane's Intelligence Review* v 9 no 12 (Dec 97) pp 531–535

[510] Sir F Galton, "Personal identification and description," in *Nature* (21/6/1888) pp 173–177

[511] Sir F Galton, *'Finger Prints'*, Macmillan, 1892

[512] HF Gaines, *'Cryptanalysis—a study of ciphers and their solution'*, Dover, ISBN 486-20097-3 (1939, 1956)

[513] T Gandy, "Brainwaves in fraud busting", *Banking Technology* (Dec 95/Jan 96) pp 20–24

[514] R Gardner, A Yasinsac, M Bishop, T Kohno, Z Hartley, J Kerski, D Gainey, R Walega, E Hollander, M Gerke, *'Software Review and Security Analysis of the Diebold Voting Machine Software'*, Floriday State University, Jul 27 2007, at `http://www.sait.fsu.edu/news/2007-07-31.shtml`

[515] S Garfinkel, *'Database Nation'*, O'Reilly and Associates (2000) ISBN 1-56592-653-6

[516] S Garfinkel, *'Design Principles and Patterns for Computer Systems That Are Simultaneously Secure and Usable'*, PhD Thesis, MIT 2005, at `http://www.simson.net/thesis/`

[517] S Garfinkel, G Spafford, *'Practical Unix and Internet Security'*, O'Reilly and Associates (1996); ISBN 1-56592-148-8

[518] W Gates, W Buffett, "The Bill & Warren Show", in *Fortune*, 20/7/1998

[519] B Gellman, D Linzer, CD Leonnig, "Surveillance Net Yields Few Suspects", in *Washington Post*, Feb 5 2006 p A01; at `http://www.washingtonpost.com/wp-dyn/content/article/2006/02/04/AR2006020401373_pf.html`

[520] General Accounting Office, USA, *'Medicare—Improvements Needed to Enhance Protection of Confidential Health Information'*, GAO/HEHS-99-140; `http://www.gao.gov/AIndexFY99/abstracts/he99140.htm`

[521] RM Gerecht, "The Counterterrorist Myth", in *Atlantic Monthly*, Jul–Aug 2001, at `http://www.theatlantic.com/doc/200107/gerecht`

[522] E German, "Problem Idents", at `http://onin.com/fp/problemidents.html`

[523] E German, "Legal Challenges to Fingerprints", at `http://www.onin.com/fp/daubert_links.html`

[524] A Gidari, JP Morgan, "Survey of State Electronic and Digital Signature Legislative Initiatives", at `http://www.ilpf.org/digsig/digrep.htm`

[525] D Gifford, A Spector, "The CIRRUS Banking Network", in *Communications of the ACM* v 28 no 8 (Aug 1985) pp 797–807

[526] D Gilbert, "If only gay sex caused global warming", *LA Times*, July 2, 2006; `http://www.latimes.com/news/opinion/sunday/commentary/la-op-gilbert2jul02,0,4254536.story?coll=la-sunday-commentary`

[527] M Gill, A Spriggs, '*Assessing the impact of CCTV*', UK Home Office Research Study 292, at `www.homeoffice.gov.uk/rds/pdfs05/hors292.pdf`

[528] J Gilmore, "Nacchio affects spy probe", in *Denver Post* Oct 20 2007; cited in "NSA solicited illegal Qwest mass wiretaps right after Bush inauguration", *Cryptography List* Oct 20 2007, at `http://www.mailarchive.com/cryptography%40metzdowd.com/msg08213.html`

[529] T Gilovich, D Griffin, D Kahneman, '*Heuristics and Biases–The Psychology of Intuitive Judgment*', Cambridge University Press 2002

[530] AA Giordano, HA Sunkenberg, HE de Pdero, P Stynes, DW Brown, SC Lee, "A Spread-Spectrum Simulcast MF Radio Network", in *IEEE Transactions on Communications* v TC-30 no 5 (May 1982) pp 1057–1070

[531] WN Goetzmann, '*Financing Civilization*', `http://viking.som.yale.edu/will/finciv/chapter1.htm`

[532] J Goguen, J Meseguer, "Security Policies and Security Models", in *Proceedings of the 1982 IEEE Computer Society Symposium on Research in Security and Privacy* pp 11–20

[533] I Goldberg, D Wagner, "Randomness and the Netscape browser", in *Dr Dobbs Journal* no 243 (Jan 96) pp 66–70

[534] L Goldberg, "Recycled Cold-War Electronics Battle Cellular Telephone Thieves", in *Electronic Design* v 44 no 18 (3 September 1996) pp 41–42

[535] O Goldreich, *'Foundations of Cryptography'*, v 1 and 2, 2001 and 2004, at `http://www.wisdom.weizmann.ac.il/~oded/foc-book.html`

[536] S Goldwasser, S Micali, "Probabilistic encryption", in *J Comp Sys Sci* v 28 (1984) pp 270–299

[537] D Gollmann, *'Computer Security'*, Wiley (1999); ISBN 0-471-97884-2

[538] D Gollmann, "What Is Authentication?", in *Security Protocols* (2000), Springer LNCS 1796 pp 65–72

[539] L Gong, *'Inside Java 2 Platform Security: Architecture, API Design, and Implementation'*, Addison-Wesley (1999); ISBN: 0-201-31000-7

[540] L Gong, DJ Wheeler, "A matrix key-distribution scheme", in *Journal of Cryptology* v 2 no 1 (1990) pp 51–59

[541] R Gonggrijp, WJ Hengeveld, A Bogk, D Engling, H Mehnert, F Rieger, P Scheffers, B Wels, "Nedap/Groenendaal ES3B voting computer–a security analysis", Oct 2006, at `http://www.wijvertrouwenstem-computersniet.nl/Nedap-en`

[542] D Goodin, "Anatomy of an eBay scam", in *The Register*, Mar 21 2007; at `http://www.theregister.co.uk/2007/03/21/ebay_fraud_anatomy/`

[543] D Goodin, "Firefox leak could divulge sensitive info", in *The Register*, Aug 13 2007; at `http://www.theregister.co.uk/2007/08/13/firefox_remote_leakage/`

[544] D Goodin, "TJX agrees to pay banks $41 m to cover Visa losses", in *The Channel Register*, Dec 3 2007; at `http://www.channelregister.co.uk/2007/12/03/tjx_settlement_agreement/print.html`

[545] D Goodin, "Ukrainian eBay scam turns Down Syndrome man into cash machine", in *The Register* Nov 8 2007, at `http://www.theregister.co.uk/2007/11/08/ebay_victims_track_their_mules/`

[546] JI Gordon, "Copyright.Protection@Internet.net", in *3W Valparaiso Journal of Law and Technology* v 1 (24/1/1999), at `http://www.wvjolt.wvu.edu/v3i1/gordon.htm`

[547] KE Gordon, RJ Wong, "Conducting Filament of the Programmed Metal Electrode Amorphous Silicon Antifuse", in *Proceedings of International Electron Devices Meeting*, Dec 93; reprinted as pp 6-3 to 6-10, *QuickLogic Data Book* (1994)

[548] MF Grady, F Parisi, *'The Law and economics of Cybersecurity'*, Cambridge University Press, 2006

[549] RM Graham, "Protection in an Information Processing Utility," in *Communications of the ACM* v 11 no 5 (May 1968) pp 365–369

[550] FT Grampp, RH Morris, "UNIX Operating System Security", *AT&T Bell Laboratories Technical Journal* v 63 no 8 (Oct 84) pp 1649–1672

[551] S Granneman, "Electronic Voting Debacle", in *The Register* Nov 18 2003; at `http://www.theregister.co.uk/2003/11/18/electronic_voting_debacle/`

[552] RD Graubart, JL Berger, JPL Woodward, *'Compartmented Mode, Workstation Evaluation Criteria, Version 1'*, Mitre MTR 10953, 1991 (also published by the Defense Intelligence Agency as document DDS-2600-6243-91)

[553] J Gray, P Helland, P O'Neil, D Shasha, "The Dangers of Replication and a Solution," in *SIGMOD Record* v 25 no 2 (1996) pp 173–182

[554] J Gray, P Syverson, "A Logical Approach to Mulilevel Security of Probabilistic Systems," in *Distributed Computing* v 11 no 2 (1988)

[555] TC Greene, "Vista security overview: too little too late", in *The Register* Feb 20 2007, at `http://www.theregister.co.uk/2007/02/20/vista_security_oversold/`

[556] T Greening, "Ask and Ye Shall Receive: A Study in Social Engineering", in *SIGSAC Review* v 14 no 2 (Apr 96) pp 9–14

[557] M Gregory, P Losocco, "Using the Flask Security Architecture to Facilitate Risk Adaptable Access Controls", in *2007 Security Enhanced Linux Symposium*, at `http://selinux-symposium.org/2007/agenda.php`

[558] A Griew, R Currell, *'A Strategy for Security of the Electronic Patient Record'*, Institute for Health Informatics, University of Wales, Aberystwyth, March 1995

[559] V Groebner, J Peck, M Kyburz, *'Who Are You?: Identification, Deception, and Surveillance in Early Modern Europe'*, Zone Books, 2007

[560] J Gross, "Keeping Patients' Details Private, Even From Kin", in *New York Times* July 3 2007

[561] D Grover, *'The protection of computer software–its technology and applications'*, British Computer Society / Cambridge University Press (1992) ISBN 0-521-42462-3

[562] D Gruhl, W Bender, "Information Hiding to Foil the Casual Counterfeiter", in *Proceedings of the Second International Workshop on Information Hiding* (Portland, Apr 98), Springer LNCS v 1525 pp 1–15

[563] LC Guillou, M Ugon, JJ Quisquater, "The Smart Card–A Standardised Security Device Dedicated to Public Cryptology", in [1171] pp 561–613

[564] R Gupta, SA Smolka, S Bhaskar, "On Randomization in Sequential and Distributed Algorithms", in *ACM Computing Surveys* v 26 no 1 (March 94) pp 7–86

[565] J Gurnsey, *'Copyright Theft'*, Aslib, 1997; ISBN 0-566-07631-4

[566] P Gutmann, "Secure Deletion of Data from Magnetic and Solid-State Memory", in *Sixth USENIX Security Symposium Proceedings* (July 1996) pp 77–89

[567] P Gutmann, "Software Generation of Practically Strong Random Numbers", in *Seventh Usenix Security Symposium Proceedings* (Jan 1998) pp 243–257

[568] P Gutmann, "Data Remanence in Semiconductor Devices", in *Usenix Security Symposium* (2001)

[569] P Gutmann, "Invalid banking cert spooks only one user in 300", *Cryptography List* May 16 2005; at `http://www.mail-archive.com/cryptography%40metzdowd.com/msg03852.html`

[570] P Gutmann, "A Cost Analysis of Windows Vista Content Protection", April 2007, at `http://www.cs.auckland.ac.nz/~pgut001/pubs/vista_cost.html`

[571] P Gutmann, "Commercial CAPTCHA-breakers for sale", *Cryptography List* Oct 22 2007, at `http://www.mail-archive.com/cryptography%40metzdowd.com/msg08203.html`; see also `http://www.lafdc.com/captcha/`

[572] S Haber, WS Stornetta, "How to time-stamp a digital document", in *Journal of Cryptology* v 3 no 2 (1991) pp 99–111

[573] S Haber, WS Stornetta, "Secure Names for Bit-Strings", in *4th ACM Conference on Computer and Communications Security* (1997) pp 28–35

[574] W Hackmann, "Asdics at war", in *IEE Review* v 46 no 3 (May 2000) pp 15–19

[575] "Chris Carey Arrested In New Zealand", in *Hack Watch News* (9/1/1999), at `http://www.iol.ie/~kooltek/legal.html`

[576] N Hager, *'Secret Power–New Zealand's Role in the International Spy Network'*, Craig Potton Publishing (1996) ISBN 0-908802-35-8

[577] JA Halderman, "Amazon's MP3 Store Wisely Forgoes Watermarks", Oct 2 2007, at `http://www.freedom-to-tinker.com/?p=1207`

[578] PS Hall, TK Garland-Collins, RS Picton, RG Lee, *'Radar'*, Brassey's New Battlefield Weapons Systems and Technology Series (v 9), ISBN 0-08-037711-4

[579] Hall of Shame, at `http://www.pluralsight.com/wiki/default.aspx/Keith.HallOfShame;` see also `http://www.threatcode.com/admin_rights.htm`

[580] H Handschuh, P Paillier, J Stern, "Probing attacks on tamper-resistant devices", in *Cryptographic Hardware and Embedded Systems–CHES 99*, Springer LNCS v 1717 pp 303–315

[581] R Hanley, "Millions in thefts plague New Jersey area", in *New York Times*, February 9, 1981, late city final edition, section A; p 1

[582] R Hanson, "Can wiretaps remain cost-effective?", in *Communications of the ACM* v 37 no 12 (Dec 94) pp 13–15

[583] V Harrington, P Mayhew, *'Mobile Phone Theft'*, UK Home Office Research Study 235, January 2002

[584] MA Harrison, ML Ruzzo, JD Ullman, "Protection in Operating Systems", in *Communications of the ACM* v 19 no 8 (Aug 1976) pp 461–471

[585] A Hassey, M Wells, "Clinical Systems Security–Implementing the BMA Policy and Guidelines", in [43] pp 79–94

[586] Health and Safety Executive, nuclear safety reports at `http://www.hse.gov.uk/nsd/`, especially *'HSE Team Inspection of the Control and Supervision of Operations at BNFL's Sellafield Site'*, `http://www.hse.gov.uk/nsd/team.htm`

[587] LJ Heath, *'An Analysis of the Systemic Security Weaknesses of the US Navy Fleet Broadcasting System 1967–1974, as Exploited by CWO John Walker'*, MSc Thesis, Georgia Tech, at `http://www.fas.org/irp/eprint/heath.pdf`

[588] T Heim, "Outrage at 500,000 DNA database mistakes", *Daily Telegraph*, Aug 28 2007

[589] N Heintze, "Scalable Document Fingerprinting", in *Second USENIX Workshop on Electronic Commerce* (1996), ISBN 1-880446-83-9 pp 191–200

[590] S Helmers, "A Brief History of anon.penet.fi–The Legendary Anonymous Remailer", *CMC Magazine*, Sep 1997; at http://www.december .com/cmc/mag/1997/sep/helmers.html

[591] D Hencke, "Child benefit workers kept out of loop on data security", in *The Guardian* Dec 15 2007, at http://politics.guardian.co.uk/ homeaffairs/story/0,,2227999,00.html

[592] E Henning, " The Stamp of Incompetence", *c't magazine*, Sep 3 2007; at http://www.heise-security.co.uk/articles/95341

[593] Sir ER Henry, '*Classification and Uses of Finger Prints*' George Rutledge & Sons, London, 1900

[594] I Herbert, "No evidence against man in child porn inquiry who 'killed himself' ", in *The Independent* Oct 1 2005, at http://news.independent .co.uk/uk/legal/article316391.ece

[595] Herodotus, '*Histories*'; Book 1 123.4, Book 5 35.3 and Book 7 239.3

[596] "Interview with David Herson - SOGIS", September 25, 1996, in *Ingeniørennet*, at http://www.ing.dk/redaktion/herson.htm

[597] A Herzberg, M Jakobsson, S Jarecki, H Krawczyk, M Yung, "Proactive Public Key and Signature Systems", *4th ACM Conference on Computer and Communications Security* (1997) pp 100–110

[598] RA Hettinga, "Credit Card Fraud Higher. Credit Card Fraud Lower", in nettime (22/3/2000), at http://www.nettime.org/nettime .w3archive/200003/msg00184.html

[599] M Hewish, "Combat ID advances on all fronts", in *International Defense Review* v 29 (Dec 96) pp 18–19

[600] Hewlett-Packard, '*IA-64 Instruction Set Architecture Guide*', at http:// devresource.hp.com/devresource/Docs/Refs/IA64ISA/index.html

[601] TS Heydt-Benjamin, DV Bailey, K Fu, A Juels, T OHare, "Vulnerabilities in First-Generation RFID-enabled Credit Cards", in *Proceedings of Eleventh International Conference on Financial Cryptography and Data Security*, 2007

[602] HM Heys, "A Tutorial on Linear and Differential Cryptanalysis", in *Cryptologia* v XXVI no 3 (Jul 2002) pp 189–221; at `www.engr.mun.ca/ ~howard/PAPERS/ldc_tutorial.ps`

[603] M Hickley, "Taliban tapping British troops' mobiles to taunt soldiers' families", in *Daily Mail*, Aug 22 2007

[604] HJ Highland "Electromagnetic Radiation Revisited", in *Computers & Security* v5 (1986) 85–93 and 181–184

[605] HJ Highland, "Perspectives in Information Technology Security", in *Proceedings of the 1992 IFIP Congress, 'Education and Society'*, IFIP A-13 v II (1992) pp 440–446

[606] TF Himdi, RS Sandhu, "Lattice-Based Models for Controlled Sharing of Confidential Information in the Saudi Hajj System", in *13th Annual Computer Security Applications Conference*, San Diego, California, December 8–12 1997; proceedings published by the IEEE Computer Society, ISBN 0-8186-8274-4; pp 164–174

[607] Eric von Hippel, "Open Source Software Projects as User Innovation Networks", Open Source Software Economics 2002 (Toulouse)

[608] Jack Hirshleifer, "Privacy: Its Origin, Function and Future", in *Journal of Legal Studies* v 9 (Dec 1980) pp 649–664

[609] Jack Hirshleifer, "From weakest-link to best-shot: the voluntary provision of public goods", in *Public Choice* v 41, (1983) pp 371–386

[610] Jack Hirshleifer, *'Economic behaviour in Adversity'*, University of Chicago Press, 1987

[611] T Hobbes, *'Leviathan, or The Matter, Forme and Power of a Common Wealth Ecclesiasticall and Civil, commonly called Leviathan'* (1651)

[612] J Hoffman, "Implementing RBAC on a Type Enforced System", in *13th Annual Computer Security Applications Conference*, San Diego, California, December 8–12 1997; proceedings published by the IEEE Computer Society, ISBN 0-8186-8274-4; pp 158–163

[613] P Hoffmann, "Microsoft Windows Root Certificate Security Issues", 2007, at `http://www.proper.com/root-cert-problem/`

[614] S Hoffmann, "Salesforce.com Responds To Phishing Scams", on *CNN*, Nov 8 2007, at `http://www.crn.com/security/202804065`

[615] G Hogben, "Security Issues and Recommendations for Online Social Networks", *ENISA Position Paper*, Oct 2007

[616] G Hoglund, G McGraw, *'Exploiting Software—How to Break Code'*, Addison Wesley 2004

[617] G Hoglund, G McGraw, *'Exploiting Online Games—Cheating Massively Distributed Systems'*, Addison-Wesley 2007

[618] P Hollinger, "Single language for barcode Babel", in *Financial Times* (25/7/2000) p 15

[619] C Holloway, "Controlling the Use of Cryptographic Keys", in *Computers and Security* v 14 no 7 (95) pp 587–598

[620] DI Hopper, "Authorities Sue Adult Web Sites", in *Washington Post* (23/8/2000); at http://www.washingtonpost.com/

[621] G Horn, B Preneel, "Authentication and Payment in Future Mobile Systems", in *ESORICS 98*, Springer LNCS v 1485, pp 277–293; journal version in *Journal of Computer Security* v 8 no 2–3 (2000) pp 183–207

[622] JD Horton, R Harland, E Ashby, RH Cooper, WF Hyslop, DG Nickerson, WM Stewart, OK Ward, "The Cascade Vulnerability Problem", in *Journal of Computer Security* v 2 no 4 (93) pp 279–290

[623] V Hougham, "Sociological Skills Used in the Capture of Saddam Hussein", in *Footnotes* (Jul/Aug 2005), at http://www.asanet.org/footnotes/julyaugust05/fn3.html

[624] House of Commons Health Committee, *'The ELectronic Patient Record'*, 6th Report of Session 2006–7, at http://www.publications.parliament.uk/pa/cm200607/cmselect/cmhealth/422/422.pdf

[625] House of Lords Science and Technology Committee, *'Personal Internet Security'*, 5th Report of Session 2006–7

[626] JD Howard, *'An Analysis Of Security Incidents On The Internet 1989–1995'*, PhD thesis (1997), Carnegie Mellon University, at http://www.cert.org/research/JHThesis/Start.html

[627] M Howard, D LeBlanc, *'Writing Secure Code'*, (second edition), Microsoft Press 2002, ISBN 0-7356-1722-8

[628] D Howell, "Counterfeit technology forges ahead", in *The Daily Telegraph* (22/3/1999), available at http://www.telegraph.co.uk:80/

[629] A Huang, *'Hacking the Xbox—An Introduction to Reverse Engineering'*, No Starch Press (2003)

[630] Q Hu, JY Yang, Q Zhang, K Liu, XJ Shen, "An automatic seal imprint verification approach", in *Pattern Recognition* v 28 no 8 (Aug 95) pp 251–266

[631] G Huber, "CMW Introduction", in *ACM SIGSAC* v 12 no 4 (Oct 94) pp 6–10

[632] N Htoo-Mosher, R Nasser, N Zunic, J Straw, "E4 ITSEC Evaluation of PRISM on ES/9000 Processors", in *19th National Information Systems Security Conference* (1996), proceedings published by NIST, pp 1–11

[633] M Hypponen, "Malware goes mobile", in *Scientific American* Nov 2006 pp 70–77

[634] "Role of Communications in Operation Desert Storm", in *IEEE Communications Magazine* (Special Issue) v 30 no 1 (Jan 92)

[635] "New England shopping mall ATM scam copied in UK", in *Information Security Monitor* v 9 no 7 (June 94) pp 1–2

[636] "Pink Death Strikes at US West Cellular", in *Information Security Monitor* v 9 no 2 (Jan 94) pp 1–2

[637] Independent Security Evaluators Inc., "Content Protection for Optical Media", May 2005, at `www.securityevaluators.com/eval/spdc_aacs_2005.pdf`

[638] Information Systems Audit and Control Association, *'Control Objectives for Information and related Technology'*, at `http://www.isaca.org/cobit.htm`

[639] Information Systems Audit and Control Association, *'Exam Preparation Materials available from ISACA'*, at `http://www.isaca.org/cert1.htm`

[640] International Atomic Energy Authority (IAEA), *'The Physical Protection of Nuclear Material and Nuclear Facilities'*, INFCIRC/225/Rev 4, `http://www.iaea.org/Publications/Documents/Infcircs/1999/infcirc225r4c/rev4_content.html`

[641] IBM, *'IBM 4758 PCI Cryptographic Coprocessor—CCA Basic Services Reference and Guide*, Release 1.31 for the IBM 4758-001, available through `http://www.ibm.com/security/cryptocards/`

[642] *IEE Electronics and Communications Engineering Journal* v 12 no 3 (June 2000)—special issue on UMTS

[643] *IEEE Carnahan Conference,* http://www.carnahanconference.com/

[644] *IEEE Spectrum,* special issue on nuclear safekeeping, v 37 no 3 (Mar 2000)

[645] "Ex-radio chief 'masterminded' TV cards scam", in *The Independent* 17/2/1998; see also "The Sinking of a Pirate", *Sunday Independent, 1/3/1998*

[646] Intel Corporation, *'Intel Architecture Software Developer's Manual– Volume 1: Basic Architecture',* Order number 243190 (1997)

[647] Intel Corporation and others, *'Advanced Access Content System (AACS)–Technical Overview (informative)',* July 21 2004, at http://www.aacsla.com/home

[648] International Electrotechnical Commission, *'Digital Audio Interface',* IEC 60958, Geneva, February 1989

[649] T Iwata, K Kurosawa, "OMAC: One-Key CBC MAC", in *Fast Software Encryption* (2003) Springer LNCS v 2887 pp 129–153

[650] C Jackson, DR Simon, DS Tan, A Barth, "An Evaluation of Extended Validation and Picture-in-Picture Phishing Attacks", *USEC 2007*; at www.usablesecurity.org/papers/jackson.pdf

[651] I Jackson, personal communication

[652] L Jackson, "BT forced to pay out refunds after free calls fraud", in *The Sunday Telegraph* (9/2/1997); at http://www.telegraph.co.uk:80/

[653] TN Jagatic, NA Johnson, M Jakobsson, F Menczer, "Social Phishing", in *Communications of the ACM* v 50 no 10 (Oct 2007) pp 94–100

[654] G Jagpal, *'Steganography in Digital Images',* undergraduate thesis, Selwyn College, Cambridge University, 1995

[655] AK Jain, R Bolle, S Pankanti, *'Biometrics–Personal Identification in Networked Society',* Kluwer (1999); ISBN 0-7923-8346-1

[656] AK Jain, L Hong, S Pankanti, R Bolle, "An Identity-Authentication System Using Fingerprints", in *Proceedings of the IEEE* v 85 no 9 (Sep 97) pp 1365–1388

[657] S Jajodia, W List, G McGregor, L Strous (editors), *'Integrity and Internal Control in Information Systems–Volume 1: Increasing the confidence in information systems',* Chapman & Hall (1997) ISBN 0-412-82600-3

[658] M Jakobsson, "Modeling and Preventing Phishing Attacks", in *Financial Cryptography 2005*, at `www.informatics.indiana.edu/markus/papers/phishing_jakobsson.pdf`

[659] M Jakobsson, S Myers, *'Phishing and Countermeasures'*, Wiley 2007

[660] M Jakobsson, Z Ramzan, *'Crimeware'*, Addison-Wesley 2008

[661] M Jay, "ACPO's intruder policy — underwritten?", in *Security Surveyor* v 26 no 3 (Sep 95) pp 10–15

[662] D Jedig, "Security by example", 2006, at `http://syneticon.net/support/security/security-by-example.html`

[663] N Jefferies, C Mitchell, M Walker, "A Proposed Architecture for Trusted Third Party Services", in *Cryptography: Policy and Algorithms*, Springer LNCS v 1029 pp 98–104

[664] R Jenkins, "Hole-in-wall thief used MP3 player", in *The Times* Nov 15 2006; at `http://www.timesonline.co.uk/article/0,,29389-2453590,00.html`

[665] A Jerichow, J Müller, A Pfitzmann, B Pfitzmann, M Waidner, "Real-Time Mixes: a Bandwidth-Efficient Anonymity Protocol", in *IEEE Journal on Special Areas in Communications* v 16 no 4 (May 98) pp 495–509

[666] John Young Architect, `http://www.jya.com`

[667] K Johnson, "One Less Thing to Believe In: Fraud at Fake Cash Machine", in *New York Times* 13 May 1993 p 1

[668] RG Johnston, ARE Garcia, "Vulnerability Assessment of Security Seals", in *Journal of Security Administration* v 20 no 1 (June 97) pp 15–27; the Vulnerability Assessment Team's papers are at `http://pearl1.lanl.gov/seals/`, backed up at `http://www.cl.cam.ac.uk/~rja14/preprints/Johnston/` for non-US readers

[669] P Jones, "Protection money", in *Computer Business Review* v 4 no 12 (Dec 96) pp 31–36

[670] RV Jones, *'Most Secret War'*, Wordsworth Editions (1978,1998) ISBN 1-85326-699-X

[671] RV Jones, *'Reflections on Intelligence'*, Octopus (1989) ISBN 0-7493-0474-X

[672] J Jonsson, B Kaliski, "Public-Key Cryptography Standards (PKCS) #1: RSA Cryptography Specifications Version 2.1", RFC 3447

[673] A Jøsang, K Johannesen, "Authentication in Analogue Telephone Access Networks", in *Pragocrypt 96*, proceedings published by CTU Publishing House, Prague, ISBN 80-01-01502-5; pp 324–336

[674] Dorothy Judd v Citibank, 435 NYS, 2d series, pp 210–212, 107 Misc.2d 526

[675] MY Jung, "Biometric Market and Industry Overview", *IBG*, Dec 8 2005; at `http://events.wcoomd.org/files/style%20elements/17-Jung-IBG%20-%20Biometric%20Market%20and%20Industry%20Overview.pdf`

[676] D Kahn, *'The Codebreakers'*, Macmillan (1967)

[677] D Kahn, *'Seizing the Enigma'*, Houghton Mifflin (1991); ISBN 0-395-42739-8

[678] D Kahn, "Soviet Comint in the Cold War", in *Cryptologia* v XXII no 1 (Jan 98) pp 1–24

[679] D Kahneman, "Maps of Bounded Rationality: a Perspective on Intuitive Judgment and Choice", Nobel Prize Lecture, 2002

[680] B Kaliski, "PKCS #7: Cryptographic Message Syntax Version 1.5", RFC 2315

[681] JB Kam, GI Davida, "A Structured Design of Substitution-Permutation Encryption Network", in *Foundations of Secure Computation*, Academic Press (1978)

[682] M Kam, G Fielding, R Conn, "Writer Identification by Professional Document Examiners", in *Journal of Forensic Sciences* v 42 (1997) pp 778–786

[683] M Kam, G Fielding, R Conn, "Effects of Monetary Incentives on Performance of Nonprofessionals in Document Examination Proficiency Tests", in *Journal of Forensic Sciences* v 43 (1998) pp 1000–1004

[684] MS Kamel, HC Shen, AKC Wong, RI Campeanu, "System for the recognition of human faces", in *IBM Systems Journal* v 32 no 2 (1993) pp 307–320

[685] MH Kang, IS Moskowitz, "A Pump for Rapid, Reliable, Secure Communications", in *1st ACM Conference on Computer and Communications*

Security, 3–5/11/93, Fairfax, Virginia; Proceedings published by the ACM, ISBN 0-89791-629-8, pp 118–129

[686] MH Kang, JN Froscher, J McDermott, O Costich, R Peyton, "Achieving Database Security through Data Replication: The SINTRA Prototype", in *17th National Computer Security Conference* (1994) pp 77–87

[687] MH Kang, IS Moskowitz, DC Lee, "A Network Pump", in *IEEE Transactions on Software Engineering* v 22 no 5 (May 96) pp 329–338

[688] MH Kang, IS Moskowitz, B Montrose, J Parsonese, "A Case Study of Two NRL Pump Prototypes", in *12th Annual Computer Security Applications Conference*, San Diego CA, December 9–13 1996; proceedings published by the IEEE, ISBN 0-8186-7606-X, pp 32–43

[689] MH Kang, JN Froscher, IS Moskowitz, "An Architecture for Multilevel Secure Interoperability", in *13th Annual Computer Security Applications Conference*, San Diego, California, December 8–12 1997; proceedings published by the IEEE Computer Society, ISBN 0-8186-8274-4; pp 194–204

[690] CS Kaplan, "Privacy Plan Likely to Kick Off Debate", in *New York Times* (28 July 2000), at `http://www.nytimes.com/`

[691] MH Kang, IS Moskowitz, S Chincheck, "The Pump: A Decade of Covert Fun", at *21st Annual Computer Security Applications Conference* (2005)

[692] PA Karger, VA Austell, DC Toll, "A New Mandatory Security Policy Combining Secrecy and Integrity", *IBM Research Report* RC 21717 (97406) 15/3/2000

[693] PA Karger, RR Schell, "Thirty Years Later': Lessons from the Multics Security Evaluation", at *ACSAC 2002* pp 119–126

[694] S Karp, "Facebook's Public Search Listing Is Problematic for Users", in *Digitalmediawire* Sep 5 2007, at `http://www.dmwmedia.com/news/2007/09/06/facebook-s-public-search-listing-is-problematic-for-users`

[695] F Kasiski, '*Die Geheimschriften und die Dechiffrier-Kunst*', Mittler & Sohn, Berlin (1863)

[696] '*KASUMI Specification*', ETSI/SAGE v 1 (23/12/1999), at `http://www.etsi.org/dvbandca/`

[697] S Katzenbeisser, FAP Petitcolas, '*Information hiding—Techniques for steganography and digital watermarking*', Artech House (2000) ISBN 1-58053-035-4

[698] C Kaufman, R Perlman, M Speciner, *'Network Security—Private Communication in a Public World'*, Prentice Hall 1995; ISBN 0-13-061466-1

[699] DT Keitkemper, SF Platek, KA Wolnik, "DNA versus fingerprints", in *Journal of Forensic Sciences* v 40 (1995) p 534

[700] GC Kelling, C Coles, *'Fixing Broken Windows: Restoring Order and Reducing Crime in Our Communities'* Martin Kessler Books (1996)

[701] L Kelly, T Young, in *Computing* Jan 25 2007; at `http://www.vnunet .com/computing/news/2173365/uk-firms-naive-usb-stick`

[702] J Kelsey, B Schneier, D Wagner, "Protocol Interactions and the Chosen Protocol Attack", in *Security Protocols—Proceedings of the 5th International Workshop* (1997) Springer LNCS v 1361 pp 91–104

[703] J Kelsey, B Schneier, D Wagner, C Hall, "Cryptanalytic Attacks on Pseudorandom Number Generators", in *Fifth International Workshop on Fast Software Encryption* (1998), Springer LNCS v 1372 pp 168–188

[704] J Kelsey, B Schneier, D Wagner, C Hall, "Side Channel Cryptanalysis of Product Ciphers," in *ESORICS 98*, Springer LNCS v 1485 pp 97–110

[705] R Kemp, N Towell, G Pike, "When seeing should not be believing: Photographs, credit cards and fraud", in *Applied Cognitive Psychology* v 11 no 3 (1997) pp 211–222

[706] R Kemmerer, "Shared Resource Matrix Methodology: An Approach to Identifying Storage and Timing Channels", in *IEEE Transactions on Computer Systems* v 1 no 3 (1983) pp 256–277

[707] R Kemmerer, C Meadows, J Millen, "Three Systems for Cryptographic Protocol Analysis", in *Journal of Cryptology* v 7 no 2 (Spring 94) pp 79–130

[708] MG Kendall, B Babington-Smith, "Randomness and Random Sampling Numbers", part 1 in *Journal of the Royal Statistical Society* v 101 pp 147–166; part 2 in *Supplement to the Journal of the Royal Statistical Society*, v 6 no 1 pp 51–61

[709] T Kendall, "Pornography, Rape, and the Internet", at *The Economics of the Software and Internet Industries* (Softint 2007), at `http://people .clemson.edu/~tkendal/internetcrime.pdf`

[710] ST Kent, MI Millett, *'Who Goes There? Authentication Through the Lens of Privacy'*, National Research Council 2003; at `http://www.nap.edu/ catalog.php?record_id=10656`

[711] JO Kephardt, SR White, "Measuring and Modeling Computer Virus Prevalence", in *Proceedings of the 1993 IEEE Symposium on Security and Privacy* pp 2–15

[712] JO Kephardt, SR White, DM Chess, "Epidemiology of computer viruses", in *IEEE Spectrum* v 30 no 5 (May 93) pp 27–29

[713] A Kerckhoffs, "La Cryptographie Militaire", in *Journal des Sciences Militaires*, 9 Jan 1883, pp 5–38; `http://www.cl.cam.ac.uk/users/fapp2/kerckhoffs/`

[714] OS Kerr, "Computer Records and the Federal Rules of Evidence", in *USA Bulletin* (Mar 2001), at `http://www.usdoj.gov/criminal/cybercrime/usamarch2001_4.htm`

[715] PJ Kerry, "EMC in the new millennium", in *Electronics and Communication Engineering Journal* v 12 no 2 pp 43–48

[716] D Kesdogan, H Federrath, A Jerichow, "Location Management Strategies Increasing Privacy in Mobile Communication", in *12th International Information Security Conference* (1996), Samos, Greece; proceedings published by Chapman & Hall, ISBN 0-412-78120-4, pp 39–48

[717] J Kilian, P Rogaway, "How to protect DES Against Exhaustive Key Search", in *Advances in Cryptology–Crypto 96* Springer LNCS v 1109 pp 252–267

[718] J King, "Bolero — a practical application of trusted third party services", in *Computer Fraud and Security Bulletin* (July 95) pp 12–15

[719] Kingpin, "iKey 1000 Administrator Access and Data Compromise", in *BugTraq* (20/7/2000), at `http://www.L0pht.com/advisories.html`

[720] DV Klein, "Foiling the Cracker; A Survey of, and Improvements to Unix Password Security", *Proceedings of the USENIX Security Workshop. (1990)*; `http://www.deter.com/unix/`

[721] RL Klevans, RD Rodman, *'Voice Recognition'*, Artech House (1997); ISBN 0-89006-927-1

[722] HM Kluepfel, "Securing a Global Village and its Resources: Baseline Security for Interconnected Signaling System # 7 Telecommunications Networks", in *First ACM Conference on Computer and Communications Security* (1993), proceedings published by the ACM , ISBN 0-89791-629-8, pp 195–212; later version in *IEEE Communications Magazine* v 32 no 9 (Sep 94) pp 82–89

[723] N Koblitz, *'A Course in Number Theory and Cryptography'*, Springer Graduate Texts in Mathematics no 114 (1987), ISBN 0-387-96576-9

[724] N Koblitz, A Menezes, "Another Look at 'Provable Security' ", in *Journal of Cryptology* v 20 no 1 (2007) pp 3–37

[725] ER Koch, J Sperber, *'Die Datenmafia'*, Rohwolt Verlag (1995) ISBN 3-499-60247-4

[726] M Kochanski, "A Survey of Data Insecurity Devices", in *Cryptologia* v IX no 1 pp 1–15

[727] P Kocher, "Timing Attacks on Implementations of Diffie-Hellman, RSA, DSS, and Other Systems", in *Advances in Cryptology–Crypto 96* Springer LNCS v 1109 pp 104–113

[728] P Kocher, "Differential Power Analysis", in *Advances in Cryptology– Crypto 99* Springer LNCS v 1666 pp 388–397; a brief version was presented at the rump session of Crypto 98

[729] P Kocher, "Design and Validation Strategies for Obtaining Assurance in Countermeasures to Power Analysis and Related Attacks", at *FIPS Physical Security Workshop*, Hawaii 2005; at `http://csrc.nist.gov/ groups/STM/cmvp/documents/fips140-3/physec/papers/physe- cpaper09.pdf`

[730] KJ Koelman, "A Hard Nut to Crack: The Protection of Technological Measures", in *European Intellectual Property Review* (2000) pp 272–288; at `http://www.ivir.nl/Publicaties/koelman/hardnut.html`

[731] T Kohno, A Stubblefield, AD Rubin, DS Wallach, "Analysis of an Electronic Voting System", Johns Hopkins TR 2003-19; also published in *IEEE Symposium on Security and Privacy* (2004)

[732] S Kokolakis, D Gritzalis, S Katsikas, "Generic Security Policies for Health Information Systems", in *Health Informatics Journal* v 4 nos 3–4 (Dec 1998) pp 184–195

[733] O Kömmerling, MG Kuhn, "Design Principles for Tamper-Resistant Smartcard Processors", in *Usenix Workshop on Smartcard Technology*, proceedings published by Usenix (1999), ISBN 1-880446-34-0 pp 9–20

[734] A Kondi, R Davis, "Software Encryption in the DoD", in *20th National Information Systems Security Conference* (1997), proceedings published by NIST, pp 543–554

[735] LD Koontz, VC Melvin, "Health Information Technology—Efforts Continue but Comprehensive Privacy Approach Needed for National Strategy", GAO, 2007; at `http://www.gao.gov/new.items/d07988t.pdf`

[736] BJ Koops, *'Crypto Law Survey'*, at `http://rechten.uvt.nl/koops/cryptolaw/;` see also his thesis *'The Crypto Controversy: A Key Conflict in the Information Society'*

[737] C Kopp, "Electromagnetic Bomb—Weapon of Electronic Mass Destruction", at `http://www.abovetopsecret.com/pages/ebomb.html`

[738] DP Kormann, AD Rubin, "Risks of the Passport Single Signon Protocol", in *Computer Networks* (July 2000); at `http://avirubin.com/vita.html`

[739] M Kotadia, "Citibank e-mail looks phishy: Consultants", *Zdnet* Nov 9 2006; at `http://www.zdnet.com.au/news/security/soa/Citibank-e-mail-looks-phishy-Consultants/0,130061744,339272126,00.htm`

[740] KPHO, "Sodomized Ex-McDonald's Employee Wins $6.1 M", KPHO, Oct 6 2007; at `http://www.kpho.com/news/14277937/detail.html`

[741] H Krawczyk, M Bellare, R Canetti, *'HMAC: Keyed-Hashing for Message Authentication'*, RFC 2104 (Feb 1997), at `http://www.faqs.org/rfcs/rfc2104.html`

[742] B Krebs, "Just How Bad Is the Storm Worm?", in *The Washington Post* Oct 1 2007; at `http://blog.washingtonpost.com/securityfix/2007/10/the_storm_worm_maelstrom_or_te.html`

[743] B Krebs, "Salesforce.com Acknowledges Data Loss", in *The Washington Post* Nov 6 2007; at `http://blog.washingtonpost.com/securityfix/2007/11/salesforcecom_acknowledges_dat.html`

[744] S Krempl, "Lauschangriff am Geldautomaten", in *Der Spiegel* Jan 8 1999; at `http://web.archive.org/web/20001031024042/http://www.spiegel.de/netzwelt/technologie/0,1518,13731,00.html`

[745] HM Kriz, "Phreaking recognised by Directorate General of France Telecom", in *Chaos Digest* 1.03 (Jan 93)

[746] I Krsul, EH Spafford, "Authorship analysis: identifying the author of a program", in *Computers and Security* v 16 no 3 (1996) pp 233–257

[747] D Kügler, " 'Man in the Middle' Attacks on Bluetooth", in *Financial Cryptography 2004*, Springer LNCS v 2742 pp 149–161

[748] MG Kuhn, "Cipher Instruction Search Attack on the Bus-Encryption Security Microcontroller DS5002FP", in *IEEE Transactions on Computers* v 47 no 10 (Oct 1998) pp 1153–1157

[749] MG Kuhn, private communication

[750] MG Kuhn, "Optical Time-Domain Eavesdropping Risks of CRT Displays" in *IEEE Symposium on Security and Privacy* (2002)

[751] MG Kuhn, "An Asymmetric Security Mechanism for Navigation Signals", in *Information Hiding 2004* Springer LNCS 3200 pp 239–252

[752] MG Kuhn, "Electromagnetic Eavesdropping Risks of Flat-Panel Displays", in *PET 2004*, at `http://www.cl.cam.ac.uk/~mgk25/pet2004-fpd.pdf`

[753] MG Kuhn, RJ Anderson, "Soft Tempest: Hidden Data Transmission Using Electromagnetic Emanations", in *Proceedings of the Second International Workshop on Information Hiding* (Portland, Apr 98), Springer LNCS v 1525 pp 126–143

[754] R Kuhn, P Edfors, V Howard, C Caputo, TS Philips, "Improving Public Switched Network Security in an Open Environment", in *Computer*, August 1993, pp 32–35

[755] S Kumar, C Paar, J Pelzl, G Pfeiffer, M Schimmler, "Breaking Ciphers with COPACOBANA–A Cost-Optimized Parallel Code Breaker", in *CHES 2006* and at `http://www.copacobana.org/`

[756] J Kuo, "Storm Drain", in *Anti-Malware Engineering Team blog*, Sep 20 2007, at `http://blogs.technet.com/antimalware/default.aspx`

[757] GD Kutz, G Aloise, JW Cooney, '*NUCLEAR SECURITY–Actions Taken by NRC to Strengthen Its Licensing Process for Sealed Radioactive Sources Are Not Effective*', GAO Report GAO-07-1038T, July 12, 2007

[758] Greg L, "ID Theft, RMT and Lineage", *Terra Nova* Jul 2007, at `http://terranova.blogs.com/terra_nova/2006/07/id_theft_rmt_nc.html#more`

[759] '*L0phtCrack 2.52 for Win95/NT*', at `http://www.l0pht.com/l0phtcrack/`

[760] J Lacy, SR Quackenbush, A Reibman, JH Snyder, "Intellectual Property Protection Systems and Digital Watermarking", in *Proceedings of the Second International Workshop on Information Hiding* (Portland, Apr 98), Springer LNCS v 1525 pp 158–168

[761] RJ Lackey, DW Upmal, "Speakeasy: The Military Software Radio", in *IEEE Communications Magazine* v 33 no 5 (May 95) pp 56–61

[762] P Ladkin, "Flight Control System Software Anomalies", `comp.risks` v 24 no 03, Aug 31 2005, at `http://www.mail-archive.com/risks@csl.sri.com/msg00319.html`

[763] Lamarr/Antheil Patent Story Home Page, `http://www.ncafe.com/chris/pat2/index.html`; contains US patent no 2,292,387 (HK Markey et al., Aug 11 1942)

[764] G Lambourne, 'The Fingerprint Story', Harrap (1984) ISBN 0-245-53963-8

[765] L Lamont, "And the real Lotto winner is . . . that man at the cash register", *Sydney Morning Herald*, May 3 2007, at `http://www.smh.com.au/articles/2007/05/02/1177788228072.html`

[766] L Lamport, "Time, Clocks and the Reordering of Events in a Distributed System", in *Communications of the ACM* v 21 no 7 (July 1978) pp 558–565

[767] L Lamport, R Shostak, M Pease, "The Byzantine Generals Problem", in *ACM Transactions on Programming Languages and Systems* v 4 no 3 (1982) pp 382–401

[768] B Lampson, "A Note on the Confinement problem", in *Communications of the ACM* v 16 no 10 (Oct 1973) pp 613–615

[769] P Lamy, J Martinho, T Rosa, MP Queluz, "Content-Based Watermarking for Image Authentication", in *Proceedings of the Third International Workshop on Information Hiding* (1999), Springer LNCS v 1768 pp 187–198

[770] S Landau, S Kent, C Brooks, S Charney, D Denning, W Diffie, A Lauck, D Miller, P Neumann, D Sobel, "Codes, Keys and Conflicts: Issues in US Crypto Policy", *Report of the ACM US Public Policy Committee*, June 1994

[771] M Landler, "Fine-Tuning For Privacy, Hong Kong Plans Digital ID", in *New York Times*, Feb 19 2002; at `http://www.nytimes.com/2002/02/18/technology/18KONG.html`

[772] R Landley, "Son of DIVX: DVD Copy Control", *Motley Fool*, `http://www.fool.com/portfolios/rulemaker/2000/rulemaker000127.htm`

[773] P Landrock, "Roles and Responsibilities in BOLERO", in *TEDIS EDI trusted third parties workshop* (1995), proceedings published as ISBN 84-7653-506-6, pp 125–135

[774] CE Landwehr, AR Bull, JP McDermott, WS Choi, *'A Taxonomy of Computer Program Security Flaws, with Examples'*, US Navy Report NRL/FR/5542-93-9591 (19/11/93)

[775] D Lane, "Where cash is king", in *Banking Technology*, Oct 92, pp 38–41

[776] J Leake, "Workers used forged passes at Sellafield", in *Sunday Times* (2/4/2000) p 6

[777] S LeBlanc, KE Register, *'Constant Battles: Why We Fight'*, St Martin's, 2003

[778] HC Lee, RE Guesslen (eds), *'Advances in Fingerprint Technology'*, Elsevier (1991) ISBN 0-444-01579-5

[779] D Leigh, "Crackdown on firms stealing personal data", in *The Guardian* Nov 15 2006; at `http://www.guardian.co.uk/crime/article/0,,1948016,00.html`

[780] AK Lenstra, HW Lenstra, *'The development of the number field sieve'*, Springer Lecture Notes in Mathematics v 1554 (1993) ISBN 0-387-57013-6

[781] AK Lenstra, E Tromer, A Shamir, W Kortsmit, B Dodson, J Hughes, P Leyland, "Factoring estimates for a 1024-bit RSA modulus", in *Asiacrypt 2003*, Springer LNCS 2894 pp 331–346

[782] K Leonard, "Face Recognition Technology: Security Enhancements v. Civil Rights", 2001 B.C. Intell. Prop. & Tech. F. 120301, at `http://www.bc.edu/bc_org/avp/law/st_org/iptf/headlines/content/2001120301.html`

[783] D Leppard, P Nuki, "BA staff sell fake duty-free goods", in *Sunday Times* Sep 12 1999; at `http://home.clara.net/brescom/Documents/BA_FAkes.htm`

[784] L Lessig, *'Code and Other Laws of Cyberspace'*, Basic Books (2000); *'Code: Version 2.0'*, Basic Books (2006); at `http://www.lessig.org/`

[785] L Lessig, *'Free Culture: The Nature and Future of Creativity'*, Penguin (2005); at `http://www.lessig.org/`

[786] NG Leveson, *'Safeware–System Safety and Computers'*, Addison-Wesley (1994) ISBN 0-201-11972-2

[787] S Levitt, SJ Dubner, *'Freakonomics: A Rogue Economist Explores the Hidden Side of Everything,'* William Morrow, 2005

[788] A Lewcock, "Bodily Power", in *Computer Business Review* v 6 no 2 (Feb 98) pp 24–27

[789] O Lewis, "Re: News: London nailbomber used the Net", post to ukcrypto mailing list, 5/6/2000, archived at `http://www.chiark.greenend.org.uk/mailman/listinfo/ukcrypto`

[790] Lexmark International, Inc., vs Static Control Components, Inc., US Court of Appeals (6th Circuit), Oct 26 2004, at `www.eff.org/legal/cases/Lexmark_v_Static_Control/20041026_Ruling.pdf`

[791] J Leyden, "Russian bookmaker hackers jailed for eight years", in *The Register* Oct 4 2006, at `http://www.theregister.co.uk/2006/10/04/russian_bookmaker_hackers_jailed/`

[792] J Leyden, "Thai police crack credit card wiretap scam", in *The Register* Aug 4 2006, at `http://www.theregister.co.uk/2006/08/04/thai_wiretap_scam/`

[793] J Leyden, "Hacked to the TK Maxx", in *The Register* Jan 19 2007; at `http://www.theregister.co.uk/2007/01/19/tjx_hack_alert/`

[794] J Leyden, "Italy tops global wiretap league", in *The Register*, Mar 7 2007; at `http://www.theregister.co.uk/2007/03/07/wiretap_trends_ss8/`

[795] J Leyden, "Feds told they need warrants for webmail", in *The Register* June 19 2007; at `http://www.theregister.co.uk/2007/06/19/webmail_wiretaps_appeal/`

[796] J Leyden, "MySpace phishing scam targets music fans", in *The Register*, Oct 14 2006; at `http://www.theregister.co.uk/2006/10/14/myspace_phishing_scam/`

[797] J Leyden, "Program Names govern admin rights in Vista, in *The Register*, Apr 23 2007; at `http://www.theregister.co.uk/2007/04/23/vista_program_naming_oddness/`

[798] CC Lin, WC Lin, "Extracting facial features by an inhibiting mechanism based on gradient distributions", in *Pattern Recognition* v 29 no 12 (Dec 96) pp 2079–2101

[799] R Linde, "Operating Systems Penetration," *National Computer Conference*, AFIPS (1975) pp 361–368

[800] JPMG Linnartz, "The 'Ticket' Concept for Copy Control Based on Embedded Signalling", *Fifth European Symposium on Research in Computer Security* (ESORICS 98), Springer LNCS 1485 pp 257–274

[801] E Linos, E Linos, G Colditz, "Screening programme evaluation applied to airport security", *British Medical Journal* v 335, Dec 22 2007 pp 1290–1292; http://www.bmj.com/cgi/content/full/335/7633/1290

[802] J Linsky and others, *'Bluetooth–simple pairing whitepaper'*, from www.bluetooth.com

[803] JPMG Linnartz, M van Dijk, "Analysis of the Sensitivity Attack Against Electronic Watermarks in Images", in [97] pp 258–272

[804] D Litchfield, C Anley, J Heasman, B Grindlay, *'The Database Hacker's Handbook: Defending Database Servers'*, Wiley 2005

[805] B Littlewood, "Predicting software reliability", in *Philosophical Transactions of the Royal Society of London* A327 (1989), pp 513–527

[806] WF Lloyd, *'Two Lectures on the Checks to Population'*, Oxford University Press (1833)

[807] Lockheed Martin, "Covert Surveillance using Commercial Radio and Television Signals", at http://silentsentry.external.lmco.com

[808] L Loeb, *'Secure Electronic Transactions–Introduction and technical reference'*, Artech House (1998) ISBN 0-89006-992-1

[809] London School of Economics & Political Science, *'The Identity Project–An assessment of the UK Identity Cards Bill & its implications'*, 2005, at www.lse.ac.uk/collections/pressAndInformationOffice/PDF/IDreport.pdf

[810] J Long, *Google Hacking Database*, at http://johnny.ihackstuff.com/ghdb.php

[811] D Longley, S Rigby, "An Automatic Search for Security Flaws in Key Management", *Computers & Security* v 11 (March 1992) pp 75–89

[812] PA Loscocco, SD Smalley, PA Muckelbauer, RC Taylor, SJ Turner, JF Farrell, "The Inevitability of Failure: The Flawed Assumption of Security in Modern Computing Environments", in *20th National Information Systems Security Conference*, proceedings published by NIST (1998 pp 303–314)

[813] PA Loscocco, SD Smalley, "Integrating Flexible Support for Security Policies into the Linux Operating System", in *Proceedings of the FREENIX Track: 2001 USENIX Annual Technical Conference (FREENIX '01)* (June 2001). See also NSA SELinux site: `http://www.nsa.gov/selinux`

[814] JR Lott, *'More Guns, Less Crime: Understanding Crime and Gun-Control Laws'*, University of Chicago Press 2000

[815] J Loughry, DA Umphress, "Information leakage from optical emanations", in *ACM Transactions on Information and System Security* v 5 no 3 (Aug 2002) pp 262–289

[816] WW Lowrance, *'Privacy and Health Research'*, Report to the US Secretary of Health and Human Services (May 1997)

[817] M Ludwig, *'The Giant Black Book of Computer Viruses'*, American Eagle Publishers (1995) ISBN 0-929408-10-1

[818] J Lukàš, J Fridrich, M Goljan, "Digital 'bullet scratches' for images", in *ICIP 05*; at `http://www.ws.binghamton.edu/fridrich/Research/ICIP05.pdf`

[819] M Lyu, *'Software Reliability Engineering'*, IEEE Computer Society Press (1995), ISBN 0-07-039400-8

[820] D Mackett, "A Pilot on Airline Security", in *Hot Air*, July 16 2007, at `http://hotair.com/archives/2007/07/16/a-pilot-on-airline-security/`

[821] Macnn, "iPhone unlock firm threatened by AT&T", Aug 25 2007, at `http://www.macnn.com/articles/07/08/25/iphone.unlock.firm.threat/`

[822] B Macq, *"Special Issue–Identification and protection of Multimedia Information"*, *Proceedings of the IEEE* v 87 no 7 (July 1999)

[823] W Madsen, "Airline passengers to be subject to database monitoring", in *Computer Fraud and Security Bulletin* (Mar 97) pp 7–8

[824] W Madsen, "Crypto AG: The NSA's Trojan Whore?", in *Covert Action Quarterly* (Winter 1998), at `http://www.mediafilter.org/caq/cryptogate/`

[825] W Madsen, "Government-Sponsored Computer Warfare and Sabotage", in *Computers and Security* v 11 (1991) pp 233–236

[826] M Maes, "Twin Peaks: The Histogram Attack on Fixed Depth Image Watermarks", in *Proceedings of the Second International Workshop on Information Hiding* (1998), Springer LNCS v 1525 pp 290–305

[827] M Magee, "HP inkjet cartridges have built-in expiry dates–Carly's cunning consumable plan", *The Inquirer*, 29 April 2003, at `http://www.theinquirer.net/?article=9220`

[828] K Maguire, "Muckraker who feeds off bins of the famous", in *The Guardian* (27/7/2000), at `http://www.guardianunlimited.co.uk/Labour/Story/0,2763,347535,00.html`

[829] S Maguire, *Debugging the Development Process*, Microsoft Press, ISBN 1-55615-650-2 p 50 (1994)

[830] F Main, "Your phone records are for sale", *Chicago Sun-Times*, Jan 5 2006, at `http://blogs.law.harvard.edu/jim/2006/01/08/your-phone-records-are-for-sale-fbi-as-reported-in-the-chicago-sun-times/`

[831] D Maio, D Maltoni, "Direct Gray-Scale Minutiae Detection in Fingerprints", in *IEEE Transactions on Pattern Analysis and Machine Intelligence* v 19 no 1 (Jan 97) pp 27–40

[832] D Maltoni, D Maio, AK Jain, S Prabhakar, '*Handbook of Fingerprint Recognition*', Springer-Verlag New York, 2003

[833] S Mangard, E Oswald, T Popp, '*Power Analysis Attacks–Revealing the Secrets of Smartcards*', Springer 2007

[834] T Mansfield, G Kelly, D Chandler, J Kane, '*Biometric Product Testing Final Report*, Issue 1.0, 19 March 2001, National Physical Laboratory; at `www.cesg.gov.uk/site/ast/biometrics/media/BiometricTest-Reportpt1.pdf`

[835] J Markoff, '*What the Dormouse Said: How the 60s Counterculture Shaped the Personal Computer*', Viking Adult (2005)

[836] L Marks, *Between Silk and Cyanide–a Codemaker's War 1941–1945*, Harper Collins (1998) ISBN 0-68486780-X

[837] L Martin, "Using Semiconductor Failure Analysis Tools for Security Analysis", FIPS Physical Security Workshop, Hawaii 2005; at `http://csrc.nist.gov/groups/STM/cmvp/documents/fips140-3/physec/papers/physecpaper11.pdf`

[838] S Mason, '*Electronic Evidence–Disclosure, Discovery and Admissibility*', LexisNexis Butterworths (2007)

[839] M Mastanduno, "Economics and Security in Statecraft and Scholarship", *International Organization* v 52 no 4 (Autumn 1998)

[840] "Reducing the Price of Convenience", B Masuda, *International Security Review* no 82 (Autumn 93) pp 45–48

[841] JM Matey, O Naroditsky, K Hanna, R Kolczynski, DJ LoIacono, S Mangru, M Tinker, TM Zappia, WY Zhao, "Iris on the Move: Acquisition of Images for Iris recognition in Less Constrained Environments", in *Proc IEEE* v 94 no 11 (Nov 2006) pp 1936–1947

[842] SA Mathieson. "Gone phishing in Halifax–UK bank sends out marketing email which its own staff identify as a fake", in *Infosecurity News*, Oct 7 2005, at `http://www.infosecurity-magazine.com/news/051007_halifax_email.htm`

[843] M Matsui, "Linear Cryptanalysis Method for DES Cipher", in *Advances in Cryptology — Eurocrypt 93*, Springer LNCS v 765 pp 386–397

[844] M Matsui, "New Block Encryption Algorithm MISTY", in *Fourth International Workshop on Fast Software Encryption* (1997), Springer LNCS v 1267 pp 54–68

[845] T Matsumoto, H Matsumoto, K Yamada, S Hoshino, "Impact of Artificial 'Gummy' Fingers on Fingerprint Systems" *Proceedings of SPIE* v 4677, Optical Security and Counterfeit Deterrence Techniques IV, 2002

[846] R Matthews, "The power of one", in *New Scientist* (10/7/1999) pp 26–30; at `http://www.newscientist.com/ns/19990710/thepowerof.html`

[847] V Matyás, "Protecting the identity of doctors in drug prescription analysis", in *Health Informatics Journal* v 4 nos 3–4 (Dec 1998) pp 205–209

[848] J Maynard Smith, G Price, "The Logic of Animal Conflict", in *Nature* v 146 (1973) pp 15–18

[849] D Mazières, MF Kaashoek, "The Design, Implementation and Operation of an Email Pseudonym Server", in *Proceedings of the 5th ACM Conference on Computer and Communications Security* (1998), `http://www.pdos.lcs.mit.edu/~dm`

[850] J McCormac. *'European Scrambling Systems–The Black Book'*, version 5 (1996), Waterford University Press, ISBN 1-873556-22-5

[851] D McCullagh, "U.S. to Track Crypto Trails", in *Wired*, 4/5/2000, at `http://www.wired.com/news/politics/0,1283,36067,00.html`; statistics at `http://www.uscourts.gov/wiretap99/contents.html`

[852] D McCullagh, R Zarate, "Scanning Tech a Blurry Picture", in *Wired*, Feb 16 2002; at `http://www.wired.com/politics/law/news/2002/02/50470`

[853] K McCurley, Remarks at IACR General Meeting. *Crypto 98*, Santa Barbara, Ca., Aug 1998

[854] D McCullough, "A Hook-up Theorem for Multi-Level Security", in *IEEE Transactions on Software Engineering* v 16 no 6 (June 1990) pp 563–568

[855] P McDaniel, K Butler, W Enck, H Hursti, S McLaughlin, P Traynor, MA Blaze, A Aviv, P Černý, S Clark, E Cronin, G Shah, M Sherr, A Vigna, R Kemmerer, D Balzarotti, G Banks, M Cova, V Felmetsger, W Robertson, F Valeur, JL Hall, L Quilter, *'EVEREST: Evaluation and Validation of Election-Related Equipment, Standards and Testing'*, Final Report, Dec 7, 2007; at `http://www.sos.state.oh.us/sos/info/EVEREST/14-AcademicFinalEVERESTReport.pdf`

[856] AD McDonald, MG Kuhn, "StegFS: A Steganographic File System for Linux", in [1022] pp 463–477

[857] D MacEoin, *'The hijacking of British Islam—How extremist literature is subverting mosques in the UK'*, Policy Exchange (2007)

[858] G McGraw, *'Software Security—Building Security In'*, Addison-Wesley, 2006

[859] G McGraw, EW Felten, *'Java Security'*, Wiley (1997) ISBN 0-471-17842-X

[860] J McGroddy, HS Lin, *'A Review of the FBI's Trilogy Information Technology Modernization Program'*, National Academies Press, 2004, at `http://www7.nationalacademies.org/cstb/pub_fbi.html`

[861] J McHugh, "An EMACS Based Downgrader for the SAT" in *Computer and Network Security*, IEEE Computer Society Press (1986) pp 228–237

[862] D McGrew, J Viega, "The Galois/Counter Mode of Operation (GCM)", Submission to NIST Modes of Operation Process, January 2004; updated May 2005

[863] J McLean, "The Specification and Modeling of Computer Security", in *Computer* v 23 no 1 (Jan 1990) pp 9–16

[864] J McLean, "Security Models," in *Encyclopedia of Software Engineering*, John Wiley & Sons (1994)

[865] J McLean, "A General Theory of Composition for a Class of 'Possibilistic' Properties,", in *IEEE Transactions on Software Engineering* v 22 no 1 (Jan 1996) pp 53–67

[866] I McKie, "Total Vindication for Shirley McKie!" (23/6/2000), at `http://onin.com/fp/mckievindication.html`

[867] I McKie, M Russell, *'Shirley McKie—The Price of Innocence'*, Birlinn, 2007; ISBN 1-84150-575-0

[868] J McMillan, "Mobile Phones Help Secure Online Banking", in *PC World*, Sep 11 2007; at `http://www.pcworld.com/printable/article/id,137057/printable.html`

[869] J McNamara, "The Complete, Unofficial TEMPEST Information Page", at `http://www.eskimo.com/~joelm/tempest.html`

[870] B McWilliams, "Sex Sites Accused of Gouging Visitors with Phone Scam", in `InternetNews.com` (7/4/2000), at `http://www.internetnews.com/bus-news/print/0,,3_337101,00.html`

[871] J Meek, "Robo Cop", in *The Guardian*, June 13 2002, at `http://www.guardian.co.uk/Archive/Article/0,4273,4432506,00.html`

[872] AJ Menezes, PC van Oorschot, SA Vanstone, *'Handbook of Applied cryptography'*, CRC Press (1997); ISBN 0-8493-8523-7; also available online at `http://www.cacr.math.uwaterloo.ca/hac/`

[873] CG Menk, "System Security Engineering Capability Maturity Model and Evaluations: Partners within the Assurance Framework", in *19th National Information Systems Security Conference* (1996) pp 76–88

[874] J Mercer, "Document Fraud Deterrent Strategies: Four Case Studies", in *Optical Security and Counterfeit Deterrence Techniques II* (1998), IS&T (The Society for Imaging Science and Technology) and SPIE (The International Society for Optical Engineering) v 3314 ISBN 0-8194-2754-3, pp 39–51

[875] R Mercuri, "Physical Verifiability of Computer Systems", *5th International Computer Virus and Security Conference* (March 1992)

[876] R Mercuri, *'Electronic Vote Tabulation Checks & Balances'*, PhD Thesis, U Penn, 2000; see `http://www.notablesoftware.com/evote.html`

[877] TS Messergues, EA Dabish, RH Sloan, "Investigations of Power Analysis Attacks on Smartcards", in *Usenix Workshop on Smartcard Technology*, pp 151–161

[878] E Messmer, "DOD looks to put pizzazz back in PKI", *Network World* Aug 15 2005; at `http://www.networkworld.com/news/2005/081505-pki.html?nl`

[879] "Gamer may face jail for £1m racket", *Metro* Oct 25 2007, at `http://www.metro.co.uk/news/article.html?in_article_id=72887&in_page_id=34`; see also "Neil Higgs, aka Mr Modchips, 'guilty' ", Oct 25 2007, at `http://www.p2pnet.net/story/13780`

[880] CH Meyer and SM Matyas, *'Cryptography: A New Dimension in Computer Data Security'*, Wiley, 1982

[881] R Meyer-Sommer, "Smartly analyzing the simplicity and the power of simple power analysis on Smartcards", in *Workshop on Cryptographic Hardware and Embedded Systems* (2000); Springer LNCS v 1965 pp 78–92

[882] J Micklethwait, A Wooldridge, *'The Witch Doctors—What the management gurus are saying, why it matters and how to make sense of it'*, Random House (1997) ISBN 0-7493-2645-X

[883] Microsoft Inc, *'Architecture of Windows Media Rights Manager'*, May 2004, at `http://www.microsoft.com/windows/windowsmedia/howto/articles/drmarchitecture.aspx`

[884] Microsoft Inc, "Sony DRM Rootkit", Nov 12 2005, at `http://blogs.technet.com/antimalware/archive/2005/11/12/414299.aspx`

[885] Microsoft Inc, *'Understanding and Configuring User Account Control in Windows Vista'*, Dec 2007, at `http://technet2.microsoft.com/WindowsVista/en/library/00d04415-2b2f-422c-b70e-b18ff918c2811033.mspx`

[886] A Midgley, "R.I.P. and NHSNet", post to `ukcrypto` mailing list, 1/7/2000, archived at `http://www.cs.ucl.ac.uk/staff/I.Brown/archives/ukcrypto/`

[887] S Mihm, *'A Nation of Counterfeiters'*, Harvard 2007

[888] S Milgram, *'Obedience to Authority: An Experimental View'*, HarperCollins, (1974, reprinted 2004)

[889] J Millen, "A Resource Allocation Model for Denial of Service Protection", in *Journal of Computer Security* v 2 no 2–3 (1993) pp 89–106

[890] B Miller, "Vital Signs of Security", in *IEEE Spectrum* (Feb 94) pp 22–30

[891] GA Miller, "The Magical Number Seven, Plus or Minus Two: Some Limits on our Capacity for Processing Information", in *Psychological Review* v 63 (1956) pp 81–97

[892] ML Miller, IJ Cox, JA Bloom, "Watermarking in the Real World: An Application to DVD" in *Sixth ACM International Multimedia Conference*

(1998); Workshop notes published by GMD–Forschungszentrum Informationstechnik GmbH. as v 41 of *GMD Report*, pp 71–76

[893] JR Minkel, "Confirmed: The U.S. Census Bureau Gave Up Names of Japanese-Americans in WW II", in *Scientific American* Mar 30 2007, at `http://www.sciam.com/article.cfm?articleID=A4F4DED6-E7F2-99DF-32E46B0AC1FDE0FE&sc=I100322`

[894] SF Mires, "Production, Distribution, and Use of Postal Security Devices and Information-Based Indicia", *Federal Register* v 65 no 191 Oct 2, 2000 pp 58682–58698; at `http://www.cs.berkeley.edu/~tygar//papers/IBIP/Production_PSD.pdf`

[895] KD Mitnick, Congressional testimony, as reported by AP (03/02/00); see also `http://www.zdnet.com/zdnn/stories/news/0,4586,2454737,00.html`and `http://news.cnet.com/category/0-1005-200-1562611.html`

[896] KD Mitnick, *'The Art of Deception: Controlling the Human Element of Security'*, John Wiley and Sons (2002)

[897] Mobile Payment Forum, *'Risks and Threats Analysis and Security Best Practices–Mobile 2-Way Messaging Systems'* (Dec 2002), at `http://www.mobilepaymentforum.org/documents/Risk_and_Threats_Analysis_and_Security_Best_Practices_Mobile_2_Way_Messaging_December_2002.pdf`

[898] B Moghaddam, A Pentland, "Probabilistic Visual Learning for Object Representation", in *IEEE Transactions on Pattern Analysis and Machine Intelligence* v 19 no 7 (July 97) pp 696–710

[899] U Möller, L Cottrell, P Palfrader, L Sassaman, "Mixmaster Protocol– Version 2", IETF draft (2003) at `http://www.abditum.com/mix-master-spec.txt`

[900] "Card fraud nets Esc6 billion', F Mollet, *Cards International* (22/9/95) p 3

[901] E Montegrosso, "Charging and Accounting Mechanisms" (3G TR 22.924 v 3.1.1), from *Third Generation Partnership Project*, at `http://www.3gpp.org/TSG/Oct_status_list.htm`

[902] J Moore, "Hacking Friendster, Part 1", Feb 5 2004, at `http://more.theory.org/archives/000106.html`; "Hacking Social Networks Part 2: Don't Search Private Data", Feb 10 2004 at `http://more.theory.org/archives/000110.html`

[903] SW Moore, RJ Anderson, R Mullins, G Taylor, J Fournier, "Balanced Self-Checking Asynchronous Logic for Smart Card Applications", in *Microprocessors and Microsystems Journal* v 27 no 9 (Oct 2003) pp 421–430

[904] R Morris, "A Weakness in the 4.2BSD Unix TCP/IP Software", Bell Labs Computer Science Technical Report no 117, February 25, 1985; at `http://www.cs.berkeley.edu/~daw/security/seq-attack.html`

[905] R Morris, Invited talk, *Crypto 95*

[906] R Morris, K Thompson, "Password security: A case history", in *Communications of the ACM* v 22 no 11 (November 1979) pp 594–597

[907] DP Moynihan, *'Secrecy–The American Experience'*, Yale University Press (1999) ISBN 0-300-08079-4

[908] C Mueller, S Spray, J Grear, "The Unique Signal Concept for Detonation Safety in Nuclear Weapons", Sand91-1269, UC-706. Available via National Technical Information Service

[909] J Mueller, *Overblown–How Politicians and the Terrorism Industry Inflate National Security Threats, and Why we Believe Them*, Simon and Schuster 2006

[910] P Mukherjee, V Stavridou, "The Formal Specification of Safety Requirements for Storing Explosives", in *Formal Aspects of Computing* v 5 no 4 (1993) pp 299–336

[911] T Mulhall, "Where Have All The Hackers Gone? A Study in Motivation, Deterrence and Crime Displacement", in *Computers and Security* v 16 no 4 (1997) pp 277–315

[912] S Mullender (ed), *'Distributed Systems'*, Addison-Wesley (1993); ISBN 0-201-62427-3

[913] SJ Murdoch, "Browser storage of passwords: a risk or opportunity?", Apr 18 2006 in *Light Blue Touchpaper*; at `http://www.lightbluetouchpaper.org/2006/04/18/browser-storage-of-passwords-a-risk-or-opportunity/`

[914] SJ Murdoch, "Hot or Not: Revealing Hidden Services by their Clock Skew", in *13th ACM Conference on Computer and Communications Security*. 2006

[915] SJ Murdoch, "Chip & PIN relay attacks", at `http://www.lightbluetouchpaper.org/2007/02/06/chip-pin-relay-attacks/`

[916] SJ Murdoch, *'Covert channel vulnerabilities in anonymity systems'*, PhD Thesis, Cambridge 2007

[917] SJ Murdoch, "Embassy email accounts breached by unencrypted passwords", Sep 10 2007; at `http://www.lightbluetouchpaper.org/2007/09/10/`

[918] SJ Murdoch, RJ Anderson, "Shifting Borders", in *Index on censorship* Dec 18 2007; at `http://www.cl.cam.ac.uk/~sjm217/papers/index07-borders.pdf`

[919] SJ Murdoch, G Danezis, "Low-Cost Traffic Analysis of Tor", in *IEEE Symposium on Security and Privacy* (2005), at `http://www.cl.cam.ac.uk/users/sjm217/papers/oakland05torta.pdf`

[920] SJ Murdoch, Piotr Zieliński, "Sampled Traffic Analysis by Internet-Exchange-Level Adversaries", at PET 2007; at `http://www.cl.cam.ac.uk/~sjm217/`

[921] JC Murphy, D Dubbel, R Benson, "Technology Approaches to Currency Security", in *Optical Security and Counterfeit Deterrence Techniques II* (1998), IS&T (The Society for Imaging Science and Technology) and SPIE (The International Society for Optical Engineering) v 3314 ISBN 0-8194-2754-3, pp 21–28

[922] K Murray, "Protection of computer programs in Ireland", in *Computer Law and Security Report* v 12 no 3 (May/June 96) pp 57–59

[923] Major General RFH Nalder, *'History of the Royal Corps of Signals'*, published by the Royal Signals Institution (1958)

[924] Shishir Nagaraja and Ross Anderson, "The Topology of Covert Conflict", *Fifth Workshop on the Economics of Information Security* (2006)

[925] E Nakashima, "Verizon Says It Turned Over Data Without Court Orders", in *The Washington Post* Oct 16 2007 p A01; at `http://www.washingtonpost.com/wp-dyn/content/article/2007/10/15/AR2007101501857.html`

[926] E Nakashima, "A Story of Surveillance – Former Technician 'Turning In' AT&T Over NSA Program", in *The Washington Post* Nov 7 2007 p D01; at `http://www.washingtonpost.com/wp-dyn/content/article/2007/11/07/AR2007110700006.html`

[927] E Nakashima, "FBI Prepares Vast Database Of Biometrics – $1 Billion Project to Include Images of Irises and Faces", in *The Washington Post*

Dec 22 2007, p A01; at `http://www.washingtonpost.com/wp-dyn/content/article/2007/12/21/AR2007122102544.html`

[928] A Narayanan, V Shmatikov, "How To Break Anonymity of the Netflix Prize Dataset" (Nov 2007) at `http://arxiv.org/abs/cs/0610105`

[929] M Nash, "MS Security VP Mike Nash Replies", on *Slashdot* Jan 26 2006, at `http://interviews.slashdot.org/interviews/06/01/26/131246.shtml`

[930] National Audit Office, *'Minister of Defence: Combat Identification'*, 2002; at `www.nao.gov.uk/publications/nao_reports/01-02/0102661.pdf`

[931] Wikipedia, *Napster*, `http://en.wikipedia.org/wiki/Napster`

[932] M Nash, R Kennett, "Implementing Security policy in a Large Defence Procurement" in *12th Annual Computer Security Applications Conference*, San Diego CA, December 9–13 1996; proceedings published by the IEEE, ISBN 0-8186-7606-X; pp 15–23

[933] National Information Infrastructure Task Force, *'Options for Promoting Privacy on the National Information Infrastructure'* (April 1997), at `http://www.iitf.nist.gov/ipc/privacy.htm`

[934] National Institute of Standards and Technology, archive of publications on computer security, `http://csrc.nist.gov/publications/history/index.html`

[935] National Institute of Standards and Technology, *'Common Criteria for Information Technology Security Evaluation'*, Version 2.0 / ISO IS 15408 (May 1998); Version 3.1 (Sep 2006 Sep 2007), at `http://www.commoncriteriaportal.org`

[936] National Institute of Standards and Technology, *'Data Encryption Standard (DES)'* FIPS 46-3, Nov 1999 incorporating upgrade to triple DES, at `http://csrc.nist.gov/publications/fips/fips46-3/fips46-3.pdf`

[937] National Institute of Standards and Technology, *'Escrowed Encryption Standard'*, FIPS 185, Feb 1994

[938] National Institute of Standards and Technology, *'Security Requirements for Cryptographic Modules'* (11/1/1994), at `http://www.itl.nist.gov/fipspubs/0-toc.htm#cs`

[939] National Institute of Standards and Technology, *'SKIPJACK and KEA Algorithms'*, 23/6/98, `http://csrc.nist.gov/encryption/skipjack-kea.htm`

[940] National Institute of Standards and Technology, *'Advanced Encryption Standard'*, FIPS 197, Nov 26, 2001

[941] National Institute of Standards and Technology, *'Digital Signature Standard (DSS)'*, FIPS 186-2, Jan 2000, with change notice Oct 2001

[942] National Institute of Standards and Technology, *'Digital Signature Standard (DSS)'*, FIPS 186-3, draft, Mar 2006

[943] National Institute of Standards and Technology, *'PBX Vulnerability Analysis—Finding Holes in Your PBX Before Somebody Else Does'*, Special Publication 800-24, at `http://csrc.nist.gov/publications/PubsSPs.html`

[944] National Institute of Standards and Technology, *'Recommendation for Block Cipher Modes of Operation'*, Special Publication 800-38A 2001 Edition, at `http://csrc.nist.gov/CryptoToolkit/modes/`

[945] National Institute of Standards and Technology, *'Recommendation for Block Cipher Modes of Operation: The CMAC Mode for Authentication'*, Special Publication 800-38B, May 2005

[946] National Institute of Standards and Technology, *'Recommendation for Block Cipher Modes of Operation: The CCM Mode for Authentication and Confidentiality'*, Special Publication 800-38C, May 2004

[947] National Institute of Standards and Technology, *'Recommendation for Block Cipher Modes of Operation: Galois/Counter Mode (GCM) and GMAC'* NIST Special Publication 800-38D, November 2007

[948] National Institute of Standards and Technology, *'Recommendation for Key Management—Part 1: General (Revised)*, Special Publication 800-57, May 2006

[949] National Institute of Standards and Technology, *'Announcing request for Candidate Algorithm Nominations for a New Cryptographic Hash Algorithm (SHA-3) Family'*, in *Federal Register* v 72 no 212, Nov 2 2007, pp 62212–20

[950] National Research Council, *'Cryptography's Role in Securing the Information Society'*, National Academy Press (1996) ISBN 0-309-05475-3

[951] National Research Council, *'For the Record: Protecting Electronic Health Information'*, National Academy Press (1997) ISBN 0-309-05697-7

[952] National Security Agency, *'The NSA Security Manual'*, at `http://www.cl.cam.ac.uk/ftp/users/rja14/nsaman.tex.gz`

[953] National Statistics, "Protocol on Data Access and Confidentiality", at http://www.statistics.gov.uk

[954] P Naur, B Randell, *'Software Engineering–Report on a Conference'*, NATO Scientific Affairs Division, Garmisch 1968

[955] R Neame, "Managing Health Data Privacy and Security", in [43] pp 225–232

[956] GC Necula, P Lee, "Safe, Untrusted Agents Using Proof-Carrying Code", in *Mobile Agents and Security*, ISBN 3-540-64792-9, pp 61–91

[957] RM Needham, "Denial of Service: An Example", in *Communications of the ACM* v 37 no 11 (Nov 94) pp 42–46

[958] RM Needham, "Naming", in [912], pp 318–127

[959] RM Needham, "The Hardware Environment", in *Proceedings of the 1999 IEEE Symposium on Security and Privacy*, IEEE Computer Society Press, p 236

[960] RM Needham, MD Schroeder, "Using Encryption for Authentication in Large Networks of Computers", in *Communications of the ACM* v 21 no 12 (Dec 78) pp 993–999

[961] A Neewitz, "Defenses lacking at social network sites", *Security Focus* Dec 31 2003, at http://www.securityfocus.com/news/7739

[962] P Neumann, *'Computer Related Risks'*, Addison-Wesley (1995); ISBN 0-201-55805-X

[963] P Neumann, *Principled Assuredly Trustworthy Composable Architectures*, CHATS Project final report (2004), at http://www.csl.sri.com/users/neumann/

[964] New South Wales Supreme Court, "RTA v. Michell (New South Wales Supreme Court, 3/24/2006)", reported in http://www.thenewspaper.com/news/10/1037.asp

[965] MEJ Newman, "The structure and function of complex networks", in *SIAM Review* v 45 no 2 (2003) pp 167–256

[966] MEJ Newman, "Modularity and community structure in networks", in *Proc. Natl. Acad. Sci. USA* v 103 pp 8577–8582 (2006); at http://arxiv.org/abs/physics/0602124

[967] Richard Newman, Sherman Gavette, Larry Yonge, RJ Anderson, "Protecting Domestic Power-line Communications", in *Symposium On Usable Privacy and Security* 2006 pp 122–132

[968] O Newman, *'Defensible Space: People and Design in the Violent City'*, MacMillan 1972

[969] J Newton, "Countering the counterfeiters", in *Cards International* (21/12/94) p 12

[970] J Newton, *'Organised Plastic Counterfeiting'*, Her Majesty's Stationery Office (1996), ISBN 0-11-341128-6

[971] N Nisan, T Roughgarden, E Tardos, VV Vazirani, *'Algorithmic Mechanism Design'*, CUP 2007

[972] DA Norman, "Cautious Cars and Cantankerous Kitchens: How Machines Take Control", at `http://www.jnd.org/`; chapter 1 of *The Design of Future Things* (due 2008)

[973] R Norton-Taylor "Titan Rain–how Chinese hackers targeted White-hall", in *The Guardian*, Sep 5 2007 p 1; at `http://www.guardian.co.uk/technology/2007/sep/04/news.internet`

[974] R v Ipswich Crown Court ex parte NTL Ltd, [2002] EWHC 1585 (Admin), at `http://www.cyber-rights.org/documents/ntl_case.htm`

[975] R v Paul Matthew Stubbs, [2006] EWCA Crim 2312 (12 October 2006), at `http://www.bailii.org/cgi-bin/markup.cgi?doc=/ew/cases/EWCA/Crim/2006/2312.html`

[976] Nuclear Regulatory Commission, `www.nrc.gov`

[977] H Nugent, "Adulterers who call 118 118 for an affair", in *The Times*, May 27 2006; at `http://www.timesonline.co.uk/article/0,,2-2198924.html`

[978] F Oberholzer, K Strumpf, "The Effect of File Sharing on Record Sales–An Empirical Analysis", June 2004; journal version F Oberholzer-Gee, K Strumpf, "The Effect of File Sharing on Record Sales: An Empirical Analysis", *Journal of Political Economy* v 115 (2007) pp 1–42

[979] AM Odlyzko, *'The history of communications and its implications for the Internet'*, at `http://www.dtc.umn.edu/~odlyzko/doc/networks.html`

[980] AM Odlyzko, "Smart and stupid networks: Why the Internet is like Microsoft", *ACM netWorker*, Dec 1998, pp 38–46, at `http://www.acm.org/networker/issue/9805/ssnet.html`

[981] AM Odlyzko, "Privacy, economics, and price discrimination on the Internet", in *ICEC '03: Proceedings of the 5th international conference on*

electronic commerce, pp 355–366; at `http://www.dtc.umn.edu/~odlyzko/doc/networks.html`

[982] AM Odlyzko, "Pricing and Architecture of the Internet: Historical Perspectives from Telecommunications and Transportation", *TPRC 2004*, at `http://www.dtc.umn.edu/~odlyzko/doc/networks.html`

[983] N Okuntsev, *'Windows NT Security'*, R&D Books (1999); ISBN 0-87930-473-1

[984] Open Net Initiative, *'Internet Filtering in China in 2004-2005: A Country Study'*, April 14, 2005, at `www.opennetinitiative.net`

[985] Open Net Initiative, *'China (including Hong Kong)'*, Country report 2006, at `www.opennetinitiative.net`

[986] Open Net Initiative, *'Pulling the Plug'*, Oct 2007, at `www.opennetinitiative.net`

[987] Open Rights Group, *'May 2007 Election Report–Findings of the Open Rights Group Election Observation Mission in Scotland and England'*, at `http://www.openrightsgroup.org/e-voting-main`

[988] R Oppliger, *'Internet and Intranet Security'*, Artech House (1998) ISBN 0-89006-829-1

[989] Oracle Inc., *'Unbreakable: Oracle's Commitment to Security'*, Oracle White Paper, Feb 2002, at `http://www.oracle.com/technology/deploy/security/pdf/unbreak3.pdf`

[990] M Orozco, Y Asfaw, A Adler, S Shirmohammadi, A El Saddik, "Automatic Identification of Participants in Haptic Systems", in *2005 IEEE Instrumentation and Measurement Technology Conference*, Ottawa, pp 888–892, at `http://www.sce.carleton.ca/faculty/adler/publications/publications.html`

[991] Organization for Economic Cooperation and Development, *'Guidelines for the Protections of Privacy and Transborder Flow of Personal Data'*, OECD Doc no C(80)58 (1981), at `http://www.oecd.org//dsti/sti/it/secur/prod/PRIV-EN.HTM`

[992] J Osen, "The Cream of Other Men's Wit: Plagiarism and Misappropriation in Cyberspace", in *Computer Fraud and Security Bulletin* (11/97) pp 13–19

[993] M Ossman, "WEP: Dead Again", in *Security Focus*: Part 1, Dec 14 2004, at `http://www.securityfocus.com/infocus/1814`, and part 2, Mar 8 2005, at `http://www.securityfocus.com/infocus/1824`

[994] DA Osvik, A Shamir, E Tromer, "Cache attacks and countermeasures: the case of AES," in *RSA Conference Cryptographers Track* 2006, LNCS 3860, pp 1–20

[995] *Out-law News*, "SWIFT broke data protection law, says Working Party", Nov 27 2006, at `http://www.out-law.com/page-7518`

[996] *Out-law News*, "SWIFT will stop some US processing in 2009", Oct 15 2007, at `http://www.out-law.com/page-8548`;

[997] A Ozment, S Schechter, "Bootstrapping the Adoption of Internet Security Protocols", at *Fifth Workshop on the Economics of Information Security Security*, 2006; at `http://www.cl.cam.ac.uk/~jo262/`

[998] A Ozment, S Schechter, "Milk or Wine: Does Software Security Improve with Age?" in *15th Usenix Security Symposium* (2006)

[999] D Page, *'Theoretical Use of Cache Memory as a Cryptanalytic Side-Channel'*, Technical Report CSTR-02-003, University of Bristol, June 2002

[1000] L Page, "Thai insurgents move to keyless-entry bombs", in *The Register* Apr 27 2007, at `http://www.theregister.co.uk/2007/04/27/ied_ew_carries_on`

[1001] G Pahl, W Beitz, *Konstruktionslehre'*; translated as *'Engineering Design: A Systematic Approach'*, Springer 1999

[1002] S Pancho, "Paradigm shifts in protocol analysis", in *Proceedings of the 1999 New Security Paradigms Workshop*, ACM (2000), pp 70–79

[1003] A Papadimoulis, "Wish-It-Was Two-Factor", Sep 20 2007, at `http://worsethanfailure.com/Articles/WishItWas-TwoFactor-.aspx`

[1004] DJ Parker, "DVD Copy Protection: An Agreement At Last?–Protecting Intellectual Property Rights In The Age Of Technology", in *Tape/Disc Magazine* (Oct 96) `http://www.kipinet.com/tdb/tdb_oct96/feat_protection.html`

[1005] DJ Parker, *'Fighting Computer crime–A New Framework for Protecting Information'*, Wiley (1998) ISBN 0-471-16378-3

[1006] A Pasick, "FBI checks gambling in Second Life virtual world", *Reuters*, Apr 4 2007, at `http://www.reuters.com/article/technologyNews/idUSN0327865820070404?feedType=RSS`

[1007] J Pastor,"CRYPTOPOST–A cryptographic application to mail processing", in *Journal of Cryptology* v 3 no 2 (Jan 1991) pp 137–146

[1008] B Patterson, letter to *Communications of the ACM* v 43 no 4 (Apr 2000) pp 11–12

[1009] R Paul, "Leaked Media Defender e-mails reveal secret government project", *Ars Technica* Sep 16 2007, at `http://arstechnica.com/news.ars/post/20070916-leaked-media-defender-e-mails-reveal-secret-government-project.html`

[1010] LC Paulson, "Inductive analysis of the Internet protocol TLS", in *ACM Transactions on Computer and System Security* v 2 no 3 (1999) pp 332–351; also at `http://www.cl.cam.ac.uk/users/lcp/papers/protocols.html`

[1011] V Paxson, "An Analysis of Using Reflectors for Distributed Denial-of-Service Attacks", in *Computer Communication Review* v 31 no 3, July 2001, at `http://www.icir.org/vern/`

[1012] B Pease, A Pease, ' *Why Men Don't Listen and Women Can't Read Maps: How We're Different and What to Do about It*', Broadway Books 2001

[1013] TP Pedersen, "Electronic Payments of Small Amounts", in *Security Protocols* (1996), Springer LNCS v 1189 pp 59–68

[1014] J Pereira, "Breaking the Code: How Credit-Card Data Went Out Wireless Door", in *The Wall Street Journal*, May 4 2007, p A1

[1015] A Perrig, '*A Copyright Protection Environment for Digital Images*', Diploma thesis, École Polytechnique Fédérale de Lausanne (1997)

[1016] P Pesic, "The Clue to the Labyrinth: Francis Bacon and the Decryption of Nature", in *Cryptologia* v XXIV no 3 (July 2000) pp 193–211

[1017] M Peters, "MTN moves to prevent SIM card swap fraud", *IOL*, Dec 30 2007, at `http://www.iol.co.za/index.php?set_id=1&click_id=79&art_id=vn20071230080257431C811594&newslett=1&em=169205a1a20080102ah`

[1018] I Peterson, "From Counting to Writing", MathLand Archives, `http://www.maa.org/mathland/mathland_2_24.html`

[1019] FAP Petitcolas, RJ Anderson, MG Kuhn, "Attacks on Copyright Marking Systems", in *Proceedings of the Second International Workshop on Information Hiding* (1998), Springer LNCS v 1525 pp 219–239

[1020] FAP Petitcolas, RJ Anderson, MG Kuhn, "Information Hiding–A Survey", in *Proceedings of the IEEE* v 87 no 7 (July 1999) pp 1062–1078

[1021] H Petroski, *'To Engineer is Human'*, Barnes and Noble Books (1994) ISBN 1-56619502-0

[1022] A Pfitzmann, *Proceedings of the Third International Workshop on Information Hiding* (1999), Springer LNCS v 1768

[1023] B Pfitzmann, "Information Hiding Terminology", in *Proceedings of the First International Workshop on Information Hiding* (1996), Springer LNCS v 1174 pp 347–350

[1024] Z Phillips, "Security Theater", in *Government Executive* Aug 1, 2007, at `http://www.govexec.com/features/0807-01/0807-01s3.htm`

[1025] GE Pickett, "How do you select the 'right' security feature(s) for your company's products?", in *Optical Security and Counterfeit Deterrence Techniques II* (1998), IS&T (The Society for Imaging Science and Technology) and SPIE (The International Society for Optical Engineering) v 3314, ISBN 0-8194-2754-3, pp 52–58

[1026] RL Pickholtz, DL Schilling, LB Milstein, "Theory of Spread Spectrum Communications–A Tutorial", in *IEEE Transactions on Communications* v TC-30 no 5 (May 1982) pp 855–884

[1027] RL Pickholtz, DB Newman, YQ Zhang, M Tatebayashi, "Security Analysis of the INTELSAT VI and VII Command Network", in *IEEE Proceedings on Selected Areas in Communications* v 11 no 5 (June 1993) pp 663–672

[1028] L Pinault, *'Consulting Demons'*, Collins 2000

[1029] RA Poisel, *'Modern Communications Jamming Principles and Techniques'*, Artech House 2003; ISBN 158053743X

[1030] D Polak, "GSM mobile network in Switzerland reveals location of its users", in *Privacy Forum Digest* v 6 no 18 (31/12/1997), at `http://www.vortex.com/privacy/priv.06.18`

[1031] *Politech* mailing list, at `http://www.politechbot.com/`

[1032] B Pomeroy, S Wiseman, "Private Desktops and Shared Store", in *Computer Security Applications Conference*, Phoenix, Arizona, (1998); proceedings published by the IEEE, ISBN 0-8186-8789-4, pp190–200

[1033] GJ Popek, RP Goldberg, "Formal Requirements for Virtualizable Third Generation Architectures", in *Communications of the ACM* v 17 no 7 (July 1974) pp 412–421

[1034] B Poser, "The Provenzano Code", in *Language Log*, Apr 21, 2006; at `http://itre.cis.upenn.edu/~myl/languagelog/archives/003049.html`

[1035] Richard Posner, "An Economic Theory of Privacy", in *Regulation* (1978) pp 19–26

[1036] Richard Posner, "Privacy, Secrecy and Reputation" in *Buffalo Law Review* v 28 no 1 (1979)

[1037] K Poulsen, "ATM Reprogramming Caper Hits Pennsylvania", in *Wired*, July 12 2007, at `http://blog.wired.com/27bstroke6/2007/07/atm-reprogrammi.html`

[1038] S Poulter, "Phone firm's whistleblower says his life has been made a misery", in *The Daily Mail* Jun 21 2007; at `http://www.dailymail.co.uk/pages/live/articles/news/news.html?in_article_id=463593&in_page_id=1770`

[1039] J Preece, H Sharp, Y Rogers, '*Interaction design: beyond human-computer interaction*', Wiley (2002)

[1040] B Preneel, PC van Oorschot, "MDx-MAC and Building Fast MACs from Hash Functions", in *Advances in Cryptology–Crypto 95*, Springer LNCS v 963 pp 1–14

[1041] RS Pressman, '*Software Engineering: A Practitioner's Approach*', McGraw-Hill (5th edition, 2000) ISBN 0-073-65578-3

[1042] V Prevelakis, D Spinellis, "The Athens Affair", *IEEE Spectrum*, July 2007, at `http://www.spectrum.ieee.org/print/5280`

[1043] G Price, '*The Interaction Between Fault Tolerance and Security*', Technical Report no 214, Cambridge University Computer Laboratory

[1044] WR Price, "Issues to Consider When Using Evaluated Products to Implement Secure Mission Systems", in *Proceedings of the 15th National Computer Security Conference*, National Institute of Standards and Technology (1992) pp 292–299

[1045] H Pringle, "The Cradle of Cash", in *Discover* v 19 no 10 (Oct 1998); `http://www.discover.com/oct_issue/cradle.html`

[1046] C Prins, "Biometric Technology Law", in *The Computer Law and Security Report* v 14 no 3 (May/Jun 98) pp 159–165

[1047] Privacy Commissioner of Canada, "Inadequate security safeguards led to TJX breach, Commissioners say", Sep 25 2007, at `http://www.privcom.gc.ca/media/nr-c/2007/nr-c_070925_e.asp`

[1048] The Privacy Exchange, `http://www.privacyexchange.org/`

[1049] A Pruneda, "Windows Media Technologies: Using Windows Media Rights Manager to Protect and Distribute Digital Media", *MSDN Magazine*, Dec 2001, at `http://msdn.microsoft.com/msdnmag/issues/01/12/DRM/`

[1050] *Public Lending Right* (PLR), at `http://www.writers.org.uk/guild/Crafts/Books/PLRBody.html`

[1051] Public Record Office, *'Functional Requirements for Electronic Record Management Systems'*, November 1999, `http://www.pro.gov.uk/recordsmanagement/eros/invest/reference.pdf`

[1052] RD Putnam, *'Bowling Alone: the Collapse and Revival of American Community'*, Simon & Schuster, 2000

[1053] T Pyszczynski, S Solomon, J Greenberg, *'In the Wake of 9/11—the Psychology of Terror'*, American Psychological Association 2003

[1054] JJ Quisquater, D Samyde, "ElectroMagnetic Analysis (EMA): Measures and Counter-Measures for Smart Cards" in *International Conference on Research in Smart Cards*, Springer LNCS v 2140 pp 200–210

[1055] Rain Forest Puppy, "Issue disclosure policy v1.1", at `http://www.wiretrip.net/rfp/policy.html`

[1056] W Rankl, W Effing, *'Smartcard Handbook'*, Wiley (1997), ISBN 0-471-96720-3; translated from the German *'Handbuch der Chpkarten'*, Carl Hanser Verlag (1995), ISBN 3-446-17993-3

[1057] ES Raymond, "The Case of the Quake Cheats", 27/12/1999, at `http://www.tuxedo.org/~esr/writings/quake-cheats.html`

[1058] ES Raymond, *'The Cathedral and the Bazaar'*, at `http://www.tuxedo.org/~esr/writings/cathedral-bazaar/`

[1059] ES Raymond, *'The Magic Cauldron'*, June 1999, at `http://www.tuxedo.org/~esr/writings/magic-cauldron/magic-cauldron.html`

[1060] J Reason, *'Human Error'*, Cambridge University Press 1990

[1061] SM Redl, MK Weber, MW Oliphant, *'GSM and Personal Communications Handbook'*, Artech House (1998) ISBN 0-89006-957-3

[1062] MG Reed, PF Syverson, DM Goldschlag, "Anonymous Connections and Onion Routing", in *IEEE Journal on Special Areas in Communications* v 16 no 4 (May 98) pp 482–494

[1063] T Reid, "China's cyber army is preparing to march on America, says Pentagon", in *The Times* Sep 7 2007; at `http://technology .timesonline.co.uk/tol/news/tech_and_web/the_web/article 2409865.ece`

[1064] "Mystery of Levy tax phone calls", C Reiss, *Evening Standard* July 5 2000 p 1; also at `http://www.thisislondon.com/`

[1065] MK Reiter, "A Secure Group Membership Protocol", *IEEE Transactions on Software Engineering* v 22 no 1 (Jan 96) pp 31–42

[1066] MK Reiter, MK Franklin, JB Lacy, RA Wright, "The Omega Key Management Service", *3rd ACM Conference on Computer and Communications Security* (1996) pp 38–47

[1067] M Reiter, AD Rubin, "Anonymous web transactions with Crowds", in *Communications of the ACM* v 42 no 2 (Feb 99) pp 32–38

[1068] J Reno, `http://www.cnn.com/2000/US/05/25/security.breaches.01/ index.html`

[1069] Reporters without Borders, *'Handbook for Bloggers and Cyber-dissidents'*, 2005, at `http://www.rsf.org/rubrique.php3?id_rubrique=542`

[1070] E Rescorla, *'SSL and TLS–Designing and Building Secure Systems'*, Addison-Wesley 2000

[1071] E Rescorla, "Is Finding Security Holes a Good Idea?", *Third Workshop on the Economics of Information Security* (2004)

[1072] *Reuters*, "No Surveillance Tech for Tampa", in *Wired* Aug 21 2003, at `http://www.wired.com/politics/law/news/2003/08/60140`

[1073] *Reuters*, "Nissan warns U.S. cellphones can disable car keys", May 24 2007, at `http://www.reuters.com/article/technologyNews/ idUSN2424455020070524?feedType=RSS&rpc=22`

[1074] D Richardson, *'Techniques and Equipment of Electronic Warfare'*, Salamander Books, ISBN 0-8601-265-8

[1075] LW Ricketts, JE Bridges, J Miletta, *'EMP Radiation and Protection Techniques'*, Wiley 1975

[1076] M Ridley, *'The Red Queen: Sex and the Evolution of Human Nature'*, Viking Books (1993); ISBN 0-1402-4548-0

[1077] RL Rivest, A Shamir, "PayWord and MicroMint: Two Simple Micro-payment Schemes", in *Security Protocols* (1996), Springer LNCS v 1189 pp 69–87

[1078] RL Rivest, A Shamir, L Adleman, "A Method for Obtaining Digital Signatures and Public-Key Cryptosystems", in *Communications of the ACM* v 21 no 2 (Feb 1978) pp 120–126

[1079] MB Robinson, "The Theoretical Development of 'CPTED': 25 years of Responses to C. Ray Jeffery", in *Advances in Criminological Theory* v 8; at `http://www.acs.appstate.edu/dept/ps-cj/vitacpted2.html`

[1080] AR Roddy, JD Stosz, "Fingerprint Features — Statistical Analysis and System Performance Estimates", in *Proceedings of the IEEE* v 85 no 9 (Sep 97) pp 1390–1421

[1081] R Rohozinski, M Mambetalieva, "Election Monitoring in Kyrgyzstan", 2005, *Open Net Initiative,* at `http://opennet.net/special/kg/`

[1082] SJ Root, *'Beyond COSO–Internal Control to Enhance Corporate Governance',* Wiley 1998

[1083] N Rosasco, D Larochelle, "How and Why More Secure Technologies Succeed in Legacy Markets: Lessons from the Success of SSH", in *WEIS 2003;* at `http://www.cl.cam.ac.uk/~rja14/econsec.html`

[1084] J Rosen, "A Watchful State", in *New York Times,* Oct 7 2001 p 38

[1085] B Ross, C Jackson, N Miyake, D Boneh, JC Mitchell, "Stronger Password Authentication Using Browser Extensions", in *Proceedings of the 14th Usenix Security Symposium, 2005;* at `http://crypto.stanford.edu/PwdHash/`

[1086] DE Ross, "Two Signatures", in `comp.risks` v 20.81: `http://catless.ncl.ac.uk/Risks/20.81.html`

[1087] "Card fraud plummets in France", M Rowe, *Banking Technology* (May 94) p 10

[1088] T Rowland, "Ringing up the wrong numbers", in *The Guardian* May 18 2006; at `http://www.guardian.co.uk/media/2006/may/18/newmedia.technology`

[1089] The Royal Society, *'Strategy options for the UK's separated plutonium',* Sep 27 2007, at `http://royalsociety.org/document.asp?latest=1&id=7080`

[1090] WW Royce, "Managing the development of Large Software Systems: Concepts and Techniques", in *Proceedings IEEE WESCON* (1970) pp 1–9

[1091] A Rubin, "Bugs in Anonymity Services", *BugTraq*, 13 Apr 1999; at
`http://www.securityportal.com/list-archive/bugtraq/1999/Apr/`
`0126.html`

[1092] HH Rubinovitz, "Issues Associated with Porting Applications to the
Compartmented Mode Workstation", in *ACM SIGSAC* v 12 no 4 (Oct
94) pp 2–5

[1093] RA Rueppel, *'Analysis and Design of Stream Ciphers'*, Springer-Verlag
(1986) ISBN 0-387-16870-2

[1094] RA Rueppel, "Criticism of ISO CD 11166 Banking: Key Management by
Means of Asymmetric Algorithms", in *Proceedings of 3rd Symposium of
State and Progress of Research in Cryptography*, Fondazione Ugo Bor-
doni, Rome 1993, pp 191–198

[1095] R Ruffin, "Following the Flow of Funds" in *Security Management*
(July 1994) pp 46–52

[1096] J Rushby, B Randell, "A Distributed Secure System", in *IEEE Computer*
v 16 no 7 (July 83) pp 55–67

[1097] B Russell, Answer to parliamentary question, *Hansard* 10 Jun 2003
column 762W, at `http://www.publications.parliament.uk/pa/`
`cm200203/cmhansrd/vo030610/text/30610w13.htm`

[1098] D Russell, GT Gangemi, *'Computer Security Basics'*, Chapter 10:
TEMPEST, O'Reilly & Associates (1991), ISBN 0-937175-71-4

[1099] J Rutkowska, " Running Vista Every Day!", *Invisible Things Blog*, Feb
2007; at `http://theinvisiblethings.blogspot.com/2007/02/`
`running-vista-every-day.html`

[1100] DR Safford, DL Schales, DK Hess, "The TAMU Security Package: An
Ongoing Response to Internet Intruders in an Academic Environment", in *Usenix Security 93*, pp 91–118

[1101] *Salon*, "The computer virus turns 25", Jul 12 2007; at `http://machinist`
`.salon.com/blog/2007/07/12/virus_birthday/index.html`

[1102] JD Saltzer, MD Schroeder, "The Protection of Information in Computer
Systems", in *Proceedings of the IEEE* v 63 no 9 (Mar 1975) pp 1278–1308

[1103] RG Saltzman, "Assuring Accuracy, Integrity and Security in National
Elections: The Role of the U.S. Congress", in *Computers, Freedom and
Privacy* (1993); at `http://www.cpsr.org/conferences/cfp93/saltman`
`.html`

[1104] J Saltzman, M Daniel, "Man freed in 1997 shooting of officer–Judge gives ruling after fingerprint revelation", in *The Boston Globe* Jan 24 2004, at `http://www.truthinjustice.org/cowans2.htm`

[1105] T Sammes, B Jenkinson, *Forensic Computing–A Practitioner's Guide'*, Springer (2000); ISBN 1-85233-299-9

[1106] R Samuels, S Stich, L Faucher, "Reason and Rationality", in *Handbook of Epistemology* (Kluwer, 1999); at `http://ruccs.rutgers.edu/ Archive-Folder/Research%20Group/Publications/Reason/ ReasonRationality.htm`

[1107] P Samuelson, "Copyright and digital libraries", in *Communications of the ACM* v 38 no 4, April 1995

[1108] P Samuelson, "Intellectual Property Rights and the Global Information Economy", in *Communications of the ACM* v 39 no 1 (Jan 96) pp 23–28

[1109] P Samuelson, "The Copyright Grab", at `http://uainfo.arizona.edu/ ~weisband/411_511/copyright.html`

[1110] Pam Samuelson and Suzanne Scotchmer, "The Law and Economics of Reverse Engineering", *Yale Law Journal* (2002)

[1111] D Samyde, SP Skorobogatov, RJ Anderson, JJ Quisquater, "On a New Way to Read Data from Memory", in *IEEE Security in Storage Workshop* (2002) pp 65–69

[1112] RS Sandhu, S Jajodia, "Polyinstantiation for Cover Stories", in *Computer Security — ESORICS 92*, LNCS v 648 pp 307–328

[1113] SANS Institute, "Consensus List of The Top Ten Internet Security Threats", at `http://www.sans.org/`, Version 1.22 June 19, 2000

[1114] G Sandoval, "Glitches let Net shoppers get free goods", in *CNET News.com*, July 5 2000; at `http://news.cnet.com/news/0-1007-200- 2208733.html`

[1115] PF Sass, L Gorr, "Communications for the Digitized Battlefield of the 21st Century", in *IEEE Communications* v 33 no 10 (Oct 95) pp 86–95

[1116] W Schachtman, "How Technology Almost Lost the War: In Iraq, the Critical Networks Are Social–Not Electronic", in *Wired*, Dec 15 2007, at `http://www.wired.com/politics/security/magazine/15-12/ff_ futurewar?currentPage=all`

[1117] M Schaefer, "Symbol Security Condition Considered Harmful", in *Proceedings of the 1989 IEEE Symposium on Security and Privacy*, pp 20–46

[1118] RR Schell, "Computer Security: The Achilles' Heel of the Electronic Air Force?", in *Air University Review*, v 30 no 2 (Jan–Feb 1979) pp 16–33

[1119] RR Schell, PJ Downey, GJ Popek, *'Preliminary notes on the design of secure military computer systems'*, Electronic Systems Division, Air Force Systems Command (1/1/1973) MCI-73-1; at `http://seclab.cs.ucdavis.edu/projects/history/papers/sche73.pdf`

[1120] DL Schilling, *'Meteor Burst Communications: Theory and Practice'*, Wiley (1993) ISBN 0-471-52212-0

[1121] DC Schleher, *'Electronic Warfare in the Information Age'*, Artech House (1999) ISBN 0-89006-526-8

[1122] D Schmandt-Besserat, *'How Writing Came About'*, University of Texas Press (1996): ISBN: 0-29277-704-3, `http://www.dla.utexas.edu/depts/lrc/numerals/dsb1.html`

[1123] ZE Schnabel, "The estimation of the total fish population in a lake", in *American Mathematical Monthly* v 45 (1938) pp 348–352

[1124] PM Schneider, "Datenbanken mit genetischen Merkmalen von Straftätern", in *Datenschutz und Datensicherheit* v 22 (6/1998) pp 330–333

[1125] B Schneier, *'Applied Cryptography'*, Wiley (1996); ISBN 0-471-12845-7

[1126] B Schneier, "Why Computers are Insecure", in `comp.risks` v 20.67: `http://catless.ncl.ac.uk/Risks/20.67.html`

[1127] B Schneier, *'Secrets and Lies : Digital Security in a Networked World'*, Wiley (2000); ISBN 0-471-25311-1

[1128] B Schneier, "Semantic Attacks: The Third Wave of Network Attacks", in *Crypto-Gram Newsletter* October 15, 2000 at `http://www.schneier.com/crypto-gram-0010.html`

[1129] B Schneier, *'Beyond Fear: Thinking Sensibly about Security in an Uncertain World'*, Copernicus Books (2003)

[1130] B Schneier, "Real-World Passwords", in *Crypto-Gram Newsletter* Dec 14, 2006; at `http://www.schneier.com/blog/archives/2006/12/realworld_passw.html`

[1131] B Schneier, "Choosing Secure Passwords", Aug 7 2007; at `http://www.schneier.com/blog/archives/2007/08/asking_for_pass.html`

[1132] B Schneier, "Secure Passwords Keep You Safer, in *Crypto-Gram Newsletter* Jan 11, 2007; at `http://www.schneier.com/blog/archives/2007/01/choosing_secure.html`

[1133] B Schneier, "The Psychology of Security", *RSA Conference* (2007), at `http://www.schneier.com/essay-155.html`

[1134] B Schneier, "The Nugache Worm/Botnet", Dec 31 2007, at `http://www.schneier.com/blog/archives/2007/12/the_nugache_wor.html`

[1135] B Schneier, D Banisar, *'The Electronic Privacy Papers–Documents on the Battle for Privacy in the Age of Surveillance'*, Wiley (1997) ISBN 0-471-12297-1

[1136] B Schneier, A Shostack, "Breaking up is Hard to Do: Modeling Security Threats for Smart Cards," in *USENIX Workshop on Smart Card Technology* 1999, pp 175–185, at `http://www.schneier.com/paper-smart-card-threats.html`

[1137] M Schnyder, "Datenfluesse im Gesundheitswesen", in *Symposium für Datenschutz und Informationssicherheit*, Zuerich, Oct 98

[1138] RA Scholtz, "Origins of Spread-Spectrum Communications", in *IEEE Transactions on Communications* v TC-30 no 5 (May 1982) pp 822–854

[1139] MD Schroeder, *'Cooperation of Mutually Suspicious Subsystems in a Computer Utility'*, MIT PhD Thesis, September 1972, also available as Project MAC Technical Report MAC TR-104, available on the web as `http://hdl.handle.net/ncstrl.mit_lcs/MIT/LCS/TR-104`

[1140] M Scorgie, "Untapped sources for accountants" in *Genizah Fragments* (The Newsletter of Cambridge University's Taylor-Schechter Genizah Research Unit) no 29 (April 1995), at `http://www.lib.cam.ac.uk/Taylor-Schechter/GF/GF29.html`

[1141] Beale Screamer, "Microsoft DRM - Technical description" and supporting documents, on *Cryptome.org*, Oct 23 2001; at `http://cryptome.org/beale-sci-crypt.htm`

[1142] W Seltzer, M Anderson, "Census Confidentiality under the Second War Powers Act (1942-1947)," Annual Meeting of the Population Association of America, Mar 30 2007, New York; at *Official Statistics and Statistical Confidentiality: Recent Writings and Essential Documents*, at `http://www.uwm.edu/%7Emargo/govstat/integrity.htm`

[1143] R Senderek, *'Key-Experiments–How PGP Deals With Manipulated Keys'*, at `http://senderek.de/security/key-experiments.html`

[1144] D Senie, "Changing the Default for Directed Broadcasts in Routers", RFC 2644, at `http://www.ietf.org/rfc/rfc2644.txt`

[1145] Chandak Sengoopta, *'Imprint of the Raj'*, Pan Macmillan 2004

[1146] A Shamir, "How to share a secret", in *Communications of the ACM* v 22 no 11 (Nov 1979) pp 612–613

[1147] A Shamir, "Identity-based cryptosystems and signature schemes", in *Proceedings of Crypto 1984*, Springer LNCS v 196, pp 47–53

[1148] A Shamir, "Research Announcement: Microprocessor Bugs Can Be Security Disasters", Nov 2007, at `http://cryptome.org/bug-attack.htm`

[1149] MI Shamos, "Electronic Voting - Evaluating the Threat", in *Computers, Freedom and Privacy* (1993); at `http://www.cpsr.org/conferences/cfp93/shamos.html`

[1150] MI Shamos, "Paper v. Electronic Voting Records–An Assessment", in *Computers, Freedom & Privacy* (Apr 2004), at `http://euro.ecom.cmu.edu/people/faculty/mshamos/paper.htm`

[1151] M Sherr, E Cronin, S Clark, M Blaze, "Signaling vulnerabilities in wiretapping systems", *IEEE Security and Privacy* v 3 no 6 (Nov/Dec 2005) pp 13–25

[1152] O Sibert, PA Porras, R Lindell, "An Analysis of the Intel 80x86 Security Architecture and Implementations" in *IEEE Transactions on Software Engineering* v 22 no 5 (May 96) pp 283–293

[1153] H Simon, '*The Sciences of the Artificial*', 3rd ed, MIT Press, 1996

[1154] Y Shachmurove, G Fishman, S Hakim, "The burglar as a rational economic agent," Technical Report CARESS Working Paper 97-07, U Penn University of Pennsylvania Center for Analytic Research in Economics and the Social Sciences, June 1997

[1155] G Shah, A Molina, M Blaze, "Keyboards and Covert Channels", in *15th USENIX Security Symposium* 2006, at `http://www.crypto.com/papers/`

[1156] Y Shaked, A Wool, "Cracking the Bluetooth PIN", 2005, at `http://www.eng.tau.ac.il/~yash/shaked-wool-mobisys05/index.html`

[1157] CE Shannon, "A Mathematical Theory of Communication", in *Bell Systems Technical Journal* v 27 (1948) pp 379–423, 623–656

[1158] CE Shannon, "Communication theory of secrecy systems", in *Bell Systems Technical Journal* v 28 (1949) pp 656–715

[1159] C Shapiro, H Varian, '*Information Rules*', Harvard Business School Press (1998), ISBN 0-87584-863-X

[1160] P Shekelle, SC Morton, EB Keeler, JK Wang, BI Chaudhry, SY Wu, WA Majica, M Maglione, EA Roth, C Rolon, D Valentine, R Shanman, SJ

Newberry, *Costs and Benefits of Health Information Technology*, DHHS June 2006; at `http://aspe.hhs.gov/daltcp/reports/2006/HITcb.htm`

[1161] M Sherr, E Cronin, S Clark, MA Blaze, "Signaling vulnerabilities in wiretapping systems", *IEEE Security and Privacy*, Nov/Dec 2005, at `http://www.crypto.com/papers/wiretapping/`

[1162] D Sherwin, "Fraud—the Unmanaged Risk", in *Financial Crime Review* v 1 no 1 (Fall 2000) pp 67–69

[1163] S Sheye, "SSL CLient Certificates–Not Securing the Web", in *Cryptomathic NewsOnInk Quarterly Newsletter* (Nov 2006), at `http://www.cryptomathic.com/Admin/Public/DWSDownload.aspx?File=%2fFiles%2fFiler%2fNewsletters%2fNewsOnInk_Nov_2006.pdf`

[1164] JF Shoch, JA Hupp, "The 'Worm' Programs–Early Experience with a Distributed Computation", *Comm ACM* v 25 no 3 (1982) pp 172–180

[1165] PW Shor, "Algorithms for Quantum Computers", in *35th Annual Symposium on the Foundations of Computer Science* (1994), proceedings published by the IEEE, ISBN 0-8186-6580-7, pp 124–134

[1166] A Shostack, P Syverson, "What Price Privacy? (and why identity theft is about neither identity nor theft)", in *Economics of Information Security*, Kluwer Academic Publishers, 2004, Chapter 11

[1167] V Shoup, "OAEP Reconsidered", IBM Zürich, Switzerland, September 18, 2001; at `http://www.shoup.net/papers/oaep.pdf`

[1168] *Luther Simjian–Inventor of the Week*, at `http://web.mit.edu/invent/iow/simjian.html`

[1169] GJ Simmons, "The Prisoners' Problem and the Subliminal Channel", in *Proceedings of CRYPTO '83*, Plenum Press (1984) pp 51–67

[1170] GJ Simmons, "How to Insure that Data Acquired to Verify Treaty Compliance are Trustworthy", GJ Simmons, *Proceedings of the IEEE* v 76 no 5 (1988; reprinted as a chapter in [1171])

[1171] GJ Simmons (ed), *'Contemporary Cryptology–The Science of Information Integrity'*, IEEE Press (1992) ISBN 0-87942-277-7

[1172] GJ Simmons, "A Survey of Information Authentication", in [1171] pp 379–439

[1173] GJ Simmons, "An Introduction to Shared Secret and/or Shared Control Schemes and Their Application", in [1171] pp 441–497

[1174] GJ Simmons, invited talk at the *1993 ACM Conference on Computer and Communications Security*, Fairfax, Virginia, Nov 3–5, 1993

[1175] GJ Simmons, 'Subliminal Channels; Past and Present', *European Transactions on Telecommunications* v 5 no 4 (Jul/Aug 94) pp 459–473

[1176] GJ Simmons, "The History of Subliminal Channels", in *IEEE Journal on Selcted Areas in Communications* v 16 no 4 (April 1998) pp 452–462

[1177] R Singel, "Encrypted E-Mail Company Hushmail Spills to Feds", in *Wired* Nov 7 2007 at `http://blog.wired.com/27bstroke6/2007/11/encrypted-e-mai.html`

[1178] R Singel, "Point, Click ... Eavesdrop: How the FBI Wiretap Net Operates", in *Wired* Aug 29 2007 at `http://www.wired.com/politics/security/news/2007/08/wiretap`

[1179] A Sipress, "Tracking Traffic by Cell Phone; Md., Va. to Use Transmissions to Pinpoint Congestion", in *Washington Post* (22/12/1999) p A01, at `http://www.washingtonpost.com/`

[1180] KS Siyan, J Casad, J Millecan, D Yarashus, P Tso, J Shoults, *'Windows NT Server 4–Professional Reference'*, New Riders Publishing (1996)

[1181] SP Skorobogatov, "Copy Protection in Modern Microcontrollers", at `http://www.cl.cam.ac.uk/~sps32/mcu_lock.html`

[1182] SP Skorobogatov, *'Low temperature data remanence in static RAM'*, Cambridge University Technical Report UCAM-CL-TR-536 (June 2002), at `http://www.cl.cam.ac.uk/techreports/UCAM-CL-TR-536.html`

[1183] SP Skorobogatov, *'Semi-invasive attacks–A new approach to hardware security analysis'*, PhD Thesis, 2004; University of Cambridge Technical Report 630, 2005; at `http://www.cl.cam.ac.uk/techreports/UCAM-CL-TR-630.html`

[1184] SP Skorobogatov, "Data Remanence in Flash Memory Devices", in *Cryptographic Hardware and Embedded Systems Workshop* (CHES-2005), Springer LNCS 3659 pp 339–353

[1185] SP Skorobogatov, "Optically Enhanced Position-Locked Power Analysis", in *CHES 2006* pp 61–75

[1186] SP Skorobogatov, "Tamper resistance and physical attacks", at *Summer School on Cryptographic Hardware, Side-Channel and Fault Attacks*, June 12–15, 2006, Louvain-la-Neuve, Belgium; slides at `http://www.cl.cam.ac.uk/~sps32`

[1187] SP Skorobogatov, RJ Anderson, "Optical Fault Induction Attacks", in *Cryptographic Hardware and Embedded Systems Workshop* (CHES 2002), Springer LNCS v 2523 pp 2–12; at `http://www.cl.cam.ac.uk/~sps32`

[1188] B Skyrms, *'Evolution of the Social Contract'* Cambridge University Press (1996)

[1189] P Slovic, ML Finucane, E Peters, DG MacGregor, "Rational Actors or Rational Fools? Implications of the Affect Heuristic for Behavioral Economics", at `http://www.decisionresearch.org/pdf/dr498v2.pdf`; revised version of "The Affect Heuristic" in *Heuristics and Biases: The Psychology of Intuitive Judgment*, Cambridge University Press (2002) pp 397–420

[1190] Smartcard Standards, `http://www.cardwerk.com/smartcards/smartcard_standards.aspx`

[1191] "Plastic Card Fraud Rises in the UK", in *Smart Card News* v 6 no 3 (Mar 97) p 45

[1192] A Smith, *'An Inquiry into the Nature and Causes of the Wealth of Nations'*, 1776; at `http://www.econlib.org/LIBRARY/Smith/smWN.html`

[1193] RE Smith, "Constructing a high assurance mail guard", in *Seventeenth National Computer Security Conference*, 11–14 October, Baltimore, Maryland; proceedings published by NIST (1994) pp 247–253

[1194] RM Smith, "Problems with Web Anonymizing Services" (15/4/1999), at `http://www.tiac.net/users/smiths/anon/anonprob.htm`

[1195] S Smith, S Weingart, *'Building a High-Performance, Programmable Secure Coprocessor'*, IBM Technical report RC 21102, available through `http://www.ibm.com/security/cryptocards/`

[1196] P Smulders, "The Threat of Information Theft by Reception of Electromagnetic Radiation from RS-232 Cables", in *Computers & Security* v 9 (1990) pp 53–58

[1197] C Soghoian, "Go Fish: Is Facebook Violating European Data Protection Rules?", on *Slight Paranoia* June 26 2007, at `http://paranoia.dubfire.net/2007/06/go-fish-is-facebook-violating-european.html`

[1198] A Solomon, "A brief history of PC virsuses", in *Computer Fraud and Security Bulletin* (Dec 93) pp 9–19

[1199] A Solomon, Seminar given at Cambridge University Computer Laboratory, 30th May 2000

[1200] D Solove, "A Taxonomy of Privacy", in *University of Pennsylvania Law Review* v 154 no 3 (2006) pp 477–560; at `http://papers.ssrn.com/abstract_id=667622`

[1201] D Solove, *'The future of reputation–gossip, rumor and privacy in the Internet'*, Caravan, 2007

[1202] P Sommer, "Intrusion Detection and Legal Proceedings", at *Recent Advances in Intrusion Detection* (RAID) 1998, at `http://www.zurich.ibm.com/~dac/Prog_RAID98/Full_Papers/Sommer_text.pdf`

[1203] DX Song, D Wagner, XQ Tian, "Timing analysis of keystrokes and SSH timing attacks," in *Proceedings of 10th USENIX Security Symposium* (2001)

[1204] R v Department of Health, ex parte Source Informatics: [2000] 2 WLR 940

[1205] South West Thames Regional Health Authority, *'Report of the Inquiry into the London Ambulance Service'* (1993), at `http://www.cs.ucl.ac.uk/staff/A.Finkelstein/las.html`

[1206] E Spafford, "The Internet worm program: an analysis", in *Computer Communications Review* v 19 no 1 (Jan 89) pp 17–57

[1207] EH Spafford, "OPUS: Preventing Weak Password Choices", in *Computers and Security* v 11 no 3 (1992) pp 273–278

[1208] M Specter, "Do fingerprints lie? The gold standard of forensic evidence is now being challenged", New York Times, May 27, 2002; at `http://www.michaelspecter.com/ny/2002/2002_05_27_fingerprint.html`

[1209] R Spencer, S Smalley, P Loscocco, M Hibler, D Andersen, J Lepreau, "The Flask Security Architecture: System Support for Diverse Security Policies," in *Proceedings of the 8th USENIX Security Symposium* (1999) pp 123–139

[1210] "Tip von Urmel", in *Spiegel Magazine* no 38 (11/9/95)

[1211] J Spolsky, "Does Issuing Passports Make Microsoft a Country?" at `http://joel.editthispage.com/stories/storyReader$139`

[1212] "Your car radio may be revealing your tastes", in *St Petersburg Times* (31/1/2000), at `http://www.sptimes.com/News/013100/Technology/Your_car_radio_may_be.shtml`

[1213] S Stamm, Z Ramzan, M Jakobsson, "Drive-By Pharming", Indiana University Department of Computer Science Technical Report TR641, 2006

[1214] M Stamp, RM Low, *'Applied Cryptanalysis'*, Wiley 2007

[1215] T Standage, *'The Victorian Internet'*, Phoenix Press (1999), ISBN 0-75380-703-3

[1216] D Standeford, "Case Could Signal Weakening Of Digital Rights Management in Europe", in *Intellectual Property Watch*, June 4 2007, at `http://www.ip-watch.org/weblog/index.php?p=639&res=1600_ff&print=0`

[1217] F Stajano, personal communication

[1218] F Stajano, RJ Anderson, "The Resurrecting Duckling: Security Issues in Ad-Hoc Wireless Networks", in *'Security Protocols–7th International Workshop'*, Springer LNCS 1796 pp 172–182

[1219] F Stajano, RJ Anderson, "The Cocaine Auction Protocol–On the Power of Anonymous Broadcast", in [1022] pp 434–447

[1220] S Staniford, D Moore, V Paxson, N Weaver, "The Top Speed of Flash Worms", in *WORM04*, at `www.icir.org/vern/papers/topspeed-worm04.pdf`

[1221] "Computer Chip Usage in Toner Cartridges and Impact on the Aftermarket: Past, Current and Future", Static Control, Inc., formerly at `http://www.scc-inc.com/special/oemwarfare/whitepaper/default.htm`, retrieved via `www.archive.org`

[1222] WA Steer, "VideoDeCrypt", at `http://www.ucl.ac.uk/~ucapwas/vdc/`

[1223] P Stein, P Feaver, "Assuring Control of Nuclear Weapons", CSIA occasional paper number 2, Harvard University 1987

[1224] J Steiner, BC Neuman, JI Schiller, "Kerberos: An Authentication Service for Open Network Systems", in *USENIX* (Winter 1988); version 5 in *'RFC 1510: The Kerberos Network Authentication Service (V5)'*; at `http://sunsite.utk.edu/net/security/kerberos/`

[1225] N Stephenson, *'Snow Crash'*, Bantam Doubleday Dell (1992), ISBN 0-553-38095-8

[1226] DR Stinson, *'Cryptography–Theory and Practice'*, CRC Press (1995); ISBN 0-8493-8521-0

[1227] *'Watching Them, Watching Us - UK CCTV Surveillance Regulation Campaign'*, at `http://www.spy.org.uk/`

[1228] R Strehle, *'Verschlüsselt–Der Fall Hans Bühler'*, Werd Verlag (1994) ISBN 3-85932-141-2

[1229] R Stross, "How to Lose Your Job on Your Own Time", in *New York Times* Dec 30 2007; at `http://www.nytimes.com/2007/12/30/business/30digi.html?ex=1356670800&en=bafd771bdcae2594&ei=5124&partner=permalink&exprod=permalink`

[1230] A Stubblefield, J Ioannidis, A Rubin, "Using the Fluhrer, Mantin, and Shamir Attack to Break WEP", in *ISOC 2002*

[1231] K Stumper, "DNA-Analysen und ein Recht auf Nichtwissen", in *Datenschutz und Datensicherheit* v 19 no 9 (Sep 95) pp 511–517

[1232] Suetonius (Gaius Suetonius Tranquillus), *'Vitae XII Caesarum'*, translated into English as *'History of twelve Caesars'* by Philemon Holland, 1606; Nutt (1899)

[1233] D Sutherland, "A Model of Information", in *9th National Computer Security Conference* (1986)

[1234] M Sutton, "How Prevalent Are SQL Injection Vulnerabilities?" *Michael Sutton's Blog*, Sep 26 2006, at `http://portal.spidynamics.com/blogs/msutton/archive/2006/09/26/How-Prevalent-Are-SQL-Injection-Vulnerabilities_3F00_.aspx`

[1235] L Sweeney, "Weaving Technology and Policy Together to Maintain Confidentiality", in *Journal of Law, Medicine and Ethics* v 25 no 2–3 (1997) pp 98–110

[1236] F Swiderski, W Snyder, *'Threat Modeling'*, Microsoft Press 2004

[1237] P Swire, "Efficient Confidentiality for Privacy, Security, and Confidential Business Information", Brookings-Wharton Papers on Financial Services (2003), at `http://ssrn.com/abstract=383180`

[1238] P Swire, "A Theory of Disclosure for Security and Competitive Reasons: Open Source, Proprietary Software, and Government Agencies", in *Houston Law Review* v 42 no 5 (Jan 2006) pp 101–148; at `http://ssrn.com/abstract_id=842228`

[1239] Symantec, *'Symantec Internet Security Threat Report—Trends for January–June 07* v 12, Sep 2007, at `www.symantec.com/threatreport/`

[1240] *Symposium On Usable Privacy and Security*, `http://cups.cs.cmu.edu/soups/2007/`

[1241] C Tavris, E Aronson, *'Mistakes were made—but not by me'*, Harcourt 2007

[1242] J Taylor, MR Johnson, CG Crawford, *'DVD Demystified'*, Third edition, McGraw-Hill 2006

[1243] J Tehranian, "An Unhurried View of Copyright Reform: Bridging the Law/Norm Gap", 2007 *Utah Law Review*, at `www.turnergreen.com/publications/Tehranian_Infringement_Nation.pdf`

[1244] S Tendler, N Nuttall, "Hackers run up £1m bill on Yard's phones", in *The Times*, 5 Aug 1996; at `http://www.the-times.co.uk/`

[1245] E Tews, RP Weinmann, A Pyshkin, "Breaking 104 bit WEP in less than 60 seconds", *Cryptology ePrint archive*, Apr 2007; at `http://eprint.iacr.org/2007/120.pdf`

[1246] L Thalheim, J Krissler, PM Ziegler, "Body Check—Biometric Access Protection Devices and their Programs Put to the Test", *c't magazine*, Nov 2002 p 114, at `http://www.heise.de/ct/english/02/11/114/`

[1247] K Thompson, "Reflections on Trusting Trust", in *Communications of the ACM* v 27 no 8 (Aug 84) pp 761–763; at `http://www.acm.org/classics/sep95/`

[1248] R Thompson, "Google Sponsored Links Not Safe", Exploit Prevention Labs Apr 24 2007, at `http://explabs.blogspot.com/2007/04/google-sponsored-links-not-safe.html`; see also J Richards, "Hackers hijack Google AdWords", *The Times*, Apr 27 2007, `http://technology.timesonline.co.uk/tol/news/tech_and_web/article1714656.ece`

[1249] J Ticehurst, "Barclays online bank suffers another blow" (11/8/2000), at `http://www.vnunet.com/News/1108767`

[1250] TimeWarner, "Carmine Caridi, Motion Picture Academy Member Who Handed Over His Awards Screeners for Illegal Duplication, Ordered to Pay $300,000 to Warner Bros. Entertainment Inc.", Nov 23 2004, at `http://www.timewarner.com/corp/newsroom/pr/0,20812,832500,00.html`

[1251] AZ Tirkel, GA Rankin, RM van Schyndel, WJ Ho, NRA Mee, CF Osborne, "Electronic Watermark", in *Digital Image Computing, Technology and Applications* (DICTA 93) McQuarie University (1993) pp 666–673

[1252] The TJX Companies, Inc., 'Form 10-k', filed with SEC, at `http://www.sec.gov/Archives/edgar/data/109198/000095013507001906/b64407tje10vk.htm`

[1253] MW Tobias, *'Locks, Safes and Security—An International Police Reference'* (second edition, 2000) ISBN 978-0-398-07079-3

[1254] MW Tobias, "Opening locks by bumping in five seconds or less: is it really a threat to physical security?", 2006, at `www.security.org`

[1255] MW Tobias, "Bumping of locks–legal issues in the United States", at www.security.org

[1256] MW Tobias, "The Medeco M3 Meets the Paper Clip: Is the security of this lock at risk?" (2007), at www.security.org

[1257] C Tomlinson, 'Rudimentary Treatise on the Construction of Locks', 1853 (excerpt), at http://www.deter.com/unix/papers/treatise_locks.html

[1258] TT Tool, 'The MIT Lock Picking Manual', 1991; at http://people.csail.mit.edu/custo/MITLockGuide.pdf

[1259] Transactional Records Access Clearinghouse, 'TRACFBI', at http://trac.syr.edu/tracfbi/index.html

[1260] A Travis, "Voice ID device to track failed asylum seekers", in The Guardian Mar 10 2006; at http://www.guardian.co.uk/uk_news/story/0,,1727834,00.html

[1261] I Traynor, "DNA database agreed for police across EU", in The Guardian, June 13 2007; at http://www.guardian.co.uk/international/story/0,,2101496,00.html

[1262] M Trombly, "Visa issues 10 'commandments' for online merchants", in Computerworld (11/8/2000), at http://www.computerworld.com/cwi/story/0,1199,NAV47_STO48487,00.html

[1263] E Tromer, 'Hardware-Based Cryptanalysis', PhD Thesis, Weizmann Institute of Science (2007), at http://www.wisdom.weizmann.ac.il/~tromer/papers/tromer-phd-dissertation.pdf

[1264] C Troncoso, G Danezis, E Kosta, B Preneel, "PriPAYD: Privacy Friendly Pay-As-You-Drive Insurance", in Workshop on Privacy in the Electronic Society (2007), at https://www.cosic.esat.kuleuven.be/publications/article-944.pdf

[1265] JD Tygar, BS Yee, N Heintze, "Cryptographic Postage Indicia", in ASIAN 96 (Springer-Verlag LNCS v 1179) pp 378–391, at www.cs.berkeley.edu/~tygar/papers/Cryptographic_Postage_Indicia/CMU-CS-96-113.pdf

[1266] R Uhlig, "BT admits staff could have fiddled system to win Concorde trip", in The Daily Telegraph (23/7/1997), at http://www.telegraph.co.uk:80/

[1267] ukcrypto mailing list, at http://www.chiark.greenend.org.uk/mailman/listinfo/ukcrypto

[1268] Underwriters' Laboratories, http://www.ul.com

[1269] J Ungoed-Thomas, A Lorenz, "French play dirty for £1bn tank deal", in *Sunday Times* (6/8/2000) p 5

[1270] United Kingdom Government, *'e-commerce@its.best.uk'*, at `http://www.e-envoy.gov.uk/2000/strategy/strategy.htm`

[1271] US Army, *'TM 31-210 Improvised Munitions Handbook'*, 1969, at `http://cryptome.org/tm-31-210.htm`

[1272] *'United States Code'*–US Federal Law, online for example at `http://www4.law.cornell.edu/uscode/`

[1273] United States Court of Appeals, District of Columbia Circuit, *United States Telecom Association v. Federal Communications Commission and United States of America*, no 99-1442, 15/8/2000, at `http://pacer.cadc.uscourts.gov/common/opinions/200008/99-1442a.txt`

[1274] UK Passport Service, *'Biometrics Enrolment Trial Report'*, May 2005; at `www.passport.gov.uk/downloads/UKPSBiometrics_Enrolment_Trial_Report.pdf`

[1275] UPI newswire item, Oklahoma distribution, November 26, 1983, Tulsa, Oklahoma

[1276] NA Van House, "Flickr and Public Image-Sharing: Distant Closeness and Photo Exhibition", at *CHI 2007* pp 2717–2722

[1277] L van Hove, "Electronic Purses: (Which) Way to Go?", in *First Monday* v 5 no 7 (June 2000) at `http://firstmonday.org/issues/issue5_7/hove/`

[1278] P Van Oorschot, M Wiener, "Parallel Collision Search with Application to Hash Functions and Discrete Logarithms", *Second ACM Conference on Computer and Communications Security*; proceedings published by the ACM, ISBN 0-89791-732-4, pp 210–218

[1279] R van Renesse, *'Optical Document Security'* (second edition), Artech House (1997) ISBN 0-89006-982-4

[1280] R van Renesse, "Verifying versus falsifying banknotes", in *Optical Security and Counterfeit Deterrence Techniques II* (1998), IS&T (The Society for Imaging Science and Technology) and SPIE (The International Society for Optical Engineering) v 3314 ISBN 0-8194-2754-3, pp 71–85

[1281] H van Vliet, *'Software Engineering–Principles and Practice'*, Wiley (second edition, 2000) ISBN 0-471-97508-7

[1282] R van Voris, "Black Box Car Idea Opens Can of Worms", in *Law news Network* (4/6/99), at `http://www.lawnewsnetwork.com/stories/ A2024-1999Jun4.html`

[1283] G Vanneste, J Degraeve, "Initial report on security requirements", in [92]

[1284] HR Varian, *'Intermediate Microeconomics – A Modern Approach'* (fifth edition), Norton (1999), ISBN 0-393-97370-0

[1285] HR Varian, "Managing Online Security Risks", in *The New York Times*, 1 June 2000; at `http://www.nytimes.com/library/financial/ columns/060100econ-scene.html`

[1286] HR Varian, "New Chips Can Keep a Tight Rein on Customers", *New York Times* July 4 2002, at `http://www.nytimes.com/2002/07/04/ business/04SCEN.html`

[1287] S Vaudenay, "FFT-Hash-II is not yet Collision-Free", *Laboratoire d'Informatique de l'Ecole Normale Supérieure report LIENS-92-17*

[1288] V Varadharajan, N Kumar, Y Mu, "Security Agent Based Distributed Authorization: An Approach', in *20th National Information Systems Security Conference*, proceedings published by NIST (1998) pp 315–328

[1289] H Varian, "Economic Aspects of Personal Privacy", in *Privacy and Self-Regulation in the Information Age*, National Telecommunications and Information Administration report, 1996

[1290] H Varian, "Managing Online Security Risks", Economic Science Column, *The New York Times*, June 1, 2000

[1291] H Varian, "New chips and keep a tight rein on consumers, even after they buy a product", *New York Times*, July 4 2002

[1292] H Varian, "System Reliability and Free Riding", in *Economics of Information Security*, Kluwer 2004 pp 1–15

[1293] H Varian, Keynote address to the Third Digital Rights Management Conference, Berlin, Germany, January 13, 2005

[1294] W Venema, "Murphy's Law and Computer Security", in *Usenix Security 96* pp 187–193

[1295] J Vijayan, "HIPAA audit at hospital riles health care IT", *Computerworld*, June 15 2007; at `http://www.computerworld.com/action/ article.do?command=viewArticleBasic&articleId=9024921`

[1296] J Vijayan, "Retail group takes a swipe at PCI, puts card companies 'on notice' ", *Computerworld* Oct 4 2007; at `http://computerworld.com/action/article.do?command=viewArticleBasic&articleId=9040958&intsrc=hm_list`

[1297] N Villeneuve, "DNS tampering in China", Jul 10 2007, at `http://www.nartv.org/2007/07/10/dns-tampering-in-china/`

[1298] B Vinck, "Security Architecture" (3G TS 33.102 v 3.2.0), from *Third Generation Partnership Project*, at `http://www.3gpp.org/TSG/Oct_status_list.htm`

[1299] B Vinck, "Lawful Interception Requirements"(3G TS 33.106 v 3.0.0), from *Third Generation Partnership Project*, at `http://www.3gpp.org/TSG/Oct_status_list.htm`

[1300] VISA International, *'Integrated Circuit Chip Card–Security Guidelines Summary*, version 2 draft 1, November 1997

[1301] A Viterbi, "Spread spectrum communications–myths and realities", in *IEEE Communications Magazine* v 17 no 3 (May 1979) pp 11–18

[1302] PR Vizcaya, LA Gerhardt, "A Nonlinear Orientation Model for Global Description of Fingerprints", in *Pattern Recognition* v 29 no 7 (July 96) pp 1221–1231

[1303] L von Ahn, personal communication, 2006

[1304] L von Ahn, M Blum, NJ Hopper, J Langford, "CAPTCHA: Using Hard AI Problems For Security", *Advances in Cryptology–Eurocrypt 2003*, Springer LNCS v 2656 pp 294–311

[1305] D Wagner, B Schneier, J Kelsey, "Cryptanalysis of the Cellular Message Encryption Algorithm", in *Advances in Cryptology–Crypto 95*, Springer LNCS v 1294 pp 527–537

[1306] D Wagner, "Cryptanalysis of Some Recently-Proposed Multiple Modes of Operation", in *Fifth International Workshop on Fast Software Encryption* (1998), Springer LNCS v 1372 pp 254–269

[1307] D Wagner, I Goldberg, M Briceno, "GSM Cloning", at `http://www.isaac.cs.berkeley.edu/isaac/gsm-faq.html`; see also `http://www.scard.org/gsm/`

[1308] D Wagner, B Schneier, "Analysis of the SSL 3.0 Protocol", in *Second USENIX Workshop on Electronic Commerce* (1996), pp 29–40; at `http://www.counterpane.com`

[1309] M Waldman, AD Rubin, LF Cranor, "Publius: A robust, tamper-evident, censorship-resistant, web publishing system", in *9th USENIX Security Symposium* (2000) pp 59–72

[1310] M Walker, "On the Security of 3GPP Networks", Invited talk at Eurocrypt 2000, at `http://www.ieee-security.org/Cipher/ConfReports/2000/CR2000-Eurocrypt.html`

[1311] G Walsh, *'Review of Policy relating to Encryption Technologies'* (1996), at `http://www.efa.org.au/Issues/Crypto/Walsh/`

[1312] KG Walter, WF Ogden, WC Rounds, FT Bradshaw, SR Ames, DG Shumway, *'Models for Secure Computer Systems'*, Case Western Reserve University, Report no 1137 (31/7/1973, revised 21/11/1973)

[1313] KG Walter, WF Ogden, WC Rounds, FT Bradshaw, SR Ames, DG Shumway, *'Primitive Models for Computer Security'*, Case Western Reserve University, Report no ESD–TR–74–117 (23/1/1974); at `http://www.dtic.mil`

[1314] E Waltz, *'Information Warfare–Principles and Operations'*, Artech House (1998) ISBN 0-89006-511-X

[1315] XY Wang, DG Feng, XJ Lai, HB Yu, "Collisions for Hash Functions MD4, MD5, HAVAL-128 and RIPEMD", IACR Cryptology ePrint Archive Report 2004/199, at `http://eprint.iacr.org/2004/199`

[1316] XY Wang, YQL Yin, HB Yu, " Collision Search Attacks on SHA1", Feb 13 2005, at `http://www.infosec.sdu.edu.cn/sha-1/shanote.pdf`

[1317] XY Wang, HB Yu, "How to Break MD5 and Other Hash Functions", in *Advances in Cryptology–Eurocrypt 2005*, at `http://www.infosec.sdu.edu.cn/paper/md5-attack.pdf`

[1318] R Want, A Hopper, V Falcao, J Gibbons, "The Active Badge Location System", in *ACM Transactions on Information Systems* v 10 no 1 (Jan 92) pp 91–102; at `http://www.cl.cam.ac.uk/research/dtg/attarchive/ab.html`

[1319] W Ware, *'Security Controls for Computer Systems: Report of Defense Science Board Task Force on Computer Security'*, Rand Report R609-1, The RAND Corporation, Santa Monica, CA (Feb 1970), available from `http://csrc.nist.gov/publications/history/index.html`

[1320] M Warner, "Machine Politics In the Digital Age", in *The New York Times* November 9, 2003; at `http://query.nytimes.com/gst/fullpage.html?res=9804E3DC1339F93AA35752C1A9659C8B63`

[1321] SD Warren, LD Brandeis, "The Right To Privacy" Harvard Law Review series 4 (1890) pp 193–195

[1322] J Warrick, "Leak Severed a Link to Al-Qaeda's Secrets", in the *Washington Post* Oct 9 2007 p A01, "U.S. Intelligence Officials Will Probe Leak of Bin Laden Video", *ibid.*, Oct 10 2007 p A13

[1323] Waste electrical and electronic equipment (WEEE) regulations 2007, at `http://www.netregs.gov.uk/netregs/275207/1631119/?version=1&lang=_e`

[1324] M Watson, "Sat-nav 'jammer' threatens to sink road pricing scheme", in *Auto Express* Aug 8th 2007; at `http://www.autoexpress.co.uk/news/autoexpressnews/209801/sat_nav_jammer.html`

[1325] RNM Watson, "Exploiting Concurrency Vulnerabilities in Kernel System Call Wrappers", in *First USENIX Workshop on Offensive Technologies* (WOOT 07), at `http://www.watson.org/~robert/2007woot/`

[1326] "Developer tortured by raiders with crowbars", M Weaver, *Daily Telegraph*, 31 October 97

[1327] W Webb, "High-tech Security: The Eyes Have It", in *EDN* (18/12/97) pp 75–78

[1328] SH Weingart, "Physical Security for the μABYSS System", in *Proceedings of the 1987 IEEE Symposium on Security and Privacy*, IEEE Computer Society Press, pp 52–58

[1329] SH Weingart, "Mind the Gap: Updating FIPS 140", at *FIPS Physical Security Workshop*, Hawaii 2005; at `http://csrc.nist.gov/groups/STM/cmvp/documents/fips140-3/physec/papers/physecpaper18.pdf`

[1330] SH Weingart, SR White, WC Arnold, GP Double, "An Evaluation System for the Physical Security of Computing Systems", in *Sixth Annual Computer Security Applications Conference*, 3–7/12/90, Tucson, Arizona; proceedings published by the IEEE (1990) pp 232–243

[1331] L Weinstein, "IDs in Color Copies–A PRIVACY Forum Special Report" in *Privacy Forum Digest*, v 8 no 18 (6 Dec 1999), at `http://www.vortex.com/privacy/priv.08.18`

[1332] L Weinstein, "The Online Medical Records Trap", Oct 4 2007, at `http://lauren.vortex.com/archive/000306.html`

[1333] L Weinstein, "Not on Track with 'Do Not Track' ", Oct 31 2007, at `http://lauren.vortex.com/archive/000326.html`

[1334] C Weissman, "Security Controls in the ADEPT-50 Time Sharing System", in *AFIPS Conference Proceedings, Volume 35, 1969 Fall Joint Computer Conference* pp 119–133

[1335] C Weissman, "BLACKER: Security for the DDN, Examples of A1 Security Engineering Trades", in *Proceedings of the 1992 IEEE Symposium on Security and Privacy* pp 286–292

[1336] G Welchman, *'The Hut Six Story'*, McGraw Hill (1982) ISBN 0-07-069180-0

[1337] B Wels, R Gonggrijp, "Bumping locks", 2006, at `http://www.toool.nl/bumping.pdf`

[1338] A Westfeld, A Pfitzmann, "Attacks on Steganographic Systems", in *Proceedings of the Third International Workshop on Information Hiding* (1999), Springer LNCS v 1768 pp 61–76

[1339] AF Westin, *'Data Protection in the Global Society'* (1996 conference report), at `http://www.privacyexchange.org/iss/confpro/aicgsberlin.html`

[1340] E Whitaker, "At SBC, It's All About 'Scale and Scope' ", in *Business Week* Nov 7 2005, at `http://www.businessweek.com/@@n34h*IUQu7KtOwgA/magazine/content/05_45/b3958092.htm`

[1341] O Whitehouse, "Bluetooth: Red fang, blue fang," in *CanSecWest/core04*, linked from "Bluetooth PIN Cracker: Be Afraid" at `http://www.symantec.com/enterprise/security_response/weblog/2006/11/bluetooth_pin_cracker_be_afrai.html`

[1342] A Whitten, JD Tygar, "Why Johnny Can't Encrypt: A Usability Evaluation of PGP 5.0", in *Eighth USENIX Security Symposium* (1999) pp 169–183

[1343] J Wildermuth, "Secretary of state casts doubt on future of electronic voting", *San Francisco Chronicle* Dec 2 2007, at `http://www.sfgate.com/cgi-bin/article.cgi?f=/c/a/2007/12/02/BASRTMOPE.DTL`

[1344] MV Wilkes, RM Needham, *'The Cambridge CAP computer and its Operating System'*, Elsevier North Holland (1979)

[1345] J Wilkins, *'Mercury; or the Secret and Swift Messenger: Shewing, How a Man May with Privacy and Speed Communicate his Thoughts to a Friend at Any Distance'*, London, Rich Baldwin (1694)

[1346] C Williams, "Surge in encrypted torrents blindsides record biz", in *The Register* Nov 8 2007, at `http://www.theregister.co.uk/2007/11/08/bittorrent_encryption_explosion/`

[1347] CL Wilson, MD Garris and CI Watson, "Matching Performance for the US-VISIT IDENT System Using Flat Fingerprints", NIST IR 7110 (May 2004), at `ftp://sequoyah.nist.gov/pub/nist_internal_reports/ir_7110.pdf`

[1348] R Wilson, "Panel unscrambles intellectual property encryption issues", *EDN* Jan 31 2007, at `http://www.edn.com/index.asp?layout=article&articleid=CA6412249`

[1349] T Wilson, "Visa Gave TJX a Pass on PCI in 2005", in *Dark Reading* Nov 12 2007, at `http://www.darkreading.com/document.asp?doc_id=138838`

[1350] FW Winterbotham, *'The Ultra Secret'*, Harper & Row (1974)

[1351] A Wolfson, 'A hoax most cruel', in *The Courier-Journal* Oct 9, 2005; at `http://www.courier-journal.com/apps/pbcs.dll/article?AID=/20051009/NEWS01/510090392`

[1352] K Wong, "Mobile Phone Fraud - Are GSM Networks Secure?", in *Computer Fraud and Security Bulletin* (Nov 96) pp 11–18

[1353] N Wong, " Judge tells DoJ 'No' on search queries", Google blog Mar 17 2006

[1354] CC Wood, "Identity token usage at American commercial banks", in *Computer Fraud and Security Bulletin* (Mar 95) pp 14–16

[1355] E Wood, *'Housing Design, A Social Theory'*, Citizens' Housing and Planning Council of New York, 1961

[1356] L Wood, "Security Feed", in *CSO*, Apr 20 2007; at `http://www2.csoonline.com/blog_view.html?CID=32865`

[1357] JPL Woodward, *'Security Requirements for System High and Compartmented Mode Workstations'* Mitre MTR 9992, Revision 1, 1987 (also published by the Defense Intelligence Agency as document DDS-2600-5502-87)

[1358] B Wright, "The Verdict on Plaintext Signatures: They're Legal", in *Computer Law and Security Report* v 14 no 6 (Nov/Dec 94) pp 311–312

[1359] B Wright, *'The Law of Electronic Commerce: EDI, Fax and Email'*, Little, Brown 1991; fourth edition (with supplement) 1994

[1360] DB Wright, AT McDaid, "Comparing system and estimator variables using data from real line-ups", in *Applied Cognitive Psychology* v 10 no 1 pp 75–84

[1361] JB Wright, *'Report of the Weaponization and Weapons Production and Military Use Working Group—Appendix F to the Report of the*

Fundamental Classification Policy Review Group', US Department of Energy Office of Scientific and Technical Information (1997), `http://www.osti.gov/opennet/app-f.html`

[1362] MA Wright, "Security Controls in ATM Systems", in *Computer Fraud and Security Bulletin*, November 1991, pp 11–14

[1363] P Wright, *'Spycatcher–The Candid Autobiography of a Senior Intelligence Officer'*, William Heinemann Australia, 1987, ISBN 0-85561-098-0

[1364] JX Yan, *'Security for Online Games'*, PhD thesis, University of Cambridge 2003

[1365] JX Yan, A Blackwell, RJ Anderson, A Grant, "The Memorability and Security of Passwords–Some Empirical Results", University of Cambridge Computer Laboratory Technical Report no 500; at `http://www.cl.cam.ac.uk/ftp/users/rja14/tr500.pdf`; also in *IEEE Security & Privacy*, Sep–Oct 2004 pp 25–29

[1366] JX Yan, S Early, RJ Anderson, "The XenoService–A Distributed Defeat for Distributed Denial of Service", at Information Survivability Workshop, Oct 2000

[1367] JX Yan, B Randell, *'Security in Computer Games: from Pong to Online Poker'*, University of Newcastle Tech Report CS-TR-889 (2005)

[1368] JX Yan, B Randell, "A systematic classification of cheating in online games", at *Proceedings of 4th ACM SIGCOMM workshop on Network and system support for games* (2005), at `http://portal.acm.org/citation.cfm?id=1103606`

[1369] T Ylönen, 'SSH–Secure Login Connections over the Internet", in *Usenix Security 96* pp 37–42

[1370] KS Yoon, YK Ham, RH Park, "Hybrid Approaches to Fractal Face Recognition Using the Hidden Markov Model and Neural Network", in *Pattern Recognition* v 31 no 3 (98) pp 283–293

[1371] G Yuval, "Reinventing the Travois: Encryption/MAC in 30 ROM Bytes", in *Fourth International Workshop on Fast Software Encryption* (1997), Springer LNCS v 1267 pp 205–209

[1372] MC Zari, AF Zwilling, DA Hess, KW Snow, CJ Anderson, D Chiang, "Personal Identification System Utilizing Low probability of Intercept (LPI) Techniques for Covert Ops", in *30th Annual IEEE Carnahan Conference on Security Technology* (1996) pp 1–6

[1373] *ZDnet*, "Software blocks images of money", Jan 12 2004, at `http://news.zdnet.co.uk/software/0,1000000121,39119018,00.htm`

[1374] K Zetter, "Scan This Guy's E-Passport and Watch Your System Crash", in *Wired*, Aug 1 2007, at http://www.wired.com/politics/security/news/2007/08/epassport

[1375] RS Zhang, XY Wang, XH Yan, XX Jiang, "Billing Attacks on SIP-Based VOIP Systems", in *WOOT 2007*

[1376] L Zhuang, F Zhou, JD Tygar, "Keyboard Acoustic Emanations Revisited" in *12th ACM Conference on Computer and Communications Security* (2005)

[1377] P Zimbardo, *'The Lucifer Effect'*, Random House (2007)

[1378] MW Zior, "A community response to CMM-based security engineering process improvement", in *18th National Information Systems Security Conference* (1995) pp 404–413

[1379] M Zviran, WJ Haga, "A Comparison of Password Techniques for Multilevel Authentication Mechanisms", in *The Computer Journal* v 36 no 3 (1993) pp 227–237

Index